Adventures in World Literature

EDITED BY

REWEY BELLE INGLIS
Formerly University High School
University of Minnesota

WILLIAM K. STEWART
Professor of Comparative Literature
Dartmouth College

REVISED EDITION EDITED BY

OSCAR JAMES CAMPBELL
Professor of Comparative Literature
Columbia University

EUNICE CHAPPELL STEARN
Central High School
Valley Stream, New York

Harcourt, Brace & World, Inc.
New York   Chicago   Atlanta   Dallas   Burlingame

Preface

ADVENTURES IN WORLD LITERATURE is the geographical sequel to *Adventures in American Literature* and *Adventures in English Literature*. The order of progress is an inevitable one. The young American begins with the literature which springs from his own environment, his native idiom, and the experience of his nation. The various sections of his own land are illuminated for him by the words of those American writers who are our best interpreters. Then the student takes a step into more difficult realms. He crosses the ocean into the old world from which the new inherits its traditions. English literature takes him not only into a distant country, but back into the far past when manners, dress, speech, daily life, education, and politics differed widely from the conditions which he perceives about him.

This gradually developing conception of humanity as a constant stream flowing between banks of varying beauty and interest is part of what we call a cultural background. Yet too often the outlook opened up to young people has stopped short with English literature, and they have never been given sufficient opportunity to look farther into the writings of other languages, through which a world point of view can be developed.

We have assumed that a student trained in our educational system who lacked the direct contact of travel would get his knowledge of the other peoples of the world from a study of foreign languages, from history, or from the universal languages — music and art. But these are all inadequate to convey that intangible something which literature possesses. Few young people study more than two foreign languages at any time. Many of them never approach even one, and often when they do, the tedious hurdling of vocabulary and grammar spoils the direct and vital thoughts the author wished to utter to his reader. Foreign literature to the immature student of a foreign language is indeed seen " through a glass darkly."

History gives him the more rapid view, but it is at best kaleidoscopic. Races and nations fall into shifting patterns as the centuries roll around. Migrations, battles, economic necessities, dynasties, and powerful individuals stand forth, but the human touch is missing. History is an airplane ride across a continent; not, like literature, a leisurely walk with a group of friends. Art is vivid, but static; music is emotional, but abstract.

Literature transcends any of these studies in its power to create sympathetic understanding because it is personal, direct, and intimate. Thus at a time when the development of world understanding is one of our great educational problems it is essential that our young people should have access to as many of the cultural sources of other nations as possible. Linguistic blockades should be broken down. Literary formulas which have marked Comparative Literature courses for advanced college upperclassmen should give way, in a book for younger students, to a presentation of literature as a human document through which one comes to sense the spirit of other peoples. To us as a nation whose life has been drawn from so many old world strains it is doubly necessary that our youth should appreciate these varied and colorful literary backgrounds.

This volume has endeavored to fulfill that purpose, and in the assembling and arrangement of material the editors have kept in mind the following guiding principles:

The Arrangement of Material. Since this book represents an ever-widening horizon for the student, who, it is assumed, has already studied American and English Literature, it was thought best to begin with the group of modern European languages, just as one might travel from the British Isles to the Continent. The grouping of the six major languages (with their branches) was a matter of careful consideration. French was placed first because that literature has been basic for the rest of Europe. This is followed by the Spanish-Portuguese and Italian sections to give unity to the Romance languages and the South-European group. German, the most central of the North-European languages, precedes the more segregated Scandinavian and Russian groups. Within each of these six sections the material is arranged chronologically to enable the student to watch the emergence of each national literature from the dim beginnings of medieval times into the illuminated power of the recent centuries. Such an arrangement also facilitates cross references in time when it is desirable to see how certain waves of fashion in writing have swept Europe as a whole.

The second part of the book covers the Greek and Roman classic literature. This gives opportunity to trace back to original sources some of the concepts which the students have found developing in modern Europe after the Renaissance. The instructor who wishes to place the course on a completely chronological basis could easily begin with Classical Literature, but such procedure is not recommended, for it postpones too far into the course that natural interest which recent literature evokes in the average student.

The third part of the book takes the student still farther afield to the Oriental races, where not only costume and custom differ, but the most fundamental conceptions of life philosophy are at variance with those to which the student has been educated. This section, though treated more sketchily than the others, may prove most provocative of thought and discussion as a finale to the course.

The Selection of Material. For each of the individual sections the editors have chosen the selections with the following questions in mind:

1. Is this material intrinsically interesting to a student of the late teens or early twenties? It was accepted as axiomatic that neither world understanding nor love of literature could be fostered through boredom, and therefore long tedious narratives without action, lengthy philosophical disquisitions, mature works of criticism, and abstruse poetry have been eliminated even though they might rank as " world classics." Some of the selections are harder than others. An instructor may shift emphasis or even eliminate the too easy or too difficult according to the maturity of his classes. The readability of the selections has been tested out both in classrooms and with volunteer groups of readers among young people of the age for which this book is intended.

2. Is this author of sufficient importance in his native literature to make him worthy of inclusion in a brief survey where only the best should be considered? It will be evident on glancing over the contents of this book that the great and significant names of each literature have found a place, and that minor writers appear very seldom, and then only perhaps to bridge a pronounced gap between centuries or illustrate some modern tendency. Where a great name is missing or represented briefly, it is because his writing lacks intrinsic appeal for the young student.

3. Does each selection give as true a picture of the work of its author as could be expected in limited space, at the same time convey the flavor of its nation or its century, and yet maintain its universal quality? This is a large order, and one that could not be met equally

well in every case; yet on the whole the selections measure up to this standard.

4. Is the translation the best one available? The compilers of a collection of translated literature have an added problem unknown to the anthologist dealing only with the language of original creation. The translator must be somewhat of an artist himself if he is to convey in another tongue the subtleties and overtones of the native idiom. Occasionally there was no choice since only one translation had been made in English, but wherever plural translations were available, the editors weighed them carefully deciding sometimes according to effectiveness as a piece of English writing (especially in poetry), sometimes according to faithful rendering of the original, and sometimes for a special purpose, such as to show the contrasting metrical effects of the Bryant and Caulfeild translations of the *Iliad* and *Odyssey*. The translators have been named at the end of each selection.

5. Is the section well balanced? The editors have endeavored, in so far as the national literature permitted, to provide a varied program of poetry, drama, fiction, and non-fiction prose, ranging from the sprightly and humorous to the serious and tragic. A chronological balance was also desired so that an uninterrupted flow of literature might be represented except where a definite hiatus was evident in the literature itself. The time balance, however, was definitely weighted toward the nineteenth and twentieth centuries throughout Modern European Literature. In the six modern European languages the proportion of literature from 1800 to the present is as follows: French, 57 per cent; Spanish, 50 per cent; Italian, 43 per cent; German, 27 per cent; Scandinavian, 81 per cent; Russian, 100 per cent. Classical and Oriental Literature are, of course, preponderantly ancient, but with considerable modern material in the Indian and Japanese sections.

The Editing of the Material. The selections are complete units as far as possible. Lyric and ballad poetry, short stories, folk tales, and essays are given entire. Where excerpts from novels, epics, and biographies have been included, care has been taken to present a distinct unit with sufficient explanation to avoid confusion in the reader's mind. Novelists have been represented by one of their short stories rather than an extract from a novel, whenever this could be adequately done. Complete long dramas are to be found in the French, Scandinavian, and Greek sections, with short plays or selected acts in many of the others.

It has been the aim of the editors to make the editorial material of sufficient intrinsic interest to warrant its inclusion with the selections as running comment. This seems especially necessary where so much of the literature has sprung from an environment unfamiliar to the student.

Each section is opened by a short history of the literature of that language. It is recommended that in taking up a new section the student read the introductory survey rapidly to block in the general outlines, but without any idea of mastering the material; then after the study of the literature has made the names meaningful, to return to the survey as a review and a more careful study of time orders and relationships. The survey should always be kept subsidiary to the appreciation of the writings themselves.

The biographical sketches of authors put emphasis only on those facts which help toward understanding the man behind the book and his significance in the world of literature. The footnotes are limited to the minimum information needed by the reader to make the text comprehensible. The study suggestions are intended to stimulate thought, to show relationships between different writers, different nations, and different arts, and to indicate opportunities for creative work growing out of the material under consideration. Since it is taken for granted that the students using this book are already familiar with American and English Literature, comparisons with our own writers are frequently pointed out. References to art and music are also interspersed. The reading lists at the end of each section, it is to be hoped, will send students to the library for further reading matter to widen their experience of various writers and nations. In compiling them, the authors have attempted to offer an appropriate representation of the literatures being studied, as well as to present writing that will appeal to students.

The editors wish to express their gratitude to the many teachers, librarians, and students of literature who, by their interest, their timely suggestions, and their willingness to " try out " material, have aided greatly in the preparation of this book. Thanks are especially due to Professor William Stuart Messer, Professor Royal Case Nemiah and Professor John Barker Stearns of Dartmouth College for assistance in preparing the bibliographies of Greek and Roman literature; to Sister Eleanore of St. Catherine's College, St. Paul, and to Miss Margaret Tupper of Washburn High School, Minneapolis, for their constructive criticisms of the Spanish section; to Professor Theodore Jorgenson of St. Olaf's College, Miss Pauline Farseth of North High School, Minneapolis, Miss Hanna Astrup Larsen and Mr. J. B. C.

Watkins of the American-Scandinavian Foundation, New York, for their invaluable help in preparing the Scandinavian section.

It is the sincere hope of the editors that the young people into whose hands this book may come will spend many hours not only profitable to the mind, but satisfying as well to that inner spirit which endlessly seeks to understand and share the experiences of all mankind.

R. B. I.
W. K. S.

NOTE ON THE REVISED EDITION

Adventures in World Literature, the standard world literature textbook for more than two decades, now appears in revised form. In bringing the book up to date, the editors have added the following new material:

(1) They have expanded each of the ten introductory surveys to the national literatures to include recent and contemporary writers, ideas, books, and literary movements.

(2) They have added, at the end of the book, a twenty-three-page section of recent world literature. Included in this section are three new selections of European and Latin American poetry, five new selections of European prose, and four new selections of Oriental poetry. Accompanying these selections are suggestions for study.

Since its original publication twenty-two years ago, *Adventures in World Literature* has been the one historical survey of its kind, embracing the entire field of foreign and classical literature. It is the editors' hope that the present edition will continue to meet the needs of the thousands of students whose major concerns include international understanding, intercultural understanding, and self-understanding.

CONTENTS

MODERN EUROPEAN LITERATURE

French Literature

CONTENTS

Spanish and Portuguese Literature

CONTENTS

Italian Literature

German Literature

Scandinavian Literature

OLD NORSE AND MEDIEVAL FOLK LITERATURE

MODERN DANISH LITERATURE

MODERN NORWEGIAN LITERATURE

Russian Literature

CLASSICAL LITERATURE

Greek Literature

Roman Literature

ORIENTAL LITERATURE
Egyptian Literature

Babylonian-Assyrian Literature

Hebrew Literature

Persian Literature

Arabic Literature

Indian Literature

Chinese Literature

RECENT WORLD LITERATURE

Recent European and Latin American Poetry

Recent European Prose

Recent Oriental Poetry

French Literature

French Literature

ALTHOUGH the French people are of mixed race, having Celtic and Germanic as well as Roman strains in their composition, it is the Roman that has counted most. The French language itself may be regarded as a modern form of Latin. The Latin genius, as it has often been called, has seemed to hover over the development of French culture and determine its destinies. It has bestowed on the French people their love of order, clarity and reasonableness, their instinctive avoidance of extremes — the very qualities which are most conspicuous in their literature. In all artistic matters the French are essentially conservative, despite the fact that they have often been initiators of new movements. Of all the modern literatures, French is the most naturally " classical."

The French have always taken ideas and esthetic matters seriously. Their literature is therefore the best from which to study literary movements. For that reason and because of its long and illustrious history and its influence on other literatures, French literature occupies, as it were, a central position.

The French have sometimes characterized themselves as possessing the *esprit gaulois* — the Gallic spirit, meaning by that a light-hearted gayety, a tendency to mock, and a refusal to take life or men too seriously. This Gallic spirit can indeed be detected all through French literature. Nevertheless, there is a fundamental earnestness in the French outlook which foreigners have too frequently been prone to overlook. As a matter of fact, most of the great French writers do not markedly display this so-called Gallic spirit.

It will be impossible in such a brief sketch as this to do justice to so rich a literature. Many important names will have to be omitted. To most foreigners, especially those of English speech, French prose with its clearness, rapidity, and grace seems superior to French poetry. The French themselves would dissent vigorously from such a judgment. Their poetry, they claim, has cadences which the outsider cannot sufficiently detect; it has all the delicacy for which its sister, French prose, is so justly renowned; and, if the poetry seems to the foreigner to be rhetorical, that is in accordance with French tradition and is acceptable to French taste.

The Middle Ages produce varied types

The earliest French literature dates from the eleventh century. The *Song of Roland*, of unknown authorship, may be looked upon as the national epic of France, comparable with *Beowulf* in England and the *Song of the Nibelungs* in Germany. It is one of many *chansons de gestes*, or songs of exploits, the subjects of which were taken, as in the *Song of Roland*, from the stories current about Charlemagne (742–814), or else from the legend of King Arthur. The chief writer of Arthurian epics, which are filled with the spirit of chivalry and courtly love, was Chrétien de Troyes (twelfth century), the most famous of French narrative poets in the Middle Ages. Courtly love was also the principal theme of the troubadours, the lyric poets of Provence in southern France, who were more distinguished for their ingenuity and artificiality than for anything distinctively personal. It is not until the end of the Middle Ages that we encounter a really great lyric poet in the person of François Villon (1431–1465?), a vagabond who had the merit of putting his heart and his life into his verse.

French prose in the Middle Ages was employed mainly in chronicles and history. There is, however, an anonymous story from the twelfth century called *Aucassin and Nicolette*, which is quite charming in an unpretentious way.

The drama in France, as in other countries of Europe, was in origin the offspring of the Church, though the two were destined much later to become bitter foes. The earliest plays were simply dramatizations of the ritual, particularly that connected with Christmas and Easter. When the plays were transferred from the church to the open air and French was substituted for Latin, the drama inevitably developed along lines of its own. Farces of a realistic, humorous, and even coarse type became popular. In these, as well as in the *fabliaux,* short narrative poems, we encounter the earliest expression of the Gallic spirit which finds nothing too sacred for satire.

The Sixteenth Century receives the impulse of the Renaissance

The Renaissance came to France in the reign of Francis I (1515–1547). The final disruption of feudalism, the introduction of the printing press, and the discovery of Italian culture were among the most important causes. It looked for a time as if the Protestant Reformation would also permeate the country, but by the end of the century the French people had definitely decided to remain Catholic. In literature the influence of the Renaissance was in the direction of classicism. A group of writers known as the Pléiade published a manifesto in 1550 which laid down the program of the school. Ronsard (1524–1585), the leading poet of the movement, was a genuine lyricist in his shorter verses. Poetic tragedies were written, carefully observing the unities of plot, time, and place, and this type of play was to flourish in France unchallenged for nearly three hundred years. But the greatest French writers of the sixteenth century used prose. Rabelais (1490?–1553) wrote long, formless works in the manner of fiction. The subject matter is grotesquely extravagant, the language is coarse and sometimes filthy, but beneath the buffoonery there is a strong undercurrent of keen satire, for Rabelais was an earnest and independent thinker. Montaigne (1533–1592), by contrast, is mature and staid, wishing to reflect on his experiences rather than live exuberantly. He is the first great essayist of modern times.

French culture of the Golden Age dominates Europe

France became thoroughly centralized in the seventeenth century, and the establishment of the French Academy, the most famous of all literary institutions, in 1635 led to the further centralization of culture. Classicism of the strictest kind was taught by Boileau (1636–1711), whose didactic poem, *The Art of Poetry*, laid down laws of composition which were considered infallible. French classicism taught the dependence of modern literature upon the ancients. The poet should avoid eccentricities and keep steadily to what is natural and reasonable. Strict rules were enjoined for verse forms and especially for the tragedy. It was within the framework of these limitations that the greatest period of French literature expressed itself. This is the Golden Age, which coincides with the long reign of Louis XIV (1643–1715). France was beyond question the leading country in Europe, both politically and culturally. In government, religion, and literature the note of authority was confidently sounded. But the classical ideals of order, clarity, sense of proportion, and good taste were, and still are, congenial to the French mind. Corneille (1606–1684) and Racine (1639–1699) wrote their great poetic tragedies in conformity with these ideals, the former dealing chiefly with the conflicts that arise out of honor, and the latter with those proceeding from love. The theologian and orator Bossuet (1627–1704) seemed to embody the spirit of authority, though posterity has accorded more attention to another religious writer, Pascal (1623–1662), who, besides being a profound thinker, is perhaps the greatest master of French prose. The less austere side of the Great Age is represented by Molière (1622–1673), the writer of the most delightful comedies of modern times, and by La Fontaine (1621–1695), whose fables in verse all French children learn. La Rochefoucauld (1613–1680) was a master of prose maxims, a form which the French have cultivated with special success.

Literature in the Golden Age was essentially aristocratic in its outlook. It was a product of the capital and the court, and its appeal was consequently limited pretty much to the cultivated few. With the diffusion of education, the widening of social sympathies, and the multiplication of interests that have taken place since then, this restricted outlook now necessarily appears as a grave shortcoming. Nevertheless, an understanding of the spirit of the Great Age and an appreciation of its masterpieces is still considered by the French to be the hall mark of true culture.

The Eighteenth Century an age of reason

The eighteenth century, particularly that portion of it between the death of Louis XIV in 1715 and the outbreak of the French Revolution in 1789, stands in startling contrast to the Great Age. It is the period of prose and of reason, the period also of general ideas, many of which were to prove destructive to existing institutions of church and state. Its spirit was critical, skeptical, and innovating. Ideas of liberty, toleration, humanitarianism, equality, and progress were advocated increasingly. Some of these ideas came from England, whose intellectual influence on France was of decisive importance during these years. The most characteristic literature of the century was of the nature of propaganda and was designed to make war on authority, dogma, and tradition. The leading writers of this " philosophic party," as it was called, were Montesquieu, Voltaire, and Diderot. Montesquieu (1689–1755) satirized many of the institutions and social customs of his country and praised the English constitution. Voltaire (1694–1778) attacked bigotry and superstition, and championed the victims of religious persecution and of political injustice. More than any other man he embodies the spirit of the age of reason. But most of his voluminous writings were too much concerned with questions of his own day to endure permanently.

Only his letters and a few of his tales are now much read. Diderot (1713-1784) was the director-in-chief of the famous *Encyclopedia*, which was designed both as a storehouse of information and as an arsenal of weapons to attack ignorance, superstition, and intolerance. In purely literary matters the taste of the age was still classical. Voltaire's poetic tragedies, for instance, were modeled largely on those of Corneille and Racine. Diderot was more of an innovator. His plays, in particular, testify to the ever-increasing importance and power of the middle class. Marivaux (1688-1763), in the earlier part of the century, and Beaumarchais (1732-1799), in the latter half, carried on the tradition of good comedy writing. Other works of pure literature unconnected with propaganda are such novels as Le Sage's *Gil Blas* (1715) and Prévost's *Manon Lescaut* (1731). Toward the close of the century the poet Chénier (1762-1794) sounded the first note of authentic lyricism that had been heard in France for many decades.

But the most significant writer of France during the eighteenth century was not Voltaire but the Swiss-born Rousseau (1712-1778). He taught the essential goodness of human nature, the rightness of our instincts, and the corruption of civilized institutions. He was the man of feeling in an age when the intellect was worshiped. He was a reformer of education, an inspirer of revolutionary ideas in government and economics, and in literature a forerunner of romanticism. He has probably had more influence on ideas than any other man of the eighteenth century.

The Romantic Movement a revolt against classicism

Between the outbreak of the French Revolution in 1789 and the final overthrow of Napoleon in 1815, the minds of Frenchmen were turned chiefly to outward events. Otherwise the full force of the Romantic Movement which was sweeping over northern Europe might have been felt earlier in France. Romanticism, however, has ideals diametrically opposed to those of French classicism. In so far as it stands for the exaltation of the emotions above reason and of the individual above society, it is not wholly suited to the French mind. It made its first appearance in the stories of Chateaubriand (1768-1848) and in Madame de Staël's interpretation of Germany as the land of romantic ideals. It found expression also in the sentimental poetry of Lamartine (1790-1869). But the real battle of romanticism in France was fought regarding poetic tragedy. The production of Victor Hugo's *Hernani* in 1830 marked the triumph of the movement.

The dramatic unities of time and place were abolished and metrical freedom was won. Victor Hugo (1802–1885) was the outstanding genius of the Romantic School and its recognized leader. He was prolific alike in poetry, drama, and fiction, but is regarded now as supreme only in lyric poetry. Other poets associated with the movement were the austere and pessimistic Vigny (1799–1863), Gautier (1811–1872), a pagan devotee of beauty and art, and Alfred de Musset (1810–1857), who best exemplifies romantic melancholy. All three also wrote novels and short stories, and Musset won a belated success with his plays. The older Dumas (1802–1870) wrote *The Three Musketeers* and other romances which have gained world fame. Mérimée (1803–1870) was a master of shorter fiction. The most famous woman writer of France, who adopted the pseudonym of George Sand (1804–1876), is seen at her best in her peasant stories. Sainte-Beuve (1804–1869), the greatest of French literary critics, showed romantic expansiveness in his hospitality to all ideas and in his unfailing endeavor to understand and interpret authors rather than to judge them.

By the middle of the nineteenth century romanticism had spent its force. It had opened fresh sources of inspiration by freeing the individual from artificial rules and conventions. It had revivified all branches of literature, but it undoubtedly left its richest legacy in poetry. Foreign influences played a big part in this renewal, especially those of Shakespeare, Scott, and Byron.

Realism develops along with science and industrialism

Romanticism was followed by realism, the attempt to depict life as it is. This was partly due to a reaction against the extravagances of romanticism, but it was also in large measure the result of the development of science and the growth of industrialism and commerce. The prevailing temper in literature was now its concern with actuality. Balzac (1799–1850) was the most prominent representative of realism in fiction. His *Human Comedy*, as he called his vast collection of novels, was the most ambitious scheme ever devised by a writer of fiction — nothing less than a complete contemporary history of his countrymen. Realism appeared also in the prose dramas of the younger Dumas and of Augier. An attempt to be objective and scientific was made even in poetry by the group of writers known as the Parnassians, the most distinguished of whom was Leconte de Lisle (1818–1894). The realists as a rule saw life without illusions and were apt to dwell on its more depressing and sordid aspects. This tendency appears in an intensified degree in the morbid poetry of Baudelaire (1821–1867), who stands somewhat apart from other writers of his day, but who was destined to have a great influence on the next generation.

With the growth of the scientific outlook, realism deepened into naturalism, which regards man as simply a part of nature to be explained by purely physical laws. Naturalism is represented in the works of the philosopher Taine (1828–1893), in Flaubert's great novel *Madame Bovary* (1857), in the short stories of Maupassant (1850–1893), in the fiction of Zola (1840–1902), and in the stories of Daudet (1840–1897).

Symbolism brings a new freedom to French poetry

Inevitably there was a reaction against the pessimism and brutality of naturalism. A movement known as *symbolism* appeared in poetry. Symbolism used subtle suggestion instead of precise statement, evoking moods and feelings by the magic of words and the cadence of verse. Verlaine (1844–1896) was the most gifted and popular of the symbolist poets. The movement is also represented in prose by the dream plays of the Belgian Maeterlinck (1862–1949), who wrote in French. As the result of the metrical experimentation and " free verse " of symbolism, French poetry is no longer as strictly traditional in form as it once was.

Contemporary French authors stress self-discovery and question tradition

Early twentieth-century French literature was eclectic, with all kinds of tendencies represented, but with no single one dominant for any great length of time. The eminent scholar Renan (1823–1892) and his disciple, the novelist Anatole France (1844–1924), believed that absolute truth is forever beyond human reach and that consequently all questions should be viewed from many sides. In contrast to this philosophy, which the French labeled " dilettantism," were the romantic and immensely popular poetic dramas of Edmond Rostand (1868–1918), especially *Cyrano de Bergerac* (first performed in 1897).

In recent years the principal interest of French authors is the development of methods that define and stabilize personality. Marcel Proust (1871–1922), in *Remembrance of Things Past,* seeks through the stimulation of memory to revitalize intense psychological experiences of his past and to relate them to a Parisian society in which the old aristocracy decays while the middle class grows in stature and authority.

Jean-Paul Sartre (1905–   ), together with many other contemporary French authors, is an exponent of *existentialism*, a philosophy based on the belief that everything extraneous to the existence of the individual is valueless. His novel *Nausea* (1938), his short story *The Wall* (1939), and his plays *The Flies* (1942) and *No Exit* (1944) illustrate this philosophy. *Nausea* is the journal of a man from whom one traditional value after another falls away. Immediate impressions make him sick. The values of words, of history, of organizations like the state all seem worthless. What is left is his essence, his freedom in an illogical world to define himself.

André Gide (1869–1951) assumed that each human being is unique; he therefore considered it of first importance for everyone to discover what he really is. His principal characters search, through self-examination, for what Gide called " sincerity." To be " sincere " is to dare to express in action one's deepest instincts, even though in so doing one breaks conventional moral laws. To Gide, even an unmotivated act is moral if it results in some measure of self-discovery. His most important novels are *The Immoralist* (1902), *Lafcadio's Adventures* (1914), and *The Counterfeiters* (1926).

André Malraux (1901–   ), believing that an individual's sense of freedom is most vital when he acts in time of crisis, sets his novels in the context of war and revolution. *The Conquerors* (1928) and *Man's Fate* (1933) deal with revolution in China; *Man's Hope* (1938) with the Civil War in Spain; *Days of Wrath* (1935) with Nazi concentration camps. In his novels Malraux adopts two different artistic methods: in some, he covers his canvas with masses of men revealed in brief flashes and with rapid changes of characters and locale; in others, the solitary individual is his subject, and he throws a glaring spotlight on significant moments of the individual's life.

Jean Cocteau (1891–   ) personifies his poetical ideas in plays, novels, films, and drawings. His two best novels, *Thomas the Impostor* and *Enfants Terribles* (*The Holy Terrors*), derive from what he calls " the mythology of childhood." The impostor is a soldier who is killed at the moment he is feigning death to avoid being shot. The " holy terrors " are a brother and a sister who live in a self-created dream world, where their perverse love for each other brings them death. Cocteau believes that life is a magical time in which the individual lives out the fables he himself creates.

Albert Camus (1913–   ), winner of the Nobel prize in 1957, shows in *The Stranger* and *The Myth of Sisyphus* that life is absurd, nothing but a series of logically unconnected present moments. In his later novels, notably *The Rebel*, although he still accepts the self-evident absurdity of life, he holds that the individual who chooses to live must devote himself to activity that will benefit his fellow men.

Jean Anouilh (1910–   ), the most honored of contemporary French dramatists, finds it comic that life is meaningless. *Ring Round the Moon* and *The Waltz of the Toreadors* present sardonically the deflation of self-important characters who are forced to accept nonsense as reality.

Paul Claudel (1868–1955), a Catholic poet and dramatist, was unlike the above pessimists. His plays *The Tidings Brought to Mary* (1910) and *The Satin Slipper* (1928) portray the universal tension between God and the world. Claudel placed a transcendant value on the language of poetry, which to him is the syntax or symbol that relates God to earthly experience.

Modern French authors can thus be regarded predominantly as rebels against traditional social and moral laws and as skeptics, who question romantic views of the value of human personality.

THE *FABLIAU* OF THE THREE HUNCHBACKS

The *fabliaux* are short humorous stories in verse, for the most part by unknown writers of the thirteenth and fourteenth centuries. About two hundred of them are in existence today. They are at the opposite pole from the courtly poetry with its artificial pictures of knights and ladies and its elaboration of the subtleties of love. They describe ordinary life and people and ridicule the absurdities and abuses of the time.

> Good Sirs, an ye would briefly hear
> A lively tale and true, give ear!
>
> Once on a time there lived in Tours
> An honest gentleman, but poor,
> Whose only daughter, passing fair,   5
> Was courted by a millionaire.
> But, as it chanced, though well-to-do,
> The lover was a hunchback too!

т. an: if.

Nor was that all — his face, alack,
Was no whit better than his back;
His hair, a mop; his head, immense;
Monstrum horrendum et ingens!
Small wonder that the girl demurred!
But when the father still decried
Her attitude as quite absurd,   15
She, all too dutiful, complied,
And found herself a hunchback's bride.

But, when the honeymoon was o'er,
Beside the faults she knew before,
The luckless lady found that he   20
Had yet one other — jealousy.
Masculine callers might have knocked
Upon his door until doomsday;
He kept it locked and double-locked —
The poor wife almost pined away.   25

At last it happed, one Christmas-tide,
Three men, three minstrels, got inside;
Three hunchbacked minstrels, bowed and bent,
Who brought to bear this argument:
Since they had humps as well as he,   30
It followed by analogy,
If he had meat on Christmas day,
And drink beside — why! so should they.
He liked their logic, strange to say,
And shared with them his festal cheer,   35
And to their songs lent willing ear,
And gave them each some farthings ten;
But afterward, right there and then,
Proffered this counsel, brief but clear:
If they should come again,   40
They wouldn't find a cheerful giver,
But *would* be chucked into the river.
And so the minstrels went their way,
Content with their successful day.

During this masculine merriment   45
The hapless wife of course was sent

12. **Monstrum horrendum et ingens:** a horrible and enormous monster.
13. **demurred:** objected.   14. **decried:** belittled.   31. **analogy:** similarity.

To comfort her as best she might.
Nevertheless, though locked from sight,
She heard their voices through the wall,
And vowed, whatever might befall,   50
She'd hear again that merry song.
Nor tarried the occasion long,
For presently her husband went
To his affairs, whereon she sent
A servant on the minstrels' track,   55
And they, not loth, came quickly back.
Inside the house again they sang,
And all the walls with merriment rang.

But while they sang, and while the dame
Listened and laughed, the husband came   60
Inopportunely back! — Alas!
Was ever wife in such a pass? —
Beside the hearth a huge box stood,
Half filled with logs of hickory wood,
With three compartments — just the size   65
For hiding guests from husbands' eyes.
And each compartment of the chest
Contained eftsoon a hunchbacked guest.
The lady slammed each heavy lid,
And thus the three were safely hid. —   70
The jealous husband came, and went,
With never a thought of discontent.

Fair Sirs, are ye prepared to hear
A thing most tragical, most drear? —
When, hardly of her husband rid,   75
The lady raised again each lid,
And those three prisoners uncovered,
She found them all completely smothered! —
Alack! no remedy avails,
All three are dead as three door-nails.   80

It was an evil plight, and yet
Her woman's wits were not upset.

68. **eftsoon: soon afterwards.**

She hailed a porter, who, it fell,
Was passing by: " I'll pay thee well,
My honest fellow, an thou ask   85
No questions, only do thy task."
" Agreed," quoth he, with ready zest;
Whereon she led him to the chest,
And, opening one compartment, showed
One lifeless hunchback. " Take this load   90
My worthy man, upon thy back —
Here, tie it up in this stout sack —
And tumble it in yonder river."
He did as bid with never a quiver,
And, once his burden overboard,   95
Returned apace for his reward.

But hold! the dame sits not, meanwhile,
Idling the time in smirk or smile.
One guest is sped — still linger twain.
The second now, with might and main,   100
She hoists and hauls upon the floor
And leaves convenient to the door.
The porter, coming for his pay,
Hunchback the First out of the way,
Stops in his tracks.   Then quick the dame: 105
" Thou churl!   Thou empty of all shame!
What meaneth pray, this foolery?
Why bring the hunchback back with thee? "
The poor wight scratched his muddled head.
" I' faith," quoth he, " I thought him dead.   110
I dropped him deep some fathom ten —
And now he turns up here again?
Alack, my lady, we're undone;
This surely is the Evil One.
But, fiend incarnate though he be,   115
I'll fix him yet, and God help me!
A pox, a murrain on his head!
I'll put him where he'll know he's dead."
Forthwith he thrust him in the sack
And took him off upon his back. —   120

---

82. fell: happened.   106. churl: ill-bred fellow.   117. murrain: plague.

The lady's task is nearly done,
Of hunchbacks there is left but one.
She drags him out upon the floor
To wait the porter as before.

Meanwhile that worthy, from the brink,   125
Was watching Hunchback Second sink.
" Unholy miscreant," muttered he,
" The river is the place for thee! "
Then hurried back to get his pay,
And found — Good Sirs, what need to say? —   130
Hunchback the Third he seized in wrath
And took once more the river path.
" Into the river for good! " cried he;
" This, I hope, is the last of thee!
Into the river, quick or dead,   135
And if I see thine ugly head,
Or uglier hump, again, thou knave,
By all the Saints, and several more,
I'll tan thee so with my good stave,
Thou'lt wish thou hadst been dead before."   140

So saying, he returned once more,
And found again the lady's door.
But, ere he entered, haply glanced
Over his shoulder. — As it chanced,
Upon his very heel-taps came   145
The hunchback husband of the dame! —
The honest porter well-nigh died.
He crossed himself nine times, and cried:
" *Dei nomine,* wretched me! "
And then continued wrathfully: 150
" God's wounds! the scurvy fellow lacks
All wit, to follow in my tracks.
Mayhap he thinks me from the country —
I never heard of such effrontery! "
On that he gripped his quarterstaff,   155
And shouted loud, with angry laugh:

---

127. miscreant: vile wretch.   135. quick: living.   143. haply: by chance.
149. Dei nomine: in God's name.   155. quarterstaff: cudgel.

" By our Holy Mother, we shall see
If I'm the fool thou thinkest me! "
One swing of his cudgel — one, no more —
One goodly rap, and all was o'er.   160
Into the sack and overboard
Went husband then without a word;
Ten fathom deep, tied in the sack,
And he, in truth, didn't come back.
At last the porter's task was done,   165
At last he was rid of the Evil One.

And so the worthy man returned
And got the wage so hardly earned.
The lady paid ungrudgingly,
And added a gratuity —   170
Who wouldn't give a sou or so,
To lose a husband quite *de trop?*

(Frederick Bliss Luquiens)

170. **gratuity:** tip.   171. **sou:** cent.   172. **de trop:** superfluous.

SUGGESTIONS FOR STUDY

1. It has been said that in the *fabliau* everything is turned into fun, immorality is not rebuked, and no sympathy is shown for its victims. To what extent is that true of this fabliau?

2. Compare " The Three Hunchbacks " with La Fontaine's " Women and Secrets " (page 83) as types of folk humor.

3. Does modern literature show any type comparable to the *fabliau?* Could this plot be used as the basis for a farce on the modern stage? Why or why not?

THE SONG OF ROLAND

The Song of Roland (eleventh century) may be called the national epic of France. It belongs to a cycle of poems celebrating the heroic achievements of Charlemagne and his twelve paladins or principal warriors, among whom Roland was the favorite hero of the French people. The author is unknown. The poem is distinguished for its straightforward simplicity and its spirit of patriotism. " Sweet France " is an expression which constantly recurs. There are about six thousand lines, linked in couplets by assonance or the similarity of sound between the last accented vowels of the adjacent lines. The hero Roland is in command of the rear-guard of Charlemagne's army on its retreat from an expedition against the Moors in Spain. He is cut off by the Moors in the pass of Roncevaux and mortally wounded.

But Rollant felt that death had made a way
Down from his head till on his heart it lay;
Beneath a pine running in haste he came,
On the green grass he lay there on his face;
His olifant and sword beneath him placed,   5
Turning his head towards the pagan race,
Now this he did, in truth, that Charles might say
(As he desired) and all the Franks his race: —
" Ah, gentle count; conquering he was slain! " —
He owned his faults often and every way,   10
And for his sins his glove to God upraised.

But Rollant feels he's no more time to seek;
Looking to Spain, he lies on a sheer peak,
And with one hand upon his breast he beats:
" *Mea culpa!* God, by Thy Virtues clean   15
Me from my sins, the mortal and the mean,
Which from the hour that I was born have been
Until this day, when life is ended here! "
Holds out his glove towards God, as he speaks;
Angels descend from heaven on that scene.   20

The count Rollant, beneath a pine he sits;
Turning his eyes towards Spain, he begins
Remembering so many divers things:
So many lands where he went conquering,
And France the Douce, the heroes of his kin,   25
And Charlemagne, his lord who nourished him.
Nor can he help but weep and sigh at this.
But his own self, he's not forgotten him,
He owns his faults, and God's forgiveness bids:
" Very Father, in Whom no falsehood is,   30
Saint Lazaron from death Thou didst remit,
And Daniel save from the lions' pit;
My soul in me preserve from all perils

5. olifant: ivory horn.   15. **Mea culpa:** my guilt.   25. **Douce:** sweet.
31. **Lazaron:** Lazarus.   See John 11.   32. **Daniel:** See Daniel 6.

And from the sins I did in life commit! "
His right-hand glove, to God he offers it;   35
Saint Gabriel from 's hand hath taken it.
Over his arm his head bows down and slips,
He joins his hands: and so is life finish'd.
God sent him down His angel cherubin,
And Saint Michael, we worship in peril;   40
And by their side Saint Gabriel alit;
So the count's soul they bare to Paradis.

(C. K. Scott-Moncrieff)

39. **Cherubin:** more commonly cherubim, the plural of cherub, an angelic being.

SUGGESTIONS FOR STUDY

1. What thoughts are uppermost in the mind of Roland as he lies dying? Compare with the death of King Arthur as told by Mallory or Tennyson.
2. Point out instances of assonance in the place of rhyme. How does the style differ from that of the English epic *Beowulf?*
3. What are some of the features common to all folk epics? Read the selection from the *Song of the Nibelungs* (see page 422) for suggestions.
4. What other national epics can you name? For special reading on epics consult the introduction and the reading lists of each nation in this volume. Guerber's *Book of the Epics* gives condensed accounts of all the major epics.

AUCASSIN AND NICOLETTE

This tender love story was written by an unknown author in the latter half of the twelfth century. With its alternations of verse and prose, it forms the connecting link between the older poetic romances and the prose fiction of a later day.

'Tis of Aucassin and Nicolette.

Who would list to the good lay
Gladness [1] of the captive gray?
'Tis how two young lovers met,
Aucassin and Nicolette,
Of the pains the lover bore
And the sorrows he outwore,
For the goodness and the grace
Of his love, so fair of face.

Sweet the song, the story sweet,
There is no man hearkens it,
No man living 'neath the sun,
So outwearied, so foredone.[2]
Sick and woeful, worn and sad,
But is healèd, but is glad
'Tis so sweet.

1 **gladness:** solace.   2 **foredone:** exhausted.

So say they, speak they, tell they the Tale:

How the Count Bougars de Valence made war on Count Garin de Biaucaire, war so great, and so marvelous, and so mortal that never a day dawned but always he was there, by the gates and walls, and barriers of the town with a hundred knights, and ten thousand men at arms, horsemen and footmen: so burned he the Count's land, and spoiled his country, and slew his men. Now the Count Garin de Biaucaire was old and frail, and his good days were gone over. No heir had he, neither son nor daughter, save one young man only; such an one as I shall tell you. Aucassin was the name of the damoiseau: [3] fair was he, goodly, and great, and featly [4] fashioned of his body, and limbs. His hair was yellow, in little curls, his eyes blue and laughing, his face beautiful and shapely, his nose high and well set, and so richly seen was he in all things good, that in him was none evil at all. But so suddenly overtaken was he of Love, who is a great master, that he would not, of his will, be dubbed knight, nor take arms, nor follow tourneys, nor do whatsoever him beseemed. Therefore his father and mother said to him:

" Son, go take thine arms, mount thy horse, and hold thy land, and help thy men, for if they see thee among them, more stoutly will they keep in battle their lives, and lands, and thine, and mine."

" Father," said Aucassin, " I marvel that you will be speaking. Never may God give me aught of my desire if I be made knight, or mount my horse, or face stour [5] and battle wherein knights smite and are smitten again, unless thou give me Nicolette, my true love, that I love so well."

" Son," said the father, " this may not be. Let Nicolette go, a slave girl she is, out of a strange land, and the captain of this town bought her of the Saracens, and carried her hither, and hath reared her and let christen the maid, and took her for his daughter in God, and one day will find a young man for her, to win her bread honorably. Herein hast thou nought to make or mend, but if a wife thou wilt have, I will give thee the daughter of a King, or a Count. There is no man so rich in France, but if thou desire his daughter, thou shalt have her."

" Faith! my father," said Aucassin, " tell me where is the place so high in all the world, that Nicolette, my sweet lady and love, would not grace it well? If she were Empress of Constantinople or of Ger-

---

3 **damoiseau:** young man.   5 **stour:** conflict.
4 **featly:** neatly.

many, or Queen of France or England, it were little enough for her; so gentle is she and courteous, and debonaire,[6] and compact of all good qualities."

Here singeth one:

Aucassin was of Biaucaire
Of a goodly castle there,
But from Nicolette the fair
None might win his heart away,
Though his father, many a day,
And his mother said him nay.
"Ha! fond child, what wouldest thou?
Nicolette is glad enow![7]
Was from Carthage cast away,

Paynims[8] sold her on a day!
Wouldst thou win a lady fair,
Choose a maid of high degree;
Such an one is meet for thee."
"Nay of these I have no care,
Nicolette is debonaire.
Her body sweet and the face of her
Take my heart as in a snare,
Loyal love is but her share
That is so sweet."

Then speak they, say they, tell they the Tale:

When the Count Garin de Biaucaire knew that he would not avail to withdraw Aucassin his son from the love of Nicolette, he went to the Captain of the city, who was his man, and spake to him saying:

" Sir Count: away with Nicolette thy daughter in God; cursed be the land whence she was brought into this country, for by reason of her do I lose Aucassin, that will neither be dubbed knight, nor do aught of the things that fall to him to be done. And wit ye well," he said, " that, if I might have her at my will, I would burn her in a fire, and yourself might well be sore adread."

" Sir," said the Captain, " this is grievous to me that he comes and goes and hath speech with her. I had bought the maiden at mine own charges, and nourished her, and baptized, and made her my daughter in God. Yea, I would have given her to a young man that should win her bread honorably. With this had Aucassin thy son naught to make or mend. But, sith[9] it is thy will and thy pleasure, I will send her into that land and that country where never will he see her with his eyes."

" Have a heed to thyself," said the Count Garin, " thence might great evil come on thee."

So parted they from each other. Now the Captain was a right rich man: so had he a rich palace with a garden in face of it; in an upper chamber thereof he let place Nicolette with one old woman to keep her company, and in that chamber put bread and meat and wine and such things as were needful. Then he let seal the door, that none

---

[6] **debonaire:** friendly, pleasant.
[7] **enow:** enough.
[8] **Paynims:** Muslims.
[9] **sith:** since.

might come in or go forth, save that there was one window, over against the garden, and strait [10] enough, where through came to them a little air.

Here singeth one:

Nicolette as ye heard tell
Prisoned is within a cell
That is painted wondrously
With colors of a far countrie,
And the window of marble wrought,
There the maiden stood in thought,
With straight brows and yellow hair
Never saw ye fairer fair!
On the wood she gazed below,
And she saw the roses blow,
Heard the birds sing loud and low,
Therefore spoke she woefully:

" Ah me, wherefore do I lie
Here in prison wrongfully:
Aucassin, my love, my knight,
Am I not thy heart's delight,
Thou that lovest me aright!
'Tis for thee that I must dwell
In the vaulted chamber cell,
Hard beset and all alone!
By our Lady Mary's Son
Here no longer will I wonn,[11]
If I may flee! "

Then speak they, say they, tell they the Tale:

Nicolette was in prison, as ye have heard soothly,[12] in the chamber. And the noise and bruit [13] of it went through all the country and all the land, how that Nicolette was lost. Some said she had fled the country, and some that the Count Garin de Biaucaire had let slay her. Whosoever had joy thereof, Aucassin had none, so he went to the Captain of the town and spoke to him, saying:

" Sir Captain, what hast thou made of Nicolette, my sweet lady and love, the thing that best I love in all the world? Hast thou carried her off or ravished her away from me? Know well that if I die of it, the price shall be demanded of thee, and that will be well done, for it shall be even as if thou hadst slain me with thy two hands, for thou hast taken from me the thing that in this world I loved the best."

" Fair Sir," said the Captain, " let these things be. Nicolette is a captive that I did bring from a strange country. Yea, I bought her at my own charges of the Saracens, and I bred her up and baptized her, and made her my daughter in God. And I have cherished her, and one of these days I would have given her a young man, to win her bread honorably. With this thou hast naught to make, but do thou take the daughter of a King or a Count. Nay more, what wouldst thou deem thee to have gained, hadst thou made her thy leman,[14] and taken her to thy bed? Plentiful lack of comfort hadst thou got

---

[10] **strait:** narrow.
[11] **wonn:** dwell.
[12] **soothly:** truly.

[13] **bruit:** fame.
[14] **leman:** sweetheart.

thereby, for in Hell would thy soul have lain while the world endures, and into Paradise wouldst thou have entered never."

"In Paradise what have I to win? Therein I seek not to enter, but only to have Nicolette. my sweet lady that I love so well. For into Paradise go none but such folk as I shall tell thee now. Thither go these same old priests, and halt old men and maimed, who all day and night cower continually before the altars, and in the crypts; [15] and such folk as wear old amices [16] and old clouted [17] frocks, and naked folk and shoeless, and covered with sores, perishing of hunger and thirst, and of cold, and of little ease. These be they that go into Paradise, with them have I naught to make. But into Hell would I fain go; for into Hell fare the goodly clerks, and goodly knights that fall in tourneys and great wars, and stout men at arms, and all men noble. With these would I liefly [18] go. And thither pass the sweet ladies and courteous that have two lovers, or three, and their lords also thereto. Thither goes the gold, and the silver, and cloth of vair, [19] and cloth of gris, [20] and harpers, and makers, [21] and the prince of this world. With these I would gladly go, let me but have with me Nicolette, my sweetest lady."

"Certes," quoth the Captain, "in vain wilt thou speak thereof, for never shalt thou see her; and if thou hadst word with her, and thy father knew it, he would let burn in a fire both her and me, and thyself might well be sore adread."

"That is even what irketh me," quoth Aucassin. So he went from the Captain sorrowing.

Here singeth one:

Aucassin did so depart
Much in dole [22] and heavy at heart
For his love so bright and dear,
None might bring him any cheer,
None might give good words to hear.
To the palace doth he fare,
Climbeth up the palace-stair,
Passeth to a chamber there,
Thus great sorrow doth he bear,
For his lady and love so fair.

"Nicolette, how fair art thou,
Sweet thy foot-fall, sweet thine eyes,
Sweet the mirth of thy replies,
Sweet thy laughter, sweet thy face,
Sweet thy lips and sweet thy brow,
And the touch of thine embrace.
All for thee I sorrow now,
Captive in an evil place,
Whence I ne'er may go my ways,
Sister, sweet friend!"

---

[15] **crypts:** vaults beneath churches.
[16] **amices:** priest's hoods or capes.
[17] **clouted:** patched.
[18] **liefly:** gladly.

[19] **vair:** squirrel fur.
[20] **gris:** gray fur.
[21] **makers:** poets.
[22] **dole:** grief.

[In a portion of the story which is omitted here, Aucassin's father promises to allow the youth to see Nicolette and talk with her after proving his worth in battle. Aucassin fights bravely and takes his country's invader captive. But the father breaks his word, and when Aucassin protests, he is thrown into a dungeon.]

Aucassin was cast into prison as ye have heard tell, and Nicolette, in another place, was in a chamber. Now it was summer time, the month of May, when days are warm, and long, and clear, and the night still and serene. Nicolette lay one night on her bed, and saw the moon shine clear through a window, yea, and heard the nightingale sing in the garden, so she minded her of Aucassin her lover whom she loved so well. Then fell she to thoughts of Count Garin de Biaucaire, that hated her to the death; therefore deemed she that there she would no longer abide, for that, if she were told of, and the Count knew whereas she lay, an ill death would he make her die. Now she knew that the old woman slept who held her company. Then she arose, and clad her in a mantle of silk she had by her, very goodly, and took napkins, and sheets of the bed, and knotted one to the other, and made therewith a cord as long as she might, so knitted it to a pillar in the window, and let herself slip down into the garden, then caught up her raiment in both hands, behind and before, and kilted up her kirtle,[23] because of dew that she saw lying deep on the grass, and so went her way down through the garden.

Her locks were yellow and curled, her eyes blue and smiling, her face featly fashioned, the nose high and fairly set, the lips more red than cherry or rose in time of summer, her teeth white and small; so slim she was in the waist that your two hands might have clipped [24] her, and the daisy flowers that brake beneath her as she went tiptoe, and that bent above her instep, seemed black against her feet, so white was the maiden. She came to the postern gate,[25] and unbarred it, and went out through the streets of Biaucaire, keeping always on the shadowy side, for the moon was shining right clear, and so wandered she till she came to the tower where her lover lay. The tower was flanked with buttresses, and she cowered under one of them, wrapped in her mantle. Then thrust she her head through a crevice of the tower that was old and worn, and so heard she Aucassin wailing within, and making dole and lament for the sweet lady he loved so well. And when she had listened to him she began to say:

---

[23] **kirtle**: skirt.
[24] **clipped**: embraced.

[25] **postern gate**: back gate.

Here one singeth:

Nicolette the bright of brow,
On a pillar leanest thou,
All Aucassin's wail dost hear
For his love that is so dear,
Then thou spakest, shrill and clear,
" Gentle knight withouten fear
Little good befalleth thee,
Little help of sigh or tear,
Ne'er shalt thou have joy of me.
Never shalt thou win me; still
Am I held in evil will

Of thy father and thy kin,
Therefore must I cross the sea,
And another land must win."
Then she cut her curls of gold,
Cast them in the dungeon hold.
Aucassin doth clasp them there,
Kissed the curls that were so fair,
Them doth in his bosom bear,
Then he wept, even as of old,
All for his love!

Then say they, speak they, tell they the Tale:

When Aucassin heard Nicolette say that she would pass into a far country, he was all in wrath.

" Fair sweet friend," quoth he, " thou shalt not go, for then wouldst thou be my death. And the first man that saw thee, and had the might withal, would take thee straightway into his bed to be his leman. And once thou camest into a man's bed and that bed not mine, wit ye well that I would not tarry till I had found a knife to pierce my heart and slay myself. Nay, verily, wait so long I would not; but would hurl myself on it so soon as I could find a wall, or a black stone, thereon would I dash my head so mightily, that the eyes would start, and my brain burst. Rather would I die even such a death, than know thou hadst lain in a man's bed, and that bed not mine."

" Aucassin," she said, " I trow thou lovest me not as much as thou sayest, but I love thee more than thou lovest me."

" Ah, fair sweet friend," said Aucassin, " it may not be that thou shouldst love me even as I love thee. Woman may not love man as man loves woman, for a woman's love lies in the glance of her eye, and the bud of her breast, and her foot's tiptoe, but the love of man is in his heart planted, whence it can never issue forth and pass away."

Now while Aucassin and Nicolette held this parley together, the town's guards came down a street, with swords drawn beneath their cloaks, for the Count Garin had charged them that if they could take her they should slay her. But the sentinel that was on the tower saw them coming, and heard them speaking of Nicolette as they went, and threatening to slay her.

" God! " quoth he, " this were great pity to slay so fair a maid!

Right great charity it were if I could say aught to her, and they perceive it not, and she should be on her guard against them, for if they slay her, then were Aucassin, my damoiseau, dead, and that were great pity."

Here one singeth:

Valiant was the sentinel,
Courteous, kind, and practiced well,
So a song did sing and tell
Of the peril that befell.
" Maiden fair that lingerest here,
Gentle maid of merry cheer,
Hair of gold, and eyes as clear
As the water in a mere,[26]
Thou, meseems, hast spoken word

To thy lover and thy lord,
That would die for thee, his dear;
Now beware the ill accord,
Of the cloaked men of the sword,
These have sworn and keep their
      word,
They will put thee to the sword
      Save thou take heed! "

Then speak they, say they, tell they the Tale:

" Ha! " quoth Nicolette, " be the soul of thy father and the soul of thy mother in the rest of Paradise, so fairly and so courteously hast thou spoken me! Please God, I will be right ware of them, God keep me out of their hands."

So she shrank under her mantle into the shadow of the pillar till they had passed by, and then took she farewell of Aucassin, and so fared till she came unto the castle wall. Now that wall was wasted and broken, and some deal mended, so she clomb thereon till she came between wall and fosse,[27] and so looked down, and saw that the fosse was deep and steep, whereat she was sore adread.

" Ah, God," saith she, " sweet Saviour! If I let myself fall hence, I shall break my neck, and, if here I abide, tomorrow they will take me and burn me in a fire. Yet liefer would I perish here than that tomorrow the folk should stare on me for a gazing-stock."

Then she crossed herself, and so let herself slip into the fosse, and when she had come to the bottom, her fair feet, and fair hands that had not custom thereof, were bruised and frayed, and the blood springing from a dozen places, yet felt she no pain nor hurt, by reason of the great dread wherein she went. But if she were in cumber [28] to win there, in worse was she to win out. But she deemed that there to abide was of none avail, and she found a pike sharpened, that they of the city had thrown out to keep the hold. Therewith made she one stepping place after another, till, with much travail,[29] she climbed the

---

26 **mere:** pond.
27 **fosse:** ditch.

28 **cumber:** difficulty.
29 **travail:** labor.

wall. Now the forest lay within two crossbow shots, and the forest was of thirty leagues this way and that. Therein also were wild beasts, and beasts serpentine, and she feared that if she entered there they would slay her. But anon she deemed that if men found her there they would hale [30] her back into the town to burn her.

Here one singeth:

Nicolette, the fair of face,
Climbed upon the coping stone,[31]
There made she lament and moan
Calling on our Lord alone
For his mercy and his grace.
" Father, king of Majesty,
Listen, for I nothing know
Where to flee or whither go.
If within the wood I fare,
Lo, the wolves will slay me there,
Boars and lions terrible,

Many in the wild wood dwell,
But if I abide the day,
Surely worse will come of it,
Surely will the fire be lit
That shall burn my body away.
Jesus, lord of Majesty,
Better seemeth it to me,
That within the wood I fare,
Though the wolves devour me there,
Than within the town to go,
    Ne'er be it so! "

Then speak they, say they, tell they the Tale:

Nicolette made great moan, as ye have heard; then commended she herself to God, and anon fared till she came unto the forest. But to go deep in it she dared not, by reason of the wild beasts, and beasts serpentine. Anon crept she into a little thicket, where sleep came upon her, and she slept till prime [32] next day, when the shepherds issued forth from the town and drove their bestial [33] between wood and water. Anon came they all into one place by a fair fountain which was on the fringe of the forest, thereby spread they a mantle, and thereon set bread. So while they were eating, Nicolette wakened, with the sound of the singing birds, and the shepherds, and she went unto them, saying, " Fair boys, our Lord keep you! "

" God bless thee," quoth he that had more words to his tongue than the rest.

" Fair boys," quoth she, " know ye Aucassin, the son of Count Garin de Biaucaire? "

" Yea, well we know him."

" So may God help you, fair boys," quoth she, " tell him there is a beast in this forest, and bid him come chase it, and if he can take it, he would not give one limb thereof for a hundred marks of gold, nay, nor for five hundred, nor for any ransom."

---

[30] **hale**: drag.
[31] **coping stone**: top stone of a wall.
[32] **prime**: sunrise.
[33] **bestial**: cattle.

Then looked they on her, and saw her so fair that they were all astonished.

" Will I tell him thereof? " quoth he that had more words to his tongue than the rest; " foul fall him who speaks of the things or tells him the tidings. These are but visions ye tell of, for there is no beast so great in this forest, stag, nor lion, nor boar, that one of his limbs is worth more than two deniers,[34] or three at the most, and ye speak of such great ransom. Foul fall him that believes your word, and him that telleth Aucassin. Ye be a Fairy, and we have none liking for your company, nay, hold on your road."

" Nay, fair boys," quoth she, " nay, ye will do my bidding. For this beast is so mighty of medicine that thereby will Aucassin be healed of his torment. And lo! I have five sols [35] in my purse, take them, and tell him: for within three days must he come hunting it hither, and, if within three days he find it not, never will he be healed of his torment."

" My faith," quoth he, " the money will we take, and if he come hither we will tell him, but seek him we will not."

" In God's name," quoth she; and so took farewell of the shepherds, and went her way.

Here one singeth:

Nicolette the bright of brow
From the shepherds doth she pass
All below the blossomed bough
Where an ancient way there was,
Overgrown and choked with grass,
Till she found the cross-roads where
Seven paths do all way fare,
Then she deemeth she will try,
Should her lover pass thereby,
If he love her loyally.
So she gathered white lilies,
Oak-leaf, that in green wood is,
Leaves of many a branch I wis,
Therewith built a lodge of green,
Goodlier was never seen,
Swore by God who may not lie,
" If my love the lodge should spy,
He will rest awhile thereby
If he love me loyally."
Thus his faith she deemed to try,
" Or I love him not, not I,
Nor he loves me! "

Then speak they, say they, tell they the Tale:

Nicolette built her lodge, of boughs, as ye have heard, right fair and feteously,[36] and wove it well, within and without, of flowers and leaves. So lay she hard by the lodge in a deep coppice [37] to know what Aucassin will do. And the cry and the bruit went abroad through all the country and all the land, that Nicolette was lost.

---

[34] **deniers:** farthings.
[35] **sols:** sous, cents.
[36] **feteously:** skilfully.
[37] **coppice:** grove of underbrush.

Some told that she had fled, and some that the Count Garin had let slay her. Whosoever had joy thereof, no joy had Aucassin. And the Count Garin, his father, had taken him out of prison, and had sent for the knights of that land, and the ladies, and let make a right great feast, for the comforting of Aucassin his son. Now at the high time of the feast, was Aucassin leaning from the gallery, all woeful and discomforted. Whatsoever men might devise of mirth, Aucassin had no joy thereof, nor no desire, for he saw not her that he loved. Then a knight looked on him, and came to him, and said:

"Aucassin, of that sickness of thine have I been sick, and good counsel will I give thee, if thou wilt hearken to me — "

"Sir," said Aucassin, "gramercy,[38] good counsel would I fain hear."

"Mount thy horse," quoth he, "and go take thy pastime in yonder forest, there wilt thou see the good flowers and grass, and hear the sweet birds sing. Perchance thou shalt hear some word, whereby thou shalt be the better."

"Sir," quoth Aucassin, "gramercy, that will I do."

He passed out of the hall, and went down the stairs, and came to the stable where his horse was. He let saddle and bridle him, and mounted, and rode forth from the castle, and wandered till he came to the forest, so rode till he came to the fountain and found the shepherds at point of noon. And they had a mantle stretched on the grass, and were eating bread, and making great joy.

Here singeth one:

There were gathered shepherds all,
Martin, Esmeric, and Hal,
Aubrey, Robin, great and small.
Saith the one, "Good fellows all,
God keep Aucassin the fair,
And the maid with yellow hair,

Bright of brow and eyes of vair,
She that gave us gold to ware,[39]
Cakes therewith to buy ye know,
Goodly knives and sheaths also,
Flutes to play, and pipes to blow,
May God him heal!"

· · · · ·

The night was fair and still, and so long he went that he came to the lodge of boughs, that Nicolette had builded and woven within and without, over and under, with flowers, and it was the fairest lodge that might be seen. When Aucassin was ware of it, he stopped suddenly, and the light of the moon fell therein.

"God!" quoth Aucassin, "here was Nicolette, my sweet lady, and this lodge builded she with her fair hands. For the sweetness of it, and for love of her, will I alight, and rest here this night long."

[38] **gramercy**: thank you.   [39] **ware**: keep.

He drew forth his foot from the stirrup to alight, and the steed was great and tall. He dreamed so much on Nicolette his right sweet lady, that he slipped on a stone, and drave his shoulder out of its place. Then knew he that he was hurt sore, natheless he bore him with what force he might, and fastened with the other hand the mare's son to a thorn. Then turned he on his side, and crept backwise into the lodge of boughs. And he looked through a gap in the lodge and saw the stars in heaven, and one that was brighter than the rest; so began he to say:

Here one singeth:

" Star, that I from far behold,
Star, the Moon calls to her fold,
Nicolette with thee doth dwell,
My sweet love with locks of gold,
God would have her dwell afar,
Dwell with him for evening star.
Would to God, whate'er befell,

Would that with her I might dwell.
I would clip her close and strait.
Nay, were I of much estate,
Some king's son desirable,
Worthy she to be my mate,
Me to kiss and clip me well,
Sister, sweet friend! "

So speak they, say they, tell they the Tale:

When Nicolette heard Aucassin, right so came she unto him, for she was not far away. She passed within the lodge, and threw her arms about his neck, and clipped and kissed him.

" Fair sweet friend, welcome be thou."

" And thou, fair sweet love, be thou welcome."

So either kissed and clipped the other, and fair joy was them between.

" Ha! sweet love," quoth Aucassin, " but now was I sore hurt, and my shoulder wried,[40] but I take no force of it, nor have no hurt therefrom since I have thee."

Right so felt she his shoulder and found it was wried from its place. And she so handled it with her white hands, and so wrought in her surgery, that, by God's will who loveth lovers, it went back into its place. Then took she flowers, and fresh grass, and leaves green, and bound these herbs on the hurt with a strip of her smock, and he was all healed.

" Aucassin," saith she, " fair sweet love, take counsel what thou wilt do. If thy father let search this forest tomorrow, and men find me here, they will slay me, come to thee what will."

" Certes, fair sweet love, therefore should I sorrow heavily, but, an if I may, never shall they take thee."

[40] **wried:** twisted awry.

Anon gat he on his horse, and his lady before him, kissing and clip-ping her, and so rode they at adventure.

Here one singeth:

Aucassin the frank, the fair,
Aucassin of the yellow hair,
Gentle knight, and true lover,
From the forest doth he fare,
Holds his love before him there,
Kissing cheek, and chin, and eyes,
But she spake in sober wise,
" Aucassin, true love and fair,
To what land do we repair? "

" Sweet my love, I take no care,
Thou art with me everywhere! "
So they pass the woods and downs,
Pass the villages and towns,
Hills and dales and open land,
Came at dawn to the sea sand,
Lighted down upon the strand,
    Beside the sea.

(Andrew Lang)

[In the remainder of the story, the lovers are captured by Saracens and carried away in separate vessels. Aucassin escapes and on his return home finds his parents dead and rules in their place. Meanwhile, Nicolette is restored to her father, the King of Carthage. But when he wishes to arrange a marriage for her, she steals away disguised as a minstrel and reaches the palace of Aucassin to whom she reveals herself. The tale ends with their happy marriage.]

SUGGESTIONS FOR STUDY

1. How much of the spirit of the Middle Ages do you find in the tale? Give some concrete examples from the incident, characterization, and language of the tale.

2. Pick out a speech of Aucassin's which anticipates the Renaissance in its pagan tone.

3. One of the distinctive marks of *Aucassin and Nicolette* is the inter-mingled verse. How much of this verse is mere comment? Where does it further the progress of the plot? Does it add to your enjoyment of the story or detract from it?

4. It has been conjectured that the unknown author of this tale was probably a wise, kind old man because of the grandfatherly indulgence with which he treats the lovers. What do you think of this suggestion?

5. How does *Aucassin and Nicolette* compare with the general run of modern love stories as to (a) credibility, (b) characterization, (c) narra-tive skill, (d) stock of ideas, (e) charm of style?

The Troubadours and the Trouvères

The troubadours of Provence in southern France and their counterparts, the trouvères of northern France, were wandering poets, who attached themselves to princes and nobles. They glorified the lady of the castle in their songs or inspired their host's subjects to deeds of loyalty. In spite of the romantic glamour that invests the age of chivalry, it must be confessed that the troubadours are often disappointing poets. Love is their perpetual theme, and the type is always the same. The lover is a feudal vassal, who worships his liege lady from a distance, while she in turn treats him with haughty indifference. This artificial situation becomes monotonous through repetition and deprives the poems of the ring of sincerity. Only a few of the poets rise above such conventions and express their natural feelings.

BERNARD DE VENTADOUR (Late Twelfth Century)

Bernard de Ventadour was of humble origin, yet because of his poetic gifts he gained the love of the Viscountess of Ventadour. Driven away from her court, he received a gracious welcome from Queen Eleanor of Guienne. His poems, of which we possess some fifty specimens, are among the best productions of the troubadours.

WHEN I BEHOLD THE LARK UPSPRING

When I behold the lark upspring
　　To meet the bright sun joyfully,
How he forgets to poise his wing,
　　In his gay spirits revelry, —
Alas! that mournful thoughts should spring　　　　5
　　E'en from that happy songster's glee!
Strange, that such gladdening sight should bring
　　Not joy, but pining care, to me!

I thought my heart had known the whole
　　Of love, but small its knowledge proved;　　　　10
For still the more my longing soul
　　Loves on, itself the while unloved:
She stole my heart, myself she stole,
　　And all I prized from me removed;

She left me but the fierce control   15
Of vain desires for her I loved.

All self-command is now gone by,
  E'er since the luckless hour when she
Became a mirror to my eye,
  Whereon I gazed complacently: 20
Thou fatal mirror! there I spy
  Love's image; and my doom shall be,
Like young Narcissus, thus to sigh,
  And thus expire, beholding thee!

                  (*E. Taylor*)

23. **Narcissus:** in Greek mythology, the beautiful youth who fell in love with his own reflection in the pool.

THIBAUD DE BLAZON (Early Thirteenth Century)

Thibaud de Blazon was attached to the service of his namesake, King Thibaud of Navarre. Twenty-seven of his songs have been preserved.

I AM TO BLAME

I am to blame! — Why should I sing?
  My lays 'twere better to forget;
Each day to others joy may bring, —
  They can but give to me regret!
Love makes my heart so full of woe,   5
  That naught can please or soothe me more,
Unless the cruel cause would show
  Less coldness than I found of yore.
Yet wherefore all my cares repeat?
Love's woes, though painful, still are sweet.   10
               I am to blame!

I am to blame! — Was I not born
  To serve and love her all my life?
Although my recompense is scorn,
  And all my care with pain is rife, —   15

15. **rife:** abundant.

Yet should I die, nor ever know
What 'tis to be beloved again;
At least, my silent life shall show
How patiently I bore my chain.
Then wherefore all my griefs repeat?   20
Love's woes, though painful, still are sweet.
                                    I am to blame!

                                    (*L. S. Costello*)

SUGGESTIONS FOR STUDY

1. Point out differences in the moods of the preceding poems.
2. What impressions do you get from these poems of the age of chivalry?
3. "Love's woes, though painful, still are sweet." What other poems
do you know which express the mingled sadness and joy of love?

FRANÇOIS VILLON (1431–1465?)

The life of Villon is obscure and ends, so far as our knowledge goes, in
total darkness. Even his family name is uncertain, the name of Villon having been adopted by him from a man who had befriended him. The little
we do know about his life is unedifying enough. He was born in Paris,
apparently, where he attended the university and received the degrees of
bachelor and master of arts. In 1455 he killed a priest in a drunken brawl
and fled to Burgundy. The following year he was pardoned for this homicide on the grounds of self-defense. But his career as a criminal had only
begun. He was implicated in several robberies, underwent imprisonment,
and finally in 1463 was condemned to be hanged, but the sentence was
commuted to banishment. Thereafter he disappears entirely from history.
It is an irony that this wasted life, which was the cause of remorse to
Villon himself, should have glorified him in the imagination of posterity
and have made him the supreme example of the Bohemian poet, "the
Vagabond King."

Villon's poetry is found in two collections, the *Little Testament* and the
Great Testament, which get their name from the mock legacies he be-
queaths to his friends. In the latter are embedded the ballads which have
made him famous. A ballad, it should be explained, does not mean here a
short narrative poem, as is usually the case in English, but is the French
ballade, that is to say, a poem of a fixed metrical structure, in which each
stanza ends with the same refrain line, and an envoy or author's message
is added at the end. In these poems there is a personal note, a genuine emotional quality, a profound sense of the beauty and brevity of life, which

will always keep them vital. Villon put his heart and his life into his verses. There was no sham about him, no hiding of anything he felt. This unmistakable ring of personality and his sense of the importance of the individual make him seem, for all the medieval atmosphere that surrounds him, like a herald of the Renaissance.

THE BALLAD OF DEAD LADIES

Tell me now in what hidden way is
  Lady Flora the lovely Roman?
Where's Hipparchia, and where is Thaïs,
  Neither of them the fairer woman?
Where is Echo, beheld of no man   5
Only heard on river and mere, —
  She whose beauty was more than human?
But where are the snows of yester-year?

Where's Héloïse, the learned nun,
  For whose sake Abeillard, I ween,   10
Lost manhood and put priesthood on?
  (From Love he won such dule and teen!)
And where, I pray you, is the Queen
Who willed that Buridan should steer
  Sewed in a sack's mouth down the Seine?   15
But where are the snows of yester-year?

White Queen Blanche, like a queen of lilies,
  With a voice like any mermaiden, —
Bertha Broadfoot, Beatrice, Alice,
  And Ermengarde the lady of Maine, —   20
And that good Joan whom Englishmen
At Rouen doomed and burned her there, —
  Mother of God, where are they then?
But where are the snows of yester-year?

2. **Flora:** Flora, Hipparchia, and Thaïs were famous Roman and Greek beauties. 6. **mere:** lake. 10. **Abeillard:** (1079–1142) a celebrated scholastic philosopher who secretly married Héloïse, one of his pupils, and was mutilated by her kinsmen. Usually spelled Abélard. 12. **dule:** grief. 12. **teen:** affliction. 14. **Buridan:** a famous fourteenth-century philosopher, who is said to have escaped drowning at the hands of one of the queens of France. 17. **Blanche:** Blanche of Castile, Mother of King Louis IX of France, better known as St. Louis. 19. **Bertha Broadfoot:** like Beatrice, Alice, and Ermengarde, she was a famous French lady of royal descent. 21. **Joan:** Joan of Arc (1412–1431), the "Maid of Orleans," who drove the English out of France and was burned at the stake in Rouen.

> Nay, never ask this week, fair lord,   25
>   Where they are gone, nor yet this year,
> Save with this much for an overword, —
>   But where are the snows of yester-year?

(D. G. Rossetti)

THE BALLAD OF THOSE CONDEMNED TO BE HANGED

> Men, brother men, that after us yet live,
>   Let not your hearts too hard against us be;
> For if some pity of us poor men ye give,
>   The sooner God shall take of you pity.
>   Here are we five or six strung up, you see,   5
> And here the flesh that all too well we fed
> Bit by bit eaten and rotten, rent and shred,
>   And we the bones grow dust and ash withal;
> Let no man laugh at us discomforted,
>   But pray to God that He forgive us all.   10

> If we call on you, brothers, to forgive,
>   Ye should not hold our prayer in scorn, though we
> Were slain by law; ye know that all alive
>   Have not wit alway to walk righteously;
>   Make therefore intercession heartily   15
> With him that of a virgin's womb was bred,
> That his grace be not as a dry well-head
>   For us, not let hell's thunder on us fall;
> We are dead, let no man harry or vex us dead,
>   But pray to God that He forgive us all.   20

> The rain has washed and laundered us all five,
>   And the sun dried and blackened; yea, perdie,
> Ravens and pies with beaks that rend and rive
>   Have dug our eyes out, and plucked off for fee
>   Our beards and eyebrows; never are we free,   25
> Not once, to rest; but here and there still sped,
> Drive at its wild will by the wind's change led,
>   More pecked of birds than fruits on garden-wall;
> Men, for God's love, let no gibe here be said;
>   But pray to God that He forgive us all.   30

22. **perdie:** truly.   23. **rive:** tear.

Prince Jesus, that of all art lord and head,
Keep us, that hell be not our bitter bed;
We have nought to do in such a master's hall.
Be not ye therefore of our fellowhead,
But pray to God that He forgive us all.   35

(*A. C. Swinburne*)

34. fellowhead: fellowship.

SUGGESTIONS FOR STUDY

1. Read both poems aloud in order to get the effect of the verse form and particularly of the recurring line. Observe that the refrain in each case sums up the essential spirit of the poem. What material differences do you observe in the two poems? Point out some of the liberties which Rossetti takes with rhyme in his translation. Do you find this objectionable or pleasing to the ear?

2. " But where are the snows of yester-year? " This line has become almost as appealing to those of English speech as the original is to the French. Why? What is the poetic value of thinking about the irrecoverable past? What other poems in the same mood can you name?

3. What do these poems reveal of the poet's personality? Since Villon has been frequently used as a character by modern writers, some additional reading on his appearance in modern literature is interesting. Especially well known are R. L. Stevenson's short story, " A Lodging for the Night," Justin McCarthy's play, " If I Were King," and C. Friml's light opera, " The Vagabond King."

FRANÇOIS RABELAIS (1490?–1553)

Rabelais is the first representative French writer after the close of the Middle Ages. He has become almost a figure of legend. Even in his own day he acquired through his writings the reputation of being a great laugher and scoffer, a great drinker and glutton, and a wanton libertine. The adjective Rabelaisian has come to mean gross, sensual and obscene. But this is quite unfair to Rabelais, who had beneath his coarse, boisterous fun a very real and sincere earnestness.

He came from the beautiful Loire valley in central France. He was trained in the monasteries but disliked most of the features of the life there. He did, however, acquire a vast learning. Like Bacon in England, he seemed to want to make all knowledge his province. He was not only an eager reader of the classics, but he also studied science, took a degree in medicine, and was for a time a practicing physician. He entered into relations with most of the eminent Frenchmen of his day, some of whom were heretics in the eyes of the Church. It is probable that only the protection of powerful friends saved him from serious persecution and perhaps martyrdom. He exemplified to the full the spirit of free inquiry so characteristic of the Renaissance.

There was in Rabelais much of the same sort of exuberance that we find in the Elizabethans. He was full of the joy of living, abounding in animal spirits, fertile in ideas, and copious in language, with an enormous vocabulary that has probably been equaled only by Victor Hugo. His writings are cast in the form of fiction. The first part of his so-called "novel," *Gargantua and Pantagruel,* deals with the life of the giant Gargantua and the remaining sections with the exploits and sayings of the giant's son, Pantagruel. This huge and shapeless work is an extravaganza with a certain amount of hidden meaning. Perhaps the nearest approach to it in English is Swift's *Gulliver's Travels.* Rabelais pictures the monks as dirty, ignorant, and superstitious. He satirizes the government of the church and the administration of the law. He criticizes the militaristic spirit. Above all, he wants education reformed by stimulating curiosity and reflection instead of cramming the memory. Rabelais felt it was safer to cover up this criticism of existing institutions with buffoonery. Besides he loved fun and nonsense for their own sake.

GARGANTUA AND PANTAGRUEL

In the first of the following passages Rabelais describes life in the Abbey of Theleme, which is a secular community where everything is just the opposite of what is found in the monasteries and convents. It represents his ideal of the intelligent, happy life. Since human nature in his eyes was fundamentally good, he resented having any fetters imposed on it. " See that you live joyously " was his motto. In the second passage Panurge is the bosom friend of Pantagruel and his companion on the long journey to consult the oracle of the Holy Bottle.

HOW THE THELEMITES WERE GOVERNED, AND OF THEIR MANNER OF LIVING

All their life was spent not in laws, statutes, or rules, but according to their own free will and pleasure. They rose out of their beds when they thought good; they did eat, drink, labor, sleep, when they had a mind to it, and were disposed for it. None did awake them, none did offer to constrain them to eat, drink, nor to do any other thing, for so had Gargantua established it. In all their rule, and strictest tie of their order, there was but this one clause to be observed: *Do what thou wilt.*

Because men that are free, well born, well bred, and conversant [1] in honest companies, have naturally an instinct and spur that prompteth them unto virtuous actions, and withdraws them from vice, which is called honor. Those same men, when by base subjection and constraint they are brought under and kept down, turn aside from that noble disposition, by which they formerly were inclined to virtue, to shake off and break that bond of servitude, agreeable with the nature of man, to long after things forbidden, and to desire what is denied us.

By this liberty they entered into a very laudable emulation,[2] to do all of them what they saw did please one. If any of the gallants or ladies should say, " Let us drink," they would all drink. If any one of them said, " Let us play," they all played. If one said, " Let us go a-walking into the fields," they went all. If it were to go a-hawking, or a-hunting, the ladies mounted upon dainty well-paced nags, seated in a stately palfrey [3] saddle, carried on their lovely fists, miniardly [4] begloved every one of them, either a sparhawk,[5] or a laneret, or a merlin, and the young gallants carried the other kinds of hawks.

So nobly were they taught, that there was neither he nor she amongst them, but could read, write, sing, play upon several musical instruments, speak five or six several languages, and compose in them all very quaintly,[6] both in verse and prose. Never were seen so valiant knights, so noble and worthy, so dextrous and skillful both on foot and a horseback, more brisk and lively, more nimble and quick, or better handling all manner of weapons, than were there. Never were seen ladies so proper and handsome, so miniard and dainty, less froward,[7] or more ready with their hand, and with their needle, in every honest and free action belonging to that sex, than were there. For this reason, when the time came, that any man of the said abbey, either at the request of his parents, or for some other cause, had a mind to go out of it, he carried along with him one of the ladies, namely her whom he had before chosen for his mistress, and they were married together. And if they had formerly in Theleme lived in good devotion and amity, they did continue therein and increase it to a greater height in their state of matrimony: and did entertain that mutual

---

[1] **conversant**: well acquainted.
[2] **emulation**: rivalry.
[3] **palfrey**: saddle horse.
[4] **miniardly**: daintily.
[5] **sparhawk**: sparrow hawk, like laneret and merlin, a bird used in falconry.
[6] **quaintly**: skillfully.
[7] **froward**: perverse.

love till the very last day of their life, in no less vigor and fervency, than at the very day of their wedding.

HOW PANURGE ASKETH COUNSEL OF PANTAGRUEL WHETHER HE SHOULD MARRY, YEA OR NO

To this Pantagruel replying nothing, Panurge prosecuted the discourse he had already broached, and therewithal fetching, as from the bottom of his heart, a very deep sigh, said, " My lord and master, you have heard the design I am upon, which is to marry. I humbly beseech you, for the affection which of a long time you have borne me, to give me your best advice therein."

Then answered Pantagruel, " Seeing you have so decreed and taken deliberation thereon, and that the matter is fully determined, what need is there of any further talk thereof, but forthwith to put into execution what you have resolved? "

" Yea, but," quoth Panurge, " I would be loath to act anything therein without your counsel had thereto."

" It is my judgment, also," quoth Pantagruel, " and I advise you to it."

" Nevertheless," quoth Panurge, " if I understood aright, that it were much better for me to remain a bachelor as I am, than to run headlong upon new hare-brained undertakings of conjugal adventure, I would rather choose not to marry."

Quoth Pantagruel: " Then do not marry."

" Yea, but," quoth Panurge, " would you have me so solitarily drive out the whole course of my life, without the comfort of a matrimonial consort? [8] You know it is written: *Vae soli!* [9] and a single person is never seen to reap the joy and solace that is found with married folks."

" Then marry, in the name of God," quoth Pantagruel.

" But if," quoth Panurge, " my wife should make me a cuckold [10] — as it is not unknown unto you, how this hath been a very plentiful year in the production of that kind of cattle — I would fly out, and grow impatient beyond all measure and mean. I love cuckolds with my heart, for they seem unto me to be of a right honest conversation, and I truly do very willingly frequent their company; but should I die for it, I would not be one of their number. That is a point for me of a too sore prickling point."

8 **consort:** spouse.
9 **Vae soli:** woe to the one who is alone.
10 **cuckold:** deceived husband.

" Then do not marry," quoth Pantagruel, " for without all contro-versy this sentence of Seneca is infallibly true: ' What thou to others shalt have done, others will do the like to thee.' "

" Do you," quoth Panurge, " aver [11] that without all exception? "

" Yes, truly," quoth Pantagruel, " without all exception."

" Ho, ho," says Panurge, " by the wrath of a little devil, his mean-ing is, either in this world or in the other which is to come. Yet seeing I can no more want a wife, than a blind man his staff — were it not a great deal better for me to apply and associate myself to some one honest, lovely, and virtuous woman? . . ."

" Marry, then, in God's name! " quoth Pantagruel.

" But if," quoth Panurge, " it were the will of God, and that my destiny did unluckily lead me to marry an honest woman, who should beat me, I would be stored with more than two third parts of the patience of Job, if I were not stark mad by it, and quite distracted with such rugged dealings. For it hath been told me, that those ex-ceeding honest women have ordinarily very wicked headpieces; there-fore it is, that their family lacketh not for good vinegar.[12] Yet in that case should it go worse with me, if I did not then in such sort bang her back and breast, so thumpingly bethwack her gillets,[13] to wit, her arms, legs, head, lights,[14] liver, and milt,[15] with her other entrails, and mangle, jag, and slash her coats, so after the cross billet [16] fashion, that the greatest devil of hell should wait at the gate for the reception of her damned soul. I could make a shift for this year to waive such molestation [17] and disquiet, and be content to lay aside that trouble, and not to be engaged in it."

" Do not marry, then," answered Pantagruel.

" Yea, but," quoth Panurge, " considering the condition wherein I now am, out of debt and unmarried; mark what I say, free from all debt in an ill hour! for, were I deeply on the score, my creditors would be but too careful of my paternity, but being quit and not married nobody will be so regardful of me, or carry toward me a love like that which is said to be in a conjugal affection. And if by some mishap I should fall sick, I would be looked to very waywardly. The wise man saith, Where there is no woman, I mean, the mother of a

---

[11] **aver:** assert.
[12] **vinegar:** from their sour disposition.
[13] **gillets:** giblets, members.
[14] **lights:** lungs.
[15] **milt:** spleen.
[16] **cross billet:** criss-cross.
[17] **molestation:** troublesome interference.

family, and wife in the union of a lawful wedlock, the crazy and diseased are in danger of being ill used, and of having much brabbling [18] and strife about them; as by clear experience hath been made apparent in the persons of popes, legates, cardinals, bishops, abbots, priors, priests, and monks: but there, assure yourself, you shall not find me."

" Marry, then, in the name of God! " answered Pantagruel.

" But if," quoth Panurge, ". . . my wife, impatient of that drooping sickness, and faint-fits of a pining languishment, should abandon me, and not only then not help and assist me in my extremity and need, but withal flout [19] at, and make sport of that my grievous distress and calamity; or peradventure, which is worse, embezzle my goods, and steal from me, as I have seen it oftentimes befall unto the lot of many other men, it were enough to undo me utterly, to fill brimful the cup of my misfortune, and make me play the mad-pate reeks [20] of Bedlam." [21]

" Do not marry, then," quoth Pantagruel.

" Yea, but," said Panurge, " I shall never by any other means come to have lawful sons and daughters, in whom I may harbor some hope of perpetuating my name and arms, and to whom also I may leave and bequeath my inheritances and purchased goods (of which latter sort you need not doubt, but that in some one or other of these mornings, I will make a fair and goodly show), that so I may cheer up and make merry, when otherwise I should be plunged into a peevish sullen mood of pensive sullenness, as I do perceive daily by the gentle and loving carriage of your kind and gracious father toward you; as all honest folks use to do at their own homes and private dwelling houses. For being free from debt, and yet not married, if casually [22] I should fret and be angry, although the cause of my grief and displeasure were never so just, I am afraid, instead of consolation, that I should meet with nothing else but scoffs, frumps,[23] gibes, and mocks at my disastrous fortune."

" Marry, then, in the name of God! " quoth Pantagruel.

(Urquhart and Motteux)

---

18 **brabbling**: bickering.
19 **flout**: mock.
20 **reeks**: pranks.

21 **Bedlam**: a madhouse.
22 **casually**: by chance.
23 **frumps**: jests.

SUGGESTIONS FOR STUDY

1. Show how the manner of living of the Thelemites was the direct opposite of that of the monks.

2. The Abbey of Theleme may be called a Utopia. What is the meaning of that word? What English author composed a book with that name? What other Utopias do you know? How do these others resemble or differ from that of Rabelais?

3. In what does the humor of the conversation between Pantagruel and Panurge consist?

4. Point out examples of Rabelais' wide vocabulary. Where does he apply to men words that belong properly only to animals? What effect is achieved by that?

MICHEL DE MONTAIGNE (1533–1592)

Michel Eyquem took the name Montaigne from his ancestral castle near Bordeaux. He was carefully educated in the classics and after studying law was made a magistrate at Bordeaux. He also saw military service and visited Paris. On the death of his father in 1568 he succeeded to the family estates. Feeling that he had had enough of active life, he resolved to devote his remaining days to study and meditation. He fitted up a tower separate from the castle and there gave himself up to the leisurely composition of his *Essays*. A sense of civic duty drew him reluctantly from this life of learned ease to serve four years as Mayor of Bordeaux.

Montaigne was the real creator of the modern literary essay. This type of essay is the prose parallel to the lyric poem. It should express the author's ideas and feelings and reflect his personality. Quite appropriately, therefore, Montaigne's *Essays* are all more or less about himself. They were written primarily for his own satisfaction and not for profit or fame. They are full of ripe worldly wisdom that springs from shrewd observation of life and remarkable knowledge of human nature. He was not a philosopher in the technical sense, but he did have a philosophy of life based on personal experience. His human tolerance was due in part to the skepticism which enabled him to see both sides of a question and so prevented him from becoming a fanatical partisan. The question, What do I know? runs like a refrain through his writings. But Montaigne did not believe in letting this skepticism affect one's actions too much. Outwardly a man should conform to custom, no matter how divergent his private opinions might be. The *Essays* are genial, almost conversational in tone, and are liberally sprinkled with quotations from the classics. They appeal chiefly to older readers, for if Rabelais expresses the exuberant youth of the French Renaissance, Montaigne represents its sober maturity.

THE AUTHOR TO THE READER

Reader, lo here a well-meaning book. It doth at the first entrance forewarn thee, that in contriving the same, I have proposed unto myself no other than a familiar and private end: I have no respect or consideration at all, either to thy service, or to my glory: my forces are not capable of any such design. I have vowed the same to the particular commodity [1] of my kinsfolks and friends: to the end, that losing me (which they are likely to do ere long) they may therein find some lineaments [2] of my conditions [3] and humors,[4] and by that means reserve more whole, and more lively foster the knowledge and acquaintance they have had of me. Had my intention been to forestall and purchase the world's opinion and favor, I would surely have adorned myself more quaintly,[5] or kept a more grave and solemn march. I desire therein to be delineated in mine own genuine, simple, and ordinary fashion, without contention, art, or study; for it is myself I portray. My imperfections shall therein be read to the life, and my natural form discerned, so far-forth as public reverence hath permitted me. For if my fortune had been to have lived among those nations, which yet are said to live under the sweet liberty of Nature's first and uncorrupted laws, I assure thee, I would most willingly have portrayed myself fully and naked. Thus, gentle Reader, myself am the groundwork of my book. It is then no reason thou shouldest employ thy time about so frivolous and vain a subject. Therefore farewell. From Montaigne, the first of March, 1580.

(John Florio)

[1] **commodity:** convenience.
[2] **lineaments:** features.
[3] **conditions:** character.
[4] **humors:** disposition.
[5] **quaintly:** ingeniously.

THE PROFIT OF ONE MAN IS THE DAMAGE OF ANOTHER

Demades [1] the Athenian condemned a man of the city, whose trade was to sell such necessaries as belonged to burials, under color,[2] he asked too much profit for them, and that such profit could not come unto him without the death of many people. This judgment seemeth

[1] **Demades:** Athenian orator of the fourth century B.C.
[2] **color:** pretense.

to be ill taken, because no man profiteth but by the loss of others, by which reason a man should condemn all manner of gain. The merchant thrives not but by the licentiousness [3] of youth; the husbandman [4] by dearth of corn; the architect but by the ruin of houses; the lawyer by suits and controversies between men; honor itself, and practice of religious ministers, is drawn from our death and vices. " No physician delighteth in the health of his own friend," saith the ancient Greek Comic; " nor no soldier is pleased with the peace of his city, and so of the rest." And which is worse, let every man sound his own conscience, he shall find, that our inward desires are for the most part nourished and bred in us by the loss and hurt of others; which when I considered, I began to think, how Nature doth not gainsay herself in this, concerning her general policy; for physicians hold, that " The birth, increase, and augmentation of everything, is the alteration and corruption of another."

What ever from its bounds doth changed pass,
That strait is death of that which erst it was.

(John Florio)

[3] **licentiousness:** extravagance.   [4] **husbandman:** farmer.

ON CORPORAL PUNISHMENT

I utterly condemn all manner of violence in the education of a young spirit, brought up to honor and liberty. There is a kind of slavishness in churlish-rigor,[1] and servility in compulsion; and I hold that that which cannot be compassed [2] by reason, wisdom, and discretion, can never be attained by force and constraint. So was I brought up, they tell me, that in all my youth I never felt rod but twice, and that very lightly. And what education I have had myself, the same have I given my children. But such is my ill hap that they die all very young; yet hath Leonora my only daughter escaped this misfortune and attained to the age of six years, and somewhat more; for the conduct of whose youth, and punishment of her childish faults (the indulgence of her mother applying itself very mildly unto it) was never other means used but gentle words.

(John Florio)

[1] **churlish-rigor:** ill-natured severity.
[2] **compassed:** reached.

SUGGESTIONS FOR STUDY

1. It is interesting to compare Montaigne's Foreword " To the Reader " with what Bacon says in the dedication of his *Essays* to the Duke of Buckingham: " I do now publish my *Essays,* which of all my other works have been most current, for that, as it seems, they come home to men's business and bosoms." What was the original meaning of the word " essay " ? How does that meaning apply to the present literary form?

2. The quotation in the second selection is from Lucretius. Explain its meaning.

3. Extend the application of the theory that the profit of one man is the damage of another to occupations other than those mentioned by Montaigne. Do you believe that it is a universal and absolute principle? Is trade, for example, necessarily a " skin game "?

4. Montaigne was one of the first men to protest against corporal punishment. What are the arguments he advances? Compare with Sir Richard Steele's famous essay on boys' schools, *Spectator,* No. 157. Debate the question whether corporal punishment may not sometimes be justified.

5. Vocabulary: foster, forestall, controversies, gainsay, augmentation, servility.

PIERRE CORNEILLE (1606–1684)

Corneille was born in Normandy. Following the traditions of his family, he was trained for the law, but his genius and taste impelled him irresistibly to the theater. After writing several indifferent comedies, he took Paris by storm in 1636 with his play *The Cid,* the first masterpiece of the classic school. It was followed by the successful tragedies *Horace, Cinna, Pompey,* and *Polyeucte,* and an enjoyable comedy *The Liar.* Corneille's triumph was completed by his admission to the Academy in 1647. His later plays were inferior in quality. He lived to see his own popularity eclipsed by that of his younger contemporary Racine.

Corneille had a strong predilection for the heroic. He celebrated in his dramas the triumph of duty over passion. He sounded the note of high courage and glorified the supremacy of the will. His interest in the theme of love was comparatively slight. These masculine qualities made him more at home with men than with women. The eloquent expression of his lofty sentiments is still prized by the French as an important incentive to the strengthening of character.

The controversy in regard to *The Cid* is the most celebrated episode in the history of the French drama. Corneille had taken his subject from a long rambling Spanish play. Although he removed various superfluities of scenes and characters and confined his plot within the required limits of time and place, he was sharply attacked for having taken too great artistic liberties. As a result of these criticisms, he saw to it that his later plays should conform more strictly to the prescribed rules. The principles of French classic tragedy, nominally based on the teachings of Aristotle, but really shaped by the Latin plays of Seneca, imposed the strictest observance of the unities of action, place, and time. The plot of a play was to be without sub-plot or minor incidents and was to be limited to a single scene and within a single day. The subjects were to be drawn from the great pages of history and legend. Style and diction were to be kept on a high level of dignity. Action, particularly of a violent nature, was practically banished. No touch of humor was permitted to mar the unity of tone. Prose was absolutely prohibited. To an English-speaking reader, accustomed to the liberties which Shakespeare took in these matters, the formality of the French classic tragedies seems very artificial. French critics, however, have not been slow to point out the advantage of concentrating interest in the characters rather than in external events. At any rate, these were the rules to which Corneille rather reluctantly submitted and which Racine obeyed with consummate ease, as though he were to the manner born.

THE CID

Cid, or Lord, was the name given to Roderick, the champion of the Spaniards against the Moors. In Corneille's play, Roderick loves Chimène but is bound by filial duty to kill her father for insulting his father. The following soliloquy expresses the dramatic conflict between love and duty in the heart of the hero.

> *Roderick.* My heart's o'erwhelmed with woe.
> A mortal stroke that mocks my tender trust
> Makes me avenger of a quarrel just,
> And wretched victim of an unjust blow.
> Though crushed in spirit, still my pride must cope   5
> With that which slays my hope.
> So near to love's fruition to be told —
> O God, the strange, strange pain! —
> My father has received an insult bold,
> The offender is the father of Chimène.   10
>
> 'Mid conflicts wild I stand.
> I lift my arm to strike my father's foe,
> But Love with mighty impulse urges " No! "
> Pride fires my heart, Affection stays my hand;

7. **fruition:** attainment.

I must be deaf to Passion's calls, or face 15
A life of deep disgrace.
Whate'er I do, fierce anguish follows me —
    O God, the strange, strange pain!
Can an affront so base unpunished be?
    But can I fight the father of Chimène? 20

    To which allegiance give? —
To tender tyranny or noble bond? —
A tarnished name or loss of pleasures fond?
    Unworthy or unhappy must I live.
[*To his sword.*]   Thou dear, stern hope of souls high-born and bold 25
And fired with love untold,
But enemy of my new dreams of bliss,
    Sword, cause of all my pain,
Was't given me to use for this, for this? —
    To save my honor, but to lose Chimène? 30

    I must seek death's dread bourne.
To weigh my duty and my love is vain.
If I avenge his death, her hate I gain,
    If I no vengeance take, I win her scorn;
Unfaithful must I prove to hope most sweet, 35
Or for that hope unmeet.
What heals my honor's wounds augments my grief,
    And causes keener pain;
Be strong, my soul!   Since death's my sole relief,
    I'll die, nor lose the love of my Chimène. 40

    What, die without redress?
Seek death — so fatal to my future fame?
Endure that Spain shall heap on me the shame
    Of one who failed in honor's sorest stress?
All for a love whose hope my frenzied heart 45
Already sees depart?
I'll list no longer to the subtle plea
    Which but renews my pain;
Come, arm of mine, my choice turns now to thee,
    Since naught, alas! can give me back Chimène. 50

31. **bourne:** boundary.   36. **unmeet:** unfit.   41. **redress:** making up for
the wrong.

Yes, love my will misled.
My father — life and name to him I owe —
Whether of grief or from a mortal blow
　　I die, my blood all pure and true I'll shed.
Too long I've dallied with a purpose weak;　　55
Now vengeance swift I seek.
The flush of shame mounts hotly to my brow,
　　That I can deem it pain
To save my father's house. I haste e'en now
　　To seek — woe's me! — the father of Chimène.　　60
　　　　　　　　　　　　　　　　[Exit RODERICK.

　　　　　　　　　　(Florence Kendrick Cooper)

MOLIÈRE (1622–1673)

World literature is much richer in good tragedies than in good comedies.
The reason for this is not far to seek. The unceasing struggle for existence,
the constant spectacle of suffering and unhappiness, the cruelty of men
and of nature, the certainty of death, all combine to make men feel instinctively the sadness of life. Even in the realm of comedy, those plays
are generally best which have a serious undertone. If a comedy is merely
witty, it seems artificial. If it is farcical, we feel that it deals with triviali-
ties and caricatures reality. The play that honestly faces life and yet
emerges with the comic spirit triumphant is consequently rare. Molière
has furnished more really good comedies than any other man. That is his
undisputed title to glory.

His real name was Jean Baptiste Poquelin, but like certain other great
French writers — Voltaire, Beaumarchais and George Sand — he is known
only by his pseudonym. He was born in Paris of a bourgeois family. His
fundamental outlook was that of his social class and was characterized by
shrewd common sense and a love of the realities of daily life. Against the
wishes of his family he decided on a theatrical career and adopted the name
Molière, which he was destined to make illustrious. After an unsuccessful
venture in Paris, he became for thirteen years an actor-manager in the
provinces, gaining not only a practical knowledge of stagecraft but also a
familiarity with all types of humanity. In 1658 he and his troupe returned
to Paris and secured the favor of King Louis XIV. His own plays were
written during the last fifteen years of his life. He died in harness while
acting in one of them.

Molière wrote some thirty plays. A distinction should be made between those on which he expended some care and those which, as an enterprising director, he merely made to order for special occasions. He is
to be judged by the former, which alone have literary or human worth.
Like Shakespeare, he took his plots where he found them and was not

particularly careful about polished workmanship. His plays often end rather artificially. What he did care about was making his characters real. A writer of comedies in Molière's day could take more liberties than a writer of tragedies. He was not so rigidly restricted by rules; he might use prose as well as verse; his vocabulary could include words which would have been considered unbecoming in tragedies. Molière rejoiced in this comparative freedom which suited his realistic method.

Among his lighter comedies, generally of a more or less farcical nature, the most enjoyable are *The Affected Misses, The Tradesman Turned Gentleman,* and *The Physician in spite of Himself.* His more serious comedies are *The Learned Ladies,* a satire on pedantry, *Tartuffe,* directed against religious hypocrisy (the central character, Tartuffe, is the most famous hypocrite in all literature), *Don Juan, The Miser,* and *The Misanthropist.* The last-named play is probably Molière's most personal utterance and is often considered to be his masterpiece. It has been pointed out that some of these serious comedies might easily have been given a tragic ending.

Of the world's greatest writers of comedies, Aristophanes supplied the political type, Shakespeare the romantic, and Molière the realistic. Molière aims at truth, but truth viewed humorously, and directed satirically. His satire is turned against all that is unreal and unnatural, whether faults of individual character or social conventions which disguise or suppress nature. The chief source of fun for him lies in what may be called the revenge of nature. If human nature is thwarted, it will get even. Examples of this abound in his plays. An old man marries a young girl; inevitably she falls in love with a youth. (Molière's own experience with a coquettish wife twenty years younger than himself finds expression here.) A man marries above his station; the union is unnatural and ends unhappily. A bourgeois pretends to a refinement which he does not possess and makes himself a laughingstock. Women feign learning or culture and only succeed in appearing ridiculous. A far-reaching philosophy of life underlies the seeming simplicity of this point of view — namely, do not try to force human nature too much; you will only make trouble for yourself and no one will be the happier. Molière believed that if that injunction were followed by parents, by the government and by society, half the misery of the world would be avoided. On the positive side, he showed the high desirability of human happiness, of good sense, moderation, and humorous tolerance.

THE PHYSICIAN IN SPITE OF HIMSELF

The medical profession was a favorite butt of Molière's satire, as it is today of Bernard Shaw's. There are at least four of his plays in which the doctors are jibed at. This was partly because he suffered from poor health himself and had never found that the doctors could do anything for him.

Partly, too, he was again directing his shafts at pretentiousness. In those days physicians wore uniforms, spoke a learned jargon which no one could understand, gave medicines which they knew little or nothing about, and in general professed to mend nature. Molière believed it was better to throw physic to the dogs and let nature have her own way.

No attempt should be made to read sense into the speeches of Sganarelle when he assumes the part of the doctor in this play. They are a meaning-less mixture of anatomical terms and dog-Latin.

The impudent and rather rascally Sganarelle appears in other plays of Molière. He is always resourceful, amusing, and full of shrewd sense. He was such an evident favorite of the author that it almost seems as if he represented Molière himself on his irresponsible side. Incidentally, Sganarelle is the ancestor of a number of characters in later French comedies, the most famous of whom is Figaro in the plays of Beaumarchais. Usually these characters are valets, who take the place which the fool or jester occupies in the Elizabethan drama.

DRAMATIS PERSONAE

GÉRONTE, *father to Lucinde*
LÉANDRE, *Lucinde's lover*
SGANARELLE, *husband to Martine*
M. ROBERT, *Sganarelle's neighbor*
LUCAS, *husband to Jacqueline*
VALÈRE, *Géronte's servant*

THIBAUT,
PERRIN, *his son* } *peasants*
LUCINDE, *Géronte's daughter*
MARTINE, *Sganarelle's wife*
JACQUELINE, *nurse at Géronte's, and Lucas' wife.*

ACT I

SCENE: *A Forest*

Scene I. SGANARELLE, MARTINE, *appearing on the stage, quarreling.*

Sganarelle. No; I tell you that I will do nothing of the kind, and that it is for me to speak, and to be master.

Martine. And I tell you that I will have you live as I like, and that I am not married to you to put up with your vagaries.[1]

Sganarelle. Oh! what a nuisance it is to have a wife! and Aristotle is perfectly right in saying that a woman is worse than a demon.

Martine. Look at Master Clever, with his silly Aristotle!

Sganarelle. Yes, Master Clever. Find me another faggot-binder who can argue upon things as I can, who has served a famous physi-

---

[1] **vagaries:** whims.

cian for six years, and who, when only a boy, knew his grammar by heart!

Martine. Plague on the arrant fool.

Sganarelle. Plague on the slut!

Martine. Cursed be the hour and the day when I took it into my head to say yes.

Sganarelle. Cursed be the cuckold [2] of a notary that made me sign my own ruination.

Martine. Certainly it well becomes you to complain on that score. Ought you not rather to thank Heaven every minute of the day that you have me for a wife? and did you deserve to marry a woman like me?

Sganarelle. It is true you did me too much honor, and I had great occasion to be satisfied with my wedding-night. Zounds! do not make me open my mouth too wide: I might say certain things . . .

Martine. What? What could you say?

Sganarelle. Enough; let us drop the subject. It is enough that we know what we know, and that you were very glad to meet with me.

Martine. What do you call very glad to meet with you? A fellow who will drive me to the hospital — a debauched, deceitful wretch, who gobbles up every farthing I have got!

Sganarelle. That is a lie: for I drink part of it.

Martine. Who sells piecemeal every stick of furniture in the house!

Sganarelle. That is living upon one's means.

Martine. Who has taken the very bed from under me!

Sganarelle. You will get up all the earlier.

Martine. In short, who does not leave me a stick in the whole house.

Sganarelle. There will be less trouble in moving.

Martine. And who from morning to night does nothing but gamble and drink!

Sganarelle. That is done in order not to get in the dumps.

Martine. And what am I to do all the while with my family?

Sganarelle. Whatever you like.

Martine. I have got four poor children on my hands.

Sganarelle. Put them down.

Martine. Who keep asking me every moment for bread.

Sganarelle. Whip them. When I have had enough to eat and to drink, every one in the house ought to be satisfied.

---

[2] **cuckold:** deceived husband.

Martine. And do you mean to tell me, you sot, that things can always go on so?

Sganarelle. Wife, let us proceed gently, if you please.

Martine. That I am to bear forever with your insolence and your debauchery?

Sganarelle. Do not let us get into a passion, wife.

Martine. And that I do not know the way to bring you back to your duty?

Sganarelle. Wife, you know that I am not very patient, and that my arm is somewhat heavy.

Martine. I laugh at your threats.

Sganarelle. My sweet wife, my pet, your skin is itching as usual.

Martine. I will let you see that I am not afraid of you.

Sganarelle. My dearest rib, you have set your heart upon a thrashing.

Martine. Do you think that I am frightened at your talk?

Sganarelle. Sweet object of my affections, I shall box your ears for you.

Martine. Sot that you are!

Sganarelle. I shall thrash you.

Martine. Walking wine-cask!

Sganarelle. I shall pummel you.

Martine. Infamous wretch!

Sganarelle. I shall curry your skin for you.

Martine. Wretch! villain! deceiver! cur! scoundrel! gallows-bird! churl! rogue! scamp! thief! . . .

Sganarelle. You will have it, will you?

[Takes a stick and beats her.

Martine. [*Shrieking*] Help! help! help! help!

Sganarelle. That is the real way of quieting you.

Scene II.[3] M. ROBERT, SGANARELLE, MARTINE.

M. Robert. Hulloa, hulloa, hulloa! Fie! What is this? What a disgraceful thing! Plague take the scamp to beat his wife so.

Martine. [*Her arms akimbo, speaks to* M. ROBERT, *and makes him draw back; at last she gives him a slap on the face.*] And I like him to beat me, I do.

[3] In French drama it is customary to indicate a new scene whenever characters enter or exit. It seldom means a change of stage setting as in English drama.

M. Robert. If that is the case, I consent with all my heart.

Martine. What are you interfering with?

M. Robert. I am wrong.

Martine. Is it any of your business?

M. Robert. You are right.

Martine. Just look at this jackanapes, who wishes to hinder husbands from beating their wives!

M. Robert. I apologize.

Martine. What have you got to say to it?

M. Robert. Nothing.

Martine. Is it for you to poke your nose into it?

M. Robert. No.

Martine. Mind your own business.

M. Robert. I shall not say another word.

Martine. It pleases me to be beaten.

M. Robert. Agreed.

Martine. It does not hurt you.

M. Robert. That is true.

Martine. And you are an ass to interfere with what does not concern you.

M. Robert. Neighbor, I ask your pardon with all my heart. Go on, thrash and beat your wife as much as you like; I shall help you, if you wish it. [*He goes towards* SGANARELLE, *who also speaks to him, makes him draw back, beats him with the stick he has been using, and puts him to flight.*]

Sganarelle. I do not wish it.

M. Robert. Ah! that is a different thing.

Sganarelle. I will beat her if I like; and I will not beat her if I do not like.

M. Robert. Very good.

Sganarelle. She is my wife, and not yours.

M. Robert. Undoubtedly.

Sganarelle. It is not for you to order me about.

M. Robert. Just so.

Sganarelle. I do not want your help.

M. Robert. Exactly so.

Sganarelle. And it is like your impertinence to meddle with other people's business. Remember that Cicero says that between the tree and the finger you should not put the bark. [*He drives him away, then comes back to his wife, and says to her, squeezing her hand:*]

Scene III. SGANARELLE, MARTINE.

Sganarelle. Come, let us make it up. Shake hands.

Martine. Yes after having beaten me thus!

Sganarelle. Never mind that. Shake hands.

Martine. I will not.

Sganarelle. Eh?

Martine. No.

Sganarelle. Come, wife!

Martine. I shall not.

Sganarelle. Come, I tell you.

Martine. I will do nothing of the kind.

Sganarelle. Come, come, come.

Martine. No; I will be angry.

Sganarelle. Bah! it is a trifle. Do.

Martine. Leave me alone.

Sganarelle. Shake hands, I tell you.

Martine. You have treated me too ill.

Sganarelle. Well! I beg your pardon; put your hand there.

Martine. I forgive you [*Aside, softly*]; but I shall make you pay for it.

Sganarelle. You are silly to take notice of it; these are trifles that are necessary now and then to keep up good feeling; and five or six strokes of a cudgel between people who love each other, only brighten the affections. There now! I am going to the wood, and I promise you that you shall have more than a hundred faggots today.

Scene IV. MARTINE, *alone*.

Go, my lad, whatever look I may put on, I shall not forget to pay you out; and I am dying to hit upon something to punish you for the blows you gave me. I know well enough that a wife has always the means of being revenged upon her husband; but that is too delicate a punishment for my gallows-bird; I want a revenge that shall strike home a little more, or it will not be satisfaction for the insult which I have received.

Scene V. VALÈRE, LUCAS, MARTINE.

Lucas. [*To* VALÈRE, *without seeing* MARTINE] I'facks we have undertaken a curious errand; and I do not know, for my part, what we shall get by it.

Valère. [*To* LUCAS, *without seeing* MARTINE] What is the use of grumbling, good foster-father? We are bound to do as our master tells us; and, besides, we have both of us some interest in the health of his daughter, our mistress; for her marriage, which is put off through her illness, will no doubt bring us in something. Horace, who is generous, is the most likely to succeed among her suitors; and although she has shown some inclination for a certain Léandre, you know well enough that her father would never consent to receive him for his son-in-law.

Martine. [*Musing on one side, thinking herself alone*] Can I not find out some way of revenging myself?

Lucas. [*To* VALÈRE] But what an idea has he taken into his head, since the doctors are quite at a loss.

Valère. [*To* LUCAS] You may sometimes find by dint of seeking, what cannot be found at once; and often in the most unlikely spots you may . . .

Martine. [*Still thinking herself alone*] Yes; I must pay him out, no matter at what cost. Those cudgel blows lie heavy on my stomach; I cannot digest them; and . . . [*She is saying all this musingly, and as she moves, she comes in contact with the two men.*] Ah, gentlemen, I beg your pardon, I did not notice you, and was puzzling my brain about something that perplexes me.

Valère. Every one has his troubles in this world, and we also are looking for something that we should be very glad to find.

Martine. Is it something in which I can assist you?

Valère. Perhaps. We are endeavouring to meet with some clever man, some special physician, who could give some relief to our master's daughter, seized with an illness which has at once deprived her of the use of her tongue. Several physicians have already exhausted all their knowledge on her behalf; but sometimes one may find people with wonderful secrets, and certain peculiar remedies, who very often succeed where others have failed; and that is the sort of man we are looking for.

Martine. [*Softly and aside*] Ah! This is an inspiration from Heaven to revenge myself on my rascal. [*Aloud*] You could never have addressed yourselves to any one more able to find what you want; and we have a man here, the most wonderful fellow in the world for desperate maladies.

Valère. Ah! for mercy's sake, where can we meet with him?

Martine. You will find him just now in that little spot yonder, where he is amusing himself in cutting wood.

Lucas. A doctor who cuts wood!

Valère. Who is amusing himself in gathering some simples,[4] you mean to say?

Martine. No; he is a strange fellow who takes a delight in this; a fantastic, eccentric, whimsical man, whom you would never take to be what he really is. He goes about dressed in a most extraordinary fashion, pretends sometimes to be very ignorant, keeps his knowledge to himself, and dislikes nothing so much every day as using the marvelous talents which God has given him for the healing art.

Valère. It is a wonderful thing that all these great men have always some whim, some slight grain of madness mixed with their learning.

Martine. The madness of this man is greater than can be imagined, for sometimes he has to be beaten before he will own his ability; and I warn you beforehand that you will not succeed, that he will never own that he is a physician, unless you take each a stick, and compel him, by dint of blows, to admit at last what he will conceal at first. It is thus that we act when we have need of him.

Valère. What a strange delusion!

Martine. That is true; but, after that, you shall see that he works wonders.

Valère. What is his name?

Martine. His name is Sganarelle. But it is very easy to recognise him. He is a man with a large black beard, and wears a ruff, and a yellow and green coat.

Lucas. A yellow and green coat! He is then a parrot-doctor?

Valère. But is it really true that he is as clever as you say?

Martine. As clever. He is a man who works miracles. About six months ago, a woman was given up by all the other physicians; she was considered dead at least six hours, and they were going to bury her, when they dragged by force the man we are speaking of to her bedside. Having seen her, he poured a small drop of something into her mouth; and at that very instant she rose from her bed, and began immediately to walk in her room as if nothing had happened.

Lucas. Ah!

Valère. It must have been a drop of liquid gold.

Martine. Possibly so. Not more than three weeks ago, a young child, twelve years old, fell from the top of the belfry, and smashed his head, arms, and legs on the stones. No sooner took they our man to it, than he rubbed the whole body with a certain ointment, which

---

4 **simples:** medicinal herbs.

he knows how to prepare; and the child immediately rose on its legs, and ran away to play at chuck-farthing.[5]

Lucas. Hah!

Valère. This man must have the universal cure-all.

Martine. Who doubts it?

Lucas. Odds-bobs! [6] that is the very man we want. Let us go quickly and fetch him.

Valère. We thank you for the service you have rendered us.

Martine. But do not fail to remember the warning I have given you.

Lucas. Hey! Zooks! leave it to us. If he wants nothing but a thrashing, we will gain our point.

Valère. [*To* Lucas] We are very glad to have met with this woman; and I conceive the best hopes in the world from it.

Scene VI. Sganarelle, Valère, Lucas.

Sganarelle. [*Singing behind the Scene*] La, la, la . . .

Valère. I hear some one singing and cutting wood.

Sganarelle. [*Coming on with a bottle in his hand, without perceiving* Valère *or* Lucas] La, la, la. . . . Really I have done enough to deserve a drink. Let us take a little breath. [*He drinks.*] This wood is as salt as the very devil. [*Sings.*]

> *How sweet to hear,*
> *My pretty flask,*
> *How sweet to hear,*
> *Your little gull, gull!*
> *No fate with mine could vie,*
> *If never you ran dry,*
> *Oh! darling little flask,*
> *But constantly were full!*

Come! Zounds! we must take care not to get the blues.

Valère. [*Softly to* Lucas] This is the very man.

Lucas. [*Softly to* Valère] I think you are right, and that we have just hit upon him.

Valère. Let us look a little closer.

---

[5] **chuck-farthing:** a kind of game of quoits with coins.

[6] **Odds-bobs:** an old-fashioned oath like odds-bodkins, zounds, zooks, etc., which occur elsewhere in the play.

Sganarelle. [*Hugging the bottle*] Ah! you little rogue! I love you, my pretty dear! [*He sings; but perceiving* LUCAS *and* VALÈRE, *who are examining him, he lowers his voice.*]

    No fate . . . with mine . . . could . . . vie,
    Is . . .

[*Seeing that they examine him more closely*] Whom the deuce do these people want?

Valère. [*To* LUCAS] It is surely he.

Lucas. [*To* VALÈRE] There he is, exactly as he has been described to us.

Sganarelle. [*Aside. At this point he puts down his bottle; and when* VALÈRE *stoops down to bow to him, he thinks that it is in order to snatch it away, and puts it on the other side. As* LUCAS *is doing the same thing as* VALÈRE, SGANARELLE *takes it up again, and hugs it to his breast, with various grimaces which make a great deal of by-play.*] They are consulting each other, while looking at me. What can be their intentions!

Valère. Sir, is not your name Sganarelle?

Sganarelle. Hey! What!

Valère. I ask you if your name is not Sganarelle.

Sganarelle. [*Turning first to* VALÈRE, *then to* LUCAS] Yes, and no. It depends on what you want with him.

Valère. We want nothing with him, but to offer him our utmost civilities.

Sganarelle. In that case my name is Sganarelle.

Valère. We are delighted to see you, Sir. We have been recommended to you for what we are in search of; and we have come to implore your help, of which we are in want.

Sganarelle. If it be anything, gentlemen, that belongs to my little trade, I am quite ready to oblige you.

Valère. You are too kind to us, Sir. But put your hat on, Sir, if you please; the sun might hurt you.

Lucas. Pray, Sir, put it on.

Sganarelle. [*Aside*] What a deal of ceremony these people use. [*He puts his hat on.*]

Valère. You must not think it strange, Sir, that we have addressed ourselves to you. Clever people are always much sought after, and we have been informed of your capacity.

Sganarelle. It is true, gentlemen, that I am the best hand in the world at making faggots.

Valère. Oh! Sir . . .

Sganarelle. I spare no pains, and make them in a fashion that leaves nothing to be desired.

Valère. That is not the question we have come about, Sir.

Sganarelle. But I charge a hundred and ten sous the hundred.

Valère. Let us not speak about that, if you please.

Sganarelle. I pledge you my word that I could not sell them for less.

Valère. We know what is what, Sir.

Sganarelle. If you know what is what, you know that I charge that price.

Valère. This is a joke, Sir, but . . .

Sganarelle. It is no joke at all, I cannot bate [7] a farthing.

Valère. Let us talk differently, please.

Sganarelle. You may find some elsewhere for less; there be faggots and faggots; but for those which I make . . .

Valère. Let us change the conversation, pray, Sir.

Sganarelle. I take my oath that you shall not have them for less, not a fraction.

Valère. Fie! Fie!

Sganarelle. No, upon my word, you shall have to pay that price. I am speaking frankly, and I am not the man to overcharge.

Valère. Ought a gentleman like you, Sir, to amuse himself with those clumsy pretences, to lower himself to talk thus? Ought so learned a man, such a famous physician as you are, wish to disguise himself in the eyes of the world and keep buried his great talents?

Sganarelle. [*Aside*] He is mad.

Valère. Pray, Sir, do not dissemble with us.

Sganarelle. What do you mean?

Lucas. All this beating about the bush is useless. We know what we know.

Sganarelle. What do you know? What do you want with me? For whom do you take me?

Valère. For what you are, a great physician.

Sganarelle. Physician yourself; I am not one, and I have never been one.

Valère. [*Aside*] Now the fit is on him. [*Aloud*] Sir, do not deny things any longer, and do not, if you please, make us have recourse to unpleasant extremities.

Sganarelle. Have recourse to what?

[7] **bate**: take off.

Valère. To certain things that we should be sorry for.

Sganarelle. Zounds! Have recourse to whatever you like. I am not a physician, and do not understand what you mean.

Valère. [*Aside*] Well, I perceive that we shall have to apply the remedy. [*Aloud*] Once more, Sir, I pray you to confess what you are.

Lucas. Odds-bobs, do not talk any more nonsense; and confess plainly that you are a physician.

Sganarelle. [*Aside*] I am getting in a rage.

Valère. What is the good of denying what all the world knows?

Lucas. Why all these funny falsehoods? What is the good of it?

Sganarelle. One word is as good as a thousand, gentlemen. I tell you that I am not a physician.

Valère. You are not a physician?

Sganarelle. No.

Lucas. You are not a physician?

Sganarelle. No, I tell you.

Valère. Since you will have it so, we must make up our minds to do it. [*They each take a stick, and thrash him.*]

Sganarelle. Hold! hold! hold, gentlemen! I will be anything you like.

Valère. Why, Sir, do you oblige us to to use this violence?

Lucas. Why do you make us take the trouble of giving you a beating?

Valère. I assure you that I regret it with all my heart.

Lucas. Upon my word I am sorry for it too.

Sganarelle. What the devil does it all mean, gentlemen? For pity's sake, is it a joke, or are you both gone out of your minds, to wish to make me out a physician?

Valère. What! you do not give in yet, and you still deny being a physician?

Sganarelle. The devil take me if I am one!

Lucas. Are you not a physician?

Sganarelle. No, plague choke me! [*They begin to thrash him again.*] Hold! hold! Well gentlemen, yes, since you will have it so, I am a physician, I am a physician — an apothecary into the bargain, if you like. I prefer saying yes to everything to being knocked about so.

Valère. Ah! that is right, Sir; I am delighted to see you so reasonable.

Lucas. It does my heart good to hear you speak in this way.

Valère. I beg your pardon with all my heart.

Lucas. I hope you will forgive me for the liberty I have taken.

Sganarelle. [*Aside*] Bless my soul! Am I perhaps myself mistaken, and have I become a physician without being aware of it?

Valère. You shall not regret, Sir, having shown us what you are; and you shall certainly be satisfied.

Sganarelle. But, tell me, gentlemen, may you not be yourselves mistaken? Is it quite certain that I am a physician?

Lucas. Yes, upon my word!

Sganarelle. Really and truly?

Valère. Undoubtedly.

Sganarelle. The devil take me if I knew it!

Valère. Nonsense! You are the cleverest physician in the world.

Sganarelle. Ha, ha!

Lucas. A physician who has cured I do not know how many complaints.

Sganarelle. The dickens I have!

Valère. A woman was thought dead for six hours; she was ready to be buried when you, with a drop of something, brought her to again, and made her walk at once about the room.

Sganarelle. The deuce I did!

Lucas. A child of twelve fell from the top of the belfry, by which he had his head, his legs, and his arms smashed; and you, with I do not know what ointment, made him immediately get up on his feet, and off he ran to play chuck-farthing.

Sganarelle. The devil I did!

Valère. In short, Sir, you will be satisfied with us, and you shall earn whatever you like, if you allow us to take you where we intend.

Sganarelle. I shall earn whatever I like?

Valère. Yes.

Sganarelle. In that case I am a physician: there is no doubt of it. I had forgotten it; but I recollect it now. What is the matter? Where am I to go?

Valère. We will conduct you. The matter is to see a girl who has lost her speech.

Sganarelle. Indeed! I have not found it.

Valère. [*Softly to* Lucas] How he loves his joke! [*To* Sganarelle] Come along, Sir!

Sganarelle. Without a physician's gown!

Valère. We will get one.

Sganarelle. [*Presenting his bottle to* Valère] You carry this:

I put my juleps in there [*turning round to* LUCAS *and spitting on the ground*]. And you, stamp on this, by order of the physician.

Lucas. Odds sniggers! this is a physician I like. I think he will do, for he is a comical fellow.

ACT II

SCENE: *A room in* GÉRONTE'S *house.*

Scene I. GÉRONTE, VALÈRE, LUCAS, JACQUELINE.

Valère. Yes, sir, I think you will be satisfied; we have brought the greatest physician in the world with us.

Lucas. Oh! Zooks! this one beats everything; all the others are not worthy to hold the candle to him.

Valère. He is a man who has performed some marvelous cures.

Lucas. Who has put dead people on their legs again.

Valère. He is somewhat whimsical, as I have told you; and at times there are moments when his senses wander, and he does not seem what he really is.

Lucas. Yes, he loves a joke, and one would say sometimes that he has got a screw loose somewhere.

Valère. But in reality he is quite scientific; and very often he says things quite beyond any one's comprehension.

Lucas. When he sets about it, he talks as finely as if he were reading a book.

Valère. He has already a great reputation hereabout, and everybody comes to consult him.

Gérente. I am very anxious to see him; send him to me quickly.

Valère. I am going to fetch him.

Scene II. GÉRONTE, JACQUELINE, LUCAS

Jacqueline. Upon my word, Sir, this one will do just the same as all the rest. I think it will be six of the one and half-a-dozen of the others; and the best medicine to give to your daughter would, in my opinion, be a handsome strapping husband, for whom she could have some love.

Gérente. Lord bless my soul, nurse dear, you are meddling with many things!

Lucas. Hold your tongue, mother Jacqueline; it is not for you to poke your nose there.

Jacqueline. I tell you, and a dozen more of you, that all these physicians do her no good; that your daughter wants something else than rhubarb and senna, and that a husband is a plaster which cures all girls' complaints.

Géronte. Would any one have her in her present state, with that affliction on her? and when I intended her to marry, has she not opposed my wishes?

Jacqueline. No wonder. You wished to give her a man whom she does not like. Why did you not give her to Monsieur Léandre, who takes her fancy? She would have been very obedient, and I vouch for it that he will take her as she is, if you but give her to him.

Géronte. Léandre is not the man we want; he has not got a fortune like the other.

Jacqueline. He has got an uncle who is so rich, and he is the heir.

Géronte. All these expectations seem to me but moonshine. Brag is a good dog, but Holdfast is a better; and we run a great risk in waiting for dead men's shoes. Death is not always at the beck and call of gentlemen heirs; and while the grass grows, the cow starves.

Jacqueline. That is all well and good, but I have always heard that in marriage, as in everything else, happiness excels riches. Fathers and mothers have this cursed habit of asking always, " How much has he got? " and " How much has she got? " And gaffer [8] Peter has married his Simonette to that lout Thomas, because he has got a few more vineyards than young Robin, for whom the girl had a fancy; and now the poor creature is as yellow as a guinea, and has not looked like herself ever since. That is a good example for you, Sir. After all, folks have but their pleasure in this world; and I would sooner give my daughter a husband whom she likes than have all the riches in the country.

Géronte. Bless me, nurse, how you chatter! Hold your tongue, let me beg of you; you take too much upon yourself, and you will spoil your milk.

Lucas. [*Slapping* GÉRONTE's *shoulder at every word*] Indeed, be silent; you are too saucy. The master does not want your speeches, and he knows what he is about. All you have got to do is to suckle your baby, without arguing so much. Our master is the girl's father, and he is good and clever enough to know what she wants.

Géronte. Gently, gently.

[8] **gaffer:** old fellow.

Lucas. [*Still slapping* GÉRONTE's *shoulder*] I wish to show her her place, and teach her the respect due to you, Sir.

Géronte. Very well. But it does not need all this gesticulating.

Scene III.   VALÈRE, SGANARELLE, GÉRONTE, LUCAS, JACQUELINE

Valère. Look out, Sir, here is our physician coming.

Géronte. [*To* SGANARELLE] I am delighted to see you, Sir, at my house, and we have very great need of you.

Sganarelle. [*In a physician's gown with a very pointed cap*] Hippocrates ⁹ says . . . that we should both put our hats on.

Géronte. Hippocrates says that?

Sganarelle. Yes.

Géronte. In which chapter, if you please?

Sganarelle. In his chapter . . . on hats.

Géronte. Since Hippocrates says so, we must obey.

Sganarelle. Doctor, having heard of the marvelous things . . .

Géronte. To whom are you speaking, pray?

Sganarelle. To you.

Géronte. I am not a physician.

Sganarelle. You are not a physician?

Géronte. Indeed I am not.

Sganarelle. Really?

Géronte. Really. [SGANARELLE *takes a stick and thrashes* GÉRONTE.] Oh! Oh! Oh!

Sganarelle. Now you are a physician; I have never taken any other degree.

Géronte. [*To* VALÈRE] What a devil of a fellow you have brought me here!

Valère. Did I not tell you that he was a funny sort of a physician?

Géronte. Yes; but I shall send him about his business with his fun.

Lucas. Do not take any notice of it, Sir. It is only his joking.

Géronte. The joking does not suit me.

Sganarelle. Sir, I beg your pardon for the liberty I have taken.

Géronte. I am your humble servant, Sir.

Sganarelle. I am sorry . . .

Géronte. It is nothing.

Sganarelle. For the cudgeling I . . .

⁹ **Hippocrates:** (460?–359? B.C.) Greek physician and writer, often called the "Father of Medicine."

Géronte. There is no harm done.

Sganarelle. Which I have had the honor to give you.

Géronte. Do not say any more about it, Sir. I have a daughter who is suffering from a strange complaint.

Sganarelle. I am delighted, Sir, that your daughter has need of my skill; and I wish, with all my heart, that you stood in the same need of it, you and all your family, in order to show you my wish to serve you.

Géronte. I am obliged to you for these kind feelings.

Sganarelle. I assure you that I am speaking from my very heart.

Géronte. You really do me too much honor.

Sganarelle. What is your daughter's name?

Géronte. Lucinde.

Sganarelle. Lucinde! Ah! a pretty name to physic! Lucinde!

Géronte. I will just see what she is doing.

Sganarelle. Who is that tall woman?

Géronte. She is my baby's nurse.

Scene IV. SGANARELLE, JACQUELINE, LUCAS.

Sganarelle. [*Aside*] The deuce! that is a fine piece of household furniture. [*Aloud*] Ah, nurse! Charming nurse! my physic is the very humble slave of your nurseship. All my nostrums,[10] all my skill, all my cleverness, is at your service; and . . .

Lucas. By your leave, M. Doctor; leave my wife alone, I pray you.

Sganarelle. What! is she your wife?

Lucas. Yes.

Sganarelle. Oh! indeed! I did not know that, but I am very glad of it for the love of both. [*He pretends to embrace* LUCAS, *but embraces the nurse.*]

Lucas. [*Pulling* SGANARELLE *away, and placing himself between him and his wife*] Gently, if you please.

Sganarelle. I assure you that I am delighted that you should be united together. I congratulate her upon having such a husband as you; and I congratulate you upon having a wife so handsome, so discreet, and so well-shaped as she is. [*He pretends once more to embrace* LUCAS, *who holds out his arms, he slips under them and embraces the nurse.*]

Lucas. [*Pulling him away again*] Do not pay so many compliments, I beg of you.

10 **nostrums:** pet remedies.

Sganarelle. Shall I not rejoice with you about such a lovely harmony?

Lucas. With me as much as you like; but a truce to compliments with my wife.

Sganarelle. I have both your happiness equally at heart; and if I embrace you to show my delight in you, I embrace her to show my delight in her. [*Same byplay*]

Lucas. [*Pulling him away for the third time*] Odds boddikins, Doctor, what capers you cut!

Scene V. GÉRONTE, SGANARELLE, LUCAS, JACQUELINE.

Géronte. My daughter will be here directly, Sir.

Sganarelle. I am awaiting her, Sir, with all my physic.

Géronte. Where is it?

Sganarelle. [*Touching his forehead*] In there.

Géronte. That is good.

Scene VI. LUCINDE, GÉRONTE, SGANARELLE, VALÈRE, LUCAS, JACQUELINE.

Sganarelle. Is this the patient?

Géronte. Yes, I have but one daughter; and I would never get over it if she were to die.

Sganarelle. Do not let her do anything of the kind. She must not die without a prescription of the physician.

Géronte. A chair here!

Sganarelle. [*seated between* GÉRONTE *and* LUCINDE] This is not at all an unpleasant patient, and I am of the opinion that she would not be at all amiss for a man in very good health.

Géronte. You have made her laugh, Sir.

Sganarelle. So much the better. It is the best sign in the world when a physician makes the patient laugh. [*To* LUCINDE] Well, what is the matter? What ails you? What is it you feel?

Lucinde. [*Replies by motions, by putting her hand to her mouth, her head, and under her chin*] Ha, hi, ho, ha!

Sganarelle. What do you say?

Lucinde. [*Continues the same motions*] Ha, hi, ho, ha, ha, hi, ho!

Sganarelle. What is that?

Lucinde. Ha, hi, ho!

Sganarelle. [*Imitating her*] Ha, hi, ho, ha, ha! I do not understand you. What sort of language do you call that?

Géronte. That is just where her complaint lies, Sir. She has become dumb, without our having been able till now to discover the cause. This accident has obliged us to postpone her marriage.

Sganarelle. And why so?

Géronte. He whom she is going to marry wishes to wait for her recovery to conclude the marriage.

Sganarelle. And who is this fool that does not want his wife to be dumb? Would to Heaven that mine had that complaint! I should take particular care not to have her cured.

Géronte. To the point, Sir. We beseech you to use all your skill to cure her of this affliction.

Sganarelle. Do not make yourself uneasy. But tell me, does this pain oppress her much?

Géronte. Yes, Sir.

Sganarelle. So much the better. Is the suffering very acute?

Géronte. Very acute.

Sganarelle. [*Turning to the patient*] Give me your hand. [*To* GÉRONTE] The pulse tells me that your daughter is dumb.

Géronte. Sir, that is what is the matter with her; ah! yes, you have found it out at the first touch.

Sganarelle. Of course!

Jacqueline. See how he has guessed her complaint.

Sganarelle. We great physicians, we know matters at once. An ignoramus would have been nonplussed, and would have told you: it is this, that, or the other; but I hit the nail on the head from the very first, and I tell you that your daughter is dumb.

Géronte. Yes; but I should like you to tell me whence it arises.

Sganarelle. Nothing is easier; it arises from loss of speech.

Géronte. Very good. But the reason of her having lost her speech, pray?

Sganarelle. Our best athorities will tell you that it is because there is an impediment in the action of her tongue.

Géronte. But, once more, your opinion upon this impediment in the action of her tongue.

Sganarelle. Aristotle on this subject says . . . a great many clever things.

Géronte. I dare say.

Sganarelle. Ah! He was a great man!

Géronte. No doubt.

Sganarelle. Yes, a very great man. [*Holding out his arm, and putting a finger of the other hand in the bend*] A man who was, by this much, greater than I. But to come back to our argument: I hold that this impediment in the action of her tongue is caused by certain humors, which among us learned men, we call peccant [11] humors; peccant — that is to say . . . peccant humors; inasmuch as the vapors formed by the exhalations of the influences which rise in the very region of diseases, coming, . . . as we may say to. . . . Do you understand Latin?

Géronte. Not in the least.

Sganarelle. [*Suddenly rising*] You do not understand Latin?

Géronte. No.

Sganarelle. [*Assuming various comic attitudes*] *Cabricias* [12] *arci thuram, catalamus, singulariter, nominativo, hœc musa,* the muse, *bonus, bona, bonum. Deus sanctus, estne oratio latinas? Etiam,* Yes. *Quare?* Why. *Quia substantivo et adjectivum, concordat in generi, numerum, et casus.*

Géronte. Ah! Why did I not study?

Jacqueline. What a clever man!

Lucas. Yes, it is so beautiful that I do not understand a word of it.

Sganarelle. Thus these vapors which I speak of, passing from the left side, where the liver is, to the right side, where we find the heart, it so happens that the lungs, which in Latin we call *armyan,* having communication with the brain, which in Greek we style *nasmus,* by means of the *vena cava,* which in Hebrew, is termed *cubile,* meet in their course the said vapors, which fill the ventricles of the omoplata; and because these said vapors . . . now understand well this argument, pray . . . and because these said vapors are endowed with a certain malignity . . . listen well to this, I beseech you.

Géronte. Yes.

Sganarelle. Are endowed with a certain malignity which is caused . . . pay attention here, if you please.

Géronte. I do.

Sganarelle. Which is caused by the acridity of these humors engendered in the concavity of the diaphragm, it happens that these vapors. . . . *Ossabandus, nequeis, nequer, potarinum, puipsa milus.* That is exactly the reason that your daughter is dumb.

Jacqueline. Ah! How well this gentleman explains all this.

[11] peccant: morbid.
[12] **Cabricias:** The Latin is incorrect or meaningless or sometimes both; so also is the medical jargon that follows.

Lucas. Why does not my tongue wag as well as his?

Géronte. It is undoubtedly impossible to argue better. There is but one thing that I cannot exactly make out: that is the whereabouts of the liver and the heart. It appears to me that you place them differently from what they are; that the heart is on the left side, and the liver on the right.

Sganarelle. Yes; this was so formerly; but we have changed all that, and we nowadays practice the medical art on an entirely new system.

Géronte. I did not know that, and I pray you pardon my ignorance.

Sganarelle. There is no harm done; and you are not obliged to be so clever as we are.

Géronte. Certainly not. But what think you, Sir, ought to be done for this complaint?

Sganarelle. What do I think ought to be done?

Géronte. Yes.

Sganarelle. My advice is to put her to bed again, and make her, as a remedy, take plenty of bread soaked in wine.

Géronte. Why so, Sir?

Sganarelle. Because there is in bread and wine mixed together a sympathetic virtue which produces speech. Do you not see that they give nothing else to parrots, and that, by eating it, they learn to speak?

Géronte. That is true. Oh, the great man! Quick, plenty of bread and wine.

Sganarelle. I shall come back tonight to see how the patient is getting on.

Scene VII. GÉRONTE, SGANARELLE, JACQUELINE.

Sganarelle. [*To* JACQUELINE] Stop a little, you. [*To* GÉRONTE] Sir, I must give some medicine to your nurse.

Jacqueline. To me, Sir? I am as well as can be.

Sganarelle. So much the worse, nurse, so much the worse. This excess of health is dangerous, and it would not be amiss to bleed you a little gently, and to administer some little soothing injection.

Géronte. But, my dear Sir, that is a method which I cannot understand. Why bleed folks when they are not ill?

Sganarelle. It does not matter, the method is salutary; and as we drink for the thirst to come, so must we bleed for the disease to come.

Jacqueline. [*Going*] I do not care a fig for all this, and I will not have my body made an apothecary's shop.

Sganarelle. You object to my remedies; but we shall know how to bring you to reason.

Scene VIII. Géronte, Sganarelle.

Sganarelle. I wish you good day.

Géronte. Stay a moment, if you please.

Sganarelle. What are you going to do?

Géronte. Give you your fee, Sir.

Sganarelle. [*Putting his hands behind him, from under his gown, while* Géronte *opens his purse*] I shall not accept it, Sir.

Géronte. Sir.

Sganarelle. Not at all.

Géronte. One moment.

Sganarelle. On no consideration.

Géronte. Pray!

Sganarelle. You are jesting.

Géronte. That is settled.

Sganarelle. I shall do nothing of the kind.

Géronte. What!

Sganarelle. I do not practice for money's sake.

Géronte. I am convinced of that.

Sganarelle. [*After having taken the money*] Are they good weight?

Géronte. Yes, Sir.

Sganarelle. I am not a mercenary physician.

Géronte. I am well aware of it.

Sganarelle. I am not actuated by interest.

Géronte. I do not for a moment think so.

Sganarelle. [*Alone, looking at the money he has received*] Upon my word, this does not promise badly; and provided . . .

Scene IX. Léandre, Sganarelle.

Léandre. I have been waiting some time for you, Sir, and I have come to beg your assistance.

Sganarelle. [*Feeling his pulse*] That is a very bad pulse.

Léandre. I am not ill, Sir; and it is not for that I am come to you.

Sganarelle. If you are not ill, why the devil do you not tell me so?

Léandre. No. To tell you the matter in a few words, my name is Léandre. I am in love with Lucinde to whom you have just paid a visit; and as all access to her is denied to me, through the ill-temper of her father, I venture to beseech you to serve me in my love affair, and to assist me in a stratagem that I have invented, so as to say a few words to her, on which my whole life and happiness absolutely depend.

Sganarelle. [*In apparent anger*] Whom do you take me for? How dare you address yourself to me to assist you in your love affair, and to wish me to lower the dignity of a physician by an affair of that kind!

Léandre. Do not make a noise, Sir!

Sganarelle. [*Driving him back*] I will make a noise. You are an impertinent fellow.

Léandre. Ah! gently, Sir.

Sganarelle. An ill-mannered jackanapes.

Léandre. Pray!

Sganarelle. I will teach you that I am not the kind of man you take me for, and that it is the greatest insolence . . .

Léandre. [*Taking out a purse*] Sir . . .

Sganarelle. To wish to employ me . . . [*taking the purse*]. I am not speaking about you, for you are a gentleman; and I should be delighted to be of any use to you; but there are certain impertinent people in this world who take folks for what they are not; and I tell you candidly that this puts me in a passion.

Léandre. I ask your pardon, Sir, for the liberty I have . . .

Sganarelle. You are jesting. What is the affair in question?

Léandre. You must know then, Sir, that this disease which you wish to cure is a feigned complaint. The physicians have argued about it, as they ought to do, and they have not failed to give it as their opinion, — this one, that it arose from the brain; that one, from the intestines; another, from the spleen; another, again, from the liver; but the fact is that love is its real cause, and that Lucinde has only invented this illness in order to free herself from a marriage with which she has been harassed. But for fear that we may be seen together, let us retire; and I will tell you as we go along, what I wish you to do.

Sganarelle. Come along, then, Sir. You have inspired me with an inconceivable interest in your love; and if all my medical science does not fail me, the patient shall either die or be yours.

ACT III

SCENE: *A spot near* GÉRONTE'S *house.*

Scene I. LÉANDRE, SGANARELLE.

Léandre. I think that I am not at all badly got up for an apothecary; and as her father has scarcely ever seen me, this change of dress
and wig is likely enough, I think, to disguise me.

Sganarelle. There is no doubt of it.

Léandre. Only I should like to know five or six big medical words
to leaven my conversation with, and to give me the air of a learned
man.

Sganarelle. Go along, go along; it is not at all necessary. The
dress is sufficient; and I know no more about it than you do.

Léandre. How is that!

Sganarelle. The devil take me if I understand anything about
medicine! You are a gentleman, and I do not mind confiding in you,
as you have confided in me.

Léandre. What! Then you are not really . . .

Sganarelle. No, I tell you. They have made me a physician in
the teeth of my protests. I have never attempted to be so learned
as that; and all my studies did not go farther than the lowest class
at school. I do not know how the idea has come to them; but when
I saw that in spite of everything they would have it that I was a
physician, I made up my mind to be so at somebody's expense. You
would not believe, however, how this error has spread, and how every
one is possessed, and believes me to be a learned man. They come
seeking me on all sides; and if things go on in this way, I am resolved
to stick to the profession all my life. I find that it is the best trade
of all; for, whether we manage well or ill, we are paid just the same.
Bad workmanship never recoils on us; and we cut the material we
have to work with pretty much as we like. A shoemaker, in making
a pair of shoes, cannot spoil a scrap of leather without having to
bear the loss; but in our business we may spoil a man without its
costing us a farthing. The blunders are never put down to us, and
it is always the fault of the fellow who dies. The best of this profession is, that there is the greatest honesty and discretion among the
dead; for you never find them complain of the physician who has
killed them.

Léandre. It is true that the dead are very honorable in that
respect.

Sganarelle. [*Seeing some people advancing towards him*] There come some people, who seem anxious to consult me. [*To* LÉANDRE] Go and wait for me near the house of your lady-love.

Scene II. THIBAUT, PERRIN, SGANARELLE.

Thibaut. Sir, we come to look for you, my son Perrin and myself.

Sganarelle. What is the matter?

Thibaut. His poor mother, whose name is Perrette, has been on a bed of sickness for the last six months.

Sganarelle. [*Holding out his hand as if to receive money*] What would you have me do to her?

Thibaut. I would like you to give me some little doctor's stuff to cure her.

Sganarelle. We must first see what is the matter with her.

Thibaut. She is ill with the hypocrisy,[13] Sir.

Sganarelle. With the hypocrisy?

Thibaut. Yes; I mean she is swollen everywhere. They say that there is a lot of seriosities in her inside, and that her liver, her belly, or her spleen, as you would call it, instead of making blood makes nothing but water. She has, every other day, the quotiguian[14] fever, with lassitude and pains in the muscles of her legs. We can hear in her throat phlegms that are ready to choke her, and she is often taken with syncoles[15] and conversions,[16] so that we think she is going off the hooks. We have got in our village an apothecary — with respect be it said — who has given her, I do not know how much stuff. But all this, as people say, was nothing but an ointment of fiddle-faddle.[17] He wanted to give her a certain drug called ametile[18] wine; but I was downright afeard that this would send her to the other world altogether; because they tell me that those big physicians kill, I do not know how many, with that new-fangled notion.

Sganarelle. [*Still holding out his hand, and moving it about to show that he wants money*] Let us come to the point, friend, let us come to the point.

Thibaut. The point is, Sir, that we have come to beg of you to tell us what we must do.

---

13 **hypocrisy:** dropsy is meant.
14 **quotiguian:** for quotidian, daily.
15 **syncoles:** for syncopes, swoons.
16 **conversions:** for convulsions.
17 **fiddle-faddle:** nonsense.
18 **ametile:** possibly camomile is meant.

Sganarelle. I do not understand you at all.

Perrin. My mother is ill, Sir, and here are two crowns which we have brought you to give us some stuff.

Sganarelle. Ah! you I do understand. There is a lad who speaks clearly, and explains himself as he should. You say that your mother is ill with the dropsy; that she is swollen all over her body; that she has a fever, with pains in the legs; that she sometimes is taken with syncopes and convulsions, that is to say with fainting fits.

Perrin. Indeed, Sir! that is just it.

Sganarelle. I understand you at once. Your father does not know what he says. And now you ask me for a remedy?

Perrin. Yes, Sir.

Sganarelle. A remedy to cure her?

Perrin. That is just what I mean.

Sganarelle. Take this then. It is a piece of cheese which you must make her take.

Perrin. A piece of cheese, Sir?

Sganarelle. Yes; it is a kind of prepared cheese, in which there is gold, coral, and pearls, and a great many other precious things.

Perrin. I am very much obliged to you, Sir, and I shall go and make her take it directly.

Sganarelle. Go, and if she dies, do not fail to bury her in the best style you can.

Scene III. *The Scene changes, and represents, as in the Second Act,
        a room in* GÉRONTE'S *house* — JACQUELINE, SGANARELLE,
        LUCAS, *at the far end of the stage.*

Sganarelle. Here is the pretty nurse. Ah! you darling nurse, I am delighted at this meeting; and the sight of you is like rhubarb, cassia, and senna to me, which purges all melancholy from my mind.

Jacqueline. Upon my word, M. Physician, it is no good talking to me in that style, and I do not understand your Latin at all.

Sganarelle. Get ill, nurse, I beg of you; get ill for my sake. I shall have all the pleasure in the world of curing you.

Jacqueline. I am your humble servant; I would much rather not be cured.

Sganarelle. How I grieve for you, beautiful nurse, in having such a jealous and troublesome husband.

Jacqueline. What am I to do, Sir? It is as a penance for my sins; and where the goat is tied down she must browse.

Sganarelle. What! Such a clod-hopper as that! a fellow who is always watching you, and will let no one speak to you!

Jacqueline. Alas! you have seen nothing yet; and that is only a small sample of his bad temper.

Sganarelle. Is it possible? and can a man have so mean a spirit as to ill-use a woman like you? Ah! I know some, sweet nurse, and who are not very far off, who would only be too glad to kiss your little feet! Why should such a handsome woman have fallen into such hands! and a mere animal, a brute, a stupid, a fool. . . . Excuse me, nurse, for speaking in that way of your husband.

Jacqueline. Oh! Sir, I know full well that he deserves all these names.

Sganarelle. Undoubtedly, nurse, he deserves them; and he also deserves that you should plant something on his head to punish him for his suspicions.

Jacqueline. It is true enough that if I had not his interest so much at heart, he would drive me to do some strange things.

Sganarelle. Indeed it would just serve him right if you were to revenge yourself upon him with some one. The fellow richly deserves it all, I tell you, and if I were fortunate enough, fair nurse, to be chosen by you . . .

[*While* SGANARELLE *is holding out his arms to embrace* JACQUE-LINE, LUCAS *passes his head under them, and comes between the two.* SGANARELLE *and* JACQUELINE *stare at* LUCAS, *and depart on opposite sides, but the doctor does so in a very comic manner.*]

Scene IV.   GÉRONTE, LUCAS.

Géronte. I say, Lucas, have not you seen our physician here?

Lucas. Indeed I have seen him, by all the devils, and my wife, too.

Géronte. Where can he be?

Lucas. I do not know; but I wish he were with the devil.

Géronte. Just go and see what my daughter is doing.

Scene V.   SGANARELLE, LÉANDRE, GÉRONTE.

Géronte. I was just inquiring after you, Sir.

Sganarelle. I have just been amusing myself in your court with expelling the superfluity of drink. How is the patient?

Géronte. Somewhat worse since your remedy.

Sganarelle. So much the better; it shows that it takes effect.

Géronte. Yes; but while it is taking effect, I am afraid it will choke her.

Sganarelle. Do not make yourself uneasy; I have some remedies that will make it all right! and I will wait until she is at death's door.

Géronte. [*Pointing to* LÉANDRE] Who is this man that is with you?

Sganarelle. [*Intimates by motions of his hands that it is an apothecary*] It is . . .

Géronte. What?

Sganarelle. He who . . .

Géronte. Oh!

Sganarelle. Who . . .

Géronte. I understand.

Sganarelle. Your daughter will want him.

Scene VI.   LUCINDE, GÉRONTE, LÉANDRE, JACQUELINE, SGANARELLE.

Jacqueline. Here is your daughter, Sir, who wishes to stretch her limbs a little.

Sganarelle. That will do her good. Go to her, M. Apothecary, and feel her pulse, so that I may consult with you presently about her complaint. [*At this point he draws* GÉRONTE *to one end of the stage, and putting one arm upon his shoulder, he places his hand under his chin, with which he makes him turn towards him, each time that* GÉRONTE *wants to look at what is passing between his daughter and the apothecary, while he holds the following discourse with him.*] Sir, it is a great and subtle question among physicians to know whether women or men are more easily cured. I pray you to listen to this, if you please. Some say " no," others say " yes." I say both " yes " and " no "; inasmuch as the incongruity of the opaque humors, which are found in the natural temperament of women, causes the brutal part to struggle for the mastery over the sensitive, we find that the conflict of their opinion depends on the oblique motion of the circle of the moon; and as the sun, which darts its beams on the concavity of the earth, meets . . .

Lucinde. [*To* LÉANDRE] No; I am not at all likely to change my feelings.

Géronte. Hark! my daughter speaks! O great virtue of the remedy! O excellent physician! How deeply am I obliged to you.

Sir, for this marvellous cure! And what can I do for you after such a service?

Sganarelle. [*Strutting about the stage, fanning himself with his hat*] This case has given me some trouble.

Lucinde. Yes, father, I have recovered my speech; but I have recovered it to tell you that I will never have any other husband than Léandre, and that it is in vain for you to wish to give me to Horace.

Géronte. But . . .

Lucinde. Nothing will shake the resolution I have taken.

Géronte. What . . .

Lucinde. All your fine arguments will be in vain.

Géronte. If . . .

Lucinde. All your talking will be of no use.

Géronte. I . . .

Lucinde. I have made up my mind about the matter.

Géronte. But . . .

Lucinde. No paternal authority can compel me to marry against my will.

Géronte. I have . . .

Lucinde. You may try as much as you like.

Géronte. It . . .

Lucinde. My heart cannot submit to this tyranny.

Géronte. The . . .

Lucinde. And I will sooner go into a convent than marry a man I do not love.

Géronte. But . . .

Lucinde. [*In a loud voice*] No. By no means. It is of no use. You waste your time. I shall do nothing of the kind. I am fully determined.

Géronte. Ah! what a torrent of words! One cannot hold out against it. [*To* SCANARELLE] I beseech you, Sir, to make her dumb again.

Sganarelle. That is impossible. All that I can do in your behalf is to make you deaf, if you like.

Géronte. I thank you. [*To* LUCINDE] Do you think . . .

Lucinde. No; all your reasoning will not have the slightest effect upon me.

Géronte. You shall marry Horace this very evening.

Lucinde. I would sooner marry death itself.

Sganarelle. [*To* GÉRONTE] Stop, for Heaven's sake! stop. Let me doctor this matter; it is a disease that has got hold of her, and I know the remedy to apply to it.

Géronte. Is it possible, indeed, Sir, that you can cure this disease of the mind also?

Sganarelle. Yes; let me manage it. I have remedies for everything; and our apothecary will serve us capitally for this cure. [*To* LÉANDRE] A word with you. You perceive that the passion she has for this Léandre is altogether against the wishes of the father; that there is no time to lose; that the humors are very acrimonious; and that it becomes necessary to find speedily a remedy for this complaint, which may get worse by delay. As for myself, I see but one, which is a dose of purgative flight, mixed, as it should be, with two drachms of matrimonium, made up into pills. She may, perhaps, make some difficulty about taking this remedy; but as you are a clever man in your profession, you must induce her to consent to it, and make her swallow the thing as best you can. Go and take a little turn in the garden with her to prepare the humors, while I converse here with her father; but, above all, lose not a moment. Apply the remedy quick! apply the specific!

Scene VII. GÉRONTE, SGANARELLE.

Géronte. What drugs are those you have just mentioned, Sir? It seems to me that I never heard of them before.

Sganarelle. They are drugs which are used only in urgent cases.

Géronte. Did you ever see such insolence as hers?

Sganarelle. Daughters are a little headstrong at times.

Géronte. You would not believe how she is infatuated with this Léandre.

Sganarelle. The heat of the blood produces those things in young people.

Géronte. As for me, the moment I discovered the violence of this passion, I took care to keep my daughter under lock and key.

Sganarelle. You have acted wisely.

Géronte. And I have prevented the slightest communication between them.

Sganarelle. Just so.

Géronte. They would have committed some folly, if they had been permitted to see each other.

Sganarelle. Undoubtedly.

Géronte. And I think she would have been the girl to run away with him.

Sganarelle. You have argued very prudently.

Géronte. I was informed, that he tried every means to get speech of her.

Sganarelle. The rascal!

Géronte. But he will waste his time.

Sganarelle. Aye! Aye!

Géronte. And I will effectually prevent him from seeing her.

Sganarelle. He has no fool to deal with, and you know some tricks of which he is ignorant. One must get up very early to catch you asleep.

Scene VIII. LUCAS, GÉRONTE, SGANARELLE.

Lucas. Odds-bobs! Sir, here is a pretty to-do. Your daughter has fled with her Léandre. It was he that played the apothecary, and this is the physician who has performed this nice operation.

Géronte. What! to murder me in this manner! Quick, fetch a magistrate, and take care that he does not get away. Ah, villain! I will have you punished by the law.

Lucas. I am afraid, Master Doctor, that you will be hanged. Do not stir a step, I tell you.

Scene IX. MARTINE, SGANARELLE, LUCAS.

Martine. [*To* LUCAS] Good gracious! what a difficulty I have had to find this place! Just tell me what has become of the physician I recommended to you?

Lucas. Here he is; just going to be hanged.

Martine. What! my husband hanged! Alas, and for what?

Lucas. He has helped some one to run away with master's daughter.

Martine. Alas, my dear husband, is it true that you are going to be hanged?

Sganarelle. Judge for yourself. Ah!

Martine. And must you be made an end of in the presence of such a crowd?

Sganarelle. What am I to do?

Martine. If you had only finished cutting our wood, I should be somewhat consoled.

Sganarelle. Leave me, you break my heart.

Martine. No, I will remain to encourage you to die; and I will not leave you until I have seen you hanged.

Sganarelle. Ah!

Scene X. Géronte, Sganarelle, Martine.

Géronte. [*To* Sganarelle] The magistrate will be here directly, and we shall put you in a place of safety where they will be answerable for you.

Sganarelle. [*On his knees, hat in hand*] Alas! will not a few strokes with a cudgel do instead?

Géronte. No; no; the law shall decide. But what do I see?

Scene XI. Géronte, Léandre, Lucinde, Sganarelle, Lucas, Martine.

Léandre. Sir, I appear before you as Léandre, and am come to restore Lucinde to your authority. We intended to run away, and get married; but this design has given away to a more honorable proceeding. I will not presume to steal away your daughter, and it is from your hands alone that I will obtain her. I must at the same time acquaint you, that I have just now received some letters informing me of the death of my uncle, and that he has left me heir to all his property.

Géronte. Really, Sir, your virtue is worthy of my utmost consideration, and I give you my daughter with the greatest pleasure in the world.

Sganarelle. [*Aside*] The physician has had a narrow escape!

Martine. Since you are not going to be hanged, you may thank me for being a physician; for I have procured you this honor.

Sganarelle. Yes, it is you who procured me, I do not know how many thwacks with a cudgel.

Léandre. [*To* Sganarelle] The result has proved too happy to harbor any resentment.

Sganarelle. Be it so. [*To* Martine] I forgive you the blows on account of the dignity to which you have elevated me; but prepare yourself henceforth to behave with great respect towards a man of my consequence; and consider that the anger of a physician is more to be dreaded than people imagine.

(*Anonymous Translation*)

SUGGESTIONS FOR STUDY

1. To what extent does the humor of *The Physician in spite of Himself* depend upon situation? How much do characterization and dialogue contribute?

2. Picture each scene of the play as you would like to see it on the stage. There is a great deal of by-play in the action, as is evidenced by the stage directions. This is more important than setting and costuming.

3. How much of the enjoyment of the play is due to the personality of Sganarelle? Characterize him as fully as you can. Do you know any characters in Shakespeare's plays who resemble him at all?

4. What is the purpose of the scene in which M. Robert tries to prevent Sganarelle from beating Martine?

5. Molière, like Shakespeare, was often careless about his plots, especially about the way his plays ended. Does the last scene here seem to you artificial or forced? If so, can you suggest a better solution?

6. Pick out passages in which the medical profession is satirized.

7. The language of the play is full of everyday idioms. Some remarks of Sganarelle have become proverbial, as for example: " There be faggots and faggots " and " We have changed all that." Notice where these occur and just how they are used.

8. Select good examples of repartee and lively dialogue.

9. Read Anatole France's one-act play *The Man Who Married a Dumb Wife,* which is based on a suggestion from Act III, Scene 6, of Molière's play.

JEAN DE LA FONTAINE (1621–1695)

La Fontaine is the prince of fabulists. We may define a fable as a tale in prose or verse, in which human emotions and actions are attributed to beasts. The fable goes back to remotest antiquity and no doubt originated in the belief of primitive man that the beasts actually could talk and reason. Fables were originally told for the sake of the story; the moral was a later addition. The East, the land of myth and legend, is the natural home of fable. The oldest specimens we possess come from India, whence they spread in all directions. The Greek Aesop is often called the father of the fable, but he is a shadowy figure, and the fables circulated under his name are sometimes identical with those found in India. The poet Phaedrus, in the first century A.D., made Latin versions of many of these tales. In the Middle Ages not only did short fables continue to be written, but long beast epics as well, in which the chief actors are the sly fox Reynard and his various enemies, whose superior strength he is able to outwit. It will thus be seen that La Fontaine had numerous predecessors in making the lower animals act like human beings.

He was born and brought up in the province of Champagne but spent the latter part of his life in Paris, where he won fame and favor by his pen and was elected to the Academy. He was of an easygoing disposition and a general favorite, as his nickname *le bonhomme*, " the good fellow," indicates. But his conduct was by no means exemplary and he gave some offense by his versified *Tales,* drawn from such sprightly sources as Boccaccio and Rabelais. Like his friend Molière, he was essentially pagan in his outlook on life. In the end, however, he made his peace with the Church.

La Fontaine was a lover of woods and fields and a close observer of the ways of animals. There was enough of the eternal child in him to indulge freely in make-believe. At the same time, he was a keen student of men, with plenty of insight into character and a lively sense of the absurd. His *Fables* were published in three installments between 1668 and 1693 and became immediately popular. They have never lost their hold on men's affections and to this day form a standard reading book of French both at home and abroad. All children in France learn them and come to appreciate and enjoy them even more after they grow up. La Fontaine's beasts are real enough in their own right, but they also represent the peasants, townsmen and nobles of his own day. The whole of seventeenth-century society is here pictured true to life. Besides, it should be observed that many of his tales are not even ostensibly beast fables but are human stories. The light, tripping movement of the lines and the variety of the meters give the final touch of grace to the amusing anecdote and the sly dig at human foibles.

Rousseau and a few others have asserted that the *Fables* are more likely to teach lessons of cunning and self-interest than of openness and generosity. La Fontaine, however, was not so much bent on laying down rules of conduct as on giving a picture of general experience. He wished to avoid a too obtrusive moral. As he put the matter himself:

> We yawn at sermons but we gladly turn
> To moral tales, and so amused we learn.

As La Fontaine has had no worthy successor, it is likely that the fable, as such, has reached its climax. But the animal story on a larger scale may have a future. The success of Joel Chandler Harris' *Uncle Remus* and Rudyard Kipling's *Jungle Book* in opening up new territory for literature warrants this belief.

THE CROW AND THE FOX

A crow sat perched upon an oak,
And in his beak he held a cheese.
A fox snuffed up the savory breeze,

And thus in honeyed accent spoke:
" O Prince of Crows, such grace of mien   5
Has never in these parts been seen.
If but your voice be half as good,
You are the Phoenix of the wood! "
The crow, beside himself with pleasure,
And in his vanity intent   10
On meriting the compliment,
Opened his beak, and dropped his treasure.
The fox was on it in a trice.
" Learn, sir," said he, " that flatterers live
On those who swallow what they say.   15
A cheese is not too much to give
For such a piece of sound advice."
The crow, ashamed to have been such easy prey,
Swore, though too late, he shouldn't catch him twice.

(Edward Marsh)

8. **Phoenix:** model of excellence.

WOMEN AND SECRETS

A secret is a heavy load;
Most women drop it on the road;
(And in this matter 'tis uncommon
To find a man who's not a woman.)

One night in bed, to test his wife,   5
" Help! " cried a husband.   " Save my life!
What *is* this pain?   Those pangs again . . .
Look!   If I haven't laid an egg! "
" An egg? "   " Yes, there, beside my leg,
New-laid and white.   Don't breathe a word   10
To living soul of what you've heard.
I couldn't face my fellow men —
I should be called the Laying Hen! "

The dame, to whom the case was new
(As many other things were too),   15
Was gulled, and swore by book and candle
Never to divulge the scandal —

A promise doomed to fade away
At the first glimmering of day,
When, weak in brains as in discretion,   20
She ups and runs across the way
To make her crony the confession.

"Oh, Mrs. Robinson," she cries,
"You'll never guess . . . . such a surprise!
John's laid an egg, four times life-size —   25
He'll beat me if you tell a creature,
So do for Heaven's sake keep it mum."
"Ah! " said the other, looking wise,
"How little do you know my nature!
Depend upon me to be dumb."   30
Relieved, the Layer's wife returns.

The neighbor's heart within her burns
Until she can the news repeat
To every gossip in the street,
Making the egg not one, but three.   35
The next said four, and whispered low —
A caution hardly needed now,
The secret having ceased to be.

From mouth to mouth, by Rumor's power,
The tale of eggs grew more and more;   40
Till that same day, by sunset hour,
The number was at least fivescore.

                                    (*Edward Marsh*)

SUGGESTIONS FOR STUDY

1. "The Crow and the Fox" belongs to the general stock of fables.
Compare it with any fable of Aesop. What does the verse form add?

2. A similar situation in which the fox uses flattery is to be found in
Chaucer's "Chaunticleer and Pertelotë," in "The Nun's Priest's Tale,"
one of *The Canterbury Tales.* "The Fox in Literature" would be an interesting subject of investigation, for there are many other examples.
What instances can you recall in the *Uncle Remus* stories of one animal
outwitting another?

3. Show in what respects "Women and Secrets" may be regarded as
a short *fabliau.* How is it related to the modern "yarn"?

LA ROCHEFOUCAULD (1613–1680)

François, Duke of La Rochefoucauld, belonged to one of the noblest families in France. In his younger days he became involved in political intrigues which resulted in the thwarting of his ambitions. This disappointment increased his natural tendency to pessimism and partly explains the almost unrelieved cynicism of his *Maxims,* which were published in 1665. Preoccupation with moral considerations was one of the most noteworthy features of the literature of the Great Age. La Rochefoucauld excelled all the other moralists in the power of concentrated expression, packing the utmost amount of meaning into the fewest possible words. His purpose was to show that all conduct could be traced back to the single motive of self-interest. He told many unpleasant truths, which most people will not admit to others and try their best to hide even from themselves. It may be added, however, that La Rochefoucauld has helped bring some of these truths into the open by the very currency which his *Maxims* have obtained in all countries. His low estimate of human nature did not differ greatly from Pascal's, but whereas the latter proclaimed the imperative need of Divine Grace as the only cure for this radical corruption, La Rochefoucauld simply shrugged his shoulders like the disillusioned man of the world that he was.

MAXIMS

Self-love is the greatest of all flatterers.

We have all of us sufficient fortitude to bear the misfortunes of others.

Neither the sun nor death can be looked at steadily.

We are never so happy, or so unhappy, as we imagine.

It is with true love as with ghosts. Every one talks of it, but few have ever seen it.

It is more disgraceful to distrust one's friends than to be deceived by them.

We are sometimes as different from ourselves as we are from others.

There are people who would never have fallen in love if they had never heard love talked about.

We would rather speak ill of ourselves than not talk of ourselves at all.

There are heroes in evil as well as in good.

It belongs only to great men to have great faults.

Hypocrisy is the homage which vice pays to virtue.

True eloquence consists in saying all that is necessary, and nothing but what is necessary.

The pleasure of love is in loving. We are happier in the passion we feel than in that which we arouse.

There are follies as catching as contagious diseases.

We think very few people sensible except those who are of our opinion.

We have more indolence in the mind than in the body.

Every one complains of his memory, and no one complains of his judgment.

Old men are fond of giving good advice, to console themselves for being no longer in a position to give bad examples.

The head is always the dupe of the heart.

(*Anonymous Translation*)

SUGGESTIONS FOR STUDY

1. Which of these Maxims do you regard as pessimistic or cynical, which as merely realistic, and which as more idealistic in tone?
2. La Rochefoucauld believed men to be actuated mainly by self-love. In which of these Maxims does he manifest this belief?
3. Do you think it is true that people are lazier mentally than physically? Consider the cases of yourself and your friends.
4. Why do people complain of their memory and not of their judgment?
5. What is the meaning of the concluding Maxim?
6. Compare the *Maxims* of La Rochefoucauld with the *Thoughts* of Pascal. Observe carefully resemblances and differences in their points of view.

BLAISE PASCAL (1623–1662)

Of all the great writers of the Great Age of French literature, Pascal is probably the one who has made the deepest impression on the English-speaking world. One of the most serious-minded of Frenchmen, with almost none of the gay Gallic spirit, he was, nevertheless, thoroughly French in the lucidity of his mind and in the clearness and elegance of his expression. He was a mathematical genius of a very high order, but his chief fame today is that of a searcher of men's hearts, whom few have equaled and none surpassed in his ability to penetrate to the very essence of human nature. The unique quality of his mind lies in its combination of two things seldom found together in such high degree — reasoning power and imaginative insight. Pascal himself called them " the spirit of geometry " and " the spirit of finesse."

He was born in the district of Auvergne in south central France, but spent most of his life in or near Paris. Except for a brief contact with the world, he lived the life of a recluse, devoting himself first to physics and mathematics and latterly to the religious life. He experienced an intense religious conversion at the age of thirty-one, after which he renounced the world entirely and spent the rest of his life in retirement. He had come under the influence of a religious movement in the Roman Catholic Church known as Jansenism, which taught the doctrine of predestination. The Jansenists were bitterly opposed by the Jesuits, who eventually brought about their suppression. The principal center of Jansenism was at Port-Royal near Paris, and it was there that Pascal spent much of his time after his conversion. He died at the early age of thirty-nine, worn out by the extreme austerities to which he had subjected himself.

Pascal has a permanent place in literature by reason of two works. His *Provincial Letters* are an attack on the principles and practices of the Jesuits, whom Pascal accused of shifty evasions and moral laxity. Of much greater interest to us today is the mass of notes which were published after his death under the title of *Thoughts*. Though very incomplete, they rightly take a high place in religious literature because of the depth of their thought, their psychological intuition and the piercing quality of their language. Pascal evidently intended them as a defense of Christianity, which for him consisted essentially of two things: the corruption of man and his redemption through Christ. He argues that Christianity is reasonable because it alone understands human nature. It is deserving of our love because it promises us happiness. Reason gets us nowhere; it leads only to doubt; and doubt, if carried far enough, destroys itself. Therefore it is the part of higher reason to obey the instinct of the heart and by faith reach what the mere intellect cannot attain to. " The heart has its reasons which reason itself does not know."

The most famous of Pascal's sayings are those which concern the nature of man. Man, he declares, is a paradox, a contradiction, partaking at one and the same time of the infinitely great and the infinitely small. He is the glory of the universe because of his power of thinking, but he is equally the shame of the universe on account of his moral degradation. The only thing, in his mind, that can solve this enigma of human nature is the Christian doctrine of the fall of man. Man was once divine, but by sin he has forfeited his high estate and abased himself to the very dust.

THOUGHTS

Men have a secret instinct which leads them to seek amusement and occupation outside of themselves, and which springs from the feeling of continual unhappiness. They also have another secret instinct — a remnant of the greatness of our original nature — which tells them that happiness is really to be found only in repose and not in distraction; and from these two opposed instincts there is formed in them a confused design, hidden from their view in the depths of their souls, which leads them to strive for repose through agitation, and always to imagine that the satisfaction which they have not will come if, surmounting certain obstacles which confront them, they can thus open for themselves the portal of rest.

Man is but a reed, — the weakest thing in nature, — but he is a reed that thinks. It is not necessary that the whole universe should arm itself to crush him. A vapor, a drop of water, is enough to kill him. But if the universe should crush him, man would still be nobler than that which slays him, for he knows that he dies; but of the advantage which it has over him the universe knows nothing. Our dignity consists, then, wholly in thought. Our elevation must come from this, not from space and time, which we cannot fill. Let us, then, labor to think well: this is the fundamental principle of morals.

The greatness of man is so obvious that it can be deduced even from his wretchedness. For that which in animals is nature, in man we call wretchedness; and by this we recognize that, his nature being now like that of the brutes, he has fallen from a better nature which once was his.

Vanity is so anchored in the heart of man that soldiers, camp-followers, cooks, and porters are boastful and wish to have admirers, and so do even the philosophers. Even those who write against fame wish for the fame of having written well, and those who read their works desire the fame of having read them. Even I who write this have, perhaps, this desire — and those, perhaps, who will read what I am writing!

What a chimera,[1] then, is man! What a novelty, monster, chaos, contradiction, prodigy![2] Judge of all things, weak earthworm, de-

---

[1] **chimera:** fantastic creature.   [2] **prodigy:** marvelous thing.

positary of truth, sewer of uncertainty and error, glory and scum of the universe!

Know, then, proud one, what a paradox [3] you are to yourself. Humble yourself, impotent reason! Be silent, imbecile nature! Understand that man infinitely transcends [4] man, and learn from your master your true condition, of which you are ignorant. Give ear to God.

The twofoldness of human nature is so obvious that some have thought that we have two souls: a single subject appears to them to be incapable of such and so sudden changes — from unbounded presumption to a horrible depression of the heart.

(Anonymous Translation)

[3] **paradox:** self-contradiction.   [4] **transcends:** surpasses.

SUGGESTIONS FOR STUDY

1. What exactly does Pascal mean by "the greatness of our original nature"?
2. Why does he regard man as the "glory and scum of the universe"?
3. Explain the statement that "man infinitely transcends man."
4. What argument does he advance to show that human dignity consists wholly in thought?
5. Would you call Pascal pessimistic or optimistic? Give reasons for your answer.

VOLTAIRE (1694–1778)

Voltaire is the pen name by which François Arouet is always known. He was the most typical man of letters of the eighteenth century, summing up in his person the opinions and attitudes of the age of reason. He was born in Paris and was educated in a Jesuit college, where he acquired the reputation of cleverness and wit, but also of impertinence. These qualities soon got him into trouble. He was twice imprisoned in the Bastille for arousing personal or political displeasure. After the second experience he departed for England, where for three years he made a careful study of English literature and thought, which resulted in the famous *Letters on the English*. When this book was suppressed, he retired to the country estate of the Marquise du Châtelet for ten years of quiet life devoted to writing and study. In 1750 he accepted the invitation of Frederick the Great of Prussia to join his court at Potsdam. After three years the visit ended in a quarrel and Voltaire then took up his residence at Ferney near

Geneva. There began the last and most interesting phase of his long and varied career. Feeling free from molestation by the authorities, he proceeded to attack political and ecclesiastical intolerance in a series of pamphlets which deeply affected public opinion. His battle cry " Crush the infamous thing! " was directed against the spirit of persecution in church and state. In 1778 he made a final visit to Paris and received an extraordinary ovation, but the physical strain proved fatal.

Voltaire has so inflamed passions both for and against him that it is not easy to form a fair estimate of either his character or his writings. Obviously he had many personal faults, but he possessed one compensating virtue — a strong sense of justice, which he manifested both in words and in deeds. His mind was uncannily active, but it was lively rather than profound. His influence on thought, enormous during his lifetime, continued to be felt in the French Revolution, of which he was one of the intellectual forerunners. His complete works fill ninety-nine volumes. Everything he wrote, especially in prose, is interesting, but not much is of significance today. For example, his poetic tragedies, which were hailed as masterpieces when they appeared, now seem like second-rate imitations of Corneille and Racine. He wrote a great deal of verse, but with the mind of a wit not the soul of a poet. His histories, notably *The Age of Louis XIV* and the *Essay on Morals and Manners,* have lasted better. But almost his only works which still give unalloyed pleasure are the satirical tales, *Candide* and *Zadig,* and many of his letters. It is probably best to regard him as a high-class journalist who swayed his own age and who occasionally achieved something of more permanent value. He was in almost every respect the opposite of his contemporary Rousseau, whose influence on his own time was equally strong and whose effect on posterity has been vastly more enduring.

LETTER TO ROUSSEAU

This famous letter was called forth by Rousseau's first book, his *Discourse on the Arts and Sciences* (1750), in which he denounced the corrupting influence of civilization and advocated a return to nature. To Voltaire this seemed like the most outrageous nonsense. His letter, for all its bantering tone, contains a serious argument and fairly bristles with historical and literary references. Most of the writers he mentions are represented in this book.

I have received, monsieur, your new book against the human race; I thank you for it. You will please men to whom you tell truths which concern them, but you will not correct them. One could not paint in stronger colors the horrors of human society, from which our ignorance and our weakness expect so many consolations. No one has ever employed so much intellect in the attempt to prove us beasts. A desire seizes us to walk on four paws, when we read your work. Nevertheless, as it is more than sixty years since I lost the habit, I feel, unfortunately, that it is impossible for me to resume it; and I leave that natural mode of walking to those who are more worthy of it than you and I. Nor can I embark to go among the savages of Canada: first because the maladies with which I am afflicted detain me near the greatest physician in Europe, and I should not find the same succor among the Missouris; secondly because war has broken out in that country, and the example of our nation has rendered the savages almost as wicked as we are. I limit myself to be a peaceful savage in the solitude which I have chosen in your country, where you ought to be.

I agree with you that literature and the sciences have sometimes been the cause of much evil. The enemies of Tasso [1] rendered his life a tissue of misfortunes; those of Galileo [2] made him groan in prison at the age of seventy years for having known the motion of the earth, and what was more shameful, they compelled him to retract. No sooner had your friends begun the *Dictionaire Encyclopédique* [3] than those who presumed to be their rivals called them deists,[4] atheists, and even Jansenists.[5]

If I dared to reckon myself among those whose labors have been recompensed by persecution alone, I should show you men in a rage to destroy me, from the day that I gave the tragedy of *Edipe;* I should show you a library of ridiculous calumnies printed against me; an ex-Jesuit priest, whom I saved from capital punishment, paying me by defamatory libels for the service which I had rendered him; I should show you a man still more culpable, printing my own work upon the *Age of Louis XIV,* with notes, in which the most brutal ignorance poured forth the most infamous impostures; . . . I should show you society infested with this kind of men, unknown to all antiquity, who, not being able to embrace an honest calling, whether that of workman or of lackey, and knowing unfortunately how to read and write, become courtiers of literature, live upon our works, steal

---

[1] **Tasso:** (1544–1595) Italian poet.

[2] **Galileo:** (1564–1642) Italian physicist and astronomer.

[3] **Dictionnaire Encylopédique:** This most famous of all encyclopedias was edited by Diderot (1713–1784). Both Voltaire and Rousseau contributed articles.

[4] **deists:** those who believed in a God but rejected Christianity.

[5] **Jansenists:** followers of Jansen (1585–1638), a Dutch theologian whose views were regarded as heretical by the Roman Catholic Church.

manuscripts, disfigure them, and sell them; . . . . I should paint you
ingratitude, imposture, and rapine pursuing me for forty years, even
to the foot of the Alps, even to the brink of my tomb. But what shall
I conclude from all these tribulations? That I ought not to complain;
that Pope,[6] Descartes,[7] Bayle,[8] Camoëns,[9] and a hundred others, have
experienced the same injustice and greater; that this destiny is that of
almost all those whom the love of letters has too powerfully influenced.

Confess, monsieur, that these are trifling private misfortunes, which
the community scarcely perceives. What does it matter to the human
race that some hornets pillage the honey of some bees? Men of letters
make a great noise about all these little quarrels; the rest of the world
does not know them, or laughs at them.

Of all the bitternesses spread over human life, these are the least
fatal. The thorns attached to literature and to the reputation which
it gives are flowers compared with other evils, which in all times have
overwhelmed the earth. Admit that neither Cicero,[10] nor Varro,[11]
nor Lucretius,[12] nor Virgil,[13] nor Horace,[14] had the least share in the
proscriptions.[15] Marius [16] was an ignorant man; the barbarous
Sylla,[17] the debauched Antony,[18] the imbecile Lepidus,[19] read little
of Plato and Socrates; and as to that tyrant without courage, Octavius
Cepias, surnamed so unworthily Augustus,[20] he was merely a detest-
able assassin while he was deprived of the society of men of letters.

Confess that Petrarch [21] and Boccaccio [22] did not cause the intes-
tine [23] troubles of Italy; confess that the badinage of Marot [24] did
not cause the massacre of St. Bartholomew,[25] nor the tragedy of *The*

---

     [6] **Pope:** (1688–1744) English poet.
     [7] **Descartes:** (1596–1650) French philosopher.
     [8] **Bayle:** (1647–1706) French writer on philosophy and science.
     [9] **Camoëns:** (1524–1580) Portuguese poet.
     [10] **Cicero:** (106–43 B.C.) Roman statesman and orator.
     [11] **Varro:** (116–27 B.C.) Roman scholar and man of letters.
     [12] **Lucretius:** (96–55 B.C.) Roman poet.
     [13] **Virgil:** (70–19 B.C.) Roman epic poet.
     [14] **Horace:** (65–8 B.C.) Roman lyric poet.
     [15] **proscriptions:** decrees of outlawry.
     [16] **Marius:** (157?–86 B.C.) Roman general and politician.
     [17] **Sylla:** (138–78 B.C.) or Sulla, Roman general and dictator.
     [18] **Antony:** (83–30 B.C.) Mark Antony, Roman politician and soldier.
     [19] **Lepidus:** (75?–13 B.C.) Roman politician.
     [20] **Augustus:** (63 B.C.–14 A.D.) Roman emperor.
     [21] **Petrarch:** (1304–1374) Italian poet and humanist.
     [22] **Boccaccio:** (1313–1375) Italian novelist and poet.
     [23] **intestine:** internal.
     [24] **Marot:** (1496–1544) French poet.
     [25] **St. Bartholomew:** massacre of the Protestants in France, August 24,
1572.

Cid [26] the trouble of the Fronde.[27] Great crimes have seldom been committed except by celebrated ignoramuses. That which makes, and will always make, of this world a vale of tears, is the insatiable cupidity and the indomitable pride of men, from Thamas Kouli-kan [28] who did not know how to read, to a clerk of the tax office who knows only how to cipher. Literature nourishes the soul, rectifies it, consoles it; it was of service to you, monsieur, at the time when you wrote against it. You are like Achilles who inveighed against glory, and like Father Malebranche [29] whose brilliant imagination wrote against imagination.

If any one ought to complain of literature, it is myself, since at all times and in all places it has served to persecute me; but we must love it, despite the abuse which is made of it, as we must love society, the agreeableness of which is corrupted by so many wicked men; as we must love our country, whatever injustice we suffer in it; as we must love and serve the Supreme Being, notwithstanding the superstitions and fanaticism which so often dishonor his worship.

M. Chappius informs me that your health is very bad: you should come to re-establish it in your native air, to enjoy liberty, to drink with me the milk of our cows, and browse our herbs. I am very philosophically, and with the most tender esteem, etc.

(Anonymous Translation)

SUGGESTIONS FOR STUDY

1. Various moods of the writer are reflected in this letter. Point out these changes.

2. The paragraph beginning " If any one " sums up Voltaire's general philosophy of life. What things does he profess to love?

3. Voltaire prided himself on his reasonableness and common sense. To what extent does he employ these in his discussion of the question at issue?

4. Who have been the real perpetrators of human misery, in Voltaire's opinion? To what extent have men of letters and of science been responsible for this misery? With what examples from the twentieth century could you uphold Voltaire's argument?

5. Rousseau did not like Voltaire's letter, regarding it as frivolous, super-

---

[26] **The Cid:** Corneille's famous tragedy first produced 1636. See pages 46–48.
[27] **The Fronde:** a civil war in France, 1648–1652.
[28] **Thamas Kouli-kan:** (1688–1747) King of Persia.
[29] **Malebranche:** (1636–1715) French philosopher.

ficial and perhaps even insincere. What reasons have you for agreeing or disagreeing with this opinion?

6. Vocabulary: calumnies, defamatory, culpable, lackey, rapine, badinage, ignoramuses, cupidity, indomitable, inveighed.

JEAN-JACQUES ROUSSEAU (1712–1778)

Rousseau was born in Geneva, Switzerland. His mother died at his birth, and the duty of rearing the child fell chiefly upon his father, whose judgment in such matters was not sound. The result was that Rousseau's sentiments and feelings were indulged at the expense of intellectual and moral discipline. At the age of sixteen he ran away to Savoy, where he was given shelter by Madame de Warens, who tried to have him trained for the Catholic priesthood. But all attempts to make him stick to regular work having failed, he was allowed to remain on Madame de Warens' estate, where he passed his time in reading, daydreaming, and composing music. In 1741 he went to Paris with the intention of devoting himself entirely to music. He had a hard struggle at first and was compelled to lead a hand-to-mouth existence. In 1750 he began his career as a writer with his *Discourse on the Arts and Sciences,* which created a furor of excitement by its denunciation of modern culture and its advocacy of a return to nature. Four years later his *Discourse on Inequality* further startled the world by its radical doctrine that all civilization is corrupt because it is based on inequalities of private possessions.

Rousseau was now a famous figure in Paris literary circles, but he did not like society and was at all times a hard man to get along with. The years 1761 and 1762 were the most fruitful of his career, for in them he wrote three of his most important books: *Julie,* his only real work of fiction, *The Social Contract,* one of the world's most influential political documents, and *Émile,* an epoch-making treatise on education. The authorities objected to the political and theological views expressed in *Émile* and ordered Rousseau's arrest. He sought refuge in Switzerland but was ill received by the inhabitants. He then accepted the invitation of the Scotch philosopher and historian, David Hume, to take up his abode in England. The visit ended in a disastrous quarrel, for Rousseau was now suffering from a mental malady which made him suspicious of everybody. He returned to France in 1767 and settled in Paris, where, poverty stricken and half insane, he passed his remaining years. He died suddenly in 1778 just a few weeks after his great rival and opposite, Voltaire. His only writing of importance during the last period of his life was his autobiography, the *Confessions,* which is now his most widely read book.

Rousseau is the greatest of romantic philosophers. The opening words of *Émile* summarize his teaching: " Everything is good coming from the hands of the Author of things, everything degenerates in the hands of man." Whatever is natural is good; every departure from nature is evil. Civilization itself is a colossal mistake, because it has perverted man by destroying his primitive simplicity and purity. Absurd as these theories sound when stated so baldly, they yet contained the democratic truth that beneath the artificial trappings of society there is an underlying humanity common to all.

Rousseau has probably influenced thought more than any other man of his time. So pervasive have his ideas become that many people who have never read a word of his writings have nevertheless felt his influence unconsciously. He was the chief intellectual cause of the French Revolution. The first sentence of *The Social Contract* challenged political despotism: " Man is born free, but everywhere he is in chains." By proclaiming the sovereignty of the people, he made himself a mighty champion of democracy. He is also claimed by the socialists as one of their forerunners because he declared private property to be the root of social injustice. The educational reforms which he advocated have affected our system of instruction all the way from kindergarten to college. In literature he heralded romanticism in his love of nature, his extreme individualism, and his assertion of the rights of the heart over those of the head.

THE CONFESSIONS

The *Confessions* were written during some of Rousseau's most agitated years, from 1765 to 1770, and give a fairly complete account of his life. They were not published until after his death. Although they unquestionably constitute one of the world's greatest autobiographies, they cannot be accepted entirely at their face value. Statements of facts, estimates of men and events, even Rousseau's judgments upon himself have to be taken with some reserve. Rousseau's announced intention is best set forth in the opening paragraphs here given. The second extract is one of the most typical of his " confessions " about himself.

I

I am commencing an undertaking, hitherto without precedent, and which will never find an imitator. I desire to set before my fellows the likeness of a man in all the truth of nature, and that man myself.

Myself alone! I know the feelings of my heart, and I know men. I am not made like any of those I have seen; I venture to believe that I am not made like any of those who are in existence. If I am not better, at least I am different. Whether Nature has acted rightly or wrongly in destroying the mould in which she cast me, can only be decided after I have been read.

Let the trumpet of the Day of Judgment sound when it will, I will present myself before the Sovereign Judge with this book in my hand. I will say boldly: " This is what I have done, what I have thought, what I was. I have told the good and the bad with equal frankness. I have neither omitted anything bad, nor interpolated anything good. If I have occasionally made use of some immaterial embellishments, this has only been in order to fill a gap caused by lack of memory. I may have assumed the truth of that which I knew might have been true, never of that which I knew to be false. I have shown myself as I was: mean and contemptible, good, high-minded and sublime, according as I was one or the other. I have unveiled my inmost self even as Thou hast seen it, O Eternal Being. Gather round me the countless host of my fellow-men; let them hear my confessions, lament for my unworthiness, and blush for my imperfections. Then let each of them in turn reveal, with the same frankness, the secrets of his heart at the foot of the Throne, and say, if he dare, *' I was better than that man! '* "

2

Would that I had finished all that I had to say about my stay at Madame de Vercellis's! But, although my condition apparently remained the same, I did not leave the house as I entered it. I carried away from it lasting recollections of crime and the insupportable weight of remorse, which, after forty years, still lies heavy on my conscience; while the bitterness of it, far from growing weaker, makes itself more strongly felt with my advancing years. Who would believe that a childish fault could have such cruel consequences? For these more than probable consequences my heart is inconsolable. I have, perhaps, caused the ruin of an amiable, honest, and estimable girl, who certainly was far more worthy than myself, and doomed her to disgrace and misery.

It is almost unavoidable that the break up of an establishment should cause some confusion in the house, and that several things should get lost; however, the servants were so honest, and the Lorenzis so watchful, that nothing was missing when the inventory was taken. Only Mademoiselle Pontal had lost a piece of old red and silver-colored ribbon. Many other things of greater value were at my disposal; this ribbon alone tempted me; I stole it, and, as I took no trouble to conceal it, it was soon found. They wanted to know how it had come into my possession. I became confused, stammered, blushed, and at last said that Marion had given it to me. Marion was a young girl from Maurienne, whom Madame de Vercellis had taken for her cook, when she left off giving dinners and discharged her own, as she had more need of good soup than of fine stews. Marion was not only pretty but had a fresh color, only found on the mountains, and, above all, there was something about her so gentle and modest, that it was impossible for any one to see her without loving her; in addition to that, she was a good and virtuous girl, and of unquestionable honesty. All were surprised when I mentioned her name. We were both equally trusted and it was considered important to find out which of us two was really the thief. She was sent for; a number of people were assembled, amongst them the Comte de la Roque. When she came, the ribbon was shown to her. I boldly accused her; she was astounded, and unable to utter a word; looked at me in a manner that would have disarmed the Devil himself, but against which my barbarous heart was proof. At last, she denied the theft firmly, but without anger, addressed herself to me, exhorted me to reflect, and not to disgrace an innocent girl who had never done me any harm; but I, with infernal impudence, persisted in my story, and declared to her face that she had given me the ribbon. The poor girl began to cry, and only said to me: " Ah! Rousseau, I thought you were a good man. You make me very unhappy, but I should not like to be in your place." That was all. She proceeded to defend herself with equal simplicity and firmness, but without allowing herself to utter the slightest reproach against me. This moderation, contrasted with my decided tone, did her harm. It did not seem natural to suppose, on the one side, such devilish impudence, and, on the other, such angelic mildness. Although the matter did not appear to be absolutely settled, they were prepossessed in my favor. In the confusion which prevailed, they did not give themselves time to get to the bottom of the affair; and the Comte de la Roque, in dismissing us both, contented himself with saying that the conscience of the guilty one would amply avenge the innocent. His prediction has been fulfilled; it fulfils itself every day.

I do not know what became of the victim of my false accusation; but it is not likely that she afterwards found it easy to get a good situation. She carried away with her an imputation upon her honesty which was in every way cruel. The theft was only a trifling one, but still it was a theft, and, what is worse, made use of to lead a young man astray; lastly, lying and obstinacy left nothing to be hoped from one in whom so many vices were united. I do not even consider misery and desertion as the greatest danger to which I exposed her. At her age, who knows to what extremes discouragement and the feeling of ill-used innocence may have carried her? Oh, if my remorse at having, perhaps, made her unhappy is unendurable, one may judge what I feel at the thought of having, perhaps, made her worse than myself!

This cruel remembrance at times so sorely troubles and upsets me, that in my sleepless hours I seem to see the poor girl coming to reproach me for my crime, as if it had been committed only yesterday. As long as I have lived quietly, it has tormented me less; but in the midst of a stormy life it robs me of the sweet consolation of persecuted innocence, it makes me feel what I think I have said in one of my books, that " Remorse goes to sleep when our fortunes are prosperous, and makes itself felt more keenly in adversity." However, I have never been able to bring myself to unburden my heart of this confession to a friend. The closest intimacy has never led me so far with any one, not even with Madame de Warens. All that I have been able to do has been to confess that I had to reproach myself with an atrocious act, but I have never stated wherein it consisted. This burden has remained to this day upon my conscience without alleviation; and I can affirm that the desire of freeing myself from it in some degree, has greatly contributed to the resolution I have taken of writing my Confessions.

I have behaved straightforwardly in the confession which I have just made, and it will assuredly be found that I have not attempted to palliate the blackness of my offence. But I should not fulfil the object of this book, if I did not at the same time set forth my inner feelings, and hesitated to excuse myself by what is strictly true. Wicked intent was never further from me than at that cruel moment; and when I accused the unhappy girl, it is singular, but it is true, that my friendship for her was the cause of it. She was present to my thoughts; I threw the blame on the first object which presented itself. I accused her of having done what I meant to do, and of having given me the ribbon, because my intention was to give it to her. When I afterwards saw her appear, my heart was torn; but the presence of so many people was stronger than repentance. I was not afraid of punishment, I was only afraid of disgrace; and that I feared more than death, more than crime, more than anything else in the world. I should have rejoiced if the earth had suddenly opened, swallowed me up and suffocated me; the unconquerable fear of shame overcame everything, and alone made me impudent. The greater my crime, the more the dread of confessing it made me fearless. I saw nothing but the horror of being recognised and publicly declared. in my own presence, a thief, liar, and slanderer. Complete embarrassment deprived me of every other feeling. If I had been allowed to recover myself I should have assuredly confessed everything. If M. de la Roque had taken me aside and said to me: "Do not ruin this poor girl; if you are guilty, confess it to me," I should have immediately thrown myself at his feet, of that I am perfectly certain. But, when I needed encouragement, they only intimidated me. And yet it is only fair to consider my age. I was little more than a child, or rather, I still was one. In youth real crimes are even more criminal than in riper years; but that which is only weakness is less so, and my offence was at bottom scarcely anything else. Thus the recollection of it afflicts me not so much by reason of the evil in itself as on account of its evil consequences. It has even done me the good of securing me for the rest of my life against every act tending to crime, by the terrible impression which I have retained of the only offence that I have ever committed; and I believe that my horror of a lie is due in great measure to my regret at having been capable myself of telling one so shameful. If it is a crime that can be expiated, as I venture to believe, it must be expiated by all the unhappiness which has overwhelmed the last years of my life, by forty years of honorable and upright conduct in difficult circumstances; and poor Marion finds so many avengers in this world, that, however great my offence against her may have been, I have little fear of dying without absolution. This is what I have to say on this matter: permit me never to speak of it again.

(John Grant)

SUGGESTIONS FOR STUDY

1. "Myself alone!" Compare Montaigne's preface to his *Essays*, page 43: "Thus, gentle Reader, myself am the groundwork of my book." What English and American writers have emphasized the value of maintaining one's individuality?

2. Read the selections in this book from the autobiographies of St. Augustine, Cellini, Goethe and Tolstoy and observe the different way each one has of proceeding with his task.

3. Rousseau says that his undertaking will never find an imitator. This prediction has not come true. There have been some equally sincere autobiographies published in recent years. Do you know any of them?

4. Illustrate the frankly confessional method of Rousseau by reference to the episode of the stolen ribbon. Does he seem to you to be trying to excuse himself in the last paragraph?

5. Rousseau has been called the father of romanticism, for his emphasis upon personality among other reasons. Where is this to be seen in the foregoing extracts?

6. Discuss the question why there are more, fuller and franker autobiographies written by men than by women.

PIERRE JEAN DE BÉRANGER (1780–1857)

French poetry does not have the singable quality of either English or German. For that reason French literature is comparatively poor in songs such as those of Burns or Heine. But an exception must be made of the songs of Béranger, which were tremendously popular in their own day and which have not yet lost their hold on men's affections. He was a stanch republican and did not hesitate to use the song as a political weapon. He no doubt contributed in this way to the Revolution of 1830, which deposed the Bourbon dynasty. By birth a man of the people and largely self-educated, he appealed to the masses by his ideas and sentiments, which were simply those of the average man. He was at his best when he sang the common sorrows of mankind. His songs, set to current tunes, reached the widest kind of an audience. Robert Louis Stevenson said of Béranger that he was the only poet of modern times who could altogether have dispensed with printing.

THE KING OF YVETOT

The lords of Yvetot, a small town in Normandy, had the title of king at one time. This song was written in 1813 and obviously contains a satirical reference to Napoleon in the fourth stanza. But Béranger came later to prefer Napoleon to the Bourbons who supplanted him after his downfall.

> There was a king of Yvetot,
>   Of whom renown hath little said,
>   Who let all thoughts of glory go,
>   And dawdled half his days a-bed;
>   And every night as night came around,   5
>   By Jenny with a nightcap crowned,
>   Slept very sound:
>   Sing ho, ho, ho! and he, he, he!
>   That's the kind of a king for me.
>
> And every day it came to pass,   10
>   That four lusty meals made he;
> And step by step, upon an ass,
>   Rode abroad, his realms to see;

And wherever he did stir,
What think you was his escort, sir?   15
   Why an old cur.
    Sing ho, ho, ho! and he, he, he!
    That's the kind of a king for me.

If e'er he went into excess,
   'Twas from a somewhat lively thirst;   20
But he who would his subjects bless,
   Odd's fish! — must wet his whistle first;
And so from every cask they got,
   Our king did to himself allot
    At least a pot.   25
    Sing ho, ho, ho! and he, he, he!
    That's the kind of a king for me.

To all the ladies of the land
   A courteous king, and kind, was he —
The reason why, you'll understand,   30
   They named him Pater Patriae.
Each year he called his fighting men,
And marched a league from home, and then
   Marched back again.
    Sing ho, ho, ho! and he, he, he!   35
    That's the kind of a king for me.

Neither by force nor false pretense,
   He sought to make his kingdom great,
And made (O princes, learn from hence)
   " Live and let live " his rule of state.   40
'Twas only when he came to die,
That his people who stood by
   Were known to cry.
    Sing ho, ho, ho! and he, he, he!
    That's the kind of a king for me.   45

The portrait of this best of kings
   Is extant still, upon a sign
That on a village tavern swings,
   Famed in the country for good wine.

31. **Pater Patriae:** father of his country.

The people in their Sunday trim,   50
Filling their glasses to the brim,
   Look up to him,
Singing " ha, ha, ha! " and " he, he, he!
That's the sort of a king for me."

                                       (*W. M. Thackeray*)

VICTOR HUGO (1802–1885)

Victor Hugo was born in Besançon in the east of France. His father, an officer in Napoleon's army, took his family with him on his expeditions, and in this way Victor in his boyhood saw Corsica, Italy, and Spain. Though irregularly educated, the future poet was extremely precocious. However, his first volumes of verse showed little departure from tradition. But from 1827 on, Hugo put himself at the head of the Romantic School which was being formed by the young literary men of France. His *Oriental Poems* (1829) were thoroughly romantic in their gorgeous coloring and intensity of passion. In these as in all his later poems he also showed astonishing skill in versification, with a range and variety of metrical effects which no other French poet had equaled. Even more striking was his conquest of the stage. When his poetic drama *Hernani* was produced in the national theater in Paris in 1830, the triumph of romanticism was officially recognized. The play violated the unities, mingled comedy with tragedy, and in every other respect repudiated the long-established traditions of the French drama. *Ruy Blas* (1838) repeated the brilliant success of *Hernani*. Meanwhile Hugo was conquering a third province of literature — the novel. *Notre Dame de Paris* (1831), in which the cathedral is the central figure, is in many ways the typical romantic novel. It is melodramatic and sensational but also undeniably picturesque and powerful. In the humanitarian novel, *Les Misérables* (1862), his most widely read book, he turned from the romance of the past to the romance of contemporary life. Since 1830 politics had divided his attention with literature. He had begun his career as a Catholic and a royalist. He now became a freethinker and a liberal. His political views grew more radical as time passed until in 1850, in consequence of his bitter opposition to Napoleon III, he was banished and for the next eighteen years lived in exile on the islands of Jersey and Guernsey. On the fall of the Empire in 1870, he returned to France, a convinced republican with strong leanings toward socialism.

Hugo's long life and prodigious vitality enabled him to produce a tremendous amount of work. It is his lyric poetry which has best stood the test of time. He is generally regarded as the greatest of French poets. His imagination, versatility, descriptive power, command of all the resources of language, and verbal music give to his verse the stamp of genius. His plays, on the other hand, now seem crude and almost childish, however effectual individual scenes may be. His novels, though maintaining their popularity, are improbable in plot and inartistic in construction. His besetting faults in whatever he wrote were pretentiousness, lack of balance, and a passion for glaring contrasts. His philosophy of life was essentially that of Rousseau. He had an optimistic faith in the goodness of human nature, a consuming hatred of injustice, and an infinite pity for all feeble and helpless creatures, the lower animals included. His vast series of poems, *The Legend of the Centuries*, which took shape during the latter part of his life, presents a panorama of human history which appeared to him to be " one single and immense movement upward toward the light."

MORE STRONG THAN TIME

Since I have set my lips to your full cup, my sweet,
Since I my pallid face between your hands have laid,
Since I have known your soul, and all the bloom of it,
And all the perfume rare, now buried in the shade;

Since it was given to me to hear one happy while,   5
The words wherein your heart spoke all its mysteries,
Since I have seen you weep, and since I have seen you smile,
Your lips upon my lips, and your eyes upon my eyes;

Since I have known above my forehead glance and gleam,
A ray, a single ray, of your star, veiled always,   10
Since I have felt the fall, upon my lifetime's stream,
Of one rose petal plucked from the roses of your days;

I now am bold to say to the swift changing hours,
Pass, pass upon your way, for I grow never old,
Fleet to the dark abysm with all your fading flowers,   15
One rose that none may pluck, within my heart I hold.

Your flying wings may smite, but they can never spill
The cup fulfilled of love, from which my lips are wet;
My heart has far more fire than you can frost to chill,
My soul more love than you can make my soul forget.   20

(Andrew Lang)

THE SOWER

Sitting in the porchway cool,
Fades the ruddy sunlight fast,
Twilight hastens on to rule —
Working hours are well-nigh past.

Shadows shoot across the lands;   5
But one sower lingers still,
Old, in rags, he patient stands, —
Looking on, I feel a thrill.

Black and high his silhouette
Dominates the furrows deep!   10
Now to sow the task is set,
Soon shall come a time to reap.

Marches he along the plain,
To and fro, and scatters wide
From his hands the precious grain;   15
Moody, I, to see him stride.

Darkness deepens. Gone the light.
Now his gestures to mine eyes
Are august; and strange — his height
Seems to touch the starry skies.   20

(*Toru Dutt*)

THE DJINNS

Djinns, or genii, in Muslim popular belief, are spirits created of
fire, and either good or evil. Hugo puts the words of the poem into the
mouth of a pious Muslim who, witnessing the approach of a storm, imagines in his terror a swarm of genii sweeping over his house. The poem
is especially noteworthy from a technical point of view.

Town, tower,
Shore, deep,
Where lower
Cliffs steep;

Waves gray,   5
Where play
Winds gay, —
All sleep.

Hark! a sound,
Far and slight,   10
Breathes around
On the night;
High and higher,
Nigh and nigher,
Like a fire   15
Roaring bright.

Now on 't is sweeping
With rattling beat,
Like dwarf imp leaping
In gallop fleet;   20
He flies, he prances,
In frolic fancies,
On wave-crest dances
With pattering feet.

Hark, the rising swell,   25
With each nearer burst!
Like the toll of bell
Of a convent cursed;
Like the billowy roar
On a storm-lashed shore, —   30
Now hushed, now once more
Maddening to its worst.

O God! the deadly sound
Of the Djinns' fearful cry!
Quick, 'neath the spiral round   35
Of the deep staircase fly!
See, see our lamplight fade!
And of the balustrade
Mounts, mounts the circling shade
Up to the ceiling high!   40

'T is the Djinns' wild streaming swarm
Whistling in their tempest-flight;
Snap the tall yews 'neath the storm,
Like a pine-flame crackling bright.
Swift and heavy, lo, their crowd   45
Through the heavens rushing loud,
Like a livid thunder-cloud
With its bolt of fiery night!

Ha! they are on us, close without!
Shut tight the shelter where we lie!   50
With hideous din the monster rout,
Dragon and vampire fill the sky!
The loosened rafter overhead
Trembles and bends like quivering reed;
Shakes the old door with shuddering dread, 55
As from its rusty hinge 't would fly!

Wild cries of hell! voices that howl and shriek!
The horrid swarm before the tempest tossed —
O Heaven! — descends my lowly roof to seek:
Bends the strong wall beneath the furious host. 60
Totters the house, as though, like dry leaf shorn
From autumn bough and on the mad blast borne,
Up from its deep foundations it were torn
To join the stormy whirl. Ah! all is lost!

O Prophet! if thy hand but now   65
Save from these foul and hellish things,
A pilgrim at thy shrine I'll bow,
Laden with pious offerings.
Bid their hot breath its fiery rain
Stream on my faithful door in vain,   70
Vainly upon my blackened pane
Grate the fierce claws of their dark wings!

They have passed! — and their wild legion
Cease to thunder at my door;
Fleeting through night's rayless region,   75
Hither they return no more.

65. **Prophet:** Mahomet.

Clanking chains and sounds of woe
Fill the forests as they go;
And the tall oaks cower low,
Bent their flaming flight before.   80

On! on! the storm of wings
Bears far the fiery fear,
Till scarce the breeze now brings
Dim murmurings to the ear;
Like locusts' humming hail,   85
Or thrash of tiny flail
Plied by the pattering hail
On some old roof-tree near.

Fainter now are borne
Fitful mutterings still;   90
As, when Arab horn
Swells its magic peal,
Shoreward o'er the deep
Fairy voices sweep,
And the infant's sleep   95
Golden visions fill.

Each deadly Djinn,
Dark child of fright,
Of death and sin,
Speeds the wild flight   100
Hark, the dull moan,
Like the deep tone
Of ocean's groan,
Afar, by night!

More and more   105
Fades it now,
As on shore
Ripple's flow, —
As the plaint
Far and faint   110
Of a saint
Murmured low.

86. flail: hand threshing instrument.

> Hark! hist!
> Around,
> I list!   115
> The bounds
> Of space
> All trace
> Efface
> Of sound.   120

(Anonymous Translation)

SUGGESTIONS FOR STUDY

1. Which of these poems have the strongest emotional appeal? Which show sympathy with the mass of humanity? Which have striking originality? Point out lines or phrases which make an especial appeal to you.

2. What is the mood of "More Strong than Time"? Show how the rich imagery of the poem intensifies the mood. Compare with Shakespeare's Sonnet 116, "Let me not to the marriage of true minds." Though the theme is similar, what marked difference is there in the total impression of the two poems? Can you name other poems on the enduring quality of true love?

3. Look at a copy of Millet's famous painting "The Sower." What have the painting and Hugo's poem in common? How does Hugo make the sower both realistic and august?

4. Show how the various stages of the situation in "The Djinns" are suggested by the movement of the lines. What English and American poems do you know in which meter and length of line are adapted to thought or mood?

5. How many different characteristics of romanticism can you find in this group of poems? Wherein do you feel kinship between Hugo and other romantic poets you know?

6. Reading hint: Besides extending your acquaintance with his poetry, you should know at least one of his two most famous novels, *Notre Dame de Paris* and *Les Misérables*. These have also been produced in moving pictures, and comparison of the effect of the story in the film and in the novel would be interesting.

ALEXANDRE DUMAS (1802–1870)

The older Dumas was a man of boundless energy whose collected works fill nearly three hundred volumes, many of them, to be sure, written with the aid of numerous assistants. Some of his plays had an importance in their day, but living interest attaches only to certain of his romances, such as *The Count of Monte Cristo* and *The Three Musketeers*. Dumas had to a supreme degree the gift of story telling. The quick movement of the narrative, the high spirits, the zest for exciting adventure, the easy style — all combine to absorb the interest of even the most hardened reader.

THE COUNT OF MONTE CRISTO

The Count of Monte Cristo is the only romance of comparatively modern times which Dumas wrote. The others are historical or pseudo-historical. Edmond Dantès, the hero of the novel, has been unjustly imprisoned for many years in the Château d'If. In the following chapter we are told how he came in contact with a fellow prisoner, Faria by name. A later chapter narrates his escape. Faria dies, and Dantès ties himself in the sack intended for the corpse. Thus he is thrown into the sea and swims to safety. He subsequently discovers a treasure and starts anew in life as the mysterious Count of Monte Cristo, who wreaks vengeance on all his persecutors.

DANTÈS IN PRISON

NO. 34 AND NO. 27

Dantès passed through all the degrees of misfortune that prisoners forgotten in their dungeon suffer. He commenced with pride, — a natural consequence of hope and a consciousness of innocence; then he began to doubt his own innocence, — a doubt which justified in some measure the governor's belief in his mental alienation; [1] and then he fell from the height of his pride, — he prayed, not yet to God, but to men. The unhappy man, who should begin by seeking the Lord, puts trust in him only after exhausting all other hopes.

Dantès prayed, then, that he might be removed from his present dungeon into another, — for a change, however disadvantageous, was still a change, and would afford him some distraction. He entreated to be allowed to walk about, to have books and instruments. Nothing was granted; no matter, he asked all the same. He accustomed himself to speak to his new jailer, although he was, if possible, more taciturn than the former; but still, to speak to a man, even though mute, was something. Dantès spoke for the sake of hearing his own voice; he had tried to speak when alone, but the sound of his voice terrified him. Often, before his captivity, Dantès's mind had revolted at the idea of those assemblages of prisoners, composed of thieves,

[1] **alienation:** insanity.

vagabonds, and murderers. He now wished to be among them, in order to see some other face besides that of his jailer, who would not speak to him; he sighed for the galleys, with their infamous costume, their chain, and the brand on the shoulder. The galley-slaves breathed the fresh air of heaven, and saw each other. They were very happy. He besought the jailer one day to let him have a companion, were it even the mad abbé.[2]

The jailer, though rude and hardened by the constant sight of so much suffering, was yet a man. At the bottom of his heart he had often compassionated the unhappy young man who suffered thus; and he laid the request of No. 34 before the governor. But the latter, as prudent as if he had been a politician, imagined that Dantès wished to conspire or attempt an escape, and refused his request. Dantès had exhausted all human resources; he then turned to God.

All the pious ideas that had been so long forgotten returned. He recollected the prayers his mother had taught him, and discovered in them a meaning until then unknown to him; for in prosperity prayers seem but a mere assemblage of words, until the day when misfortune comes to explain to the unhappy sufferer the sublime language by which he invokes the pity of Heaven! He prayed, not with fervor but with rage. He prayed aloud, no longer terrified at the sound of his voice. Then he fell into a species of trance. He saw God listening to every word he uttered; he laid every action of his life before the Almighty, proposed tasks to accomplish, and at the end of every prayer introduced the entreaty oftener addressed to man than to God, " Forgive us our trespasses as we forgive them that trespass against us." Spite of the earnest prayers, Dantès remained a prisoner.

Then a gloomy feeling took possession of him. He was simple, and without education; he could not, therefore, in the solitude of his dungeon and of his thoughts, reconstruct the ages that had passed, reanimate the nations that had perished, and rebuild the ancient cities that imagination renders so vast and stupendous, and that pass before our eyes, illuminated by the fires of heaven. He could not do this, his past life was so short, his present so melancholy, and his future so doubtful. Nineteen years of light to reflect upon in eternal darkness! No distraction could come to his aid; his energetic spirit, that would have exulted in thus revisiting the past, was imprisoned like an eagle in a cage. He clung to one idea, — that of his happiness, destroyed without apparent cause by an unheard-of fatality; he con-

---

[2] **abbé**: priest.

sidered and reconsidered this idea, devoured it (so to speak) as Ugolino,[3] devours the skull of the Archbishop Roger in the Inferno of
Dante.

Rage succeeded to asceticism. Dantès uttered blasphemies that
made his jailer recoil with horror, dashed himself furiously against
the walls of his prison; he turned his fury against everything around
him, and especially against himself, against the least thing that annoyed him, — a grain of sand, a straw, or a breath of air. He said
to himself that it was the enmity of man, and not the vengeance of
Heaven, that had thus plunged him into the deepest misery. He devoted these unknown persecutors to the most horrible tortures he
could imagine, and found them all insufficient, because after torture
came death, and after death, if not repose, at least that insensibility
that resembles it.

By dint of constantly dwelling on the idea that repose was death,
and that in order to punish cruelly other tortures than death must be
invented, he began to reflect on suicide. Unhappy he who on the brink
of misfortune broods over these ideas! The idea of suicide is one of
those dead seas that seem clear and smooth to the eye; but he who
unwarily ventures within its embrace finds himself entangled in a
quagmire that attracts and swallows him. Once thus ensnared, unless the protecting hand of God snatch him thence, all is over, and
his struggles but tend to hasten his destruction. This state of mental
anguish is, however, less terrible than the sufferings that precede and
the punishment that perhaps awaits it; it is a sort of consolation that
points to the yawning abyss, at the bottom of which is darkness.

Edmond found some solace in this idea. All his sorrows, all his
sufferings, with their train of gloomy spectres, fled from his cell when
the angel of death seemed about to enter. Dantès reviewed with composure his past life, and looking forward with terror to his future,
chose that middle line that seemed to afford him a refuge.

" Sometimes," said he, " in my voyages, when I was still a man,
free and powerful, and commanded other men, I have seen the heavens
become overcast, the sea rage and foam, the storm arise, and like a
monstrous bird cover the sky with its wings. Then I felt that my
vessel was a vain refuge, for like a feather in the hand of a giant, it
trembled and shook before the tempest. Soon the fury of the waves
and the sight of the sharp rocks announced the approach of death,

---

[3] **Ugolino**: Ugolino, his two sons and his grandson were imprisoned by the
treachery of Archbishop Roger and starved to death. The horrible punishment
of the traitor is described in Canto XXXIII of Dante's *Inferno*.

and death then terrified me; and I used all my skill and intelligence as a man and a sailor in a struggle against the Almighty! I did so because I was happy; because a return to life was a return to enjoyment; because I had not courted that death, had not chosen it; because this repose on a bed of rocks and seaweed seemed terrible; because I was unwilling that I, a creature made in the image of God, should serve for food to the gulls and ravens. But now it is different. I have lost all that bound me to life; death smiles and invites me to repose. I die after my own manner, I die exhausted and broken-spirited, as I fall asleep after one of those evenings of despair and rage when I have paced three thousand times round my cell."

No sooner had this idea taken possession of him than he became more composed; he arranged his couch to the best of his power, ate and slept little, and found this existence almost supportable, because he felt he could throw it off at pleasure, like a worn-out garment. He had two means of dying, — one was to hang himself with his handkerchief to the stanchions [4] of the window; the other to refuse food and starve himself. But the former project was repugnant to him. Dantès had always entertained a horror of pirates, who are hung up to the yardarm; he would not die by what seemed an infamous death. He resolved to adopt the second, and began that day to execute his resolve. Nearly four years had passed away; at the end of the second he had fallen again into ignorance of dates, from which the inspector had lifted him.

Dantès had said, " I wish to die," and had chosen the manner of his death; and fearful of changing his mind, he had taken an oath so to die. " When my morning and evening meals are brought," thought he, " I will cast them out of the window, and I shall be believed to have eaten them."

He kept his word; twice a day he cast out, by the barred aperture, the provisions his jailer brought him, — at first gaily, then with deliberation, and at last with regret. Nothing but the recollection of his oath gave him strength to proceed. Hunger rendered these viands, once so repugnant, appetizing to the eye and exquisite to the sense of smell; sometimes he held the plate in his hand for an hour at a time, and gazed on the morsel of bad meat, of tainted fish, of black and mouldy bread. The deeper instincts of self-preservation yet strove within him, and occasionally vanquished his resolve; then his dungeon seemed less sombre, his condition less desperate. He was still young, — he was only four or five and twenty; he had nearly

[4] **stanchions**: upright supports.

fifty years to live. In that vast space of time what unforeseen events might not open his prison door, and restore him to liberty? Then he raised to his lips the repast that, like a voluntary Tantalus [5] he had refused himself; but he thought of his oath, and that generous nature had too great fear of despising himself to be able to break his oath. He persisted, then, rigorous and pitiless, until at last he had not sufficient force to cast his supper out of the loophole. The next morning he could not see or hear; the jailer feared he was dangerously ill. Edmond hoped he was dying.

The day passed away thus. Edmond felt a species of stupor creeping over him; the gnawing pain at his stomach had ceased; his thirst had abated; when he closed his eyes he saw myriads of lights dancing before them, like the meteors that play about the marshes. It was the twilight of that mysterious country called Death!

Suddenly, about nine o'clock in the evening, Edmond heard a hollow sound in the wall against which he was lying.

So many loathsome animals inhabited the prison that their noise did not in general awake him; but now, whether abstinence had quickened his faculties, or whether the noise was really louder than usual, or whether in that supreme moment everything gained in significance, Edmond raised his head and listened. It was a continual scratching, as if made by a huge claw, a powerful tooth, or some iron instrument attacking the stones.

Although weakened, the young man's brain instantly recurred to the idea that haunts all prisoners, — liberty! It seemed to him that Heaven had at length taken pity on him, and had sent this noise to warn him on the very brink of the abyss. Perhaps one of those beloved ones he had so often thought of was thinking of him, and striving to diminish the distance that separated them.

No, no! doubtless he was deceived, and it was but one of those dreams that hover at the gate of death!

Edmond still heard the sound. It lasted about three hours; he then heard a noise of something falling, and all was silent.

Some hours afterwards it began nearer and more distinct; Edmond became already interested in that labor, which afforded him companionship. Suddenly the jailer entered.

During the week in which he was forming his resolution to die, and the four days since he began to put his resolve into execution, Ed-

---

[5] **Tantalus**: In Greek mythology, Tantalus was punished in the lower world for his offense against the gods by having food and drink placed forever beyond his reach. This myth is the origin of the English word " tantalize."

mond had not spoken to this man, had not answered him when he inquired what was the matter with him, and had turned his face to the wall when he looked too curiously at him; but now the jailer might hear this noise, and taking alarm, might put an end to it, thus destroying a ray of something like hope that soothed his last moments.

The jailer brought him his breakfast. Dantès raised himself up, and began to speak on all possible subjects, — on the bad quality of his food, on the coldness of his dungeon, grumbling and complaining in order to have an excuse for speaking louder, and wearying the patience of the jailer, who that very day had solicited some broth and white bread for his prisoner, and had brought it to him.

Fortunately the jailer fancied that Dantès was delirious; and placing his food on the rickety table, he withdrew. Free at last, Edmond again eagerly listened. The noise began again, and was now so distinct that he could hear it without effort.

"There can be no doubt," thought he; "it is some prisoner who is striving to obtain his freedom. Oh, if I were with him how I would help!"

Suddenly a cloud darkened that dawn of hope in a mind so used to misfortune that it could scarcely understand hope; the idea possessed him that the noise arose from the workmen the governor had ordered to repair the neighboring dungeon.

It was easy to ascertain this; but how could he risk the question? It was easy to call his jailer's attention to the noise, and watch his countenance as he listened; but might he not by this means betray precious hopes for a short-lived satisfaction? Unfortunately, Edmond's brain was still so feeble that he could not bend his thoughts to anything in particular.

He saw but one means of restoring lucidity and clearness to his judgment. He turned his eyes towards the soup his jailer had brought him, rose, staggered towards it, raised the vessel to his lips, and drank off the contents with an indescribable sensation of comfort; then he had the courage to abstain. He had heard that shipwrecked persons had died through having eagerly devoured too much food. Edmond replaced on the table the bread he was about to devour, and returned to his couch; he no longer wished to die. He soon felt that his ideas became again collected; he could think, and strengthen his thoughts by reasoning. Then he said to himself, "I must put this to the test, but without compromising anybody. If it is a workman, I need but knock against the wall, and he will cease to work in order to find out who is knocking and why he does so; but as his occupation is sanctioned by the governor, he will soon resume it. If, on the contrary, it is a prisoner, the noise I make will alarm him; he will cease, and not resume until he thinks every one is asleep."

Edmond rose again, but this time his legs did not tremble, and his eyes were free from mists; he advanced to a corner of his dungeon, detached a stone loosened by the moisture, and with it knocked against the wall at the place where the noise was most audible. He struck thrice; at the first blow the sound ceased, as if by magic.

Edmond listened intently. An hour passed, two hours passed, and no sound was heard from the wall, — all was silent there.

Full of hope Edmond swallowed a few mouthfuls of bread, drank some water, and thanks to the excellence of his constitution, found himself well-nigh recovered.

The day passed away in utter silence; night came without the noise having recommenced.

" It is a prisoner! " said Edmond, joyfully.

The night passed in unbroken silence. Edmond did not close his eyes.

In the morning the jailer brought his rations — he had already devoured those of the previous day; he ate these, listening anxiously for the sound, walking round and round his cell shaking the iron bars of the loophole, restoring by exercise vigor and agility to his limbs, and preparing himself thus for what might lie before him. At intervals he listened for a recurrence of the noise, and grew impatient at the prudence of the prisoner, who did not guess he had been disturbed by a captive as anxious for liberty as himself.

Three days passed, — seventy-two mortal hours, reckoned minute by minute!

At length, one evening just after the jailer's last visit, as for the hundredth time Dantès placed his ear against the wall, he fancied that he heard an almost imperceptible movement among the stones. He recoiled from the wall, walked up and down his cell to collect his thoughts, and replaced his ear at the same spot.

There could be no doubt that something was taking place on the other side; the prisoner had discovered the danger, and to continue his work in greater security, had substituted the lever for the chisel.

Encouraged by this discovery, Edmond determined to assist the indefatigable laborer. He began by moving his bed, behind which it seemed to him the work of deliverance was going on, and sought with his eyes for something with which he might pierce the wall, penetrate the cement, and displace a stone.

He saw nothing. He had no knife or sharp instrument; the grating of his window alone was of iron, and he had too often assured himself of its solidity. All his furniture consisted of a bed, a chair, a table, a pail, and a jug. The bed had iron clamps; but they were screwed to the wood, and it would have required a screw-driver to take them off. The table and chair had nothing that would serve; the pail had had a handle, but that had been removed. There remained but one resource, which was to break the jug, and with one of the sharp fragments attack the wall. He let the jug fall on the floor, and it broke in pieces. He concealed two or three of the sharpest fragments in his bed, leaving the rest on the floor. The breaking of his jug was too natural an accident to excite suspicion. He had all the night to work in, but in the darkness he could not do much, and he soon perceived that his instrument was blunted against something hard; he pushed back his bed, and awaited the day. With hope, patience had returned to him.

All night he heard the subterranean workman, who continued to mine his way. The day came; the jailer entered. Dantès told him the jug had fallen from his hand in drinking, and the jailer went grumbling to fetch another, without giving himself the trouble to remove the fragments of the broken one. He returned speedily, recommended the prisoner to be more careful, and departed.

Dantès heard joyfully the key grate in the lock; he listened until the sound of steps died away, and then, hastily displacing his bed, saw by the faint light that penetrated into his cell that he had labored uselessly the previous evening in attacking the stone instead of removing the plaster that surrounded it. The damp had rendered it friable, and he saw joyfully the plaster detach itself, — in small morsels, it is true; but at the end of half an hour he had scraped off a handful. A mathematician might have calculated that in two years, supposing that the rock was not encountered, a passage twenty feet long and two feet broad might be formed. The prisoner reproached himself with not having thus employed the hours which he had passed in prayers and despair. In the six years — as he reckoned — of his imprisonment, what might he not have accomplished?

In three days Dantès had succeeded, with the utmost precaution, in removing the cement and exposing the stone. The wall was formed of rough stones, to give solidity to which were imbedded at intervals blocks of hewn stone. It was one of these he had uncovered, and which he must remove from its socket. He strove to do so with his nails, but they were too weak; the fragments of the jug, inserted in the opening, broke, and after an hour of useless toil he paused. Was he to be thus stopped at the beginning, and was he to wait inactive until his neighbor, weary, perhaps, with toil, had accomplished everything? Suddenly an idea occurred to him; he smiled, and the perspiration dried on his forehead.

The jailer always brought Dantès's soup in an iron saucepan; this saucepan contained the soup of a second prisoner,— for Dantès had remarked that it was either quite full or half empty, according as the turnkey gave it to himself or his companion first. The handle of this saucepan was of iron; Dantès would have given ten years of his life in exchange for it.

The jailer poured the contents of this saucepan into Dantès's plate, who, after eating his soup with a wooden spoon, washed the plate, which thus served for every day. In the evening Dantès placed his plate on the ground near the door; the jailer, as he entered, stepped on it and broke it. This time he could not blame Dantès. He had done wrong in leaving it there, but the jailer was at fault in not noticing where he stepped.

The jailer therefore contented himself with grumbling. Then he looked about him for something to pour the soup into; Dantès whole furniture consisted of one plate, — there was no alternative.

" Leave the saucepan," said Dantès; " you can take it away when you bring me my breakfast." This advice was to the jailer's taste, as it spared him the necessity of ascending, descending, and ascending again. He left the saucepan.

Dantès was beside himself with joy. He rapidly devoured his food, and after waiting an hour, lest the jailer should change his mind and return, he removed his bed, took the handle of the saucepan, inserted the point between the hewn stone and rough stones of the wall, and employed it as a lever. A slight oscillation showed Dantès that his plan was a good one. At the end of an hour the stone was extricated from the wall, leaving a cavity of a foot and a half in diameter.

Dantès carefully collected the plaster, carried it into the corners of his cell, and covered it with earth. Then, wishing to make the best use of this night, in which chance, or rather his own stratagem, had placed so precious an instrument in his hands, he continued to work without ceasing. At the dawn of day he replaced the stone, pushed his bed against the wall, and lay down. The breakfast consisted of a piece of bread; the jailer entered and placed the bread on the table.

" Well, you do not bring me another plate," said Dantès.

" No," replied the turnkey, " you destroy everything. First you break your jug, then you make me break your plate; if all the prisoners followed your example the government would be ruined. I shall leave you the saucepan and pour your soup into that; under that arrangement you will perhaps avoid breaking dishes."

Dantès raised his eyes to heaven and clasped his hands beneath the coverlid. He felt more gratitude for the possession of this piece of iron than he had ever felt for anything. He had however remarked that the prisoner on the other side had ceased to labor. No matter, this was a greater reason for proceeding; if his neighbor would not come to him, he would go to him. All day he toiled on untiringly, and by the evening he had succeeded in extracting ten handfuls of plaster and fragments of stone. When the hour for his jailer's visit arrived, Dantès straightened the handle of the saucepan and put that receptacle in its accustomed place. The turnkey poured into it the customary ration of soup and meat, or rather of soup and fish, for it was a fast day; three times a week the prisoners were made to fast. This would have been a method of reckoning time, had not Dantès long ceased to do so. Having poured out the soup, the turnkey retired. Dantès wished to ascertain whether his neighbor had really ceased to work. He listened; all was silent, as it had been for the last three days. Dantès sighed; it was evident that his neighbor distrusted him. However, he toiled on all the night without being discouraged; but after two or three hours he encountered an obstacle. The iron made no impression, but glided on a smooth surface; Dantès touched it with his hands, and found it was a beam. This beam crossed, or rather blocked up, the hole Dantès had made; it was necessary, therefore, to dig above or under it. The unhappy young man had not expected this obstacle. "Oh, my God! my God!" murmured he, "I have so earnestly prayed to thee that I hoped my prayers had been heard. After having deprived me of my liberty, after having denied to me the repose of death, after having recalled me to existence, — my God! have pity on me, and do not let me die in despair!"

"Who talks of God and despair at the same time?" said a voice that seemed to come from beneath the earth, and deadened by the distance, sounded hollow and sepulchral in the young man's ears. Edmond's hair stood on end, and he recoiled on his knees.

"Ah!" said he, "I hear a human voice." He had not heard any one speak save his jailer for four or five years; and to a prisoner the jailer is not a man, — he is a living door added to his door of oak, a barrier of flesh and blood added to his barriers of iron.

"In the name of Heaven," cried Dantès, "speak again, though the sound of your voice terrifies me: who are you?"

" Who are you? " said the voice.

" An unhappy prisoner," replied Dantès, who made no hesitation in answering.

" Of what country? "

" A Frenchman."

" Your name? "

" Edmond Dantès."

" Your profession? "

" A sailor."

" How long have you been here? "

" Since the 28th of February, 1815."

" Your crime? "

" I am innocent."

" But of what are you accused? "

" Of having conspired to aid the emperor's return."

" What! the emperor's return! The emperor is no longer on the throne, then? "

" He abdicated at Fontainebleau in 1814, and was sent to the island of Elba. But how long have you been here that you are ignorant of all this? "

" Since 1811."

Dantès shuddered; this man had been four years longer than himself in prison.

" Do not dig any more," said the voice; " only tell me how high up is your excavation? "

" On a level with the floor."

" How is it concealed? "

" Behind my bed."

" Has your bed been moved since you have been a prisoner? "

" No."

" What does your chamber open on? "

" A corridor."

" And the corridor? "

" On the court."

" Alas! " murmured the voice.

" Oh, what is the matter? " cried Dantès.

" I am deceived; and the imperfection of my plans has ruined all. An error of a line in the plan has been equivalent to fifteen feet in reality, and I took the wall you are mining for the wall of the fortress."

" But then you would be close to the sea? "

" That is what I hoped."

" And supposing you had succeeded? "

" I should have thrown myself into the sea, gained one of the islands near here, — the Isle de Daume or the Isle de Tiboulen, — and then I should have been safe."

" Could you have swum so far? "

" Heaven would have given me strength; and now all is lost! "

" All? "

" Yes; stop up your excavation carefully. Do not work any more; and wait until you hear from me."

" Tell me, at least, who you are."

" I am — I am No. 27."

" You mistrust me, then? " said Dantès. He fancied he heard a bitter laugh proceed from the unknown.

" Oh, I am a Christian," cried Dantès, guessing instinctively that this man meant to abandon him. " I swear to you by Christ that I will let them kill me rather than suffer your executioners and mine to get a glimpse of the truth; but in the name of Heaven, do not deprive me of your presence, do not withdraw your voice from me, or I swear to you — for I have reached the end of my endurance — that I will dash my brains out against the wall, and you will have my death to reproach yourself with."

" How old are you? Your voice is that of a young man? "

" I do not know my age, for I have not counted the years I have been here. All I know is that I was just nineteen when I was arrested, the 28th of February, 1815."

" Not quite twenty-six! " murmured the voice; " at that age one cannot be a traitor."

" Oh, no, no! " cried Dantès. " I swear to you again, rather than betray you I will let them hew me to pieces! "

" You have done well to speak to me and entreat me, for I was about to form another plan, and leave you; but your age reassures me. I will come again to you. Expect me."

" When? "

" I must calculate our chances; I will give you the signal."

" But you will not leave me; you will come to me, or you will let me go to you. We will escape together, and if we cannot escape we will talk, — you of those whom you love, and I of those whom I love. You must love somebody? "

" No, I am alone in the world."

" Then you will love me. If you are young, I will be your comrade; if you are old, I will be your son. I have a father, who is seventy, if he yet lives; I love only him and a young girl called Mercédès. My father has not yet forgotten me, I am sure; but God alone knows if she loves me still. I shall love you as I loved my father."

" It is well," returned the voice; " tomorrow."

These few words were uttered with an accent that left no doubt of his sincerity. Dantès rose, buried the fragments with the same precaution as before, and pushed back his bed against the wall. He then gave himself up to his happiness. He would no longer be alone; he was perhaps about to regain his liberty. At the worst, if he remained a prisoner, he would have a companion; and captivity that is shared is but half captivity.

All day Dantès walked up and down his cell, his heart bounding with joy. From time to time his joy stifled him; he sat down on his bed, pressing his hand on his breast. At the slightest noise he bounded towards the door. Once or twice the fear crossed his mind that he might be separated from this unknown, whom he loved already. In that case his resolution was formed; when the jailer moved his bed and stooped to examine the opening, he would kill him with his water-jug. He would be condemned to die, but he was already about to die of grief and despair when this miraculous noise recalled him to life.

The jailer came in the evening; Dantès was on his bed. It seemed to him that thus he better guarded the unfinished opening. Doubtless there was a strange expression in his eyes, for the jailer said, " Come, are you going mad again? "

Dantès did not answer; he feared that the emotion of his voice would betray him. The jailer retired, shaking his head. The night came; Dantès hoped that his neighbor would profit by the silence to address him, but he was mistaken. The next morning, however, just as he removed his bed from the wall, he heard three knocks; he threw himself on his knees.

" Is it you? " said he; " I am here."

" Is your jailer gone? "

" Yes," said Dantès; " he will not return until the evening. We have twelve hours of liberty."

" I can work, then? " said the voice.

" Oh, yes, yes; this instant, I entreat you! "

In an instant the portion of the floor on which Dantès (half-buried in the opening) was leaning his two hands, began to yield under him; he cast himself back, while a mass of stones and earth disappeared in a hole that opened beneath the aperture he himself had formed. Then from the bottom of this passage, the depth of which it was impossible to measure, he saw appear, first the head, then the shoulders, and lastly the body of a man, who sprang lightly into his cell.

(*Anonymous Translation*)

SUGGESTIONS FOR STUDY

1. By what means does the author make the situation and feeling of Dantès especially vivid? Is the main emphasis put on external conditions or on the mental state of the prisoner?

2. Where in this chapter is suspense particularly great? What setbacks maintain the suspense?

3. Is the situation credible throughout, or do you find details which you think impossible in actual life? If so, do you think the author was justified in using them? Why, or why not?

4. If you have seen the film version of the book, discuss how closely the picture has followed this chapter of the novel.

5. Compare this picturing of a prison situation with other famous descriptions in literature, such as Byron's " Prisoner of Chillon " and those in Dickens's *A Tale of Two Cities*. *The Count of Monte Cristo* and Hugo's *Les Misérables* are similar in having a hero who remolds his life after an unjust imprisonment. If you have read both these books discuss the difference in the treatment of the situation.

ALFRED DE MUSSET (1810–1857)

Musset, poet, dramatist, and novelist, was a Parisian by birth and a thorough city man in all his tastes and habits. A very precocious youth, he had already made himself known as a poet by the time the Romantic School, with which he was associated, celebrated its great triumph in 1830. His best work was produced between 1835 and 1840. Dissipation undermined his health and hastened his death.

Musset was the most personal of poets. His sole concern was with the life of his own heart, and that meant for him love. His range was therefore narrow, but he made up for it by the intensity of his feeling. He conceived his happiness to have been wrecked by his hopeless passion for the novelist Aurore Dupin (George Sand). The grief and rankling disappointment of this experience inspired some of his best verse, notably the group of poems called *The Nights*. It also caused him to write the autobiographical novel *Confession of a Child of the Century*, in which he painfully analyzed himself and his passion. Romantic exaltation of love thus led to an equally romantic melancholy. There was perhaps something unmanly in the attitude, but it was at least bitterly sincere.

His plays show the same preoccupation with the emotion of love, which he sometimes handles with delicate bantering, but more often with tragic intensity. Whether in prose or verse, these plays with their sparkling dialogues make delightful reading and go surprisingly well on the stage. Among the best of them are *Marianne's Caprices* and *Love Is No Trifling Matter.*

PALE STAR OF EVEN

Pale star of even, on thy distant quest
    Lifting thy radiant brow from twilight's veil,
From out thy azure palace in the west,
    What seest thou in the dale?
The storm recedes, the winds are lulled to rest,   5
    The shivering trees weep on the grass beneath,
The evening butterfly, with gilded crest,
    Flits o'er the fragrant heath.
What seekest thou on Nature's sleeping breast?
    Down toward the mountains thou art sinking fast,   10
Sinking and smiling, sweet and pensive guest;
    Thy tremulous gaze has almost looked its last.

Sad, silvery tear on evening's mantle brown,
    Slow gliding downward to the verdant steep,
The shepherd sees thee, as across the down   15
    He homeward leads his lingering flock of sheep.
Star, at this silent hour so strangely fair,
    Through boundless night, O, whither dost thou go?
To seek beside the shore a reedy lair,
    Or like a pearl, sink in the gulf below?   20
O, if thy glowing tresses thou must wet
    In ocean's brine, fair star, if thou must die,
Ere thou forsake us, stay a moment yet;
    Sweet star of love! ah, do not leave the sky!

(S. B. Wister)

A LAST WORD

Thing of a day!   Fret out thy little hour;
  Whence thy unceasing plaint, thy bitter cry?
And why in tears consume thy spirit's power?
  Immortal is thy soul, thy tears will dry.

Thy heart is racked and wrung by love betrayed,   5
  Beneath the strain 't will break, or cease to feel;
Thou prayest God to hasten to thine aid;
  Immortal is thy soul, thy heart will heal.

By longing and regret thy life is torn,
  The past shuts out the future from thine eye;   10
Grieve not for yesterday, — await the morn;
  Immortal is thy soul, time passes by.

Thy form is bent beneath oppressive thought,
  Thy brow is burdened, and thy limbs give way;
O, bow the knee! fall prostrate, thing of naught!   15
  Immortal is thy soul, death frees thy clay.

Thy mouldering form its mother-earth will feed,
  Thy glory, name, and memory must die,
But not thy love, if thou hast loved indeed,
  Thy deathless soul will cherish it on high.   20

                                   (*S. B. Wister*)

SUGGESTIONS FOR STUDY

1. State in a few words of your own the essential idea of each poem.

2. To whom is " A Last Word " addressed?   Is its tone hopeful or sad?
What other poems on immortality do you know?   Compare the beliefs expressed in them with Musset's idea.

3. What lines in either of the poems most clearly express romantic melancholy?

CHARLES BAUDELAIRE (1821–1867)

Baudelaire published only one volume of verse, *The Flowers of Evil*
(1857), for which he was prosecuted on the ground of its being morally
offensive.   The atmosphere of his poetry is unwholesome because of his

perverse dwelling on unnatural and repulsive subjects. But his rich imagination and the haunting music of his verse have greatly influenced later poets. He bears a certain resemblance to Edgar Allan Poe, of whom he was an enthusiastic admirer and an admirable translator.

SPLEEN

I'm like some king in whose corrupted veins
Flows aged blood; who rules a land of rains;
Who, young in years, is old in all distress;
Who flees good counsel to find weariness
Among his dogs and playthings, who is stirred   5
Neither by hunting-hound nor hunting-bird;
Whose weary face emotion moves no more
E'en when his people die before his door.
His favorite Jester's most fantastic wile
Upon that sick, cruel face can raise no smile;   10
The courtly dames, to whom all kings are good,
Can lighten this young skeleton's dull mood
No more with shameless toilets. In his gloom
Even his lilied bed becomes a tomb.
The sage who takes his gold essays in vain   15
To purge away the old corrupted strain,
His baths of blood, that in the days of old
The Romans used when their hot blood grew cold,
Will never warm this dead man's bloodless pains,
For green Lethean water fills his veins.   20

(*F. P. Sturm*)

20. Lethean: of Lethe, the river of forgetfulness.

SUNSET

Fair is the sun when first he flames above,
   Flinging his joy down in a happy beam;
And happy he who can salute with love
   The sunset far more glorious than a dream.
Flower, stream, and furrow! — I have seen them all   5
   In the sun's eye swoon like one trembling heart —
Though it be late let us with speed depart
   To catch at least one last ray ere it fall!

But I pursue the fading god in vain,
For conquering Night makes firm her dark domain,   10
Mist and gloom fall, and terrors glide between,
And graveyard odors in the shadow swim,
And my faint footsteps on the marsh's rim,
Bruise the cold snail and crawling toad unseen.

(F. P. Sturm)

SUGGESTIONS FOR STUDY

1. The word " spleen," in the sense of melancholy, was once in common usage in England and is still often employed by French and German writers. Show how the title is applicable to the present poem.

2. Indicate from specific passages in both poems the morbid character of Baudelaire's imagination.

3. For certain resemblances to " Sunset " read Poe's story " The Fall of the House of Usher." Do you note a resemblance in any of Poe's poems?

4. Though " Sunset " is a sonnet, in what way does it depart from typical sonnet form?

PROSPER MÉRIMÉE (1803–1870)

Mérimée was an archaeologist who professed to regard his literary work as of secondary importance. But he is rightly remembered for his novelettes and short stories, for he had to a remarkable degree the gift of narration. Among the best of these are " Colomba," a tale of the Corsican vendetta, and " Carmen," a story of the Spanish gypsies. The latter furnished the subject of Bizet's famous opera. Mérimée grew up under the influence of romanticism, which can be seen in his fondness for foreign settings and for dramatic happenings, especially deeds of violence. These qualities are well exemplified in " Mateo Falcone." On the other hand, he was classical in the restraint and impersonality of his style, while his lack of illusions and his skill in making even the unusual appear credible align him with the realists. He was the first man to introduce the Russian novelists to the French public.

MATEO FALCONE

As you leave Porto Vecchio and journey northwest, towards the interior of the island, you find that the ground rises rather rapidly; and after a three hours' jaunt along winding paths, obstructed by huge boulders, and sometimes interrupted by ravines, you find yourself on the edge of a very extensive *maquis*.[1] The *maquis* is the home of the Corsican shepherd and of all those who are at odds with the law. You must know that the Corsican farmer, to save himself the trouble of fertilizing his land, sets fire to a certain amount of woodland. If the fire spreads farther than is necessary, so much the worse; come what come may, he is quite sure of obtaining a good harvest by planting the ground fertilized by the ashes of the trees it formerly bore. When the ripe grain is gathered, — for they leave the straw, which it would require some labor to collect, — the roots which are left unburned in the ground put forth in the following spring very vigorous shoots, which reach a height of seven or eight feet in a few years. It is this species of dense underbrush which is called *maquis*. It consists of trees and bushes of different kinds, mingled together as God pleases. Only with hatchet in hand can man open a path through it; and there are some *maquis* so dense and thick that even the wild sheep cannot break through.

If you have killed a man, betake yourself to the *maquis* of Porto Vecchio, and you can live there in safety with a good rifle, powder, and shot. Do not forget a brown cloak provided with a hood, to serve as a covering and as a mattress. The shepherds will give you milk, cheese, and chestnuts, and you will have no reason to fear the law, or the dead man's kindred, except when you are forced to go down into the town to replenish your stock of ammunition.

Mateo Falcone, when I was in Corsica, in 18—, had his home about half a league from this *maquis*. He was a rather wealthy man for that country; living nobly — that is to say, without working — on the produce of his flocks, which were driven to pasture here and there upon the mountains by shepherds, a sort of nomadic people. When I saw him, two years subsequent to the episode I am about to relate, he seemed to me to be not more than fifty years old at most. Imagine a small, but sturdily built man, with curly hair as black as jet, aquiline nose, thin lips, large bright eyes, and a complexion of the hue of a boot-flap. His skill in marksmanship was considered extraordinary, even in his country, where there are so many good shots. For example, Mateo would never fire at a wild sheep with buckshot; but he would bring one down at a hundred and twenty yards with a bullet in the head or the shoulder, as he pleased. He used his weapons as readily at night as by day, and I was told of this instance of his skill, which will seem incredible perhaps to those who have not traveled in Corsica. A candle was placed at a distance of

---

[1] **maquis:** underbrush.

twenty-four yards, behind a piece of transparent paper as large as a plate. He took aim, then the candle was extinguished, and, a minute later, in absolute darkness, he fired and hit the paper three times out of four.

With such transcendent talent, Mateo Falcone had won a great reputation. He was said to be as true a friend as he was a dangerous enemy; always ready to oblige, and generous to the poor, he lived at peace with all the world in the district of Porto Vecchio. But the story was told of him, that at Corte, where he married his wife, he had disposed very summarily of a rival who was reputed to be as redoubtable in war as in love; at all events, Mateo was given credit for a certain rifle shot which surprised the aforesaid rival as he was shaving in front of a little mirror that hung at his window. When the affair was forgotten, Mateo married. His wife, Giuseppa, gave him at first three daughters (which caused him to fret and fume), and finally a son, whom he named Fortunato; he was the hope of the family, the heir to the name. The daughters were well married; their father could at need rely upon the daggers and carbines of his sons-in-law. The son was only ten years old, but he already gave rich promise for the future.

On a certain day in autumn, Mateo left the house early, with his wife, to inspect one of his flocks at a clearing in the *maquis*. Fortunato would have liked to go with them, but the clearing was too far; moreover, some one must stay behind to watch the house; so the father refused. We shall see whether he had reason to repent.

He had been absent several hours, and little Fortunato was lying placidly in the sun, watching the blue mountains, and thinking that, on the following Sunday, he was going to the town to dine with his uncle the *caporal*,[2] when he was suddenly interrupted in his meditations by the report of a firearm. He rose and turned towards the plain from which the sound came. Other reports followed, at unequal intervals, coming constantly nearer. At last, on a path leading from the plain to Mateo's house, appeared a man wearing a pointed cap such as the mountaineers wear, with a long beard, clad in rags, and hardly able to drag himself along, using his rifle as a cane. He had received a bullet in the thigh.

That man was a bandit, who, having started under cover of the darkness to go to the town for powder, had fallen into an ambush of Corsican voltigeurs.[3] After a stout defense he had succeeded in beating a retreat, hotly pursued, and firing from one rock after an-

[2] **caporal**: magistrate.   [3] **voltigeurs**: militiamen.

other. But he was only a little in advance of the soldiers, and his wound made it impossible to reach the *maquis* before he was overtaken.

He went up to Fortunato and said:

" You are Mateo Falcone's son? "

" Yes."

" I am Gianetto Sanpiero. I am pursued by the yellow collars.[4] Hide me, for I can't go any further."

" What will my father say if I hide you without his leave? "

" He will say that you did well."

" Who knows? "

" Hide me quick; they're coming."

" Wait till my father comes home."

" Wait? damnation! They will be here in five minutes. Come, hide me, or I'll kill you."

Fortunato replied with the utmost coolness:

" Your gun's empty, and there ain't any cartridges left in your *carchera*."[5]

" I have my stiletto."[6]

" But can you run as fast as I can? "

He gave a leap and placed himself out of danger.

" You are not Mateo Falcone's son! Will you let me be arrested in front of your house? "

The child seemed to be moved.

" What will you give me if I hide you? " he said, drawing nearer.

The bandit felt in a leather pocket that hung from his belt and took out a five-franc piece, which he had kept in reserve, no doubt, to buy powder. Fortunato smiled at sight of the silver; he seized it and said to Gianetto:

" Don't be afraid."

He instantly dug a great hole in a haystack that stood near the house. Gianetto crept into it, and the child covered him so as to let him have a little air to breathe, but so that it was impossible to suspect that the hay concealed a man. He conceived also an ingeniously crafty idea, worthy of a savage. He took a cat and her kittens and placed them on the haystack, to make it appear that it had not been disturbed recently. Then, noticing marks of blood on the path near the house, he carefully covered them with dirt, and, when that was done, lay down again in the sun with the most perfect tranquillity.

A few minutes later, six men in brown uniform with yellow facings

---

[4] **yellow collars:** The uniform of the voltigeurs consisted of a brown coat with a yellow collar.   [5] **carchera:** wallet.   [6] **stiletto:** dagger.

commanded by an adjutant halted in front of Mateo's door. This adjutant was distantly related to the Falcones. (It is well known that in Corsica degrees of kinship are followed out much farther than elsewhere.) His name was Tiodoro Gamba; he was an active officer, greatly feared by the bandits, several of whom he had already run to earth.

"Good-day, my young cousin," he said to Fortunato, walking to where he lay; "how you've grown! Did you see a man pass by just now?"

"Oh! I ain't as tall as you yet, cousin," replied the child, with a stupid expression.

"That will come. But tell me, didn't you see a man pass?"

"Didn't I see a man pass?"

"Yes, a man with a black velvet pointed cap and a red and yellow embroidered jacket?"

"A man in a pointed cap and a red and yellow embroidered jacket?"

"Yes; answer at once, and don't repeat my questions."

"Monsieur le curé [7] passed our door this morning, on his horse Piero. He asked me how papa was and I told him — "

"Ah! you little scamp, you are playing sly! Tell me quick which way Gianetto went; for he's the man we're looking for, and I am certain he took this path."

"Who knows?"

"Who knows? I know that you saw him."

"Does a fellow see people pass when he's asleep?"

"You weren't asleep, good-for-nothing; the shots woke you."

"Do you think, cousin, that your guns make such a great noise? My father's carbine makes a lot more."

"May the devil take you, you infernal rascal! I am perfectly sure you saw Gianetto. Perhaps you have hidden him even. Come, boys; go into the house, and see if our man isn't there. He was only going on one foot, and he knows too much, the villain, to try to get to the *maquis* at that gait. Besides, the marks of blood stopped here."

"What will papa say?" queried Fortunato, with a mocking laugh. "What will he say when he knows that you went into his house when he was away?"

"You good-for-nothing!" said Adjutant Gamba, taking him by the ear, "do you know that it rests with me to make you change your

[7] **curé:** priest.

tune? Perhaps, if I give you twenty blows or so with the flat of my sabre, you will conclude to speak."

But Fortunato continued to laugh sneeringly.

" My father is Mateo Falcone! " he said with emphasis.

" Do you know, you little scamp, that I can take you to Corte or to Bastia? I'll make you sleep in a dungeon, on straw, with irons on your feet, and I'll have you guillotined, if you don't tell me where Gianetto Sanpiero is."

The child laughed heartily at this absurd threat.

" My father's Mateo Falcone," he repeated.

" Adjutant," said one of the voltigeurs in an undertone, " let us not get into a row with Mateo."

Gamba was evidently perplexed. He talked in a low tone with his soldiers, who had already searched the whole house. It was not a very long operation, for a Corsican's cabin consists of a single square room. The furniture consists of a table, benches, chests, and household and hunting implements. Meanwhile little Fortunato patted his cat, and seemed to derive a wicked enjoyment from the embarrassment of the voltigeurs and his cousin.

A soldier approached the haystack. He saw the cat and thrust his bayonet carelessly into the hay, shrugging his shoulders, as if he realized that it was an absurd precaution. Nothing stirred; and the child's face did not betray the slightest excitement.

The adjutant and his squad were at their wit's end; they were already glancing meaningly toward the plain, as if proposing to return whence they came, when their leader, convinced that threats would have no effect on Falcone's son, determined to make one last effort, and to try the power of caresses and gifts.

" You seem to be a very wide-awake youngster, cousin," said he. " You will go far. But you are playing a low game with me; and if I wasn't afraid of distressing my cousin Mateo, deuce take me if I wouldn't carry you off with me! "

" Bah! "

" But, when my cousin returns, I'll tell him the story, and he'll give you the lash till the blood comes, to punish you for lying."

" And then? "

" You will see. But, I say, be a good boy, and I'll give you something."

" And I'll give you a piece of advice, cousin: if you stay here any longer, Gianetto will be in the *maquis,* and then it will take more than one fox like you to catch him."

The adjutant took a silver watch from his pocket, worth perhaps thirty francs; and observing that little Fortunato's eyes sparkled as he looked at it, he said, holding it up at the end of its steel chain:

" Rascal! you'd like to have a watch like this hanging round your neck, and you'd stroll through the streets of Porto Vecchio, as proud as a peacock; and people would ask you: ' What time is it? ' and you'd say: ' Look at my watch! ' "

" When I'm big, my uncle the *caporal* will give me a watch."

" Yes; but your uncle's son has got one now — not such a fine one as this, to be sure. Still, he's younger than you."

The child sighed.

" Well! would you like this watch, my little cousin? "

Fortunato, with his eye fixed on the watch, resembled a cat to which a whole chicken is presented. As the beast feels sure that he is being made a fool of, he dares not touch it with his claws, and he turns his eyes away from time to time to avoid the risk of yielding to temptation; but he licks his chops every instant, and seems to say to his master: " What a cruel joke this is! "

But Adjutant Gamba seemed to be in earnest in his offer of the watch. Fortunato did not put out his hand; but he said with a bitter smile:

" Why do you make sport of me? "

" By God! I am not joking. Just tell me where Gianetto is, and this watch is yours."

Fortunato smiled an incredulous smile; and, fastening his black eyes on the adjutant's, he strove to read therein how far he should put faith in his words.

" May I lose my epaulets," [8] cried the adjutant, " if I don't give you the watch on that condition! My comrades are witnesses; and I can't go back on my word."

As he spoke, he held the watch nearer and nearer, so that it almost touched the child's pale cheek. His face betrayed the battle that was taking place in his mind between covetousness and respect for the duties of hospitality. His bare breast rose and fell violently, and he seemed on the point of suffocation. Meanwhile the watch swung to and fro, turned, and sometimes touched the end of his nose. At last, by slow degrees, his right hand rose toward the watch; the ends of his fingers touched it; and he felt the full weight of it on his hand, but still the adjutant did not let go the end of the chain. The face

[8] **epaulets:** ornamental shoulder pieces worn by officers.

was sky-blue, the case newly polished — in the sun it shone like fire. The temptation was too great.

Fortunato raised his left hand, too, and pointed with his thumb, over his left shoulder, to the haystack against which he was leaning. The adjutant understood him instantly. He let go the end of the chain; Fortunato realized that he was the sole possessor of the watch. He sprang up with the agility of a stag, and ran some yards away from the haystack, which the voltigeurs began at once to demolish.

They soon saw the hay begin to move; and a man covered with blood came forth, dagger in hand; but when he tried to raise himself, his stiffened wound prevented him from standing erect. He fell. The adjutant threw himself upon him and tore his stiletto from his hand. In a trice he was securely bound, despite his resistance.

Gianetto, lying on the ground and corded like a bundle of sticks, turned his head toward Fortunato, who had drawn near.

" Son of ——! " he said, with more scorn than anger.

The child tossed him the piece of silver which he had received from him, feeling that he no longer deserved it; but the outlaw seemed to pay no heed to that movement. He said to the adjutant, as coolly as possible:

" I can't walk, my dear Gamba; you will have to carry me to the town."

" You ran faster than a kid just now," retorted the cruel victor; " but never fear; I am so pleased to have caught you, that I would carry you on my back a whole league without getting tired. However, my boy, we'll make a litter for you with some branches and your cloak; and we shall find horses at Crespoli's farm."

" Good," said the prisoner; " just put a little straw on your litter, too, so that I can be more comfortable."

While the voltigeurs busied themselves, some in making a sort of litter with chestnut branches, others in dressing Gianetto's wound, Mateo Falcone and his wife suddenly appeared at a bend in the path leading to the *maquis*. The woman was stooping painfully beneath the weight of an enormous bag of chestnuts, while her husband sauntered along, carrying nothing save one rifle in his hand and another slung over his shoulder; for it is unworthy of a man to carry any other burden than his weapons.

At sight of the soldiers, Mateo's first thought was that they had come to arrest him. But why that thought? Had Mateo any difficulties to adjust with the authorities? No. He enjoyed an excellent reputation. He was, as they say, a person of good fame; but he was a Corsican and a mountaineer; and there are few Corsican mountain-eers who, by carefully searching their memory, cannot find some trifling peccadillo [9] — such as a rifle shot, a dagger thrust, or other bagatelle.[10]   Mateo's conscience was clearer than most, for he had not aimed his rifle at a man for more than ten years; but he was prudent none the less, and he placed himself in a position to make a stout defense, if need be.

"Wife," he said to Giuseppa, "put down your bag and be ready." She instantly obeyed. He gave her the gun that he carried slung over his shoulder, which might be in his way. He cocked the one he had in his hand, and walked slowly toward his house, skirting the trees that lined the path, and ready, at the slightest hostile demon-stration, to jump behind the largest trunk, where he could fire without exposing himself. His wife followed at his heels, holding his spare gun and his cartridge-box. A good housewife's work, in case of a fight, is to load her husband's weapons.

The adjutant, on the other hand, was greatly disturbed to see Mateo advance thus with measured steps, with rifle raised and finger on trigger.

"If by any chance," he thought, "Mateo proves to be related to Gianetto, or if he is his friend and should take it into his head to defend him, the charges of his two rifles would reach two of us, as sure as a letter reaches its address; and suppose he should draw a bead on me, notwithstanding our relationship! "

In his perplexity he adopted an extremely courageous course — he went forward alone toward Mateo, to tell him what had happened, accosting him as an old acquaintance; but the short distance that separated them seemed to him terribly long.

"Hallo! my old comrade," he cried; "how goes it, old fellow? It's me, Gamba, your cousin."

Mateo, without a word in reply, halted, and as the other spoke he raised the barrel of his gun slowly, so that it was pointed at the sky when the adjutant met him.

"Good-day, brother," said the adjutant, "it's a long while since I saw you."

"Good-day, brother."

"I looked in to say good-day to you and Cousin Pepa as I passed. We have had a long jaunt today; but we ought not to complain of fatigue, as we have made a famous capture. We have caught Gianetto Sanpiero."

---

[9] **peccadillo:** small offense.   [10] **bagatelle:** trifle.

" God be praised! " cried Giuseppa. " He stole a milch goat from us last week."

Those words made Gamba's heart glad.

" Poor devil! " said Mateo, " he was hungry."

" The rascal defended himself like a lion," continued the adjutant, slightly mortified; " he killed one of my men, and, not content with that, he broke Corporal Chardon's arm; but there's no great harm done; he was only a Frenchman. After that, he hid himself so completely that the devil himself couldn't have found him. If it hadn't been for my little cousin, Fortunato, I could never have unearthed him."

" Fortunato! " cried Mateo.

" Fortunato! " echoed Giuseppa.

" Yes, Gianetto was hidden under the haystack yonder; but my little cousin showed me the trick. And I'll tell his uncle the *caporal*, so that he'll send him a handsome present for his trouble. And his name and yours will be in the report I shall send the advocate-general."

" Malediction! " muttered Mateo.

They had joined the squad. Gianetto was already lying on the litter, ready to start. When he saw Mateo with Gamba, he smiled a strange smile; then, turning towards the door of the house, he spat on the threshold, saying:

" House of a traitor! "

Only a man who had made up his mind to die would have dared to utter the word traitor as applying to Falcone. A quick thrust of the stiletto, which would not have needed to be repeated, would have paid for the insult instantly. But Mateo made no other movement than to put his hand to his forehead, like a man utterly crushed.

Fortunato had gone into the house when he saw his father coming. He soon reappeared with a mug of milk, which he handed to Gianetto with downcast eyes.

" Away from me! " shouted the outlaw in a voice of thunder. Then, turning to one of the voltigeurs, " Comrade," he said, " give me a drink."

The soldier placed his gourd in his hands, and the outlaw drank the water given him by a man with whom he had recently exchanged rifle shots. Then he asked that his hands might be bound so that they would be folded on his breast, instead of behind his back.

" I like to lie comfortably," he said.

They readily gratified him; then the adjutant gave the signal for departure, bade adieu to Mateo, who made no reply, and marched down at a rapid pace towards the plain.

Nearly ten minutes passed before Mateo opened his mouth. The child glanced uneasily, now at his mother and now at his father, who, leaning upon his gun, gazed at him with an expression of intense wrath.

" You begin well! " said Mateo at last, in a voice which, although calm, was terrifying to one who knew the man.

" Father! " cried the child stepping forward, with tears in his eyes, as if to throw himself at his feet.

But Mateo cried:

" Away from me! "

And the child stopped and stood still, sobbing, a few steps from his father.

Giuseppa approached. She had spied the watch chain, one end of which protruded from Fortunato's shirt.

" Who gave you that watch? " she asked in a harsh tone.

" My cousin the adjutant."

Falcone seized the watch, and hurled it against a stone, breaking it into a thousand pieces.

" Woman," he said, " is this child mine? "

Giuseppa's brown cheeks turned a brick red.

" What do you say, Mateo? Do you know who you're talking to? "

" Well, this child is the first of his race that ever did an act of treachery."

Fortunato's sobs and hiccoughs redoubled in force, and Falcone still kept his lynx-eyes fastened on him. At last he struck the butt of his gun on the ground, then threw it over his shoulder again and started back toward the *maquis,* calling to Fortunato to follow him. The child obeyed.

Giuseppa ran after Mateo and grasped his arm.

" He is your son," she said in a trembling voice, fixing her black eyes on her husband's, as if to read what was taking place in his mind.

" Let me alone," replied Mateo, " I am his father."

Giuseppa embraced her son and entered her cabin, weeping. She fell on her knees before an image of the Virgin and prayed fervently. Meanwhile Falcone walked some two hundred yards along the path, and did not stop until they reached a narrow ravine into which he descended. He sounded the earth with the butt of his rifle, and found it soft and easy to dig. It seemed to him a suitable spot for his design.

" Fortunato, go and stand by that big stone."

The child did what he ordered, then knelt.

" Say your prayers."

" Father, father, don't kill me! "

" Say your prayers! " Mateo repeated, in a terrible voice.

The child, stammering and sobbing, repeated the *Pater* [11] and the *Credo*.[12] The father, in a loud voice, said *Amen!* at the end of each prayer.

" Are those all the prayers you know? "

" I know the *Ave Maria*,[13] too, father, and the litany [14] my aunt taught me."

" That's very long, but no matter."

The child finished the litany in a feeble voice.

" Have you finished? "

" Oh, father! mercy! forgive me! I won't do it again! I will pray so hard to my uncle the *caporal* that he'll forgive Gianetto! "

He continued to speak; Mateo had cocked his gun, and he took aim at him, saying:

" May God forgive you! "

The child made a desperate effort to rise and grasp his father's knees; but he had not time. Mateo fired, and Fortunato fell stark dead.

Without glancing at the body, Mateo returned to his house to fetch a spade, in order to bury his son. He had taken only a few steps, when he met Giuseppa, who was running after them, terrified by the report.

" What have you done? " she cried.

" Justice."

" Where is he? "

" In the ravine. I am going to bury him. He died the death of a Christian; I will have a mass sung for him. Send word to my son-in-law Tiodoro Bianchi to come and live with us."

(Anonymous Translation)

SUGGESTIONS FOR STUDY

1. What does Mateo Falcone's code of honor consist of? What do you think of it?

---

[11] **Pater:** Lord's Prayer.
[12] **Credo:** creed, beginning in Latin with *credo*, I believe.
[13] **Ave Maria:** Hail, Mary.   [14] **litany:** series of supplications.

2. How much of the atmosphere of Corsica does Mérimée manage to impart to the story?   Point out significant bits of local color.

3. Does the author seem to you to reveal his sympathies?

4. Examine " Mateo Falcone " carefully for the technique of the short story.   Does it meet the requirements of Poe's definition of the short story?   Is the situation handled dramatically?   Would it lend itself to stage presentation?

5. Vocabulary: replenish, nomadic, aquiline, summarily, redoubtable, malediction.

ALPHONSE DAUDET (1840–1897)

Daudet was born at Nîmes in southern France, passed a rather dreary childhood, served for a short time as assistant teacher in a boys' school, where he was wretchedly unhappy, and then at the age of seventeen joined his older brother in Paris.   He started as a hack writer but was rescued from this precarious life by his appointment as one of the secretaries of the Duke de Morny, an influential minister of Napoleon III.   Literary fame came to him abundantly with the publication of his novels in the eighteen-seventies.

Of all French writers of fiction during the last seventy-five years, Daudet is probably the one who appeals most to the English-speaking world.   His books have such broad humanity about them that the author wins our personal affection as well as our admiration.   In many respects he resembles Dickens, by whom he was unquestionably influenced.   He has the same gift of laughter and tears.   His characters are very much alive.   His stories never drag.   And to put the finishing touch on it, he writes with a charm that is peculiarly his own.   Among his best novels are *Little What's His Name, Froment Junior and Risler Senior, Jack* and *Sapho*.   Three of his most popular stories are humorous extravaganzas dealing with the mock adventures of a boastful southern Frenchman named Tartarin, who is one of the most successful literary creations of the century.   Equally enjoyable are Daudet's short stories, of which " The Siege of Berlin " is a good specimen.

THE SIEGE OF BERLIN

In order to understand this story properly some knowledge of the background is necessary.   The Franco-German War, which broke out in the summer of 1870, proved a series of disastrous defeats for the French armies and ended in the overthrow of the Empire of Napoleon III and the capture of Paris.   In the opening days of the war the French people were cheered by false reports of victory until the true state of affairs became only too evident to them.

We were going up Avenue des Champs-Élysées with Dr. V——, asking the shell-riddled walls, and the sidewalks torn up by grape-shot, for the story of the siege of Paris, when, just before we reached the Rond-point de l'Étoile, the doctor stopped and, pointing to one of the great corner houses so proudly grouped about the Arc de Tri-omphe, said to me:

" Do you see those four closed windows up there on that balcony? In the early days of August, that terrible August of last year,[1] so heavily laden with storm and disasters, I was called there to see a case of apoplexy. It was the apartment of Colonel Jouve, a cuiras-sier [2] of the First Empire,[3] an old enthusiast on the subject of glory and patriotism, who had come to live on the Champs-Élysées, in an apartment with a balcony, at the outbreak of the war. Guess why? In order to witness the triumphant return of our troops. Poor old fellow! The news of Wissembourg [4] reached him just as he was leaving the table. When he read the name of Napoleon at the foot of that bulletin of defeat, he fell like a log.

" I found the former cuirassier stretched out at full length on the carpet, his face covered with blood, and as lifeless as if he had re-ceived a blow on the head from a poleaxe. He must have been very tall when he was standing; lying there, he looked enormous. Hand-some features, magnificent teeth, a fleece of curly white hair, eighty years with the appearance of sixty. Beside him was his grand-daughter, on her knees and bathed in tears. She looked like him. One who saw them side by side might have taken them for two beau-tiful Greek medallions, struck from the same die, one of which was old and earth-colored, a little roughened on the edges, the other resplendent and clean-cut, in all the brilliancy and smoothness of a fresh impression.

" The child's grief touched me. Daughter and granddaughter of soldiers, her father was on MacMahon's [5] staff, and the image of that tall old man stretched out before her evoked in her mind another im-age no less terrible. I comforted her as best I could, but in reality I had little hope. We had to do with a case of complete paralysis of one side, and at eighty years of age few people recover from it. For

---

[1] **last year:** 1870.

[2] **cuirassier:** horse soldier wearing a breastplate.

[3] **First Empire:** that of Napoleon I (1804–1815). The Second Empire is that of Napoleon III (1852–1870).

[4] **Wissembourg:** or Weissenburg in Alsace, where the Germans gained the first victory of the war.

[5] **MacMahon:** (1808–1893) famous general, afterwards President of the French Republic.

three days the patient lay in the same state of inanition and stupor. Then the news of Reichshofen [6] reached Paris. You remember in what a strange way it came. Up to the evening, we all believed in a great victory, twenty thousand Prussians killed and the Prince Royal a prisoner. I know not by what miracle, what magnetic current, an echo of that national rejoicing sought out our poor deaf-mute in the depths of his paralysis; but the fact is that on that evening, when I approached his bed, I did not find the same man there. His eye was almost clear, his tongue less heavy. He had the strength to smile at me, and he stammered twice:

" ' Vic-to-ry! '

" And as I gave him details of the grand exploit of MacMahon, I saw that his features relaxed and his face lighted up.

" When I left the room, the girl was waiting for me at the door, pale as death. She was sobbing.

" ' But he is saved! ' I said, taking her hands.

" The unhappy child hardly had the courage to reply. The true report of Reichshofen had been placarded; MacMahon in retreat, the whole army crushed. We gazed at each other in consternation. She was in despair, thinking of her father. I trembled, thinking of the old man. He certainly could not stand this fresh shock. And yet what were we to do? Leave him his joy, and the illusions which had revived him? But in that case we must lie.

" ' Very well, I will lie! ' said the heroic girl, quickly wiping away her tears; and with radiant face she entered her grandfather's chamber.

" It was a hard task that she had undertaken. The first few days she had no great difficulty. The good man's brain was feeble, and he allowed himself to be deceived like a child. But with returning health his ideas became clearer. We had to keep him posted concerning the movement of the armies, to draw up military bulletins for him. Really, it was pitiful to see that lovely child leaning night and day over her map of Germany, pinning little flags upon it, and struggling to lay out a glorious campaign: Bazaine [7] besieging Berlin, Frossard in Bavaria, MacMahon on the Baltic. For all this she asked my advice, and I assisted her as well as I could; but it was the grandfather who was especially useful to us in that imaginary invasion. He had conquered Germany so many times under the First Empire! He knew all the strokes beforehand: ' Now this is where

---

[6] **Reichshofen:** town in Alsace and the scene of a German victory.
[7] **Bazaine:** (1811–1888), French marshal.

they will go. Now this is what they will do'; and his anticipations were always realized, which did not fail to make him very proud.

" Unluckily it was of no avail for us to take cities and win battles; we never went quickly enough for him. That old man was insatiable! Every day, when I arrived, I learned of some new military exploit.

" ' Doctor, we have taken Mayence,' [8] the girl would say to me, coming to meet me with a heart-broken smile, and I would hear through the door a joyous voice shouting to me:

" ' They are getting on! They are getting on! In a week we shall be in Berlin! '

" At that moment the Prussians were only a week's march from Paris. We asked ourselves at first if it would be better to take him into the provinces; but as soon as we were outside the city, the state of the country would have told him everything, and I considered him still too weak, too much benumbed by his great shock, to let him know the truth. So we decided to remain.

" The first day of the investment [9] of Paris, I went up to their rooms, I remember, deeply moved, with that agony at the heart which the closed gates, the fighting under the walls, and our suburb turned into frontiers, gave us all. I found the good man seated on his bed, proud and jubilant.

" ' Well,' he said, ' so the siege has begun! '

" I gazed at him in blank amazement.

" ' What, colonel! you know? '

" His granddaughter turned towards me:

" ' Why, yes; doctor, that's the great news. The siege of Berlin has begun.'

" As she said this, she plied her needle with such a sedate and placid air! How could he have suspected anything? He could not hear the guns of the forts. He could not see our unfortunate Paris, all in confusion and dreadful to behold. What he saw from his bed was a section of the Arc de Triomphe, and in his room, about him, a collection of bric-a-brac of the First Empire, well adapted to maintain his illusion. Portraits of marshals, engravings of battles, the King of Rome [10] in a baby's dress, tall consoles [11] adorned with copper trophies, laden with imperial relics, medals, bronzes, a stone from St. Helena [12] under a globe; several miniatures representing the

---

[8] **Mayence:** or Mainz, a city on the Rhine.
[9] **investment:** siege.
[10] **King of Rome:** son of Napoleon I.   [11] **consoles:** brackets.
[12] **St. Helena:** an island in the South Atlantic to which Napoleon was exiled in 1815.

same lady all becurled, in a ball dress of yellow, with leg-of-mutton sleeves and bright eyes; — and all these things: consoles, King of Rome, marshals, yellow ladies, with the high-necked, short-waisted dresses, the bestarched stiffness, which was the charm of 1806. Gallant colonel! It was that atmosphere of victories and conquests, even more than anything we could say to him, that made him believe so innocently in the siege of Berlin.

" From that day our military operations were much simplified. To take Berlin was only a matter of patience. From time to time, when the old man was too much bored, we would read him a letter from his son — an imaginary letter, of course, for nothing was allowed to enter Paris, and since Sedan,[18] MacMahon's aide-de-camp had been sent to a German fortress. You can imagine the despair of that poor child, without news from her father, knowing that he was a prisoner, in need of everything, perhaps sick, and she obliged to represent him as writing joyful letters, a little short, perhaps, but such as a soldier on the field might be expected to write, always marching forward through a conquered country. Sometimes her strength gave way; then they were without news for weeks. But the old man became anxious, could not sleep. Thereupon a letter from Germany would speedily arrive, which she would bring to his bedside and read joyously, forcing back her tears. The colonel would listen religiously, smile with a knowing air, approve, criticize, and explain to us the passages that seemed a little confused. But where he was especially grand was in the replies that he sent to his son. ' Never forget that you are a Frenchman,' he would say to him. ' Be generous to those poor people. Don't make the invasion too hard for them.' And there were recommendations without end, admirable preachments upon respect for the proprieties, the courtesy which should be shown to the ladies, a complete code of military honor for the use of conquerors. He interpersed also some general considerations upon politics, the conditions of peace to be imposed upon the vanquished. Thereupon I must say that he was not exacting.

" ' A war indemnity, and nothing more. What is the use of taking their provinces? Is it possible to turn Germany into France? '

" He dictated this in a firm voice; and one was conscious of such candor in his words, of such a noble, patriotic faith, that it was impossible not to be moved while listening to him.

" Meanwhile the siege went on — not the siege of Berlin, alas!

---

[18] **Sedan:** a town of northern France where the French experienced the most crushing defeat of the war.

It was the time of intense cold, of the bombardment, of epidemics, and of famine. But, thanks to our care, to our efforts, to the unwearying affection which multiplied itself about him, the old man's serenity was not disturbed for an instant. To the very end I was able to obtain white bread and fresh meat for him. There was none for anybody but him, to be sure; and you can imagine nothing more touching than those breakfasts of the grandfather, so innocently selfish — the old man seated on his bed, fresh and smiling, with a napkin at his chin, and his granddaughter beside him, a little pale because of privations, guiding his hand, helping him to drink, and to eat all those forbidden good things. Then, enlivened by the repast, in the comfort of his warm room, the winter wind whistling outside and the snow eddying about his windows, the ex-cuirassier would recall his campaigns in the north, and would describe to us for the hundredth time that terrible retreat [14] from Russia, when they had nothing to eat but frozen biscuit and horseflesh.

"' Do you understand that, my love? We had horseflesh! '

"I rather think that she did understand it. For two months she had had nothing else. From that day, however, as the period of convalescence drew near, our task about the patient became more difficult. That numbness of all his senses, of all his members, which had served us so well hitherto, began to disappear. Two or three times, the terrible volleys from Porte Maillot had made him jump, with his ears pricked up like a hunting dog; we were obliged to invent a final victory of Bazaine under the walls of Berlin, and guns fired in his honor at the Invalides. [15] Another day when his bed had been moved to the window he saw large numbers of National Guards collected on Avenue de la Grande Armée.

"' What are all those troops? ' asked the good man; and we heard him mutter between his teeth:

"' Poorly set up! Poorly set up! '

"That was all; but we understood that we must take great precautions thenceforth. Unluckily we did not take enough.

"One evening when I arrived, the girl came to me in great trouble.

"' They are to march into the city tomorrow,' she said.

"Was the grandfather's door open? In truth, on thinking it over afterwards, I remembered that his face wore an extraordinary expression that night. It is probable that he had overheard us. But we were talking of the Prussians; and the good man was thinking of

---

[14] retreat: during the winter of 1812–1813.
[15] Invalides: Veterans' Home in Paris.

the French, of that triumphal entry which he had been awaiting so long — MacMahon marching down the avenue amid flowers and flourishes of trumpets, his son beside him, and he, the old colonel, on his balcony, in full uniform, saluting the torn flags and the eagles blackened by powder.

"Poor Father Jouve! He had imagined doubtless that we intended to prevent him from witnessing that parade of our troops, in order to avoid too great excitement. So he was very careful not to mention it to any one; but the next day, at the very hour when the Prussian battalions entered hesitatingly upon the long road which leads from Porte Maillot to the Tuileries, the window up there opened softly, and the colonel appeared on the balcony, with his helmet, his long sword, all the glorious old array of one of Milhaud's cuirassiers. I wonder still what effort of the will, what sudden outburst of life had placed him thus upon his feet and in his harness. This much is sure, that he was there, standing behind the rail, amazed to find the broad avenues so silent, the blinds of the houses closed, Paris as gloomy as a huge lazaretto,[16] flags everywhere, but such strange flags, white with little crosses, and no one to go to meet our soldiers.

" For a moment he might have thought that he was mistaken.

" But no! Yonder, behind the Arc de Triomphe, there was a confused rumbling, a black line approaching in the rising sunlight. Then, little by little, the points of the helmets gleamed, the little drums of Jena began to beat, and beneath the Arc de Triomphe, while the heavy tramp of the regiments and the clashing of the sabers beat time, Schubert's *Triumphal March* burst forth!

" Thereupon in the deathlike silence of the square, a cry rang out, a terrible cry: ' To arms! To arms! The Prussians! ' and the four uhlans [17] of the vanguard saw up yonder, on the balcony, a tall old man wave his arms, stagger, and fall. That time, Colonel Jouve was really dead."

(Anonymous Translation)

SUGGESTIONS FOR STUDY

1. Discuss the question whether Colonel Jouve's granddaughter and doctor were justified in deceiving him.

2. What do you learn about the mental and physical sufferings of the Parisians during the war?

3. The principal weakness of many short stories is that they have no

---

[16] **lazaretto:** hospital.   [17] **uhlans:** cavalrymen armed with lances.

particular significance beyond the immediate incident which they narrate. Does the present story throw any light on character or on human relations?

4. Compare it with " Mateo Falcone " as to interest, local color, character drawing, suspense. In what way does each story pivot around the idea of duty?

GUY DE MAUPASSANT (1850–1893)

Maupassant is the great French master of the short story. He was born in Normandy, learned to write under the tutelage of the novelist Flaubert, who was such a severe disciplinarian that by the time Maupassant began to publish he was already a finished artist. He died hopelessly insane.

Maupassant wrote more than two hundred short stories, many of which are as nearly perfect as can be in conception and technique. His sole aim was to depict life as he saw it without letting his vision be disturbed by sympathies or moral scruples. Like most of the extreme realists, he had a low estimate of human nature and seemed to prefer to dwell on the evil and depressing aspects of life. His style is exceedingly simple and direct. Superfluities of plot and of diction alike are pruned away. He gave an impetus to the development of the short story in all countries.

THE PIECE OF STRING

On all the roads about Goderville the peasants and their wives were coming toward the town, for it was market day. The men walked at an easy gait, the whole body thrown forward with every movement of their long, crooked legs, misshapen by hard work, by the bearing down on the plough which at the same time causes the left shoulder to rise and the figure to slant; by the mowing of the grain, which makes one hold his knees apart in order to obtain a firm footing; by all the slow and laborious tasks of the fields. Their starched blue blouses, glossy as if varnished, adorned at the neck and wrists with a bit of white stitchwork, puffed out about their bony chests like balloons on the point of taking flight, from which protruded a head, two arms, and two feet.

Some of them led a cow or a calf at the end of a rope. And their wives, walking behind the beast, lashed it with a branch still covered with leaves, to hasten its pace. They carried on their arms great baskets, from which heads of chickens or of ducks were thrust forth. And they walked with a shorter and quicker step than their men, their stiff, lean figures wrapped in scanty shawls pinned over their flat breasts, their heads enveloped in a white linen cloth close to the hair, with a cap over all.

Then a *char-à-bancs* [1] passed, drawn by a jerky-paced nag, with two men seated side by side shaking like jelly, and a woman behind, who clung to the side of the vehicle to lessen the rough jolting.

On the square at Goderville there was a crowd, a medley of men and beasts. The horns of the cattle, the high hats, with a long, hairy nap, of the wealthy peasants, and the headdresses of the peasant women, appeared on the surface of the throng. And the sharp, shrill, high-pitched voices formed an incessant, uncivilized uproar, over which soared at times a roar of laughter from the powerful chest of a sturdy yokel, [2] or the prolonged bellow of a cow fastened to the wall of a house.

There was an all-pervading smell of the stable, of milk, of the dung-hill, of hay, and of perspiration — that acrid, disgusting odor of man and beast peculiar to country people.

Master Hauchecorne, of Bréauté, had just arrived at Goderville, and was walking toward the square, when he saw a bit of string on the ground. Master Hauchecorne, economical like every true Norman, thought that it was well to pick up everything that might be of use; and he stooped painfully, for he suffered with rheumatism. He took the piece of slender cord from the ground, and was about to roll it up carefully, when he saw Master Malandain, the harness maker, standing in his doorway and looking at him. They had formerly had trouble on the subject of a halter, and had remained at odds, being both inclined to bear malice. Master Hauchecorne felt a sort of shame at being seen thus by his enemy, fumbling in the mud for a bit of string. He hurriedly concealed his treasure in his blouse, then in his breeches pocket; then he pretended to look on the ground for something else, which he did not find; and finally he went on toward the market, his head thrust forward, bent double by his pains.

He lost himself at once in the slow-moving, shouting crowd, kept in a state of excitement by the interminable bargaining. The peasants felt of the cows, went away, returned, sorely perplexed, always afraid of being cheated, never daring to make up their minds, watching the vendor's eye, striving incessantly to detect the tricks of the man and the defect in the beast.

The women, having placed their great baskets at their feet, took out their fowls, which lay on the ground, their legs tied together, with frightened eyes and scarlet combs.

They listened to offers, adhered to their prices, short of speech and impassive of face; or else, suddenly deciding to accept the lower price

---

[1] **char-à-bancs:** long vehicle with many seats.   [2] **yokel:** rustic.

offered, they would call out to the customer as he walked slowly away:

"All right, Mast' Anthime. You can have it."

Then, little by little, the square became empty, and when the Angelus [3] struck midday those who lived too far away to go home betook themselves to the various inns.

At Jourdain's the common room was full of customers, as the great yard was full of vehicles of every sort — carts, cabriolets,[4] *chars-à-bancs*, tilburies,[5] unnamable carriages, shapeless, patched, with their shafts reaching heavenward like arms, or with their noses in the ground and their tails in the air.

The vast fireplace, full of clear flame, cast an intense heat against the backs of the row on the right of the table. Three spits were revolving, laden with chickens, pigeons, and legs of mutton; and a delectable odor of roast meat, and of gravy dripping from the browned skin, came forth from the hearth, stirred the guests to merriment, and made their mouths water.

All the aristocracy of the plough ate there, at Mast' Jourdain's, the innkeeper and horse trader — a shrewd rascal who had money.

The dishes passed and were soon emptied, like the jugs of yellow cider. Every one told of his affairs, his sales, and his purchases. They inquired about the crops. The weather was good for green stuffs, but a little wet for wheat.

Suddenly a drum rolled in the yard, in front of the house. In an instant everybody was on his feet, save a few indifferent ones; and they all ran to the door and windows, with their mouths still full and napkins in hand.

Having finished his long tattoo, the public crier shouted in a jerky voice, making his pauses in the wrong places:

"The people of Goderville, and all those present at the market are informed that between — nine and ten o'clock this morning on the Beuzeville — road, a black leather wallet was lost, containing five hundred — francs, and business papers. The finder is requested to carry it to — the mayor's office at once, or to Master Fortuné Houlbrèque of Manneville. A reward of twenty francs will be paid."

Then he went away. They heard once more in the distance the muffled roll of the drum and the indistinct voice of the crier.

Then they began to talk about the incident, reckoning Master Houlbrèque's chance of finding or not finding his wallet.

[3] **Angelus:** bell rung at morning, noon and sunset to announce devotional exercise.   [4] **cabriolets:** two-wheeled carriages, usually with a canopy.
[5] **tilburies:** light two-wheeled carriages without tops.

And the meal went on.

They were finishing their coffee when the corporal of gendarmes appeared in the doorway.

He inquired:

" Is Master Hauchecorne of Bréauté here? "

Master Hauchecorne, who was seated at the farther end of the table, answered:

" Here I am."

And the corporal added:

" Master Hauchecorne, will you be kind enough to go to the mayor's office with me? Monsieur the mayor would like to speak to you."

The peasant, surprised and disturbed, drank his *petit verre* [6] at one swallow, rose, and even more bent than in the morning, for the first steps after each rest were particularly painful, he started off, repeating:

" Here I am, here I am."

And he followed the brigadier.

The mayor was waiting for him, seated in an armchair. He was the local notary, a stout, solemn-faced man, given to pompous speeches.

" Master Hauchecorne," he said, " you were seen this morning, on the Beuzeville road, to pick up the wallet lost by Master Houlbrèque of Manneville."

The rustic, dumbfounded, stared at the mayor, already alarmed by this suspicion which had fallen upon him, although he failed to understand it.

" I, I — I picked up that wallet? "

" Yes, you."

" On my word of honor, I didn't even so much as see it."

" You were seen."

" They saw me, me? Who was it saw me? "

" Monsieur Malandain, the harness maker."

Thereupon the old man remembered and understood; and flushing with anger, he cried:

" Ah! he saw me, did he, that sneak? He saw me pick up this string, look, m'sieu' mayor."

And fumbling in the depths of his pocket, he produced the little piece of cord.

But the mayor was incredulous and shook his head.

---

[6] **petit verre:** small glass.

" You won't make me believe, Master Hauchecorne, that Monsieur Malandain, who is a man deserving of credit, mistook this string for a wallet."

The peasant, in a rage, raised his hand, spit to one side to pledge his honor, and said:

" It's God's own truth, the sacred truth, all the same, m'sieu mayor. I say it again, by my soul and my salvation."

" After picking it up," rejoined the mayor, " you hunted a long while in the mud, to see if some piece of money hadn't fallen out."

The good man was suffocated with wrath and fear.

" If anyone can tell — if anyone can tell lies like that, to ruin an honest man! If anyone can say — "

To no purpose did he protest; he was not believed.

He was confronted with Monsieur Malandain, who repeated and maintained his declaration. They insulted each other for a whole hour. At his own request, Master Hauchecorne was searched. They found nothing on him. At last the mayor, being sorely perplexed, discharged him, but warned him that he proposed to inform the prosecuting attorney's office and to ask for orders.

The news had spread. On leaving the mayor's office, the old man was surrounded and questioned with serious or bantering curiosity, in which, however, there was no trace of indignation. And he began to tell the story of the string. They did not believe him. They laughed.

He went his way, stopping his acquaintances, repeating again and again his story and his protestations, showing his pockets turned inside out, to prove that he had nothing.

They said to him:

" You old rogue, *va!* "[7]

And he lost his temper, lashing himself into a rage, feverish with excitement, desperate because he was not believed, at a loss what to do, and still telling his story.

Night came. He must needs go home. He started with three neighbors, to whom he pointed out the place where he had picked up the bit of string; and all the way he talked of his misadventure.

During the evening he made the circuit of the village of Bréauté, in order to tell everybody about it. He found none but incredulous listeners.

He was ill over it all night.

The next afternoon, about one o'clock, Marius Paumelle, a farm

[7] **va:** get out.

hand employed by Master Breton, a farmer of Ymauville, restored the wallet and its contents to Master Houlbrèque of Manneville.

The man claimed that he had found it on the road; but, being unable to read, he had carried it home and given it to his employer.

The news soon became known in the neighborhood; Master Hauchecorne was informed of it. He started out again at once, and began to tell his story, now made complete by the dénouement.[8]   He was triumphant.

"What made me feel bad," he said, "wasn't so much the thing itself, you understand, but the lying. There's nothing hurts you so much as being blamed for lying."

All day long he talked of his adventure; he told it on the roads to people who passed; at the wine-shop to people who were drinking; and after church on the following Sunday. He even stopped strangers to tell them about it. His mind was at rest now, and yet something embarrassed him, although he could not say just what it was. People seemed to laugh while they listened to him. They did not seem convinced. He felt as if remarks were made behind his back.

On Tuesday of the next week, he went to market at Goderville, impelled solely by the longing to tell his story.

Malandain, standing in his doorway, began to laugh when he saw him coming. Why?

He accosted a farmer from Criquetot, who did not let him finish, but poked him in the pit of his stomach, and shouted in his face: "Go on, you old fox!" Then he turned on his heel.

Master Hauchecorne was speechless, and more and more disturbed. Why did he call him "old fox"?

When he was seated at the table, in Jourdain's Inn, he set about explaining the affair once more.

A horse trader from Montivilliers called out to him:

"Nonsense, nonsense, you old dodger! I know all about your string!"

"But they've found the wallet!" faltered Hauchecorne.

"None of that, old boy; there's one who finds it, and there's one who carries it back. I don't know just how you did it, but I understand you."

The peasant was fairly stunned. He understood at last. He was accused of having sent the wallet back by a confederate, an accomplice.

He tried to protest. The whole table began to laugh.

[8] **dénouement:** final solution.

He could not finish his dinner, but left the inn amid a chorus of jeers.

He returned home, shamefaced and indignant, suffocated by wrath, by confusion, and all the more cast down because, with his Norman cunning, he was quite capable of doing the thing with which he was charged, and even of boasting of it as a shrewd trick. He had a confused idea that his innocence was impossible to establish, his craftiness being so well known. And he was cut to the heart by the injustice of the suspicion.

Thereupon he began once more to tell of the adventure, making the story longer each day, adding each time new arguments, more forcible protestations, more solemn oaths, which he devised and prepared in his hours of solitude, his mind being wholly engrossed by the story of the string. The more complicated his defense and the more subtle his reasoning, the less he was believed.

" Those are a liar's reasons," people said behind his back.

He realized it; he gnawed his nails, and exhausted himself in vain efforts.

He grew perceptibly thinner.

Now the jokers asked him to tell the story of " The Piece of String " for their amusement, as a soldier who has seen service is asked to tell about his battles. His mind, attacked at its source, grew feebler.

Late in December he took to his bed.

In the first days of January he died, and in the delirium of the death agony, he protested his innocence, repeating:

" A little piece of string — a little piece of string — see, here it is, m'sieu' mayor."

(George Burnham Ives)

SUGGESTIONS FOR STUDY

1. Which of the following adjectives best applies to this story — tragic, ironic, or pathetic? Give your reasons for your choice. How is the outcome prepared for step by step? Would any other ending have been plausible?

2. What is Maupassant's opinion of the peasants and townspeople of Normandy?

3. Compare this story with Mérimée's " Mateo Falcone " in regard to setting, tone, construction, and general interest.

4. Vocabulary: vendor, impassive, delectable, bantering, protestations, incredulous, engrossed.

5. Read " The Diamond Necklace " and other stories from Maupassant's *The Odd Number*. Show how they illustrate his concentration on essential details and his clear-cut endings. What American short-story writers resemble him in this?

ÉMILE ZOLA (1840–1902)

Zola was the most celebrated exponent of Naturalism in literature. Naturalism may be described as scientific realism. It claims that man and his activities can be explained as the product of natural forces, and that it is the business of literature to show this by examples. It is thus based on a philosophy of materialism which denies the freedom of the will. Zola, who was a man of tremendous energy, tried to demonstrate these theories in a series of twenty novels to which he gave the collective title of *The Rougon-Macquart Family*. He wished to trace the history of this family in its two main branches during the Second Empire (1852–1870) and to show the workings of heredity and environment in its different members. Each novel gives a story complete in itself, though many of the characters necessarily reappear in other books of the series. Zola's scheme is second only to Balzac's *Human Comedy* in the vastness of its scope and has the advantage of being more closely connected. The series amounts to a study of degeneracy. There is a hereditary taint in the blood of the Rougons and the Macquarts which breeds disease, crime and insanity. The stories are frequently coarse and repulsive. Certain of them stand out, however, as being unusually powerful: *The Dram Shop,* an epic of alcoholism; *Master and Man,* a story of life in the mines; *The Soil,* a brutal picture of the peasants, and *The Downfall,* which portrays the collapse of the Second Empire in the Franco-Prussian War (1870). For many years these novels were the most read, the most discussed and the most purchased books in France. Now that naturalism as a dominant movement in literature is dead, it is evident to us that Zola's theories and practice suffered from certain grave defects. He stressed too much the ugly and sordid side of life. He was too sure of his materialistic explanation of human beings. And so far from being scientifically impartial, he was a man of strong sympathies and antipathies which he allowed to color his books. He constantly denounced romanticism and idealism as giving a false picture of life, but in his last books he showed a romantic enthusiasm for ideals of his own. That is the reason why Maupassant, who was content simply to depict life as he saw it, seems the more consistent naturalist.

Zola wrote only a few short stories. " The Attack on the Mill " is one of the best of these. It is realistic without being revolting.

THE ATTACK ON THE MILL

I

It was high holiday at Father Merlier's mill on that pleasant sum‑ mer afternoon. Three tables had been brought out into the garden and placed end to end in the shadow of the great elm, and now they were awaiting the arrival of the guests. It was known throughout the length and breadth of the land that that day was to witness the be‑ trothal of old Merlier's daughter Françoise, to Dominique, a young man who was said to be not overfond of work, but whom never a woman for three leagues of the country around could look at without sparkling eyes, such a well-favored young fellow was he.

That mill of Father Merlier's was truly a very pleasant spot. It was situated right in the heart of Rocreuse, at the place where the main road makes a sharp bend. The village has but a single street, bordered on either side by a row of low, whitened cottages, but just there where the road curves, there are broad stretches of meadow‑ land, and huge trees, which follow the course of the Morelle and cover the low grounds of the valley with a most delicious shade. All Lorraine has no more charming bit of nature to show. To right and left dense forests, great monarchs of the wood, centuries old, rise from the gentle slopes and fill the horizon with a sea of verdure, while away towards the south extends the plain, of wondrous fertility and check‑ ered almost to infinity with its small enclosures, divided off from one another by their live hedges. But what makes the crowning glory of Rocreuse is the coolness of this verdurous nook, even in the hottest days of July and August. The Morelle comes down from the woods of Gagny, and it would seem as if it gathered to itself on the way all the delicious freshness of the foliage beneath which it glides for many a league; it brings down with it the murmuring sounds, the glacial, solemn shadows of the forest. And that is not the only source of coolness; there are running waters of all kinds singing among the copses; one cannot take a step without coming on a gushing spring, and as he makes his way along the narrow paths he seems to be tread‑ ing above subterranean lakes that seek the air and sunshine through the moss above and profit by every smallest crevice at the roots of trees or among the chinks and crannies of the rocks, to burst forth in fountains of crystalline clearness. So numerous and so loud are the whispering voices of these streams that they silence the song of the bullfinches. It is as if one were in an enchanted park, with cascades falling on every side.

The meadows below are never athirst. The shadows beneath the gigantic chestnut trees are of inky blackness, and along the edges of the fields long rows of poplars stand like walls of rustling foliage. There is a double avenue of huge plane trees ascending across the fields towards the ancient castle of Gagny, now gone to rack and ruin. In this region, where drought is never known, vegetation of all kinds is wonderfully rank; it is like a flower garden down there in the low ground between those two wooded hills, a natural garden where the lawns are broad meadows and the giant trees represent colossal beds. When the noonday sun pours down his scorching rays the shadows lie blue upon the ground, the glowing vegetation slumbers in the heat, while every now and then a breath of icy coldness passes under the foliage.

Such was the spot where Father Merlier's mill enlivened with its cheerful clack nature run riot. The building itself, constructed of wood and plaster, looked as if it might be coeval [1] with our planet. Its foundations were in part washed by the Morelle, which here expands into a clear pool. A dam, a few feet in height, afforded sufficient head of water to drive the old wheel, which creaked and groaned as it revolved, with the asthmatic wheezing of a faithful servant who has grown old in her place. Whenever Father Merlier was advised to change it, he would shake his head and say that like as not a young wheel would be lazier and not so well acquainted with its duties, and then he would set to work and patch up the old one with anything that came to hand, old hogshead staves, bits of rusty iron, zinc or lead. The old wheel only seemed the gayer for it, with its odd profile, all plumed and feathered with tufts of moss and grass, and when the water poured over it in a silver tide its gaunt black skeleton was decked out with a gorgeous display of pearls and diamonds.

That portion of the mill which was bathed by the Morelle had something of the look of a barbaric arch that had been dropped down there by chance. A good half of the structure was built on piles; the water came in under the floor, and there were deep holes, famous throughout the whole country for the eels and huge crawfish that were to be caught there. Below the fall the pool was as clear as a mirror, and when it was not clouded by foam from the wheel one could see troops of great fish swimming about in it with the slow, majestic move-

---

[1] coeval: of the same age.

ment of a squadron. There was a broken stairway leading down to the stream, near a stake to which a boat was fastened, and over the wheel was a gallery of wood. Such windows as there were were arranged without any attempt at order. The whole was a quaint conglomeration of nooks and corners, bits of wall, additions made here and there as afterthoughts, beams and roofs, that gave the mill the aspect of an old dismantled citadel; but ivy and all sorts of creeping plants had grown luxuriantly, and kindly covered up such crevices as were too unsightly, casting a mantle of green over the old dwelling. Young ladies who passed that way used to stop and sketch Father Merlier's mill in their albums.

The side of the house that faced the road was less irregular. A gateway in stone afforded access to the principal courtyard, on the right and left hand of which were sheds and stables. Beside a well stood an immense elm that threw its shade over half the court. At the further end, opposite the gate, stood the house surmounted by a dovecote, the four windows of its first floor in a symmetrical line. The only vanity that Father Merlier ever allowed himself was to paint this façade [2] every ten years. It had just been freshly whitened at the time of our story, and dazzled the eyes of all the village when the sun lighted it up in the middle of the day.

For twenty years had Father Merlier been mayor of Rocreuse. He was held in great consideration on account of his fortune; he was supposed to be worth something like eighty thousand francs, the result of patient saving. When he married Madeleine Guillard, who brought him the mill as her dowry, his entire capital lay in his two strong arms, but Madeleine had never repented of her choice, so manfully had he conducted their joint affairs. Now his wife was dead, and he was left a widower with his daughter Françoise. Doubtless he might have set himself down to take his rest, and suffered the old mill wheel to sleep among its moss, but he would have found idleness too irksome and the house would have seemed dead to him. He kept on working still for the pleasure of it. In those days Father Merlier was a tall old man, with a long, silent face, on which a laugh was never seen, but beneath which there lay, none the less, a large fund of good-humor. He had been elected mayor on account of his money, and also for the impressive air that he knew how to assume when it devolved on him to marry a couple.

Françoise Merlier had just completed her eighteenth year. She was small, and for that reason was not accounted one of the beauties

---

[2] **façade:** front of a building.

of the country. Until she reached the age of fifteen she had been even homely: the good folks of Rocreuse could not see how it was that the daughter of Father and Mother Merlier, such a hale, vigorous couple, had such a hard time of it in getting her growth. When she was fifteen, however, though still remaining delicate, a change came over her and she took on the prettiest little face imaginable. She had black hair, black eyes, and was red as a rose withal; her mouth was always smiling, there were delicious dimples in her cheeks, and a crown of sunshine seemed to be ever resting on her fair, candid forehead. Although small as girls went in that region, she was far from being thin; she might not have been able to raise a sack of wheat to her shoulder, but she became quite plump as she grew older, and gave promise of becoming eventually as well rounded and appetizing as a partridge. Her father's habits of taciturnity had made her reflective while yet a young girl; if she always had a smile on her lips it was in order to give pleasure to others. Her natural disposition was serious.

As was no more than to be expected, she had every young man in the countryside at her heels as a suitor, more even for her money than her attractiveness, and she had made a choice at last, a choice that had been the talk and scandal of the entire neighborhood.

On the other side of the Morelle lived a strapping young fellow who went by the name of Dominique Penquer. He was not to the manor born; ten years previously he had come to Rocreuse from Belgium to receive the inheritance of an uncle who had owned a small property on the very borders of the forest of Gagny, just facing the mill and distant from it only a few musket shots. His object in coming was to sell the property, so he said, and return to his own home again; but he must have found the land to his liking, for he made no move to go away. He was seen cultivating his bit of field and gathering the few vegetables that afforded him an existence. He fished, he hunted; more than once he was near coming in contact with the law through the intervention of the keepers. This independent way of living, of which the peasants could not very clearly see the resources, had in the end given him a bad name. He was vaguely looked on as nothing better than a poacher. At all events he was lazy, for he was frequently found sleeping in the grass at hours when he should have been at work. Then, too, the hut in which he lived, in the shade of the last trees of the forest, did not seem like the abode of an honest young man; the old women would not have been surprised at any time to hear that he was on friendly terms with the wolves in the ruins of Gagny. Still, the young girls would now and then venture to stand up for him, for he was altogether a splendid specimen of manhood, was this individual of doubtful antecedents, tall and straight as a young poplar, with a milk-white skin and ruddy hair and moustaches that seemed to be of gold when the sun shone on them. Now one fine morning it came to pass that Françoise told Father Merlier that she loved Dominique, and that never would she consent to marry any other young man.

It may be imagined what a knockdown blow it was that Father Merlier received that day! As was his wont, he said never a word; his countenance wore its usual reflective look, only the fun that used to bubble up from within no longer shone in his eyes. Françoise, too, was very serious, and for a week father and daughter scarcely spoke to each other. What troubled Father Merlier was to know how that rascal of a poacher had succeeded in bewitching his daughter. Dominique had never shown himself at the mill. The miller played the spy a little, and was rewarded by catching sight of the gallant, on the other side of the Morelle, lying among the grass and pretending to be asleep. Françoise could see him from her chamber window. The thing was clear enough; they had been making sheep's-eyes at each other over the old mill wheel, and so had fallen in love.

A week slipped by; Françoise became more and more serious. Father Merlier still continued to say nothing. Then, one evening, of his own accord, he brought Dominique to the house, without a word. Françoise was just setting the table. She made no demonstration of surprise; all she did was to add another plate, but her laugh had come back to her, and the little dimples appeared again upon her cheeks. Father Merlier had gone that morning to look for Dominique at his hut on the edge of the forest, and there the two men had had a conference, with closed doors and windows, that lasted three hours. No one ever knew what they said to each other; the only thing certain is that when Father Merlier left the hut he already treated Dominique as a son. Doubtless the old man had discovered that he whom he had gone to visit was a worthy young fellow, even though he did lie in the grass to gain the love of young girls.

All Rocreuse was up in arms. The women gathered at their doors and could not find words strong enough to characterize Father Merlier's folly in thus receiving a ne'er-do-well into his family. He let them talk. Perhaps he thought of his own marriage. Neither had he possessed a penny to his name at the time he married Madeleine and her mill, and yet that had not prevented him from being a good husband to her. Moreover, Dominique put an end to their tittle-tattle by setting to work in such strenuous fashion that all the countryside was amazed. It so happened just then that the boy of the mill drew an unlucky number and had to go for a soldier, and Dominique would not hear of their engaging another. He lifted sacks, drove the cart, wrestled with the old wheel when it took an obstinate fit and refused to turn, and all so pluckily and cheerfully that people came from far and near merely for the pleasure of seeing him. Father Merlier laughed his silent laugh. He was highly elated that he had read the youngster aright. There is nothing like love to hearten up young men.

In the midst of all that laborious toil Françoise and Dominique fairly worshipped each other. They had not much to say, but their tender smiles conveyed a world of meaning. Father Merlier had not said a word thus far on the subject of their marriage, and they had both respected his silence, waiting until the old man should see fit to give expression to his will. At last, one day, toward the middle of July, he had had three tables laid in the courtyard, in the shade of the big elm, and had invited his friends of Rocreuse to come that afternoon and drink a glass of wine with him. When the courtyard was filled with people, and every one there had a full glass in his hand, Father Merlier raised his own high above his head and said:

" I have the pleasure of announcing to you that Françoise and this lad will be married in a month from now, on St. Louis' fête-day." [3]

Then there was a universal touching of glasses, attended by a tremendous uproar; every one was laughing. But Father Merlier, raising his voice above the din, again spoke:

" Dominique, kiss your wife that is to be. It is no more than customary."

And they kissed, very red in the face, both of them, while the company laughed louder still. It was a regular fête; they emptied a small cask. Then, when only the intimate friends of the house remained, conversation went on in a calmer strain. Night had fallen, a starlit night, and very clear. Dominique and Françoise sat on a bench, side by side, and said nothing. An old peasant spoke of the war that the Emperor [4] had declared against Prussia. All the lads of the village were already gone off to the army. Troops had passed through the place only the night before. There were going to be hard knocks.

" Bah! " said Father Merlier, with the selfishness of a man who is quite happy, " Dominique is a foreigner; he won't have to go — and, if the Prussians come this way, he will be here to defend his wife."

The idea of the Prussians coming there seemed to the company an

[3] St. Louis' fête-day: August 25.
[4] Emperor: Napoleon III.

exceedingly good joke. The army would give them one good conscientious thrashing, and the affair would be quickly ended.

" I have seen them before, I have seen them before," the old peasant repeated, in a low voice.

There was silence for a little, then they all touched glasses once again. Françoise and Dominique had heard nothing; they had managed to clasp hands behind the bench in such a way as not to be seen by the others, and this condition of affairs seemed so beatific to them that they sat there mute, their gaze lost in the darkness of the night.

What a magnificent, balmy night! The village lay slumbering on either side of the white road as peacefully as a little child. The deep silence was undisturbed save by the occasional crow of a cock in some distant barnyard acting on a mistaken impression that dawn was at hand. Perfumed breaths of air, like long-drawn sighs, came down from the great woods that lay around and above, sweeping softly over the roofs, as if caressing them. The meadows, with their black intensity of shadow, took on a dim, mysterious majesty of their own, while all the springs, all the brooks and watercourses that gurgled in the darkness, might have been taken for the cool and rhythmical breathing of the sleeping country. Every now and then the old dozing mill wheel seemed to be dreaming like a watchdog that barks uneasily in his slumber; it creaked, it talked to itself, rocked by the fall of the Morelle, whose current gave forth the deep, sustained music of an organ pipe. Never was there a more charming or happier nook, never did a deeper peace come down to cover it.

2

One month later, to a day, on the eve of the fête of Saint Louis, Rocreuse was in a state of alarm and dismay. The Prussians had beaten the Emperor, and were advancing on the village by forced marches. For a week past, people passing along the road had brought tidings of the enemy: " They are at Lormières, they are at Nouvelles "; and by dint of hearing so many stories of the rapidity of their advance, Rocreuse woke up every morning in the full expectation of seeing them swarming out of Gagny wood. They did not come, however, and that only served to make the affright the greater. They would certainly fall upon the village in the nighttime, and put every soul to the sword.

There had been an alarm the night before, a little before daybreak. The inhabitants had been aroused by a great noise of men tramping upon the road. The women were already throwing themselves upon their knees and making the sign of the cross, when some one, to whom it happily occurred to peep through a half-opened window, caught sight of red trousers. It was a French detachment. The captain had forthwith asked for the mayor, and, after a long conversation with Father Merlier, had remained at the mill.

The sun shone bright and clear that morning, giving promise of a warm day. There was a golden light floating over the woodland, while in the low grounds white mists were rising from the meadows. The pretty village, so neat and trim, awoke in the cool dawning, and the country, with its streams and its fountains, was as gracious as a freshly plucked bouquet. But the beauty of the day brought gladness to the face of no one; the villagers had watched the captain, and seen him circle round and round the old mill, examine the adjacent houses, then pass to the other bank of the Morelle, and from thence scan the country with a field glass. Father Merlier, who accompanied him, appeared to be giving explanations. After that the captain had posted some of his men behind walls, behind trees or in hollows. The main body of the detachment had encamped in the courtyard by the mill. So there was going to be a fight, then? And when Father Merlier returned they questioned him. He spoke no word, but slowly and sorrowfully nodded his head. Yes, there was going to be a fight.

Françoise and Dominique were there in the courtyard, watching him. He finally took his pipe from his lips and gave utterance to these few words:

" Ah! my poor children, I shall not be able to marry you today! "

Dominique, with lips tight set and an angry frown upon his forehead, raised himself on tiptoe from time to time and stood with eyes bent on Gagny wood, as if he would have been glad to see the Prussians appear and end the suspense they were in. Françoise, whose face was grave and very pale, was constantly passing back and forth, supplying the needs of the soldiers. They were preparing their soup in a corner of the courtyard, joking and chaffing one another while awaiting their meal.

The captain appeared to be highly pleased. He had visited the chambers and the great hall of the mill that looked out on the stream. Now, seated beside the well, he was conversing with Father Merlier.

" You have a regular fortress here," he was saying.

" We shall have no trouble in holding it until evening. The bandits are late; they ought to be here by this time."

The miller looked very grave. He saw his beloved mill going up in flame and smoke, but uttered no word of remonstrance or complaint, considering that it would be useless. He only opened his mouth to say:

" You ought to take steps to hide the boat; there is a hole behind the wheel fitted to hold it. Perhaps you may find it of use to you."

The captain gave an order to one of his men. This captain was a tall, fine-looking man of about forty, with an agreeable expression of countenance. The sight of Dominique and Françoise seemed to afford him much pleasure; he watched them as if he had forgotten all about the approaching conflict. He followed Françoise with his eyes as she moved about the courtyard, and his manner showed clearly enough that he thought her charming. Then, turning to Dominique:

" You are not with the army, I see, my boy? " he abruptly asked.

" I am a foreigner," the young man replied.

The captain did not seem particularly pleased with the answer; he winked his eyes and smiled. Françoise was doubtless a more agreeable companion than a musket would have been. Dominique, noticing his smile, made haste to add:

" I am a foreigner, but I can lodge a rifle bullet in an apple at five hundred yards. See, there's my rifle behind you."

" You may find use for it," the captain drily answered.

Françoise had drawn near; she was trembling a little, and Dominique, regardless of the bystanders, took and held firmly clasped in his own the two hands that she held forth to him, as if committing herself to his protection. The captain smiled again, but said nothing more. He remained seated, his sword between his legs, his eyes fixed on space, apparently lost in dreamy reverie.

It was ten o'clock. The heat was already oppressive. A deep silence prevailed. The soldiers had sat down in the shade of the sheds in the courtyard and begun to eat their soup. Not a sound came from the village, where the inhabitants had all barricaded their houses, doors and windows. A dog, abandoned by his master, howled mournfully upon the road. From the woods and the near-by meadows, that lay fainting in the heat, came a long-drawn, whispering, soughing sound, produced by the union of what wandering breaths of air there were. A cuckoo called. Then the silence became still.

And all at once, upon that lazy, sleepy air, a shot rang out. The captain rose quickly to his feet, the soldiers left their half-emptied plates. In a few seconds all were at their posts; the mill was occupied from top to bottom. And yet the captain, who had gone out through the gate, saw nothing: to right and left the road stretched away, desolate and blindingly white in the fierce sunshine. A second report was heard, and still nothing to be seen, not even so much as a shadow; but just as he was turning to re-enter he chanced to look over toward Gagny and there beheld a little puff of smoke floating away on the tranquil air, like thistledown. The deep peace of the forest was apparently unbroken.

"The rascals have occupied the wood," the officer murmured. "They know we are here."

Then the firing went on, and became more and more continuous between the French soldiers posted about the mill and the Prussians concealed among the trees. The bullets whistled over the Morelle without doing any mischief on either side. The firing was irregular; every bush seemed to have its marksman, and nothing was to be seen save those bluish smoke wreaths that hung for a moment on the wind before they vanished. It lasted thus for nearly two hours. The officer hummed a tune with a careless air. Françoise and Dominique, who remained in the courtyard, raised themselves to look out over a low wall. They were more particularly interested in a little soldier who had his post on the bank of the Morelle, behind the hull of an old boat; he would lie face downward on the ground, watch his chance, deliver his fire, then slip back into a ditch a few steps in his rear to reload, and his movements were so comical, he displayed such cunning and activity, that it was difficult for any one watching him to refrain from smiling. He must have caught sight of a Prussian, for he rose quickly and brought his piece to the shoulder, but before he could discharge it he uttered a loud cry, whirled completely around in his tracks and fell backward into the ditch, where for an instant his legs moved convulsively, just as the claws of a fowl do when it is beheaded. The little soldier had received a bullet directly through his heart. It was the first casualty of the day. Françoise instinctively seized Dominique's hand and held it tight in a convulsive grasp.

"Come away from there," said the captain. "The bullets reach us here."

As if to confirm his words a slight, sharp sound was heard up in the old elm, and the end of a branch came to the ground, turning over and over as it fell, but the two young people never stirred, riveted to the spot as they were by the interest of the spectacle. On the edge of the wood a Prussian had suddenly emerged from behind a tree, as an actor comes upon the stage from the wings, beating the air with his arms and falling over upon his back. And beyond that there was no movement: the two dead men appeared to be sleeping in the bright sunshine; there was not a soul to be seen in the fields on which the heat lay heavy. Even the sharp rattle of the musketry had ceased. Only the Morelle kept on whispering to itself with its low, musical murmur.

Father Merlier looked at the captain with an astonished air, as if to inquire whether that were the end of it.

" Here comes their attack," the officer murmured. " Look out for yourself! Don't stand there! "

The words were scarcely out of his mouth when a terrible discharge of musketry ensued. The great elm was riddled, its leaves came eddying down as thick as snowflakes. Fortunately, the Prussians had aimed too high. Dominique dragged, almost carried, Françoise from the spot, while Father Merlier followed them shouting:

" Get into the small cellar, the walls are thicker there."

But they paid no attention to him; they made their way to the main hall, where ten or a dozen soldiers were silently waiting, watching events outside through the chinks of the closed shutters. The captain was left alone in the courtyard, where he sheltered himself behind the low wall, while the furious fire was maintained uninterruptedly. The soldiers whom he had posted outside only yielded their ground inch by inch; they came crawling in, however, one after another, as the enemy dislodged them from their positions. Their instructions were to gain all the time they could, taking care not to show themselves, in order that the Prussians might remain in ignorance of the force they had opposed to them. Another hour passed, and as a sergeant came in, reporting that there were now only two or three men left outside, the officer took his watch from his pocket, murmuring:

" Half-past two. Come, we must hold out for four hours yet."

He caused the great gate of the courtyard to be tightly secured, and everything was made ready for an energetic defense. The Prussians were on the other side of the Morelle; consequently there was no reason to fear an assault at the moment. There was a bridge indeed, a mile and a quarter away, but they were probably unaware of its existence, and it was hardly to be supposed that they would attempt to cross the stream by fording. The officer, therefore, simply caused the road to be watched; the attack, when it came, was to be looked for from the direction of the fields.

The firing had ceased again. The mill appeared to lie there in the sunlight, void of all life. Not a shutter was open, not a sound came from within. Gradually, however, the Prussians began to show themselves at the edge of Gagny wood. Heads were protruded here and there; they seemed to be mustering up their courage. Several of the soldiers within the mill brought up their pieces to an aim, but the captain shouted:

"No, no; not yet; wait. Let them come nearer."

They displayed a great deal of prudence in their advance, looking at the mill with a distrustful air; they seemed hardly to know what to make of the old structure, so lifeless and gloomy, with its curtain of ivy. Still they kept on advancing. When there were fifty of them or so in the open, directly opposite, the officer uttered one word:

"Now!"

A crashing, tearing discharge burst from the position, succeeded by an irregular, dropping fire. Françoise, trembling violently, involuntarily raised her hands to her ears. Dominique, from his position behind the soldiers, peered out upon the field, and when the smoke drifted away a little, counted three Prussians extended on their backs in the middle of the meadow. The others had sought shelter among the willows and the poplars. And then commenced the siege.

For more than an hour the mill was riddled with bullets; they beat and rattled on its old walls like hail. The noise they made was plainly audible as they struck the stonework, were flattened and fell back into the water; they buried themselves in the woodwork with a dull thud. Occasionally a creaking sound would announce that the wheel had been hit. Within the building the soldiers husbanded their ammunition, firing only when they could see something to aim at. The captain kept consulting his watch every few minutes, and as a ball split one of the shutters in halves and then lodged in the ceiling:

"Four o'clock," he murmured. "We shall never be able to hold the position."

The old mill, in truth, was gradually going to pieces beneath that terrific fire. A shutter that had been perforated again and again, until it looked like a piece of lace, fell off its hinges into the water, and had to be replaced by a mattress. Every moment, almost, Father Merlier exposed himself to the fire in order to take account of the damage sustained by his poor wheel, every wound of which was like a bullet in his own heart. Its period of usefulness was ended this time for certain; he would never be able to patch it up again. Dominique had besought Françoise to retire to a place of safety, but she was determined to remain with him; she had taken a seat behind a great oaken clothespress, which afforded her protection. A ball struck the press, however, the sides of which gave out a dull hollow sound, whereupon Dominique stationed himself in front of Françoise. He had as yet taken no part in the firing, although he had his rifle in his hand; the soldiers occupied the whole breadth of the windows, so that he could not get near them. At every discharge the floor trembled.

" Look out! look out! " the captain suddenly shouted.

He had just descried a dark mass emerging from the wood. As soon as they gained the open they set up a telling platoon fire. It struck the mill like a tornado. Another shutter parted company, and the bullets came whistling in through the yawning aperture. Two soldiers rolled upon the floor; one lay where he fell and never moved a limb; his comrades pushed him up against the wall because he was in their way. The other writhed and twisted, beseeching some one to end his agony, but no one had ears for the poor wretch; the bullets were still pouring in, and every one was looking out for himself and searching for a loophole whence he might answer the enemy's fire. A third soldier was wounded; that one said not a word, but with staring haggard eyes sank down beneath a table. Françoise, horror-stricken by the dreadful spectacle of the dead and dying men, mechanically pushed away her chair and seated herself on the floor, against the wall; it seemed to her that she would be smaller there and less exposed. In the meantime men had gone and secured all the mattresses in the house; the opening of the window was partially closed again. The hall was filled with débris of every description, broken weapons, dislocated furniture.

" Five o'clock," said the captain. " Stand fast, boys. They are going to make an attempt to pass the stream."

Just then Françoise gave a shriek. A bullet had struck the floor, and, rebounding, grazed her forehead on the ricochet.[5] Dominique looked at her, then went to the window and fired his first shot, and from that time kept on firing uninterruptedly. He kept on loading and discharging his piece mechanically, paying nc attention to what was passing at his side, only pausing from time to time to cast a look at Françoise. He did not fire hurriedly, or at random, moreover, but took deliberate aim. As the captain had predicted, the Prussians were skirting the belt of poplars and attempting the passage of the Morelle, but each time one of them showed himself he fell with one of Dominique's bullets in his brain. The captain, who was watching the per-- formance, was amazed: he complimented the young man, telling him that he would like to have more marksmen of his skill. Dominique did not hear a word he said. A ball struck him in the shoulder, another raised a contusion [6] on his arm. And still he kept on firing.

[5] **ricochet:** rebound.   [6] **contusion:** bruise.

There were two more deaths. The mattresses were torn to shreds and no longer availed to stop the windows. The last volley that was poured in seemed as if it would carry away the mill bodily, so fierce it was. The position was no longer tenable. Still, the officer kept repeating:

" Stand fast. Another half-hour yet."

He was counting the minutes, one by one. He had promised his commanders that he would hold the enemy there until nightfall, and he would not budge a hair's breadth before the moment that he had fixed for his withdrawal. He maintained his pleasant air of good-humor, smiling at Françoise by way of reassuring her. He had picked up the musket of one of the dead soldiers and was firing away with the rest.

There were but four soldiers left in the room. The Prussians were showing themselves *en masse* on the other side of the Morelle, and it was evident that they might now pass the stream at any moment. A few moments more elapsed; the captain was as determined as ever, and would not give the order to retreat, when a sergeant came running into the room, saying:

" They are on the road; they are going to take us in the rear."

The Prussians must have discovered the bridge. The captain drew out his watch again.

" Five minutes more," he said. " They won't be here within five minutes."

Then exactly at six o'clock he at last withdrew his men through a little postern [7] that opened on a narrow lane, whence they threw themselves into the ditch, and in that way reached the forest of Sauval. The captain took leave of Father Merlier with much politeness, apologizing profusely for the trouble he had caused. He even added:

" Try to keep them occupied for a while. We shall return."

While this was occurring Dominique had remained alone in the hall. He was still firing away, hearing nothing, conscious of nothing; his sole thought was to defend Françoise. The soldiers were all gone, and he had not the remotest idea of the fact; he aimed and brought down his man at every shot. All at once there was a great tumult. The Prussians had entered the courtyard from the rear. He fired his last shot, and they fell upon him with his weapon still smoking in his hand.

It required four men to hold him; the rest of them swarmed about

[7] **postern:** back door.

him, vociferating like madmen in their horrible dialect. Françoise
rushed forward to intercede with her prayers. They were on the
point of killing him on the spot, but an officer came in and made
them turn the prisoner over to him. After exchanging a few words
in German with his men he turned to Dominique and said to him
roughly, in very good French:

"You will be shot in two hours from now."

3

It was the standing regulation, laid down by the German staff, that
every Frenchman not belonging to the regular army, taken with arms
in his hands, should be shot. Even the *compagnies franches* [8] were
not recognized as belligerents. It was the intention of the Germans,
in making such terrible examples of the peasants who attempted to
defend their firesides, to prevent a rising *en masse,* which they
greatly dreaded.

The officer, a tall, square man about fifty years old, subjected Dominique to a brief examination. Although he spoke French fluently,
he was unmistakably Prussian in the stiffness of his manner.

"You are a native of this country."

"No, I am a Belgian."

"Why did you take up arms? These are matters with which you
have no concern."

Dominique made no reply. At this moment the officer caught
sight of Françoise where she stood listening, very pale; her slight
wound had marked her white forehead with a streak of red. He
looked from one to the other of the young people and appeared to
understand the situation: he merely added:

"You do not deny having fired on my men?"

"I fired as long as I was able to do so," Dominique quietly replied.

The admission was scarcely necessary, for he was black with powder, wet with sweat, and the blood from the wound in his shoulder
had trickled down and stained his clothing.

"Very well," the officer repeated. "You will be shot two hours
hence."

Françoise uttered no cry. She clasped her hands and raised them
above her head in a gesture of mute despair. Her action was not
lost upon the officer. Two soldiers had led Dominique away to an
adjacent room, where their orders were to guard him and not lose sight

[8] **compagnies franches:** independent companies.

of him. The girl had sunk upon a chair; her strength had failed her, her legs refused to support her; she was denied the relief of tears, it seemed as if her emotion was strangling her. The officer continued to examine her attentively, and finally addressed her:

"Is that young man your brother?" he inquired.

She shook her head in negation. He was as rigid and unbending as ever, without the suspicion of a smile on his face. Then, after an interval of silence, he spoke again:

"Has he been living in the neighborhood long?"

She answered yes, by another motion of the head.

"Then he must be well acquainted with the woods about here?"

This time she made a verbal answer. "Yes, sir," she said, looking at him with some astonishment.

He said nothing more, but turned on his heel, requesting that the mayor of the village should be brought before him. But Françoise had risen from her chair, a faint tinge of color on her cheeks, believing that she had caught the significance of his questions, and with renewed hope she ran to look for her father.

As soon as the firing had ceased Father Merlier had hurriedly descended by the wooden gallery to have a look at his wheel. He adored his daughter and had a strong feeling of affection for Dominique, his son-in-law who was to be; but his wheel also occupied a large space in his heart. Now that the two little ones, as he called them, had come safe and sound out of the fray, he thought of his other love, which must have suffered sorely, poor thing, and bending over the great wooden skeleton, he was scrutinizing its wounds with a heartbroken air. Five of the buckets were reduced to splinters, the central framework was honeycombed. He was thrusting his fingers into the cavities that the bullets had made to see how deep they were and reflecting how he was ever to repair all that damage. When Françoise found him he was already plugging up the crevices with moss and such débris as he could lay his hands on.

"They are asking for you, father," said she.

And at last she wept as she told him what she had just heard. Father Merlier shook his head. It was not customary to shoot people like that. He would have to look into the matter. And he reentered the mill with his usual placid, silent air. When the officer made his demand for supplies for his men, he answered that the people of Rocreuse were not accustomed to be ridden roughshod, and that nothing would be obtained from them through violence; he was willing to assume all the responsibility, but only on condition that he was allowed to act independently. The officer at first appeared to take umbrage [9] at this easy way of viewing matters, but finally gave way before the old man's brief and distinct representations. As the latter was leaving the room the other recalled him to ask:

" Those woods there, opposite, what do you call them? "

" The woods of Sauval."

" And how far do they extend? "

The miller looked him straight in the face. "I do not know," he replied.

And he withdrew. An hour later the subvention [10] in money and provisions that the officer had demanded was in the courtyard of the mill. Night was coming on; Françoise followed every movement of the soldiers with an anxious eye. She never once left the vicinity of the room in which Dominique was imprisoned. About seven o'clock she had a harrowing emotion; she saw the officer enter the prisoner's apartment, and for a quarter of an hour heard their voices raised in violent discussion. The officer came to the door a moment and gave an order in German which she did not understand, but, when twelve men came and formed in the courtyard with shouldered muskets, she was seized with a fit of trembling and felt as if she should die. It was all over then; the execution was about to take place. The twelve men remained there ten minutes; Dominique's voice kept rising higher and higher in a tone of vehement denial. Finally the officer came out, closing the door behind him with a vicious bang and saying:

" Very well; think it over. I give you until tomorrow morning."

And he ordered the twelve men to break ranks by a motion of his hand. Françoise was stupefied. Father Merlier, who had continued to puff away at his pipe while watching the platoon with a simple, curious air, came and took her by the arm with fatherly gentleness. He led her to her chamber.

" Don't fret," he said to her; " try to get some sleep. Tomorrow it will be light and we shall see more clearly."

He locked the door behind him as he left the room. It was a fixed principle with him that women are good for nothing, and that they spoil everything whenever they meddle in important matters. Françoise did not lie down, however; she remained a long time seated on her bed, listening to the various noises in the house. The German soldiers quartered in the courtyard were singing and laughing; they must have kept up their eating and drinking until eleven o'clock, for

---

[9] **umbrage:** offense. [10] **subvention:** contribution.

the riot never ceased for an instant. Heavy footsteps resounded from time to time through the mill itself, doubtless the tramp of the guards as they were relieved. What had most interest for her were the sounds that she could catch in the room that lay directly under her own; several times she threw herself prone upon the floor and applied her ear to the boards. That room was the one in which they had locked up Dominique. He must have been pacing the apartment, for she could hear for a long time his regular, cadenced tread passing from the wall to the window and back again; then there was a deep silence; doubtless he had seated himself. The other sounds ceased too; everything was still. When it seemed to her that the house was sunk in slumber she raised her window as noiselessly as possible and leaned out.

Without, the night was serene and balmy. The slender crescent of the moon, which was just setting behind Sauval wood, cast a dim radiance over the landscape. The lengthening shadows of the great trees stretched far athwart the fields in bands of blackness, while in such spots as were unobscured the grass appeared of a tender green, soft as velvet. But Françoise did not stop to consider the mysterious charm of the night. She was scrutinizing the country and looking to see where the Germans had posted their sentinels. She could clearly distinguish their dark forms outlined along the course of the Morelle. There was only one stationed opposite the mill, on the far bank of the stream, by a willow whose branches dipped in the water. Françoise had an excellent view of him; he was a tall young man, standing quite motionless with face upturned toward the sky, with the meditative air of a shepherd.

When she had completed her careful inspection of localities she returned and took her former seat upon the bed. She remained there an hour absorbed in deep thought. Then she listened again; there was not a breath to be heard in the house. She went again to the window and took another look outside, but one of the moon's horns was still hanging above the edge of the forest, and this circumstance doubtless appeared to her unpropitious, for she resumed her waiting. At last the moment seemed to have arrived; the night was now quite dark; she could no longer discern the sentinel opposite her, the land-scape lay before her black as a sea of ink. She listened intently for a moment, then formed her resolve. Close beside her window was an iron ladder made of bars set in the wall, which ascended from the mill wheel to the granary at the top of the building, and had formerly served the miller as a means of inspecting certain portions of the gearing, but a change having been made in the machinery the ladder had long since become lost to sight beneath the thick ivy that covered all that side of the mill.

Françoise bravely climbed over the balustrade of the little balcony in front of her window, grasped one of the iron bars and found herself suspended in space. She commenced the descent; her skirts were a great hindrance to her. Suddenly a stone became loosened from the wall and fell into the Morelle with a loud splash. She stopped, benumbed with fear, but reflection quickly told her that the waterfall, with its continuous roar, was sufficient to deaden any noise that she could make, and then she descended more boldly, putting aside the ivy with her foot, testing each round of her ladder. When she was on a level with the room that had been converted into a prison for her lover she stopped. An unforeseen difficulty came near depriving her of all her courage; the window of the room beneath was not situated directly under the window of her bedroom; there was a wide space between it and the ladder, and when she extended her hand it only encountered the naked wall.

Would she have to go back the way she came and leave her project unaccomplished? Her arms were growing very tired; the murmuring of the Morelle, far down below, was beginning to make her dizzy. Then she broke off bits of plaster from the wall and threw them against Dominique's window. He did not hear; perhaps he was asleep. Again she crumbled fragments from the wall, until the skin was peeled from her fingers. Her strength was exhausted, she felt that she was about to fall backward into the stream, when at last Dominique softly raised his sash.

"It is I," she murmured. "Take me quick; I am about to fall." Leaning from the window he grasped her and drew her into the room, where she had a paroxysm of weeping, stifling her sobs in order that she might not be heard. Then, by a supreme effort of the will she overcame her emotion.

"Are you guarded?" she asked in a low voice.

Dominique, not yet recovered from his stupefaction at seeing her there, made answer by simply pointing toward his door. There was a sound of snoring audible on the outside; it was evident that the sentinel had been overpowered by sleep and had thrown himself upon the floor close against the door in such a way that it could not be opened without arousing him.

"You must fly," she continued earnestly. "I came here to bid you fly and say farewell."

But he seemed not to hear her. He kept repeating:

"What, it is you, is it you? Oh, what a fright you gave me! You might have killed yourself." He took her hands, he kissed them again and again. "How I love you, Françoise! You are as courageous as you are good. The only thing I feared was that I might die without seeing you again; but you aïe here, and now they may shoot me when they will. Let me but have a quarter of an hour with you and I am ready."

He had gradually drawn her to him; her head was resting on his shoulder. The peril that was so near at hand brought them closer to each other, and they forgot everything in that long embrace.

"Ah, Françoise!" Dominique went on in low, caressing tones, "today is the fête of Saint Louis, our wedding day that we have been waiting for so long. Nothing has been able to keep us apart, for we are both here, faithful to our appointment, are we not? It is now our wedding morning."

"Yes, yes," she repeated after him, "our wedding morning."

They shuddered as they exchanged a kiss. But suddenly she tore herself from his arms; the terrible reality arose before her eyes.

"You must fly, you must fly," she murmured breathlessly. "There is not a moment to lose." And as he stretched out his arms in the darkness to draw her to him again, she went on in tender, beseeching tones: "Oh, listen to me, I entreat you. If you die, I shall die. In an hour it will be daylight. Go, go at once; I command you to go."

Then she rapidly explained her plan to him. The iron ladder extended downward to the wheel; once he had got so far he could climb down by means of the buckets and get into the boat, which was hidden in a recess. Then it would be an easy matter for him to reach the other bank of the stream and make his escape.

"But are there no sentinels?" said he.

"Only one, directly opposite here, at the foot of the first willow."

"And if he sees me, if he gives the alarm?"

Françoise shuddered. She placed in his hand a knife that she had brought down with her. They were silent.

"And your father — and you," Dominique continued. "But no, it is not to be thought of; I must not fly. When I am no longer here those soldiers are capable of murdering you. You do not know them. They offered to spare my life if I would guide them into Sauval forest. When they discover that I have escaped, their fury will be such that they will be ready for every atrocity."

The girl did not stop to argue the question. To all the considerations that he adduced to her, her one simple answer was: " Fly. For the love of me, fly. If you love me, Dominique, do not linger here a single moment longer."

She promised that she would return to her bedroom; no one should know that she had helped him. She concluded by folding him in her arms and smothering him with kisses, in an extravagant outburst of passion. He was vanquished. He put only one more question to her:

" Will you swear to me that your father knows what you are doing, and that he counsels my flight? "

" It was my father who sent me to you," Françoise unhesitatingly replied.

She told a falsehood. At that moment she had but one great, overmastering longing, to know that he was in safety, to escape from the horrible thought that the morning's sun was to be the signal for his death. When he should be far away, then calamity and evil might burst upon her head; whatever fate might be in store for her would seem endurable, so that only his life might be spared. Before and above all other considerations, the selfishness of her love demanded that he should be saved.

" It is well," said Dominique; " I will do as you desire."

No further word was spoken. Dominique went to the window to raise it again. But suddenly there was a noise that chilled them with affright. The door was shaken violently; they thought that some one was about to open it; it was evidently a party going the rounds who had heard their voices. They stood by the window, close locked in each other's arms, awaiting the event with anguish unspeakable. Again there came the rattling at the door, but it did not open. Each of them drew a deep sigh of relief; they saw how it was. The soldier lying across the threshold had turned over in his sleep. Silence was restored indeed, and presently the snoring began again.

Dominique insisted that Françoise should return to her room first of all. He took her in his arms, he bade her a silent farewell, then helped her to grasp the ladder, and himself climbed out in turn. He refused to descend a single step, however, until he knew that she was in her chamber. When she was safe in her room she let fall, in a voice scarce louder than a whisper, the words:

" Au revoir. I love you! "

She kneeled at the window, resting her elbows on the sill, straining her eyes to follow Dominique. The night was still very dark. She looked for the sentinel, but could see nothing of him; the willow alone was dimly visible, a pale spot upon the surrounding blackness. For a moment she heard the rustling of the ivy as Dominique descended, then the wheel creaked, and there was a faint splash which told that the young man had found the boat. This was confirmed when, a minute later, she descried the shadowy outline of the skiff on the gray bosom of the Morelle. Then a horrible feeling of dread seemed to clutch her by the throat. Every moment she thought she heard the sentry give the alarm; every faintest sound among the dusky shadows seemed to her overwrought imagination to be the hurrying tread of soldiers, the clash of steel, the click of musket locks. The seconds slipped by, however, the landscape still preserved its solemn peace. Dominique must have landed safely on the other bank. Françoise no longer had eyes for anything. The silence was oppressive. And she heard the sound of trampling feet, a hoarse cry, the dull thud of a heavy body falling. This was followed by another silence, even deeper than that which had gone before. Then, as if conscious that Death had passed that way, she became very cold in presence of the impenetrable night.

4

At early daybreak the repose of the mill was disturbed by the clamor of angry voices. Father Merlier had gone and unlocked Françoise's door. She descended to the courtyard pale and very calm, but, when there, could not repress a shudder upon being brought face to face with the body of a Prussian soldier that lay on the ground beside the well, stretched out upon a cloak.

Around the corpse the soldiers were shouting and gesticulating angrily. Several of them shook their fists threateningly in the direction of the village. The officer had just sent a summons to Father Merlier to appear before him in his capacity as mayor of the commune.

" Here is one of our men," he said, in a voice that was almost unintelligible from anger, " who was found murdered on the bank of the stream. The murderer must be found, so that we may make a salutary example of him, and I shall expect you to co-operate with us in finding him."

" Whatsoever you desire," the miller replied, with his customary impassiveness. " Only it will be no easy matter."

The officer stooped down and drew aside the skirt of the cloak which concealed the dead man's face, disclosing as he did so a frightful wound. The sentinel had been struck in the throat and the weapon had not been withdrawn from the wound. It was a common kitchen knife, with a black handle.

" Look at that knife," the officer said to Father Merlier. " Perhaps it will assist us in our investigation."

The old man had started violently, but recovered himself at once; not a muscle of his face moved as he replied:

" Every one about here has knives like that. Like enough your man was tired of fighting and did the business himself. Such things have happened before now."

" Be silent! " the officer shouted in a fury. " I don't know what it is that keeps me from setting fire to the four corners of your village."

His anger fortunately kept him from noticing the great change that had come over Françoise's countenance. Her feelings had compelled her to sit down upon the stone bench beside the well. Do what she would she could not remove her eyes from the body that lay stretched upon the ground, almost at her feet. He had been a tall, handsome young man in life, very like Dominique in appearance, with blue eyes and yellow hair. The resemblance went to her heart. She thought that perhaps the dead man had left behind him in his German home some sweetheart who would weep for his loss. And she recognized her knife in the dead man's throat. She had killed him.

The officer, meantime, was talking of visiting Rocreuse with some terrible punishment, when two or three soldiers came running in. The guard had just that moment ascertained the fact of Dominique's escape. The agitation caused by the tidings was extreme. The officer went to inspect the locality, looked out through the still open window, saw at once how the event had happened, and returned in a state of exasperation.

Father Merlier appeared greatly vexed by Dominique's flight. " The idiot! " he murmured; " he has upset everything."

Françoise heard him, and was in an agony of suffering. Her father, moreover, had no suspicion of her complicity. He shook his head, saying to her in an undertone:

" We are in a nice box now! "

" It was that scoundrel! it was that scoundrel! " cried the officer. " He has got away to the woods; but he must be found, or the village shall stand the consequences." And addressing himself to the miller: " Come, you must know where he is hiding? "

Father Merlier laughed in his silent way, and pointed to the wide stretch of wooded hills.

" How can you expect to find a man in that wilderness? " he asked.

" Oh! there are plenty of hiding places that you are acquainted with. I am going to give you ten men; you shall act as guide to them."

" I am perfectly willing. But it will take a week to beat up all the woods of the neighborhood."

The old man's serenity enraged the officer; he saw, indeed, what a ridiculous proceeding such a hunt would be. It was at that moment that he caught sight of Françoise where she sat, pale and trembling, on her bench. His attention was aroused by the girl's anxious attitude. He was silent for a moment, glancing suspiciously from father to daughter and back again.

" Is not that man," he at last coarsely asked the old man, " your daughter's lover? "

Father Merlier's face became ashy pale, and he appeared for a moment as if about to throw himself on the officer and throttle him. He straightened himself up and made no reply. Françoise had hidden her face in her hands.

" Yes, that is how it is," the Prussian continued; " you or your daughter have helped him to escape. You are his accomplices. For the last time, will you surrender him? "

The miller did not answer. He had turned away and was looking at the distant landscape with an air of indifference, just as if the officer were talking to some other person. That put the finishing touch to the latter's wrath.

" Very well, then! " he declared, " you shall be shot in his stead."

And again he ordered out the firing party. Father Merlier was as imperturbable as ever. He scarcely did so much as shrug his shoulders; the whole drama appeared to him to be in very doubtful taste. He probably believed that they would not take a man's life in that unceremonious manner. When the platoon was on the ground he gravely said:

" So, then, you are in earnest? Very well, I am willing it should be so. If you feel you must have a victim, it may as well be I as another."

But Françoise arose, greatly troubled, stammering: " Have mercy, sir; do not harm my father. Kill me instead of him. It was I who helped Dominique to escape; I am the only guilty one."

" Hold your tongue, my girl," Father Merlier exclaimed. " Why do you tell such a falsehood? She passed the night locked in her room, sir; I assure you that she does not speak the truth."

" I am speaking the truth," the girl eagerly replied. " I got down by the window; I incited Dominique to fly. It is the truth, the whole truth."

The old man's face was very white. He could read in her eyes that she was not lying, and her story terrified him. Ah, those children! those children! how they spoiled everything, with their hearts and their feelings! Then he said angrily:

" She is crazy; do not listen to her. It is a lot of trash she is telling you. Come, let us get through with this business."

She persisted in her protestations; she kneeled, she raised her clasped hands in supplication. The officer stood tranquilly by and watched the harrowing scene.

" *Mon Dieu!* " he said at last, " I take your father because the other has escaped me. Bring me back the other man, and your father shall have his liberty."

She looked at him for a moment with eyes dilated by the horror which his proposal inspired in her.

" It is dreadful," she murmured. " Where can I look for Dominique now? He is gone; I know nothing beyond that."

" Well, make your choice between them; him or your father."

" Oh, my God! how can I choose? Even if I knew where to find Dominique I could not choose. You are breaking my heart. I would rather die at once. Yes, it would be more quickly ended thus. Kill me, I beseech you, kill me — "

The officer finally became weary of this scene of despair and tears. He cried:

" Enough of this! I wish to treat you kindly; I will give you two hours. If your lover is not here within two hours, your father shall pay the penalty he has incurred."

And he ordered Father Merlier away to the room that had served as a prison for Dominique. The old man asked for tobacco, and began to smoke. There was no trace of emotion to be described on his impassive face. Only when he was alone he wept two big tears that coursed slowly down his cheeks. His poor, dear child, what a fearful trial she was enduring!

Françoise remained in the courtyard. Prussian soldiers passed back and forth, laughing. Some of them addressed her with coarse pleasantries which she did not understand. Her gaze was bent upon the door through which her father had disappeared, and with a slow movement she raised her hand to her forehead, as if to keep it from bursting. The officer turned sharply on his heel, and said to her:

" You have two hours. Try to make use of them."

She had two hours. The words kept buzzing, buzzing in her ears. Then she went forth mechanically from the courtyard; she walked straight ahead with no definite end. Where was she to go? what was she to do? She did not even endeavor to arrive at any decision, for she felt how utterly useless were her efforts. And yet she would have liked to see Dominique; they could have come to some understanding together, perhaps they might hit on some plan to extricate them from their difficulties. And so, amid the confusion of her whirling thoughts, she took her way downward to the bank of the Morelle, which she crossed below the dam by means of some stepping-stones which were there. Proceeding onward, still involuntarily, she came to the first willow, at the corner of the meadow, and stooping down, beheld a sight that made her grow deathly pale — a pool of blood. It was the spot. And she followed the track that Dominique had left in the tall grass; it was evident that he had run, for the footsteps that crossed the meadow in a diagonal line were separated from one another by wide intervals. Then, beyond that point, she lost the trace, but thought she had discovered it again in an adjoining field. It led her onward to the border of the forest, where the trail came abruptly to an end.

Though conscious of the futility of the proceeding, Françoise penetrated into the wood. It was a comfort to her to be alone. She sat down for a moment, then, reflecting that time was passing, rose again to her feet. How long was it since she left the mill? Five minutes, or a half-hour? She had lost all idea of time. Perhaps Dominique had sought concealment in a clearing that she knew of, where they had gone together one afternoon and eaten hazelnuts. She directed her steps toward the clearing; she searched it thoroughly. A blackbird flew out, whistling his sweet and melancholy note; that was all. Then she thought that he might have taken refuge in a hollow among the rocks where he went sometimes with his gun, but the spot was untenanted. What use was there in looking for him? She would never find him, and little by little the desire to discover the hiding place became a passionate longing. She proceeded at a more rapid pace. The idea suddenly took possession of her that he had climbed into a tree, and thenceforth she went along with eyes raised aloft and called him by name every fifteen or twenty steps, so that he might know she was near him. The cuckoos answered her; a breath of air that rustled the leaves made her think that he was there and coming down to her. Once she even imagined that she saw him; she stopped with a sense of suffocation, with a desire to run away. What was she to say to him? Had she come there to take him back with her and have him shot? Oh! no, she would not mention those things; she would tell him that he must fly, that he must not remain in the neighborhood. Then she thought of her father awaiting her return, and the reflection caused her most bitter anguish. She sank upon the turf, weeping hot tears, crying aloud:

" My God! My God! why am I here! "

It was a mad thing for her to have come. And, as if seized with sudden panic, she ran hither and thither, she sought to make her way out of the forest. Three times she lost her way, and had begun to think she was never to see the mill again, when she came out on the meadow, directly opposite Rocreuse. As soon as she caught sight of the village she stopped. Was she going to return alone?

She was standing there when she heard a voice calling her name, softly:

" Françoise, Françoise! "

And she beheld Dominique raising his head above the edge of a ditch. Just God! she had found him.

Could it be, then, that Heaven willed his death? She suppressed a cry that rose to her lips, and slipped into the ditch beside him.

" You were looking for me? " he asked.

" Yes," she replied bewilderedly, scarcely knowing what she was saying.

" Ah! what has happened? "

She stammered, with eyes downcast: " Why, nothing; I was anxious, I wanted to see you."

Thereupon, his fears alleviated, he went on to tell her how it was that he had remained in the vicinity. He was alarmed for them. Those rascally Prussians were not above their vengeance on women and old men. All had ended well, however, and he added, laughing:

" The wedding will be put off for a week, that's all."

He became serious, however, upon noticing that her dejection did not pass away.

" But what is the matter? You are concealing something from me."

" No, I give you my word I am not. I am tired; I ran all the way here."

He kissed her, saying it was imprudent for them both to talk there any longer, and was about to climb out of the ditch in order to return to the forest. She stopped him; she was trembling violently.

" Listen, Dominique; perhaps it will be as well for you to stay here, after all. There is no one looking for you; you have nothing to fear."

"Françoise, you are concealing something from me," he said again.

Again she protested that she was concealing nothing. She only liked to know that he was near her. And there were other reasons still that she gave in stammering accents. Her manner was so strange that no consideration could now have induced him to go away. He believed, moreover, that the French would return presently. Troops had been seen over towards Sauval.

"Ah! let them make haste; let them come as quickly as possible," she murmured fervently.

At that moment the clock of the church at Rocreuse struck eleven; the strokes reached them, clear and distinct. She arose in terror; it was two hours since she had left the mill.

"Listen," she said, with feverish rapidity, "should we need you, I will go up to my room and wave my handkerchief from the window."

And she started off homeward on a run, while Dominique, greatly disturbed in mind, stretched himself at length beside the ditch to watch the mill. Just as she was about to enter the village Françoise encountered an old beggar man, Father Bontemps, who knew every one and everything in that part of the country. He saluted her; he had just seen the miller, he said, surrounded by a crowd of Prussians; then, making numerous signs of the cross and mumbling some inarticulate words, he went his way.

"The two hours are up," the officer said when Françoise made her appearance.

Father Merlier was there, seated on the bench beside the well. He was smoking still. The young girl again proffered her supplication, kneeling before the officer and weeping. Her wish was to gain time. The hope that she might yet behold the return of the French had been gaining strength in her bosom, and amid her tears and sobs she thought she could distinguish in the distance the cadenced tramp of an advancing army. Oh! if they would but come and deliver them all from their fearful trouble!

"Hear me, sir: grant us an hour, just one little hour. Surely you will not refuse to grant us an hour!"

But the officer was inflexible. He even ordered two men to lay hold of her and take her away, in order that they might proceed undisturbed with the execution of the old man. Then a dreadful conflict took place in Françoise's heart. She could not allow her father to be murdered in that manner! no, no, she would die in company with Dominique rather; and she was just darting away in the direction of her room in order to signal to her *fiancé,* when Dominique himself entered the courtyard.

The officer and his soldiers gave a great shout of triumph, but he, as if there had been no soul there but Françoise, walked straight up to her. He was perfectly calm, and his face wore a slight expression of sternness.

"You did wrong," he said. "Why did you not bring me back with you? Had it not been for Father Bontemps I should have known nothing of all this. Well, I am here, at all events."

5

It was three o'clock. The heavens were piled high with great black clouds, the tail end of a storm that had been raging somewhere in the vicinity. Beneath the coppery sky and ragged scud [11] the valley of Rocreuse, so bright and smiling in the sunlight, became a grim chasm, full of sinister shadows. The Prussian officer had done nothing with Dominique beyond placing him in confinement, giving no indication of his ultimate purpose in regard to him. Françoise, since noon, had been suffering unendurable agony; notwithstanding her father's entreaties, she would not leave the courtyard. She was waiting for the French troops to appear, but the hours slipped by, night was approaching, and she suffered all the more since it appeared as if the time thus gained would have no effect on the final result.

About three o'clock, however, the Prussians began to make their preparation for departure. The officer had gone to Dominique's room and remained closeted with him for some minutes, as he had done the day before. Françoise knew that the young man's life was hanging in the balance; she clasped her hands and put up fervent prayers. Beside her sat Father Merlier, rigid and silent, declining, like the true peasant he was, to attempt any interference with accomplished facts.

"Oh! my God! my God!" Françoise exclaimed, "they are going to kill him!"

The miller drew her to him, and took her on his lap as if she had been a little child. At this juncture the officer came from the room, followed by two men conducting Dominique between them.

"Never, never," the latter exclaimed. "I am ready to die."

[11] **scud:** drifting clouds.

"You had better think the matter over," the officer replied. "I shall have no trouble in finding some one else to render us the service which you refuse. I am generous with you; I offer you your life. It is simply a matter of guiding us across the forest to Montredon; there must be paths."

Dominique made no answer.

"Then you persist in your obstinacy?"

"Shoot me, and let's have done with it," he replied.

Françoise, in the distance, entreated her lover with clasped hands; she was forgetful of all considerations save one — she would have had him commit a treason. But Father Merlier seized her hands, that the Prussians might not see the wild gestures of a woman whose mind was disordered by her distress.

"He is right," he murmured, "it is best for him to die."

The firing party was in readiness. The officer still had hopes of bringing Dominique over, and was waiting to see him exhibit some signs of weakness. Deep silence prevailed. Heavy peals of thunder were heard in the distance, the fields and woods lay lifeless beneath the sweltering heat. And it was in the midst of this oppressive silence that suddenly the cry arose:

"The French; the French!"

It was a fact; they were coming. The line of red trousers could be seen advancing along the Sauval road, at the edge of the forest. In the mill the confusion was extreme; the Prussian soldiers ran to and fro, giving vent to guttural cries. Not a shot had been fired as yet.

"The French! the French!" cried Françoise, clapping her hands for joy. She was like a woman possessed. She had escaped from her father's embrace and was laughing boisterously, her arms raised high in the air. They had come at last, then, and had come in time, since Dominique was still there, alive!

A crash of musketry that rang in her ears like a thunderclap caused her to suddenly turn her head. The officer had muttered, "We will finish this business first," and, with his own hands pushing Dominique up against the wall of a shed, had given the command to the squad to fire. When Françoise turned, Dominique was lying on the ground, pierced by a dozen bullets.

She did not shed a tear; she stood there like one suddenly rendered senseless. Her eyes were fixed and staring, and she went and seated herself beneath the shed, a few steps from the lifeless body. She looked at it wistfully; now and then she would make a movement with her hands in an aimless, childish way. The Prussians had seized Father Merlier as a hostage.

It was a pretty fight. The officer, perceiving that he could not retreat without being cut to pieces, rapidly made the best disposition possible of his men; it was as well to sell their lives dearly. The Prussians were now the defenders of the mill, and the French were the attacking party. The musketry fire began with unparalleled fury; for half an hour there was no lull in the storm. Then a deep report was heard, and a ball carried away a main branch of the old elm. The French had artillery; a battery, in position just beyond the ditch where Dominique had concealed himself, commanded the main street of Rocreuse. The conflict could not last long after that.

Ah! the poor old mill! The cannon balls raked it from wall to wall. Half the roof was carried away; two of the walls fell in. But it was on the side toward the Morelle that the damage was most lamentable. The ivy, torn from the tottering walls, hung in tatters, débris of every description floated away upon the bosom of the stream, and through a great breach Françoise's chamber was visible, with its little bed, the snow-white curtains of which were carefully drawn. Two balls struck the old wheel in quick succession, and it gave one parting groan; the buckets were carried away down stream, the frame was crushed into a shapeless mass. It was the soul of the stout old mill parting from the body.

Then the French came forward to carry the place by storm. There was a mad hand-to-hand conflict with the bayonet. Under the dull sky the pretty valley became a huge slaughter pen; the broad meadows looked on in horror, with their great isolated trees and their rows of poplars, dotting them with shade, while to right and left the forest was like the walls of a tilting-ground enclosing the combatants, and in Nature's universal panic the gentle murmur of the springs and watercourses sounded like sobs and wails.

Françoise had not stirred from the shed where she remained hanging over Dominique's body. Father Merlier had met his death from a stray bullet. Then the French captain, the Prussians being exterminated and the mill on fire, entered the courtyard at the head of his men. It was the first success that he had gained since the breaking out of the war, so, all inflamed with enthusiasm, drawing himself up to the full height of his lofty stature, he laughed pleasantly, as a handsome cavalier like him might laugh. Then, perceiving poor idiotic Françoise where she crouched between the corpses of her father and her intended, among the smoking ruins of the mill, he saluted her gallantly with his sword, and shouted:

" Victory! Victory! "

(*Anonymous Translation*)

SUGGESTIONS FOR STUDY

1. What sort of picture does Zola paint of the mill and its surroundings in the opening paragraphs? What is his purpose in dwelling on this description?

2. What are the motives which actuate Françoise during the course of events? Would she have liked Dominique to save his life at the price of giving information to the Prussians?

3. What is the net effect of Zola's picture of warfare? Which leaves the stronger impression on you — the heroism of Dominique or the horror of the end?

4. Comment on the effectiveness of the last paragraph of the story. Why are the words of the French officer so striking?

5. Compare " The Attack on the Mill " with Daudet's " The Siege of Berlin " as glimpses of the Franco-Prussian War. What other stories of modern warfare do you know? How do they affect your attitude toward war in general?

6. Vocabulary: verdurous, taciturnity, beatific, casualty, débris, belligerents, athwart, unpropitious, paroxysm, imperturbable, impassive, extricate, inflexible, sinister.

ANATOLE FRANCE (1844–1924)

Anatole France, whose real name was Jacques Anatole Thibault, was the leading French writer during the quarter of a century preceding the World War. He was born in Paris and was the son of a bookseller. Always an eager reader, he acquired in time a great fund of curious learning with which to salt his writings. But he took an even keener interest in human nature, which he never idealized but regarded with an ironical indulgence. His masters in thinking were Voltaire and Renan. During the first part of his career he seemed to be a universal skeptic, caring only for the intellectual amusement which life afforded him. In his later years his sense of justice impelled him to take an active interest in politics. Most of his work is cast in the form of fiction, which serves, however, chiefly as a vehicle for his opinions. He was primarily a critic of literature, of human activities and of social institutions. Literary criticism he called " the adventures of a soul among masterpieces." Its function, he asserted, was merely to express personal tastes, not to pronounce judgment. He ridiculed mercilessly the pretentions of philosophy, theology and science to arrive at absolute truth. In public affairs he strongly opposed nationalism, militarism and clerical domination. His philosophy of life is most directly expressed in his *Garden of Epicurus*. His most interesting "novels" (in which the story is nearly always subordinate to the ideas) are *Crime of Sylvester Bonnard, Thais, The Red Lily, Penguin Island, The Gods Are Athirst* and *The Revolt of the Angels*. He also wrote some delightful books of reminiscences. His style is a model of clarity, grace and wit. His influence, which at its highest was very great, declined during the last ten years of his life. He has been called "the fine flower of the Latin genius," and in truth no other country but France could have produced him. The American writer who most nearly resembles him is Mr. James Branch Cabell.

CRAINQUEBILLE, THE MAJESTY OF JUSTICE

This short story, which was published in 1903, was suggested to Anatole France by the Dreyfus case, the most celebrated political "affair" in the history of the present French Republic. Alfred Dreyfus, an officer in the French army, was charged in 1894 with having revealed military secrets to the Germans, was declared guilty of treason before a court martial and was condemned to life imprisonment. Many responsible people became convinced that he was innocent and had been made the scapegoat of others. Public opinion forced a second trial of Dreyfus in 1899, at which he was again found guilty but received a much lighter sentence and was actually pardoned within a few months. Finally in 1906 he was completely absolved of the charge and was restored to his rank in the army. He served in the World War and died in 1935. The Dreyfus case divided the French people into two bitterly hostile parties — the militarists, including the royalists and many conservatives, and the anti-militarists who were stanch adherents of the Republic. Anatole France was of course on the side of Dreyfus. But, he seems to ask in this little story, what chance has a poor Crainquebille, a Dreyfus without money or influence, to secure justice in our modern society? The satirical intention is obvious throughout.

CRAINQUEBILLE'S MISADVENTURE

Up and down the town went Jérôme Crainquebille, costermonger,[1] pushing his barrow before him and crying: "Cabbages! Turnips! Carrots!" When he had leeks he cried: "Asparagus!" For leeks are the asparagus of the poor. Now it happened that on October 20, at noon, as he was going down the Rue Montmartre, there came

---

[1] **costermonger**: man who sells vegetables, etc., from a barrow in the street.

out of her shop the shoemaker's wife, Madame Bayard. She went up to Crainquebille's barrow and scornfully taking up a bundle of leeks, she said:

" I don't think much of your leeks. What do you want a bundle? "

" Sevenpence halfpenny, mum, and the best in the market! "

" Sevenpence halfpenny for three wretched leeks? "

And disdainfully she cast the leeks back into the barrow.

Then it was that Constable 64 came and said to Crainquebille: " Move on."

Moving on was what Crainquebille had been doing from morning till evening for fifty years. Such an order seemed right to him, and perfectly in accordance with the nature of things. Quite prepared to obey, he urged his customer to take what she wanted.

" You must give me time to choose," she retorted sharply.

Then she felt all the bundles of leeks over again. Finally, she selected the one she thought the best, and held it clasped to her bosom as saints in church pictures hold the palm of victory.

" I will give you sevenpence. That's quite enough; and I'll have to fetch it from the shop, for I haven't anything on me."

Still embracing the leeks, she went back into the shop, whither she had been preceded by a customer, carrying a child.

Just at this moment Constable 64 said to Crainquebille for the second time:

" Move on."

" I'm waiting for my money," replied Crainquebille.

" And I'm not telling you to wait for your money; I'm telling you to move on," retorted the constable grimly.

Meanwhile, the shoemaker's wife in her shop was fitting blue slippers on to a child of eighteen months, whose mother was in a hurry. And the green heads of the leeks were lying on the counter.

For the half century that he had been pushing his barrow through the streets, Crainquebille had been learning respect for authority. But now his position was a peculiar one: he was torn asunder between what was his due and what was his duty. His was not a judicial mind. He failed to understand that the possession of an individual's right in no way exonerated him from the performance of a social duty. He attached too great importance to his claim to receive sevenpence, and too little to the duty of pushing his barrow and moving on, for ever moving on. He stood still.

For the third time Constable 64 quietly and calmly ordered him to move on. Unlike Inspector Montauciel, whose habit it is to threaten constantly but never to take proceedings, Constable 64 is slow to threaten and quick to act. Such is his character. Though somewhat sly he is an excellent servant and loyal soldier. He is as brave as a lion and as gentle as a child. He knows naught save his official instructions.

" Don't you understand when I tell you to move on? "

To Crainquebille's mind his reason for standing still was too weighty for him not to consider it sufficient. Wherefore, artlessly and simply he explained it:

" Good Lord! Don't I tell you that I am waiting for my money."

Constable 64 merely replied:

" Do you want me to summons you? If you do you have only to say so."

At these words Crainquebille slowly shrugged his shoulders, looked sadly at the constable, and then raised his eyes to heaven, as if he would say:

" I call God to witness! Am I a lawbreaker? Am I one to make light of the by-laws and ordinances which regulate my ambulatory [2] calling? At five o'clock in the morning I was at the market. Since seven, pushing my barrow and wearing my hands to the bones, I have been crying: ' Cabbages! Turnips! Carrots! ' I am turned sixty. I am worn out. And you ask me whether I have raised the black flag of rebellion. You are mocking me and your joking is cruel."

Either because he failed to notice the expression on Crainquebille's face, or because he considered it no excuse for disobedience, the constable inquired curtly and roughly whether he had been understood.

Now, just at that moment the block of traffic in the Rue Montmartre was at its worst. Carriages, drays, carts, omnibuses, trucks, jammed one against the other, seemed indissolubly welded together. From their quivering immobility proceeded shouts and oaths. Cabmen and butchers' boys grandiloquent [3] and drawling insulted one another from a distance, and omnibus conductors, regarding Crainquebille as the cause of the block, called him " a dirty leek."

Meanwhile, on the pavement the curious were crowding round to listen to the dispute. Then the constable, finding himself the centre of attention, began to think it time to display his authority:

" Very well," he said, taking a stumpy pencil and a greasy notebook from his pocket.

Crainquebille persisted in his idea, obedient to a force within. Be-

[2] **ambulatory:** walking.
[3] **grandiloquent:** using pompous language.

sides, it was now impossible for him either to move on or to draw back. The wheel of his barrow was unfortunately caught in that of a milkman's cart.

Tearing his hair beneath his cap he cried:

" But don't I tell you I'm waiting for my money! Here's a fix! *Misère de misère!* " [4]

By these words, expressive rather of despair than of rebellion, Constable 64 considered he had been insulted. And, because to his mind all insults must necessarily take the consecrated, regular, traditional, ritual form so to speak of *Mort aux vaches*, [5] thus the offender's words were heard and understood by the constable.

" Ah! You said: *Mort aux vaches*. Very good. Come along."

Stupefied with amazement and distress, Crainquebille opened his great rheumy [6] eyes and gazed at Constable 64. With a broken voice proceeding now from the top of his head and now from the heels of his boots, he cried, with his arms folded over his blue blouse:

" I said ' *Mort aux vaches* '? I? . . . Oh! "

The tradesmen and errand boys hailed the arrest with laughter. It gratified the taste of all crowds for violent and ignoble spectacles. But there was one serious person who was pushing his way through the throng; he was a sad-looking old man, dressed in black, wearing a high hat; he went up to the constable and said to him in a low voice very gently and firmly:

" You are mistaken. This man did not insult you."

" Mind your own business," replied the policeman, but without threatening, for he was speaking to a man who was well dressed.

The old man insisted calmly and tenaciously. And the policeman ordered him to make his declaration to the Police Commissioner.

Meanwhile Crainquebille was explaining:

" Then I did say ' *Mort aux vaches!* ' Oh! . . ."

As he was thus giving vent to his astonishment, Madame Bayard, the shoemaker's wife, came to him with sevenpence in her hand. But Constable 64 already had him by the collar; so Madame Bayard, thinking that no debt could be due to a man who was being taken to the police-station, put her sevenpence into her apron pocket.

Then, suddenly beholding his barrow confiscated, his liberty lost, a gulf opening beneath him and the sky overcast, Crainquebille murmured:

" It can't be helped! "

---

[4] misère de misère: wretched misery.
[5] **Mort aux vaches**: Down with the cops! [6] rheumy: watery.

Before the Commissioner, the old gentleman declared that he had been hindered on his way by the block in the traffic, and so had witnessed the incident. He maintained that the policeman had not been insulted, and that he was laboring under a delusion. He gave his name and profession: Dr. David Matthieu, chief physician at the Ambroise-Paré Hospital, officer of the Legion of Honor. At another time such evidence would have been sufficient for the Commissioner. But just then men of science [7] were regarded with suspicion in France.

Crainquebille continued under arrest. He passed the night in the lockup. In the morning he was taken to the Police Court in the prison van.

He did not find prison either sad or humiliating. It seemed to him necessary. What struck him as he entered was the cleanliness of the walls and of the brick floor.

" Well, for a clean place, yes, it is a clean place. You might eat off the floor."

When he was left alone, he wanted to draw out his stool; but he perceived that it was fastened to the wall. He expressed his surprise aloud:

" That's a queer idea! Now there's a thing I should never have thought of, I'm sure."

Having sat down, he twiddled his thumbs and remained wrapped in amazement. The silence and the solitude overwhelmed him. The time seemed long. Anxiously he thought of his barrow, which had been confiscated with its load of cabbages, carrots, celery, dandelion and lettuce. And he wondered, asking himself with alarm: " What have they done with my barrow? "

On the third day he received a visit from his lawyer, Maître Lemerle, one of the youngest members of the Paris Bar.

Crainquebille endeavoured to tell him his story; but it was not easy, for he was not accustomed to conversation. With a little help he might perhaps have succeeded. But his lawyer shook his head doubtfully at everything he said; and, turning over his papers, muttered:

" Hm! Hm! I don't find anything about all this in my brief."

Then, in a bored tone, twirling his fair moustache he said:

" In your own interest it would be advisable, perhaps, for you to confess. Your persistence in absolute denial seems to me extremely unwise."

[7] **men of science:** The scientists of France were nearly all on the side of Dreyfus.

And from that moment Crainquebille would have made confession if he had known what to confess.

CRAINQUEBILLE BEFORE THE MAGISTRATES

President Bourriche devoted six whole minutes to the examination of Crainquebille. This examination would have been more enlightening if the accused had replied to the questions asked him. But Crainquebille was unaccustomed to discussion; and in such a company his lips were sealed by reverence and fear. So he was silent: and the President answered his own question; his replies were staggering. He concluded: " Finally, you admit having said, ' *Mort aux vaches.*' "

" I said, '*Mort aux vaches!*' because the policeman said, ' *Mort aux vaches!*' so then I said ' *Mort aux vaches!*' "

He meant that, being overwhelmed by the most unexpected of accusations, he had in his amazement merely repeated the curious words falsely attributed to him, and which he had certainly never pronounced. He had said, " *Mort aux vaches!*" as he might have said, " I capable of insulting anyone! how could you believe it? "

President Bourriche put a different interpretation on the incident.

" Do you maintain," he said, " that the policeman was, himself, the first to utter the exclamation? "

Crainquebille gave up trying to explain. It was too difficult.

" You do not persist in your statement. You are quite right," said the President.

And he had the witness called.

Constable 64, by name Bastien Matra, swore he spoke the truth and nothing by the truth. Then he gave evidence in the following terms:

" I was on my beat on October 20, at noon, when I noticed in the Rue Montmartre a person who appeared to be a hawker, unduly blocking the traffic with his barrow opposite No. 328. Three times I intimated to him the order to move on, but he refused to comply. And when I gave him warning that I was about to charge him, he retorted by crying: ' *Mort aux vaches!*' Which I took as an insult."

This evidence, delivered in a firm and moderate manner, the magistrates received with obvious approbation. The witnesses for the defense were Madame Bayard, shoemaker's wife, and Dr. David Matthieu, chief physician to the Hospital Ambroise Paré, officer of the Legion of Honor. Madame Bayard had seen nothing and heard nothing. Dr. Matthieu was in the crowd which had gathered round the policeman, who was ordering the costermonger to move on. His evidence led to a new episode in the trial.

"I witnessed the incident," he said, "I observed that the constable had made a mistake; he had not been insulted. I went up to him and called his attention to the fact. The officer insisted on arresting the costermonger, and told me to follow him to the Commissioner of Police. This I did. Before the Commissioner, I repeated my declaration.

"You may sit down," said the President. "Usher, recall witness Matra."

"Matra, when you proceeded to arrest the accused, did not Dr. Matthieu point out to you that you were mistaken? "

"That is to say, Monsieur le Président, that he insulted me."

"What did he say? "

"He said, '*Mort aux vaches!*' "

Uproarious laughter arose from the audience.

"You may withdraw," said the President hurriedly.

And he warned the public that if such unseemly demonstrations occurred again he would clear the court. Meanwhile, Counsel for the defense was haughtily fluttering the sleeves of his gown, and for the moment it was thought that Crainquebille would be acquitted.

Order having been restored, Maître Lemerle rose. He opened his pleading with a eulogy of policemen: " those unassuming servants of society who, in return for a trifling salary, endure fatigue and brave incessant danger with daily heroism. They were soldiers once, and soldiers they remain; soldiers, that word expresses everything. . . ."

From this consideration Maître Lemerle went on to descant [8] eloquently on the military virtues. He was one of those, he said, who would not allow a finger to be laid on the army, on that national army, to which he was so proud to belong.

The President bowed. Maître Lemerle happened to be lieutenant in the Reserves. He was also nationalist candidate for Les Vielles Haudriettes. He continued:

"No, indeed, I do not esteem lightly the invaluable services unassumingly rendered, which the valiant people of Paris receive daily from the guardians of the peace. And had I beheld in Crainquebille, gentlemen, one who had insulted an ex-soldier, I should never have consented to represent him before you. My client is accused of having said: '*Mort aux vaches!*' The meaning of such an expression is

[8] descant: talk freely.

clear. If you consult the dictionary you will find: ' *Vachard,* a slug-gard, an idler, one who stretches himself out lazily like a cow instead of working. *Vache,* one who sells himself to the police; spy.' *Mort aux vaches* is an expression employed by certain people. But the question resolves itself into this: how did Crainquebille say it? And, further, did he say it at all? Permit me to doubt it, gentlemen.

" I do not suspect Constable Matra of any evil intention. But, as we have said, his calling is arduous. He is sometimes harassed, fatigued, overdone. In such conditions he may have suffered from an aural[9] hallucination. And, when he comes and tells you, gentle-men, that Dr. David Matthieu, officer of the Legion of Honor, chief physician at the Ambroise-Paré Hospital, a gentleman and a prince of science, cried: ' *Mort aux vaches,*' then we are forced to believe that Matra is obsessed,[10] and if the term be not too strong, suffering from the mania of persecution.

" And even if Crainquebille did cry: ' *Mort aux vaches,*' it remains to be proved whether such words on his lips can be regarded as an offense. Crainquebille is the natural child of a costermonger, de-praved by years of drinking and other evil courses. Crainquebille was born alcoholic. You behold him brutalized by sixty years of poverty. Gentlemen, you must conclude that he is irresponsible."

Maître Lemerle sat down. Then President Bourriche muttered a sentence condemning Jérôme Crainquebille to pay fifty francs fine and to go to prison for a fortnight. The magistrates convicted him on the strength of the evidence given by Constable Matra.

As he was being taken down the long dark passage of the Palais, Crainquebille felt an intense desire for sympathy. He turned to the municipal guard who was his escort and called him three times: " 'Cipal![11] . . . 'cipal! . . . Eh! 'cipal! " And he sighed: " If anyone had told me only a fortnight ago that this would happen! "

Then he reflected:

" They speak too quickly, these gentlemen. They speak well, but they speak too quickly. You can't make them understand you. . . . 'cipal, don't you think they speak too quickly? "

But the soldier marched straight on without replying or turning his head.

Crainquebille asked him: " Why don't you answer me? "

9 aural: pertaining to hearing.   10 obsessed: excessively preoccupied.
11 'Cipal: Crainquebille's way of saying " municipal."

The soldier was silent. And Crainquebille said bitterly: " You would speak to a dog. Why not to me? Do you never open your mouth? Is it because your breath is foul? " . . .

CRAINQUEBILLE SUBMITS TO THE LAWS OF THE REPUBLIC

Having been taken back to his prison, Crainquebille sat down on his chained stool, filled with astonishment and admiration. He, himself, was not quite sure whether the magistrates were mistaken. The tribunal had concealed its essential weakness beneath the majesty of form. He could not believe that he was in the right, as against magistrates whose reasons he had not understood: it was impossible for him to conceive that anything could go wrong in so elaborate a ceremony. For, unaccustomed to attending Mass or frequenting the Élysée,[12] he had never in his life witnessed anything so grand as a police court trial. He was perfectly aware that he had never cried " *Mort aux vaches!* " That for having said it he should have been sentenced to a fortnight's imprisonment seemed to him an august mystery, one of those articles of faith to which believers adhere without understanding them, an obscure, striking, adorable and terrible revelation.

This poor old man believed himself guilty of having mystically offended Constable 64, just as the little boy learning his first Catechism believes himself guilty of Eve's sin. His sentence had taught him that he had cried " *Mort aux vaches!* " He must, therefore, have cried " *Mort aux vaches!* " in some mysterious manner, unknown to himself. He was transported into a supernatural world. His trial was his apocalypse.[13]

If he had no very clear idea of the offense, his idea of the penalty was still less clear. His sentence appeared to him a solemn and superior ritual, something dazzling and incomprehensible, which is not to be discussed, and for which one is neither to be praised nor pitied. If at that moment he had seen President Bourriche, with white wings and a halo round his forehead, coming down through a hole in the ceiling, he would not have been surprised at this new manifestation of judicial glory. He would have said: " This is my trial continuing! "

On the next day his lawyer visited him:

" Well, my good fellow, things aren't so bad after all! Don't be

---

[12] **Élysée:** the official residence of the President of the French Republic.
[13] **apocalypse:** revelation.

discouraged. A fortnight is soon over. We have not much to complain of."

" As for that, I must say the gentlemen were very kind, very polite: not a single rude word. I shouldn't have believed it. And the *cipal* was wearing white gloves. Did you notice? "

" Everything considered, we did well to confess."

" Perhaps."

" Crainquebille, I have a piece of good news for you. A charitable person, whose interest I have elicited on your behalf, gave me fifty francs for you. The sum will be used to pay your fine."

" When will you give me the money? "

" It will be paid into the clerk's office. You need not trouble about it."

" It does not matter. All the same I am very grateful to this person." And Crainquebille murmured meditatively: " It's something out of the common that's happening to me."

" Don't exaggerate, Crainquebille. Your case is by no means rare, far from it."

" You couldn't tell me where they've put my barrow? "

CRAINQUEBILLE IN THE LIGHT OF PUBLIC OPINION

After his discharge from prison, Crainquebille trundled his barrow along the Rue Montmartre, crying: " Cabbages, turnips, carrots! " He was neither ashamed nor proud of his adventure. The memory of it was not painful. He classed it in his mind with dreams, travels and plays. But, above all things, he was glad to be walking in the mud, along the paved streets, and to see overhead the rainy sky as dirty as the gutter, the dear sky of the town. At every corner he stopped to have a drink; then, gay and unconstrained, spitting in his hands in order to moisten his horny palms, he would seize the shafts and push his barrow. Meanwhile a flight of sparrows, as poor and as early as he, seeking their livelihood in the road, flew off at the sound of his familiar cry: " Cabbages, turnips, carrots! " An old housewife, who had come up, said to him as she felt his celery:

" What's happened to you, Père Crainquebille? We haven't seen you for three weeks. Have you been ill? You look rather pale."

" I'll tell you, M'ame Mailloche, I've been doing the gentleman."

Nothing in his life changed, except that he went oftener to the pub,[14] because he had an idea it was a holiday and that he had made

---

[14] **pub:** public house, saloon.

the acquaintance of charitable folk. He returned to his garret rather gay. Stretched on his mattress he drew over him the sacks borrowed from the chestnut-seller at the corner which served him as blankets, and he pondered: " Well, prison is not so bad; one has everything one wants there. But all the same one is better at home."

His contentment did not last long. He soon perceived that his customers looked at him askance.

" Fine celery, M'ame Cointreau! "

" I don't want anything."

" What! nothing! do you live on air, then? "

And M'ame Cointreau without deigning to reply returned to the large bakery of which she was the mistress. The shopkeepers and caretakers, who had once flocked round his barrow all green and blooming, now turned away from him. Having reached the shoemaker's, at the sign of l'Ange Gardien,[15] the place where his adventures with justice had begun, he called:

" M'ame Bayard, M'ame Bayard, you owe me sevenpence half-penny from last time."

But M'ame Bayard, who was sitting at her counter, did not deign to turn her head.

The whole of the Rue Montmartre was aware that Père Crainquebille had been in prison, and the whole of the Rue Montmartre gave up his acquaintance. The rumor of his conviction had reached the Faubourg and the noisy corner of the Rue Richer. There, about noon, he perceived Madame Laure, a kind and faithful customer, leaning over the barrow of another costermonger, young Martin. She was feeling a large cabbage. Her hair shone in the sunlight like masses of golden threads loosely twisted. And young Martin, a nobody, a good-for-nothing, was protesting with his hand on his heart that there were no finer vegetables than his. At this sight Crainquebille's heart was rent. He pushed his barrow up to young Martin's, and in a plaintive broken voice said to Madame Laure: " It's not fair of you to forsake me."

As Madame Laure herself admitted, she was no duchess. It was not in society that she had acquired her ideas of the prison van and the police-station. But can one not be honest in every station in life? Every one has his self respect; and one does not like to deal with a man who has just come out of prison. So the only notice she took of Crainquebille was to give him a look of disgust. And the old costermonger resenting the affront shouted:

[15] **l'Ange Gardien: The Guardian Angel**

" Dirty wench, go along with you."

Madame Laure let fall her cabbage and cried:

" Eh! Be off with you, you bad penny. You come out of prison and then insult folk! "

If Crainquebille had had any self-control he would never have reproached Madame Laure with her calling.   He knew only too well that one is not master of one's fate, that one cannot always choose one's occupation, and that good people may be found everywhere. He was accustomed discreetly to ignore her customers' business with her; and he despised no one.   But he was beside himself.   Three times he called Madame Laure drunkard, wench, harridan.[16]   A group of idlers gathered round Madame Laure and Crainquebille.   They exchanged a few more insults as serious as the first; and they would soon have exhausted their vocabulary, if a policeman had not suddenly appeared, and at once, by his silence and immobility, rendered them as silent and as motionless as himself.   They separated.   But this scene put the finishing touch to the discrediting of Crainquebille in the eyes of the Faubourg Montmartre and the Rue Richer.

RESULTS

The old man went along mumbling:

" For certain she's a hussy, and none more of a hussy than she."

But at the bottom of his heart that was not the reproach he brought against her.   He did not scorn her for being what she was.   Rather he esteemed her for it, knowing her to be frugal and orderly.   Once they had liked to talk together.   She used to tell him of her parents who lived in the country.   And they had both resolved to have a little garden and keep poultry.   She was a good customer.   And then to see her buying cabbages from young Martin, a dirty, good-for-nothing wretch; it cut him to the heart; and when she pretended to despise him, that put his back up, and then. . . . !

But she, alas! was not the only one who shunned him as if he had the plague.   Every one avoided him.   Just like Madame Laure, Madame Cointreau the baker, Madame Bayard of l'Ange Gardien scorned and repulsed him.   Why! the whole of society refused to have anything to do with him.

So because one had been put away for a fortnight one was not good enough even to sell leeks!   Was it just?   Was it reasonable to make a decent chap die of starvation because he had got into difficulties

---

[16] harridan: vixen.

with a cop? If he was not to be allowed to sell vegetables then it was all over with him. Like a badly doctored wine he turned sour. After having had words with Madame Laure, he now had them with every one. For a mere nothing he would tell his customers what he thought of them and in no ambiguous terms, I assure you. If they felt his wares too long he would call them to their faces chatterer, soft head. Likewise at the wine-shop he bawled at his comrades. His friend, the chestnut-seller, no longer recognized him; old Père Crainquebille, he said, had turned into a regular porcupine. It cannot be denied: he was becoming rude, disagreeable, evil-mouthed, loquacious. The truth of the matter was that he was discovering the imperfections of society; but he had not the facilities of a Professor of Moral and Political Science for the expression of his ideas concerning the vices of the system and the reforms necessary; and his thoughts evolved devoid of order and moderation.

Misfortune was rendering him unjust. He was taking his revenge on those who did not wish him ill and sometimes on those who were weaker than he. One day he boxed Alphonse, the wine-seller's little boy, on the ear, because he had asked him what it was like to be sent away.[17] Crainquebille struck him and said:

" Dirty brat! it's your father who ought to be sent away instead of growing rich by selling poison."

A deed and a speech which did him no honor; for, as the chestnut-seller justly remarked, one ought not to strike a child, neither should one reproach him with a father whom he has not chosen.

Crainquebille began to drink. The less money he earned the more brandy he drank. Formerly frugal and sober, he himself marveled at the change.

" I never used to be a waster," he said. " I suppose one doesn't improve as one grows old."

Sometimes he severely blamed himself for his misconduct and his laziness:

" Crainquebille, old chap, you ain't good for anything but liftin' your glass."

Sometimes he deceived himself and made out that he needed the drink.

" I must have it now and then; I must have a drop to strengthen me and cheer me up. It seems as if I had a fire in my inside; and there's nothing like the drink for quenching it."

It often happened that he missed the auction in the morning and

[17] sent away: put in jail.

so had to provide himself with damaged fruit and vegetables on credit. One day, feeling tired and discouraged, he left his barrow in its shed, and spent the livelong day hanging round the stall of Madame Rose, the tripe-seller, or lounging in and out of the wine-shops near the market. In the evening, sitting on a basket, he medi-tated and became conscious of his deterioration. He recalled the strength of his early years: the achievements of former days, the arduous labors and the glad evenings; those days quickly passing, all alike and fully occupied; the pacing in the darkness up and down the Market pavement, waiting for the early auction; the vegetables carried in armfuls and artistically arranged in the barrow; the piping hot black coffee of Mère Théodore swallowed standing, and at one gulp; the shafts grasped vigorously; and then the loud cry, piercing as cock crow, rending the morning air as he passed through the crowded streets. All that innocent, rough life of the human pack-horse came before him. For half a century, on his travelling stall, he had borne to townsfolk worn with care and vigil the fresh harvest of kitchen gardens. Shaking his head he sighed:

"No! I'm not what I was. I'm done for. The pitcher goes so often to the well that at last it comes home broken. And then I've never been the same since my affair with the magistrates. No, I'm not the man I was."

In short he was demoralized. And when a man reaches that con-dition he might as well be on the ground and unable to rise. All the passers-by tread him under foot.

THE FINAL RESULT

Poverty came, black poverty. The old costermonger who used to come back from the Faubourg Montmartre with a bag full of five-franc pieces, had not a single coin now. Winter came. Driven out of his garret, he slept under the carts in a shed. It had been raining for days; the gutters were overflowing, and the shed was flooded.

Crouching in his barrow, over the pestilent water, in the company of spiders, rats and half-starved cats, he was meditating in the gloom. Having eaten nothing all day and no longer having the chestnut-seller's sacks for a covering, he recalled the fortnight when the Gov-ernment had provided him with food and clothing. He envied the prisoners' fate. They suffer neither cold nor hunger, and an idea occurred to him:

" Since I know the trick why don't I use it? "

He rose and went out into the street. It was a little past eleven. The night was dark and chill. A drizzling mist was falling, colder and more penetrating than rain. The few passers-by crept along under cover of the houses.

Crainquebille went past the Church of Saint-Eustache and turned into the Rue Montmartre. It was deserted. A guardian of the peace stood on the pavement, by the apse [18] of the church. He was under a gas-lamp, and all around fell a fine rain looking reddish in the gas-light. It fell on to the policeman's hood. He looked chilled to the bone; but, either because he preferred to be in the light or because he was tired of walking he stayed under the lamp, and perhaps it seemed to him a friend, a companion. In the loneliness of the night the flickering flame was his only entertainment. In his immobility he appeared hardly human. The reflection of his boots on the wet pavement, which looked like a lake, prolonged him downwards and gave him from a distance the air of some amphibious monster half out of water. Observed more closely he had at once a monkish and a military appearance. The coarse features of his countenance, magnified under the shadow of his hood, were sad and placid. He wore a thick mustache, short and gray. He was an old copper, a man of some twoscore years. Crainquebille went up to him softly, and in a weak hesitating voice, said: " *Mort aux vaches!* "

Then he awaited the result of those sacred words. But nothing came of them. The constable remained motionless and silent, with his arms folded under his short cloak. His eyes were wide open; they glistened in the darkness and regarded Crainquebille with sadness, vigilance and scorn.

Crainquebille, astonished, but still resolute, muttered:

" *Mort aux vaches!* I tell you."

There was a long silence in the chill darkness and the falling of the fine penetrating rain. At last the constable spoke:

" Such things are not said. . . . For sure and for certain they are not said. At your age you ought to know better. Pass on."

" Why don't you arrest me? " asked Crainquebille.

The constable shook his head beneath his dripping hood:

" If we were to take up all the addlepates who say what they oughtn't to, we should have our work cut out! . . . And what would be the use of it? "

Overcome by such magnanimous disdain, Crainquebille remained

18 **apse:** semicircular end of the nave of a church.

for some time stolid and silent, with his feet in the gutter. Before going, he tried to explain:

" I didn't mean to say: *Mort aux vaches!* to you. It was not for you more than for another. It was only an idea."

The constable replied sternly but kindly:

"Whether an idea or anything else it ought not to be said, because when a man does his duty and endures much, he ought not to be insulted with idle words. . . . I tell you again to pass on."

Crainquebille, with head bent and arms hanging limp, plunged into the rain and the darkness.

(Winifred Stephens)

SUGGESTIONS FOR STUDY

1. How much irony can you detect in the story? Where is it irony of situation and where irony of language?

2. Note carefully indications of the author's social sympathies. What is the general implication of Crainquebille's plight? Could such a situation happen in America? Discuss.

3. What can you learn from the story about the street life of Paris? How much of this is typical of a large American city? How much distinctly French?

4. "Crainquebille" has also appeared in dramatic form. What elements of good drama do you find in it? Try turning it into a play for class production.

EDMOND ROSTAND (1868-1918)

Rostand was the most successful author of poetic dramas that French literature had seen since the days of Hugo and his circle. He captivated the imagination with dashing romance and charmed the ear with musical verse. His "heroic comedy" *Cyrano de Bergerac* was greeted with unparalleled enthusiasm on its production in 1897. It was believed by many that it would usher in a new era of romanticism, but this expectation was not realized. *L'Aiglon* (*The Eaglet*) (1900) which deals with the pathetic fate of the great Napoleon's frail son, and *Chanticleer* (1910), in which the characters are farmyard fowls and domestic animals, were less dazzlingly triumphant.

CYRANO DE BERGERAC

The historical Cyrano de Bergerac was a novelist and soldier of the seventeenth century. Rostand represents him in the play as boastful but valiant, grotesquely ugly but inimitably witty and possessing the soul of a poet. He loves his beautiful cousin Roxane, who in turn loves a handsome but unimaginative youth. Cyrano hides his heartbreak, writes poetic love letters for his rival to deliver, and thereby sacrifices himself to the lovers. The famous duelling scene which is reproduced here is from the first act. Cyrano has just broken up the performance of a play because he objects to one of the actors.

A Meddler. [*Hurries up to* CYRANO] But what a scandal! Montfleury —
The great Montfleury! Did you know the Duc
De Candale was his patron? Who is yours?
   Cyrano. No one.
   The Meddler. No one — no patron?
   Cyrano. I said no.
   The Meddler. What, no great lord, to cover with his name — 5
   Cyrano. [*With visible annoyance*] No, I have told you twice.
     Must I repeat?
No, sir, no patron — [*his hand on his sword*] But a patroness!
   The Meddler. And when do you leave Paris?
   Cyrano. That's as may be.
   The Meddler. The Duc de Candale has a long arm.
   Cyrano. Mine
Is longer [*drawing his sword*] by three feet of steel.
   The Meddler Yes, yes, 10
But do you dream of daring —
   Cyrano. I do dream
Of daring . . .
   The Meddler. But —
   Cyrano. You may go now.
   The Meddler. But —
   Cyrano. You may go —
Or tell me why are you staring at my nose!
   The Meddler. [*In confusion*] No — I —
   Cyrano. [*Stepping up to him*] Does it astonish you?
   The Meddler. [*Drawing back*] Your grace
Misunderstands my —
   Cyrano. Is it long and soft 15
And dangling, like a trunk?
   The Meddler. [*Same business*] I never said —
   Cyrano. Or crooked, like an owl's beak?
   The Meddler. I —
   Cyrano. Perhaps

A pimple ornaments the end of it?
   The Meddler. No —
   Cyrano.   Or a fly parading up and down?
What is this portent?
   The Meddler.   Oh! —
   Cyrano.   This phenomenon?   20
   The Meddler. But I have been careful not to look —
   Cyrano.   And why
Not, if you please?
   The Meddler. Why —
   Cyrano.   It disgusts you, then?
   The Meddler. My dear sir —
   Cyrano.   Does its color appear to you
Unwholesome?
   The Meddler. Oh, by no means!
   Cyrano.   Or its form
Obscene?
   The Meddler. Not in the least —
   Cyrano.   Then why assume   25
This deprecating manner? Possibly
You find it just a trifle large?
   The Meddler.   [*Babbling*] Oh no! —
Small, very small, infinitesimal —
   Cyrano. [*Roars*]   What!
How? You accuse me of absurdity?
Small — *my nose?* Why —
   The Meddler.   [*Breathless*] My God —
   Cyrano.   Magnificent, 30
My nose! . . . You pug, you knob, you button-head,
Know that I glory in this nose of mine,
For a great nose indicates a great man —
Genial, courteous, intellectual,
Virile, courageous — as I am — and such   35
As you — poor wretch — will never dare to be
Even in imagination. For that face —
That blank, inglorious concavity
Which my right hand finds — [*He strikes him.*]
   The Meddler.   Ow!
   Cyrano.   — on top of you,
Is as devoid of pride, of poetry,   40

    20. **portent:** marvelous thing. 26. **deprecating:** disapproving.

Of soul, of picturesqueness, of contour,
Of character, of NOSE in short — as that
[*Takes him by the shoulders and turns him around, suiting the action
to the word.*]
Which at the end of that limp spine of yours
My left foot —

   The Meddler.   [*Escaping*] Help!   The Guard!
   Cyrano.   Take notice, all

Who find this feature of my countenance   45
A theme for comedy!   When the humorist
Is noble, then my custom is to show
Appreciation proper to his rank —
More heartfelt . . . and more pointed. . . .

   De Guiche. [*Who has come down from the stage, surrounded by
      the Marquis*]   Presently

This fellow will grow tiresome.

   Valvert. [*Shrugs*]   Oh, he blows   50
His trumpet!

   De Guiche. Well — will no one interfere?
   Valvert. No one? [*Looks round*] Observe. I myself will pro-
    ceed
To put him in his place.
[*He walks up to* CYRANO, *who has been watching him, and stands
    there, looking him over with an affected air.*]
                  Ah . . . your nose . . . hem! . . .
Your nose is . . . rather large!

   Cyrano. [*Gravely*]   Rather.
   Valvert. [*Simpering*]   Oh well —
   Cyrano. [*Coolly*] Is that all?
   Valvert. [*Turns away, with a shrug*] Well, of course —
   Cyrano.   Ah, no, young sir!   55
You are too simple. Why, you might have said —
Oh, a great many things! *Mon dieu*, why waste
Your opportunity? For example, thus: —
AGGRESSIVE: I, sir, if that nose were mine,
I'd have it amputated — on the spot!   60
FRIENDLY: How do you drink with such a nose?
You ought to have a cup made specially.
DESCRIPTIVE: 'Tis a rock — a crag — a cape —
A cape? say rather, a peninsula!
INQUISITIVE: What is that receptacle —   65

A razor-case or a portfolio?
KINDLY: Ah, do you love the little birds
So much that when they come and sing to you,
You give them this to perch on?   INSOLENT:
Sir, when you smoke, the neighbors must suppose   7c
Your chimney is on fire.   CAUTIOUS: Take care —
A weight like that might make you topheavy.
THOUGHTFUL: Somebody fetch my parasol —
Those delicate colors fade so in the sun!
PEDANTIC: Does not Aristophanes   75
Mention a mythologic monster called
Hippocampelephantocamelos?
Surely we have here the original!
FAMILIAR: Well, old torchlight!   Hang your hat
Over that chandelier — it hurts my eyes.   8o
ELOQUENT: When it blows, the typhoon howls,
And the clouds darken.   DRAMATIC: When it bleeds —
The Red Sea!   ENTERPRISING: What a sign
For some perfumer!   LYRIC: Hark — the horn
Of Roland calls to summon Charlemagne! —   85
SIMPLE: When do they unveil the monument?
RESPECTFUL: Sir, I recognize in you
A man of parts, a man of prominence —
RUSTIC: Hey?   What?   Call that a nose?   Na, na —
I be no fool like what you think I be —   9c
That there's a blue cucumber!   MILITARY:
Point against cavalry!   PRACTICAL: Why not
A lottery with this for the grand prize?
Or — parodying Faustus in the play —
" Was this the nose that launched a thousand ships   95
And burned the topless towers of Ilium? "
These, my dear sir, are things you might have said
Had you some tinge of letters, or of wit
To color your discourse.   But wit, — not so,
You never had an atom — and of letters,   100
You need but three to write you down — an Ass.
Moreover, — if you had the invention, here
Before these folk to make a jest of me —

75. **Aristophanes:** (445?–385? B.C.) Greek writer of comedies.   85. **Roland:** one of the twelve Peers of Charlemagne and hero of the old French epic, the *Song of Roland.*   94. **Faustus:** hero of Marlowe's play *Doctor Faustus.* 96. **Ilium:** Troy.   The reference in Marlowe is to Helen of Troy.

Be sure you would not then articulate
The twentieth part of half a syllable 105
Of the beginning! For I say these things
Lightly enough myself, about myself,
But I allow none else to utter them.

    De Guiche. [*Tries to lead away the amazed* VALVERT.] Vicomte
    — come.

    Valvert. [*Choking*] Oh — These arrogant grand airs! —
A clown who — look at him — not even gloves! 110
No ribbons — no lace — no buckles on his shoes —

    Cyrano. I carry my adornments on my soul.
I do not dress up like a popinjay;
But inwardly, I keep my daintiness.
I do not bear with me, by any chance, 115
An insult not yet washed away — a conscience
Yellow with unpurged bile — an honor frayed
To rags, a set of scruples badly worn.
I go caparisoned in gems unseen,
Trailing white plumes of freedom, garlanded 120
With my good name — no figure of a man,
But a soul clothed in shining armor, hung
With deeds for decorations, twirling — thus —
A bristling wit, and swinging at my side
Courage, and on the stones of this old town 125
Making the sharp truth ring, like golden spurs!

    Valvert. But —

    Cyrano. But I have no gloves! A pity too!
I had one — the last one of an old pair —
And lost that. Very careless of me. Some
Gentleman offered me an impertinence. 130
I left it — in his face.

    Valvert. Dolt, bumpkin, fool,
Insolent puppy, jobbernowl!

    Cyrano. [*Removes his hat and bows*] Ah, yes?
And I — Cyrano-Savinien-Hercule
De Bergerac!

    Valvert. [*Turns away*] Buffoon!

    Cyrano. [*Cries out as if suddenly taken with a cramp*] Oh!

    Valvert. [*Turns back*] Well, what now?

---

113. **popinjay:** parrot. 119. **caparisoned:** bedecked. 131. **dolt:** blockhead.
132. **jobbernowl:** stupid person.

Cyrano. [*With grimaces of anguish*] I must do something to   135
    relieve these cramps —
This is what comes of lack of exercise —
Ah! —
    Valvert. What is all this?
    Cyrano.   My sword has gone to sleep!
    Valvert. [*Draws*] So be it!
    Cyrano.   You shall die exquisitely.
    Valvert. [*Contemptuously*] Poet!
    Cyrano.   Why yes, a poet, if you will;
So while we fence, I'll make you a Ballade   140
Extempore.
    Valvert. A Ballade?
    Cyrano.   Yes. You know
What that is?
    Valvert.   I —
    Cyrano.   The Ballade, sir, is formed
Of three stanzas of eight lines each —
    Valvert.   Oh, come!
    Cyrano. And a refrain of four.
    Valvert.   You —
    Cyrano.   I'll compose
One, while I fight with you; and at the end   145
Of the last line — thrust home!
    Valvert.   Will you?
    Cyrano.   I will.
[*Declaims*] " *Ballade of the duel at the Hôtel de Bourgogne*
          Between de Bergerac and a Boeotian."
    Valvert. [*Sneering*] What do you mean by that?
    Cyrano.   Oh, that? The title.
    The Crowd. [*Excited*] Come on —
               A circle —
                    Quiet —
                  Down in front!   150

[TABLEAU. *A ring of interested spectators in the center of the floor,
the Marquis and the Officers mingling with the citizens and common folk. Pages swarming up on men's shoulders to see better;
the Ladies in the boxes standing and leaning over. To the right,*

---

148. **Boeotian:** native of Boeotia, a Greek district whose inhabitants were
derided by the Athenians as dull.

De Guiche *and his following; to the left,* Le Bret, Cuigy, Ragueneau, *and others of* Cyrano's *friends.*]

Cyrano. [*Closes his eyes for an instant.*] Stop . . . Let me choose my rimes. . . . Now!
Here we go — [*He suits the action to the word, throughout the following:*]

> *Lightly I toss my hat away,*
> *Languidly over my arm let fall*
> *The cloak that covers my bright array —*   155
> *Then out swords, and to work withal!*
> *A Launcelot, in his Lady's hall . . .*
> *A Spartacus, at the Hippodrome! . . .*
> *I dally awhile with you, dear jackal,*
> *Then, as I end the refrain, thrust home.*   160

> [*The swords cross — the fight is on.*]

> *Where shall I skewer my peacock? . . . Nay,*
> *Better for you to have shunned this brawl! —*
> *Here, in the heart, thro' your ribbons gay?*
> *— In the belly, under your silken shawl?*
> *Hark, how the steel rings musical!*   165
> *Mark how my point floats, light as the foam,*
> *Ready to drive you back to the wall,*
> *Then, as I end the refrain, thrust home!*

> *Ho, for a rime! . . . You are white as whey —*
> *You break, you cover, you cringe, you . . . crawl!*   170
> *Tac! — and I parry your last essay:*
> *So may the turn of a hand forestall*
> *Life with its honey, death with its gall;*
> *So may the turn of my fancy roam*
> *Free, for a time, till the rimes recall,*   175
> *Then, as I end the refrain, thrust home!*

[*He announces solemnly.*]

---

157. **Launcelot:** or Lancelot, the most famous of the knights of King Arthur and the secret lover of Queen Guenevere. 158. **Spartacus:** leader of the rebellion of the gladiators against Rome, 73–71 B.C. 158. **Hippodrome:** circus where the gladiatorial fights took place. 161. **skewer:** pierce.

REFRAIN

Prince! Pray God, that is Lord of all,
Pardon your soul, for your time has come!
Beat — pass — fling you aslant, asprawl —
Then, as I end the refrain . . .
[*He lunges;* VALVERT *staggers back and falls into the arms of his friends.* CYRANO *recovers, and salutes.*]

— *Thrust home!*   180

(*Brian Hooker*)

SUGGESTIONS FOR STUDY

1. *Cyrano de Bergerac* is one of the most successful of modern plays, partly because of its picturesqueness and romantic appeal, but chiefly because of the personality of the hero. Show how these three things are manifest in the scene you have read. If you have seen a stage presentation of the play, discuss it from these angles. This scene lends itself to class dramatization.

2. Notice how Cyrano fights the duel with his pointed wit as well as his sword. What other characters in literature do you know who combine keenness of intellect and depth of feeling with bravery and physical prowess? What Shakespearean character "capitalizes" his grotesque appearance as Cyrano does?

3. What is the structure of the *ballade?* Compare this one with those of Villon, p. 34. Although it is a French verse form, you will find good examples of it in the writings of certain English poets like Austin Dobson and Andrew Lang. Try writing a *ballade.* How does it compare in difficulty of composition with a sonnet?

4. For further reading: (a) the entire play, with special attention to the development of Cyrano's character; (b) other plays of Rostand, especially *The Eaglet;* (c) a comparison of some of the different translations of the famous "Nose" speech.

Recent French Poetry

A few specimens of French poetry of the last fifty years or so are given here in the admirable translations of Mr. Ludwig Lewisohn. Though they differ considerably from one another in subject, treatment, and tone, they have in common a certain note of modernity. Perhaps the most striking characteristic of this more recent poetry is the rejection of declamation, rhetoric, wordiness and stereotyped imagery — all of which are denounced as the besetting sins of French verse from the seventeenth century onward. Probably the French poet is now more at liberty to fashion his own idiom and express his real self than at any previous time. Undeniably this new freedom has led to a certain amount of obscurity, which has been increased by the tendency to imitate the vague and elusive effects of music. Much of the newer poetry does not yield its meaning at a first reading — it is, indeed, not the intention of the poet that it should. But the French mind is pre-eminently clear and the French language itself an instrument of precision. Given these two things, it is reasonably certain that French poetry will never become willfully unintelligible.

PAUL VERLAINE (1844–1896)

Paul Verlaine recalls Villon in the vagabondage of his life and in the personal quality of his poetry. He was born in Metz (annexed to Germany in 1871 and reunited to France in 1919) and was educated in Paris. His addiction to drink nearly wrecked his career at the outset. In 1873 he was sentenced to two years of imprisonment for trying to kill the young poet Rimbaud with whom he had been traveling in England and Belgium. His conversion to Catholicism took place in prison. It made him a mystic but did not enable him to mend his ways. Much of his later life in Paris was spent between the slums and the hospitals.

Verlaine was the best of the French symbolist poets. The intellectual content of his verse is slight. His intention was not to communicate a thought but to evoke a mood. He wanted to suggest feelings through the medium of sound, especially the sound of vowels. The Parnassians, under whose influence he had begun writing, had tried to be as objective in their representation of things as a sculptor or a painter. Verlaine, on the contrary, sought his model in music. His finest volume bears the significant title *Songs without Words*. Only the subtlest of verbal harmonies could suffice to render the ebb and flow of emotions — the feelings of longing, regret and imaginative pathos, the sense of the inexpressible and the infinite which stirred in his heart. The magic with which he did this in his native language cannot be reproduced even in the most skillful of translations.

MY FAMILIAR DREAM

Often a strange and poignant dream is mine
Of an unknown lady whom I love and who
Loves me, forever one yet other, too,
And constant only in her love divine.

Only for her my heart's confusions shine,   5
Only for her, alas, who can gaze through
My enigmatic soul, who heals the dew
On my pale forehead with her tears benign.
Is she dark, russet, blonde? Her name! Who knows?
Sweet and sonorous as the name of those   10
Beloved ones whom life to exile drove.
Her eyes are with a marble calmness filled,
And her grave voice holds the faint echo of
The cadence of dear voices that are stilled.

(Ludwig Lewisohn)

LATE WISDOM

Above the roof, the sky expands
So blue, so calm;
Above the roof a tall tree stands
And rocks its palm.

The bell that in the sky you see   5
Chimes sweet and faint,
A bird in the familiar tree
Sings its low plaint.

Dear God, dear God, life glides on there
In tranquil wise.   10
That peaceful murmur comes from where
The city lies.

O you who stand here full of tears
That flow and flow,
What have you done with the lost years   15
Of long ago?

(Ludwig Lewisohn)

JEAN ARTHUR RIMBAUD (1854–1891)

Jean Arthur Rimbaud was a poet and adventurer who had a puzzling career. He ceased to write poetry at the age of nineteen and after various ups and downs became one of the pioneers of French commercial expan-

sion in Africa, a venture which in the end proved financially rewarding.
Verlaine, thinking him dead, published his poems in 1886. Rimbaud never
knew the sensation which his work produced in literary circles, nor would
he probably have cared if he had known. He is regarded today as an important forerunner of symbolism, while the veil of mystery over his life
of course adds greatly to his power of fascination.

THE SLEEPER OF THE VALLEY

There's a green hollow where a river sings
Silvering the torn grass in its glittering flight,
And where the sun from the proud mountain flings
Fire — and the little valley brims with light.
A soldier young, with open mouth, bare head,   5
Sleeps with his neck in dewy water cress,
Under the sky and on the grass his bed,
Pale in the deep green and the light's excess.
He sleeps amid the iris and his smile
Is like a sick child's slumbering for a while.   10
Nature, in thy warm lap his chilled limbs hide!
The perfume does not thrill him from his rest.
He sleeps in sunshine, hand upon his breast,
Tranquil — with two red holes in his right side.

(Ludwig Lewisohn)

ÉMILE VERHAEREN (1855–1916)

Émile Verhaeren, the greatest lyric poet of Belgium, was French
only in his language; in thought and in feeling he was Flemish. A social
thinker with advanced views, he believed that modern poetry should express
and interpret modern life and not seek to escape from it. He found significance and beauty even in the factories in which his own highly industrialized
country abounds. In subject matter and in his use of free verse he shows
kinship with Walt Whitman.

THE MILL

Deep in gray dusk the mill turns faltering,
Under a somber, melancholy sky,
It turns and turns; its earth-hued wheel drifts by
Endlessly feeble and heavy and lingering.

Since dawn its arms in plaintive gesture rise   **5**
Heavenward and fall in turn; behold them there
Drooping again deep through the blackening air
And utter silence of a world that dies.

Over the hamlets a cold day foredone
Slumbers; the clouds are weary of voyaging;   10
To the black woods the massive shadows cling;
To an horizon dead the roads run on.

Some beechen huts, upon the roadway's hem,
Squat in a wretched circle; on their wall
And window a feeble blotch of light lets fall   15
A copper lamp hanging in one of them.

And in the empty vast of plain and skies
These poor, pinched hovels fix their glances vain
From under lids of broken window-pane
On the old mill that turns and turns and dies.   20

(Ludwig Lewisohn)

HENRI DE RÉGNIER (1864–1936)

Henri de Régnier came of an ancient and noble family and was thoroughly aristocratic in his outlook and interests. He gained recognition very early as a poet and writer of fiction. Although like the other symbolists he took metrical liberties, he possessed a Greek clarity and serenity.

ON THE SHORE

Rest on the shore and take in your two hands,
And let them slip out grain by grain, the sands
Whose paler hue the sun turns into gold;
Then, ere you close your eyes, once more behold
Harmonious ocean and transparent sky,
And when you feel most faintly, by and by,   5
That in your lightened hand is not a grain,
Consider ere you lift your lids again
That life takes from us and gives evermore
Our fleeting sands to the eternal shore.   10

(Ludwig Lewisohn)

FRANCIS JAMMES (1868–1938)

Francis Jammes was born in the Pyrenees. He wrote about the simple
life of the countryside. Like Wordsworth he did not hesitate to use in his
poetry the commonest words in the commonest order. His love of the
humbler things of life and his unaffected piety set him apart from most
literary men of his time.

THAT THOU ART POOR . . .

That thou art poor I see:
So plain thy little dress.
Dear heart of gentleness,
My grief I offer thee.

But thou art lovelier   5
Than others; very sweet
Thy fragrant lips to meet
That my slow pulses stir.

And thou art poor and true
And kind as the poor be,   10
Wouldst have me give to thee
Kisses and roses too?

For but a lass thou art,
And books have made thee dream,
And olden stories deem   15
That arbors charm the heart,

Roses and mulberries
And flowers of the plain,
Of which the poets feign,
And boughs of rustling trees.   20

Yes thou art poor, I see:
So plain thy little dress.
Dear heart of gentleness,
My grief I offer thee.

(Ludwig Lewisohn)

PAUL FORT (1872-   )

Paul Fort has been one of the chief experimenters in contemporary French poetry. Much of his prolific verse has been written as prose, but with pronounced rhythms and intermittent rhymes. This arrangement, which seems like affectation to many people, is defended by Fort and his friends on the score of being more "natural"—that is, less hampered by the trammels of artificial stanzas. Certainly his sentences flow freely without losing their music. Fort is one of the most joyous of modern poets.

BELL OF DAWN

Faint music of a bell which dawn brings to my ear, made my heart young again here at the break of day.

Faint bell-like music which through dewy dawn I hear ringing so far, so near, changed all I hope and fear.

What, shall I after this survive my dear-brought bliss, music by which my soul's far youth recovered is?

Chiming so far away, so lonely and withdrawn, O little singing air in the fresh heart of dawn,

You flee, return and ring; seeking like love to stray, you tremble in my heart here at the break of day.

Ah, can life ever be of such serenity, so peaceful, mild and fair as is this little air?

So simple yet so sweet as, over meadows borne, this little tune that thrills all the fresh heart of morn?

(*Ludwig Lewisohn*)

SUGGESTIONS FOR STUDY

1. Characterize briefly each of the seven poems in regard to subject matter and versification.

2. Which poems do you find most easily intelligible? Which seem to you difficult? Which poems do you like best? Can you give reasons for your preference?

3. In Verlaine's "My Familiar Dream" explain the words, "forever one yet other, too." How is the title "Late Wisdom" applicable to the

second poem?   Can you account for the sequence of thought from the third to the fourth stanza of that poem?

4. The details of description in " The Mill " are for the most part ugly. Is, nevertheless, a beautiful poem made out of this unpromising material? If so, how is this accomplished?   What other examples can you give from literature of beauty wrought from ugliness?   What has been the attitude of modern art toward this principle?   Illustrate by examples.

5. Comparing Fort's poem with Régnier's, what do you think is gained and what lost by the abandonment of orthodox verse forms?   Compare with English " free verse."   Who are its leading exponents on both sides of the Atlantic?

6. Vocabulary: poignant, enigmatic, sonorous, cadence, plaint, fain, feign.

ROMAIN ROLLAND (1866–1944)

Rolland was born in France but lived in Switzerland after 1914.   When World War I broke out in that year, his pacifism and international outlook found expression in an article entitled " Above the Conflict," which was denounced by many Frenchmen as treasonable.   His monumental novel *Jean-Christophe*, in ten volumes (1904–1912), is frequently regarded as the best product of French fiction during the early twentieth century.   It is a biographical novel about a musical genius of heroic character.   The book contains discussions of modern intellectual and artistic movements and of national differences.   It won for him the Nobel prize for literature in 1915.   Rolland's scholarly interests in the history of music and painting resulted in his excellent studies of Beethoven and Michelangelo.   He also wrote sympathetic books about Tolstoy and Mahatma Gandhi, both of whom, like Rolland himself, denounced all forms of violence and preached the doctrine of nonresistance.

JEAN–CHRISTOPHE MEETS HASSLER

Jean-Christophe Krafft spends the first twenty years of his life in a little town on the Rhine; the rest of the book pictures his mature life in France.   The following incident of his childhood shows the budding of a musical genius.   Melchior is his father, Jean Michel his grandfather, both musicians.

Some time after that a musical event brought even more excitement into Jean-Christophe's thoughts.   François Marie Hassler, the author of the first opera which had so bowled him over, was to visit the town. He was to conduct a concert consisting of his compositions.   The town was excited. The young musician was the subject of violent discussion in Germany, and for a fortnight he was the only topic of conversation. It was a different matter when he arrived. The friends of Melchior and old Jean Michel continually came for news, and they went away with the most extravagant notions of the musician's habits and eccentricities. The child followed these narratives with eager attention. The idea that the great man was there in the town, breathing the same air as himself, treading the same stones, threw him into a state of dumb exaltation. He lived only in the hope of seeing him.

Hassler was staying at the Palace as the guest of the Grand Duke. He hardly went out, except to the theater for rehearsals, to which Jean-Christophe was not admitted, and as he was very lazy, he went to and fro in the Prince's carriage. Therefore, Jean-Christophe did not have many opportunities of seeing him, and he only succeeded once in catching sight of him as he drove in the carriage. He saw his fur coat, and wasted hours in waiting in the street, thrusting and jostling his way to right and left, and before and behind, to win and keep his place in front of the loungers. He consoled himself with spending half his days watching the windows of the Palace which had been pointed out as those of the master. Most often he only saw the shutters, for Hassler got up late, and the windows were closed almost all morning. This habit had made well-informed persons say that Hassler could not bear the light of day, and lived in eternal night.

At length Jean-Christophe was able to approach his hero. It was the day of the concert. All the town was there. The Grand Duke and his Court occupied the great royal box, surmounted with a crown supported by two chubby cherubims. The theater was in gala array. The stage was decorated with branches of oak and flowering laurel. All the musicians of any account made it a point of honor to take their places in the orchestra. Melchior was at his post, and Jean Michel was conducting the chorus.

When Hassler appeared, there was loud applause from every part of the house, and the ladies rose to see him better. Jean-Christophe devoured him with his eyes. Hassler had a young, sensitive face, though it was already rather puffy and tired-looking; his temples were bald, and his hair was thin on the crown of his head; for the rest, fair, curly hair. His blue eyes looked vague. He had a little fair mustache and an expressive mouth, which was rarely still, but twitched with a thousand imperceptible movements. He was tall, and held himself badly — not from awkwardness, but from weariness or boredom. He conducted capriciously and lithely, with his whole awkward body swaying, like his music, with gestures, now caressing, now sharp and jerky. It was easy to see that he was very nervous and his music was the exact reflection of himself. The quivering and jerky life of it broke through the usual apathy of the orchestra. Jean-Christophe breathed heavily; in spite of his fear of drawing attention to himself, he could not stand still in his place; he fidgeted, got up, and the music gave him such violent and unexpected shocks that he had to move his head, arms, and legs, to the great discomfort of his neighbors, who warded off his kicks as best they could. The whole audience was enthusiastic, fascinated by the success, rather than by the compositions. At the end there was a storm of applause and cries, in which the trumpets in the orchestra joined, German fashion, with their triumphant blare in salute of the conqueror. Jean-Christophe trembled with pride, as though these honors were for himself. He enjoyed seeing Hassler's face light up with childish pleasure. The ladies threw flowers, the men waved their hats, and the audience rushed for the platform. Every one wanted to shake the master's hand. Jean-Christophe saw one enthusiast raise the master's hand to his lips, another steal a handkerchief that Hassler had left on the corner of his desk. He wanted to reach the platform also, although he did not know why, for if at that moment he had found himself near Hassler, he would have fled at once in terror and emotion. But he butted with all his force, like a ram, among the skirts and legs that divided him from Hassler. He was too small; he could not break through.

Fortunately, when the concert was over, his grandfather came and took him to join in a party to serenade Hassler. It was night, and torches were lighted. All the musicians of the orchestra were there. They talked only of the marvelous compositions they had heard. They arrived outside the Palace, and took up their places without a sound under the master's windows. They took on an air of secrecy, although everybody, including Hassler, knew what was to come. In the silence of the night they began to play certain famous fragments of Hassler's compositions. He appeared at the window with the Prince, and they roared in his honor. Both bowed. A servant came from the Prince to invite the musicians to enter the Palace. They passed through great rooms, with frescoes representing naked men with helmets; they were of a reddish color, and were making gestures of defiance. The sky was covered with great clouds like sponges. There were also men and women of marble clad in waist-cloths made of iron. The guests walked on carpets so thick that their tread was inaudible, and they came at length to a room which was as light as day, and there were tables laden with drinks and good things.

The Grand Duke was there, but Jean-Christophe did not see him; he had eyes only for Hassler. Hassler came towards them; he thanked them. He picked his words carefully, stopped awkwardly in the middle of a sentence, and extricated himself with a quip which made everybody laugh. They began to eat. Hassler took four or five musicians aside. He singled out Jean-Christophe's grandfather, and addressed very flattering words to him: he recollected that Jean Michel had been one of the first to perform his works, and he said that he had often heard tell of his excellence from a friend of his who had been a pupil of the old man's. Jean-Christophe's grandfather expressed his gratitude profusely; he replied with such extraordinary eulogy that, in spite of his adoration of Hassler, the boy was ashamed. But to Hassler they seemed to be pleasant and in the rational order. Finally, the old man, who had lost himself in his rigmarole,[1] took Jean-Christophe by the hand, and presented him to Hassler. Hassler smiled at Jean-Christophe, and carelessly patted his head, and when he learned that the boy liked his music, and had not slept for several nights in anticipation of seeing him, he took him in his arms and plied him with questions. Jean-Christophe, struck dumb and blushing with pleasure, dared not look at him. Hassler took him by the chin and lifted his face up. Jean-Christophe ventured to look. Hassler's eyes were kind and smiling; he began to smile too. Then he felt so happy, so wonderfully happy in the great man's arms, that he burst into tears. Hassler was touched by this simple affection, and was more kind than ever. He kissed the boy and talked to him tenderly. At the same time he said funny things and tickled him to make him laugh; and Jean-Christophe could not help laughing through his tears. Soon he became at ease, and answered Hassler readily, and of his own accord he began to whisper in his ear all his small ambitions, as though he and Hassler were old friends; he told him how he wanted to be a musician like Hassler, and, like Hassler, to make beautiful things, and to be a great man. He, who was always ashamed, talked confidently; he did not know what he was saying; he was in a sort of ecstasy. Hassler smiled at his prattling and said:

"When you are a man, and have become a good musician, you shall come and see me in Berlin. I shall make something of you."

Jean-Christophe was too delighted to reply.

---

[1] **rigmarole:** rambling talk.

Hassler teased him.

" You don't want to? "

Jean-Christophe nodded his head violently five or six times, mean-ing " Yes."

" It is a bargain, then? "

Jean Christophe nodded again.

" Kiss me, then."

Jean-Christophe threw his arms round Hassler's neck and hugged him with all his strength.

" Oh, you are wetting me! Let go! Your nose wants wiping! "

Hassler laughed, and wiped the boy's nose himself, a little self-consciously, though he was quite jolly. He put him down, then took him by the hand and led him to a table, where he filled his pockets with cake, and left him, saying:

" Good-bye! Remember your promise."

Jean-Christophe swam in happiness. The rest of the world had ceased to exist for him. He could remember nothing of what had happened earlier in the evening; he followed lovingly Hassler's every expression and gesture. One thing that he said struck him. Hassler was holding a glass in his hand; he was talking, and his face suddenly hardened, and he said:

" The joy of such a day must not make us forget our enemies. We must never forget our enemies. It is not their fault that we are not crushed out of existence. It will not be our fault if that does not happen to them. That is why the toast I propose is that there are people whose health . . . we will not drink! "

Everybody applauded and laughed at this original toast. Hassler had laughed with the others and his good-humored expression had returned. But Jean-Christophe was put out by it. Although he did not permit himself to criticise any action of his hero, it hurt him that he had thought ugly things, when on such a night there ought to be nothing but brilliant thoughts and fancies. But he did not examine what he felt, and the impression that it made was soon driven out by his great joy and the drop of champagne which he drank out of his grandfather's glass.

On the way back the old man never stopped talking; he was de-lighted with the praise that Hassler had given him; he cried out that Hassler was a genius such as had not been known for a century. Jean-Christophe said nothing, locking up in his heart his intoxication of love. *He* had kissed him. *He* had held him in his arms! How good *he* was! How great!

" Ah," he thought in bed, as he kissed his pillow passionately, " I would die for him — die for him! "

The brilliant meteor which had flashed across the sky of the little town that night had a decisive influence on Jean-Christophe's mind. All his childhood Hassler was the model on which his eyes were fixed, and to follow his example the little man of six decided that he also would write music. To tell the truth, he had been doing so for long enough without knowing it, and he had not waited to be conscious of composing before he composed.

Everything is music for the born musician. Everything that throbs, or moves, or stirs, or palpitates — sunlit summer days, nights when the wind howls, flickering light, the twinkling of the stars, storms, the song of birds, the buzzing of insects, the murmuring of trees, voices, loved or loathed, familiar fireside sounds, a creaking door, blood moving in the veins in the silence of the night — everything that is is music; all that is needed is that it should be heard. All the music of creation found its echo in Jean-Christophe. Everything that he saw, everything that he felt, was translated into music without his being conscious of it. He was like a buzzing hive of bees. But no one noticed it, himself least of all.

(Gilbert Cannan)

SUGGESTIONS FOR STUDY

1. What evidence have you from this selection that music was already the all-absorbing thing for Jean-Christophe? How old was he at the time? Does this seem a consistent picture of a child of that age? Discuss in the light of your observation of children.

2. Show how Jean-Christophe idealized Hassler both as man and as musician. What was the one thing which Hassler said or did that disconcerted him? What sort of impression does Hassler make on you? How does his personality compare with that of famous musicians you have heard?

3. When did hero-worship begin with you? Who were your first heroes? Do you still have any? Do you regard hero-worship as a natural and praiseworthy thing? Discuss outstanding examples of hero-worship in the modern world.

ANDRÉ MAUROIS (1885–)

Maurois is the leading French representative of " the new biography " which aims primarily at human interest. He was an interpreter during the World War. Since then he has made a special study of English life and literature. He gained a wide audience by his *Ariel, the Life of Shelley* (1923). His lives of Disraeli and Byron appeared four years later. *The Edwardian Era* (1933) presents a panorama of the reign of Edward VII of England (1901–1910). His books have been especially popular in England and America. They combine skillful narrative with charm of manner.

The following selections are from his *Byron* (1927), in all respects one of his most satisfactory books.

BYRON

THE BOY

At the age of nine he had discovered that one can find an infinite happiness merely in a presence. Returning to Aberdeen, he fell in love with his cousin, Mary Duff, a little girl with hazel eyes and dark brown hair. He admired her features; he could conceive of nothing more beautiful. He liked to walk with her, to sit beside her, to caress her gently. All his thoughts now were of his cousin's face, his cousin's gowns; he could not sleep; he talked of nothing but Mary Duff. When parted from her, he pestered his mother to write to Mary Duff, and love made this child so compelling that, willy-nilly, Catherine Byron had to shrug her shoulders and become her son's amanuensis.[1]

How passionate he was, and how shy! At the thought of his game leg[2] and his hobbling gait, he felt ridiculous and ashamed. He would have liked to hide away — to vanish. Sentimental, tender and dreamy, he would suddenly, for no visible reason, turn fierce. Sometimes after a long silence he made a gesture of brutality that seemed quite inexplicable. One day at table he snatched up a knife and pressed it so hard against his chest that his mother was terrified. The origins of these extravagances were the harder to guess at because of his spiteful memory, tenacious of grievances for a very long time. The cause of one of these outbursts was often an incident of several weeks back.

THE MAN

It is always interesting to observe, in the course of a life, the gradual information of the stony strata which, hardened by time, will shape and limit a man's character. On the ancestral basis of Gordon[3] violence and Byron sensuality, there had been laid a physical

[1] amanuensis: one who writes from dictation.
[2] game leg: Byron had a clubfoot.
[3] Gordon: his mother's family name.

deposit, in an infirmity inspiring hatred of the world and a beauty giving the means of avenging himself. On the gloomy and narrow religion taught by his first Scottish masters, there had been superimposed, but without destroying the first, the Voltairean deism [4] of the Cambridge undergraduates, and on the ingenuous sentimentalism of adolescence, a strongly ironical humor. The view of the universe which now graced this inner landscape was simple. This world had been created, for no object known to ourselves, by a God who seemed indifferent to our ills. Moved by their passions, men pursued either agreeable sensations, which was wise, or fame, which was foolish. Empires rose and sank like the waves of the sea. All was vanity, save pleasure.

This teaching had been strongly confirmed by his journeying in the Orient.[5] Go where he might, Byron found life a stern business, vice omnipresent, and death both easy and close at hand. The fatalism of Islam had reinforced his own. Its treatment of women had satisfied him. The multiplicity of religions was proof of their weakness. He brought back doubts, as solid as acts of faith. His long solitude had taught him some truths regarding himself. He knew now that he was happy only as an outlaw, and had loved those lands where he cared not about anybody and where none had cared about him. Distance had taught him contempt. How could you grow excited over a pedant's [6] hostile essay when the Atlantic and the Mediterranean rolled between you and him, when the thunder of hyperborean [7] reviews was dulled by the moaning of the Hellespont? [8] Henceforth he would know that, if things went askew with him in England, a fortnight of sea would bring him to white islands beneath a sky for ever blue.

THE DEATH OF BYRON

During this Easter day he was still able to read a few letters, and even to translate one written in Greek by the deputy Luriottis. In the late afternoon all who were at his bedside realized that the end was drawing near. Fletcher and Gamba had to go out; they were in

[4] **deism:** belief in a God coupled with rejection of Christianity. Its foremost advocate was Voltaire.

[5] **Orient:** Byron visited the Near East during the years 1809–1811.

[6] **pedant:** one who parades his learning. A hostile criticism of Byron and his poetry appeared in an unsigned article in the *Edinburgh Review* for January 1808.

[7] **hyperborean:** from the extreme north. The *Edinburgh Review* is meant.

[8] **Hellespont:** the Dardanelles, the strait uniting the Sea of Marmora with the Aegean.

tears. Tita remained, because Byron was holding his hand, but he turned away his head to hide his tears. Byron gazed at him fixedly and said in Italian, half smiling: " *Oh questa è una bella scena!* "⁹ Immediately after that he fell into delirium, and began calling out, now in Italian, now in English, as if he were advancing to the attack: " Forward! Courage! Follow my example! Don't be afraid! "

In his lucid moments he realized that he was dying, and said to Fletcher: " It is now nearly over, I must tell you all without losing a moment."

" Shall I go, my lord, and fetch pen, ink and paper? "

" Oh, my God! No, you will lose too much time, and I have it not to spare, for my time is now short. Now, pay attention! You will be provided for." Fletcher begged him to turn to things of more consequence, and Byron went on: " Oh! my poor dear child! My dear Ada! My God! Could I but have seen her! Give her my blessing! And my dear sister Augusta, and her children — and you will go to Lady Byron,¹⁰ and say, — tell her everything — you are friends with her."

At that moment he seemed to be deeply affected. His voice failed, and Fletcher could now only catch a word here and there. Byron went on very seriously, mumbling unintelligible sentences for some time. Then he raised his voice. " Fletcher," he said, " now if you do not execute every order which I have given you, I will torment you hereafter if possible."

He knew well how timorous and superstitious Fletcher was, and this threat was certainly the last flickering gleam of his humor. In consternation, his servant replied that he had not grasped a single word of what his lordship had said.

" Oh, my God! " said Byron, " then all is lost, for it is now too late! Can it be possible you have not understood me? . . ."

" No, my lord, but I pray you to try and inform me once more."

" How can I? It is now too late, and all is over! "

" Not our will, but God's be done! " said Fletcher.

And Byron, with a fresh effort went on: " Yes, not mine be done — but I will try . . ."

Several times he struggled to speak, but could only keep on repeating: " My wife! My child! My sister! — You know all — You must say all — You know my wishes. . . ."

After that it became difficult to understand him. He uttered names

⁹ " **Oh questa è una bella scena:** " " Oh, this is a beautiful scene."
¹⁰ **Lady Byron:** his wife from whom he had separated in 1816.

and figures, speaking one moment in English and the next in Italian. Sometimes he said: " Poor Greece, — poor town — my poor servants! " — and then: " Why was I not aware of this sooner? " and another time: " My hour is come! I do not care for death — but why did I not go home before I came here." And later he said: " *Io lascio qualche cosa di caro nel mundo* " — " I am leaving something dear in the world. . . ."

About six in the evening he said: " I want to go to sleep now," and turning over, he fell into a sleep from which he never awoke. He seemed powerless to move a limb, but the onlookers observed symptoms of suffocation, and a rattle in his throat. Every now and then Fletcher and Tita raised his head, but he seemed to feel nothing. The doctors applied leeches [11] to dispel this lethargy. Blood trickled down his face. For twenty-four hours he remained in this condition. On the evening of the 19th, in the twilight, Fletcher was keeping watch beside his master and saw him open his eyes, then shut them instantly. " My God! " he said, " I fear his lordship is gone. . . ." The doctors felt the pulse. " You are right," they said. " He is gone."

A few moments before, a terrible storm had broken over Missolonghi. Night was falling; lightning and thunderclaps came one on top of another in the gloom. Far off, across the lagoon, the fleeting gleam of flashes lit up the dark outlines of the island. A scudding rain lashed the windows of the houses. The fatal tidings had not yet reached the Greek soldiers and shepherds who had taken refuge indoors; but like their ancestors they believed that the death of a hero came heralded by portents, and as they listened to the prodigious fury of this thunder, they murmured to each other: " Byron is dead."

(Hamish Miles)

SUGGESTIONS FOR STUDY

1. Read a brief account of Byron's life to get a unified picture of the whole.

2. What elements in Byron's character does Maurois attribute to heredity and what to environment? How did Byron at the age of nine foreshadow the mature Byron?

3. What effect did travel have on Byron's state of mind? What reflection of his many travels do we find in his writings? Name characters in Byron's poems who illustrate the attitude of the poet himself according to Maurois' sentence, " He knew now that he was happy only as an outlaw."

4. Show from the third selection how Byron affected those who came

[11] **leeches:** bloodsucking worms, formerly used medicinally for bleeding.

into contact with him. What seemed uppermost in his last thoughts? Read Byron's last poem inscribed " On this day I have completed my thirty-sixth year." What light does this throw on his mental state at the time of his death?

5. Byron is held in higher esteem on the Continent of Europe than he is in the English-speaking countries. Can you suggest any reasons for this?

READING LIST

TRANSLATIONS FROM FRENCH LITERATURE

Poetry

Villon, François: *Poems* (Modern Library)

Ronsard, Pierre de: *Songs and Sonnets,* trans. by C. H. Page

La Fontaine, Jean de: *Fables,* trans. by Edward Marsh

Lang, Andrew: *Ballads and Lyrics of Old France*

Carrington, Henry: *Anthology of French Poetry* (10th to 19th centuries)

Lewisohn, Ludwig: *The Poets of Modern France*

Boni, Albert: *Modern Book of French Verse in English Translation*

Savage, R. C.: *Casements* (50 modern French poems)

Shipley, J. T.: *Modern French Poetry*

Drama

Corneille, Pierre: *The Cid*

Molière: *Comedies* (French Classics for English Readers), trans. by C. H. Page

Beaumarchais: *The Barber of Seville*
The Marriage of Figaro

Hugo, Victor: *Ruy Blas*
Hernani

Sandeau, Jules: *Mlle. de la Seiglière*

Rostand, Edmond: *Cyrano de Bergerac*

L'Aiglon (*The Eaglet*)
Chanticleer

Maeterlinck, Maurice: *The Blue Bird*
Pelléas and Mélisande

Fiction

Rabelais (French Classics for English Readers), ed. by C. H. Page

Voltaire: *Candide*
Zadig

Hugo, Victor: *Notre-Dame de Paris*
Les Misérables
Toilers of the Sea
Ninety-Three

Dumas, Alexandre: *The Three Musketeers*
The Count of Monte Cristo
The Black Tulip
The Queen's Necklace

Mérimée, Prosper: *Colomba*
Carmen

Le Sage, Alain René: *Gil Blas*

Sand, George: *The Devil's Pool*

Balzac, Honoré: *Eugénie Grandet*
Old Goriot
The Country Doctor

Loti, Pierre: *The Iceland Fisherman*

Daudet, Alphonse: *Letters from My Mill*
Tartarin of Tarascon
Tartarin on the Alps

Maupassant, Guy de: *Best Short Stories* (Modern Library)
The Odd Number
France, Anatole: *Little Pierre*
The Bloom of Life
The Crime of Sylvestre Bonnard
The Gods Are Athirst
Rolland, Romain: *Jean-Christophe*
Duhamel, Georges: *Papa Pasquier*
Schweikert, H. C. (ed.): *French Short Stories*

Non-Fiction Prose

Montaigne, Michel de: *Essays* (French Classics for English Readers), selected by Adolphe Cohn.
Pascal, Blaise: *Thoughts*
La Rochefoucauld, François de: *Maxims*
Sainte-Beuve, Charles Augustin: *Causeries du Lundi,* trans. by E. J. Trechmann
Vallery-Radot, Louis *Pasteur: His Life and Labors*
Maurois, André: *Ariel, the Life of Shelley*
Byron
Disraeli
Michelet, Jules: *Life of Joan of Arc*

BOOKS ABOUT FRANCE

English Fiction

Dickens, Charles: *A Tale of Two Cities*
Scott, Sir Walter: *Quentin Durward*
Doyle, Sir Arthur Conan: *The Refugees*
Davis, William Stearns: *The Whirlwind*
Weyman, Stanley: *The Red Cockade*
D'Orczy, Emmiska: *The Scarlet Pimpernel*

History of Literature

Sedgwick, H. D.: *France: A Short History of Its Politics, Literature, and Art*
Strachey, Lytton: *Landmarks in French Literature*
Nitze, W. A. and Dargan, E. P.: *History of French Literature*
Churchman, P. H.: *French Literature in Outline*
Wright, C. H. C.: *History of French Literature*

Guyer, F. E.: *The Main Stream of French Literature*

Art and Music

Wilenski, R. H.: *French Painting*
Bryant, Lorinda: *French Pictures and Their Painters*
Pennell, Elizabeth: *French Cathedrals*
Hervey, A.: *Masters of French Music*

Travel, Social Life and Customs

Huddleston, S.: *France and the French*
Slocombe, G.: *The Heart of France*
Laughlin, C. E.: *So You're Going to Paris*
Jerrold, Laurence: *France, Her People and Her Spirit*
Siegfried, André: *France, A Study in Nationality*
James, Henry: *A Little Tour in France*
Stevenson, R. L.: *Travels with a Donkey*

Spanish and Portuguese Literature

Spanish and Portuguese Literature

PERHAPS more than any other country of Europe, Spain spells romance to the average American — a sun-drenched land, outside the major conflicts of European politics, and symbolized by mantillas and matadors, castanets and conquistadors. But that is like judging the United States entirely by its skyscrapers, steel-magnates, baseball, and bank bandits. There is much more beneath the surface.

Spanish peninsula shows variety of natural scenery and racial characteristics

The Spanish peninsula is somewhat smaller than the state of Texas, but it has about six times the population. Its people are much less unified in race and disposition than the French. Its scenery is more diversified than that of France. The surface of the country is so cut up by mountain ranges that before the days of modern travel facilities, one province had difficult access to another and the tendency was for local differences of manners, customs, language and even character traits to remain strongly marked. Local patriotism also has often been a greater motivating force than national patriotism, and even today when unification has been apparently established, these loyalties to the individual provinces are still pronounced. Thus the student of Spanish life comes to realize that within this comparatively small country we find such widely contrasting types as the poetic, meditative, often melancholy Galicians of the northwest, and the practical, independent, businesslike Basques and Catalonians of the northeast. Or again, the Castilians living on the tawny plains and plateaus of central Spain have a corresponding austerity, determination, and pride quite in contrast to the light-hearted, lazy gayety of the southern Andalusians in their fertile sunny valleys.

A glance at the mingling of races which history has brought about will show cause for many of these differences aside from geographical influence. The beginnings of historical time show a race called

Iberians mingled with the Berbers of North Africa. Phoenicians, Greeks, and Carthaginians also left their imprint along the Mediterranean coast. From the sixth to the fourth centuries B.C. Celts from the north invaded Galicia and Portugal. Finally the all-absorbing Romans annexed the Spanish peninsula to their Empire. During the early centuries of the Christian era Spain contributed much to Latin literature especially through Seneca, Lucan, and Quintilian.

Spain's power as a kingdom marked by ups and downs

But when the barbarian Goths from the north swept the Roman empire in the fifth century A.D., Spain was not exempt. The Vandals practiced the art of destruction so effectively as to contribute the term *vandalism* to our language. They in turn were ousted by the Visigoths who maintained supremacy up to 711, when the last and most picturesque invasion of the Spanish peninsula began. At that time the Moors from Africa crowded in from the south, pushed the Visigoths back into the mountains, and for more than seven hundred years continued their flourishing kingdom with various dynasties centered at Cordova, Granada, and other cities even as far north as Toledo. This was the period of exotic civilization celebrated by Washington Irving in *The Alhambra*.

But during the centuries of Muslim power, the small Christian states were gathering strength for their final conflict, and under the united leadership of Castile and Aragon evicted the Moors in 1492. This victory, combined with the opening up of a new world across the Atlantic in the same year, ushered in the period of Spain's greatest glory. During the sixteenth century she was a world power, with a brilliant court at Madrid and a group of colonies growing up across the sea. But her peak of power was reached in the middle of the century. With the defeat of the " Invincible Armada " by England, Spain began to give way before her northern rival. With the advent of the Protestant Reformation, Spain, in bending all her efforts to defend Catholicism against heresy, restricted her thought and weakened her resources. As the Bourbon kings in the eighteenth century extended the power of France, Spain practically lost her individuality. During the nineteenth century she sacrificed all her colonies and went through the internal confusion of Napoleonic domination, civil wars, attempts at republics, and returns to monarchy.

Spanish, a Romance language, extends to New World

Now as to how this affected language and literature. Present-day Spanish is distinctly a Romance language, that is, one based on Latin, the tongue of the Romans. The régimes of the Visigoths and the Moors introduced some new words, but surprisingly few in view of their long sway. Among the Christian provinces there arose several distinct dialects, three of which have produced a definite literature of their own. On the west developed the Portuguese, and on the east the Catalan. The central provinces from the fifteenth century have adopted Castilian as the standard and that is the basis of what we call Spanish language. Various dialectical forms are still found in the popular speech of other provinces. Strangely enough, many of these dialects have flourished in the New World while fading at home. Spanish is the official language of the South and Central American countries, and in the nineteenth and twentieth centuries the Spanish literature produced on this side of the water has been increasing in importance. The strangest sub-language in Spain is the Basque, spoken by the people of the Pyrenees mountains who claim to be the oldest unalloyed stock of southern Europe. Their speech is not a Romance language, but the nearest we have to the ancient Iberian tongue spoken on the peninsula before the advent of the Romans.

Epic of the Cid celebrates national hero

Just when Spanish as a language distinct from Latin was first used in literature we cannot tell. There remains a wealth of folk lore and balladry handed down by word of mouth and not put into writing till many, many years after its composition. The oldest piece of writing that we have is the *Cid* which dates back to about 1140, and is only one of several epics produced in the heroic age. The others, however, have been lost and the condition of the *Cid* manuscript, a fourteenth-century copy of the earlier text, shows that it too might soon have gone to pieces without special preservation. This epic of 3735 lines was first published with elaborate commentaries in 1779. It gives a full account in rhymed verse of the adventures of Ruy (or Rodrigo) Diaz, a powerful vassal of Alfonso VI. How much of the account is historical and how much fictitious is hard to say. Rodrigo undoubtedly recaptured Valencia from the Moors, who called him the Cid (Lord), but the stories of his difficulties with his cowardly sons-in-law and his exacting overlord are questionable. He remains the great central figure of Spanish legend, comparable to Roland of France and Arthur of England. Sir Walter Scott, Robert Southey, and Washington Irving have all written about the Cid for English readers. Corneille immortalized him in French drama. (See page 46.) Similar in heroic quality and more interesting reading than the rather bare chronicle of the *Cid* are the many ballads of the Middle Ages.

Drama and poetry develop in the middle centuries

Drama too had its beginning during these centuries, first with the short religious acts or *autos* performed in churches, then developing through such forms as the dialogue verses of wandering *jongleurs* (minstrels), and the improvised comedies, similar to the Italian, with the stock characters of Pantalone, Arlecchino, and Pulcinella, or, as we know them in English, Pantaloon, Harlequin, and Punch.

The first author to emerge as an individual from the mass of anonymous writings was the poet-monk Gonzalo de Berceo (1180?–1250?), and undoubtedly the greatest Spanish poet of the middle ages was Juan Ruiz, Archpriest of Hita (1283?–1350?). Most of the writers of the thirteenth, fourteenth, and fifteenth centuries were priests or princes, and one king, Alfonso the Wise (1251–1284), stands out like Alfred of England as an author, translator, and patron of literature. These were the centuries, also, of the ballads, the romances of chivalry, the pastoral novel, and the stilted courtly lyrics.

Literary glory crowns sixteenth and seventeenth centuries

It was not until the sixteenth century, however, that Spanish literature reached its full flowering and produced prose and poetry of greater interest to the modern reader. Saint Teresa (1515–1582) with her exquisite lyrics of religious devotion and her prolific letters is an outstanding woman of all time.

Another representative of the church, Luis de Leon (1527?–1591?) was a typical Renaissance scholar, a teacher at the University of Salamanca, a writer of direct, unpedantic prose, and of such spiritual and musical poems that some critics call him the greatest lyric poet of Spain.

In contrast to the exalted writing of these religious recluses we find the picaresque novel, celebrating the escapades of clever rogues and revealing the life of the dregs of society. This was a Spanish contribution soon adopted by other European literatures. After this form was introduced in the anonymous *Lazarillo de Tormes* (1554), it found a notable successor in the *Guzman de Alfarache* of Mateo Alemán (1547–1613?). A dozen other writers of picaresque novels during the sixteenth and seventeenth centuries might be named.

But the glory of the novel in the Golden Age came when Miguel de Cervantes (1547–1616) gave the world one of its masterpieces in *Don Quixote,* which marks the turn from the extravagances of medieval romance to the humor and realism of everyday life.

The spirit of the Renaissance made inevitable a great flood of secular poetry in addition to the religious lyrics already mentioned. Much of it, as in the other countries of Europe, turned to a highly artificial style, full of subtleties, hidden meanings, elaborate figures of speech, and flowery words. As in England such style was called euphuism from the book *Euphues,* so in Spain it was christened Gongorism from the poet who most practiced it, Luis de Góngora (1561–1627). Though in early life he had written delightfully vigorous poetry, in the late thirties he turned from a popular audience to find favor with the ultra-cultivated, and much of his writing became so stilted and affected that it is practically unintelligible today. Its influence, however, was felt well into the eighteenth century.

As in England, the culmination of the drama came in the sixteenth and early seventeenth centuries. The founder of dramatic art was Lope de Rueda (1510?–1565?) who according to Cervantes " drew the *comedia* from its swaddling clothes." This goldsmith of Seville became an actor-manager-playwright, and in his years of wandering over Spain practiced all four professions, writing about twenty plays of various types. His followers in the drama were legion, but two stand head and shoulders above the rest — Lope de Vega and Calderón.

Lope de Vega and Calderón write prolific drama

Lope de Vega (1562–1635) was the most productive and versatile of all dramatists. He wrote hundreds of three-act plays based on history — both Spanish and foreign — mythology, medieval romance, pastoral themes, plots of Italian and Spanish novels, his own observation of contemporary manners, the Bible, and the lives of saints, to say nothing of innumerable one-act plays and dialogues. His best work is in the Spanish historical play and the comedy of manners. His history is sometimes inaccurate as to facts, but his creation of personalities from mere historical names, his understanding of mob psychology, and his sense of dramatic values have produced a body of historical material without parallel. His plays of contemporary life imitated the style of the " cloak and sword " drama in which the theme was a love intrigue resulting in a duel, the whole bristling with masks, mistaken identity, concealed listeners, bribed servants, discovered letters, unexpected returns and other machinery of the romantic drama. While Lope de Vega did not invent all this himself, so powerfully did he stamp it upon the Spanish stage that scarcely a playwright after his day dared break away from the style until the advent of Benavente at the end of the nineteenth century.

Pedro Calderón de la Barca (1600–1681) crystallized the " cloak and sword " drama which had been already popularized. The point of honor was carried to an extreme that is ridiculous to the modern mind. It was to protect the reputation of himself and his family name rather than because of any actual love that the jealous husband or stern father brought terrible vengeance upon often innocent victims. Besides these plays Calderón is significant as " the poet of Heaven," through the *auto sacramental,* or little act in honor of the Holy Sacrament, performed on a movable platform on Corpus Christi day much as the miracle plays had been in England at an earlier time. Calderón's seventy *autos* represent the high point of religious fervor during the century of the Spanish Inquisition.

Classicism weakens, Romanticism strengthens Spanish writing

The eighteenth century, called the " Neo-Classic " age, marks a decided decline in Spanish literature, since French standards of disciplined expression and observance of narrow literary rules sat ill upon the fiery, independent Spanish disposition. No really great writers stand out, but Tomás de Iriarte (1750–1791) may serve to represent a number of authors who made reputations according to the French model.

When the Romantic Revival followed upon the heels of classicism throughout Europe, it seemed in Spain more of a return to a time-honored mode after a brief vacation than a new movement. The Spaniard had always been a romanticist at heart. Of the many writers of the early nineteenth century, it will suffice to name only a few who present some point of special interest. José de Espronceda (1808–1842), for a time an exile in England, became the Spanish Byron, resembling him in his dandyism, his pessimism, and his political idealism. He also wrote an historical novel which is a close imitation of Scott's *Ivanhoe*. In contrast to this aristocrat, we have the picturesque bohemian, José Zorrilla (1817–1893), the idol of the populace, " the last of the troubadours." His play *Don Juan* had the widest vogue on both sides of the Atlantic of any nineteenth-century Spanish drama.

The lyrics of Gustavo Adolfo Bécquer (1836–1870) are thought to resemble those of Heine, the German romanticist, in sensitive sadness. His prose legends are like those of Washington Irving in their charm and delicacy of style.

Fiction the favorite in modern Spanish

Modern realism in Spain is saved from the morbid, depressing atmosphere of Russian realism and the repulsiveness of French and Italian naturalism by its sense of humor and its preoccupation with regional differences. During the late nineteenth and twentieth centuries, fiction has held the center of interest. José María de Pereda (1833–1906) pictured the lives of simple farmers and fishermen of the Montaña district and was an advocate of the simple life based on a kind of feudal relationship between aristocrat and peasant. Benito Pérez Galdós (1843–1920), more than any other modernist, was a representative of all Spain rather than of a single region. His fifty-six historical novels give us the past in all its pageantry. His novels of social reform attack — without bitterness — political dishonesty, religious bigotry, and the inadequacy of the educational system: Emilia Pardo Bazán (1852–1921), the most noted woman writer of modern Spain, was a literary critic and a daring portrayer of degeneracy.

Throughout the nineteenth century, drama based on the old " cloak and sword " model flourished mildly, with José Echegaray (1832–1916) holding the center of the playwriting stage. The change brought about by Jacinto Benavente is discussed on page 289.

Spanish-American literature shows vigor and variety

Another development of the present century is the rise of Spanish-American literature. Aside from Brazil, which speaks Portuguese, the chief Central and South American countries use Spanish. The greatest impetus to modern Spanish poetry· came from the Nicaraguan, Rubén Darío (1867–1916).·; In his day the literatures of the two sides of the Atlantic were closely associated, though political ties had been severed. Said Darío, " I am a Spaniard of South America and a South American of Spain." But conditions are changing. South Americans resent having their literature looked upon merely as an offshoot of the main trunk, but wish it to be considered as a twin growth springing from the common roots of language and past literature.

Modern Spanish-American literature is necessarily regional. The differences of the twenty-one Latin-American countries in terrain, in population, and in social and economic features are all reflected in the works of the important authors. The racial variety in the fictional characters is striking. The sympathies of most of the writers are for the poor, the maltreated, and the exploited. Most of the writers are distinctly leftist.

The two best-known South American poets, Gabriela Mistral (1889–1957) and Pablo Neruda (1904–   ), are Chileans. Mistral's most popular collections of verse, *Lullabies, Children's Songs,* and *White Clouds,* are recited and sung everywhere in South America. A devout Catholic, she shows a maternal feeling for the poor and distressed. She was awarded the Nobel prize in 1945. Neruda was transformed from a romantic to a Communist poet by the Spanish Civil War. His collection *Spain in the Heart* was such effective propaganda that it was distributed to soldiers in the Republican Army. In 1953 he received the Stalin Peace Prize.

Gustavo Martínez Zuviría (1883–   ), a professor of political economy who writes under the pseudonym Hugo Wast, is the most important novelist of Argentina. His principal works are *Black Valley, Stone Desert* (a trilogy dealing with the struggle for Argentinian independence), and *The House of the Ravens.* These novels are powerful, somber, and melodramatic.

Another Argentinian novelist, Manuel Gálvez (1882–   ), is mostly concerned with the submerged classes. *The Normal-School Teacher* is a realistic picture of the semi-arid region of northwest Argentina and of the people on the different social levels. His other important novels are *The Shadow of the Monastery* and *Scenes of the Paraguayan War.*

Ciro Alegría (1909–   ), representing Peru, has an international reputation that rests on his novels, *The Golden Serpent, The Hungry Dogs,* and *Broad and Alien Is the World.* His best work has been praised as tragedy representative of the poor and helpless everywhere.

The Mexican novelist, Mariano Azuela (1873–1952), was a physician in Villá's army and so naturally a partisan of the revolution. *The Under Dogs,* his most popular work, dramatizes two years of revolutionary struggle. In *Disillusioned,* in which he vividly portrays the intolerable conditions in a Mexican town, he explains the brutality of those who rose against their cruel masters.

Rómulo Gallegos (1884–   ), the distinguished Venezuelan novelist, interprets life in the vast region drained by the Orinoco and its tributaries. His masterpiece, *Doña Bárbara,* is widely regarded as the best of contemporary Spanish-American novels.

Recent literature reflects Spanish intensity and regional variety

Although the distinguishing characteristic of most modern Spanish literature is its intensity, its range and diversity reflect the different tempers of the various regions of the country.

José Ortega y Gasset (1883–1955) and Miguel de Unamuno (1864–1936) exerted a formative influence upon Spain's intellectual life. Ortega y Gasset, in *The Revolt of the Masses,* fights the destructive influence of the masses upon civilized values. In *Invertebrate Spain* he recognizes his country's decadence and urges it to regain its position in the main current of European life. Unamuno, the author of poems, plays, novels, and essays, in his greatest work, *The Tragic Sense of Life,* urges every man to destroy all of his traditional faiths so that he can then devote all his energy to hunger for immortality. His novels, the best of which are *Three Exemplary Novels and a Prologue,* are products of a similar desperate urgency.

Ramón Pérez de Ayala (1880–   ) endows his realistic treatment of strange, fantastic events with lyrical emotion. His main novels are *The Travails of Urbano and Simona, The Fox's Paw,* and *Tiger Juan.*

By far the most important lyric poet of modern Spain is Federico García Lorca (1899–1936). His *Gypsy Ballads* are recited everywhere in Andalusia and sung by the common people. After spending a year in New York City, he wrote *The Poet in New York,* a collection of poems showing his distaste for the city. His best plays, *Yerma, Blood Wedding,* and *The House of Bernardo Alba,* are tense tragedies of passion, self-denial, and death.

Known as the poet's poet for his experimentation with styles and forms, Juan Ramón Jiménez (1881–   ) has had a tremendous influence upon young poets. His favorite themes are *nada* (nothing) and illusion.

The gay side of Andalusian life is reflected in the plays of the Quintero brothers, Serafín (1871–1938) and Joaquín (1873–1944). The two best are *Love Passes By* and *Doña Clarines.*

Gregorio Martínez Sierra (1881–1947), a devout Catholic, is the author of the plays *The Cradle Song* and *The Kingdom of God*. His quaint *Take Two from One* presents characters of the world of make-believe who cannot survive in reality.

Spain's chief contributions to world culture have been — in addition to her powerful art — a wealth of mystic poetry, a vivacious body of prose fiction, and a prolific drama of marked individuality.

COPLAS

The reputation of Spain as a land of song is justified by the tremendous number of little four-line songs called *coplas*, which have sprung up like field flowers, without literary cultivation or known authorship.

1

What do you wash your face
        with?
    It looks so fresh.
I wash it with clear water,
    God does the rest.

2

Your white face is like a garden,
    Which under snow lies.
And in it three flowers uncov-
        ered:
    Your mouth and your eyes.

3

When I saw you coming,
I said to my heart;
What a pretty little stone
To stumble on!

4

When I come on a visit
    To Mary's house,
The hill which I must walk up
    Seems to go down.
    And when I go,
The hill which I walk down
    Seems to go up.

5

At your stairway tomorrow
    I will put up a sign
Of six words which will say,
    "This way to heaven you
        climb."

6

"Give me your love or I kill
        you "
Say a pair of black eyes.
A pair of blue eyes say
"Give me your love or I die."

7

I dreamt last night
That the Moors were killing
        me,
And it was your beautiful eyes
Looking at me angrily.

8

They say that black is sad.
    I say that isn't true,
For you, my love, have black
        eyes,
    And my happiness is you.

9

You have blue eyes,
Eyes the color of heaven,
And to heaven you shall give account
Of the evil you do with them.

10

Sweet lover, oh, sweet lover,
  When thee I sight,
Even my own eyelashes
  Are in my light.

11

Your eyes are full of sweetness,
  Your lips are full of fear,
And while your lips breathe:
  " Leave me! "
  Your eyes cry out: " Come
  here! "

12

I am like an apple,
  You are an apricot;
I have a heart inside me,
  — Only a stone you've got!

13

Before he embarks on shipboard
  A man should always pray,
And twice when he'd be a soldier,
  And thrice on his marriage
  day.

14

Like the rails of the railway
Are your love and my love,
For they go together, each close
  to the other
All the way, all the way.

15

Like two trees we are
  By fate separated.
The road is between,
  But the boughs are mated.

16

In the garden of my queen
I was the gardener,
And in time for rose-gathering
Came another gardener.

17

Goodbye, and go with God,
Go with God, love of mine,
See that you do not drink water
At the spring of oblivion.

18

Give me your hand. We shall go
To the place where you wept,
And we shall gather between us
The pearls which you there shed.

19

Your love is like a pool
And mine is like a spring.
The sun comes out, the pool dries
  up,
But the spring remains.

20

He who would care to sing well
  Let him sing when grieved at
  heart.
Though he know nothing of singing
  Grief will take the place of art.

(Numbers 5, 8, 9 are translated by *Margaret Tupper*;
11, 12, 13 by *Havelock Ellis*; all the others by *S. de Madariaga*)

Ancient Spanish Ballads

Like the English and Scotch ballads, those of Spain represent the legends of popular heroes and other song stories handed down by word of mouth through many generations. But publication of Spanish ballads first occurred in 1510, over two hundred years before Percy's *Reliques* perpetuated the English ballad in print, and while the most exhaustive collection shows about twelve hundred different versions of English ballads, there are known to be about two thousand Spanish versions. In fact they are the largest and perhaps the oldest body of popular poetry of all Europe. These ballads fall into several major groups: (1) the legends of great Spanish heroes such as Bernardo del Carpio and the Cid, (2) the Moorish ballads, (3) miscellaneous romantic and pastoral stories, (4) the stories of saints.

THE LAMENTATION OF DON RODERICK

Don Roderick (the Anglicized form of Ruy or Rodrigo) was a Gothic king of the eighth century, not to be confused with Rodrigo Diaz, hero of the epic *The Cid*. Historically Rodrigo was a usurper of the throne. The rightful heir probably called in the Moors, who defeated Rodrigo, and forced him to flee. Legend has embroidered the meager facts with elaborate details of marriages, miracles, and military exploits. Some legends apparently kill him off soon after his defeat by the Moors, by such varied methods as dying in battle, drowning in a river, being devoured by wild beasts, and entering a tomb full of serpents for the salvation of his soul.

This ballad, one of the oldest and best known of the Rodrigo stories, represents the plight of the defeated king after the Moorish victory. The situation resembles that of King Arthur after the disruption of his kingdom.

The hosts of Don Rodrigo were scattered in dismay,
When lost was the eighth battle, nor heart nor hope had they;
He, when he saw that field was lost, and all his hope was flown,
He turned him from his flying host, and took his way alone.

His horse was bleeding, blind, and lame, — he could no farther 5
    go;
Dismounted, without path or aim, the king stepped to and fro;
It was a sight of pity to look on Roderick,
For, sore athirst and hungry, he staggered, faint and sick.

All stained and strewed with dust and blood, like to some smouldering
    brand
Plucked from the flame, Rodrigo showed: — his sword was in his   10
    hand,
But it was hacked into a saw of dark and purple tint;
His jewelled mail had many a flaw, his helmet many a dint.

He climbed unto a hill-top, the highest he could see,
Thence all about of that wide rout his last long look took he;
He saw his royal banners, where they lay drenched and torn,   15
He heard the cry of victory, the Arab's shout of scorn.

He looked for the brave captains that led the hosts of Spain,
But all were fled except the dead, and who could count the slain?
Where'er his eye could wander, all bloody was the plain,
And, while thus he said, the tears he shed ran down his cheeks 20
    like rain: —

" Last night I was the King of Spain, — today no king am I;
Last night fair castles held my train, — tonight where shall I lie?
Last night a hundred pages did serve me on the knee, —
Tonight not one I call mine own — not one pertains to me.

Oh, luckless, luckless was the hour, and cursèd was the day,   25
When I was born to have the power of this great seignory!
Unhappy me that I should see the sun go down tonight!
O Death, why now so slow art thou, why fearest thou to smite?

                             (*J. G. Lockhart*)

THE FLIGHT FROM GRANADA

    The Moors first entered Spain in 711 and for more than seven hundred
years maintained flourishing kingdoms in the south of the peninsula.
Naturally, legendary literature of the medieval period is full of the conflict
between Moors and Christians. Both sides were split up into small kingdoms with considerable internal strife. Ultimate victory could go only to
the side which became a united group. This the Spaniards accomplished
with the marriage of Ferdinand of Aragon and Isabel of Castile in 1469,
and the Moors lost their last foothold at Granada in 1492, the year of the
discovery of America. In actual history the defeated Boabdil did not flee
in the dramatic manner recounted in this ballad, but received Ferdinand

and Isabel at the gates of the city, craved their protection, and was assigned a residence in Spain with a revenue for maintaining it. It was later that his wounded pride caused him to withdraw to Barbary. The ballad version, however, makes a better story.

There was crying in Granada when the sun was going down, —
Some calling on the Trinity — some calling on Mahoun!
Here passed away the Koran, — there, in the Cross was borne, —
And here was heard the Christian bell, — and there the Moorish horn.

Te Deum Laudamus! was up the Alcala sung;   5
Down from the Alhambra's minarets were all the crescents flung;
The arms thereon of Aragon they with Castile's display;
One king comes in in triumph, — one weeping goes away.

Thus cried the weeper, while his hands his old white beard did tear,
" Farewell, farewell, Granada! thou city without peer!   10
Woe! Woe! thou pride of Heathendom!   Seven hundred years and
   more
Have gone since first the faithful thy royal scepter bore!

" Thou wert the happy mother of an high renownèd race;
Within thee dwelt a haughty line that now go from their place;
Within thee fearless knights did dwell, who fought with mickle 15
   glee
The enemies of proud Castile — the bane of Christientie!

" The mother of fair dames wert thou, of truth and beauty rare,
Into whose arms did courteous knights for solace sweet repair;
For whose dear sakes the gallants of Afric made display
Of might in joust and battle on many a bloody day.   20

" Here gallants held it little thing for ladies' sake to die,
Or for the Prophet's honor and pride of Soldanry, —
For here did valor flourish and deeds of warlike might
Ennobled lordly palaces, in which was our delight.

2. **Mahoun:** Mahomet. 3. **Koran:** sacred book of Islam. 5. **Te Deum Laudamus:** We praise thee, O Lord. 5. **Alcala:** the Moorish fortress. 6. **Alhambra:** the palace within the fortress. 15. **mickle:** much. 22. **Soldanry:** realm of the Sultan.

" The gardens of thy Vega, its fields and blooming bowers, — 25
Woe! Woe! I see their beauty gone, and scattered all their flowers!
No reverence can he claim, the King that such a land hath lost, —
On charger never can he ride, nor be heard among the host;

" But in some dark and dismal place, where none his face may see,
There weeping and lamenting, alone that King should be." — 30

Thus spoke Granada's King as he was riding to the sea,
About to cross Gibraltar's Strait away to Barbary;
Thus he in heaviness of soul unto his Queen did cry
(He had stopped and ta'en her in his arms, for together they did
    fly).

" Unhappy King! whose craven soul can brook " (she made 35
    reply)
" To leave behind Granada — who hast not the heart to die!
Now for the love I bore thy youth, thee gladly could I slay!
For what is life to leave when such a crown is cast away? "

(J. G. Lockhart)

25. **Vega:** fertile plain south of Granada.

THE BALLAD OF COUNT ARNALDOS

This ballad, probably dating back to the sixteenth century, is one of the
best known of those outside the historical group. It is to be found in
several English translations, but this one adheres more closely to the
original than the others, for instance, in the strange mixture of tenses and
in the medieval tone conveyed in the words of the Count and the Mariner.
The mystic quality is typical of Spanish literature. Who is this strange
mariner? What the power behind his song? The interpretation is left
to the reader.

Have ye ever heard such marvel as to Count Arnaldos fell
By the sea-shore on St. John's Day, even as I here will tell?
Lo! with falcon at his gauntlet forth unto the hunt he hied,
And a gallant ship saw speeding — landwards o'er the water wide.
Sails it bore of finest satin, silken cordage, goodly gear, 5
And the mariner who steered it sang a song as he drew near;
Sings a song that calms the billows, soothes the wind to peace pro-
    found,

2. **St. John's Day:** June 24, a day when it was supposed that miracles
were most likely to occur

Lures the fish from deepest ocean, makes them sport and swim
    around,
Calls the circling birds to gather on the masthead painted gay.
Thereon spake the Count Arnaldos, ye shall hear what he will   10
    say:
" Gentle mariner, I prithee, rede me now thy song, perdie."
And the mariner gave answer, even in this wise spake he:
" Unto none I'll rede my ditty save to him that sails with me."

(Ida Farnell)

11. **rede:** explain, interpret.   11. **perdie:** a mild oath often found in
medieval literature.

SUGGESTIONS FOR STUDY

1. What varied moods are illustrated in the coplas? What light do they
throw on Spanish character? Select the coplas which seem to you especially original in idea or treatment. Try your hand at composing some
coplas.

2. In what ways do the Spanish ballads remind you of English ballads?
How true are they to typical ballad measure? to common characteristics
of the English ballad, such as refrain, conversation, and indirect narration
by suggestion?

3. Compare the situation of Don Roderick with that of King Arthur in
The Passing of Arthur.

4. As background for " The Flight from Granada," read Washington
Irving's description of the palace in *The Alhambra,* and his account of the
defeat of the Moors in *The Conquest of Granada.*

5. "The Ballad of Count Arnaldos" has been frequently translated.
Read the version in Lockhart's *Ancient Spanish Ballads* and Walsh's
Hispanic Anthology. What difference in effect do these translations have?
How do you interpret the mariner's reply in the last line?

The Folk Tale

Spanish and Portuguese literature is rich in folk tales, as well as in folk
poetry. The comic element is marked in these tales. Often the fun turns
upon the theme of the clever rogue outwitting the gullible fool, as in the
Portuguese story of " The Oil Merchant's Donkey." This germ of ridicule
found in the early tales later grew into an extended treatment of roguery
in the picaresque novel (see page 253). Even when the Spanish tale has
a moral, it often drives the point home with a smile.

THE OIL MERCHANT'S DONKEY (Portuguese)

Once upon a time two students, walking along the high road, met an oil merchant leading a donkey loaded with jars full of oil. The students, being very poor and just then reduced to their last penny, were glad to fall in with such a lucky find; so they agreed together to steal the donkey with its burden, and take them to a neighboring fair and sell them both.

While the poor man trudged along contentedly, holding the reins of this beast, which trotted behind him, one of the students quietly and cleverly slipped the donkey's bridle off its head and put it over his own, while his companion seized the donkey and marched off with it, unperceived by the owner. The student who now occupied the place of the donkey, wishing to call the merchant's attention to himself, suddenly came to a standstill. Great was the astonishment and stupefaction of the merchant when, on turning round, he found he was leading a man instead of his donkey. "Dear Master," said the witty student in an affectionate tone, "I can never thank you sufficiently for having so often beaten me with your cudgel, as by that means you have gradually dispelled the enchantment that has held me bound so many years under the shape of a donkey."

When the bewildered merchant heard these words he took his hat off to the student, and said very humbly, "I have lost in you, sir, as a donkey, my only means of support; but as it cannot be helped I must have patience, and Providence will no doubt help me some other way. Being what you are, no longer a donkey but a man, I beg a thousand pardons and trust you will forgive me my treatment of you. But when you consider what a stubborn, slow, and stupid beast you were, what else could you expect? Sometimes you nearly drove me mad by your waywardness and tricks, and then, hardly knowing what I was doing, I have taken up my cudgel and beaten you. But then you must remember how often I rewarded you with a handful of hay, or a piece of bread, when you behaved well and worked hard."

"My good man, rest assured that I forgive you all the hard treatment I ever received from you," replied the student, "and the only favor I ask of you now is to let me go in peace, for you must allow it would be a great hardship for a man to be driven about like a donkey."

The poor oil merchant, seeing no other remedy for his misfortune, consented to release the man, and before long they parted company, each going his own way.

When the oil merchant found himself alone, without his ass and his jars of oil, he lamented his sad lot, and wished he had never come across an enchanted donkey. He made up his mind to go and see his godfather, to tell him what had occurred, by which he was left without the means of earning his living, and to ask him at the same time to lend him some money to buy another donkey at the next fair.

His godfather was sorry to hear of his sad plight and readily lent him the money required.

The oil merchant, much comforted, went to the fair next day. He had not been there long when he saw his own beast held by a student, who, though he was the man that had carried away the beast, was unknown to him. The merchant, believing that the man had again transformed himself into a donkey, went up to the student and asked to be allowed to tell the donkey a secret, which was only intended for it to hear.

The student, though much amused at the poor man's simplicity, replied with a grave face that he was at liberty to tell his donkey as many secrets as he chose, as he would not interfere in the least.

Then the merchant went up to the donkey, put his mouth close to its ear, and cried with a loud voice these words: " I tell you what, donkey, those that do not now know what you are, are welcome to buy you if they choose."

(*H. Monteiro*)

JUAN RUIZ (1283?–1350?)

The first poet of Spain to have any distinct personality beyond a mere name is Juan Ruiz, Archpriest of Hita, whose life is partly contemporaneous with Chaucer's, and who in his writing depicts the corruption in the Church, which Chaucer satirizes. To judge by his own lively poems he was more of a pagan than an ecclesiastic, loving the pleasures of the table and the gayeties of social life with hearty vitality. His monumental work, which is really a collection of miscellaneous poems, is given various titles, the commonest being *The Book of Divine Love,* but therein one finds the most space devoted to profane love affairs. There are also humorous fables similar to Aesop's, songs for begging students, and a curious allegory celebrating the combat between Lord Carnival and Lady Lent. Here the Lord marshals his forces of capon, rabbit, bacon, and beef, armed with cooking pots and saucepans. The Lady's army consists of fish, oysters, lobsters, and crabs. Though temporarily victorious for forty days, the Lady is finally defeated on Easter and Lord Carnival welcomes Lord Love to celebrate the victory.

The book as a whole is written with distinction of style and gives the most vivid picture of life in medieval Spain that we have. It was written during the thirteen years that the priest was imprisoned by his ecclesiastical superiors, for just what reasons we are not told.

Though we know little else of the events of his life we have a clear portrait of the man in his own words: a large rawboned frame, beady black eyes and bushy eyebrows, full red lips and a deep voice — a composite picture of Chaucer's monk and friar.

ON THE POWER OF MONEY

In this poem the Archpriest speaks out boldly on one of the main sources of corruption in the medieval Church, but the universal frailty of human nature where money is concerned makes the subject pertinent to modern life in general.

The ignorant churl that knoweth naught but how to plow the earth,
By money gaineth wisdom, gaineth rank and gentle birth;
The fuller are the money-bags, the greater is his worth,
But none may count him master when of gold there is a dearth.

If thou but have great store of gold all will with thee be well;   5
And with the Pope's full favor thou wilt in gladness dwell;
For gold they'll sell thee Paradise, thy soul's salvation sell;
For gold a man may win him grace, and 'scape the pains of Hell.

Whilom I saw in Rome's high court, of holiness the seat,
That all with full great humbleness the man of riches greet;   10
I saw that all men honored him, and bowed before his feet,
And paid him homage as, methought, to royal state were meet.

I marked how gold made abbots, and eke priors and bishops high,
Archbishops, doctors, patriarchs, and gave great dignity;
Marked how good gold for witless clerks a benefice might buy,   15
Converting every lie to truth, and every truth to lie.

7. **sell thee Paradise:** The selling of "indulgences" which were supposed to bring forgiveness of sins was one of the great abuses of the fourteenth century. 9. **Whilom:** Once. 13. **eke:** also. 15. **for witless clerks a benefice might buy:** might buy a church position for stupid clergymen.

Behold, howbeit of God they prate, full many a monk and friar
By worldliness and avarice will prove himself a liar;
And when death striketh down the rich, with greed that naught can
    tire,
To win from him their goods and pelf, lo, one and all conspire!   20

(Ida Farnell)

SAINT TERESA (1515–1582)

Not only is Saint Teresa considered the greatest woman writer of Spanish literature, but she also has the distinction of being the earliest woman writer of consequence in any modern European nation. Remember that in England no woman appeared on the literary horizon before the last half of the seventeenth century; but two hundred years before Lady Mary Wortley Montagu, this Spanish nun was writing charming letters, four hundred of which have been preserved; and three hundred years before Christina Rossetti, she produced lyric poetry of delicate beauty. Because so much of her writing is autobiographic, we can picture her more clearly than almost any other medieval woman. We see the romantic quality of her childhood at Avila, when she ran away at the age of seven to seek martyrdom, her moments of depression and exaltation as a girl, her entering the Carmelite order at nineteen, her human sympathy, sense of humor, and executive ability which eventually promoted her to the position of Mother Superior, her coping with the infinite details of founding seventeen nunneries, and her wisdom in advising her correspondents. In contrast to this evident practical common sense, she had the poetic quality of the mystic. One of her long works shows the soul passing through seven chambers of a mystic castle to the final sanctuary of Divine Love. Some of her short lyrics in their simplicity and sincerity have a universal appeal. She was canonized in 1622.

LINES WRITTEN IN HER BREVIARY

Let nothing disturb thee,
Nothing affright thee;
All things are passing;
God never changeth;
Patient endurance
Attaineth to all things;
Who God possesseth
In nothing is wanting;
Alone God sufficeth.

(Henry W. Longfellow)

IF, LORD, THY LOVE FOR ME IS STRONG

If, Lord, Thy love for me is strong
As this which binds me unto Thee,
What holds me from Thee, Lord, so long,
What holds Thee, Lord, so long from me?

O soul in God hidden from sin,   5
— Lord, I would see Thee, who thus choose Thee.
What fears can yet assail thee now?
—All that I fear is but to lose Thee.

Love's whole possession I entreat,
Lord, make my soul Thine own abode,   10
And I will build a nest so sweet
It may not be too poor for God.

O soul in God hidden from sin,
What more desires for thee remain,
Save but to love and love again,   15
And, all on flame with love within,
Love on, and turn to love again?

(Arthur Symons)

SUGGESTIONS FOR STUDY

1. What two different aspects of the medieval Church are represented by Juan Ruiz and Saint Teresa?

2. Enumerate some of the things money could do, according to Ruiz. Find examples in Chaucer's "Prologue" which confirm his picture of fourteenth-century corruption. When did reaction against this situation come to a definite head? Point out examples in modern life of the undue power of money either in religious or in secular organizations.

3. What general similarity is there in the two poems by Saint Teresa? Which is more intense, which more philosophic? Which appeals to you as the more beautiful poem? Compare her with some of the modern mystic poets, such as Emily Dickinson, Francis Thompson, Alice Meynell, Katharine Tynan, Rabindranath Tagore (see page 1169), and Kahlil Gibran.

4. Do not confuse this Saint Teresa with the other one, called Little Flower, (1873–97). Look up the difference between the two. There are about half a dozen biographies of the Spanish Teresa in English.

LUIS DE CAMOËNS (1524–1580)

The greatest luminary of Portuguese literature is Luis de Camoëns, an aristocrat and courtier of Lisbon. Students of English literature may be particularly interested in Camoëns because of Elizabeth Barrett Browning's devotion to his poetry, which eventually suggested to her the title " Sonnets from the Portuguese " to disguise the highly personal quality of her own sonnets to her husband.

Camoëns' one great love affair, celebrated in many sonnets, was with Dona Catharina de Attayda on whose account he was banished from the court. Thereafter he led an adventurous and for the most part disastrous life. In a naval engagement near Gibraltar he lost the sight of one eye. His father died as the result of a shipwreck, and he himself reached India on the only surviving ship of an entire squadron. In India he incurred the wrath of some officials because of a satire on their maladministration, and as a result was sent to China with a government position which proved both easy and remunerative. During this one and only peaceful period of his life he produced his great epic poem, *The Lusiad,* which he had contemplated ever since his first banishment years before. Unfortunately he accepted an invitation to return to India, and from that time ill-luck dogged his steps. In a shipwreck he lost all his possessions except the precious manuscript of *The Lusiad.* He was falsely accused and imprisoned by his enemies. In order to return to Portugal to present his poem to the king he joined the train of a nobleman who made life intolerable for him. The king was so much engrossed in his African wars that he was in no mood to appreciate poetry and gave Camoëns an inadequate pension, though the poem was widely heralded as a work of genius. Finally, with broken health and no means of livelihood, the poor poet sank into such poverty that he was maintained only by the begging of his faithful servant, and even the shroud in which he was buried was a gift of charity. Is it any wonder that a note of sadness runs through his many sonnets and songs?

ON THE DEATH OF CATHARINA DE ATTAYDA

It was far off in India and many years after Camoëns had last seen Catharina that he heard of her death. Many of his most beautiful sonnets were written in commemoration of this lady who, like Dante's Beatrice, was an inspiring but unattainable love.

> While, pressed with woes from which it cannot flee,
> My fancy sinks, and slumber seals my eyes,
> Her spirit hastens in my dreams to rise,
> Who was in life but as a dream to me.

O'er the drear waste, so wide no eye can see   5
How far its sense-evading limit lies,
I follow her quick step; but, ah, she flies!
Our distance widening by fate's stern decree.
" Fly not from me, kind shadow! " I exclaim; —
She, with fixed eyes, that her soft thoughts reveal,   10
And seem to say, " Forbear thy fond design," —
She flies. I call her, but her half-formed name
Dies on my faltering tongue; — I wake, and feel
Not e'en one short delusion can be mine.

(Richard Garnett)

ON REVISITING CINTRA AFTER THE DEATH
OF CATHARINA

Apparel of green woods and meadows gay;
    Clear and fresh waters innocent of stain,
    Wherein the field and grove are found again,
As from high rocks ye take your downward way;
And shaggy peaks, and ordered disarray   5
    Of crags abrupt, know that ye strive in vain,
    Till grief consent, to soothe the eye of pain,
Shown the same scene that Pleasure did survey.
Nor as erst seen am I beheld by you,
    Rejoiced no more by fields of pleasant green,   10
    Or lively runnels laughing as they dart;
Sown be these fields with seeds of ruth and rue,
    And wet with brine of welling tears, till seen
    Sere with the herb that suits the broken heart.

(Richard Garnett)

9. **erst:** formerly.   12. **ruth and rue:** regret and disappointment.

CHANGES

Time and the mortal will stand never fast;
    Estrangèd fates man's confidence estrange;
    Aye with new quality imbued, the vast
World seems but victual of voracious change.

New endless growth surrounds on every side,   5
    Such as we deemed not earth could ever bear,
Only doth sorrow for past woe abide,
    And sorrow for past good, if good it were.
Now Time with green hath made the meadows gay,
    Late carpeted with snow by winter frore,   10
And to lament hath turned my gentle lay;
    Yet of all change this chiefly I deplore,
The human lot, transformed to ill alway,
    Not chequered with rare blessing as of yore.

                                        (*Richard Garnett*)

            10. frore: frozen.

SUGGESTIONS FOR STUDY

1. What experiences of Camoëns' life are reflected in these sonnets? Is the tone emotional or philosophical? What connection between nature and the human experience is brought out in these sonnets?

2. Compare the mood of these poems with that in the poems of Musset (page 123). Where in the poems of Burns, Tennyson, Poe, Longfellow, and others do you find mourning for a lost loved one? What poems of Wordsworth are suggested by " On Revisiting Cintra "? Read some of Mrs. Browning's " Sonnets from the Portuguese " which were indirectly named from these. What striking difference is there in the experience back of the two sonnet sequences?

3. From what country did the sonnet originally come (see page 326)? Compare the dates of Camoëns with those of Petrarch (page 342), and of Wyatt and Surrey, who introduced the sonnet into England. Review the differences between the Petrarchan and Shakespearean sonnet forms. What use does the translator of Camoëns make of these? Point out lines in which he has succeeded in giving the flavor of Elizabethan sonnets to his translation.

MATEO ALEMÁN (1547–1613?)

As the son of a prison doctor, and twice in jail himself for debt, Mateo Alemán had ample opportunity for contacts with criminals, which he turned to good account in his writing. On the other hand, he studied at three important Spanish universities and for twenty years held a position in the Auditor's office of Madrid.

In 1599 he published part of his novel *Guzman de Alfarache,* which made such popular appeal that fifteen editions were printed within the next fifteen years. When another man tried to capitalize this popularity with a spurious second part, Alemán issued his own second part at Lisbon, and in the same year, curiously enough, he wrote a pious life of St. Anthony of Padua.

The knowledge of Italy shown in his books leads to the inference that he had at one time gone a-soldiering to that country, but there is no real proof. However, there is proof that he went to Mexico in 1608 to seek his fortune and that he published two books while there, but whether they or the gold of the Aztec's produced the coveted fortune we shall never learn, for no records show what became of him.

GUZMAN DE ALFARACHE

The Picaresque Novel

The Spanish word *picaro* means a lively rogue who lives by trickery, roves from place to place in search of adventure, and is entirely unconventional in his habits. In the middle of the sixteenth century there appeared in Spain an anonymous book called *The Life of Lazarillo de Tormes* with such a rogue for its hero. This was the first of a long line of " picaresque " novels, not confined alone to Spain but spreading to other countries, so that we find one of Shakespeare's contemporaries, Thomas Nash, writing *Jack Wilton,* the first English picaresque novel, and a Frenchman, Le Sage, producing the famous *Gil Blas* in the eighteenth century. Two outstanding novels of modern times follow in general the picaresque model: Mark Twain's *Huckleberry Finn* and Hervey Allen's *Anthony Adverse.* It is evident from the nature of the hero of a picaresque novel that the plot will consist merely of a loosely strung series of episodes, that the style will be lively, and that considerable satire on human foibles will be evident.

One of the best examples of the Spanish picaresque novels is *Guzman de Alfarache* in which the author not only presents the experiences of his hero, but also appends to each episode a long moral, probably to mollify the church authorities who had banned " Lazarillo." These morals have been scored by some critics as tedious and hailed by others as cleverly written sermonettes, which serve as antidotes to Guzman's rascality. The adventurer figures in many rôles throughout the pages of the book — as kitchen-boy, beggar, soldier, lover, thief, student, merchant, rich man, and finally as a convict sentenced to the galleys for having defrauded a wealthy widow. In the seclusion of imprisonment he finds opportunity to write his memoirs and warn others against following his course.

This chapter shows how Guzman rose from a street beggar to a cardinal's trusted servant. As in so many picaresque novels the incident plays up both knavery and the gullibility of people of rank. One can see why the authorities looked askance at such books.

GUZMAN AND MY LORD CARDINAL

Having roused myself early one fine morning, according to custom, I went and seated myself at the door of a cardinal, concerning whom I had heard an excellent character, being one of the most charitably disposed in Rome. I had taken the trouble of getting one of my legs swelled, on which, notwithstanding what had passed, was to be seen a new ulcer, one that might set at defiance the most penetrating eye or probe of a surgeon. I had not this time omitted to have my face as pale as death; and thus, filling the air with horrible lamentations while I was asking alms, I moved the souls of the different domestics who came in and out to take pity upon me. They gave me something; but I was yet only beating up for game — it was their master I wanted. He at length made his appearance — I redoubled my cries and groans — I writhed in anguish; and I then accosted him in these terms: " Oh! most noble Christian! thou friend of Christ and his afflicted ones! Have pity upon me, a poor wretched sinner. Behold me cut down in the flower of my days. May your excellency be touched with my extreme misery, for the sake of the sufferings of our dear Redeemer."

The cardinal, who was really a pious man, stopped; and, after looking at me earnestly, turned to his attendants. " In the name of Christ, take this unhappy being, and bear him into my own apartments! Let the rags that cover him be exchanged for fine linen. Put him into a good bed — nay, into my own — and I will go into another room. I will tend on him, for in him do I verily see what must have been the sufferings of our Savior."

He was obeyed; and, oh, charity! how didst thou shame those lordly prelates who think Heaven in debt to them, if they do but look down on some poor wretch; while my good cardinal, not content with what he had done, ordered two surgeons to attend, recommending them to do all in their power to ease my agony, and to examine and cure my leg; after which they should be well recompensed. He then, bidding me be of good cheer, left me, to pursue his affairs; and the surgeons, to make the best of my case.

They declared at once that it was useless, and that gangrene had already commenced. So seriously did they pronounce this, that, though I knew the effect was solely produced by staining my leg with a certain herb, I almost felt alarmed for the consequence. They then took out their case of instruments, called for a caldron of hot water, for some fine linen, and a poultice. While these were in preparation, they questioned me as to the origin of my disease, how long I had had it, etc., etc. Moreover, whether I drank wine, and what was my usual diet? To these, and to a hundred such interrogatories, I replied not a word; so great was my alarm at the terrific processes that appeared to be going on, in order to restore me to my pristine health and soundness. I was infinitely perplexed, not knowing to what saint to have recourse, for I was apprehensive there might not be a single one in heaven inclined to interfere in behalf of so thorough-paced a rascal. I recalled to mind the lesson I had so lately been taught at Gaerta,[1] and had my misgivings that I might not escape even on such good terms as I had done there.

The surgeons ranked high in their profession; and, after having curiously turned round my leg about twenty times, retired into another room to discuss the result of their observations. I remained in a state of horror not to be described; for it had got into my head that they would decide upon amputation; to learn which I crept softly towards the door to listen, fully resolved to reveal the imposture in so dreadful an alternative.

" Sir," said one, " we may consult here forever, to little purport; he has got St. Anthony's fire." [2]

" No such thing," replied the other, " he has no more fire in his leg than I have in my hand. We might easily remove it in a couple of days."

" You cannot be serious," said the first speaker. " By St. Comus, I know something of ulcers; and here, I maintain it, we have a gangrene."

" No, no, friend," replied the second, " we have no ulcer. We have a rogue to deal with. Nothing is the matter with him. I know the whole history of his ulcer, and how it was made. It is by no means very rare, for I know the herbs with which the impostor has prepared it, and the ingenious method in which they have been applied."

The other seemed quite confounded at this assertion; but, ashamed of owning himself a dupe, he persisted in his former opinion; on which a pretty warm colloquy would have ensued, had not the more ingenious of the two had the sense to recommend first to examine the leg, and to end the dispute afterwards. " Look a little deeper into the matter," said he, " and you will see the fellow's knavery."

---

[1] **Gaerta**: In this little Italian town, the mayor, having found that Guzman was an imposter, had him given thirty lashes and turned out of town.

[2] **St. Anthony's fire**: erysipelas, a skin disease, supposed to be healed by St. Anthony.

" With all my heart.   I will confess you are right, when I see there is no ulcer, or rather gangrene."

" That is not enough," replied his colleague.   " In acknowledging your error, you must also admit I am entitled to at least a third more fees than yourself."

" By no means," retorted the other.   " I have eyes to detect imposture as well as you, and I am of opinion we ought to divide the good cardinal's fees fairly between us."

The dispute now waxed warm, and rather than give up his point, each declared that he would make the cardinal acquainted with the whole business.

In this dilemma I did not hesitate a moment.   There was no time to lose.   Escape was impossible.   I rushed into the presence of the faculty, and threw myself at their feet.   With well-dissembled grief I thus addressed them: " Alas! my dear sirs, take pity upon an unfortunate fellow creature.   Think, gentlemen, *homo sum; nihil humani,*[3] *etc.*   I am mortal like yourselves — you know the hard-heartedness of the great, and how the poor and forlorn are compelled to assume the most horrible shapes in order to soften their hardness; and in doing this what risks and sufferings do we not encounter, and all for so small a remuneration.   Besides, what advantage will you get by exposing such a poor miserable sinner?   You will certainly lose your fees, which you need not do if you will let us understand each other. You may rely on my discretion; the fear of consequences will keep me silent, and we may each benefit in our respective professions."

Upon this the men of physic again consulted, and at length came to the resolution of pocketing their fees, *secundum artem.*[4]   Being all of one mind, we now begged to be ushered into the presence of the cardinal, and the surgeons then ordered me to be placed upon a couch, at the side of which they made an immense display of chirurgical[5] instruments, dressings, etc. — again consulted, and after wrapping my leg in a great number of bandages, they desired that I might be put into a warm bed.   His excellency, meanwhile, was full of anxiety to learn the state of my health, and whether there were any hopes of recovery.

" My lord," replied one of the surgeons, " the patient is in a de-

---

[3] **Homo sum, nihil humani:** " I am a man, and nothing that concerns a man do I deem a matter of indifference to me." — Terence.   Guzman quotes only the first few words.

[4] **secundum artem:** according to art; i.e., according to the custom of their profession.

[5] **chirurgical:** surgical.

plorable situation, gangrene has already begun. Still, with time and care, there is a chance that he might recover, please God, but it will be a long affair."

" And he is fortunate," said his coadjutor, " in having fallen into our hands. Another day, and he was lost forever. But no doubt Providence must have directed him to the door of your excellency."

This account seemed to please the cardinal. It gave him occasion to display the truest Christian charity, and he desired that neither time nor skill might be spared in the endeavor to restore me to health. He also directed that I should be supplied with everything; and the surgeons on their part pledged themselves to do all that art could effect, and each of them to pay me a visit at least twice in the day; it being necessary to detect the slightest change that might occur in my present condition. They then withdrew, not a little to my consolation; for I could not but regard them while present, in the light of two executioners, who might fall upon me at any moment, or publish my imposition to the world. So far from this, however, they made me keep my apartment for three months, which to me seemed like so many ages, so difficult is it to give up the habit of gambling — or begging, with the tone of freedom they seem to include. In vain was I daintily lodged and fed, like his excellency himself; the *ennui* [6] I felt was intolerable. I was incessantly beseeching the doctors to take pity on me, and bring the farce to a close, until they were at length compelled to yield to my importunity.

They left off dressing my leg, and, on its being reduced to its natural size, they acquainted the good cardinal with the fact, who was in raptures at the performance, under his auspices, of so great a cure. He rewarded them handsomely, and came to congratulate me on the miraculous event; and having acquitted myself well in his frequent visits to me, in regard both to my opinions and my principles, he imbibed a real kindness for me; and to give me a further proof of it, he gave me the situation of one of his confidential attendants — a species of honor I was too deeply sensible of to be able to refuse.

(*Thomas Roscoe*)

SUGGESTIONS FOR STUDY

1. Which deceivers do you consider more to be condemned, Guzman or the doctors? Why? How do you feel toward the cardinal? In modern life are there impostors comparable to Guzman? Discuss.

6 **ennui**: boredom.

2. If you have read *Gil Blas, Huckleberry Finn,* or other famous picaresque novels, recall incidents of imposture from them. Point out situations in well-known novels of Dickens and other authors, which border on the picaresque. See O. Henry's collection of stories, *The Gentle Grafter,* for American types of the *picaro.* Compare the character of the cardinal with that of the bishop who befriended Jean Valjean in *Les Misérables.*

3. Are picaresque novels advisable reading for young people? Discuss.

4. Vocabulary: gangrene, interrogatories, pristine, imposture, colloquy, importunity.

MIGUEL DE CERVANTES (1547-1616)

Comparison of Cervantes and Shakespeare is inevitable. Each is the greatest literary name in his own country; each has been the subject of endless research to piece out the details of his life; and by strange coincidence, both men died on the same day, April 23, 1616. Marked differences, however, are apparent. Shakespeare was essentially a dramatist, but Cervantes was always unsuccessful in his attempted stage plays and won his fame through the novel. Shakespeare excelled in both comedy and tragedy, while Cervantes' best writing was in the marked vein of humor, however much philosophy and human frailty might lie beneath the surface. Shakespeare, as far as we have records, lived an outwardly uneventful life, while Cervantes' actual experiences make a narrative of high adventure.

He was born in Alcalá de Henares, near Madrid. Again, as in the case of Shakespeare, the year and place are determined only by the baptismal record. His father was a surgeon, better provided with noble ancestors than with coin in purse. The boy's education is largely a matter of conjecture — probably as meager as Shakespeare's. But facts begin to emerge when we find that at twenty-two he was in Italy, first in the train of a papal legate and later as a soldier. In the famous naval battle of Lepanto in 1571, in which the Muslims were finally defeated by the Christians, Cervantes was wounded, and as his left hand was permanently disabled he was often called thereafter "the cripple of Lepanto." However, he remained in active service for the next four years, and then started back home with his brother. Not far from their destination the ship was attacked by Moorish pirates and Cervantes was borne off to Algiers as a Christian slave to be held for ransom. Through some letters he carried addressed to persons of high rank in Spain, the Algerians gained a false impression of his importance. This was unfortunate in one way, for they set his ransom at a figure too high for his indigent family to meet; but fortunate in another, for he avoided the ill treatment of his fellow slaves, and in spite of five unsuccessful attempts at escape in which he was always the ringleader, he was not given the brutal punishment customary for that offense. Finally, after five years, the ransom was met and the prisoner returned to Spain only to lead a rather miserable life, beset by financial difficulties, and frustrated in his literary aspirations. He wanted to be a great poet and dramatist; but, as he later wrote, he " had more experience in reverses than in verses." To eke out a living he at one time held a government job in which he bought provisions for the famous Spanish Armada. But when he was nearing sixty that elusive literary acclaim finally came his way, for the publication of the first part of *Don Quixote* in 1605 was an immediate success and was followed by numerous editions, translations, and attentions from patrons. Later he published a collection of novelettes called *Exemplary Novels,* and a second part of *Don Quixote* after a fraudulent second part had been issued by another writer.

It is more true of Cervantes than of most of the world's preëminent authors that his fame rests on a single book. Even so, someone has said that his life was greater than his book. It was the fact that through six decades of poverty and misfortune he could preserve his noble qualities of courage, humor, tolerance, and human sympathy that enabled him to distill from them in his late years the masterpiece which has made his name memorable.

DON QUIXOTE

As o'er the laughter-moving page
Thy readers, O Cervantes, bend,
What shouts of mirth, through age on age,
From every clime of earth ascend!

Thus William Cullen Bryant opened his commemorative poem to Cervantes. The laughter in the pages of *Don Quixote* springs largely from the contrast between the romantic ideals of chivalry and the practical everyday life of Spain in the seventeenth century. Cervantes had witnessed this transition in his own life. The battle of Lepanto in 1571 was one of the last great combats in the mode of chivalry, with its brilliant pageantry and cumbersome galleys. In 1588 the Invincible Armada, magnificent in medieval trappings, had been ignominiously scattered by the smaller British craft. Cervantes, a "modernist" of the seventeenth century, could look back at the days that had gone by and laugh at them, not with bitter cynicism, but with permeating love of human kind.

The story is a long plotless narrative of the adventures of an elderly knight, Don Quixote, whose brain has become warped by much reading of the romances of chivalry. He attempts to live literally the life of an armed knight on horseback journeying about the country in search of noble adventure. His inner vision causes him to misinterpret most of what he sees about him in a ludicrous fashion. His servant, Sancho Panza, a practical, unimaginative fellow, is enlisted as his accompanying squire, and willy-nilly must participate in the ridiculous encounters from which he is constantly trying to dissuade his master. Part I is frankly a satire on the romances of knight-errantry. Part II has more underlying serious-ness in its picturing of human nature, and the end shows some undue haste to get the poor old Don killed and wind up the story. There has been considerable controversy among critics as to whether the book was purely humorous in purpose or intended as a great allegory of human life. To some, the reading into the story of a serious motive spoils the whole im-pression of vital merriment which is its great charm. To others, the alle-gory of human ideal and aspiration constantly frustrated by the trivial and the prosaic, lifts the book to the plane of greatness. Its fundamental truth lies in its varied types of characters, drawn so evidently from life that the book is in marked contrast to the stilted figures fashionable in other literature of that day.

In his poem, "Lepanto," G. K. Chesterton closes with these lines:

Cervantes on his galley sets the sword back in the sheath . . .
And he sees across a weary land a struggling road in Spain,
Up which a lean and foolish knight forever rides in vain,
And he smiles, but not as Sultans smile, and settles back the blade . . .

Not with a smile of deceit, or of complacency, or of triumph known to sovereigns, but with a smile of kindly understanding, with a rueful smile at the futility of outworn ideals, he sends his lean knight along the highway.

DON QUIXOTE AND THE LIONS

Wherein is shown the furthest and highest point which the unexampled courage of Don Quixote reached or could reach; together with the happily achieved adventure of the lions.

When the author of this great history comes to relate what is set down in this chapter, he says he would have preferred to pass it over in silence, fearing it would not be believed, because here Don Quixote's madness reaches the confines of the greatest that can be conceived, and even goes a couple of bowshots beyond the greatest. But after all, though still under the same fear and appre-hension, he has recorded it without adding to the story or leaving out a particle of the truth, and entirely disregarding the charges of falsehood that might be brought against him; and he was right, for the truth may run fine but will not break, and always rises above falsehood as oil above water; and so, going on with his story, he says that when Don Quixote called out to Sancho to bring him his helmet, Sancho was buying some curds [1] the shepherds agreed to

1 **curds:** thickened milk forming thin cheese.

sell him, and flurried by the great haste his master was in did not know what to do with them or what to carry them in; so, not to lose them, for he had already paid for them, he thought it best to throw them into his master's helmet, and acting on this bright idea he went to see what his master wanted with him. He, as he approached, exclaimed to him, " Give me that helmet, my friend, for either I know little of adventures, or what I observe yonder is one that will, and does, call upon me to arm myself."

He of the green gaban,[2] on hearing this, looked in all directions, but could perceive nothing, except a cart coming towards them with two or three small flags, which led him to conclude it must be carrying treasure of the King's and he said so to Don Quixote. He, however, would not believe him, being always persuaded and convinced that all that happened to him must be adventures and still more adventures; so he replied to the gentleman. " He who is prepared has his battle half fought; nothing is lost by my preparing myself, for I know by experience that I have enemies, visible and invisible, and I know not when, or where, or at what moment, or in what shapes they will attack me "; and turning to Sancho he called for his helmet; and Sancho, as he had no time to take out the curds, had to give it just as it was. Don Quixote took it, and without perceiving what was in it thrust it down in hot haste upon his head; but as the curds were pressed and squeezed, the whey began to run all over his face and beard, whereat he was so startled that he cried out to Sancho, " Sancho, what's this? I think my head is softening, or my brains are melting, or I am sweating from head to foot! If I am sweating it is not indeed from fear. I am convinced beyond a doubt that the adventure which is about to befall me is a terrible one. Give me something to wipe myself with, if thou hast it, for this profuse sweat is blinding me."

Sancho held his tongue, and gave him a cloth, and gave thanks to God at the same time that his master had not found out what was the matter. Don Quixote then wiped himself, and took off his helmet to see what it was that made his head feel so cool, and seeing all that white mash inside his helmet he put it to his nose, and as soon as he had smelt it he exclaimed, " By the life of my lady Dulcinea del Toboso,[3] but it is curds thou hast put here, thou treacherous, impudent, ill-mannered squire! "

[2] **gaban:** a tunic. The knight wearing this is Don Diego de Miranda, an acquaintance made on the journey.

[3] **Dulcinea del Toboso:** a county girl, whom Don Quixote regarded as his chosen lady after the manner of knight-errantry.

To which, with great composure and pretended innocence, Sancho replied, " If they are curds let me have them, your worship, and I'll eat them; but let the devil eat them, for it must have been he who put them there. I dare to dirty your worship's helmet! You have guessed the offender finely! Faith, sir, by the light God gives me, it seems I must have enchanters too, that persecute me as a creature and limb of your worship, and they must have put that nastiness there in order to provoke your patience to anger and make you baste [4] my ribs as you are wont to do. Well, this time, indeed, they have missed their aim, for I trust to my master's good sense to see that I have got no curds or milk, or anything of the sort; and that if I had, it is in my stomach I would put it and not in the helmet."

" May be so," said Don Quixote. All this the gentleman was observing, and with astonishment, more especially when, after having wiped himself clean, his head, face, beard, and helmet, Don Quixote put it on, and settling himself firmly in his stirrups, easing his sword in the scabbard, and grasping his lance, he cried, " Now, come who will, here am I, ready to try conclusions with Satan himself in person! "

By this time the cart with the flags had come up, unattended by any one except the carter on a mule, and a man sitting in front. Don Quixote planted himself before it and said, " Whither are you going, brothers? What cart is this? What have you got in it? What flags are those? "

To this the carter replied, " The cart is mine. What is in it is a pair of fine caged lions, which the governor of Oran is sending to court as a present to his Majesty; and the flags are our lord the King's, to show that what is here is his property."

" And are the lions large? " asked Don Quixote.

" So large," replied the man who sat at the door of the cart, " that larger, or as large, have never crossed from Africa to Spain; I am the keeper, and I have brought over others, but never any like these. They are male and female; the male is in that first cage and the female in the one behind, and they are hungry now, for they have eaten nothing today, so let your worship stand aside, for we must make haste to the place where we are to feed them."

Hereupon, smiling slightly, Don Quixote exclaimed, " Lion-whelps to me! to me whelps of lions, and at such a time! Then, by God! those gentlemen who send them here shall see if I am a man to be

4 **baste:** beat.

frightened by lions. Get down, my good fellow, and as you are the keeper open the cages, and turn me out those beasts, and in the midst of this plain I will let them know who Don Quixote of La Mancha is, in spite and in the teeth of the enchanters who send them to me."

"So, so," said the gentleman to himself at this; "our worthy knight has shown of what sort he is; the curds, no doubt, have softened his skull and brought his brains to a head."

At this instant Sancho came up to him, saying, "Señor, for God's sake do something to keep my master, Don Quixote, from tackling these lions; for if he does they'll tear us all to pieces here."

"Is your master then so mad," asked the gentleman, "that you believe and are afraid he will engage such fierce animals?"

"He is not mad," said Sancho, "but he is venturesome."

"I will prevent it," said the gentleman; and going over to Don Quixote, who was insisting upon the keeper's opening the cages, he said to him, "Sir knight, knights-errant should attempt adventures which encourage the hope of a successful issue, not those which entirely withhold it; for valor that trenches upon temerity savors rather of madness than of courage; moreover, these lions do not come to oppose you, nor do they dream of such a thing; they are going as presents to his Majesty, and it will not be right to stop them or delay their journey."

"Gentle sir," replied Don Quixote, "you go and mind your tame partridge and your bold ferret, and leave every one to manage his own business; this is mine, and I know whether these gentlemen the lions come to me or not"; and then turning to the keeper he exclaimed, "By all that's good, sir scoundrel, if you don't open the cages this very instant, I'll pin you to the cart with this lance."

The carter, seeing the determination of this apparition in armor, said to him, "Please your worship, for charity's sake, señor, let me unyoke the mules and place myself in safety along with them before the lions are turned out; for if they kill them on me I am ruined for life, for all I possess is this cart and mules."

"O man of little faith," replied Don Quixote, "get down and unyoke; you will soon see that you are exerting yourself for nothing, and that you might have spared yourself the trouble."

The carter got down and with all speed unyoked the mules, and the keeper called out at the top of his voice, "I call all here to witness that against my will and under compulsion I open the cages and let the lions loose, and that I warn this gentleman that he will be accountable for all the harm and mischief which these beasts may do, and for my salary and dues as well. You, gentlemen, place yourselves in safety before I open, for I know they will do me no harm."

Once more the gentleman strove to persuade Don Quixote not to do such a mad thing, as it was tempting God to engage in such a piece of folly. To this, Don Quixote replied that he knew what he was about. The gentleman in return entreated him to reflect, for he knew he was under a delusion.

" Well, señor," answered Don Quixote, " if you do not like to be a spectator of this tragedy, as in your opinion it will be, spur your flea-bitten mare and place yourself in safety."

Hearing this, Sancho with tears in his eyes entreated him to give up an enterprise compared with which the one of the windmills,[5] and the awful one of the fulling mills,[6] and, in fact, all the feats he had attempted in the whole course of his life, were cakes and fancy bread. " Look ye, señor," said Sancho, " there's no enchantment here, nor anything of the sort, for between the bars and chinks of the cage I have seen the paw of a real lion, and judging by that I reckon the lion such a paw could belong to must be bigger than a mountain."

" Fear, at any rate," replied Don Quixote, " will make him look bigger to thee than half the world. Retire, Sancho, and leave me; and if I die here thou knowest our old compact; thou wilt repair to Dulcinea — I say no more." To these he added some further words that banished all hope of his giving up his insane project. He of the green gaban would have offered resistance, but he found himself ill-matched as to arms, and did not think it prudent to come to blows with a madman, for such Don Quixote had shown himself to be in every respect; and the latter, renewing his commands to the keeper and repeating his threats, gave warning to the gentleman to spur his mare, Sancho his Dapple, and the carter his mules, all striving to get away from the cart as far as they could before the lions broke loose. Sancho was weeping over his master's death, for this time he firmly believed it was in store for him from the claws of the lions; and he cursed his fate and called it an unlucky hour when he thought of taking service with him again; but with all his tears and lamentations he did not forget to thrash Dapple so as to put a good space between himself and the cart. The keeper, seeing that the fugitives were now some distance off, once more entreated and warned Don Quixote as he had entreated and warned him before; but he replied that he heard him, and that he

---

⁵ **windmills**: Don Quixote had been injured while attempting to tilt with the revolving arms of a windmill.

⁶ **fulling mills**: cloth mills.

need not trouble himself with any further warnings or entreaties, as they would be fruitless, and bade him make haste.

During the delay that occurred while the keeper was opening the first cage, Don Quixote was considering whether it would not be well to do battle on foot, instead of on horseback, and finally resolved to fight on foot, fearing that Rocinante [7] might take fright at the sight of the lions. He therefore sprang off his horse, flung his lance aside, braced his buckler on his arm, and drawing his sword, advanced slowly with marvelous intrepidity and resolute courage, to plant himself in front of the cart, commending himself with all his heart, first to God, and then to his lady Dulcinea.

It is to be observed, that on coming to this passage, the author of this veracious history breaks out into exclamations. " O doughty Don Quixote! high mettled past extolling! Mirror, wherein all the heroes of the world may see themselves! Second and modern Don Manuel de Leon,[8] once the glory and honor of Spanish knighthood! In what words shall I describe this dread exploit, by what language shall I make it credible to ages to come, what eulogies are there unmeet for thee, though they be hyperboles piled on hyperboles! On foot, alone, undaunted, high-souled, with but a simple sword, and that no trenchant blade of the Perrillo [9] brand, a shield, but no bright polished steel one, there stoodst thou, biding and awaiting the two fiercest lions that Afric's forests ever bred! Thy own deeds be thy praise, O valiant Manchegan,[10] and here I leave them as they stand, wanting the words wherewith to glorify them! "

Here the author's outburst came to an end, and he proceeded to take up the thread of his story, saying that the keeper, seeing that Don Quixote had taken up his position, and that it was impossible for him to avoid letting out the male without incurring the enmity of the fiery and daring knight, flung open the doors of the first cage, containing, as has been said, the lion, which was now seen to be of enormous size, and grim and hideous mien. The first thing he did was to turn round in the cage in which he lay, and protrude his claws, and stretch himself thoroughly. He next opened his mouth, and yawned very leisurely, and with near two palms'-length of tongue that he had thrust forth, he licked the dust out of his eyes and washed

---

[7] **Rocinante:** Don Quixote's " steed," in reality a broken old nag.

[8] **Don Manuel de Leon:** a fourteenth-century knight who fought against the Moors.

[9] **Perrillo:** a famous brand of sword made in Toledo, with a little dog (perrillo) cut on the blade as a trademark.

[10] **Manchegan:** a native of La Mancha, Don Quixote's home.

his face. Having done this, he put his head out of the cage and looked all round with eyes like glowing coals, a spectacle and demeanor to strike terror into temerity itself. Don Quixote merely observed him steadily, longing for him to leap from the cart and come to close quarters with him, when he hoped to hew him in pieces.

So far did his unparalleled madness go; but the noble lion, more courteous than arrogant, not troubling himself about silly bravado, after having looked all round, as has been said, turned about and presented his hind-quarters to Don Quixote, and very coolly and tranquilly lay down again in the cage. Seeing this, Don Quixote ordered the keeper to take a stick to him and provoke him to make him come out.

" That I won't," said the keeper; " for if I anger him, the first he'll tear to pieces will be myself. Be satisfied, sir knight, with what you have done, which leaves nothing more to be said on the score of courage, and do not seek to tempt fortune a second time. The lion has the door open; he is free to come out or not to come out; but as he has not come out so far, he will not come out today. The greatness of your worship's courage has been fully manifested already; no brave champion, so it strikes me, is bound to do more than challenge his enemy and wait for him on the field; if his adversary does not come, on him lies the disgrace, and he who waits for him carries off the crown of victory."

" That is true," said Don Quixote; " close the door, my friend, and let me have, in the best form thou canst, what thou hast seen me do, by way of certificate; to wit, that thou didst open for the lion, that I waited for him, that he did not come out, that I still waited for him, and that still he did not come out, and lay down again. I am not bound to do more. Enchantments avaunt, and God uphold the right, the truth, and true chivalry! Close the door as I bade thee, while I make signals to the fugitives that have left us, that they may learn this exploit from my lips."

The keeper obeyed, and Don Quixote, fixing on the point of his lance the cloth he had wiped his face with after the deluge of curds, proceeded to recall the others, who still continued to fly, looking back at every step, all in a body, the gentleman bringing up the rear. Sancho, however, happening to observe the signal of the white cloth, exclaimed, " May I die, if my master has not overcome the wild beasts, for he is calling to us."

They all stopped, and perceived that it was Don Quixote who was making signals, and shaking off their fears to some extent, they approached slowly until they were near enough to hear distinctly Don Quixote's voice calling to them. They returned at length to the cart, and as they came up, Don Quixote said to the carter, " Put your mules to once more, brother, and continue your journey; and do thou, Sancho, give him two gold crowns for himself and the keeper, to compensate for the delay they have incurred through me."

" That will I give with all my heart," said Sancho; " but what has become of the lions? Are they dead or alive? "

The keeper, then, in full detail, and bit by bit, described the end of the contest, exalting to the best of his power and ability the valor of Don Quixote, at the sight of whom the lion quailed, and would not and dared not come out of the cage, although he had held the door open ever so long; and showing how, in consequence of his having represented to the knight that it was tempting God to provoke the lion in order to force him out, which he wished to have done, he very reluctantly, and altogether against his will, had allowed the door to be closed.

" What dost thou think of this, Sancho? " said Don Quixote. " Are there any enchantments that can prevail against true valor? The enchanters may be able to rob me of good fortune, but of fortitude and courage they can not."

Sancho paid the crowns, the carter put to, the keeper kissed Don Quixote's hands for the bounty bestowed upon him, and promised to give an account of the valiant exploit to the King himself, as soon as he saw him at court.

" Then," said Don Quixote, " if his Majesty should happen to ask who performed it, you must say THE KNIGHT OF THE LIONS; for it is my desire that into this the name I have hitherto borne of Knight of the Rueful Countenance be from this time forward changed, altered, transformed, and turned; and in this I follow the ancient usage of knights-errant, who changed their names when they pleased, or when it suited their purpose."

The cart went its way, and Don Quixote, Sancho, and he of the green gaban went theirs. All this time, Don Diego de Miranda had not spoken a word, being entirely taken up with observing and noting all that Don Quixote did and said, and the opinion he formed was that he was a man of brains gone mad, and a madman on the verge of rationality. The first part of his history had not yet reached him, for, had he read it, the amazement with which his words and deeds filled him would have vanished, as he would then have understood the nature of his madness; but knowing nothing of it, he took him to be rational one moment, and crazy the next, for what he said was sensible, elegant, and well expressed, and what he did, absurd, rash, and foolish; and said he to himself, " What could be madder than putting on a helmet full of curds, and then persuading one's self that enchanters are softening one's skull; or what could be greater rashness and folly than wanting to fight lions tooth and nail? "

Don Quixote roused him from these reflections and this soliloquy by saying, "No doubt, Señor Don Diego de Miranda, you set me down in your mind as a fool and a madman, and it would be no wonder if you did, for my deeds do not argue anything else. But for all that, I would have you take notice that I am neither so mad nor so foolish as I must have seemed to you. A gallant knight shows to advantage bringing his lance to bear adroitly upon a fierce bull under the eyes of his sovereign, in the midst of a spacious plaza; a knight shows to advantage arrayed in glittering armor, pacing the lists before the ladies in some joyous tournament, and all those knights show to advantage that entertain, divert, and, if we may say so, honor the courts of their princes by warlike exercises, or what resemble them; but no greater advantage than all these does a knight-errant show when he traverses deserts, solitudes, cross-roads, forests, and mountains, in quest of perilous adventures, bent on bringing them to a happy and successful issue, all to win a glorious and lasting renown. To greater advantage, I maintain, does the knight-errant show bringing aid to some widow in some lonely waste, than the court knight dallying with some city damsel. All knights have their own special parts to play. Let the courtier devote himself to the ladies; let him add luster to his sovereign's court by his liveries; let him entertain poor gentlemen with the sumptuous fare of his table; let him arrange joustings, marshal tournaments, and prove himself noble, generous, and magnificent, and above all a good Christian, and so doing he will fulfill the duties that are especially his. But let the knight-errant explore the corners of the earth and penetrate the most intricate labyrinths; at each step let him attempt impossibilities; on desolate heaths let him endure the burning rays of the midsummer sun, and the bitter inclemency of the winter winds and frosts; let no lions daunt him, no monsters terrify him, no dragons make him quail; for to seek these, to attack those, and to vanquish all, are in truth his main duties. I, then, as it has fallen to my lot to be a member of knight-errantry, cannot avoid attempting all that to me seems to come within the sphere of my duties. Thus it was my bounden duty to attack those lions that I just now attacked, although I knew it to be the height of rashness; for I know well what valor is, that it is a virtue that occupies a place between two vicious extremes, cowardice and temerity; but it will be a lesser evil for him who is valiant to rise till he reaches the point of rashness, than to sink until he reaches the point of cowardice; for, as it is easier for the prodigal than for the miser to become generous, so it is easier for a rash man to prove truly valiant than for a coward to rise to true valor; and believe me, Señor Don Diego, in attempting adventures it is better to lose by a card too many than by a card too few; for to hear it said, ' such a knight is rash and daring,' sounds better than ' such a knight is timid and cowardly.' ''

" I protest, Señor Don Quixote," said Don Diego, " everything you have said and done is proved correct by the test of reason itself; and I believe, if the laws and ordinances of knight-errantry should be lost, they might be found in your worship's breast as in their own proper depository and muniment-house; [11] but let us make haste, for it grows late, and reach my village and house, where you shall take rest after your late exertions; for if they have not been of the body they have been of the spirit, and these sometimes tend to produce bodily fatigue."

" I take the invitation as a great favor and honor, Señor Don Diego," replied Don Quixote; and pressing forward at a better pace than before, at about two in the afternoon they reached the village and house of Don Diego, or, as Don Quixote called him, " The Knight of the Green Gaban."

(John Ormsby)

SUGGESTIONS FOR STUDY

1. Where does the Don impress you as simply a ridiculous, half-mad old man? Where does his conduct show elements of nobility and idealism? Does the author's interpolation on page 265 add to or detract from this impression?

2. Characterize Sancho. Where does he play up to the imagination of his master and where fight against it? If the story is to be regarded as an allegory of life, what would Sancho represent?

3. Compare these two characters with other famous master-and-servant combinations, such as Mr. Pickwick and Sam Weller, Shylock and Launcelot Gobbo, Petruchio and Grumio.

4. Does the humor of this episode lie primarily in the characters, the action, or the language? Or is it a balance of all three? Comment on the

[11] **muniment-house:** fortification.

contrast between the language of Don Quixote and that of the other characters. Does it strain your credulity to believe that the lions ignored the Don? Would this scene be effective on the screen? Discuss.

5. Vocabulary: intrepidity, eulogy, hyperboles.

LUIS DE GÓNGORA (1561–1627)

Original in everything, this native of Cordova set aside his father's name of Argote and assumed his mother's maiden name of Góngora. The reason is unknown, but one critic maintains that it was because he preferred the sound of the word. As a youth he attended the University of Salamanca and later took holy orders. At one time his conduct was under investigation, the charges being that he talked to his neighbors during church service, received actors at his house, attended bullfights, and wrote poetry on secular subjects. He defended himself in sprightly manner and escaped with a reprimand. The most significant thing in his life, however, was his sudden change in middle life from a simple, vivacious style, illustrated by the poem below, to an intricate and flowery style designed for the understanding of only the most cultured. Thus "gongorism" infected Spanish literature as "euphuism," which it somewhat resembled, did English literature. The chief earmarks of this style are abuse of Latin and Greek words, innumerable classical references, extravagant figures of speech and stilted sentence structure, all producing a combination so obscure as to require the services of a commentary. Even such antagonistic authors as Lope de Vega became tarred with the same stick. Eventually when simplicity of manner returned to literary favor the term "gongorism" became a word of reproach.

LET ME GO WARM

Let me go warm and merry still;
And let the world laugh, an' it will.

Let others muse on earthly things, —
The fall of thrones, the fate of kings,
And those whose fame the world doth fill;   5
Whilst muffins sit enthroned in trays,
And orange-punch in winter sways
The merry scepter of my days; —
And let the world laugh, an' it will.

2. an': if.

He that the royal purple wears   10
From the golden plate a thousand cares
   Doth swallow as a gilded pill;
On feasts like these I turn my back,
Whilst puddings in my roasting-jack
Besides the chimney hiss and crack; —   15
   And let the world laugh, an' it will.

And when the wintry tempest blows,
And January's sleets and snows
   Are spread o'er every vale and hill,
With one to tell a merry tale   20
O'er roasted nuts and humming ale,
I sit, and care not for the gale; —
   And let the world laugh, an' it will.

Let merchants traverse seas and lands,
For silver mines and golden sands;   25
   Whilst I beside some shadowy rill,
Just where its bubbling fountain swells,
Do sit and gather stones and shells,
And hear the tale the blackbird tells; —
   And let the world laugh, an' it will.   30

For Hero's sake the Grecian lover
The stormy Hellespont swam over:
   I cross, without the fear of ill,
The wooden bridge that slow bestrides
The Madrigal's enchanting sides,   35
Or barefoot wade through Yepes' tides; —
   And let the world laugh, an' it will.

But since the Fates so cruel prove,
That Pyramus should die of love,
   And love should gentle Thisbe kill;   40
My Thisbe be an apple-tart,
The sword I plunge into her heart
The tooth that bites the crust apart; —
   And let the world laugh, an' it will.

                    (Anonymous Translation)

31. **Grecian lover:** Leander, who was drowned while swimming across the Hellespont to see Hero. 35, 36. **Madrigal** and **Yepes:** small Spanish streams. 39, 40. **Pyramus** and **Thisbe:** ill-fated lovers, whose suicides resulted from a mischance at their appointed meeting.

LOPE DE VEGA (1562–1635)

Lope de Vega holds the world's record for literary output. In a life crowded with romantic episodes, he found time to turn out an incredible amount of writing, much of which has been lost. His most important writing lies in the field of drama, and the estimate of his number of full-length plays is fifteen hundred according to his own record, or eighteen hundred according to his friend and biographer. Besides these there are many short dramatic pieces, lyrics, narrative poems, novels, novelettes, religious meditations, and a history. It has been said that he could write verse as rapidly as a business man dictates letters. His biographer tells an anecdote of his collaborating with Lope de Vega on a play in which each was to have half of an act ready by a certain time. Lope rose at five, wrote his half of the act in verse, composed one hundred and fifty lines of lyric poetry, ate his breakfast and had been working in his garden for an hour when the friend arrived at eleven o'clock that same morning.

Naturally such writing, rich and varied as it is, shows the effect of haste. There is considerable repetition of plot and incident, and little real study of human nature. Though he did not originate, he securely established the " cloak and sword " drama. Love intrigues and duels on a point of honor form the basis of these melodramatic plays. The estimate of his contemporaries that he was the greatest writer of Spain is not borne out by modern criticism, which prefers flesh and blood people to fine figures spouting heroics.

The incidents of Lope de Vega's life are colorful enough. Born in Madrid of humble parents, he showed such precocity — for example, reading Latin at five and writing plays at twelve — that he was sent to the university by a patron. Later he was banished for misconduct, he fought duels, he eloped, he joined the Invincible Armada, he married twice, losing both wives and his son by death, he became a priest and figured in the Inquisition, he continued to write voluminously for the theater, he died after seventy-three years packed as full of living as ever a man has had.

A SONG OF THE VIRGIN MOTHER

As ye go through these Palm-trees,
O holy angels,
Sith sleepeth my child here
Still ye the branches.

O Bethlehem palm-trees   5
That move to the anger

3. **sith:** since.

Of winds in their fury,
Tempestuous voices,
Make ye no clamor,
Run ye less swiftly,   10
Sith sleepeth the child here
Still ye your branches.

He the divine child
Is here a-wearied
Of weeping the earth-pain,   15
Here for his rest would he
Cease from his mourning,
Only a little while,
Sith sleepeth this child here
Stay ye the branches.   20

Cold be the fierce winds,
Treacherous round him.
Ye see that I have not
Wherewith to guard him,
O angels, divine ones   25
That pass us a-flying,
Sith sleepeth my child here
Stay ye the branches.

(Ezra Pound)

TOMORROW

Lord, what am I, that, with unceasing care,
Thou didst seek after me, — that thou didst wait,
Wet with unhealthy dews, before my gate,
And pass the gloomy nights of winter there?
O, strange delusion, that I did not greet   5
Thy blest approach! and, O, to heaven how lost,
If my ingratitude's unkindly frost
Has chilled the bleeding wounds upon thy feet!
How oft my guardian angel gently cried,
" Soul, from thy casement look, and thou shalt see   10
How he persists to knock and wait for thee! "
And, O, how often to that voice of sorrow,
" Tomorrow we will open," I replied!
And when the morrow came, I answered still,
    " Tomorrow."   15

(Henry W. Longfellow)

SUGGESTIONS FOR STUDY

1. Point out marked difference in the moods of the three preceding poems. Which shows the new spirit of the Renaissance? How? Which still have a medieval flavor?

2. How does the meter of each of these lyrics suit the mood? The translators are both poets themselves. Show how the different metrical effects in their translations correspond to fundamental differences in their original poetry. Which sonnet form is used in "Tomorrow"? Another translation of "Let Me Go Warm" by Clinton is to be found in Northrup's *History of Spanish Literature*.

3. If you are not familiar with the stories of Hero and Leander, Pyramus and Thisbe, look them up in any book on Greek mythology. Read Shakespeare's burlesque on the latter story in Act V of *A Midsummer Night's Dream*. Compare the mood of Góngora's poem with R. L. Stevenson's "The Vagabond." What similarities and differences are there in the two poets' requirements for happiness?

4. What different impression do you gain of Lope de Vega from these two poems and the account of his life? During which part of his life do you imagine these were written?

PEDRO CALDERÓN DE LA BARCA (1600–1681)

With Calderón the Golden Age of Spanish literature saw the last of its great writers. He was the son of a nobleman from the north of Spain who held a position in the treasury department at Madrid, at the time of Pedro's birth. The boy was well educated, first at a Jesuit school, then at the University of Salamanca, where he proved himself a brilliant scholar. His young manhood followed the typical pattern of the day — attachment to the households of various noblemen and campaigns in Italy and Flanders up to 1635, when he was summoned to the court at Madrid as a successor to Lope de Vega. For the next fifteen years he lived the life of a courtier and playwright, his vogue being distinctly with the upper classes rather than the populace. His natural religious and philosophical bent led him in the early fifties to become a priest, after which he ceased to write secular comedy, but produced numerous *autos* to be played in honor of the Holy Sacrament. These little allegories somewhat resemble the morality plays of English literature in their use of abstract characters pointing a moral.

In contrast to Lope de Vega's output, Calderón's seems meager, but in comparison with English writers his one hundred and twenty full plays, eighty *autos* and twenty or more short pieces sound prodigious. Many more of his plays than of Lope de Vega's have been translated into English. Like his predecessor, he wrote historical dramas and "cloak and sword" plays. The latter were so ingeniously worked out in plot with such disregard of genuine human emotion or character study that they seem to a modern mind quite removed from actual life. Goethe said that his characters were like bullets all cast in the same mold. Calderón's great power lies in the poetry and philosophy underlying his dramas. Quotable lines and memorable passages abound in his works. Where he used the raw materials of Lope de Vega's plays as he did in one of his best, *The Mayor of Zalamea*, he has undoubtedly produced a more finished creation than his source.

LIFE IS A DREAM

One of the most celebrated of Caledrón's plays, *Life Is a Dream*, is based on the conflicting ideas of predestination and free will. As a child, Segismundo, the hero, has been isolated from human life by his father because of evil prophecies as to his future. An attempt to return him to court in youth proves that the prophecies about his character had foundation, and he is sent back to his tower in a drugged condition. When he wakens from his stupor he is convinced that his experience at the palace has been a dream. After a popular uprising has put Segismundo on the throne, his fear that he will again awake and find this life a dream causes him to overcome his evil nature and defeat the sinister prophecies. In the following famous passage (as often memorized by Spanish students as Hamlet's soliloquy is by English ones) the prince shows his mental confusion on the relation between dreams and life.

A dream it was in which I found myself.
And you that hail me now, then hailed me king,
In a brave palace that was all my own,
Within, and all without it, mine; until,
Drunk with excess of majesty and pride,   5
Methought I towered so big and swelled so wide
That of myself I burst the glittering bubble
Which my ambition had about me blown
And all again was darkness. Such a dream
As this, in which I may be walking now,   10
Dispensing solemn justice to you shadows,
Who make believe to listen; but anon
Kings, princes, captains, warriors, plume and steel,
Ay, even with all your airy theater,
May flit into the air you seem to rend   15
With acclamations, leaving me to wake

In the dark tower; or dreaming that I wake
From this that waking is; or this and that,
Both waking and both dreaming; such a doubt
Confounds and clouds our mortal life about.   20
But whether wake or dreaming, this I know
How dreamwise human glories come and go;
Whose momentary tenure not to break,
Walking as one who knows he soon may wake,
So fairly carry the full cup, so well   25
Disordered insolence and passion quell,
That there be nothing after to upbraid
Dreamer or doer in the part he played;
Whether tomorrow's dawn shall break the spell,
Or the last trumpet of the Eternal Day,   30
When dreaming, with the night, shall pass away.

                                        (*Edward Fitzgerald*)

SUGGESTIONS FOR STUDY

1. Have you ever experienced a feeling of unreality in the material things about you? Discuss.

2. Various aspects of the question, " What is reality? " enter into several of Shakespeare's famous speeches. Reread Hamlet's " To be or not to be," Macbeth's " dagger speech," Jacques' " All the world's a stage " (*As You Like It*), Prospero's " We are such stuff as dreams are made on " (*The Tempest*), and show how they have something in common with Segismundo's soliloquy.

TOMÁS DE IRIARTE (1750–1791)

The eighteenth century was conspicuously sterile in Spanish literature. After the giants of the seventeenth century, Cervantes, Lope de Vega, and Calderón, the writers of the next hundred years seem mere pigmies, imitating the French preciseness, which did not sit well upon the Spanish temperament. *The Oxford Book of Spanish Verse* includes only four poets for the whole century. Of these Tomás de Iriarte, a native of the island of Tenerife, is the most interesting to the modern reader through his animal fables which suggest the French model of La Fontaine, but yet have individuality and humor of their own, with a neatness of phrase typical of the eighteenth century.

Tomás had a rather unhappy life. First embroiled in literary quarrels which the eighteenth century took so seriously, then condemned to secret penance by the Inquisition for teaching infidel principles, and finally pursued by the gout in old age, he may be forgiven for the vinegar in some of his poetry, such as " The Ass and the Flute."

THE ASS AND THE FLUTE

From the *Fábulas literarias*

You must know that this ditty,
  This little romance,
Be it dull, be it witty,
  Arose from mere chance.

Near a certain inclosure,   5
  Not far from a manse,
An ass, with composure,
  Was passing by chance.

As he went along prying,
  With sober advance,   10
A shepherd's flute lying,
  He found there by chance.

Our amateur started
  And eyed it askance,
Drew nearer, and snorted   15
  Upon it by chance.

The breath of the brute, Sir,
  Drew music for once;
It entered the flute, Sir,
  And blew it by chance.   20

" Ah! " cried he, in wonder,
  " How comes this to pass?
Who will now dare to slander
  The skill of an ass? "

And asses in plenty   25
  I see at a glance,
Who, one time in twenty,
  Succeed by mere chance.

                                    (*T. Roscoe*)

SUGGESTIONS FOR STUDY

1. Compare this with the Fable of La Fontaine (page 82) and other animal fables you know. Can you give any concrete examples to prove the point of the fable?

2. How does the style of this poem reflect the general fashion of the eighteenth century? Does its tone remind you of any English writers of that time? If so, discuss. What is the effect of the recurring phrase at the end of each stanza? How do you like the sound of the same rhyme running through the entire poem?

JOSÉ ZORRILLA (1817–1893)

" I shot up," says Zorrilla of himself, " like a poisonous herb beside the tomb of an evil doer." This describes his dramatic gesture which made the public of Madrid aware of his existence. Larra, a well-known writer of the day, had committed suicide at the age of twenty-eight. At the funeral Zorrilla, a down-at-the-heels youth of twenty, rushed forward and read a highly emotional tribute to the deceased. Zorrilla was bohemian in his taste, prolific in his writing, and unfortunate in his marriage. His wife, a woman old enough to be his mother, proved so difficult a companion that he sacrificed the success of his playwriting to go abroad, spending considerable time in Mexico. On his return at about the age of fifty he was honored by election to the Spanish Academy, but his best writing days were over.

He is one of the chief Spanish representatives of the Romantic Movement which swept Europe in the early nineteenth century. His dramas did for history in Spain what Scott's novels did in England — made it relive as a glorious pageant. Zorrilla turned largely to seventeenth-century writers for his themes. One of his best plays is *Don Juan* based on the play of Tirso de Molina, a contemporary of Lope de Vega. This character has been handed down in Spanish literature from generation to generation and still appears in various guises in modern works. Zorrilla's play is the most popular version of them all, and is still acted annually on All Souls' Day (November 2) in Spain and most Spanish-speaking countries.

THE BULL AND THE PICADOR

If one were enumerating the elements which go to make up the " local color " of Spain, bullfighting would inevitably appear on the list, since only Spanish-speaking countries have taken up this sport to any extent, but with them it has become the national pastime. When Northerners express distaste for it as a brutalizing sport, the Spaniards retort that it is no more so than prize fighting and hunting in which Americans and English indulge. Bullfighting plays a major part in the novel of Blasco Ibáñez called *Blood and Sand,* and in *Death in the Afternoon* by the American, Ernest Hemingway. It enters incidentally into many other pieces, especially the story of Carmen, which most Americans know through the opera.

> Pawing the earth, and snorting in his rage
> The Bull is tossing up the torrid sand;
> The while the horseman's eye serene and bland
> Seeks out a point for his red lance to gauge.
> Steadied to take the charge, the fight to wage,   5
> The picador holds his impatient stand;
> His face, for all its blackness, whiter fanned
> To anger as the bull obstructs the stage.
> He hesitates; the Spaniard jeers at him;
> He shakes his horned front; he tears the earth,   10
> Heaving great breaths and straining every limb;
> The taunter urges him to prove his worth;
> Sudden he charges, fails, and bellows grim,
> His shoulder bleeding, the great crowd in mirth!

> *(Thomas Walsh)*

SUGGESTIONS FOR STUDY

1. How does this description make you feel toward a bullfight? Would you say the situation was treated romantically or realistically? Does the attitude of the crowd at the end seem natural or strange to you?

2. Does a sonnet seem to you an appropriate medium for such a description? Why or why not?

3. Zorrilla has been compared to Byron. How does this poem resemble the description of the Roman gladiatorial contest in *Childe Harold's Pilgrimage*? What romantic hero of Spain did both poets use in a major work? What other points of similarity do you find in their lives?

PEDRO ANTONIO DE ALARCÓN (1833–1891)

The short story in Spain has played an insignificant rôle compared to the novel. While American literature can show dozens of names which have won literary reputation primarily through the short story, Spanish literature has scarcely any. But Pedro Antonio de Alarcón might be considered one of those exceptions to the common pattern, for his short stories and novelettes excel his longer attempts.

He was a native of colorful Andalusia in southern Spain. Though in early life a radical, he later developed a more conservative political view, and became minister to the Scandinavian countries and Councilor of State. Alarcón was neither a thoroughgoing romanticist nor a pronounced realist. In subject matter he was more like the former, with rampant imagination and impossible situations, but his style had a brilliant incisiveness which bore a more modern note. He knew how to tell a good tale with a rich vein of wit and no mawkish sentimentality. *The Three-Cornered Hat*, his masterpiece, and one of the greatest humorous stories in any language, is a picture of Andalusian life, while *The Child of the Ball* is the best known of his later novels, which concerned themselves more with political problems. In the short historical story he holds his supreme position unchallenged.

THE GYPSY'S PROPHECY

I don't remember what day of August in the year 1816 it was that there came to the doors of the captain-general of Granada a certain ragged and uncouth gypsy, seventy years of age, by trade a sheep-shearer, by name Heredia, astride of a lean and shambling black donkey whose whole equipment consisted of a halter about its neck. The man, immediately on dismounting, said:

" I want to see the captain-general."

Needless to say such presumption awoke in turn the resistance of the sentinel, the laugh of the orderlies, and the doubt and hesitancy of the *aides-de-camp*,[1] before he was brought to the notice of the Most Excellent Señor Don Eugenio Portocarrero, then captain-general of the ancient kingdom of Granada; but as that dignitary was a man of kindly disposition, and already knew of Heredia, renowned for his tricks, his bargains, and his love for his neighbor's goods, order was given to let the gypsy enter.

Once within the office, he fell on his knees, exclaiming, " Blessed be Mary, Most Holy, and long life to your honor, ruler of this little world."

" Get up and leave off ceremony and say to me what you have to tell," replied the count with seeming severity.

Heredia at once drew a long face, and said, " Well, my lord, I have come that the thousand *reales* [2] may be given me."

" What thousand *reales?* "

---

[1] **aides-de-camp:** officers who transmit the general's orders.
[2] **reales:** Spanish coins worth about five cents each.

" Those offered a few days ago by prociamation to any one bringing information about Parrón."

" Indeed!   You knew him, then? "

" No, sir."

" Well? "

" I know him now."

" How? "

" Very simply; I tracked him, I saw him, I bring the information, I claim the reward."

" Are you sure you have seen him? " said the captain-general, with an interest that overcame his doubt.

The gypsy burst out laughing, and said: " It's very evident that your honor thinks ' this gypsy is like them all, and wants to cheat me.'   May God never forgive me if I lie!   I saw Parrón yesterday."

" But do you realize the importance of what you are saying?   Do you know that for years we have pursued this monster, this bloody bandit, whom nobody knows or has ever seen?   Do you know that every day, in different parts of the *sierra*,[3] he robs wayfarers and then shoots them, for, as he says, dead men tell no tales; and by this means only has he escaped being brought to justice?   Finally, do you know that to see Parrón means death? "

The gypsy laughed again, and said: " Doesn't your honor know that what a gypsy cannot do, no one on earth can?   Does any one know when our laughing or crying is real?   Does your honor know a fox as tricky as we are?   I repeat, general, that not only have I seen Parrón, but I have talked with him."

" Where? "

" On the road to Tózar."

" Give me proof."

" Listen, your honor!   Yesterday morning, eight days since, my donkey and I fell into the hands of some robbers.   They bound me fast, and led me through some bewildering hollows till we came to the clearing where the bandits camped; a cruel suspicion laid hold on me. ' Can these be Parrón's people? '   I was constantly asking myself; ' If so, there's no remedy, for this devil has decreed that eyes that have seen his face shall never see another.'

" While I was thus cogitating, there approached me a man, strangely but elegantly dressed, who, slapping me on the shoulder, said, ' Friend!   I am Parrón! '

" To hear this and fall backward was one and the same thing.   The

---

[3] **sierra:** an irregular ridge of mountains and rocks.

bandit burst out laughing. I arose trembling, fell on my knees, and cried out in every tone of voice I could muster, ' Blessed be thy soul, king of men! Who would not have known thee by the princely bearing God has given thee! May there be mothers to bear more such sons! Let me kiss you, my son! May this little gypsy die in torment if he was not wishing to meet you and tell your fortune, and kiss your lordly hands. Behold me at your service. Do you want to know how to trade dead donkeys for live ones? Do you want to sell your old horses for the price of young ones? Do you want to teach French to a mule? ' "

The Count of Montijo could not suppress a laugh. Then he asked, " And what said Parrón to all this; what did he do? "

" The same as your honor, he laughed with all his might."

" And you? "

" I, my lord, laughed too, while tears as big as oranges ran down my cheeks."

" Proceed! "

" Presently he held out his hand to me, and said, ' Friend, you are the only man of talent that has fallen into my power; all the others have had the bad taste to annoy me by weeping and wailing and the like nonsense, which puts me into a bad humor; you, alone, have made me laugh, and if it were not for these tears — '

" ' What? Good Lord, they are for joy! '

" ' I believe it. Devil knows it's the first time for six or seven years that I have laughed; truth is, I haven't wept either. But let us hasten. Eh, boys? '

" For Parrón to say this, and for me to be surrounded by a ring of blunderbusses [4] was quicker than a wink. ' Lord, have mercy on me! ' I began to screech.

" ' Halt! ' cried Parrón. ' We are not ready for this yet. I called you to find out what you took from this man.'

" ' A donkey with his hide on.'

" ' Any money? '

" ' Three *duros* [5] and seventy *reales*.'

" ' Now, then, leave us alone,' and they all withdrew.

" ' Now, tell me my fortune,' said the robber, extending his hand to me. I took hold of it and thought a moment. I knew I was in a position to speak freely, so I said to him, with all the conviction of

---

[4] **blunderbusses:** obsolete short guns capable of firing several balls at once.
[5] **duros:** dollars.

my heart: ' Parrón, sooner or later, whether you take my life or leave it to me, you will die on the gallows! '

" ' I know that already,' answered the bandit with perfect calmness. ' Tell me when! '

" I began to consider. This man, said I to myself, is going to free me; tomorrow I'll be in Granada, and peach [6]; the next day they'll take him; then the trial will begin. ' Do you ask when? ' I said, aloud. ' Then, take notice, it will be during next month.'

" Parrón shuddered and so did I, fearing my love of fortune-telling would be my death.

" ' Look you, gypsy,' replied Parrón, very deliberately, ' you will remain in my power, and if by the end of next month they do not hang me, I will hang you, as sure as they hanged my father. If I die by that time, you will go free.'

" ' Much obliged,' said I to myself, ' to pardon me after death,' and I repented for having made the time so short. We stayed at the aforesaid camp, and I was locked up in a cave, while Parrón mounted his mare and took the track through the bushes."

" All right," said the Count, " I understand, Parrón is dead; you are free; and therefore you know his whereabouts."

" Quite the contrary, my general! Parrón is alive! And now comes the blackest part of my story.

" A week passed without the captain coming to see us, and, as far as I could make out, he had not shown himself in the neighborhood since the evening I told his fortune; a thing not at all extraordinary, as my guards told me. For, do you know, the chief goes to hell occasionally, and doesn't return till it suits him. The fact is, we know nothing whatever of him during these long absences. About this time, by force of entreaty, and having told the fortunes of the band, prognosticating freedom from hanging and comfortable old age for all, I had succeeded in getting them to take me out of the cave, evenings, and bind me to a tree, for I was smothering with heat in the cell. Needless to say, there was a pair of watchers continually at my side.

" One evening, about six o'clock, the robbers who had been on ' duty ' by command of Parrón's lieutenant returned to camp, bringing with them a miserable reaper, forty to fifty years old, manacled, and crying fit to break one's heart. ' Give me back my twenty *duros!* ' he said. ' Ah, if you only knew what it cost me to earn them: a whole summer's reaping in the sun! A whole summer away from

[6] **peach:** inform the authorities.

wife and children! and so I scraped together by my toil and self-denial this sum, that we might live this winter, and that on reaching home I might embrace them, and pay the debts the unfortunate ones have contracted, so that they might live. Ought I to lose this money, which is a fortune to me? Pity, gentlemen! Give me my twenty *duros* for the sake of the most Holy Mary of Sorrows! '

" A mocking laugh answered the plaints of the old man. Bound as I was to the tree I shook with horror! For gypsies, too, have families.

" ' Don't be a fool! ' finally said a bandit, going to the reaper. ' You do wrong in thinking of money when more important matters should occupy your thoughts.'

" ' How? ' said the reaper, not supposing there could be a greater misfortune than his children going without bread.

" ' You are in Parrón's hands.'

" ' Parrón? I don't know him — never heard of him; I come a long way; I belong in Alicante,[7] and was reaping in Sevilla.' [8]

" ' But, my friend, Parrón means death. Everyone that falls into our hands must die; therefore, make your will in two minutes, and your peace with God in the next two. Make ready! Aim! You have four minutes.'

" ' I am going to improve them. Hear me for pity's sake.'

" ' Speak.'

" ' I have six children and one unfortunate — widow, I will say, since I must die, for I read in your eyes that you are worse than wild beasts — yes, worse — for beasts of the same species do not destroy each other. Oh! pardon! I know not what I say. Gentlemen, some one of you must be a father! Is there not a father among you? Do you know what it is to have children starving all winter? Do you know what it is for a mother to see the children of her blood die, crying, " I am hungry; I am cold "? Gentlemen, I don't want to live without them; for what would life be to me? — a chain of toil and privation. But I must live for my children's sake — oh, my children, children of my heart! '

" The father dragged himself along the ground and turned his face to the robbers. Such a face! It seemed like one of those saints that King Nero [9] threw to the tigers, as the preachers say. The robbers

---

[7] **Alicante:** town on the coast about 200 miles northeast of Granada.

[8] **Sevilla:** town about 150 miles west of Granada.

[9] **Nero:** Roman emperor (37–68 A.D.) famous for persecution of early Christians.

felt something stir within their breasts; then they looked at one another, and, seeing all were of one accord, one made bold to say — ”

" What said he? " asked the captain-general, deeply affected by the story.

" He said, ' Comrades, what we are about to do must never be known to Parrón.'

" ' Never! Never! ' muttered the rest of the bandits.

" ' Go thy way, good man,' said another, almost weeping, and I made signs to the reaper that he should instantly go.

" ' Quick! March! ' they said, and all turned their backs. The reaper held out his hand beseechingly.

" ' Aren't you satisfied? ' growled one. ' Do you want your money, besides? Go! Go! Do not try our patience! '

" The poor father went away weeping, and soon was out of sight.

" Perhaps a half hour later, which was taken up by the bandits swearing one another not to tell the captain they had freed a man, there suddenly appeared Parrón, leading the reaper alongside his mare.

" The bandits fell back astounded. Parrón dismounted, leisurely, unslung his two-barrelled carbine,[10] and aiming at his comrades said, ' Fools! Idiots! I know not why I do not shoot every one of you! Quick! give back to this man the twenty *duros* you took from him! ' The robbers produced the money and gave it to the reaper, who cast himself at the feet of the bandit chief who had so kind a heart.

" Parrón said to him, ' By the peace of God! without your directions I never should have found them. Now, you see you mistrusted me without cause. I have fulfilled my promise — you have your twenty *duros*. Now be off! '

" The reaper kissed him again and again, and departed full of joy; but he had gone hardly fifty paces when his benefactor called him anew, and the poor man hastened to retrace his steps.

" ' What is your command? ' said he, anxious to do a service to him who had restored happiness to his family.

" ' Do you know Parrón? ' asked the man himself.

" ' I know him not.'

" ' You mistake,' said the chief, ' I am he! '

" The reaper stood stupefied. Parrón brought his carbine to his cheek and fired both barrels at the reaper, who fell rolling on the ground.

" ' May you be accursed,' were the only words he spoke. During

---

[10] **carbine:** a short, light musket.

the terror that blinded me, I felt the tree to which I was bound quiver slightly, and knew my bonds were loose. One of the balls after having wounded the reaper, hit the cord which held me fast, and cut it. I concealed my freedom and waited a chance for escape. Meantime, Parrón, pointing to the reaper, said to his men, ' Now you can rob him. You pack of idiots! you lot of fools! to free this man that he might go as he did, howling along the highway! Fortunately it was I that met him, and learned what had happened, for had it been the soldiers, he would have shown them the way to this camp, same as he did to me, and we would all have been in prison by this. See the result of robbing and not killing; but enough of preaching, bury this body before it rot.'

" While the robbers were digging a grave, Parrón was lunching, with his back to me. Little by little I moved from the tree, and slipped down into a hollow nearby. It was already night, and shielded by the darkness, I set out with all haste. By the starlight I found my donkey, who was quietly feeding, tied to an ash tree. I mounted him and never stopped till I got here. Therefore, my Lord, give me the thousand *reales*, and I will put you on Parrón's track, who, by the by, has kept my three-and-a-half *duros*."

The gypsy, having given a description of the bandit, afterward received the promised reward, and departed from the general's office, leaving the count and a person then present, from whom I had these details, utterly confounded. It remains to be seen whether Heredia guessed aright when he foretold Parrón's destiny.

Fifteen days after the scene we have just described took place, about nine in the morning, a large crowd of idlers attended the assembling of two companies of soldiers in the streets of San Juan de Dios and part of that of San Felipe, in the aforesaid capital city, who, about a half-hour later, were to set out in quest of Parrón, the description of his hiding-place, his person, and his comrades having finally been approved by the Count of Montijo. The interest and excitement of the public was extraordinary, and none the less so was the soberness with which the soldiers took leave of families and friends before starting on so important an expedition, such fear had Parrón aroused throughout the old kingdom of Granada.

" Seems we are ready to fall in," said one soldier to his comrade.
" But I don't see Cabo-López."
" That's strange, too, for he was always on hand first of any when there was talk of hunting Parrón. He hated him with all his heart."

"So, don't you know what has happened?" said a third one, joining in the talk.

"Hello! this must be our new man. How do you like our company?"

"Very well, indeed," answered the one inquired of, a man of pale complexion and fine shape, which was partly hidden by the uniform.

"What were you saying?" asked the first.

"Ah yes! Cabo-López is dead," replied the pale-faced one.

"Manuel! What are you talking about? This can't be. I, myself, saw López this morning, surely as I see you now."

He called Manuel coolly said, "Half an hour ago Parrón killed him."

"Parrón! Where?"

"Right here in Granada. They found López's dead body on the Dog's Hill."

All kept silence except Manuel, who began to whistle a patriotic air.

"Eleven soldiers gone in six days," said a sergeant. "Parrón means to exterminate us! But how comes it that he is in Granada? Aren't we going to look for him in the Sierra-de-Loja?"

Manuel ceased whistling, and said with his usual recklessness, "An old woman, who saw the deed, says, that since he killed López, she hopes if we look for him we may have the pleasure of seeing him."

"Comrade! aren't you pretty bold to speak of Parrón with such contempt?"

"Well, is Parrón more than a man!" asked Manuel with a shrug.

Just then "Fall in!" was shouted by various tongues. The two companies formed and roll call was begun.

Now it happened that at the moment Heredia was going by, and, like every one else, stopped to admire the soldiery.

It seemed as if Manuel, the new soldier, gave a start, and fell back a little so as to hide behind his comrades, when Heredia caught sight of him, gave a yell, and, jumping as if he had stepped on a viper, started to run up San Yeronimos Street.

Manuel raised his musket and aimed at the gypsy, but another soldier was quick enough to strike the gun up, and the shot was spent in the air.

"He's crazy! Manuel has gone mad! A soldier has lost his wits!" was shouted in succession by the lookers-on, and officers, sergeants, and countrymen fell on the man, who was struggling to escape, and whom, after they had subdued him, they plied with ques-

tions, accusations, and insults which drew from him no response whatever. Meantime, Heredia had been seized by some passers-by, who,
seeing him running and hearing the musket-shot, took him for a male-
factor.

" Lead me to the captain-general," said the gypsy; " I must speak
to the Count of Montijo."

" Count of Montijo, indeed! Whom have you killed? " asked his
captors. " Here comes the guard and they'll know what to do with
you."

" I think so, too," said Heredia, " but be careful not to let Parrón
kill me."

" What do you mean by Parrón? What's the man talking about? "

" Come and you will see," and, so saying, the gypsy made them
take him to the commandant of the platoon, and pointing to Manuel,
he said: " Commandant, this is Parrón, and I am the gypsy who two
weeks ago gave a description of him to the Count of Montijo."

" Parrón! Parrón is taken! A soldier proved to be Parrón! "
shouted the crowd.

" No doubt about it," said the commandant, reading the order
given him by the captain-general. " We certainly have been very
stupid; but who would have thought of looking for the robber chief
among the very soldiers that were searching for him? "

" Fool that I am," Parrón was saying to himself, regarding the
gypsy with eyes like a wounded lion's. " He is the only man to whom
I ever granted life. I deserve what has happened."

The week following, Parrón was executed, and so the gypsy's
prophecy was literally fulfilled.

SUGGESTIONS FOR STUDY

1. In what sense might this be called a romantic story? How does the
picture of Parrón depart from the romantic treatment of bandits? What
other elements of realism do you observe?

2. Did you find the method of narration by story within story confusing? How else might the story have been handled? Discuss.

3. If you were preparing this story for dramatic presentation, would
you have the first part told by the gypsy or acted directly? Why? Into
how many scenes would the play fall? What dramatic elements do you
find throughout the story?

4. How does this story compare with other bandit tales you have read?
With the typical American " Western " story? With the modern " crime "
story?

JACINTO BENAVENTE (1866–1954)

As in the seventeenth century Spain had two great dramatists, Lope de Vega and Calderón, so in the last one hundred years she has again found two outstanding playwrights. José Echegaray held the center of the stage in the seventies and eighties with plays that were technically excellent, but, to present-day notions, bombastic and full of forced emotionalism. Some of his plays were acted throughout Europe and America, and he was the first Spanish writer to win the Nobel prize.

But from the advent of Benavente in the nineties, Echegaray's reputation began to wane. The new playwright had a keen insight into character, a ready wit, and a determined avoidance of hackneyed situations which made the older writer's characters seem like straw figures. Benavente's plays are modern in every way. The backgrounds are big hotels, railroad trains, and homes of the newest mode. The mockery with which he uncovers pretense and abuses of all sorts reminds one in some ways of George Bernard Shaw, though his plays are better constructed and less talky than Shaw's. Benavente is more successful in picturing the wealthy aristocratic classes of Madrid among whom his own life was cast, than in his plays of peasants or small townspeople. The tone of his plays is urbane, cosmopolitan, and sophisticated. Many of them center around a general theme such as the high cost of living, the corruption of politics, or the folly of struggling " to keep up with the Joneses," as we say in America.

In sharp contrast to these comedies of actuality, we have from his pen a group of fantasies, some of which are classed as children's plays but have an underlying significance far over the heads of children. For instance, one of the best known, " The Prince Who Learned Everything Out of Books," shows a young prince taking literally the fairy stories on which he has been educated. But it needs an adult mind to appreciate the satire of having the ogre prove to be a social oppressor, and of making one king boast of his twenty-five-year friendship for another king with only three wars between them. Perhaps Benavente inherited some of his interest in children from his physician father, who specialized in children's diseases.

The author's versatility is astonishing. He wrote occasional melodramas, historical plays, and farces, in addition to his more typical fantasy and social satire. Of the hundred and fifty plays he produced, about a score have been translated into English. At the time Echegaray received the Nobel prize, some of the younger generation were skeptical of his deserving it, but when it was given to Benavente in 1922 there was supreme satisfaction expressed throughout Spain.

NO SMOKING

This farce, one of the few translated one-act plays of Benavente, is typical of his modern settings, his sense of " situation," and his lively dialogue. It gives, however, little conception of the cumulative power of his full-length plays.

The one-act play has received more attention in Spain than in most countries. In some Spanish cities there are theaters devoted entirely to this form, and in all the theaters short plays are used as curtain raisers and entr'actes for full-length dramas. This prolongs the program beyond what we are accustomed to, and the audience comes and goes during the intervals, much as in our "movie" houses. The climate of Spain also affects the theater program, for with the universal *siesta* during the heat of the afternoon and dinner postponed till about nine o'clock, one goes to the theater at ten and stays as long as desired during a series of plays lasting into the early morning hours. The Spanish are an essentially dramatic people, and their love for the theater has resulted in a tremendous body of drama. Though most of this is of no lasting value, Spain has contributed her share, or perhaps more, to the list of the world's great dramatists.

In reading this play, the student must picture the European train, which differs from our typical railroad coach. Each car consists of a series of compartments accommodating eight or ten people. These compartments open directly upon the station platform, and there is no means of moving from one into another except when the train is standing in a station. Since the platform is level with the compartment floor, it is easy to step out for exercise and to get food and drink from the platform lunch wagons and water carriers. While the train is moving, the conductor can go from one compartment to another on a narrow step running alongside the car.

Characters

A Lady	A Conductor
A Young Lady	Several Voices
A Gentleman	

A compartment in a first-class railway carriage. The GENTLE-MAN *is seated alone when the curtain rises.*

A Voice. [*Outside*] Three minutes! The train stops three minutes! —

Another Voice. Water! Fresh water! Who wants water?

Another Voice. Here, girl! Water!

The Lady *and the* Young Lady *enter.*

Lady. Hurry up; it only stops a minute. I thought we'd die in that compartment. — See if we have everything. One, two — Where's the basket? The basket! —

Young Lady. Here it is, mamma.

Lady. Gracious! What a fright you did give me! The one thing, too, your Aunt asked us to bring with us — She would always have insisted that we lost it on purpose. — Good afternoon.

Gentleman. Good afternoon. — I beg your pardon. But as I was riding alone, although it says " No Smoking " —

Lady. For goodness' sake, don't stop upon our account! Smoke as much as you want to — it doesn't bother me, or my daughter, either. We are used to it. Her poor father, my first husband, — he is now in glory, — was never without a cigar in his mouth. He bit off one to light it with the butt of the other. — And my second husband, who now rests in peace, they were alike as two buttons; you could scarcely tell the difference. — I had a difficulty at one time myself, a suffocating feeling, all stuffed up here, — terrible distress, — and the doctors were telling me that it was asthma and that it wasn't asthma — Well, I smoked them myself — aromatic cigarettes — which didn't do me any good, either, by the way. I can say that. So you see as far as we are concerned — My dear, what on earth are you doing with that basket? Don't you see that you've got it with the holes against the wall, and the poor animal will be smothered to death? It's a cat; yes, sir, an aunt of my daughter — she requested us to bring it with us, as a favor to her — She is my sister-in-law — It began to howl the moment the conductor came after the tickets — And this poor child had to sit there and sing and laugh so as to drown it — so the conductor couldn't tell who was howling. I should say it was a favor!

A Voice. [*Outside*] All aboard! Passengers who are going will please take the train!

Lady. They are afraid of leaving us behind. However, we are off now — But you needn't think you are inconveniencing us. You can't annoy us by smoking. Before we changed we were traveling in the ladies' compartment, and we transferred to this one as soon as we could because there were people in it one simply couldn't travel with; they were out of the question. You would think that people who traveled first class would have manners, that they would know something. But not a bit of it! Believe me, if you want to find out what people are like, you have to play cards with them, or watch them eat, or go traveling. You'll find out then soon enough. There was a woman in that compartment — I say she was a woman because I don't know what else to call her — with her companion — she must have been her companion; she was with her anyway — well, I can tell you I was mortified. I was ashamed — such a conversation! Between the two of them! It was just as if they had been in their own parlor! As far as that goes, you know, speaking for myself, a widow twice, it was nothing to me; but before my daughter! — I had to make her sit with her head out of the window all the way. It was pretty chilly for her. You can see for yourself she has taken cold. And she's got a cinder in her eye, too — worse luck! — Her eyes are the best part of her.

Young Lady. For mercy's sake, mamma! What will this gentleman think? I hope you don't mind mamma.

Lady. Keep quiet, for heaven's sake! Such women! And they didn't stop there. One of them, tired of gabbling, I suppose, takes out a book if you please, and settles herself down to read. — And what a book! There was a woman on the cover in her chemise, fanning herself.

Gentleman. Evidently hot —

Lady. You needn't tell me it was hot.

[*The* GENTLEMAN, *with a detached air, reaches for a book which has been lying on the seat beside him.*]

Gentleman. You can't always be sure. Sometimes the publishers — so as to attract attention — And then it turns out that there is nothing in the book, after all.

Lady. You needn't tell me. Why, didn't she begin to laugh right out loud, and the other one wanted to know what she was laughing at? And she started in to read to her, at the top of her voice. It was too much for me this time. There we sat in that compartment, helpless, wondering what was coming next. I made up my mind I'd have to ask them to show some consideration for the girl. I'd better have held my tongue! How they did go for us! I didn't ring the alarm and stop the train because I was too excited. It isn't safe to travel with people who begin to gabble and talk the minute they lay eyes on you, and tell you all their private affairs just as if you were one of the family. People ought to be careful what they say. The very least that happens is that they tell you some scandal or dishonesty or something of the sort about Mr. So and So — that he is this way or that he is that way, and the next thing you know he turns out to be your father. And a person who would talk like that about your father, what wouldn't he say about your uncle or your cousins or any one else in the family? And there you are!

The CONDUCTOR *enters.*

Conductor. Good afternoon.

Lady. The tickets, child! What have you done with the tickets?

Young Lady. Why, you have them, mamma!

Lady. No, my dear; I gave them to you — the last time they came round. I am so sorry — [*The cat begins to howl.*] My dear! [*The* YOUNG LADY *begins to sing.*] I can't find them; you must have them! What's that? Ah, yes! Of course! Wait a minute. Here they are —

Conductor. Thank you. Good afternoon. [*He goes out.*]

Young Lady. What did you ask me for? You know perfectly well that I couldn't stop singing.

Lady. I wonder what that animal has against the conductor? I told you it was a nuisance; now judge for yourself. If it wasn't that my relations with my sister-in-law are a little bit strained — you understand — I don't want to give her a chance to talk — Well, the fact is she wasn't pleased because I married a second time. Just as if I would forget my first husband any sooner on that account! Put yourself in my place. Suppose you have been a widow of twenty-six without any visible means of support, and the man who was in love with you, without any offense to his predecessor, without reflecting upon his merits in the least, was the best man in the world — I ought to have known, though, that it couldn't last. Something was sure to happen — Good Lord! What's the matter?

Gentleman. We are coming to a tunnel.

Lady. Horrors! [*They pass into a tunnel. After a moment they come out.*] Don't look at that gentleman. I was the one who pinched you on the arm —

Gentleman. Madam!

Lady. But that wasn't all. My sister-in-law is of a very domineering disposition. She is the moneyed member of the family, and, naturally, she expects everybody to bow down before her. She wants them to grovel. Well, that isn't my style. If I say anything she doesn't like, we have an explosion! Now, she has set herself on marrying my daughter to a nephew of hers about whom we know absolutely nothing. It is a delicate subject. A woman only marries once; at least, the first time that's all that she counts on. She plans no further ahead. She says he is a nice fellow, but I have made inquiries — Look out of the window, my dear — I hear he is very fond of the ladies. But what of that? All men are alike.

Young Lady. Mamma! Mamma! Look at all the little rabbits!

Lady. Don't talk to me about little rabbits. You can take your head in now. We were discussing your fiancé.

Young Lady. What does this gentleman think?

Lady. He thinks the same as I do. He says that without knowing him thoroughly — And he is perfectly right —

Gentleman. [*Aside*] Where did this woman get the idea that I said anything?

Lady. Are we coming to a stop?

Young Lady. Yes. We're stopping now. That was a long run, mamma.

Gentleman. I believe I will get out and stretch myself for a moment. With your permission, ladies —

Lady. Be sure you have time enough.

Gentleman. Yes. The engine takes in water. [*The* GENTLEMAN *goes out.*]

A Voice. [*Outside*] Two minutes! The train stops two minutes!

Another Voice. Water! Who wants water?

Another Voice. Buy your cinnamon cakes! Cinnamon cakes!

Young Lady. Mamma, I want some cinnamon cakes.

Lady. Didn't I tell you, when you were traveling to be careful what you eat? We've had spice enough already. We're a great deal better off in this compartment. That seems to be a very nice gentleman. He is probably taking a vacation — I think we saw him in Madrid one afternoon with a fat lady, that day we were at the Lyric to see *The Iron Ring.* Don't you remember the woman who sat in front of us with the big hat so that you couldn't see? She cried through all the sad parts.

Young Lady. I don't remember, mamma.

Lady. When I get a good look at a person I never forget — I'll ask him when he comes back.

Voices. All aboard! Passengers who are going will please take the train!

Lady. Goodness, there's the bell! — The gentleman hasn't come back — See if he's on the platform — Can't you see him?

Young Lady. No.

Lady. Here! Stop! Don't start the train! There's a gentleman missing! — I wonder where he can be? The train is moving — He's left — What can the matter be? Too bad. What a pity!

Young Lady. He hasn't moved to another compartment. Here are his things.

Lady. Of course he hasn't. We had better throw them out of the window. He can pick them up on the platform. It's the best we can do.

Young Lady. Yes! It's the best.

Lady. Help me! Hurry up!

Young Lady. There they go!

Lady. They belong to a gentleman who has lost the train! Keep them for him! He'll be out in a minute! — Didn't he know that the train doesn't wait for anybody? I am so sorry!

Young Lady. We forgot the book.

Lady. Never mind; it's all right. It won't be like the other, anyhow — What a pity!

Young Lady. [*Looking at the book*] What a pity!

Lady. If there isn't another train today and his family should be waiting for him and he should be ashamed to let them know — I hate to think of it! It's too horrible for words!

Young Lady. [*Giggling*] Too horrible!

Lady. God bless me! It's too bad. While he was here, we had an escort, as it were. We were having a very agreeable conversation. It was easy to see he had acquired a great deal of information.

Young Lady. He was very good looking. Listen, mamma; where did you say that you pinched me in the tunnel? On the arm?

Lady. What do you want to know that for?

Young Lady. Nothing. Because it hurts.

Lady. I am so nervous; I'm always afraid of those tunnels. You never can tell what is going to happen in a tunnel! However, it's too late now for regrets! — Don't you feel hungry?

Young Lady. I should say I do. It always gives me an appetite to ride on the train.

Lady. If you traveled more maybe you'd pick up faster. Now, you look like half a Philopena — Hand me down the basket — Better see how the cat is.

Young Lady. Hello, kitty! Puss! Puss! My, what eyes! They shine like fire!

Lady. I'm thankful it hasn't given us any trouble, though. It's time to eat.

Young Lady. Another stop.

Lady. Good. We can spread the things out now.

A Voice. One minute! One minute!

Another Voice. Water! Who wants water?

Lady. These breaded chops ought to taste good. Spread the paper for a cloth — Give me a napkin — Don't upset the wine bottle —·

The GENTLEMAN *reënters.*

Gentleman. I beg your pardon, ladies —
Lady. Eh?
Young Lady. Oh!
Lady. What! You again?
Gentleman. Yes, I was riding in the smoking car.
Lady. But weren't you left behind?
Young Lady. We thought —
Gentleman. But my luggage? How is this?
Lady. Oh! — I beg your pardon!
Young Lady. You see —
Lady. We thought you had missed the train, and, so as to oblige you —
Young Lady. We threw it out of the window —
Gentleman. But who told you to do that?
Lady. To accommodate you —
Young Lady. How were we to suppose —
Gentleman. But what am I to do now? The devil! These women — I ought to have known that you would be up to something!
Lady. If you are going to take it like this, sir —
Gentleman. How the devil do you expect me to take it?
Lady. Why didn't you tell us what you were going to do?
Gentleman. Every time I go out do I have to hold up my hand to you? If you weren't irresponsible —
Lady. I don't allow gentlemen to call me irresponsible; nor my daughter, either. Where are your manners?
Gentleman. Madam! Would you recognize them?
Lady. You don't know what you are talking about. You are the one who is irresponsible.
Gentleman. I?
Lady. Yes! You're mad! You're crazy!
Young Lady. Why, mamma!
Voice. Passengers who are going will please take the train! All aboard!
Lady. You can telegraph when we get to the next station.
Gentleman. I can, can I? — My bags! My bags!
Lady. A lady ought never to travel without a private compartment.
Gentleman. Oh, travel in the dog-car!
Lady. I? In the dog-car?

Gentleman. Chained.

Young Lady. Mamma! Mamma!

All talk at the same time.

Curtain.

(*John Garrett Underhill*)

SUGGESTIONS FOR STUDY

1. What is your reaction to this play according to the first test of a farce: " Is it funny? " Would this be effective on the stage? Is it adapted to classroom dramatization? Why, or why not?

2. Exaggeration is legitimate in farce. Is the lady exaggerated beyond credibility, or is she true to a certain type of character? Is the gentleman merely a lay figure, or does the part need a good actor?

3. Make a plan for the staging and costuming of this play. What difficulties of staging by amateurs would this farce present? How might this be overcome?

4. Read some of the one-act plays of the Quintero brothers, who have specialized in this form. " A Sunny Morning " is to be found in several general collections of plays. Compare the Spanish with American one-act plays which you know.

5. A study of the technique of the one-act play, and the writing of original plays would be appropriate at this point for those especially interested.

6. Read some of Benavente's long plays, especially *The Bonds of Interest.* Observe the modern note and the social significance of these plays.

RUBÉN DARIO (1867–1916)

The greatest impetus to modern Spanish poetry came from our side of the Atlantic in the person of Rubén Darío, a native of Nicaragua. His autobiography written shortly before his death gives in somewhat highly colored style the details of his life. At thirteen his first poem was published and a year later he did some journalistic writing which led to newspaper work in various South American cities. In 1892 he went to Spain to represent Nicaragua at the Columbus Centenary, and there came in contact with Spanish writers, who had already become acquainted with his volume of prose and verse called *Azul* (1888). Some critics have considered that this book marked the real beginning of modern Spanish poetry. Later volumes of poetry, criticism and travel sketches appeared in Buenos Aires, Paris, and Madrid. Darío was a true cosmopolite who spent much of his time in travel, lived in Paris for long periods, and at various times held diplomatic posts.   Finally he returned to his native city, León, in order to spend his last days there.

Not only was Darío the first of the modern Spanish school of poetry, but he is generally conceded to be the greatest.   In delicacy of imagery, charm of vocabulary, and flexibility of meter he is unrivaled.   He loves rich backgrounds, gorgeous fabrics, epicurean viands.   Love, music, the passing of youth are his themes.

The qualities of his poetry are so intimately bound up with the rhythm of the Spanish language that they can never be appreciated in translation.

SONATINA

The Princess mourns — Why is the Princess sighing?
Why from her lips are song and laughter dying?
  Why does she droop upon her chair of gold?
Hushed is the music of her royal bower;
Beside her in a vase, a single flower   5
  Swoons and forgets its petals to unfold.

The fool in scarlet pirouettes and flatters,
Within the hall the silly dueña chatters;
  Without, the peacock's regal plumage gleams.
The Princess heeds them not; her thoughts are veering   10
Out through the gates of Dawn, past sight and hearing,
  Where she pursues the phantoms of her dreams.

Is it a dream of China that allures her,
Or far Golconda's ruler who conjures her
  But to unveil the laughter of her eyes?   15
He of the island realms of fragrant roses,
Whose treasure flashing diamond hoards discloses,
  And pearls of Ormuz, rich beyond surmise?

Alas!   The Princess longs to be a swallow,
To be a butterfly, to soar, to follow   20
  The ray of light that climbs into the sun;
To greet the lilies, lost in Springtime wonder,
To ride upon the wind, to hear the thunder
  Of ocean waves where monstrous billows run.

8. dueña: a chaperon, by whom a young Spanish girl of quality must always be accompanied.   14. Golconda: a town in India, once a famous diamond market.   18. Ormuz: a small island in the Persian gulf, once a rich seaport.

Her silver distaff fallen in disfavor,   25
Her magic globe shorn of its magic savor,
    The swans that drift like snow across the lake,
The lotus in the garden pool are mourning;
The dahlias and the jasmin flowers adorning
    The palace gardens, sorrow for her sake.   30

Poor little captive of the blue-eyed glances!
A hundred negroes with a hundred lances,
    A hound, a sleepless dragon, guard her gates.
There in the marble of her palace prison
The little Princess of her roving vision,   35
    Caught in her gold and gauzes, dreams and waits.

" Oh " (sighs the Princess), " Oh, to leave behind me
My marble cage, the golden chains that bind me,
    The empty chrysalis the moth forsakes!
To fly to where a fairy Prince is dwelling ——   40
O radiant vision past all mortal telling,
    Brighter than April, or the day that breaks! "

" Hush, little Princess," whispers the good fairy,
" With sword and goshawk; on his charger airy,
    The Prince draws near the lover without blame.   45
Upon his winged steed the Prince is fleeting,
The conqueror of Death, to bring you greeting,
    And with his kiss to touch your lips to flame! "

(John Pierrepont Rice)

44. **goshawk:** goose hawk, a bird used for hunting like a falcon.

TO ROOSEVELT

Like many South Americans Darío felt considerable hostility toward the United States for our so-called imperialism, and shortly after the establishment of the State of Panama he wrote a poem to Theodore Roosevelt, then President, in which his pent-up bitterness burst forth in strong terms. Later he realized that the evils, which undoubtedly existed, were to be laid at the door of a few politicians rather than the President himself. The poem, however, had great vogue among the South Americans and is interesting to us as affording a chance to " see ourselves as others see us." It is considerably longer than the selection given here, but continues in the same vein.

I

'Tis only with the Bible or with Walt Whitman's verse,
That you, the mighty hunter, are reached by other men.
You're primitive and modern, you're simple and complex, —
A veritable Nimrod with aught of Washington.
You are the United States;   5
You are the future foe
Of free America that keeps its Indian blood,
That prays to Jesus Christ, and speaks in Spanish still.
You are a fine example of a strong and haughty race;
You're learned and you're clever; to Tolstoy you're opposed;   10
And whether taming horses or slaying savage beasts,
You seem an Alexander and Nebuchadnezzar too.
(As madmen today are wont to say,
You're a great professor of energy.)
You seem to be persuaded   15
That life is but combustion,
That progress is eruption,
And where you send the bullet
You bring the future.

2

The United States are rich, they're powerful and great   20
(They join the cult of Mammon to that of Hercules),
And when they stir and roar, the very Andes shake. . . .

But our America, which since the Ancient times . . .
Has had its native poets; which lives on fire and light,
On perfumes and on love; our vast America,   25
The land of Montezuma, the Inca's mighty realm,
Of Christopher Columbus the fair America,
America the Spanish, the Roman Catholic, . . .
O men of Saxon eyes and fierce, barbaric soul,

4. **Nimrod:** a famous hunter of Biblical times, Genesis 10:8–9. 10. **Tolstoy:** Russian novelist and philosopher (1828–1910), who believed that a simple life of toil developed the highest character (see page 811). 12. **Alexander:** Greek conqueror of the world in the fourth century B.C. 12. **Nebuchadnezzar:** Babylonian conqueror of the sixth century B.C. 2 Chronicles 36:6–10. 21. **Mammon:** god of riches. 21. **Hercules:** Greek mythical hero of prodigious strength. 22. **Andes:** mountain range of South America, here representing the South American states. 26. **Montezuma:** last Aztec emperor of Mexico (1480?–1520). 26. **Incas:** original Indian race of South America.

This land still lives and dreams, and loves and stirs! 30
    Take care!
The daughter of the Sun, the Spanish land, doth live!
And from the Spanish lion a thousand whelps have sprung!
'Tis need, O Roosevelt, that you be God himself . . .
Before you hold us fast in your grasping, iron claws. 35

And though you count on all, one thing is lacking: God!

                         (*Elijah Clarence Hills*)

SUGGESTIONS FOR STUDY

1. What is the significance of the title, " Sonatina "? What similarity do you see between this poem and those of Keats and Swinburne? Read Oscar Wilde's story, " The Birthday of the Infanta," for a prose picture of similar poetic quality. What symbolical interpretation might be put on this poem?

2. Read up on the situation between the United States and Nicaragua at the time of the building of the Panama Canal. When since then have relations been strained? Considering the relative size and power of the two countries, can you sympathize with Darío's feeling? What in his picture of the United States seems false to you? What light does this poem throw on the whole subject of patriotism and international hostility?

3. What entirely different aspects of Darío's personality and poetic quality does each of these poems give you? How do the meter and the imagery of each fit the mood?

VICENTE BLASCO IBÁÑEZ (1867–1928)

Like many other modern Spanish writers, Blasco Ibáñez was in his youth concerned with revolutionary politics to such an extent that he was imprisoned and exiled. On his return he founded a radical newspaper, for which he began to write serial novels. His early stories, which many critics consider his most artistic work, were pictures of life — largely the life of fishermen — in his native Valencia. These were usually tragic tales in which the struggles of humble people against heavy odds formed the chief subject. Not satisfied with the narrow locale of his stories, the author set about to become the mouthpiece for the entire peninsula. In rapid succession he focused attention on the cathedral of Toledo, the trade unions of Bilbao, the riffraff of Madrid, the peasants of Andalusia, the bullfights of Seville. Then he started out for South America with intent to picture each nation in a separate novel, but the World War interrupted this ambition after the first one was completed on Argentina. But with the journalist's knack of seizing an opportunity he produced a novel on the war, *The Four Horsemen of the Apocalypse,* which established his reputation in the United States.

Probably his name is the best known to Americans among all the modern Spanish writers, though he was by no means as careful a literary craftsman as many. But he became less nationalistic and more cosmopolitan than any of the others. From the Mediterranean to California he ranged for his scenes, and his latest books became animated geographies, well suited to production in the movies but lacking in literary finesse. The great vogue of his many novels brought him a large fortune. With characteristic impetuosity he decided to build along the Riviera a pretentious Roman villa, with a pillared dining room overlooking the sea. But the plans were too hastily laid. On the day of his first great banquet the supporting cliff crumbled and the great structure collapsed. This incident has been cited by one critic as an allegory of Blasco Ibáñez's literary fame.

IN THE SEA

At two o'clock in the morning there was a knock at the door of the cabin.

" Antonio!   Antonio! "

Antonio jumped out of bed. It was his godfather, his fishing companion, who was notifying him to make ready for the sea.

He had slept but little that night. At eleven he was still chatting with Rufina, his poor wife, who tossed restlessly about on the bed, talking about their affairs. Things could not possibly be worse. What a summer! The season before the tunnies had raced through the Mediterranean in endless shoals. Every day two or three hundred *arrobas* [1] of them were killed; money circulated like a blessing from God, and those who, like Antonio, attended strictly to business, had saved some of their money — freed themselves from the position of common sailors, bought a boat and went fishing on their own account.

The little harbor was filled. A veritable fleet occupied it every night, leaving scarcely any room in which to move about; but with the increase in the number of boats had come a scarcity of fish.

The nets drew up only seaweed or little fish — small fry, which were wasted in the frying-pan. The tunnies this year had taken another route, so that no one had succeeded in hauling one into his boat.

[1] **arrobas:** an arroba is twenty-five pounds.

Rufina was frightened by this situation. They had no money in the house; they were in debt at the baker's and at the store; and Señor Tomás, a retired sea captain, master of the village because of the money he loaned at usurious rates, threatened them continually unless they paid *something* on the fifty *duros* [2] (with interest) which he had let them have to complete that neat, swift-sailing boat which had eaten up all of their small savings.

Antonio, while dressing, awakened his son, a cabin-boy nine years old, who accompanied him on his fishing trips and did a man's work.

"Let's hope that today you'll have more luck," murmured the woman from the bed. "In the kitchen you'll find the basket with food. — Yesterday they didn't want to give me credit at the store. — And what a dog's life!"

"Silence, woman. The sea is bad, but God will provide. Only yesterday several men saw a tunny going along by himself — an old one that according to reckoning weighs more than thirty *arrobas*. Just imagine if we should catch him! seventy *duros* at least!"

And the fisherman finished his preparations, thinking of that large fish which, isolated from its shoal, had through force of habit returned to the same water as the year before.

By this time little Antonio was up and ready to go, with the seriousness that comes from the satisfaction of earning one's bread at an age when other boys are still playing. On one shoulder he carried the provision basket and in his hand a basket of pilchards, the favorite fish of the tunny and the best bait with which to entice them.

Father and son left the cabin and proceeded along the shore until they came to the jetty. The godfather was waiting for them in the boat, getting the sail ready.

The fleet set out in the darkness, a moving palisade of masts. Upon the boats scurried the dark silhouettes of the crews; the silence was broken by the falling of masts on the decks, the creaking of pulleys, and the flapping of sails as they were unfurled in the darkness like enormous sheets.

The straight streets of the village extended almost to the water. On each side were white cottages in which summer boarders found lodgings, men and women who came from inland in search of the sea. Near the wharf was a large ungainly structure with its window aglow like furnaces, projecting furrows of light over the restless waters.

It was the Casino. Antonio gave it a look of hatred. How those

2 **duros**: dollars.

people sat up all night! Very likely they were gambling now. If they had to rise early to earn their living!

"Hoist! Hoist the sail! The others are getting far ahead of us."

The godfather and Antonio pulled at the ropes and slowly the lateen sail [3] rose, trembling as it was filled by the wind.

The boat at first crept along slowly over the calm surface of the bay, and then the waves began to roll and the vessel began to pitch. They were beyond the headland, on the open sea. Before them the dark infinite in which the stars twinkled; on every side, on the black sea, boats and more boats which drew away like sharp-pointed phantoms as they glided over the waves.

The godfather looked at the horizon.

"Antonio, the wind is shifting."

"I notice it."

"We're going to have a heavy sea."

"I know it. But forward! Let's get ahead of all those who are cluttering up the sea."

And the boat, instead of following those that kept along the coast, continued with its prow forward in the open sea.

Day broke. The sun, red and jagged like an enormous sealing-wafer, traced a triangle of fire over the sea, and the waters seethed as though reflecting a conflagration.

Antonio grasped the helm, his companion was near the mast, and the boy was at the prow exploring the sea. From the stern and sides hung a number of lines which dragged the bait along in the water. From time to time a tug and up came a fish which flopped about and glistened like animated tin. But they were little things — nothing.

And so the hours passed, the vessel always straight ahead, now suddenly listing as it leaped from some high wave, far enough to show its red belly. It was hot, and little Antonio slipped down the hatchway to take a drink from the water-keg placed in the narrow hold.

At ten o'clock they had lost sight of land; behind them, over the stern, they could see only the distant sails of the other vessels, resembling the fins of white fishes.

"But Antonio!" exclaimed the godfather. "Are we going to Oran? [4] If the fish don't wish to show themselves it's the same here as farther out."

---

[3] lateen sail: a triangular sail fastened to a low mast, common in the Mediterranean.
[4] Oran: town on the north coast of Africa.

Antonio shifted the helm and the boat began a different tack, but without turning toward land.

" Now," he said cheerfully, " let's take a bite of lunch. Godfather, bring the basket. The fish will appear when it suits them."

There was a huge chunk of bread for each of them and a raw onion, which they crushed with a blow of the fist on the gunwale.

The wind was blowing strong and the boat listed roughly over the large high waves.

" Pa! " shouted little Antonio from the prow. " A big fish; very big. — A tunny! "

The onions and the bread rolled toward the stern and the two men rushed to the side of the ship.

Yes, it was a tunny, a huge one, big-bellied, powerful, dragging its black velvet back along near the surface of the water. Perhaps it was the lone tunny about which there had been so much talk among the fishermen. It swam powerfully; with a quick contraction of its strong tail it passed from one side of the boat to the other, and as promptly as it was lost to view it reappeared again instantaneously.

Antonio grew red with excitement and hastily cast into the sea a line with a hook thick as a finger.

The waters seethed and the boat listed as if some colossal giant were pulling it over, holding it back in its course and trying to capsize it. The deck reeled as though fleeing from under the feet of the crew, and the mast creaked under the strain of the swollen sail. But presently the obstacle gave way and the boat, bounding back, resumed its course.

The line, a moment before rigid and taut, now hung slack and useless. They pulled at it and drew the hook to the surface. It was broken in the middle, in spite of its size.

The godfather shook his head sadly.

" Antonio, that animal is stronger than we. Let him go, and let us be thankful that the hook broke. A little more and we should have gone down."

" Let him go? " shouted the skipper. " The devil! Do you know how much that fish is worth? This isn't the time for scruples and fears. At him! At him! "

By changing the tack the boat spun round to the spot where the encounter had taken place.

He replaced the broken hook with an enormous new one, and to this he attached several pilchards. Without letting go of the helm he grasped a sharp-pointed boat-hook. A feeble blow he was going to give that stupid, lusty beast if he came within range!

The line hung almost straight down from the stern. Once more the boat trembled, but this time in a frightful manner. The tunny was well caught and pulled at the firm hook in such a way as to hold the vessel back and made it do a crazy dance on the waves.

The water seemed to boil. Foam and bubbles rose to the surface in a troubled whirl, as if in the depths of the sea a struggle between giants was going on. Suddenly the boat, as though seized by a hidden hand, listed so far that the water inundated it to the middle of the deck.

That wrench threw the crew prostrate. Antonio, torn away from the helm, thought that he must be in the sea. A creaking sound, and then the boat recovered its normal position. The line had broken, and at the same moment the tunny appeared at the vessel's side, near the surface of the water, its powerful tail beating the sea into masses of foam. Ah, the rascal! At last he was within range! And furiously, as if he were dealing with an implacable enemy, Antonio delivered several blows with the boat-hook, burying the iron in that viscous hide. The water was stained with blood and the animal went down in a red whirlpool.

Antonio breathed again. Luckily they had gotten rid of him. The whole affair lasted but a few seconds, but a little more and they would have gone to the bottom.

He looked at the deck, which was drenched, and at his godfather, who was clutching the foot of the mast, pale, but tranquil as usual.

" I thought that we were about to drown, Antonio. I even swallowed some water. Cursed animal! But you gave him some stout blows. You'll see him come floating up in a little while."

" And the boy? "

The father asked this question with uneasiness, anxiously, as though fearing the reply.

The child was not on the deck. Antonio went down the hatchway hoping to find the boy in the hold. He plunged into the water up to his knees; the sea had flooded the hold. But who thought anything of that? He groped about at random in the dark narrow space, encountering only the water-keg and the spare fishing-tackle.

He returned to the deck like a madman.

" The boy! The boy! My little Antonio! "

The godfather twisted his face sorrowfully. Hadn't they been on the point of going down? Overwhelmed by a heavy sea the boy must have gone down to the bottom like a ball of lead. The old fisherman, although he thought this, said nothing.

Far off, on the spot where the boat had almost foundered in the waves, a black object was floating.

" There he is! "

And the father threw himself into the water, swimming vigorously, while his companion lowered the sail.

He swam and swam, but he nearly exhausted his strength only to be convinced that the object was an oar stripped from his own boat.

As the waves bore him on their crests he raised his body out of the water in order to see farther. Water on all sides. On the sea there were only himself, the approaching boat, and a curving blackness which had just risen to the surface, with dreadful contortions, staining the sea with blood.

The tunny was dead. — A fine thing to bother about now! The life of his only son, his little Antonio, in exchange for that beast! God! That one had to earn his living in this way!

He swam around for more than an hour, thinking every time he touched anything that the body of his son was about to rise up from beneath his legs. He even imagined the shadows of the waves to be the corpse of his child floating upon the water.

He would have preferred to remain there — to die with his son. His godfather had to fish him out and place him in the boat as though he were a rebellious child.

" What shall we do, Antonio? "

There was no reply.

" You mustn't take it that way, man. Such is life. The child died where all of our people have died — where we ourselves shall die. It's only a question of sooner or later. — But now, we are still living — and must not forget that we are poor folk."

And preparing two running knots he fastened the rope around the body of the tunny so that the boat took it in tow, tingeing the foaming water a bloody red.

The wind favored them, but the boat was flooded and sailed badly; the two men, therefore, being sailors above all else, forgot the tragedy, and with scoops in hand they bent over into the hold and threw out scoopfuls of water into the sea.

So the hours passed. That rude labor dulled the senses of Antonio and kept him from thinking. But from his eyes rolled tears and more tears, which, mingling with the water from the hold, fell into the sea upon the tomb of the son.

The vessel now sailed with growing speed, feeling that it was becoming empty on the inside.

The little harbor came into view, with its aggregation of small white cottages gilded by the late afternoon sun.

The sight of land woke in Antonio the grief and terror which had lain dormant.

" What will my wife say? What will my Rufina say? " groaned the wretched man.

And he trembled like all energetic and bold men who at home are slaves to their families.

The rhythm of merry waltzes was borne across the water like a caress. The wind from the shore greeted the boat with lively, joyous melodies. It was the music being played on the promenade in front of the Casino. Underneath the flattened palms paraded by, like the colored beads of a rosary, the silk parasols, the straw hats, the bright showy clothes of all the summer folk.

The children, dressed in white and red, were jumping about and running after their playthings, or forming merry circles as they wheeled about in colorful rings.

On the wharf there was a crowd of the fisherfolk. Their vision, accustomed to the vastness of the sea, had already recognized what the vessel was towing in. But Antonio had eyes only for the end of the jetty where a tall woman, darkly erect, was standing by herself on a large rock, her skirts fluttering in the wind.

They reached the wharf. What an ovation! Every one wanted to see the huge animal at close range. The fishermen cast envious looks from their boats. The urchins, naked and brick-colored from the sun, threw themselves headlong into the water in order to touch the enormous tail.

Rufina made her way through the people until she reached her husband who, with bowed head and a stupid expression, was listening to the felicitations of his friends.

" And the child? Where is the child? "

The poor man bowed his head still lower. He let it sink between his shoulders as if he wished to make it disappear in order to hear nothing, to see nothing.

" But where is little Antonio? "

And Rufina, with eyes blazing as if she were going to devour her husband, seized him by the front of his shirt and rudely shook the brawny man. However, she soon let him go and burst out into frightful cries.

"Ah, Lord! — He is dead! My little Antonio is drowned! He is in the sea!"

"Yes, wife," said her husband slowly, his senses dulled, stammering as though the tears were choking him. "Misfortune has come upon us. The child is dead; he is with his grandfather; he is where I shall be some day. The sea feeds us, only to devour us in the end.— But what can we do? Not all of us are born to be bishops."

But his wife no longer heard him. She was on the ground, overcome by a nervous crisis, and kicked about violently in her agony, tearing her hair and clawing her face.

"My son! My little Antonio!"

Some neighbors from the fishermen's quarter ran to her assistance. Well they knew what this was; nearly all of them had passed through similar crises. They lifted her up and supporting her in their strong arms they proceeded toward her cabin.

Several of the men handed a glass of wine to Antonio, who was still weeping. In the meantime the godfather, dominated by the brutal egoism of life, was bravely haggling with the fish-buyers who wanted to acquire the splendid catch.

It was nightfall. The water, gently rippling, assumed the color of gold.

At intervals, each time further away, were heard the despairing cries of that poor woman, disheveled and crazy, as her friends took her home.

"My little Antonio! My son!"

And under the palm trees the showy clothes, the happy smiling faces, continued their promenade, a whole world that had not felt the misfortune which happened so close to it, that had not cast a glance upon this drama of poverty. The elegant, rhythmical, voluptuous waltz, the hymn of light-headed folly, was borne harmoniously over the waters, caressing with its breath the eternal beauty of the sea.

(H. C. Schweikert)

SUGGESTIONS FOR STUDY

1. Show several ways in which contrast has been effectively used in this story. How does it accentuate the tragedy?

2. Point out the details which add vividness to the picture of the sea or the life of fishermen. Are there any which would not be true of American sea life?

3. Compare this story with the Irish classic. *Riders to the Sea.* Note

especially differences in the two mothers. Which woman's method of receiving the news makes the deeper impression on you? What stories or
poems do you know which picture tragedies of seafolk along the American
coast? Discuss in comparison with this.

4. For further reading of Blasco Ibáñez: *The Four Horsemen of the
Apocalypse* and *Blood and Sand*.

PÍO BAROJA (1872–   )

From among the Basques, those distinctive people of the Pyrenees, who
have retained their own language and racial characteristics, comes Pío
Baroja, one of the most widely read modern Spanish novelists. Before
turning to literature as a profession he practiced medicine, and later owned
a bakery in Madrid. Most of his novels were written in groups of three,
each trilogy dealing with a different subject, such as Basque life, contrasting notions of government, Madrid street life, the Carlist War.
Recent editions recognize nine distinct series. Baroja is a prolific writer,
having kept up an average of almost a novel a year since his first in 1900.
His interest lies largely in studies of the proletariat. While this brings
him close to the picaresque novel so characteristic of Spain, his books
nevertheless are far removed in spirit from the gayety and abounding
heartiness of the picaresque. Baroja is one of the few Spanish writers
who lacks humor. Instead he presents the tragedies of poverty, superstition, and general economic and governmental conditions which thrust
people down into abject life. He is especially sensitive to abuse of children and animals and seems to be constantly seeking the causes of human
misery. His style is direct, bare of ornamentation, and highly condensed,
but at the same time his selection of concrete detail and his use of specific
rather than general terms produce descriptive effects of tremendous power.
In the type of life which he depicts, Baroja may be compared with the
French Zola and the Russian Gorki.

THE ABYSS

This story is typical of Baroja's work in three ways: it is laid in the
mountains of the Basque country; it pictures the life of humble people;
it strikes at superstition and human stupidity.

The landscape was stern, harsh and unsmiling. Away to the far
horizon, beneath a sky aflame with reddened clouds, the mountain
chain of the Sierra lay spread like a bluish wall of lead, with its peaks
crowned by fantastic rocks and the slopes below them mottled with
white stripes of snow.

The goatherd and his grandson were grazing their herd of goats in the mountains on the higher slopes of the Pedrizas, where the peak of the Corneja rears itself erect like some gigantic sentinel hewn in granite.

A cloak of yellow stuff hung from the goatherd's shoulders, rawhide leggings encased his limbs to the knees, a goatskin cap covered his head; and in his hand, horny as the claw of a bird, he grasped a white rough crook of hawthorn. He was a man uncouth and primitive. His cheeks, rough as the bark of an old oak, were partly covered by a sprouting beard several days old, whitish and dirty.

His assistant, a ruddy, freckled youth, followed by his mastiff wherever he went, made the welkin ring as he traced dizzying circles with his sling in the air above his head, and gayly gave answer to the distant voices of other goatherds and cowmen. His shouts, strident as the neighing of a horse, ended in a clear, long, silvery trill of bantering laughter, which the mountain echoes gave back over and over again.

From the mountain heights the goatherd and his grandson looked out over treeless hills and slopes and bare meadows, with here and there the dark, round patches of thickets of broom, thickly strewn with violets and purple with flowering thyme and lavender.

At the foot of the mountain, beside the bed of a torrent full of dry leaves, grew bushes with dark green foliage and copses of stunted swamp oaks.

Evening was falling, and a light breeze went wandering. The sun sank slowly behind the peaks of the mountains. Reddish snakes and dragons swam in the iridescent blue sea of the sky. As the sun went down the clouds paled and lost their color, and the snakes and dragons were transformed into immense crocodiles and gigantic cetaceans.[1] The mountains folded themselves out of sight in the distance, and the depths of the valleys seemed to assume added width and profundity as the twilight deepened.

Afar off could be heard the tinkling of cowbells as the cattle made their way down the paths, the barking of dogs, the sighing of the breeze; and all these sounds, linked with the indefinable murmuring of the hills, echoed in the utter desolation of the landscape like mysterious voices born of the solitude and the silence.

" Let us go down, my boy," said the goatherd; " the sun is setting."

His assistant ran nimbly from side to side, waving his arms, wielding his crook, beating on the ground, shouting and throwing stones,

---

[1] cetaceans: whales.

until the goats were rounded up in a nook on the mountainside. The old man took a tally of them. A buck with a big bell round his neck put himself at the head of them as their guide, and the herd started to descend toward the plain. As it set out over the grass it seemed like a dark wave sweeping across a green sea. The cheerful tinkling of bells re-echoed, monotonous in its rhythm.

" Did you make sure that the buck of Mother Remedios is with the herd, boy? " asked the goatherd.

" Yes, Grandfather, I saw him," replied the boy.

" We'll have to keep an eye on that animal; for may the evil spirits carry me away if I haven't taken a dislike to the beast."

" And why is that, Grandfather? "

" Don't you know that Mother Remedios is famed all through the countryside as a witch? "

" And is it true, Grandfather? "

" So the sacristan said when he was here the other day. They say, too, that she carries off people and cattle, and that she gives philters.[2] And she's said to have been seen flying through the air to a witches' Sabbath." [3]

The goatherd told his grandson more about what they had to say in the village about the old woman, and, engaged in this conversation, the two of them descended the mountain, from the track to the path, and from the path to the road, until they stopped at the gate of an enclosure.

Thence, far below, was to be seen the deep valley, shot with the brilliant silver thread of the river, and they could just make out on its bank the village swathed in mist. A little distance away, on the ridge of a hill, stood out the ruined castle of the old lords of the countryside.

" Open the gate, boy! " shouted the goatherd to his assistant.

The boy unfastened the staples of the fence, and the goats began to stream into the enclosure, jostling one another on their way. Amid the jostling one of the animals took fright, swerved out of its course, and stampeded at full speed down the mountainside.

" Stop him! It's Mother Remedios' goat! " cried the helper.

" After him, after him, boy! " shouted the old man. He called up his mastiff and sent him in pursuit of the fugitive beast. " Fetch him, Lobo, go and fetch him! " The dog briefly barked obedience, and set off like an arrow.

---

[2] **philters:** magic drinks.
[3] **witches' Sabbath:** a midnight orgy of witches and devils.

The buck leaped from rock to rock like an india-rubber ball. From time to time he turned to look back, standing stiff and erect, with his black horns outlined against the sky and his long beard bristling like the Devil. Taking cover among the thickets of bramble and genista,[4] he jumped and bounded on his way.

After him sped the dog, slowly gaining on him. The young goatherd followed the two of them, fully realizing that there was no time to lose; for a little way ahead the steep slope of the mountain ended in a sheer precipice. As he reached it he saw the buck, racing madly with the dog after him, head for a heap of rocks and disappear among them.

In the midst of the rocks was a cave, which some claimed to be bottomless. Fearing that the animal had fallen down it, the boy ventured to peer over the edge of the abyss. On a moss-grown shelf in its wall stood the buck.

Sprawling on his face on the brink of the gulf, the youth tried to lasso him with a rope; but, finding these efforts fruitless, he went back to where his master was waiting and told him what had happened.

" Curse the beast! " muttered the old man. " We'll see about him in a minute; but first we must get the herd into the fold."

Between the two of them they herded the goats inside, and then the goatherd and his grandson went down to the precipice and approached the edge of the abyss. The buck was still standing on the grass ledge. Above him stood the dog, growling softly.

" Give me a hand, Grandfather. I'll go down," said the helper.

" Be careful, my boy. I'm afraid you may fall down."

" I'll be all right, Grandfather."

The boy parted the brushwood at the mouth of the cave, sat down on the edge, squirmed himself round until he was hanging by his hands over the abyss, and groped with his feet in its wall until he found a foothold. Then, holding on with one hand, he grasped one of the beast's horns with the other and tried to pull it up.

As he felt the tug, the animal gave such a tremendous leap backward that he lost his footing. He fell, and in his fall he dragged the boy with him to the bottom of the abyss. Not a cry, or a groan, or the slightest sound came from the depths.

The old man peered down into the cave.

" Grandson, Grandson! " he shouted wildly. Not a sound was to be heard. " Grandson, Grandson! " With the sighing of the wind

4 **genista:** a spiny shrub with yellow flowers.

there seemed to mingle a plaintive wailing that rose from the floor of the cave.

Half crazy in his consternation, the goatherd stood for some moments irresolute; then it occurred to him to seek help from the other goatherds, and he set off at a run toward the castle.

It seemed but a stone's throw away; but it took him half an hour to reach it, even though he cut across country. The ruined castle, standing above the sheer drop of its hill, was in ogival [5] style. The gathering darkness hid the devastation of its ruin, and in its twilight setting it appeared to draw itself proudly erect until it assumed fantastic proportions.

The old man stumbled on his way. The night was closing in, and the sky was strewn with stars. The Evening Star, shining with its silver light, appeared over a mountain, a soft and dreaming eye that looked down upon the valley.

By a narrow causeway the old man climbed to the castle, dared its ruined ramparts, and through a Gothic doorway penetrated into a courtyard full of fallen stones, a frame of four crumbling walls, the sole remains of the old seignioral mansion.

In the dusk of the stairway of the tower, beneath a shelter fashioned of stakes and straw, he saw by the light of a smoking torch ten or a dozen men, rude shepherds and goatherds, gathered around a charcoal fire. In broken phrases the old man told them what had happened. The men sprang to their feet, one of them picked up a rope from the ground, and they sallied forth from the castle. With the old man leading the way they hastened to the precipice that yawned below the cave.

And as they went, there loomed large and awful in the imagination of the goatherds the fact that it should have been the buck of the old witch that had dragged the young man down into the abyss.

" What if this beast were the Devil? " suggested one of them.

" It might well be," replied another. They looked at one another with frightened eyes.

The moon had risen. Heavy black clouds, like a herd of monsters, grazed across the sky. There was a muted tinkling of bells. The watch fires of the shepherds blazed in the distance.

They reached the precipice, and with thumping hearts they neared the abyss. One of them lit an armful of dry brushwood and flung it into the mouth of the cavern. The flare illuminated its frowning walls, with all their crevices and juttings of rock. A cloud of startled bats rose and fluttered in the air.

[5] **ogival**: having pointed arches.

" Who's going down? " asked the old man in a hushed voice.

There was no eagerness to volunteer, but finally a youth declared that, if nobody else dared, he would go down himself. They tied the rope round his waist, gave him a lighted spruce bough as a torch, which he held in one hand, and he advanced to the abyss and disappeared over the edge. Little by little the men above paid out the rope. The cave must be very deep, for more and more of the rope ran out without the youth signaling that he had reached the bottom.

Suddenly the rope was shaken violently and shouts were heard from the depths of the abyss. The men above rapidly hauled in the rope, and the youth was dragged over the edge, more dead than alive. In his hand he held the extinguished torch.

" What did you see? What did you see? " they asked him all at once.

" I saw the Devil! He was all crimson — all crimson! "

His terror communicated itself to all the other goatherds.

" Will nobody go down? " murmured the old man in despair. " Are you going to let my poor grandson die? "

" That's all very well, Grandfather; but can't you see that this is a cave of demons? " one of them protested. " Go down yourself if you want to."

Resolutely the old man tied the rope round his waist and approached the verge of the black pit. Just at this moment there was heard a vague, far-off murmuring, like the voice of some supernatural being. The knees of the old man knocked together.

" I daren't," he whispered, " I daren't go down either "; and he began to sob bitterly.

Silently, somberly, the goatherds stared at the old man. As their flocks went down toward the village, the shepherds in charge of them approached the group that stood at the mouth of the cave. When they heard what had happened they offered a silent prayer, crossed themselves many times, and went their way down the mountainside.

Men and women gathered around the goatherds, exchanging whispered comments with bated breath. Held there by curiosity, one and all they gazed into the black mouth of the cavern and listened to that vague, distant, and mysterious murmuring that issued from it.

The night was now pitch dark; but still they stood there, seized in the grip of wonder. Suddenly there was heard the sound of a bell, and the people streamed away to a height to see what was coming.

They saw the parish priest climbing the mountain, accompanied by his sacristan, carrying a torch. A goatherd had met him on the road and told him what had happened.

At the sight of the viaticum,[6] men and women lit torches and they all knelt down. By the blood-red light of the brands the priest was seen to approach the abyss slowly. The old goatherd went on sobbing convulsively. With head bowed upon his breast, the priest began to recite the prayers for the dead. In a chorus of sad psalmody men and women murmured the responses. The smoking torches spluttered and crackled; and from time to time, in a momentary silence, there was heard that mysterious moaning that arose, vague and distant, out of the depths of the cave.

When the prayers were ended the priest withdrew, and all the men and women followed him, helping the old man's tottering feet to bear him away from that spot accursed. . . .

And for three days, and for three nights, there was heard a wailing and a moaning, vague, distant, and mysterious, that issued from the bottom of the abyss.

(*W. B. Wells*)

[6] **viaticum**: Holy Communion when given to the dying.

SUGGESTIONS FOR STUDY

1. What does this story show of Baroja's attitude toward superstition? Where is the note of superstition first introduced? How is it gradually intensified to a dramatic climax?

2. Point out examples which prove Baroja's style to be especially graphic. Show his poetic sensitiveness to nature, to mood, to human suffering.

3. How does Shakespeare's treatment of witchcraft in *Macbeth* differ markedly from Baroja's?

4. Vocabulary: thyme, iridescent, seignioral, sacristan, psalmody.

ENRIQUE GONZÁLEZ MARTÍNEZ (1871–   )

Typical of Spanish literature on the American side of the Atlantic is Enrique González Martínez, a native of Guadalajara, Mexico, who is held in high repute in all the Spanish American countries. He has led an active life outside of literature both in politics and in the academic world where he has been a professor of physiology. The note that he sounds again and again is that the poet of a new world must not ape the conventional subjects and phrases of traditional poetry from abroad, but must draw directly from the life he sees, though it be bare, rough, and supposedly unpoetic. In this he resembles the Imagists of our country in the second decade of this century, who derided the trite and pretty-pretty poetry of the late nineteenth century and demanded " brittle " images.

In " The Prayer of the Barren Rock," González Martínez concludes:

> And since I am denied the friendly flowers,
>> The fragrant beds of moss, the singing stream,
>> Lord, let the nesting eagles mate and scream
> Above my mountain towers.

> Yet by my loneliness would I express,
>> As in a symbol, that exalted mood
>> Which in impassioned, Godlike solitude
> Finds everlastingness.

THROTTLE THE SWAN

This poem is a pertinent statement of the poet's creed of realism, though expressed through the symbol of the swan and the owl. It is a curious fact that the swan was frequently to be found in the poetry of Rubén Darío, a somewhat older and even more influential South American poet. Perhaps this poem represents the reaction of González Martínez against that particular poet and others of his contemporaries.

> Wring the neck of the lying-feathered swan
> That gives a white note to the fountain's blue.
> Its prettiness is well enough but on
> The soul of things it can't say much to you.

> Make away with every speech and every fashion   5
> In which life's latent rhythm does not live;
> Only Life itself adore with passion,
> And make Life feel the homage that you give.

> Observe the sober owl that takes his flight
> From the Olympian refuge Pallas made,   10
> And gets himself in silence to that tree.
> Although he has no swan's grace, you can see
> His restless profile sharp against the shade,
> Interpreting the mystery of night.

> *(Muna Lee)*

10. **Olympian:** Mount Olympus was the home of the Greek gods. **Pallas:** Greek goddess of wisdom to whom the owl was sacred.

ANTONIO MACHADO (1875–   )

Now that Rubén Darío has died, it is rather generally conceded that
Antonio Machado is the greatest living Spanish poet. He comes from a
distinguished family of Seville, his father being a well-known authority on
folklore and his older brother also a noteworthy poet. But though a native
of southern Spain, Antonio Machado has little of the light-heartedness of
the typical Southerner. Instead, he finds his greater poetic inspiration in
the rugged landscapes of Castile, which emphasize the stern necessities of
peasant life. He is less concerned with the metrical perfection of his
poetry than with the emotion expressed. He says, " Poetry, for me, consists more in the reaction of a delicate nature to objects than in harmony
of words or in color and design." He is inclined to solitude and meditation, and has published a much smaller body of poetry than many of his
contemporaries. But the quality is superb.

POEMS

I

A frail sound of a tunic trailing
across the infertile earth,
and the sonorous weeping
of the old bells.

The dying embers   5
of the horizon smoke.
White ancestral ghosts
go lighting the stars.

— Open the balcony-window. The hour
of illusion draws near. . . .   10
The afternoon has gone to sleep
and the bells dream.

2

Figures in the fields against the sky!
Two slow oxen plow
on a hillside early in autumn,
and between the black heads bent down
under the weight of the yoke,   5

hangs and sways a basket of reeds,
a child's cradle;
And behind the yoke stride
a man who leans towards the earth
and a woman who, into the open furrows,   10
throws the seed.
Under a cloud of carmine and flame,
in the liquid green gold of the setting,
their shadows grow monstrous.

3

Naked is the earth
and the soul howls to the wan horizon
like a hungry she-wolf.
                                   What do you seek,
poet, in the sunset?   5
Bitter going, for the path
weighs one down, the frozen wind,
and the coming night and the bitterness
of distance. . . . On the white path
the trunks of frustrate trees show black,   10
on the distant mountains
there is gold and blood. The sun dies. . . .
                                   What do you seek,
poet, in the sunset?
                              (*John Dos Passos*)

SUGGESTIONS FOR STUDY

1. In " Throttle the Swan " how might the significance of the swan and
the owl be conveyed in a brief phrase? Has the rebellion against old-
world traditional poetry had its advocates in the United States as well as
in the Spanish-speaking countries? Discuss.

2. In what ways does Machado show himself a modern poet? Do any
of his poems remind you of some in the French section? If so, discuss.
Which of his poems emphasize the picture, the mood, the inner significance? How do you interpret the last poem?

READING LIST

TRANSLATIONS FROM THE SPANISH

Poetry

Madariaga, Salvador de: *Spanish Folk Songs*

Ellis, Havelock: *Sonnets with Folk Songs*

Lockhart, J. G.: *Ancient Spanish Ballads*

Walsh, Thomas: *Hispanic Anthology*

Farnell, Ida: *Spanish Prose and Poetry*

Drama

Calderón, P.: *Eight Dramas of Calderon*, trans. by Edward Fitzgerald

Benavente, Jacinto: *Plays.* 4 volumes. Especially, *The Bonds of Interest, The Prince Who Learned Everything Out of Books, The Governor's Wife*

Alvarez Quintero, S. and J.: *A Sunny Morning*
The Women's Town
By Their Words Ye Shall Know Them

Clark, B. H.: *Masterpieces of Modern Spanish Drama*

Turrell, C. A.: *Contemporary Spanish Dramatists*

Martinez Sierra, G.: *Cradle Song*

Fiction

Alarcón, P. A. de: *The Three-Cornered Hat*
Moors and Christians (short stories)

Blasco Ibáñez, Vicente: *The Cabin Blood and Sand*

The Shadow of the Cathedral
The Four Horsemen of the Apocalypse
Our Sea (Mare Nostrum)
The Last Lion and Other Tales (short stories)
The Old Woman of the Movies (short stories)

Becquer, G. A.: *Romantic Legends of Spain*

Cervantes, M. de: *Don Quixote*

Espina, Concha: *Mariflor*

Perez Galdos, B.: *Trafalgar*
Doña Perfecta

Palacio Valdez, Armando: *Marta and Maria*

Perez de Ayala, Ramon: *Prometheus and Other Tales and Poems*

Valera, Juan: *Pepita Jimenez*

Valle-Inclan, R. del: *The Tyrant*

Spence, Lewis: *Legends and Romances of Spain* (Contains stories of *Guzman* and *Don Quixote*.)

MacMichael, C. B.: *Short Stories from the Spanish*

Wells, W. B.: *Great Spanish Short Stories*

Trend, J. B.: *Spanish Short Stories of the Sixteenth Century*

Frank, W. D.: *Tales from the Argentine*

Non-Fiction Prose

Farnell, Ida: *Spanish Prose and Poetry*

Taylor, Susette M.: *The Humor of Spain*

Unamuno, M de: *Essays and Soliloquies*

BOOKS ABOUT SPAIN

Fiction

Irving, Washington: *The Alhambra*

Crawford, F. Marion: *In the Palace of the King*

Wilde, Oscar: *The Birthday of the Infanta*

Frank, Bruno: *A Man Called Cervantes* (trans. from the German)

Criticisms and History of Literature

Bell, Aubrey: *Contemporary Spanish Literature*

Fitzmaurice Kelly, James: *New History of Spanish Literature*
The Relation between Spanish and English Literature
Some Masters of Spanish Verse

Ford, J. D. M.: *Main Currents of Spanish Literature*

Hume, Martin: *Spanish Influence on English Literature*

Laborde, E. D.: *History of Spanish Literature*

Mérimée, E.: *History of Spanish Literature*, trans. by S. G. Morley

Northrup, George T.: *Introduction to Spanish Literature*

Starkie, Walter W.: *Modern Spain and Its Literature*

Warren, L. A.: *Modern Spanish Literature*
Spanish-American Literature

Hague, Eleanor: *Spanish-American Folk-Songs*

Coester, Alfred: *Literary History of Spanish-America*

Goldberg, Isaac: *Studies in Spanish-American Literature*

Craig, G. D.: *Modernist Trend in Spanish American Poetry*

On Cervantes

Ybarra, T. R.: *Cervantes*

Ryner, Han: *The Ingenious Hidalgo* (trans. from the French)

Frank, B.: *A Man Called Cervantes* (trans. from the German)

Tomas, Mariano: *Life and Misadventures of Miguel de Cervantes* (trans. from the Spanish)

Lowell, James R.: *Essay on Cervantes*

Kester, Paul: *Don Quixote, a Dramatization of the Novel*

Art and Music

Tatlock, R. R.: *Spanish Art*

Caffin, C. H.: *The Story of Spanish Painting*

Dieulafoy, M. A.: *Art in Spain and Portugal*

Post, C. R.: *History of Spanish Painting* (6 vols.)

Trend, J. B.: *Music in The History of Spain*

Van Vechten, C.: *The Music of Spain*

Travel, Social Life and Custom

Bailey, V. H.: *New Trails in Old Spain*

Bates, Katherine Lee: *Spanish Highways and Byways*

Bell, Aubrey: *A Pilgrim in Spain*

Clarke, Keith: *The Spell of Spain*

Gordon, J.: *A Donkey Trip through Spain*

Hill, Cecilia: *Moorish Towns in Spain*

Dos Passos, John: *Rosinante to the Road Again*

Phillips, H. A.: *Meet the Spaniards*

Peixotte, E.: *Through Spain and Portugal*

Trend, J. B.: *A Picture of Modern Spain*

BOOKS ABOUT SPAIN

Italian Literature

Italian Literature

THOUGH Italy did not exist in a national sense until 1860, the Italians look upon it as the oldest civilized country in the world and upon themselves as the direct heirs of Roman culture. In the mind of an educated Italian there is always the consciousness of two things back of him or at present surrounding him: ancient Rome with its grandeur and the Roman Catholic Church with its spiritual sway. He feels that his country once dominated the world politically and to some extent still dominates it spiritually. Rome is now and always the Eternal City, the center and hearth of civilization.

So strong was the Latin tradition in Italy that for a long time the Italian language was not considered a suitable vehicle for literature. Literature in the vernacular was consequently later in beginning than was the case with certain other European countries. However, Italian literature has had a continuous history since the thirteenth century, though not without various ups and downs.

Italians characterized by strong artistic tastes

The Italians differ from us, morally and esthetically, in some important respects. They are distinguished for certain qualities, which because of their persistence may fairly be called national traits. They are very concretely minded and gifted with a strong artistic sense which delights in form, color, and sound. With this sensuous nature goes a ready reaction to pleasant surroundings — a light-hearted gayety under favorable conditions. They are not so much given to brooding or introspection as are the northern peoples. Their love of the concrete shows itself in their disinclination to speculative philosophy and in their strong sense of facts. They are not troubled as a rule by a Puritanic conscience. There is much in them that we sometimes call paganism; but it would be a capital mistake to suppose them incapable of deep religious feeling — St. Francis of Assisi, St. Thomas Aquinas, and Dante would alone refute that notion.

The Italian spirit has expressed itself to the greatest advantage in painting, music, literature, and in certain branches of both the natural and the social sciences. The greatest development in painting the world has ever seen took place in Italy from the thirteenth to the seventeenth century. Italian pictorial art has, to be sure, achieved comparatively little since then; but that fact cannot diminish the glory of the great period of Leonardo, Michelangelo, Raphael and Titian. The first two of these master artists have also a place in literature. Modern music arose in Italy after the decline in painting. Our musical terms — *concerto, sonata, allegro, andante,* and many others, — are still Italian. The opera is an Italian invention. In music also the leadership passed later to other countries, though recent Italian music is once more claiming the attention of the world.

The Renaissance and Italian poetic forms influence all Europe

Italy also gave the world that very complex thing we call the Renaissance, which had its finest growth in Florence. Florence, incidentally, has produced more great men than any other city except Athens. The Renaissance, starting as the revival of classical scholarship and the gradual substitution of humanistic studies for medieval theology, was destined in due time to give rise to science, freedom of thought, and representative government, and thus to color the whole modern outlook on life.

Italian literature is particularly rich in poetry; the drama and fiction are not so well represented. Perhaps it is form even more than substance that is emphasized. Certain it is that in poetry the beauty and sonority of the Italian language and its natural rhyming facilities have given rise to new verse forms which have often been the envy and despair of the foreign imitator or translator. Many literary forms and literary fashions have come from Italy, such as the sonnet, the pastoral poem, certain types of prose fiction, and the movement known as neo-classicism. We have only to think of Chaucer, Spenser, Shakespeare and Milton to perceive the great debt which English literature alone owes to Italian.

Italian literature rises rapidly after the thirteenth century

We see the first beginnings of Italian literature at the court of Frederick II in Sicily in the thirteenth century. The Sicilian group of poets imitated the troubadours of southern France. The ever-recurring theme was the love of a vassal for his liege lady, so far above him as to be indifferent to his protestations, so remote and cold as to remain a lifeless abstraction. This sort of poetry was taken up on the mainland of Italy in the province of Tuscany and was there given a somewhat different turn. The poets of the "sweet new style," as it was called, spiritualized love and made it an ennobling influence. In fact love and nobility of heart became for them inseparable. This conception of love had an important influence on Dante (1265–1321), the greatest literary genius of Italy and one of the world's supreme poets. His *Divine Comedy* is the acknowledged masterwork of Italian literature. In view of its comparatively late beginnings, the rapid rise of Italian literature is most extraordinary. Within a century the three greatest names in the history of Italian letters appear — Dante, Petrarch (1304–1374) and Boccaccio (1313–1375). Dante represents all that is best in the Middle Ages. Petrarch, who has been called "the first modern man," inaugurates the Renaissance and excels in lyric poetry. Boccaccio, like Petrarch, was a poet and humanist, but his fame rests chiefly on his *Decameron,* perhaps the most famous collection of prose tales in the world. The tendency toward paganism which became an increasing mark of the Italian Renaissance is already noticeable in him.

The Renaissance reaches its climax in the sixteenth century

After this great triumvirate there was a lull in Italian literature for some time, but it flourished with renewed vigor in the early sixteenth century. It is impossible to convey in a few words an adequate idea of the teeming intellectual and artistic life in Italy at the time of the High Renaissance — that is, around the year 1500. Literature represents only a fraction of this energy, but in literature alone many noteworthy things were achieved. Ariosto (1474–1533) and, half a century later, Tasso (1544–1595) carried the romantic epic of Boiardo and other predecessors to more glorious heights, the former in a worldly and satirical mood, the latter with greater concentration on his theme and a more truly poetical and religious spirit. Machiavelli wrote his famous treatise on statecraft, the *Prince,* and Castiglione his dialogue, the *Courtier,* on the ideals and qualities of a gentleman — both destined to be influential all over Europe on the conduct and morals of men. Other prose writers of note were Cellini with his celebrated autobiography and Vasari with his *Lives of the Painters.* The Italian drama, which as in other countries had arisen from the liturgy of the church, began to put forth comedies and tragedies. One of the most interesting features of this new theater was the *commedia dell' arte,* in which the personages were stock characters and the dialogue was largely extemporized. Molière, the great French writer of comedies, was much influenced by this type of play. The style spread into Spain and up to England, where the names of these popular stock characters became Anglicized to Harlequin, Columbine, and Pantaloon. They still figure on the English and American stage in pantomimes and fantasies.

Italian culture has never exerted so much influence abroad as it did during the early sixteenth century. Even things which now seem artificial and tiresome like the pastoral poem found many imitators in other countries. Italian classical scholars by their interpretation of Aristotle's *Poetics* laid the foundations of the neo-classic movement, which through France was to dominate European literature during the seventeenth century and later.

The creative spirit declines under political and religious censorship

Following this great outburst of Italian literature there came a long period of decline. For upwards of two hundred years little was produced that seems of value today. It was a period of foreign political domination, with first Spain and then Austria as the alien tyrant. It was also a time of religious reaction which was hostile to independent thinking. The censorship weighed heavily upon writers. Both the poet-philosopher Bruno (1548–1600) and Italy's greatest scientist, the physicist Galileo (1564–1642), suffered persecution at the hands of the Church, the former by death at the stake, the latter by imprisonment and threat of torture. Literary academies flourished but did not foster originality. The poet Marini (1569–1625) had his brief day of popularity. His stilted, far-fetched, ornate style of writing was known as Marinism and had many features in common with Euphuism in England and Preciosity in France.

Patriotism and romanticism combine in literary revival

After the middle of the eighteenth century Italy began to shake off her national and literary lethargy. Fresh intellectual influences came from France and England. The chief gain was in the field of the drama. Metastasio (1698–1782) wrote many music dramas in verse which were the forerunners of the modern opera. Goldoni (1707–1793), strongly influenced by Molière, wrote the best prose comedies which Italy has produced, and Alfieri (1749–1803) the best tragedies in verse. Alfieri was also an ardent patriot, and we now begin to see Italy's national consciousness reawakened and that desire for unity and independence asserted which was to be of decisive importance in the nineteenth century.

Meanwhile impulses from the Romantic Movement which was sweeping over northern Europe began to be felt in Italy. Foscolo (1778–1827) was one of the first writers to exemplify romantic melancholy in his fiction and poetry. He is akin to Thomas Gray in English poetry. Italian romanticism, however, acquired a peculiarly national stamp. The chief aim of all the writers was to develop the national character. The story of the struggle for Italian unification does not properly belong here. Only one of the men actively implicated in the political movement has a place in literature — Mazzini (1805–1872). But it is well to remember that the Risorgimento, as this struggle for liberty and union is called, is rightly regarded by the Italians as the most glorious episode in their history. The two greatest writers of the first half of the nineteenth century were unquestionably Manzoni (1785–1873) and Leopardi (1798–1837). The former was celebrated as a lyric and dramatic poet; he is even more secure in his fame as the writer of the historical romance *The Betrothed*, which is the finest novel in Italian literature. Leopardi was a poet and pessimist. His life, which was one of the unhappiest in all literary annals, would alone account for his sadness, but this melancholy was deepened by his despair of his country's fortunes. He is the greatest Italian lyric poet since Petrarch. His prose dialogues give the most systematic exposition of his hopeless creed.

Contemporary writers receive international recognition

The foremost literary man of the later century was the poet and scholar Carducci (1836–1907), who opposed romanticism and tried to revive many features of classical poetry. He was strongly opposed to the Church. Realism with idealistic tendencies made its appearance in the novels of Fogazzaro (1842–1911) and a more drastic sort of realism in the stores of Verga (1840–1922).

One of the most famous of contemporary Italian authors was Gabriele d'Annunzio (1863–1938), a master of form in whatever he wrote — poetry, drama, or fiction. Other Italian writers who achieved an international reputation before World War II are the controversial writer Papini and the dramatist Pirandello.

Italian literature since World War II is realistic and anti-fascist

Recent Italian literature is an expression of regional realism and hostility to fascism. Benedetto Croce (1866–1952), the world-famous critic and philosopher, in a political *Manifesto* issued in 1936, assembled with savage eloquence the arguments against fascism. They have been the lifeblood of most literature written since Mussolini's seizure of power.

Grazia Deledda (1875–1936), who won the Nobel prize in 1926, in her best-known novel, *Elias Portolu,* uses the primitive customs and superstitions of Sardinian peasants to illustrate their difficulty in distinguishing right from wrong.

Ignazio Silone (1900–   ), himself a revolutionary, through his re-creation of peasant life in his novel *Bread and Wine,* shows how fascism preys on poverty and produces moral decay. In another novel, *The School for Dictators,* with bitter irony he shows tyrants how to seize and hold power.

The novel *Christ Stopped at Eboli* by Carlo Levi (1902–   ) is an appalling revelation of subhuman existence. It is an exiled doctor's report of the near starvation, poverty, and hopelessness of the inhabitants of a barren wilderness between Calabria and Apulia. The one force that binds these wretches into a community is hatred for the state that has for centuries forgotten them.

Other revolutionary writers have abandoned stark realism for a poetic interpretation of peasant life. Of these, one of the greatest is Cesare Pavese (1908–1950). In *The Moon and the Bonfires,* a tale of the pointless violence of peasants in Piedmont, he manages to give the local situation a universal significance. The hero, returning from an imaginary journey to America to find the old destroyed and the new not yet born, turns from his despair not to Communism but to revelations of the eternal in the lives of simple men — to the hills, to the rivers, and to the magic bonfires lit to make the fields fertile.

Corrado Alvaro (1895–   ), in *Man Is Strong,* presents the natives of Calabria in the prevailing realistic manner. In other novels, notably *Brief Youth,* he displays delicate sensibility in describing the emotional growth of a boy in a Calabrian village.

Alberto Moravia (1907–   ), pseudonym of Alberto Pincherle, is neither a revolutionary nor a regionalist. He is an expert traditional realist, influenced by Freud and Dostoevsky in his treatment of middle-class Roman society. Yet in novels like *The Conformist* he lays bare the shabby influence of the social and political changes wrought by fascism upon businessmen.

Opposing Communism with easy humor, Giovanni Guareschi (1908–   ) is well known for his Don Camillo stories that spoof "isms," but the sharpness of the political attack is largely softened by the delightful humor.

The predominant feature of recent Italian literature, whatever the literary method, is its exclusive concern with some phase of contemporary life stirred into tragic activity by fascism.

SAINT FRANCIS OF ASSISI (1182–1226)

The most lovable of all the saints in the calendar was christened Giovanni Bernardone but as a boy received the nickname Francis. He was born in the hill town of Assisi in Umbria. After a care-free youth, a severe illness turned his thoughts to religion. He renounced all his worldly possessions, took Lady Poverty as his bride, and modeled his life as closely as possible on that of Christ. He now founded the order of the Franciscan friars, undertook to carry the Gospel to the Muslims, and made a pilgrimage to the Holy Land. His transparently pure character and wholehearted devotion so captivated the popular imagination that a plentiful crop of legends grew up about him. These stories were afterwards written by his disciples in the collection known as *The Little Flowers of St. Francis*, a book which is widely read in Italy where Francis is still emphatically the saint of the people. One of his most endearing traits was his love of all creatures. His preaching to the birds and his taming of the wolf were favorite subjects of early Italian painters. This joyous love of all things is artlessly expressed in his hymn "The Canticle of the Creatures," which the French critic Renan called "the loveliest piece of religious poetry since the time of the Evangelists." The most famous touch of the supernatural in connection with St. Francis is the miracle of the Stigmata. He is said to have received and retained on his body the marks of Christ's wounds.

THE LITTLE FLOWERS OF ST. FRANCIS

THE CONVERSION OF THE WOLF OF GUBBIO

In the days when St. Francis abode in the city of Gubbio, a huge wolf, terrible and fierce, appeared in the neighborhood, and not only devoured animals but men also; in such wise that all the citizens went in great fear of their lives, because ofttimes the wolf came close to the city. And when they went abroad, all men armed themselves as were they [1] going forth to battle; and even so, none who chanced on the wolf alone could defend himself; and at last it came to such a pass that for fear of this wolf no man durst leave the city walls. Wherefore St. Francis had great compassion for the men of that city,

[1] **as were they:** as if they were.

and purposed to issue forth against that wolf, albeit [2] the citizens, with one accord, counseled him not to go. But he, making the sign of holy cross, and putting all his trust in God, set forth from the city with his companions; but they, fearing to go farther, St. Francis went his way alone towards the place where the wolf was. And lo! the said wolf, in the sight of much folk that had come to behold the miracle, leapt towards St. Francis with gaping jaws; and St. Francis, drawing nigh, made to him the sign of most holy cross and called him, speaking thus, " Come hither, friar [3] wolf; I command thee in the name of Christ that thou do hurt neither to me nor to any man." Marvelous to tell! no sooner had St. Francis made the sign of holy cross than the terrible wolf closed his jaws and stayed his course; no sooner was the command uttered than he came, gentle as a lamb, and laid himself at the feet of St. Francis.

Then St. Francis speaks to him thus, " Friar wolf, thou workest much evil in these parts, and hast wrought grievous ill, destroying and slaying God's creatures without His leave; and not only hast thou slain and devoured the beasts of the field, but thou hast dared to destroy and slay men made in the image of God; wherefore thou art worthy of the gallows as a most wicked thief and murderer; all folk cry out and murmur against thee, and all this city is at enmity with thee. But, friar wolf, fain would I make peace with them and thee, so that thou injure them no more; and they shall forgive thee all thy past offenses, and neither man nor dog shall pursue thee more." Now when St. Francis had spoken these words, the wolf, moving his body and his tail and his ears, and bowing his head, made signs that he accepted what had been said, and would abide thereby.

Then said St. Francis, " Friar wolf, since it pleaseth thee to make and observe this peace, I promise to obtain for thee, so long as thou livest, a continual sustenance from the men of this city, so that thou shalt no more suffer hunger, for well I ween that thou hast wrought all this evil to satisfy thy hunger. But after I have won this favor for thee, friar wolf, I desire that thou promise me to do hurt neither to man nor beast. Dost thou promise me this? " And the wolf bowed his head and gave clear token that he promised these things. And St. Francis said, " Friar wolf, I desire that thou pledge thy faith to me to keep this promise, that I may have full trust in thee." And when St. Francis held forth his hand to receive this pledge, the wolf lifted up his right paw and gently laid it in the hand of St

----

[2] **albeit:** although.   [3] **friar: brother.**

Francis, giving him thereby such token of good faith as he could. Then said St. Francis, " Friar wolf, I command thee in the name of Jesus Christ to come with me; fear naught, and we will go and confirm this peace in the name of God." And the wolf, obedient, set forth by his side even as a pet lamb; wherefore, when the men of the city beheld this, they marvelled greatly.

And anon [4] this miracle was noised about the whole city, and all folk, great and small, men and women, old and young, flocked to the market-place to see the wolf with St. Francis. And when all the people were gathered together there, St. Francis stood forth and preached to them, saying, among other things, how that for their sins God had suffered such calamities to befall them, and how much more perilous were the flames of hell which the damned must endure everlastingly than was the ravening [5] of a wolf that could only slay the body; and how much more to be feared were the jaws of hell, since that for fear of the mouth of a small beast such multitudes went in fear and trembling. " Turn ye, then, dearest children, to God, and do fitting penance for your sins, and so shall God free you from the wolf in this world and from eternal fire in the world to come."

And having made an end of his sermon, St. Francis said, " Hark ye, my brethren, friar wolf, here before you, hath promised and pledged his faith to me never to injure you in anything whatsoever, if you will promise to provide him daily sustenance; and here stand I, a bondsman for him, that he will steadfastly observe this pact of peace." Then the people with one voice promised to feed him all his days. And St. Francis, before all the people, said to the wolf, " And thou, friar wolf, dost promise to observe the conditions of this peace before all this people, and that thou wilt injure neither man nor beast nor any living creature? " And the wolf knelt down and bowed his head, and with gentle movements of tail and body and ears, showed by all possible tokens his will to observe every pact of peace. Says St. Francis, " I desire, friar wolf, that even as thou didst pledge thy faith to me without the city gates to hold fast to thy promise, so here, before all this people, thou shalt renew thy pledge, and promise thou wilt never play me, thy bondsman false." Then the wolf, lifting up his right paw, placed it in the hand of St. Francis. Whereat, what with this act and the others aforesaid, there was such marvel and rejoicing among all the people — not only at the strangeness of the miracle, but because of the peace made with the wolf — that they all began to cry aloud to heaven, praising and

---

[4] **anon:** presently. [5] **ravening:** devouring.

blessing God, who had sent St. Francis to them, by whose merits they had been freed from the cruel wolf.

And the said wolf lived two years in Gubbio, and was wont to enter like a tame creature into the houses from door to door, doing hurt to no one and none doing hurt to him. And he was kindly fed by the people; and as he went about the city never a dog barked at him. At last, after two years, friar wolf died of old age; whereat the citizens grieved much, for when they beheld him going thus tamely about the city, they remembered better the virtues and holiness of St. Francis.

(*T. Okey*)

SUGGESTIONS FOR STUDY

1. What aspects of the Middle Ages are revealed in this tale? Find instances where the language adds to the medieval tone.

2. What impression do you get of the character of St. Francis? To confirm or modify this first impression read other stories of his treatment of animals in the *Little Flowers*. How did the rules and labors of the Franciscan order correspond to the character of St. Francis?

3. Read one of the recent interesting biographies of St. Francis, such as those by Gilbert Chesterton and M. F. Egan, or the biographical essays on St. Francis in G. Bradford's *Saints and Sinners*, J. A. Myers' *Fighters of Fate*, and L. F. Abbott's *Twelve Great Modernists*. Lives of St. Francis by three Italian writers of note: Papini, Sabatini, and Salvatorelli, have recently been translated into English. Numerous short plays have been written on his life, notably three volumes of them by Lawrence Housman. *The Wolf of Gubbio* by Josephine P. Peabody dramatizes the story told above.

4. The career and character of St. Francis greatly influenced the art of Giotto (1276?–1337?), one of the first great Italian painters. Find in histories of art illustrations of Giotto's frescoes in the church of Assisi. What mood or spirit do the art and the stories of medieval life have in common? See also W. M. Conway's *Early Tuscan Art,* and the famous book of drawings, *St. François d'Assise,* by Boutet de Monvel.

MARCO POLO (1254–1324)

Marco Polo, the most celebrated of medieval travelers, was born in Venice. At the age of seventeen he accompanied his father and uncle to the court of Kublai Khan, the founder of the Mongol dynasty in China, where he was treated with extraordinary favor. He learned the language and customs of the country and was sent by the emperor on various diplomatic missions. After a sojourn of many years in China, the Polos started on the long journey back to Europe, finally reaching Venice in 1295. Shortly after this, Marco was taken prisoner in a naval battle between the Venetians and the Genoese. He utilized his captivity to put into shape the notes he had gathered on his travels. This material he dictated to a fellow prisoner and the result is the book now known as the *Travels of Marco Polo*. Little is known about his subsequent life. The nickname of " Marco Millions " was apparently given him because of his frequent use of grand numerical expressions. The American dramatist Eugene O'Neill has written an interesting play with that title.

Marco Polo's book was written in French and later was translated into Italian. It is the first authentic account by a European of China or the Far East. It had an undoubted effect on exploration. It is known, for instance, that Christopher Columbus, who possessed a Latin version of the book, was confirmed by it in his determination to reach Asia by crossing the Atlantic. It was long supposed that the *Travels* were filled with fabrications and exaggerations, but modern investigation has established the trustworthiness of much of the account. The prologue says: " Ye shall find in this book all kinds of wonderful things. . . . Some things there be indeed which the author beheld not; but these he heard from men of credit and veracity."

THE TRAVELS OF MARCO POLO

THE OLD MAN OF THE MOUNTAIN

Having spoken of this country, mention shall now be made of the old man of the mountain. The district in which his residence lay obtained the name of Mulehet, signifying in the language of the Saracens, the place of heretics, and his people that of Mulehetites, or holders of heretical tenets; as we apply the term of Patharini to certain heretics amongst Christians. The following account of this chief, Marco Polo testifies to having heard from sundry persons. He was named Alo-eddin, and his religion was that of Mahomet. In a beautiful valley enclosed between two lofty mountains, he had formed a luxurious garden, stored with every delicious fruit and every fragrant shrub that could be procured. Palaces of various sizes and forms were erected in different parts of the grounds, ornamented with works in gold, with paintings, and with furniture of rich silks. By means of small conduits contrived in these buildings, streams of wine, milk, honey, and some of pure water, were seen to flow in every direction. The inhabitants of these palaces were elegant and beautiful damsels, accomplished in the arts of singing, playing upon all sorts of musical instruments, dancing, and especially those of dalliance and amorous allurement. Clothed in rich dresses they were seen continually sporting and amusing themselves in the garden and pavilions, their female guardians being confined within doors and never suffered to appear. The object which the chief had in view in forming a garden of this fascinating kind, was this: that Mahomet having promised to those who should obey his will the enjoyments of Paradise, where every species of sensual gratification should be found, in the society of beautiful nymphs, he was desirous of its being understood by his followers that he also was a prophet and the compeer of Mahomet, and had the power of admitting to Paradise such as he should choose to favor. In order that none without his licence might find their way into this delicious valley, he caused a strong and inexpugnable castle to be erected at the opening of it, through which the entry was by a secret passage.

At his court, likewise, this chief entertained a number of youths, from the age of twelve to twenty years, selected from the inhabitants of the surrounding mountains, who showed a disposition for martial exercises, and appeared to possess the quality of daring courage. To them he was in the daily practice of discoursing on the subject of the paradise announced by the prophet, and of his own power of granting admission; and at certain times he caused opium to be administered to ten or a dozen of the youths; and when half dead with sleep he had them conveyed to the several apartments of the palaces in the garden. Upon awakening from this state of lethargy, their senses were struck with all the delightful objects that have been described, and each perceived himself surrounded by lovely damsels, singing, playing, and attracting his regards by the most fascinating caresses, serving him also with delicate viands and exquisite wines; until intoxicated with excess of enjoyment amidst actual rivulets of milk and wine, he believed himself assuredly in Paradise, and felt an unwillingness to relinquish its delights. When four or five days had thus been passed, they were thrown once more into a state of somnolency, and carried out of the garden. Upon their being introduced to his presence, and questioned by him as to where they had been, their answer was, " In Paradise, through the favor of your highness "; and then before the whole court, who listened to them with eager curiosity and astonishment, they gave a circumstantial account of the scenes to which they had been witnesses. The chief thereupon addressing them, said: " We have the assurances of our prophet that he who defends his lord shall inherit Paradise, and if you show yourselves devoted to the obedience of my orders, that happy lot awaits you." Animated to enthusiasm by words of this nature, all deemed themselves happy to receive the commands of their master, and were forward to die in his service.

The consequence of this system was, that when any of the neighboring princes, or others, gave umbrage to this chief, they were put to death by these his disciplined assassins; none of whom felt terror at the risk of losing their own lives, which they held in little estimation, provided they could execute their master's will. On this account his tyranny became the subject of dread in all the surrounding countries. He had also constituted two deputies or representatives of himself, of whom one had his residence in the vicinity of Damascus, and the other in Kurdistan; and these pursued the plan he had established for training their young dependents. Thus there was no person, however powerful, who, having become exposed to the enmity of the old man of the mountain, could escape assassination. His territory being situated within the dominions of Ulau (Hulagu), the brother of the grand khan (Mangu), that prince had information of his atrocious practices, as above related, as well as of his employing people to rob travelers in their passage through his country, and in the year 1262 sent one of his armies to besiege this chief in his castle. It proved, however, so capable of defence, that for three years no impression could be made upon it; until at length he was forced to surrender from the want of provisions, and being made prisoner was put to death. His castle was dismantled, and his garden of paradise destroyed. And from that time there has been no old man of the mountain.

(William Marsden)

SUGGESTIONS FOR STUDY

1. Comment on the credibility of the story. Does Marco Polo vouch for its truth? How does Marco Polo impress you as a narrator? Compare him with other famous travelers whose accounts you have read.

2. For further reading: (a) Coleridge's poem, "Kubla Khan," which was indirectly inspired by Marco Polo's narrative; (b) Eugene O'Neill's play, *Marco Millions;* (c) Don Byrne's story, *Messer Marco Polo;* (d) Other early travel books such as Mandeville's *Travels* and Hakluyt's *Voyages,* famous in English literature.

3. Vocabulary: heretics, tenets, lethargy, viands, somnolency, dismantled, dalliance, compeer, inexpugnable, umbrage.

DANTE (1265–1321)

Dante Alighieri, like many other famous Italians, is almost entirely known by his first name. He was born in Florence of a family which belonged to the lesser nobility. He passed through the regular curriculum of medieval education, learning Latin, but no Greek, studying profoundly theology and philosophy, and acquiring a love of art, music, and poetry. He married the daughter of one of the most prominent families of Florence and in 1300 entered public life. Becoming involved in the dispute between the two political factions, the Guelphs and the Ghibellines, he was banished from the city in 1302. From that time until his death he was an exile and a wanderer, always hoping to be allowed to return to Florence, yet refusing to go back under humiliating conditions. We know few definite details of these years, except that he was in many different places and seems to have journeyed as far as Paris. His final refuge was at Ravenna on the east coast of Italy, where he died and was buried. The sadness of Dante is proverbial. An exile from his native city, separated from family and friends, forced to live on the bounty of others, disappointed in his patriotic hopes, he yet transmuted his very sufferings into immortal poetry. But his sadness was not pessimism, for he never lost faith in God or doubted the triumph of right.

The most interesting of Dante's works, after the *Divine Comedy*, is the little book, part prose and part poetry, called the *New Life*. It gives an account of his love for Beatrice Portinari, a young girl of Florence, whom he saw only a few times and who probably knew little of him. She became for him the ideal of womanhood, to be worshiped from afar. His love for her was entirely Platonic and later grew to be a symbol of the spiritual life. It was in her honor that he wrote the *Divine Comedy*, in which he represents her as his guide through Paradise.

Another work of importance for the understanding of Dante is his Latin treatise *On Monarchy*, which sums up his theory of world politics. Dante was a Ghibelline who believed in the separation of church and state and in the independence of the emperor in his relations to the pope. The pope should be the spiritual ruler of Christendom and the emperor the temporal ruler. The sovereignty of each in his own sphere was to be universal, but neither should interfere with the functions of the other.

THE DIVINE COMEDY

The *Divine Comedy*, one of the most splendid monuments of world poetry, sums up all that was best in the thought and spirit of the Middle Ages. It is a visionary journey through the unseen world which medieval Christianity believed in — Hell, Purgatory, and Paradise. It is constructed with deliberate symmetry. After an introductory canto, there are thirty-three cantos for each of the three parts. Moreover, each part has approximately the same number of lines and each ends with the word " stars." The poem is an epic, with Dante himself, symbolizing the human soul, as the hero. His guide through the Inferno and the Purgatorio is Virgil, who typifies human wisdom. In the Paradiso, Beatrice, representing divine wisdom, becomes his guide, until he is at last permitted to see the celestial vision of the Godhead under the guidance of St. Bernard who signifies mystic contemplation. Dante believed that the earth was the center of the universe and that the heavenly bodies revolved about it. Hell, he thought, was in the interior of the earth, while the mount of Purgatory rose from the surface of the southern hemisphere.

The *Divine Comedy* has always at least two meanings: the literal meaning, taking the narrative at its face value, and a figurative sense, which is sometimes twofold. Viewed figuratively, the poem may be called a spiritual allegory of the destinies of the human race. It is not a national poem after the fashion of *The Song of Roland,* the *Cid,* or the *Song of the Nibelungs,* which deal with national heroes, but it is full of references to Italian history and to people who lived in Dante's own time. Dante's conceptions and concerns have necessarily lost much of their significance for us today, but the imaginative poetry remains. The *Divine Comedy* is a mystical poem, culminating in what is perhaps the finest mystical vision in all literature. It is also a political poem; and although the immediate questions which exercised Dante no longer vex us, we can at least sympathize with his ideal of unity and peace for Christendom. And finally it is a love poem — a point that is often forgotten. Love is the supreme Christian virtue; it is by love that the world is redeemed; it is " love which moves the sun and the other stars " (the last line of the poem). The poem was first inspired by Dante's love for Beatrice and it is all suffused with the spirit of this love.

The *Divine Comedy* was written during Dante's exile. The vision which he is supposed to have had is usually dated at Easter time in the year 1300.

INSCRIPTION OVER THE GATE OF HELL

When Dante and his guide Virgil approach the entrance to the Inferno they read the following words over the portal. The last line has become famous.

" Through me you pass into the city of woe;
Through me you pass into eternal pain;
Through me among the people lost for aye.
Justice the founder of my fabric moved;
To rear me was the task of Power divine,   5

5. **Power:** Power, Wisdom, and Love are the special attributes of the Father, Son, and Holy Spirit respectively.

Supremest Wisdom, and primeval Love.
Before me things create were none, save things
Eternal, and eternal I endure.
All hope abandon, ye who enter here."

(*H. F. Cary*)

PAOLO AND FRANCESCA

In the second circle of Hell Dante and Virgil encounter the spirits of those " who loved not wisely but too well." Virgil has just been naming these to Dante as the following passage begins. The two spirits, borne along to them by the wind, are those of lovers slain within Dante's own lifetime. Francesca, married to a nobleman of Rimini, fell in love with her husband's younger brother, Paolo, himself a married man. They were killed by the outraged husband in 1285.

When I had heard my sage instructor name
Those dames and knights of antique days, o'erpowered
By pity, well-nigh in amaze my mind
Was lost; and I began: " Bard! willingly
I would address those two together coming,   5
Which seem so light before the wind." He thus:
" Note thou, when nearer they to us approach.
Then by that love which carries them along,
Entreat; and they will come." Soon as the wind
Swayed them towards us, I thus framed my speech: 10
" O wearied spirits! come, and hold discourse
With us, if by none else restrained." As doves
By fond desire invited, on wide wings
And firm, to their sweet nest returning home,
Cleave the air, wafted by their will along;   15
Thus issued, from that troop where Dido ranks,
They, through the ill air speeding; with such force
My cry prevailed, by strong affection urged.
" O gracious creature and benign! who go'st
Visiting, through this element obscure,   20
Us, who the world with bloody stain imbrued;
If, for a friend, the King of all, we owned,
Our prayer to him should for thy peace arise,

1. **instructor:** Virgil.   16. **Dido:** queen of Carthage, who broke faith with the memory of her husband for the sake of Aeneas. The story is told in Book IV of the *Aeneid*.   21. **imbrued:** stained.

Since thou hast pity on our evil plight.
Of whatsoe'er to hear or to discourse   25
It pleases thee, that will we hear, of that
Freely with thee discourse, while e'er the wind,
As now, is mute. The land, that gave me birth,
Is situate on the coast, where Po descends
To rest in ocean with his sequent streams.   30
   " Love, that in gentle heart is quickly learnt,
Entangled him by that fair form, from me
Ta'en in such cruel sort, as grieves me still;
Love, that denial takes from none beloved,
Caught me with pleasing him so passing well,   35
That, as thou seest, he yet deserts me not.
Love brought us to one death; Caïna waits
The soul, who split our life." Such were their words;
At hearing which, downward I bent my looks,
And held them there so long, that the bard cried: 40
" What art thou pondering? " I in answer thus:
" Alas! by what sweet thoughts, what fond desire,
Must they at length to that ill pass have reached! "
   Then turning, I to them my speech addressed,
And thus began: " Francesca! your sad face   45
Even to tears my grief and pity moves.
But tell me; in the time of your sweet sighs,
By what, and how Love granted, that ye knew
Your yet uncertain wishes? " She replied:
" No greater grief than to remember days   50
Of joy, when misery is at hand. That kens
Thy learn'd instructor. Yet so eagerly
If thou art bent to know the primal root,
From whence our love gat being, I will do
As one, who weeps and tells his tale. One day,   55
For our delight we read of Lancelot,
How him love thralled. Alone we were, and no
Suspicion near us. Oft-times by that reading
Our eyes were drawn together, and the hue
Fled from our altered cheek. But at one point   60

---

28. **land:** Ravenna. 30. **sequent:** tributary. 31. **gentle:** noble. 35. **passing:** very. 37. **Caïna:** named after Cain, is the first division of the ninth circle of Hell, in which the treacherous murderers of their kindred are punished. 52. **instructor:** Virgil. 56. **Lancelot:** a knight of King Arthur and the lover of Queen Guenevere. 57. **thralled:** made captive.

Alone we fell. When of that smile we read,
The wished smile, so rapturously kissed
By one so deep in love, then he, who ne'er
From me shall separate, at once my lips
All trembling kissed. The book and writer both   65
Were love's purveyors. In its leaves that day
We read no more." While thus one spirit spake,
The other wailed so sorely, that heart-struck
I, through compassion fainting, seemed not far
From death, and like a corse fell to the ground.   70

(*H. F. Cary*)

70. **corse**: corpse.

SUGGESTIONS FOR STUDY

1. How is the symbolism of the Trinity worked into the inscription over the gate of Hell?

2. What makes Francesca's narrative so moving that Dante swoons? What advantage is gained by its emotional restraint, especially in the last lines?

3. Lines 50–51 contain one of the most famous quotations from Dante. Compare Tennyson's sentiment in " Locksley Hall ":

" This is truth the poet sings,
That a sorrow's crown of sorrows is remembering happier things."

Would you say from your own experience that this is true? If so, can you suggest a reason?

4. The story of Paolo and Francesca has been popular alike with artists and poets. It has been painted by Ary Scheffer, George F. Watts, Dante Gabriel Rossetti, and others. It has received dramatic treatment in modern times by the contemporary Italian writer Gabriele d'Annunzio and the English poet Stephen Phillips (1868–1915). What dramatic possibilities do you see in the story?

5. What other pairs of lovers, famous in life or literature, do you know besides Paolo and Francesca?

FRANCESCO PETRARCA (1304–1374)

Petrarch, as he is always called in English, is famous both as a poet and as a scholar. He was born in the town of Arezzo, but since his father had been exiled from Florence for political reasons, we may number Petrarch among the sons of that illustrious city. In 1313 the family moved to

Avignon in southern France, which had been the residence of the pope for several years. In this cosmopolitan atmosphere Petrarch grew up. He received a legal training but was attracted to a life of study and writing. Securing powerful patrons, he traveled widely in search of ancient manuscripts. In this way he was the real initiator of the revival of learning and has won the title of " the first modern scholar." Indeed, the Renaissance may be said to have been ushered in when he was crowned poet laureate with solemn pomp by a Roman senator on the Capitol Hill in 1341. From that time on he was chiefly the guest of princes and an ambassador to royal courts. In 1369 he retired from active life and in 1374 was found dead in his library.

Petrarch's services as the founder of humanism and the inaugurator of the Renaissance are too great to be forgotten. But a more living interest attaches to his Italian poetry, which he himself valued far less than his Latin verse, now no longer read. Nearly all of this Italian poetry is concerned with his love for Laura, whom he first saw in a church at Avignon in 1327. Her identity is not certain, but she was apparently a married woman with whom he had a respectful and not very intimate friendship. The impression she made on him is comparable to that which Beatrice made on Dante. She was for him not so much a mortal woman as the embodiment of his ideal, though he speaks of her with more ardor and less in the spirit of distant worship than Dante does of Beatrice. His three hundred sonnets and six long poems called *Triumphs* are all addressed to her.

SONNETS

The sonnet as a verse form originated in Italy in the early thirteenth century. Petrarch brought it to perfection. From him it radiated all over Europe, Wyatt and Surrey being responsible for its introduction into England. The Petrarchan sonnet, which is the prevalent form, is divided into two parts, of eight lines (octave) and six lines (sestet) respectively. The two parts produce the impression of question and answer, situation and result, cause and effect. The Shakespearean sonnet, with its division into three quatrains and a couplet, is quite different in spirit. The compactness and unity of the sonnet make it an admirable vehicle for the expression of a single idea or sentiment. But really good sonnets are hard to write. That is the chief reason why the unpoetic eighteenth century, " the age of prose," produced so few. With the poetic revival associated with the Romantic Movement, the sonnet again became a favored verse form.

> The stars, the elements, and Heaven have made
> With blended powers a work beyond compare;
> All their consenting influence, all their care,

To frame one perfect creature lent their aid.
Whence Nature views her loveliness displayed   5
With sun-like radiance sublimely fair;
Nor mortal eye can the pure splendor bear:
Love, sweetness, in unmeasured grace arrayed.
The very air illumed by her sweet beams
Breathes purest excellence; and such delight   10
That all expression far beneath it gleams.
No base desire lives in that heavenly light,
Honor alone and virtue! — fancy's dreams
Never saw passion rise refined by rays so bright.

                                        (*Capel Lofft*)

High birth in humble life, reserved yet kind,
On youth's gay flower ripe fruits of age and rare,
A virtuous heart, therewith a lofty mind,
A happy spirit in a pensive air;
Her planet, nay, heaven's king, has fitly shrined   5
All gifts and graces in this lady fair,
True honor, purest praises, worth refined,
Above what rapt dreams of best poets are.
Virtue and Love so rich in her unite,
With natural beauty dignified address,   10
Gestures that still a silent grace express,
And in her eyes I know not what strange light,
That makes the noonday dark, the dusk night clear,
Bitter the sweet, and e'en sad absence dear.

                                        (*Charles M. Macgregor*)

SUGGESTIONS FOR STUDY

1. Express the thought of each of the poems in simple, straightforward language.

2. Compare these with some of Shakespeare's sonnets, especially numbers 18, 27, 39, 47, 53, as a tribute to a loved one. In the second Petrarch sonnet, what lines suggest parts of Wordsworth's " She Was a Phantom of Delight "?

3. How does the Petrarchan sonnet differ in form from the Shakespearean? What English and American poets have excelled in the sonnet? what Portuguese poet? (See page 250.)

LETTER TO POSTERITY

While leading a leisurely existence in this region I received, remarkable as it may seem, upon one and the same day, letters both from the Senate at Rome and the Chancellor of the University of Paris, pressing me to appear in Rome and Paris, respectively, to receive the poet's crown of laurel. In my youthful elation I convinced myself that I was quite worthy of this honor; the recognition came from eminent judges, and I accepted their verdict rather than that of my own better judgment. I hesitated for a time which I should give ear to, and sent a letter to Cardinal Giovanni Colonna, of whom I have already spoken, asking his opinion. He was so near that, although I wrote late in the day, I received his reply before the third hour on the morrow. I followed his advice, and recognized the claims of Rome as superior to all others. My acceptance of his counsel is shown by my twofold letter to him on that occasion, which I still keep. I set off accordingly; but although, after the fashion of youth, I was a most indulgent judge of my own work, I still blushed to accept in my own case the verdict even of such men as those who summoned me, despite the fact that they would certainly not have honored me in this way, had they not believed me worthy.

So I decided, first to visit Naples, and that celebrated king and philosopher, Robert, who was not more distinguished as a ruler than as a man of culture. He was, indeed, the only monarch of our age who was the friend at once of learning and of virtue, and I trusted that he might correct such things as he found to criticize in my work. The way in which he received and welcomed me is a source of astonishment to me now, and, I doubt not, to the reader also, if he happens to know anything of the matter. Having learned the reason of my coming, the King seemed mightily pleased. He was gratified, doubtless, by my youthful faith in him, and felt, perhaps, that he shared in a way the glory of my coronation, since I had chosen him from all others as the only suitable critic. After talking over a great many things, I showed him my *Africa*,[1] which so delighted him that he asked that it might be dedicated to him in consideration of a handsome reward. This was a request that I could not well refuse, nor, indeed, would I have wished to refuse it, had it been in my power. He then fixed a day upon which we could consider the object of my visit. This occupied us from noon until evening, and the time proving too

[1] **Africa:** Petrarch's Latin epic.

short, on account of the many matters which arose for discussion, we passed the two following days in the same manner. Having thus tested my poor attainments for three days, the King at last pronounced me worthy of the laurel. He offered to bestow that honor upon me at Naples, and urged me to consent to receive it there, but my veneration for Rome prevailed over the insistence of even so great a monarch as Robert. At length, seeing that I was inflexible in my purpose, he sent me on my way accompanied by royal messengers and letters to the Roman Senate, in which he gave enthusiastic expression to his flattering opinion of me. This royal estimate was, indeed, quite in accord with that of many others, and especially with my own, but today I cannot approve either his or my own verdict. In his case, affection and the natural partiality to youth were stronger than his devotion to truth.

On arriving at Rome, I continued, in spite of my unworthiness, to rely upon the judgment of so eminent a critic, and, to the great delight of the Romans who were present, I who had been hitherto a simple student received the laurel crown. This occasion is described elsewhere in my letters, both in prose and verse. The laurel, however, in no way increased my wisdom, although it did arouse some jealousy — but this is too long a story to be told here.

(James Harvey Robinson)

SUGGESTIONS FOR STUDY

1. Why did Petrarch prefer to be crowned in Rome rather than in Paris or Naples?

2. What light does this letter throw on the character and personality of the writer?

3. Visualize as well as you can the scene in which Petrarch is crowned with solemn pomp on the Capitol Hill. What does this ceremony indicate of the attitude toward poetry at that time? Have we anything in modern life which at all corresponds to it? If so, what?

GIOVANNI BOCCACCIO (1313–1375)

Boccaccio, novelist, poet and humanist, was the illegitimate son of a French mother and an Italian father. His birthplace is uncertain — it may have been either Paris or Florence: at any rate he was by citizenship a Florentine. His father apprenticed him to a merchant and later had him study law, but the love of literature was already the ruling passion of

Boccaccio's life. Some of his happiest years were spent in Naples, where he became enamored of Maria, King Robert's daughter, celebrated in poems and prose romances under the name of "Fiammetta." His intimate friendship with Petrarch began in 1350. From that time on Boccaccio occupied a prominent position in the early Renaissance. He studied the ancient classics diligently, sought eagerly for new manuscripts, and established a chair of Greek in the University of Florence. He had been frankly pagan during most of his life but toward the end experienced religion sufficiently to take holy orders.

Boccaccio's masterpiece the *Decameron* (1352) is perhaps the most celebrated collection of stories in the world. The name is derived from two Greek words meaning "ten days." A party of ten people gather in a villa near Florence to escape the plague which is raging in the city. To help pass the time, they agree that each one of them shall tell a story every day. As the party lasts for ten days, there are a hundred tales in all. The tone of the stories varies from tragedy and pathos to the coarsest humor. Like Chaucer, whose *Canterbury Tales* were written just a few years later, Boccaccio was a realist with a keen relish for the pageantry of human life. The sources of the stories are also varied. A few are from the classics, others from folklore, still others from actual happenings. Some of the more licentious tales, especially those in which women and priests are satirized, are taken from French *fabliaux*. Boccaccio has had many imitators but no equals. He has furnished material for countless later writers, including Chaucer and Shakespeare, Molière and La Fontaine, Hans Sachs and Lessing.

THE TALE OF THE FALCON

There dwelt at Florence a young gentleman named Federigo, son of Filippo Alberighi, who in feats of arms and gentility surpassed all the youth in Tuscany: this gentleman was in love with a lady called Madame Giovanna, one of the most agreeable women in Florence, and, to gain her affection, he used to be continually making tilts, balls, and such diversions; lavishing away his money in rich presents, and everything that was extravagant. But she, as just and reputable as she was fair, made no account either of what he did for her sake, or of himself. Living in this manner, his wealth soon began to waste, till at last he had nothing left but a very small farm, the income of which was a most slender maintenance, and a single hawk, one of the best in the world. Yet loving still more than ever, and finding that he could subsist no longer in the city in the manner he would choose to live, he retired to his farm, where he went out a-fowling [1] as often as the

---

[1] **a-fowling**: bird hunting.

weather would permit, and bore his distress patiently, and without ever making his necessity known to anybody.

Now, one day it happened that, as he was reduced to the last extremity, the husband of this lady chanced to fall sick, who, being very rich, left all his substance to an only son, who was almost grown up, and, if the son should die without issue, he then ordered that it should revert to his lady, whom he was extremely fond of; and, when he had disposed thus of his fortune, he died. She now, being left a widow, retired, as our ladies usually do during the summer season, to a house of hers in the country, near to that of Federigo: whence it happened that her son soon became acquainted with him, and they used to divert themselves together with dogs and hawks; when he, having often seen Federigo's hawk fly, and being strangely taken with it, was desirous of having it, though the other valued it to that degree, that the youth knew not how to ask for it. This being so, the young spark [2] soon fell sick, which gave his mother great concern, as he was her only child; and she ceased not to attend on and comfort him, often requesting, if there was any particular thing which he fancied, to let her know it, and promising to procure it for him if it were possible. The young gentleman, after many offers of this kind, at last said, "Madam, if you could contrive for me to have Federigo's hawk, I should soon be well." She was in some suspense at this, and began to consider how best to act. She knew that Federigo had long entertained a liking for her, without the least encouragement on her part; therefore she said to herself, "How can I send or go to ask for this hawk, which I hear is the very best of its kind, and which alone maintains him in the world? Or how can I offer to take away from a gentleman all the pleasure that he has in life?" Being in this perplexity, though she was very sure of having it for a word, she stood without making any reply, till at last the love of her son so far prevailed, that she resolved at all events to make him easy, and not send, but go herself, to bring it. She then replied, "Son, set your heart at rest, and think only of your recovery, for I promise you that I will go tomorrow for it the first thing I do." This afforded him such joy, that he immediately showed signs of amendment.

The next morning she went, by way of a walk, with another lady in company, to his little cottage to inquire for him. At that time, as it was too early to go out upon his diversion, he was at work in his garden. Hearing, therefore, that his mistress inquired for him at the door, he ran thither, surprised and full of joy; whilst she, with a great

---

[2] **spark:** gay fellow.

deal of complaisance,[3] went to meet him; and after the usual compliments, she said, " Good morning to you, sir; I am come to make you some amends for what you have formerly done on my account; what I mean is, that I have brought a companion to take a neighborly dinner with you today."

He replied, with a great deal of humility, " Madam, I do not remember ever to have received any harm by your means, but rather so much good that, if I was worth anything at any time, it was due to your singular merit, and the love I had for you; and most assuredly this courteous visit is more welcome to me than if I had all that I have wasted returned to me to spend over again; but you are come to a very poor host."

With these words he showed her into his house, seeming much out of countenance, and from thence they went into the garden, when, having no company for her, he said, " Madam, as I have nobody else, please to admit this honest woman, a laborer's wife, to be with you, whilst I set forth the table."

He, although his poverty was extreme, was never so sensible of his having been extravagant as now; but finding nothing to entertain the lady with, for whose sake he had treated thousands, he was in the utmost perplexity, cursing his evil fortune, and running up and down like one out of his wits. At length, having neither money nor anything he could pawn, and wishing to give her something, at the same time that he would not make his case known, even so much as to his own laborer, he espied his hawk upon the perch, which he seized, and, finding it very fat, judged it might make a dish not unworthy of such a lady. Without further thought, then, he pulled the hawk's head off, and gave it to a girl to truss [4] and roast carefully, whilst he laid the cloth, having a small quantity of linen yet left; and then he returned, with a smile on his countenance, into the garden to her, telling her that what little dinner he was able to provide was now ready. She and her friend, therefore, entered and sat down with him, he serving them all the time with great respect, when they ate the hawk. After dinner was over, and they had sat chatting a little together, she thought it a fit time to tell her errand, and she spoke to him courteously in this manner: —

" Sir, if you call to mind your past life, and my resolution, which perhaps you may call cruelty, I doubt not but you will wonder at my presumption, when you know what I am come for; but if you had

---

3 **complaisance:** obligingness.
4 **truss:** fasten the wings before cooking.

children of your own, to know how strong our natural affection is towards them, I am very sure you would excuse me. Now, my having a son forces me, against my own inclinations and all reason whatsoever, to request a thing of you, which I know you value extremely, as you have no other comfort or diversion left in your small circumstances; I mean your hawk, which my son has taken such a fancy to that, unless I bring him back with me, I very much fear that he will die of his disorder. Therefore I entreat you, not for any regard you have for me (for in that respect you are no way obliged to me), but for that generosity with which you have always distinguished yourself, that you would please to let me have him; by which means you will save my child's life, and lay him under perpetual obligations."

Federigo, hearing the lady's request, and knowing it was out of his power to serve her, began to weep before he was able to make a word of reply. This she first thought was his great concern to part with his favorite bird, and that he was going to give her a flat denial; but, after she had waited a little for his answer, he said, " Madam, ever since I have fixed my affections upon you, fortune has still been contrary to me in many things; but all the rest is nothing to what has now come to pass. You are here to visit me in this my poor mansion, and whither in my prosperity you would never deign to come; you also entreat a small present from me, which it is no way in my power to give, as I am going briefly to tell you. As soon as I was acquainted with the great favor you intended to do me, I thought it proper, considering your superior merit and excellency, to treat you, according to my ability, with something more nice and valuable than is usually given to other persons, when, calling to mind my hawk, which you now request, and its goodness, I judged it a fit repast for you, and you have had it roasted. Nor could I have thought it better bestowed, had you not now desired it in a different manner, which is such a grief to me, that I shall never be at peace as long as I live "; and upon saying this, he produced its feathers, feet, and talons. She began now to blame him for killing such a bird to entertain any woman with; secretly praising the greatness of his soul, which poverty had no power to abase.

Thus, having no further hopes of obtaining the hawk, she thanked him for the respect and good-will he had showed toward her, and returned full of concern to her son; who, either out of grief for the disappointment, or through the violence of his disorder, died in a few days. She continued sorrowful for some time; but, being left rich, and young, her brothers were very pressing with her to marry again which, though against her inclinations, yet finding them still importunate, and remembering Federigo's great worth, and the late instance of his generosity, in killing such a bird for her entertainment, she said, " I should rather choose to continue as I am; but since it is your desire that I take a husband, I will have only Federigo degli Alberighi."

They smiled contemptuously at this, and said, " You simple woman! what are you talking of? He is not worth one farthing in the world."

She replied, " I believe it, brothers, to be as you say: but know, *that I would sooner have a man that stands in need of riches, than riches without a man.*"

They, hearing her resolution and well knowing his generous temper, gave her to him with all her wealth; and he, seeing himself possessed of a lady whom he had so dearly loved, and such a vast fortune, lived in all true happiness with her, and was a better manager of his affairs for the time to come.

(Thomas Wright)

SUGGESTIONS FOR STUDY

1. What was it precisely that won the affection of Madame Giovanna? What do you think of the casual treatment of the death of the child? What does Giovanna's concluding speech reveal in regard to her character?

2. It has been said that most of the tales in the *Decameron* are realistic in setting and detail and romantic in general effect. To what extent is that true of the present story?

3. Read Longfellow's version, " The Falcon of Sir Frederigo," in *Tales of a Wayside Inn.* How closely does he follow Boccaccio's story? Which version appeals to you more? Why?

4. Discuss the question whether " The Falcon " could be expanded into a novel.

LEONARDO DA VINCI (1452–1519)

Of all the great men of genius that the Italian Renaissance produced, Leonardo was the most universal in his range. He was a painter, sculptor, architect, engineer and musician. He was also an investigator in all the mathematical and natural sciences. He seems to have taken all knowledge for his province, except the study of government, which somehow did not interest him. It has been remarked that he combined three distinct powers: the shaping or artistic, the contriving or mechanical, and the reasoning or philosophical. He was born at Vinci in the Florentine territory. By the age of twenty-six he was a master painter. Florence and Milan were the chief scenes of his restless activities, though the last two and a half years of his life were spent in a castle on the Loire, whither he had gone at the invitation of Francis I of France. He was chronologically the first of the four greatest artists of Italy — Leonardo, Michelangelo, Raphael, and Titian.

Until fairly recent years the only writing of Leonardo's that was known was the *Treatise on Painting,* a clear and concise encyclopedia of art. His unpublished manuscripts were considered of little value, besides being almost illegible. Contemporary scholars, however, have succeeded in deciphering them and have found a number of things of unusual interest. These *Note Books,* as they are called, contain jottings on all kinds of matters relating to nature, art, and human life, and even some excursions into prophecy. They reveal in particular how Leonardo anticipated by the intuitions of genius many of the most remarkable discoveries and theories of modern science.

NOTE BOOKS

The eye, which is called the window of the soul, is the chief means whereby the understanding may most fully and abundantly appreciate the infinite works of nature; and the ear is the second inasmuch as it acquires its importance from the fact that it hears the things which the eye has seen. If you historians, or poets, or mathematicians had never seen things with your eyes you would be ill able to describe them in your writings. And if you, O poet, represent a story by depicting it with your pen, the painter with his brush will so render it as to be more easily satisfying and less tedious to understand. If you call painting " dumb poetry," then the painter may say of the poet that his art is " blind painting." Consider then which is the more grievous affliction, to be blind or be dumb! Although the poet has as wide a choice of subjects as the painter, his creations fail to afford as much satisfaction to mankind as do paintings, for while poetry attempts with words to represent forms, actions, and scenes, the painter employs the exact images of the forms in order to reproduce these forms. Consider, then, which is more fundamental to man, the name of man or his image? The name changes with change of country; the form is unchanged except by death.

. . . .

The painter will produce pictures of little merit if he takes the works of others as his standard; but if he will apply himself to learn from the objects of nature he will produce good results. This we see was the case with the painters who came after the time of the Romans, for they continually imitated each other, and from age to age their art steadily declined.

. . . .

Men shall walk without moving, they shall speak with those who are absent; they shall hear those who do not speak. It shall seem to men that they see new destructions in the sky, and flames descending therefrom shall seem to have taken flight and to flee away in terror; they shall hear creatures of every kind speaking human language; they shall run in a moment in person to divers parts of the world without movement; amidst the darkness they shall see the most radiant splendors.

. . . .

O marvel of mankind — what frenzy has thus impelled you? You shall hold converse with animals of every species and they with you in human language. You shall behold yourselves falling from great heights without injury; the torrents shall bear you with them as they mingle in their rapid course.

. . . .

Thou, O God, dost sell unto us all good things at the price of labor.

In life beauty perishes, not in art.

As a well-spent day brings happy sleep, so life well used brings happy death.

Life well spent is long.

While I thought I was learning how to live, I was learning how to die.

The natural desire of good men is knowledge.

Nature never breaks her own law.

Intellectual passion drives out sensuality.

We support life by the death of others.

(Edward McCurdy)

SUGGESTIONS FOR STUDY

1. Why does Leonardo put painting higher than poetry? What arguments could be advanced for the superiority of poetry?

2. Which is the most precious of the physical senses, in your opinion? Give reasons for your answer.

3. Which of Leonardo's prophecies have been fulfilled? How?

4. If you disagree with any of the short statements, explain your view of the subject. What is the meaning of the last two statements? What do you understand by a " law of nature "?

5. Procure a book containing illustrations of Leonardo's paintings and statues. The volume in the series *Klassiker der Kunst* (*Classics of Art*) is complete and inexpensive. The titles are given in English as well as German. Merezhkovsky's famous novel *The Romance of Leonardo da Vinci* gives a full picture of the painter's time. See also Vasari's account, page 364.

NICOLO MACHIAVELLI (1469–1527)

Machiavelli, Italy's most celebrated writer on government, was a native of Florence. He played a conspicuous part in the public life of his city, helping to organize its military forces and going on diplomatic missions. The overthrow of the republican government in 1512 compelled his retirement to private life. He devoted his time thereafter to study and writing and produced his *History of Florence,* a successful prose comedy *Mandragola,* and his epoch-making treatise *The Prince.*

Machiavelli's chief concern was politics. Taking men as he found them with all their imperfections, he produced in *The Prince* to inquire how, under these circumstances, a ruler should govern. Unhappily for his future reputation, Machiavelli chose as his model prince the cruel and unscrupulous Cesare Borgia (1476–1507) and furthermore sprinkled his book with statements which, taken by themselves, sound cynical and immoral. Necessity knows no law, nothing succeeds like success, the end justifies the means, the only crime is a blunder — such seems to be his plain drift. But it should be remembered that Machiavelli was describing actual, not ideal, conditions, and that he was animated by a fervent desire to see his country at all costs united under native rule. It is chiefly as a great patriot that he is revered in Italy today. Mussolini has called *The Prince* " the statesman's supreme guide."

OF CRUELTY AND CLEMENCY, AND WHETHER IT IS BETTER TO BE LOVED OR FEARED

I say that every Prince should desire to be accounted merciful and not cruel. Nevertheless, he should be on his guard against the abuse of this quality of mercy. Cesare Borgia was reputed cruel, yet his cruelty restored Romagna,[1] united it, and brought it to order and obedience; so that if we look at things in their true light, it will be

---

[1] **Romagna:** an ancient province of Italy.

seen that he was in reality far more merciful than the people of Florence, who, to avoid the imputation of cruelty, suffered Pistoja to be torn to pieces by factions.

A Prince should therefore disregard the reproach of being thought cruel where it enables him to keep his subjects united and obedient. For he who quells disorder by a very few signal examples will in the end be more merciful than he who from too great leniency permits things to take their course and so to result in rapine and bloodshed; for these hurt the whole State, whereas the severities of the Prince injure individuals only.

And for a new Prince, of all others, it is impossible to escape a name for cruelty, since new States are full of dangers. Wherefore Virgil, by the mouth of Dido,[2] excuses the harshness of her reign on the plea that it was new, saying:

> A fate unkind, and newness in my reign
> Compel me thus to guard a wide domain.

Nevertheless, the new Prince should not be too ready of belief, nor too easily set in motion; nor should he himself be the first to raise alarms; but should so temper prudence with kindliness that too great confidence in others shall not throw him off his guard, nor groundless distrust render him insupportable.

And here comes in the question whether it is better to be loved rather than feared, or feared rather than loved. It might perhaps be answered that we should wish to be both; but since love and fear can hardly exist together, if we must choose between them, it is far safer to be feared than loved. For of men it may generally be affirmed that they are thankless, fickle, false, studious to avoid danger, greedy of gain, devoted to you while you are able to confer benefits upon them, and ready, as I said before, while danger is distant, to shed their blood, and sacrifice their property, their lives, and their children for you; but in the hour of need they turn against you. The Prince, therefore, who without otherwise securing himself builds wholly on their professions is undone. For the friendships which we buy with a price, and do not gain by greatness and nobility of character, though they be fairly earned are not made good, but fail us when we have occasion to use them.

Moreover, men are less careful how they offend him who makes himself loved than him who makes himself feared. For love is held

---

[2] **Dido:** queen of Carthage, who figures prominently in Book IV of Virgil's *Aeneid*.

by the tie of obligation, which, because men are a sorry breed, is broken on every whisper of private interest; but fear is bound by the apprehension of punishment which never relaxes its grasp.

Nevertheless a Prince should inspire fear in such a fashion that if he do win love he may escape hate. For a man may very well be feared and yet not hated, and this will be the case so long as he does not meddle with the property or with the women of his citizens and subjects. And if constrained to put any to death, he should do so only when there is manifest cause or reasonable justification. But, above all, he must abstain from the property of others. For men will sooner forget the death of their father than the loss of their patrimony.[3] Moreover, pretexts for confiscation are never to seek,[4] and he who has once begun to live by rapine[5] always finds reasons for taking what is not his; whereas reasons for shedding blood are fewer, and sooner exhausted.

But when a Prince is with his army, and has many soldiers under his command, he must needs disregard the reproach of cruelty, for without such a reputation in its Captain, no army can be held together or kept under any kind of control. Among other things remarkable in Hannibal[6] this has been noted, that having a very great army, made up of men of many different nations and brought to fight in a foreign country, no dissension ever arose among the soldiers themselves, nor any mutiny against their leader, either in his good or in his evil fortunes. This we can only ascribe to the transcendent[7] cruelty, which, joined with numberless great qualities, rendered him at once venerable and terrible in the eyes of his soldiers; for without this reputation for cruelty these other virtues would not have produced the like results.

Unreflecting writers, indeed, while they praise his achievements, have condemned the chief cause of them; but that his other merits would not by themselves have been so efficacious we may see from the case of Scipio,[8] one of the greatest Captains, not of his own time only but of all times of which we have record, whose armies rose against him in Spain for no other cause than his too great leniency in allowing them a freedom inconsistent with military strictness. With which

[3] **patrimony:** property inherited from one's father.
[4] **never to seek:** never hard to find.
[5] **rapine:** plundering.
[6] **Hannibal:** (247?–183 B.C.) Carthaginian general who invaded Italy.
[7] **transcendent:** surpassing.
[8] **Scipio:** (237–183? B.C.) Publius Cornelius Scipio, the elder, was a Roman general who defeated the Carthaginians.

weakness Fabius Maximus [9] taxed him in the Senate House, calling him the corrupter of the Roman Soldiery. Again, when the Locrians [10] were shamefully outraged by one of his lieutenants, he neither avenged them, nor punished the insolence of his officer; and this from the natural easiness of his disposition. So that it was said in the Senate by one who sought to excuse him, that there were many who knew better how to refrain from doing wrong themselves than how to correct the wrong-doing of others. This temper, however, must in time have marred the name and fame even of Scipio, had he continued in it, and retained his command. But living as he did under the control of the Senate, this hurtful quality was not merely disguised, but came to be regarded as a glory.

Returning to the question of being loved or feared, I sum up by saying, that since his being loved depends upon his subjects, while his being feared depends upon himself, a wise Prince should build on what is his own, and not on what rests with others. Only, as I have said, he must do his utmost to escape hatred.

[9] **Fabius Maximus:** Roman general of the third century B.C. who opposed Hannibal.
[10] **Locrians:** inhabitants of the town of Locri in southern Italy.

SUGGESTIONS FOR STUDY

1. Discuss Machiavelli's estimate of men. Locke, Rousseau, Jefferson, and other political philosophers have had a much higher opinion of human nature. What are your own beliefs on the subject?

2. Consider that Machiavelli wrote for the instruction of Princes, not for ordinary citizens. What difference does this make in the application of his principles? Is it justifiable to have one code for rulers and another for private citizens?

3. Machiavelli is said to have separated political science from ethics. What does such a statement mean? Show from the chapter you have read why he has acquired the reputation of immorality.

4. It has been said that political morality is lower than personal morality, and national morality lower than either. Discuss this statement.

5. What rulers in the world today seem to follow Machiavelli's advice? Discuss.

MICHELANGELO (1475–1564)

Michelangelo Buonarroti was a sculptor, painter and architect of genius, who has probably been the most influential figure in modern art. He was born near Florence and divided his time and activity between that city and Rome. His poetry, consisting chiefly of sonnets, was written in his later years and was inspired by his friendship for Vittoria Colonna, a poetess of merit, and for a young Roman nobleman, in whom he saw the ideal of youthful beauty. These sonnets, often rugged in form, are interesting as a revelation of the inner life of the great artist. Many of them have a philosophic content and are filled with his interpretations of the Christian religion, Platonism, and the nature of art.

The ceiling of the Sistine Chapel in the Vatican is Michelangelo's masterpiece of painting. It took four and a half years of toil under the most uncomfortable physical conditions to complete the work.

ON THE PAINTING OF THE SISTINE CHAPEL

TO GIOVANNI DA PISTOJA

I've grown a goiter by dwelling in this end —
  As cats from stagnant streams in Lombardy,
  Or in what other land they hap to be —
  Which drives the belly close beneath the chin;
My beard turns up to heaven; my nape falls in,   5
  Fixed on my spine; my breast-bone visibly
  Grows like a harp; a rich embroidery
  Bedews my face from brush-drops thick and thin.
My loins into my paunch like levers grind;
  My buttock like a crupper bears my weight;   10
  My feet unguided wander to and fro;
In front my skin grows loose and long; behind,
  By bending it becomes more taut and strait;
  Crosswise I strain me like a Syrian bow:
    Whence false and quaint, I know,   15
Must be the fruit of squinting brain and eye;
  For ill can aim the gun that bends awry.
    Come then, Giovanni, try
To succor my dead pictures and my frame;
Since foul I fare and painting is my shame.   20

                              (*John Addington Symonds*)

1. **goiter:** diseased enlargement of a gland in the neck. 10. **crupper:** strap that passes under a horse's tail.

SUGGESTIONS FOR STUDY

1. Show how this poem reveals the knowledge of anatomy for which Michelangelo was famous.

2. What was his mood when he wrote it? Under what circumstances have you had similar feelings?

3. Comment on the form of the poem. Wherein does it resemble a sonnet?

4. Examine a book with illustrations of Michelangelo's statues and paintings. The volume in the series *Klassiker der Kunst* is recommended. How in general does his work differ from Leonardo's?

5. Michelangelo has been the subject of countless biographies. English translations have been made of three studies by notable European writers: Romain Rolland, *Michelangelo;* Emil Ludwig, in *Three Titans;* Papini, in *Laborers in the Vineyard.* His own letters and papers have been edited by R. W. Carden.

BENVENUTO CELLINI (1500–1571)

Cellini was a sculptor and goldsmith of genius and the author of one of the few world-famous autobiographies. Except for five years spent at the court of Francis I of France, his life was divided between his birthplace Florence and Rome. His vivid autobiography carries the story of his life down to 1562. It has the supreme merit of candor in regard to himself. Cellini was a bully and a braggart, sensual and violent, with neither temperamental restraints nor moral scruples. He admits in his *Life* to all kinds of crimes, theft and homicide included. He was sensitive only to beauty and its creation in art. Other values counted for nothing. The Italy of the Renaissance willingly overlooked all such moral delinquencies in a great artist. Cellini's *Life* is thus more than a personal confession; it is a revelation of the age in which he lived.

AUTOBIOGRAPHY OF CELLINI

The following is Cellini's account of the casting of the bronze statue of Perseus. This statue, which is his masterpiece, now stands in one of the public squares of Florence.

Accordingly I strengthened my heart, and with all the forces of my body and my purse, employing what little money still remained to me, I set to work. First I provided myself with several loads of pinewood from the forest of Serristori, in the neighborhood of Montelupo. While these were on their way, I clothed my Perseus with the clay which I had prepared many months beforehand, in order that it might be duly seasoned. After making its clay tunic (for that is the term used in this art) and properly arming it and fencing it with iron girders, I began to draw the wax out by means of a slow fire. This melted and issued through numerous air-vents I had made; for the more there are of these, the better will the mould fill. When I had finished drawing off wax, I constructed a funnel-shaped furnace all round the model of my Perseus. It was built of bricks, so interlaced, the one above the other, that numerous apertures were left for the fire to exhale at. Then I began to lay on wood by degrees, and kept it burning two whole days and nights. At length when all the wax was gone, and the mould was well baked, I set to work at digging the pit in which to sink it. This I performed with scrupulous regard to all the rules of art. When I had finished that part of my work, I raised the mould by windlasses [1] and stout ropes to a perpendicular position, and suspending it with the greatest care one cubit [2] above the level of the furnace, so that it hung exactly above the middle of the pit, I next lowered it gently down into the very bottom of the furnace, and had it firmly placed with every possible precaution for its safety. When this delicate operation was accomplished, I began to bank it up with the earth I had excavated; and, ever as the earth grew higher, I introduced its proper air-vents, which were little tubes of earthenware, such as folk use for drains and such-like purposes. At length, I felt sure that it was admirably fixed, and that the filling-in of the pit and the placing of the air-vents had been properly performed. I also could see that my work-people understood my method, which differed very considerably from that of all the other masters in the trade. Feeling confident, then, that I could rely upon them, I next turned to my furnace, which I had filled with numerous pigs [3] of copper and other bronze stuff. The pieces were piled according to the laws of art, that is to say, so resting one upon the other that the flames could play freely through them, in order that the metal might heat and liquefy the sooner. At last I called out heartily to set the furnace going. The logs of pine were heaped in, and, what with the unctuous [4] resin of the wood and the good draught I had given, my furnace worked so well that I was obliged to rush from side to side to keep it going. The labor was more than I could stand; yet I forced myself to strain every nerve and muscle. To increase my anxieties, the workshop took fire, and we were afraid lest the roof should fall upon our heads; while, from the garden, such a storm of wind and rain kept blowing in, that it perceptibly cooled the furnace.

Battling thus with all these untoward circumstances for several

---

[1] **windlasses:** machines for hoisting.   [3] **pigs:** oblong masses of metal.
[2] **cubit:** about 20 inches.   [4] **unctuous:** oily.

hours, and exerting myself even beyond the measure of my powerful constitution, I could at last bear up no longer, and a sudden fever, of the utmost possible intensity, attacked me. I felt absolutely obliged to go and fling myself upon my bed.

No sooner had I got to bed, than I ordered my servant-maids to carry food and wine for all the men into the workshop; at the same time I cried: "I shall not be alive tomorrow." They tried to encourage me, arguing that my illness would pass over, since it came from excessive fatigue. In this way I spent two hours battling with the fever, which steadily increased, and calling out continually: "I feel that I am dying." My housekeeper, who was named Mona Fiore da Castel del Rio, a very notable manager and no less warm hearted, kept chiding me for my discouragement; but, on the other hand, she paid me every kind attention which was possible. However, the sight of my physical pain and moral dejection so affected her, that, in spite of that brave heart of hers, she could not refrain from shedding tears; and yet, so as she was able, she took good care that I should not see them. While I was thus terribly afflicted, I beheld the figure of a man enter my chamber, twisted in his body into the form of the letter S. He raised a lamentable, doleful voice, like one who announced their last hour to men condemned to die upon the scaffold, and spoke these words: "O Benvenuto! your statue is spoiled, and there is no hope whatever of saving it."

No sooner had I heard the shriek of that wretch than I gave a howl which might have been heard from the sphere of flame. Jumping from my bed, I seized my clothes and began to dress. The maids, and my lad, and every one who came around to help me, got kicks or blows of the fist, while I kept crying out in lamentation: "Ah! traitors! enviers! This is an act of treason, done by malice prepense! [5] But I swear by God that I will sift it to the bottom, and before I die will leave such witness to the world of what I can do as shall make a score of mortals marvel."

When I got my clothes on, I strode with soul bent on mischief toward the workshop; there I beheld the men, whom I had left erewhile [6] in such high spirits, standing stupefied and downcast. I began at once and spoke; "Up with you! Attend to me! Since you have not been able or willing to obey the directions I gave you, obey me now that I am with you to conduct my work in person. Let no one contradict me, for in cases like this we need the aid of hand and hearing, not advice."

[5] prepense: intentional.　　　　　　[6] erewhile: shortly before.

When I had uttered these words, a certain Maestro Alessandro Lastricati broke silence and said: " Look you, Benvenuto, you are going to attempt an enterprise which the laws of art do not sanction, and which cannot succeed." I turned upon him with such fury and so full of mischief, that he and all the rest of them exclaimed with one voice: " On then! Give orders! We will obey your least commands, so long as life is left in us." I believe they spoke thus feelingly because they thought I must fall shortly dead upon the ground.

I went immediately to the furnace, and found that the metal was all curdled; an accident which we express by " being caked." I told two of the hands to cross the road, and fetch from the house of the butcher Capretta, a load of young oak-wood, which had lain dry for above a year; this wood had been previously offered me by Madame Ginevre, wife of the said Capretta. So soon as the first armfuls arrived, I began to fill the grate beneath the furnace. Now oak-wood of that kind heats more powerfully than any other sort of tree; and for this reason, where a slow fire is wanted, as in the case of gun-foundry,[7] alder or pine is preferred. Accordingly, when the logs took fire, oh! how the cake began to stir beneath that awful heat, to glow and sparkle in a blaze! At the same time I kept stirring up the channels, and sent men upon the roof to stop the conflagration, which had gathered force from the increased combustion in the furnace; also I caused boards, carpets, and other hangings to be set up against the garden, in order to protect us from the violence of the rain. When I had thus provided against these several disasters, I roared out first to one man and then to another: " Bring this thing here! Take that thing there! " At this crisis, when the whole gang saw the cake was on the point of melting, they did my bidding, each fellow working with the strength of three. I then ordered half a pig of pewter to be brought, which weighed about sixty pounds, and flung it into the middle of the cake inside the furnace. By this means, and by piling on wood and stirring now with pokers and now with iron rods, the curdled mass rapidly began to liquefy. Then, knowing I had brought the dead to life again, against the firm opinion of those ignoramuses, I felt such vigor fill my veins, that all those pains of fever, all those fears of death, were quite forgotten.

All of a sudden an explosion took place, attended by a tremendous flash of flame, as though a thunderbolt had formed and been discharged among us. Unwonted and appalling terror astonished every one, and me more even than the rest. When the din was over and the

---

[7] **gun-foundry:** process of casting guns.

dazzling light extinguished, we began to look each other in the face. Then I discovered that the cap of the furnace had blown up, and the bronze was bubbling over from its source beneath. So I had the mouths of my mould immediately opened, and at the same time drove in the two plugs which kept back the molten metal. But I noticed that it did not flow as rapidly as usual, the reason being probably that the fierce heat of the fire we kindled had consumed its base alloy. Accordingly I sent for all my pewter platters, porringers,[8] and dishes, to the number of some two hundred pieces, and had a portion of them cast, one by one into the channels, the rest into the furnace. This expedient succeeded, and every one could now perceive that my bronze was in the most perfect liquefaction, and my mould was filling; whereupon they all with heartiness and happy cheer assisted and obeyed my bidding, while I, now here, now there, gave orders, helped with my own hands, and cried aloud: "O God! Thou that by Thy glory didst ascend to heaven! " . . . even thus in a moment my mould was filled; and seeing my work finished, I fell upon my knees, and with all my heart gave thanks to God.

(Anonymous Translation)

SUGGESTIONS FOR STUDY

1. What characteristics of Cellini appear most prominently in this narrative? Point out the dramatic elements in the account.

2. Study a picture of the statue. It is available in small print as well as in art books. Read the story of Perseus in a Greek mythology. How does the statue suggest the story? For what other great work in bronze is Cellini especially famous?

3. Horace Walpole declared that Cellini's *Life* was "more amusing than any novel." Do you feel the same interest? What biographies or autobiographies do you know which hold your attention as a good work of fiction would do?

4. Among other notable passages in Cellini's *Life* are the narrative of how he returned to Florence to find his family dead of the plague, the romance about his conjuring up legions of devils in the Colosseum in Rome and the story of the mad castellan. Read as much of the book as you can.

5. How do you reconcile Cellini's many professions of piety and gratitude to God with his notorious immorality?

6. Vocabulary: exhale, untoward (note the correct pronunciation), chiding, unwonted, alloy.

[8] **porringers**: small basins.

GIORGIO VASARI (1511-1574)

Vasari was a painter and architect who is chiefly known as a biographer of artists. His world-renowned *Lives of the Painters, Sculptors and Architects* constitute one of the best series of biographies in the world. These *Lives* are, moreover, the principal source of our knowledge about the artists of the Italian Renaissance. The first edition of this work appeared in 1550; a second edition, enlarged and improved, was issued in 1568. It has been widely translated and has become a part of our general cultural inheritance. Vasari may be termed the father of modern art history and criticism. His tastes were broad and his judgments on individual artists acute and fairly impartial. There may be inaccuracies of fact and a certain amount of hearsay and gossip, but the *Lives* are pleasantly written and full of human as well as historical interest. The estimates which Vasari give of Leonardo, Michelangelo, and Raphael are perhaps the most interesting.

LEONARDO DA VINCI, PAINTER AND SCULPTOR OF FLORENCE (1452-1519)

The heavens often rain down the richest gifts on human beings, naturally, but sometimes with lavish abundance bestow upon a single individual beauty, grace and ability, so that, whatever he does, every action is so divine that he distances all other men, and clearly displays how his genius is the gift of God and not an acquirement of human art. Men saw this in Leonardo da Vinci, whose personal beauty could not be exaggerated, whose every movement was grace itself and whose abilities were so extraordinary that he could readily solve every difficulty. He possessed great personal strength, combined with dexterity, and a spirit and courage invariably royal and magnanimous, and the fame of his name so spread abroad that, not only was he valued in his own day, but his renown has greatly increased since his death.

This marvelous and divine Leonardo was the son of Piero da Vinci. He would have made great profit in learning had he not been so capricious and fickle, for he began to learn many things and then gave them up. Thus in arithmetic, during the few months that he studied it, he made such progress that he frequently confounded his master by continually raising doubts and difficulties. He devoted some time to music, and soon learned to play the lyre, and, being filled with a lofty and delicate spirit, he could sing and improvise divinely with it. Yet though he studied so many different things, he never neglected design and working in relief, those being the things which appealed to his fancy more than any other. When Ser [1] Piero perceived this, and knowing the boy's soaring spirit, he one day took some of his drawings to Andrea del Verrocchio,[2] who was his close friend, and asked his opinion whether Leonardo would do anything by studying design. Andrea was so amazed at these early efforts that he advised Ser Piero to have the boy taught. So it was decided that Leonardo should go to Andrea's workshop. The boy was greatly delighted, and not only practiced his profession, but all those in which design has a part. Possessed of a divine and marvelous intellect, and being an excellent geometrician, he not only worked in sculpture, doing some heads of women smiling, which were casts, and children's heads also, executed like a master, but also prepared many architectural plans and elevations, and he was the first, though so young, to propose to canalize the Arno from Pisa to Florence. He made designs for mills, fulling machines, and other engines to go by water, and as painting was to be his profession he studied drawing from life. He would make clay models of figures, draping them with soft rags dipped in plaster, and then would draw them patiently on thin sheets of cambric or linen, in black and white, with the point of the brush. He did these admirably, as may be seen by specimens in my book of designs. He also drew upon paper so carefully and well that no one has ever equalled him. I have a head in grisaille [3] which is divine. The grace of God so possessed his mind, his memory and intellect formed such a mighty union, and he could so clearly express his ideas in discourse, that he was able to confound the boldest opponents. Every day he made models and designs for the removal of mountains with ease and to pierce them to pass from one place to another, and by means of levers, cranes and winches [4] to raise and draw heavy weights; he devised a method for cleansing ports, and to raise water from great depths, schemes which his brain never ceased to evolve. Many designs for these notions are scattered about, and I have seen numbers of them. He spent much time in making a regular design of a series of knots so that the cord may be traced from one end to the other, the whole filling a round space. There is a fine engraving of this most difficult design, and in the middle are the words: *Leonardus Vinci Academia.*[5] Among these models and designs there was one which

---

[1] **Ser**: Sir.
[2] **Verrocchio**: (1435–1488) Florentine painter and sculptor.
[3] **grisaille**: decorative painting in gray.
[4] **winches**: hoisting-machines.
[5] **Leonardus Vinci Academia**: (Latin) the Academy of Leonardo da Vinci.

he several times showed to many able citizens who then ruled Florence, of a method of raising the church of S. Giovanni and putting steps under it without it falling down. He argued with so much eloquence that it was not until after his departure that they recognized the impossibility of such a feat.

His charming conversation won all hearts, and although he possessed nothing and worked little, he kept servants and horses of which he was very fond, and indeed he loved all animals, and trained them with great kindness and patience. Often, when passing places where birds were sold, he would let them out of their cages and pay the vendor the price asked. Nature had favored him so greatly that in whatever his brain or mind took up he displayed unrivaled divinity, vigor, vivacity, excellence, beauty and grace. His knowledge of art, indeed, prevented him from finishing many things which he had begun, for he felt that his hand would be unable to realize the perfect creations of his imagination, as his mind formed such difficult, subtle and marvelous conceptions that his hands, skillful as they were, could never have expressed them. His interests were so numerous that his inquiries into natural phenomena led him to study the properties of herbs and to observe the movements of the heavens, the moon's orbit and the progress of the sun.

Leonardo was placed, as I have said, with Andrea del Verrocchio in his childhood by Ser Piero, and his master happened to be painting a picture of St. John baptizing Christ. For this Leonardo did an angel holding some clothes, and, although quite young, he made it far better than the figures of Andrea. The latter would never afterwards touch colors, chagrined that a child should know more than he. Leonardo was next employed to draw a cartoon [6] of the Fall for a portière in tapestry, to be made in Flanders of gold and silk, to send to the King of Portugal. Here he did a meadow in grisaille, with the lights in white lead, containing much vegetation and some animals, unsurpassable for finish and naturalness. There is a fig-tree, the leaves and branches beautifully foreshortened [7] and executed with such care that the mind is amazed at the amount of patience displayed. There is also a palm-tree, the rotundity of the dates being executed with great and marvelous art, due to the patience and ingenuity of Leonardo. This work was not carried farther, and the cartoon is now in Florence in the fortunate house of Ottaviano de'

---

[6] **cartoon of the Fall:** drawing on stout paper as a design for a tapestry, picturing the Fall of Man in the Garden of Eden.
[7] **foreshortened:** shortened by drawing in perspective.

Medici the Magnificent, to whom it was given not long ago by Leonardo's uncle.

It is said that when Ser Piero was at his country-seat he was requested by a peasant of his estate to get a round piece of wood painted for him at Florence, which he had cut from a fig-tree on his farm. Piero readily consented, as the man was very skillful in catching birds and fishing, and was very useful to him in such matters. Accordingly Piero brought the wood to Florence and asked Leonardo to paint something upon it, without telling him its history. Leonardo, on taking it up to examine it one day, found it warped, badly prepared and rude, but with the help of fire he made it straight, and giving it to a turner, had it rendered soft and smooth instead of being rough and rude. Then, after preparing the surface in his own way, he began to cast about what he should paint on it, and resolved to do the Medusa [8] head to terrify all beholders. To a room, to which he alone had access, Leonardo took lizards, newts,[9] maggots, snakes, butterflies, locusts, bats, and other animals of the kind, out of which he composed a horrible and terrible monster, of poisonous breath, issuing from a dark and broken rock, belching poison from its open throat, fire from its eyes, and smoke from its nostrils, of truly terrible and horrible aspect. He was so engrossed with the work that he did not notice the terrible stench of the dead animals, being absorbed in his love for art. His father and the peasant no longer asked for the work, and when it was finished Leonardo told his father to send for it when he pleased, as he had done his part. Accordingly Ser Piero went to his rooms one morning to fetch it. When he knocked at the door Leonardo opened it and told him to wait a little, and, returning to his room, put the round panel in the light on his easel, and having arranged the window to make the light dim, he called his father in. Ser Piero, taken unaware, started back, not thinking of the round piece of wood, or that the face which he saw was painted, and was beating a retreat when Leonardo detained him and said, " This work has served its purpose; take it away, then, as it has produced the effect intended." Ser Piero indeed thought it more than miraculous, and he warmly praised Leonardo's idea. He then quietly went and bought another round wheel with a heart transfixed by a dart painted upon it, and gave it to the peasant, who was grateful to Piero all his life. Piero took Leonardo's work secretly to Florence and sold it to

---

[8] **Medusa**: in Greek mythology, one of the Gorgons, winged creatures with hair of writhing snakes.
[9] **newts**: salamanders.

some merchants for 100 ducats,[10] and in a short time it came into the hands of the Duke of Milan, who bought it of them for 300 ducats.

Leonardo was so delighted when he saw curious heads, whether bearded or hairy, that he would follow about any one who had thus attracted his attention for a whole day, acquiring such a clear idea of him that when he went home he would draw the head as well as if the man had been present. In this way many heads of men and women came to be drawn, and I have several such pen-and-ink drawings in my book, so often referred to. Among them is the head of Amerigo Vespucci,[11] a fine old man, drawn in carbon, and that of Scaramuccia, the gipsy captain, which afterwards belonged to M. Donato Valdambrini of Arezzo, canon of S. Lorenzo, left to him by Giambullari. He began a picture of the Adoration of the Magi,[12] containing many beautiful things, especially heads, which was in the house of Amerigo Benci, opposite the loggia [13] of the Peruzzi, but which was left unfinished like his other things.

On the death of Giovan. Galeazzo, Duke of Milan, and the accession of Ludovico Sforza in the same year, 1493, Leonardo was invited to Milan with great ceremony by the duke to play the lyre, in which that prince greatly delighted. Leonardo took his own instrument, made by himself in silver, and shaped like a horse's head, a curious and novel idea to render the harmonies more loud and sonorous, so that he surpassed all the musicians who had assembled there. Besides this he was the best reciter of improvised rhymes of his time. The duke, captivated by Leonardo's conversation and genius, conceived an extraordinary affection for him. He begged him to paint an altarpicture of the Nativity, which was sent by the duke to the emperor. Leonardo then did a Last Supper for the Dominicans at S. Maria delle Grazie in Milan, endowing the heads of the Apostles with such majesty and beauty that he left that of Christ unfinished, feeling that he could not give it that celestial divinity which it demanded. This work left in such a condition has always been held in the greatest veneration by the Milanese and by other foreigners, as Leonardo has seized the moment when the Apostles are anxious to discover who would betray their Master. All their faces are expressive of love, fear, wrath, or grief at not being able to grasp the meaning

[10] **100 ducats:** about 228 dollars.

[11] **Vespucci:** (1451–1512) merchant and explorer who gave the name of America to the new world. The common form of his first name is Amerigo.

[12] **Magi:** the wise men of the East who brought offerings to the infant Christ.

[13] **loggia:** open-sided arcade.

of Christ, in contrast to the obstinacy, hatred, and treason of Judas, while the whole work, down to the smallest details, displays incredible diligence, even the texture of the tablecloth being clearly visible so that actual cambric would not look more real. It is said that the prior incessantly importuned Leonardo to finish the work, thinking it strange that the artist should pass half a day at a time lost in thought. He would have desired him never to lay down the brush, as if he were digging a garden. Seeing that his importunity produced no effect, he had recourse to the duke, who felt compelled to send for Leonardo to inquire about the work, showing tactfully that he was driven to act by the importunity of the prior. Leonardo, aware of the acuteness and discretion of the duke, talked with him fully about the picture, a thing which he had never done with the prior. He spoke freely of his art, and explained how men of genius really are doing most when they work least, as they are thinking out ideas and perfecting the conceptions, which they subsequently carry out with their hands. He added that there were still two heads to be done, that of Christ, which he would not look for on the earth, and felt unable to conceive the beauty of the celestial grace that must have been incarnate in the divinity. The other head was that of Judas, which also caused him thought, as he did not think he could express the face of a man who could resolve to betray his Master, the Creator of the world, after having received so many benefits. But he was willing in this case to seek no farther, and for lack of a better he would do the head of the importunate and tactless prior. The duke was wonderfully amused, and laughingly declared that he was quite right. Then the poor prior, covered with confusion, went back to his garden and left Leonardo in peace, while the artist indeed finished his Judas, making him a veritable likeness of treason and cruelty. The head of Christ was left unfinished, as I have said. The nobility of this painting, in its composition and the care with which it was finished, induced the King of France to wish to take it home with him. Accordingly he employed architects to frame it in wood and iron, so that it might be transported in safety, without any regard for the cost, so great was his desire. But the king was thwarted by its being done on the wall, and it remained with the Milanese.

While engaged upon the Last Supper, Leonardo painted the portrait of Duke Ludovico, with Maximilian, his eldest son, at the top of this same refectory, where there is a Passion in the old style. At the other end he did the Duchess Beatrice with Francesco, her other son, both of whom afterwards became Dukes of Milan, the portraits being marvelous. While thus employed, Leonardo suggested that the duke should set up a bronze horse of colossal size with the duke upon it in memory of himself. But he began it on such a scale that it could never be done. Such is the malice of man when stirred by envy that there are some who believe that Leonardo, as with so many of his things, began this with no intention of completing it, because its size was so great that extraordinary difficulties might be foreseen in having it cast all in one piece. And it is probable that many have formed this opinion from the result, since so many of his things have been left unfinished. However, we can readily believe that his great and extraordinary talents suffered a check from being too venturesome, and that the real cause was his endeavor to go on from excellence to excellence and from perfection to perfection. In truth, those who have seen Leonardo's large clay model aver that they never beheld anything finer or more superb. It was preserved until the French came to Milan with King Louis of France, and broke it all to pieces. Thus a small wax model, considered perfect, was lost, as well as a book of the anatomy of horses, done by him. He afterwards devoted even greater care to the study of the anatomy of men, aiding and being aided by M. Marcantonio della Torre, a profound philosopher, who then professed at Padua and wrote upon the subject. I have heard it said that he was one of the first who began to illustrate the science of medicine, by the learning of Galen,[14] and to throw true light upon anatomy, up to that time involved in the thick darkness of ignorance. In this he was marvelously served by the genius, work and hands of Leonardo, who made a book about it with red crayon drawings outlined with the pen, in which he foreshortened and portrayed with the utmost diligence. He did the skeleton, adding all the nerves and muscles, the first attached to the bone, the others keeping it firm and the third moving, and in the various parts he wrote notes in curious characters, using his left hand, and writing from right to left, so that it cannot be read without practice, and only at a mirror. A great part of the sheets of this anatomy is in the hands of M. Francesco de Melzo, a nobleman of Milan, who was a lovely child in Leonardo's time, who was very fond of him, and being now a handsome and courteous old man, he treasures up these drawings with a portrait of Leonardo. Whoever succeeds in reading these notes of Leonardo will be amazed to find how well that divine spirit has reasoned of the arts, the muscles, the nerves and veins, with the greatest diligence in all things. N. N., a painter of Milan, also possesses some writings of Leonardo, written in the same way, which treat of painting and of the methods

---

[14] **Galen:** Greek physician of the second century A.D.

of design and color. Not long ago he came to Florence to see me, wishing to have the work printed. He afterwards went to Rome to put it in hand, but I do not know with what result.

Leonardo returned to Florence, where he found that the Servite friars had allotted to Filippino [15] the picture of the high altar of the Nunziata. At this Leonardo declared that he should like to have done a similar thing. Filippino heard this, and being very courteous, he withdrew. The friars, wishing Leonardo to paint it, brought him to their house, paying all his expenses and those of his household. He kept them like this for a long time, but never began anything. At length he drew a cartoon of the Virgin and St. Anne with a Christ, which not only filled every artist with wonder, but, when it was finished and set up in the room, men and women, young and old, flocked to see it for two days, as if it had been a festival, and they marveled exceedingly. The face of the Virgin displays all the simplicity and beauty which can shed grace on the Mother of God, showing the modesty and humility of a Virgin contentedly happy, in seeing the beauty of her Son, whom she tenderly holds in her lap. As she regards it the little St. John at her feet is caressing a lamb, while St. Anne smiles in her great joy at seeing her earthly progeny become divine, a conception worthy of the great intellect and genius of Leonardo. This cartoon, as will be said below, afterwards went to France. He drew Ginevra, the wife of Amerigo Benci, a beautiful portrait, and then abandoned the work of the friars, who recalled Filippino, though he was prevented from finishing it by death.

For Francesco del Giocondo Leonardo undertook the portrait of Mona [16] Lisa, his wife, and left it incomplete after working at it for four years. This work is now in the possession of Francis, King of France, at Fontainebleau. This head is an extraordinary example of how art can imitate Nature, because here we have all the details painted with great subtlety. The eyes possess that moist luster which is constantly seen in life, and about them are those livid reds and hair which cannot be rendered without the utmost delicacy. The lids could not be more natural, for the way in which the hairs issue from the skin, here thick and there scanty, and following the pores of the skin. The nose possesses the fine delicate reddish apertures seen in life. The opening of the mouth, with its red ends, and the scarlet cheeks seem not color but living flesh. To look closely at her throat

---

[15] **Filippino:** painter friar celebrated in Browning's poem "Fra Lippo Lippi."

[16] **Mona:** Madonna, My Lady. The portrait of Mona Lisa is now in the Louvre in Paris.

you might imagine that the pulse was beating. Indeed, we may say that this was painted in a manner to cause the boldest artists to despair. Mona Lisa was very beautiful, and while Leonardo was drawing her portrait he engaged people to play and sing, and jesters to keep her merry, and remove that melancholy which painting usually gives to portraits. This figure of Leonardo's has such a pleasant smile that it seemed rather divine than human, and was considered marvelous, an exact copy of Nature.

Leonardo had a high spirit and was most generous in every action. It is said that when he went to the bank for the monthly provision that he used to receive from Piero Soderini, the cashier wanted to give him some rolls of farthings, but he would not take them, saying that he was not a painter for farthings. Learning that Piero Soderini accused him of deceiving him and that murmurs rose against him, Leonardo with the help of his friends collected the money and took it back, but Piero would not accept it. He went to Rome with Duke Giuliano de' Medici on the election of Leo X., who studied philosophy and especially alchemy.[17] On the way he made a paste with wax and constructed hollow animals which flew in the air when blown up, but fell when the wind ceased. On a curious lizard found by the vine-dresser of Belvedere he fastened scales taken from other lizards, dipped in quicksilver, which trembled as it moved, and after giving it eyes, a horn and a beard, he tamed it and kept it in a box. All the friends to whom he showed it ran away terrified. He would often dry and purge the guts of a wether and make them so small that they might be held in the palm of the hand. In another room he kept a pair of smith's bellows, and with these he would blow out one of the guts until it filled the room, which was a large one, forcing anyone there to take refuge in a corner. The fact that it had occupied such a little space at first only added to the wonder. He perpetrated many such follies, studied mirrors and made curious experiments to find oil for painting and varnish to preserve the work done. At this time he did a small picture for M. Baldassare Turini of Pescia, the datary[18] of Leo, of the Virgin and Child, with infinite diligence and art. But today it is much spoiled either by neglect or because of his numerous fanciful mixtures and the coloring. In another picture he represented a little child, marvelously beautiful and graceful, both works being now at Pescia in the possession of M. Giulio Turini. It is said that. on being commissioned by the Pope to do a work, he straightway be-

17 **alchemy:** the chemistry of the Middle Ages.
18 **datary:** officer of the Pope's court.

gan to distil oil and herbs to make the varnish, which induced Pope Leo to say: " This man will never do anything, for he begins to think of the end before the beginning! "

There was no love lost between him and Michelagnolo [19] Buonarroti, so that the latter left Florence owing to their rivalry, Duke Giuliano excusing him by saying that he was summoned by the Pope to do the façade of S. Lorenzo. When Leonardo heard this, he left for France, where the king had heard of his works and wanted him to do the cartoon of St. Anne in colors. But Leonardo, as was his wont, gave him nothing but words for a long time. At length, having become old, he lay sick for many months, and seeing himself near death, he desired to occupy himself with the truths of the Catholic Faith and the holy Christian religion. Then, having confessed and shown his penitence with much lamentation, he devoutly took the Sacrament out of his bed, supported by his friends and servants, as he could not stand. The king arriving, for he would often pay him friendly visits, he sat up in bed from respect, and related the circumstances of his sickness, showing how greatly he had offended God and man in not having worked in his art as he ought. He was then seized with a paroxysm, the harbinger of death, so that the king rose and took his head to assist him and show him favor as well as to alleviate the pain. Leonardo's divine spirit, then recognizing that he could not enjoy a greater honor, expired in the king's arms, at the age of seventy-five. The loss of Leonardo caused exceptional grief to those who had known him, because there never was a man who did so much honor to painting. By the splendor of his magnificent mien he comforted every sad soul, and his eloquence could turn men to either side of a question. His personal strength was prodigious, and with his right hand he could bend the clapper of a knocker or a horseshoe as if they had been of lead. His liberality warmed the hearts of all his friends, both rich and poor, if they possessed talent and ability. His presence adorned and honored the most wretched and bare apartment. Thus Florence received a great gift in the birth of Leonardo, and its loss in his death was immeasurable.

SUGGESTIONS FOR STUDY

1. Make a list of the various things which Vasari finds to praise in Leonardo. Does he mention any of the latter's shortcomings? Give some examples of his remarkable inventiveness. Which of these show his sense

[19] **Michelagnolo:** the commoner form of the name is Michelangelo.

of humor? Compare with some of the prophecies from his *Notebooks*, page 352.

2. How do both this account and the selection from Cellini's autobiography illustrate the engrossing power of great art?

3. What impressions do you gain of the Italy of Leonardo's time?

4. Study copies of " The Last Supper " and the " Mona Lisa." Dc the descriptions and comments of Vasari help you to appreciate these pictures? Both paintings have had interesting histories since Vasari's time. In some art history read accounts of the attempts to restore the crumbling " Last Supper," and the theft of " Mona Lisa."

5. Vocabulary: vendor, rotundity, importuned, incarnate, aver, progeny, façade, paroxysm, harbinger, prodigious.

ALESSANDRO MANZONI (1785–1873)

Manzoni, poet and novelist, was born and reared in Milan, which remained his headquarters throughout his long life. He had been a freethinker in his youth but became converted to Catholicism and thereafter was the strongest individual force in Italy on the side of positive Christianity. His literary work was virtually accomplished by 1830 but his religious and ethical influence continued until his death. Manzoni sums up the romantic movement in Italy, especially on its spiritual side, though he was also an innovator in form. His poetic drama, *The Count of Carmagnola* (1819), violated all the classical conventions and came in for some sharp criticism from the literary conservatives. But his ode, " The Fifth of May," on the death of Napoleon in 1821, received universal applause and has remained to this day one of the most popular Italian poems. His masterpiece was the three-volume novel *The Betrothed* (1825–26), a historical romance of Milan in the seventeenth century. It gave Manzoni a European reputation and has deservedly remained the most famous of Italian novels. He was influenced to undertake this work by the example of Sir Walter Scott, but it may be truthfully said that he surpassed his model. Manzoni's death was mourned by the whole nation to whose service he had so unselfishly devoted himself. The celebrated composer Verdi wrote his beautiful *Requiem* to honor his memory.

THE FIFTH OF MAY

Napoleon died in exile at St. Helena on the fifth of May 1821. He had previously been exiled to Elba but escaped in the spring of 1815 to resume the throne of France and fight at Waterloo.

He was. — As motionless he lay,
First mingled with the dead,

The relics of the senseless clay,
Whence such a soul had fled, —
The Earth astounded holds her breath, 5
Struck with the tidings of his death.
    She pauses the last hour to see
Of the dread Man of Destiny;
Nor knows she when another tread,
Like that of the once mighty dead, 10
Shall such a footprint leave impressed
As his, in blood, upon her breast.

I saw him blazing on his throne,
Yet hailed him not — by restless fate
Hurled from the giddy summit down — 15
Resume again his lofty state;
Saw him at last for ever fall,
Still mute amid the shouts of all.
    Free from base flattery, when he rose —
From baser outrage, when he fell; 20
Now his career has reached its close,
My voice is raised, the truth to tell,
And o'er his exiled urn will try
To pour a strain that shall not die.

From Alps to Pyramids were thrown 25
His bolts, from Scylla to the Don,
From Manzanares to the Rhine,
From sea to sea, unerring hurled;
And ere the flash had ceased to shine,
Burst on their aim, — and shook the world. 30
    Was this true glory? — The high doom
Must be pronounced by times to come.
For us, we bow before His throne,
Who willed, in gifting mortal clay
With such a spirit, to display 35
A grander impress of his own.

His was the stormy, fierce delight
To dare adventure's boldest scheme;

26. **Scylla:** the rocky shore of the mainland on the Straits of Messina.
27. **Manzanares:** a town in Spain.

The soul of fire, that burned for might,
And could of naught but empire dream;   40
And his the indomitable will
That dream of empire to fulfil,
    And to a greatness to attain
'T were madness to have hoped to gain:
All these were his; nor these alone —   45
Flight, victory, exile, and the throne —
Twice in the dust by thousands trod,
Twice on the altar as a god.

Two ages stood in arms arrayed,
Contending which should victor be.   50
He spake: — his mandate they obeyed,
And bowed to hear their destiny.
He stepped between them, to assume
The mastery, and pronounce their doom,
    Then vanished, and inactive wore   55
Life's remnant out on that lone shore.
What envy did his palmy state,
What pity his reverses move,
Object of unrelenting hate,
And unextinguishable love!   60

As beat innumerable waves
O'er the last floating plank that saves
One sailor from the wreck, whose eye
Intently gazes o'er the main,
Far in the distance to descry   65
Some speck of hope, — but all in vain;
    Did countless waves of memory roll
Incessant, thronging on his soul.
Recording, for a future age,
The tale of his renown,   70
How often on the immortal page
His hand sank weary down!

Oft on some sea-beat cliff alone
He stood, — the lingering daylight gone,
And pensive evening come at last, —   75
With folded arms, and eyes declined;
While, O, what visions on his mind

Came rushing — of the past!
   The rampart stormed, — the tented field, —
His eagles glittering far and wide, —   80
His columns never taught to yield, —
His cavalry's resistless tide,
Watching each motion of his hand,
Swift to obey the swift command.

Such thoughts, perchance, last filled his breast,   85
And his departing soul oppressed,
To tempt it to despair;
Till from on high a hand of might
In mercy came to guide its flight
Up to a purer air, —   90
   Leading it, o'er hope's path of flowers,
To the celestial plains,
Where greater happiness is ours
Than even fancy feigns,
And where earth's fleeting glories fade   95
Into the shadow of a shade.

Immortal, bright, beneficent,
Faith, used to victories, on thy roll
Write this with joy; for never bent
Beneath death's hand a haughtier soul;   100
Thou from the worn and pallid clay
Chase every bitter word away,
   That would insult the dead.
His holy crucifix, whose breath
Has power to raise and to depress,   105
Send consolation and distress,
Lay by him on that lovely bed
And hallowed it in death.

                    (*F. C. Gray*)

SUGGESTIONS FOR STUDY

1. If your only knowledge of Napoleon came from this poem, what impression would you have of him? In which stanza does Manzoni characterize Napoleon most fully? How far does he venture to judge him?

2. Explain the historical reference of lines 47–48; also lines 49–54.

3. In what other pieces of literature has Napoleon figured?

GIACOMO LEOPARDI (1798–1837)

Leopardi, poet and pessimist, was born in the town of Recanati in the Abruzzi Mountains of noble but impoverished parents. Circumstances combined to make his life one of the unhappiest on record. Delicate and high-strung from birth, he developed his precocious genius at the cost of his physical health and mental balance. By the age of sixteen he was already a distinguished scholar, and at twenty-one he put himself in the front rank of Italian poets of his day. But ill-health wrecked every chance of a normally happy life. For years he was half blind, sleepless, and tortured by incessant pain. The only wonder is that he accomplished as much as he did in productive scholarship and creative writing. Much of his time was spent in his dull birthplace, with intervals of visits to Rome, Bologna, and Florence. In 1833 he repaired to Naples in the vain hope of improving his health. He died there before completing his thirty-ninth year.

Leopardi was the finest Italian lyric poet since Petrarch. His poems, few in number, consist principally of odes and meditative soliloquies, classically perfect in construction and style. They voice his conviction of the sadness of life and his shame at his country's degradation, which was a contributing cause of that sadness. But the clearest exposition of his pessimism is found in his prose *Dialogues*. Pessimism, in the philosophical sense, is the belief that evil predominates over good in the scheme of things, and that this condition is irremediable. Leopardi universalized his own unhappiness. He proclaimed misery to be the common lot imposed by the cruelty of nature herself. It is interesting to compare his utterances, on the one hand, with those of poets like Byron and Musset, who were infected with romantic melancholy, and on the other hand, with the writings of Schopenhauer, who claimed he had proved pessimism philosophically.

DIALOGUE BETWEEN A NATURAL PHILOSOPHER [1] AND A METAPHYSICIAN [2]

Natural Philosopher. Eureka! [3] Eureka!

Metaphysician. What is it? What have you found?

Nat. Phil. The art of long life.

Met. And the book that you carry?

Nat. Phil. Explains my theory. This invention of mine will give me eternal life. Others may live long, but I shall live for ever. I mean that I shall acquire immortal fame.

---

[1] **Natural Philosopher:** scientist.
[2] **Metaphysician:** philosopher.
[3] **Eureka:** I have found it.

Met. Follow my advice. Get a leaden casket; enclose therein your book; bury it; and leave in your will directions where it may be found, with instructions to your heirs not to exhume [4] the book until they shall have discovered the art of living a happy life.

Nat. Phil. And meanwhile?

Met. Meanwhile your invention will be good for nothing. It were far better if it taught the art of living briefly.

Nat. Phil. That has already been known a long time. The discovery was not a difficult one.

Met. At any rate I prefer it to yours.

Nat. Phil. Why?

Met. Because if life be not happy, as hitherto it has not been, it were better to endure a short term of it than a long one.

Nat. Phil. No, no. I differ from you. Life is a good in itself, and is naturally desired and loved by every one.

Met. So men think. But they are deceived. Similarly people deceive themselves in thinking that colors are attributes of the objects colored; whereas really they are not qualities of objects, but of light. I assert that man loves and desires nothing but his own happiness. He therefore loves his life only inasmuch as he esteems it the instrument or subject of his happiness. Hence it is happiness that he always loves, and not life; although he very often attributes to the one the affection he has for the other. It is true that this illusion and that relating to colors are both natural. But as a proof that the love of life in men is unnatural, or rather unnecessary, think of the many people that in olden times preferred to die rather than live. In our own time too many people often wish for death, and some kill themselves. Now such things could not occur if man naturally loved life itself. The love of happiness, on the contrary, is innate [5] in every living being; indeed the world would perish before they ceased loving and seeking it in every possible form. And as for your assertion that life in itself is a good thing, I challenge you to prove your words by any arguments you please, whether of physics or metaphysics. Personally I am of opinion that a happy life is undoubtedly a good thing. But this is because of the happiness, not the life. An unhappy life is therefore an evil. And since it is ordained that human life should be inseparable from unhappiness, I leave you to draw your own conclusions.

Nat. Phil. Let us drop the subject, if you please; it is too melancholy. Answer me one question candidly, and without such subtleties.

---

⁴ **exhume:** dig up.   ⁵ **innate:** inborn.

If man had the power to live for ever, I mean in this life and not after death, do you think he would be happy?

Met. Allow me to answer you by a fable. Moreover, as I have never tasted immortality, I cannot reply to you from experience. Besides, I have never by any chance met an immortal, the very existence of whom is a mere matter of legend. If Cagliostro [6] were alive, he could perhaps enlighten you, since he was said to have lived for several centuries. But he is now dead, like his contemporaries.

To return to the fable. The wise Chiro, who was a god, in time became so wearied of his life, that he asked permission from Jove to die. This was granted to him; so he died. If immortality wrought such an effect on the gods, how would it be with men? The Hyperboreans, an unknown but famous people, whose country is inaccessible by sea or land, were, it is said, rich in all manner of things, and possessed a race of asses of peculiar beauty, which they used to offer as sacrifices. They had the power, unless I am mistaken, of living for ever, and knew nothing of fatigues, cares, wars, discords, or crimes. Yet we learn that after several thousand years of life, they all killed themselves by jumping from a certain rock into the sea, where they were drowned. Here is another legend. The brothers Biton and Cleobus, at a festival, when the mules were not ready, attached themselves to the chariot of their mother, who was a priestess of Juno, and drew her to the temple. Touched by their devotion, the priestess asked Juno to reward her sons for their piety by the greatest gift possible for men to receive. The goddess caused them both to die peacefully within an hour, instead of giving them immortality, as they had expected.

The same happened to Agamede and Trophonius. When these two men had finished the temple of Delphi, they begged Apollo to reward them. The god asked them to wait seven days, at the end of which time he would do so. On the seventh night he sent them a sweet sleep from which they have never awakened. They are so satisfied with their recompense that they have asked nothing more.

On the subject of legends, here is one which introduces a question I would have you answer. I know that by you and your colleagues human life is generally considered to be, as a rule, of an uniformly average duration: this in all countries and under all climates. But Pliny [7] relates that the men of some parts of India and Ethiopia do

[6] **Cagliostro:** an Italian physician of the eighteenth century who claimed to perform miracles.

[7] **Pliny:** a Roman naturalist who perished in the eruption of Vesuvius 79 A.D. See page 1087.

not exceed the age of forty years. They who die at this age are considered very old. Their children marry at seven years of age; and this
statement is verified by the custom in Guinea, the Deccan,[8] and elsewhere in the torrid zone. Now, regarding it as true that these people
do not live more than forty years (and this as a natural limit, and not
due to artificial circumstances), I ask you whether you imagine their
lot ought to be considered more or less happy than that of others?

Nat. Phil. Undoubtedly, more miserable, since they die so soon.

Met. I am of the contrary opinion for the very same reason. But
that does not matter. Give me your attention for a moment. I deny
that life itself, *i.e.*, the mere sensation of existence, has anything pleasurable or desirable in its nature. But we all wish for the other thing,
also called life; I mean strength, and numerous sensations. Thus,
all activity, and every strong and lively passion, provided it be neither
disagreeable nor painful, pleases us simply because it is strong and
lively, although it possess no other pleasurable attributes.

Now these men, whose life normally lasts only forty years, that is,
half the time granted by nature to other men, would experience every
moment an intensity of life, twice as strong as ours, because their
growth, maturity, and decline are accomplished twice as rapidly as
with us. Their energy of life therefore ought to be twice as intense as
ours at every moment of their existence. And to this greater intensity
there must correspond a more lively activity of the will, more vivacity
and animation. Thus they experience in less time the same quantity
of life as we have. And the fewer years that these favored people
spend on the earth are so well filled that there is no sensible [9] vacuum;
whereas this same quantity of life is insufficient to vivify a term twice
as long. Their actions and sensations, diffused over so limited a
space, can duly occupy all their existence; but our longer life is constantly divided by protracted intervals devoid of all activity and
lively passion. And since existence itself is in no sense desirable, but
only in so far as it is happy; and since good or evil fortune is not
measurable by the number of our days; I conclude that the life of
these people, though shorter than ours, is much the richer in pleasures, or what are so called. Their life must then be preferable to
ours, or even to that of the earliest kings of Assyria, Egypt, China,
India, and other countries, who are said to have lived thousands of
years. So that, far from being desirous of immortality, I am content
to leave it to fishes, which are by Leeuwenhoek [10] believed to be im-

---

[8] **Deccan:** the southern part of India.   [9] **sensible:** perceptible.
[10] **Leeuwenhoek:** (1632–1723) a Dutch scientist.

mortal, provided they are neither eaten by us nor their fellows. Instead of delaying the development of the body, in order to lengthen life, as Maupertuis [11] proposed, I would rather accelerate it until the duration of our life was as short as that of the insects called ephemerals; which insects, although the most aged does not live beyond a single day, nevertheless preside over three generations before they die. If it were so, then there would at least be no time for ennui.[12]

What do you think of my reasoning?

Nat. Phil. It does not persuade me. I know that you love metaphysics, whereas I for my part hold to physics. To your subtleties I oppose simple common sense, which is sufficient for me. Thus, I venture to assert, without appealing to the microscope, that life is better than death. Judging between the two, I would give the apple to the former, without troubling them to strip for the contest.

Met. And I would do the same. But when I call to mind the custom of those barbarians, who, for every unhappy day of their lives, used to throw a black stone into a quiver, and for every happy day a white one, I cannot help thinking how few white stones compared to the black ones would be found therein on the death of the proprietor of the quiver. Personally, I should like to have now all the stones representing the days of life yet remaining to me, and permission to separate them, throwing away all the black ones and retaining only those that were white; even though the number of the latter was exceedingly small, and their color a doubtful white.

Nat. Phil. Many people, on the contrary, would be glad to increase the number of their black stones, even though they were blacker than they naturally would be; because they always, in their minds, dread the last as the blackest of all. And such people, of whom I am one, will really be able to add many stones to their normal quantity, if they follow out the instructions contained in my book.

Met. Every one thinks and works in his own way. Death also will not fail to do the same. But if you wish, in prolonging man's life, really to be of service to him, discover an art to increase the number and strength of sensations, and their effects. This would be a genuine augmentation [13] of human life, for it would fill up those long intervals of time, during which we vegetate rather than live. You could then boast of having truly prolonged human life; and without having sought after the impossible, or used violence to natural laws;

[11] **Maupertuis:** a French scientist of the eighteenth century.
[12] **ennui:** boredom.
[13] **augmentation:** enlargement.

rather, by having strengthened them. For does it not seem as though the ancients were more full of life than we are, in spite of the many and great dangers by which they were surrounded, and which generally shortened their existence?

You will thus render a real service to man, whose life is, I will not say more happy, but certainly less unhappy, when it is better occupied and more violently agitated, without pain or discomfort. When, on the other hand, existence is so full of idleness and ennui as to be justly termed empty, the saying of Pyrrhus,[14] " there is no difference between life and death," is literally realized. Were this saying true, I should be in no slight terror of death.

But finally, unless life be active and vigorous, it is not true life, and death is far preferable to it.

(Charles Edwards)

[14] **Pyrrhus:** King of Epirus, who invaded Italy and won some victories over the Romans in the third century B.C.

SUGGESTIONS FOR STUDY

1. Summarize the argument of the metaphysician. Can you find any flaws in it? Give reasons for your answer.

2. Which speaker in the dialogue seems to voice the opinions of Leopardi? With which do you agree? Why?

3. What is the essential difference between vegetating and really living? Is the life span tending to increase or decrease at the present time? What bearing does this dialogue have on the question of the proper use of leisure time much discussed today?

ODE TO ITALY

My native land, I see the walls and arches,
The columns and the statues, and the lonely
Towers of our ancestors,
But not their glory, not
The laurel and the steel that of old time   5
Our great forefathers bore. Disarmèd now,
Naked thou showest thy forehead and thy breast!
O me, how many wounds,
What bruises and what blood! How do I see thee,
Thou loveliest Lady! Unto Heaven I cry,   10
And to the world: " Say, say,

Who brought her unto this? " To this and worse,
For both her arms are loaded down with chains,
So that, unveiled and with disheveled hair,
She crouches all forgotten and forlorn,   15
Hiding her beautiful face
Between her knees, and weeps.
Weep, weep, for well thou may'st, my Italy!
Born, as thou wert, to conquest,
Alike in evil and in prosperous sort!   20
    If thy sweet eyes were each a living stream,
Thou could'st not weep enough
For all thy sorrow and for all thy shame.
For thou wast queen, and now thou art a slave.
Who speaks of thee or writes,   25
That thinking on thy glory in the past
But says, " She was great once, but is no more."
Wherefore, oh wherefore? Where is the ancient strength,
The valor and the arms, the constancy?
Who rent the sword from thee?   30
Who hath betrayed thee? What art, or what toil,
Or what o'erwhelming force,
Hath stripped thy robe and golden wreath from thee?
How didst thou fall, and when,
From such height unto a depth so low?   35
Doth no one fight for thee, no one defend thee,
None of thy own? Arms, arms! For I alone
Will fight and fall for thee.
Grant me, O Heaven, my blood
Shall be as fire unto Italian hearts!   40
    Where are thy sons? I hear the sound of arms,
Of wheels, of voices, and of drums;
In foreign fields afar
Thy children fight and fall.
Wait, Italy, wait! I see, or seem to see,   45
A tumult as of infantry and horse,
And smoke and dust, and the swift flash of swords
Like lightning among clouds.
Wilt thou not hope? Wilt thou not lift and turn
Thy trembling eyes upon the doubtful close?   50
For what, in yonder fields,
Combats Italian youth? O gods, ye gods,

Oh, misery for him who dies in war,
Not for his native shores and his beloved,
His wife and children dear,   55
But by the foes of others
For others' cause, and cannot dying say
" Dear land of mine,
The life thou gavest me I give thee back."

(*W. D. Howells*)

SUGGESTIONS FOR STUDY

1. Show where this poem reveals not only the habitual sadness of Leopardi's mind but also his imaginative power.

2. When Leopardi wrote this poem, Italy was divided and partly ruled by foreigners. He longed for national unity and independence. What was to him the worst feature of Italy's plight? If he were living today how do you think he would feel toward the present government of Italy?

3. How would you define pessimism? What other poets do you know who might be called pessimists? Who are some of the optimists among the English and American poets?

GIUSEPPE MAZZINI (1805–1872)

Mazzini was the prophet of Italian unification and one of the most famous political agitators of the nineteenth century. In 1831 he founded the Young Italy movement, which aimed at the overthrow of all the existing Italian governments and the union of the entire country as a republic. As a result, he was exiled and eventually made his way to England, which was to be his headquarters for many years. With tireless energy he continued his agitation for the liberation and unification of his country, and by preparing men's minds for these things helped bring them to pass, though the monarchical form of the new free and united Italy, which was set up in 1861, did not please him.

The Duties of Man, his most popular work, was for many years used as a textbook in the Italian schools. Mazzini, though looked upon as a radical in his day, had no sympathy with the materialistic doctrines of socialism. His desire was to proclaim ideals and duties instead of self-interest and rights.

THE DUTIES OF MAN

TO THE ITALIAN WORKINGMEN

I want to speak to you of your duties. I want to speak to you, as my heart dictates to me, of the most sacred things which we know — of God, of Humanity, of the Fatherland, of the Family. Listen to me with love, even as I shall speak to you with love. My words are words of conviction matured by long years of sorrow and of observation and of study. The duties which I am going to point out to you I strive and shall strive as long as I live to fulfil, to the utmost of my power. I may make mistakes, but my heart is true. I may deceive myself, but I will not deceive you. Hear me therefore as a brother; judge freely among yourselves, whether it seems to you that I speak the truth; abandon me if you think that I preach what is false; but follow me and do according to my teaching if you find me an apostle of truth. To be mistaken is a misfortune to be pitied; but to know the truth and not to conform one's actions to it is a crime which Heaven and Earth condemn.

Why do I speak to you of your *duties* before speaking to you of your *rights?* Why in a society in which all, voluntarily or involuntarily, oppress you, in which the exercise of all the rights which belong to man is constantly denied you, in which misery is your lot, and what is called happiness is for other classes of men, why do I speak to you of self-sacrifice and not of conquest; of virtue, moral improvement, education, and not of material *well-being?* This is a question which I must answer before going further, because here precisely lies the difference between our school and many others which are being preached today in Europe; because, moreover, it is a question which rises readily in the indignant mind of the suffering workingman.

We are poor, enslaved, unhappy; speak to us of better material conditions, of liberty, of happiness. Tell us if we are doomed to suffer forever, or if we too may enjoy in our turn. Preach Duty to our masters, to the classes above us which treat us like machines, and monopolize the blessings which belong to all. To us speak of rights; speak of the means of vindicating them; speak of our strength. Wait till we have a recognized existence; then you shall speak to us of duties and of sacrifice. This is what many of our workingmen say, and follow teachers and associations which respond to their desires. They forget one thing only, and that is, that the doctrine which they invoke has been preached for the last fifty years without producing the slightest material improvement in the condition of the working people.

For the last fifty years whatever has been done for the cause of progress and of good against absolute governments and hereditary aristocracies has been done in the name of the Rights of Man; in the name of liberty as the means, and of well-being as the object of existence. All the acts of the French Revolution and of the revolutions which followed and imitated it were consequences of a Declaration of the Rights of Man. All the works of the philosophers [1] who prepared it were based upon a theory of liberty, and upon the need of making known to every individual his own rights. All the revolutionary schools preached that man is born for happiness, that he has the right to seek it by all the means in his power, that no one has the right to impede him in this search, and that he has the right of overthrowing all the obstacles which he may encounter on his path. And the obstacles were overthrown; liberty was conquered. It endured for years in many countries; in some it still endures. Has the condition of the people improved? Have the millions who live by the daily labor of their hands gained the least fraction of the well-being hoped for and promised to them? . . .

And nevertheless, in these last fifty years, the sources of social wealth and the sum of material blessings have steadily increased. Production has doubled. Commerce, amid continual crises, inevitable in the utter absence of organization, has acquired a greater force of activity and a wider sphere for its operations. Communication has almost everywhere been made secure and rapid, and the price of commodities has fallen in consequence of the diminished cost of transport. And, on the other hand, the idea of rights inherent in human nature is today generally accepted; accepted in word and, hypocritically, even by those who seek to evade it in deed. Why, then, has the condition of the people not improved? Why is the consumption of products, instead of being divided equally among all the members of the social body in Europe, concentrated in the hands of a small number of men forming a new aristocracy? Why has the new impulse given to industry and commerce produced, not the well-being of the many, but the luxury of the few?

The answer is clear to those who will look a little closely into things. Men are creatures of education, and act only according to the principle of education given to them. The men who have promoted revo-

---

[1] philosophers: for example, Locke in England and Rousseau in France.

lutions hitherto have based them upon the idea of the rights belonging to the individual; the revolutions conquered liberty — individual liberty, liberty of teaching, liberty of belief, liberty of trade, liberty in everything and for everybody. But of what use was the recognition of their rights to those who had no means of exercising them? What did liberty of teaching mean to those who had neither time nor means to profit by it, or liberty of trade to those who had nothing to trade with, neither capital nor credit? In all the countries where these principles were proclaimed society was composed of a small number of individuals who possessed the land, the credit, the capital, and of vast multitudes of men who had nothing but their own hands and were forced to give the labor of them to the former class, on any terms, in order to live, and forced to spend the whole day in material and monotonous toil. For these, constrained to battle with hunger, what was liberty but an illusion and a bitter irony? To make it anything else it would have been necessary for the men of the well-to-do classes to consent to reduce the hours of labor, to increase the remuneration, to institute free and uniform education for the masses, to make the instruments of labor accessible to all, and to provide a bonus fund for the workingman endowed with capacity and good intentions. But why should they do it? Was not *well-being* the supreme object in life? Were not material blessings desirable before all other things? Why should they lessen their own enjoyment for the advantage of others? Let those who could, help themselves. When society has secured to everybody who can use them the free exercise of the rights belonging to human nature, it does all that is required of it. If there be any one who is unable from the fatality of his own circumstances to exercise any of these rights, he must resign himself and not blame others.

It was natural that they should say thus, and thus, in fact, they did say. And this attitude of mind towards the poor in the classes privileged by fortune soon became the attitude of every individual towards every other. Each man looked after his own rights and the improvement of his own condition without seeking to provide for others; and when his rights clashed with those of others, there was war; not a war of blood, but of gold and of cunning; a war less manly than the other, but equally destructive; cruel war, in which those who had the means and were strong relentlessly crushed the weak or the unskilled. In this continual warfare, men were educated in egoism and in greed for material welfare exclusively. Liberty of belief destroyed all community of faith. Liberty of education produced moral anarchy.

Men without a common tie, without unity of religious belief and of aim, and whose sole vocation was enjoyment, sought every one his own road, not heeding if in pursuing it they were trampling upon the heads of their brothers — brothers in name and enemies in fact. To this we are come today, thanks to the theory of *rights*.

Certainly rights exist; but where the rights of an individual come into conflict with those of another, how can we hope to reconcile and harmonize them, without appealing to something superior to all rights? And where the rights of an individual, or of many individuals, clash with the rights of the Country, to what tribunal are we to appeal? If the right to *well-being*, to the greatest possible well-being, belongs to every living person, who will solve the difficulty between the workingman and the manufacturer? If the right to existence is the first and inviolable right of every man, who shall demand the sacrifice of that existence for the benefit of other men? Will you demand it in the name of Country, of Society, of the multitude of your brothers? What is Country, in the opinion of those of whom I speak, but the place in which our individual rights are most secure? What is Society but a collection of men who have agreed to bring the strength of the many in support of the rights of each? And after having taught the individual for fifty years that Society is established for the purpose of *assuring to him the exercise of his rights,* would you ask him to sacrifice them all to Society, to submit himself, if need be, to continuous toil, to prison, to exile, for the sake of improving it? After having preached to him everywhere that the object of life is *well-being,* would you all at once bid him give up well-being and life itself to free his country from the foreigner, or to procure better conditions for a class which is not his own? After having talked to him for years of *material* interests, how can you maintain that, finding wealth and power in his reach, he ought not to stretch out his hand to grasp them, even to the injury of his brothers?

Italian Workingmen, this is not a chance thought of my mind, without a foundation in fact. It is history, the history of our own times, a history the pages of which drip with blood, the blood of the people. . . . Who shall say to a man, *Go on struggling for your rights,* when to struggle for them costs him dearer than to abandon them?

And even in a society constituted on a juster basis than our own, who shall convince a believer in the theory of *rights* solely that he has to work for the common purpose and devote himself to the development of the social *idea?* Suppose he should rebel; suppose he should feel himself strong and should say to you: *I break the social compact,*[2] *my inclinations, my faculties, call me elsewhere; I have a sacred and inviolable right to develop them, and I choose to be at war with everybody:* what answer can you give him while he keeps to his theory of rights? What right have you, because you are a majority, to compel his obedience to laws which do not accord with his desires and with his individual aspirations? What right have you to punish him if he violates them? Rights belong equally to every individual; the fact of living together in a community does not create a single one. Society has greater strength, not more rights, than the individual. How, then, are you going to prove to the individual that he must merge his will in the will of those who are his brothers, whether in the Country or in the wider fellowship of Humanity? By means of the executioner, of the prison? Societies existing up till now have used such means. But that is war, and we want peace; that is tyrannical repression, and we want education.

Education, we have said; and this is the great word which sums up our whole doctrine. The vital question agitating our century is a question of education. What we have to do is not to establish a new order of things by violence. An order of things so established is always tyrannical even when it is better than the old. *We have to overthrow by force the brute force which opposes itself today to every attempt at improvement,* and then propose for the approval of the nation, free to express its will, what we believe to be the best order of things and by every possible means educate men to develop it and act in conformity with it. The theory of *rights* enables us to rise and overthrow obstacles, but not to found a strong and lasting accord between all the elements which compose the nation. With the theory of happiness, of *well-being,* as the primary aim of existence we shall only form egoistic men, worshipers of the material, who will carry the old passions into the new order of things and corrupt it in a few months. We have therefore to find a principle of education superior to any such theory, which shall guide men to better things, teach them constancy in self-sacrifice and link them with their fellow men without making them dependent on the ideas of a single man or on the strength of all. And this principle is Duty. We must convince men that they, sons of one only God, must obey one only law, here on earth; that each one of them must live, not for himself, but for others;

[2] **social compact:** the social compact or social contract was a general agreement on which society was supposed to be founded. One of Rousseau's most influential books was called the *Social Contract.*

that the object of their life is not to be more or less happy, but to make themselves and others better; that to fight against injustice and error for the benefit of their brothers is not only a *right,* but a *duty;* a duty not to be neglected without sin, — the duty of their whole life.

Italian Workingmen, my Brothers! understand me fully. When I say that the knowledge of their *rights* is not enough to enable men to effect any appreciable or lasting improvement, I do not ask you to renounce these rights; I only say that they cannot exist except as a consequence of duties fulfilled, and that one must begin with the latter in order to arrive at the former. And when I say that by proposing *happiness, well-being,* or *material* interest as the aim of existence, we run the risk of producing egoists, I do not mean that you should never strive after these things. I say that material interests pursued alone, and not as a means, but as an end, lead always to this most disastrous result. When under the Emperors, the old Romans asked for nothing but *bread* and *amusements,* they became the most abject race conceivable, and after submitting to the stupid and ferocious tyranny of the Emperors they basely fell into slavery to the invading Barbarians. In France and elsewhere the enemies of all social progress have sown corruption and tried to divert men's minds from ideas of change by furthering the development of *material* activity. And shall we help the enemy with our own hands? Material improvement is essential, and we shall strive to win it for ourselves; but not because the one thing necessary for man is to be well fed and housed, but rather because you cannot have a sense of your own dignity or any moral development while you are engaged, as at the present day, in a continual duel with want. You work ten or twelve hours a day: how can you find *time* to educate yourselves? Most of you earn hardly enough to keep yourselves and your families: how can you then find *means* to educate yourselves? The uncertainty of your employment and the frequent interruptions in it cause you to alternate between too much work and periods of idleness: how are you to acquire habits of order, regularity, and assiduity? The scantiness of your earnings does away with any hope of saving enough to be useful some day to your children, or to your own old age: how are you to educate yourselves into habits of economy? Many of you are compelled by poverty to separate your children, we will not say from the careful bringing-up — what sort of bringing-up can the poor wives of workingmen give their children? — but from the love and the watchful eye of their mothers, and to send them out, for the sake of a few halfpence, to unwholesome labor in factories: how, in such conditions, can family affection unfold itself and be ennobled? You have not the rights of citizens, nor any participation, by election or by vote, in the laws which regulate your actions and your life: how should you feel the pride of citizenship or have any zeal for the State, or sincere affection for the laws? Justice is not dealt out to you with the same equal hand as to the other classes: whence, then, are you to learn respect and love for justice? Society treats you without a shadow of sympathy: whence are you to learn sympathy with society? You need, then, a change in your material conditions to enable you to develop morally; you need to work less so as to have some hours of your day to devote to the improvement of your minds; you need a sufficient remuneration of your labor to put you in a position to accumulate savings, and so set your minds at rest about the future, and to purify yourselves above all of every sentiment of *retaliation,* every impulse of revenge, every thought of injustice towards those who have been unjust to you. You must strive, then, for this change, and you will obtain it, but you must strive for it as a *means,* not as an *end;* strive for it from a sense of *duty,* not only as a *right;* strive for it in order to make yourselves better, not only to make yourselves *materially* happy. If not, what difference would there be between you and your tyrants? They are tyrants precisely because they do not think of anything but *well-being,* pleasure and power.

To make yourselves better; this must be the aim of your life. You cannot make yourselves permanently less unhappy except by improving yourselves. Tyrants will arise by the thousand among you, if you fight only in the name of material interests, or of a particular organization. A change of social organization makes little difference if you and the other classes keep the passions and the egoism of today; organizations are like certain plants which yield poison or remedies according to the way in which they are administered. Good men make bad organizations good, and bad men make good organizations bad. You have got to improve the classes which, voluntarily or involuntarily, oppress you today, and convince them of their duties; but you will never succeed in this unless you begin by making yourselves better as far as possible.

When therefore you hear men who preach the necessity of a social transformation telling you that they can accomplish it by invoking your *rights* only, be grateful to them for their good intentions, but distrustful of the outcome. The ills of the poor man are known, in part at least, to the well-to-do classes; *known* but not *felt.* In the general indifference born of the absence of a common faith; in the egoism, inevitably resulting from the continual preaching through so many years of the doctrine of material *well-being,* those who do not suffer have grown accustomed little by little to consider these ills as a sad necessity of the social order and to leave the trouble of remedying them to the generations to come. The difficulty is not to convince them, but to shake them out of inertia and to induce them, when they are convinced, to *act,* to associate themselves, to unite with you in brotherly fellowship for the purpose of creating such a social organization as shall put an end, as far as the conditions of humanity allow, to your ills and to their own fears. Now, this is a work of faith, of faith in the mission which God has given to the human creature here upon earth; of faith in the responsibility weighing upon all those who do not fulfil that mission, and in the duty which bids every one work continually, and with self-sacrifice, for the cause of Truth. All possible theories of rights and of material *well-being* can only lead you to attempts which, so long as they remain isolated and dependent on your strength only, will not succeed, but can only bring about the worst of social crimes, a civil war between class and class.

Italian Workingmen, my Brothers! When Christ came and changed the face of the world, He did not speak of rights to the rich, who had no need to conquer them; nor to the poor, who would perhaps have abused them, in imitation of the rich. He did not speak of utility or of self-interest to a people whom utility and self-interest had corrupted. He spoke of Duty, He spoke of Love, of Sacrifice, of Faith: He said that *they only should be first among all who had done good to all by their work.* And these thoughts, breathed into the ear of a society which had no longer any spark of life, reanimated it, conquered the millions, conquered the world, and caused the education of the human race to progress a degree. Italian Workingmen! we live in an epoch like Christ's. We live in the midst of a society rotten as that of the Roman Empire, and feel in our souls the need of reviving and transforming it, of associating all its members and its workers in one single faith, under one single law, and for one purpose; the free and progressive development of all the faculties which God has planted in His creatures. We seek the reign of God upon earth as in heaven, or better, that the earth shall be a preparation for heaven, and society an endeavor towards a progressive approach to the Divine Idea.

But every act of Christ's represented the faith which He preached, and round Him there were apostles who embodied in their acts the faith which they had accepted. Be such as they, and you will conquer. Preach Duty to the men of the classes above you, and fulfil, as far as possible, your own duties; preach virtue, sacrifice, love; and be yourselves virtuous and prompt to self-sacrifice and love. . . .

(Anonymous Translation)

SUGGESTIONS FOR STUDY

1. Why does Mazzini place Duty above rights? Read Wordsworth's " Ode to Duty " for a somewhat similar conception.

2. What are the " inalienable rights " of men, according to our Declaration of Independence? Does Mazzini mean the same thing by " rights "? Do you believe that the assertion of " rights " leads to selfishness? Discuss. Would Mazzini have approved of Mussolini's emphasis on duty to the state to the exclusion of individual rights?

3. Is Mazzini a convincing writer? What would you say of his clarity of ideals, logical development of argument, use of climax?

4. What similarity do you see between labor problems of a hundred years ago and those of today? Discuss whether Mazzini's message has value for the American workingman of today.

GIOSUE CARDUCCI (1836–1907)

Carducci was the most talented and influential Italian poet between Leopardi and D'Annunzio. For more than forty years he was professor of Italian literature in Bologna, where his authority as scholar and critic attracted many students. He caused a considerable scandal in 1865 by his sonorous *Hymn to Satan*. Satan symbolized for him science and the freedom of thought; he was " the banner-bearer of the great reformers and innovators in all ages." Carducci was opposed to romanticism, which he regarded as unsuited to his countrymen. He preferred to emphasize the classical tradition in Italian culture and in some of his poems even sought to reproduce the rhythm of Latin meters. His spirit was pagan and anti-clerical. " Other gods die," he wrote, " the divinities of Greece know no setting." Ardently patriotic and a convinced liberal in his political views, he modified his early republicanism enough to accept the Italian monarchy. His poems are distinguished for their vigor of thought and expression and their metrical variety. He received the Nobel prize in 1906.

THE OX

I love thee, pious ox; a gentle feeling
Of vigor and of peace thou givest my heart.
How solemn, like a monument, thou art!

Over wide fertile fields thy calm gaze stealing,
Unto the yoke with grave contentment kneeling, 5
To man's quick work thou dost thy strength impart,
He shouts and goads, and, answering thy smart,
Thou turn'st on him thy patient eyes appealing.
From thy broad nostrils, black and wet, arise
Thy breath's soft fumes; and on the still air swells, 10
Like happy hymn, thy lowing's mellow strain.
In the grave sweetness of thy tranquil eyes
Of emerald, broad and still, reflected dwells
All the divine green silence of the plain.

(*Frank Sewall*)

SUGGESTIONS FOR STUDY

1. The ox has often been taken as a symbol of strength or patience or even of stupidity. Why does Carducci love the ox? How does this poem suggest the poet's conservative attitude toward life?

2. What other poems about farm animals do you know?

GABRIELE D'ANNUNZIO (1863–1938)

D'Annunzio, poet, dramatist, and novelist, became Italy's most conspicuous man of letters after the last decade of the nineteenth century. He was born in the mountainous district of the Abruzzi. Frankly a pagan and a voluptuary, he was regarded, before 1915, as a pronounced egoist and a writer of brilliant but somewhat unwholesome books. From 1915 to 1921, however, he surprised the world by showing himself a man of romantic action. Not only was he largely instrumental in bringing his country into World War I on the side of the Allies, but he also displayed incredible bravery as an aviator. After the war he led an unauthorized expedition and seized the city of Fiume, which he wished to annex to Italy. For fifteen months he held out in defiance of the world, until he was forced to yield by the Italian government. In 1924 the King of Italy made him a prince.

D'Annunzio was perhaps an unequaled master of word painting. As a lord of language he may be compared to Victor Hugo, but he is utterly without Hugo's humanitarianism. His creed was ever beauty for beauty's sake, art for art's sake. The only thing he recognized as higher than himself was Italy. His genius is really lyrical. No one can contest his command of rhythm, sense of music, and splendor of vocabulary. Among his novels may be mentioned *The Child of Pleasure,* more or less a picture of himself, *The Virgin of the Rocks,* which shows the influence

of Nietzsche's doctrine of the superman, and *The Flame of Life,* a glorification of Venice as the city of poetry, beauty and love. His best-known
plays are *The Dead City,* masterly in construction and atmosphere but
most unpleasant in theme, *Francesca da Rimini* and *The Daughter of Jorio.*

SONNETS

I

At times, exhausted by the pains austere
Of long night-labors with success uncrowned,
I lean upon my books, and hear
The sea that bellows through the night profound;
And in the northern wind a sudden fear   5
Destroys each fairest dream my heart has found,
When all my sweetest visions disappear,
And doubt and cold and the void have hemmed me round.

Then think I often of a great ship lost,
With shattered keel, in the whirlwind's storm and stress,   10
Alone 'twixt sea and heaven, from land afar;

I think of the shipwrecked men that, tempest-tossed,
Helpless and hopeless in their last distress,
Despairing cling to the last remaining spar.

II

Again! again! on the remaining mast
Like a living bunch of fruit on the tempest swayed,
The shipwrecked men upon the whirlwind cast
Utter their desperate cries and shout for aid.
In vain! in vain! The black hull sinks at last,   5
A horrid bier, by vain hopes undelayed,
Deep in the roaring waves where, dense and vast,
A bank of seaweed lurks in silent shade.

The cuttlefish shall watch with hungry eyes,
With horrible eyes, with yellowish eyes and grim,   10
That tragic agony of life that dies;

Then, in a play of shadows strange and dim,
Entwined around men's bodies serpent-wise,
Long tentacles shall seize each human limb.

(Greene)

SUGGESTIONS FOR STUDY

1. Show how the second of these sonnets follows logically upon the first. Discuss the poet's use of vivid detail. How is his imagined picture influenced by his mood?

2. Read the famous description of a fight with a cuttlefish in Victor Hugo's novel *Toilers of the Sea,* by which D'Annunzio was evidently influenced. What do you find in these poems that suggest passages from Coleridge's " The Rime of the Ancient Mariner," from Cowper's " The Castaway "? Where else have shipwrecks or other sea disasters been treated in well-known literature?

LUIGI PIRANDELLO (1867–1936)

Pirandello became internationally famous as a dramatist, and was awarded the Nobel prize in 1934. The success of his plays rather obscured the reputation of his fiction. But he was writing novels and short stories for nearly twenty years before he turned to the drama, and the plots of many of his plays were taken from his tales. He was born in Sicily, studied philosophy in Germany, and later lived in Rome, where he had a theater of his own. His novel *The Late Mattia Pascal* (1904) first attracted notice. It is the story of a man who shammed being dead and then tried in vain to begin life over again amid changed surroundings and under an assumed name. Among Pirandello's most original plays are *Right You Are (If You Think So)*, *Six Characters in Search of an Author, Henry IV,* and *Tonight We Improvise*. He is concerned mainly with the problem of human personality. Is a man what he believes himself to be, or what others think he is, or, if neither of these, what is he really? Pirandello found it impossible to answer these questions, since personality, like everything else in life, is not an absolutely fixed thing but is relative and variable. He proclaimed the necessity of illusion, but equally its vanity. At bottom, then, he was pessimistic, but not too gloomy to have a sense of humor, as the following little story shows.

THE JAR

The olive crop was a bumper one that year: the trees had flowered luxuriantly the year before, and, though there had been a long spell of misty weather at the time, the fruit had set well. Lollo Zirafa had a fine plantation on his farm at Primosole. Reckoning that the five old jars of glazed earthenware which he had in his wine cellar would not suffice to hold all the oil of that harvest, he had placed an order well beforehand at Santo Stefano di Camastra, where they are made. His new jar was to be of greater capacity — breast-high and pot-bellied; it would be the mother superior to the little community of five other jars.

I need scarcely say that Don Lollo Zirafa had had a dispute with the potter concerning this jar. It would indeed be hard to name any one with whom he had not picked a quarrel; for every trifle — be it merely a stone that had fallen from his boundary wall, or a handful of straw — he would shout out to the servants to saddle his mule, so that he could hurry to the town and file a suit. He had half ruined himself, because of the large sums he had had to spend on court fees and lawyers' bills, bringing actions against one person after another, which always ended in his having to pay the costs of both sides. People said that his legal adviser grew so tired of seeing him appear two or three times a week that he tried to reduce the frequency of his visits by making him a present of a volume which looked like a prayer book; it contained the judicial code — the idea being that he should take the trouble to see for himself what the rights and wrongs of the case were before hurrying to bring a suit.

Previously, when anyone had a difference with him, they would try to make him lose his temper by shouting out: " Saddle the mule! " but now they changed it to: " Go and look up your pocket code! " Don Lollo would reply: " That I will and I'll break the lot of you, you swine! "

In course of time, the new jar, for which he had paid the goodly sum of four florins,[1] duly arrived; until room could be found for it in the wine cellar, it was lodged in the crushing-shed for a few days. Never had there been a finer jar. It was quite distressing to see it lodged in that foul den, which reeked of stale grape juice and had that musty smell of places deprived of light and air.

It was now two days since the harvesting of the olives had begun, and Don Lollo was almost beside himself, having to supervise not only the men who were beating down the fruit from the trees, but also a number of others who had come with mule loads of manure to be deposited in heaps on the hillside, where he had a field in which he was going to sow beans for the next crop. He felt that it was really more than one man could manage. He was at his wits' ends whom to attend to. Cursing like a trooper, he vowed he would exterminate, first this man and then that, if an olive — one single olive — was missing. He almost talked as if he had counted them one by one, on his trees. Then he would turn to the muleteers and utter the direst

---

[1] **florins:** A florin is equivalent to about a dollar.

threats as to what would happen, if any one heap of manure were not exactly the same size as the others. A little white cap on his head, his sleeves rolled up and his shirt open at the front, he rushed here, there, and everywhere; his face was a bright red and poured with sweat, his eyes glared about him wolfishly, while his hands rubbed angrily at his shaven chin, where a fresh growth of beard always sprouted the moment the razor had left it.

At the close of the third day's work, three of the farm hands — rough fellows with dirty, brutish faces — went to the crushing-shed; they had been beating the olive trees and went to replace their ladders and poles in the shed. They stood aghast at the sight of the fine new jar in two pieces, looking for all the world as if some one had caught hold of the bulging front and cut it off with a sharp sweep of the knife.

" Oh, my God! look! look! "

" How on earth has that happened? "

" My holy aunt! When Don Lollo hears of it! The new jar! What a pity, though! "

The first of the three, more frightened than his companions, proposed to shut the door again at once and to sneak away very quietly, leaving their ladders and poles outside leaning up against the wall; but the second took him up sharply.

" That's a stupid idea! You can't try that on Don Lollo. As like as not he'd believe we broke it ourselves. No, we will stay here! "

He went out of the shed and, using his hands as a trumpet, called out:

" Don Lollo! Oh! Don LOLLOOOOO! "

When the farmer came up and saw the damage, he fell into a towering passion. First he vented his fury on the three men. He seized one of them by the throat, pinned him against the wall, and shouted:

" By the Virgin's blood, you'll pay for that! "

The other two sprang forward in wild excitement, fell upon Don Lollo and pulled him away. Then his mad rage turned against himself; he stamped his feet, flung his cap on the ground, and slapped his cheeks, bewailing his loss with screams suited only for the death of a relation.

" The new jar! A four-florin jar! Brand new! "

Who could have broken it? Could it possibly have broken of itself? Certainly some one must have broken it, out of malice or from envy at his possession of such a beauty. But when? How? There was no sign of violence. Could it conceivably have come in a broken condition from the pottery? No, it rang like a bell on its arrival.

As soon as the farm hands saw that their master's first outburst of rage was spent, they began to console him, saying that he should not take it so to heart, as the jar could be mended. After all, the break was not a bad one, for the front had come away all in one piece; a clever riveter could repair it and make it as good as new. Zi' [2] Dima Licasi was just the man for the job: he had invented a marvelous cement made of some composition which he kept a strict secret — miraculous stuff! Once it had set, you couldn't loosen it, even with a hammer. So they suggested that, if Don Lollo agreed, Zi' Dima Licasi should turn up at daybreak and — as sure as eggs were eggs — the jar would be repaired and be even better than a new one.

For a long time Don Lollo turned a deaf ear to their advice — it was quite useless, there was no making good the damage — but in the end he allowed himself to be persuaded, and punctually at daybreak Zi' Dima Licasi arrived at Primosole, with his outfit in a basket slung on his back. He turned out to be a misshapen old man with swollen crooked joints, like the stem of an ancient Saracen olive tree. To extract a word from him, it looked as if you would have to use a pair of forceps on his mouth. His ungraceful figure seemed to radiate discontent or gloom, due perhaps to his disappointment that no one had so far been found willing to do justice to his merits as an inventor. For Zi' Dima Licasi had not yet patented his discovery; he wanted to make a name for it first by its successful application. Meanwhile he felt it necessary to keep a sharp lookout, lest some one steal the secret of his process.

" Let me see that cement of yours," began Don Lollo in a distrustful tone, after examining him from head to foot for several minutes.

Zi' Dima declined, with a dignified shake of the head.

" You'll see its results."

" But, will it hold? "

Zi' Dima put his basket on the ground and took out from it a red bundle composed of a large cotton handkerchief, much the worse for wear, wrapped round and round something. He began to unroll it very carefully, while they all stood round watching him with close attention. When at last, however, nothing came to light save a pair of spectacles with bridge and sides broken and tied up with string, there was a general laugh. Zi' Dima took no notice, but wiped his fingers before handling the spectacles, then put them on and, with much solemnity, began his examination of the jar, which had been brought outside onto the threshing floor. Finally he said:

[2] **zi' or zio**: uncle.

" It'll hold."

" But I can't trust cement alone," Don Lollo stipulated. " I must have rivets as well."

" I'm off," Zi' Dima promptly replied, standing up and replacing his basket on his back.

Don Lollo caught hold of his arm:

" Off? Where to? You've got no more manners than a pig! . . . Just look at this pauper putting on an air of royalty! . . . Why! you wretched fool, I've got to put oil in that jar, and don't you know that oil oozes? Yards and yards to join together, and you talk of using cement alone! I want rivets — cement and rivets. It's for me to decide."

Zi' Dima shut his eyes, closed his lips tightly and shook his head. People were all like that — they refused to give him the satisfaction of turning out a neat bit of work, performed with artistic thoroughness and proving the wonderful virtues of his cement.

" If," he said, " the jar doesn't ring as true as a bell once more. . . ."

" I won't listen to a word," Don Lollo broke in. " I want rivets! I'll pay you for cement and rivets. How much will it come to? "

" If I use cement only . . ."

" My God! what an obstinate fellow! What did I say? I told you I wanted rivets. We'll settle the terms after the work is done. I've no more time to waste on you."

And he went off to look after his men.

In a state of great indignation Zi' Dima started on the job and his temper continued to rise as he bored hole after hole in the jar and in its broken section — holes for his iron rivets. Along with the squeaking of his tool went a running accompaniment of grunts which grew steadily louder and more frequent; his fury made his eyes more piercing and bloodshot and his face became green with bile. When he had finished that first operation, he flung his borer angrily into the basket and held the detached portion up against the jar to satisfy himself that the holes were at equal distances and fitted one another; next he took his pliers and cut a length of iron wire into as many pieces as he needed rivets, and then called to one of the men who were beating the olive trees to come and help him.

" Cheer up, Zi' Dima! " said the laborer, seeing how upset the old man looked.

Zi' Dima raised his hand with a savage gesture. He opened the tin which contained the cement and held it up towards heaven, as if offering it to God, seeing that men refused to recognize its value. Then he began to spread it with his finger all round the detached portion and along the broken edge of the jar. Taking his pliers and the iron rivets he had prepared, he crept inside the open belly of the jar and instructed the farm hand to hold the piece up, fitting it closely to the jar as he had himself done a short time previously. Before starting to put in the rivets, he spoke from inside the jar:

" Pull! Pull! Tug at it with all your might! . . . You see it doesn't come loose. Curses on people who won't believe me! Knock it! Yes, knock it! . . . Doesn't it ring like a bell, even with me inside it? Go and tell your master that! "

" It's for the top-dog to give orders, Zi' Dima," said the man with a sigh, " and it's for the under-dog to carry them out. Put the rivets in. Put 'em in."

Zi' Dima began to pass the bits of iron through the adjacent holes, one on each side of the crack, twisting up the ends with his pliers. It took him an hour to put them all in, and he poured with sweat inside the jar. As he worked, he complained of his misfortune, and the farm hand stayed near, trying to console him.

" Now help me to get out," said Zi' Dima, when all was finished.

But large though its belly was, the jar had a distinctly narrow neck — a fact which Zi' Dima had overlooked, being so absorbed in his grievance. Now, try as he would, he could not manage to squeeze his way out. Instead of helping him, the farm hand stood idly by, convulsed with laughter. So there was poor Zi' Dima, imprisoned in the jar which he had mended and — there was no use in blinking at the fact — in a jar which would have to be broken to let him out, and this time broken for good.

Hearing the laughter and shouts, Don Lollo came rushing up. Inside the jar Zi' Dima was spitting like an angry cat.

" Let me out," he screamed, " for God's sake! I want to get out! Be quick! Help! "

Don Lollo was quite taken aback and unable to believe his own ears.

" What? Inside there? He's riveted himself up inside? "

Then he went up to the jar and shouted out to Zi' Dima:

" Help you? What help do you think I can give you? You stupid old dodderer, what d'you mean by it? Why couldn't you measure it first? Come, have a try! Put an arm out . . . that's it! Now the head! Up you come! . . . No, no, gently! . . . Down again . . . . Wait a bit! . . . Not that way . . . Down, get down . . . How on earth could you do such a thing? . . . What about my jar now? . . .

" Keep calm!   Keep calm! " he recommended to all the onlookers, as if it was they who were becoming excited and not himself. . . . " My head's going round!   Keep calm!   This is quite a new point! Get me my mule! "

He rapped the jar with his knuckles.   Yes, it really rang like a bell once again.

" Fine!   Repaired as good as new. . . . You wait a bit! " he said to the prisoner; then instructed his man to be off and saddle the mule. He rubbed his forehead vigorously with his fingers, and continued:

" I wonder what's the best course.   That's not a jar, it's a contrivance of the devil himself. . . . Keep still!   Keep still! " he exclaimed, rushing up to steady the jar, in which Zi' Dima, now in a towering passion, was struggling like a wild animal in a trap.

" It's a new point, my good man, which the lawyer must settle.   I can't rely on my own judgment. . . . Where's that mule?   Hurry up with the mule! . . . I'll go straight there and back.   You must wait patiently; it's in your own interest. . . . Meanwhile, keep quiet, be calm!   I must look after my own rights.   And, first of all, to put myself in the right, I fulfil my obligation.   Here you are!   I am paying you for your work, for a whole day's work.   Here are your five lire.[3] Is that enough? "

" I don't want anything," shouted Zi' Dima.   " I want to get out! "

" You shall get out, but meanwhile I, for my part, am paying you. There they are — five lire."

He took the money out of his waistcoat pocket and tossed it into the jar, then enquired in a tone of great concern:

" Have you had any lunch? . . . Bread and something to eat with it, at once! . . . What!   You don't want it?   Well, then, throw it to the dogs!   I shall have done my duty when I've given it to you."

Having ordered the food, he mounted and set out for the town. His wild gesticulations made those who saw him galloping past think that he might well be hastening to shut himself up in a lunatic asylum.

As luck would have it, he did not have to spend much time in the anteroom before being admitted to the lawyer's study; he had, however, to wait a long while before the lawyer could finish laughing after the matter had been related to him.   Annoyed at the amusement he caused, Don Lollo said irritably:

" Excuse me, but I don't see anything to laugh at.   It's all very well for your Honor, who is not the sufferer, but the jar is my property."

---

[3] **lire:** A lira at that time was worth about twenty cents.

The lawyer, however, continued to laugh and then made him tell the story all over again, just as it had happened, so that he could raise another laugh out of it.

" Inside, eh? So he's riveted himself inside? " And what did Don Lollo want to do? . . . " To ke . . . to ke . . . keep him there inside — ha! ha! ha! . . . keep him there inside, so as not to lose the jar? "

" Why should I lose it? " cried Don Lollo, clenching his fists. " Why should I put up with the loss of my money, and have people laughing at me? "

" But don't you know what that's called? " said the lawyer at last. " It's called ' wrongful confinement.' "

" Confinement? Well, who's confined him? He's confined himself! What fault is that of mine? "

The lawyer then explained to him that the matter gave rise to two cases: on the one hand he, Don Lollo, must straightway liberate the prisoner, if he wished to escape from being prosecuted for wrongful confinement; while, on the other hand, the riveter would be responsible for making good the loss resulting from his lack of skill or his stupidity.

" Ah! " said Don Lollo, with a sigh of relief. " So he'll have to pay me for my jar? "

" Wait a bit," remarked the lawyer. " Not as if it were a new jar, remember! "

" Why not? "

" Because it was a broken one, badly broken, too."

" Broken! No, Sir. Not broken. It's perfectly sound now and better than ever it was — he says so himself. And if I have to break it again, I shall not be able to have it mended. The jar will be ruined, Sir! "

The lawyer assured him that that point would be taken into account and that the riveter would have to pay the value which the jar had in its present condition.

" Therefore," he counselled, " get the man himself to give you an estimate of its value first."

" I kiss your hands," Don Lollo murmured, and hurried away.

On his return home towards evening, he found all his laborers engaged in a celebration around the inhabited jar. The watch dogs joined in the festivities with joyous barks and capers. Zi' Dima had not only calmed down, but had even come to enjoy his curious adventure and was able to laugh at it, with the melancholy humor of the unfortunate.

Don Lollo drove them all aside and bent down to look into the jar.

" Hallo! Getting along well? "

" Splendid! An open-air life for me! " replied the man. " It's better than in my own house."

" I'm glad to hear it. Meanwhile I'd just like you to know that that jar cost me four florins when it was new. How much do you think it is worth now? "

" With me inside it? " asked Zi' Dima.

The rustics laughed.

" Silence! " shouted Don Lollo. " Either your cement is of some use or it is of no use. There is no third possibility. If it is of no use, you are a fraud. If it is of some use, the jar, in its present condition, must have a value. What is that value? I ask for your estimate."

After a space for reflection, Zi' Dima said:

" Here is my answer: if you had let me mend it with cement only — as I wanted to do — first of all I should not have been shut up inside it and the jar would have had its original value, without any doubt. But spoilt by these rivets, which had to be done from inside, it has lost most of its value. It's worth a third of its former price, more or less."

" One-third? That's one florin, thirty-three cents."

" Maybe less, but not more than that."

" Well," said Don Lollo. " Promise me that you'll pay me one florin — thirty-three cents."

" What? " asked Zi' Dima, as if he did not grasp the point.

" I will break the jar to let you out," replied Don Lollo. " And — the lawyer tells me — you are to pay me its value according to your own estimate — one florin thirty-three."

" I? Pay? " laughed Zi' Dima, " I'd sooner stay here till I rot! "

With some difficulty he managed to extract from his pocket a short and peculiarly foul pipe and lighted it, puffing out the smoke through the neck of the jar.

Don Lollo stood there scowling. The possibility that Zi' Dima would no longer be willing to leave the jar had not been foreseen either by himself or by the lawyer. What step should he take now? He was on the point of ordering them to saddle the mule, but reflected that it was already evening.

" Oh ho! " he said. " So you want to take up your abode in my jar! I call upon all you men as witnesses to his statement. He refuses to come out, in order to escape from paying. I am quite prepared to break it. Well, as you insist on staying there, I shall take proceedings against you tomorrow for unlawful occupancy of the jar and for preventing me from my rightful use of it."

Zi' Dima blew out another puff of smoke and answered calmly:

"No, your Honor. I don't want to prevent you at all. Do you think I am here because I like it? Let me out and I'll go away gladly enough. But as for paying, I wouldn't dream of it, your Honor."

In a sudden access of fury Don Lollo made to give a kick at the jar but stopped in time. Instead he seized it with both hands and shook it violently, uttering a hoarse growl.

"You see what fine cement it is," Zi' Dima remarked from inside.

"You rascal!" roared Don Lollo. "Whose fault is it, yours or mine? You expect me to pay for it, do you? You can starve to death inside first. We'll see who'll win."

He went away, forgetting all about the five lire which he had tossed into the jar that morning. But the first thing Zi' Dima thought of doing was to spend that money in having a festive evening, in company with the farm hands, who had been delayed in their work by that strange accident, and had decided to spend the night at the farm, in the open air, sleeping on the threshing floor. One of them went to a neighboring tavern to make the necessary purchases. The moon was so bright that it seemed almost day — a splendid night for their carousal.

Many hours later Don Lollo was awakened by an infernal din. Looking out from the farmhouse balcony, he could see in the moonlight what looked like a gang of devils on his threshing floor; his men, all roaring drunk, were holding hands and performing a dance round the jar, while Zi' Dima, inside it, was singing at the top of his voice.

This time Don Lollo could not restrain himself, but rushed down like a mad bull and, before they could stop him, gave the jar a push which started it rolling down the slope. It continued on its course, to the delight of the intoxicated company, until it hit an olive tree and cracked in pieces, leaving Zi' Dima the winner in the dispute.

(Arthur and Henrie Mayne)

SUGGESTIONS FOR STUDY

1. Show how some of the characteristics of the Italian countryside and the habits of the people are brought out in the story.

2. What is the type of humor? Is it pure comedy, farce, tragi-comedy or satire? Is the fun due chiefly to the character types or to the situation?

3. What marked dramatic elements do you see in "The Jar"? Read

the dramatized form of this story. Does the story gain or suffer by the change? Would it be adapted to amateur presentation?

4. What contrast do you find between this and the other selections in the Italian section? How does it compare with humorous selections in the French and Spanish sections? With humorous stories in American literature?

READING LIST

TRANSLATIONS FROM ITALIAN LITERATURE

Poetry

Dante, *The Divine Comedy*, trans. by H. F. Cary and also by J. B. Fletcher

Petrarch, F.: *Sonnets*, trans. by Joseph Auslander

Leopardi, G.: *Poems*, trans. by Geoffrey L. Bickersteth

Carducci, G.: *Poems*, trans. by Frank Sewall

De'Lucchi, Lorna (ed. and trans.): *Anthology of Italian Poems*

Everett, William: *The Italian Poets since Dante*

Rendel, Romilda: *An Anthology of Italian Lyrics from the Thirteenth Century to Present Day*

Drama

Goldberg, Isaac (trans.): *Plays of the Italian Theater*

Machiavelli, N.: *Mandragola*

Goldoni, C.: *The Mistress of the Inn*

Pirandello, L.: *One Act Plays*, ed. by Arthur Livingstone

Biography, Essays, etc.

Vasari, G.: *Lives of the Painters*

Cellini, B., *Autobiography*

Machiavelli, N.: *The Prince*

Castiglione, B.: *The Book of the Courtier*

Leopardi, G.: *Essays, Dialogues and Thoughts,* trans. by James Thomson

Papini, G.: *The Failure* (a spiritual autobiography)
Four-and-Twenty Minds
Life of Christ

Mussolini, B.: *My Autobiography*

Fiction

Manzoni, A.: *The Betrothed*

Fogazzaro, A.: *The Patriot, The Saint*

Amicis, E. de: *Heart, a Schoolboy's Diary*

Verga, G.: *Little Novels of Sicily*

D'Annunzio, G.: *Tales of My Native Town*

Pirandello, L.: *The Late Mattia Pascal*
Better Think Twice About It (short stories)
Horse in the Moon (short stories)
The Naked Truth (short stories)

Italian Short Stories from the 13th to the 20th Centuries (Everyman's Library)

Tettoello, Decio: *Great Italian Short Stories*

Stories by Foreign Authors: Italian

BOOKS ABOUT ITALY

Fiction

Eliot, George: *Romola*

Merezhkovski, D.: *The Romance of Leonardo da Vinci*

History, Literature, and Biography

Sedgwick, H. D.: *A Short History of Italy*

McClellan, G. B.: *Modern Italy: a Short History*

Sichel, E. H.: *The Renaissance*

Symonds, J. A.: *The Renaissance in Italy*, 5 vols.

Sanctis, Francesco de: *History of Italian Literature*, 2 vols.

Kuhns, O.: *Great Poets of Italy*

Collinson, M. L.: *Modern Italian Literature*

Chesterton, G. K.: *St. Francis of Assisi*

Grandgent, C. H.: *Dante*

Rolland, Romain: *The Life of Michelangelo*

Thayer, W. R.: *The Life and Times of Cavour*

Trevelyan, G. M.: *Garibaldi and the Making of Italy*

Art, Music, and Popular Drama

Mather, F. J.: *History of Italian Painting*

Berenson, B.: *Italian Painters of the Renaissance*

Faure, Élie: *The Italian Renaissance*

Seeley, E. L.: *Artists of the Italian Renaissance*

Kimball and Edgell: *A History of Architecture*

Streatfield, R. A.: *Masters of Italian Music*

Walker, Conway: *Early Italian and French Opera*
Modern French and Italian Opera

Lea, Kathleen M.: *Italian Popular Comedy*

Nicoll, Alardyce: *Masks, Mimes, and Miracles*

Duchartre, P. L.: *The Italian Comedy*

Travel, Social Life and Customs

Bagot, R.: *Italians of Today*

Coote, C. R.: *Italian Town and Country Life*

Lucas, E. V.: *A Wanderer in Rome*
A Wanderer in Florence

Mason, Caroline A.: *The Spell of Italy*

Smith, F. Hopkinson: *Gondola Days*

German Literature

German Literature

G ERMAN literature includes, properly speaking, all the writing done
in the German language. This tongue is considerably more wide-
spread than the boundaries of present-day Germany. It is spoken,
for example, by several million people in Austria and Switzerland.
Remember, further, that Germany did not exist as a nation until
1871. The fact that the German-speaking peoples were for centuries
badly divided, politically and otherwise, made their literature less unified and more irregular in its development than either English or
French.

German may be called a cousin-language of English. Its two chief
branches are Low and High German. These terms refer to the alti-
tude of the country. The former is spoken in the lowlands — that is,
the parts which lie to the north, while the latter is the language of
the southern highlands. Since the time of Luther (early sixteenth
century), High German has become the standard literary language
and Low German has sunk to the level of a dialect.

The German mind has found its most congenial expression in lyric
poetry, music, philosophy, and scientific research. In German literature poetry far surpasses prose in quality, whereas the opposite seems
to be the case with French literature. It does not appear that German literature can equal English or French in either drama or fiction.
Nevertheless, taking German literature as a whole, and especially its
poetry, we may say that it reflects admirably the ideals and inner-
most aspirations of the German people.

German literature falls into three chronological periods

It is customary to distinguish three periods in German literature —
Old High German (to the twelfth century), Middle High German
(twelfth to fourteenth centuries), and New High German (after the
fourteenth century). In the first of these periods there was evidently
a good deal of alliterative verse, for in Germany as elsewhere poetry

preceded prose. But nearly all of this has been lost. The only important thing that has survived is a fragment of the *Song of Hildebrand,* which dates from about 800. The influence of Christianity is seen in a Low German poem of this time called the *Heliand* or *Savior,* a paraphrase of the Gospels.

The Middle High German period produces a rich literature

From the Middle High German period, on the other hand, a very large amount of poetry has survived, considered by many critics the finest body of literature in the Europe of the Middle Ages. The best of it is from the early part of the thirteenth century. Both epic and lyric poetry are well represented. The former consists of folk epics and court epics. The folk epics are of unknown authorship and reproduce the legends current among the common people. The two most famous of these are the *Song of the Nibelungs* and *Gudrun,* which have sometimes been compared to the *Iliad* and the *Odyssey,* respectively, in Greek literature. They bear a closer relationship, however, to the great Scandinavian epics, since many of the characters are practically identical. In the case of the court epics the authors are conscious literary artists who chose their subjects from the stories of chivalry current in Western Europe. The best-known court epics are *Tristan* by Gottfried von Strassburg and *Parzival* by Wolfram von Eschenbach.

The lyric poetry of the Middle High German period, like the court epics, was influenced by French models. The theme was chivalrous love and the poets were therefore called Minnesingers, from the old German word *Minne* which meant " love." By all odds the most attractive of them was Walther von der Vogelweide, who by reason of his spontaneity and sincerity deserves to be considered the greatest of all medieval lyric poets.

Prolonged stagnation of literature results from social and religious upheaval

Linguistically, the New German period dates from the fourteenth century, but after the thirteenth century there was a marked decline in literature. The period of creation was followed by one of stagnation. One may say that the literature of Germany from 1300 to 1500 reflects in a general way the break-up of the feudal system and the rise of the burgher class. Little that is memorable was produced during these two centuries, though mention should be made of the low German poem *Reynard the Fox,* the most humorous and realistic of all the beast tales. There took place also at this time the beginnings of the drama, which in Germany as in the other countries of Europe developed out of the liturgy of the Church.

Conditions seemed favorable for a revival of literature when the Renaissance reached Germany toward the close of the fifteenth century, largely through the agency of Erasmus. But the Renaissance was speedily overlaid there by the Protestant Reformation begun by Luther in 1517. Luther by his translation of the Bible gave the German people a standard literary language, but he also brought religious discord, which along with political strife was destined to set German culture back for two more centuries. Almost the only writer of Luther's day who is still read with pleasure is Hans Sachs (1494–1576), whose Shrovetide plays are full of quaint humor and charming naturalness.

The final outcome of religious dissension was the Thirty Years' War (1618–1648), perhaps the most devastating war of modern times, which left the German states so weakened that it took them at least a hundred years to recover. German civilization and culture reached their lowest ebb. Such literature as existed was for the most part a feeble imitation of the French. It was mechanical in its emphasis on literary rules and wholly devoid of genuine inspiration or of vital concern to the people. We call such literature pseudo-classic, because it was falsely supposed to follow Greek and Latin models, whereas in reality it saw them through the eyes of the French. This French influence had to be thrown off before Germany could develop a truly national literature.

Rise of German states gives new impetus to literature

Modern German literature dates from about the middle of the eighteenth century. Previous to that, there are few writers who can be read with interest or profit, unless we turn back to the great Middle High German poetry of the thirteenth century. By 1750 the German states had recovered in great measure from the effects of the Thirty Years' War, and one of them, Prussia, was rapidly becoming a European power of the first magnitude. Four men are regarded as the founders of modern German literature: Klopstock (1724–1803), Wieland (1733–1813), Herder (1744–1803), and Lessing (1729–1781). Klopstock showed in his long epic in blank verse, *The Messiah,* that a German poet could be original. Wieland contributed fanciful poetry and the psychological novel. Lessing, the greatest of the four, threw off the critical authority of the French and wrote the first good comedy and the first good tragedy in German literature. Herder, who was strongly imbued with the idea of historical development and consequently of the necessary differences among peoples, called particular attention to the interest and value of the folk song and of other treasures of the German heritage. Partly as a resultant of all these forces, but chiefly through Herder's emphasis on national consciousness, there arose a youth movement in literature known as the "Storm and Stress." The young writers of Germany between 1770 and 1780 threw off all restraints, and in their longing to be original instituted a sort of literary revolution. But it was a short-lived affair. Apart from the poet Bürger, who had undoubted talent, the only writers of the "Storm and Stress" who are still generally remembered are the young Goethe and the young Schiller, and they both speedily outgrew the mood of the movement.

Goethe (1749-1832) and Schiller (1759-1805) are Germany's greatest writers. Goethe is regarded by the Germans as a world genius, worthy of rank beside Homer, Dante, and Shakespeare. He is supreme as a lyric poet. His masterpiece, the dramatic poem *Faust*, is the greatest single work in German literature. But Goethe was also a novelist, a scientist, and a penetrating critic of life and men. Schiller is still the most popular of German writers. His best works are the poetic dramas of his last years. He is perhaps the most outstanding idealist in all literature.

The German mind welcomes romanticism

The Romantic Movement, which swept over Europe toward the close of the eighteenth and at the beginning of the nineteenth centuries, found a favorable atmosphere in Germany. The "Storm and Stress" movement a generation earlier may indeed be considered a preliminary phase of this romanticism. The essence of romanticism seems to be an exaltation of the personal and emotional elements in human nature rather than the social and intellectual. But German romanticism was also to develop certain characteristics of its own. It was strongly under the influence of transcendental philosophy, which asserted that the human mind had the power to transcend or go beyond experience, and could grasp great truths by intuition, besides by material evidence. This philosophy took its start with Kant (1724-1804). The latter's successors, Fichte and Schelling, were in direct contact with the German Romantic School, which was formed in 1798. The leaders of the School were the brothers Schlegel; its most original genius was the poet-novelist Novalis. Perhaps the most enduring work of the group is to be found in translations made from foreign literatures. The translation of Shakespeare, notably, made him into a German classic.

But the most pleasing productions of German romanticism came from other and younger writers, such as the lyric poet Eichendorff and the dramatist Kleist. Still later poets, like Uhland, who is pre-eminent in ballads (short narrative poems), and Mörike, exhibit many of the better qualities of romanticism.

Realism follows on the heels of romanticism

Romanticism in Germany as in other countries was succeeded by realism or the attempt to portray life as it is. The poet Heine (1797–1856) best represents the transition from romanticism to realism. His lyrics have become world famous. But Heine is probably more appreciated abroad than he is in Germany, where his Jewish birth and his French sympathies have alienated many readers. The drama-tist Hebbel (1813–1863) introduced modern psychology into his char-acter studies. He is probably the most important dramatic theorist of the nineteenth century. The Austrian Grillparzer (1791–1872) wrote a number of successful poetic dramas. Realism also made its appearance in fiction, for example in Freytag's novel *Debit and Credit* (1854), in the stories of the Low German writer Fritz Reuter, and in the novelettes of the Swiss author Keller (1819–1890). In the decades of the 1860's and 1870's the pessimism of the philosopher Schopenhauer left its unmistakable mark on literature.

Modern German literature swayed by various 'isms

Beginning about 1885 a new rebellion on the part of the younger generation took place. The demand this time was for closer observa-tion of actuality and for a keener appreciation of social problems. Influences came from writers like Flaubert and Zola in France, Ibsen in Norway, and Tolstoy in Russia. The movement is sometimes called naturalism, which in literature may be defined as realism with scientific pretensions. But it had other and very different character-istics as well, such as symbolism, according to which the superficial sense of the thing expressed is never the true meaning. The chief writers of the new movement were Hauptmann (1862–1946) and Sudermann. The former became Germany's leading dramatist. Sudermann (1857–1928) gained his first successes by his realistic plays in prose, though some of his best work was in fiction. The philosopher Nietzsche (1844–1900), who taught the doctrine of the will to power, gained a strong sway over the younger German writers and swept away the influence of Schopenhauer's pessimism.

During and after World War I, still other changes took place in the temper of German literature. For a time the movement known as *expressionism* pervaded poetry, drama, and fiction. It demanded full freedom for the writer to express his own moods in his own way, regardless of recognized conventions or even of intelligibility. But this tendency did not last long, and in recent years German writers have returned to more traditional modes of utterance. Prominent among twentieth-century authors are the novelist Jakob Wassermann (1873–1934) and the poet Rainer Maria Rilke (1875–1926).

Turmoil in the Fatherland is reflected by recent German literature

Recent German literature treats with its distinctive accent many of the favorite subjects of other European authors.

One note persistently struck is that of pessimism verging on despair. Oswald Spengler (1880–1936), in his gigantic historical work *The Decline of the West,* laid some of the foundations of this movement. He maintains that European civilization, having exhausted in its youth its spiritual resources, has become sick unto death.

At least one very influential poet, Stefan George (1868–1933), adopted Spengler's point of view, particularly in *The Star of the Covenant.* He advocated, as a substitute for decadent democracy, the establishment of a closely knit political order devoted to worship of the soil and the blood, under a dominant leader, like Hitler. Hugo von Hofmannsthal (1874–1929) produced realistic re-creations of Greek stories. In *Electra* and *Oedipus and the Sphinx* he strips the myths of their religious grandeur by showing the characters to be the victims of primitive violence and brutality.

Franz Kafka (1883–1924) in *The Castle, The Trial,* and *Metamorphosis* paints shocking pictures of the plight of the individual isolated from normal life by hostile social pressures and banished to the prison of his disturbed mind. His torture is expressed in the terrors and frustrations of a nightmare.

Georg Kaiser (1878–1945) exhibits his revolutionary methods of play construction most strikingly in his trilogy, *The Coral, Gas I,* and *Gas II.* The action dramatizes man's frantic efforts to free himself from the machine and the materialistic values it has created.

Erich Maria Remarque (1898–   ) expresses in his work the view that war and its results imprison and dehumanize the individual.

In his best novel, *All Quiet on the Western Front,* he describes in repulsive detail the horrors of existence in the trenches of World War I. His works present different phases of the defeat of man's spirit by powers both outside and within him.

The two writers who represent the idealistic reaction from the pessimistic realists are Franz Werfel (1890–1945) and Hermann Hesse (1877–   ). Their literary methods are radically different. Werfel, poet, novelist, and playwright, shows how man can preserve his spiritual integrity from the assaults of a hostile world. His major works are the novel *We Are,* the collection of poems *Mirror Man,* and the stirring play *Goat Song.* In this strange symbolical tragedy, he shows the cleansing effects of revolution. In the ruinous course of revolution, man exhausts his destructive energies, leaving his mind open only to simplicity and tenderness. Hermann Hesse, avoiding violence, turns to self-analysis, confession, and meditation. His most important novels, *Steppenwolf* and *Magister Ludi,* illustrate his conviction that man can find peace and security only by establishing communion with the God who dwells deep within his soul and with that God's mystical closeness to Nature.

Thomas Mann (1875–1955), the greatest of modern German novelists, shows deep understanding of the problems, both emotional and intellectual, of his characters. In *Buddenbrooks,* he treats with equal skill the individuals of four generations of a family of merchant princes. In *The Magic Mountain,* his greatest work, he presents the attitudes of the members of an international collection of patients in a sanitorium for consumptives.

Most modern German literature reflects in different ways the social and political turmoil that afflicted the Fatherland for half a century.

The Household Tale

The folk tale which follows is taken from the famous collection made by the brothers Grimm in the early nineteenth century. The tales themselves are incalculably older. Many of them belong to the common stock of the Indo-European peoples and are presumably as ancient as the myths of the race. Jacob Grimm (1785–1863) and Wilhelm Grimm (1786–1859) were primarily scholars who collected these tales in order to store up material for students of folklore and not to provide amusement for children. They wrote down every story exactly as they heard it, adding nothing of their own. In this way they founded the science of folklore, but incidentally they furnished a book which has made its way into almost every civilized household and delighted the hearts of innumerable children

the world over. Most American boys and girls first learn the tales or
" Cinderella " and of " Little Red Riding-Hood " from the version of the
Grimm brothers. But some of the stories gathered by the worthy scholars,
though familiar enough in Germany, are by no means as well known in
our country. One of the more characteristic of these tales is reproduced
here.

GAMBLING HANSEL

This story, or some variant of it, is current in many parts of Germany.

Once upon a time there was a man who did nothing but gamble,
and for that reason people never called him anything but Gambling
Hansel, and as he never ceased to gamble, he played away his house
and all that he had. Now the very day before his creditors were to
take his house from him, came the Lord and St. Peter, and asked
him to give them shelter for the night. Then Gambling Hansel said,
" For my part, you may stay the night, but I cannot give you a bed
or anything to eat." So the Lord said he was just to take them in,
and they themselves would buy something to eat, to which Gambling
Hansel made no objection. Thereupon St. Peter gave him three
groschen,[1] and said he was to go to the baker's and fetch some bread.
So Gambling Hansel went, but when he reached the house where the
other gambling vagabonds were gathered together, they, although
they had won all that he had, greeted him clamorously, and said,
" Hansel, do come in."

" Oh," said he, " do you want to win the three groschen, too? "
On this they would not let him go. So he went in, and played away
the three groschen also.

Meanwhile St. Peter and the Lord were waiting, and as he was so
long in coming, they set out to meet him. When Gambling Hansel
came, however, he pretended that the money had fallen into the
gutter, and kept raking about in it all the while to find it, but our
Lord already knew that he had lost it in play. St. Peter again gave
him three groschen, and now he did not allow himself to be led away
once more, but fetched them the loaf. Our Lord then inquired if he
had no wine, and he said, " Alack, sir, the casks are all empty! "
But the Lord said he was to go down into the cellar, for the best
wine was still there. For a long time he would not believe this, but
at length he said, " Well, I will go down, but I know that there is none
there." When he turned the tap, however, lo and behold, the best

---

[1] **groschen**: nickels.

of wine ran out! So he took it to them, and the two passed the night there.

Early next day our Lord told Gambling Hansel that he might beg three favors. The Lord expected that he would ask to go to Heaven; but Gambling Hansel asked for a pack of cards with which he could win everything, for dice with which he would win everything, and for a tree whereon every kind of fruit would grow, and from which no one who had climbed up, could descend until he bade him do so. The Lord gave him all that he had asked, and departed with St. Peter.

And now Gambling Hansel at once set about gambling in real earnest, and before long he had gained half the world. Upon this St. Peter said to the Lord, " Lord, this thing must not go on. He will win, and thou lose, the whole world. We must send Death to him." When Death appeared, Gambling Hansel had just seated himself at the gaming-table, and Death said, " Hansel, come out a while."

But Gambling Hansel said, " Just wait a little until the game is done, and in the meantime get up into that tree out there, and gather a little fruit that we may have something to munch on our way." Thereupon Death climbed up, but when he wanted to come down again, he could not, and Gambling Hansel left him up there for seven years, during which time no one died.

So St. Peter said to the Lord, " Lord, this thing must not go on. People no longer die; we must go ourselves." And they went themselves, and the Lord commanded Hansel to let Death come down. So Hansel went at once to Death and said to him, " Come down," and Death took him directly and put an end to him. They went away together and came to the next world, and then Gambling Hansel made straight for the door of Heaven, and knocked at it.

" Who is there? "

" Gambling Hansel."

" Ah, we will have nothing to do with him! Begone! "

So he went to the door of Purgatory, and knocked once more.

" Who is there? "

" Gambling Hansel."

" Ah, there is quite enough weeping and wailing here without him. We do not want to gamble, just go away again."

Then he went to the door of Hell, and there they let him in. There was, however, no one at home but old Lucifer and the crooked devils who had just been doing their evil work in the world. And no sooner was Hansel there than he sat down to gamble again. Lucifer, however, had nothing to lose but his mis-shapen devils, and Gambling Hansel won them from him, as with his cards he could not fail to do. And now he was off again with his crooked devils, and they went to Hohenfuert and pulled up a hop-pole, and with it went to Heaven and began to thrust the pole against it, and Heaven began to crack. So again St. Peter said, " Lord, this thing cannot go on; we must let him in, or he will throw us down from Heaven." And they let him in.

But Gambling Hansel instantly began to play again, and there was such a noise and confusion that there was no hearing what they themselves were saying. Therefore St. Peter once more said, " Lord, this cannot go on; we must throw him down, or he will make all Heaven rebellious." So they went to him at once, and threw him down, and his soul broke into fragments, and went into the gambling vagabonds who are living this very day.

SUGGESTIONS FOR STUDY

1. Compare the story with the folk tale in the Spanish section (page 245) as examples of folk humor. Do you know of any American stories similar in situation or in general tone?

2. Show how the story follows the popular pattern of folk tales in having a series of parallel occurrences, like rungs of a ladder, leading up to the climax. How does such a construction help the survival of a tale?

3. Comment on the effectiveness of the ending of the story. Could you suggest a better one?

The Epic

THE SONG OF THE NIBELUNGS

The national epic of Germany was composed by an unknown poet about the year 1200. But earlier ballads and lays evidently furnished the material. The theme itself is found among all the Teutonic peoples and has received literary treatment in the Scandinavian countries. The story of the poem is about the murder of Siegfried and the revenge of his widow upon the murderers.

Siegfried is the ideal hero — strong, handsome, fearless, and transparently honest and sincere. He is also the richest man in the world, for he has wrested from the dwarfs their hoard of gold. The name Nibelungs — " People of the Mist " — goes with the successive possessors of this gold: first the dwarfs, then Siegfried, and finally the Burgundians. It is noteworthy also that possession of the treasure brings doom with it. Siegfried, in addition to all his natural advantages, has certain magic properties. For example, he is invulnerable, except in one spot in the middle of his back. When the poems begin, he is a prince living on the lower Rhine. He woos and weds the Princess Kriemhild, sister of King Gunther of the Burgundians, whose court is farther up the river. Gunther, in turn, woos a distant princess named Brunhild, but he has to rely on the secret assistance of Siegfried in order to win her. Brunhild discovers, too late, the deception that has been practiced upon her, and in her fury she incites Gunther's chief vassal, Hagen, to kill Siegfried by treachery. In the second half of the poem, Kriemhild marries Etzel, King of the Huns, whose country lies along the middle stretch of the Danube. After the lapse of some time, she invites the chieftains of the Burgundians to her court and there has them massacred one and all, she herself perishing in the final slaughter. "That is the Nibelungs' woe."

The author's sympathies shift in rather curious fashion as the story proceeds. At the outset, he quite obviously takes Siegfried as his hero, but in the second half he is just as plainly on the side of the Burgundians, who are, after all, Germans fighting against an overwhelming horde of barbaric Huns. So Hagen, the villain of the first part, virtually emerges as the hero. As a matter of fact, Hagen is psychologically the most complicated and interesting character in the poem — experienced, crafty, disillusioned, but also grim and relentless in his undertakings.

The poem breathes the spirit of the heroic age. Actions and personages seem projected on a scale much larger than real life. The German poet Heine once remarked that to watch these gigantic but shadowy figures in action was like seeing Cologne Cathedral and Notre-Dame dancing together in the moonlight!

The legendary events of the poem may be dated in the fifth century, since Etzel is evidently the historical Attila. The Burgundians are nominally Christians, but it is easy to see that beneath the thin veneer of Christianity they are still pagans at heart, filled with the joy of sensuous life and the lust of power. We may learn much from this national epic about the mental outlook of these early Germans and their scale of values. This is particularly true in regard to their most cherished virtue — *Treue* or loyalty, and the question as to what loyalty should bid one do. There are also good examples of German humor scattered through the poem and a very striking expression of German pessimism in the closing stanzas:

"Joy to sorrow turneth ever at the last." The language of the *Song of the Nibelungs* differs from modern German somewhat as the language of Chaucer differs from modern English. The translation follows faithfully the meter and rhyme-scheme of the original.

THE MURDER OF SIEGFRIED

The plot to murder Siegfried was devised by Hagen with the acquiescence of King Gunther. After a hunting expedition, during which every one was sure to become thirsty, it was arranged that there should be a foot race between Siegfried and Hagen to a spring in the woods. While Siegfried was stooping over to drink, Hagen was to pierce his back with his spear.

When now they would go thither   to where the linden spread,
Spake of Tronje Hagen: " To me hath oft been said,
That none could follow after   Kriemhild's nimble knight
Or vie with him in running;   would that he'd prove it to our sight! "

Then spake of Netherland   bold Siegfried speedily: 5
" That may ye well have proof of,   will ye but run with me
In contest to the fountain.   When that the same be done,
To him be given honor   who the race hath fairly won."

" Now surely make we trial,"   quoth Hagen the thane.
Thereto the doughty Siegfried: " I too will give you gain,   10
Afore your feet at starting   to lay me in the grass."
When that he had heard it,   thereat how joyous Gunther was!

And spake again the warrior: " And ye shall further hear:
All my clothing likewise   will I upon me wear,
The spear and shield full heavy   and hunting-dress I'll don."   15
His sword as well as quiver   had he full quickly girded on.

Doffed they their apparel   and aside they laid it then;
Clothed in white shirts only   saw you there the twain.
Like unto two wild panthers   they coursed across the green;
Yet first beside the fountain   was the valiant Siegfried seen.   20

No man in feats of valor   who with him had vied.
The sword he soon ungirded   and quiver laid aside;
The mighty spear he leanèd   against the linden-tree;
Beside the running fountain   stood the knight stately to see.

To Siegfried naught was lacking   that doth good knight adorn.   25
Down the shield then laid he   where did flow the burn,

2. **Tronje:** Hagen's birthplace.   10. **doughty:** valiant.   26. **burn:** brook.

Yet howsoe'er he thirsted   no whit the hero drank
Before had drunk the monarch;   therefor he earned but evil thank.

There where ran clear the water   and cool from out the spring,
Down to it did bend him   Gunther the king.   30
And when his thirst was quenchèd   rose he from thence again;
Eke the valiant Siegfried,   how glad had he done likewise then.

For his courtesy he suffered.   Where bow and sword there lay,
Both did carry Hagen   from him thence away,
And again sprang quickly thither   where the spear did stand;   35
And for a cross the tunic   of the valiant knight he scanned.

As there the noble Siegfried   to drink o'er the fountain bent,
Through the cross he pierced him,   that from the wound was sent
The blood nigh to bespatter   the tunic Hagen wore.
By hand of knight such evil   deed shall wrought be nevermore.   40

The spear he left projecting   where it had pierced the heart.
In terror as that moment   did Hagen never start
In flight from any warrior   he ever yet had found.
Soon as the noble Siegfried   within him felt the mighty wound,

Raging the knight full doughty   up from the fountain sprang,   45
The while from 'twixt his shoulders   stood out a spearshaft long.
The prince weened to find there   his bow or his sword;
Then in sooth had Hagen   found the traitor's meet reward.

When from the sorely wounded   knight his sword was gone,
Then had he naught to 'venge him   but his shield alone.   50
This snatched he from the fountain   and Hagen rushed upon,
And not at all escape him   could the royal Gunther's man.

Though he nigh to death was wounded   he yet such might did wield
That out in all directions   flew from off the shield
Precious stones a many;   the shield he clave in twain.   55
Thus vengeance fain had taken   upon his foe the stately thane.

Beneath his hand must Hagen   stagger and fall to ground.
So swift the blow he dealt him,   the meadow did resound.

32. eke: also.   38. cross: Kriemhild had sewed a cross on the vulnerable
spot on Siegfried's back when Hagen had promised her he would protect him.
47. weened: thought.

Had sword in hand been swinging,   Hagen had had his meed,
So sorely raged he stricken;   to rage in sooth was mickle need.   60

Faded from cheek was color,   no longer could he stand,
And all his might of body   soon complete had waned,
As did a deathly pallor   over his visage creep.
Full many a fairest lady   for the knight anon must weep.

So sank amid the flowers   Kriemhild's noble knight,   65
While from his wound flowed thickly   the blood before the sight.
Than gan he reviling   — for dire was his need —
Who had thus encompassed   his death by this same faithless deed.

Then spake the sorely wounded: " O ye base cowards twain,
Doth then my service merit   that me ye thus have slain?   70
To you I e'er was faithful   and so am I repaid.
Alas, upon your kindred   now have ye shame eternal laid.

" By this deed dishonored   hereafter evermore
Are their generations.   Your anger all too sore
Have ye now thus vented   and vengeance ta'en on me.   75
With shame henceforth be parted   from all good knight's company."

All the hunters hastened   where he stricken lay,
It was in sooth for many   of them a joyless day.
Had any aught of honor,   he mourned that day, I ween,
And well the same did merit   the knight high-spirited and keen.   80

As there the king of Burgundy   mourned that he should die,
Spake the knight sore wounded: " To weep o'er injury,
Who hath wrought the evil   hath smallest need, I trow.
Reviling doth he merit,   and weeping may he well forego."

Thereto quoth grim Hagen: " Ye mourn, I know not why;   85
This same day hath ended   all our anxiety.
Few shall we find henceforward   for fear will give us need,
And well is me that from his   mastery we thus are freed."

" Light thing is now thy vaunting,"   did Siegfried then reply.
" Had I e'er bethought me   of this thy infamy   90

59. **meed:** reward. 60. **mickle:** great. 67. **gan:** began. 81. **king:** Gunther is meant.

Well had I preservèd   'gainst all thy hate my life.
Me rueth naught so sorely   as Lady Kriemhild my wife.

" Now may God have mercy   that to me a son was born,
That him alack! the people   in times to come shall spurn,
That those he nameth kinsmen   have done the murderer's deed.   95
An had I breath," spake Siegfried,   " to mourn o'er this I well had
      need."

Then spake, in anguish praying,   the hero doomed to die:
" An wilt thou, king, to any   yet not good faith deny,
In all the world to any,   to thee commended be
And to thy loving mercy   the spouse erstwhile was wed to me.   100

" Let it be her good fortune   that she thy sister is;
By all the princely virtues,   I beg thee pledge me this.
For me long time my father   and men henceforth must wait;
Upon a spouse was never   wrought, as mine, a wrong so great."

All around the flowers   were wetted with the blood   105
As there with death he struggled.   Yet not for long he could,
Because the deadly weapon   had cut him all too sore;
And soon the keen and noble   knight was doomed to speak no more.

When the lords perceivèd   how that the knight was dead,
Upon a shield they laid him   that was of gold full red,   110
And counsel took together   how of the thing should naught
Be known, but held in secret   that Hagen the deed had wrought.

Then spake of them a many: " This is an evil day.
Now shall ye all conceal it   and all alike shall say,
When as Kriemhild's husband   the dark forest through   115
Rode alone a-hunting,   him the hand of robber slew."

Then spake of Tronje Hagen: " Myself will bring him home.
In sooth I reck but little   if to her ears it come,
Who my Lady Brunhild   herself hath grieved so sore.
It maketh me small worry,   an if she weep for evermore."   120

(G. H. Needler)

---

92. **me rueth nought:** I regret nothing.   96. **an:** if.   118. **reck:** care.

SUGGESTIONS FOR STUDY

1. Point out indications of Siegfried's physical prowess, bravery, and generosity. How does he compare with Roland of France and Arthur of England as a heroic figure?

2. What sort of impression does Hagen make upon you? What part does Gunther seem to play in the episode?

3. What is the effect of the lengthened last half-line of the stanzas? How does the metrical form remind you of Anglo-Saxon poetry? What marked differences are there?

4. How does the language contribute to the archaic atmosphere of the story? Select some of the most striking examples.

The Folk Song

Folk songs are poems which have their origin among the common people and express their sentiments. They exist in all countries, but since the method of their transmission is oral, they tend to disappear as reading increases. Folk songs are almost always anonymous. While each one must have been originally the product of an individual poet, it was regarded as common property in the sense that any one felt free to make changes in it. It expressed collective rather than individual feelings. The language and metrical structure are simple, with frequent refrains, repetitions and stereotyped formulas. The general effect is one of artlessness, sometimes of crudity. The great period of the German folk song was from the middle of the fourteenth to the middle of the sixteenth century. After the Renaissance folk songs came to be regarded with contempt. It was to the credit of the romanticists that they rediscovered them and detected in them a fresh spontaneity and a direct, hearty expression of feeling. Bishop Percy's famous collection, *Reliques of Ancient English Poetry* (1765) exerted an important influence in Germany. Herder, stimulated by it, gathered folk songs from all countries and aroused Goethe's interest in the subject. In 1805 Arnim and Brentano published a valuable collection of German folk songs called *The Boy's Magic Horn.* Most of the best German poets since Goethe have tried to recapture in their own verse something of the authentic spirit of the folk song.

THE HEMLOCK TREE

This artless song is sung to the tune of "Maryland, My Maryland."

O Hemlock tree! O hemlock tree! how faithful are thy branches!
    Green not alone in summer time,
    But in the winter's frost and rime!
O Hemlock tree! O hemlock tree! how faithful are thy branches!

O maiden fair! O maiden fair! how faithless is thy bosom! 5
    To love me in prosperity,
    And leave me in adversity!
O maiden fair! O maiden fair! how faithless is thy bosom!

The nightingale, the nightingale, thou tak'st for thine example!
    So long as summer laughs she sings; 10
    But in the autumn spreads her wings.
The nightingale, the nightingale, thou tak'st for thine example!

The meadow brook, the meadow brook, is mirror of thy falsehood!
    It flows so long as falls the rain,
    In drought its springs soon dry again. 15
The meadow brook, the meadow brook, is mirror of thy falsehood!

                              (H. W. Longfellow)

THE DEAD BRIDEGROOM

The return of the dead lover to his sweetheart is a popular theme in folklore. This ballad should be compared with Bürger's " William and Helen " (see page 460) and with the English ballad " Sweet William's Ghost." Washington Irving's " The Specter Bridegroom " deals with a similar subject.

    There went a boy so stilly,
        To the window small went he:
    " Art thou within, my fair sweetheart?
        Rise up and open to me."

    " We well may speak together, 5
        But I may not open to thee;
    For I have plighted my faith to one,
        And want no other but he."

    " The one to whom thou'rt plighted,
        Fair sweetheart, I am he; 10
    Reach me thy snow-white little hand,
        And then perhaps thou'lt see."

    " But nay! thou smellest of the earth;
        And thou art Death, I ween! "
    " Why should I not smell of the earth, 15
        When I have lain therein?

" Wake up thy father and mother,
Wake up thy friends so dear;
The chaplet green shalt thou ever wear,
Till thou in heaven appear."   20

(*Anonymous Translation*)

WOLFRAM VON ESCHENBACH (1160?–1220?)

We know little about Wolfram except that he was a Bavarian knight in
straitened circumstances, who frequented the courts of central and
southern Germany and professed to be prouder of his feats of arms than
of his poetic gifts. His *Parzival,* probably the most original poem of
medieval Germany, was composed about the year 1200. Its originality
consists, not so much in its subject matter, which is partly derived from
the *Perceval* of Chrétien de Troyes, as in the author's spiritual and ethical
interpretation of it. The theme is the quest of the Holy Grail. Wolfram
converts this into a symbolic narrative of man's upward struggle from
darkness to light. He does not teach ascetic renunciation of the world,
but fulfillment of duty in the world. He exalts chastity and loyalty as the
supreme virtues. The poem is long and has its obscurities as well as its
more inspired passages. The hero is represented as a sort of saintly
simpleton or wise fool, an ignoramus who blunders sadly but comes out
all right in the end, as befits his guilelessness.

The boyhood of Parzival is described in the following passage. His
mother, Queen Herzeleide, brings him up in ignorance of the world and of
warfare because she has lost her husband on a military expedition.

PARZIVAL'S BOYHOOD

Then full sore were her people grievèd, for they held it an evil thing,
And a training that ill beseemèd the son of a mighty king.
But his mother kept him hidden in the woodland valleys wild,
Nor thought in her love and sorrow how she wronged the kingly child.
No knightly weapon she gave him, save such as in childish play   5
He wrought himself from the bushes that grew on his lonely way,
A bow and arrows he made him, and with these, in thoughtless glee,
He shot at the birds as they caroled o'erhead in the leafy tree.

But when the feathered songster of the woods at his feet lay dead,
In wonder and dumb amazement he bowed down his golden head,   10
And in childish wrath and sorrow tore the locks of his sunny hair;

(For I wot well of all earth's children was never a child so fair
As this boy, who afar in the desert from the haunts of mankind did
    dwell,
Who bathed in the mountain streamlet, and roamed o'er the rock-
    strewn fell!)
Then he thought him well how the music, which his hand had   15
    for ever stilled,
Had thrilled his soul with its sweetness, and his heart was with sorrow
    filled,
And the ready tears of childhood flowed forth from their fountains
    free
As he ran to his mother weeping, and bowed him beside her knee.
" What aileth thee, child? " quoth the mother, " but now wast thou
    gay and glad " —
But, childlike, he gave no answer, scarce wist he what made him   20
    sad!

But Queen Herzeleide watched him through the sunny summer days,
Till beneath a tree she saw him stand silent, with upturned gaze,
And a look of joyful rapture in the radiant childish eyes,
As he listed the bird, that, soaring, sang clear through the cloudless
    skies;
And the mother's heart was troubled, and her wrath waxed to   25
    fever heat,
She would brook in his love no rival — not even God's singers sweet!
So she sent forth in haste her servants, with many a cunning snare
To capture the singers whose music made joyful the woodlands fair.
Then, alas! for the birds, who struggled in the cruel snare in vain,
Yet some few burst their bonds, and joyful, brake forth into song   30
    again!

Then the boy spake, " Now sweet my mother, why trouble the birds
    so sore?
Forsooth they can ne'er have harmed thee, ah, leave them in peace
    once more! "
And his mother kissed him gently, " Perchance I have wrought a
    wrong,
Of a truth, the dear God who made them, He gave unto them their
    song,

      12. wot: know; the past tense is wist. 14. fell: mountain.

And I would not that one of his creatures should sorrow because   35
    of me."
But the boy looked up in wonder, " God, Mother?   Who may God
    be? "
" My son, He is light beyond all light, brighter than summer's day,
And He bare a Man's Face, that we men might look on His Face
    alway!
Art thou ever in need of succor? call on Him in thine hour of ill,
And be sure He will fail thee never, but will hear thee, and help   40
    thee still.
Yet one there is dwelleth in darkness, and I wot men may fear him
    well,
For his home is the house of falsehood, and his kingdom the realm of
    Hell!
Turn thy mind away from him ever, nor waver betwixt the twain,
For he who doubteth, his labor shall ever be wrought in vain."

Thus his mother read him the riddle, the myst'ry of day and   45
    night,
The dread and the doom of darkness, and the glory and grace of light!
Then javelin in hand he hastened through the forest pathways wild,
And the deer sprang up from their thickets, and fled from the daunt·
    less child;
But clear-eyed and eager-footed he hastened upon their track,
And full oft with a hornèd trophy, at even he hied him back.   50
Little cared he for rain or sunshine, summer's storm or winter's snow,
And daily in strength and beauty all men might behold him grow;
Till at length no beast so mighty through the forest wild did roam,
If it fell 'neath his shaft, unaided, on his shoulder he bore it home!

It chanced through a woodland thicket one morn as he took his   55
    way,
And brake from o'erhanging bushes full many a leafy spray,
That a pathway steep and winding rose sharply his track anear,
And the distant beat of horse-hoofs fell strange on his wondering
    ear.
Then the boy grasped his javelin firmly and thought what the sound
    might be;
" Perchance 'tis the devil cometh!   Well, I care not if it be he!   60
Methinks I can still withstand him, be he never so fierce and grim,
Of a truth my lady mother she is o'er-much afraid of *him!* "

              39. **succor:** aid.

As he stood there for combat ready, behold, in the morning light,
Three knights rode into the clearing, in glittering armor bright;
From head to foot were they armèd, each one on his gallant steed,   65
And the lad as he saw their glory thought each one a god indeed!
No longer he stood defiant, but knelt low upon his knee,
And cried, " God, Who helpest all men, I pray Thee have thought
   for me! "

Then wroth was the foremost rider as the lad barred his further way,
And he spake out, " This stupid *Waleis* will hinder our work to-   70
   day! "
(Now here would I give to the Waleis the fame we Bavarians hold;
They are duller than e'en our people, yet manly in strife and bold.
And in sooth were one born in both countries such marvel of strength
   and skill
Would he hide in himself that I think me their fame he might well
   fulfil!)

Then there rode swift with hanging bridle, in costly harness   75
   dight,
With plumed and jewelled helmet another gallant knight;
Swiftly he came as thirsting to challenge in mortal fight
The foe who sped far before him, who had done him a sore despite;
For two knights from out his kingdom a maiden had borne away,
And he held it a deed most shameful and one he must needs re-   80
   pay;
For the maiden's sorrow grieved him, and fain would he ease her
   pain:
(And the three knights who rode before him were part of his warlike
   train.)
He rode a Spanish war-horse, and his shield had fierce conflict seen,
And Karnachkarnanz did they call him (he was Ulterleg's count I
   ween).

Then he cried to his knights, " Why loiter? who barreth our on-   85
   ward way? "
And straight on the lad did he ride there, who deemed him a god
   alway,
For ne'er had he seen such glory; his harness shone fair with dew,
And on either foot the stirrups with golden bells rang true.

   70. **Waleis:** inhabitant of Valois, a district in the northeast of France.
75. dight: clad.

And their length was e'en as fitting, and with bells did each strong
    arm ring,
As he stirred himself, or his sword-blade in battle aloft would   90
    swing.
And the hero was swift in seeking the guerdon of knightly prize,
So he rode here, the prince, and had decked him in a fair and won-
    drous wise.

Then spake this flower of all knighthood, " Say, boy, did they pass
    thy way?
Two knights who have shamed their knighthood, nay, *robbers* I ween
    are they,
For they bear a maiden with them, and she rideth against her   95
    will! "
Yet the boy, though he spake with a man's tongue, as a god must
    account him still;
For he thought how Queen Herzeleide had told him that God was
    Light
And dwelleth in Light for ever; and so to his dazzled sight
This knight, in his shining armor in the glow of the summer's day,
Was the God of his mother's lesson, and he knelt him again to   100
    pray.

But the prince he spake full gently, " Fain am I to do God's will,
And yet for no God I hold me, but a sinful mortal still.
Nay, wert thou more clear of vision, thou wouldst see, an thou sawest
    aright,
No Lord of the host of Heaven, but only a humble knight! "

" Knight? " quoth the boy in answer, "Nay! I wot not what   105
    that may be,
Is thy strength not of God, but of knighthood, then I would such were
    given to me! "
" Then wend thy way to King Arthur, an thou camest unto his court,
A noble knight he would make thee, ashamed and afeared for naught,
For sure, now I look upon thee, thou com'st of a noble strain."
Then his knights they turned their bridles, and gazed at the boy   110
    again.
Full well might they look and wonder, at the work that God's Hand
    had wrought.
For they say, who tell this story, that never could human thought

        91. guerdon: reward.   **103. an:** if.

Have dreamed of aught so goodly, since ever the world began,
For of all men beloved by women, was there never so fair a man!

Loud they laughed as the boy spake further, " Good knight,   115
    what may these be —
These rings that so close around thee, above and below I see? "
Then he handled, with curious finger, the armor the knight did bear,
His coat of mail close-linkèd as behovèd a knight to wear;
And he spake as he looked on the harness, " My mother's maidens
    string
On their chains, and around their fingers, full many a shining   120
    ring,
But they cling not so close to each other as these rings that here I
    see,
I cannot force them asunder; what good are they then to thee? "

Then the prince drew forth from its scabbard his shining blade so
    keen,
" Now see, he who fights against me, must withstand my sword I
    ween;
And lest he, on his part, should slay me, it is fit that with mail   125
    and shield,
I ward me against his spear-thrusts, and the blows that his arm may
    wield."
Swiftly the lad made answer, " Little good would it do the deer
An their coats were e'en such as thine is, they would fall still beneath
    my spear."

Full wroth were the knights and scornful that their lord thus long
    had talked
With this lad with the face of an angel, and the speech as of   130
    one distraught;
Then the prince he spake full gently, " God keep thee in His good
    grace,
I would that my shield's bright mirror might show me as fair a face!
Nay, an the Giver of all gifts but gave thee wit enow
To match with a mien so goodly, full rich wert thou then I trow!
May He keep all sorrow from thee, and thy life be a summer's   135
    day — "
And with that he turned his bridle, and wended once more his way.

(Jessie L. Weston)

---

130. distraught: demented.   133. enow: enough.

SUGGESTIONS FOR STUDY

1. What impression do you get of the budding character of Parzival?
2. What other descriptions of the innocent wonder of childhood do you know?
3. Wagner's opera *Parzival* is based on Wolfram's poem. What other modern operas do you know which were inspired by medieval literature?
4. What English authors have dealt with the subject of the Holy Grail?

WALTHER VON DER VOGELWEIDE
(1165?–1230?)

Walther, as he is frequently called for short, is the outstanding figure among the Minnesingers, the German poets of chivalrous love. He was also probably the greatest of all medieval lyric poets. He was born in southern Tyrol and belonged to the lesser nobility. His poverty forced him to earn his living as a wandering minstrel or gleeman. In this capacity he traversed most of Germany and had counts, dukes, and emperors for patrons. Many of his poems are of a political nature. He took an active part in the affairs of his country, hoping to allay sectional jealousies and thereby prevent civil strife. The Emperor Frederick II gave him a small pension.

The German Minnesingers took over the conception of chivalrous love from the trouvères and the troubadours of France. But chivalrous love was something very different from love as we understand it. It was more a matter of the imagination and the senses than of the heart. In most cases the mistress was a high-placed lady whom the lover was rarely privileged to meet. Sometimes she was entirely indifferent to his protestations and pleas. It was a constant wooing and a constant refusal. There was something artificial and insincere about the whole situation. Through repetition it readily degenerated into a mere literary convention. That is why these love songs, if read in large numbers, are so tiresome to us today.

It is Walther's supreme merit that he was able to rise above conventionalities which seemed to him inane. He believed that love (*Minne*) should be genuine and natural. " The bliss of two hearts is Minne," he says in one of his poems. " If both share equally, then Minne is there. One heart alone cannot hold her." Woman is a nobler title than Lady. Grace may mean more than beauty. Country girls dancing on the meadows are often more charming to him than fine ladies at court.

Walther was also very patriotic and never tired of singing the praises and glory of his beloved Germany, where, as he says, the best men and the fairest women are to be found. Like most poets he rejoiced in nature, particularly in the fresh beauty of the springtime. Above all, he was deeply religious. In one of his poems he calls for a renewal of spiritual life, which shall sweep away selfishness and indifference and unite Christendom in the fervor of a new crusade. Altogether he was a manly, lovable figure and a most sweet singer.

WHEN FROM THE SOD THE FLOWERETS SPRING

When from the sod the flowerets spring,
  And smile to meet the sun's bright ray,
When birds their sweetest carols sing,
  In all the morning pride of May,
What lovelier than the prospect there?   5
Can earth boast any thing more fair?
To me it seems an almost heaven,
So beauteous to my eyes that vision bright is given.

But when a lady chaste and fair,
  Noble, and clad in rich attire,   10
Walks through the throng with gracious air,
  As sun that bids the stars retire, —
Then, where are all thy boastings, May?
What hast thou beautiful and gay,
Compared with that supreme delight?   15
We leave thy loveliest flowers, and watch that lady bright.

Wouldst thou believe me, — come and place
  Before thee all this pride of May;
Then look but on my lady's face,
  And which is best and brightest say;   20
For me, how soon (if choice were mine)
This would I take, and that resign,
And say, " Though sweet thy beauties, May,
I'd rather forfeit all than lose my lady gay! "

                                                   (*E. Taylor*)

MARTIN LUTHER (1483–1546)

The name and fame of Luther, the leader of the Protestant Reformation in Germany, belong much more to the history of public events and to theological controversy than to the history of literature. Nevertheless, Luther rendered an indirect service of inestimable value to German literature by supplying his country with a standard literary language. He accomplished this feat by his translation of the Bible. Thereafter the various

Low German dialects gradually disappeared from writing. The vocabulary which Luther employed remains to this day the stock vocabulary of the German people. He furnished countless writers with imagery and phrases which have persisted ever since. The only other translation of the Bible that can be compared in importance to Luther's is the Authorized or King James version in English. Luther also wrote a number of hymns, of which the one here given is the most famous. It has been aptly called " the battle hymn of the Reformation." The first line was suggested by the opening words of Psalm 46. The rugged quality of the verse is apparent, even in translation.

PSALM

A safe stronghold our God is still,
　A trusty shield and weapon;
He'll help us clear from all the ill
　That hath us now o'ertaken.
　　The ancient Prince of Hell   5
　　Hath risen with purpose fell;
　　Strong mail of craft and power
　　He weareth in this hour;
　On earth is not his fellow.

With force of arms we nothing can;   10
　Full soon were we down-ridden,
But for us fights the proper Man,
　Whom God himself hath bidden.
　　Ask ye, Who is this same?
　　Christ Jesus is his name,   15
　　The Lord Zebaoth's Son.
　　He, and no other one
　Shall conquer in the battle.

And were this world all devils o'er
　And watching to devour us,   20
We lay it not to heart so sore,
　Not they can overpower us.
　　And let the Prince of Ill
　　Look grim as e'er he will,
　　He harms us not a whit.   25
　　For why? His doom is writ,
　A word shall quickly slay him.

16. Lord Zebaoth: Lord of Hosts. The form Sabaoth is commoner.

God's word, for all their craft and force,
One moment will not linger,
But, spite of Hell, shall have its course;   30
'Tis written by his finger.
    And though they take our life,
    Goods, honor, children, wife,
    Yet is their profit small.
    These things shall vanish all,   35
The City of God remaineth.

                         (*Thomas Carlyle*)

HANS SACHS (1494–1576)

Hans Sachs, the cobbler-poet, is best remembered today as an important character in Wagner's music drama, *The Mastersingers of Nürnberg*. He was indeed the last of the mastersingers, those burgher poets who established a guild of poetry and music with a fully developed apprenticeship system. But no one reads any longer the mechanically constructed poetry of the guild. Hans Sachs looked on the world with wondering, childlike eyes and transformed all that he saw, heard or read into verse, which he turned out as industriously as he cobbled shoes. Of his appallingly large output, a few Shrovetide plays may still be enjoyed. These are appropriate to the spirit of the carnival season just before Lent. They are artlessly written with a homely realism and a humor that now seems to us quaint. Taken collectively, they mirror faithfully the everyday life of the sixteenth century.

THE HORSE THIEF

[December 27, 1553]

Characters

GANGEL DÖTSCH ⎫
STEFFEL LÖLL   ⎬ *farmers*
LINDEL FRITZ   ⎭
UL VON FRISING, *the horse thief*

SCENE. *Fünsing*

The three FARMERS *come in.*

Dötsch. We elders have been chosen — we,
As wiser than the rest — to be
Judges for the community,
How best to hang our thief, who lies

Waiting in jail. No one denies   5
He should be hung. He brought us loss,
And stole from me my good gray horse.
 Löll. Why counsel long? He is a thief;
There is none questions that belief.
Hang him at once, nor feed him more;   10
In jail he eats of food great store.
 Fritz. Odds-bobs! friend Löll, thou tak'st the word
Out of my mouth; delay's absurd.
He is not worth three kreuzers; why
Waste food on such as he? say I.   15
 Dötsch. If you think so, what do you say
To Monday next for hanging-day?
 Löll. Oh, neighbors, think you of my rye;
Close to the gallows it doth lie;
If now we hang him all my grain   20
Will thus be spoiled; the thing is plain;
They will so crowd upon my field
To see the hanging, it will yield
No crop to me; for, trampled flat,
It so is ruined. Think of that!   25
 Fritz. Our neighbor, Steffel Löll, is wise;
I have a field that also lies
On the left side — it came to me
By an inheritance — so we
Will lose our crops; for, doubt it not,   30
They all will trample round the spot,
Excited, as they all will be,
To see the horse-thief on the tree.
 Dötsch. Yes, neighbors; now we all must say
That not at once be hanging-day;   35
After the reaping time is past
The hanging-day will come at last.
 Löll. That will be best; I think we may
Decide on these three weeks' delay.
 Fritz. But think of this! For three weeks more   40
We still must feed him from our store;
These thieves are very hungry, so
What he will eat no man doth know! —

---

12. **Odds-bobs:** an ancient oath, probably a corruption of the words God's
body. The form Odds-Bodkins occurs later. 14. **kreuzers:** cents.

Odds-bobs! my friends, his keeper says
He cost ten kreuzers in eight days.   45
    Dötsch. Why should we fill his basket? Why
Simply fat up a thief to die?
Cut down his food till he be thin;
To keep him fat is sure a sin;
Besides it were a lighter thing   50
To give a thin thief his last swing.
    Löll. Neighbors, attend!   It comes to me —
Here in my head — a remedy,
By which our thief no cost will be,
If we can do it skillfully: 55
Set the thief free; but make him swear,
Within four weeks he will repair
Back to the jail on hanging-day;
And do this thing without delay.
So will he find himself in food;   60
While, unto us, is understood
We reap the grain the gallows round,
That all in readiness be found:
No grain to trample, fields all mown;
Thus will the hanging be well shown.   65
    Fritz. This is, for all, the wisest plan;
Our Steffel is a prudent man.
We save our crops; we save our food;
We win the horse-thief's gratitude,
For he may in the sunshine stay.   70
My Gangel Dötsch, what dost thou say?
    Dötsch. First ask the thief if this will be
Agreeable to him; if he
Will take this oath. If he agree,
Then let him run. In meantime we   75
Can harvest all conveniently.
Löll, wilt thou go and bring the man,
That we may let him know our plan?
Look that he doth not steal away;
For stealing is to him but play.   80

STEFFEL LÖLL *goes out.*

    Fritz. Look now, my Gangel, good advice
Hath Steffel given; the man is wise.

Dötsch. From Steffel I looked not for it;
Nor thought the man had so much wit.

Fritz. My Gangel Dötsch, this should'st thou know,   85
He hath more wit than he doth show;
Is crafty; and the world hath seen;
Wider abroad he oft hath been
Than any Fünsinger. 'Twas he
Advised the church should plastered be   90
With loam. If Munich were his town
He had won wealth and high renown,
A solid burgher; and his wit
Had made him in the senate sit.

STEFFEL LÖLL *brings in the thief fastened with a rope, by
which he is led.*

Dötsch. Now, Ul of Frising, listen well,   95
While I the village orders tell;
We have decided to delay
Thy hanging four weeks from today;
In the meantime thou shalt go free,
And take what pleasure suiteth thee,   100
Where'er it be, but must not stay
Longer than these four weeks away,
And come back on thy hanging-day.

Löll. And thou must swear an oath, to be
Held fast to what we now agree.   105
While thou dost think of it aside,
Thy oath and answer we abide.

The three FARMERS *go out.*

Ul von Frising. Now, by the saint of thieves, I swear
I never dreamed that anywhere
There were such fools! But Fünsing sure   110
Is full of asses — asses pure! —
Asses whose folly never sleeps,
But still its candle lighted keeps!
Caught in the act, why should they stay
My hanging? — wherefore thus delay?   115
Twice have they sentenced me, and now
They set me free on my own vow —
An oath — what is it? made to break,

As mine will be for my neck's sake.
An old-time proverb says, " To swear 120
Is easier beyond compare
Than digging turnips." It will be
Hard finding oath too big for me.
If I come back at their set day,
Hang me for thief and fool they may. 125
I will this town's acquaintance drop
Rather than fill a raven's crop —
Pshaw! I will come on some dark night,
And when again there cometh light
These three wise men will miss some things 130
That, in the night, have taken wings.
So easy on these fools to play
A trick, one's wit is thrown away.

The three FARMERS *come in.*

Dötsch. Say, Ul of Frising; shall it be
That thou wilt swear, and then go free? 135
Ul von Frising. Dear men of Fünsing, fortunate
Is your wise town in men so great
Of wisdom. I, submissive, bow
Before this sentence, and will now
Make my full oath to do your will, 140
And all your wise commands fulfill.
When you have reaped your crop of grain
I will be duly back again
So promptly there will no delay
By me postpone my hanging-day; 145
But now, indeed, I must confess,
That, if you send me moneyless
Into the world, I then must steal;
So to your justice I appeal.
If, for such crime, they hang me high, 150
My oath to you I must deny.
How then my conduct would you scan?
" Surely he is no honest man."
Or if, for weeks, about I go
Begging my bread, this thing would show 155
No credit to you; men would say,
" They cannot find, till hanging-day,

Food for their thieves." Fünsing would be
A name for scorn and raillery.
  Fritz. Neighbors, 'tis true. Can we afford   160
To have the country's scornful word?
So should we be for ever shamed;
And a mean man, Fünsinger named.
There is, indeed, a better plan:
Let us take care of this good man;   165
Let each of us a kreuzer give;
On thirty kreuzers he can live;
I will collect it, and will lend
The half a gulden to our friend.
There is the sum. Two fingers raise;   170
Swear thou wilt come in thirty days,
That we may hang thee from the tree,
Example to all thieves like thee.

UL VON FRISING *holds up two fingers, and swears.*

  Ul von Frising. So! I will do it. Oath and word
I freely give as you have heard;   175
And take my red cap; it is small,
But is my pledge, and is my all.
Whenever this red cap you see,
Proof of my sworn fidelity,
Know I will come, without a doubt,   180
Upon the day my time is out.
Yes; I, poor wretch, as best I may,
Will come upon my hanging-day.
  Dötsch. And, Ul, consider well that we
Will have no foolish trick from thee.   185
If, after reaping, thou should'st stay —
Were it, indeed, for but one day —
Thy ears cropped to thy head will be
Before we hang thee on the tree,
In punishment for perjury.   190
All this we tell thee openly.
  Ul von Frising. Ah, spare yourselves anxiety!
Think you my cap I now should leave
As pledge, if I would thus deceive
Your honest faith? Oh, trust in me!   195
I swear it by my honesty!

Dötsch. Go quickly, friend! We are agreed;
And all good luck attend thy need;
But come thou back with equal speed.

UL VON FRISING *goes quickly off.*

Fritz. The cap is worth nine kreuzers, so   200
This thief most honest faith did show,
Leaving his cap. The pledge with me
Shall stay. I keep it carefully;
And if I should this red cap wear,
The thief, at least, will little care;   205
When he comes back, for it I'll trade
Unless too great a price is made.
   Dötsch. We must, to all the village, tell
How we arranged this thing so well;
The people will be pleased to know   210
That the affair we managed so;
No wisdom surely could have won
Better result than ours has done.

The three FARMERS *go off.*
UL VON FRISING *comes on wearing a blue coat.*

Ul von Frising. The Fünsingers had many a fear
That I should never re-appear;   215
Yet here I am for spoil and fun.
Their reaping yet is hardly done.
But I have so much honesty
I do not feel that I am free.
Last night I stole our Lindel's goat   220
And Steffel's beautiful new coat —
No one would doubt that it is mine,
The fit is so exact and fine —
I picked up sundry other things,
Each one of which, at Munich, brings   225
A price; so there I soon must go,
Its lucky market favors so.
The Fünsingers still have my cap —
Oh, I could steal it! but mayhap
My luck would turn; for I should feel it   230
Scarcely an honest act to steal it.
I pledged the thing; and I might make

A blunder, that red cap to take.
Perhaps I might no more be free,
But have the irons eating me —   235
After the reaping I may stay,
From Fünsing, many months away,
And let the farmers wait for me.
I still must pilfer — it may be
That there will come quite suddenly   240
At last a dark, unlucky day,
When I for many thefts must pay —
Pooh! Let me put such folly down!
Though I must die, I cannot drown!
I know that I am ravens' food,   245
And from all other deaths made good.
A proverb says, " The gallows-tree
From other deaths doth guarantee."

UL von Frising *goes out, and* Lindel Fritz *and* Gangel
Dötsch *come in.*

Fritz. The reaping done, 'tis hanging-day,
And Ul, the thief, is still away;   250
If one day longer he remain
He gets not back his cap again;
Whate'er he say, his fault is plain.
Dötsch. Here cometh Steffel Löll this way;
He may, perhaps, have news to say;   255
He was in Munich yesterday;
Ask him what word he brings, I pray.

Steffel Löll *comes in.*

What news, my Löll? Come, pay it down
Didst see our horse-thief in the town?
Löll. Yes; late at evening he was there.   260
Fritz. When to his hanging doth he fare?
On yesterday his time was out;
What is the lazy man about?
Löll. Lindel, he is a busy man;
One gets a word in as one can;   265
For to him many traders ran.
Dötsch. What had this horse-thief then to sell?
Löll. More — oh, much more — than I can tell!

Some odds and ends, house-furnishings,
This good blue coat and other things. 270
He had for sale an old gray goat;
I would have bought it, but this coat
Took all my coin.   It seemed to me,
His goat was like one owned by thee,
Shaggy like thine, and with one horn; 275
No liker pair were ever born.

    Fritz. Odds-Bodkins!   Then that goat was mine;
For mine is lost; and each like sign
Is proof to any honest sight.
Listen, good friends!   All is not right! 280
This thief hath come to us by night.
My Steffel Löll, why didst thou fail
To have him put in city jail?

    Löll. If they had hanged him, then I pray,
Had we not lost our hanging-day? 285

    Fritz. I swear that thou didst share with him
The goat and coat!   Look not so grim!
Thou hast no look of innocence,
To cover up thy vile offence.

    Löll. Thou liest in thy throat, thou knave! 290
It was twelve kreuzers that I gave.

    Dötsch. The coat is dirty, full of beer
And feathers.   Why not sweep it clear?
                          [The coat is swept.

    Löll. The coat fits well; I have another
As like to this as any brother; 295
Now I shall dress so fine each day
That I the nobleman can play.
        [Still brushing the coat and examining it very closely.
Body and brains!   How can it be!
He sold my own old coat to me!
It is, indeed, beyond belief, 300
Buying one's own coat from a thief!

    Dötsch. My Steffel, how didst find this thing?

    Löll. See! by this worn and tagless string.
How the thief mocked me!   By a price
So low he made his art entice 305
Me into thoughtless, foolish trust
Filling my eyes with blinding dust

So that I had no sense to know
It was my coat that he did show.
But on this thief a trick I played   310
That made me better of the trade.
   Dötsch. Pray how could such a trick be made?
   Löll. When none was looking then at me
I thrust a pair of gloves — you see —
In the coat pocket. Hurriedly   315
The people pressed around us, so
There was no one to see or know;
Thence I escaped with gloves of twice
The value of the coat's low price.
   Fritz. Here one thief from another steals.   320
   Löll. Not steals! When one with rascal deals,
From any loss himself he shields.
   Fritz. I find no truer word than steals.
   Löll. There was a pitchfork once made way
From my house into thine; one day   325
I found it there. " Steal and give back ";
My mouth did not the proverb lack;
And dost thou now forget the smack
I gave thee then, my Lindel Fritz?
But there are proverbs worse than this.   330
   Fritz. Why speak of such an ancient thing
That chanced a year ago? To bring
Such slander up is false and vile,
And doth so much thy tongue defile
That I will beat thy wicked face,   335
And drive such liar from the place.
   Löll. Strike, fool! and find thy master then,
Thou pest of true and honest men!

       Gangel Dötsch *goes between them.*

   Dötsch. Hey! would you fight, you foolish ones?
Batter your flesh? and break your bones?   340
What would you gain? the surgeon first,
And then the bailiff — which is worst?
Bite off your words, both one and other,
And cease at once this senseless pother.
   Fritz. That he should dare to call me thief!   345
It is a thing beyond belief!

344. pother: fuss.

Can any one believe his lie
That he is honester than I?

   Dötsch. I do believe that either one
Is good as other; and all done;   350
Fitting companions are you two;
What either doth, you both may do.

   Löll. My Gangel, strong is thine own lot
In honesty! Hast thou forgot? ——

   Dötsch. Cry not dishonesty at me!   355
A foolish clamor that would be.
Thou think'st upon the iron chain
That from thy wagon had been ta'en;
Did I not pay thee for it, fool?
Shut up thy mouth, and let it cool!   360
When we have long been reconciled,
To raise the question now is wild;
Thou temptest me thy face to beat,
Make thee a calf that cannot bleat.

   Löll. Strike, my dear Gangel! I fear not   365
Thy wrath, nor have that chain forgot.

   Fritz. Ho, for a fight! — The green is clear!
For blood and wounds let no one fear!
Ho! some shall skip the green plot o'er
As if they heard a lion roar!   370
   [*The three* FARMERS *draw their swords and drive each other around
and off, fighting furiously.*

UL VON FRISING *comes in.*

   Ul von Frising. Like a thieves' quarrel this appears:
They pulled each others' beards and ears;
They cut and hacked in angry fight;
And each now lies in bloody plight —
Lies while the grinning surgeon sews   375
The gaping wounds of many blows.
Our Lindel Fritz hath a great crack
Extending down one half his back;
Dötsch's great head is slashed and split;
A cap of plasters covers it;   380
And his jaws chatter so, his teeth
Like dice are rattling underneath;
And Löll is bleeding while they seek
To stop the veins in face and cheek;

His nose and teeth are chopped away;   385
He will not speak for many a day.
After the quarrel, on the ground
Once more my red cap I have found,
Lost in the battle, it would seem;
So I my pledge again redeem;   390
For I, in proper time, am here
To keep my oath, it would appear;
But for my deeds I need not fear.
I am as honest as the rest,
Who all are robbers self-confessed.   395
" As is the stable, so the cow ";
We prove the proverb truly now.
Therefore I risk these Fünsing men.
Where all are thieves, what reason then
For hanging any one for theft?   400
If this were done who would be left?
The thing is simple; let it pass,
And drink together, glass to glass,
In Fünsing village, where, indeed,
Of gallows-tree there is no need;   405
But, like with like, we bear life's cracks
Like honest men.

> So says Hans Sachs.
>
> *(William Leighton)*

SUGGESTIONS FOR STUDY

1. Does the humor of the play seem to you anything more than merely farcical? Give reasons for your answer. What is the essential difference between a farce and a comedy?

2. Describe the meter and the rhyme scheme. What is the general effect of each? Do you think the play gains or loses by being in verse?

3. What characters in Spanish fiction resemble Ul von Frising? Point out selections in the folklore of both the Spanish and German sections which resemble this farce in theme. Can you think of any examples in early literature where dishonesty is treated seriously rather than satirically?

4. How would this farce lend itself to amateur presentation? Plan the stage setting and costumes. Where would " stage business " play an important part? Compare it in this respect with *A Doctor in Spite of Himself* and *No Smoking.*

GOTTHOLD EPHRAIM LESSING (1729–1781)

Lessing was the liberator of German literature from French domination, and in this sense may be called the founder of modern German literature. He was the foremost critic of his time and one of the greatest of all critics. He not only pulled down, but he also laid the foundations of something new and better. In his creative work, he gave his country its first good comedy and its first good tragedy. Born in Saxony, the son of a Lutheran minister, he received an excellent education and became famous for his scholarship, especially in the ancient classics. For a time he was critic and adviser of the national theater in Hamburg. During the last years of his life he acted as librarian to the Duke of Brunswick. Lessing was a manly, generous soul, who inspired many men, both in his own day and later, in the devoted search for truth — a quest in which he himself never faltered or compromised. He was a master of clear, vigorous prose and much dreaded as an opponent in controversies.

Lessing's dramatic criticism is contained in his *Letters on Literature* and *Hamburg Dramaturgy*. In these he attacked the slavish observance of the unities in the French classic drama by showing that they were based on a misunderstanding of Aristotle. He praised Shakespeare at the expense of Corneille, Racine and Voltaire. Above all, he urged the Germans to develop a national literature of their own. In all these matters, his learning and eloquence carried the day. His essay "Laocoön" is a valuable contribution to esthetics. In it he distinguishes the respective fields of sculpture and painting on the one hand and poetry on the other.

NATHAN THE WISE

Very different from Lessing's other works is *Nathan the Wise*, a dramatic poem, intended to enforce the lesson of religious toleration. By choosing as his setting one of the crusades, he was able to bring Christianity, Judaism and Islam into contact with one another. Nathan, an ideally wise and good man, is a portrait of Lessing's friend, the philosopher Moses Mendelssohn. In the central scene of the play, Saladin, the Muslim Sultan, urged by his sister Sittah, questions Nathan, who is a Jew, about the true religion. The story of the three rings, which Nathan then proceeds to tell, is taken from Boccaccio's *Decameron*.

SITTAH, SALADIN, AND NATHAN

SCENE. *An audience room in the Sultan's palace*

Saladin. [*Giving directions at the door*] Here, introduce the Jew, whene'er he comes, —
He seems in no great haste.

Sittah. May be, at first,
He was not in the way.
 Saladin. Ah, sister, sister!
 Sittah. You seem as if a combat were impending.
 Saladin. With weapons that I have not learned to wield. — 5
Must I disguise myself? I use precautions?
I lay a snare? When, where gained I that knowledge?
And this, for what? To fish for money, — money, —
For money from a Jew. And to such arts
Must Saladin descend, at last, to come at   10
The least of little things?
 Sittah. Each little thing,
Despised too much, finds methods of revenge.
 Saladin. 'Tis but too true. And if this Jew should prove
The fair, good man, as once the dervis painted —
 Sittah. Then difficulties cease. A snare concerns 15
The avaricious, cautious, fearful Jew;
And not the good, wise man; for he is ours
Without a snare. Then the delight of hearing
How such a man speaks out; with what stern strength
He tears the net, or with what prudent foresight 20
He one by one undoes the tangled masses!
That will be all to boot.
 Saladin. That I shall joy in.
 Sittah. What, then, should trouble thee? For if he be
One of the many only, a mere Jew,
You will not blush, to such a one to seem   25
A man as he thinks all mankind to be.
One that to him should bear a better aspect
Would seem a fool, — a dupe.
 Saladin. So that I must
Act badly, lest the bad think badly of me?
 Sittah. Yes; if you call it acting badly, brother, 30
To use a thing after its kind.
 Saladin. There's nothing,
That woman's wit invents, it can't embellish.
 Sittah. Embellish? —
 Saladin. But their fine-wrought filagree
In my rude hand would break. It is for those

---

14. **dervis:** more commonly dervish, a Muslim friar. 32. **embellish:** beautify.
33. **filagree:** delicate metal openwork

That can contrive them to employ such weapons; 35
They ask a practiced wrist. But chance what may,
Well as I can ——
    Sittah. Trust not yourself too little.
I answer for you, if you have the will.
Such men as you would willingly persuade us
It was their swords, their swords alone, that raised them. 40
The lion's apt to be ashamed of hunting
In fellowship of the fox; — 'tis of his fellow,
Not of the cunning, that he is ashamed.
    Saladin. You women would so gladly level man
Down to yourselves! — Go, I have got my lesson. 45
    Sittah. What! must I go?
    Saladin. Had you the thought of staying?
    Sittah. In your immediate presence not, indeed;
But in the by-room.
    Saladin. You could like to listen.
Not that, my sister, if I may insist.
Away! the curtain rustles, — he is come. 50
Beware of staying, — I'll be on the watch. —

[*While* SITTAH *retires through one door,* NATHAN *enters at another,*
and SALADIN *seats himself.*]

Draw nearer, Jew; yet nearer; here, quite by me,
Without all fear.
    Nathan. Remain that for thy foes!
    Saladin. Your name is Nathan?
    Nathan. Yes.
    Saladin. Nathan the Wise?
    Nathan. No.
    Saladin. If not thou, the people calls thee so. 55
    Nathan. May be, the people.
    Saladin. Fancy not that I
Think of the people's voice contemptuously,
I have been wishing much to know the man
Whom it has named the Wise.
    Nathan. And if it named
Him so in scorn? If wise meant only prudent; 60
And prudent, one who knows his interest well?
    Saladin. Who knows his real interest, thou must mean.
    Nathan. Then were the interested the most prudent;
Then wise and prudent were the same.

Saladin.   I hear
You proving what your speeches contradict.   65
You know man's real interests, which the people
Knows not, — at least, have studied how to know them.
That alone makes the sage.
    Nathan.   Which each imagines
Himself to be.
    Saladin.   Of modesty enough!
Ever to meet it, where one seeks to hear   70
Dry truth, is vexing. Let us to the purpose; —
But, Jew, sincere and open ——
    Nathan.   I will serve thee
So as to merit, Prince, thy further notice.
    Saladin.   Serve me? — how?
    Nathan.   Thou shalt have the best I bring, —
Shalt have them cheap.
    Saladin.   What speak you of? — your wares?   75
My sister shall be called to bargain with you
For them (so much for the sly listener) ; — I
Have nothing to transact now with the merchant.
    Nathan.   Doubtless, then, you would learn what, on my journey,
I noticed of the motions of the foe,   80
Who stirs anew. If unreserved I may ——
    Saladin.   Neither was that the object of my sending;
I know what I have need to know already.
In short, I willed your presence ——
    Nathan.   Sultan, order.
    Saladin.   To gain instruction quite on other points.   85
Since you are a man so wise, — tell me, which law,
Which faith, appears to you the better?
    Nathan.   Sultan,
I am a Jew.
    Saladin.   And I a Mussulman:
The Christian stands between us. Of these three
Religions only one can be the true.   90
A man like you remains not just where birth
Has chanced to cast him, or, if he remains there,
Does it from insight, choice, from grounds of preference.
Share, then, with me your insight, —let me hear
The grounds of preference, which I have wanted   95
The leisure to examine, — learn the choice
These grounds have motived, that it may be mine.

In confidence I ask it. How you startle,
And weigh me with your eye! It may well be
I'm the first sultan to whom this caprice,   100
Methinks not quite unworthy of a sultan,
Has yet occurred. Am I not? Speak, then, — speak.
Or do you, to collect yourself, desire
Some moments of delay? I give them you. —
(Whether she's listening? — I must know of her   105
If I've done right. —)   Reflect, — I'll soon return.

[SALADIN *steps into the room to which* SITTAH *had retired.*]

Nathan. Strange! How is this? What wills the sultan of me?
I came prepared with cash, — he asks truth. Truth?
As if truth, too, were cash, — a coin disused,
That goes by weight, — indeed, 'tis some such thing; —   110
But a new coin, known by the stamp at once,
To be flung down and told upon the counter,
It is not that. Like gold in bags tied up,
So truth lies hoarded in the wise man's head,
To be brought out. — Which, now, is this transaction,   115
Which of us plays the Jew? He asks for truth, —
Is truth what he requires, his aim, his end?
That this is but the glue to lime a snare
Ought not to be suspected, — 'twere too little.
Yet what is found too little for the great?   120
In fact, through hedge and pale to stalk at once
Into one's field beseems not, — friends look round,
Seek for the path, ask leave to pass the gate. —
I must be cautious. Yet to damp him back,
And be the stubborn Jew, is not the thing;   125
And wholly to throw off the Jew, still less.
For, if no Jew, he might with right inquire,
Why not a Mussulman? — Yes, — that may serve me.
Not children only can be quieted
With stories. — Ha! he comes; — well, let him come.   130
  Saladin [*returning*].   So there the field is clear. — I'm not too
    quick?
Thou hast bethought thyself as much as need is? —
Speak, no one hears.
  Nathan. Might the whole world but hear us!

118. lime: smear.   121. pale: fence.

Saladin. Is Nathan of his cause so confident?
Yes, that I call the sage, — to veil no truth; 135
For truth to hazard all things, life and goods.
   Nathan. Ay, when 'tis necessary, and when useful.
   Saladin. Henceforth I hope I shall with reason bear
One of my titles, — " Betterer of the world
And of the law."
   Nathan. In truth, a noble title. 140
But, Sultan, ere I quite unfold myself,
Allow me to relate a tale.
   Saladin. Why not?
I always was a friend of tales well told.
   Nathan. Well told, — that's not precisely my affair.
   Saladin. Again so proudly modest? — Come, begin. 145
   Nathan. In days of yore, there dwelt in East a man
Who from a valued hand received a ring
Of endless worth; the stone of it an opal,
That shot an ever changing tint; moreover,
It had the hidden virtue him to render 150
Of God and man beloved, who, in this view,
And this persuasion, wore it. Was it strange
The Eastern man ne'er drew it off his finger,
And studiously provided to secure it
For ever to his house? Thus he bequeathed it, 155
First, to the most belovèd of his sons, —
Ordained that he again should leave the ring
To the most dear among his children, — and,
That without heeding birth, the favorite son,
In virtue of the ring alone, should always 160
Remain the lord o' th' house. — You hear me, Sultan?
   Saladin. I understand thee, — on.
   Nathan. From son to son,
At length this ring descended to a father
Who had three sons alike obedient to him;
Whom, therefore, he could not but love alike. 165
At times seemed this, now that, at times the third
(Accordingly as each apart received
The overflowings of his heart) most worthy
To heir the ring, which, with good-natured weakness,
He privately to each in turn had promised. 170
This went on for a while. But death approached,
And the good father grew embarrassed. So

To disappoint two sons, who trust his promise,
He could not bear. What's to be done? He sends
In secret to a jeweler, of whom,   175
Upon the model of the real ring,
He might bespeak two others, and commanded
To spare nor cost nor pains to make them like,
Quite like the true one. This the artist managed.
The rings were brought, and e'en the father's eye   180
Could not distinguish which had been the model.
Quite overjoyed, he summons all his sons,
Takes leave of each apart, on each bestows
His blessing and his ring, and dies. — Thou hear'st me?
   Saladin. I hear, I hear. Come, finish with thy tale; —   185
Is it soon ended?
   Nathan. It is ended, Sultan;
For all that follows may be guessed of course.
Scarce is the father dead, each with his ring
Appears, and claims to be the lord o' th' house.
Comes question, strife, complaint, — all to no end;   190
For the true ring could no more be distinguished
Than now can — the true faith.
   Saladin. How, how? — is that
To be the answer to my query?
   Nathan. No,
But it may serve as my apology;
If I can't venture to decide between   195
Rings which the father got expressly made,
That they might not be known from one another.
   Saladin. The rings, — don't trifle with me; I must think
That the religions which I named can be
Distinguished, e'en to raiment, drink, and food.   200
   Nathan. And only not as to their grounds of proof.
Are not all built alike on history,
Traditional, or written? History
Must be received on trust, — is it not so?
In whom now are we likeliest to put trust?   205
In our own people surely, in those men
Whose blood we are, in them who from our childhood
Have given us proofs of love, who ne'er deceived us,
Unless 'twere wholesomer to be deceived.
How can I less believe in my forefathers   210
Than thou in thine? How can I ask of thee

To own that thy forefathers falsified,
In order to yield mine the praise of truth?
The like of Christians.

   Saladin. By the living God!
The man is in the right, — I must be silent.   215

   Nathan. Now let us to our rings return once more.
As said, the sons complained. Each to the judge
Swore from his father's hand immediately
To have received the ring, as was the case,
After he had long obtained the father's promise   220
One day to have the ring, as also was.
The father, each asserted, could to him
Not have been false; rather than so suspect
Of such a father, willing as he might be
With charity to judge his brethren, he   225
Of treacherous forgery was bold to accuse them.

   Saladin. Well, and the judge, — I'm eager now to hear
What thou wilt make him say. Go on, go on.

   Nathan. The judge said, " If ye summon not the father
Before my seat, I cannot give a sentence.   230
Am I to guess enigmas? Or expect ye
That the true ring should here unseal its lips?
But hold, — you tell me that the real ring
Enjoys the hidden power to make the wearer
Of God and man beloved; let that decide.   235
Which of you do two brothers love the best?
You're silent. Do these love-exciting rings
Act inward only, not without? Does each
Love but himself? Ye're all deceived deceivers, —
None of your rings is true. The real ring,   240
Perhaps, is gone. To hide or to supply
Its loss, your father ordered three for one."

   Saladin. O, charming, charming!

   Nathan. " And," the judge continued,
" If you will take advice, in lieu of sentence,
This is my counsel to you, — to take up   245
The matter where it stands. If each of you
Has had a ring presented by his father,
Let each believe his own the real ring.
'Tis possible the father chose no longer
To tolerate the one ring's tyranny;   250
And certainly, as he much loved you all,

And loved you all alike, it could not please him,
By favoring one, to be of two the oppressor.
Let each feel honored by this free affection
Unwarped of prejudice; let each endeavor   255
To vie with both his brothers in displaying
The virtue of his ring; assist its might
With gentleness, benevolence, forbearance,
With inward resignation to the Godhead;
And if the virtues of the ring continue   260
To show themselves among your children's children,
After a thousand thousand years, appear
Before this judgment-seat, — a greater one
Than I shall sit upon it, and decide." —
So spake the modest judge.

    Saladin. God!

    Nathan. Saladin,   265
Feel'st thou thyself this wiser, promised man?

    Saladin. I, dust, — I, nothing, — God?

[*Precipitates himself upon* NATHAN *and takes hold of his hand,
which he does not quit the remainder of the scene.*]

    Nathan. What moves thee, Sultan?

    Saladin. Nathan, my dearest Nathan, 'tis not yet
The judge's thousand thousand years are past, —
His judgment-seat's not mine. Go, go, but love me.   270

                                 (*W. Taylor*)

SUGGESTIONS FOR STUDY

1. What is the lesson of the story of the three rings? How should true religion prove itself?

2. Show from this scene why Nathan deserved his reputation for wisdom.

3. Account for Saladin's change of attitude toward Nathan. In general, which is the more effective way of convincing an opponent — logical argument or illustrative story? Discuss.

4. A fine portrayal of Saladin's character is to be found in Sir Walter Scott's novel *The Talisman*. Do you get the same impression of him from Scott and Lessing? Read a historical account of him to determine whether he has been romanticized by literature.

5. How does Nathan compare with well-known Jewish characters in English and American literature? Of what Biblical character does he remind you?

IMMANUEL KANT (1724-1804)

Kant is the greatest of German philosophers and the one from whom all subsequent philosophic thinking proceeds. He was born, spent all his life, and died in the small university town of Königsberg in East Prussia. There is something almost ludicrous in the contrast between his uneventful, secluded existence and the sweep of his philosophy which penetrated to the very limits of the knowable. Kant was the great philosophic defender of the ideas of God, the freedom of the will, and the immortality of the soul. In his *Critique of Pure Reason* (1781) he showed that those ideas could not be rationally demonstrated, but in the *Critique of Practical Reason* he restored them as moral certainties reached through our experience in life. His writing was dry and abstract and without any literary graces. Only the contemplation of the solemn majesty of man's moral nature could arouse him to eloquence. Two things there were, he said, which filled him with awe: the starry heavens above him and the moral law within him. His best-known formulation of the law of duty is: " Act as if the principles by which you act were by your will to be made a universal law of nature." He called this law " the categorical imperative." Thomas Carlyle has expounded the idea eloquently in his spiritual autobiography *Sartor Resartus*.

A GOOD WILL

Nothing in the whole world, or even outside of the world, can possibly be regarded as good without limitation except a *good will*. No doubt it is a good and desirable thing to have intelligence, sagacity, judgment, and other intellectual gifts, by whatever name they may be called; it is also good and desirable in many respects to possess by nature such qualities as courage, resolution, and perseverance; but all these gifts of nature may be in the highest degree pernicious and hurtful, if the will which directs them, or what is called the *character*, is not itself good. The same thing applies to *gifts of fortune*. Power, wealth, honor, even good health, and that general well-being and contentment with one's lot which we call *happiness*, give rise to pride and not infrequently to insolence, if a man's will is not good; nor can a reflective and impartial spectator ever look with satisfaction upon the unbroken prosperity of a man who is destitute of the ornament of a pure and good will. A good will would therefore seem to be the indispensable condition without which no one is even worthy to be happy.

A man's will is good, not because the consequences which flow from it are good, nor because it is capable of attaining the end which it seeks, but it is good in itself, or because it wills the good. By a good will is not meant mere well-wishing; it consists in a resolute employment of all the means within one's reach, and its intrinsic value is in no way increased by success or lessened by failure.

This idea of the absolute value of mere will seems so extraordinary that, although it is endorsed even by the popular judgment, we must subject it to careful scrutiny.

If nature had meant to provide simply for the maintenance, the well-being, in a word the happiness, of beings which have reason and will, it must be confessed that, in making use of their reason, it has hit upon a very poor way of attaining its end. As a matter of fact, the very worst way a man of refinement and culture can take to secure enjoyment and happiness is to make use of his reason for that purpose. Hence there is apt to arise in his mind a certain degree of *misology,* or hatred of reason. Finding that the arts which minister to luxury, and even the sciences, instead of bringing him happiness, only lay a heavier yoke on his neck, he at length comes to envy, rather than to despise, men of less refinement, who follow more closely the promptings of their natural impulses, and pay little heed to what reason tells them to do or to leave undone. It must at least be admitted, that one may deny reason to have much or indeed any value in the production of happiness and contentment, without taking a morose or ungrateful view of the goodness with which the world is governed. Such a judgment really means that life has another and a much nobler end than happiness, and that the true vocation of reason is to secure that end.

The true object of reason then, in so far as it is practical, or capable of influencing the will, must be to produce a will which is *good in itself,* and not merely good *as a means* to something else. This will is not the only or the whole good, but it is the highest good, and the condition of all other good, even of the desire for happiness itself. It is therefore not inconsistent with the wisdom of nature that the cultivation of reason which is essential to the furtherance of its first and unconditioned object, the production of a good will, should, in this life at least, in many ways limit, or even make impossible, the attainment of happiness, which is its second and conditioned object.

(John Watson)

SUGGESTIONS FOR STUDY

1. What is the difference between a good will and mere well-wishing? In what sense is the term " good will " commonly interpreted today? Give examples.

2. Why does Kant think reason is a poor means of attaining happiness? Can you illustrate this from your own experience?

3. "Life has another and a much nobler end than happiness." Explain what is meant.

4. Rousseau used to think highly of himself because he had a kind heart and meant well. What would Kant say about such a person?

5. If you find any statements in this essay which seem to you debatable, discuss them pro and con.

GOTTFRIED AUGUST BÜRGER (1748-1794)

Bürger was associated for a number of years with the University of Göttingen as student and teacher. His dissipated habits and lack of moral balance wrecked his life. But in his poetry he revealed to his generation some long-neglected values. His ballads are among the finest in the German language. The weird and haunting "Lenore" (1773) may be said to have opened a new era in ballad poetry and to have contributed mightily to the "renascence of wonder" which was a mark of romanticism. The return of a dead lover to his grieving sweetheart is a common enough theme in folk songs of all countries. The old Scotch ballad "Sweet William's Ghost," which Bürger found in Percy's *Reliques,* gave him the immediate impulse to write "Lenore." Sir Walter Scott in his translation of Bürger's poem bestowed on the heroine the more familiar name of Helen. Among Bürger's other ballads are "The Wild Huntsman," "The Brave Man" and "Emperor and Abbot."

WILLIAM AND HELEN

From heavy dreams fair Helen rose,
  And eyed the dawning red:
"Alas, my love, thou tarriest long!
  O art thou false or dead?"—

With gallant Fred'rick's princely power   5
  He sought the bold Crusade;
But not a word from Judah's wars
  Told Helen how he sped.

With Paynim and with Saracen
  At length a truce was made,   10
And ev'ry knight returned to dry
  The tears his love had shed.

9. **Paynim:** pagan.   9. **Saracen:** Arab.

Our gallant host was homeward bound
    With many a song of joy;
Green waved the laurel in each plume,   15
    The badge of victory.

And old and young, and sire and son,
    To meet them crowd the way,
With shouts, and mirth, and melody,
    The debt of love to pay.   20

Full many a maid her true-love met,
    And sobbed in his embrace,
And flutt'ring joy in tears and smiles
    Arrayed full many a face.

Nor joy nor smile for Helen sad;   25
    She sought the host in vain;
For none could tell her William's fate,
    If faithless, or if slain.

The martial band is past and gone;
    She rends her raven hair,   30
'And in distraction's bitter mood
    She weeps with wild despair.

" O rise, my child," her mother said,
    " Nor sorrow thus in vain;
A perjured lover's fleeting heart   35
    No tears recall again." —

" O mother, what is gone, is gone;
    What's lost, for ever lorn.
Death, death alone can comfort me;
    O had I ne'er been born!   40

" O break, my heart, O break at once!
    Drink my life-blood, Despair!
No joy remains on earth for me,
    For me in heaven no share." —

38. lorn: gone.

" O enter not in judgment, Lord! "   45
　　The pious mother prays;
" Impute not guilt to thy frail child!
　　She knows not what she says.

" O say thy pater noster, child!
　　O turn to God and grace!   50
His will, that turn'd thy bliss to bale,
　　Can change thy bale to bliss." —

" O mother, mother, what is bliss?
　　O mother, what is bale?
My William's love was heaven on earth,   55
　　Without it earth is hell.

" Why should I pray to ruthless Heaven,
　　Since my loved William's slain?
I only prayed for William's sake,
　　And all my prayers were vain." —   60

" O take the sacrament, my child,
　　And check these tears that flow;
By resignation's humble prayer,
　　O hallowed be thy woe! " —

" No sacrament can quench this fire,   65
　　Or slake this scorching pain;
No sacrament can bid the dead
　　Arise and live again.

" O break, my heart, O break at once!
　　Be thou my god, Despair!   70
Heaven's heaviest blow has fallen on me,
　　And vain each fruitless prayer." —

" O enter not in judgment, Lord,
　　With thy frail child of clay!
She knows not what her tongue has spoke;   75
　　Impute it not, I pray!

49. **pater noster:** Our Father, the opening words of the Lord's Prayer.

" Forbear, my child, this desperate woe,
    And turn to God and grace;
Well can devotion's heavenly glow
    Convert thy bale to bliss." —   80

" O mother, mother, what is bliss?
    O mother, what is bale?
Without my William what were heaven,
    Or with him what were hell? " —

Wild she arraigns the eternal doom,   85
    Upbraids each sacred power,
Till, spent, she sought her silent room,
    All in the lonely tower.

She beat her breast, she wrung her hands,
    Till sun and day were o'er,   90
And through the glimmering lattice shone
    The twinkling of the star.

Then, crash! the heavy drawbridge fell
    That o'er the moat was hung;
And, clatter! clatter! on its boards   95
    The hoof of courser rung.

The clank of echoing steel was heard
    As off the rider bounded;
And slowly on the winding stair
    A heavy footstep sounded.   100

And hark! and hark! a knock — Tap! tap!
    A rustling stifled noise; —
Door-latch and tinkling staples ring; —
    At length a whispering voice.

" Awake, awake, arise, my love!   105
    How, Helen, dost thou fare?
Wak'st thou, or sleep'st? laugh'st thou, or weep'st?
    Hast thought on me, my fair? " —

85. **arraigns**: accuses.   87. **spent**: exhausted.   96. **courser**: swift horse.

" My love! my love! — so late by night! —
  I waked, I wept for thee: 110
Much have I borne since dawn of morn;
  Where, William, could'st thou be? " —

" We saddle late — from Hungary
  I rode since darkness fell;
And to its bourne we both return   115
  Before the matin-bell." —

" O rest this night within my arms,
  And warm thee in their fold!
Chill howls through hawthorn bush the wind: —
  My love is deadly cold."   120

" Let the wind howl through hawthorn bush!
  This night we must away;
The steed is wight, the spur is bright;
  I cannot stay till day.

" Busk, busk, and boune!   Thou mount'st behind   125
  Upon my black barb steed.
O'er stock and stile, a hundred miles,
  We haste to bridal bed." —

" Tonight — tonight a hundred miles! —
  O dearest William, stay!   130
The bell strikes twelve — dark, dismal hour!
  O wait, my love, till day! " —

" Look here, look here — the moon shines clear —
  Full fast I ween we ride;
Mount and away! for ere the day   135
  We reach our bridal bed.

" The black barb snorts, the bridle rings;
  Haste, busk, and boune, and seat thee!
The feast is made, the chamber spread,
  The bridal guests await thee." —   140

---

115. **bourne:** boundary.   116. **matin-bell:** bell calling to early morning
prayer.   123. **wight:** swift.   125. **busk:** get ready.   125. **boune:** prepare.
126. **barb:** Barbary. whence a fine breed of horse comes.

Strong love prevailed: she busks, she bounes,
    She mounts the barb behind,
And round her darling William's waist
    Her lily arms she twined.

And, hurry! hurry! off they rode, 145
    As fast as fast might be;
Spurned from the courser's thundering heels
    The flashing pebbles flee.

And on the right, and on the left,
    Ere they could snatch a view, 150
Fast, fast each mountain, mead, and plain
    And cot, and castle, flew.

" Sit fast — dost fear? — The moon shines clear —
    Fleet goes my barb — keep hold!
Fear'st thou? " — " O no! " she faintly said; 155
    " But why so stern and cold?

" What yonder rings? what yonder sings?
    Why shrieks the owlet gray? " —
" 'Tis death-bells' clang, 'tis funeral song,
    The body to the clay. 160

" With song and clang, at morrow's dawn,
    Ye may inter the dead.
Tonight I ride, with my young bride,
    To deck our bridal bed.

" Come with thy choir, thou coffined guest, 165
    To swell our nuptial song!
Come, priest, to bless our marriage feast!
    Come all, come all along! " —

Ceased clang and song; down sunk the bier;
    The shrouded corpse arose: 170
And, hurry! hurry! all the train
    The thundering steed pursues.

152. cot: cottage.

And, forward! forward! on they go;
   High snorts the straining steed;
Thick pants the rider's laboring breath,   175
   As headlong on they speed.

" O William, why this savage haste?
   And where thy bridal bed? " —
" 'Tis distant far, low, damp, and chill,
   And narrow, trustless maid." —   180

" No room for me? " — " Enough for both; —
   Speed, speed, my barb, thy course! "
O'er thundering bridge, through boiling surge,
   He drove the furious horse.

Tramp! tramp! along the land they rode,   185
   Splash! splash! along the sea;
The scourge is wight, the spur is bright,
   The flashing pebbles flee.

Fled past on right and left how fast
   Each forest, grove, and bower!   190
On right and left fled past how fast
   Each city, town, and tower!

" Dost fear? dost fear? The moon shines clear,
   Dost fear to ride with me? —
Hurrah! hurrah! the dead can ride! " —   195
   " O William, let them be! —

" See there, see there! What yonder swings
   And creaks 'mid whistling rain? " —
" Gibbet and steel, th' accursed wheel;
   A murderer in his chain. —   **200**

" Hollo! thou felon, follow here;
   To bridal bed we ride;
And thou shalt prance a fetter dance
   Before me and my bride." —

   203. fetter dance: a dance with the limbs shackled.

And, hurry! hurry! clash, clash, clash!   205
   The wasted form descends;
And fleet as wind through hazel bush
   The wild career attends.

Tramp! tramp! along the land they rode,
   Splash! splash! along the sea;   210
The scourge is red, the spur drops blood,
   The flashing pebbles flee.

How fled what moonshine faintly showed!
   How fled what darkness hid!
How fled the earth beneath their feet,   215
   The heaven above their head!

" Dost fear? dost fear?   The moon shines clear,
   And well the dead can ride;
Does faithful Helen fear for them? " —
   " O leave in peace the dead! " —   220

" Barb! barb! methinks I hear the cock;
   The sand will soon be run:
Barb! barb! I smell the morning air;
   The race is well-nigh done." —

Tramp! tramp! along the land they rode,   225
   Splash! splash! along the sea;
The scourge is red, the spur drops blood,
   The flashing pebbles flee.

" Hurrah! hurrah! well ride the dead;
   The bride, the bride is come;   230
And soon we reach the bridal bed,
   For, Helen, here's my home." —

Reluctant on its rusty hinge
   Revolved an iron door,
And by the pale moon's setting beam   235
   Were seen a church and tower.

With many a shriek and cry whiz round
   The birds of midnight, scared;
And rustling like autumnal leaves
   Unhallowed ghosts were heard.   240

O'er many a tomb and tombstone pale
   He spurred the fiery horse,
Till sudden at an open grave
   He checked the wondrous course.

The falling gauntlet quits the rain,   245
   Down drops the casque of steel,
The cuirass leaves his shrinking side,
   The spur his gory heel.

The eyes desert the naked skull,
   The mold'ring flesh the bone,   250
Till Helen's lily arms entwine
   A ghastly skeleton.

The furious barb snorts fire and foam,
   And, with a fearful bound,
Dissolves at once in empty air,   255
   And leaves her on the ground.

Half seen by fits, by fits half heard,
   Pale specters flit along,
Wheel round the maid in dismal dance,
   And howl the funeral song;   260

" E'en when the heart's with anguish cleft,
   Revere the doom of Heaven,
Her soul is from her body reft;
   Her spirit be forgiven! "

                               (Sir Walter Scott)

247. **cuirass:** body armor.   263. **reft:** torn away.

SUGGESTIONS FOR STUDY

1. Observe the successive tokens of death in the ballad and the growing terror of Helen as she perceives them.

2. Point out specific instances of onomatopoeia; i.e., words which imitate sounds.

3. What is the "moral lesson" of the poem? What is the "moral lesson" of Coleridge's "The Rime of the Ancient Mariner," with which Bürger's ballad has been compared? How important are they compared with the descriptive power of the poems?

4. Compare this story with the ballad "The Dead Bridegroom" (page 427) and with Irving's story "The Specter Bridegroom," as to general tone and dramatic quality.

5. Vocabulary: perjured, impute, ruthless, forbear, upbraids.

JOHANN WOLFGANG VON GOETHE (1749–1832)

Goethe, Germany's greatest poet, was such a many-sided genius that it is impossible in this brief sketch to do more than indicate a few of his most important activities and accomplishments. He was born at Frankfort of a well-to-do and respectable family. His father, who supervised his early education, trained him in the languages and in the appreciation of art and music. In 1765 he went to Leipzig to study law and there he composed his first plays, two comedies in the French manner. After a severe illness which interrupted his studies for many months, he proceeded to the University of Strassburg to complete his law course. His stay at Strassburg is chiefly memorable for his meeting with the critic Herder, who changed the whole current of his ideas regarding literature. Herder deprecated the imitation of French authors and directed Goethe's attention to Homer, Shakespeare, Ossian and the folk song. Under his influence Goethe began his real career as a writer. His irregularly constructed prose play, *Götz von Berlichingen* (1773), the hero of which is the last of the free barons, gave him a national reputation. It was immediately followed by his first novel, *The Sorrows of Werther* (1774), a tragic love story, which spread his fame all over Europe. These are the chief works of his youthful " Storm and Stress " period.

In 1775 Goethe moved to Weimar, which was destined to be his home for the rest of his life. He went there as the companion and adviser of the young Duke and gradually became involved in administrative work until at last he was virtually prime minister. The sobering responsibility of office helped cure him of his early romantic turbulence. Its effect can be seen in the restraint and poise of the dramas he wrote in his middle period: *Iphigenia, Egmont,* and *Tasso.* Henceforth he sought his ideal in the moderation and balance of the Greeks, and this tendency was increased by his momentous sojourn in Italy from 1786 to 1788, during which he devoted himself to the study of classical art. He also became greatly interested in the natural sciences, especially biology, geology, and optics, and was able to make several interesting contributions to knowledge. His friendship with Schiller, begun in 1794, was not only a beautiful thing in itself, but was also mutually stimulating in a literary way. The novel *William Meister's Apprenticeship* and the idyllic poem *Hermann and Dorothea,* one of his most popular works, belong to these years. Goethe had twenty-seven more years to live after the death of Schiller in 1805. This last period of his life was one of increasing loneliness but of unremitting activity as well. His greatest work, the first part of the poetic drama *Faust,* was given to the world in 1808; the second part appeared just a few months before his death. His last novel of importance was *The Elective Affinities* (1809).

Goethe once remarked that all his writings were fragments of one great confession. He felt an inward compulsion to give literary expression to every significant experience he underwent. This is particularly true of his many love affairs, each one of which was accompanied by an outburst of lyric poetry. His life and writings form an organic unit. Even those novels and plays which seem most objective are saturated with his personality and his inner life. It is this " confessional " quality, together with his native gift of song, which has made him incomparable as a lyric poet. His commanding position in modern literature is due principally to these short poems and to the first part of *Faust.*

Goethe's religion consisted in a reverence for the divinity which he saw in all things. He had an optimistic confidence in everything that was natural, including the impulses of man. In practical conduct he taught the gospel of the upward struggle:

> " That men may rise on stepping stones
>   Of their dead selves to higher things."

POETRY AND TRUTH FROM MY LIFE

Goethe's autobiography was published in three parts, 1811–1814. It begins with the author's birth and carries the story of his life down to the year 1775. It may be supplemented with other autobiographical writings like the *Italian Journey.* Goethe chose the peculiar title of *Poetry and Truth* because he wished to indicate that, with all the desire in the world to be strictly truthful, he could not guarantee that he was not viewing his youth through a haze of romantic illusion.

The following selection narrates the beginning of his first adult love affair in 1770 when he was a law student at Strassburg. He and Frederica parted when Goethe took his degree in the summer of 1771. Many of his most delightful lyrics were inspired by her.

My fellow-boarder, Weyland, would from time to time enliven his quiet, laborious life by visiting his friends and relatives in the country (for he was a native of Alsace), and did me many a good turn on my little excursions, by introducing me to various places and families, sometimes in person, sometimes by letters of introduction. He had often spoken to me of a country clergyman who lived near Drusenheim, six leagues from Strassburg, in possession of a good living, an intelligent wife, and attractive daughters. He always spoke warmly of the hospitality and charming character of this family. This was more than sufficient to attract a young knight who had already accustomed himself to spend all his leisure days and hours on horseback and in the open air. So we decided to take this excursion, and my friend had to promise that when he introduced me he would say neither good nor ill of me, would treat me with perfect indifference, and allow me to make my appearance somewhat poorly and negligently, if not meanly, attired. He consented in the hope of some amusement.

It is a pardonable whim in men of consequence occasionally to conceal their external advantages, so as to allow their own inner human nature free scope. That is why there is always something so attractive in the incognito [1] of princes, and the adventures which result from it; they appear as disguised divinities, who are entitled to place a double value on all the good offices shown to them as individuals, and are in such a position that they can either make light of what is disagreeable or avoid it. That Jupiter should be well pleased in his incognito with Philemon [2] and Baucis, and Henry the Fourth [3] with his peasants after a day's hunting, is quite in the course of nature, and we approve it; but that a young man of no importance or reputation should take it into his head to amuse himself by assuming an incognito, might be construed by many as an unpardonable piece of arrogance. Yet since it is not here a question of the praise or blame attaching to such thoughts and actions, but rather of their actual occurrence, we will on this occasion, for the sake of our own amusement, pardon the youngster his self-conceit; and the more so, as I must here allege, that from youth upwards, a love of disguising myself had been implanted in me by my stern father himself.

On this occasion, partly by cast-off clothes of my own, partly by borrowed garments and by the way of dressing my hair, I had, if not disfigured myself, yet at least made myself look so odd, that my friend could not help laughing as we went, especially as I knew how to imitate to perfection the bearing and gestures of the clumsy horse-

---

[1] **incognito:** assumption of disguise.
[2] **Philemon:** Philemon and his wife Baucis were an aged couple who gave hospitality to Jupiter in their humble cottage.
[3] **Henry the Fourth:** (1553–1610) King of France.

men, generally known as "Latin riders." The fine road, the splendid weather and the near neighborhood of the Rhine, put us in the best of humors. At Drusenheim we stopped a moment, he to make himself spruce,[4] and I to rehearse my part, from which I was afraid I might now and then lapse. The country here has the characteristics of all the open, level parts of Alsace. We rode by a pleasant footpath through the meadows, soon reached Sesenheim, left our horses at the tavern, and walked leisurely towards the parsonage. "Do not be taken aback," said Weyland, showing me the house from a distance, " because it looks like a miserable old farm-house; it is all the younger inside." We stepped into the courtyard; the look of the whole delighted me; for it had exactly that charm which we call picturesqueness, and which had so enthralled me in Dutch art. The effect which time exercises on all human handiwork was plainly visible. House, barn, and stable were just at that point of dilapidation where, indecisive and doubtful between preserving and rebuilding, the owner often neglects the one without being able to accomplish the other.

As in the village, so in the courtyard, all was quiet and deserted. We found the father, a retiring yet friendly little man, quite alone, for the family were in the fields. He bade us welcome, and offered us some refreshment, which we declined. My friend hurried away to look after the ladies, and I remained alone with our host. " You are perhaps surprised," said he, " to find me in such poor quarters in a wealthy village, and with a lucrative living; but," he continued, " it all comes from irresolution. It has been promised me long ago by the parish, and even by persons in authority, that the house shall be rebuilt; many plans have been already drawn up, examined and altered, none of them entirely rejected, and none carried into execution. This has gone on so many years, that I scarcely know how to control my impatience." I made him an answer such as I thought likely to sustain his hopes, and to encourage him to push the matter on more vigorously. He then proceeded to describe most confidentially the personages on whom such things depended, and though he was no great delineator of character, I could easily understand how the whole business had come to be delayed. The tone of friendly intimacy in the man was characteristic; he talked to me as if he had known me for ten years, while there was nothing in his look from which I could have suspected that he was directing any attention to me. At last my friend came in with the mother. She seemed

---

[4] **spruce:** neat.

to look at me with quite different eyes. Her countenance was regular, and intelligent in expression; she must have been beautiful in her youth. Her figure was tall and spare, but not more so than became her years, and when seen from behind, she still looked youthful and attractive. The elder daughter then came bounding in; she inquired after Frederica, just as both the others had also done. The father assured them that he had not seen her since the three of them had gone out together. His daughter went out again to look for her sister; the mother brought us some refreshment, and Weyland continued his conversation with the husband and wife, which turned entirely on common acquaintances and experiences; for it is usual, when friends meet after some length of time, for them to ask and receive information on the whole circle of their acquaintanceship. I listened, and learned what I might expect from these new connections.

The elder daughter came hastily back into the room, uneasy at not having found her sister. They were anxious about her, and blamed her for one bad habit and another; only the father said, with calm composure, " Let her alone; she will come back all right." At this instant she actually appeared at the door; and then indeed a lovely star arose in this rural firmament. Both daughters still wore German dress, as it was then called, and this almost obsolete national costume became Frederica particularly well. A short, white, full skirt, with a flounce, not too long to reveal the neatest little feet and ankles; a tight white bodice and a black taffeta apron, — thus she stood on the boundary between town and peasant girl. Slender and light, she tripped along with buoyant step, and her neck seemed almost too delicate to bear the weight of the thick, fair plaits on the neat little head. The look of her merry, cheerful blue eyes was frank and free, and her pretty turned-up nose peered as freely into the air as if there could be no care in the world; her straw hat hung on her arm, and thus, at the first glance, I had the delight of seeing and appreciating her at once in her full grace and loveliness.

I now began to act my character in moderation, half ashamed of playing a joke on such good people. I had plenty of time to observe them well, for the girls continued the previous conversation, and that with animation and humor. All neighbors and relations were again discussed, and there seemed, to my imagination, such a swarm of uncles and aunts and cousins, comers and goers, godparents and guests, that I felt transported into the liveliest of worlds. All the members of the family had addressed a few words to me, the mother looked at me every time she came in or went out, but Frederica was the first to enter into conversation with me, asking me, as I took up and glanced through some music that was lying about, if I played too? When I told her I did, she asked me to play something; but the father would not allow this, for he maintained that it was proper that the guest should be first entertained with some music or song.

She played several things with some skill, and in the usual country style, and on a harpsichord,[5] too, that the schoolmaster should have tuned long ago, if he had only had time. She was next to sing a song, one in a tender, melancholy strain, and here she failed. She rose and said, smiling, or rather with that look of happy serenity which was a characteristic of her face, " If I sing badly, I cannot lay the blame on the harpsichord or the schoolmaster; but let us go out of doors; then you shall hear my Alsatian and Swiss songs; they sound much better."

During supper-time, an idea which had already struck me, filled my mind to such a degree, that I grew meditative and silent, though the sprightliness of the elder sister, and the charm of the younger, roused me repeatedly from my reveries. My astonishment at finding myself actually transported into the very midst of the Wakefield [6] family was beyond all expression. The father, indeed, could not be compared with that excellent man; but where will you find his like? On the other hand, all the dignity there peculiar to the husband, here appeared in the wife. To see her was to reverence and fear her. She bore the traces of a wise upbringing in her quiet, easy, cheerful, and engaging manner.

If the elder daughter had not Olivia's far-famed beauty, yet she was well made, lively, and rather impetuous; she seemed full of activity, and lent a helping hand to her mother in all things. But it was by no means difficult to put Frederica in the place of Primrose's Sophia; for little is said of the latter, but it is only taken for granted that she is sweetly lovable; and this girl was really so. Now as like occupations and like conditions, wherever they occur, produce similar, if not the same effects, so here too many things were talked about, and many things happened, which had already taken place in the Wakefield family. But when at last a younger son, long announced and impatiently expected by the father, sprang into the room, and boldly sat himself down by us, taking but little notice of the guests, I could scarcely help exclaiming, " And Moses too! "

[5] **harpsichord:** keyboard instrument with strings plucked by quill or leather points.

[6] **Wakefield:** Oliver Goldsmith's novel *The Vicar of Wakefield* (1766) seemed to Goethe to supply in its pictures of the Primrose family many striking resemblances to the Alsatian clergyman's family.

The conversation at table gave us further insight into this country and family circle, for their talk turned on various droll incidents which had happened at different times. Frederica, who sat by me, took the opportunity to describe to me different localities in the neighborhood which it was worth while to visit. As one story always calls forth another, I was better able to join in the conversation, with several anecdotes of my own, and as, in addition, there was no stint of good country wine, I stood in danger of forgetting my rôle. My more prudent friend, seeing this, took advantage of the beautiful moonlight, and proposed a walk, to every one's satisfaction. He gave his arm to the elder, I to the younger, and thus we went through the broad meadows, paying more attention to the heavens above us than to the earth, stretching away in the darkness at our feet. But Frederica's talk savored little of moonlight; the clearness of her words turned night into day, and there was nothing in what she said to indicate or excite feeling, except that her conversation included me more than it had done, since she described to me her own position, as well as the neighborhood and her acquaintances, in the light in which I should probably become acquainted with them; for she hoped, she added, I would prove no exception, but would visit them again, as all strangers gladly did who had once been to see them.

It was very pleasant to me to listen in silence to the description she gave of the little world in which she moved, and of the persons whom she particularly valued. The picture of her life which I gained from her words was at once so clear and so attractive that it produced a marvelous effect on me; for I felt both a deep regret that I had not lived with her sooner, and at the same time a positively painful feeling of envy towards all who had hitherto had the good fortune to be near her. I followed closely, as if I had a right to do so, all her descriptions of men, whether under the names of neighbors, cousins, or godparents, and my conjectures inclined now this way and now that; but how could I discover anything in my complete ignorance of all the circumstances? At last she became more and more talkative, and I more and more silent. It was so pleasant to listen to her, and as I could only hear her voice, while her face, as well as the rest of the world, floated dimly in the twilight, it seemed to me as if I saw into her heart, which could not but be pure, since it could open out to me with such unconstrained directness.

When my companion retired with me to the guest-chamber, which was prepared for us, he at once, with self-complacency, broke out into exclamations of amusement, and took great credit to himself for having surprised me so much with this counterpart of the Primrose family. I chimed in with his humor and expressed my gratitude. "Upon my word," he cried, "the story is quite complete. The two families may very well be compared, and the gentleman in disguise here may assume the honor of passing for Mr. Burchell; [7] moreover, since scoundrels are not so necessary in common life as in novels, I will for this time undertake the rôle of the nephew, and behave myself better than he did." However, I immediately changed this conversation, pleasant though it might be to me, and asked him, first, to tell on his honor, if he really had not betrayed me? His hearty disavowal quite convinced me. They had indeed inquired, he said, after the merry, boon companion who boarded at the same house with him in Strassburg, and of whom they had heard all sorts of marvelous nonsense. I now passed on to other questions: Had she ever been in love? Was she now in love? Was she engaged? He replied to all in the negative. "Really," I replied, "such natural cheerfulness is inconceivable to me. Had she loved and lost, and again recovered herself, or had she been betrothed,— in both these cases I could account for it."

Thus we chatted together far into the night, and I was awake again at dawn. My desire to see her once more seemed irresistible; but while I dressed, I was horrified at the disgraceful wardrobe I had so wantonly selected. Each article of clothing I put on made me seem more despicable in my own eyes; for everything had been selected to produce this effect. My hair I might perhaps have set to rights; but when at last I struggled into the worn-out, borrowed gray coat, and saw what a ridiculous appearance the shortness of the sleeves gave me, I fell into despair, all the more as, in the small looking-glass, I could see myself only piecemeal, and each part looked more ridiculous than the other.

During this process my friend awoke, and with the satisfaction of a good conscience, and in pleasurable anticipation of the coming day, beamed at me from under the quilted silk of our counterpane. I had long been envying him his fine clothes, as they hung over the chair, and had he been of my size, I would have carried them off before his eyes, changed my dress outside, and hurrying into the garden, left my accursed husk for him; he would have been good-humored enough to get into my clothes, and thus the tale would have come to a merry ending early in the morning. But that was not now to be thought of, nor did there seem to be any other feasible solution. To reappear

[7] **Mr. Burchell:** a character in *The Vicar of Wakefield* who turned out to be a baronet.

before Frederica in the figure which my friend could fittingly describe
as that of an industrious and gifted but poor student of theology, —
before Frederica, who the evening before had spoken so kindly to my
disguised self, — that was altogether impossible. There I stood,
vexed and thoughtful, summoning all my powers of invention; but
they deserted me! However, when my friend, luxuriously stretched
upon his pillows, after fixing his eyes upon me for a while, burst
suddenly into a loud laugh, and exclaimed, " No! there's no denying
it, you look disgraceful! " I replied impetuously, " And I know what
I will do. Good-bye, and make my excuses! "

" Are you mad? " he cried, springing out of bed and trying to
detain me. But I was already out of the door, down the stairs, out
of the house and yard, and off to the inn; in an instant my horse was
saddled, and I rushed off mad with vexation, galloping towards Drusenheim, then through it, and on beyond.

As I now thought myself safe, I rode more slowly, and then began
to feel how infinitely against my will it was to go away. But I resigned myself to my fate, called up the memory of last night's walk
with perfect calm, and cherished the secret hope of seeing her soon
again. But this quiet resignation soon changed into impatience
again. I now determined to ride rapidly to the town, change my
dress, and take a good, fresh horse, for then, so my passion led me
to believe, I could at all events return by dinner time, or, which was
more probable, by dessert, or even towards evening, and entreat my
forgiveness.

I was just about to put spurs to my horse to execute this plan,
when another, and, as seemed to me, a very happy idea passed through
my mind. In the inn at Drusenheim, the day before, I had noticed
a son of the landlord very neatly dressed, and had seen him again
early this morning, busy with his farm work, as he greeted me from
his courtyard. He was of my figure, and had for the moment even
reminded me of myself. I waited for no second thoughts. I had
hardly turned my horse round, when I was back in Drusenheim;
I took him to the stables, and in a few words put my proposal before
the fellow, namely, that he should lend me his clothes, as I had a
merry jest on hand at Sesenheim. Before I had finished my sentence he agreed with enthusiasm, delighted that I should wish to
make some sport for the young ladies; they were, he said, such
delightful girls, especially Miss Riekchen,[8] and the parents, too,
liked things to go merrily and brightly at all times. He considered

---

[8] **Riekchen:** diminutive of Frederica.

me attentively, and as from my appearance he might well take me for a poor starveling, he said, " If you want to get into favor, this is the right way." In the meanwhile we had been getting on fast with our change of dress, though, as a matter of fact, he was making a poor bargain in trusting his holiday clothes to me on the strength of mine; but he was honest-hearted, and, moreover, had my horse in his stable. I was soon sufficiently presentable, put on a consequential air, while my friend apparently gazed on his counterpart with complacency. " Done, Sir Brother! " said he, giving me his hand, which I shook heartily, " don't come too near my girl; she might make a mistake! "

My hair, now restored to its full growth, he easily parted in imitation of his, and looking at him, several times it occurred to me that it would be a good jest to blacken my eyebrows with a burnt cork, and bring them nearer together in imitation of his.

" Now, have you no business at the parsonage," I said, as he handed me his be-ribboned hat, " so that I might announce myself there quite naturally? "

" Certainly," he replied, " but then you will have to wait two hours. A woman has been confined in our house; I will offer to carry the cake [9] to the parson's wife, and you can take it over. Pride must pay its penalty, and so must a joke."

I resolved to wait, but these two hours seemed unending, and I was dying of impatience when the third hour had come and gone before the cake came out of the oven. At last I got it quite hot, and hastened away with my credentials, the sun shining brightly on me, and escorted some way by my counterpart, who promised to come after me in the evening and bring me my clothes. But this I firmly declined, and stipulated that I should bring his garments back myself.

I had not ridden far with my present, which I carried in a neatly-knotted napkin, when, in the distance, I saw my friend coming towards me with the two ladies. My heart beat more uneasily than it should have done under such a coat. I stood still, took breath and tried to consider how I should begin; and now I first remarked that the disposition of the ground was very much in my favor; for they were walking on the other side of the brook, and this, together with the strips of meadow through which it ran, kept the two footpaths pretty far apart. When they were just opposite to me, Frederica, who had already seen me a long way off, cried, " George, what are you bringing there? " I had enough sense to take off my hat and

9 **cake**: a christening cake.

cover my face with it, while I held the cake in its napkin well up in front of me. " A christening cake! " she cried; " how is your sister? "

" Quite well," said I, trying to talk in a strange dialect, if not exactly in Alsatian.

" Take it to the house! " said the elder sister, " and if you do not find my mother, give it to the maid; but wait for us, we shall soon be back, — do you hear? "

I hurried on in the happy hope that, as the beginning had been so lucky, all the rest would follow suit, and soon reached the parsonage. There was no one to be found in house or kitchen; not wanting to disturb the old gentleman, whom I supposed busy in the study, I sat down on the bench before the door, the cake beside me, and covered my face with my hat.

I can rarely remember feeling a pleasanter sensation. To sit once more on this threshold, which, a short time before, I had crossed stumbling in despair; to have already seen her once more, to have heard her dear voice again so soon after my grief had pictured a long separation, to be expecting her every moment and to await a discovery at which my heart throbbed, but which was, in this ambiguous case, a discovery without shame; for this was, to begin with, a merrier prank than any of those they had laughed at so much yesterday. Love and necessity are the best of masters; they were both acting in concert here, and their pupil was not unworthy of them.

But the maid came stepping out of the barn. " Well! did the cakes turn out all right? " she cried to me; " how is your sister? "

" All right," I said, and pointed to the cake without looking up.

She took up the napkin, muttering, " Now what's the matter with you again today? Has Bärbchen [10] been kind to some one else again? But you should not make us pay the penalty. A pretty couple you will make if you carry on so! " Her loud voice called the pastor to the window to ask what was the matter. She pointed him out to me; I stood up and turned towards him; but still kept my hat over my face. He spoke a few kind words to me, and asked me to stop a while, so I turned towards the garden, and was just going in, when the pastor's wife called to me as she went through the yard gate. I availed myself of the fact that the sun was shining straight in my eyes to keep on sheltering behind my hat, and gave her a loutish scrape; [11] but she passed on into the house, telling me not to go before I had eaten something. I now walked up and down the

---

[10] **Bärbchen:** Barbara, George's sweetheart.
[11] **loutish scrape:** awkward bow.

garden; everything had hitherto been most successful, yet I breathed hard and fast as I realized that the young people must soon be back again. But the mother came up to me most unexpectedly, and was just going to ask me a question, when she looked me in the face, and seeing what I could conceal no longer, the words stuck in her throat. " I look for George," she said, after a pause, " and whom do I find? Is it you, young gentleman? How many shapes have you, then? "

" In earnest only one," I replied; " in jest as many as you like."

" I will not spoil the jest," she smiled; " go out behind the garden into the meadow until it strikes twelve, then come back, when you will find I have started the fun."

I did as she told me; but as I was going along the meadows, beyond the hedges of the village gardens, some country people came towards me on the footpath, and put me in some embarrassment. I turned aside into a little wood, on the top of a hill near by, intending to hide myself there till the appointed time. Yet what was my astonishment when I entered it; for there before me was a neat little clearing, with benches, each of which afforded a charming view of the countryside. First the village and the steeple, then Drusenheim, and behind it the woody islands of the Rhine; in the opposite direction the Vosges mountains, and last the Strassburg minster.[12] All these shining pictures were set in leafy frames, so that it would be hard to imagine anything brighter or more delightful. I sat down on one of the benches, and noticed on the largest tree an oblong little board with the inscription, " Frederica's Rest." It never occurred to me that I might have come to disturb this rest; for a budding passion has this lovely characteristic, that, as it is unconscious of its origin, so it has no conception of an end, and, being itself full of joy and gladness, can have no presentiment that it may also be the cause of grief.

I had scarcely had time to look about me and was losing myself in sweet reveries, when I heard somebody coming; it was Frederica herself. " George, what are you doing here? " she cried from a distance.

" Not George! " I cried, running towards her, " but one who craves forgiveness of you a thousand times."

She looked at me in astonishment, but soon collected herself, and said, fetching a deep breath, " You horrid man, how you frighten me! "

" The first disguise has led me into a second," I exclaimed; " the former would have been unpardonable had I had any idea whom

[12] minster: cathedral.

I was going to see; but this one you will certainly forgive, for it is the garb of those whom you always treat with kindness."

Her pale cheeks had flushed a lovely rosy red. " You shall not be worse off than George, at any rate! But let us sit down! I confess the fright you gave me has made me shaky." I sat down beside her, in great agitation. " We know everything already, as far as what happened this morning, from your friend," she said, " now tell me the rest."

She did not need to ask me twice, for I described to her my horror at the figure I cut yesterday, and my rushing from the house, so comically, that she burst into hearty, rippling laughter; then I went on to what followed, with all modesty indeed, yet with sufficient passion for my words to pass for a declaration of love under the guise of a story. At last I sealed my joy at finding her again, by a kiss upon her hand, which she let lie in mine. If she had provided all the conversation during last night's moonlight walk, I now, on my part, richly repaid the debt. The pleasure of seeing her again, and being able to say to her all that I had kept back yesterday, was so great that, in my eloquence, I did not notice how thoughtful and silent she had grown. She drew several deep breaths, and over and over again I begged her pardon for the fright I had given her.

How long we may have sat there, I have no idea; but suddenly we heard some one call " Riekchen, Riekchen." It was her sister's voice. " Now we shall have sport," she said, restored to perfect cheerfulness; " she is coming on my side," she added, bending so as to half conceal me; " turn away, so that she may not recognize you at once." The sister came towards us, but not alone; Weyland was with her, and both, when they saw us, stood still, as if petrified.

The sight of flames bursting fiercely from a peaceful roof, or the meeting of a monster whose deformity is at the same time revolting and terrifying, would not strike us with such fierce horror as that which seizes us when, unexpectedly, we see with our own eyes what we should have believed morally impossible. " How is this? " cried the elder, with all the haste of one in terror. " How is this? you and George, hand-in-hand! What am I to understand by this? "

" Dear sister," Frederica hesitatingly replied, " poor fellow, — he is begging something of me; he has something to beg of you too, but you must forgive him beforehand."

" I do not understand — I cannot understand —— " said her sister, shaking her head and looking at Weyland, who, with his usual calm, stood looking on in silence.

Frederica rose and drew me after her. " No hesitating! " she cried, " but pardon given as soon as asked! "

" Now do! " I said, stepping nearer to her; " I have need of pardon! "

She drew back with a loud shriek, and covered with blushes; then she threw herself on the grass, laughing immoderately, and as though she would never stop. Weyland smiled, well pleased. " You are a splendid fellow," he said, and shook me by the hand. He was not usually demonstrative, but his handshake had something hearty and enlivening about it; yet he was sparing of this also.

When we had recovered and collected ourselves a little, we set out to return to the village. On the way I learned how this singular meeting had taken place. Frederica had separated from the other two to rest in her little nook for a moment before dinner, and when the other two returned to the house, the mother had sent them to call Frederica as quickly as possible, because dinner was ready.

The elder sister showed the most extravagant delight, and when she learned that the mother had already discovered the secret, she exclaimed, " Now we have still to play the trick on my father, my brother, the man-servant, and the maid." When we reached the garden-hedge, Frederica insisted upon going first into the house with my friend. The maid was busy in the kitchen-garden, and Olivia (for so the elder sister shall be called in these pages) called out to her, " Stop; I have something to tell you! "

She left me standing by the hedge and went to the maid. I saw they were speaking very earnestly. Olivia pretended to her that George had quarrelled with Barbara, and was now anxious to marry her. The girl was by no means displeased; I was now called up, and was to confirm what had been said. The pretty, plump lass cast down her eyes, and kept them so until I had got quite close to her. But when, suddenly, she saw a strange face, she too gave vent to a loud scream and ran away. Olivia bade me run after her and hold her fast, so that she should not get into the house and make a noise; while she herself meant to go in and see what her father was doing. On the way Olivia met the servant-boy, who was in love with the maid; in the meantime I had hurried after the girl, and held her fast. " Just think! what good luck! " cried Olivia; " it's all over with Barbara, and George is to marry Liese."

" I have expected that long enough," said the good fellow, and stood nursing his vexation.

I had given the maid to understand that all we had to do was to deceive the father. We went up to the lad, who turned and tried to get away; but Liese brought him back, and he, too, when undeceived, gave vent to the most extraordinary contortions. We went together to the house. The table was laid, and the father already in the room. Olivia, keeping me behind her, stepped to the threshold, and said, " Father, have you any objection to George's dining with us today? but you must let him keep his hat on."

" Oh, very well! " said the old gentleman, " but why such an unusual thing? Has he hurt himself? "

She dragged me forward as I was with my hat on. " No! " she said, leading me into the room, " but he has a bird-cage under it, and the birds might fly out and make a dreadful fuss; for they are all loose."

The father was amused at the joke, without precisely knowing what it meant. This instant she took off my hat, scraped and bowed and made me do the same. The old man looked at me and recognized me, but without losing his clerical self-possession. " Fie, fie, Sir Candidate! " [13] he exclaimed, raising a threatening finger at me; " you have changed saddles very quickly, and in the course of a night I have lost an assistant, who only yesterday promised me so faithfully that he would often take my pulpit for me on week-days." He then laughed heartily, bade me welcome, and we sat down to table.

Moses came in much later; for, being the youngest and most spoilt, he had got into the habit of not hearing the dinner-bell. Besides, he took little notice of the company, not even when he contradicted them. To make more sure of him, they had put me, not between the sisters, but at the end of the table, where George often used to sit. As he came in at the door behind me, he gave me a hearty clap on the shoulder, and said, " Good appetite, George! "

" Many thanks, squire! " I replied. The strange voice and the strange face startled him.

" Well, don't you think," cried Olivia, " that he looks very like his brother? "

" Yes, from behind," replied Moses, who managed to recover his composure immediately, " everyone does." He did not look at me again, but gave himself up with zeal to devouring the courses, to make up for lost time. Then he was pleased to go out, as he often did, and busied himself in the yard or garden. At dessert the real George came in, and helped to make matters still more lively. They began to banter him on his jealousy, and blamed him for making

[13] **Candidate:** theological student.

another rival of me; but he was modest and clever enough to get out of his difficulties, and, in a half-confused manner, succeeded in mixing up himself, his sweetheart, his counterpart, and the young ladies with each other, to such a degree, that at last nobody could tell about whom he was talking, and they were only too glad to leave him to consume a glass of wine and a bit of his own cake in peace.

At table there was some talk of going for a walk; but the suggestion did not appeal much to me in my peasant's clothes. However, the ladies, early that very morning, when they learned who had run away in such a desperate hurry, had remembered that a fine hunting-coat belonging to a cousin of theirs, who sometimes wore it when he was visiting there, was hanging in the clothes-press. But I declined it, joking to all appearance, yet in reality from a feeling of vanity, not wishing to spoil, by impersonating the cousin, the good impression I had made as the peasant. The father had gone to take his afternoon-nap; the mother, as usual, was busy with her housekeeping. But my friend proposed that I should tell them some story, and I immediately consented. We went into a spacious arbor, and I gave them a tale which I have since worked out in writing under the title of *The New Melusina*.[14] . . .

(*Anonymous Translation*)

SUGGESTIONS FOR STUDY

1. What impression do you get from these pages of the personality of the young Goethe? Why does he assume a disguise? Why does he later repent of it? Why does he then disguise himself a second time? Which parts of the whole episode were particularly amusing to you?

2. Describe the appearance and disposition of Frederica. In what ways does she resemble a modern American girl? In what ways differ from one?

3. What brief descriptive touches make the young brother seem especially real?

4. If you read *The Vicar of Wakefield* you will be able to work out for yourself the parallel between the two families. Can you name another of Goldsmith's works in which an intentional disguise opens up a love affair?

5. Compare Goethe's manner of narrating his reminiscences with Rousseau's manner in the *Confessions*. Which is the more objective way of procedure? An interesting comparison may be made also with Benvenuto Cellini's autobiography, and modern biographies. What in Goethe's first meeting with Frederica is similar to Benjamin Franklin's first encounter with his future wife?

[14] **The New Melusina:** Goethe's version of a well-known medieval romance.

WANDERER'S NIGHT SONG

Thou that from the heavens art,
    Every pain and sorrow stillest,
And the doubly wretched heart
    Doubly with refreshment fillest,
I am weary with contending!   5
    Why this rapture and unrest?
Peace descending,
    Come, ah, come into my breast!

(H. W. Longfellow)

O'ER ALL THE HILLTOPS

O'er all the hilltops
    Is quiet now,
In all the treetops
    Hearest thou
Hardly a breath;   5
    The birds are asleep in the trees.
Wait; soon like these
    Thou, too, shalt rest.

(H. W. Longfellow)

THE FISHER

The water rolled, the water swelled;
    A fisher sat thereby,
And quietly his angle held;
    Chilled to his heart was he.
The water in dreamy motion kept,   5
    As he sat in dreamy mood;
A wave hove up — and a damsel stepped,
    All dripping, from the flood.

She sang to him, she spake to him:
    " Why wilt thou lure away   10
My sweet brood by thy human art
    To the deadly light of day?

Ah! knewest thou how light of heart
  The little fishes live,
Thou wouldst come down, all as thou art,   15
  And thy true life receive.

" Bathes not the sun with all his skies?
  Bathes not the moon by night,
To breathe my dew awhile, and rise
  All smiling doubly bright?   20
And tempt thee not the deep, deep skies,
  Here spread in watery blue?
And tempt thee not thine own dark eyes
  Down through th' eternal dew? "

The water rolled, the water swelled;   25
  It wetted his bare feet;
A something through his bosom thrilled;
  He seemed his love to meet.
She spake to him, she sang to him;
  With him 'twas quickly o'er: 30
Half drew she him, half sank he in,
  And never was seen more.

                          (*J. S. Dwight*)

THE LOVED ONE EVER NEAR

I think of thee, when the bright sunlight shimmers
      Across the sea;
When the clear fountain in the moonbeam glimmers,
      I think of thee.

I see thee, if far up the pathway yonder   5
      The dust be stirred;
If faint steps o'er the little bridge to wander
      At night be heard.

I hear thee, when the tossing waves' low rumbling
      Creeps up the hill;   10
I go to the lone wood and listen, trembling,
      When all is still.

I am with thee, wherever thou art roaming, —
    And thou art near!
The sun goes down, and soon the stars are coming: 15
    Would thou wert here!

                  (*J. S. Dwight*)

TO THE MOON

Fillest hill and vale again,
    Still, with softening light!
Loosest from the world's cold chain
    All my soul tonight!

Spreadest round me, far and nigh,   5
    Soothingly, thy smile;
From thee, as from friendship's eye,
    Sorrow shrinks the while.

Every echo thrills my heart; —
    Glad and gloomy mood,   10
Joy and sorrow, both have part
    In my solitude.

River, river, glide along!
    I am sad, alas!
Fleeting things are love and song, —   15
    Even so they pass!

I have had and I have lost
    What I long for yet;
Ah! why will we, to our cost,
    Simple joys forget?   20

River, river, glide along,
    Without stop or stay!
Murmur, whisper to my song,
    In melodious play, —

Whether on a winter's night   25
    Rise thy swollen floods,
Or in spring thou hast delight
    Watering the young buds.

Happy he, who, hating none,
  Leaves the world's dull noise,   30
And, with trusty friend alone,
  Quietly enjoys

What, for ever unexpressed,
  Hid from common sight,
Through the mazes of the breast   35
  Softly steals by night!

                   (*J. S. Dwight*)

THE PARTING

Let mine eyes tell all at parting,
  For my lips they never can!
Hard! how hard! These tears keep starting,
  Yet I thought I was a man.

No more fond remembered blisses   5
  Love's sweet tokens now command;
Cold seem all thy burning kisses,
  Faint the pressure of thy hand.

Once, it seemed a heavenly treasure,
  One mere kiss snatched on the wing!   10
As we feel a startling pleasure
  Finding violets first in Spring.

But no more of love's fond trances,
  No more roses plucked for thee.
Spring-time smiles, my dearest Frances: 15
  Ah! 'tis Autumn drear to me!

                  (*J. S. Dwight*)

THE ELF KING

In this, the most popular of Goethe's ballads, use is made of the wide-spread belief that elves, fairies and other semi-supernatural creatures do not possess souls and can obtain them only by wresting them from human beings. Notice carefully in each instance whether it is the father, the child or the Elf King who speaks. The musical setting of Schubert is famous.

Who is it that rides through the night and the rain?
A father it is; he is riding amain —
His son he is holding close in his arm
To shield him from cold, to keep him from harm.

" Son, why do you hide your face in fear? "
" O father, my father, I see coming near
The Elf King wearing his crown and train."
" It's a vision, my child, that you see through the rain."

" Beautiful boy, come go with me —
Many a game I'll play with thee;
Flowers bright in our garden sway;
My mother's gown is golden and gay."

" Father, O father, do you not hear
What the Elf King's whispering in my ear? "
" Quiet, my son, you must not mind;
It's only the rustle of leaves in the wind."

" Beautiful boy, come go with me.
My lovely daughters shall wait on thee;
Gaily they'll dance — ring upon ring —
Nightly they'll dance for thee and sing."

" Father, O father! Look! — over there
Wait the Elf King's daughters with streaming hair."
" I see over there at the edge of day
Naught but the willows sere and gray."

" Beautiful boy, I love you so,
I'll take you by force, if you will not go."
The boy cries out in wild alarm,
" O father, the Elf King! He's done me harm! "

The father shudders; he rides with speed;
He flies through the night in terror and need;
He reaches the courtyard in anguished dread,
But there in his arms — the boy — is dead!

(Sophia H. Patterson)

SUGGESTIONS FOR STUDY

1. Which of these poems would you classify as ballads and which as pure lyrics? What do you think of their singing quality? How do they compare in this respect with the lyrics of Robert Burns?

2. How much use is made in these poems of folklore material? Which one seems most like a folk song? Where does the supernatural play a part? Of what other famous poems are you reminded by " The Fisher "?

3. To whom or what is the first poem addressed? In which poems is mood especially emphasized? Follow the successive moods of the poet in " To the Moon."

4. Which of the poems are the most personal? Is it the sadness or the joy of his experiences that Goethe dwells on most?

5. Read the Scandinavian ballad " Sir Olof's Bridal " (in Longfellow's *Prose and Poetry of Europe*) in conjunction with " The Elf King." Wherein do the stories differ? Which is the more powerful and dramatic? Why? What other stories do you know of people spirited away by supernatural beings?

6. The musical settings which Goethe has inspired are as famous in music as the poems are in literature. Schubert especially has helped to immortalize these songs. His settings for the two " Wanderer's Night Songs " (in *Fifty Songs by Schubert*) are simple enough to be well rendered by an amateur. " The Elf King " (" Erlkönig " in the same book), a favorite concert piece of dramatic contraltos, is too difficult for the average singer, but appears in phonograph record.

FAUST

The story of a man who sells his soul to the devil belongs to general folklore. In the early sixteenth century this story became attached to a certain Dr. Faust, a quack physician of Germany who pretended to work miracles. A chapbook was published in 1587 by an anonymous author recounting, as a dire warning, the wicked life and awful end of this presumptuous man. Translated into English, this book supplied material for Christopher Marlowe's tragedy of *Dr. Faustus* (1589). So well was Marlowe's play received in Germany that it gave rise to a German drama popular on the stage for over a hundred years. Eventually it became a puppet play, in which form it attracted Goethe, who in his boyhood had possessed a set of puppets of his own. The poet recognized the story as having possibilities for a great dramatic epic.

Goethe's *Faust* is in a unique way his life work. He began it as a young man and did not complete it until the year before he died. Since he used it as the repository of his most cherished thoughts, it reveals the successive

phases through which his philosophy of life passed. It is divided into two
parts. Part I is a complete drama in itself and is Goethe's universally
recognized masterpiece. Part II, on the other hand, is an allegorical play,
dealing with the salvation of Faust's soul through altruistic action. The
difficulty of the symbolism and the lack of dramatic movement distinguish
it far from Part I, which is largely concerned with the love story of Faust
and Margaret.

PROLOGUE IN HEAVEN

THE LORD. THE HEAVENLY HOSTS. *Afterwards* MEPHISTOPHELES.

The THREE ARCHANGELS *come forward.*

Raphael. The Sun, in ancient guise, competing
With brother spheres in rival song,
With thunder-march, his orb completing,
Moves his predestined course along;
His aspect to the powers supernal   5
Gives strength, though fathom him none may;
Transcending thought, the works eternal
Are fair as on the primal day.
   Gabriel. With speed, thought baffling, unabating,
Earth's splendor whirls in circling flight;   10
Its Eden-brightness alternating
With solemn, awe-inspiring night;
Ocean's broad waves in wild commotion,
Against the rocks' deep base are hurled;
And with the spheres, both rock and ocean   15
Eternally are swiftly whirled.
   Michael. And tempests roar in emulation
From sea to land, from land to sea,
And raging form, without cessation,
A chain of wondrous agency,   20
Full in the thunder's path careering,
Flaring the swift destructions play;
But, Lord, thy servants are revering
The mild procession of thy day.
   The Three. Thine aspect to the powers supernal   25
Gives strength, though fathom thee none may;
And all thy works, sublime, eternal,
Are fair as on the primal day.
   Mephistopheles. Since thou, O Lord, approachest us once more,
And how it fares with us, to ask art fain,   30

Since thou hast kindly welcomed me of yore,
Thou see'st me also now among thy train.
Excuse me, fine harangues I cannot make,
Though all the circle look on me with scorn;
My pathos soon thy laughter would awake,   35
Hadst thou the laughing mood not long forsworn.
Of suns and worlds I nothing have to say,
I see alone mankind's self-torturing pains.
The little world-god still the selfsame stamp retains,
And is as wondrous now as on the primal day.   40
Better he might have fared, poor wight,
Hadst thou not given him a gleam of heavenly light;
Reason he names it, and doth so
Use it, than brutes more brutish still to grow.
With deference to your grace, he seems to me   45
Like any long-legged grasshopper to be,
Which ever flies, and flying springs,
And in the grass its ancient ditty sings.
Would he but always in the grass repose!
In every heap of dung he thrusts his nose.   50
    The Lord. Hast thou naught else to say? Is blame
In coming here, as ever, thy sole aim?
Does nothing on the earth to thee seem right?
    Mephistopheles. No, Lord! I find things there, as ever, in sad
        plight.
Men, in their evil days, move my compassion;   55
Such sorry things to plague is nothing worth.
    The Lord. Know'st thou my servant, Faust?
    Mephistopheles.   The doctor?
    The Lord.   Right.
    Mephistopheles. He serves thee truly in a wondrous fashion.
Poor fool! His food and drink are not of earth.
An inward impulse hurries him afar,   60
Himself half conscious of his frenzied mood;
From heaven claimeth he the fairest star,
And from the earth craves every highest good,
And all that's near, and all that's far,
Fails to allay the tumult in his blood.   65
    The Lord. Though in perplexity he serves me now,
I soon will lead him where more light appears;
When buds the sapling, doth the gardener know

That flowers and fruit will deck the coming years.

   Mephistopheles. What wilt thou wager? Him thou yet shall   70
    lose,
If leave to me thou wilt but give,
Gently to lead him as I choose!

   The Lord. So long as he on earth doth live,
So long 'tis not forbidden thee.
Man still must err, while he doth strive.   75

   Mephistopheles. I thank you; for not willingly
I traffic with the dead, and still aver
That youth's plump blooming cheek I very much prefer.
I'm not at home to corpses; 'tis my way,
Like cats with captive mice to toy and play.   80

   The Lord. Enough! 'tis granted thee! Divert
This mortal spirit from his primal source;
Him, canst thou seize, thy power exert
And lead him on thy downward course,
Then stand abashed, when thou perforce must own,   85
A good man in his darkest aberration,
Of the right path is conscious still.

   Mephistopheles. 'Tis done! Full soon thou'lt see my exultation;
As for my bet no fears I entertain.
And if my end I finally should gain,   90
Excuse my triumphing with all my soul.
Dust he shall eat, ay, and with relish take,
As did my cousin, the renownèd snake.

   The Lord. Here too thou'rt free to act without control;
I ne'er have cherished hate for such as thee.   95
Of all the spirits who deny,
The scoffer is least wearisome to me.
Ever too prone is man activity to shirk,
In unconditioned rest he fain would live;
Hence this companion purposely I give,   100
Who stirs, excites, and must, as devil, work.
But ye, the genuine sons of heaven, rejoice!
In the full living beauty still rejoice!
May that which works and lives, the ever-growing,
In bonds of love enfold you, mercy-fraught,   105
And Seeming's changeful forms, around you flowing,
Do ye arrest, in ever-during thought! [*Heaven closes, the* ARCH-
    ANGELS *disperse.*]

Mephistopheles. [*Alone*] The ancient one I like sometimes to see,
And not to break with him am always civil;
'Tis courteous in so great a lord as he,   110
To speak so kindly even to the devil.

(*Anna Swanwick*)

SUGGESTIONS FOR STUDY

1. Contrast the opening speech of Mephistopheles with those of the three Archangels. In what mood does he address the Lord? What is his opinion of the Lord? (See especially lines 29–36 and 108–112.) The Lord's opinion of him? (See lines 95–97.)

2. Point out the difference between the Lord and Mephistopheles in their attitude toward mankind in general and Faust in particular. Why does the Lord permit Mephistopheles to do as he wishes with Faust?

3. Further reading: Compare the treatment of the Faust story in its three most famous forms — Goethe's dramatic poem, Marlowe's tragedy, *Dr. Faustus*, Gounod's opera, *Faust*. Much of the music of the last is available in phonograph records. Read Book I or more of Milton's *Paradise Lost* and compare Satan and Mephistopheles.

FRIEDRICH VON SCHILLER (1759–1805)

Schiller was a poet and dramatist, and in a lesser degree a historian and critic. His name is usually coupled with that of Goethe. The two men formed a beautiful and fruitful friendship during the last eleven years of Schiller's life and reigned supreme on the German Olympus. Yet Schiller has by no means the universal significance of Goethe, nor has he made the same appeal to other countries. He voiced admirably the ideals and aspirations of his own age. But it should be remembered that he is in many respects the greatest of German dramatists, as he is certainly the one whose plays are most often produced. His writings, popularized by school and theater, have been a great educative force.

The course of his career was very different from that of Goethe, the child of fortune. Schiller had a hard struggle against poverty and ill health. Born at Marbach in Württemberg, he early conceived a hatred of social injustice and tyrannical government and vented his feelings in the prose melodramas *The Robbers* and *Intrigue and Love,* both of them typical "Storm and Stress" products. Less turbulent emotionally and more temperate in language was the poetic drama *Don Carlos,* in which we see Schiller well on the way toward the classic idealism of his later years. He was appointed professor of history in the University of Jena in 1789. Ten years later he moved to Weimar in order to be near Goethe. The poetic dramas of his last period represent him at his best. They include the trilogy *Wallenstein, Mary Stuart, The Maid of Orleans,* and the ever-popular *William Tell.* Among Schiller's minor poems, the fine ballads deserve particular mention.

Schiller was an undaunted idealist both in theory and in practice. He held to the ultimate values of the true, the good, and the beautiful as tenaciously as Plato. He had faith in God, in the moral law, and in the immortality of the soul. Like Rousseau, he trusted the essential goodness of human nature. He believed in liberty, both individual and national, and in justice. He exalted love, marriage and family life. He proclaimed all these ideals with an enthusiastic optimism. There was something un-critical, as later dramatists like Ibsen were to show. In view of the strange vicissitudes of their history, it is worth noting that the Germans have had as their favorite poet such an uncompromising idealist.

WILLIAM TELL

William Tell has always been Schiller's most popular play, effective alike on the stage and as a drama to read. The legendary Tell is taken as a typical representative of the Swiss people who are collectively the real hero of the play. Before the following scene opens, the leaders of the Swiss, goaded to desperation by the oppressive measures of the Austrian ruler, have formed a conspiracy to rise in rebellion when the opportune moment comes. They hope for the adherence of Tell, who so far has not openly joined them. Gessler, the Austrian governor, sets up a cap on a pole as a symbol of his authority and orders all passers-by to salute it.

Scene III

A meadow near Altdorf. Trees in the foreground. At the back of the stage a cap upon a pole. The prospect is bounded by the Bannberg, which is surmounted by a snow-capped mountain.

FRIESSHARDT *and* LEUTHOLD *on guard.*

Friess. We keep our watch in vain. There's not a soul
Will pass, and do obeisance to the cap.
But yesterday the place swarmed like a fair;
Now the whole green looks like a very desert,
Since yonder scarecrow hung upon the pole.   5

Leuth. Only the vilest rabble show themselves,
And wave their tattered caps in mockery at us.
All honest citizens would sooner make
A tedious circuit over half the town,

2. obeisance: salutation of respect.

Than bend their backs before our master's cap.   10
   Friess. They were obliged to pass this way at noon,
As they were coming from the Council House.
I counted then upon a famous catch,
For no one thought of bowing to the cap.
But Rosselmann, the priest, was even with me.   15
Coming just then from some sick penitent,
He stands before the pole, — raises the Host —
The Sacrist, too, must tinkle with his bell, —
When down they dropped on knee — myself and all
In reverence to the Host, but not the cap.   20
   Leuth. Hark ye, companion, I've a shrewd suspicion,
Our post's no better than the pillory.
It is a burning shame, a trooper should
Stand sentinel before an empty cap,
And every honest fellow must despise us   25
To do obeisance to a cap, too! Faith,
I never heard an order so absurd!
   Friess. Why not, an't please thee, to an empty cap?
Thou'st ducked, I'm sure, to many an empty sconce.
[HILDEGARD, MECHTHILD, *and* ELSBETH *enter with their children,*
                         and station themselves around the pole.
   Leuth. And thou art an officious, sneaking knave,   30
That's fond of bringing honest folks to trouble.
For my part, he that likes may pass the cap: —
I'll shut my eyes and take no note of him.
   Mech. There hangs the Viceroy! Your obeisance, children!
   Els. I would to God he'd go, and leave his cap!   35
The country would be none the worse for it.
   Friess. [*Driving them away*] Out of the way! Confounded pack
      of gossips!
Who sent for you? Go, send your husbands here,
If they have courage to defy the order.
[TELL *enters with his crossbow, leading his son* WALTER *by the hand.*
   They pass the hat without noticing it, and advance to the front
   of the stage.
   Walt. [*Pointing to the Bannberg*] Father, is't true, that on   40
    the mountain there,
The trees, if wounded with a hatchet, bleed?

17. **Host:** the consecrated bread.   18. **Sacrist:** or sacristan, official who
keeps the utensils of a church.   28. **an:** if.   29. **sconce:** head.

Tell.   Who says so, boy?

Walt.   The master herdsman, father!
He tells us, there's a charm upon the trees,
And if a man shall injure them, the hand
That struck the blow will grow from out the grave.   45

Tell.   There is a charm about them — that's the truth.
Dost see those glaciers yonder — those white horns —
That seem to melt away into the sky?

Walt.   They are the peaks that thunder so at night,
And send the avalanches down upon us.   50

Tell.   They are; and Altdorf long ago had been
Submerged beneath these avalanches' weight,
Did not the forest there above the town
Stand like a bulwark to arrest their fall.

Walt.   [*After musing a little*] And are there countries with   55
   no mountains, father?

Tell.   Yes, if we travel downwards from our heights,
And keep descending in the rivers' courses,
We reach a wide and level country, where
Our mountain torrents brawl and foam no more,
And fair large rivers glide serenely on.   60
All quarters of the heaven may there be scanned
Without impediment.   The corn grows there
In broad and lovely fields, and all the land
Is fair as any garden to the view.

Walt.   But, father, tell me, wherefore haste we not   65
Away to this delightful land, instead
Of toiling here, and struggling as we do?

Tell.   The land is fair and bountiful as Heaven;
But they who till it never may enjoy
The fruits of what they sow.

Walt.   Live they not free,   70
As you do, on the land their fathers left them?

Tell.   The fields are all the bishop's or the king's.

Walt.   But they may freely hunt among the woods?

Tell.   The game is all the monarch's — bird and beast.

Walt.   But they, at least, may surely fish the streams?   75

Tell.   Stream, lake, and sea, all to the king belong.

Walt.   Who is this king, of whom they're so afraid?

Tell.   He is the man who fosters and protects them.

Walt.   Have they not courage to protect themselves?

Tell. The neighbor there dare not his neighbor trust.   80
Walt. I should want breathing room in such a land.
I'd rather dwell beneath the avalanches.
Tell. 'Tis better, child, to have these glacier peaks
Behind one's back, than evil-minded men!

[They are about to pass on.
Walt. See, father, see the cap on yonder pole!   85
Tell. What is the cap to us? Come, let's begone.

[As he is going, FRIESSHARDT, *presenting his pike, stops him.*
Friess. Stand, I command you, in the Emperor's name!
Tell. *[Seizing the pike]* What would ye? Wherefore do ye stop
    my path?
Friess. You've broke the mandate, and must go with us.
Leuth. You have not done obeisance to the cap.   90
Tell. Friend, let me go.
Friess.   Away, away to prison!
Walt. Father to prison? Help! *[Calling to the side scene]* This
    way, you men!
Good people, help! They're dragging him to prison!

*[*ROSSELMANN, *the Priest, and the* SACRISTAN, *with three other men,*
                                                              enter.
Sacris. What's here amiss?
Ross.   Why do you seize this man?
Friess. He is an enemy of the King — a traitor.   95
Tell. *[Seizing him with violence]* A traitor, I!
Ross.   Friend, thou art wrong. 'Tis Tell.
An honest man, and worthy citizen.
Walt. *[Descries* FURST *and runs up to him]* Grandfather, help,
    they want to seize my father!
Friess. Away to prison!
Furst. *[Running in]*   Stay, I offer bail.
For God's sake, Tell, what is the matter here?   100

*[*MELCHTHAL *and* STAUFFACHER *enter.*
Leuth. He has contemned the Viceroy's sovereign power
Refusing flatly to acknowledge it.
Stauff. Has Tell done this?
Melchthal.   Villain, thou knowest 'tis false!
Leuth. He has not made obeisance to the cap.
Furst. And shall for this to prison? Come, my friend,   105
Take my security, and let him go.

101. **contemned:** despised.

Friess. Keep your security for yourself — you'll need it,
We only do our duty. Hence with him.

Melchthal. [*To the country people*] This is too bad — shall we
stand by, and see them
Drag him away before our very eyes? 110

Sacris. We are the strongest. Don't endure it, friends.
Our countrymen will back us to a man.

Friess. Who dares resist the governor's commands?

Other Three Peasants. [*Running in*] We'll help you. What's
the matter? Down with them!

[HILDEGARD, MECHTHILD *and* ELSBETH *return.*]

Tell. Go, go, good people, I can help myself. 115
Think you, had I a mind to use my strength,
These pikes of theirs should daunt me?

Melchthal. [*To* FRIESSHARDT] Only try —
Try, if you dare, to force him from amongst us.

Furst and Stauff. Peace, peace, friends!

Friess. [*Loudly*] Riot! Insurrection, ho!

[*Hunting horns without.*]

Women. The Governor!

Friess. [*Raising his voice*] Rebellion! Mutiny! 120

Stauff. Roar, till you burst, knave!

Ross. and Melchthal. Will you hold your tongue?

Friess. [*Calling still louder*] Help, help, I say, the servants of
the law!

Furst. The Viceroy here! Then we shall smart for this!

[*Enter* GESSLER *on horseback, with a falcon on his wrist;* RUDOLPH
DER HARRAS, BERTHA, *and* RUDENZ, *and a numerous train of
armed attendants, who form a circle of lances round the whole
stage.*

Har. Room for the Viceroy!

Gessl. Drive the clowns apart.
Why throng the people thus? Who calls for help? 125

[*General silence.*

Who was it? I will know. [FRIESSHARDT *steps forward.*
And who art thou?
And why hast thou this man in custody?

[*Gives his falcon to an attendant.*

Friess. Dread sir, I am a soldier of your guard,
And stationed sentinel beside the cap;
This man I apprehended in the act 130

Of passing it without obeisance due,
So I arrested him, as you gave order,
Whereon the people tried to rescue him.

   Gessl. [*After a pause*] And do you, Tell, so lightly hold your
     king,
And me, who act as his viceregent here, 135
That you refuse the greeting to the cap
I hung aloft to test your loyalty?
I read in this a disaffected spirit.

   Tell. Pardon me, good my lord! The action sprung
From inadvertence, — not from disrespect. 140
Were I discreet, I were not William Tell.
Forgive me now — I'll not offend again.

   Gessl. [*After a pause*] I hear, Tell, you're a master with the
     bow, —
And bear the palm away from every rival.

   Walt. That must be true, sir! At a hundred yards 145
He'll shoot an apple for you off the tree.

   Gessl. Is that boy thine, Tell?

   Tell.   Yes, my gracious lord.

   Gessl. Hast any more of them?

   Tell.   Two boys, my lord.

   Gessl. And, of the two, which dost thou love the most?

   Tell. Sir, both the boys are dear to me alike. 150

   Gessl. Then, Tell, since at a hundred yards thou canst
Bring down the apple from the tree, thou shalt
Approve thy skill before me. Take thy bow —
Thou hast it there at hand — and make thee ready
To shoot an apple from the stripling's head! 155
But take this counsel, — look well to thine aim,
See, that thou hitt'st the apple at the first,
For, shouldst thou miss, thy head shall pay the forfeit.

                      [*All give signs of horror.*
   Tell. What monstrous thing, my lord, is this you ask?
That I, from the head of mine own child! — No, no! 160
It cannot be, kind sir, you meant not that —
God, in His grace, forbid! You could not ask
A father seriously to do that thing!

   Gessl. Thou art to shoot an apple from his head!
I do so desire — command it so.

           140. inadvertence: lack of attention.

Tell.   What I!   165
Level my crossbow at the darling head
Of mine own child? No — rather let me die!
   Gessl. Or thou must shoot, or with thee dies the boy.
   Tell. Shall I become the murd'rer of my child!
You have no children, sir — you do not know   170
The tender throbbings of a father's heart.
   Gessl. How now, Tell, so discreet upon a sudden
I had been told thou wert a visionary, —
A wanderer from the paths of common men.
Thou lov'st the marvellous. So have I now   175
Culled out for thee a task of special daring.
Another man might pause and hesitate; —
Thou dashest at it, heart and soul, at once.
   Bertha. Oh, do not jest, my lord, with these poor souls!
See, how they tremble, and how pale they look,   180
So little used are they to hear thee jest.
   Gessl. Who tells thee that I jest? [*Grasping a branch above his
      head*] Here is the apple.
Room there, I say! And let him take his distance —
Just eighty paces, — as the custom is, —
Not an inch more or less! It was his boast,   185
That at a hundred he could hit his man.
Now, archer, to your task, and look you miss not!
   Har. Heavens! this grows serious — down, boy, on your knees,
And beg the governor to spare your life.
   Furst. [*Aside to* MELCHTHAL, *who can scarcely restrain his im-
      patience*] Command yourself, — be calm, I beg of you!   190
   Bertha. [*To the governor*] Let this suffice you, sir! It is inhuman
To trifle with a father's anguish thus.
Although this wretched man had forfeited
Both life and limb for such a slight offence,
Already has he suffered tenfold death.   195
Send him away uninjured to his home;
He'll know thee well in future; and this hour
He and his children's children will remember.
   Gessl. Open a way there — quick! Why this delay?
Thy life is forfeited; I might dispatch thee,   200
And see I graciously repose thy fate
Upon the skill of thine own practiced hand.
No cause has he to say his doom is harsh,

Who's made the master of his destiny.
Thou boastest of thy steady eye. 'Tis well!
Now is a fitting time to show thy skill.   205
The mark is worthy, and the prize is great.
To hit the bull's eye in the target; — that
Can many another do as well as thou;
But he, methinks, is master of his craft,   210
Who can at all times on his skill rely,
Nor lets his heart disturb or eye or hand.

   Furst. My lord, we bow to your authority;
But oh, let justice yield to mercy here.
Take half my property, nay, take it all,   215
But spare a father this unnatural doom!

   Walt. Grandfather, do not kneel to that bad man!
Say, where am I to stand? I do not fear;
My father strikes the bird upon the wing,
And will not miss now when 'twould harm his boy!   220

   Stauff. Does the child's innocence not touch your heart?

   Ross. Bethink you, sir, there is a God in heaven,
To whom you must account for all your deeds.

   Gessl. [*Pointing to the boy*] Bind him to yonder lime tree
straight!

   Walt.   Bind me?
No, I will not be bound! I will be still,   225
Still as a lamb — nor even draw my breath!
But if you bind me, I can not be still.
Then I shall writhe and struggle with my bonds.

   Har. But let your eyes at least be bandaged, boy!

   Walt. And why my eyes? No! Do you think I fear   230
An arrow from my father's hand? Not I!
I'll wait it firmly, nor so much as wink!
Quick, father, show them that thou art an archer!
He doubts thy skill — he thinks to ruin us.
Shoot then, and hit, though but to spite the tyrant!   235
    [*He goes to the lime tree, and an apple is placed on his head.*

   Melchthal. [*To the country people*] What! Is this outrage to
    be perpetrated
Before our very eyes? Where is our oath?

   Stauff. 'Tis all in vain. We have no weapons here;

237. **oath:** Melchthal and others had taken an oath to resist the tyranny
of the Austrian governor.

And see the wood of lances that surrounds us!

Melchthal. Oh! would to Heaven that we had struck at 240
once!

God pardon those, who counseled the delay!

Gessl. [*To* TELL] Now to thy task! Men bear not arms for
nought.

'Tis dangerous to carry deadly weapons,
And on the archer oft his shaft recoils.

This right, these haughty peasant churls assume, 245
Trenches upon their master's privileges.

None should be armed, but those who bear command.

It pleases you to wear the bow and bolt; —
Well, — be it so. I will provide the mark.

Tell. [*Bends the bow, and fixes the arrow*] A lane there! Room!

Stauff. What, Tell? You would — no, no! 250
You shake — your hand's unsteady — your knees tremble.

Tell. [*Letting the bow sink down*] There's something swims
before my eyes!

Women. Great Heaven!

Tell. Release me from this shot! Here is my heart!
[*Tears open his breast.*

Summon your troopers — let them strike me down!

Gessl. I do not want thy life, Tell, but the shot. 255
Thy talent's universal! Nothing daunts thee!
Thou canst direct the rudder like the bow!
Storms fright not thee, when there's a life at stake.
Now, savior, help thyself, — thou savest all!

[TELL *stands fearfully agitated by contending emotions, his hands
moving convulsively, and his eyes turning alternately to the governor and Heaven. Suddenly he takes a second arrow from his
quiver, and sticks it in his belt. The governor watches all these
motions.*

Walt. [*Beneath the lime tree*] Come, father, shoot! I'm not
afraid!

Tell. It must be! 260
[*Collects himself and levels the bow.*

Rud. [*Who all the while has been standing in a state of violent
excitement, and has with difficulty restrained himself, advances*]
My lord, you will not urge this matter further.
You will not. It was surely but a test.

---

245. **churls:** ill-mannered fellows. 246. **trenches:** encroaches.

You've gained your object. Rigor pushed too far
Is sure to miss its aim, however good,
As snaps the bow that's all too straitly bent.   265
   Gessl. Peace, till your counsel's asked for!
   Rud.   I will speak!
Ay, and I dare! I reverence my king;
But acts like these must make his name abhorred.
He sanctions not this cruelty. I dare
Avouch the fact. And you outstep your powers   270
In handling thus an unoffending people.
   Gessl. Ha! thou grow'st bold, methinks!
   Rud.   I have been dumb
To all the oppressions I was doomed to see.
I've closed mine eyes, that they might not behold them,
Bade my rebellious, swelling heart be still,   275
And pent its struggles down within my breast.
But to be silent longer, were to be
A traitor to my king and country both.
   Bertha. [*Casting herself between him and the governor*] Oh
      Heavens! you but exasperate his rage!
   Rud. My people I forsook — renounced my kindred —   280
Broke all the ties of nature, that I might
Attach myself to you. I madly thought,
That I should best advance the general weal,
By adding sinews to the Emperor's power.
The scales have fallen from mine eyes — I see   285
The fearful precipice on which I stand.
You've led my youthful judgment far astray, —
Deceived my honest heart. With best intent,
I had well nigh achieved my country's ruin.
   Gessl. Audacious boy, this language to thy lord?   290
   Rud. The Emperor is my lord, not you! I'm free
As you by birth, and I can cope with you
In every virtue that beseems a knight.
And if you stood not here in that King's name
Which I respect e'en where 'tis most abused,   295
I'd throw my gauntlet down, and you should give
An answer to my gage in knightly fashion.
Ay, beckon to your troopers! Here I stand;
But not like these   [*Pointing to the people.*
         — unarmed. I have a sword,

270. **avouch:** affirm.   297. **gage:** challenge.

And he that stirs one step —

Stauff. [*Exclaims*] The apple's down! 300

[*While the attention of the crowd has been directed to the spot where* BERTHA *had cast herself between* RUDENZ *and* GESSLER, TELL *has shot.*

Ross. The boy's alive!

Many voices. The apple has been struck!

[WALTER FURST *staggers, and is about to fall.* BERTHA *supports him.*

Gessl. [*Astonished*] How? Has he shot? The madman!

Bertha. Worthy father!

Pray you, compose yourself. The boy's alive.

Walt. [*Runs in with the apple*] Here is the apple, father! Well I knew,

You would not harm your boy.

[TELL *stands with his body bent forward, as though he would follow the arrow. His bow drops from his hand. When he sees the boy advancing, he hastens to meet him with open arms, and embracing him passionately sinks down with him quite exhausted. All crowd round them deeply affected.*

Bertha. Oh, ye kind Heavens! 305

Furst. [*To father and son*] My children, my dear children!

Stauff. God be praised!

Leuth. Almighty powers! That was a shot indeed!

It will be talked of to the end of time.

Har. This feat of Tell, the archer, will be told 310

While yonder mountains stand upon their base.

[*Hands the apple to* GESSLER.

Gessl. By Heaven! the apple's cleft right through the core.

It was a master shot, I must allow.

Ross. The shot was good. But woe to him, who drove

The man to tempt his God by such a feat! 315

Stauff. Cheer up, Tell, rise! You've nobly freed yourself,

And now may go in quiet to your home.

Ross. Come, to the mother let us bear her son!

[*They are about to lead him off.*

Gessl. A word, Tell.

Tell. Sir, your pleasure?

Gessl. Thou didst place

A second arrow in thy belt — nay, nay! 320

I saw it well — what was thy purpose with it?

Tell. [*Confused*] It is a custom with all archers, Sir.

Gessl. No, Tell, I cannot let that answer pass.

There was some other motive, well I know.
Frankly and cheerfully confess the truth; — 325
Whate'er it be, I promise thee thy life,
Wherefore the second arrow?

   Tell.   Well, my lord,
Since you have promised not to take my life,
I will, without reserve, declare the truth.

[*He draws the arrow from his belt, and fixes his eyes sternly upon the
governor.*

If that my hand had struck my darling child,   330
This second arrow I had aimed at you,
And, be assured, I should not then have missed.

   Gessl. Well, Tell, I promised thou shouldst have thy life;
I gave my knightly word, and I will keep it.
Yet, as I know the malice of thy thoughts,   335
I will remove thee hence to sure confinement,
Where neither sun nor moon shall reach thine eyes.
Thus from thy arrows I shall be secure.
Seize on him, guards, and bind him!   [*They bind him.*

   Stauff.   How, my Lord —
How can you treat in such a way a man,   340
On whom God's hand has plainly been revealed?

   Gessl. Well, let us see if it will save him twice!
Remove him to my ship; I'll follow straight.
In person I will see him lodged at Küssnacht.

   Ross. You dare not do't. Nor durst the Emperor's self   345
So violate our dearest chartered rights.

   Gessl. Where are they? Has the Emp'ror confirmed them?
He never has. And only by obedience
Need you expect to win that favor from him.
You are all rebels 'gainst the Emp'ror's power, —   350
And bear a desperate and rebellious spirit.
I know you all — I see you through and through.
Him do I single from amongst you now,
But in his guilt you all participate.
The wise will study silence and obedience.   355

   [*Exit, followed by* BERTHA, RUDENZ, HARRAS, *and attendants.*
                 FRIESSHARDT *and* LEUTHOLD *remain.*

   Furst. [*In violent anguish*] All's over now! He is resolved, to
     bring
Destruction on myself and all my house.

Stauff. [*To* TELL] Oh, why did you provoke the tyrant's rage?

Tell. Let him be calm who feels the pangs I felt.

Stauff. Alas! alas! Our every hope is gone.   360
With you we all are fettered and enchained.

Country People. [*Surrounding* TELL] Our last remaining comfort
goes with you!

Leuth. [*Approaching him*] I'm sorry for you, Tell, but must obey.

Tell. Farewell!

Walt. [*Clinging to him in great agony*] Oh, father, father, my
dear father!

Tell. [*Pointing to Heaven*] Thy father is on high — appeal   365
to him!

Stauff. Hast thou no message, Tell, to send thy wife?

Tell. [*Clasping the boy passionately to his breast*] The boy's uninjured; God will succor me!

[*Tears himself suddenly away, and follows the soldiers of the guard.*

(*Theodore Martin*)

SUGGESTIONS FOR STUDY

1. Note the various indications in this scene of Tell's character and of
his reputation among the people.

2. Does the fact that Tell was a mythical character make any difference
in the interest you take in the story? Discuss the question whether
imaginary people and scenes may not be as "real" to us as those which
have actually existed.

3. By what devices does Schiller enlist our sympathies for the Swiss
against the Austrian governor?

4. The Italian musician Rossini (1792–1868) composed an opera on
Schiller's *William Tell*. Get a phonograph record of the well-known over-
ture to this opera.

5. Vocabulary: mandate, daunt, viceregent, cope.

KNIGHT TOGGENBURG

This ballad, glorifying poetic chivalry, was apparently of Schiller's own
invention. It brings out the contrast between earthly love and religious
devotion which constantly agitated people in the days of the Crusades.

" Knight, to love thee like a sister
Vows this heart to thee;
Ask no other warmer feeling, —
That were pain to me.

Tranquil would I see thy coming,   5
  Tranquil see thee go;
What that starting tear would tell me
  I must never know."

He with silent anguish listens,
  Though his heart-strings bleed;   10
Clasps her in his last embraces,
  Springs upon his steed,
Summons every faithful vassal
  From his Alpine home,
Binds the cross upon his bosom,   15
  Seeks the Holy Tomb.

There full many a deed of glory
  Wrought the hero's arm;
Foremost still his plumage floated
  Where the foemen swarm;   20
Till the Muslim, terror-stricken,
  Quailed before his name.
But the pang that wrings his bosom
  Lives at heart the same.

One long year he bears his sorrow,   25
  But no more can bear;
Rest he seeks, but, finding never,
  Leaves the army there;
Sees a ship by Joppa's haven,
  Which with swelling sail   30
Wafts him where his lady's breathing
  Mingles with the gale.

At her father's castle portal,
  Hark! his knock is heard;
See! the gloomy gate uncloses   35
  With the thunder-word:
" She thou seek'st is veiled for ever,
  Is the bride of Heaven;
Yester eve the vows were plighted, —
  She to God is given."   40

Then his old ancestral castle
  He for ever flees;
Battle-steed and trusty weapon
  Never more he sees.
From the Toggenburg descending,   45
  Forth unknown he glides;
For the frame once sheathed in iron
  Now the sackcloth hides.

There beside that hallowed region
  He hath built his bower,   50
Where from out the dusky lindens
  Looked the convent tower;
Waiting from the morning's glimmer
  Till the day was done,
Tranquil hope in every feature,   55
  Sat he there alone.

Gazing upward to the convent,
  Hour on hour he passed,
Watching still his lady's lattice,
  Till it oped at last, —   60
Till that form looked forth so lovely,
  Till the sweet face smiled,
Down into the lonesome valley,
  Peaceful, angel-mild.

Then he laid him down to slumber,   65
  Cheered by peaceful dreams,
Calmly waiting till the morning
  Showed again its beams.
Thus for days he watched and waited,
  Thus for years he lay,   70
Happy if he saw the lattice
  Open day by day; —

If that form looked forth so lovely,
  If the sweet face smiled
Down into the lonesome valley,   **75**
  Peaceful, angel-mild.

There a corse they found him sitting
Once when day returned,
Still his pale and placid features
To the lattice turned.   80

(Anonymous Translation)

LUDWIG UHLAND (1787–1862)

Uhland, poet and scholar, was born in the university town of Tübingen
in the section of southwestern Germany known as Swabia. He and his
poet friends were often referred to as the Swabian School, though they
had no formal organization and no hard and fast doctrines. They represented the healthier side of romanticism. Uhland's poetical creed is
summed up in his statement: " I never had any leaning toward poetry as
something dissociated from the life of the people and expressing only
individual sentiments; whatever attracted me had its roots in the people,
their customs and religion." This being the case, he did not write personal
poetry like his great contemporary Heine, but was at his best in ballads,
or short narrative poems, most of which are medieval in setting and
theme. Though no innovator, he was a most conscientious literary artist,
revising his work with infinite pains. As a ballad writer he deserves to
rank with Bürger and Schiller.

THE LUCK OF EDENHALL

Uhland's own statement about the source of this legendary ballad is as
follows: " At Edenhall, in Cumberland, the mansion of the knightly family
of Musgrave for many centuries, is carefully preserved in a leathern case
an old painted drinking glass which, according to the tradition of the
neighborhood, was long ago left by fairies near a well not far from the
house, with an inscription along with it to this effect:

> ' If this glass either break or fall
> Farewell the luck of Edenhall.' "

Of Edenhall the youthful lord
    Bids sound the festal trumpet's call;
He rises at the banquet board,
    And cries, 'mid the drunken revelers all,
    " Now bring me the Luck of Edenhall! "   5

The butler hears the words with pain, —
  The house's oldest seneschal, —
Takes slow from its silken cloth again
  The drinking-glass of crystal tall;
  They call it *The Luck of Edenhall.*   10

Then said the lord, " This glass to praise,
  Fill with red wine from Portugal! "
The graybeard with trembling hand obeys;
  A purple light shines over all;
  It beams from the Luck of Edenhall.   15

Then speaks the lord, and waves it light, —
  " This glass of flashing crystal tall
Gave to my sires the Fountain-Sprite;
  She wrote it, *If this glass doth fall,*
  Farewell then, O Luck of Edenhall!   20

" 'Twas right a goblet the fate should be
  Of the joyous race of Edenhall!
We drink deep draughts right willingly;
  And willingly ring, with merry call,
  Kling! klang! to the Luck of Edenhall! "   25

First rings it deep, and full, and mild,
  Like to the song of a nightingale;
Then like the roar of a torrent wild;
  Then mutters, at last, like the thunder's fall,
  The glorious Luck of Edenhall.   30

" For its keeper takes a race of might
  The fragile goblet of crystal tall;
It has lasted longer than is right
  Kling! klang! with a harder blow than all
  Will I try the Luck of Edenhall! "   35

As the goblet, ringing, flies apart,
  Suddenly cracks the vaulted hall;
And through the rift the flames upstart;
  The guests in dust are scattered all
  With the breaking Luck of Edenhall!   40

     7. **seneschal:** steward.

In storms the foe, with fire and sword!
  He in the night had scaled the wall;
Slain by the sword lies the youthful lord,
  But holds in his hand the crystal tall,
  The shattered Luck of Edenhall.   45

On the morrow the butler gropes alone,
  The graybeard, in the desert hall;
He seeks his lord's burnt skeleton;
  He seeks in the dismal ruin's fall
  The shards of the Luck of Edenhall.   50

" The stone wall," saith he, " doth fall inside;
  Down must the stately columns fall;
Glass is this earth's Luck and Pride;
  In atoms shall fall this earthly ball,
  One day, like the Luck of Edenhall! "   55

                              (*H. W. Longfellow*)

      50. **shards:** fragments.

THE CASTLE BY THE SEA

This ballad is the poet's own invention. It is told in the form of a
dialogue.

        Hast thou seen that lordly castle,
          That castle by the sea?
        Golden and red above it
          The clouds float gorgeously.

        And fain it would stoop downward   5
          To the mirrored wave below;
        And fain it would soar upward
          In the evening's crimson glow.

        Well have I seen that castle,
          That castle by the sea,   10
        And the moon above it standing,
          And the mist rise solemnly.

The winds and the waves of ocean,
   Had they a merry chime?
Didst thou hear, from those lofty chambers,   15
   The harp and the minstrel's rhyme?

The winds and the waves of ocean,
   They rested quietly;
But I heard on the gale a sound of wail,
   And tears came to mine eye.   20

And sawest thou on the turrets
   The king and his royal bride,
And the wave of their crimson mantles,
   And the golden crown of pride?

Led they not forth, in rapture,   25
   A beauteous maiden there,
Resplendent as the morning sun,
   Beaming with golden hair?

Well saw I the ancient parents,
   Without the crown of pride;   30
They were moving slow, in weeds of woe;
   No maiden was by their side!

                    (*H. W. Longfellow*)

31. **weeds:** garments.

SUGGESTIONS FOR STUDY

1. What is the character of the youthful lord in the "Luck of Eden-hall"? Why does he defy fate? What is the effect of the fifth line in each stanza?

2. Infer the situation in "The Castle by the Sea" from the conversa-tion of the two speakers.

3. What in general do these ballads have in common with those by Bürger, Goethe, and Schiller? With English ballads?

ARTHUR SCHOPENHAUER (1788–1860)

Schopenhauer, distinguished philosopher and essayist, was born in Dan-zig. His father was a prosperous merchant of the patrician class, his mother a novelist. The father left Danzig when it was annexed to Prussia in 1795 and moved to Hamburg. Arthur accompanied him on frequent business trips through Germany and abroad and in this way acquired a knowledge of the world and a facility in modern languages. But having no taste for business, he resumed his studies and received the degree of doctor of philosophy in 1813. Subsequent attempts to teach philosophy in the University of Berlin proved a dismal failure. In 1831 he moved to Frankfort where he lived in seclusion for the rest of his life. He had published his great philosophical work *The World as Will and Idea* in 1819, but it had attracted no attention. Public recognition did not come to him until his *Essays* appeared in 1851.

Schopenhauer is the most persuasive preacher of pessimism that Europe has ever listened to. He taught that the fundamental thing in the universe is the will to live. But since this will is instinctive and not a matter of reasoned choice, life does not and cannot bring happiness. Men may escape momentarily from the misery of existence by forgetting themselves in the contemplation of beauty and art, and more lastingly by suppressing selfish desires and practicing altruism. Schopenhauer profoundly affected German literature during twenty years or so following his death, partly because of his stylistic ability, which is a rare thing among German philosophers. He has also greatly influenced certain schools of psychology. His successor in these matters was Nietzsche.

ON THINKING FOR ONESELF

As the richest library unarranged is not so useful as a very moderate one well arranged, so the greatest amount of erudition,[1] if it has not been elaborated by one's own thought, is worth much less than a far smaller amount that has been well thought over. For it is through the combination on all sides of that which one knows, through the comparison of every truth with every other, that one assimilates one's own knowledge and gets it into one's power. One can only think out what one knows; hence one should learn something; but one only knows what one has thought.

One can only apply oneself of set purpose to reading and learning, but not to thinking proper. The latter must, that is, be stimulated and maintained, like fire by a draught of air, by some interest in the subject itself, which may be either a purely objective or a merely subjective one. The latter is only present in the case of our personal interest, but the former only for thinking heads by nature, for which thought is as natural as breath, but which are very rare. For this reason it is so little the case with most scholars.

The distinction between the effect which thinking for oneself, and that which reading has upon the mind, is inconceivably great, hence it perpetually increases the original diversity of heads, by virtue of

----

[1] **erudition:** learning.

which a man is driven to the one or to the other. Reading imposes thoughts upon the mind which are as foreign and heterogeneous [2] to the direction and mood which it has for the moment, as the seal is to the wax on which it impresses its stamp. The mind suffers thereby an entire compulsion from without, to think now this, now that, for which it has no desire, and no capacity. In thinking for itself, on the other hand, it follows its own natural impulse, as either external circumstance or some recollection has determined it for the moment. Perceptual surroundings, namely, do not impress one definite thought upon the mind as reading does, but merely give it material and occasion to think that which is according to its nature and present disposition. Hence much reading deprives the mind of all elasticity, as a weight continually pressing upon it does a spring, and the most certain means of never having any original thoughts is to take a book in hand at once, at every spare moment. This practice is the reason why scholarship makes most men more unintelligent and stupid than they are by nature, and deprives their writings of all success; they are, as Pope says —

> " For ever reading, never to be read."
>
> " Dunciad," iii, 194.

Scholars are those who have read in books; but thinkers, geniuses, enlighteners of the world, and benefactors of the human race, are those who have directly read in the book of the world.

At bottom it is only our own fundamental conceptions which have truth and life, for it is they alone that one thoroughly and correctly understands. Alien thoughts that we read are the remnants of another's meal, the cast-off clothes of a strange guest.

The alien thought arising within us is related to our own as the impression in stone of a plant of the early world is to the blooming plant of spring.

Reading is a mere surrogate [3] for original thought. In reading, one allows one's own thoughts to be guided by another in leading-strings. Besides, many books are only good for showing how many false paths there are, and how seriously one may miss one's way if one allows oneself to be guided by them; but he whom genius guides, he, that is, who thinks for himself, thinks of free will, thinks correctly — he has the compass to find out the right way. One should only read when the source of original thoughts fails, which is often enough the case even with the best heads. But to scare away one's

---

[2] heterogeneous: diverse in character.
[3] surrogate: substitute.

own original thoughts for the sake of taking a book in the hand is a sin against the Holy Ghost. In this case, one resembles a man who runs away from free nature in order to look at a herbarium,[4] or to contemplate a beautiful landscape in an engraving.

Even if sometimes one may find with ease in a book a truth or an insight already given, which one has worked out slowly, and with much trouble, by one's own thinking and combining; it is yet worth a hundred times more when one has attained it through one's original thought. Only then does it become as integral part, as living member, one with the whole system of our thoughts; only then does it stand in complete and firm cohesion with them, is understood in all its grounds and consequences, bears the color, the shade, the stamp of our whole mode of thought, and this because it has come at the precise time that the need for it was present, and therefore sits firmly, secure from dispossession. Here accordingly Goethe's verse,

> "What thou hast inherited from thy fathers
> Acquire it, in order to possess it,"

finds its most perfect application and explanation. The self-thinker, namely, learns the authorities for his opinions afterwards, when they serve merely to confirm him in them and for his own strengthening. The book-philosopher, on the other hand, starts from them, in that he constructs a whole for himself out of the alien opinions he has read up, which then resembles an automaton that has been put together of foreign material, while the former resembles a living man. For in this case it has arisen like the living man, since the outer world has impregnated the thinking mind which has carried it, and given it birth.

Truth that has only been learnt cleaves to us like a limb that has been stuck on — a false tooth, a waxen nose, or at best like a genuine one of alien flesh. But that which has been acquired by original thought resembles the natural limb; it alone really belongs to us. On this rests the distinction between the thinker and the mere scholar. Hence the intellectual acquirement of the self-thinker is like a fine painting, which stands out lifelike with accurate light and shade, well-balanced tone, and complete harmony of color. The intellectual acquirement of the mere scholar, on the contrary, resembles a large palette full of bright colors, systematically arranged, indeed, but without harmony, cohesion, and significance.

Reading means thinking with an alien head, not one's own. But to original thought, from which a coherent whole, even if not a strictly

----

[4] **herbarium:** collection of dried plants.

rounded-off system, seeks to develop itself, nothing is more injurious than too great an influx of foreign thoughts through continual reading. For these, each sprung from another mind, belonging to another system, bearing another color, never of themselves flow together to form a whole of thought, of knowledge, of insight, and conviction, but rather set up a Babylonian [5] confusion of tongues in the head, and rob the mind which has been filled with them of all clear insight, and thus almost disorganize it. This state is noticeable with many scholars, and the result is that they are behind many unlearned persons in healthy understanding, accurate judgment, and practical tact, the latter having always subordinated to and incorporated with their own thought what has come to them from without, through experience, conversation, and a little reading. The scientific *thinker* does this in a greater degree. Although he needs much knowledge, and therefore must read much, his mind is nevertheless strong enough to master all this, to assimilate it, to incorporate it into the system of thoughts, and so to subordinate it to the organically coherent whole of a magnificent insight, which is always growing. In this, his own thinking, like the ground bass of the organ, perpetually dominates all, and is never drowned by foreign tones, as is the case with merely polyhistorical [6] heads, in which, as it were, musical fragments from all keys run into one another, and the fundamental note is no more to be heard.

People who have occupied their life with reading, and who have derived their wisdom from books, resemble those who have acquired a correct knowledge of a country from many descriptions of travel. Such persons can give information about much, but at bottom they have no coherent, clear, fundamental knowledge of the structure of the country. Those, on the contrary, who have occupied their life with thought, resemble persons who have themselves been in that country. They alone know, properly speaking, what is in question, since they know the things there in their connection, and are truly at home in them.

(Belfort Bax)

SUGGESTIONS FOR STUDY

1. Schopenhauer's essay implies a contrast between thinking for oneself and reading. Do you believe the two things are incompatible? How should one read in order still to retain one's originality of thinking?

[5] **Babylonian:** the reference is to the Tower of Babel, Genesis 11.
[6] **polyhistorical:** knowing many facts.

2. Do you believe most people read too much or too little? What are your own habits in this regard?

3. *What* one reads is also very important. Enumerate the things you prefer to read and the things you avoid. Can you justify your likes and dislikes?

4. Explain the meaning of the lines from Goethe. Compare the general idea of the essay with Emerson's " Self-Reliance."

5. Vocabulary: integral, dispossession, automaton, impregnated, cohesion, influx, incorporate.

HEINRICH HEINE (1797–1856)

Heine is the greatest German lyric poet since Goethe. He was also master of a clear, brilliant and witty prose style, which has served as a model for higher journalistic writing. But his prose works were too much concerned with local and temporary matters to endure permanently, whereas his poems are for all times and places. He was born at Düsseldorf on the Rhine of Jewish parents. A rich uncle in Hamburg gave him a start in business, for which, however, Heine showed no aptitude, and he was then allowed to study law at various German universities. But his stay in Hamburg was important for his inner life and for his poetry, because he fell in love with his cousin and this unrequited passion was the stock subject of his early verse. In 1825, having taken his degree in law, he was nominally converted to Christianity, in which he had no real belief, for the sake of easing his public career. His *Book of Songs* met with an enthusiastic reception in 1827. He also made his mark as a prose writer with his *Travel Pictures*.

A bitter opponent of all autocratic governments, he felt ill at ease in Germany and in 1831 moved to Paris, which was to be his home for the rest of his life. Paris seemed to him the capital of the civilized world and for a number of years he was thoroughly happy there, associating on friendly terms with the leading writers, artists and musicians. He accepted a pension from the French government and married a French wife. Some of his best prose writings of those years were devoted to an attempt to bring about a better mutual understanding between Germany and France. In 1845 the first signs of a spinal disease appeared, and three years later he took to what he called his " mattress grave " for the rest of his life. His sufferings not only brought him a sort of spiritual purification but actually increased his poetic powers. He is buried in the Montmartre cemetery in Paris.

Heine has been bitterly attacked by German nationalists on account of his alleged disloyalty. He has been called cynical, malicious, and insincere. In point of fact, his character is much less admirable than his genius. But

Heine was an internationalist and a political liberal, professing genuinely to be " a valiant soldier in humanity's war of liberation."

After all, it is by his poems that Heine is to be judged, and here the world (at least the world outside Germany) has united to pay him homage. He had begun as a romanticist, but he was a very modern man in his thoughts and feelings. The result is that he added to his inheritance from romanticism a clarity of perception and a firm hold on reality that were not at all in the tradition of his predecessors. His shift of moods is often disconcerting. He can be tender, melancholy, ironical and gay, sometimes within the compass of a single poem. Like Byron, by whom he was influenced, he occasionally mocks his own sentiments. But each lyric of his is crystal clear and displays some facet of his many-sided personality. Except in his fine North Sea poems with their free rhythms, he used chiefly the simple meters of the folk song. Most of his more popular poems have been set to music.

FAREWELL TO HAMBURG

This poem is typical of many which Heine wrote in his earlier days about his unhappy love for his cousin.

> Lovely cradle of my sorrow,
>   Lovely tomb where peace might dwell,
> Smiling town, we part tomorrow;
>   I must leave, and so farewell.
>
> Farewell threshold, where still slowly   5
>   Her belovèd footstep stirs;
> Farewell to that hushed and holy
>   Spot where first my eyes met hers.
>
> Had you never caught or claimed me,
>   Fairest, heart's elected queen,   10
> Wretchedness would not have maimed me
>   In its toils — as you have seen.
>
> Never have you found me grieving
>   For your heart with loud despair;
> All I asked was quiet living,   15
>   Quietly to breathe your air.
>
> But you drove me forth with scourging,
>   Bitter words and lashing scorn;
> Madness in my soul is surging,
>   And my heart is flayed and torn.   20

And I take my staff and stumble
　　On a journey, far from brave;
Till my head droops and I tumble
　　In some cool and kindly grave.

(Louis Untermeyer)

A PINE TREE STANDS SO LONELY

This little poem is symbolical of the separation of lovers.

A pine tree stands so lonely
　　In the North where the high winds blow,
He sleeps; and the whitest blanket
　　Wraps him in ice and snow.

He dreams — dreams of a palm-tree   5
　　That far in an Orient land,
Languishes, lonely and drooping,
　　Upon the burning sand.

(Louis Untermeyer)

THE LORELEY

The Loreley (or Lorelei) is a rocky cliff on the Rhine, at the foot of
which there are dangerous rapids. The popular legend arose that a siren,
seated on the rock, enticed sailors and fishermen to their destruction. This
is Heine's best-known poem, and with its familiar musical setting, it has
become part of the song tradition of the world.

I cannot tell why this imagined
　　Sorrow has fallen on me;
The ghost of an unburied legend
　　That will not let me be.

The air is cool and twilight   5
　　Flows down the quiet Rhine;
A mountain alone in the high light
　　Catches the faltering shine.

One rosy peak half gleaming
　　Reveals, enthroned in air,   10
A goddess, lost in dreaming,
　　Who combs her golden hair.

With a golden comb she is combing
   Her hair, as she sings a song;
Heard and reheard through the gloaming,   15
   It hurries the night along.

The boatman has heard what has bound him
   In throes of a strange, wild love.
He is blind to the reefs that surround him
   Who sees but the vision above.   20

And lo, the wild waters are springing —
   The boat and the boatman are gone . . .
Then silence. And this with her singing,
   The Loreley has done.
                    (Louis Untermeyer)

TO MY SISTER

My child, we once were children,
   Two children, blithe and gay,
We used to crawl up to the hen-house
   And hide ourselves under the hay.

We cackled and crowed whenever   5
   People passed down the road —
" Kikerikee! " They thought it
   Was really the cocks that crowed.

The boxes in our courtyard
   We draped with what we could find,   10
And lived in them together,
   A home of the cosiest kind.

Our neighbor's cat came often
   To visit us in our bower;
We met her with bows and curtsies   15
   And compliments by the hour.

Politely we asked how her health was,
   In the course of a friendly chat.
(We've said the same things since then
   To many a grave old cat.)   20

And often like old folk we gossiped,
   Aping their serious ways;
Complaining how things were better
   In " the dead and dear old days."

How Love and Faith and Honor   25
   Were lost without regret;
How coffee was so expensive,
   And money so hard to get! . . .

Gone are the plays of childhood,
   And all things seem a wraith —   30
Time and the world and money,
   And Love and Honor and Faith.

                                         (Louis Untermeyer)

            30. wraith: ghost.

I PASS YOUR LITTLE WINDOW

This poem was addressed to a little English girl.

I pass your little window
   The mornings that are fair,
And I am thrilled, my darling,
   Whene'er I see you there.

Your deep brown eyes disturb me,   5
   They question and condole,
" Who art thou and what ails thee,
   O pale and wandering soul? "

I am a German poet,
   In German lands I shine;   10
And where great names are mentioned
   They're sure to speak of mine.

As for my sickness, darling,
   It's rather a common sign . . .
And where great griefs are mentioned   15
   They're sure to speak of mine.

                                         (Louis Untermeyer)

CHILD, YOU ARE LIKE A FLOWER

This song has been set to music oftener than any other poem on record. For this reason it is more easily recognized by most people under its German title, " Du Bist Wie Eine Blume."

Child, you are like a flower
　So sweet and pure and fair;
I look at you and sadness
　Comes on me, like a prayer.

I must lay my hands on your forehead　　　　5
　And pray God to be sure
To keep you forever and always
　So sweet and fair — and pure.

(Louis Untermeyer)

YOU'VE PEARLS AND YOU'VE DIAMONDS

You've pearls and you've diamonds, my dearest,
　You've all that most mortals revere;
And oh, your blue eyes are the fairest —
　What else could you ask for, my dear?

Upon those blue eyes, my dearest,　　　　5
　I've written for many a year
A host of immortal poems —
　What else could you ask for, my dear?

And with those blue eyes, my dearest,
　You wrought a bright torture here,　　　　10
And lightly you led me to ruin —
　What else could you ask for, my dear?

(Louis Untermeyer)

BY THE SEA

Heine, like Byron and Swinburne in England, was a great lover of the sea. His North Sea poems, in blank verse and with irregular lines, are among his most original works.

By the sea, by the dreary, night-colored sea,
　A young man stands;

His heart full of anguish, his head full of doubts.
And with pale lips he questions the billows:
" Oh, solve me the riddle of Life,   5
The torturing, deathless riddle
Which has cracked so many heads,
Heads in hieroglyphic bonnets,
Heads in black birettas and turbans,
Heads in weighty wigs and a thousand other   10
Poor, perspiring heads of people —
Tell me, what is Man?   And what's his meaning?
Where does he come from?   Where is he going?
Who dwells up there among the golden stars?

The billows are whispering their eternal whispers.   15
The wind blows on, the clouds go sailing;
The stars keep twinkling, indifferent and cold.
And a fool waits for his answer.

                        (*Louis Untermeyer*)

8. **hieroglyphic:** symbolic figure used in Egyptian writing.   9. **birettas:** square caps, such as those worn by Roman Catholic clerics.

LIGHTLY SWINGING BELLS ARE RINGING

Lightly swinging bells are ringing
    With a soft insistence;
Tinkle, tiny tunes of Spring,
    Tinkle through the distance.

Fill the air and run to where   5
    All the flowers grow sweeter.
If you see a Rosebud there
    Tell her that I greet her!

                        (*Louis Untermeyer*)

THE WEAVERS

This poem was occasioned by a strike of the Silesian weavers which was bloodily suppressed.   The contemporary German dramatist, Gerhart Hauptmann, has a famous play on the same subject.

From darkened eyes no tears are falling;
Gnashing our teeth, we sit here calling:

" Germany, listen, ere we disperse,
We weave your shroud with a triple curse —
   We weave, we are weaving!   5

" A curse to the false god that we prayed to,
And worshiped in spite of all, and obeyed, too.
We waited and hoped and suffered in vain;
He laughed at us, sneering, for all of our pain —
   We weave, we are weaving!   10

" A curse to the king, and a curse to his coffin,
The rich man's king whom our plight could not soften;
Who took our last penny by taxes and cheats,
And let us be shot like the dogs in the streets —
   We weave, we are weaving!   15

" A curse to the Fatherland, whose face is
Covered with lies and foul disgraces;
Where the bud is crushed as it leaves the seed,
And the worm grows fat on corruption and greed —
   We weave, we are weaving!   20

" The shuttle flies in the creaking loom;
And night and day we weave your doom —
Old Germany, listen, ere we disperse,
We weave your shroud with a triple curse.
   We weave — we are weaving! "   25

(Louis Untermeyer)

WHERE?

This was one of Heine's last poems.

Where shall I, the wander-wearied,
   Find my haven and my shrine?
Under palms will I be buried?
   Under lindens on the Rhine?

Shall I lie in desert reaches,   5
   Buried by a stranger's hand?
Or upon the well-loved beaches,
   Covered by the friendly sand?

Well, what matter! God has given
Wider spaces there than here.   10
And the stars that swing in heaven
Shall be lamps above my bier.

(Louis Untermeyer)

SUGGESTIONS FOR STUDY

1. What varying moods do you find in this group of poems? Which poem expresses the greatest variety of moods within itself? In which of the poems does Heine show self-pity? Conceit? Humanitarian spirit? What would you infer regarding his religious beliefs?

2. Which of these poems do you regard as the most powerful? The most delicate? The most musical? Give reasons where possible.

3. What do you observe of Heine's versification? In what way are you reminded of Burns, Wordsworth, Emily Dickinson?

4. Compare " The Loreley " with Goethe's " The Fisher," page 485, and with other stories of mermaids and sirens.

5. As far as possible listen to musical settings of Heine's poetry. See collections of German songs, folk songs, songs by Schubert and by Schumann, and lists of phonograph records.

GOTTFRIED KELLER (1819–1890)

Keller was a Swiss-German novelist. The Swiss have no separate language. The great majority speak German, the rest either French or Italian. French-speaking Switzerland has produced one literary genius of the first importance — Rousseau. Keller has by no means the epoch-making significance of Rousseau, but he is the most original of Swiss-German authors, as well as one of the best writers of the shorter type of fiction to be found anywhere. He studied art and philosophy in Germany but spent most of his life in his native Zurich, where he was for some years city registrar. His long novel *Green-coated Henry,* from which the following episode is taken, is to a great extent autobiographical and follows somewhat the pattern of Goethe's *Wilhelm Meister.* He is seen at his best in his novelettes of Swiss provincial life contained in such collections as *The People of Seldwyla.* These stories vary greatly in tone from the deep pathos and tragedy of " A Village Romeo and Juliet " to the delightful humor of " Clothes Make the Man." Keller was a realist with the gift of imagination. He tells his stories with gusto and with a shrewd eye for character.

LITTLE MERET

After my father died, my mother felt that we were absolutely dependent upon the " God of the widows and fatherless," and so it seemed to her that we, of all others, should take pains to neglect no religious ceremony or service. She resolved to have grace at meals. So, one Sunday noon when we sat down to the table, she recited a little old prayer used by the common people, and bade me say it over after her. How surprised she was when I stammered out the first words, and then suddenly stopped, and could go no further.

The food was steaming on the table, there was not a sound in the room, my mother was waiting, but I did not speak. She repeated her command, but it was no use, I only sat there, dumb and overwhelmed with humiliation, and she let it pass for that time as a simple child's whim.

But on the next day the episode was repeated, and now she was really troubled, and asked me, " Why won't you pray? Are you ashamed to? " That was truly the case, but I could not answer " yes," because after all I was not ashamed in the way she meant. The food on the table was no longer food; in my eyes it was a sacrificial meal, the folding of the hands and the solemn prayer before the smoking dishes had turned into a ceremony from which I felt an unconquerable aversion. I was not such a hardened sinner that I was ashamed to confess my religion before the world, as the priests say, — and how should I be afraid of my mother, from whose mildness I never dreamed of concealing anything? It was simply that I could not bear to speak aloud to the Almighty God; and from that day I have never been able, even in the remotest solitude, to pray aloud.

" Then you shall not eat until you have prayed," my mother said, and I climbed down from my chair, and went away into the corner, where I stood, feeling very sad, and a little defiant. My mother sat still in her place, and made a pretence of eating. And I felt a sort of dismal tension between us, which made my heart very heavy. Soon my mother got up from the table and began to carry out the dishes. She went back and forth in silence, but when it was almost time for me to go to school, she brought my dinner in again. She was wiping her eyes as if she had gotten something in them, and she said, " Here is something for you to eat, you wilful child! " And then I, too, burst into sobs and tears, but the food tasted very good when my crying fit was over. As I was walking back to school I did not fail to send up to God a happy sigh of thanksgiving for this deliverance and reconciliation.

Years afterwards when I was visiting in my parents' native village, this episode in my childhood was vividly recalled to me by the story of a child who had lived there more than a hundred years before.

In one corner of the churchyard was a small stone tablet with nothing on it but a scarcely distinguishable coat of arms, and the date, 1713. The people called the spot beside it the " witch child's grave," and they told all sorts of strange stories about her. She was a city child, and belonged to a noble family, but she was banished to this country parsonage, in which at that time a severe and pious clergyman lived, in the hope that he could cure her of her godlessness, and mysterious, precocious witchcraft. But he had not succeeded. For one thing he had never been able to make her speak the three names of the Holy Trinity. She had continued in this stubborn godlessness, and died miserably. She was an extraordinarily lovely and intelligent little girl, of the tender age of seven years, but all the same she was a most wicked witch. She laid her spell upon grown men especially, so that if they so much as looked at the little child they fell desperately in love with her, and stirred up all sorts of disturbances on her account.

She made mischief with the birds, enticed all the village doves to the parsonage, and even bewitched the pious gentleman himself, so that he caught them, and ate them roasted, to his own hurt. She charmed the fish in the river, sitting all day long on the bank, and dazzling the wise old trout, until they swam round and round her unceasingly, their backs flashing in the sunlight.

The old women used the legend of this child-witch to frighten the children, when they were naughty, adding all sorts of fabrications. But there really hung in the parsonage an old dim oil-painting, which preserves the likeness of this strange child.

It is a portrait of a wonderfully beautiful little girl. She wears a bluish green damask gown. Her wide, flaring skirt hides her feet. A golden chain is twisted around her waist, and hangs down to the floor in front. On her head she wears a crown-shaped headdress of shimmering gold and silver tinsel, interwoven with silk threads and pearls. She holds in her hand a child's skull and a white rose.

I have never seen anywhere such a beautiful, spiritual, lovable child's face. It is pointed, not plump, and it wears an expression of great sadness. The mournful shining dark eyes look out at you, as if beseeching you for help, while around the firmly closed lips there hovers the suggestion of a roguish smile.

The child's heavy suffering has given her whole face a look of maturity and womanliness, which stirs you with an involuntary longing to see the living child, — to be able to take her into your arms and cherish her.

The real story is this.

The little girl belonged to a highly aristocratic and orthodox family. She showed a stubborn aversion to prayer, and worship of every sort . . . tore up the prayer books they gave her to learn from . . . covered her head with the bedclothes when they tried to make her say her prayers . . . and shrieked with terror, when they took her into the cold dark church, saying she was afraid of the black man in the pulpit.

She was the child of an unhappy first marriage, and might easily have been the cause of unpleasantness in any case. So the family made the experiment, since no measures they took against this mysterious stubbornness were of any avail, of giving the child into the care of this minister, who was widely famed for his strict orthodoxy.

If the child was a source of sorrow and disgrace in the eyes of her own family, much more was she regarded by this severe dogmatic man as possessed of an infernal spirit, against which he must enter upon a deadly warfare. He shaped his conduct accordingly.

An old diary has been preserved in the parsonage, which was kept by the pious clergyman himself. On its old gilt-edged leaves are some entries which tell of his experiences, and of the fate of this unhappy child.

THE DIARY

" Today, received the first quarter's payment from the honorable and God-fearing Frau [1] M., immediately receipted it, and dispatched my report.

" Further dispensed to little Meret her weekly punishment which fell due upon this day. I increased the severity of the aforesaid punishment, inasmuch as I laid her upon a settle, and chastised her with a fresh switch, not without inward lamentations and beseechings of the Lord that He would bring this sorrowful undertaking to a favorable conclusion. The child, for a truth, cried piteously, and humbly begged for pardon, but none the less, she continued in her stiff-neckedness, and threw the hymn book I had given her to learn from upon the floor. I then allowed her a few minutes' respite, and put her under arrest in the dark smoke-shed, where she whimpered and complained, — afterwards became quiet, then suddenly began to sing and make jubilation, not otherwise than after the manner of the three holy men in the fiery furnace.[2] Went to the smoke-house and lis-

[1] **Frau:** Mrs.
[2] **fiery furnace:** The story of the three Jews who were cast into the fiery furnace but escaped unhurt is told in the third chapter of Daniel.

tened, and discovered that she was singing the psalms in meter, namely the very songs she had just refused to learn; but in such a vain and worldly fashion, after the manner of nurses' lullabies or children's rhymes, that I was forced to look upon this behavior as a new piece of wantonness and a fresh device of the devil's."

Further:

" A most lamentable letter has arrived from Madame, who is truly a most excellent person and well-grounded in the faith. She had wet the afore-mentioned letter with her tears; and she also communicated to me her honored husband's great anxiety over the little Meret's case. And it is truly a great calamity which has come upon this highly reputable and exalted family, and one might be of the opinion (speaking with due respect) that the sins of the Sir grandpapa on the father's side, who was a great wanton and light-minded cavalier, are being atoned for by this unhappy creature. Have changed my mode of dealing with the child and will now try the starvation treatment. Also I have had a little dress of coarse sackcloth made by my worthy consort's [3] own hands, and forbidden little Meret to wear any other garment, inasmuch as this penitent's garb is the most fitting for her. Obstinacy on the same point.

" Found myself forced to debar the little Demoiselle [4] from all dealings and intercourse with the country children, because she ran away into the woods with the aforesaid children. While there she bathed in the pond, hung up the penitent's dress I had devised for her on the branch of a tree, and stirred up her companions to bold and unseemly mirth. — Severe punishment.

" Today a great scandal and vexation. There came to the house a great strapping fellow, young Mullerhans, and took me to task for my treatment of little Meret, claiming that he hears her crying and screaming every day; and I was dealing with him, when in came the good-for-nothing young schoolmaster, threatening to bring a complaint against me. And he forthwith fell upon the wicked creature, and caressed and fondled her. I straightway made the schoolmaster to be arrested and brought before the magistrate. Must take like measures against Mullerhans, though same is rich and influential. Am almost forced to believe, myself, that the child is a witch, as the country people say she is, only such a belief is contrary to all reason. At all events the devil has taken possession of her and I have a woeful undertaking on my hands.

" This week we have entertained in the house a painter sent hither

---

[3] consort's: wife's.
[4] Demoiselle: Miss.

by Madame to paint the portrait of the little Miss. The afflicted family do not wish to receive the creature again, but they desire to preserve a likeness of her, as a sorrowful memorial, and a useful object of penitential contemplation, and also on account of the child's great beauty. The gentleman is exceeding set on the idea. My honored spouse serves to the painter two pints of wine every day, but he does not seem to get enough, for he goes to the ' Red Lion ' every evening to play with the Chirurgeon.[5] This painter is a haughty individual, and for this reason I often set before him a partridge or a pike, which shall be duly noted in Madame's quarterly account. He began by paying court to the little Miss, and she soon showed such a foolish attachment to him that I was forced to request him not to interfere with my mode of procedure. When they brought the child her Sabbath array (which we had preserved with all care) for the picture, and put on her girdle and headdress, she gave evidence of the greatest delight, and straightway began to dance about. But her joy was soon turned to mourning, when in accordance with the command of her mamma I caused a man's skull to be brought and placed in the child's hand, which skull she at first refused to take and being compelled, she held it with trembling and weeping, not otherwise than if it were a piece of red-hot iron. The painter assured us he could paint the skull without a model, inasmuch as it belonged to the first rudiments of his art: — But would not yield, seeing that Madame had written: ' In whatever the child suffers, we suffer also. If we have been given an opportunity for doing penance by permitting her to suffer, we perform this penance for her sake. Therefore your reverence will not omit the execution of any commands we shall give in regard to her care and her education. If, as I pray the Almighty and Compassionate God, she should sometime, either in this world or the next, be enlightened and redeemed, she would, without doubt, greatly rejoice that a good share had already been performed of her penance for the hardness of heart it has pleased the Infinite Father to bring upon her.'

" With these excellent words before my eyes, I resolved to impose a serious penance upon the child by means of the skull.

" In the end they procured a small, light child's skull, since the painter complained that the large one was too heavy for the little hands, in consideration of the rules for proportion of his art. She held this skull without making any complaint. The painter added a white rose which I could well suffer, since it may serve as an edifying symbol.

[5] **Chirurgeon:** surgeon.

" Today have received a sudden counter-order in regard to the portrait, and am not to expedite same to the city, but am to keep it in my own house. It is a sinful waste, for the painter had done a highly excellent piece of work, being quite carried away by the child's beauty. If I had only known in the beginning, the man might have painted my own presentment [6] upon the canvas for the money, even if I had been obliged to charge him nothing for the handsome victuals we have given him, but to let them serve as additional compensation for my portrait.

" Further notice has come to me, namely: to suspend all worldly instruction, especially the instruction in the French language, seeing that the child will never have any occasion for such knowledge; also my wife is to make an end of the lessons on the spinet.[7] The child is greatly grieved. From this time forth she is to be treated as a simple foundling, and our only care is to be that she makes no open disturbance.

" Day before yesterday the little Meret ran away, and threw us into the greatest distress of mind, until at noon today she was spied at the top of Beech Hill, where she was sitting, warming herself in the sun, having taken off her sackcloth garment. She had all unbraided her hair, and set on her head a wreath of beech leaves, and hung a scarf of ditto over her body; also she had beside her on the ground a pile of fine strawberries, off which she had dined very pleasantly and sufficiently. When she caught sight of us she started for the woods again, but she was ashamed of her nakedness, and stopped to put on her dress, so was luckily captured. She is sick and seems to be out of her head, for she is not able to give any intelligible answers.

" Little Meret is better, but she grows more and more strange. Is stupid and silent most of the time. The opinion of the medical man is that she will become demented or idiotic, and will soon be no longer susceptible to medical treatment. He promised to put her on her feet again if we would place her in his house. But it is my observation that the Monsieur Surgeon is concerned only with the large bill he can present for board, and with the presents that Madame will make. Accordingly I answered him to this effect, that the Lord seemed to be nearing the accomplishments of His purposes for His creature, and human hands might not and dared not intermeddle with the Divine plans. As is assuredly the truth."

After an interval of five or six months comes the following entry:

[6] presentment: likeness.
[7] spinet: a musical instrument with a keyboard.

" The child seems to enjoy excellent health in her imbecile condition, and has gotten the most shining red cheeks. She stays all day now in the bean vines, where she is out of our sight; and what is more, no one troubles about her, as long as she makes no disturbance.

" Little Meret has arranged a little salon for herself in the middle of the vines, — so we have discovered, — and there she receives visits from the farmers' children, who smuggle in fruit for her, and other food, which she buries very neatly, and keeps for further use. We have also found buried here the little child's skull; it has been lost for a long time, and so could not be returned to the sexton. She has enticed sparrows and other birds to the place, and tamed them, so that they have already done great hurt to the garden. And yet I cannot shoot into the garden any more, because she stays there. In the same way she has bewitched a poisonous snake, which has made its way through the hedge, and taken up its abode with her. Finally, — to make conclusion, we have taken her into the house again, and now keep her in confinement.

" Little Meret has lost her red cheeks, and the doctor states that in his opinion she is not much longer for this world. Have dispatched a letter to the parents.

" This morning before daylight poor little Meret must have left her bed, slipped out into the garden, and passed away there, for we found her dead in a little hollow she had dug out in the ground, apparently for the sake of concealing herself. She was quite stiff, her hair and gown wet and heavy with the dew which lay in shining drops on her pink cheeks, just as on an apple blossom. And we were filled with horror; and I have been thrown into great confusion and embarrassment today by the arrival of their excellencies from the city, just after my consort had departed for K. to purchase some provisions and delicacies for their fitting entertainment. Hardly knew which end my head was on, and there was great scurrying and running about, and the maids had to wash and dress the little corpse, and all at the same time prepare a suitable luncheon. Finally I had the fresh ham baked that my spouse put to pickle eight days ago, and had Jacob catch three of the tame trout, which still occasionally come to the garden, although the sainted (?!) Meret had not been allowed to go down to the water for some time. Have happily with these dishes managed to set before them a respectable meal, and Madame seemed to find it to her taste.

" We have been exceeding mournful, and passed more than two hours in prayer and meditation upon death, also in melancholy discourse upon the unhappy illness of the dead girl, for we must now believe, to our great consolation, that both mind and body have always been mortally diseased. Then we talked of her otherwise highly brilliant disposition, of her frequent graceful sallies [8] and fancies, and we could not reconcile it all in our earthly short-sightedness. To-morrow morning they will give the child Christian burial. The presence of the distinguished parents at this time is very fortunate, since otherwise the deacons would probably have made objections.

" This has been the strangest, the most frightful day I have ever spent, not only since I have been concerned with this unhappy creature, but in my whole otherwise peaceful existence. When the hour had come and it had struck ten, we went in procession behind the body to the churchyard, while Sigrist rang the children's chimes, which he did not do with much diligence, for he rang most piteously, and the sound was blown away by strong and disagreeable wind. The sky was all dark and overcast, and the churchyard deserted except for our little company. But outside all the country people were gathered, and they stuck their heads over the wall in great curiosity. When the little coffin was being let down into the grave a strange cry was heard from inside the coffin, so that we were most violently terrified, and the grave-digger took to his heels. But the surgeon, who had run up, unfastened the lid, and took it off, and the dead child sat up like a live person, and crawled out of the grave all of a tremble, and stood and looked at us. And as at the same time the rays of Phoebus [9] broke through the clouds in a most strange and lurid manner, the girl, in her brocade and glittering crown, looked like a fairy or a kobold's [10] child. The lady, her mamma, immediately fell into a severe fainting fit, and Herr von M. sank to the ground weeping. I myself could not move from astonishment and terror and at the instant almost believed in witchcraft.

" But the little girl soon recovered herself and rushed away from the graveyard, and out through the village like a cat, so that all the people flew home in terror, and bolted their doors. School was just out, and a throng of children on the streets. And when the little brats saw the thing, they could not be kept back, but a whole troop of them ran after the corpse and followed it, and after them ran the schoolmaster with his ferrule.[11] But she had twenty paces advantage, and did not stop until she reached Beech Hill, and there she

---

[8] **sallies:** lively remarks.
[9] **Phoebus:** the sun, so called from Phoebus Apollo who was god of the sun.
[10] **kobold:** a domestic spirit, often mischievous.
[11] **ferrule:** a rod tipped with metal

fell down lifeless, whereupon the children gathered around the body and stroked and caressed it, but to no avail.

" All this we heard of by report, inasmuch as we, in dire straits, took refuge in the parsonage and waited there in deep desolation until they brought the body home again. They placed it on a mattress, and the gentlefolk started immediately for home, leaving behind them a little stone on which there is engraved simply the family arms and the date.

" Now the child again lies as if dead, and we are not able to go to our beds because of our fear. The doctor is sitting beside her, and he is now of the opinion that she has at last entered into rest.

" Today, after various experiments, the doctor declared her to be dead, beyond a doubt, and she has now been laid away, and nothing more has happened."

(L. R. Smith)

SUGGESTIONS FOR STUDY

1. What do you make out of the character of Meret? How did she win people's hearts? Why was the clergyman unable to understand her?

2. Do you think there is anything incredible about the story? Give reasons for your answer.

3. Why should Meret have gained the reputation of being a witch? Could such a situation have arisen in America at that time? Read about the life and writings of Cotton Mather. Compare with " The Abyss," page 310.

4. What do you learn from the story in regard to the bringing up of children? How have general ideas on this subject changed in the last century?

5. Compare this story with Dickens' pictures of sensitive or mistreated children in *David Copperfield, Oliver Twist, Dombey and Son,* and other novels. Where else in literature have similar pictures of children appeared?

6. Vocabulary: tension, precocious, fabrication, dogmatic, respite, edifying, expedite.

HERMANN SUDERMANN (1857–1928)

The two most conspicuous leaders in the revolt of the younger literary men of Germany toward the close of the eighteen-eighties were Gerhart Hauptmann and Hermann Sudermann. Both came into prominence the same year, 1889, and each in his separate way continued to be in the vanguard of the new movement for many years. It used to be alleged that Hauptmann was the poet and thinker whose dramatic resources were scanty, while Sudermann was the born dramatist with nothing to say! Neither statement is strictly correct. It is true that Sudermann's strong point was his accomplished technique. His plays were uniformly effective on the stage and were further memorable because they supplied favorite parts for star actresses. The protests against conventional and artificial standards with which they are filled earned for him temporarily the title of "The German Ibsen." But with the decreasing restrictions of society. the problems he raised became less significant, so that his later plays are already forgotten. Among his earlier dramas, *Honor* (1889), *Magda* (1893), and *The Joy of Living* (1902) can still evoke our interest.

His work in fiction gives greater promise of permanence. During what he called his "bread-and-cheese" existence in Berlin, before he made a success in the theater, he had tried his hand at writing stories. His first novel, *Dame Care* (1887), became his most popular work after his plays had made him famous. It is autobiographical to the extent of reflecting his early struggle with poverty in his East Prussian birthplace. *Regina* (1888) is an exciting story, the scene of which is also laid in East Prussia. Other works of fiction are the humorous *Iolanthe's Wedding* (1892), *The Song of Songs* (1908) and *Lithuanian Stories* (1917). His autobiography, *The Book of My Youth* (1923), has considerable human interest.

THE GOOSE–HERD

My dear man, I've been listening to you now for a long while and you fill me with astonishment. You usually show — more than I do myself — an honest wish to take things as they are. Then whence all of a sudden, in making these nice observations of human emotions, do you draw this idealistic illusion of yours?

It seems to me your levelling-down democratic sentiment has been playing you a naughty trick again. You maintain, if I understand you correctly, that there is not a profound difference in the way the various social classes feel and express their feelings; while, as a matter of fact, life proves the very reverse every day. Oh, it would be beautiful as a dream if you were right. The ideals of brotherhood and equality that I, the bred-in-the-bone aristocrat — that is what you say I am — must necessarily consider mere figments [1] of the brain, would then be reality, or, rather, have already become reality; because the bit of knowledge more or less cannot possibly produce an organic difference in men's natures.

No, no, dear sir, it is the cleavage in the way they feel, more than all differences in wealth, rank, and learning, that separates the upper from the lower classes; so much so that they go through the world to-

[1] figments: invented statements.

gether each without comprehension of what the other does, like citizens of different globes. Woe to him who hopes to leap the gap!

You don't believe me? You shake your head? Oh, my dear man, I am speaking from experience. Alas, alas! If I could tell you — but why shouldn't I? Night is falling outside, the November storm is howling, and today I celebrated the advent of my thirtieth gray hair — quite the atmosphere for conjuring up a picture of light, spring and youth.

Let me close my eyes, and you listen to me like a good little boy. I want to tell you of my first love. Do you know who my first love was? A goose-herd, a real, out-and-out goose-herd. I am not joking. I have wept bitter tears over the wrong he did me, and that when I had long been a grown-up, highly respectable young lady.

To be sure, when he first set my heart afire, I was still of the age when my highest ideal of happiness was to go barefoot. I was eight years old, he ten. I was the daughter of the lord of the castle, he, the son of our smith.

Mornings, when I took breakfast on the verandah with my mother and big brother, he used to pass by with his geese and disappear in the direction of the pasture. At first he stared up at us with naïve astonishment, it never occurring to him to raise his cap. Then my brother impressed it upon him that it was proper to give the family a decent greeting, and from that time on he always called up a " Good mornin' to you " like a lesson learned by heart and with a long sweep of his cap.

If my brother happened to be in a good humor, I received permission to take a roll down to him, and he always snatched it out of my hand with a certain greedy anxiety, as if there were danger of my withdrawing it at the last moment.

What did he look like? I can still see him as if he were right there in front of me. His straight flaxen hair hung down over his sun-burned cheeks like a thatched roof, with his blue eyes peering from underneath, jolly and cunning. He wore his ragged trousers rolled up over his knees, and always carried an osier [2] switch, into which, along the green bark, he had cleverly cut white spirals.

It was upon this switch that my childish covetousness first fastened itself. How fascinating to hold in my hand a marvelous piece of work like that, so different from all my toys! And when I pictured to myself being allowed to chase geese with it and to go barefoot, the pinnacle of earthly happiness had been reached.

---

[2] osier: willow.

And it was this same switch that brought us into human contact. One morning at breakfast, as I saw him going by so cheerily, I could no longer restrain my desire. I furtively put together the pieces of the roll spread with honey that I was eating and asked hurriedly to be excused, and ran after him.

When he saw me coming, he stopped and looked at me wonderingly. But as soon as he caught sight of the roll in my hand, a gleam of comprehension shot into his eyes.

" Will you give me your switch? " I asked.

" Why? " he asked back, and put one foot up to rub the calf of his other leg.

" Because I want it," I said defiantly, then added more gently, " I'll give you my roll spread with honey for it."

He let his eyes rest longingly on the piece of deliciousness, and then finally observed, " No, I have to have it for the geese, but I'll cut another one like it for you."

" Can you do that? "

I was all astonishment.

" Oh, that's nothing," he pooh-poohed. " I can make flutes, too, and jumping jacks."

I was so completely carried off my feet that I handed him the roll on the spot. He bit into it with gusto, and, not honoring me with another glance, he drove his feathered flock off before him.

I looked after him, envy in my heart. *He* was allowed to shepherd geese, but *I* had to go up to Mademoiselle and learn French. Yes, I thought, how unequal fortune's favors are.

That evening he brought me the switch he promised to make. It was even more beautiful than I had dared to hope in my wildest dreams. There were the white spirals that had so fascinated me in the original, and more than that, the butt end was topped with a knob, on which a human countenance — whether mine or his, I could not unriddle — was depicted by two dots and two dashes at right angles.

From that time on we were friends. I shared with him all the goodies that fell to me, the spoiled little darling, from every side. In return, he bestowed upon me the artistic products of his skilful fingers, reed pipes, little boxes, houses, toy utensils, and, best of all, his famous jumping jacks.

Our meetings took place every evening behind the goose coops, and there we exchanged gifts. I looked forward the whole day to these meetings, my thoughts constantly engaged by my young hero. I saw him on the sunny pasture lying in the grass, blowing his reed pipes, while I was torturing myself with horrid vowels. And the yearning grew ever stronger within me to partake of that bliss which is called minding geese.

When I told him of my feelings, he burst out laughing.

" Why don't you come along, then? " he said.

That tipped the scales, and without a second's reflection, " All right," I said, " I'll go along tomorrow."

" Don't forget to bring something to eat along," my friend forewarned me.

Luck was with me. Mademoiselle's headache came at the very opportune moment, and the French lesson was dispensed with. Feverish with joy and excitement, I sat at the breakfast table waiting for him to go by. My pockets were stuffed with goodies of all sorts, which I had wheedled out of Mademoiselle, and beside me lay the switch, which I looked forward to swinging that day in the strict fulfillment of my duty.

Ah, there he was coming. His blue eyes glanced up at me slily as he bellowed his " Good mornin' to you " at us; and the instant I could slip away without attracting attention I was off after him.

" What have you brought along? " was his first question.

" Two little ginger cakes, three cervelat [3] sandwiches, a roll cut in two with sardelles [4] between, and a piece of gooseberry pie," said I, spreading out my glories.

He fell upon them at once, while I with carefully concealed glee proudly drove the geese along.

After passing through the fir woods, the first part of which was somewhat familiar to me from my previous walks, we came to regions less and less well known. Stunted undergrowth rose on each side of the way, making an uncanny thicket, and then, all of a sudden, the broad, boundless heath opened up to my vision.

Oh, how lovely it was, how lovely! As far as the eye reached, a sea of grass and gaily colored flowers. Molehills covered with turf stretched away in long rows like motionless waves. The hot air quivered, fairly dancing on the breezy heath, while the buzzing of the bees made the accompaniment. And high up in the deep blue heavens stood the golden sun.

At the edge of the woods was a marsh with gleaming puddles of grayish yellow, thickish water. The refuse of the geese floated on the surface, and roundabout on the ground — so moist that great bubbles gushed up between the clumps of grass — were thousands of fine

[3] **cervelat**: sausage.
[4] **sardelles**: sardines.

tracks of the geese's feet, making the whole spot look like a patterned rug.

This was the flock's paradise. Here we made halt, and while the geese settled themselves comfortably in the puddles, we chased about on the heath, shouting and laughing, caught yellow butterflies, and picked blueberries.

Then we played husband and wife; Elsie, the tamest of the geese, was our child. We kissed and whipped the poor creature almost to death, but it finally succeeded, after prodigious efforts, in making its escape from our clutches. Next, I prepared the meals for my husband. I untied my white apron, spread it on the ground for a table-cloth, and placed on it the remnants of the food I had brought along. He sat down to the repast pompously, and when I saw the rapidity with which he finished up one bit after the other, I nearly jumped out of our little home for joy.

The hours passed as in a dream. Higher and higher rose the sun, until its rays came burning down on us perpendicularly. My head began to spin, and a dull lassitude came over me. Also, I experienced considerable hunger, but my spouse had already consumed everything. The inside of my mouth was dry, my lips were feverish. To cool them, I held moist blades of grass against them.

Suddenly, from beyond the woods, from way far away, came the ringing of a bell. I knew what it meant. It was the summons to the midday meal, which called me to table, too. And if they missed me! Oh, God, what would become of me?

I threw myself on the grass and began to cry bitterly, while my companion, meaning to comfort me, passed his rough hands over my face and neck.

Suddenly I jumped up and made a dash for the woods, as though pursued by the furies. It must have been about two hours that I strayed about in the undergrowth crying. Then I caught the sound of voices calling my name, and a few moments later I was in my brother's arms.

The next morning my poor friend appeared in the part of abductor and seducer before the high criminal court of the lord of the manor. He seemed to take it for granted that he was to be the scapegoat and was in for a flogging, and he made not the slightest attempt to shift part of the blame from himself. He accepted the chastisement my brother inflicted upon him with the greatest calm. Then he rubbed his aching back against a porch column, smiling dolefully, and, after that, hastily made off, while I, sobbing aloud, rolled on the floor.

From that day on I loved him. I plotted a thousand wiles and schemes for meeting him secretly. I nabbed edibles like a magpie, so that he might regale himself with the fruits of my pilferings. I fairly oppressed him with the profusion of fond attentions, with which I tried to wipe out of existence those frightful blows of my brother's whip.

He accepted my love calmly and rewarded me for it by a devotion that was moving and an appetite that was sound.

Fate separated us six months later.

My mother had been ailing for some time, and the physician now recommended her living in the south. She put the estate entirely in my brother's charge and moved to the Riviera, taking me along.

.   .   .   .   .   .

Nine years were to elapse before I came back home. The return was sadder than ever I should have dreamed. In Berlin, where I had lived after my mother's death, a tricky nervous trouble had taken hold of me and kept me confined to bed for many weeks. The doctors wrestled with death and saved my life, but the blooming young girl had become a pale, weak shadow. My physician recommended the country and pine-needle baths, and so I was bundled on to the train and transported to my brother's estate.

I must have presented a pretty pitiful spectacle, because when I reached the house and was lifted out of the carriage, I saw tears in the old domestics' eyes.

It is a peculiar feeling to know you are back home again after long wanderings, especially if you have gone through as much trouble as I had. A rare softness takes hold of you, and you try to blot out forever the joy and the suffering imposed by an alien world. You try to be a child again and conjure up long lost magic out of the grave.

As I leaned back in my reclining chair and let my tired eyes roam over the familiar fields, one shade after another came alive again, and the first one in the motley throng was — my dear, flaxen-haired goose-herd.

" What has become of him? " I asked my brother, and was rejoiced by the good news that he had grown up into a fine, good-looking young man and could already fully take the place of his father, the smith.

I felt my heart throbbing. I tried to scold myself for my folly, but with poor success. The dear old memories were not to be dismissed, and finally I yielded myself up to them unrestrainedly and pictured the manner of our seeing each other again in all the glowing colors of fairy tale romance.

A few days after my arrival I was allowed to take my first drive. I was lifted into a carriage, driven to the woods, and then set down on a soft, mossy, peaceful little spot, which I had selected deliberately. From it you could see the smithy in which the companion of my childhood dwelt.

My brother wanted to stay with me, but I begged him not to let me keep him from his work, and assured him that the little girl sent along to wait on me was quite enough protection. Besides, what was there to be afraid of in these peaceful home woods? So, the coachman drove my brother back to his office on the estate, and they were to call for me again in two hours. Then I dismissed the little girl, too, telling her to go hunt strawberries but to stay near by. She ran off happily.

I was alone at last! Now I could dream to my heart's content. The fir trees rustled overhead, and from the smithy came the dull blows of the hammer. Brightly glowed the fire in the forge, and every now and then a dark figure glided in front of it. That must be he.

I did not tire following the movements of his arms. I admired his strength and trembled for him when the sparks flew about his body.

The two hours went by unnoticed, and in the midst of my dreamy meditations I was surprised by my brother coming to call for me.

" Well, did it seem a long time? " my brother asked gaily.

I shook my head, smiling, and tried to get up, but sank back wearily.

" Hm, hm," said my brother, reflecting. " I didn't bring the coachman back, thinking I could carry you to the carriage by myself, but the seat is high, and I couldn't get you up without hurting you. See here, Grete," — he turned to my little companion, who had come running at the sound of the carriage — " you go run down to 'the smith, the young one, you know, and tell him he should come and help me here."

He tossed a penny on the ground and the little maid, radiant with delight, picked it up before going for the smith.

I felt the blood rush to my cheeks. I was to see him again, here, on this spot. He was to act the Samaritan [5] to me. I sat there waiting, my hand pressed to my pounding heart, until — until —

There he was coming! Yes, that was he! How strong, how handsome he had grown to be! Heavy flaxen hair about his smoke-blackened face, and a thick growth of light down around his powerful

---

[5] **Samaritan**: see the parable of the good Samaritan, Luke 10.

chin. Young Siegfried [6] must have looked like that while serving his apprenticeship with the wicked Mime.

He clutched awkwardly at his little cap, tipped back on his neck so jauntily, while I held out my hand smiling and said, " How do you do? "

" Very well," he replied with an embarrassed laugh, and carefully wiped his grimy fingers on his leather apron before taking my hand.

" Help me lift the lady into the carriage," said my brother.

He wiped his hands again, and caught hold of me — none too gently — under the armpits, and the two of them, my brother taking me by my feet, lifted me up on to the carriage cushions.

" Thanks, thanks," I said and gave him a smile.

He stood at the carriage door, shyly twisting his cap and looking from one to the other of us uncertainly.

" He still has something on his heart," I said to myself. " Why not? At the sight of me old memories have been awakened. He wants to talk to me of the blissful days when in childish innocence we watched the geese together. Ah, he doesn't trust himself — his lord's presence — I ought to come to his assistance a little."

" Well," I said, giving him a friendly, encouraging look straight in his eyes, " what are you thinking of? "

My brother at this turned from his horses, with which he had been busy, and said, thrusting his hand into his pocket:

" Oh, you're waiting for your tip."

I felt as though some one had struck me in the face.

" For goodness' sake, Max," I stammered, my blood going hot and cold.

But my brother did not hear me and handed him — actually dared to — a dime.

I was already seeing my childhood friend dashing the coin back in my brother's face. I exerted all my strength to raise myself and stretch my hands out so as to prevent violence — but what was that? No, impossible! And yet I saw it with my own eyes. He took the money — he said, " Thank you " — he bowed — he walked away!

And I? I stared after him as though he were an evil spirit, then sank back on the cushions with a weary sigh.

That, my dear friend, was the way I said good-bye to my youthful dream.

(Adele S. Seltzer)

---

[6] **Siegfried:** the hero of the *Song of the Nibelungs.* According to one of the Scandinavian legends, he was apprenticed in his youth to the mastersmith Mime, whom he slew because of his treachery.

SUGGESTIONS FOR STUDY

1. What was the discussion which gave rise to the story? What is the narrator trying to show?

2. What caused the girl's disillusionment? Is this ending convincing to you?

3. What inferences can you draw from the story regarding the gap between the social classes in Germany? Would there have been any difference if the story had occurred in this country?

RAINER MARIA RILKE (1875–1926)

Rilke is one of the most admired of the more recent German poets. He was born in Prague. In the course of extensive travels he frequented artistic circles in various countries and was for a time secretary of the famous French sculptor Rodin. His melodious poetry is concerned mainly with problems of the soul, especially his search for God.

CLOUD

Thou cloud that floats above the golden grain,
I love the spaces where thy gray veils stream;
Before the sickle of the moon shall wane
Thou wilt descend as softly falling rain
And wake the harvest fields from out their dream.

(Jessie Lamont)

PRAYER OF THE MAIDENS TO MARY

So dark, O Virgin, are our days,
Our nights so full of dread,
We reach in youthful awkward ways
Out to the roses red.

Mary, be mild to us, Thine own.
We blossom from Thy blood,
And no one else save Thee alone
Our pain hath understood.

Thy soul hath known this maiden woe.
To Thee this longing came;
It seems as chill as winter's snow,
And is aflame — aflame —

(Jessie Lamont)

EMIL LUDWIG (1881–1948)

Ludwig was born in Breslau of a Jewish family. He secured an international audience through a series of vividly written biographies which show insight into character and lay emphasis on psychological motives instead of outward happenings. In addition to his *Napoleon* (1924), he wrote lives of Goethe, Bismarck, and the Emperor William II. His book of shorter biographies, called *Genius and Character,* includes Leonardo da Vinci.

NAPOLEON

THE CORONATION

Napoleon Bonaparte (1769–1821), born in the island of Corsica, had risen by his military genius to be master of France. He was made First Consul for life in 1802, but for the greater glory of himself, his relatives, and his possible descendants, he wished to obtain the imperial title.

On December 2, 1804, in Notre-Dame,[1] an abundance of precious stones reflects the light of a myriad candles, so that the place looks more like a banqueting hall than a church. Everything has been prepared for weeks beforehand. A skillful museum director has even produced a colorable imitation of Charlemagne's[2] scepter. Ancient parchments from the days of the Roi Soleil[3] had been consulted, to insure that the crowning of this revolutionist should vie in every respect with that of the legitimate monarchs of France. Ségur[4] had studied the etiquette of the occasion with the utmost care; Isabey[5] had rehearsed the whole affair with an array of dolls; the old palace, Paris, France, were in fever.

The Emperor is in a pleasant humor. Early in the morning he makes sure that Josephine's crown is a good fit. The great procession drives to the cathedral. Napoleon, robed in an antique imperial mantle, strides to the high altar leading the empress by the hand. Josephine's charm helps to divest the great moment of a certain sense of embarrassment. Surrounded by attendant cardinals, the pope is seated, waiting. The organ peals forth.

Then, when the appointed instant has come, and all are expecting

---

[1] **Notre-Dame:** famous Gothic cathedral in Paris.

[2] **Charlemagne:** (742–814) the first sovereign to be crowned Holy Roman Emperor.

[3] **Roi Soleil:** "King Sun," Louis XIV, whose reign (1643–1715) coincides with the most illustrious period of French history and literature.

[4] **Ségur:** (1756–1805) French playwright.

[5] **Isabey:** (1767–1855) French painter.

this man who has never bowed the knee to any one, to kneel before
the Holy Father, Napoleon, to the amazement of the congregation,
seizes the crown, turns his back on the pope and the altar, and, standing upright as always, crowns himself in the sight of France. Then
he crowns his kneeling wife.

None but the pope had known his intentions. Informed at the
eleventh hour, Pius had lacked the courage to threaten immediate
departure. Now, all he could do was to anoint and bless the two
sinners. Moreover, the crown on the Emperor's head is not a Christian crown at all, but a small pagan circlet of golden laurel leaves.
All who describe the occasion agree in saying that the Emperor was
pale but handsome. He resembled Emperor Augustus; and from
now onwards, as if by some mystical power, his features grew more
and more like those of the first emperor of Rome.

Thus, in this symbolical hour, Napoleon reduces to mockery the
legitimate formalities he is affecting to copy. Furthermore, he
makes a laughing-stock of the pope, who will not forget the slight.
In an instant the cloud of Bourbon [6] reminiscence has been scattered;
the flavor of imitation and parody has vanished; and on the steps
of a temple there stands a soldier, a Roman imperator,[7] whom a dozen
years before this day no one had ever heard of, who since then has
performed no miracles but only done deeds, and has now crowned
himself with the golden laurels of these deeds. But his mantle is
broidered with golden bees, the emblem of activity.

Several incidents show that he has not, throughout this day of his
coronation, wholly surrendered to the mood of a man who has made
his own destiny.

When he was seated on the throne, crown on head, with the pope in
front of him, he said in a low aside to his brother: " Joseph, if only
Father could see this! " The remark, poignant at such an hour in
the mouth of a man who was never wont to speak of his father, is
fundamentally natural. The perfect simplicity, the unsophisticated
innocence, of his course of action, lead his mind back to his origin.
Memories of family feuds on the island, of the pride and ambition of
the Corsican clans, direct his thoughts toward the stock from which
he has sprung.

Semblance never holds his attention, which always reaches out to
the core of reality. Thus he is not bewildered even in this amazing
hour. When he wants to whisper something to his uncle, who stands

---

[6] **Bourbon:** the Bourbon dynasty had occupied the throne of France from
1589 to 1792.   [7] **imperator:** emperor.

just in front of him during Mass, he gives the cardinal a gentle dig in the back with his scepter. As soon as all is over, and, alone with Josephine, he goes in to dinner, he says with a sigh of relief: " Thank God we're through with it! A day on the battle-field would have pleased me better! " At their little dinner he tells her to keep on her crown, as if he and she were poet and actress, for, he says, she is charming, his little Creole [8] woman, as empress. Thus, in the most natural way in the world, he unmasks the whole masquerade, and we are at ease once more as we see the son of the revolution [9] laughing his own empire to scorn.

The freedom of spirit shown by the foregoing petty details is splendidly illuminated by an admission he made the same evening, when, to a confidant, he summed up the whole matter with skeptical emotion: " No, Decrès,[10] I have come into the world too late. There is nothing great left for me to do. I do not deny that I have had a fine career, but what a difference between me and the heroes of antiquity. Look at Alexander, for instance. After he had conquered Asia, he declares himself to be the son of Jupiter, and the whole East believes him, save only his mother and Aristotle and a handful of Athenian pedants. But if I, nowadays, were to declare myself the son of the Father Eternal, every fishwife would laugh in my face. There is nothing great left for me to do."

This was said a few hours after he had crowned himself emperor; said quite simply and quite truthfully. Is it not plain why the East has always allured him, and will continue to allure him? By nature he is endowed with immense powers, and is overburdened by their incredible weight. Nothing can be adequate to his aspirations, now that he has learned how readily people obey the man who can command obedience by his skill and by his deeds. He is strong in his own strength; what does Voltaire's enlightenment, what does Rousseau, matter to him? How can he wish to establish democracy, to install popular government, when he knows the weakness of the popular instincts, and all the corruptness of the leaders of the people? To expand his sway, to spread his name widely and ever more widely, to leave more record of himself in the book of universal history than that half page of which he spoke a few years ago, to sacrifice life itself to the little golden circlet on his head, to do these

[8] **Creole:** a descendant of non-aboriginal races born and settled in the West Indies. Josephine was born in the island of Martinique.

[9] **son of the revolution:** Only the great French Revolution of 1789 could have enabled Napoleon to come to the top.

[10] **Decrès:** (1762–1820) French admiral.

things without enjoyment and without leisure and without pause —
this is all that life now offers.

When, during these days, the sketch for an imperial seal is laid
before him, and he sees a lion couchant,[11] he draws his pen across the
picture, and writes in the margin: " An eagle volant." [12]

IN EXILE

After his defeat at Waterloo in 1815, Napoleon was banished to the
island of St. Helena, where he died six years later.

" No one but myself can be blamed for my fall. I have been my
own greatest enemy, the cause of my own disastrous fate."

This admission, the profoundest of all those made by the exile,
shows that Napoleon has completely outgrown the cloudy Caesarist
fancies of his middle period. Had he been a believing Christian, the
confession would have rounded off his atonement upon the rock.
His sense of responsibility, however, is not directed toward God but
only toward himself, and therefore the utterance represents a great
man's final settlement of accounts with destiny. But, at the same
time, it is a last outburst of defiance, for his overweening self-esteem
made it impossible for him to admit that there were any greater
forces in the world than his own. Napoleon alone could overthrow
Napoleon.

The remark was not the outcome of transient depression. During
the closing years of his power, he had again and again spoken to his
intimates about his faults and errors; now, upon the island, such
admissions are frequent. Some of them are ardent, and some of
them are cold; for even in these self-examinations there is an alternation between fantasy and realism. From time to time, we have the
heartfelt cry of a penitent: " When I close my eyes, all my mistakes
parade themselves before me, like figures in a nightmare." Or,
again: " I wanted too much. . . . I strung the bow too tightly, and
trusted too much in my good fortune."

(Eden and Cedar Paul)

[11] **couchant:** lying down.   [12] **volant:** flying.

SUGGESTIONS FOR STUDY

1. What was natural and what was imitative and artificial in Napoleon's
conduct during and after the coronation? What was the significance of
his act of crowning himself?

2. By virtue of what qualities had he risen to power? Why did he feel

the lure of the East? What was the height of his ambition at the time of his coronation?

3. How did he finally explain his downfall? How was this explanation consistent with his general character?

4. Sir J. R. Seeley's *Short History of Napoleon I* is recommended to those who find Ludwig's *Napoleon* too long.

5. Compare this coronation scene with other famous ones, such as that of Charles II in Samuel Pepy's *Diary* and that of Queen Victoria in the biography by Lytton Strachey. How do Americans, without the excuse of royalty, satisfy the human craving for pageantry?

6. Vocabulary: myriad, parody, poignant, semblance, confident, pedants, overweening.

READING LIST

TRANSLATIONS FROM GERMAN LITERATURE

Poetry

The translations of the lyrics and ballads of Goethe and Uhland in Longfellow's Complete Works are recommended.

Heine, H.: *Poems*, trans. by Louis Untermeyer

Deutsch, B. and Yarmolinski, A.: *Contemporary German Poetry*

Drama

Lessing, G. E.: *Minna von Barnhelm*
Emilia Galotti
Nathan the Wise

Goethe, J. W. von: *Faust*, Part I, trans. by Anna Swanwick

Schiller, F. von: *The Maid of Orleans*
William Tell

Hebbel, F.: *Three Plays*, trans. by Allen and Fairley

Hauptmann, G.: *Lonely Lives*
Assumption of Hannele
The Sunken Bell

Schnitzler, A.: *Anatol*

Sudermann, H.: *Magda*
The Joy of Living

Fiction

Grimm, Jakob and Wilhelm: *Domestic Tales*

Hoffmann, E. T. A.: *Weird Tales*

Keller, Gottfried: *The People of Seldwyla*

Meyer, C. F.: *The Saint*

Auerbach, B.: *On the Heights*

Sudermann, H.: *Dame Care*
Iolanthe's Wedding
Regina

Hauptmann, G.: *The Heretic of Soana*

Mann, T.: *Buddenbrooks*
Death in Venice
The Magic Mountain
Joseph and His Brethren
Young Joseph

Schnitzler, A.: *Fräulein Else*
Little Novels

Wassermann, J.: *The Mauritius Case*

Zweig, S.: *Conflicts*

Remarque, E. M.: *All Quiet on the Western Front*
The Road Back

Fallada, H.: *Little Man, What Now?*

Franck, Bruno: *A Man Called Cervantes*

Werfel, Franz: *The Forty Days of Musa Dagh*

Cerf, B. A.: *Great German Short Novels and Stories*

Melville and Hargreaves: *Great German Short Stories*

Stories by Foreign Authors: German

Non-Fiction Prose

Goethe, J. W. von: *Poetry and Truth from My Life*

Ludwig, E.: *Genius and Character Napoleon Bismarck*

Zweig, S.: *Marie Antoinette Mary Queen of Scotland and the Isles*

Wassermann, J.: *Bula Matari* (Life of Henry M. Stanley)

BOOKS ABOUT GERMAN LIFE AND ARTS

Fiction

Davis, W. S.: *God Wills It*

Irving, Washington: *The Specter Bridegroom*
Tales of a Traveler

Reade, Charles: *The Cloister and the Hearth*

Biography

Froude, J. A.: *Life and Letters of Erasmus*

Smith, P.: *Life and Letters of Martin Luther*

Robertson, J. G.: *Goethe*

Thomas, Calvin: *Schiller*

Browne, Lewis: *That Man Heine*

Rolland, Romain: *Beethoven, The Creator*

Davenport, Marcia: *Mozart*

History, Criticism, Literature

Richard, Ernest: *History of German Civilization*

Francke, Kuno: *History of German Literature*

Robertson, J. G.: *The Literature of Germany*

Priest, G. M.: *Germany Since 1740*

Bithell, J.: *Germany*

Eloesser, A.: *Modern German Literature*

Heller, Otto: *Studies in Modern German Literature*

Hewett, T. H. N.: *The Modern German Novel*

Hosmer, J. K.: *A Short History of German Literature*

Art and Music

Dickinson, Helen A.: *German Masters of Art*

Singer, H. W.: *Stories of the German Artists*
The Art of the Netherlands and Germany (500 University Prints bound in one vol.)

Elson, L. C.: *The History of German Song*

Walker, Conway: *The Art Song and Its Composers*
German and Russian Opera

Maitland, J. A. F.: *Masters of German Music*

Travel, Social Life and Customs

Holzwarth, F. J.: *German Students' Manual of Literature, Lands, and People of Germany*

Scandinavian Literature

Scandinavian Literature

THE lure of the Scandinavian countries for the tourist lies in the strange alternation of midnight sun and noonday dark, in the majestic scenery of mountain and fjord, the rich rolling farm lands, the pattern of lakes and forests, the cities built on little clusters of islands, rivaling Venice in their natural beauty. The student of literature finds much of this reflected in the writings of these countries, Norway, Sweden, and Denmark, for the lives of the people are inevitably colored by the condition of their background. The long period of gloom in the winter months and the hard conditions of wresting a livelihood from stony soil and turbulent seas have given to north-Scandinavian literature a certain seriousness — even austerity. The reader feels the latent power in the people beneath their somewhat inarticulate exterior. In contrast we find in south-Scandinavian writing the gayety, charm, and humor of the prosperous farm lands where the peasant tradition had produced native costumes, music, dances, songs, and stories of unusual picturesqueness. On the whole the literature reveals to us a race of people thoughtful, practical, earnest, self-reliant — holding education and their state religion, the Lutheran Church, in great respect. Besides these good qualities we may also find pictured that characteristic stubbornness, repression, and sullen jealousy which contrasts with the more spontaneous and emotional outbursts of southern Europeans.

Scandinavian literature is produced by three distinct nations

The relations among the nations composing the Scandinavian group have been somewhat intricate and need not be dwelt upon at length, but a few outstanding facts in their history will give helpful background in interpreting their literature. Before the tenth century the Scandinavians were Viking sea pirates speaking approximately the same language in the three countries. After that a gradual development into three distinct languages is evident, showing the influence of their various political affiliations. When in the last quarter of the ninth century Harold the Fairhaired consolidated most of Norway under his control, the disgruntled chieftains who would not acknowledge him withdrew to Iceland, and active colonization went on for about sixty years. These Northmen intermingling with a small group of Irish Celts already on the island formed a race whose great significance in Scandinavian literature will be shown later. Denmark, being nearest to old European culture, was the first to be Christianized in the ninth century. Norway adopted Christianity in the late tenth century, but Sweden not till the early twelfth. The various unions and separations which have complicated the histories of the three countries may be easily seen in the following graph:

	1300	1400	1500	1600	1700	1800	1900
DENMARK	D+N	D+N+S	D+N			D	→ D
NORWAY	1319 1397		1523			1814	→ N
SWEDEN			S			S+N 1905	→ S

Early Medieval literature has remarkable development

From a chronological point of view, Scandinavian literature is like a two-pronged fork. After the rich literature of the early middle ages, chiefly in Old Norse, there is a wide hiatus until the writings of the late eighteenth century emerge, later to develop into a modern literature of great power in three distinct languages. The traditional literature of the Old Norse is of great interest to us because it is so closely akin to our earliest epic *Beowulf*, which the Jutes probably brought with them from Denmark. Through the first migration of the Jutes in the fifth century and the later settlements of the Danes in the ninth, England acquired a great inflow of Scandinavian custom and tradition. Even the Normans had originally been Northmen. That our days of the week are named after old Norse gods illustrates the close union of our past with that of the Scandinavians.

Though the legends of Odin, Thor, and other gods and heroes, which all children read today, were the common property of the continental Norsemen, it is to remote Iceland that we owe our present knowledge of them. Long after traces of the old writings had been lost elsewhere, it was discovered in the middle of the seventeenth century that a great body of material had been preserved on this island. Since the spoken language there still resembled to a great extent the Old Norse, it was easy to translate these writings into modern tongues. The Icelandic manuscripts include (1) the Elder or Poetic Edda containing about thirty-eight poems of ancient composition, but put in writing supposedly about the thirteenth century; (2) the Younger or Prose Edda by Snorri Sturluson, of the fourteenth century, summing up and repeating in prose many of the same legends of gods and heroes as appeared in the Poetic Edda; (3) many sagas or family tales which were carefully preserved by Icelandic chiefs as a basis of the aristocratic organization of their society. Of these sagas the most famous are Sturluson's *Heimskringla* (*Circuit of the World*) about early kings and saints, and the *Volsunga Saga*, about Sigurd the Volsung, whose story had been told also in the Eddas. Sigurd is the Norse name of Siegfried, the hero of the *Song of the Nibelungs* (page 420) and the similarity of the two stories illustrates the common origin of the early Gothic tribes. William Morris gave a masterly English version of the old story in his poem *Sigurd the Volsung*. Thomas Gray is another English poet who made great use of the Norse legends, and in America Longfellow popularized Viking literature through his " The Saga of King Olaf " and " The Skeleton in Armor."

Other important remains of the Middle Ages are the popular ballads, in which Denmark excelled the other countries of this group, *Chronicle of Denmark and Norway* by Saxo (1200) and the religious writings of the Swedish St. Birgitta (1302?-1373). The barren centuries from the fourteenth to the eighteenth were preoccupied with the Reformation and the struggle of political self-determination. With the eighteenth century French classicism and the early glimmerings of romanticism penetrated to the Scandinavian countries. Ludvig Holberg (Danish, 1684-1754) with his brilliant satirical comedies illustrates the classic influence, while Carl Michael Bellman (Swedish, 1740-1795) illustrates the Rousseau influence.

Romantic movement awakens modern literature in Denmark

But it was Adam Gottlob Oehlenschläger (1779-1850) who gave the great impetus to romanticism and with him modern Danish literature is said to begin. His reputation, however, was largely national rather than international. It was Hans Christian Andersen (1805-1875) with his simple yet subtle fairy tales who made the rest of Europe aware that Danish authors existed. Today his poems, dramas, and novels lie unread, but his tales remain immortal. In contrast to Andersen's appeal to the fancy, his only fellow countryman of the mid-century who attained international reputation was the literary critic Georg Brandes (1842–1927), author of the monumental work *Main Currents in Nineteenth-Century Literature*. Johannes Vilhelm Jensen (1873–1950) was a leading figure in the fight for a realistic Danish literature, against Brandes' influential dictum that literature should "put problems into debate." Jensen was awarded the Nobel prize in 1944 for his six-volume epic *The Long Journey*. It traces the history of the Cimbrians, a Teutonic race which overran all Europe, from the Ice Age to the time of Columbus. Jensen was also a lyric poet of distinction and a successful dramatist. He exhibits both of these talents in his admirable translation of *Hamlet* into Danish.

Political independence gives impetus to Norwegian literature

Up to her separation from Denmark in 1814, Norway produced no distinctive literature of her own; but with a new national consciousness, creative work began to flourish. Henrik Wergeland (1808–1845) and Johan Sebastian Welhaven (1807–1873) carried on a literary feud for many years. The first represented an emotional, nationalistic, and idealistic attitude toward literature; the second, a more witty, classical, and international point of view. Another picturesque figure of the day was Wergeland's sister, the brilliant Camilla Collett (1813–1895), who wrote the novel *The Governor's Daughters*. From 1841 to 1851 Asbjörnsen and Moe were publishing their Norwegian folk tales, so important in the perpetuation of early Medieval literature.

Ibsen and Björnson bring Norwegian literature to its climax

With Henrik Ibsen (1828–1906) and Björnstjerne Björnson (1832–1910), modern Norwegian literature reached full flower and became international in reputation. Ibsen exerted more influence outside his own country than did any late nineteenth-century dramatist of any other nation. It was largely because of Ibsen that English and American drama emerged from mere light entertainment or mawkish sentimentality into mature treatment of significant problems. In his earlier dramas Ibsen used the ancient national themes of saga and folklore. The plays of his middle years treat the problems of the individual against the background of society of his own day. The tragedies of his late years are highly symbolic and have caused much controversy as to their true interpretation.

In contrast to the gloomy intensity of Ibsen's writings, those of

Björnson are buoyant and heartening. Instead of criticizing and probing humanity, he seems to touch it with the gentleness of profound understanding or invigorate it with vital energy. His dramas show an interesting scheme of linking the heroic past to the realistic present by treating similar human problems in pairs of plays for the two periods. Unlike Ibsen he was distinguished also in the fields of fiction and poetry, both epic and lyric. His strong patriotic feeling is evident throughout his work, and one of his poems became the national hymn of Norway.

A third contemporary and friend of these two has had great reputation as a novelist in his own country but has never been so well known abroad, though his best works have been translated into English. This is Jonas Lie (1833–1908), whose fifteen volumes include both short stories and novels. *The Pilot and His Wife* is typical of his excellent sea stories. *Go Ahead!*, a tale of an isolated northern region where everything stagnates for fresh air, symbolizes his desire to permeate Norway with intellectual currents from the rest of Europe. Lie is said by critics to have created the modern Norwegian novel, which came to its full fruitage in the twentieth century.

The novel the outstanding type in present Norwegian literature

Today the novel is the preëminent form of writing in Norway, poetry and drama being distinctly in the background since Björnson's death. Among the many excellent novelists, three are outstanding in international reputation: Hamsun, Bojer, and Sigrid Undset.

Knut Hamsun (1860–1952) established his reputation with *Hunger* (1890) presented as a psychological situation, not just as a realistic treatment of famine conditions as current in the fiction of that day. His long series of novels plays many variations on the general theme of the lonely spirit seeking the satisfaction of his inner life in forest seclusion or farm toil. In 1917 Hamsun won the Nobel prize for *The Growth of the Soil,* his masterpiece of peasant life.

Johan Bojer (1872–   ) somewhat resembles Hamsun in style but emphasizes the social rather than the solitary psychology of man. *The Great Hunger* (1916), *The Last of the Vikings* (1921), and *The Emigrants* are his best-known novels.

The transplanted Norwegian peasant from the American point of view is represented in *Giants in the Earth* (1924), written in the Norwegian language by the American Ole E. Rölvaag (1876–1931).

The peasant theme has also been ably handled by Olav Duun, a writer of the far north, whose work is discussed later.

Sigrid Undset (1882–1949) was not only Norway's chief woman writer, but among all the recent Scandinavian writers she undoubtedly has the greatest world reputation. Her monumental trilogy *Kristin Lavransdatter*, the first book of which was published in 1920, brought her the Nobel prize in 1928 after it was completed and translated into fourteen foreign languages. This was followed by a tetralogy, *The Master of Hestviken*. Both the trilogy and the tetralogy are family tales of the Middle Ages which are, in their majestic sweep, reminiscent of the early sagas. In later books Sigrid Undset turned to modern backgrounds, but continued to follow her favorite theme of the psychology of marriage and family life.

The novelist Johan Falkberget (1879–   ) takes a sympathetic view of the grim lives of people living in a small mining town on a barren plateau near the Swedish border. His three-volume cycle *Christianus Sextus* relates the history of a copper mine from the early eighteenth century to the present.

Johan Nordahl Grieg (1902–1943), poet, dramatist, and novelist, in all his work speaks for the downtrodden. His important early novel *The Ship Sails On* lays bare the hardships endured by common sailors. His play *Our Honor and Our Might*, written under Communist influence, attacks the greed of Norwegian shipowners during World War I. Later, his was an important role in his country's resistance to Hitler's invasion. His lyrics, especially *Norway in Our Hearts*, helped maintain his countrymen's enthusiasm for the Allied cause. He was killed while a member of the crew of an American bomber over Berlin.

Until 1850 all modern Norwegian literature was written in Danish. Since then, many young patriots have written in a synthetic Norwegian dialect, called *Landsmaal*. The greatest of writers in this dialect is Olav Duun (1876–1939). His notable work *The People of Juvik* traces in six volumes the history of four generations of a family of peasant landowners in northern Norway. This ambitious product has been called the most complete picture of peasant life in modern times. Duun's narrative style, in its simplicity and directness, has been compared to that of the sagas.

Swedish literature emphasizes poetry

In contrast to the seriousness and introspection of Norwegian literature, that of Sweden presents on the whole a lighter and more lyrical touch. The gentler aspects of nature with foothills, rivers, lakes, and rich farm land have given grace to Swedish writers just as the rugged mountains and fjords have lent austerity to the Norwegian. Poetry has been the great medium of Sweden; tragedy and novel that of Norway. Whether Sweden produced an ancient literature comparable to the Old Norse, but now lost, is a matter of conjecture. Her first extant local writing comes with the folk ballads, which are quite distinct from those of Denmark, though not so numerous. The great period of Gustavus Adolphus (seventeenth century), which brought Sweden into European prominence, produced literary names, but they were merely imitators of the all-pervading French classicism.

Native Scandinavian genius could flower only from the seeds of the romantic movement of the late eighteenth century. Percy's *Reliques* (1765) in England greatly influenced the northern countries, and the discovery of ancient Scandinavian records stirred the creative impulse of Esaias Tegnér (1782–1846) to make the old heroes live again in his modern epic *Frithjof's Saga.* Erik Geijer (1783–1847) added to the general romantic fervor with his original poems, his collection of Swedish ballads, and his prose *Chronicles of Sweden.* Johan Runeberg (1804–1877), Finnish but writing in Swedish, contributed the quaintness and humor of native characters in his richly varied *Ensign Stål's Stories.*

Carl Snoilsky (1841–1903), on the other hand, has been called " the last of Sweden's classicists," and his carefully molded poems contrast with the popular abrupt style derived from the manner of the Eddas. Gustaf Fröding (1860–1911) shows the contrast of exuberant joy and twilight melancholy in his melodious verse. Erik Axel Karlfeldt (1864–1931) glorified the scenery and the peasant families of his native province. For his *Dalecarlian Paintings in Rhyme,* a unique series of Bible stories, he was awarded the Nobel prize in 1931.

Sweden also has great names in fiction and drama

Verner von Heidenstam (1859–1940), Nobel prize winner of 1916, was the chief link between the poets and the novelists, for he excelled in both fields. His cosmopolitan background influenced the subject matter and polished style of his poetry; his interest in national history is reflected in his greatest novel *The Charles Men.*

Sweden's fiction writers are less given to long novels than are Norway's, and have done more with the short story. One of the greatest Scandinavian short-story writers is Per Hallström (1866–   ), whose many volumes attest his unusual talent in that field. Hjalmar

Söderberg (1869–1941) was also outstanding for his brilliant and witty " short shorts."

Selma Lagerlöf (1858–1940), more than any other Swedish writer of fiction, has been translated into many tongues and is well known to Americans for her short stories, her autobiography *Mårbacka,* and her novels, among which *Gösta Berling* established her reputation.

In drama Sweden has had one great name, August Strindberg (1849–1912), a troubled genius whose mental rebellions and inconsistencies are at variance with the placid, romantic flow of Swedish literature. His dramas, powerful, often unpleasant, but never platitudinous, reflect his own inner conflicts. He also wrote poetry, short stories, and novels, but will inevitably be known as a dramatist.

Contemporary Swedish literature analyzes war, society, and personality

The most interesting figure in contemporary Swedish literature is Pär Fabian Lagerkvist (1891–   ), poet, novelist, and dramatist, and winner of the Nobel prize in 1951. His novels, *The Hangman, The Dwarf,* and *Barabbas,* are mixtures of fantasy and cruel satire. Each in its peculiar way reveals all that is brutal and twisted in modern man. In *Barabbas,* we see and feel the crucifixion through the criminal whom Pilate reprieved instead of Jesus. The criminal represents careless, morally confused Everyman who finds Christianity hard to understand and harder to practice. His plays, *Let Man Live, The Man without a Soul,* and *Victory in the Dark,* written under Strindberg's influence, reveal the method and intensity of a true master.

Hjalmar Bergman (1883–1930) has been called the Swedish Dickens. His drama *The Swidenholm Family* is about an amusing collection of artists and their hangers-on. His novel *God's Orchard,* full of abnormal characters, betrays the influence of Freud and the life-long mental depression from which Bergman suffered.

Gustaf Hellström (1882–1953) wrote novels that imitate the ample manner of Dickens. His novel *Lacemaker Lekholm Has an Idea* is the history of three generations of a typical Swedish middle-class family. The irony with which the author seasons his realism makes this one of the best of the many Scandinavian genealogical novels.

Sigfrid Siwertz, (1882–   ), a writer of novels and short stories, in *Selambs,* reveals the influence of Zola by tracing degeneracy through five members of the same family.

The only Finnish writer of international reputation is Frans Eemil Sillanpää (1888–   ), who received the Nobel prize in 1939. His *Meek Heritage,* written just after the close of the 1918 Civil War between the Whites and the Reds, describes, without taking sides, the horror of the struggle. To him the conflict is an expression of the tragedy of elemental man. *The Maid Silja* treats the same war in a more imaginative fashion. Silja represents innocent, uncorrupted humanity caught willy-nilly in the struggle. *People in a Summer Night* discloses an entirely different aspect of Sillanpää's art — his mystical attitude toward nature. His collections of short stories, *My Dear Fatherland, Of and To My Own,* and *From the Level of the Earth,* form a priceless collection of vignettes of Finnish life.

Viewed as a whole the Scandinavian countries, once they reëstablished contact with the ancients, produced a modern literature of highly individual character. It is simple, direct, and without pretense. Like waters, rocks, and soil, it is elemental.

The Old Norse Literature

Far removed from the rest of Europe is Iceland, a wild volcanic island that was discovered by a Viking around 860 A.D. Its center towered into mountains seven thousand feet high, its coast was notched by deep fjords, but between the two vegetation flourished during the short summer season. It therefore offered a pleasant and secure refuge to certain lords of Norway who resented the domination of Harold the Fairhaired. His attempts at consolidating Norway at the end of the ninth century caused many of his fellow Northmen to emigrate to Iceland. In Iceland the old Norse customs, the aristocratic family lines, the very language remained practically unchanged well up to modern times. In the seventeenth century certain professors of the University of Copenhagen discovered that in Iceland, skalds (bards), long since suppressed by monastic rule on the Continent, still recited songs of their ancestors at public gatherings. With scarcely any change in the spoken tongue during eight hundred years, it was easy for scholars to translate the old manuscripts and the oral traditions into modern Scandinavian languages.

The ancient literature falls into two types — Eddas and Sagas. The Eddas are collections of stories celebrating the legendary gods and heroes; the Sagas are family histories.

THE POETIC EDDA

There are two Eddas in the Old Norse, the Poetic and the Prose. The Poetic Edda is sometimes called the Elder because it is the earlier of the two ancient manuscripts dating back to the thirteenth century, found in a remote corner of Iceland. The exact meaning of the term *edda* has long been debated by scholars. The first theory was that because of its relation to the word "great-grandmother" it meant tales handed down by word of mouth in the family circle. Later this theory was rejected in favor of the idea that the word meant "poesy." The newest theory is that it is derived from Oddi, the place where the old manuscript was read by Snorri Sturluson and that he therefore refers to it as the "Book of Oddi," which in process of time became Edda.

The authorship, too, has been disputed. The Elder Edda was long attributed to a certain Bishop Saemund; but after that was disproved, the Elder Edda remained an orphan without an author.

This Edda consists of many stories of the gods and heroes of Norse mythology. They are told in an abrupt, alliterative meter, adapted to the chanting of the skalds accompanied by their harps. The meter resembles that of *Beowulf*. Professional skalds played an important part in Icelandic life, since they were both the libraries and the newspapers of the early times; and it is through their amazing memories that so much ancient lore has been handed down. Some of these stories are earlier than the year 1000, though most of them were recorded between the eleventh and the thirteenth centuries. Since the metrical form and archaic expressions make the stories hard to follow for the average reader, the selection here given is part of the High Song of Odin. This piece of sound advice on the wise conduct of life as the ordinary man lived it was in marked contrast to the fantastic stories of gods and giants found in the rest of the narrative. It is put into the mouth of Odin, who was not only the chief god but also the wisest. In fact, legend had it that he had sacrificed one eye for the gift of wisdom. Perhaps this was a symbol of the price paid by human sages in the days before oculists and electricity.

The order of the stanzas here given has been rearranged from the original to give some continuity of idea, and the captions have been added.

HIGH SONG OF ODIN THE OLD

From the *Poetic Edda*

FRIENDSHIP

With weapons and garments,
As best may be fitting
Give thou thy friends pleasure.
By gifts interchanged
Is friendship made surest;   5
If the heart proffers them.

Let a man towards his friend,
Ever be friendly,
And with gifts make return for gifts.
With thy cheerful friend   10
Be thou cheerful;

With thy guileful friend on thy
   guard.

Let a man towards his friend
Ever be friendly;
Towards him and his friend.   15
But with an enemy's friend
Can no man
Be friendly.

If thou hast a friend
Whom thou canst confide in   20
And wouldst have joy of his
   friendship,
Then, mingle thy thoughts with
   his,
Give gifts freely,
And often be with him.

THE FOOLISH MAN

No better burden   25
Bears a man on his journey
Than mickle wisdom.
No worse provision
Takes a man on his journey
Than frequent drunkenness.   30

Ale is not so good
As people have boasted
For the children of men.
For less and still less,
As more he drinketh,   35
Knows man himself.

The gluttonous man,
Though he may not know it,
Eats his life's sorrow;
Lust of drink, often   40
Makes the fool foolish
When he comes mid the prudent.

A foolish man
Lies awake the night through
And resolves on many   45
   things.
Thus is he weary
When the day cometh;
The old care remaineth.

A foolish man
Thinks all are friendly   50
Who meet him with smiles.
But few he findeth
Who will aid his cause
When to the Ting he cometh.

A foolish man   55
Thinks all are friendly
Who meet him with smiles;
Nor knows he the difference
Though they laugh him to scorn
When he sits 'mong the   60
   knowing ones.

A foolish man
Thinks he knows everything
When he needs not the knowl-
   edge.
But he knows not
How to make answer   65
When he is questioned.

A foolish man,
When he comes into company
Had better keep silence.
No one remarketh   70
How little he knows
Till he begins talking.

27. **mickle:** much. 54. **Ting:** the assembly or local governing body of the
early Norsemen.

THE WISE MAN

Good understanding
Ought all to possess, —
But not too much wisdom.   75
Those human beings
Whose lives are the brightest,
Know much and know it well.

Good understanding,
Ought all to possess,   80
But not too much knowledge.
For the heart of a wise man

Seldom is gladdened
By knowledge of all things.

Good understanding   85
Ought all to possess,
But not too much knowledge.
Let no one beforehand
Inquire his own fortune.
The gladdest heart knoweth   90
    it not.

(William and Mary Howitt)

THE PROSE EDDA

The Younger or Prose Edda, dating about 1350, has been definitely proved to be the work of one man, Snorri Sturluson, the greatest Icelandic historian. This man was a strange paradox. The son of a hotheaded chieftain of West Iceland, Snorri inherited his father's turbulent disposition and added to it tremendous personal ambition to which he was willing to sacrifice the interests and sometimes the lives of his own family. He even negotiated to betray his country into the hands of the Norwegian king. Whether conscience or expediency restrained him is hard to say, but he proved too dilatory to suit the king and was secretly murdered by royal order. In contrast to this unpleasant picture of him seen through the eyes of his nephew-biographer, his literary remains prove him to be a tireless antiquarian and a graphic writer. His study of the Poetic Edda resulted in his composition of the Prose Edda, which might be called a textbook for skalds, as the first part contains the mythological tales of the earlier work retold in prose, evidently intended as a source book for bards. The second and third parts are technical explanations of the figures of speech, verse forms, and grammatical rules used in poetry. The first part is naturally the most interesting. Since the authorized translation follows the archaic form of the original too closely for the comfort of the average reader, the story here given is one of the many adaptations. Thor is the god of thunder — like Zeus in his wielding of thunderbolts, like Hercules in his physical prowess. Loki is the mischief maker among the gods — crafty like Mercury and deformed like Vulcan. The gods and giants were deadly enemies, and so when the two gods went to Jötunheim, land of the giants, they showed great daring. Some of the later tales show the final defeat of the gods at the hands of the giants. This was called " the twilight of the gods." The German form of the phrase — *Götterdäm-merung* — is the title of the last of Wagner's famous " Ring " operas pic-turing the Teutonic myths.

THE JOURNEY OF THOR AND LOKI TO JÖTUNHEIM

Thor and Loki with their servants, Thjalfi and Roska, swam over the deep sea and reached the land of the giants. After a short time they came to a wood, through which they traveled the whole day until it became dark. Thjalfi was a quick walker, and carried Thor's provision-bag. But it was no easy matter to find lodging for the night. They sought about in the darkness, and at length found a house which was very spacious. At the side was an entrance as wide as the house itself, and there they took up their night quarters. At midnight, however, they perceived a great earthquake; the earth reeled under them and the house shook. Then up rose Thor and called to his companions. They sought about and found a side build-ing to the right, into which they went. Thor placed himself at the door; the rest went and sat down further in and were very much afraid. Thor kept his hammer in his hand ready to defend them. Then they heard a terrible noise and roaring. As it began to dawn, Thor went out and saw a man lying in the wood not far from them. He was by no means small, and he slept and snored loudly. Then Thor understood what the noise was which they heard in the night. He buckled on his belt of power by which he increased his divine strength. At the same instant the man awoke and rose up. It is said that Thor was so much astonished that he did not dare to slay him with his hammer, but inquired his name. He called himself Skrymer. " Thy name," said he, " I need not ask, for I know that thou art Asar [1]-Thor; but what hast thou done with my glove? "

Skrymer stooped and took up his glove, and Thor saw that it was the house in which they had passed the night, and that the outbuild-ing was the thumb. Skrymer asked Thor if he would allow him to accompany him, to which he consented. Skrymer then opened his wallet and began to eat his breakfast. Thor and his companions did the same. Skrymer proposed that they should put all their provisions together, to which Thor also consented. Then Skrymer put them all together in a bag, threw it upon his back, and marched on the whole day at a great pace.

In the evening they encamped under a huge oak, and Skrymer said

[1] **Asar:** God.

to Thor, " I will now go to sleep. You can take the bag and eat your suppers." Then slept Skrymer and snored outrageously. Thor took the provision-bag and attempted to open it; but it is related, however improbable it may seem, that he could neither untie a single knot, nor loosen a single string. When he saw that it was all in vain, then he became angry, seized the hammer with both hands, and at one stride advanced to where Skrymer lay, and struck him on the head. Skrymer awoke and asked if a leaf had fallen on his head, and also whether they had supped and were ready to lie down. Thor answered that they would now go to rest. Then they went and lay down under another tree, for they were afraid to sleep there. But at midnight Thor heard Skrymer snoring so terribly that it thundered through the wood. He arose, lifted his hammer high in the air, and struck him in the midst of his locks, so that he could see the head of the hammer was buried in his skull. At the same moment Skrymer awoke, and asked, " What is that? Has an acorn fallen on my head, or what is the matter, Thor? "

Thor stepped hastily back, and answered that he was but just awake; that it was but midnight, and therefore proper to go to sleep again. In his mind, he resolved that if he could but get one more stroke at him, the giant should never see him again; and he now lay and watched for Skrymer being soundly asleep. A little before day this was the case. Thor strode to him, lifted his hammer, and gave him such a blow on the temples that the hammer sunk into his head up to the very handle. Skrymer rose, stroked his chin, and said, " There must many birds roost in the tree above me. It seemed to me as I awoke that some moss fell down on me out of the boughs. But art thou awake, Thor? It is time for you to arise and dress yourselves, for you have now a long journey to the castle which is called Utgaard. I have heard you whisper amongst yourselves that you do not think me small, but you will find larger men when you come to Utgaard. I will give you some good counsel; don't show any lofty airs. The courtiers of Utgaard-Loki [2] would by no means put up with it in such little fellows as you are; but rather than that turn home again, for it will become you better. But if you will persist in your journey, hold to the east. My way lies northward toward the mountains that you see over yonder." Skrymer took the provision-sack on his back, and disappeared in the wood; and it is not said whether Thor wished ever to see him again.

[2] **Utgaard-Loki:** king of the giants, not to be confused with Loki, the companion of Thor.

Thor now went on with his attendants till it was noon, when they saw a castle standing on a great plain; and it was so high, that with all their endeavors they could scarcely see over it. They advanced to the castle. There was a gate to the entrance which was locked. Thor endeavored to open it, but could not; and to get into the castle, they were obliged to creep through the bars of the gate. They then saw a vast palace, and went up to it. The doors were open; they entered, and saw a multitude of men, of whom the greater number were immensely large, sitting on two benches. After this, they advanced into the presence of the King, Utgaard-Loki, and saluted him. He scarcely deigned to give them a look, and said, smiling, " It is late to inquire after true tidings from a great distance, but is it not Ek-Thor that I see? Yet you are really bigger than I imagined. What are the exploits that you can perform? For no one is tolerated amongst us who cannot distinguish himself by some art or accomplishment."

" Then," said Loki, " I understand an art, of which I am prepared to give proof; and that is, that no one here can dispose of his food as I can."

Then answered Utgaard-Loki, " Truly, that is an art, if thou canst achieve it, which we will now see."

He called from the bench a man called Logi, to contend with Loki. They set a trough in the middle of the hall, filled with meat. Loki placed himself at one end, and Logi at the other. Both ate the best they could, and they met in the middle of the trough. Loki had picked the meat from the bones; Logi had eaten meat, bones, and trough altogether. All agreed that Loki was beaten.

Then asked Utgaard-Loki what art the young man understood. Thjalfi answered that he would run a race with anyone that Utgaard-Loki would appoint. Utgaard-Loki answered that that was a good attempt; but added that he must be very swift if he thought to win in that art, but they would see. Utgaard-Loki arose and went out. There was a very good race-ground on a level field. Utgaard-Loki called a young man, named Hugi, and bade him run with Thjalfi. The first time they ran, Hugi was so much in advance, that at the turning of the course he met Thjalfi. Then said Utgaard-Loki, " Thou must put forth all thy speed, Thjalfi, if thou hopest to win; though this I say to thee, that hitherto no one has come here who was fleeter of foot than thou."

They now ran a second time, but when Hugi came to the end, and turned himself around, there was Thjalfi a good arrow-shot behind.

"Well run, both of you! " said Utgaard-Loki, " but I think Thjalfi will hardly win the race, but that the third course will show."

They ran the third time, but when Hugi reached the goal, Thjalfi had scarcely reached the middle. All agreed that this was decisive.

Then asked Utgaard-Loki of Thor, what were the feats that he would attempt, corresponding to the fame that went abroad of him. Thor answered that first he would contend in drinking with any of his people. Utgaard-Loki said, " Very good," went into his palace, and bade his cup-bearer bring out the horn from which his courtiers were accustomed to drink. Immediately appeared the cup-bearer and placed the horn in Thor's hand. Utgaard-Loki then said that to empty that horn at one pull was well done; some drained it at twice; but that he was a wretched drinker who could not exhaust it at the third draught. Thor looked at the horn and thought that it was not large, though it was tolerably long. He was very thirsty, lifted it to his mouth, and reveled in the thought that there was no necessity this time to make many breaths of it. When he could drink no more, he took the horn from his mouth, and saw to his astonishment, that there was little less in it than before.

Utgaard-Loki said, " Well hast thou drunk, yet not much. I should never have believed that Asar-Thor could have drunk more; however, of this I am confident, thou wilt empty it at the second time."

Thor drank again as much as he could, but saw that the point of the horn did not rise as he expected, and when he withdrew the horn from his mouth, it seemed to him that it had sunk less this time than the first, but the horn might now be carried without spilling.

Then said Utgaard-Loki, " How is this, Thor? If thou dost not reserve thyself purposely for the third draught, thine honor must be lost. Yet it seems to me that if thou shalt empty the horn at the third time, the draught must be the greatest. But how canst thou be regarded as a great man, as the Asar look upon thee, if thou dost not distinguish thyself in other ways more than thou hast done in this? "

Then was Thor angry, put the horn to his mouth, drank with all his might, and strained himself to the utmost; and when he looked into the horn, it was now somewhat lessened. He gave up the horn and would not drink any more. Now said Utgaard-Loki, " Now is it clear that thy strength is not so great as we supposed. Wilt thou try some other game, for we see that thou canst not succeed in this? "

Thor answered, " I will now try something else, but I wonder who among the Asar, could call that a little drink? What play will you propose? "

Utgaard-Loki answered, " Young men think it mere play to lift my cat from the ground, and I would never have proposed this to Asar-Thor, if I did not perceive that thou art much less man than I had thought thee."

Thereupon sprang an uncommonly great gray cat upon the floor. Thor advanced, took the cat around the body, and lifted it up. The cat bent its back in the same degree as Thor lifted; and when Thor had lifted it with one foot from the ground and was not able to lift it any higher, said Utgaard-Loki, " The game has terminated just as I expected. The cat is very great, and Thor is low and small compared with the great men who are here with us."

Then said Thor, " Little as you call me, I challenge any one to wrestle with me, for now I am angry."

Utgaard-Loki answered, looking round on the benches, " I see no one here who would not deem it play to wrestle with thee; but let us call hither the old Ella, my nurse. With her shall Thor prove his strength, if he will. She has given men a fall who appeared far stronger than Thor is."

On this, there entered the hall an old woman, and Utgaard-Loki said she should wrestle with Thor. In short the contest went so, that the more Thor exerted himself, the firmer she stood. And now began the old woman to exert herself, and Thor to give way, and severe struggles followed. It was not long before Thor was brought down on one knee. Then Utgaard-Loki stepped forward, bade them cease the strife, and said that Thor should attempt nothing more at his court. It was now drawing toward night. Utgaard-Loki showed Thor and his companions their lodging, where they were well accommodated.

As soon as it was light the next morning, up rose Thor and his companions, dressed themselves, and prepared to set out. Then came Utgaard-Loki, and ordered the table to be set, where there wanted no good provisions, either meat or drink. When they had breakfasted, they set out on their way. Utgaard-Loki accompanied them out of the castle, but at the parting he asked Thor how the journey had gone off; whether he had found any man more mighty than himself. Thor answered that the enterprise had brought him much dishonor, it was not to be denied, and that he should esteem himself a man of no account, which much mortified him.

Utgaard-Loki replied, " Now will I tell thee the truth, since thou art out of my castle, where, so long as I live and reign, thou shalt never re-enter; and whither, believe me, thou hadst never come, if

I had known before what might thou possessed, and that wouldst so nearly plunge us into great trouble. False appearances have I created for thee, so that the first time when thou metst the man in the wood it was I. And when thou wouldst open the provision-sack, I had laced it together with an iron band so that thou couldst not find the means to undo it. After that, thou struck at me three times with the hammer. The first stroke was the weakest, and it had been my death had it hit me. Thou saw by my castle a rock with three deep square holes, of which one was very deep. Those were the marks of thy hammer. The rock I placed in the way of the blow, without thy perceiving it.

"So also in the games, when thou contended with my courtiers. When Loki made his assay the fact was this: he was very hungry, and ate voraciously. He who was called Logi, that was fire, which consumed the trough as well as the meat. But Hugi (Mind) that was my thought with which Thjalfi ran a race, and it was impossible for his to match it in speed. When thou drank from the horn, and thought that its contents grew no less, it was notwithstanding a great marvel, such as I never believed could take place. The one end of the horn stood in the sea, which thou didst not perceive, and when thou comest to the shore thou wilt see how much the ocean has diminished by what thou hast drunk. It is even said to be ebb.

"Farther," said he, "most remarkable did it seem to me that thou lifted the cat, and in truth, all became terrified when they saw that thou lifted one foot from the ground. For it was no cat, as it seemed to thee, but the veritable Midgaard's Serpent,[3] which lies around all lands. Scarcely had he length that his tail and head might reach the earth, and thou lifted him so high up that it was but a little way to heaven. That was a marvelous wrestling that thou wrestled with Ella (Old-Age), for never has there been any one, nor shall there ever be, let him approach what great age he will, that Ella shall not overcome.

"Now must we part, and it is best for us on both sides that you do not often come to me; but if it should so happen, I shall defend my castle with such other arts that you shall not be able to effect anything against me."

When Thor heard this discourse he grasped his hammer and lifted it into the air; but as he was about to strike, he saw Utgaard-Loki

[3] **Midgaard's Serpent:** Midgaard was the earth, which the Scandinavians pictured as a flat disc around which a great serpent was coiled.

nowhere. Then he turned back to the castle to destroy it, but saw only beautiful and wide plains, and no castle. . . .

And now I know that no one can tell you anything more true of this journey of Thor's.

(William and Mary Howitt)

SUGGESTIONS FOR STUDY

1. Explain the importance of Iceland in connection with Old Norse literature. Distinguish between the Elder and Younger Eddas as to subject matter, authorship, and general style. What evidence do you find in the selections from the Eddas that they are the work of a Northern rather than a Southern people?

2. How does the verse form compare with that of *Beowulf?* With that of the *Song of the Nibelungs*, page 420? Where do you find repetition, almost like a refrain?

3. Compare the High Song of Odin with other famous examples of wisdom such as the Book of Proverbs in the Bible, the Sayings of Poor Richard, the Analects of Confucius (see page 1184). Do you find certain kinds of advice common to several of them? Which have the greatest originality of expression?

4. What light does the story of Thor and Loki throw upon the ancient Scandinavians' attitude toward nature? Their sense of humor? Qualities they admired in a hero? What points of comparison can you find with *Beowulf*, with the *Odyssey*, with *Paul Bunyan?*

5. After extending your reading on the old Norse gods (see reading list, page 738), can you note any general distinction between the Scandinavian conception of deities and that of the Greeks? Work out parallels among the individual gods and goddesses.

6. An interesting study is the comparison of the story common to Scandinavian and German epic, told in the *Volsunga Saga* in the former and the *Song of the Nibelungs* in the latter language. Good brief accounts are given in Guerber's *Book of the Epic*. See also selection on page 420. Modern reappearances of the heroes are in William Morris' *Sigurd the Volsung* and Wagner's " Ring " operas.

HEIMSKRINGLA

The Sagas were family histories, which the Icelanders cherished dearly because of their strong family pride and their love of doughty heroism. The term *saga* has long been familiar to English readers and appears in several titles, ranging from Longfellow's " The Saga of King Olaf," which is a poetic adaptation of an Old Norse story, to Galsworthy's *The Forsyte*

Saga, which has nothing to do with the Scandinavians but gives an English family history.

Countless Icelandic Sagas have been found, some anonymous, others with definite names attached. Snorri Sturluson, author of the Prose Edda, is also responsible for two of the best sagas — *Heimskringla* (*Circuit of the World*), which gives a detailed and comparatively accurate history of old Norse kings, and *Volsunga Saga*, the story of Sigurd, best known to most Americans in its German form because of Wagner's operas. Some maintain, however, that though the characters in these operas are German in name, they are in spirit more closely akin with the shadowy but powerful Norse figures than with the more humanized persons of the *Song of the Nibelungs*.

The great significance of *Heimskringla* is that it is the first historical document in a Teutonic language to go beyond mere chronology and show cause and effect, kingly responsibility and social significance of events.

The following dialogue from *Heimskringla* shows its frequent dramatic power. The two brothers here pictured were the sons of King Magnus Barefoot of the eleventh century. When the father was killed in Iceland, the kingdom, instead of descending to one heir as in England, was given to the joint rule of his three sons, Eystein the eldest being only fourteen. The youngest child soon died, but Eystein and Sigurd ruled jointly for many years. The two men were entirely different types. Eystein was of medium size, blue-eyed, handsome, good-natured and highly intelligent, with a special gift for law and government. Sigurd, on the other hand, was tall and athletic, red-haired, homely, and though generous and upright, he had a morose disposition which developed into actual insanity toward the end of his life. When the whole of Europe was aroused to unite with the First Crusade, it was natural that Sigurd should go to Palestine at the head of sixty ships and ten thousand warriors, while Eystein stayed home to govern the country. He proved an excellent organizer and his reign was one of the most benign and prosperous the country had ever known.

The difference in the two brothers was bound to result in strained relations between them after Sigurd's return. Remember in reading this passage that boasting bouts were a favorite amusement among early Norse heroes. It was no more bad taste at that time to outdo your opponent in recounting achievements, than it would be today to beat him in a game of golf.

KING EYSTEIN AND KING SIGURD

King Eystein and King Sigurd went both in spring to guest-quarters in the Uplands; and each was entertained in a separate house, and the houses were not very distant from each other. The bonder,[1] however, thought it more convenient that both should be entertained together by turns in each house; and thus they were both at first in the house of King Eystein. But in the evening, when the people began to drink, the ale was not good; so that the guests were very quiet and still. Then said King Eystein, " Why are the people so silent? It is more usual in drinking parties that people are merry, so let us fall upon some jest over our ale that will amuse people; for surely, brother Sigurd, all people are well pleased when they talk cheerfully."

Sigurd replies, bluntly, " Do you talk as much as you please, but give me leave to be silent."

Eystein says, " It is a common custom over the ale-table to compare one person with another, and now let us do so." Then Sigurd was silent.

" I see," says King Eystein, " that I must begin this amusement. Now I will take thee, brother, to compare myself with, and will make it appear so as if we had both equal reputation and property, and that there is no difference in our birth and education."

Then King Sigurd replies, " Do you remember that I was always able to throw you on your back, when I pleased, although you are a year older? "

Then King Eystein replied, " But I remember that you were not so good at the games which require agility."

Sigurd: " Do you remember that I could drag you under water, when we swam together, as often as I pleased? "

Eystein: " But I could swim as far as you, and could dive as well as you; and I could skate so well that nobody could beat me, and you could no more do it than an ox."

Sigurd: " Methinks it is a more useful and suitable accomplishment for a chief to be expert at his bow; and I think you could scarcely draw my bow, even if you took your foot to help."

Eystein: " I am not strong at the bow as you are, but there is less difference between our shooting at a target; and I can run on ski much better than you, and in former times that was held a great accomplishment."

Sigurd: " It appears to me much better for a chief who is to be the superior of other men, that he is conspicuous in a crowd, and strong and powerful in weapons above other men; easily seen, and easily known, where there are many together."

Eystein: " It is not less a distinction and an ornament that a man

---

[1] **bonder**: farmers.

is of a handsome appearance, so as to be easily known from others on that account; and this appears to me to suit a chief best, because the best ornament is allied to beauty. I am moreover more knowing in the law than you, and on every subject my words flow more easily than yours."

Sigurd: "It may be that you know more law-quirks, for I have something else to do: neither will any deny you a smooth tongue. But there are many who say that your words are not to be trusted; that what you promise is little to be regarded; and that you talk just according to what those who are about you say, which is not kingly."

Eystein: "This is because, when people bring their cases before me, I wish first to give every man that satisfaction in his affair which he desires; but afterwards comes the opposite party, and then there is something to be given or taken away very often, in order to mediate between them, so that both may be satisfied. It often happens too that I promise whatever is desired of me, that all may be joyful about me. It would be an easy matter for me to do as you do — to promise evil to all; and I never hear any complain of your not keeping this promise to them."

Sigurd: "It is the conversation of all that the expedition I made out of the country was a princely expedition, while you in the meantime sat at home like your father's daughter."

Eystein: "Now you betake yourself to your cudgel. I would not have brought up this conversation if I had not known what to reply on this point. I can truly say that I equipped you from home like a sister, before you went upon this expedition."

Sigurd: "You must have heard that on this expedition I was in many a battle in the Saracens' land, and gained the victory in all; and you must have heard of the many valuable articles I acquired, the like of which were never seen before in this country, and I was the most respected wherever the most gallant men were; and, on the other hand, you cannot conceal that you have only a home-bred reputation. I went to Palestine, and I came to Apulia; but I did not see you there, brother. I gave Roger the Great the title of king; I won seven battles and you were in none of them. I was at our Lord's grave; but did not see you there, my brother. On this expedition I went all the way to Jordan, where our Lord was baptized, and swam across the river; but did not see you there. On the edge of the river-bank there was a bush of willows, and there I twisted a knot of willows which is waiting you there; for I said this knot thou shouldst untie, and fulfil the vow,[2] brother, that is bound up in it."

Eystein: "It is but little I have to set up against this. I have heard that you had several battles abroad, but it was more useful for the country what I was doing in the meantime here at home. In the north at Vaage I built fish-houses, so that all the poor people could earn a livelihood, and support themselves. I built there a priest's house, and endowed a church, where before all the people almost were heathen; and on this account I think all these people will remember that Eystein was once king of Norway. The road from Drontheim goes over the Dovrefjelds, and many people had to sleep out of doors, and made a very severe journey; but I built hospices, and supported them with money; and all travelers know that Eystein has been king in Norway. Out at Agdaness was a barren waste, and no harbor, and many a ship was lost there; and now there is a good harbor, and ship-station, and a church also built there. Then I raised beacons on all the high fjelds,[3] of which all the people in the interior enjoy the benefit. In Bergen I built a royal hall, and the church of the Apostles, with a stair between the two; so that all the kings who come after me will remember my name. I built Michael's church, and founded a monastery beside it. I settled the laws, brother, so that every man can obtain justice from his fellow-man; and according as these are observed the country will be the better governed. I raised a tower in the sound of Sinsholm.[4] The Jemteland people are again joined to this kingdom, and more by prudence and kind words than by force and war. Now although all this that I have reckoned up be but small doings, yet I am not sure if the people of the country have not been better served by it than by your killing bluemen[5] for the devil in the land of the Saracens, and sending them to hell. Now if you prize yourself on your good deeds, I think the places I have raised for chaste people of God will serve me not less for my soul's salvation. So if you tied a knot for me, I will not go to untie it; and if I had been inclined to tie a knot for thee, thou wouldst not have been king of Norway at my return to this country, when with a single ship thou camest into my fleet.

---

2 **vow:** Making a vow to accomplish some devout act was common in the Middle Ages. Here it has the force of a challenge or dare.

3 **fjelds:** hills or promontories.

4 **Sinsholm:** This is the only one of the localities mentioned which cannot be identified. The tower was probably a lighthouse.

5 **bluemen:** a common Scandinavian way of designating dark-skinned races, much as we say "blacks."

Now let men of understanding judge what thou hast above me, and thou wilt discover that here in Norway there are men equal to thee." Thereupon both were silent, and there was anger on both sides. More things passed between the brothers, from which it appeared that each of them would be greater than the other; however, peace was preserved between them as long as they lived.

(*Samuel Laing*)

SUGGESTIONS FOR STUDY

1. With which of the two brothers do your sympathies lie? Is this because your own interests tend in that direction? Do we find similar types among rulers today? Give examples. What two types of college students might be represented by these two brothers? Discuss.

2. Point out how this dialogue is a comment on the whole philosophy of government as well as an allegory of life. Link it to present-day problems.

3. Write a similar dialogue between two modern men, either well-known characters, or college students. Assume for the time being that boasting is socially permissible.

4. Would you recommend boasting bouts as a social pastime? In what ways do men match themselves against each other today? Do these have advantages or disadvantages compared with boasting? Is boasting really a defunct art?

5. Where in *Beowulf* and other older literature do we find heroes proclaiming their achievements in competition? How does Sigurd resemble Richard I of England?

Old Ballads

The great wealth of old Danish balladry might have been lost to the modern world had it not been for a heavy snowstorm. It happened in 1586 that Queen Sophia of Denmark was forced by this storm to spend some days in the little town of Knutstrup. Here she passed the time in conversation with the pastor, Andrew Söffrensön, a man of great literary learning. One of their conversations turned on the subject of Danish ballads, which had never been assembled and put in print. As a result of the Queen's interest, the pastor edited a collection of a hundred ballads. A century later this collection was reëdited and doubled by another clergyman, and ever since, the number of printed ballads has been increasing, until now Denmark has one of the richest ballad collections in Europe. Sweden also has an extensive balladry. Norwegian literature tends more toward the prose folk tale.

Though these old poems remind one in many ways of the Scottish ballads, yet they have a distinct quality of their own. They put more emphasis on battle, and on mythical creatures such as trolls, dragons, serpents, and giants, but they also show pictures of actual men and women with their loves and joys and sorrows. Many of these ballads grew out of the social order of chivalry of the middle ages when the ring dance became fashionable both in the castle and on the village green. The leader singing the stanza summoned dancers, a few at a time, into the central ring. The refrain which often had nothing to do with the story was sung by the entire group as they danced in a circle. Such a refrain is illustrated in the following ballad, and would have been sung at the end of each stanza.

This ballad has a particularly modern note in the expressed independence of the girl. Kerstin is a favorite character in Danish ballads reappearing again and again. Whether these stories are all based on some one legendary Kerstin, or whether that was simply a common girl's name (modern Christine) it is hard to say.

SPEECH AND REJOINDER

A DANISH BALLAD

Many a fair young gentleman
Was seated at the Queen's board,
And they fell into pleasant converse
With many a jesting word.
Under the linden-tree you shall await me.   5

They did not talk of churches,
Of convents nought they said;
But they talked of lady-mothers
Who daughters had to wed.
Under the linden-tree you shall await me.   10

Then spake the gay Sir Peter,
So proudly and off-hand:
" I will have the maiden
Who has both house and land.

" I will have the maiden   15
Who sews silk-work so neat.
She will I never marry
Who gads about the street!

" I will have the maiden
Who the table well can lay;   20
She will I never marry
Who has too much to say! "

There sate the lovely maidens,
And never spake a word,
None save the little Kerstin   25
Who waited at the Queen's board.

" If I were grown a woman,
And lovers came to woo,
So help me, God in heaven,
I never would marry you!   30

" To sit alone in my chamber
And sew, and shape so neat,
Whilst you on your horse went riding
All up and down the street.

" To sit alone in my chamber   35
And duly the table lay
Whilst you stood up in the diet,
Yet had not a word to say.

" To go alone in my chamber
And set the chairs by the wall,   40
Whilst you sate with lords and princes,
Yet had not a thought at all! "

With that uprose Sir Peter,
The words were quick to his tongue:
" Now I have found the maiden   45
Whom I have sought so long! "

In the Queen's court was there rejoicing,
And merriment great beside;
The Queen gave away the maiden,
Sir Peter from her took his bride.   50
Under the linden-tree you shall await me.

(*William and Mary Howitt*)

37. **diet:** legislative assembly.

THE ROYAL CHILDREN

A SWEDISH BALLAD

I went forth on a Midsummer day,
When the grass and flowers spring;
And the King's daughter was plighting her faith
With the handsome son of a King.

" Ah! how shall I come to thee again, 5
For the way is hard to trace? "
" We will put a light in the lanthorn,
When thou swimmest to this place."

It was the wicked witch-woman,
She heard each word was said; 10
" And I'll make an end of all your love
Ere many hours shall have fled."

It was the wicked witch-woman,
God grant she come to no good;
She put out the light in the lanthorn, 15
And the King's son sank in the flood.

The maiden clothed her in scarlet-white,
Likewise in the scarlet-blue;
Then up she went to the chamber high,
Where her father slept, she knew. 20

" And hearken now, dear father of mine,
To what I say this night;
And let me unto the garden go,
To pluck the lilies white."

" And if thou wilt go to the garden, 25
To pluck the lilies each one,
So take thy youngest sister with thee,
That thou go not alone."

" My youngest sister she is so small,
That little to her is known; 30
She plucks up the weeds and the lilies alike,
And leaves the grass alone.

7. **lanthorn:** lantern.

" And hearken now, dear father of mine,
And hearken to me this night;
May I go down to the wild sea-shore,　　　　　　　35
To pluck the lilies white? "

" If thou wilt go to the wild sea-shore,
To pluck the lilies each one,
Then take with thee thy youngest brother,
That thou go not alone."　　　　　　　　　40

" My youngest brother he is so little,
He nothing can understand;
He will shoot at all the little birds
That come to the wild sea-strand."

The maiden clothed her in scarlet-white,　　　45
Likewise in the scarlet-dun;
And down she went to the wild sea-shore,
Where a fisherman sate alone.

" And hearken to me, thou good fisherman,
And give me answer true;　　　　　　　50
Hast thou not seen a King's own son
Lying dead on the waters blue? "

" Here have I fished through the live-long night,
Here have I fished with care,
And here have I found the King's noble son,　55
Nor ever saw corpse so fair.

" His stockings were worked with silver,
His shoes were buckled with gold;
And, so sure as God is in heaven,
He smiled with his lips so cold! "　　　　　60

The maiden took the corpse in her arms,
And kissed it with lips so red;
A sorrowful sight was it to see
The two on the earth lie dead.

　　　　　　　　　　　(*William and Mary Howitt*)

SUGGESTIONS FOR STUDY

1. How does " The Royal Children " resemble the Greek story of Hero and Leander?

2. How do these ballads show that human nature was much the same in medieval times as today? Which of the two ballads sounds more modern?

3. Wherein do these ballads resemble the old English and Scottish ballads? Review typical ballad measure, and find out whether these depart from it in any way. Compare them with the Spanish ballads (page 240) and the German ballads (page 427) as to vigor, rapid movement, use of conversation, type of story.

The Folk Tale

With the great romantic movement of the early nineteenth century and the patriotic impetus of a new independent government, the Norwegians fervently pursued the study of their past literature. One of the important milestones in the study was the publication of Norwegian fairy and folk tales by two friends, Asbjörnsen and Moe, who did for Norway what the Grimm Brothers had done for Germany. Peter Asbjörnsen and Jörgen Moe became acquainted at school in their middle teens. Financial reverses in both families separated them, but after an interval of several years they came together again and developed common interest in the problem of folk lore. In 1841 they published the first small volume of fairy tales, which met with such approbation, including that of the Grimm Brothers, that they decided to continue making additions in each of the next three years, and a complete revision in 1851. This has remained the standard collection of Norwegian folk tales, and has had pronounced influence on the literature of the country ever since.

Rich with the color of the mountains and woods, teeming with the mythological creations of primitive minds, and simmering with the racy humor of the peasant, these stories are classics of their kind. Their humor, especially, is illustrated by the following tale, so universal in its theme that by changing the housekeeping details we have the ingredients for a modern short comedy in the movies.

THE HUSBAND WHO WAS TO MIND THE HOUSE

Once on a time there was a man, so surly and cross he never thought his wife did anything right in the house. So, once evening, in hay-making time, he came home, scolding and swearing, and showing his teeth and making a dust.

" Dear love, don't be so angry; there's a good man," said his goody;

"tomorrow let's change our work. I'll go out with the mowers and mow, and you shall mind the house at home."

Yes! the husband thought that would do very well. He was quite willing, he said.

So, early next morning, his goody took a scythe over her neck, and went out into the hay-field with the mowers, and began to mow; but the man was to mind the house, and do the work at home.

First of all, he wanted to churn the butter; but when he had churned a while, he got thirsty, and went down to the cellar to tap a barrel of ale. So, just when he had knocked in the bung, and was putting the tap into the cask, he heard overhead the pig come into the kitchen. Then off he ran up the cellar steps, with the tap in his hands, as fast as he could, to look after the pig, lest it should upset the churn; but when he got up, and saw the pig had already knocked the churn over, and stood there, rooting and grunting amongst the cream which was running all over the floor, he got so wild with rage that he quite forgot the ale-barrel, and ran at the pig as hard as he could. He caught it, too, just as it ran out of doors, and gave it such a kick, that piggy lay for dead on the spot. Then all at once he remembered he had the tap in his hand; but when he got down to the cellar, every drop of ale had run out of the cask.

Then he went into the dairy and found enough cream left to fill the churn again, and so he began to churn, for butter they must have at dinner. When he had churned a bit, he remembered that their milking cow was still shut up in the byre, and hadn't had a bit to eat or a drop to drink all the morning, though the sun was high. Then all at once he thought 'twas too far to take her down to the meadow, so he'd just get her up on the house-top — for the house, you must know, was thatched with sods, and a fine crop of grass was growing there. Now their house lay close up against a steep down, and he thought if he laid a plank across to the thatch at the back he'd easily get the cow up.

But still he couldn't leave the churn, for there was his little babe crawling about the floor, and "if I leave it," he thought, "the child is sure to upset it." So he took the churn on his back, and went out with it; but then he thought he'd better first water the cow before he turned her out on the thatch; so he took up a bucket to draw water out of the well; but as he stooped down at the well's brink, all the cream ran out of the churn over his shoulders, and so down into the well.

Now it was near dinner-time, and he hadn't even got the butter yet; so he thought he'd best boil the porridge, and filled the pot with water and hung it over the fire. When he had done that, he thought the cow might perhaps fall off the thatch and break her legs or her neck. So he got up on the house to tie her up. One end of the rope he made fast to the cow's neck and the other he slipped down the chimney and tied round his own thigh; and he had to make haste, for the water now began to boil in the pot, and he had still to grind the oatmeal.

So he began to grind away; but while he was hard at it, down fell the cow off the house-top after all, and as she fell, she dragged the man up the chimney by the rope. There he stuck fast; and as for the cow, she hung half-way down the wall, swinging between heaven and earth, for she could neither get down nor up.

And now the goody had waited seven lengths and seven breadths [1] for her husband to come and call them home to dinner; but never a call they had. At last she thought she'd waited long enough, and went home. But when she got there and saw the cow hanging in such an ugly place, she ran up and cut the rope in two with her scythe. But as she did this, down came her husband out of the chimney; and so when his old dame came inside the kitchen, there she found him standing on his head in the porridge pot.

(Sir G. W. Dasent)

SUGGESTIONS FOR STUDY

1. What do we learn from this tale of the mode of living and personality of Norwegian peasants?

2. Would this story lend itself to presentation on the stage or screen? Why or why not? Try writing a version either in narrative or dramatic form with the scene in a modern American home.

3. Read some of the Scandinavian folk tales dealing with trolls and other supernatural beings. Which do you enjoy more, the realistic or the fantastic tale? Why?

4. Compare this with the Spanish and German folk tales in this book What points of resemblance are evident?

[1] **seven lengths and seven breadths:** that is, across the field they were mowing.

Modern Danish Literature

ADAM GOTTLOB OEHLENSCHLÄGER (1779–1850)

Considered the greatest poet of Denmark, Oehlenschläger represents for that country the far-flung romantic tendency which gripped Europe at the beginning of the nineteenth century. As a boy he had an unusual life, for his father, an organist of German extraction, was made superintendent of the royal summer palace not far from the capital, Copenhagen. Here in the summer, according to his own account, young Adam admired the aristocracy with their elegant costumes; in the autumn he made friends with the swarm of bricklayers, carpenters, painters, and plumbers who came to refurnish the palace for the next season; and in the winter he roamed about the empty castle, building his own castles in the air. With his father he spent the long evenings reading before the fire, and estimated that he read about three hundred volumes before leaving the palace at the age of twelve to go to school.

During his school days he developed an ambition to go on the stage, but a short experience with acting convinced him that he had better drop it and study law at the university. But that too failed to win his heart, and largely through the influence of certain literary friends he began writing. His first poem, "The Golden Horns," was based on the theft from the Chamber of Arts of two antique golden drinking horns, which the thief melted down for their gold. The poet made his poem a plea for romance as opposed to materialism, and this is supposed to have opened up the whole romantic movement in Denmark. His great poetic dramas — *Aladdin*, based on the Arabian Nights story, *Hakon Jarl*, on an old Scandinavian legend, *Correggio*, on the life of the Italian painter — and dozens of other poems, long and short, show his versatility and virility.

Three times he narrowly escaped death, once by slipping into an Italian cataract, once by just missing the fall of a heavy piece of scenery in the theater, and once by stepping into a trapdoor. Throughout his life he traveled a great deal, and on one visit to Sweden he was formally crowned with laurel, in the Lund Cathedral, by the poet Tegnér, who hailed him "the northern king of song." More than anyone else he brought to life the old Scandinavian legends and established Danish national spirit.

SONG

Behind black woods the pale
Moonlight is sifting.
To God the nightingale
Her song is lifting.

The low tones float and linger,   5
Blend and expire,
And I hear the brook's white finger
Plucking her lyre.

In the wood there is one flower
Death has chosen;   10
(Soon, soon, perhaps, my hour!)
Its heart is frozen.
Let the last flower die.
From clods that smother
Its seeds, toward a fairer sky   15
Rises another.

O Darkness! perhaps soon
Here in the deathless
Path of thy summer moon,
I shall lie breathless.   20
Though the shadow of death is blue,
Smile, thou immortal!
And bear my last sigh through
Dawn's scarlet portal.

                              (*Robert Silliman Hillyer*)

SUGGESTIONS FOR STUDY

1. What elements of romanticism do you find in this poem?
2. Of what English or American poets of the early nineteenth century
are you reminded in reading it? Did you find poems in earlier sections of
this book written in the same general mood? If so, did they correspond
to this in the approximate time of writing?

HANS CHRISTIAN ANDERSEN (1805-1875)

" My life has been a lovely story, happy and full of incident." This
is the opening sentence of Hans Christian Andersen's autobiography, yet
many of the mere facts of his life sound unfortunate enough. His father
was a poor shoemaker of Odense on one of the Danish islands, his mother
an uneducated woman. The father died during his son's childhood and
the boy's education was obtained through friends and the public scholar-
ships for talented poor boys. He had theatrical ambitions but failed
miserably in his early attempts. One of his patrons ridiculed his peculiari-

ties of manner in a way unendurable to anyone as sensitive as Andersen always was. Yet in retrospect his life was a "lovely story" because he lived largely in the realm of his fancy and had the guileless and transparent nature of a child. He loved the excitement of travel and was constantly on the go. He loved to collect on every occasion little mementos, which his friends regarded as rubbish. He loved to interview great writers of all nations and boast about these acquaintances. He loved praise and shrank from the slightest censure. Like a child he was naïvely egocentric. Because he was child-in-man he could write fairy tales as no one else in the world could, and that is why every nation has translated them and read them, so that no Danish writer is known abroad so well as Hans Christian Andersen. Of course, being ambitious, he wrote romances and poetic dramas and comedies and operas and travel books and his autobiography, but except for the last, which reveals his unique personality, none of them count for much today. On his seventieth birthday Denmark gave him a celebration such as only a super-child should have — a public holiday, recognition from the royal family, a statue in Copenhagen to perpetuate his name. From the excitement of this day he never rallied, but died four months later.

THE EMPEROR'S NEW CLOTHES

Many of Andersen's tales are more than mere imaginative fancy, but have behind them a significance or a sly dig at human nature which would be far over the head of the child reader. That is why adults appreciate him and why his reputation outstrips that of the average writer for children. Such a tale is the one which follows — quaint and original, yet satirizing the pretenses of sophisticated life and the social insecurity which makes people afraid of the truth. Andersen himself in his view of life is like the boy at the end of the story, without guile, without repression.

Many years ago there lived an Emperor, who was so excessively fond of grand new clothes that he spent all his money upon them, that he might be very fine. He did not care about his soldiers, nor about the theater, and only liked to drive out and show his new clothes. He had a coat for every hour of the day; and just as they say of a king, " He is in council," so they always said of him, " The Emperor is in the wardrobe."

In the great city in which he lived it was always very merry; every day came many strangers; one day two rogues came: they gave themselves out as weavers, and declared they could weave the finest stuff any one could imagine. Not only were their colors and patterns, they said, uncommonly beautiful, but the clothes made of the stuff possessed the wonderful quality that they became invisible to any one who was unfit for the office he held, or was incorrigibly stupid.

" Those would be capital clothes! " thought the Emperor. " If I wore those, I should be able to find out what men in my empire are not fit for the places they have; I could tell the clever from the dunces. Yes, the stuff must be woven for me directly! "

And he gave the two rogues a great deal of cash in hand, that they might begin their work at once.

As for them, they put up two looms, and pretended to be working; but they had nothing at all on their looms. They at once demanded the finest silk and the costliest gold; this they put into their own pockets, and worked at the empty looms till late into the night.

" I should like to know how far they have got on with the stuff," thought the Emperor. But he felt quite uncomfortable when he thought that those who were not fit for their offices could not see it. He believed, indeed, that he had nothing to fear for himself, but yet he preferred first to send someone else to see how matters stood. All the people in the city knew what peculiar power the stuff possessed, and all were anxious to see how bad or how stupid their neighbors were.

" I will send my honest old Minister to the weavers," thought the Emperor. " He can judge best how the stuff looks, for he has sense, and no one understands his office better than he."

Now the good old Minister went out into the hall where the two rogues sat working at the empty looms.

" Mercy on us! " thought the old Minister, and he opened his eyes wide. " I cannot see anything at all! " But he did not say this.

Both the rogues begged him to be so good as to come nearer, and asked if he did not approve of the colors and the pattern. Then they pointed to the empty loom, and the poor old Minister went on opening his eyes; but he could see nothing, for there was nothing to see.

" Mercy! " thought he, " can I indeed be so stupid? I never thought that, and not a soul must know it. Am I not fit for my office? No, it will never do for me to tell that I could not see the stuff."

" Don't you say anything to it? " asked one, as he went on weaving.

" Oh, it is charming — quite enchanting! " answered the old Minister, as he peered through his spectacles. " What a fine pattern, and what colors! Yes, I shall tell the Emperor that I am very much pleased with it."

" Well, we are glad of that," said both weavers; and then they named the colors, and explained the strange pattern. The old Minister listened attentively, that he might be able to repeat it when the Emperor came. And he did so.

Now the rogues asked for more money, and silk and gold, which they declared they wanted for weaving. They put all into their own pockets, and not a thread was put upon the loom; they continued to work at the empty frames as before.

The Emperor soon sent again, dispatching another honest officer of the court, to see how the weaving was going on, and if the stuff would soon be ready. He fared just like the first: he looked and looked, but, as there was nothing to be seen but the empty looms, he could see nothing.

" Is not that a pretty piece of stuff? " asked the two rogues; and they displayed and explained the handsome pattern which was not there at all.

" I am not stupid! " thought the man: " it must be my good office, for which I am not fit. It is funny enough, but I must not let it be noticed." And so he praised the stuff which he did not see, and expressed his pleasure at the beautiful colors and charming pattern. " Yes, it is enchanting," he told the Emperor.

All the people in the town were talking of the gorgeous stuff. The Emperor wished to see it himself while it was still upon the loom. With a whole crowd of chosen men, among whom were also the two honest statesmen who had already been there, he went to the two cunning rogues, who were now weaving with might and main without fiber or thread.

" Is not that splendid? " said the two statesmen, who had already been there once. " Does not your majesty remark the pattern and the colors? " And they pointed to the empty loom, for they thought that the others could see the stuff.

" What's this? " thought the Emperor. " I can see nothing at all! That is terrible. Am I stupid? Am I not fit to be Emperor? That would be the most dreadful thing that could happen to me. Oh, it is very pretty!" he said aloud. " It has our highest approbation." And he nodded in a contented way, and gazed at the empty loom, for he would not say that he saw nothing. The whole suite whom he had with him looked and looked, and saw nothing, any more than the rest; but, like the Emperor, they said, " That is pretty! " and counseled him to wear the splendid new clothes for the first time at the great procession that was presently to take place. " It is splendid, excellent! " went from mouth to mouth. On all sides there seemed to be general rejoicing, and the Emperor gave the rogues the title of Imperial Court Weavers.

The whole night before the morning on which the procession was to take place, the rogues were up, and kept more than sixteen candles burning. The people could see that they were hard at work, completing the Emperor's new clothes. They pretended to take the stuff down from the loom; they made cuts in the air with great scissors; they sewed with needles without thread; and at last they said, " Now the clothes are ready! "

The Emperor came himself with his noblest cavaliers; and the two rogues lifted up one arm as if they were holding something, and said, " See, here are the trousers! here is the coat! here is the cloak! " and so on. " It is as light as a spider's web: one would think one had nothing on; but that is just the beauty of it."

" Yes," said all the cavaliers; but they could not see anything, for nothing was there.

" Will your Imperial Majesty please to condescend to take off your clothes? " said the rogues; " then we will put on you the new clothes here in front of the great mirror."

The Emperor took off his clothes, and the rogues pretended to put on him each new garment as it was ready; and the Emperor turned round and round before the mirror.

" Oh, how well they look! how capitally they fit! " said all. " What a pattern! what colors! That *is* a splendid dress! "

" They are standing outside with the canopy which is to be borne above your Majesty in the procession! " announced the head Master of the Ceremonies.

" Well, I am ready," replied the Emperor. " Does it not suit me well? " And then he turned again to the mirror, for he wanted it to appear as if he contemplated his adornment with great interest.

The two chamberlains, who were to carry the train, stooped down with their hands towards the floor, just as if they were picking up the mantle; then they pretended to be holding something in the air. They did not dare to let it be noticed that they saw nothing.

So the Emperor went in procession under the rich canopy and every one in the streets said, " How incomparable are the Emperor's new clothes! what a train he has to his mantle! how it fits him! " No one would let it be perceived that he could see nothing, for that would have shown that he was not fit for his office, or was very stupid. No clothes of the Emperor's had ever had such a success as these.

" But he has nothing on! " a little child cried out at last.

" Just hear what the innocent says! " said the father; and ᴜᴎe whispered to another what the child had said.

" But he has nothing on! " said the whole people at length. That touched the Emperor, for it seemed to him that they were right; but he thought within himself, " I must go through with the procession." And so he held himself a little higher, and the chamberlains held on tighter than ever, and carried the train which did not exist at all.

(Mrs. Edward Lucas)

SUGGESTIONS FOR STUDY

ɪ. What human traits are satirized in this story? Is the point of the story still applicable today? Discuss.

2. What in this story could not be fully appreciated by the child reader? Why not?

3. Try to condense the point of the story into a wise saying which could be put at the end in the style of the fable.

4. Read others of Andersen's Tales, especially "The Ugly Duckling," which has autobiographical interest. How do they differ from the ordinary run of fairy or folk tales? Have you observed anything comparable to them in the other sections of this book?

5. The names of Hans Christian Andersen and the Grimm Brothers are often associated. In what ways did their work show a marked difference? What Scandinavians are a better parallel to the Grimms in their literary contributions?

HOLGER DRACHMANN (1846–1908)

Outstanding among the young writers who were influenced by the critic Georg Brandes is Holger Drachmann, a vivid personality and versatile writer of novels, plays, and most important of all, lyric poetry. Drachmann's father was a navy physician, and the inherited sea fever showed itself in the son's early career as a marine painter of talent. This interest took him on a trip around the British Isles. Here he faced for the first time the poverty and misery of the London dock district and became a radical social reformer. The influence of Brandes's lectures fanned his new enthusiasm into poetry. His long poem, *English Socialists*, with its graphic detail and vigorous style made the public aware of a new light on the literary horizon. Two volumes of poetry were followed by two novels, a book of travels, a fairy-tale poem, an epic, and numerous short stories of sailor life, then three more volumes of poetry, all within the decade of the seventies. The eighties brought forth a long fairy poem, a fairy comedy, *Once upon a Time,* still popular in Denmark, an Oriental play, two novels, and two more volumes of lyrics. He continued producing actively up to 1904, and his last fragments of poems were published posthumously. He was one of the most prolific writers Denmark has known, and at the end of the century was hailed as the poet-king of the nation.

Drachmann was effervescent of disposition, moved by numerous enthusiasms, and full of creative fervor. He sang like the ancient skalds. He loved freedom, individualism, the heroic. His poems were often careless and buoyant, never wooden and banal. He translated Byron and admired Rousseau. Like both of them, he never quite lost sight of himself as the center of interest about which his art gravitated.

VALBORG SONG

Hello there! take your ragged hat
Old as the hills and tattered,
Toss it up to the ceiling first,
Then down to the floor, well battered.
High to fly, — that's all we know   5
When Pegasus is saddled,
But the vicious ass soon throws you off,
He's old and his brains are addled.
And tomorrow is Valborg's Day!

Whoa! hold still there, little horse!   10
You've been standing too long idle.
Once mounted I'll ride to Heaven's Inn
And throw the porter the bridle.
The sun is shining and clear as a gem,
Clouds melt as the day grows older; —   15
" Well, well," says the porter, " and whom have we here
With a fiddle slung from his shoulder! "
And tomorrow is Valborg's Day!

Fiddler I am by bent and trade,
But I borrowed these and my fine old hat,   20
As for strings, I don't own any,
For I haven't a single penny.

6. **Pegasus:** in Greek mythology, the winged horse symbolizing poetic inspiration.   9. **Valborg's Day:** Danish festival on May 1, in honor of St. Walpurgis, an English princess who became head of a convent in Swabia, and died about 780.

My fiddle dangles in rose-red bands,
And my hat has a heron feather,
But I pawned to a Jew the clasp that held   25
The hat and the plume together.
And tomorrow is Valborg's Day!

My sweetheart tied the red ribbons on,
And behind my ear she kissed me;
I can hear her voice wherever I go,   30
Wherever the bypaths twist me.
A voice that whispers: flit far and wide,
And if you know the way there,
Fly even to Heaven's merry Inn, —
But don't forget me and stay there!   35
And tomorrow is Valborg's Day!

                        (*Robert Silliman Hillyer*)

LUDVIG HOLSTEIN (1864–   )

Reflecting the warmth and natural beauty of his native island of Southern Sealand, Holstein's many volumes of poetry show a mind at peace
with life. His first book of poems in 1895 was in its simple directness a
marked contrast to the prevalent affected style of that day. The next
year his romantic drama *Tove* reiterated the theme of the medieval
legends dear to the heart of all Danish poets. Almost twenty years of
silence followed, but the next five were marked by three volumes of lyrics
whose titles show Holstein's devotion to nature: *Leaves, Moss and Mould,
Apple Time*. So much of his poetry glows with the health-giving qualities
of sunlight and fresh air that the following little picture seems symbolical
of the man himself. He transmuted the commonplace into poet's gold.

SUNLIGHT IN THE ROOM

In my room the light and sprightly
Sunmotes leap and twinkle brightly;
Jacob's ladder climbs the glory
Of the sun king's territory.

Angels mounting, intertwining,   5
Where the million motes are shining;

3. **Jacob's ladder:** The sloping rays of the sun remind the poet of the
ladder sloping to heaven in Jacob's dream, Genesis 28:10–15.

Smoke from my cigar entangles
With its spiraled blue their spangles.

Look, the light glows through the ruddy
Red begonia; we could study   10
In those flowers and in those hairy
Leaves each vein and capillary.

All the picture frames conspire
To enkindle golden fire,
And the lampshade on the narrow   15
Shelf shoots out a ruby arrow.

Even the chair's green velvet cover,
Half in sun, half darkened over,
Is a forest-bounded meadow
Slowly yielding to the shadow.   20

You, my tiny wife, sit quiet
In the sunlight's playful riot,
Lulled by dusk, amused by fancies
Of these mutable romances.

(Robert Silliman Hillyer)

12. **capillary:** a tiny vein.

SUGGESTIONS FOR STUDY

1. Contrast the moods of " Valborg Day " and " Sunlight in the Room."
Point out specific details which create these moods. What poems in English do you know which show either of these moods?

2. Where do you find in these touches of originality which set them
off from other poems? Do you find lines in either of them which suggest
that they probably suffer in translation? If so, where?

Modern Norwegian Literature

HENRIK IBSEN (1828–1906)

Of all Norwegian writers, Ibsen has undoubtedly had the widest influence outside his own country. He is preëminently a world-figure, one of
the giants in the great renaissance of drama which swept Europe in the
late nineteenth century.

The first fifteen years of his life were spent at his birthplace, Skien, not far from the capital Kristiania.[1] The witty tongue of his Scandinavian father and the serious, meditative bent of his German mother can both be traced in the son, though in these early years the latter seemed the predominant trait. The boy spent much of his time in his own room, and a bond of genuine sympathy between him and his parents seemed lacking. At fifteen, he left his home to make his own way as a druggist's apprentice at Grimstad, a small town further south, and after that he apparently saw very little of his family. Later he continued his education at the capital in a strange Latin school commonly known as the "Student Factory" where older men and youths of all classes of society came for rapid preparation to enter the university. Here he became acquainted with Björnson, and the violinist Ole Bull. Through the latter he was given the position of instructor and dramatic author at the national theater at Bergen, with opportunity to study stage production in Copenhagen and Dresden, and so he gave up the idea of attending the university. The six years at Bergen were important not only in making him conversant with practical stage technique and launching him into actual dramatic writing, but also in acquainting him with the daughter of a Lutheran minister who later became his wife. Then for about seven years he was associated with theaters of Kristiania, or lived on small government pensions until he left Norway in disgust because his country had not stood by Denmark in her war with Germany. For more than twenty-five years (from 1864–1891) Ibsen stayed in various foreign countries, Italy being his favorite. Practically all of his important plays were written during the years of his voluntary exile and were acted in other countries before ever being presented in Norway. Only about four or five of his plays were written during the last fifteen years of his life, which he spent once more in Kristiania. By this time his fame abroad was assured; his fortune was reputed to be one of the greatest in Norway; and his position of honor among his countrymen, who had once looked askance at his plays, was completely established.

Ibsen's many dramas fall into three general groups. In his early years he was engrossed with national legend. The culmination of that interest comes in *Peer Gynt,* one of the major poetic dramas of the world's literature. The hero Peer Gynt irresponsible, extravagant, rollicking, and without aim or focus in his life finally returns to the faithful Solveig who has waited a lifetime for him. The beautiful suite, written for the play by Grieg containing such favorites as "Anitra's Dance" and "The Death of Ase," is one of the happy combinations of great music with great drama. Another poetic drama, *Brand,* picturing the opposite type of hero, the

---

[1] **Kristiania:** now Oslo. After Norway became independent of Denmark, in 1814, there was a growing demand to change the capital, which had been named for King Christian of Denmark, back to the old original name of Oslo. The official change, however, was not effective until 1925. Throughout this section, the name which was in current use at the time referred to is the one employed.

earnest, dogmatic man who demands " all or nothing " in every situation, is considered by some Ibsen's greatest play.

In the second period of his writing, he turns to the prose drama of social problems, and here we find the plays which brought Ibsen into the limelight of controversy, and which are his most permanent contribution to stage production, even though in some cases the theme is now rather out of date. Four major plays attacked various forms of hypocrisy. *The Pillars of Society* aimed at that which builds social position on a foundation of lies. *The Doll's House* opened up the question of woman's relation to her home and to society at large, and aroused a torrent of argument especially in England. *Ghosts* with its unvarnished treatment of heredity brought down much abusive language on the head of the author. *An Enemy of the People* was an answer to his opponents in showing the evils of concealing hidden sources of corruption. Then strangely enough in his next play *The Wild Duck* he turned against his previous themes and presented the tragedy resulting from undue insistence on truth telling.

After that he turned from social problems to plays of personal tragedy, many of which tended to become overly symbolical and difficult to interpret. Of these *Hedda Gabler* is one of the best known and most adaptable to stage presentation.

Ibsen has been widely studied in America especially in those states where the Scandinavian population is large. Both professional companies and amateur college groups have essayed a number of different Ibsen plays in recent years. The modern theater-goer is astounded to think what storms of vituperation were aroused by these dramas in the eighties and nineties.

AN ENEMY OF THE PEOPLE

No ghosts haunting deserted castles ever caused such consternation as Ibsen's *Ghosts,* where the evil forces of heredity haunted the life of a certain family. Especially in England, but also in Norway, the press outdid itself in heaping abuse upon a man who would discuss such subjects on the stage. Unpleasant though the play is, a person of today on reading the criticisms of half a century ago finds it hard to understand the evidently sincere horror expressed in those days. So far have the last fifty years brought us in frankness of discussion. Ibsen, in spite of all his independence, was not indifferent to this criticism. His method of turning the other cheek was to turn out another play. The critics could slap it if they wished, but their hands would tingle with the blow. So in *An Enemy of the People,* which came out the next year, the hero is really Ibsen in disguise, and the resentment of the townspeople at the Doctor's revelation of the corruption in the springs which fed their prosperity, represents the agitation of a much larger world at the author's revelations.

It is interesting to see what Ibsen himself has to say in two letters to

Georg Brandes about the play. The first was written a few months before its appearance, the second a few months after:

1. "Björnson says: 'The majority is always right.' And as a practical politician he is bound, I suppose, to say so. I, on the contrary, must of necessity say: 'The minority is always right.' Naturally I am not thinking of the minority of stagnationists who are left behind by the great middle party which with us is called Liberal; but I mean that minority which leads the van, and pushes on to points which the majority has not yet reached. I mean: That man is right who has allied himself most closely with the future."

2. "I maintain that a fighter in the intellectual vanguard can never collect a majority round him. In ten years the majority will, possibly, occupy the standpoint which Dr. Stockmann held at the public meeting. But during these ten years the Doctor will not have been standing still; he will still be at least ten years ahead of the majority. He can never have the majority with him. As regards myself, at least, I am conscious of incessant progression. At the point where I stood when I wrote each of my books, there now stands a tolerably compact crowd; but I myself am no longer there; I am elsewhere; farther ahead, I hope."

And so he was — always a step beyond the majority.

DRAMATIS PERSONAE

DR. THOMAS STOCKMANN, *Medical Officer of the Municipal Baths*

MRS. STOCKMANN, *his wife*

PETRA, *their daughter, a teacher*

EJLIF } *their sons (aged*
MORTEN } *thirteen and ten respectively)*

PETER STOCKMANN, *the Doctor's elder brother; Mayor of the Town and Chief Constable, Chairman of the Baths' Committee, etc., etc.*

MORTEN KIIL, *a tanner (Mrs. Stockmann's adoptive father)*

HOVSTAD, *editor of the* People's Messenger

BILLING, *sub-editor*

CAPTAIN HORSTER

ASLAKSEN, *a printer*

Men of various conditions and occupations, some few women, and a troop of schoolboys — the audience at a public meeting.

The action takes place in a coast town in southern Norway.

ACT I

SCENE. DR. STOCKMANN'S *sitting room. It is evening. The room is plainly but neatly appointed and furnished. In the right-hand wall are two doors; the farther leads out to the hall, the nearer to the doctor's study. In the left-hand wall, opposite the door leading to the hall, is a door leading to the other rooms occupied by the family. In the middle of the same wall stands the stove,[1] and, farther forward, a couch with a looking-glass hanging over it and an oval table in front of it. On the table, a lighted lamp, with a lamp-shade. At the back of the room, an open door leads to the dining room.*

BILLING *is seen sitting at the dining table, on which a lamp is burning. He has a napkin tucked under his chin, and* MRS. STOCKMANN *is standing by the table handing him a large plateful of roast beef. The other places at the table are empty, and the table somewhat in disorder, a meal having evidently recently been finished.*

Mrs. Stockmann. You see, if you come an hour late, Mr. Billing, you have to put up with cold meat.

Billing. [*As he eats*] It is uncommonly good, thank you — remarkably good.

Mrs. Stockmann. My husband makes such a point of having his meals punctually, you know —

Billing. That doesn't affect me a bit. Indeed, I almost think I enjoy a meal all the better when I can sit down and eat all by myself and undisturbed.

Mrs. Stockmann. Oh, well, as long as you are enjoying it — [*Turns to the hall door, listening.*] I expect that is Mr. Hovstad coming, too.

Billing. Very likely.

PETER STOCKMANN *comes in. He wears an overcoat and his official hat, and carries a stick.*

Peter Stockmann. Good evening, Katherine.

Mrs. Stockmann. [*Coming forward into the sitting room*] Ah, good evening — is it you? How good of you to come up and see us!

Peter Stockmann. I happened to be passing, and so — [*Looks into the dining room.*] But you have company with you, I see.

Mrs. Stockmann. [*A little embarrassed*] Oh, no — it was quite by chance he came in. [*Hurriedly*] Won't you come in and have something, too?

Peter Stockmann. I! No, thank you. Good gracious — hot meat at night![2] Not with my digestion.

---

[1] stove: The Scandinavian stove is a tall porcelain structure often beautifully colored, standing close to the wall, more like a high mantel than a typical American stove.

[2] hot meat at night: Dinner was eaten in the middle of the day.

Mrs. Stockmann. Oh, but just once in a way —

Peter Stockmann. No, no, my dear lady; I stick to my tea and bread and butter. It is much more wholesome in the long run — and a little more economical, too.

Mrs. Stockmann. [*Smiling*] Now you mustn't think that Thomas and I are spendthrifts.

Peter Stockmann. Not you, my dear; I would never think that of you. [*Points to the Doctor's study.*] Is he not at home?

Mrs. Stockmann. No, he went out for a little turn after supper — he and the boys.

Peter Stockmann. I doubt if that is a wise thing to do. [*Listens.*] I fancy I hear him coming now.

Mrs. Stockmann. No, I don't think it is he. [*A knock is heard at the door.*] Come in! [HOVSTAD *comes in from the hall.*] Oh, it is you, Mr. Hovstad!

Hovstad. Yes, I hope you will forgive me, but I was delayed at the printer's. Good evening, Mr. Mayor.

Peter Stockmann. [*Bowing a little distantly*] Good evening. You have come on business, no doubt.

Hovstad. Partly. It's about an article for the paper.

Peter Stockmann. So I imagined. I hear my brother has become a prolific contributor to the *People's Messenger*.

Hovstad. Yes, he is good enough to write in the *People's Messenger* when he has any home truths to tell.

Mrs. Stockmann. [*To* HOVSTAD] But won't you — ? [*Points to the dining room.*]

Peter Stockmann. Quite so, quite so. I don't blame him in the least, as a writer, for addressing himself to the quarters where he will find the readiest sympathy. And, besides that, I personally have no reason to bear any ill will to your paper, Mr. Hovstad.

Hovstad. I quite agree with you.

Peter Stockmann. Taking one thing with another, there is an excellent spirit of toleration in the town — an admirable municipal spirit. And it all springs from the fact of our having a great common interest to unite us — an interest that is in an equally high degree the concern of every right-minded citizen —

Hovstad. The Baths, yes.

Peter Stockmann. Exactly — our fine, new, handsome Baths. Mark my words, Mr. Hovstad — the Baths will become the focus of our municipal life! Not a doubt of it!

Mrs. Stockmann. That is just what Thomas says.

Peter Stockmann. Think how extraordinarily the place has developed within the last year or two! Money has been flowing in, and there is some life and business doing in the town. Houses and landed property are rising in value every day.

Hovstad. And unemployment is diminishing.

Peter Stockmann. Yes, that is another thing. The burden of the poor rates has been lightened, to the great relief of the propertied classes; and that relief will be even greater if only we get a really good summer this year, and lots of visitors — plenty of invalids, who will make the Baths talked about.

Hovstad. And there is a good prospect of that, I hear.

Peter Stockmann. It looks very promising. Inquiries about apartments and that sort of thing are reaching us every day.

Hovstad. Well, the doctor's article will come in very suitably.

Peter Stockmann. Has he been writing something just lately?

Hovstad. This is something he wrote in the winter; a recommendation of the Baths — an account of the excellent sanitary conditions here. But I held the article over, temporarily.

Peter Stockmann. Ah — some little difficulty about it, I suppose?

Hovstad. No, not at all; I thought it would be better to wait till the spring, because it is just at this time that people begin to think seriously about their summer quarters.

Peter Stockmann. Quite right; you were perfectly right, Mr. Hovstad.

Hovstad. Yes, Thomas is really indefatigable when it is a question of the Baths.

Peter Stockmann. Well — remember, he is the Medical Officer to the Baths.

Hovstad. Yes, and what is more, they owe their existence to him.

Peter Stockmann. To him? Indeed! It is true I have heard from time to time that some people are of that opinion. At the same time I must say I imagined that I took a modest part in the enterprise.

Mrs. Stockmann. Yes, that is what Thomas is always saying.

Hovstad. But who denies it, Mr. Stockmann? You set the thing going and made a practical concern of it; we all know that. I only meant that the idea of it came first from the doctor.

Peter Stockmann. Oh, ideas — yes! My brother has had plenty of them in his time — unfortunately. But when it is a question of putting an idea into practical shape, you have to apply to a man of different mettle, Mr. Hovstad. And I certainly should have thought that in this house at least —

Mrs. Stockmann. My dear Peter —

Hovstad. How can you think that — ?

Mrs. Stockmann. Won't you go in and have something Mr. Hovstad? My husband is sure to be back directly.

Hovstad. Thank you, perhaps just a morsel. [*Goes into the dining room.*]

Peter Stockmann. [*Lowering his voice a little*] It is a curious thing that these farmers' sons never seem to lose their want of tact.

Mrs. Stockmann. Surely it is not worth bothering about! Cannot you and Thomas share the credit as brothers?

Peter Stockmann. I should have thought so; but apparently some people are not satisfied with a share.

Mrs. Stockmann. What nonsense! You and Thomas get on so capitally together. [*Listens.*] There he is at last, I think. [*Goes out and opens the door leading to the hall.*]

Dr. Stockmann. [*Laughing and talking outside*] Look here — here is another guest for you, Katherine. Isn't that jolly! Come in, Captain Horster; hang your coat up on this peg. Ah, you don't wear an overcoat. Just think, Katherine; I met him in the street and could hardly persuade him to come up! [CAPTAIN HORSTER *comes into the room and greets* MRS. STOCKMANN. *He is followed by* DR. STOCKMANN.] Come along in, boys. They are ravenously hungry again, you know. Come along, Captain Horster; you must have a slice of beef. [*Pushes* HORSTER *into the dining room.* EJLIF *and* MORTEN *go in after them.*]

Mrs. Stockmann. But, Thomas, don't you see — ?

Dr. Stockmann. [*Turning in the doorway*] Oh, is it you, Peter? [*Shakes hands with him.*] Now that is very delightful.

Peter Stockmann. Unfortunately I must go in a moment —

Dr. Stockmann. Rubbish! There is some toddy just coming in. You haven't forgotten the toddy, Katherine?

Mrs. Stockmann. Of course not; the water is boiling now. [*Goes into the dining room.*]

Peter Stockmann. Toddy, too!

Dr. Stockmann. Yes, sit down and we will have it comfortably.

Peter Stockmann. Thanks, I never care about an evening's drinking.

Dr. Stockmann. But this isn't an evening's drinking.

Peter Stockmann. It seems to me — [*Looks toward the dining room.*] It is extraordinary how they can put away all that food.

Dr. Stockmann. [*Rubbing his hands*] Yes, isn't it splendid to see young people eat? They always have an appetite, you know! That's as it should be. Lots of food — to build up their strength! They are the people who are going to stir up the fermenting forces of the future, Peter.

Peter Stockmann. May I ask what they will find here to "stir up," as you put it?

Dr. Stockmann. Ah, you must ask the young people that — when the time comes. We shan't be able to see it, of course. That stands to reason — two old fogies, like us —

Peter Stockmann. Really, really! I must say that is an extremely odd expression to —

Dr. Stockmann. Oh, you mustn't take me too literally, Peter. I am so heartily happy and contented, you know. I think it is such an extraordinary piece of good fortune to be in the middle of all this growing, germinating life. It is a splendid time to live in! It is as if a whole new world were being created around one.

Peter Stockmann. Do you really think so?

Dr. Stockmann. Ah, naturally you can't appreciate it as keenly as I. You have lived all your life in these surroundings, and your impressions have got blunted. But I, who have been buried all these years in my little corner up north, almost without ever seeing a stranger who might bring new ideas with him — well, in my case it has just the same effect as if I had been transported into the middle of a crowded city.

Peter Stockmann. Oh, a city — !

Dr. Stockmann. I know, I know; it is all cramped enough here, compared with many other places. But there is life here — there is promise — there are innumerable things to work for and fight for; and that is the main thing. [*Calls.*] Katherine, hasn't the postman been here?

Mrs. Stockmann. [*From the dining room*] No.

Dr. Stockmann. And then to be comfortably off, Peter! That is something one learns to value, when one has been on the brink of starvation, as we have.

Peter Stockmann. Oh, surely —

Dr. Stockmann. Indeed I can assure you we have often been very hard put to it, up there. And now to be able to live like a lord! To-day, for instance, we had roast beef for dinner — and, what is more, for supper too. Won't you come and have a little bit? Or let me show it you, at any rate? Come here —

Peter Stockmann. No, no — not for worlds!

Dr. Stockmann. Well, but just come here then. Do you see, we have got a table-cover?

Peter Stockmann. Yes, I noticed it.

Dr. Stockmann. And we have got a lamp-shade too. Do you see? All out of Katherine's savings! It makes the room so cozy. Don't you think so? Just stand here for a moment — no, no, not there — just here, that's it! Look now, when you get the light on it all together — I really think it looks very nice, doesn't it?

Peter Stockmann. Oh, if you can afford luxuries of this kind —

Dr. Stockmann. Yes, I can afford it now. Katherine tells me I earn almost as much as we spend.

Peter Stockmann. Almost — yes!

Dr. Stockmann. But a scientific man must live in a little bit of style. I am quite sure an ordinary civil servant spends more in a year than I do.

Peter Stockmann. I dare say. A civil servant — a man in a well-paid position —

Dr. Stockmann. Well, any ordinary merchant, then! A man in that position spends two or three times as much as —

Peter Stockmann. It just depends on circumstances.

Dr. Stockmann. At all events I assure you I don't waste money unprofitably. But I can't find it in my heart to deny myself the pleasure of entertaining my friends. I need that sort of thing, you know. I have lived for so long shut out of it all, that it is a necessity of life to me to mix with young, eager, ambitious men, men of liberal and active minds; and that describes every one of those fellows who are enjoying their supper in there. I wish you knew more of Hovstad —

Peter Stockmann. By the way, Hovstad was telling me he was going to print another article of yours.

Dr. Stockmann. An article of mine?

Peter Stockmann. Yes, about the Baths. An article you wrote in the winter.

Dr. Stockmann. Oh, that one! No, I don't intend that to appear just for the present.

Peter Stockmann. Why not? It seems to me that this would be the most opportune moment.

Dr. Stockmann. Yes, very likely — under normal conditions. [*Crosses the room.*]

Peter Stockmann. [*Following him with his eyes*] Is there anything abnormal about the present conditions?

Dr. Stockmann. [*Standing still*] To tell you the truth, Peter, I can't say just at this moment — at all events, not tonight. There may be much that is very abnormal about the present conditions — and it is possible there may be nothing abnormal about them at all. It is quite possible it may be merely my imagination.

Peter Stockmann. I must say it all sounds most mysterious. Is there something going on that I am to be kept in ignorance of? I should have imagined that I, as Chairman of the governing body of the Baths —

Dr. Stockmann. And I should have imagined that I — Oh, come, don't let us fly out at one another, Peter.

Peter Stockmann. Heaven forbid! I am not in the habit of flying out at people, as you call it. But I am entitled to request most emphatically that all arrangements shall be made in a business-like manner, through the proper channels, and shall be dealt with by the legally constituted authorities. I can allow no going behind our backs by any roundabout means.

Dr. Stockmann. Have I ever at any time tried to go behind your backs.

Peter Stockmann. You have an ingrained tendency to take your own way, at all events; and that is almost equally inadmissible in a well-ordered community. The individual ought undoubtedly to acquiesce in subordinating himself to the community —or, to speak more accurately, to the authorities who have the care of the community's welfare.

Dr. Stockmann. Very likely. But what the deuce has all this to do with me?

Peter Stockmann. That is exactly what you never appear to be willing to learn, my dear Thomas. But, mark my words, some day you will have to suffer for it — sooner or later. Now I have told you. Goodby.

Dr. Stockmann. Have you taken leave of your senses? You are on the wrong scent altogether.

Peter Stockmann. I am not usually that. You must excuse me now if I — [*Calls into the dining room.*] Good night, Katherine. Good night, gentlemen. [*Goes out.*]

Mrs. Stockmann. [*Coming from the dining room*] Has he gone?

Dr. Stockmann. Yes, and in such a bad temper.

Mrs. Stockmann. But, dear Thomas, what have you been doing to him again?

Dr. Stockmann. Nothing at all. And, anyhow, he can't oblige me to make my report before the proper time.

Mrs. Stockmann. What have you got to make a report to him about?

Dr. Stockmann. Hm! Leave that to me, Katherine. — It is an extraordinary thing that the postman doesn't come.

HOVSTAD, BILLING, *and* HORSTER *have risen from the table and come into the sitting room.* EJLIF *and* MORTEN *come in after them.*

Billing. [*Stretching himself*] Ah! — one feels a new man after a meal like that.

Hovstad. The mayor wasn't in a very sweet temper to-night, then?

Dr. Stockmann. It is his stomach; he has a wretched digestion.

Hovstad. I rather think it was us two of the *People's Messenger* that he couldn't digest.

Mrs. Stockmann. I thought you came out of it pretty well with him.

Hovstad. Oh yes; but it isn't anything more than a sort of truce.

Billing. That is just what it is! That word sums up the situation.

Dr. Stockmann. We must remember that Peter is a lonely man, poor chap. He has no home comforts of any kind; nothing but ever-lasting business. And all that infernal weak tea wash that he pours into himself! Now then, my boys, bring chairs up to the table. Aren't we going to have that toddy, Katherine?

Mrs. Stockmann. [*Going into the dining room*] I am just get-ting it.

Dr. Stockmann. Sit down here on the couch beside me, Captain Horster. We so seldom see you — Please sit down, my friends. [*They sit down at the table.* MRS. STOCKMANN *brings a tray, with a spirit-lamp, glasses, bottles, etc., upon it.*]

Mrs. Stockmann. There you are! This is arrack, and this is rum, and this one is the brandy. Now every one must help himself.

Dr. Stockmann. [*Taking a glass*] We will. [*They all mix them-selves some toddy.*] And let us have the cigars. Ejlif, you know where the box is. And you, Morten, can fetch my pipe. [*The two boys go into the room on the right.*] I have a suspicion that Ejlif pockets a cigar now and then! — but I take no notice of it. [*Calls out.*] And my smoking-cap too, Morten. Katherine, you can tell him where I left it. Ah, he has it. [*The boys bring the various things.*] Now, my friends. I stick to my pipe, you know. This one has seen plenty of bad weather with me up north. [*Touches glasses with them.*] Your good health! Ah, it is good to be sitting snug and warm here.

Mrs. Stockmann. [*Who sits knitting*] Do you sail soon, Captain Horster?

Horster. I expect to be ready to sail next week.

Mrs. Stockmann. I suppose you are going to America?

Horster. Yes, that is the plan.

Mrs. Stockmann. Then you won't be able to take part in the coming election.

Horster. Is there going to be an election?

Billing. Didn't you know?

Horster. No, I don't mix myself up with those things.

Billing. But do you not take an interest in public affairs?

Horster. No, I don't know anything about politics.

Billing. All the same, one ought to vote, at any rate.

Horster. Even if one doesn't know anything about what is going on?

Billing. Doesn't know! What do you mean by that? A community is like a ship; every one ought to be prepared to take the helm.

Horster. Maybe that is all very well on shore; but on board ship it wouldn't work.

Hovstad. It is astonishing how little most sailors care about what goes on on shore.

Billing. Very extraordinary.

Dr. Stockmann. Sailors are like birds of passage; they feel equally at home in any latitude. And that is only an additional reason for our being all the more keen, Hovstad. Is there to be anything of public interest in tomorrow's *Messenger?*

Hovstad. Nothing about municipal affairs. But the day after tomorrow I was thinking of printing your article —

Dr. Stockmann. Ah, devil take it — my article! Look here, that must wait a bit.

Hovstad. Really? We had just got convenient space for it, and I thought it was just the opportune moment —

Dr. Stockmann. Yes, yes, very likely you are right; but it must wait all the same. I will explain to you later.

PETRA *comes in from the hall, in hat and cloak and with a bundle of exercise books under her arm.*

Petra. Good evening.

Dr. Stockmann. Good evening, Petra; come along. [*Mutual greetings;* PETRA *takes off her things and puts them down on a chair by the door.*]

Petra. And you have all been sitting here enjoying yourselves, while I have been out slaving!

Dr. Stockmann. Well, come and enjoy yourself, too!

Billing. May I mix a glass for you?

Petra. [*Coming to the table*] Thanks, I would rather do it; you always mix it too strong. But I forgot, father — I have a letter for you. [*Goes to the chair where she has laid her things.*]

Dr. Stockmann. A letter? From whom?

Petra. [*Looking in her coat pocket*] The postman gave it to me just as I was going out —

Dr. Stockmann. [*Getting up and going to her*] And you only give it to me now!

Petra. I really had not time to run up again. There it is!

Dr. Stockmann. [*Seizing the letter*] Let's see, let's see, child! [*Looks at the address.*] Yes, that's all right!

Mrs. Stockmann. Is it the one you have been expecting so anxiously, Thomas?

Dr. Stockmann. Yes, it is. I must go to my room now and — Where shall I get a light, Katherine? Is there no lamp in my room again?

Mrs. Stockmann. Yes, your lamp is already lit on your desk.

Dr. Stockmann. Good, good. Excuse me for a moment — [*Goes into his study.*]

Petra. What do you suppose it is, mother?

Mrs. Stockmann. I don't know; for the last day or two he has always been asking if the postman has not been.

Billing. Probably some country patient.

Petra. Poor old dad! — he will overwork himself soon. [*Mixes a glass for herself.*] There, that will taste good!

Hovstad. Have you been teaching in the evening school again today?

Petra. [*Sipping from her glass*] Two hours.

Billing. And four hours of school in the morning —

Petra. Five hours.

Mrs. Stockmann. And you have still got exercises to correct, I see.

Petra. A whole heap, yes.

Horster. You are pretty full up with work, too, it seems to me.

Petra. Yes — but that is good. One is so delightfully tired after it.

Billing. Do you like that?

Petra. Yes, because one sleeps so well then.

Morten. You must be dreadfully wicked, Petra.

Petra. Wicked?

Morten. Yes, because you work so much. Mr. Rörlund says work is a punishment for our sins.

Ejlif. Pooh, what a duffer you are, to believe a thing like that!

Mrs. Stockmann. Come, come, Ejlif!

Billing. [*Laughing*] That's capital!

Hovstad. Don't you want to work as hard as that, Morten?

Morten. No, indeed I don't.

Hovstad. What do you want to be, then?

Morten. I should like best to be a viking.

Ejlif. You would have to be a pagan then.

Morten. Well, I could become a pagan, couldn't I?

Billing. I agree with you, Morten! My sentiments, exactly.

Mrs. Stockmann. [*Signaling to him*] I am sure that is not true, Mr. Billing.

Billing. Yes, I swear it is! I am a pagan, and I am proud of it. Believe me, before long we shall all be pagans.

Morten. And then shall be allowed to do anything we like?

Billing. Well, you see, Morten —

Mrs. Stockmann. You must go to your room now, boys; I am sure you have some lessons to learn for tomorrow.

Ejlif. I should like so much to stay a little longer —

Mrs. Stockmann. No, no; away you go, both of you. [*The boys say good night and go into the room on the left.*]

Hovstad. Do you really think it can do the boys any harm to hear such things?

Mrs. Stockmann. I don't know; but I don't like it.

Petra. But you know, mother, I think you really are wrong about it.

Mrs. Stockmann. Maybe, but I don't like it — not in our own home.

Petra. There is so much falsehood both at home and at school. At home one must not speak, and at school we have to stand and tell lies to the children.

Horster. Tell lies?

Petra. Yes; don't you suppose we have to teach them all sorts of things that we don't believe?

Billing. That is perfectly true.

Petra. If only I had the means I would start a school of my own, and it would be conducted on very different lines.

Billing. Oh, bother the means — !

Horster. Well if you are thinking of that, Miss Stockmann, I shall be delighted to provide you with a schoolroom. The great big old house my father left me is standing almost empty; there is an immense dining room downstairs —

Petra. [*Laughing*] Thank you very much; but I am afraid nothing will come of it.

Hovstad. No, Miss Petra is much more likely to take to journalism, I expect. By the way, have you had time to do anything with that English story you promised to translate for us?

Petra. No, not yet; but you shall have it in good time.

DR. STOCKMANN *comes in from his room with an open letter in his hand.*

Dr. Stockmann. [*Waving the letter*] Well, now the town will have something new to talk about, I can tell you!

Billing. Something new?

Mrs. Stockmann. What is this?

Dr. Stockmann. A great discovery, Katherine.

Hovstad. Really?

Mrs. Stockmann. A discovery of yours?

Dr. Stockmann. A discovery of mine. [*Walks up and down.*] Just let them come saying, as usual, that it is all fancy and a crazy man's imagination! But they will be careful what they say this time, I can tell you!

Petra. But, father, tell us what it is.

Dr. Stockmann. Yes, yes — only give me time, and you shall know all about it. If only I had Peter here now! It just shows how we men can go about forming our judgments, when in reality we are as blind as any moles —

Hovstad. What are you driving at, Doctor?

Dr. Stockmann. [*Standing still by the table*] Isn't it the universal opinion that our town is a healthy spot?

Hovstad. Certainly.

Dr. Stockmann. Quite an unusually healthy spot, in fact — a place that deserves to be recommended in the warmest possible manner either for invalids or for people who are well —

Mrs. Stockmann. Yes, but my dear Thomas —

Dr. Stockmann. And we have been recommending it and praising it — I have written and written, both in the *Messenger* and in pamphlets —

Hovstad. Well, what then?

Dr. Stockmann. And the Baths — we have called them the " main artery of the town's lifeblood," the " nerve-center of our town," and the devil knows what else —

Billing. " The town's pulsating heart " was the expression I once used on an important occasion —

Dr. Stockmann. Quite so. Well, do you know what they really are, these great, splendid, much-praised Baths, that have cost so much money — do you know what they are?

Hovstad. No, what are they?

Mrs. Stockmann. Yes, what are they?

Dr. Stockmann. The whole place is a pesthouse!

Petra. The Baths, father?

Mrs. Stockmann. [*At the same time*] Our Baths!

Hovstad. But, Doctor —

Billing. Absolutely incredible!

Dr. Stockmann. The whole Bath establishment is a whited, poisoned sepulcher, I tell you — the gravest possible danger to the public health! All the nastiness up at Mölledal, all that stinking filth is infecting the water in the conduit-pipes leading to the reservoir; and the same cursed, filthy poison oozes out on the shore to —

Horster. Where the bathing-place is?

Dr. Stockmann. Just there.

Hovstad. How do you come to be so certain of all this, Doctor?

Dr. Stockmann. I have investigated the matter most conscientiously. For a long time past I have suspected something of the kind. Last year we had some very strange cases of illness among the visitors — typhoid cases, and cases of gastric fever —

Mrs. Stockmann. Yes, that is quite true.

Dr. Stockmann. At the time, we supposed the visitors had been infected before they came; but later on, in the winter, I began to have a different opinion; and so I set myself to examine the water, as well as I could.

Mrs. Stockmann. Then that is what you have been so busy with?

Dr. Stockmann. Indeed I have been busy, Katherine. But here I had none of the necessary scientific apparatus; so I sent samples, both of the drinking-water and of the sea-water, up to the University, to have an accurate analysis made by a chemist.

Hovstad. And have you got that?

Dr. Stockmann. [*Showing him the letter*] Here it is! It proves the presence of decomposing organic matter in the water — it is full of infusoria.[3] The water is absolutely dangerous to use, either internally or externally.

Mrs. Stockmann. What a mercy you discovered it in time!

Dr. Stockmann. You may well say so.

Hovstad. And what do you propose to do now, Doctor?

Dr. Stockmann. To see the matter put right — naturally.

Hovstad. Can that be done?

Dr. Stockmann. It must be done. Otherwise the Baths will be absolutely useless and wasted. But we need not anticipate that; I have a very clear idea what we shall have to do.

Mrs. Stockmann. But why have you kept this all so secret, dear?

Dr. Stockmann. Do you suppose I was going to run about the town gossiping about it, before I had absolute proof? No, thank you. I am not such a fool.

Petra. Still, you might have told us —

Dr. Stockmann. Not a living soul. But tomorrow you may run round to the old Badger —

Mrs. Stockmann. Oh, Thomas! Thomas!

Dr. Stockmann. Well, to your grandfather, then. The old boy will have something to be astonished at! I know he thinks I am cracked — and there are lots of other people think so too, I have noticed. But now these good folks shall see — they shall just see — ! [*Walks about, rubbing his hands.*] There will be a nice upset in the town, Katherine; you can't imagine what it will be. All the conduit-pipes will have to be relaid.

Hovstad. [*Getting up*] All the conduit-pipes — ?

Dr. Stockmann. Yes, of course. The intake is too low down; it will have to be lifted to a position much higher up.

Petra. Then you were right after all.

Dr. Stockmann. Ah, you remember, Petra — I wrote opposing the plans before the work was begun. But at that time no one would listen to me. Well, I am going to let them have it, now! Of course I have prepared a report for the Baths Committee; I have had it ready for a week, and was only waiting for this to come. [*Shows the letter.*] Now it shall go off at once. [*Goes into his room and comes back with some papers.*] Look at that! Four closely written sheets! — and the letter shall go with them. Give me a bit of paper, Katherine — something to wrap them up in. That will do! Now

---

[3] **infusoria**: microscopic bacteria.

give it to — to — [*stamps his foot*] — what the deuce is her name? — give it to the maid, and tell her to take it at once to the Mayor.

MRS. STOCKMANN *takes the packet and goes out through the dining room.*

Petra. What do you think Uncle Peter will say, father?

Dr. Stockmann. What is there for him to say? I should think he would be very glad that such an important truth has been brought to light.

Hovstad. Will you let me print a short note about your discovery in the *Messenger?*

Dr. Stockmann. I shall be very much obliged if you will.

Hovstad. It is very desirable that the public should be informed of it without delay.

Dr. Stockmann. Certainly.

Mrs. Stockmann. [*Coming back*] She has just gone with it.

Billing. Upon my soul, Doctor, you are going to be the foremost man in the town!

Dr. Stockmann. [*Walking about happily*] Nonsense! As a matter of fact I have done nothing more than my duty. I have only made a lucky find — that's all. Still, all the same —

Billing. Hovstad, don't you think the town ought to give Dr. Stockmann some sort of testimonial?

Hovstad. I will suggest it, anyway.

Billing. And I will speak to Aslaksen about it.

Dr. Stockmann. No, my good friends, don't let us have any of that nonsense. I won't hear of anything of the kind. And if the Baths Committee should think of voting me an increase of salary, I will not accept it. Do you hear, Katherine? — I won't accept it.

Mrs. Stockmann. You are quite right, Thomas.

Petra. [*Lifting her glass*] Your health, father!

Hovstad and *Billing.* Your health, Doctor! Good health!

Horster. [*Touches glasses with* DR. STOCKMANN] I hope it will bring you nothing but good luck.

Dr. Stockmann. Thank you, thank you, my dear fellows! I feel tremendously happy! It is a splendid thing for a man to be able to feel that he has done a service to his native town and to his fellow-citizens. Hurrah, Katherine! [*He puts his arms around her and whirls her round and round, while she protests with laughing cries. They all laugh, clap their hands, and cheer the* DOCTOR. *The boys put their heads in at the door to see what is going on.*]

ACT II

SCENE. *The same. The door into the dining room is shut. It is
morning.*

MRS. STOCKMANN, *with a sealed letter in her hand, comes in from the
dining room, goes to the door of the* DOCTOR'S *study, and peeps in.*
Mrs. Stockmann. Are you in, Thomas?

Dr. Stockmann. [*From within his room*] Yes, I have just come
in. [*Comes into the room.*] What is it?

Mrs. Stockmann. A letter from your brother.

Dr. Stockmann. Aha, let us see! [*Opens the letter and reads:*]
"I return herewith the manuscript you sent me " — [*reads on in a
low murmur*]. Hm! —

Mrs. Stockmann. What does he say?

Dr. Stockmann. [*Putting the papers in his pocket*] Oh, he only
writes that he will come up here himself about midday.

Mrs. Stockmann. Well, try to remember to be at home this time.

Dr. Stockmann. That will be all right; I have got through all my
morning visits.

Mrs. Stockmann. I am extremely curious to know how he takes it.

Dr. Stockmann. You will see he won't like its having been I, and
not he, that made the discovery.

Mrs. Stockmann. Aren't you a little nervous about that?

Dr. Stockmann. Oh, he really will be pleased enough, you know.
But, at the same time, Peter is so confoundedly afraid of any one's
doing any service to the town except himself.

Mrs. Stockmann. I will tell you what, Thomas — you should be
good-natured, and share the credit of this with him. Couldn't you
make out that it was he who set you on the scent of this discovery?

Dr. Stockmann. I am quite willing. If only I can get the thing
set right. I — [MORTEN KIIL *puts his head in through the door
leading from the hall, looks round in an inquiring manner, and
chuckles*].

Morten Kiil. [*Slyly*] Is it — is it true?

Mrs. Stockmann. [*Going to the door*] Father! — is it you?

Dr. Stockmann. Ah, Mr. Kiil — Good morning, good morning!

Mrs. Stockmann. But come along in.

Morten Kiil. If it is true, I will; if not, I am off.

Dr. Stockmann. If what is true?

Morten Kiil. This tale about the water-supply. Is it true?

Dr. Stockmann. Certainly it is true. But how did you come to hear it?

Morten Kiil. [*Coming in*] Petra ran in on her way to the school —

Dr. Stockmann. Did she?

Morten Kiil. Yes; and she declares that — I thought she was only making a fool of me, but it isn't like Petra to do that.

Dr. Stockmann. Of course not. How could you imagine such a thing!

Morten Kiil. Oh well, it is better never to trust anybody; you may find you have been made a fool of before you know where you are. But it is really true, all the same?

Dr. Stockmann. You can depend upon it that it is true. Won't you sit down? [*Settles him on the couch.*] Isn't it a real bit of luck for the town —

Morten Kiil. [*Suppressing his laughter*] A bit of luck for the town?

Dr. Stockmann. Yes, that I made the discovery in good time.

Morten Kiil. [*As before*] Yes, yes, yes! — But I should never have thought you the sort of man to pull your own brother's leg [4] like this!

Dr. Stockmann. Pull his leg!

Mrs. Stockmann. Really, father dear —

Morten Kiil. [*Resting his hands and his chin on the handle of his stick and winking slyly at the* Doctor] Let me see, what was the story? Some kind of beast that had got into the water-pipes, wasn't it?

Dr. Stockmann. Infusoria — yes.

Morten Kiil. And a lot of these beasts had got in, according to Petra — a tremendous lot.

Dr. Stockmann. Certainly; hundreds of thousands of them, probably.

Morten Kiil. But no one can see them — isn't that so?

Dr. Stockmann. Yes; you can't see them.

Morten Kiil. [*With a quiet chuckle*] Damme — it's the finest story I have ever heard!

Dr. Stockmann. What do you mean?

Morten Kiil. But you will never get the Mayor to believe a thing like that.

Dr. Stockmann. We shall see.

Morten Kiil. Do you think he will be fool enough to — ?

[4] **pull your own brother's leg:** slang for " get money out of him."

Dr. Stockmann. I hope the whole town will be fools enough.

Morten Kiil. The whole town! Well, it wouldn't be a bad thing. It would just serve them right, and teach them a lesson. They think themselves so much cleverer than we old fellows. They hounded me out of the council; they did, I tell you — they hounded me out. Now they shall pay for it. You pull their legs too, Thomas!

Dr. Stockmann. Really, I —

Morten Kiil. You pull their legs! [*Gets up.*] If you can work it so that the Mayor and his friends all swallow the same bait, I will give ten pounds to a charity — like a shot!

Dr. Stockmann. That is very kind of you.

Morten Kiil. Yes, I haven't got much money to throw away, I can tell you; but if you can work this, I will give five pounds to a charity at Christmas.

HOVSTAD *comes in by the hall door.*

Hovstad. Good morning! [*Stops.*] Oh, I beg your pardon —

Dr. Stockmann. Not at all; come in.

Morten Kiil. [*With another chuckle*] Oho! — is he in this, too?

Hovstad. What do you mean?

Dr. Stockmann. Certainly he is.

Morten Kiil. I might have known it! It must get into the papers. You know how to do it, Thomas! Set your wits to work. Now I must go.

Dr. Stockmann. Won't you stay a little while?

Morten Kiil. No, I must be off now. You keep up this game for all it is worth. You won't repent it; I'm damned if you will!

He goes out; MRS. STOCKMANN *follows him into the hall.*

Dr. Stockmann. [*Laughing*] Just imagine — the old chap doesn't believe a word of all this about the water-supply.

Hovstad. Oh, that was it, then?

Dr. Stockmann. Yes, that was what we were talking about. Perhaps it is the same thing that brings you here?

Hovstad. Yes, it is. Can you spare me a few minutes, Doctor?

Dr. Stockmann. As long as you like, my dear fellow.

Hovstad. Have you heard from the Mayor yet?

Dr. Stockmann. Not yet. He is coming here later.

Hovstad. I have given the matter a great deal of thought since last night.

Dr. Stockmann. Well?

Hovstad. From your point of view, as a doctor and a man of science, this affair of the water-supply is an isolated matter. I mean, you do not realize that it involves a great many other things.

Dr. Stockmann. How do you mean? — Let us sit down, my dear fellow. No, sit here on the couch. [HOVSTAD *sits down on the couch,* DR. STOCKMANN *on a chair on the other side of the table.*] Now then. You mean that — ?

Hovstad. You said yesterday that the pollution of the water was due to impurities in the soil.

Dr. Stockmann. Yes, unquestionably it is due to that poisonous morass up at Mölledal.

Hovstad. Begging your pardon, Doctor, I fancy it is due to quite another morass altogether.

Dr. Stockmann. What morass?

Hovstad. The morass that the whole life of our town is built on and is rotting in.

Dr. Stockmann. What the deuce are you driving at, Hovstad?

Hovstad. The whole of the town's interests have, little by little, got into the hands of a pack of officials.

Dr. Stockmann. Oh, come! — they are not all officials.

Hovstad. No, but those that are not officials are at any rate the officials' friends and adherents; it is the wealthy folk, the old families in the town, that have got us entirely in their hands.

Dr. Stockmann. Yes, but after all they are men of ability and knowledge.

Hovstad. Did they show any ability or knowledge when they laid the conduit-pipes where they are now?

Dr. Stockmann. No, of course that was a great piece of stupidity on their part. But that is going to be set right now.

Hovstad. Do you think that will be all such plain sailing?

Dr. Stockmann. Plain sailing or no, it has got to be done, anyway.

Hovstad. Yes, provided the press takes up the question.

Dr. Stockmann. I don't think that will be necessary, my dear fellow. I am certain my brother —

Hovstad. Excuse me, doctor; I feel bound to tell you I am inclined to take the matter up.

Dr. Stockmann. In the paper?

Hovstad. Yes. When I took over the *People's Messenger* my idea was to break up this ring of self-opinionated old fossils who had got hold of all the influence.

Dr. Stockmann. But you know you told me yourself what the result had been; you nearly ruined your paper.

Hovstad. Yes, at the time we were obliged to climb down a peg or two, it is quite true; because there was a danger of the whole project of the Baths coming to nothing if they failed us. But now the scheme has been carried through, and we can dispense with these grand gentlemen.

Dr. Stockmann. Dispense with them, yes; but we owe them a great debt of gratitude.

Hovstad. That shall be recognized ungrudgingly. But a journalist of my democratic tendencies cannot let such an opportunity as this slip. The bubble of official infallibility must be pricked. This superstition must be destroyed, like any other.

Dr. Stockmann. I am whole-heartedly with you in that, Mr. Hovstad; if it is a superstition, away with it!

Hovstad. I should be very reluctant to bring the Mayor into it, because he is your brother. But I am sure you will agree with me that truth should be the first consideration.

Dr. Stockmann. That goes without saying. [*With sudden emphasis*] Yes, but — but —

Hovstad. You must not misjudge me. I am neither more self-interested nor more ambitious than most men.

Dr. Stockmann. My dear fellow — who suggests anything of the kind?

Hovstad. I am of humble origin, as you know; and that has given me opportunities of knowing what is the most crying need in the humbler ranks of life. It is that they should be allowed some part in the direction of public affairs, Doctor. That is what will develop their faculties and intelligence and self-respect —

Dr. Stockmann. I quite appreciate that.

Hovstad. Yes — and in my opinion a journalist incurs a heavy responsibility if he neglects a favorable opportunity of emancipating the masses — the humble and oppressed. I know well enough that in exalted circles I shall be called an agitator, and all that sort of thing; but they may call me what they like. If only my conscience doesn't reproach me, then —

Dr. Stockmann. Quite right! Quite right, Mr. Hovstad. But all the same — devil take it! [*A knock is heard at the door.*] Come in! [ASLAKSEN *appears at the door. He is poorly but decently dressed, in black, with a slightly crumpled white neckcloth; he wears gloves and has a felt hat in his hand.*]

Aslaksen. [*Bowing*] Excuse my taking the liberty, Doctor —

Dr. Stockmann. [*Getting up*] Ah, it is you, Aslaksen!

Aslaksen. Yes, doctor.

Hovstad. [*Standing up*] Is it me you want, Aslaksen?

Aslaksen. No; I didn't know I should find you here. No, it was the Doctor I —

Dr. Stockmann. I am quite at your service. What is it?

Aslaksen. Is what I heard from Mr. Billing true, sir — that you mean to improve our water-supply?

Dr. Stockmann. Yes, for the Baths.

Aslaksen. Quite so, I understand. Well, I have come to say that I will back that up by every means in my power.

Hovstad. [*To the* DOCTOR] You see!

Dr. Stockmann. I shall be very grateful to you, but —

Aslaksen. Because it may be no bad thing to have us small trades-men at your back. We form, as it were, a compact majority in the town — if we choose. And it is always a good thing to have the majority with you, Doctor.

Dr. Stockmann. That is undeniably true; but I confess I don't see why such unusual precautions should be necessary in this case. It seems to me that such a plain, straightforward thing —

Aslaksen. Oh, it may be very desirable, all the same. I know our local authorities so well; officials are not generally very ready to act on proposals that come from other people. That is why I think it would not be at all amiss if we made a little demonstration.

Hovstad. That's right.

Dr. Stockmann. Demonstration, did you say? What on earth are you going to make a demonstration about?

Aslaksen. We shall proceed with the greatest moderation, Doctor. Moderation is always my aim; it is the greatest virtue in a citizen — at least, I think so.

Dr. Stockmann. It is well known to be a characteristic of yours, Mr. Aslaksen.

Aslaksen. Yes, I think I may pride myself on that. And this matter of the water-supply is of the greatest importance to us small tradesmen. The Baths promise to be a regular gold-mine for the town. We shall all make our living out of them, especially those of us who are householders. That is why we will back up the project as strongly as possible. And as I am at present Chairman of the Householders' Association —

Dr. Stockmann. Yes — ?

Aslaksen. And, what is more, local secretary of the Temperance Society — you know, sir, I suppose, that I am a worker in the temperance cause?

Dr. Stockmann. Of course, of course.

Aslaksen. Well, you can understand that I come into contact with a great many people. And as I have the reputation of a temperate and law-abiding citizen — like yourself, Doctor — I have a certain influence in the town, a little bit of power, if I may be allowed to say so.

Dr. Stockmann. I know that quite well, Mr. Aslaksen.

Aslaksen. So you see it would be an easy matter for me to set on foot some testimonial, if necessary.

Dr. Stockmann. A testimonial?

Aslaksen. Yes, some kind of an address of thanks from the townsmen for your share in a matter of such importance to the community. I need scarcely say that it would have to be drawn up with the greatest regard to moderation, so as not to offend the authorities — who, after all, have the reins in their hands. If we pay strict attention to that, no one can take it amiss, I should think!

Hovstad. Well, and even supposing they didn't like it —

Aslaksen. No, no, no; there must be no discourtesy to the authorities, Mr. Hovstad. It is no use falling foul of those upon whom our welfare so closely depends. I have done that in my time, and no good ever comes of it. But no one can take exception to a reasonable and frank expression of a citizen's views.

Dr. Stockmann. [*Shaking him by the hand*] I can't tell you, dear Mr. Aslaksen, how extremely pleased I am to find such hearty support among my fellow citizens. I am delighted — delighted! Now, you will take a small glass of sherry, eh?

Aslaksen. No, thank you; I never drink alcohol of that kind.

Dr. Stockmann. Well, what do you say to a glass of beer, then?

Aslaksen. Nor that either, thank you, Doctor. I never drink anything as early as this. I am going into town now to talk this over with one or two householders, and prepare the ground.

Dr. Stockmann. It is tremendously kind of you, Mr. Aslaksen; but I really cannot understand the necessity for all these precautions. It seems to me that the thing should go of itself.

Aslaksen. The authorities are somewhat slow to move, Doctor. Far be it from me to seem to blame them —

Hovstad. We are going to stir them up in the paper tomorrow, Aslaksen.

Aslaksen. But not violently, I trust, Mr. Hovstad. Proceed with moderation, or you will do nothing with them. You may take my advice; I have gathered my experience in the school of life. Well, I must say goodby, Doctor. You know now that we small tradesmen are at your back at all events, like a solid wall. You have the compact majority on your side, Doctor.

Dr. Stockmann. I am very much obliged, dear Mr. Aslaksen. [*Shakes hands with him.*] Goodby, goodby.

Aslaksen. Are you going my way, toward the printing-office, Mr. Hovstad?

Hovstad. I will come later; I have something to settle up first.

Aslaksen. Very well. [*Bows and goes out;* STOCKMANN *follows him into the hall.*]

Hovstad. [*As* STOCKMANN *comes in again*] Well, what do you think of that, Doctor? Don't you think it is high time we stirred a little life into all this slackness and vacillation and cowardice?

Dr. Stockmann. Are you referring to Aslaksen?

Hovstad. Yes, I am. He is one of those who are floundering in a bog — decent enough fellow though he may be, otherwise. And most of the people here are in just the same case — seesawing and edging first to one side and then to the other, so overcome with caution and scruple that they never dare to take any decided step.

Dr. Stockmann. Yes, but Aslaksen seemed to me so thoroughly well-intentioned.

Hovstad. There is one thing I esteem higher than that; and that is for a man to be self-reliant and sure of himself.

Dr. Stockmann. I think you are perfectly right there.

Hovstad. That is why I want to seize this opportunity, and try if I cannot manage to put a little virility into these well-intentioned people for once. The idol of Authority must be shattered in this town. This gross and inexcusable blunder about the water-supply must be brought home to the mind of every municipal voter.

Dr. Stockmann. Very well; if you are of opinion that it is for the good of the community, so be it. But not until I have had a talk with my brother.

Hovstad. Anyway, I will get a leading article ready; and if the Mayor refuses to take the matter up —

Dr. Stockmann. How can you suppose such a thing possible?

Hovstad. It is conceivable. And in that case —

Dr. Stockmann. In that case I promise you — Look here, in that case you may print my report — every word of it.

Hovstad. May I? Have I your word for it?

Dr. Stockmann. [*Giving him the MS*] Here it is; take it with you. It can do no harm for you to read it through, and you can give it back later on.

Hovstad. Good, good! That is what I will do. And now goodby, Doctor.

Dr. Stockmann. Goodby, goodby. You will see everything will run quite smoothly, Mr. Hovstad — quite smoothly.

Hovstad. Hm! — we shall see. [*Bows and goes out.*]

Dr. Stockmann. [*Opens the dining-room door and looks in.*] Katherine! Oh, you are back, Petra?

Petra. [*Coming in*] Yes, I have just come from the school.

Mrs. Stockmann. [*Coming in*] Has he not been here yet?

Dr. Stockmann. Peter? No. But I have had a long talk with Hovstad. He is quite excited about my discovery. I find it has a much wider bearing than I at first imagined. And he has put his paper at my disposal if necessity should arise.

Mrs. Stockmann. Do you think it will?

Dr. Stockmann. Not for a moment. But at all events it makes me feel proud to know that I have the liberal-minded, independent press on my side. Yes, and — just imagine — I have had a visit from the Chairman of the Householders' Association!

Mrs. Stockmann. Oh! What did he want?

Dr. Stockmann. To offer me his support too. They will support me in a body if it should be necessary. Katherine — do you know what I have behind me?

Mrs. Stockmann. Behind you? No, what have you behind you?

Dr. Stockmann. The compact majority.

Mrs. Stockmann. Really? Is that a good thing for you, Thomas?

Dr. Stockmann. I should think it was a good thing. [*Walks up and down rubbing his hands.*] By Jove, it's a fine thing to feel this bond of brotherhood between oneself and one's fellow citizens!

Petra. And to be able to do so much that is good and useful, father!

Dr. Stockmann. And for one's own native town into the bargain, my child!

Mrs. Stockmann. That was a ring at the bell.

Dr. Stockmann. It must be he, then. [*A knock is heard at the door.*] Come in!

Peter Stockmann. [*Comes in from the hall.*] Good morning.

Dr. Stockmann. Glad to see you, Peter!

Mrs. Stockmann. Good morning, Peter. How are you?

Peter Stockmann. So so, thank you. [*To* DR. STOCKMANN] I received from you yesterday, after office hours, a report dealing with the condition of the water at the Baths.

Dr. Stockmann. Yes. Have you read it?

Peter Stockmann. Yes, I have.

Dr. Stockmann. And what have you to say to it?

Peter Stockmann. [*With a sidelong glance*] Hm! —

Mrs. Stockmann. Come along, Petra. [*She and* PETRA *go into the room on the left.*]

Peter Stockmann. [*After a pause*] Was it necessary to make all these investigations behind my back?

Dr. Stockmann. Yes, because until I was absolutely certain about it —

Peter Stockmann. Then you mean that you are absolutely certain now?

Dr. Stockmann. Surely you are convinced of that.

Peter Stockmann. Is it your intention to bring this document before the Baths Committee as a sort of official communication?

Dr. Stockmann. Certainly. Something must be done in the matter — and that quickly.

Peter Stockmann. As usual, you employ violent expressions in your report. You say, amongst other things, that what we offer visitors in our Baths is a permanent supply of poison.

Dr. Stockmann. Well, can you describe it any other way, Peter? Just think — water that is poisonous, whether you drink it or bathe in it! And this we offer to the poor sick folk who come to us trustfully and pay us at an exorbitant rate to be made well again!

Peter Stockmann. And your reasoning leads you to this conclusion, that we must build a sewer to draw off the alleged impurities from Mölledal and must relay the water-conduits.

Dr. Stockmann. Yes. Do you see any other way out of it? I don't.

Peter Stockmann. I made a pretext this morning to go and see the town engineer, and, as if only half seriously, broached the subject of these proposals as a thing we might perhaps have to take under consideration some time later on.

Dr. Stockmann. Some time later on!

Peter Stockmann. He smiled at what he considered to be my extravagance, naturally. Have you taken the trouble to consider what your proposed alterations would cost? According to the information I obtained, the expenses would probably mount up to fifteen or twenty thousand pounds.[5]

Dr. Stockmann. Would it cost so much?

Peter Stockmann. Yes; and the worst part of it would be that the work would take at least two years.

Dr. Stockmann. Two years? Two whole years?

Peter Stockmann. At least. And what are we to do with the Baths in the meantime? Close them? Indeed we should be obliged to. And do you suppose any one would come near the place after it had got about that the water is dangerous?

Dr. Stockmann. Yes, but Peter, that is what it is.

Peter Stockmann. And all this at this juncture — just as the Baths are beginning to be known. There are other towns in the neighborhood with qualifications to attract visitors for bathing purposes. Don't you suppose they would immediately strain every nerve to divert the entire stream of strangers to themselves? Unquestionably they would; and then where should we be? We should probably have to abandon the whole thing, which has cost us so much money — and then you would have ruined your native town.

Dr. Stockmann. I — should have ruined — !

Peter Stockmann. It is simply and solely through the Baths that the town has before it any future worth mentioning. You know that just as well as I.

Dr. Stockmann. But what do you think ought to be done, then?

Peter Stockmann. Your report has not convinced me that the condition of the water at the Baths is as bad as you represent it to be.

Dr. Stockmann. I tell you it is even worse! — or at all events it will be in summer, when the warm weather comes.

Peter Stockmann. As I said, I believe you exaggerate the matter considerably. A capable physician ought to know what measures to take — he ought to be capable of preventing injurious influences or of remedying them if they become obviously persistent.

Dr. Stockmann. Well? What more?

Peter Stockmann. The water-supply for the Baths is now an established fact, and in consequence must be treated as such. But probably the Committee, at its discretion, will not be disinclined to consider the question of how far it might be possible to introduce certain improvements consistently with a reasonable expenditure.

Dr. Stockmann. And do you suppose that I will have anything to do with such a piece of trickery as that?

[5] **fifteen or twenty thousand pounds:** from $75,000 to $100,000.

Peter Stockmann. Trickery!!

Dr. Stockmann. Yes, it would be a trick — a fraud, a lie, a downright crime toward the public, toward the whole community!

Peter Stockmann. I have not, as I remarked before, been able to convince myself that there is actually any imminent danger.

Dr. Stockmann. You have! It is impossible that you should not be convinced. I know I have represented the facts absolutely truthfully and fairly. And you know it very well, Peter, only you won't acknowledge it. It was owing to your action that both the Baths and the water-conduits were built where they are; and that is what you won't acknowledge — that damnable blunder of yours. Pooh! — do you suppose I don't see through you?

Peter Stockmann. And even if that were true? If I perhaps guard my reputation somewhat anxiously, it is in the interests of the town. Without moral authority I am powerless to direct public affairs as seems, to my judgment, to be best for the common good. And on that account — and for various other reasons, too — it appears to me to be a matter of importance that your report should not be delivered to the Committee. In the interests of the public, you must withhold it. Then, later on, I will raise the question and we will do our best, privately; but nothing of this unfortunate affair — not a single word of it — must come to the ears of the public.

Dr. Stockmann. I am afraid you will not be able to prevent that now, my dear Peter.

Peter Stockmann. It must and shall be prevented.

Dr. Stockmann. It is no use, I tell you. There are too many people that know about it.

Peter Stockmann. That know about it? Who? Surely you don't mean those fellows on the *People's Messenger?*

Dr. Stockmann. Yes, they know. The liberal-minded, independent press is going to see that you do your duty.

Peter Stockmann. [*After a short pause*] You are an extraordinarily independent man, Thomas. Have you given no thought to the consequences this may have for yourself?

Dr. Stockmann. Consequences? — for me?

Peter Stockmann. For you and yours, yes.

Dr. Stockmann. What the deuce do you mean?

Peter Stockmann. I believe I have always behaved in a brotherly way to you — have always been ready to oblige or to help you?

Dr. Stockmann. Yes, you have, and I am grateful to you for it.

Peter Stockmann. There is no need. Indeed, to some extent I was forced to do so — for my own sake. I always hoped that, if I helped to improve your financial position, I should be able to keep some check on you.

Dr. Stockmann. What!! Then it was only for your own sake — !

Peter Stockmann. Up to a certain point, yes. It is painful for a man in an official position to have his nearest relative compromising himself time after time.

Dr. Stockmann. And do you consider that I do that?

Peter Stockmann. Yes, unfortunately, you do, without even being aware of it. You have a restless, pugnacious, rebellious disposition. And then there is that disastrous propensity of yours to want to write about every sort of possible and impossible thing. The moment an idea comes into your head, you must needs go and write a newspaper article or a whole pamphlet about it.

Dr. Stockmann. Well, but is it not the duty of a citizen to let the public share in any new ideas he may have?

Peter Stockmann. Oh, the public doesn't require any new ideas. The public is best served by the good old-established ideas it already has.

Dr. Stockmann. And that is your honest opinion?

Peter Stockmann. Yes, and for once I must talk frankly to you. Hitherto I have tried to avoid doing so, because I know how irritable you are; but now I must tell you the truth, Thomas. You have no conception what an amount of harm you do yourself by your impetuosity. You complain of the authorities, you even complain of the government — you are always pulling them to pieces; you insist that you have been neglected and persecuted. But what else can such a cantankerous [6] man as you expect?

Dr. Stockmann. What next! Cantankerous, am I?

Peter Stockmann. Yes, Thomas, you are an extremely cantankerous man to work with — I know that to my cost. You disregard everything that you ought to have consideration for. You seem completely to forget that it is I you have to thank for your appointment here as medical officer to the Baths —

Dr. Stockmann. I was entitled to it as a matter of course! — I and nobody else! I was the first person to see that the town could be made into a flourishing watering-place, and I was the only one who saw it at that time. I had to fight single-handed in support of the idea for many years; and I wrote and wrote —

Peter Stockmann. Undoubtedly. But things were not ripe for

_____

[6] **cantankerous:** disagreeable, complaining.

the scheme then — though, of course, you could not judge of that in your out-of-the-way corner up north. But as soon as the opportune moment came I — and the others — took the matter into our hands —

Dr. Stockmann. Yes, and made this mess of all my beautiful plan. It is pretty obvious now what clever fellows you were!

Peter Stockmann. To my mind the whole thing only seems to mean that you are seeking another outlet for your combativeness. You want to pick a quarrel with your superiors — an old habit of yours. You cannot put up with any authority over you. You look askance at any one who occupies a superior official position; you regard him as a personal enemy, and then any stick is good enough to beat him with. But now I have called your attention to the fact that the town's interests are at stake — and, incidentally, my own too. And therefore I must tell you, Thomas, that you will find me inexorable with regard to what I am about to require you to do.

Dr. Stockmann. And what is that?

Peter Stockmann. As you have been so indiscreet as to speak of this delicate matter to outsiders, despite the fact that you ought to have treated it as entirely official and confidential, it is obviously impossible to hush it up now. All sorts of rumors will get about directly, and everybody who has a grudge against us will take care to embellish these rumors. So it will be necessary for you to refute them publicly.

Dr. Stockmann. I! How? I don't understand.

Peter Stockmann. What we shall expect is that, after making further investigations, you will come to the conclusion that the matter is not by any means as dangerous or as critical as you imagined in the first instance.

Dr. Stockmann. Oho! — so that is what you expect!

Peter Stockmann. And, what is more, we shall expect you to make public profession of your confidence in the Committee and in their readiness to consider fully and conscientiously what steps may be necessary to remedy any possible defects.

Dr. Stockmann. But you will never be able to do that by patching and tinkering at it — never! Take my word for it, Peter; I mean what I say, as deliberately and emphatically as possible.

Peter Stockmann. As an officer under the Committee, you have no right to any individual opinion.

Dr. Stockmann. [*Amazed*] No right?

Peter Stockmann. In your official capacity, no. As a private person, it is quite another matter. But as a subordinate member of the staff of the Baths, you have no right to express any opinion which runs contrary to that of your superiors.

Dr. Stockmann. This is too much! I, a doctor, a man of science, have no right to — !

Peter Stockmann. The matter in hand is not simply a scientific one. It is a complicated matter, and has its economic as well as its technical side.

Dr. Stockmann. I don't care what it is! I intend to be free to express my opinion on any subject under the sun.

Peter Stockmann. As you please — but not on any subject concerning the Baths. That we forbid.

Dr. Stockmann. [*Shouting*] You forbid — ! You! A pack of —

Peter Stockmann. *I* forbid it — I, your chief; and if I forbid it, you have to obey.

Dr. Stockmann. [*Controlling himself*] Peter — if you were not my brother —

Petra. [*Throwing open the door*] Father, you shan't stand this!

Mrs. Stockmann. [*Coming in after her*] Petra, Petra!

Peter Stockmann. Oh, so you have been eavesdropping.

Mrs. Stockmann. You were talking so loud, we couldn't help —

Petra. Yes, I was listening.

Peter Stockmann. Well, after all, I am very glad —

Dr. Stockmann. [*Going up to him*] You were saying something about forbidding and obeying?

Peter Stockmann. You obliged me to take that tone with you.

Dr. Stockmann. And so I am to give myself the lie, publicly?

Peter Stockmann. We consider it absolutely necessary that you should make some such public statement as I have asked for.

Dr. Stockmann. And if I do not — obey?

Peter Stockmann. Then we shall publish a statement ourselves to reassure the public.

Dr. Stockmann. Very well; but in that case I shall use my pen against you. I stick to what I have said; I will show that I am right and that you are wrong. And what will you do then?

Peter Stockmann. Then I shall not be able to prevent your being dismissed.

Dr. Stockmann. What — ?

Petra. Father — dismissed!

Mrs. Stockmann. Dismissed!

Peter Stockmann. Dismissed from the staff of the Baths. I shall be obliged to propose that you shall immediately be given notice, and shall not be allowed any further participation in the Baths' affairs.

Dr. Stockmann. You would dare to do that!

Peter Stockmann. It is you that are playing the daring game.

Petra. Uncle, that is a shameful way to treat a man like father!

Mrs. Stockmann. Do hold your tongue, Petra!

Peter Stockmann. [*Looking at* PETRA] Oh, so we volunteer our opinions already, do we? Of course. [*To* MRS. STOCKMANN] Katherine, I imagine you are the most sensible person in this house. Use any influence you may have over your husband, and make him see what this will entail for his family as well as —

Dr. Stockmann. My family is my own concern and nobody else's!

Peter Stockmann. — For his own family, as I was saying, as well as for the town he lives in.

Dr. Stockmann. It is I who have the real good of the town at heart! I want to lay bare the defects that sooner or later must come to the light of day. I will show whether I love my native town.

Peter Stockmann. You, who in your blind obstinacy want to cut off the most important source of the town's welfare?

Dr. Stockmann. The source is poisoned, man! Are you mad? We are making our living by retailing filth and corruption! The whole of our flourishing municipal life derives its sustenance from a lie!

Peter Stockmann. All imagination — or something even worse. The man who can throw out such offensive insinuations about his native town must be an enemy to our community.

Dr. Stockmann. [*Going up to him*] Do you dare to —!

Mrs. Stockmann. [*Throwing herself between them*] Thomas!

Petra. [*Catching her father by the arm*] Don't lose your temper, father!

Peter Stockmann. I will not expose myself to violence. Now you have had a warning; so reflect on what you owe to yourself and your family. Goodby. [*Goes out.*]

Dr. Stockmann. [*Walking up and down*] Am I to put up with such treatment as this? In my own house, Katherine! What do you think of that!

Mrs. Stockmann. Indeed it is both shameful and absurd, Thomas —

Petra. If only I could give uncle a piece of my mind —

Dr. Stockmann. It is my own fault. I ought to have flown out at him long ago! — shown my teeth! — bitten! To hear him call me an enemy to our community! Me! I shall not take that lying down, upon my soul!

Mrs. Stockmann. But, dear Thomas, your brother has power on his side —

Dr. Stockmann. Yes, but I have right on mine, I tell you.

Mrs. Stockmann. Oh yes, right — right. What is the use of hav-ing right on your side if you have not might?

Petra. Oh, mother! — how can you say such a thing!

Dr. Stockmann. Do you imagine that in a free country it is no use having right on your side? You are absurd, Katherine. Besides, haven't I the liberal-minded, independent press to lead the way, and the compact majority behind me? That is might enough, I should think!

Mrs. Stockmann. But, good heavens, Thomas, you don't mean to — ?

Dr. Stockmann. Don't mean to what?

Mrs. Stockmann. To set yourself up in opposition to your brother.

Dr. Stockmann. In God's name, what else do you suppose I should do but take my stand on right and truth?

Petra. Yes, I was just going to say that.

Mrs. Stockmann. But it won't do you any earthly good. If they won't do it, they won't.

Dr. Stockmann. Oho, Katherine! Just give me time, and you will see how I will carry the war into their camp.

Mrs. Stockmann. Yes, you carry the war into their camp, and you get your dismissal — that is what you will do.

Dr. Stockmann. In any case I shall have done my duty toward the public — toward the community. I, who am called its enemy!

Mrs. Stockmann. But toward your family, Thomas? Toward your own home! Do you think that is doing your duty toward those you have to provide for?

Petra. Ah, don't think always first of us, mother.

Mrs. Stockmann. Oh, it is easy for you to talk; you are able to shift for yourself, if need be. But remember the boys, Thomas; and think a little, too, of yourself, and of me —

Dr. Stockmann. I think you are out of your senses, Katherine! If I were to be such a miserable coward as to go on my knees to Peter and his damned crew, do you suppose I should ever know an hour's peace of mind all my life afterwards?

Mrs. Stockmann. I don't know anything about that; but God

preserve us from the peace of mind we shall have, all the same, if you go on defying him! You will find yourself again without means of subsistence, with no income to count upon. I should think we had had enough of that in the old days. Remember that, Thomas; think what that means.

Dr. Stockmann. [*Collecting himself with a struggle and clenching his fists*] And this is what this slavery can bring upon a free, honorable man! Isn't it horrible, Katherine?

Mrs. Stockmann. Yes, it is sinful to treat you so, it is perfectly true. But, good heavens, one has to put up with so much injustice in this world. — There are the boys, Thomas! Look at them! What is to become of them? Oh, no, no, you can never have the heart — [EJLIF *and* MORTEN *have come in while she was speaking, with their schoolbooks in their hands.*]

Dr. Stockmann. The boys — ! [*Recovers himself suddenly.*] No, even if the whole world goes to pieces, I will never bow my neck to this yoke! [*Goes toward his room.*]

Mrs. Stockmann. [*Following him*] Thomas — what are you going to do!

Dr. Stockmann. [*At his door*] I mean to have the right to look my sons in the face when they are grown men. [*Goes into his room.*]

Mrs. Stockmann. [*Bursting into tears*] God help us all!

Petra. Father is splendid! He will not give in. [*The boys look on in amazement;* PETRA *signs to them not to speak.*]

ACT III

SCENE. *The editorial office of the* People's Messenger. *The entrance door is on the left-hand side of the back wall; on the right-hand side is another door with glass panels through which the printing room can be seen. Another door in the right-hand wall. In the middle of the room is a large table covered with papers, newspapers, and books. In the foreground on the left a window, before which stands a desk and a high stool. There are a couple of easy chairs by the table, and other chairs standing along the wall. The room is dingy and uncomfortable; the furniture is old, the chairs stained and torn.*

In the printing room the compositors are seen at work, and a printer is working a hand-press. HOVSTAD *is sitting at the desk, writing.* BILLING *comes in from the right with* DR. STOCKMANN'S *manuscript in his hand.*

Billing. Well, I must say!

Hovstad. [*Still writing*] Have you read it through?

Billing. [*Laying the MS on the desk*] Yes, indeed I have.

Hovstad. Don't you think the Doctor hits them pretty hard?

Billing. Hard? Bless my soul, he's crushing! Every word falls like — how shall I put it? — like the blow of a sledge hammer.

Hovstad. Yes, but they are not the people to throw up the sponge at the first blow.

Billing. That is true; and for that reason we must strike blow upon blow until the whole of this aristocracy tumbles to pieces. As I sat in there reading this, I almost seemed to see a revolution in being.

Hovstad. [*Turning round*] Hush! — Speak so that Aslaksen cannot hear you.

Billing. [*Lowering his voice*] Aslaksen is a chicken-hearted chap, a coward; there is nothing of the man in him. But this time you will insist on your own way, won't you? You will put the Doctor's article in?

Hovstad. Yes, and if the Mayor doesn't like it —

Billing. That will be the devil of a nuisance.

Hovstad. Well, fortunately, we can turn the situation to good account, whatever happens. If the Mayor will not fall in with the Doctor's project, he will have all the small tradesmen down on him — the whole of the Householders' Association and the rest of them. And if he does fall in with it, he will fall out with the whole crowd of large shareholders in the Baths, who up to now have been his most valuable supporters —

Billing. Yes, because they will certainly have to fork out a pretty penny —

Hovstad. Yes, you may be sure they will. And in this way the ring will be broken up, you see, and then in every issue of the paper we will enlighten the public on the Mayor's incapability on one point and another, and make it clear that all the positions of trust in the town, the whole control of municipal affairs, ought to be put in the hands of the Liberals.

Billing. That is perfectly true! I see it coming — I see it coming; we are on the threshold of a revolution! [*A knock is heard at the door.*]

Hovstad. Hush! [*Calls out.*] Come in! [DR. STOCKMANN *comes in by the street door.* HOVSTAD *goes to meet him.*] Ah, it is you, Doctor! Well?

Dr. Stockmann. You may set to work and print it, Mr. Hovstad!

Hovstad. Has it come to that, then?

Billing. Hurrah!

Dr. Stockmann. Yes, print away. Undoubtedly it has come to that. Now they must take what they get. There is going to be a fight in the town, Mr. Billing!

Billing. War to the knife, I hope! We will set our knives to their throats, Doctor!

Dr. Stockmann. This article is only a beginning. I have already four or five more sketched out in my head. Where is Aslaksen?

Billing. [*Calls into the printing room*] Aslaksen, just come here for a minute!

Hovstad. Four or five more articles, did you say? On the same subject?

Dr. Stockmann. No — far from it, my dear fellow. No, they are about quite another matter. But they all spring from the question of the water-supply and the drainage. One thing leads to another, you know. It is like beginning to pull down an old house, exactly.

Billing. Upon my soul, it's true; you find you are not done till you have pulled all the old rubbish down.

Aslaksen. [*Coming in*] Pulled down? You are not thinking of pulling down the Baths surely, Doctor?

Hovstad. Far from it, don't be afraid.

Dr. Stockmann. No, we meant something quite different. Well, what do you think of my article, Mr. Hovstad?

Hovstad. I think it is simply a masterpiece —

Dr. Stockmann. Do you really think so? Well, I am very pleased, very pleased.

Hovstad. It is so clear and intelligible. One need have no special knowledge to understand the bearing of it. You will have every enlightened man on your side.

Aslaksen. And every prudent man too, I hope?

Billing. The prudent and the imprudent — almost the whole town.

Aslaksen. In that case we may venture to print it.

Dr. Stockmann. I should think so!

Hovstad. We will put it in tomorrow morning.

Dr. Stockmann. Of course — you must not lose a single day. What I wanted to ask you, Mr. Aslaksen, was if you would supervise the printing of it yourself.

Aslaksen. With pleasure.

Dr. Stockmann. Take care of it as if it were a treasure! No misprints — every word is important. I will look in again a little later; perhaps you will be able to let me see a proof. I can't tell you how eager I am to see it in print, and see it burst upon the public —

Billing. Burst upon them — yes, like a flash of lightning!

Dr. Stockmann. — And to have it submitted to the judgment of my intelligent fellow-townsmen. You cannot imagine what I have gone through today. I have been threatened first with one thing and then with another; they have tried to rob me of my most elementary rights as a man —

Billing. What! Your rights as a man!

Dr. Stockmann. — They have tried to degrade me, to make a coward of me, to force me to put personal interests before my most sacred convictions —

Billing. That is too much — I'm damned if it isn't.

Hovstad. Oh, you mustn't be surprised at anything from that quarter.

Dr. Stockmann. Well, they will get the worst of it with me; they may assure themselves of that. I shall consider the *People's Messenger* my sheet anchor now, and every single day I will bombard them with one article after another, like bombshells —

Aslaksen. Yes, but —

Billing. Hurrah! — It is war, it is war!

Dr. Stockmann. I shall smite them to the ground — I shall crush them — I shall break down all their defenses, before the eyes of the honest public! That is what I shall do!

Aslaksen. Yes, but in moderation, Doctor — proceed with moderation —

Billing. Not a bit of it, not a bit of it! Don't spare the dynamite!

Dr. Stockmann. Because it is not merely a question of water-supply and drains now, you know. No — it is the whole of our social life that we have got to purify and disinfect —

Billing. Spoken like a deliverer!

Dr. Stockmann. All the incapables must be turned out, you understand — and that in every walk of life! Endless vistas have opened themselves to my mind's eye today. I cannot see it all quite clearly yet, but I shall in time. Young and vigorous standard-bearers — those are what we need and must seek, my friends; we must have new men in command at all our outposts.

Billing. Hear, hear!

Dr. Stockmann. We only need to stand by one another, and it will all be perfectly easy. The revolution will be launched like a ship that runs smoothly off the stocks. Don't you think so?

Hovstad. For my part I think we have now a prospect of getting the municipal authority into the hands where it should lie.

Aslaksen. And if only we proceed with moderation, I cannot imagine that there will be any risk.

Dr. Stockmann. Who the devil cares whether there is any risk or not! What I am doing, I am doing in the name of truth and for the sake of my conscience.

Hovstad. You are a man who deserves to be supported, Doctor.

Aslaksen. Yes, there is no denying that the Doctor is a true friend to the town — a real friend to the community, that he is.

Billing. Take my word for it, Aslaksen, Dr. Stockmann is a friend of the people.

Aslaksen. I fancy the Householders' Association will make use of that expression before long.

Dr. Stockmann. [*Affected, grasps their hands.*] Thank you, thank you, my dear stanch friends. It is very refreshing to me to hear you say that; my brother called me something quite different. By Jove, he shall have it back, with interest! But now I must be off to see a poor devil. — I will come back, as I said. Keep a very careful eye on the manuscript, Aslaksen, and don't for worlds leave out any of my notes of exclamation! Rather put one or two more in! Capital, capital! Well, goodby for the present — goodby, goodby! [*They show him to the door, and bow him out.*]

Hovstad. He may prove an invaluably useful man to us.

Aslaksen. Yes, so long as he confines himself to this matter of the Baths. But if he goes farther afield, I don't think it would be advisable to follow him.

Hovstad. Hm! — that all depends —

Billing. You are so infernally timid, Aslaksen!

Aslaksen. Timid? Yes, when it is a question of the local authorities, I am timid, Mr. Billing; it is a lesson I have learned in the school of experience, let me tell you. But try me in higher politics, in matters that concern the government itself, and then see if I am timid.

Billing. No, you aren't, I admit. But this is simply contradicting yourself.

Aslaksen. I am a man with a conscience, and that is the whole matter. If you attack the government, you don't do the community any harm, anyway; those fellows pay no attention to attacks, you see — they go on just as they are, in spite of them. But *local* authorities are different; they *can* be turned out, and then perhaps you may get an ignorant lot into office who may do irreparable harm to the householders and everybody else.

Hovstad. But what of the education of citizens by self-government — don't you attach any importance to that?

Aslaksen. When a man has interests of his own to protect, he cannot think of everything, Mr. Hovstad.

Hovstad. Then I hope I shall never have interests of my own to protect!

Billing. Hear, hear!

Aslaksen. [*With a smile*] Hm! [*Points to the desk.*] Mr. Sheriff Stensgaard was your predecessor at that editorial desk.

Billing. [*Spitting*] Bah! That turncoat.

Hovstad. I am not a weathercock — and never will be.

Aslaksen. A politician should never be too certain of anything, Mr. Hovstad. And as for you, Mr. Billing, I should think it is time for you to be taking in a reef or two in your sails, seeing that you are applying for the post of secretary to the Bench.

Billing. I — !

Hovstad. Are you, Billing?

Billing. Well, yes — but you must clearly understand I am only doing it to annoy the bigwigs.[7]

Aslaksen. Anyhow, it is no business of mine. But if I am to be accused of timidity and of inconsistency in my principles, this is what I want to point out: my political past is an open book. I have never changed, except perhaps to become a little more moderate, you see. My heart is still with the people; but I don't deny that my reason has a certain bias toward the authorities — the local ones, I mean. [*Goes into the printing room.*]

Billing. Oughtn't we to try and get rid of him, Hovstad?

Hovstad. Do you know any one else who will advance the money for our paper and printing bill?

Billing. It is an infernal nuisance that we don't possess some capital to trade on.

Hovstad. [*Sitting down at his desk*] Yes, if we only had that, then —

Billing. Suppose you were to apply to Dr. Stockmann?

Hovstad. [*Turning over some papers*] What is the use? He has nothing.

_____
[7] **bigwigs:** slang for important officials.

Billing. No, but he has a warm man in the background, old Morten Kiil — " the Badger," as they call him.

Hovstad. [*Writing*] Are you so sure *he* has anything?

Billing. Good Lord, of course he has! And some of it must come to the Stockmanns. Most probably he will do something for the children, at all events.

Hovstad. [*Turning half round*] Are you counting on that?

Billing. Counting on it? Of course I am not counting on anything.

Hovstad. That is right. And I should not count on the secretaryship to the Bench either, if I were you; for I can assure you — you won't get it.

Billing. Do you think I am not quite aware of that? My object is precisely *not* to get it. A slight of that kind stimulates a man's fighting power — it is like getting a supply of fresh bile — and I am sure one needs that badly enough in a hole-and-corner place like this, where it is so seldom anything happens to stir one up.

Hovstad. [*Writing*] Quite so, quite so.

Billing. Ah, I shall be heard of yet! — Now I shall go and write the appeal to the Householders' Association. [*Goes into the room on the right.*]

Hovstad. [*Sitting at his desk, biting his penholder, says slowly*] Hm! — that's it, is it? [*A knock is heard.*] Come in! [PETRA *comes in by the outer door.* HOVSTAD *gets up.*] What, you! — here?

Petra. Yes, you must forgive me —

Hovstad. [*Pulling a chair forward*] Won't you sit down?

Petra. No, thank you; I must go again in a moment.

Hovstad. Have you come with a message from your father, by any chance?

Petra. No, I have come on my own account. [*Takes a book out of her coat pocket.*] Here is the English story.

Hovstad. Why have you brought it back?

Petra. Because I am not going to translate it.

Hovstad. But you promised me faithfully —

Petra. Yes, but then I had not read it. I don't suppose you have read it either?

Hovstad. No, you know quite well I don't understand English; but —

Petra. Quite so. That is why I wanted to tell you that you must find something else. [*Lays the book on the table.*] You can't use this for the *People's Messenger.*

Hovstad. Why not?

Petra. Because it conflicts with all your opinions.

Hovstad. Oh, for that matter —

Petra. You don't understand me. The burden of this story is that there is a supernatural power that looks after the so-called good people in this world and makes everything happen for the best in their case — while all the so-called bad people are punished.

Hovstad. Well, but that is all right. That is just what our readers want.

Petra. And are you going to be the one to give it to them? For myself, I do not believe a word of it. You know quite well that things do not happen so in reality.

Hovstad. You are perfectly right; but an editor cannot always act as he would prefer. He is often obliged to bow to the wishes of the public in unimportant matters. Politics are the most important thing in life — for a newspaper, anyway; and if I want to carry my public with me on the path that leads to liberty and progress, I must not frighten them away. If they find a moral tale of this sort in the serial at the bottom of the page, they will be all the more ready to read what is printed above it; they feel more secure, as it were.

Petra. For shame! You would never go and set a snare like that for your readers; you are not a spider!

Hovstad. [*Smiling*] Thank you for having such a good opinion of me. No; as a matter of fact that is Billing's idea and not mine.

Petra. Billing's!

Hovstad. Yes; anyway he propounded that theory here one day. And it is Billing who is so anxious to have that story in the paper; I don't know anything about the book.

Petra. But how can Billing, with his emancipated views —

Hovstad. Oh, Billing is a many-sided man. He is applying for the post of secretary to the Bench, too, I hear.

Petra. I don't believe it, Mr. Hovstad. How could he possibly bring himself to do such a thing?

Hovstad. Ah, you must ask him that.

Petra. I should never have thought it of him.

Hovstad. [*Looking more closely at her*] No? Does it really surprise you so much?

Petra. Yes. Or perhaps not altogether. Really, I don't quite know —

Hovstad. We journalists are not worth much, Miss Stockmann.

Petra. Do you really mean that?

Hovstad. I think so sometimes.

Petra. Yes, in the ordinary affairs of everyday life, perhaps; I can understand that. But now, when you have taken a weighty matter in hand —

Hovstad. This matter of your father's, you mean?

Petra. Exactly. It seems to me that now you must feel you are a man worth more than most.

Hovstad. Yes, today I do feel something of that sort.

Petra. Of course you do, don't you? It is a splendid vocation you have chosen — to smooth the way for the march of unappreciated truths, and new and courageous lines of thought. If it were nothing more than because you stand fearlessly in the open and take up the cause of an injured man —

Hovstad. Especially when that injured man is — ahem! — I don't rightly know how to —

Petra. When that man is so upright and so honest, you mean?

Hovstad. [*More gently*] Especially when he is your father, I meant.

Petra. [*Suddenly checked*] That?

Hovstad. Yes, Petra — Miss Petra.

Petra. Is it *that*, that is first and foremost with you? Not the matter itself? Not the truth? — not my father's big generous heart?

Hovstad. Certainly — of course — that, too.

Petra. No, thank you; you have betrayed yourself, Mr. Hovstad, and now I shall never trust you again in anything.

Hovstad. Can you really take it so amiss in me that it is mostly for your sake — ?

Petra. What I am angry with you for, is for not having been honest with my father. You talked to him as if the truth and the good of the community were what lay nearest to your heart. You have made fools of both my father and me. You are not the man you made yourself out to be. And that I shall never forgive you — never!

Hovstad. You ought not to speak so bitterly, Miss Petra — least of all now.

Petra. Why not now, especially?

Hovstad. Because your father cannot do without my help.

Petra. [*Looking him up and down*] Are you that sort of man, too? For shame!

Hovstad. No, no, I am not. This came upon me so unexpectedly — you must believe that.

Petra. I know what to believe. Goodby.

Aslaksen. [*Coming from the printing room, hurriedly and with an air of mystery*] Damnation, Hovstad! — [*Sees* PETRA.] Oh, this is awkward —

Petra. There is the book; you must give it to some one else. [*Goes toward the door.*]

Hovstad. [*Following her*] But, Miss Stockmann —

Petra. Goodby. [*Goes out.*]

Aslaksen. I say — Mr. Hovstad —

Hovstad. Well, well! — what is it?

Aslaksen. The Mayor is outside in the printing room.

Hovstad. The Mayor, did you say?

Aslaksen. Yes, he wants to speak to you. He came in by the back door — didn't want to be seen, you understand.

Hovstad. What can he want? Wait a bit — I will go myself. [*Goes to the door of the printing room, opens it, bows, and invites* PETER STOCKMANN *in.*] Just see, Aslaksen, that no one —

Aslaksen. Quite so. [*Goes into the printing room.*]

Peter Stockmann. You did not expect to see me here, Mr. Hovstad?

Hovstad. No, I confess I did not.

Peter Stockmann. [*Looking around*] You are very snug in here — very nice, indeed.

Hovstad. Oh —

Peter Stockmann. And here I come, without any notice, to take up your time!

Hovstad. By all means, Mr. Mayor. I am at your service. But let me relieve you of your — [*Takes* STOCKMANN's *hat and stick and puts them on a chair.*] Won't you sit down?

Peter Stockmann. [*Sitting down by the table*] Thank you. [HOVSTAD *sits down.*] I have had an extremely annoying experience to-day, Mr. Hovstad.

Hovstad. Really? Ah well, I expect with all the various business you have to attend to —

Peter Stockmann. The Medical Officer of the Baths is responsible for what happened today.

Hovstad. Indeed? The Doctor?

Peter Stockmann. He has addressed a kind of report to the Baths Committee on the subject of certain supposed defects in the Baths.

Hovstad. Has he, indeed?

Peter Stockmann. Yes — has he not told you? I thought he said —

Hovstad. Ah, yes — it is true he did mention something about —

Aslaksen. [*Coming from the printing room*] I ought to have that copy —

Hovstad. [*Angrily*] Ahem! — there it is on the desk.

Aslaksen. [*Taking it*] Right.

Peter Stockmann. But look there — that is the thing I was speaking of!

Aslaksen. Yes, that is the Doctor's article, Mr. Mayor.

Hovstad. Oh, is *that* what you were speaking about?

Peter Stockmann. Yes, that is it. What do you think of it?

Hovstad. Oh, I am only a layman — and I have only taken a very cursory glance at it.

Peter Stockmann. But you are going to print it?

Hovstad. I cannot very well refuse a distinguished man —

Aslaksen. I have nothing to do with editing the paper, Mr. Mayor —

Peter Stockmann. I understand.

Aslaksen. I merely print what is put into my hands.

Peter Stockmann. Quite so.

Aslaksen. And so I must — [*Moves off toward the printing room.*]

Peter Stockmann. No, but wait a moment, Mr. Aslaksen. You will allow me, Mr. Hovstad?

Hovstad. If you please, Mr. Mayor.

Peter Stockmann. You are a discreet and thoughtful man, Mr. Aslaksen.

Aslaksen. I am delighted to hear you think so, sir.

Peter Stockmann. And a man of very considerable influence.

Aslaksen. Chiefly among the small tradesmen, sir.

Peter Stockmann. The small tax-payers are the majority — here as everywhere else.

Aslaksen. That is true.

Peter Stockmann. And I have no doubt you know the general trend of opinion among them, don't you?

Aslaksen. Yes, I think I may say I do, Mr. Mayor.

Peter Stockmann. Yes. Well, since there is such a praiseworthy spirit of self-sacrifice among the less wealthy citizens of our town —

Aslaksen. What?

Hovstad. Self-sacrifice?

Peter Stockmann. It is pleasing evidence of a public-spirited feeling, extremely pleasing evidence. I might almost say I hardly expected it. But you have a closer knowledge of public opinion than I.

Aslaksen. But, Mr. Mayor —

Peter Stockmann. And indeed it is no small sacrifice that the town is going to make.

Hovstad. The town?

Aslaksen. But I don't understand. Is it the Baths — ?

Peter Stockmann. At a provisional estimate, the alterations that the Medical Officer asserts to be desirable will cost somewhere about twenty thousand pounds.

Aslaksen. That is a lot of money, but —

Peter Stockmann. Of course it will be necessary to raise a municipal loan.

Hovstad. [*Getting up*] Surely you never mean that the town must pay — ?

Aslaksen. Do you mean that it must come out of the municipal funds? — out of the ill-filled pockets of the small tradesmen?

Peter Stockmann. Well, my dear Mr. Aslaksen, where else is the money to come from?

Aslaksen. The gentlemen who own the Baths ought to provide that.

Peter Stockmann. The proprietors of the Baths are not in a position to incur any further expense.

Aslaksen. Is that absolutely certain, Mr. Mayor?

Peter Stockmann. I have satisfied myself that it is so. If the town wants these very extensive alterations, it will have to pay for them.

Aslaksen. But, damn it all — I beg your pardon — this is quite another matter, Mr. Hovstad!

Hovstad. It is, indeed.

Peter Stockmann. The most fatal part of it is that we shall be obliged to shut the Baths for a couple of years.

Hovstad. Shut them? Shut them altogether?

Aslaksen. For two years?

Peter Stockmann. Yes, the work will take as long as that — at least.

Aslaksen. I'm damned if we will stand that, Mr. Mayor! What are we householders to live upon in the meantime?

Peter Stockmann. Unfortunately that is an extremely difficult question to answer, Mr. Aslaksen. But what would you have us do? Do you suppose we shall have a single visitor in the town, if we go about proclaiming that our water is polluted, that we are living over a plague spot, that the entire town —

Aslaksen. And the whole thing is merely imagination?

Peter Stockmann. With the best will in the world, I have not been able to come to any other conclusion.

Aslaksen. Well, then, I must say it is absolutely unjustifiable of Dr. Stockmann — I beg your pardon, Mr. Mayor —

Peter Stockmann. What you say is lamentably true, Mr. Aslaksen. My brother has unfortunately always been a headstrong man.

Aslaksen. After this, do you mean to give him your support, Mr. Hovstad?

Hovstad. Can you suppose for a moment that I — ?

Peter Stockmann. I have drawn up a short *résumé* [8] of the situation as it appears from a reasonable man's point of view. In it I have indicated how certain possible defects might suitably be remedied without outrunning the resources of the Baths Committee.

Hovstad. Have you got it with you, Mr. Mayor?

Peter Stockmann. [*Fumbling in his pocket*] Yes, I brought it with me in case you should —

Aslaksen. Good Lord, there he is!

Peter Stockmann. Who? My brother?

Hovstad. Where? Where?

Aslaksen. He has just gone through the printing room.

Peter Stockmann. How unlucky! I don't want to meet him here, and I had still several things to speak to you about.

Hovstad. [*Pointing to the door on the right*] Go in there for the present.

Peter Stockmann. But — ?

Hovstad. You will only find Billing in there.

Aslaksen. Quick, quick, Mr. Mayor — he is just coming.

Peter Stockmann. Yes, very well; but see that you get rid of him quickly. [*Goes out through the door on the right, which* ASLAKSEN *opens for him and shuts after him.*]

Hovstad. Pretend to be doing something, Aslaksen. [*Sits down and writes.* ASLAKSEN *begins foraging among a heap of newspapers that are lying on a chair.*]

Dr. Stockmann. [*Coming in from the printing room*] Here I am again. [*Puts down his hat and stick.*]

Hovstad. [*Writing*] Already, Doctor? Hurry up with what we were speaking about, Aslaksen. We are very pressed for time today.

Dr. Stockmann. [*To* ASLAKSEN] No proof for me to see yet, I hear.

[8] résumé: summary.

Aslaksen. [*Without turning round*] You couldn't expect it yet, Doctor.

Dr. Stockmann. No, no; but I am impatient, as you can understand. I shall not know a moment's peace of mind till I see it in print.

Hovstad. Hm! — It will take a good while yet, won't it, Aslaksen?

Aslaksen. Yes, I am almost afraid it will.

Dr. Stockmann. All right, my dear friends; I will come back. I do not mind coming back twice if necessary. A matter of such great importance — the welfare of the town at stake — it is no time to shirk trouble. [*Is just going, but stops and comes back.*] Look here — there is one thing more I want to speak to you about.

Hovstad. Excuse me, but could it not wait till some other time?

Dr. Stockmann. I can tell you in half a dozen words. It is only this: When my article is read tomorrow and it is realized that I have been quietly working the whole winter for the welfare of the town —

Hovstad. Yes, but, Doctor —

Dr. Stockmann. I know what you are going to say. You don't see how on earth it was any more than my duty — my obvious duty as a citizen. Of course it wasn't; I know that as well as you. But, my fellow citizens, you know — ! Good Lord, think of all the good souls who think so highly of me — !

Aslaksen. Yes, our townsfolk have had a very high opinion of you so far, Doctor.

Dr. Stockmann. Yes, and that is just why I am afraid they — Well, this is the point; when this reaches them, especially the poorer classes, and sounds in their ears like a summons to take the town's affairs into their own hands for the future —

Hovstad. [*Getting up*] Ahem! Doctor, I won't conceal from you the fact —

Dr. Stockmann. Ah! — I knew there was something in the wind! But I won't hear a word of it. If anything of that sort is being set on foot —

Hovstad. Of what sort?

Dr. Stockmann. Well, whatever it is — whether it is a demonstration in my honor, or a banquet, or a subscription list for some presentation to me — whatever it is, you must promise me solemnly and faithfully to put a stop to it. You, too, Mr. Aslaksen; do you understand?

Hovstad. You must forgive me, Doctor, but sooner or later we must tell you the plain truth —

He is interrupted by the entrance of Mrs. Stockmann, *who comes in from the street door.*

Mrs. Stockmann. [*Seeing her husband*] Just as I thought!

Hovstad. [*Going toward her*] You, too, Mrs. Stockmann?

Dr. Stockmann. What on earth do *you* want here, Katherine?

Mrs. Stockmann. I should think you know very well what I want.

Hovstad. Won't you sit down? Or perhaps —

Mrs. Stockmann. No, thank you; don't trouble. And you must not be offended at my coming to fetch my husband; I am the mother of three children, you know.

Dr. Stockmann. Nonsense! — we know all about that.

Mrs. Stockmann. Well, one would not give you credit for much thought for your wife and children today; if you had had that, you would not have gone and dragged us all into misfortune.

Dr. Stockmann. Are you out of your senses, Katherine! Because a man has a wife and children, is he not to be allowed to proclaim the truth — is he not to be allowed to be an actively useful citizen — is he not to be allowed to do a service to his native town?

Mrs. Stockmann. Yes, Thomas — in reason.

Aslaksen. Just what I say. Moderation in everything.

Mrs. Stockmann. And that is why you wrong us, Mr. Hovstad, in enticing my husband away from his home and making a dupe of him in all this.

Hovstad. I certainly am making a dupe of no one —

Dr. Stockmann. Making a dupe of me! Do you suppose I should allow myself to be duped!

Mrs. Stockmann. It is just what you do. I know quite well you have more brains than any one in the town, but you are extremely easily duped, Thomas. [*To* Hovstad.] Please to realize that he loses his post at the Baths if you print what he has written —

Aslaksen. What!

Hovstad. Look here, Doctor —

Dr. Stockmann. [*Laughing*] Ha — ha! — just let them try! No, no — they will take good care not to. I have got the compact majority behind me, let me tell you!

Mrs. Stockmann. Yes, that is just the worst of it — your having any such horrid thing behind you.

Dr. Stockmann. Rubbish, Katherine! — Go home and look after your house and leave me to look after the community. How can you be so afraid, when I am so confident and happy? [*Walks up and down, rubbing his hands.*] Truth and the People will win the fight, you may be certain! I see the whole of the broad-minded middle class marching like a victorious army — ! [*Stops beside a chair.*] What the deuce is that lying there?

Aslaksen. Good Lord!

Hovstad. Ahem!

Dr. Stockmann. Here we have the topmost pinnacle of authority! [*Takes the Mayor's official hat carefully between his finger tips and holds it up in the air.*]

Mrs. Stockmann. The Mayor's hat!

Dr. Stockmann. And here is the staff of office too. How in the name of all that's wonderful — ?

Hovstad. Well, you see —

Dr. Stockmann. Oh, I understand. He has been here trying to talk you over. Ha — ha! — he made rather a mistake there! And as soon as he caught sight of me in the printing room — [*Bursts out laughing.*] Did he run away, Mr. Aslaksen?

Aslaksen. [*Hurriedly*] Yes, he ran away, Doctor.

Dr. Stockmann. Ran away without his stick or his — Fiddlesticks! Peter doesn't run away and leave his belongings behind him. But what the deuce have you done with him? Ah! — in there, of course. Now you shall see, Katherine!

Mrs. Stockmann. Thomas — please don't — !

Aslaksen. Don't be rash, Doctor. [DR. STOCKMANN *has put on the Mayor's hat and taken his stick in his hand. He goes up to the door, opens it, and stands with his hand to his hat at the salute.* PETER STOCKMANN *comes in, red with anger.* BILLING *follows him.*]

Peter Stockmann. What does this tomfoolery mean?

Dr. Stockmann. Be respectful, my good Peter. I am the chief authority in the town now. [*Walks up and down.*]

Mrs. Stockmann. [*Almost in tears*] Really, Thomas!

Peter Stockmann. [*Following him about*] Give me my hat and stick.

Dr. Stockmann. [*In the same tone as before*] If you are chief constable, let me tell you that I am the Mayor — I am the master of the whole town, please understand!

Peter Stockmann. Take off my hat, I tell you. Remember it is part of an official uniform.

Dr. Stockmann. Pooh! Do you think the newly-awakened, lionhearted people are going to be frightened by an official hat? There is going to be a revolution in the town tomorrow, let me tell you. You thought you could turn me out; but now I shall turn you out — turn you out of all your various offices. Do you think I cannot? Listen to me. I have triumphant social forces behind me. Hovstad and Billing will thunder in the *People's Messenger,* and Aslaksen will take the field at the head of the whole Householders' Association —

Alsaksen. That I won't, Doctor.

Dr. Stockmann. Of course you will —

Peter Stockmann. Ah! — may I ask then if Mr. Hovstad intends to join this agitation?

Hovstad. No, Mr. Mayor.

Aslaksen. No, Mr. Hovstad is not such a fool as to go and ruin his paper and himself for the sake of an imaginary grievance.

Dr. Stockmann. [*Looking round him*] What does this mean?

Hovstad. You have represented your case in a false light, Doctor, and therefore I am unable to give you my support.

Billing. And after what the Mayor was so kind as to tell me just now, I —

Dr. Stockmann. A false light! Leave that part of it to me. Only print my article; I am quite capable of defending it.

Hovstad. I am not going to print it. I cannot and will not and dare not print it.

Dr. Stockmann. You dare not? What nonsense! — You are the editor; and an editor controls his paper, I suppose!

Aslaksen. No, it is the subscribers, Doctor.

Peter Stockmann. Fortunately, yes.

Aslaksen. It is public opinion — the enlightened public — householders and people of that kind; they control the newspapers.

Dr. Stockmann. [*Composedly*] And I have all these influences against me?

Aslaksen. Yes, you have. It would mean the absolute ruin of the community if your article were to appear.

Dr. Stockmann. Indeed!

Peter Stockmann. My hat and stick, if you please. [Dr. Stockmann *takes off the hat and lays it on the table with the stick.* Peter Stockmann *takes them up.*] Your authority as Mayor has come to an untimely end.

Dr. Stockmann. We have not got to the end yet. [*To* Hovstad.] Then it is quite impossible for you to print my article in the *People's Messenger?*

Hovstad. Quite impossible — out of regard for your family as well.

Mrs. Stockmann. You need not concern yourself about his family, thank you, Mr. Hovstad.

Peter Stockmann. [*Taking a paper from his pocket*] It will be sufficient, for the guidance of the public, if this appears. It is an official statement. May I trouble you?

Hovstad. [*Taking the paper*] Certainly; I will see that it is printed.

Dr. Stockmann. But not mine. Do you imagine that you can silence me and stifle the truth? You will not find it so easy as you suppose. Mr. Aslaksen, kindly take my manuscript at once and print it as a pamphlet — at my expense. I will have four hundred copies — no, five — six hundred.

Aslaksen. If you offered me its weight in gold, I could not lend my press for any such purpose, Doctor. It would be flying in the face of public opinion. You will not get it printed anywhere in the town.

Dr. Stockmann. Then give it back to me.

Hovstad. [*Giving him the MS.*] Here it is.

Dr. Stockmann. [*Taking his hat and stick*] It shall be made public all the same. I will read it out at a mass meeting of the townspeople. All my fellow citizens shall hear the voice of truth!

Peter Stockmann. You will not find any public body in the town that will give you the use of their hall for such a purpose.

Aslaksen. Not a single one, I am certain.

Billing. No, I'm damned if you will find one.

Mrs. Stockmann. But this is too shameful! Why should every one turn against you like that?

Dr. Stockmann. [*Angrily*] I will tell you why. It is because all the men in this town are old women — like you; they all think of nothing but their families, and never of the community.

Mrs. Stockmann. [*Putting her arm into his*] Then I will show them that an — an old woman can be a man for once. I am going to stand by you, Thomas!

Dr. Stockmann. Bravely said, Katherine! It shall be made public — as I am a living soul! If I can't hire a hall, I shall hire a drum, and parade the town with it and read it at every street corner.

Peter Stockmann. You are surely not such an arrant fool as that!

Dr. Stockmann. Yes, I am.

Aslaksen. You won't find a single man in the whole town to go with you.

Billing. No, I'm damned if you will.

Mrs. Stockmann. Don't give in, Thomas. I will tell the boys to go with you.

Dr. Stockmann. That is a splendid idea!

Mrs. Stockmann. Morten will be delighted; and Ejlif will do whatever he does.

Dr. Stockmann. Yes, and Petra! — and you, too, Katherine!

Mrs. Stockmann. No, I won't do that, but I will stand at the window and watch you; that's what I will do.

Dr. Stockmann. [*Puts his arms around her and kisses her.*] Thank you, my dear! Now you and I are going to try a fall,[9] my fine gentlemen! I am going to see whether a pack of cowards can succeed in gagging a patriot who wants to purify society! [*He and his wife go out by the street door.*]

Peter Stockmann. [*Shaking his head seriously*] Now he has sent *her* out of her senses, too.

ACT IV

SCENE. *A big old-fashioned room in* CAPTAIN HORSTER'S *house. At the back folding doors, which are standing open, lead to an anteroom. Three windows in the left-hand wall. In the middle of the opposite wall a platform has been erected. On this is a small table with two candles, a water-bottle and glass, and a bell. The room is lit by lamps placed between the windows. In the foreground on the left there is a table with candles and a chair. To the right is a door and some chairs standing near it. The room is nearly filled with a crowd of townspeople of all sorts, a few women and schoolboys being amongst them. People are still streaming in from the back, and the room is soon filled.*

First Citizen. [*Meeting another*] Hullo, Lamstad! You here, too?

Second Citizen. I go to every public meeting, I do.

Third Citizen. Brought your whistle, too, I expect!

Second Citizen. I should think so. Haven't you?

Third Citizen. Rather! And old Evensen said he was going to bring a cow-horn, he did.

Second Citizen. Good old Evensen! [*Laughter among the crowd.*]

Fourth Citizen. [*Coming up to them*] I say, tell me what is going on here tonight.

Second Citizen. Dr. Stockmann is going to deliver an address attacking the Mayor.

Fourth Citizen. But the Mayor is his brother.

⁹ **try a fall:** come to open struggle

First Citizen. That doesn't matter; Dr. Stockmann's not the chap to be afraid.

Third Citizen. But he is in the wrong; it said so in the *People's Messenger.*

Second Citizen. Yes, I expect he must be in the wrong this time, because neither the Householders' Association nor the Citizens' Club would lend him their hall for his meeting.

First Citizen. He couldn't even get the loan of the hall at the Baths.

Second Citizen. No, I should think not.

A Man in Another Part of the Crowd. I say — who are we to back up in this?

Another Man, Beside Him. Watch Aslaksen, and do as he does.

Billing. [*Pushing his way through the crowd, with a writing case under his arm*] Excuse me, gentlemen — do you mind letting me through? I am reporting for the *People's Messenger.* Thank you very much! [*He sits down at the table on the left.*]

A Workman. Who was that?

Second Workman. Don't you know him? It's Billing, who writes for Aslaksen's paper.

CAPTAIN HORSTER *brings in* MRS. STOCKMANN *and* PETRA *through the door on the right.* EJLIF *and* MORTEN *follow them in.*

Horster. I thought you might all sit here; you can slip out easily from here, if things get too lively.

Mrs. Stockmann. Do you think there will be a disturbance,

Horster. One can never tell — with such a crowd. But sit down, and don't be uneasy.

Mrs. Stockmann. [*Sitting down*] It was extremely kind of you to offer my husband the room.

Horster. Well, if nobody else would —

Petra. [*Who has sat down beside her mother*] And it was a plucky thing to do, Captain Horster.

Horster. Oh, it is not such a great matter as all that.

HOVSTAD *and* ASLAKSEN *make their way through the crowd.*

Aslaksen. [*Going up to* HORSTER] Has the Doctor not come yet?

Horster. He is waiting in the next room. [*Movement in the crowd by the door at the back.*]

Hovstad. Look — here comes the Mayor!

Billing. Yes, I'm damned if he hasn't come after all!

PETER STOCKMANN *makes his way gradually through the crowd, bows courteously, and takes up a position by the wall on the left. Shortly afterwards* DR. STOCKMANN *comes in by the right-hand door. He is dressed in a black frock coat, with a white tie. There is a little feeble applause, which is hushed down. Silence is obtained.*

Dr. Stockmann. [*In an undertone*] How do you feel, Katherine?

Mrs. Stockmann. All right, thank you. [*Lowering her voice*] Be sure not to lose your temper, Thomas.

Dr. Stockmann. Oh, I know how to control myself. [*Looks at his watch, steps on to the platform, and bows.*] It is a quarter past — so I will begin. [*Takes his MS. out of his pocket.*]

Aslaksen. I think we ought to elect a chairman first.

Dr. Stockmann. No, it is quite unnecessary.

Some of the Crowd. Yes — yes!

Peter Stockmann. I certainly think, too, that we ought to have a chairman.

Dr. Stockmann. But I have called this meeting to deliver a lecture, Peter.

Peter Stockmann. Dr. Stockmann's lecture may possibly lead to a considerable conflict of opinion.

Voices in the Crowd. A chairman! A chairman!

Hovstad. The general wish of the meeting seems to be that a chairman should be elected.

Dr. Stockmann. [*Restraining himself*] Very well — let the meeting have its way.

Aslaksen. Will the Mayor be good enough to undertake the task?

Three Men. [*Clapping their hands*] Bravo! Bravo!

Peter Stockmann. For various reasons, which you will easily understand, I must beg to be excused. But fortunately we have amongst us a man who, I think, will be acceptable to you all. I refer to the President of the Householders' Association, Mr. Aslaksen.

Several Voices. Yes — Aslaksen! Bravo, Aslaksen! [DR. STOCKMANN *takes up his MS. and walks up and down the platform.*]

Aslaksen. Since my fellow citizens choose to entrust me with this duty, I cannot refuse. [*Loud applause.* ASLAKSEN *mounts the platform.*]

Billing. [*Writing*] " Mr. Aslaksen was elected with enthusiasm."

Aslaksen. And now, as I am in this position, I should like to say a few brief words. I am a quiet and peaceable man, who believes in discreet moderation, and — and — in moderate discretion. All my friends can bear witness to that.

Several Voices. That's right! That's right, Aslaksen!

Aslaksen. I have learned in the school of life and experience that moderation is the most valuable virtue a citizen can possess —

Peter Stockmann. Hear, hear!

Aslaksen. — And, moreover, that discretion and moderation are what enable a man to be of most service to the community. I would therefore suggest to our esteemed fellow citizen, who has called this meeting, that he should strive to keep strictly within the bounds of moderation.

A Man by the Door. Three cheers for the Moderation Society!

A Voice. Shame!

Several Voices. Sh! — Sh!

Aslaksen. No interruptions, gentlemen, please! Does any one wish to make any remarks?

Peter Stockmann. Mr. Chairman.

Aslaksen. The Mayor will address the meeting.

Peter Stockmann. In consideration of the close relationship in which, as you all know, I stand to the present Medical Officer of the Baths, I should have preferred not to speak this evening. But my official position with regard to the Baths and my solicitude for the vital interests of the town compel me to bring forward a motion. I venture to presume that there is not a single one of our citizens present who considers it desirable that unreliable and exaggerated accounts of the sanitary condition of the Baths and the town should be spread abroad.

Several Voices. No, no! Certainly not! We protest against it!

Peter Stockmann. Therefore I should like to propose that the meeting should not permit the Medical Officer either to read or to comment on his proposed lecture.

Dr. Stockmann. [*Impatiently*] Not permit — ! What the devil — !

Mrs. Stockmann. [*Coughing*] Ahem! — ahem!

Dr. Stockmann. [*Collecting himself*] Very well. Go ahead!

Peter Stockmann. In my communication to the *People's Messenger,* I have put the essential facts before the public in such a way that every fair-minded citizen can easily form his own opinion. From it you will see that the main result of the Medical Officer's proposals — apart from their constituting a vote of censure on the leading men of the town — would be to saddle the ratepayers with an unnecessary expenditure of at least some thousands of pounds. [*Sounds of disapproval among the audience, and some catcalls.*]

Aslaksen. [*Ringing his bell*] Silence, please, gentlemen! I beg to support the Mayor's motion. I quite agree with him that there is something behind this agitation started by the Doctor. He talks about the Baths; but it is a revolution he is aiming at — he wants to get the administration of the town put into new hands. No one doubts the honesty of the Doctor's intentions — no one will suggest that there can be any two opinions as to that. I myself am a believer in self-government for the people, provided it does not fall too heavily on the ratepayers. But that would be the case here; and that is why I will see Dr. Stockmann damned — I beg your pardon — before I go with him in the matter. You can pay too dearly for a thing sometimes; that is my opinion. [*Loud applause on all sides.*]

Hovstad. I, too, feel called upon to explain my position. Dr. Stockmann's agitation appeared to be gaining a certain amount of sympathy at first; so I supported it as impartially as I could. But presently we had reason to suspect that we had allowed ourselves to be misled by misrepresentation of the state of affairs —

Dr. Stockmann. Misrepresentation — !

Hovstad. Well, let us say a not entirely trustworthy representation. The Mayor's statement has proved that. I hope no one here has any doubt as to my liberal principles; the attitude of the *People's Messenger* toward important political questions is well known to every one. But the advice of experienced and thoughtful men has convinced me that in purely local matters a newspaper ought to proceed with a certain caution.

Aslaksen. I entirely agree with the speaker.

Hovstad. And, in the matter before us, it is now an undoubted fact that Dr. Stockmann has public opinion against him. Now, what is an editor's first and most obvious duty, gentlemen? Is it not to work in harmony with his readers? Has he not received a sort of tacit mandate to work persistently and assiduously for the welfare of those whose opinions he represents? Or is it possible I am mistaken in that?

Voices from the Crowd. No, no! You are quite right!

Hovstad. It has cost me a severe struggle to break with a man in whose house I have been lately a frequent guest — a man who till today has been able to pride himself on the undivided goodwill of his fellow citizens — a man whose only, or at all events whose essential, failing is that he is swayed by his heart rather than his head.

A Few Scattered Voices. That is true! Bravo, Stockmann!

Hovstad. But my duty to the community obliged me to break with him. And there is another consideration that impels me to oppose him, and, as far as possible, to arrest him on the perilous course he has adopted; that is, consideration for his family —

Dr. Stockmann. Please stick to the water-supply and drainage!

Hovstad. — Consideration, I repeat, for his wife and his children, for whom he has made no provision.

Morten. Is that us, mother?

Mrs. Stockmann. Hush!

Aslaksen. I will now put the Mayor's proposition to the vote.

Dr. Stockmann. There is no necessity! Tonight I have no intention of dealing with all that filth down at the Baths. No; I have something quite different to say to you.

Peter Stockmann. [*Aside*] What is coming now?

A Drunken Man. [*By the entrance door*] I am a ratepayer! And therefore I have a right to speak, too. And my entire — firm — inconceivable opinion is —

A Number of Voices. Be quiet, at the back there!

Others. He is drunk! Turn him out! [*They turn him out.*]

Dr. Stockmann. Am I allowed to speak?

Aslaksen. [*Ringing his bell*] Dr. Stockmann will address the meeting.

Dr. Stockmann. I should like to have seen any one, a few days ago, dare to attempt to silence me as has been done tonight! I would have defended my sacred rights as a man, like a lion! But now it is all one to me; I have something of even weightier importance to say to you. [*The crowd presses nearer to him,* Morten Kiil *conspicuous among them.*]

Dr. Stockmann. [*Continuing*] I have thought and pondered a great deal, these last few days — pondered over such a variety of things that in the end my head seemed too full to hold them —

Peter Stockmann. [*With a cough*] Ahem!

Dr. Stockmann. — But I got them clear in my mind at last, and then I saw the whole situation lucidly. And that is why I am standing here tonight. I have a great revelation to make to you, my fellow citizens! I will impart to you a discovery of a far wider scope than the trifling matter that our water-supply is poisoned and our medicinal Baths are standing on pestiferous soil.

A Number of Voices. [*Shouting*] Don't talk about the Baths! We won't hear you! None of that!

Dr. Stockmann. I have already told you that what I want to speak about is the great discovery I have made lately — the discovery that all the sources of our *moral* life are poisoned and that the whole fabric of our civic community is founded on the pestiferous soil of falsehood.

Voices of Disconcerted Citizens. What is that he says?

Peter Stockmann. Such an insinuation — !

Aslaksen. [*With his hand on his bell*] I call upon the speaker to moderate his language.

Dr. Stockmann. I have always loved my native town as a man only can love the home of his youthful days. I was not old when I went away from here; and exile, longing, and memories cast as it were an additional halo over both the town and its inhabitants. [*Some clapping and applause.*] And there I stayed, for many years, in a horrible hole far away up north. When I came into contact with some of the people that lived scattered about among the rocks, I often thought it would of been more service to the poor half-starved creatures if a veterinary doctor had been sent up there, instead of a man like me. [*Murmurs among the crowd.*]

Billing. [*Laying down his pen*] I'm damned if I have ever heard — !

Hovstad. It is an insult to a respectable population!

Dr. Stockmann. Wait a bit! I do not think any one will charge me with having forgotten my native town up there. I was like one of the eider-ducks brooding on its nest, and what I hatched was — the plans for these Baths. [*Applause and protests.*] And then when fate at last decreed for me the great happiness of coming home again — I assure you, gentlemen, I thought I had nothing more in the world to wish for. Or rather, there was one thing I wished for — eagerly, untiringly, ardently — and that was to be able to be of service to my native town and the good of the community.

Peter Stockmann. [*Looking at the ceiling*] You chose a strange way of doing it — ahem!

Dr. Stockmann. And so, with my eyes blinded to the real facts, I reveled in happiness. But yesterday morning — no, to be precise, it was yesterday afternoon — the eyes of my mind were opened wide, and the first thing I realized was the colossal stupidity of the authorities — [*Uproar, shouts, and laughter.* MRS. STOCKMANN *coughs persistently.*]

Peter Stockmann. Mr. Chairman!

Aslaksen. [*Ringing his bell*] By virtue of my authority — !

Dr. Stockmann. It is a petty thing to catch me up on a word, Mr. Aslaksen. What I mean is only that I got scent of the unbelievable piggishness our leading men had been responsible for down at the Baths. I can't stand leading men at any price! — I have had enough of such people in my time. They are like billy-goats in a young plantation; they do mischief everywhere. They stand in a free man's way, whichever way he turns, and what I should like best would be to see them exterminated like any other vermin — [*Uproar*]

Peter Stockmann. Mr. Chairman, can we allow such expressions to pass?

Aslaksen. [*With his hand on his bell*] Doctor — !

Dr. Stockmann. I cannot understand how it is that I have only now acquired a clear conception of what these gentry are, when I had almost daily before my eyes in this town such an excellent specimen of them — my brother Peter — slow-witted and hidebound in prejudice — [*Laughter, uproar, and hisses.* MRS. STOCKMANN *sits coughing assiduously.* ASLAKSEN *rings his bell violently.*]

The Drunken Man. [*Who has got in again*] Is it me he is talking about? My name's Petersen, all right — but devil take me if I —

Angry Voices. Turn out that drunken man! Turn him out. [*He is turned out again.*]

Peter Stockmann. Who was that person?

First Citizen. I don't know who he is, Mr. Mayor.

Second Citizen. He doesn't belong here.

Third Citizen. I expect he is a navvy [10] from over at — [*The rest is inaudible.*]

Aslaksen. He had obviously had too much beer. — Proceed, Doctor; but please strive to be moderate in your language.

Dr. Stockmann. Very well, gentlemen, I will say no more about our leading men. And if any one imagines, from what I have just said, that my object is to attack these people this evening, he is wrong — absolutely wide of the mark. For I cherish the comforting conviction that these parasites — all these venerable relics of a dying school of thought — are most admirably paving the way for their own extinction; they need no doctor's help to hasten their end. Nor is it folk of that kind who constitute the most pressing danger to the community. It is not they who are most instrumental in poisoning the sources of our moral life and infecting the ground on which we stand. It is not

---

[10] **navvy:** excavator.

they who are the most dangerous enemies of truth and freedom amongst us.

Shouts from All Sides. Who then? Who is it? Name! Name!

Dr. Stockmann. You may depend upon it I shall name them! That is precisely the great discovery I made yesterday. [*Raises his voice.*] The most dangerous enemy of truth and freedom amongst us is the compact majority — yes, the damned compact Liberal majority — that is it! Now you know! [*Tremendous uproar. Most of the crowd are shouting, stamping, and hissing. Some of the older men among them exchange stolen glances and seem to be enjoying themselves.* MRS. STOCKMANN *gets up, looking anxious.* EJLIF *and* MORTEN *advance threateningly upon some schoolboys who are playing pranks.* ASLAKSEN *rings his bell and begs for silence.* HOVSTAD *and* BILLING *both talk at once, but are inaudible. At last quiet is restored.*]

Aslaksen. As chairman, I call upon the speaker to withdraw the ill-considered expressions he has just used.

Dr. Stockmann. Never, Mr. Aslaksen! It is the majority in our community that denies me my freedom and seeks to prevent my speaking the truth.

Hovstad. The majority always has right on its side.

Billing. And truth too, by God!

Dr. Stockmann. The majority *never* has right on its side. Never, I say! That is one of these social lies against which an independent, intelligent man must wage war. Who is it that constitute the majority of the population in a country? Is it the clever folk or the stupid? I don't imagine you will dispute the fact that at present the stupid people are in an absolutely overwhelming majority all the world over. But, good Lord! — you can never pretend that it is right that the stupid folk should govern the clever ones! [*Uproar and cries*] Oh, yes — you can shout me down, I know! but you cannot answer me. The majority has *might* on its side — unfortunately; but *right* it has *not.* I am in the right — I and a few other scattered individuals. The minority is always in the right. [*Renewed uproar*]

Hovstad. Aha! — so Dr. Stockmann has become an aristocrat since the day before yesterday!

Dr. Stockmann. I have already said that I don't intend to waste a word on the puny, narrow-chested, short-winded crew whom we are leaving astern. Pulsating life no longer concerns itself with them. I am thinking of the few, the scattered few amongst us, who have absorbed new and vigorous truths. Such men stand, as it were, at the outposts, so far ahead that the compact majority has not yet been able to come up with them; and there they are fighting for truths that are too newly-born into the world of consciousness to have any considerable number of people on their side as yet.

Hovstad. So the Doctor is a revolutionary now!

Dr. Stockmann. Good heavens — of course I am, Mr. Hovstad! I propose to raise a revolution against the lie that the majority has the monopoly of the truth. What sort of truths are they that the majority usually supports? They are truths that are of such advanced age that they are beginning to break up. And if a truth is as old as that, it is also in a fair way to become a lie, gentlemen. [*Laughter and mocking cries.*] Yes, believe me or not, as you like; but truths are by no means as long-lived as Methuselah [11] — as some folk imagine. A normally-constituted truth lives, let us say, as a rule seventeen or eighteen, or at most twenty years; seldom longer. But truths as aged as that are always worn frightfully thin, and nevertheless it is only then that the majority recognizes them and recommends them to the community as wholesome moral nourishment. There is no great nutritive value in that sort of fare, I can assure you; and, as a doctor, I ought to know. These " majority truths " are like last year's cured meat — like rancid, tainted ham; and they are the origin of the moral scurvy that is rampant in our communities.

Aslaksen. It appears to me that the speaker is wandering a long way from his subject.

Peter Stockmann. I quite agree with the Chairman.

Dr. Stockmann. Have you gone clean out of your senses, Peter? I am sticking as closely to my subject as I can; for my subject is precisely this, that it is the masses, the majority — this infernal compact majority — that poisons the sources of our moral life and infects the ground we stand on.

Hovstad. And all this because the great, broad-minded majority of the people is prudent enough to show deference only to well-ascertained and well-approved truths?

Dr. Stockmann. Ah, my good Mr. Hovstad, don't talk nonsense about well-ascertained truths! The truths of which the masses now approve are the very truths that the fighters at the outposts held to in the days of our grandfathers. We fighters at the outposts nowadays no longer approve of them; and I do not believe there

[11] **Methuselah:** The oldest man in the Bible. He lived 969 years, Genesis 5:27.

is any other well-ascertained truth except this, that no community can live a healthy life if it is nourished only on such old marrowless truths.

Hovstad. But instead of standing there using vague generalities, it would be interesting if you would tell us what these old marrowless truths are, that we are nourished on. [*Applause from many quarters.*]

Dr. Stockmann. Oh, I could give you a whole string of such abominations; but to begin with I will confine myself to one well-approved truth, which at bottom is a foul lie, but upon which nevertheless Mr. Hovstad and the *People's Messenger* and all the *Messenger's* supporters are nourished.

Hovstad. And that is — ?

Dr. Stockmann. That is, the doctrine you have inherited from your forefathers and proclaim thoughtlessly far and wide — the doctrine that the public, the crowd, the masses, are the essential part of the population — that they constitute the People — that the common folk, the ignorant and incomplete element in the community, have the same right to pronounce judgment and to approve, to direct and to govern, as the isolated, intellectually superior personalities in it.

Billing. Well, damn me if ever I —

Hovstad. [*At the same time, shouting out*] Fellow citizens, take good note of that!

A Number of Voices [*Angrily*]. Oho! — we are not the People! Only the superior folk are to govern, are they!

A Workman. Turn the fellow out, for talking such rubbish!

Another. Out with him!

Another. [*Calling out*] Blow your horn, Evensen! [*A horn is blown loudly, amidst hisses and an angry uproar.*]

Dr. Stockmann. [*When the noise has somewhat abated*] Be reasonable! Can't you stand hearing the voice of truth for once? I don't in the least expect you to agree with me all at once; but I must say I did expect Mr. Hovstad to admit I was right, when he had recovered his composure a little. He claims to be a freethinker —

Voices. [*In murmurs of astonishment*] Freethinker, did he say? Is Hovstad a freethinker?

Hovstad. [*Shouting*] Prove it, Dr. Stockmann! When have I said so in print?

Dr. Stockmann. [*Reflecting*] No, confound it, you are right! — you have never had the courage to. Well, I won't put you in a hole, Mr.

Hovstad. Let us say it is I that am the freethinker, then. I am going to prove to you, scientifically, that the *People's Messenger* leads you by the nose in a shameful manner when it tells you that you — that the common people, the crowd, the masses, are the real essence of the People. That is only a newspaper lie, I tell you! The common people are nothing more than the raw material of which a People is made. [*Groans, laughter, and uproar.*] Well, isn't that the case? Isn't there an enormous difference between a well-bred and an ill-bred strain of animals? Take, for instance, a common barn-door hen. What sort of eating do you get from a shriveled up old scrag of a fowl like that? Not much, do you! And what sort of eggs does it lay? A fairly good crow or a raven can lay pretty nearly as good an egg. But take a well-bred Spanish or Japanese hen, or a good pheasant or a turkey — then you will see the difference. Or take the case of dogs, with whom we humans are on such intimate terms. Think first of an ordinary common cur — I mean one of the horrible, coarse-haired, low-bred curs that do nothing but run about the streets. Compare one of these curs with a poodle whose sires for many generations have been bred in a gentleman's house, where they have had the best of food and had the opportunity of hearing soft voices and music. Do you not think that the poodle's brain is developed to quite a different degree from that of the cur? Of course it is. It is puppies of well-bred poodles like that, that showmen train to do incredibly clever tricks — things that a common cur could never learn to do even if it stood on its head. [*Uproar and mocking cries.*]

A Citizen. [*Calls out.*] Are you going to make out we are dogs, now?

Another Citizen. We are not animals, Doctor!

Dr. Stockmann. Yes but, bless my soul, we *are*, my friend! It is true we are the finest animals any one could wish for; but, even amongst us, exceptionally fine animals are rare. There is a tremendous difference between poodle-men and cur-men. And the amusing part of it is, that Mr. Hovstad quite agrees with me as long as it is a question of four-footed animals —

Hovstad. Yes, it is true enough as far as they are concerned.

Dr. Stockmann. Very well. But as soon as I extend the principle and apply it to two-legged animals, Mr. Hovstad stops short. He no longer dares to think independently, or to pursue his ideas to their logical conclusion; so he turns the whole theory upside down and proclaims in the *People's Messenger* that it is the barn-door hens and street curs that are the finest specimens in the menagerie. But that is always the way, as long as a man retains the traces of common origin and has not worked his way up to intellectual distinction.

Hovstad. I lay no claim to any sort of distinction. I am the son of humble countryfolk, and I am proud that the stock I come from is rooted deep among the common people he insults.

Voices. Bravo, Hovstad! Bravo! Bravo!

Dr. Stockmann. The kind of common people I mean are not only to be found low down in the social scale; they crawl and swarm all around us — even in the highest social positions. You have only to look at your own fine, distinguished Mayor! My brother Peter is every bit as plebeian as any one that walks in two shoes — [*Laughter and hisses.*]

Peter Stockmann. I protest against personal allusions of this kind.

Dr. Stockmann. [*Imperturbably*] — And that, not because he is, like myself, descended from some old rascal of a pirate from Pomerania or thereabouts — because that is who we are descended from —

Peter Stockmann. An absurd legend. I deny it!

Dr. Stockmann. — But because he thinks what his superiors think and holds the same opinions as they. People who do that are, intellectually speaking, common people; and that is why my magnificent brother Peter is in reality so very far from any distinction — and consequently also so far from being liberal-minded.

Peter Stockmann. Mr. Chairman — !

Hovstad. So it is only the distinguished men that are liberal-minded in this country? We are learning something quite new! [*Laughter*]

Dr. Stockmann. Yes, that is part of my new discovery, too. And another part of it is that broad-mindedness is almost precisely the same thing as morality. That is why I maintain that it is absolutely inexcusable in the *People's Messenger* to proclaim, day in and day out, the false doctrine that it is the masses, the crowd, the compact majority, that have the monopoly of broad-mindedness and morality — and that vice and corruption and every kind of intellectual depravity are the result of culture, just as all the filth that is draining into our Baths is the result of the tanneries up at Mölledal! [*Uproar and interruptions.* Dr. Stockmann *is undisturbed, and goes on, carried away by his ardor, with a smile.*] And yet this same *People's Messenger* can go on preaching that the masses ought to be elevated to higher conditions of life! But, bless my soul, if the *Messenger's* teaching is to be depended upon, this very raising up the masses would mean nothing more or less than setting them straightway upon the paths of depravity! Happily the theory that culture demoralizes is only an old falsehood that our forefathers believed in and we have inherited. No, it is ignorance, poverty, ugly conditions of life, that do the devil's work! In a house which does not get aired and swept every day — my wife Katherine maintains that the floor ought to be scrubbed as well, but that is a debatable question — in such a house, let me tell you, people will lose within two or three years the power of thinking or acting in a moral manner. Lack of oxygen weakens the conscience. And there must be a plentiful lack of oxygen in very many houses in this town, I should think, judging from the fact that the whole compact majority can be unconscientious enough to wish to build the town's prosperity on a quagmire [12] of falsehood and deceit.

Aslaksen. We cannot allow such a grave accusation to be flung at a citizen community.

A Citizen. I move that the Chairman direct the speaker to sit down.

Voices. [*Angrily*] Hear, hear! Quite right! Make him sit down.

Dr. Stockmann. [*Losing his self-control*] Then I will go and shout the truth at every street corner! I will write it in other towns' newspapers! The whole country shall know what is going on here!

Hovstad. It almost seems as if Dr. Stockmann's intention were to ruin the town.

Dr. Stockmann. Yes, my native town is so dear to me that I would rather ruin it than see it flourishing upon a lie.

Aslaksen. This is really serious. [*Uproar and catcalls.* MRS. STOCKMANN *coughs, but to no purpose; her husband does not listen to her any longer.*]

Hovstad. [*Shouting above the din*] A man must be a public enemy to wish to ruin a whole community.

Dr. Stockmann. [*With growing fervor*] What does the destruction of a community matter, if it lives on lies! It ought to be razed to the ground, I tell you! All who live by lies ought to be exterminated like vermin! You will end by infecting the whole country; you will bring about such a state of things that the whole country will deserve to be ruined. And if things come to that pass, I shall say from the bottom of my heart: Let the whole country perish, let all these people be exterminated!

Voices from the Crowd. That is talking like an out-and-out enemy of the people!

Billing. There sounded the voice of the people, by all that's holy!

[12] **quagmire:** disease-breeding marsh.

The Whole Crowd. [*Shouting*] Yes, yes! He is an enemy of the people! He hates his country! He hates his own people!

Aslaksen. Both as a citizen and as an individual, I am profoundly disturbed by what we have had to listen to. Dr. Stockmann has shown himself in a light I should never have dreamed of. I am unhappily obliged to subscribe to the opinion which I have just heard my estimable fellow citizens utter; and I propose that we should give expression to that opinion in a resolution. I propose a resolution as follows: " This meeting declares that it considers Dr. Thomas Stockmann, Medical Officer of the Baths, to be an enemy of the people." [*A storm of cheers and applause. A number of men surround the* DOCTOR *and hiss him.* MRS. STOCKMANN *and* PETRA *have got up from their seats.* MORTEN *and* EJLIF *are fighting the other schoolboys for hissing; some of their elders separate them.*]

Dr. Stockmann. [*To the men who are hissing him*] Oh, you fools! I tell you that —

Aslaksen. [*Ringing his bell*] We cannot hear you now, Doctor. A formal vote is about to be taken; but, out of regard for personal feelings, it shall be by ballot and not verbal. Have you any clean paper, Mr. Billing?

Billing. I have both blue and white here.

Aslaksen. [*Going to him*] That will do nicely; we shall get on more quickly that way. Cut it up into small strips — yes, that's it. [*To the meeting*] Blue means no; white means yes. I will come round myself and collect votes. [PETER STOCKMANN *leaves the hall.* ASLAKSEN *and one or two others go round the room with the slips of paper in their hats.*]

First Citizen. [*To* HOVSTAD] I say, what has come to the Doctor? What are we to think of it?

Hovstad. Oh, you know how headstrong he is.

Second Citizen. [*To* BILLING] Billing, you go to their house — have you ever noticed if the fellow drinks?

Billing. Well I'm hanged if I know what to say. There are always spirits on the table when you go.

Third Citizen. I rather think he goes quite off his head sometimes.

First Citizen. I wonder if there is any madness in this family?

Billing. I shouldn't wonder if there were.

Fourth Citizen. No, it is nothing more than sheer malice; he wants to get even with somebody for something or other.

Billing. Well certainly he suggested a rise in his salary on one occasion lately, and did not get it.

The Citizens. [*Together*] Ah! — then it is easy to understand how it is!

The Drunken Man. [*Who has got amongst the audience again*] I want a blue one, I do! And I want a white one, too!

Voices. It's that drunken chap again! Turn him out!

Morten Kiil. [*Going up to* DR. STOCKMANN] Well, Stockmann, do you see what these monkey tricks of yours lead to?

Dr. Stockmann. I have done my duty.

Morten Kiil. What was that you said about the tanneries at Mölledal?

Dr. Stockmann. You heard well enough. I said they were the source of all the filth.

Morten Kiil. My tannery, too?

Dr. Stockmann. Unfortunately your tannery is by far the worst.

Morten Kiil. Are you going to put that in the papers?

Dr. Stockmann. I shall conceal nothing.

Morton Kiil. That may cost you dear, Stockmann. [*Goes out.*]

A Stout Man. [*Going up to* CAPTAIN HORSTER, *without taking any notice of the ladies*] Well, Captain, so you lend your house to enemies of the people?

Horster. I imagine I can do what I like with my own possessions, Mr. Vik.

The Stout Man. Then you can have no objections to my doing the same with mine.

Horster. What do you mean, sir?

The Stout Man. You shall hear from me in the morning. [*Turns his back on him and moves off.*]

Petra. Was that not your owner, Captain Horster?

Horster. Yes, that was Mr. Vik, the shipowner.

Aslaksen. [*With the voting-papers in his hands, gets up on the platform and rings his bell*] Gentlemen, allow me to announce the result. By the votes of every one here except one person —

A Young Man. That is the drunk chap!

Aslaksen. By the votes of every one here except a tipsy man, this meeting of citizens declares Dr. Thomas Stockmann to be an enemy of the people. [*Shouts of applause*] Three cheers for our ancient and honorable citizen community! [*Renewed applause*] Three cheers for our able and energetic Mayor, who has so loyally suppressed the promptings of family feeling! [*Cheers*] The meeting is dissolved. [*Gets down.*]

Billing. Three cheers for the Chairman!

The Whole Crowd. Three cheers for Aslaksen! Hurrah!

Dr. Stockmann. My hat and coat, Petra! Captain, have you room on your ship for passengers to the New World?

Horster. For you and yours we will make room, Doctor.

Dr. Stockmann. [*As* PETRA *helps him into his coat*] Good. Come, Katherine! Come, boys!

Mrs. Stockmann. [*In an undertone*] Thomas, dear, let us go out by the back way.

Dr. Stockmann. No back ways for me, Katherine. [*Raising his voice*] You will hear more of this enemy of the people, before he shakes the dust off his shoes upon you! I am not so forgiving as a certain Person; I do not say: " I forgive you, for ye know not what ye do." [13]

Aslaksen. [*Shouting*] That is a blasphemous comparison, Dr. Stockmann!

Billing. It is, by God! It's dreadful for an earnest man to listen to.

A Coarse Voice. Threatens us now, does he!

Other Voices. [*Excitedly*] Let's go and break his windows! Duck him in the fjord! [14]

Another Voice. Blow your horn, Evensen! Pip, pip! [*Hornblowing, hisses, and wild cries.* DR. STOCKMANN *goes out through the hall with his family,* HORSTER *elbowing a way for them.*]

The Whole Crowd. [*Howling after them as they go*] Enemy of the People! Enemy of the People!

Billing. [*As he puts his paper together*] Well, I'm damned if I go and drink toddy with the Stockmanns tonight! [*The crowd press toward the exit. The uproar continues outside; shouts of " Enemy of the People! " are heard from without.*]

ACT V

SCENE. DR. STOCKMANN'S *study. Bookcases and cabinets containing specimens line the walls. At the back is a door leading to the hall; in the foreground on the left, a door leading to the sitting room. In the right-hand wall are two windows, of which all the panes are broken. The* DOCTOR'S *desk, littered with books and papers, stands in the middle of the room, which is in disorder. It is morning.*

[13] " I forgive you, etc." : words of Christ on the Cross.
[14] fjord: long narrow inlets of the ocean along the coast of Norway.

Dr. Stockmann, *in dressing-gown, slippers, and a smoking-cap, is bending down and raking with an umbrella under one of the cabinets. After a while he rakes out a stone.*

Dr. Stockmann. [*Calling through the open sitting-room door*] Katherine, I have found another one.

Mrs. Stockmann. [*From the sitting room*] Oh, you will find a lot more yet, I expect.

Dr. Stockmann. [*Adding the stone to a heap of others on the table*] I shall treasure these stones as relics. Ejlif and Morten shall look at them every day, and when they are grown up they shall inherit them as heirlooms. [*Rakes about under a bookcase.*] Hasn't — what the deuce is her name? — the girl, you know — hasn't she been to fetch the glazier [15] yet?

Mrs. Stockmann. [*Coming in*] Yes, but he said he didn't know if he would be able to come today.

Dr. Stockmann. You will see he won't dare to come.

Mrs. Stockmann. Well, that is just what Randine thought — that he didn't dare to, on account of the neighbors. [*Calls into the sitting room.*] What is it you want, Randine? Give it to me. [*Goes in, and comes out again directly.*] Here is a letter for you, Thomas.

Dr. Stockmann. Let me see it. [*Opens and reads it.*] Ah! — of course.

Mrs. Stockmann. Who is it from?

Dr. Stockmann. From the landlord. Notice to quit.

Mrs. Stockmann. Is it possible? Such a nice man —

Dr. Stockmann. [*Looking at the letter*] Does not dare do otherwise, he says. Doesn't like doing it, but dare not do otherwise — on account of his fellow citizens — out of regard for public opinion. Is in a dependent position — dare not offend certain influential men —

Mrs. Stockmann. There, you see, Thomas!

Dr. Stockmann. Yes, yes, I see well enough; the whole lot of them in the town are cowards; not a man among them dares do anything for fear of the others. [*Throws the letter on the table.*] But it doesn't matter to us, Katherine. We are going to sail away to the New World, and —

Mrs. Stockmann. But, Thomas, are you sure we are well advised to take this step?

Dr. Stockmann. Are you suggesting that I should stay here, where they have pilloried [16] me as an enemy of the people — branded me —

---

[15] **glazier:** glass mender.
[16] **pilloried:** persecuted. The old pillory confining arms, legs, and neck, is referred to only metaphorically.

broken my windows! And just look here, Katherine — they have torn a great rent in my black trousers, too!

Mrs. Stockmann. Oh, dear! — and they are the best pair you have!

Dr. Stockmann. You should never wear your best trousers when you go out to fight for freedom and truth. It is not that I care so much about the trousers, you know; you can always sew them up again for me. But that the common herd should dare to make this attack on me, as if they were my equals — that is what I cannot, for the life of me, swallow!

Mrs. Stockmann. There is no doubt they have behaved very ill to you, Thomas; but is that sufficient reason for our leaving our native country for good and all?

Dr. Stockmann. If we went to another town, do you suppose we should not find the common people just as insolent as they are here? Depend upon it, there is not much to choose between them. Oh, well, let the curs snap — that is not the worst part of it. The worst is, that from one end of this country to the other every man is the slave of his party. Although, as far as that goes, I daresay it is not much better in the free West either; the compact majority, and liberal public opinion, and all that infernal old bag of tricks are probably rampant there too. But there things are done on a larger scale, you see. They may kill you, but they won't put you to death by slow torture. They don't squeeze a free man's soul in a vice, as they do here. And, if need be, one can live in solitude. [*Walks up and down.*] If only I knew where there was a virgin forest or a small South Sea island for sale, cheap —

Mrs. Stockmann. But think of the boys, Thomas!

Dr. Stockmann. [*Standing still*] What a strange woman you are, Katherine! Would you prefer to have the boys grow up in a society like this? You saw for yourself last night that half the population are out of their minds; and if the other half have not lost their senses, it is because they are mere brutes, with no sense to lose.

Mrs. Stockmann. But, Thomas dear, the imprudent things you said had something to do with it, you know.

Dr. Stockmann. Well, isn't what I said perfectly true? Don't they turn every idea topsy-turvy? Don't they make a regular hotch-potch of right and wrong? Don't they say that the things I know are true, are lies? The craziest part of it all is the fact of these " liberals," men of full age, going about in crowds imagining that they are the broad-minded party! Did you ever hear anything like it, Katherine!

Mrs. Stockmann. Yes, yes, it's mad enough of them, certainly; but — [PETRA *comes in from the sitting room.*] Back from school already?

Petra. Yes. I have been given notice of dismissal.

Mrs. Stockmann. Dismissal?

Dr. Stockmann. You, too?

Petra. Mrs. Busk gave me my notice; so I thought it was best to to go at once.

Dr. Stockmann. You were perfectly right, too!

Mrs. Stockmann. Who would have thought Mrs. Busk was a woman like that!

Petra. Mrs. Busk isn't a bit like that, mother; I saw quite plainly how it hurt her to do it. But she didn't dare do otherwise, she said; and so I got my notice.

Dr. Stockmann. [*Laughing and rubbing his hands*] She didn't dare do otherwise, either! It's delicious!

Mrs. Stockmann. Well, after the dreadful scenes last night —

Petra. It was not only that. Just listen to this, father!

Dr. Stockmann. Well?

Petra. Mrs. Busk showed me no less than three letters she received this morning —

Dr. Stockmann. Anonymous, I suppose?

Petra. Yes.

Dr. Stockmann. Yes, because they didn't dare to risk signing their names, Katherine!

Petra. And two of them were to the effect that a man, who has been our guest here, was declaring last night at the Club that my views on various subjects are extremely emancipated —

Dr. Stockmann. You did not deny that, I hope?

Petra. No, you know I wouldn't. Mrs. Busk's own views are tolerably emancipated, when we are alone together; but now that this report about me is being spread, she dare not keep me on any longer.

Mrs. Stockmann. And some one who had been a guest of ours! That shows you the return you get for your hospitality, Thomas!

Dr. Stockmann. We won't live in such a disgusting hole any longer. Pack up as quickly as you can, Katherine; the sooner we can get away, the better.

Mrs. Stockmann. Be quiet — I think I hear some one in the hall. See who it is, Petra.

Petra. [*Opening the door*] Oh, it's you, Captain Horster! Do come in.

Horster. [*Coming in*] Good morning. I thought I would just come in and see how you were.

Dr. Stockmann. [*Shaking his hand*] Thanks — that is really kind of you.

Mrs. Stockmann. And thank you, too, for helping us through the crowd, Captain Horster.

Petra. How did you manage to get home again?

Horster. Oh, somehow or other. I am fairly strong, and there is more sound than fury about these folk.

Dr. Stockmann. Yes, isn't their swinish cowardice astonishing? Look here; I will show you something! There are all the stones they have thrown through my windows. Just look at them! I'm hanged if there are more than two decently large bits of hard stone in the whole heap; the rest are nothing but gravel — wretched little things. And yet they stood out there bawling and swearing that they would do me some violence; but as for *doing* anything — you don't see much of that in this town.

Horster. Just as well for you this time, Doctor!

Dr. Stockmann. True enough. But it makes one angry all the same; because if some day it should be a question of a national fight in real earnest, you will see that public opinion will be in favor of taking to one's heels, and the compact majority will turn tail like a flock of sheep, Captain Horster. That is what is so mournful to think of; it gives me so much concern, that — No, devil take it, it is ridiculous to care about it! They have called me an enemy of the people, so an enemy of the people let me be!

Mrs. Stockmann. You will never be that, Thomas.

Dr. Stockmann. Don't swear to that, Katherine. To be called an ugly name may have the same effect as a pin-scratch in the lung. And that hateful name — I can't get quit of it. It is sticking here in the pit of my stomach, eating into me like a corosive acid. And no magnesia will remove it.

Petra. Bah! — you should only laugh at them, father.

Horster. They will change their minds some day, Doctor.

Mrs. Stockmann. Yes, Thomas, as sure as you are standing here.

Dr. Stockmann. Perhaps, when it is too late. Much good may it do them! They may wallow in their filth then and rue the day when they drove a patriot into exile. When do you sail, Captain Horster?

Horster. Hm! — that was just what I had come to speak about —

Dr. Stockmann. Why, has anything gone wrong with the ship?

Horster. No; but what has happened is that I am not to sail in it.

Petra. Do you mean that you have been dismissed from your command?

Horster. [*Smiling*] Yes, that's just it.

Petra. You, too.

Mrs. Stockmann. There, you see, Thomas!

Dr. Stockmann. And that for the truth's sake! Oh, if I had thought such a thing possible —

Horster. You mustn't take it to heart; I shall be sure to find a job with some shipowner or other, elsewhere.

Dr. Stockmann. And that is this man Vik — a wealthy man, independent of every one and everything — ! Shame on him!

Horster. He is quite an excellent fellow otherwise; he told me himself he would willingly have kept me on, if only he had dared —

Dr. Stockmann. But he didn't dare? No, of course not.

Horster. It is not such an easy matter, he said, for a party man —

Dr. Stockmann. The worthy man spoke the truth. A party is like a sausage machine; it mashes up all sorts of heads together into the same mincemeat — fatheads and blockheads, all in one mash!

Mrs. Stockmann. Come, come, Thomas dear!

Petra. [*To* HORSTER] If only you had not come home with us, things might not have come to this pass.

Horster. I do not regret it.

Petra. [*Holding out her hand to him*] Thank you for that!

Horster. [*To* DR. STOCKMANN] And so what I came to say was that if you are determined to go away, I have thought of another plan —

Dr. Stockmann. That's splendid! — if only we can get away at once.

Mrs. Stockmann. Hush! — wasn't that some one knocking?

Petra. That is uncle, surely.

Dr. Stockmann. Aha! [*Calls out.*] Come in!

Mrs. Stockmann. Dear Thomas, promise me definitely — [PETER STOCKMANN *comes in from the hall.*]

Peter Stockmann. Oh, you are engaged. In that case, I will —

Dr. Stockmann. No, no, come in.

Peter Stockmann. But I wanted to speak to you alone.

Mrs. Stockmann. We will go into the sitting room in the mean-while.

Horster. And I will look in again later.

Dr. Stockmann. No, go in there with them, Captain Horster; I want to hear more about —

Horster. Very well, I will wait, then. [*He follows* MRS. STOCK-MANN *and* PETRA *into the sitting room.*]

Dr. Stockmann. I dare say you find it rather drafty here today. Put your hat on.

Peter Stockmann. Thank you, if I may. [*Does so.*] I think I caught cold last night; I stood and shivered —

Dr. Stockmann. Really? I found it warm enough.

Peter Stockmann. I regret that it was not in my power to prevent those excesses last night.

Dr. Stockmann. Have you anything particular to say to me besides that?

Peter Stockmann. [*Taking a big letter from his pocket*] I have this document for you, from the Baths Committee.

Dr. Stockmann. My dismissal?

Peter Stockmann. Yes, dating from today. [*Lays the letter on the table.*] It gives us pain to do it; but, to speak frankly, we dared not do otherwise on account of public opinion.

Dr. Stockmann. [*Smiling*] Dared not? I seem to have heard that word before, today.

Peter Stockmann. I must beg you to understand your position clearly. For the future you must not count on any practice whatever in the town.

Dr. Stockmann. Devil take the practice! But why are you so sure of that?

Peter Stockmann. The Householders' Association is circulating a list from house to house. All right-minded citizens are being called upon to give up employing you; and I can assure you that not a single head of a family will risk refusing his signature. They simply dare not.

Dr. Stockmann. No, no; I don't doubt it. But what then?

Peter Stockmann. If I might advise you, it would be best to leave the place for a little while —

Dr. Stockmann. Yes, the propriety of leaving the place *has* occurred to me.

Peter Stockmann. Good. And then, when you have had six months to think things over, if, after mature consideration, you can persuade yourself to write a few words of regret, acknowledging your error —

Dr. Stockmann. I might have my appointment restored to me, do you mean?

Peter Stockmann. Perhaps. It is not at all impossible.

Dr. Stockmann. But what about public opinion, then? Surely you would not dare to do it on account of public feeling.

Peter Stockmann. Public opinion is an extremely mutable thing. And, to be quite candid with you, it is a matter of great importance to us to have some admission of that sort from you in writing.

Dr. Stockmann. Oh, that's what you are after, is it! I will just trouble you to remember what I said to you lately about foxy tricks of that sort!

Peter Stockmann. Your position was quite different then. At that time you had reason to suppose you had the whole town at your back —

Dr. Stockmann. Yes, and now I feel I have the whole town *on* my back — [*Flaring up.*] I would not do it if I had the devil and his dam on my back — ! Never, never, I tell you!

Peter Stockmann. A man with a family has no right to behave as you do. You have no right to do it, Thomas.

Dr. Stockmann. I have no right! There is only one single thing in the world a free man has no right to do. Do you know what that is?

Peter Stockmann. No.

Dr. Stockmann. Of course you don't, but I will tell you. A free man has no right to soil himself with filth; he has no right to behave in a way that would justify his spitting in his own face.

Peter Stockmann. This sort of thing sounds extremely plausible, of course; and if there were no other explanation for your obstinacy — But as it happens there is.

Dr. Stockmann. What do you mean?

Peter Stockmann. You understand very well what I mean. But, as your brother and as a man of discretion, I advise you not to build too much upon expectations and prospects that may so very easily fail you.

Dr. Stockmann. What in the world is all this about?

Peter Stockmann. Do you really ask me to believe that you are ignorant of the terms of Mr. Kiil's will?

Dr. Stockmann. I know that the small amount he possesses is to go to an institution for indigent old workpeople. How does that concern me?

Peter Stockmann. In the first place, it is by no means a small amount that is in question. Mr. Kiil is a fairly wealthy man.

Dr. Stockmann. I had no notion of that!

Peter Stockmann. Hm! — hadn't you really? Then I suppose you had no notion, either, that a considerable portion of his wealth will come to your children, you and your wife having a liferent of the capital. Has he never told you so?

Dr. Stockmann. Never, on my honor! Quite the reverse; he has consistently done nothing but fume at being so unconscionably heavily taxed. But are you perfectly certain of this, Peter?

Peter Stockmann. I have it from an absolutely reliable source.

Dr. Stockmann. Then, thank God, Katherine is provided for — and the children too! I must tell her this at once — [*Calls out.*] Katherine, Katherine!

Peter Stockmann. [*Restraining him*] Hush, don't say a word yet!

Mrs. Stockmann. [*Opening the door*] What is the matter?

Dr. Stockmann. Oh, nothing; you can go back. [*She shuts the door.* DR. STOCKMANN *walks up and down in his excitement.*] Provided for! — Just think of it, we are all provided for! And for life! What a blessed feeling it is to know one is provided for!

Peter Stockmann. Yes, but that is just exactly what you are not. Mr. Kiil can alter his will any day he likes.

Dr. Stockmann. But he won't do that, my dear Peter. The " Badger " is much too delighted at my attack on you and your wise friends.

Peter Stockmann. [*Starts and looks intently at him.*] Ah, that throws a light on various things.

Dr. Stockmann. What things?

Peter Stockmann. I see that the whole thing was a combined maneuver on your part and his. These violent, reckless attacks that you have made against the leading men of the town, under the pretense that it was in the name of truth —

Dr. Stockmann. What about them?

Peter Stockmann. I see that they were nothing else than the stipulated price for that vindictive old man's will.

Dr. Stockmann. [*Almost speechless*] Peter — you are the most disgusting plebeian I have ever met in all my life.

Peter Stockmann. All is over between us. Your dismissal is irrevocable — we have a weapon against you now. [*Goes out.*]

Dr. Stockmann. For shame! For shame! [*Calls out.*] Katherine, you must have the floor scrubbed after him! Let — what's her name — devil take it, the girl who has always got soot on her nose —

Mrs. Stockmann. [*In the sitting room*] Hush, Thomas, be quiet!

Petra. [*Coming to the door*] Father, grandfather is here, asking if he may speak to you alone.

Dr. Stockmann. Certainly he may. [*Going to the door.*] Come in, Mr. Kiil. [MORTEN KIIL *comes in.* DR. STOCKMANN *shuts the door after him.*] What can I do for you? Won't you sit down?

Morten Kiil. I won't sit. [*Looks around.*] You look very comfortable here today, Thomas.

Dr. Stockmann. Yes, don't we!

Morten Kiil. Very comfortable — plenty of fresh air. I should think you have got enough today of that oxygen you were talking about yesterday. Your conscience must be in splendid order today, I should think.

Dr. Stockmann. It is.

Morten Kiil. So I should think. [*Taps his chest.*] Do you know what I have got here?

Dr. Stockmann. A good conscience, too, I hope.

Morten Kiil. Bah! — No, it is something better than that. [*He takes a thick pocketbook from his breast pocket, opens it, and displays a packet of papers.*]

Dr. Stockmann. [*Looking at him in astonishment*] Shares in the Baths?

Morten Kiil. They were not difficult to get today.

Dr. Stockmann. And you have been buying — ?

Morten Kiil. As many as I could pay for.

Dr. Stockmann. But, my dear Mr. Kiil — consider the state of the Baths' affairs!

Morten Kiil. If you behave like a reasonable man, you can soon set the Baths on their feet again.

Dr. Stockmann. Well, you can see for yourself that I have done all I can, but — They are all mad in this town!

Morten Kiil. You said yesterday that the worst of this pollution came from my tannery. If that is true, then my grandfather and my father before me, and I myself, for many years past, have been poisoning the town like three destroying angels. Do you think I am going to sit quiet under that reproach?

Dr. Stockmann. Unfortunately I am afraid you will have to.

Morten Kiil. No, thank you. I am jealous of my name and reputation. They call me " the Badger," I am told. A badger is a kind of pig, I believe; but I am not going to give them the right to call me that. I mean to live and die a clean man.

Dr. Stockmann. And how are you going to set about it?

Morten Kiil. You shall cleanse me, Thomas.

Dr. Stockmann. I!

Morten Kiil. Do you know what money I have bought these shares with? No, of course you can't know — but I will tell you. It is the money that Katherine and Petra and the boys will have when I am gone. Because I have been able to save a little bit after all, you know.

Dr. Stockmann. [*Flaring up*] And you have gone and taken Katherine's money for *this!*

Morten Kiil. Yes, the whole of the money is invested in the Baths now. And now I just want to see whether you are quite stark, staring mad, Thomas! If you still make out that these animals and other nasty things of that sort come from my tannery, it will be exactly as if you were to flay broad strips of skin from Katherine's body, and Petra's, and the boys'; and no decent man would do that — unless he were mad.

Dr. Stockmann. [*Walking up and down*] Yes, but I *am* mad; I *am* mad!

Morten Kiil. You cannot be so absurdly mad as all that, when it is a question of your wife and children.

Dr. Stockmann. [*Standing still in front of him*] Why couldn't you consult me about it, before you went and bought all that trash?

Morten Kiil. What is done cannot be undone.

Dr. Stockmann. [*Walks about uneasily.*] If only I were not so certain about it — ! But I am absolutely convinced that I am right.

Morten Kiil. [*Weighing the pocketbook in his hand*] If you stick to your mad idea, this won't be worth much, you know. [*Puts the pocketbook in his pocket.*]

Dr. Stockmann. But, hang it all! it might be possible for science to discover some prophylactic,[17] I should think — or some antidote of some kind —

Morten Kiil. To kill these animals, do you mean?

Dr. Stockmann. Yes, or to make them innocuous.

Morten Kiil. Couldn't you try some ratsbane?

Dr. Stockmann. Don't talk nonsense! They all say it is only imagination, you know. Well, let it go at that! Let them have their

17 **prophylactic:** disinfectant.

own way about it! Haven't the ignorant, narrow-minded curs reviled me as an enemy of the people? — and haven't they been ready to tear the clothes off my back too?

Morten Kiil. And broken all your windows to pieces!

Dr. Stockmann. And then there is my duty to my family. I must talk it over with Katherine; she is great on those things.

Morten Kiil. That is right; be guided by a reasonable woman's advice.

Dr. Stockmann. [*Advancing toward him*] To think you could do such a preposterous thing! Risking Katherine's money in this way, and putting me in such a horribly painful dilemma! When I look at you, I think I see the devil himself —

Morten Kiil. Then I had better go. But I must have an answer from you before two o'clock — yes or no. If it is no, the shares go to a charity, and that this very day.

Dr. Stockmann. And what does Katherine get?

Morten Kiil. Not a halfpenny. [*The door leading to the hall opens, and* HOVSTAD *and* ASLAKSEN *make their appearance.*] Look at those two!

Dr. Stockmann. [*Staring at them*] What the devil! — have *you* actually the face to come into my house?

Hovstad. Certainly.

Aslaksen. We have something to say to you, you see.

Morten Kiil. [*In a whisper*] Yes or no — before two o'clock.

Aslaksen. [*Glancing at* HOVSTAD] Aha! [MORTEN KIIL *goes out.*]

Dr. Stockmann. Well, what do you want with me? Be brief.

Hovstad. I can quite understand that you are annoyed with us for our attitude at the meeting yesterday —

Dr. Stockmann. Attitude, do you call it? Yes, it was a charming attitude! I call it weak, womanish — damnably shameful!

Hovstad. Call it what you like, we could not do otherwise.

Dr. Stockmann. You *dared* not do otherwise — isn't that it?

Hovstad. Well, if you like to put it that way.

Aslaksen. But why did you not let us have word of it beforehand? — just a hint to Mr. Hovstad or to me?

Dr. Stockmann. A hint? Of what?

Aslaksen. Of what was behind it all.

Dr. Stockmann. I don't understand you in the least.

Aslaksen. [*With a confidential nod*] Oh yes, you do, Dr. Stockmann.

Hovstad. It is no good making a mystery of it any longer.

Dr. Stockmann. [*Looking first at one of them and then at the other*] What the devil do you both mean?

Aslaksen. May I ask if your father-in-law is not going round the town buying up all the shares in the Baths?

Dr. Stockmann. Yes, he has been buying Baths shares today; but —

Aslaksen. It would have been more prudent to get some one else to do it — some one less nearly related to you.

Hovstad. And you should not have let your name appear in the affair. There was no need for any one to know that the attack on the Baths came from you. You ought to have consulted me, Dr. Stockmann.

Dr. Stockmann. [*Looks in front of him; then a light seems to dawn on him and he says in amazement:*] Are such things conceivable? Are such things possible?

Aslaksen. [*With a smile*] Evidently they are. But it is better to use a little *finesse*,[18] you know.

Hovstad. And it is much better to have several persons in a thing of that sort; because the responsibility of each individual is lessened, when there are others with him.

Dr. Stockmann. [*Composedly*] Come to the point, gentlemen. What do you want?

Aslaksen. Perhaps Mr. Hovstad had better —

Hovstad. No, you tell him, Aslaksen.

Aslaksen. Well, the fact is that, now we know the bearings of the whole affair, we think we might venture to put the *People's Messenger* at your disposal.

Dr. Stockmann. Do you dare do that now? What about public opinion? Are you not afraid of a storm breaking upon our heads?

Hovstad. We will try to weather it.

Aslaksen. And you must be ready to go off quickly on a new tack, Doctor. As soon as your invective has done its work —

Dr. Stockmann. Do you mean, as soon as my father-in-law and I have got hold of the shares at a low figure?

Hovstad. Your reasons for wishing to get the control of the Baths are mainly scientific, I take it.

Dr. Stockmann. Of course; it was for scientific reasons that I persuaded the old " Badger " to stand in with me in the matter. So we will tinker at the conduit-pipes a little, and dig up a little bit of

[18] **finesse**: diplomacy.

the shore, and it shan't cost the town a sixpence. That will be all right — eh?

Hovstad. I think so — if you have the *People's Messenger* behind you.

Aslaksen. The Press is a power in a free community, Doctor.

Dr. Stockmann. Quite so. And so is public opinion. And you, Mr. Aslaksen — I suppose you will be answerable for the House-holders' Association?

Aslaksen. Yes, and for the Temperance Society. You may rely on that.

Dr. Stockmann. But, gentlemen — I really am ashamed to ask the question — but, what return do you — ?

Hovstad. We should prefer to help you without any return whatever, believe me. But the *People's Messenger* is in rather a shaky condition; it doesn't go really well; and I should be very unwilling to suspend the paper now, when there is so much work to do here in the political way.

Dr. Stockmann. Quite so; that would be a great trial to such a friend of the people as you are. [*Flares up.*] But I am an enemy of the people, remember! [*Walks about the room.*] Where have I put my stick? Where the devil is my stick?

Hovstad. What's that?

Aslaksen. Surely you never mean — ?

Dr. Stockmann. [*Standing still*] And suppose I don't give you a single penny of all I get out of it? Money is not very easy to get out of us rich folk, please to remember!

Hovstad. And you please to remember that this affair of the shares can be represented in two ways!

Dr. Stockmann. Yes, and you are just the man to do it. If I don't come to the rescue of the *People's Messenger,* you will certainly take an evil view of the affair; you will hunt me down, I can well imagine — pursue me — try to throttle me as a dog does a hare.

Hovstad. It is a natural law; every animal must fight for its own livelihood.

Aslaksen. And get its food when it can, you know.

Dr. Stockmann. [*Walking about the room*] Then you go and look for yours in the gutter; because I am going to show you which is the strongest animal of us three! [*Finds an umbrella and brandishes it above his head.*] Ah, now — !

Hovstad. You are surely not going to use violence!

Aslaksen. Take care what you are doing with that umbrella.

Dr. Stockmann. Out of the window with you, Mr. Hovstad!

Hovstad. [*Edging to the door*] Are you quite mad!

Dr. Stockmann. Out of the window, Mr. Aslaksen! Jump, I tell you! You will have to do it, sooner or later.

Aslaksen. [*Running round the writing-table*] Moderation, Doctor — I am a delicate man — I can stand so little — [*Calls out.*] Help, help!

MRS. STOCKMANN, PETRA, *and* HORSTER *come in from the sitting room.*

Mrs. Stockmann. Good gracious, Thomas. What is happening?

Dr. Stockmann. [*Brandishing the umbrella*] Jump out, I tell you! Out into the gutter!

Hovstad. An assault on an unoffending man! I call you to witness, Captain Horster. [*Hurries out through the hall.*]

Aslaksen. [*Irresolutely*] If only I knew the way about here — [*Steals out through the sitting room.*]

Mrs. Stockmann. [*Holding her husband back*] Control yourself, Thomas!

Dr. Stockmann. [*Throwing down the umbrella*] Upon my soul, they have escaped after all.

Mrs. Stockmann. What did they want you to do?

Dr. Stockmann. I will tell you later on; I have something else to think about now. [*Goes to the table and writes something on a calling-card.*] Look there, Katherine; what is written there?

Mrs. Stockmann. Three big *Noes;* what does that mean?

Dr. Stockmann. I will tell you that, too, later on. [*Holds out the card to* PETRA.] There, Petra; tell sooty-face to run over to the " Badger's " with that, as quick as she can. Hurry up! [PETRA *takes the card and goes out to the hall.*]

Dr. Stockmann. Well, I think I have had a visit from every one of the devil's messengers today! But now I am going to sharpen my pen till they can feel its point; I shall dip it in venom and gall; I shall hurl my ink-pot at their heads!

Mrs. Stockmann. Yes, but we are going away, you know, Thomas.

PETRA *comes back.*

Dr. Stockmann. Well?

Petra. She has gone with it.

Dr. Stockmann. Good. — Going away, did you say? No, I'll be hanged if we are going away! We are going to stay where we are, Katherine!

Petra. Stay here?

Mrs. Stockmann. Here, in the town?

Dr. Stockmann. Yes, here. This is the field of battle — this is where the fight will be. This is where I shall triumph! As soon as I have had my trousers sewn up I shall go out and look for another house. We must have a roof over our heads for the winter.

Horster. That you shall have in my house.

Dr. Stockmann. Can I?

Horster. Yes, quite well. I have plenty of room, and I am almost never at home.

Mrs. Stockmann. How good of you, Captain Horster!

Petra. Thank you!

Dr. Stockmann. [*Grasping his hand*] Thank you, thank you! That is one trouble over! Now I can set to work in earnest at once. There is an endless amount of things to look through here, Katherine! Luckily I shall have all my time at my disposal; because I have been dismissed from the Baths, you know.

Mrs. Stockmann. [*With a sigh*] Oh yes, I expected that.

Dr. Stockmann. And they want to take my practice away from me, too. Let them! I have the poor people to fall back upon, any-way — those that don't pay anything; and, after all, they need me most. But, by Jove, they will have to listen to me; I shall preach to them in season and out of season, as it says somewhere.

Mrs. Stockmann. But, dear Thomas, I should have thought events had showed you what use it is to preach.

Dr. Stockmann. You are really ridiculous, Katherine. Do you want me to let myself be beaten off the field by public opinion and the compact majority and all that devilry? No, thank you! And what I want to do is so simple and clear and straightforward. I only want to drum into the heads of these curs the fact that the liberals are the most insidious enemies of freedom — that party programs strangle every young and vigorous truth — that considerations of ex-pediency turn morality and justice upside down — and that they will end by making life here unbearable. Don't you think, Captain Horster, that I ought to be able to make people understand that?

Horster. Very likely; I don't know much about such things myself.

Dr. Stockmann. Well, look here — I will explain! It is the party leaders that must be exterminated. A party leader is like a wolf, you see — like a voracious wolf. He requires a certain number of smaller victims to prey upon every year, if he is to live. Just look at Hovstad and Aslaksen! How many smaller victims have they not put an end to — or at any rate maimed and mangled until they are fit for nothing except to be Householders or subscribers to the *People's Messenger!* [*Sits down on the edge of the table.*] Come here, Katherine — look how beautifully the sun shines today! And this lovely spring air I am drinking in!

Mrs. Stockmann. Yes, if only we could live on sunshine and spring air, Thomas.

Dr. Stockmann. Oh, you will have to pinch and save a bit — then we shall get along. That gives me very little concern. What is much worse is, that I know of no one who is liberal-minded and high-minded enough to venture to take up my work after me.

Petra. Don't think about that, father; you have plenty of time before you. — Hullo, here are the boys already!

EJLIF *and* MORTEN *come in from the sitting room.*

Mrs. Stockmann. Have you got a holiday?

Morten. No; but we were fighting with the other boys between lessons —

Ejlif. That isn't true; it was the other boys were fighting with us.

Morten. Well, and then Mr. Rörlund said we had better stay at home for a day or two.

Dr. Stockmann. [*Snapping his fingers and getting up from the table*] I have it! I have it, by Jove! You shall never set foot in the school again!

The Boys. No more school!

Mrs. Stockmann. But, Thomas —

Dr. Stockmann. Never, I say. I will educate you myself; that is to say, you shan't learn a blessed thing —

Morten. Hooray!

Dr. Stockmann. — But I will make liberal-minded and high-minded men of you. You must help me with that, Petra.

Petra. Yes, father, you may be sure I will.

Dr. Stockmann. And my school shall be in the room where they insulted me and called me an enemy of the people. But we are too few as we are; I must have at least twelve boys to begin with.

Mrs. Stockmann. You will certainly never get them in this town.

Dr. Stockmann. We shall. [*To the boys.*] Don't you know any street urchins — regular ragamuffins — ?

Morten. Yes, father, I know lots!

Dr. Stockmann. That's capital! Bring me some specimens of

them. I am going to experiment with curs, just for once; there may be some exceptional heads amongst them.

Morten. And what are we going to do, when you have made liberal-minded and high-minded men of us?

Dr. Stockmann. Then you shall drive all the wolves out of the country, my boys!

EJLIF *looks rather doubtful about it;* MORTEN *jumps about crying* " Hurrah! "

Mrs. Stockmann. Let us hope it won't be the wolves that will drive you out of the country, Thomas.

Dr. Stockmann. Are you out of your mind, Katherine? Drive me out! Now — when I am the strongest man in the town!

Mrs. Stockmann. The strongest — now?

Dr. Stockmann. Yes, and I will go so far as to say that now I am the strongest man in the whole world.

Morten. I say!

Dr. Stockmann. [*Lowering his voice*] Hush! You mustn't say anything about it yet; but I have made a great discovery.

Mrs. Stockmann. Another one?

Dr. Stockmann. Yes. [*Gathers them round him, and says confidentially:*] It is this, let me tell you — that the strongest man in the world is he who stands most alone.

Mrs. Stockmann. [*Smiling and shaking her head*] Oh, Thomas, Thomas!

Petra. [*Encouragingly, as she grasps her father's hands*] Father!

(*R. Farquharson Sharp*)

SUGGESTIONS FOR STUDY

1. Point out how the first act defines the major characters. What difference between the brothers is at once evident? Trace these differences through the play showing how they become more marked as the plot develops. How do you feel toward each of the brothers? Record speeches of the Doctor which are evident examples of Ibsen's putting his own message into the mouth of that character.

2. *Act I.* What point in the first act would you designate as the exciting force introducing the real action of the play? What speeches of the Doctor at the end of this act prove to have strong ironic force when we later find how his discovery is received? At the end of this act what question is left in the mind of the reader or spectator to continue his interest?

3. *Act II.* List the various reactions of the characters to the news about the Baths. How is each the natural result of his or her personality and relation to the Doctor or to the community? Where does Mrs. Stockmann's reaction change? Why? Do you sympathize with the reason for her change? From the speeches of Aslaksen and Peter Stockmann in this act select sentences which express common theories or attitudes toward community life. Debate those which give room for difference of opinion.

4. *Act III.* Toward the beginning of the act, what title is given the Doctor in marked contrast to the title of the play? What is the ironic force of this? Where else is a forecast made which later seems ironic? Show how the changed attitude of each character toward the Doctor results from self-interest. How at the end of the act is the audience left in suspense?

5. *Act IV.* (a) How is the mood of the audience at the hall conveyed to the reader at the outset? Trace the change in the audience — how caused and how manifested? Compare this act with Act III of *Julius Caesar* in which Anthony sways the populace. Galsworthy's play *The Mob* is another good example of the instability of the public. Can you name others in literature? What principles of mob psychology can you deduce from these and from your own observations of crowds?

(b) Comment on Aslaksen as a chairman. Point out steps by which the Doctor is led to alter his lecture entirely. How is suspense maintained throughout the act? Why do you think the drunken man was introduced? At what point does the climax of the play come?

(c) Discuss the Doctor's speech as representing Ibsen's views, comparing with his letter quoted in the introduction. Is Ibsen an advocate of democracy? How would you have felt if you had been one of the audience in the scene?

6. *Act V.* Show all the ways in which the Doctor and his family are ostracized. Point out speeches which indicate that the Doctor's desperation has made him satirical. What is the worst blow that comes to him? What makes him change his mind about leaving the country? Comment on Dr. Stockmann's last speech.

7. How in this play does Ibsen show up either weakness, hypocrisy, or malice in officialdom, the middle-class majority, radical politics, romantic fiction, the fickle public? What application of the principles involved in this play can be made to present-day situations?

8. George Bernard Shaw was one of the chief defenders and promoters of Ibsen in England. Can you name any of his plays in which he attacks the ideas of the compact majority? How is his method of attack radically different from Ibsen's?

9. Vocabulary: askance, inexorable, insinuation, subsistence, cursory, colossal, parasites, plebeian, corrosive, magnesia, indigent, maneuver, vindictive, irrevocable, antidote, ingenious, preposterous, insidious, voracious.

BJÖRNSTJERNE BJÖRNSON (1832–1910)

The little parish of Kvikne high in the mountains of West Norway, where for more than half the year the landscape is white with snow, is the birthplace of Björnstjerne Björnson. Here his father was the rector, the only one who had been able to succeed in this district of great rough peasants and ex-miners. One of the boy's early recollections was seeing a village giant, who had been threatening his father in his own study, thrown bodily down the stairs. Undoubtedly the father's physical as much as his spiritual strength enabled him to hold his congregation together. The son inherited his father's prowess, and by the time he had finished what schooling various small parishes afforded, he was a great rawboned fellow with a peak of red hair brushed back from his forehead. This gave his fellow students at Kristiania, where he went to prepare for college, the idea of calling him " Romsdalshorn," the name of a mountain near his home. A picturesque incident of his student days is his purchasing of a twelve-year-old boy from an abusive organ grinder. He induced the students in his house to adopt the boy and bring him up on the coöperative plan, and by this experiment the waif was eventually turned into a successful chemist.

Björnson began his writing while he was still in college. A quotation from one of his editorials in the college magazine is typical of the man: "When the fresh currents of life do not flow in through the open window, ruffle the leaves of the student's book, blow the dust from off it, and at times make one lose the open place, then study will acquire a weary page-for-page step, bringing no health to the soul." Throughout his career the "fresh currents of life" flowed through his acts and his writing. His dramatic criticisms in the papers and later his management of a Bergen theater did much to free the Norwegian stage from the dominance of French and Danish traditions. His early stories of peasant life rang true, for he understood, as no writer before him had, the natural reserve and inarticulateness of the mountain people. He believed that the past and the present should each help to illuminate the other, and to this end he paired historical poetic drama with modern plays. His problem novels and plays touched on vital issues of the newspaper and business world. His active political life, which made him leader of the Republican party for almost thirty years, was largely concerned with making Norway conscious of its own national life as distinct from Sweden. In whatever phase of writing or activity he took up we feel the vital freshness of the air currents.

Of the many works of Björnson only a few can here be mentioned as examples of his different types. Of his peasant novels, *Synnöve Solbakken* (name of the heroine) brought his first fame and *Arne* established it. Among his legendary plays *Between the Battles* pictures a strong-willed king of the twelfth century, *Halte-Hulda*, the powerful unscrupulous woman of the old sagas. Of the modern plays two titles *The Editor* and *A Bankruptcy* suggest the nature of the problems he handles.

The names of Björnson and Ibsen are inevitably linked together. They were the two greatest Norwegian writers of their period, they were lifelong acquaintances — though their friendship was marred by temporary periods of antagonism — and their families were bound together by the marriage of Björnson's daughter and Ibsen's son. Though practically all Björnson's writings have been translated into English, he has never been as conspicuous an influence in the English world as Ibsen. Probably several reasons have caused this comparative indifference. The very intenseness of his nationalism would tend to give him less universal appeal than Ibsen. No critic-champion fought his battles on English soil as Shaw and others did for Ibsen, nor was his work as provocative of battles in the first place. Lastly, the peculiar idiom and quality of style which in his native language make Björnson fascinating are much harder than Ibsen's manner to reproduce in another language. Because of the intense vitality of Björnson's poetry he has been compared with Browning in English literature and Walt Whitman in America. Björnson and Whitman in fact held each other in mutual admiration. Whitman said: "I was particularly interested in the Norwegian Björnson. He sent me his picture once. It is that of a Viking: powerful, inflexible, clean: a face of humanity, purpose: a face of the ideal. Norway has made her best men much bigger than her own size — has made them men of world dimensions." Björnson can truly be said to have lived up to his own definition of a poet: "The poet radiates joy from the whole of his person, gives out words like sunlight, helps to arrange life. To be able to say words at the right time, words that flame — that is to be a poet."

LIFE AND SONG

Björnson is regarded by Norwegians as the poetic spokesman of their country. Their national hymn is his composition, as well as many other patriotic poems for various occasions. In addition, of course, he has written much of a general nature, although his complete volume of verse is small. His themes were, on the whole, vigorous and inspiring. In the following poem, he seems to be apologizing to his Muse for having so little recorded poetry to offer, but the poem contains, after all, the "quintessence of Björnsonism" if one may paraphrase Shaw's title about Ibsen. Björnson *did* live in the thick of life and he *is* considered "the best bard for his nation."

I lived far more than e'er I sang;
Thought, ire, and mirth unceasing rang
Around me, where I guested;

To be where life's loud battles call
For me was well-nigh more than all
　　My pen on page arrested.

What's true and strong has growing-room,
And will perhaps eternal bloom,
　　Without black ink's salvation;
And he will be, who least it planned,
But in life's surging dared to stand,
　　The best bard for his nation.

(Arthur H. Palmer)

THE BROTHERS

To all intents and purposes, this is a short story and is often published as such, but it is really a chapter of the novel *A Happy Boy*. It is, however, distinct from the main plot of the book. It is introduced to explain the past history of Baard, who as the schoolmaster of Oivind, the " happy boy," is to play a part in the narrative.

The schoolmaster's name was Baard, and he had a brother named Anders. They thought a great deal of each other, enlisted together, lived together in town, went through the war together, served in the same company, and both rose to the rank of corporal. When they came home from the war, people said they were two fine, stalwart fellows.

Then their father died. He left much personal property, which it was difficult to divide, and therefore they said to each other that they would not let this come between them, but would put the property up at auction, that each might buy what he wanted, and both share the proceeds. And it was so done.

But the father had owned a large gold watch, which had come to be known far and wide, for it was the only gold watch people in those parts had ever seen. When this watch was put up, there were many wealthy men who wanted it, but when both brothers began to bid, all the others desisted. Now Baard expected that Anders would let him have it, and Anders expected the same of Baard. They bid in turn, each trying the other out, and as they bid they looked hard at each other. When the watch had gone up to twenty dollars, Baard began to feel that this was not kind of his brother, and bid over him until he almost reached thirty. When Anders did not withdraw even then, Baard felt that Anders no longer remembered how good he had often been to him, and that he was furthermore the elder of the two; and the watch went over thirty. Anders still kept on. Baard then raised the price to forty dollars with one bound, and no longer looked at his brother. It grew very still in the auction room; only the bailiff repeated the figures quietly. Anders thought, as he stood there, that if Baard could afford to go to forty dollars, so could he, and if Baard begrudged him the watch, he might as well take it, and bid over him. This to Baard seemed the greatest disgrace that had ever befallen him; he bid fifty dollars in a low voice. There were many people there, and Anders said to himself that he would not let his brother mock him before them all, and again raised the bid. Baard burst out laughing.

"One hundred dollars and my brotherhood into the bargain," he said, as he turned on his heel, and left the room.

A little later, as he stood saddling the horse he had just bought at the auction, a man came out to him.

"The watch is yours; Anders gave in."

The instant he heard the news, there welled up in him a sense of remorse; he thought of his brother and not of the watch. The saddle was already in place, but he paused, his hand on his horse, uncertain whether to mount. Many people came out, Anders among them, and when he saw his brother, with horse saddled, ready to leave, he little knew what Baard was turning over in his mind.

"Thanks for the watch, Baard," he shouted over to him. "You shall never see the day when your brother shall tread on your heels!"

"Nor you the day I shall darken your doors again!" Baard answered, his face pale, as he swung himself on his horse.

After that day neither of them ever set foot in the home where they had both lived with their father.

Anders married into a crofter's family, not long afterwards, but he did not invite Baard to the wedding. Nor did Baard go to the church. The first year he was married, Anders lost his only cow. It was found dead one morning on the north side of the house, where it had been tethered, and no one could explain what it had died of. Other misfortunes befell him, and he fared from bad to worse. But the heaviest blow came when his hayloft and all it contained burned down one night in the dead of winter. No one knew how the fire had started.

"This has been done by some one who wishes me ill," Anders said, and all that night he wept. He became a poor man, and he lost all inclination to work.

The evening after the fire, Baard appeared at his brother's house. Anders lay on his bed, but sprang up as Baard entered.

" What do you want here? " he asked, then stopped short, and stood staring fixedly at his brother.

Baard waited a little before he answered.

" I want to help you, Anders; you're in a bad way."

" I'm faring no worse than you wished me to fare! Go — else I'm not sure I can master myself."

" You're mistaken, Anders; I regret — "

" Go, Baard, or God have mercy on us both."

Baard drew back a step.

" If you want the watch," he said in a trembling voice, " you can have it."

" Go, Baard! " shrieked his brother, and Baard, unwilling to stay any longer, left.

In the meanwhile Baard had fared thus. As soon as he heard of his brother's misfortunes, he had suffered a change of heart, but pride held him back. He felt urged to go to church, and there he vowed many a good resolve, but he lacked strength to carry them out. He frequently went so far that he could see the house, but either some one was just coming out, or there were strangers there, or Anders stood chopping wood outside — there was always something in the way.

But one Sunday, late in the winter, he again went to church, and that Sunday Anders too was there. Baard saw him. He had grown pale and thin, and he wore the same clothes he had worn when the brothers were together, although now they were old and patched. All through the service Anders looked steadily at the minister. To Baard it seemed that he was kind and gentle, and he recalled their childhood days, and what a good boy Anders had been. That day Baard even went to communion, and he made a solemn vow to God that he would make up with his brother, come what might. This resolution swept through his soul as he drank the wine, and when he arose he felt an impulse to go over and take a seat beside him, but there was some one in the way, and Anders did not look up. After the service there was still something in the way; there were too many people about; Anders' wife was with him, and her he did not know. He decided it would be better to seek Anders in his home and have a quiet talk with him.

When evening came, he set out. He went right up to the door. Then he paused, and as he stood there listening, he heard his name mentioned; it was the wife speaking.

" He went to communion this morning," she was saying. " I am sure he was thinking of you."

" No, it wasn't of me he was thinking," Anders replied. " I know him, he thinks only of himself."

For a long time nothing was said, and Baard sweat, as he stood there, although it was a cold night. The wife inside was busy with a kettle; the fire on the hearth crackled and hissed; a child cried now and then, and Anders rocked it. At length the wife spoke again.

" I believe you are both thinking of each other though you won't admit it."

" Let us talk of something else," Anders answered.

After a little he got up to go out. Baard had to hide in the wood-shed; but then Anders, too, came to the shed to get an armful of wood. From where he stood in the corner Baard could see him clearly. He had taken off his threadbare Sunday clothes, and put on his uni-form, just like Baard's own. These they had promised each other never to wear, but to pass on as heirlooms to their children. Anders' was now patched and worn out, so that his strong, well-built frame seemed bundled in rags, while at the same time Baard could hear the gold watch ticking in his own pocket. Anders went over to the brush-wood, but instead of bending down immediately to gather up his load, he leaned back against a pile of wood, and looked up at the sky glim-mering brightly with stars. Then he sighed heavily and muttered to himself, " Well — well — well — oh, Lord, oh, Lord! "

As long as he lived, Baard never forgot those words. He wanted to step forward then, but the brother coughed, and it seemed so diffi-cult. No more was needed to hold him back. Anders took his armful of fagots, and as he went out, brushed past Baard so close that the twigs struck him in the face.

For fully ten minutes more he stood rooted to the spot, and it is doubtful how much longer he might have stayed, had not a chill, on top of the emotional stress, seized him, and set him shivering through and through. Then he went out. He frankly confessed to himself that he was too cowardly to enter now; wherefore he conceived an-other plan. From an ash barrel, which stood in the corner he had just left, he selected some bits of charcoal, found a pitch pine splinter, went up into the hayloft, closed the door, and struck a light. When he had lit the torch he searched about for the peg on which Anders hung his lantern when he came out early in the morning to thresh. Baard then took his gold watch and hung it on the peg, put out his light, and left. He felt so relieved in his mind that he raced over the snow like a youngster.

The day following he heard that the hayloft had burned down during the night. Presumably sparks had flown from the torch he had used while hanging up the watch.

This so overwhelmed Baard that all that day he kept to himself as though he were ill, brought out his hymnbook, and sang until the people in the house thought something was wrong with him. But in the evening he went out. It was bright moonlight. He went over to his brother's place, dug around in the charred ruins of the fire, and found, sure enough, a little lump of melted gold — all that remained of the watch.

It was with this in his hand that he had gone in to his brother, anxious to explain everything, and to sue for peace. But how he fared that evening has already been told.

A little girl had seen him digging in the ashes; some boys, on their way to a dance, had observed him go down toward his brother's the Sunday evening in question; and the people where he lived explained how strangely he had acted on the Monday following. And inasmuch as every one knew that he and his brother were bitter enemies, these details were reported to the authorities and an inquiry instituted. No one could prove anything against him, yet suspicion hovered around him. He could now less than ever approach his brother.

Anders had thought of Baard when the hayloft burned, but had said nothing. When he had seen him enter his house, the following evening, pale and strange, he had forthwith thought: He is smitten with remorse, but for such a terrible outrage against his brother there can be no forgiveness. Since then he heard how people had seen Baard go down towards his home the evening of the fire, and although nothing was brought to light at the inquiry, he felt convinced that his brother was the guilty one.

They met at the hearing, Baard in his good clothes, Anders in his worn-out rags. Baard looked at his brother as he entered, and Anders was conscious, in his inmost heart, of an anxious pleading in his eyes. He doesn't want me to say anything, thought Anders; and when he was asked whether he suspected his brother of the deed he answered loudly and decisively, " No! "

Anders took to drinking heavily after that day, and it was not long before he was in a bad way. Even worse, however, fared Baard, although he did not drink; he was so changed that people hardly knew him.

Then late one evening a poor woman entered the little room Baard rented and asked him to come with her. He recognized her; it was his brother's wife. Baard understood at once what her errand was, turned deathly pale, dressed himself, and followed her without a word. A pale glimmer shone from Anders' window, now flickering, now vanishing, and this light they followed, for there was no path across the snow. When Baard again stood in the doorway, he was met with a strange odor which almost made him ill. They went in. A little child sat eating charcoal over by the hearth, its face all black, but it looked up and laughed and showed its white teeth. It was his brother's child.

Over on the bed, with all sorts of clothes over him, lay Anders, pale, emaciated, his forehead high and smooth, and he stared at his brother with hollow eyes. Baard's knees trembled. He sat down at the foot of the bed and burst into uncontrollable weeping. The sick man looked at him intently and said nothing. At length he asked his wife to go out, but Baard motioned for her to remain. And then the two brothers began to talk to each other. They explained everything, from the day they bid for the watch down through the years to this day when they finally met again. Baard ended by taking out the lump of gold, which he always carried about him, and it came to light in the course of their talk that never for one single day in all these years had they been really happy.

Anders did not say much, for he had little strength, but Baard watched by the bedside as long as Anders was ill.

" Now I am perfectly well," Anders said one morning, on awakening. " Now, brother, we shall live together always, just as in the old days, and never leave each other."

But that day he died.

The widow and the child Baard took home with him, and they were henceforth well taken care of. But what the brothers had talked of at the bedside came out through the walls and the night, and became generally known to all the people in the valley. Baard grew to be the most highly respected man among them. They all honored him as one who had had a great sorrow and had found peace again, or as one who had returned after a long absence. And Baard grew in strength of mind by reason of all their friendliness. He became a godly man, and wishing to be of some use, as he said, the old corporal turned schoolmaster. What he impressed upon the children, first and last, was love, and himself he practiced it till the children came to love him as a playmate and a father.

(Anders Orbeck)

SUGGESTIONS FOR STUDY

1. Show how with each incident the gulf between the brothers becomes harder to cross. What in their conduct seems typical of men of Northern races rather than Southern? How would a quarrel between South Europeans have probably been carried on?

2. Do you sympathize with one brother any more than with the other? If so, which one? Why?

3. Read Björnson's story "The Father," found in many collections. By what quality of style does the author increase the poignancy of these two stories? Which of the two is, to your mind, the more moving? Why?

4. In what way does the situation in "The Brothers" resemble that in "King Eystein and King Sigurd," and also in *An Enemy of the People?* What other stories do you know that turn on the strained relations between two brothers or two sisters? Why does such a situation offer greater dramatic possibilities than a quarrel between friends?

KNUT HAMSUN (1859–1952)

In the nineties when Ibsen and Björnson were approaching old age, there arose on the literary horizon of Norway a young man who represented the mental unrest and the rebellion of youth. During his lifetime he became revered throughout the world as the dean of modern Norwegian literature. Knut Hamsun was born into a peasant family of Gudbrandsdal in north Norway. His father, unlike his substantial, home-loving neighbors, was a wanderer, and this roving spirit was transmitted to his eight children. Several unhappy years spent by young Knut in the home of a stern uncle tended to emphasize his solitary and restless disposition. After trying various occupations, he eventually, like so many other young Norwegians, landed in America. During the eighties he spent considerable time in Minneapolis and also in Chicago, where he was a street-car conductor. But he disliked this country intensely and later wrote an arraignment of intellectual life in America, which antagonized his fellow countrymen on this side of the ocean.

Back in Kristiania once more, he attempted unsuccessfully to live by free-lance writing, until his own painful experiences set forth in the remarkable book *Hunger* (1890) brought him wide recognition. This direct, first-person narrative of the effects of hunger on a man's whole being opened up an unusual series of books in each of which some solitary hero — a wanderer, a recluse, a misfit in society, a remote peasant — seeks satisfaction of his inmost personality in forest or farm. Usually the particular slant of the story developed from his own experience at the time. *Pan* and *Victoria* are the love stories of young men, and he later named his own daughter Victoria from this most noble of his heroines. *The Growth of the Soil* (1917), considered his masterpiece, resulted from six years spent on his north-country estate after his second marriage. That same year he bought an estate in south Norway near Grimstad, scene of Ibsen's youth, and there he passed the rest of his life, developing his property, rearing his four children, and writing numerous books in the secluded peasant's cottage which he used for a study and in which he attained the uninterrupted solitude his spirit demanded.

THE SOLITARY HUNTER

From *Pan*

This novel, written in 1894, has been called the greatest prose lyric in Norwegian literature. It represents young Lieutenant Glahn's record of his summer in the woods of the far north, a summer colored in his memory by an unhappy love affair. The title *Pan,* the Greek nature-god, suggests the poetic quality permeating the book. The following selection combines parts of several chapters. In order to give a condensed impression of the young man's love of the woods, and to avoid confusion in the reader's mind, passages introducing other characters in the plot have been omitted.

These last few days I have been thinking and thinking of the Nordland summer, with its endless day. Sitting here thinking of that, and of a hut I lived in, and of the woods behind the hut. And writing things down, by way of passing the time; to amuse myself, no more. The time goes very slowly; I cannot get it to pass as quickly as I would, though I have nothing to sorrow for, and live as pleasantly as could be. I am well content withal, and my thirty years are no age to speak of. . . .

Two years ago I remember, the time passed quickly — beyond all comparison more quickly than time now. A summer was gone before I knew. Two years ago it was, in 1855. I will write of it just to amuse myself — of something that happened to me, or something I dreamed. Now, I have forgotten many things belonging to that time, by having scarcely thought of them since. But I remember that the nights were very light. And many things seemed curious and unnatural. Twelve months to the year — but night was like day, and never a star to be seen in the sky. And the people I met were strange, and of a different nature from those I had known before; sometimes a single night was enough to make them blossom out from childhood into the full of their glory, ripe, and fully grown. No witchery in this; only I had never seen the like before. No.

In a white, roomy home down by the sea, I met with one who busied my thoughts for a little time. I do not always think of her now; not any more. No; I have forgotten her. But I think of all the other things; the cry of the sea birds, my hunting in the woods, my nights, and all the warm hours of that summer. After all, it was only the merest accident I happened to meet her; save for that, she would never have been in my thoughts for a day.

From the hut where I lived I could see a confusion of rocks and reefs and islets, and a little of the sea, and a bluish mountain peak or so; behind the hut was the forest. A huge forest it was; and I was glad and grateful beyond measure for the scent of roots and leaves, the thick smell of the fir sap, that is like the smell of marrow. Only the forest could bring all things to calm within me; my mind was strong and at ease. Day after day I tramped over the wooded hills with Aesop at my side, and asked no more than leave to keep on going there day after day, though most of the ground was covered still with snow and soft slush. I had no company but Aesop — Aesop, my dog that I afterwards shot.

Often in the evening, when I came back to the hut after being out shooting all day, I could feel that kindly, homely feeling trickling through me from head to foot — a pleasant little inward shivering. And I would talk to Aesop about it, saying how comfortable we were. "There, now we'll get a fire going, and roast a bird on the hearth," I would say; "what do you say to that?" And when it was done and we both had fed, Aesop would slip away to his place behind the hearth, while I lit a pipe and lay down on the bench for a while listening to the dead soughing of the trees. There was a slight breeze bearing down toward the hut, and I could hear quite clearly the clutter of a grouse far away on the ridge behind. Save for that, all was still.

And many a time I fell asleep there as I lay, just as I was, fully dressed and all, and did not wake till the sea birds began calling. And then, looking out of the window, I could see the big white building of the trading station, the landing stage at Sirilund, the store where I used to get my bread. And I would lie there a while, wondering how I came to be there, in a hut on the fringe of a forest, away up in the Nordland.

Then Aesop over by the hearth would shake out his long, slender body, rattling his collar, and yawning and wagging his tail, and I would jump up, after those three or four hours of sleep, fully rested and full of joy in everything — everything.

Many a night passed just that way.

Rain and storm — 'tis not such things that count. Many a time some little joy can come along on a rainy day, and make a man turn off somewhere to be alone with his happiness — stand up somewhere and look out straight ahead, laughing quietly now and again, and looking round. What is there to think of? One clear pane in a window, a ray of sunlight on the pane, the sight of a little brook, or maybe a blue strip of sky between the clouds. It needs no more than that.

At other times even quite unusual happenings cannot avail to lift a man from dulness and poverty of mind; one can sit in the middle of a ballroom and be cool, indifferent, unaffected by anything. Sorrow and joy are from within oneself. . . .

I was never short of game those days, but shot all I cared to — a hare, a grouse, a ptarmigan — and when I happened to be down near the shore and came within range of some sea bird or other, I shot it too. It was a pleasant time; the days grew longer and the air clearer; I packed up things for a couple of days and set off up into the hills, up to the mountain peaks. I met reindeer Lapps, and they gave me cheese — rich little cheeses tasting of herbs. I went up that way more than once. Then, going home again, I always shot some bird or other to put in my bag. I sat down and put Aesop on the lead. Miles below me was the sea; the mountain sides were wet and black with the water running down them, dripping and trickling always with the same little sound. That little sound of the water far up on the hills has shortened many an hour for me when I sat looking about. Here, I thought to myself, is a little endless song trickling away all to itself and no one ever hears it, and no one ever thinks of it, and still it trickles on nevertheless, to itself, all the time, all the time! And I felt that the mountains were no longer quite deserted as long as I could hear that little trickling song. Now and again something would happen; a clap of thunder shaking the earth, a mass of rock slipping loose and rushing down towards the sea, leaving a trail of smoking dust behind. Aesop turned his nose to the wind at once, sniffing in surprise at the smell of burning that he could not understand. When the melting of the snow had made rifts in the hillside, a shot, or even a sharp cry, was enough to loosen a great block and send it tumbling down. . . .

An hour might pass or perhaps more — the time went so quickly. I let Aesop loose, slung my bag over the other shoulder, and set off toward home. It was getting late. Lower down in the forest, I came unfailingly upon my old, well-known path, a narrow ribbon of a path, with the strangest bends and turns. I followed each one of them, taking my time — there was no hurry. No one was waiting for me at home. Free as a lord, a ruler, I could ramble about there in the peaceful woods, just as idly as I pleased. All the birds were silent; only the grouse was calling far away — it was always calling. . . .

It was evening now. I went home and lit a fire, roasted a bird and had a meal. Tomorrow there would be another day. . . .

All things quiet and still. I lay that evening looking out of the window. There was a fairy glimmer at that hour over wood and field; the sun had gone down and dyed the horizon with a rich red light that stood there still as oil. The sky all open and clear, I stared into that clear sea, and it seemed as if I were lying face to face with the uttermost depth of the world, my heart beating tensely against it, and at home there. God knows, I thought to myself, God knows why the sky is dressed in gold and mauve tonight, if there is not some festival going on up there in the world, some great feast with music from the stars, and boats gliding along river ways. It looks so! — And I closed my eyes, and followed the boats, and thoughts and thoughts floated through my mind. . . .

So more than one day passed.

I wandered about, noting how the snow turned to water, how the ice loosed its hold. Many a day I did not even fire a shot, when I had food enough in the hut — only wandered about in my freedom and let the time pass. Whichever way I turned, there was always just as much to see and hear — all things changing a little every day. Even the osier thickets and the juniper stood waiting for the spring. One day I went out to the mill; it was still icebound, but the earth around it had been trampled through many and many a year, showing how men and more men had come that way with sacks of corn on their shoulders, to be ground. It was like walking among human beings to go there; and there were many dates and letters cut in the walls. Well, well. . . .

The woods more yellow still. It is drawing towards autumn now; a few more stars have come in the sky, and from now on the moon looks like a shadow of silver dipped in gold. There is no cold; nothing, only a cool stillness and a flow of Life in the woods. Every tree stands in silent thought. The berries are ripe.

Then — the twenty-second of August and the three iron nights.[1]

---

[1] **iron nights:** a literal translation of the word used by Norwegians to designate the August nights when the early frosts come.

The first iron night; at nine the sun sets. A dull darkness settles over the earth, a star or so can be seen; two hours later there is a glow of the moon. I wander up in the woods with my gun and my dog. I light a fire, and the light of the flames shines in between the fir-trunks. There is no frost.

" The first iron night! " I say. And a confused, passionate delight in the time and the place sends a strange shiver through me. . . .

" Hail, men and beasts and birds, to the lonely night in the woods, in the woods! Hail to the darkness and God's murmuring between the trees, to the sweet, simple melody of silence in my ears, to green leaves and yellow! Hail to the life-sound I hear; a snout against the grass, a dog sniffing over the ground! A wild hail to the wildcat lying crouched, sighting and ready to spring on a sparrow in the dark, in the dark! Hail to the merciful silence upon earth, to the stars and the half-moon; ay, to them and to it! " . . .

I rise and listen. No one has heard me. I sit down again.

" Thanks for the lonely night, for the hills, the rush of the darkness and the sea through my heart! Thanks for my life, for my breath, for the boon of being alive tonight; thanks from my heart for these! Hear, east and west, oh, hear. It is the eternal God. This silence murmuring in my ears is the blood of all Nature seething; it is God weaving through the world and me. I see a glistening gossamer thread in the light of my fire; I hear a boat rowing across the harbor; the northern lights flare over the heavens to the north. By my immortal soul I am full of thanks that it is I who am sitting here! "

Silence. A fir cone falls dully to the ground. A fir cone fell! I think to myself. The moon is high, the fire flickers over the half-burned brands and is dying. And in the late night I wander home.

The second iron night; the same stillness and mild weather. My soul is pondering. I walk mechanically over to a tree, pull my cap deep down over my eyes, and lean against that tree, with hands clasped behind my neck. I gaze and think; the flame from my fire dazzles my eyes, and I do not feel it. I stand in that stupor for a while, looking at the fire; my legs fail me at first, and grow tired; thoroughly stiff, I sit down. Not till then do I think of what I have been doing. Why should I stare so long at the fire? . . .

The third iron night, a night of extremest tension. If only there were a little frost! Instead, still heat after the sun of the day; the night is like a lukewarm marsh. I light my fire. . . . I lie down closer to the fire and look at the flames. A pine cone falls from the branch; a dry twig or so falls too. The night is like a boundless depth. I close my eyes.

After an hour, my senses begin swinging in a certain rhythm. I am ringing in tune with the great stillness — ringing with it. I look at the half-moon; it stands in the sky like a white scale, and I have a feeling of love for it; I can feel myself blushing. " It is the moon! " I say softly and passionately; " it is the moon! " and my heart strikes toward it in a soft throbbing. So for some minutes. It is blowing a little; a stranger wind comes to me, a mysterious current of air. What is it? I look round, but see no one. The wind calls me, and my soul bows acknowledging the call; and I feel myself lifted into the air, pressed to an invisible breast; my eyes are dewed, I tremble — God is standing near, watching me. Again several minutes pass. I turn my head round; the stranger wind is gone, and I see something like the back of a spirit wandering silently in through the woods. . . .

I struggle a short while with a heavy melancholy; I was worn out with emotion; I am deathly tired, and I sleep.

When I awoke the night was past. Alas, I had been going about for a long time in a sad state, full of fever, on the verge of falling down stricken with some sickness or other. Often things had seemed upside down. I had been looking at everything through inflamed eyes. A deep misery had possessed me.

It was over now.

(W. W. Worster)

SUGGESTIONS FOR STUDY

1. Characterize Lieutenant Glahn from the evidence of his own account. How does he resemble the average young American who goes out hunting? How differ from him?

2. Compare Glahn's reactions to the woods with those of Henry Thoreau in *Walden*. Can you detect a marked difference in the style of the two books? Compare also with other accounts of forest life which you have read.

3. Select passages in which the lyrical quality is especially marked. Walt Whitman was one of the few American poets whom Hamsun liked to read. Can you explain this?

4. Write an account of your own experience with some aspect of nature, trying to keep a unified mood throughout.

5. Of the many novels by Hamsun, the four mentioned on pages 690–691 are especially recommended for further reading. How does each present a different aspect of Hamsun's favorite subject — the solitary man?

OLE E. RÖLVAAG (1876–1931)

Does Rölvaag belong to Norwegian or to American literature? That is a difficult question to answer, for he holds a unique position in the literatures of both nations. He presents the one example of an American writing in America about the American scene and producing an American best seller which nevertheless was written in Norwegian and published in Norway three years before a translation into English was made. And this is the way it happened:

Rölvaag was born in a tiny settlement on the island of Dönna in Helgeland, only a short distance south of the Arctic circle, where fishing was the chief industry. The long months of darkness shortened the school year to nine weeks, and so in seven years of schooling the boy had only the equivalent of about two years in American education. And the school was seven miles away! At the age of fourteen he was taken out of school because his father did not consider him worth educating. For the next six years he was in the fishing fleet visiting annually the Lofoten Islands, scene of Poe's story " A Descent into the Maelstrom." But he was reading widely all during his boyhood. Cooper's *The Last of the Mohicans* was his first novel. Dickens, Scott, and Bulwer-Lytton were also favorites. Once he walked fourteen miles to another village to get a copy of *Ivanhoe*. He longed to go to America to escape the narrowness, gloom, and frightful storms of the fisherman's life, but the uncle in South Dakota to whom he applied delayed two years before sending him a ticket. Then after the ticket arrived the master of the fishing fleet, whom the boy greatly admired, offered to buy him the best fishing boat on the market if he would stay in Norway. It was a temptation, but after hours of meditation America won. The youth of twenty reached New York with only a dime to his name, and a single loaf of bread lasted him to South Dakota. After a few years farming wearied him. He returned to school life, was graduated from St. Olaf College in Minnesota at twenty-eight, and after a year of advanced study in Norway returned to that college to teach Norwegian. Here he remained for twenty-five years, retiring in 1931, as he said " to read and write a great deal," but within four months he was dead of a heart attack.

Rölvaag's writing was all done in Norwegian because he could create more naturally in that language, though he spoke English fluently. His first work, *Letters from America* (1912), was largely autobiographical. Several novels and textbooks followed, all published in this country. In 1924–1925 his two consecutive novels *In Those Days* and *Founding the Kingdom* were published in Norway and ran into many editions. The next year Rölvaag was decorated as a Knight of St. Olaf by the King of Norway. In 1927 the two books were translated into English as one novel, with the title *Giants in the Earth*. It was immediately recognized by Americans as a masterpiece — a story of American pioneers of the Northwest told in the slow-moving, psychological manner of the European novel. In the few remaining years of his life Rölvaag published three other novels, *Peder Victorious,* a sequel to the preceeding book, *Pure Gold* and *Their Father's God,* all of which are translated; but none quite equaled the power of the earlier novel. Rölvaag once said, "If I could write in such a way that I could leave one true story, told in living pictures, behind me, I would be very happy." This wish has certainly been fulfilled in *Giants in the Earth.*

GIANTS IN THE EARTH

In 1923 O. E. Rölvaag read in a Norwegian paper that Johan Bojer was soon to visit the United States to assemble material for a great novel on the Norwegian-American immigrants. His creative faculties were immediately stimulated by this, for he felt that the real story could never be told by an outsider after a short inspection. It must come from within the country, from one who had shared the immigrant point of view. A year's leave of absence from his college gave him the opportunity to plan his story and to visit Bojer in Norway. To his relief he found that the other writer viewed his tale from a different angle, and so he felt free to proceed with his own plan. Bojer's novel, known in English as *The Emigrants,* was published just a month after the first part of Rölvaag's. The very spelling of the title shows that Bojer saw his story from the Norwegian viewpoint entirely. A similar title for Rölvaag's novel would have been spelled *The Immigrants.* However the similarity of certain passages in the two books might have caused unpleasant suspicions of plagiarism had not both been in the press at the same time. The two novels read together give a full picture of the whole immigration problem.

The following selection from *Giants in the Earth* is the opening chapter describing the long trek across the empty prairies. It is a prose poem in itself and establishes the mood of the entire book, which combines the slow movement of the ox-cart, the poetic beauty of the prairie night, and the feeling of inevitable fate, typified by the constant "Tish-ah!" of the prairie grass. Per Hansa, the father, capable, practical, yet driven ever by his dream; Beret, the gentle daughter of civilization, who cannot become adjusted to the barren existence of the prairie and whose mind eventually snaps; the little group of settlers with whom their lot is closely united, each differentiated in marked ways from the other — all these make us feel by the end of the book that we have partaken of life with them. The title of the book is taken from the sixth chapter of Genesis, "There were giants in the earth in those days." Its subtitle is "A Saga of the Prairie." These simple people do indeed take on the gigantic qualities of the old saga heroes seen through the mists of the past.

TOWARD THE SUNSET

I

Bright, clear sky over a plain so wide that the rim of the heavens cut down on it around the entire horizon. . . . Bright, clear sky, today, tomorrow, and for all time to come.

. . . And sun! And still more sun! It set the heavens afire every morning; it grew with the day to quivering golden light — then softened into all the shades of red and purple as evening fell. . . . Pure color everywhere. A gust of wind, sweeping across the plain, threw into life waves of yellow and blue and green. Now and then a dead black wave would race over the scene . . . a cloud's gliding shadow . . . now and then. . . .

It was late afternoon. A small caravan was pushing its way through the tall grass. The track that it left behind was like the wake of a boat — except that instead of widening out astern it closed in again.

" Tish-ah! " said the grass. . . . " Tish-ah, tish-ah! " . . . Never had it said anything else — never would it say anything else. It bent resiliently under the trampling feet; it did not break, but it complained aloud every time — for nothing like this had ever happened to it before. . . . " Tish-ah, tish-ah! " it cried, and rose up in surprise to look at this rough, hard thing that had crushed it to the ground so rudely, and then moved on.

A stocky, broad-shouldered man walked at the head of the caravan. He seemed shorter than he really was, because of the tall grass around him and the broad-brimmed hat of coarse straw which he wore. A few steps behind him followed a boy of about nine years of age. The boy's blond hair was clearly marked against his brown, sunburnt neck; but the man's hair and neck were of exactly the same shade of brown. From the looks of these two, and still more from their gait, it was easy to guess that here walked father and son.

Behind them a team of oxen jogged along; the oxen were drawing a vehicle which once upon a time might have been a wagon, but which now, on account of its many and grave infirmities, ought long since to have been consigned to the scrap heap — exactly the place, in point of fact, where the man had picked it up. Over the wagon box long willow saplings had been bent, in the form of arches in a church chancel — six of them in all. On these arches, and tied down to the body on each side, were spread first of all two hand-woven blankets, that might well have adorned the walls of some manor house in the olden times; on top of the blankets were thrown two sheepskin robes, with the wool side down, which were used for bed-coverings at night. The rear of the wagon was stowed full of numberless articles, all the way up to the top. A large immigrant chest at the bottom of the pile, very long and high, devoured a big share of the space; around and above it were piled household utensils, tools, implements, and all their clothing.

Hitched to this wagon and trailing behind was another vehicle, homemade and very curious-looking, so solidly and quaintly constructed that it might easily have won a place in any museum. Indeed, it appeared strong enough to stand all the jolting from the Atlantic to the Pacific. . . . It, too, was a wagon, after a fashion; at least, it had been intended for such. The wheels were made from pieces of plank fitting roughly together; the box, considerably wider than that of the first wagon, was also loaded full of provisions and household gear, covered over with canvas and lashed down securely. Both wagons creaked and groaned loudly every time they bounced over a tussock or hove out of a hollow. . . . " Squeak, squeak! " said the one. . . . " Squeak, squeak! " answered the other. . . . The strident sound broke the silence of centuries.

A short distance behind the wagons followed a brindle cow. The caravan moved so slowly that she occasionally had time to stop and snatch a few mouthfuls, though there was never a chance for many at a time. But what little she got in this way she sorely needed. She had been jogging along all day, swinging and switching her tail, the rudder of the caravan. Soon it would be night, and then her part of the work would come — to furnish milk for che evening porridge, for all the company up ahead.

Across the front end of the box of the first wagon lay a rough piece of plank. On the right side of this plank sat a woman with a white kerchief over her head, driving the oxen. Against her thigh rested the blond head of a little girl, who was stretched out on the plank and sleeping sweetly. Now and then the hand of the mother moved across the child's face to chase away the mosquitoes, which had begun to gather as the sun lowered. On the left side of the plank, beyond the girl, sat a boy about seven years old — a well-grown lad, his skin deeply tanned, a certain clever, watchful gleam in his eyes. With hands folded over one knee, he looked straight ahead.

This was the caravan of Per Hansa, who with his family and all his earthly possessions was moving west from Fillmore County, Minnesota, to Dakota Territory. There he intended to take up land and build himself a home; he was going to do something remarkable out there, which should become known far and wide. No lack of opportunity in that country, he had been told! . . . Per Hansa himself strode ahead and laid out the course; the boy Ole, or *Olamand,* followed closely after, and explored it. Beret, the wife, drove the oxen and took care of little Anna Marie, pet-named *And-Ongen* (which means " The Duckling "), who was usually bubbling over with happiness. Hans Kristian, whose everyday name was *Store-Hans* (meaning " Big Hans," to distinguish him from his godfather, who was also named Hans, but who, of course, was three times his size), sat there on the wagon, and saw to it that every one attended to business. . . . The cow Rosie trailed behind, swinging and switching her tail, following the caravan farther and farther yet into the endless vista of the plain.

" Tish-ah, tish-ah! " cried the grass. . . . " Tish-ah, tish-ah! " . . .

II

The caravan seemed a miserably frail and Lilliputian [1] thing as it crept over the boundless prairie toward the sky line. Of road or trail there lay not a trace ahead; as soon as the grass had straightened up again behind, no one could have told the direction from which it had come or whither it was bound. The whole train — Per Hansa with his wife and children, the oxen, the wagons, the cow, and all — might just as well have dropped down out of the sky. Nor was it at all impossible to imagine that they were trying to get back there again; their course was always the same — straight toward the west, straight toward the sky line. . . .

Poverty-stricken, unspeakably forlorn, the caravan creaked along, advancing at a snail's pace, deeper and deeper into a bluish-green infinity — on and on, and always farther on. . . . It steered for Sunset Land! . . .

For more than three weeks now, and well into the fourth, this caravan had been crawling across the plain. . . . Early in the journey it had passed through Blue Earth; it had left Chain Lakes behind; and one fine day it had crept into Jackson, on the Des Moines River. But that seemed ages ago. . . . From Jackson, after a short lay-up, it had pushed on westward — always westward — to Wor-

1 **Lilliputian:** little; derived from the island of Lilliput in *Gulliver's Travels,* where the inhabitants were only six inches tall.

thington, then to Rock River. . . . A little west of Rock River, Per Hansa had lost the trail completely. Since then he had not been able to find it again; at this moment he literally did not know where he was, nor how to get to the place he had to reach. But Split Rock Creek must lie out there somewhere in the sun; if he could only find that landmark, he could pick his way still farther without much trouble. . . . Strange that he hadn't reached Split Rock Creek before this time! According to his directions, he should have been there two or three days ago; but he hadn't seen anything that even looked like the place. . . . Oh, my God! If something didn't turn up soon! . . . My God! . . .

The wagons creaked and groaned. Per Hansa's eyes wandered over the plain. His bearded face swung constantly from side to side as he examined every inch of ground from the northeast to the southwest. At times he gave his whole attention to that part of the plain lying between him and the western sky line; with head bent forward and eyes fixed and searching, he would sniff the air, like an animal trying to find the scent. Every now and then he glanced at an old silver watch which he carried in his left hand; but his gaze would quickly wander off again, to take up its fruitless search of the empty horizon.

It was now nearing six o'clock. Since three in the afternoon he had been certain of his course; at that time he had taken his bearings by means of his watch and the sun. . . . Out here one had to get one's cross-bearings from the very day itself — then trust to luck. . . .

For a long while the little company had been silent. Per Hansa turned halfway around, and without slackening his pace spoke to the boy walking behind.

" Go back and drive for a while now, Ola.[2] . . . You must talk to mother, too, so that it won't be so lonesome for her. And be sure to keep as sharp a lookout as you can."

" I'm not tired yet! " said the boy, loath to leave the van.

" Go back, anyway! Maybe you're not, but I can feel it beginning to tell on me. We'll have to start cooking the porridge pretty soon. . . . You go back, and hold her on the sun for a while longer."

" Do you think we'll catch up with them tonight, Dad? " The boy was still undecided.

" Good Lord, no! They've got too long a start on us. . . . Look sharp, now! If you happen to see anything suspicious, sing out! "

[2] **Ola:** Ole is here changed to Ola to represent the spoken sound of the vowel.

. . . Per Hansa glanced again at his watch, turned forward, and strode steadily onward.

Ole said no more; he stepped out of the track and stood there waiting till the train came up. Then Store-Hans jumped down nimbly, while the other climbed up and took his seat.

"Have you seen anything?" the mother asked in an anxious voice.

"Why, no . . . not yet," answered the boy, evasively.

"I wonder if we shall ever see them again," she said, as if speaking to herself, and looked down at the ground. "This seems to be taking us to the end of the world . . . beyond the end of the world!"

Store-Hans, who was still walking beside the wagon, heard what she said and looked up at her. The buoyancy of childhood shone in his brown face. . . . Too bad that mother should be so scared! . . .

"Yes, Mother, but when we're both steering for the sun, we'll both land in the same place, won't we? . . . The sun is a sure guide, you know!"

These were the very words which he had heard his father use the night before; now he repeated them. To Store-Hans the truth of them seemed as clear as the sun itself; in the first place, because dad had said it, and then because it sounded so reasonable.

He hurried up alongside his father and laid his hand in his — he always felt safer thus.

The two walked on side by side. Now and then the boy stole a glance at the face beside him, which was as stern and fixed as the prairie on which they were walking. He was anxious to talk, but couldn't find anything to say that sounded grown-up enough; and so he kept quiet. At last, however, the silence grew too heavy for him to bear. He tried to say indifferently, just like his father:

"When I'm a man and have horses, I'm going to make a road over these plains, and . . . and put up some posts for people to follow. Don't you think that'll be a good idea?"

A slight chuckle came from the bearded face set toward the sun.

"Sure thing, Store-Hans — you'll manage that all right. . . . I might find time to help you an hour or two, now and then."

The boy knew by his father's voice that he was in a talkative mood. This made him so glad, that he forgot himself and did something that his mother always objected to; he began to whistle, and tried to take just as long strides as his father. But he could only make the grass say: "Swish-sh, swish-sh!"

On and on they went, farther out toward Sunset Land — farther into the deep glow of the evening.

The mother had taken little Anna up in her lap and was now leaning backward as much as she could; it gave such relief to her tired muscles. The caresses of the child and her lively chatter made her forget for a moment care and anxiety, and that vague sense of the unknown which bore in on them so strongly from all directions. . . . Ole sat there and drove like a full-grown man; by some means or other he managed to get more speed out of the oxen than the mother had done — she noticed this herself. His eyes were searching the prairie far and near.

Out on the sky line the huge plain now began to swell and rise, almost as if an abscess were forming under the skin of the earth. Although this elevation lay somewhat out of his course, Per Hansa swung over and held straight toward the highest part of it.

The afternoon breeze lulled, and finally dropped off altogether. The sun, whose golden luster had faded imperceptibly into a reddish hue, shone now with a dull light, yet strong and clear; in a short while, deeper tones of violet began to creep across the red. The great ball grew enormous; it retreated farther and farther into the empty reaches of the western sky; then it sank suddenly. . . . The spell of evening quickly crowded in and laid hold of them all; the oxen wagged their ears; Rosie lifted her voice in a long moo, which died out slowly in the great stillness. At the moment when the sun closed his eye, the vastness of the plain seemed to rise up on every hand — and suddenly the landscape had grown desolate; something bleak and cold had come into the silence, filling it with terror. . . . Behind them, along the way they had come, the plain lay dark green and life-less, under the gathering shadow of the dim, purple sky.

Ole sat motionless at his mother's side. The falling of evening had made such a deep impression on him that his throat felt dry; he wanted to express some of the emotions that overwhelmed him, but only choked when he tried.

" Did you ever see anything so beautiful! " he whispered at last, and gave a heavy sigh. . . . Low down in the northwest, above the little hill, a few fleecy clouds hovered, betokening fair weather; now they were fringed with shining gold, which glowed with a mellow light. As if they had no weight, they floated lightly there. . . .

The mother drew herself forward to an upright position. She still held the child in her lap. Per Hansa and Store-Hans were walking in the dusk far up ahead. For the last two days Per had kept well in advance of the caravan all the time; she thought she knew the reason why.

"Per," she called out, wearily, " aren't we going to stop soon? " " Pretty soon." . . . He did not slacken his pace.

She shifted the child over into the other arm and began to weep silently. Ole saw it, but pretended not to notice, though he had to swallow big lumps that were forcing themselves up in his throat; he kept his eyes resolutely fixed on the scene ahead.

" Dad," he shouted after a while, " I see a wood over there to the westward! "

" You do, do you? A great fellow you are! Store-Hans and I have seen that for a long time now."

" Whereabouts is it? " whispered Store-Hans, eagerly.

" It begins down there on the slope to the left, and then goes around on the other side," said his father. " Anyway, it doesn't seem to be much of a wood."

" D'you think they are there? "

" Not on your life! But we're keeping the right course, anyhow."

" Have the others been this way? "

" Of course they have — somewhere near, at any rate. There's supposed to be a creek around here, by the name of Split Rock Creek, or whatever they call it in English."

" Are there any people here, do you think? "

" People? Good Lord, no! There isn't a soul around these parts."

The somber blue haze was now closing rapidly in on the caravan. One sensed the night near at hand; it breathed a chill as it came.

At last Per Hansa halted. " Well, I suppose we can't drive any farther today. We and the animals would both drop pretty soon." With these words he faced the oxen, held his arms straight out like the horizontal beam of a cross, shouted a long-drawn " Whoa! " — and then the creaking stopped for that day.

III

The preparations for the night were soon made; each had his own task and was now well used to it. Store-Hans brought the wood; it lay strapped under the hind wagon and consisted of small logs and dry branches from the last thicket they had passed.

Ole got the fireplace ready. From the last wagon he brought out two iron rods, cleft in one end; these he drove into the ground and then went back to the wagon for a third rod, which he laid across the other two. It was also his duty to see that there was water enough in the keg, no matter where they happened to stop; for the rest of it, he was on hand to help his mother.

The father tended to the cattle. First he lifted the yoke off the oxen and turned them loose; then he milked Rosie and let her go also. After that he made up a bed for the whole family under the wagon.

While the mother waited for the pot to boil she set the table. She spread a home-woven blanket on the ground, laid a spoon for each one on it, placed a couple of bowls for the milk, and fetched the dishes for the porridge. Meanwhile she had to keep an eye on And-Ongen, who was toddling about in the grass near by. The child stumbled, laughed, lay there a moment chattering to herself, then got up, only to trip on her skirt and tumble headlong again. Her prattling laughter rang on the evening air. Now and then the voice of the mother would mingle with it, warning the child not to stray too far.

Store-Hans was the first to get through with his task; he stood around a while, but, finding nothing more to do, he strolled off westward. He was itching to know how far it was to the hill out there; it would be great fun to see what things looked like on the other side! . . . Now he started off in that direction. Perhaps he might come across the others? They surely must be somewhere. Just think, if he could only find them! He would yell and rush in on them like an Indian — and then they would be scared out of their senses! . . . He had gone quite far before he paused to look back. When he did so, the sight sent a shiver over him; the wagons had shrunk to two small specks, away off on the floor of a huge, dusky room. . . . I'd better hurry at once, he thought; mother will surely have the porridge ready by this time! His legs had already adopted the idea of their own accord. But thoughts of his mother and the porridge didn't quite bring him all the feeling of safety he needed; he hunted through his mind for a few strains of a hymn, and sang them over and over in a high-pitched, breaking voice, until he had no more breath left to sing with. . . . He didn't feel entirely safe until the wagons had begun to assume their natural size once more.

The mother called to them that supper was ready. On the blanket stood two dishes of porridge—a large dish for the father and the two boys, a smaller one for the mother and And-Ongen. The evening milk was divided between two bowls, and set before them; Rosie, poor thing, was not giving much these days! The father said that he didn't care for milk this evening, either; it had a tangy taste, he thought;

and he drank water with his porridge. But when Ole also began to complain of the tangy taste and asked for water, the father grew stern and ordered him to go ahead and get that drop of milk down as quick as he could! There was nothing else on the table but milk and porridge.

Suddenly Ole and Store-Hans flared up in a quarrel; one blamed the other for eating too close to the edge, where the porridge was coolest. The father paused in his meal, listening to them a moment, then chuckled to himself. Taking his spoon and cutting three lines through the crust of the porridge, he quickly settled the matter between them.

" There you are! Here, Store-Hans, is your land; now take it and be satisfied. Ola, who is the biggest, gets another forty. . . . Shut up your mouths, now, and eat! " Per Hansa himself got the smallest share that evening.

Aside from this outbreak it was quiet at the table. A spell of silence lay upon them and they were not able to throw it off. . . . As soon as the father had eaten he licked his spoon carefully, wiped it off on his shirt-sleeve, and threw it on the blanket. The boys did likewise as they finished; but And-Ongen wanted to tuck her spoon in her dress and keep it there till morning.

They sat around in the same silence after they were done. Then she who was the smallest of them repeated in a tiny voice:

" Thanks to Thee, Our Lord and Maker. . . .

" Now I want to go to sleep in your lap! " she said, after the Amen. She climbed up into her mother's lap and threw her arms around her neck.

" Oh, how quickly it grows dark out here! " the mother murmured.

Per Hansa gave a carefree shrug of his shoulders. " Well," he said, dryly, " the sooner the day's over, the sooner the next day comes! "

But now something seemed to be brewing back there over the prairie whence they had come. Up from the horizon swelled a supernatural light — a glow of pale yellow and transparent green, mingled with strange touches of red and gold. It spread upward as they watched; the colors deepened; the glow grew stronger, like the witching light of a fen fire.

All sat silently gazing. It was And-Ongen, hanging around her mother's neck, who first found her voice.

" Oh, look! . . . She is coming up again! "

In solemn grandeur the moon swung up above the plain. She

had been with them many nights now; but each time she seemed as wonderful a sight as ever. Tonight a hush fell on their spirits as they watched her rise — just as the scene had hushed them the evening before, far away to the eastward somewhere on the plain. The silvery beams grew stronger; the first pale fen fire began to shimmer and spread; slowly the light mellowed into a mist of green and yellow and blue. And-Ongen exclaimed that the moon was much bigger tonight; but it had seemed bigger the night before also. Store-Hans again solemnly told her the reason for it — that the moon had to grow, just as she did! This seemed to her quite logical; she turned to her mother and asked whether the moon had milk and porridge every evening, too.

Per Hansa had been sitting on the tongue of the wagon, smoking his pipe. Now he got up, knocked out the ashes carefully, put his pipe in his pocket, and wound up his watch. These duties done, he gave the order to turn in for the night.

A little while later they all lay under the quilts, gazing off into the opalescent glow. When the mother thought that the children had gone to sleep she asked, soberly:

" Do you suppose we'll ever find the others again? "

" Oh yes — I'm sure of it . . . if they haven't sunk through the ground! "

This was all Per Hansa said. He yawned once or twice, long and heavily, as if he were very sleepy, and turned away from her.

. . . After that she said no more, either.

(O. E. Rölvaag and Lincoln Colcord)

SUGGESTIONS FOR STUDY

1. What qualities of a prose poem do you find in this description? What phrases toward the beginning immediately inform the reader that this is wild uninhabited country?

2. At what points does the author leave his objective picture and suddenly dip into the mind of some character? What can you say of this as a modern method of story telling?

3. Prove that Rölvaag is a realist as well as a poet in this selection. What details are particularly good in his treatment of the children?

4. Compare the poetic treatment of these peasants with the peasant pictures of Victor Hugo's " The Sower," page 104 and Machado's second poem, page 318. Read also the opening chapter of Hamsun's *Growth of the Soil* and Book II, especially chapters 1, 2, and 5 of Boyer's *The Emigrants* for the same quality of " primal things " running through Norwegian literature.

5. Vocabulary: resiliently, tussock, tangy.

SIGRID UNDSET (1882–1949)

Sigrid Undset takes her place among the great women novelists of the world: Jane Austen and George Eliot of England, George Sand of France, Selma Lagerlöf of Sweden, Edith Wharton and Willa Cather of the United States. She has been translated into fourteen different languages and in 1928 she was given the Nobel prize for her " powerful delineation of medieval life " in *Kristin Lavransdatter*.

Her mother was Danish, her father Norwegian. She was born in Denmark, grew up in Oslo, and later made her home in Norway — in a thousand-year-old country house in the Lillehammer valley. As a little girl her reading was surprisingly mature. At eleven she was reading Ibsen's *Ghosts*, Strindberg, Zola, and other authors far beyond the average child's interests. After graduating from the Women's College at Oslo, she spent ten years in secretarial work and began to publish fiction in 1907. Her greatest novels show the influence of the Norwegian tradition, being series of related stories tracing the life of a family, somewhat as the ancient sagas did. To the sagas, also, she went for the subject matter of her great trilogy, *Kristin Lavransdatter,* which makes the fourteenth-century characters so real that the reader is living among them rather than viewing them from the distance of six centuries. Her antiquarian knowledge recalls that of Sir Walter Scott, but her modern psychological treatment produces a totally different effect from that of Scott's novels.

This is the novel which the public in general seems still to consider her best, but Sigrid Undset's own preference was for the tetralogy, *The Master of Hestviken,* which centers about a man of medieval Norway, as the first had about a woman. Her later books *The Wild Orchid* and *The Burning Bush* are modern in their setting. They form a sequence in the life of Paul Selmer, the first title signifying earthly love, the second heavenly love. Paul becomes a Catholic in the second book, an experience reflecting a spiritual struggle and decision of the author's own life. Her *Saga of Saints* is a collection of eight short biographies of Norwegian saints ranging from the ninth century when Christianity was introduced into Norway up to the present century. The more Sigrid Undset became engrossed in doctrinal and ecclesiastical matters the less her books appealed from a literary point of view. Her perpetuated fame will unquestionably rest on *Kristin Lavransdatter* and *The Master of Hestviken,* which in vitality of style and searching psychological insight are undoubted masterpieces.

KRISTIN LAVRANSDATTER

THE BURNING OF THE CHURCH

Sigrid Undset's masterpiece, *Kristin Lavransdatter*, is a story of Norway in the fourteenth century in which the medieval characters are painted with lifelike reality. The power of the book may be glimpsed in this scene of the burning of the church, an episode which may be understood without a complete reading of the tale. All that is necessary to know is that this was the church in which Kristin, the heroine of the story, was to have been married. Lavrans is her father; Ragnfrid, her mother; Erlend, her betrothed; Sira Eirik, the priest. The place names are local names near Jörundgaard, Lavrans' estate in southern Norway.

Toward evening the whole load stood ready, firmly bound under the wagon-tilt. Erlend was to set forth early the next morning.

He stood with Kristin leaning over the courtyard gate, looking northward to where a blue-black storm-cloud filled the Dale. Thunder was rolling far off in the mountains — but southward the green fields and the river lay in yellow, burning sunshine.

" Mind you the storm that day in the woods at Gerdarud? " he asked softly, playing with her fingers.

Kristin nodded and tried to smile. The air was so heavy and close — her head ached, and at every breath she took her skin grew damp with sweat.

Lavrans came across to the two as they stood by the gate, and spoke of the storm. 'Twas but rarely it did much harm down here in the parish — but God knew if they should not hear of cattle and horses killed up in the mountains.

It was black as night above the church up on the hillside. A lightning flash showed them a troop of horses standing uneasily huddled together on the green-sward outside the church gate. Lavrans thought they could scarce belong here in the parish — rather must they be horses from Dovre that had been running loose up on the hills below Jetta; but yet he had a mind to go up and look at them, he shouted through a peal of thunder — there might be some of his among them —

A fearful lightning-flash tore the darkness above the church — the thunder crashed and bellowed so as to deafen them to all other sounds. The fluster of horses burst asunder, scattering over the hill-slopes beneath the mountain-ridge. All three of them crossed themselves —

Then came another flash; it was as though the heavens split asunder right above them, a mighty snow-white flame swooped down upon them — the three were thrown against each other, and stood with shut, blinded eyes, and a smell in their nostrils as of burning stone — while the crashing thunder rent their ears.

" Saint Olav, help us! " said Lavrans in a low voice.

" Look! the birch — the birch," shouted Erlend; the great birch-tree in the field near by seemed to totter — and a huge bough parted from the tree and sank to the ground, leaving a great gash in the trunk.

" Think you 'twill catch fire — Jesus Kristus! The church-roof is alight! " shouted Lavrans.

They stood and gazed — no — yes! Red flames were darting out among the shingles beneath the ridge-turret.

Both men rushed back across the courtyard. Lavrans tore open the doors of all the houses he came to and shouted to those inside; the house-folk came swarming out.

" Bring axes, bring axes — timber axes," he cried, " and bill-hooks " — he ran on to the stables. In a moment he came out leading Gulsveinen by the mane; he sprang on the horse's bare back and dashed off up the hill, with the great broad-axe in his hand. Erlend rode close behind him — all the men followed; some were a-horseback, but some could not master the terrified beasts, and giving up, ran on afoot. Last came Ragnfrid and all the women on the place with pails and buckets.

None seemed to heed the storm any longer. By the light of the flashes they could see folk streaming out of the houses further down the valley. Sira Eirik was far up the hill already, running with his house-folk behind him. There was a thunder of horses' hoofs on the ridge below — some men galloped past, turning white, appalled faces toward their burning church.

It was blowing a little from the south-east. The fire had a strong hold on the north wall; on the west the entrance door was blocked already. But it had not caught yet on the south side nor on the apse.[1]

Kristin and the women from Jörundgaard came into the graveyard south of the church at a place where the fence was broken.

The huge red glare lighted up the grove of trees north of the church and the green by it where there were bars to tie the horses to. None could come thither for the glowing heat — the great cross stood alone out there, bathed in the light of the flames. It looked as though it lived and moved.

Through the hissing and roar of the flames sounded the thudding of axes against the staves of the south wall. There were men in the

---

[1] apse: the eastern or altar side of a church.

cloister-way [2] hewing and hammering at the wall, while others tried to tear down the cloister itself. Some one called out to the Jörund-gaard women that Lavrans and a few other men had followed Sira Eirik into the church, and now 'twas high time to cut a passage through the south wall — small tongues of flame were peeping out among the shingles here too; and should the wind go round or die down, the fire would take hold on the whole church.

To think of putting out the fire was vain; there was no time to make a chain down to the river; but at Ragnfrid's bidding the women made a line and passed water along from the little beck [3] that ran by the roadside — it was but little to throw on the south wall and over the men working there. Many of the women sobbed and wept the while, in terror for the men who had made their way into the burning building, and in sorrow for their church.

Kristin stood foremost in the line of women handing along the pails — she gazed breathless at the burning church — they were both there, inside — her father — and surely Erlend too.

The torn-down pillars of the cloister-way lay in a tangled mass of timber and shingles from its roof. The men were attacking the inner wall of staves now with all their might — a group of them had lifted up a great log and were battering the wall with it.

Erlend and one of his men came out of the little door in the south wall of the choir, carrying between them the great chest from the sacristy [4] — the chest Eirik was used to sit on when he heard confession. Erlend and the man flung the chest out into the churchyard.

He shouted out something, but Kristin could not hear; he dashed on at once into the cloister-way. Nimble as a cat he seemed as he ran — he had thrown off his outer garments and had naught on him but shirt, breeches and hose.

The others took up his shout — the choir and the sacristy were burning; none could pass from the nave [5] to the south door any longer — the fire had blocked both ways of escape. Some of the staves in the wall had been splintered by the ram — Erlend had seized a fire-hook and with it he tugged and wrenched at the wreckage of the staves — he and those with him tore a hole in the side of the church, while other folks cried to take care, for the roof might fall and shut in the men inside: the shingle roof on this side too was burning hard now, and the heat had grown till 'twas scarce to be borne.

[2] **cloister-way:** a covered walk following the walls of the building.
[3] **beck:** a small brook.
[4] **sacristy:** a room for the sacred vessels and vestments.
[5] **nave:** the main body of a church built in the form of a cross.

Erlend burst through the hole and helped out Sira Eirik. The priest came bearing the holy vessels from the altars in the skirt of his gown.

A young boy followed, with one hand over his face and the other holding the tall processional cross lance-wise in front of him. Lavrans came next. He kept his eyes shut against the smoke — he staggered under the weight of the great crucifix, which he bore in his arms; it was much taller than the man himself.

Folk ran forward and helped them out and into the churchyard. Sira Eirik stumbled and fell on his knees, and the altar vessels rolled out down the slope. The silver dove flew open and the Host [6] fell out — the priest took it up, brushed the soil off it and kissed it, sobbing aloud; he kissed the gilded head, too, that had stood on the altar with shreds of the nails and hair of Saint Olav in it.

Lavrans Björgulfsön still stood holding up the Holy Rood. [7] His arm lay along the arms of the cross; his head was bowed against the shoulder of the Christ-figure; it seemed as though the Redeemer bent his fair, sorrowful face over the man to pity and to comfort.

The roof on the north side of the church had began to fall in by bits — a burning piece from a falling beam was hurled outwards and struck the great bell in the belfry by the churchyard gate. The bell gave out a deep sobbing note, which died in a long wail that was drowned in the roaring of the flames.

None had paid heed to the weather all this time — the whole had lasted indeed no long time, but whether short or long scarce any could have told. The thunder and lightning had passed now far down the Dale; the rain, that had began some time back, fell ever the more heavily, and the wind had died down.

But of a sudden it was as though a sheet of flame shot up from the groundsill of the building — a moment, and with a mounting roar the fire had swallowed up the church from end to end.

The people scattered, rushing away to escape the devouring heat. Erlend was at Kristin's side on the instant, dragging her away down the hill. The whole man smelt of burning — when she stroked his head and face her hand came away full of burnt hair.

They could not hear each other's voices for the roaring of the fire. But she saw that his eyebrows were burnt off to the roots; he had burns on his face, and great holes were burnt in his shirt. He laughed as he dragged her along with him after the others.

All the folk followed the old priest as he went weeping, with Lavrans Björgulfsön bearing the crucifix.

---

[6] **Host:** the bread used in the Mass.　　　　[7] **Rood:** cross.

At the foot of the churchyard Lavrans set the Rood from him up against a tree, and sank down to a seat on the wreckage of the fence. Sira Eirik was sitting there already — he stretched out his arms toward the burning church:

" Farewell, farewell, thou Olav's-Church; God bless thee, thou my Olav's-Church; God bless thee for every hour I have chanted in thee and said Mass in thee — thou Olav's-Church, good-night, good-night — "

The church-folk wept aloud with their priest. The rain streamed down on the groups of people, but none thought of seeking shelter. Nor did it seem to check the fierce burning of the tarred woodwork — brands and glowing shingles were tossed out on every side. Then, suddenly, the ridge-turret crashed down into the fiery furnace, sending a great shower of sparks high into the air.

Lavrans sat with one hand over his face; the other arm lay in his lap, and Kristin saw that the sleeve was all bloody from the shoulder down, and blood ran down over his fingers. She went to him and touched his arm.

" Not much is amiss, methinks — there fell somewhat on my shoulder," he said, looking up. He was white to the lips. " Ulvhild," [8] he murmured in anguish, gazing into the burning pile.

Sira Eirik heard the word and laid a hand on his shoulder:

" 'Twill not wake your child, Lavrans — she will sleep none the less sound for the burning above her bed. She hath not lost her soul's home, as we others have lost ours this night."

(*Charles Archer and J. S. Scott*)

SUGGESTIONS FOR STUDY

1. Is there anything in this account to show that the scene takes place in the fourteenth century? What in it illustrates the author's power to make the past seem like the present? For comparison consider a similar situation, the burning of Torquilstone in Scott's *Ivanhoe*.

2. What evidence can you find in this narrative of the author's dramatic power, poetic feeling, human sympathy? Compare her in these respects with the preceding Norwegian writers. Can you discover elements which distinguish the Norwegian writers as a group from those of previous sections in this volume?

3. Write an actual or imaginary account of a great fire, considering carefully the part to be played by human beings.

[8] **Ulvhild:** Lavrans' little daughter who was buried beneath the floor of the church.

HERMAN WILDENVEY (1886–)

The Norwegians have laid emphasis on prose narrative to so great an extent that poetry has remained decidedly in the background compared with Swedish literature. In this century, however, there has been a revival of lyric poetry — best expressed in the work of Herman Wildenvey, whom Knut Hamsun calls " Norway's greatest lyric poet of our times." He has completely won the younger generation by the vivacity and drollery of his verse. Sometimes this expresses pure fun; at other times it is the surface glitter shielding the really poignant experiences of a sensitive nature. His technical skill and his original slant on life distinguish him among contemporary poets, and with nineteen volumes (including a novel and some short stories, plays and essays) published between 1907 and 1930, he has proved himself a prolific writer as well as a meticulous one.

Wildenvey's own life has had its thrilling passages. He was born on a farm at Eiker near Oslo. Like Rölvaag, he longed for the adventure of the new world, and was enabled to satisfy his desire through the help of an uncle in this country. Wildenvey crossed the ocean on the steamer *Norge* which was shipwrecked on the north coast of Scotland, and only one hundred and eighty out of nine hundred and eighty passengers were rescued in small fishing boats. It seemed that the boy's life had been saved for some great purpose; so on reaching Minnesota he entered a theological seminary in St. Paul. In a short time, however, both the instructors and the student himself decided that the ministry was not the purpose for which he had been saved, and he departed. Several years of adventure read like a story book — vagabonding, shipping from San Francisco on a German freighter just three days before the earthquake, cruising around South America for a year, and finally returning to Norway to be praised by the critics as a coming man upon the publication of his first volume *Bonfires*. After that he settled down to a literary life near Oslo. His wife, Gisken Wildenvey, is a novelist.

FEBRUARY DIALOGUE

Wildenvey's originality is evident in the following poem with its short abrupt rhythm and unexpected rhymes, all of which the translation has reproduced as faithfully as possible in another language. The reader should picture the scene as taking place on top of Holmenkollen, a mountain about eight miles northwest of Oslo. Here there is a hotel which is a favorite dining place because of its view over the city and harbor. It is also famous as the center of the Norwegian winter sports, having the highest ski jump in the world. Every February a national ski contest is held there which attracts as many as seventy-five thousand people. Evidently from the first stanza this had been a poor winter for skiing.

They are two:
" What month is it, Mary? "
" Don't you know?   You do! "
" February? "
·" Queer.   So short."   5
" Very."
" And bare."
" Yes, and rare —
No snow, no sport."

The Holmenkollen car   10
Stops, and there they are.
She is young and fair and bright.
He's all right.

How lovely to walk
And not talk   15
While snowstars mild and meek
Melt against mouth and
    cheek. . . .

" Look sharp now."
" Get going."
" Snow."   20
" It's snowing."
They smile. . . .
Silence for quite a while.

It is one of those nights
Pastel blue: 25
The city in view,
The city lights,
The fjord,
Hills and heights. . . .
A way   30
And they
And not a word.

Enchanted and hushed all;
Over the path the snowstars fall.
Looking back   35
He sees their track —
Hers like a bird's
Beside his. . . .
How thrilling it is! . . .
And no words.   40

She stopped and said,
" Do you love me, Fred? "
" Yes."
" But do you love me? " he says.
" No."   45
" Oh."

After all how lovely to walk
And not talk
While snowstars, small and meek,
Melt on the flaming cheek.   50
They walk, breathing deep:
" Is it leap year this year? "
" It's a cheap year, my dear."
" Sheep! "

That was a damned smart sen- 55
    tence.
But she'll be repaid:
She'll be brought to repentance
For what she just said.

He tried in vain to be clever —
No use whatever.   60

Then stopping, she said,
" Do you love me, Fred? "
" No."

10. **Holmenkollen:** *Holm* means harbor, and *kollen* a mountain; hence, a
mountain overlooking the harbor   28. **fjord:** a deep inlet of the ocean inclosed by high cliffs.

" You said Yes a minute ago."

" But you said No."   65

" I meant Yes."

" So did I — I confess."

No doubt, so did Mary,

So sweet and so cruel,

Who made Fred an April fool 70

In February.

(Joseph Auslander)

NATURE

I saw from a garden gate like snow
Chrysanthemums blooming white.
I was not looking as far as I know,
For poems to write.

But poets are poets and flowers flowers   5
In gardens that father the wish —
I dreamed a dream-something in those magic hours
Chrysanthemumish.

There suddenly sprouted, or seemed to sprout,
A bark from the blossoms uncanny,   10
And lo, a little white poodle bloomed out,
One blossom of many.

A poodle in the chrysanthemum bed,
All white and woolly and curly!
Sure, a botanical quadruped —   15
It looked like that surely!

Or else the white botanical glitter
Of blossoms, albeit not yelping,
Seemed animal blooms, a whole damned litter,
A soft woolly whelping!   20

Woolgathering words you well may say —
Heaven knows they will not bear shouting
Like those of Goethe. . . . O Wildenvey!
O white poodle sprouting!

(Joseph Auslander)

23. **Wildenvey:** The poet's name literally means "wild way," so there is a certain pun involved here.

SUGGESTIONS FOR STUDY

1. What qualities in these poems bring out the originality of Wildenvey both in subject matter and in technical form? Can you see why he would be particularly hard to translate?

2. In " February Dialogue " how are the short lines particularly suited to the situation? Would a Spanish love affair, for example, be carried on in the same style of dialogue? How is the young man made especially real by the very brevity of what is said about him? Explain the joke, lines 52–54.

3. In "Nature," point out expressions which are in themselves unexpected and comical, thus adding flavor to the quaint idea of the poem.

4. Read other poems of Wildenvey's in his volume *Owls to Athens,* translated by Joseph Auslander. Some of the serious poems are highly noteworthy, but it is the droll touch which distinguishes Wildenvey.

Modern Swedish Literature

ESAIAS TEGNÉR (1782–1846)

Sweden's greatest poet, according to some critics, is Esaias Tegnér, a native of Värmland, one of the most beautiful and romantic parts of the country. He was the son of a clergyman who died when the boy was only nine years old; but fortunately an excellent friend of the family took him into his household and saw to it that he went to the University of Lund for an education worthy of his talents. Much of Tegnér's life was closely identified with Lund, for he was advanced through various positions from humble tutor to Professor of Greek Literature. In fact the last half of Tegnér's life piled one honor upon another. He was elected to the Swedish Academy; he rose rapidly in the church until he was made bishop of Wexio; and he was elected Knight Commander of the Order of the North Star. He was in demand as a public speaker, and famed in private conversation for his repartee. We have it on one authority that his *bon-mots* traveled over the whole kingdom.

Tegnér's first reputation as a poet was made with his long poem " Svea " (Sweden), which won him the coveted Academy prize at the age of twenty-nine. It is a vigorous call to an effeminate age weakly following French models, to return to the ideals of their ancestors and develop national manhood and glory. His greatest poem is *Frithiof's Saga,* a series of twenty-four cantos each in a different meter, based on an Old Norse saga. This is the romantic tale of the hero Frithiof who is separated from his beloved Ingeborg by the ambitions and treacheries of her brothers, but finally after many years united to her. This poem, perhaps the most famous of any single modern Scandinavian poem, has been translated into many languages, there being twenty-one different versions in English alone.

Since *Frithiof's Saga* cannot be adequately represented by a short selection, this poem serves to suggest Tegnér's poetic skill and scholarly background. Even if one does not know the languages here described, it is interesting to observe whether the flavor of the original tongues clings to the translations in this book.

THE LANGUAGES

Greek

Language of beauty and taste, thou native tongue of the Muses,
All the Olympian train, Pythia uttered but Greek.
Graceful as draperies fold on a youthful Athenian maiden,
Showest thou feelings and thoughts, givest thou beauty its form.

Latin

Sharp is thy voice and strong as the clashing of swords, duly tem-   5
    pered,
Hard as the warrior behooves, rings thy imperial sound.
Proud, unpliable, poor, but from ruins mighty and awful,
Rulest thou nations and thoughts, givest thou order and form.

Italian

Language of pleasure and love, most musical daughter of Latin,
Song is thy essence and life, music an echo of thee,   10
Great prima donna, remain and in melody sweet and enchanting
Sing of thy longings and dreams, sing of fair Italy's hope.

French

Flattering, fickle coquette, thy prattle how soft and alluring,
Often thy lisping is sweet, always genteel and polite.
Should we perchance no more proclaim thee as queen among sisters, 15
Still in a sociable chat gladly we listen to thee.
Spare us, we pray thee, thy song, it is like the dance of the deafmutes,
Busy, indeed, are their feet, only they do not keep time.

2. **Olympian train**: the Greek gods who lived on Mount Olympus.   2. **Pythia**: the Delphic oracle.   6. **behooves**: needs.   11. **prima donna**: literally, first lady; the leading woman singer in an opera.

German

Strong-limbed, healthy, robust as a maiden raised in the forest,
Beautiful, flexible, rich, only too wide is thy mouth,   20
Put in thy motion more life, lest ere the close of a sentence
We its beginning forget; speed is essential to wit.

English

Speech for the stammering made, thy words in a state embryonic
Strike at the kernel of things, give us their sense with despatch,
Time in thy busy domain was early conceived to be money,   25
Money is dear to thy folk; therefore thy words were made short.
Steam, impetuous steam, keeps England's machinery running.
Pity an engine improved cannot be geared to thy tongue.

Swedish

Language of heroes and bards, how manly, how noble thou movest,
Royal and bold is thy march, clear as from metal thy sound.   30
Dwell on the mountaintop thou, where thunder and storm sing in
    chorus,
Lowland, valley and cave were not intended for thee.
Look in the lake, thy image behold and from masculine features
Wash every outlandish stain, wash, and be truly thyself.

SUGGESTIONS FOR STUDY

1. Contrast the Greek and Latin languages. After you have studied the section on Ancient European Classics, reread these stanzas to see whether your general impression of the two literatures agrees with this. If you have studied Latin, explain what the poet means by "proud, unpliable, poor." In what way is the last line true of the relation between Latin and the other languages of Europe?

2. What general similarity is suggested between Italian and French? What marked difference in the rhythmic qualities of the two? What does he think of French poetry? Is this explained by the comment on French versification, pages 3 and 4? What is especially appropriate about calling Italian a *prima donna?* Explain line 15. What language is the present "queen" as far as international communication is concerned?

3. If you know German, comment on his description. If you do not, find some one who does to explain from the middle of line 20 on.

4. It is hard to realize how English sounds to a foreigner. What does he mean by the opening phrase? How does he account for the shortness

of English words? Does he mean this seriously? From what original source do the short words in English usually come? From what languages do the longer words usually come? Does English have a tendency to shorten up words coming from other languages? If so, illustrate.

5. Is Tegnér prejudiced in favor of his own language? If you know Swedish or have heard it used, do you agree with him? What does he mean by the last line? How does this show the influence of the romantic movement in Scandinavian countries?

AUGUST STRINDBERG (1849–1912)

Most complex, most enigmatical, most translated, most analyzed, and most world renowned of Swedish writers is August Strindberg, the only outstanding dramatist whom that country has produced. A psychologist would probably explain the mental conflicts and inconsistencies of his mature life by the unfortunate home atmosphere of his childhood, which we find pictured in some of his autobiographical works. His father and mother represented wide social inequality, his father being a Stockholm merchant of an established family, his mother a former barmaid. Though August's own mother understood him little, his stepmother did even less, and the boy was terribly afraid of his father. Hard times, a large family, insufficient food, unsympathetic elders, interrupted schooling — all had their effect on a naturally nervous disposition prone to hysterical anger and spells of depression. Strindberg's whole life shows intense mental and spiritual conflict, which is reflected in the probing into human motives evident throughout his works. A frequent shifting of attitude is also evident throughout his career. During the eighties he espoused the cause of socialism and as a follower of Rousseau preached the return to nature and the value of the simple peasantry. But his apparent love of humanity was strangely contradicted by a pronounced antagonism to woman in opposition to the attitudes of Ibsen and Björnson and the great movement for emancipation of women. Whether this hostility developed from his own unfortunate experiences in three unhappy marriages or whether the failure of these marriages was largely due to his attitude it is hard to say. Then from socialism he turned directly away to the theory of the superman, that the masses of inferior beings must be dominated by the superior personality. In the nineties after separation from his second wife he spent a distressing period of groping through the sciences, occultism, and other " isms," which terminated in a sudden conversion to mystical religion. Now he began to write religious drama, historical drama, parables, fairy tales — all showing faith in God and humanity. Yet before his death he seemed to run through the whole mental cycle again, repeating some of the cynicism and pessimism of his early days. Thus it will be seen how little of the man can be judged from any one work.

His output was prodigious. In the forty years between his first and last play he produced more than fifty plays, many of which were tried out in the little theater, seating only one hundred and fifty and built for him by his friends. This alone would have represented a life work, but in addition he wrote a number of novels, several volumes of short stories, three or four autobiographical books and some poetry. Much of his work is unpleasant reading, upsetting, confusing, at times verging on the insane, but as in the turbulence of a great waterfall there is latent power impossible to the placid river of the plain, so in Strindberg there lies power unfelt in the writing of those " whose sails were never to the tempest given."

HALF A SHEET OF PAPER

The last moving van had gone; the tenant, a young man with a mourning-band around his hat, wandered through the empty rooms to see if anything had been left behind. No, nothing had been forgotten, nothing. He went out into the corridor, determined never to think again of all he had passed through in this apartment. But there, on the wall, near the telephone, was a slip of paper covered with writing. The entries were in several handwritings; some quite legible, in black ink; some, pencil scrawls in black and red and blue. There stood recorded the whole beautiful romance that had been lived in the short space of two years. All that he had resolved to forget was written there — a bit of human history on half a sheet of paper.

He took the sheet down. It was a piece of sun-yellow scratch paper that casts a sheen. He laid it on the mantel of the fireplace in the living room, and, bending over, he began to read.

First stood her name: Alice — the most beautiful name he knew, because it was the name of his sweetheart. Beside it was a number, 15,111 — It looked like a chant number on the hymnboard in church.

Underneath was scribbled: The Bank. It was there his work lay, the sacred work which for him had meant bread, home, family — the foundations of life. A heavy black line had been drawn across the number, for the bank had failed, and he had been taken on at another, after a short period of much anxiety.

Then followed the livery stable and the florist — That was when they were engaged, and he had a pocketful of money.

The furniture dealer — The decorator — They furnish their apartment. Express Bureau — They move in. Opera House Box-Office, 50,50 — They are newly married and go to the opera on Sunday evenings. Their most delightful hours are those spent there, sitting quietly, while their hearts commune in the beauty and harmony of the fairyland on the other side of the footlights.

Here followed the name of a man (crossed out) a friend who had risen high, but who fell — dazzled by prosperity — fell irremediably, and had to flee the country. So ephemeral is that will-o'-the-wisp, Success!

Now something new came into the lives of the couple. Entered with a pencil in a woman's hand stands The Sister. What sister? Ah! the one with the long gray cloak and the sweet, sympathetic face, who comes so softly and never goes through the drawing room, but takes the corridor way to the bedroom. Below her name is written: Dr. L——

Here first appeared on the list a relative — Mother. That is his mother-in-law, who had discreetly kept away so as not to disturb the newly married. But now she has been called, and comes gladly, since she is needed.

Then came some entries in red and blue pencil. Employment Agency. The maid has left, and a new one must be engaged. The Apothecary — H-m! It begins to look dark. The dairy — Milk is ordered, sterilized milk. The grocer, the butcher, and others. The household affairs are being conducted by telephone. Then the mistress of the house is not at her usual post? No. She is confined to her bed.

That which followed he could not read, for it grew dim before his eyes, as it must for the drowning man at sea who would look through salt water. But there it stood recorded, in plain, black letters: The undertaker.

That tells enough! — a larger and a smaller casket. And in parenthesis was written: " Of dust."

There is nothing more. It ended in dust, the way of all flesh.

He took up the sun-yellow paper, kissed it, folded it carefully, and put it in his breast pocket.

In two minutes he had relived two years of his life.

But he was not bowed down as he walked out. On the contrary, he carried his head high, like a proud and happy man, for he knew that to him it had been to hold for a little the best that life can bestow on man. How many there were, alas! who had not had this.

(Velma Swanson Howard)

SUGGESTIONS FOR STUDY

1. What is there in the way in which this story is told that makes it particularly moving? Is it the kind of story you would have expected from Strindberg after reading about his life?

2. What other pieces in the Scandinavian section show the art of suggesting intensity of emotion through simple restrained language? Do you find this same method among the other literatures or does it seem a Scandinavian manner? Do you find this laconic quality in English and American literature? If so, cite examples.

SELMA LAGERLÖF (1858–1940)

Like Tegnér, Selma Lagerlöf was born in Värmland, noted for its beautiful lakes and its picturesque native culture of song, dance, quaint constume, and social hospitality. In *Mårbacka* Miss Lagerlöf has pictured this life of her childhood with delightful detail. We learn how the grandmother's wondrous tales colored the imagination of the little girl and how the legends and ghost stories of the old housekeeper continued in the same vein after the grandmother's death. It is not surprising, then, that the fairy-tale manner runs through much of Miss Lagerlöf's writing. Her fame began with *The Saga of Gösta Berling,* a loosely constructed tale woven from the romantic stories she had heard in her childhood and in marked contrast to the coldly realistic novels current at the time of its publication. *Jerusalem,* an entirely different type of novel, portrays a group of peasants journeying to the Holy Land as a result of a religious revival. *The Wonderful Adventures of Nils,* a picture of Sweden as seen by a little elf-boy, is considered a children's classic here in the United States. It was largely on the strength of these books, though she had written many others, that she was given the Nobel prize in 1909, a double honor since she was the first Swedish author to receive this award offered by her own countryman.

Five years later she was again honored by election to the Swedish Academy — the only woman to hold membership. Some considered the novel published in that same year, *The Emperor of Portugallia,* to be her best work. All her writing is marked by simplicity, dignity, and idealism. Extensive translation into foreign languages has made her probably the most widely read Swedish author.

THE STORY OF A STORY

The following is an account written by Selma Lagerlöf in answer to a request from some young people to tell how she came to write *The Saga of Gösta Berling.* It combines in small compass the autobiographical manner of *Mårbacka* and the fanciful quality of her stories.

Once there was a story that wanted to be told and sent out in the world. This was very natural, inasmuch as it knew that it was already as good as finished. Many, through remarkable deeds and strange events, had helped create it; others had added their straws in it by again and again relating these things. What it lacked was merely a matter of being joined together, so that it could travel comfortably through the country. As yet it was only a confused jumble of stories — a big, formless cloud of adventures rushing hither and thither like a swarm of stray bees on a summer's day, not knowing where they will find some one who can gather them into a hive.

The story that wanted to be told had sprung up in Värmland, and you may be sure that it circled over many mills and manors, over many parsonages and many homes of military officers, in the beautiful province, peering through the windows and begging to be cared for. But it was forced to make many futile attempts, for everywhere it was turned away. Anything else was hardly to be expected. People had many things of much more importance to think of.

Finally the story came to an old place called Mårbacka. It was a little homestead, with low buildings overshadowed by giant trees. At one time it had been a parsonage, and it was as if this had set a certain stamp upon the place which it could not lose. They seemed to have a greater love for books and reading there than elsewhere, and a certain air of restfulness and peace always pervaded it. There rushing with duties and bickering with servants were never met with, nor was hatred or dissension given house room, either. One who happened to be a guest there was not allowed to take life too seriously, but had to feel that his first duty was to be light-hearted and believe that for one and all who lived on this estate our Lord managed everything for the best.

As I think of the matter now, I apprehend that the story of which I am speaking must have lingered thereabouts a great many years during its vain longing to be told. It seems to me as though it must have enwrapped the place, as a mist shrouds a mountain summit, now and then letting one of the adventures of which it consisted rain down upon it.

They came in the form of strange ghost stories about the superintendent of the foundries, who always had black bulls hitched to his wagon when he drove home at night from a revel. And in his home the Evil One himself used to sit in the rocker and rock while the wife sat at the piano and played. They came as true stories from the neighboring homestead, where crows had persecuted the mistress until she didn't dare venture outside the door; from the Captain's house, where they were so poor that everything had to be borrowed; from the little cottage down by the church, where there lived a lot of young and old girls who had all fallen in love with the handsome organ builder.

Sometimes the dear adventures came to the homestead in an even more tangible form. Aged and poverty-stricken army officers would drive up to the doorstep behind rickety old horses and in rickety carryalls. They would stop and visit for weeks, and in the evenings, when the toddy had put courage into them, they would talk of the time when they had danced in stockingless shoes, so that their feet would look small, of how they had curled their hair and dyed their mustaches. One of them told how he had tried to take a pretty young girl back to her sweetheart and how he had been hunted by wolves on the way; another had been at the Christmas feast where an angered guest had flung all the hazel hens at the wall because some one had made him believe they were crows; a third had seen the old gentleman who used to sit at a plain board table and play Beethoven.

But the story could reveal its presence in still another way. In the attic hung the portrait of a lady with powdered hair, and when any one walked past it he was reminded that it was a portrait of the beautiful daughter of the Count, who had loved her brother's young tutor, and had called to see him once when she was an old gray-haired lady and he an old married man. In the lumber room were heaped up bundles of documents containing deeds of purchase and leases signed by the great lady, who once ruled over seven foundries which had been willed to her by her lover. If one entered the church, one saw in a dusty little cabinet under the pulpit the chest filled with infidel manuscripts, which was not to be opened until the beginning of the new century. And not very far from the church is the river, at the bottom of which rests a pile of sacred images that were not allowed to remain in the pulpit and chancel they once had ornamented.

It must have been because so many legends and traditions hovered around the farm that one of the children growing up there longed to become a narrator. It was not one of the boys. They were not at home very much, for they were away at their schools almost the whole year; so the story did not get much of a hold upon them. But it was one of the girls — one who was delicate and could not romp and play like other children, but found her greatest enjoyment in reading and hearing stories about all the great and wonderful things which had happened in the world.

However, at the start it was not the girl's intention to write about the stories and legends surrounding her. She hadn't the remotest idea that a book could be made of these adventures, which she had so often heard related that to her they seemed the most commonplace things in the world. When she tried to write, she chose material from her books, and with fresh courage she strung together stories of the Sultans in *Thousand and One Nights,* Walter Scott's heroes, and Snorri Sturluson's *Kings of Romance.*

Surely it is needless to state that what she wrote was the least original and the crudest that has ever been put upon paper. But this very naturally she herself did not see. She went about at home on the quiet farm, filling every scrap of paper she could lay her hands on with verse and prose, with plays and romances. When she wasn't writing, she sat and waited for success. And success was to consist in this: Some stranger who was very learned and influential, through some rare freak of fortune, was to come and discover what she had written and find it worth printing. After that, all the rest would come of itself.

Meanwhile nothing of the sort happened. And when the girl had passed her twentieth year, she began to grow impatient. She wondered why success did not come her way. Perhaps she lacked knowledge. She probably needed to see a little more of the world than the homestead in Värmland. And seeing that it would be a long time before she could earn her livelihood as an author, it was necessary for her to learn something — find some work in life — that she might have bread while she waited for herself. Or maybe it was simply this — that the story had lost patience with her. Perhaps it thought thus: "Since this blind person does not see that which lies nearest her eyes, let her be forced to go away. Let her tramp upon gray stone streets; let her live in cramped city rooms with no other outlook than gray stone walls; let her live among people who hide everything that is unusual in them and who appear to be all alike. It may perchance teach her to see that which is waiting outside the gate of her home — all that lives and moves between the stretch of blue hills which she has every day before her eyes."

And so, one autumn, when she was two-and-twenty, she traveled up to Stockholm to begin preparing herself for the vocation of teacher.

The girl soon became absorbed in her work. She wrote no more, but went in for studies and lectures. It actually looked as though the story would lose her altogether.

Then something extraordinary happened. This same autumn,

after she had been living a couple of months amidst gray streets and house walls, she was walking one day up Malmskillnad Street with a bundle of books under her arm. She had just come from a lecture on the history of literature. The lecture must have been about Bellman [1] and Runeberg,[2] because she was thinking of them and of the characters that live in their verses. She said to herself that Runeberg's jolly warriors and Bellman's happy-go-lucky roisterers were the very best material a writer could have to work with. And suddenly this thought flashed upon her: Värmland, the world in which you have been living, is not less remarkable than that of Fredman [3] or Fänrik Stål.[4] If you can only learn how to handle it, you will find that your material is quite as good as theirs.

This is how it happened that she caught her first glimpse of the story. And the instant she saw it, the ground under her seemed to sway. The whole long Malmskillnad Street from Hamn Street Hill to the firehouse rose toward the skies and sank again — rose and sank. She stood still a long while, until the street had settled itself. She gazed with astonishment at the passers-by, who walked calmly along, apparently oblivious to the miracle that had taken place.

At that moment the girl determined that she would write the story of Värmland's Cavaliers, and never for an instant did she relinquish the thought of it; but many and long years elapsed before the determination was carried out.

In the first place she had entered upon a new field of labor, and she lacked the time needful for the carrying out of a great literary work. In the second place she had failed utterly in her first attempts to write the story.

During these years many things were constantly happening which helped mould it. One morning, on a school holiday, she was sitting at the breakfast table with her father, and the two of them talked of old times. Then he began telling of an acquaintance of his youth, whom he described as the most fascinating of men. This man brought joy and cheer with him wherever he went. He could sing; he composed music; he improvised verse. If he struck up a dance, it was not alone the young folk who danced, but old men and old women, high and low. If he made a speech, one had to laugh or cry, whichever he wished. If he drank himself full, he could play and

---

[1] **Bellman**: Carl Michael Bellman (1740–1795) Swedish poet of the early romantic movement.
[2] **Runeberg**: John Ludwig Runeberg (1804–1877) Finnish poet.
[3] **Fredman**: a character in Bellman's poems.
[4] **Fänrik Stål**: a character in Runeberg's poems.

talk better than when he was sober, and when he fell in love with a woman, it was impossible for her to resist him. If he did foolish things, one forgave him; if he was sad at times, one wanted to do anything and everything to see him glad again. But any great success in life he had never had, despite his wealth of talents. He had lived mostly at the foundries in Värmland as private tutor. Finally he was ordained a minister. This was the highest that he had attained.

After this conversation she could see the hero of her story better than heretofore, and with this a little life and action came into it. One fine day a name was given to the hero and he was called Gösta Berling. Whence he got the name she never knew. It was as if he had named himself.

Another time, she came home to spend the Christmas holidays. One evening the whole family went off to a Christmas party a good distance from home in a terrible blizzard. It turned out to be a longer drive than one would have thought. The horse ploughed his way ahead at a walking pace. For several hours she sat there in the sleigh in the blinding snowstorm and thought of the story. When they arrived finally, she had thought out her first chapter. It was the one about the Christmas night at the smithy.

What a chapter! It was her first and for many years her only one. It was first written in verse, for the original plan was that it should be a romance cycle, like *Fänrik Stål's Sagas*.[5] But by degrees this was changed, and for a time the idea was that it should be written as drama. Then the Christmas night was worked over to go in as the first act. But this attempt did not succeed, either; at last she decided to write the story as a novel. Then the chapter was written in prose. It grew enormously long, covering forty written pages. The last time it was rewritten it took up only nine.

After a few more years came a second chapter. It was the story of the Ball at Borg and of the wolves that hunted Gösta Berling and Anna Stjernhök.

In the beginning this chapter was not written with the thought that it could come into the story, but as a sort of chance composition to be read at a small social gathering. The reading, however, was postponed, and the novelette was sent to *Dagny*. After a time the story was returned as unavailable for the magazine. It was in reality not available anywhere. As yet it was altogether lacking in artistic smoothness.

Meanwhile the author wondered to what purpose this unluckily

5 **Fänrik Stål's Sagas:** *Stories of Ensign Stål* by Runeberg.

born novelette could be turned. Should she put it into the story? To be sure, it was an adventure by itself — and ended. It would look odd among the rest, which were better connected. Perhaps it wouldn't be such a bad idea, she thought then, if all the chapters of the story were like this one — almost finished adventures. This would be difficult to carry out, but it might possibly be done. There would doubtless be gaps in the continuity here and there, but that should give to the book great strength and variety.

Now two important matters were settled: The story was to be a novel, and each chapter should be complete in itself. But nothing much had been gained hereby. She who had been fired with the idea of writing the story of Värmland's Cavaliers when she was two-and-twenty, at this stage was nearing the thirties and had not been able to write more than two chapters. Where had the years gone? She had been graduated from the Teachers' College and for several years past had been a teacher at Landskrona.[6] She had become interested in much and had been occupied with many things, but the story was just as unwritten. A mass of material had certainly been collected, but why was it so hard for her to write it down? Why did the inspiration never come to her? Why did the pen glide so slowly over the paper? She certainly had her dark moments at that time! She began to think that she never would finish her novel. She was that servant who buried his talent in the ground [7] and never tried to use it.

As a matter of fact, all this occurred during the eighties, when stern Realism was at its height. She admired the great masters of that time, never thinking that one could use any other style in writing than the one they employed. For her own part, she liked the Romanticists better, but Romanticism was dead, and she was hardly the one to think of reviving its form and expression! Although her brain was filled to overflowing with stories of ghosts and mad love, of wondrously beautiful women and adventure-loving cavaliers, she tried to write about it in calm, realistic prose. She was not very clear-visioned. Another would have seen that the impossible was impossible.

Once she wrote a couple of chapters in another style. One was a scene from Svartsjö churchyard; the other was about the old philosopher, Uncle Eberhard, and his infidel manuscripts. She scribbled them mostly in fun, with many ohs and ahs in the prose, which made

---

[6] **Landskrona:** city on southwest coast of Sweden.

[7] **buried his talent in the ground:** for the parable of the talents see Matthew 25: 14–30.

it almost rhythmical. She perceived that in this vein she could write. There was inspiration in this — she could feel it. But when the two short chapters were finished, she laid them aside. They were only written in fun. One could not write a whole book in that vein.

But now the story had been waiting long enough. It thought, no doubt, as it did at the time when it sent her out in the world: " Again I must send this blinded person a great longing which will open her eyes."

The longing came over her in this manner: The homestead where she had grown up was sold. She journeyed to the home of her childhood to see it once again before strangers should occupy it.

The evening before she left there, perhaps nevermore to see the dear old place, she concluded in all meekness and humility to write the book in her own way and according to her own poor abilities. It was not going to be any great masterwork, as she had hoped. It might be a book at which people would laugh, but anyway she would write it — write it for herself, to save for herself what she could still save of the home — the dear old stories, the sweet peace of the care-free days, and the beautiful landscape with the long lakes and the many-hued blue hills.

But for her, who had hoped that she might yet learn to write a book people would care to read, it seemed as though she had re-linquished the very thing in life she had been most eager to win. It was the hardest sacrifice she had made thus far.

A few weeks later, she was again at her home in Landskrona, seated at her writing-desk. She began writing — she didn't know exactly what it was to be — but she was not going to be afraid of the strong words, the exclamations, the interrogations, nor would she be afraid to give herself with all her childishness and all her dreams! After she had come to this decision, the pen began to move almost by itself. This made her quite delirious. She was carried away with enthusi-asm. Ah, this was writing! Unfamiliar thoughts and things, or, rather, things she never had surmised were stored away in her brain, crowded down upon the paper. The pages were filled with a haste of which she had never dreamed. What had hitherto required months — no, years — to work out, was now accomplished in a couple of hours. That evening she wrote the story of the young countess' tramp over the ice on River Löven, and the flood at Ekeby.

The following afternoon she wrote the scene in which the gouty ensign, Rutger von Örneclou, tries to raise himself in bed to dance the Cachuca, and on the evening of the next day appeared the story of the old Mamsell who went off to visit the parsimonious Broby clergyman.

Now she knew for certain that in this style she could write the book; but she was just as certain that no one would have the patience to read it through.

However, not many chapters let themselves be written like this — in one breath. Most of them required long and arduous labor, and there were only little snatches of time in the afternoons which she could devote to authorship. When she had been writing about half a year, reckoning from the day when she had gone in for romanticism with a vengeance, about a dozen chapters were written. At this rate the book would be finished in three or four years.

It was in the spring of this year, 1890, that *Idun* invited prize competitors to send in short novelettes of about one hundred printed pages. This was an outlet for a story that wanted to be told and sent into the world. It must have been the story itself that prompted her sister to suggest to her that she make use of this opportunity. Here, at last, was a way of finding out if her story was so hopelessly bad! If it received the prize, much would be gained; if it didn't, she simply stood in exactly the same position as before.

She had nothing against the idea, but she had so little faith in herself that she couldn't come to any conclusion.

Finally, just eight days before the time for submitting manuscripts had expired, she decided to take from the novel five chapters which were sufficiently well connected to pass for a novelette, and chance it with these. But the chapters were far from ready. Three of them were loosely written, but of the remaining two there was barely an outline. Then the whole thing must be legibly copied, of course. To add to this, she was not at home just then, but was visiting her sister and brother-in-law, who still lived in Värmland. And one who has come to visit with dear friends for a short time cannot spend the days at a writing desk. She wrote therefore at night, sitting up the whole week until four in the mornings.

Finally there were only twenty-four hours of the precious time left, and there were still twenty pages to be written.

On this the last day they were invited out. The whole family were going on a little journey to be gone for the night. Naturally, she had to accompany the rest. When the party was over and the guests dispersed, she sat up all night writing in the strange place.

At times she felt very queer. The place where she was visiting was the very estate on which the wicked Sintram had lived. Fate, in a singular way, had brought her there on the very night when she must write about him who sat in the rocker and rocked.

Now and then she looked up from her work and listened in the direction of the drawing room for the possible sound of a pair of rockers in motion. But nothing was heard. When the clock struck six the next morning, the five chapters were finished.

Along in the forenoon they traveled home on a little freight steamer. There her sister did up the parcel, sealed it with sealing wax, which had been brought from home for this purpose, wrote the address, and sent off the novelette.

This happened on one of the last days in July. Toward the end of August *Idun* contained a notice to the effect that something over twenty manuscripts had been received by the editors, but that one or two among them were so confusedly written they could not be counted in.

Then she gave up waiting for results. She knew, of course, which novelette was so confusedly written that it could not be counted in.

One afternoon in November she received a curious telegram. It contained simply the words " Hearty Congratulations," and was signed by three of her college classmates.

For her it was a terribly long wait until dinnertime of the following day, when the Stockholm papers were distributed. When the paper was in her hands, she had to search long without finding anything. Finally, on the last page she found a little notice in fine print which told that the prize had been awarded to her.

To another it might not have meant so much, perhaps, but for her it meant that she could devote herself to the calling which all her life she had longed to follow.

There is but little to add to this: The story that wanted to be told and sent out in the world was now fairly near its destination. Now it was to be written, at least, even though it might take a few years more before it was finished.

She who was writing it had gone up to Stockholm around Christmas time, after she had received the prize.

The editor of *Idun* volunteered to print the book as soon as it was finished.

If she could ever find time to write it!

The evening before she was to return to Landskrona, she spent with her loyal friend, Baroness Adlersparre, to whom she read a few chapters aloud.

" Esselde " listened, as only she could listen, and she became interested. After the reading she sat silently and pondered. " How long will it be before all of it is ready? " she asked finally.

" Three or four years."

Then they parted.

The next morning, two hours before she was to leave Stockholm, a message came from " Esselde " bidding her come to her before the departure.

The old Baroness was in her most positive and determined mood. " Now you must take a leave of absence for a year and finish the book. I shall procure the money."

Fifteen minutes later the girl was on her way to the Principal of the Teachers' College to ask her assistance in securing a substitute.

At one o'clock she was happily seated in the railway carriage. But now she was going no farther than Sörmland, where she had good friends who lived in a charming villa.

And so they — Otto Gumaelius and his wife — gave her the freedom of their home — freedom to work, and peace, and the best of care for nearly a year, until the book was finished.

Now, at last, she could write from morning till night. It was the happiest time of her life.

But when the story was finished at the close of the summer, it looked queer. It was wild and disordered, and the connecting threads were so loose that all the parts seemed bent upon following their old inclination to wander off, each in its own way.

It never became what it should have been. Its misfortune was that it had been compelled to wait so long to be told. If it was not properly disciplined and restrained, it was mostly because the author was so overjoyed in the thought that at last she had been privileged to write it.

(*Velma Swanson Howard*)

SUGGESTIONS FOR STUDY

1. Why do you think Selma Lagerlöf wrote her autobiographical sketch in the third person? Do you like this way of writing about oneself? Do you see anything in the style that suggests the author's " fairy-tale manner "?

2. How do you like her picture of her childhood home? What details make it vivid? For an extended picture of this Swedish country home read *Mårbacka*.

3. Is it characteristic of a young writer to want to write about distant romantic subjects rather than those which have been close at hand since

childhood? Prove from what you know of English and American novels that the masterpiece of an author is pretty likely to have grown out of his experiences in early life.

4. What other light do you get on the stages which a story may go through in an author's mind before it reaches its final state? Do you consider this sketch encouraging or discouraging for an ambitious young writer to read?

5. Read *The Saga of Gösta Berling*. Does the previous reading of " The Story of a Story " add to the interest of the novel? Would you have noticed the loose construction if she had not mentioned it in this account? Read some of Selma Lagerlöf's short stories especially in the volume *The Girl of the Marshcroft*.

6. What differences do you notice between Miss Lagerlöf's work and that of Sigrid Undset? Which writer appeals to you more? Why? How does she compare in your mind with women novelists of England and America?

CARL SNOILSKY (1841–1903)

Count Carl Snoilsky was a nobleman of Polish descent, born in Stockholm, and trained for the Swedish diplomatic service. During 1864–1865 he was in Madrid and Paris on diplomatic missions. His early tastes were epicurean, and his cultural interests were especially centered in Italy. As he grew older, however, he turned with the fashion toward realism and his later poems are based on observations of the life about him. During his later life he was chief librarian of the Royal Library at Stockholm. His seven volumes of verse show him to be a poet of imagination and skill in handling words. Because of his restraint and balance he has been called by one critic " the last of the Swedish classicists." His translation of Goethe into Swedish was also one of his significant works.

BIRDS ON A TELEGRAPH WIRE

On yonder taut aerial wire,
    A bridge where thought is speeding,
A merry little sparrow-choir
    Sits careless and unheeding.

They chirp through life as in a dream,   5
    They sport there, never knowing
Of that unbroken, silent stream
    That through the wire is flowing.

Though thought goes by in endless round,
    The sparrows no more hear it   10

Than we may catch the whispered sound
From the dim World of Spirit.

Our questions find no sure reply,
   Though deep and wondrous answers
To all we ask are flitting by   15
   Like waves of airy dancers.

Scarce in our clay-dim nature rings
   An echo of their brooding,
When softly murmur the twin strings
   Called Memory and Foreboding.   20

(Charles Wharton Stork)

OLD CHINA

A great collector was the Saxon king,
His craze for china had some bounds, until
He sent his royal guard to do the will
Of Prussia's lord — to get a bowl of Ming!
Five hundred men with guns and swords to swing,   5
Such could the Prussian use with right good skill:
Men supple in maneuver, deft in drill,
In war a wall — for that blue Chinese thing!
Five hundred men with all their gear intact!
Why, since the world began, so mad an act —   10
No doubt you all agree — was heard of never.
Since then a generation has passed o'er:
Five hundred gallant hearts now bear no more;
The ancient bowl — 'tis there as good as ever.

(Charles Wharton Stork)

4. **Ming:** a Chinese dynasty of the fourteenth to seventeenth centuries, famous for its beautiful china.

ERIK AXEL KARLFELDT (1864–1931)

Picturesque Dalecarlia, where rustic scenery and colorful peasant customs vie with each other to produce the thing we call " charm," has been made vocal through Erik Karlfeldt. Since he confined himself to poetry, he is not so well known abroad as those writers whose prose is more easily conveyed in another tongue. Between 1895 and 1927 he published six volumes of poems. Most of these celebrate his native province — its patriotic reminiscences of the wars against the Danes in the sixteenth century, its merry folk dances, its famous wedding ceremonials, its peasant family pride, its beauty of prosperous farmland and foliaged hills. The character of Fridolin is the medium through whom Karlfeldt's lyrical strains are uttered, and many of his most exuberant poems are in the volumes *Fridolin's Songs* (1898) and *Fridolin's Pleasure Garden* (1901). But Karlfeldt's rich vein of humor is one of the most individual things about him, and nowhere is it better illustrated than in a volume called *Dalecarlian Pictures in Rhyme* (1901). Here he looks at the old paintings of Bible stories hanging in peasant houses and conveys quaintly and naïvely the stories of Adam and Eve, Noah, Jonah, Elijah, and other Old Testament heroes with all the anachronisms and absurdities of the old peasant artists. But Karlfeldt becomes a modernist in his last three volumes, deserts Dalecarlia, and shows us the longings and dissatisfactions of the soul of man. The following poem is in his earlier manner.

SONG AFTER HARVEST

Fridolin dances free,
And full of sweet wine is he, —
Of the berry's juice, and the wheat-field's dower,
And the whirl of the waltz-melodie.
With the tails of his long coat over his arm　　　　　5
He dances full many a partner warm,
Till she leans on his breast like a drooping flower,
Overcome by his manly charm.

Fridolin dances free,
He is filled with the memory　　　　　10
Of his sire and grandsire who danced there long
Before to that old melodie.
Ye sleep now, ye sires, on the festival night,
And stilled is the hand that could fiddle with might,
For your life — like your day — is a murmuring song　　　　　15
Which echoes a wistful delight.

But Fridolin dances free, —
Your son, and a brave lad he;
He can talk in the peasant style with a churl,
And in Latin to men of degree.　　　　　20

His scythe goes sharp through the harvest's gold,
He is proud of the store that his granaries hold,
Toward the moon's red saucepan he tosses his girl
Like a man of your stalwart mold.

(*Charles Wharton Stork*)

SUGGESTIONS FOR STUDY

1. What seems ironic to Snoilsky in the birds sitting on the telegraph wire? How does he compare this to human life? Explain the last stanza. Compare Untermeyer's "Lines on a Telegraph Pole" to a poem on a related subject. Which do you consider the better poem? Why?

2. In "Old China" explain the agreement between the Saxon and Prussian king. Which, to the average man, had the better bargain? Do you think the poet agrees with this point of view? How are the preferences of the two kings to some extent symbolical of the people they represent? In what way does this sonnet suggest Shelley's sonnet "Ozymandias"? Does Lamb's essay "Old China" resemble this poem which bears the same name?

3. How is "Song after Harvest" typical of the Swedish folk dance? Look at pictures of peasant costume and dancing. If you have seen Swedish folk dances either in life or in the movies, explain the last two lines. In what way do lines 19–20 typify the Scandinavian ideal? Have you read anything of the habits and personalities of the Scandinavian monarchs of the present which would bear this out? Compare the mood of this poem with "Valborg Song," page 591.

READING LIST

TRANSLATIONS FROM SCANDINAVIAN LITERATURE

Old Norse

The Poetic Edda, trans. by Henry A. Bellows

The Saga of the Volsungs, trans. by Margaret Schlauch

Sturluson, Snorri: *Heimskringla; The Olaf Sagas* (Everyman's Library)

The Norse Kings' Sagas (Everyman's Library)

The Lives of the Norse Kings, trans. by Erling Monsen

The Saga of Grettir the Strong

The Story of Burnt Njal

The Laxdaela Saga, trans. by Thorsten Veblen

Munch, P. A.: *Norse Mythology*

Poetry

Björnson, B.: *Poems and Songs,* trans. by A. H. Palmer

Tegnér, E.: *Frithiof's Saga*

Wildenvey, H.: *Owls to Athens,* trans. by Joseph Auslander

Anthology of Swedish Lyrics, trans. by Charles Stork
Selections from Modern Swedish Poetry, trans. by C. D. Locock
Book of Danish Verse, trans. by S. F. Damon and R. S. Hillyer

Drama

Ibsen, Henrik: *Plays*
Especially *Peer Gynt*
A Doll's House
Pillars of Society
Björnson, B.: *Three Comedies,* trans. by R. F. Sharp
Holberg, Ludvig: *Comedies by Holberg*
Strindburg, August: *Easter*
Simoon (one-act play)

Fiction

Danish

Andersen, Hans C.: *Fairy Tales and Stories*
Jensen, Johannes: *The Long Journey* (1 vol. ed.)
Nexö, Martin A.: *Pelle the Conqueror* (1 vol. ed.)
Lie, Jonas: *Weird Tales from Northern Seas*

Norwegian

Asbjornson, P. and Moe, J.: *Norwegian Fairy Tales*
Björnson, B.: *Sunny Hill (Synnöve Solbakken)*
A Happy Boy
Arne
Hamsun, Knut: *Hunger*
Victoria

Pan
The Growth of the Soil
Bojer, Johan: *The Great Hunger*
The Emigrants
Dunn, Olav: *The People of Juvik*
Rölvaag, O. E.: *Giants in the Earth*
Undset, Sigrid: *Kristin Lavransdatter*

Swedish

Lagerlöf, Selma: *The Story of Gösta Berling*
Jerusalem
The Emperor of Portugallia
The Girl from the Marshcroft (short stories)
Von Heidenstam, W.: *The Charles Men*
Söderberg, Hjalmar: *Selected Short Stories*
Martinsson, Harry: *Cape Farewell*
Hallström, Per: *Short Stories,* trans. by F. J. Fielden
Collections of short stories ed. by Hanna A. Larsen:
Denmark's Best Stories
Norway's Best Stories
Told in Norway
Sweden's Best Stories
Modern Swedish Masterpieces, trans. by C. W. Stork

Non-Fiction Prose

Lagerlöf, Selma: *Mårbacka* (autobiography)
Brandes, Georg: *Reminiscences of My Childhood and Youth*
Creative Spirits of the Nineteenth Century

BOOKS ABOUT SCANDINAVIAN COUNTRIES

Criticism and History of Literature

Larsen, Hanna A.: *Scandinavian Literature* (brief outline)

Jorgenson, Theodore: *History of Norwegian Literature*

Gröndahl, I. and Raknes, O.: *Chapters in Norwegian Literature*

Topsöe-Jensen, H. G.: *Scandinavian Literature from Brandes to Our Day*

Howitt, William and Mary: *Literature and Romance of Northern Europe*

Horn, F. W.: *History of the Literature of the Scandinavian North*

Shaw, G. B.: *The Quintessence of Ibsenism*

Lee, Jeanette: *The Ibsen Secret*

Monkhouse, Allan: *Ibsen's Social Plays*

Boyesen, H. H.: *Commentary on the Writings of Henrik Ibsen*

Moses, Montrose: *Henrik Ibsen, The Man and His Plays*

Longfellow, H. W.: *Frithiof's Saga* (in *Driftwood*)

Art and Music

Laurin, C., Hannover, E., and Thiis, J.: *Scandinavian Art*

Wettergren, Erik: *The Modern Decorative Art of Sweden*

Werrenrath, Reinald: *One Hundred Modern Scandinavian Songs*

Travel, Social Life and Customs

Williams, Mary W.: *Social Scandinavia in the Viking Age*

Franck, Harry A.: *A Scandinavian Summer*

Desmond, Shaw: *The Soul of Denmark*

Holland, H. C.: *Denmark*

Hammer, S. C.: *Norway*

Medill, Robert: *Norwegian Towns and People*

Heathcote, Dudley: *Sweden*

Whyte, Frederic: *A Wayfarer in Sweden*

Medill, Robert: *Sweden and Its People*

Rothery, Agnes: *Sweden, the Land and the People*

Chapman, Olive M.: *Across Iceland*

Russian Literature

Russian Literature

RUSSIA, the largest of the European countries, is the least European of them all. In fact Russians have often spoken of a journey west as " going to Europe," as if they themselves were quite outside that continent. The great stretches of Siberia have tied Russia to the East as no other European nation has been, and the Oriental element is a force that must be reckoned with in understanding Russian character. Complex indeed is the pattern of peoples designed to live under one government. It is said that there are one hundred and eighty nationalities in the present Soviet Union. When we add to the complexity the great problem of widespread illiteracy, against which such valiant struggles have been made in this century, we realize how different is the social background of Russian literature from that of other European nations. In fact Russia was so far behind the others that she was just emerging from semi-barbarism during the eighteenth century when the Western nations were rising to a climax of elegance and polish after several centuries of increasing refinements of life. This retardation was largely because of the great Mongolian invasions of the thirteenth century which destroyed the budding civilization and crowded the Slavs westward. For the next four centuries church and state bent their efforts toward the expulsion of the Tartars from Europe. A great change began with Peter the Great (1672–1725) who not only laid a firm foundation for an expanding empire, but systematically established contacts with the rest of Europe and thus leavened his country with Western civilization.

Russian literature a blend of Oriental and Occidental traits

We can feel in Russian life and character two great conflicting undercurrents — that which draws toward Western ideas and standards, vigorous, progressive and materialistic — and that which draws toward the Oriental mood of inertia, contemplation, and resignation to things as they are. What with this basic inner conflict, a natural tendency toward introspection, a frankness of self-revelation, and undue sensitiveness to suffering, the Russians have produced a body of literature which tends toward the morbid, the pessimistic, and the tragic, but which in its very power derived from searching the depths of human experience is one of the greatest literatures of Europe. Another marked characteristic of Russian writing is its realism, in contrast to the strong romantic quality of much Western literature. Russian books turn their searchlights on the daily lives of men and women. They throw no glamour over life, nor wrench it from its moorings to satisfy prescribed rules of plot or style. Hence the simple directness and formlessness of most Russian novels and dramas. It is evident too that much of the important fiction of this country is bound up either directly or indirectly with the political and social struggles which have racked the Russian people for two centuries. The reason for this is not only that these conflicts formed an integral part of living which could not be ignored, but also that with strict censorship stifling all freedom of speech on such matters, Russians have often been driven to make public their views through the thin disguise of fiction. The speeches of a nihilist character in a great novel could convey what no pamphlet could get into print. These three characteristics then are distinctive for Russian literature: pessimism, realism, and social significance.

For the general Western reader Russian literature may be said to begin with the nineteenth century. This does not mean a total lack of writing in the language before that time. In fact a detailed history of Russian literature devotes a large volume to the works produced before 1800, and bristles with the many-syllabled names of many authors. But these are of interest only to advanced scholars or native Russians and are seldom translated into foreign tongues.

Russia lacks great national epic but tales abound

Of the early literature the most appealing part is the folklore which gives the rich flavor of native peasant life. The continued primitiveness of country life in modern times made it easy to assemble folk tales and songs when interest in such things became current in the nineteenth century, for in remote districts wandering bards were still going from village to village to sing of the ancient heroes as in medieval centuries. While there are numerous heroes, many of whom are Oriental characters redressed in Russian garments, there is no one great epic comparable to those of other European nations. The nearest is the *Lay of Igor's Raid,* based on an expedition which actually happened in 1185. This Prince Igor has also figured prominently in Russian music and ballet. The poem rises to heights of imaginative language in the description of the march across the steppes, the battle in which Nature too takes part, and the lament of Igor's wife waiting anxiously at home. The prose folk tales show certain patterns common to those of other nations — the poor peasant who by his wits comes to marry a princess, the supposed fool who proves wiser than his practical brothers, the prince who performs impossible feats to win the hand of the princess, the tyrannical master who meets his just deserts, the animal who outwits other animals or man. Animals, in fact, especially the wolf and bear, play an unusually large part in Russian tales. Songs there are in abundance, many of them with ancient music. They still play an active part in the celebration of holidays, weddings, and burials. This body of folk literature together with a great number of annals constitutes the production of the centuries preceding the Mongol invasion of 1223. From then to the time of Ivan the Terrible (1529) writing was confined entirely to the monasteries and to religious subjects, or translations of foreign materials. Ivan introduced printing and himself headed a group of writers who produced satire and history. Religious drama assumed an important place during the late sixteenth and seventeenth centuries.

Peter the Great establishes education and simpler alphabet

In the early eighteenth century Peter the Great gave a new impetus to writing by establishing a simpler alphabet and encouraging works of an educational nature, but he was not particularly interested in artistic literature. During this century the writers were distinctly the products of Western education, and their work was largely imitative of French and German styles. The only one who seems worthy of special mention here is Lomonosov (1711–1765) a poor priest, son of a fisherman, who was selected, because of his abilities, to be sent to Germany for education. Upon his return he was the only native Russian to be elected to the exclusive and largely German Academy of St. Petersburg. In addition to important experimentation in physics and chemistry, he worked out a Russian grammar, various forms of versification, and practically a new literary language. Pushkin called him a university in himself.

Pushkin the first great name of Russian literature

With Pushkin (1799–1837) the modern literature of Russia really begins. In versatility, poetic insight and real power of word picturing he has not been excelled in the poetry of his land. He broke definitely with the followers of the French classic school, and in his first long poem " Ruslan and Ludmila " told a native fairy tale with so much charm that the stilted and artificial pseudo-classic style met permanent defeat in the public mind. This simple and honest style, to which Wordsworth offers the best parallel in English poetry, remained in all Pushkin's later writing. His masterpiece, *Eugene Onegin*, tells the story of a society dandy who scorns the love of Tatiana, a poetically inclined young country girl, only to fall in love with her years later when he meets her in the court circles of St. Petersburg as the wife of an old general. Tatiana's pathetic speech of regret for the past when happiness would have been so possible and so near is one of the most famous passages among Russian classics. The story forms the basis of an opera by Tschaikovsky; in fact, most of Pushkin's long poems have been used for opera by Russian composers. Pushkin's treatments of earlier history in *Boris Gudonov* and *The Bronze Horseman* further stamped him as the mouthpiece of the nation, and his limning of local scenery endeared him to a nature-loving people. He is universally regarded as the foundation stone of modern Russian literature.

Lermontov writes in the Byronic manner

Second to Pushkin among the early poets stands Lermontov (1814–1841), a more extravagant romanticist than the former and somewhat comparable to the English Byron in his love of the exotic and the dramatically heroic. His most famous long poem *The Demon* portrays what one critic has called " the least convincing devil ever conceived by a poet." Rather it is a powerful and rebellious spirit, hovering about the rocky crags of the Caucasus mountains, who falls in love with a beautiful peasant girl. The fantastic nature of this plot is offset by the grandeur of the mountain scenery which has never been more impressively described. Rebellion against environment is also the theme of *A Novice,* in which a youth brought up in a monastery tries to escape to his early mountain home, but after three days of ecstatic joy in his forest liberty he is fatally wounded by a leopard. Lermontov's poetry has unusual melodiousness and liquid flow in addition to emotional fervor, but there is an artificial, operatic quality which marks it as inferior to the genuineness of Pushkin's.

Gogol mimics life in a great novel and a great comedy

Both of these men also attempted novels in prose, but in that field they were far excelled by Gogol (1809–1852), whose inventive gift for creating multitudes of vivid characters has been compared to that of Dickens. He was a born mimic, and so caught and held the colloquial mannerisms of his men and women as well as their physical peculiarities that he is especially difficult to translate. In the novel *Dead Souls* the hero is an ingenious " gentle grafter " whose plan to people his imaginary estate with the names of dead serfs gives the author a chance to send him touring the countryside. This comes the nearest to the Spanish " picaresque " novel (the lively adventures of a quick-witted rogue) that Russian literature has produced. Rogues of another sort create the stage fun of *The Government Inspector,* the outstanding and almost unique comedy of Russian drama. Here the roguery of incompetency, inaction, and indifference to duty is stirred to consternation at the thought of discovery, and thus proves its own undoing. Among Gogol's short stories, " The Overcoat " is the most notable. It portrays a poor clerk whose long-standing wish to own an overcoat is fulfilled only to have the coat stolen the first day he wears it. This story was paid the tribute of imitation in a long series of pathetic stories about poor clerks.

Three masters of the Russian novel remain preëminent

In the middle of the nineteenth century we come to the golden age of the Russian novel. There is no question as to the three names at the top of the list of novelists though there has been considerable ink expended by critics as to which one or two out of the three can be placed above the others of the triad. The birth dates of these three men — Turgenev, 1818, Dostoevsky, 1821, and Tolstoy, 1828 — show how closely contemporaneous they were. Dostoevsky had a slight head start on the others in publication, for his *Poor Folk* was enthusiastically received in 1846; but his nine years of isolation in Siberia removed him from the scene temporarily, and it was Turgenev who laid the earliest permanent reputation with his *A Sportsman's Sketches* of 1850. Tolstoy's *Childhood* brought him some recognition in 1852, but it was not till his *Sevastopol Stories* of the Crimean War were published in 1855 that his name was as well known as Turgenev's. Since Turgenev lived abroad for so many years and was translated earlier than the other two, his reputation in the Western countries long preceded theirs. But so too it waned earlier, and today Turgenev seems more dated by the sentiment and refinement of his style, less powerful and universal than the other two.

Turgenev pictures women and serfs with poetic insight

In the works of Turgenev we find a wistful and poetical quality in the descriptions, especially of landscapes and of the women characters who are for the most part delightful though somewhat idealized creatures. Maurice Baring the English critic says, " He has the magic that water gives to the reflected images of trees, hills and woods." Turgenev was in love with the Russian language and the painstaking care with which he managed its subtleties and rhythms cannot of course be fully appreciated in translation. He also crystallizes more than the other two novelists the political unrest of the day and the desperation of human beings faced by social forces which they cannot change or control. His influence on reform policies was greater than he realized at the time of writing. *A Sportsman's Sketches* were not written with direct intent to free the serfs, nor *Fathers and Sons* to christen the " Nihilist " party, yet such results followed in their wake. Turgenev is the great reflector of his age.

Tolstoy reveals the inner life under emotional stress

Tolstoy, too, paints on a large canvas but is more concerned with the psychological development of his characters. Our ability to look into the hidden mental processes of each person gives us a feeling of oneness with the experience of each. His style is simpler, more transparent than Turgenev's. We are not aware of a well-turned phrase or a sudden loveliness of cadence between us and the story, but we see the characters almost as in a picture without the intervention of words. The author's knack of vivifying a face or a whole personality through some selected physical detail which is repeatedly introduced leads to this impression of clarity. In Tolstoy's earlier works — *Sevastopol Stories, The Cossacks,* and *War and Peace* — the lives of the characters are enmeshed in the net of military life or of open warfare; in the later ones — *Anna Karenina, The Kreutzer Sonata,* and *Resurrection* — it is love and the expiation of sin which bring about the human struggle. A pronounced moral purpose is evident in most of Tolstoy's books, especially the later ones. Many of his short stories, in fact, are parables to mold human attitudes toward right and wrong.

Dostoevsky draws powerful picture of human derelicts

Dostoevsky had a long struggle to win the public acclaim which came so quickly to his two great contemporaries. He returned to Petersburg in 1859. In the score of years between then and his death he produced about nine long books besides numerous miscellaneous writings, but he was constantly in financial straits, and far-reaching popularity did not come to him until a few years before his death. In fact it was not until the nineties that his fame abroad began to equal that of the other two men, then, in the minds of some critics at least, to overtop Turgenev's. The names of Dostoevsky's great books are for the most part suggestive of the human derelicts from whose ranks he drew practically all his characters. — *Humiliated and Insulted* (in some translations called *Downtrodden and Oppressed*), *The House of the Dead, Memoirs from Underground, Crime and Punishment, The Gambler, The Idiot, The Devils.* Only in his last and greatest book does he choose the noncommittal title *The Brothers Karamazov.* However much Dostoevsky may be criticized for the formlessness and prolixity of his novels, for the fantastic quality of his plots, for the misery, disease or insanity with which all his characters are warped, the fact remains that he wrote with terrifying power, and invested his gruesome situations with human sympathy and spiritual significance beyond that of any other writer.

Minor novelists and poets show varying aspects of Russian life

Out of the many other mid-century writers only a few can be mentioned. Goncharov (1812–1891) produced, among his several novels, one classic called *Oblomov* in which the central character, an aristocrat completely enervated by his irresponsible and luxurious life, sank into " dressing-gown laziness." The character so held the mirror up to a recognized national failing that it created a new term for indolence, which might be translated *oblomovism.*

The poets of the day must in this brief history be limited to three. Count Alexey Tolstoy (1817–1875) may be called the comic relief in the tragedy of Russian literature. He seems to be about the only important author since 1800 who led a normal, happy, uneventful life, unmarred by devastating inner conflict or melancholy. Consequently he could write in a hearty, humorous vein and produce either nonsense verse or truly joyous lyrics quite in contrast to the tone of his contemporaries. His versatility showed itself in his attempts at both novel and drama, but it is for his clever and lightly satirical verse that his name will be perpetuated. Fet (1820–1892) is unique among his contemporaries in that his fanciful love lyrics show no trace of interest in social reform, for he was definitely opposed to liberal ideas. In contrast, Nekrasov (1821–1877) is one of the first men to bring proletarian life into poetry. Because of increasing appreciation of the common people and of a ruggedly original style, Nekrasov is more highly regarded by moderns than he was by his contemporaries.

Short story supplants novel at turn of the century

With the nineties we come to the three modernists, Chekhov, Gorki, and Andreyev, all of whom illustrate the turn toward the short story instead of the long novel of the earlier day, and the awakened interest in drama. Chekhov (1860–1904) continued the tradition of Gogol in his humor with a wry satirical twist, and portrayed the middle classes of the city, a group which had had scant attention before his day. Gorki (1868–1936) followed Nekrasov and Dostoevsky in picturing social derelicts, but the devil-may-care virility of his tramps created an entirely different emotional tone from the compassion and Christian resignation to misfortune which permeate Dostoevsky's narratives. Andreyev (1871–1919) adopted into prose and drama the element of symbolism which had characterized much of the poetry of the nineties and early nineteen hundreds, and thus definitely broke away from the established tradition of realism.

Of the early symbolists, Sologub (1863–1927) is the best known through English translation; of the later ones Blok (1880–1921) and Bely (1880–1934) stand above the others. Blok's long poem called *The Twelve*, which depicts a group of Red soldiers harrying the bourgeois in the early days of the Revolution, is probably the most famous single poem written since that event.

Russian Revolution splits writers into two camps

After the Revolution, Russian literature was definitely split into two parts: that produced by the exiled intelligentsia, and that produced within the Soviet Union. Among the exiles two interesting personalities were Merezhkovsky, outstanding critic of pre-Revolutionary days, author of the well-known *Romance of Leonardo da Vinci*, and his wife, Zinaida Hippius, poet and journalist. But topping all the exiled Russians in literary importance was Bunin, poet, novelist, and short-story writer, whose winning of the Nobel prize in 1933 brought him into the limelight.

Russian " artists in uniform " express Soviet realism

Post-Revolutionary works of Russian literature are predominantly expressions of " Soviet realism." Authors have sought to simplify and intensify the picture of the Soviet man by presenting him with " unvarnished " truth. At first they merely continued and modified some of the methods of pre-Revolutionary realists.

Gorki, for example, in *Decadence* (1925) presented in his familiar, gloomy, matter-of-fact fashion the decay of a bourgeois family through three generations. Alexey Tolstoy (1882–1945) continued to employ the epic amplitude of pre-Revolutionary novels like *War and Peace.* In *The Way Through Hell,* he paints on a huge canvas the futile life of the intelligentsia during the Revolution. His vast historical novel *Peter the Great* is an important piece of Soviet realism by virtue of its vivid descriptions of the horrors of serfdom.

Ilya Ehrenburg (1891–   ), prolific novelist, essayist, and, above all, journalist, writes novels that are political pamphlets seasoned with melodrama. His *Trust D E* (1923) is a fantasy picturing the destruction of Europe through the invasion of crass American culture. His *The Fall of Paris* (1941) is a Communist-biased analysis of France's collapse at the beginning of World War II.

Yevgeny Zamyatin (1884–1937) looked with clear but hostile eyes on Soviet policy. *The Fires of St. Dominic* is a bitter attack on the secret police. His utopian novel *We,* set in the twenty-sixth century, is a satire of the mechanized, standardized life every Soviet citizen must live.

Leonid Leonov (1899–   ), in his long, formless novels, seasons his realism with an interest, like Dostoevsky's, in strange, unpredictable individuals. His *Badgers* (1924) deals with a peasant uprising against the government. In *Sot* (1929) and *Skutarevsky* (1931) he continues to dramatize the conflict between the new and the old Russia.

The realism of Boris Pilnyak (1894–   ) is cool, but deliberately cruel. His *Hollow Arabia* describes starving peasants driven to eating each other because of the devastation of civil war. In *The Volga Flows to the Caspian Sea,* he shows the difference between a model Communist city built to house workers on a gigantic dam and the old town Kolomna where pigs wallow in the mud of its main street.

Mikhail Sholokhov (1905–   ), popular for his writings about the Don Cossack region, depicts in *And Quiet Flows the Don* peasants caught in the new order of the anonymity of the collective farm.

His novels *Tales of the Don* and *Seeds of Tomorrow* are skillful journalistic descriptions of the same region.

The growing freedom of writers is strikingly shown by the amazing popularity of the recent novel *Not by Bread Alone* (1956) by Vladimir Dudintsev. Its main theme is the hounding of an inventor without important political connections and the neglect of his valuable invention by stupid bureaucrats.

Although Russian writers continue to be " artists in uniform " (Max Eastman's phrase), they are less and less thwarted by political censorship. They have thus been able, more and more, to turn from crude propaganda to studies of individuals in a Soviet society.

The Russian Folk Tale

Russian literature, like that of other northern European nations, is rich in folk tales and folk songs. The most famous collection of *skaska,* as the folk tales are called, that by Afanasief, contains three hundred and thirty-two distinct stories, some with several versions. Three other good collections bring the total number of stories somewhat above five hundred, exclusive of the tales of South Russia, which are in a different dialect.

Many of these tales show distinctly that they come from the Orient and have simply taken on Russian names and customs as a veneer. These are usually the more fantastic stories of magic and mystery. More indigenous to the country are the many animal tales in which, with characteristic Russian realism, the beasts of the northern forests, from the bear to the ermine, are often made most convincingly human. The many narratives of peasant life show recurring notes similar to German and Scandinavian stories, such as the triumph of the younger son over his brothers, of the serf over the cruel master, of the guileless peasant over the wise men of the court. Humor plays a prominent part in the peasant tales, turning, as one writer puts it, upon " the incorrigible folly of man and the inflexible obstinacy of woman." Some of these have given rise to proverbs. For instance, the Russian version of a situation which appears in different guise among other nations shows the husband and wife disputing over whether his beard has been shaved or only cut. Enraged at her insistence that he has cut it, the husband throws the wife into a pond, but as she goes under the water she raises her arm and makes a motion of cutting with her fingers. This has given rise to the common Russian proverb: " If you say ' shaved ' she'll say ' cut.' "

The following story also pokes fun at a certain traditional weakness of woman which has resulted in the proverb: " Women have long hair and short wits." Afanasief gives other versions of this same tale, in one of which the lord causes the husband to be divorced from his supposedly mad wife and married to a young and beautiful one.

FISH IN THE FOREST

In tilling the ground a laborer found a treasure, and carrying it home, said to his wife, " See! Heaven has sent us a fortune. But where can we conceal it? " She suggested he should bury it under the floor, which he did accordingly. Soon after this the wife went out to fetch water, and the laborer reflected that his wife was a dreadful gossip, and by tomorrow night all the village would know their secret. So he removed the treasure from its hiding-place and buried it in his barn, beneath a heap of corn. When the wife came back from the well, he said to her quite gravely, " Tomorrow we shall go to the forest to seek fish; they say there's plenty there at present."

" What! fish in the forest? " she exclaimed.

" Of course," he rejoined; " and you'll see them there."

Very early next morning he got up, and took some fish, which he had concealed in a basket. He went to the grocer's and bought a quantity of sweet cakes. He also caught a hare and killed it. The fish and cakes he disposed of in different parts of the wood, and the hare he hooked on a fishing-line, and then threw it in the river. After breakfast he took his wife with him into the wood, which they had scarcely entered when she found a pike, then a perch, and then a roach, on the ground. With many exclamations of surprise, she gathered up the fish and put them in her basket.

Presently they came to a pear-tree, from the branches of which hung sweet cakes. " See! " she cried. " Cakes on a pear-tree! "

" Quite natural," replied he; " it has rained cakes, and some have remained on this tree; travelers have picked up the rest." Continuing their way to the village, they passed near a stream.

" Wait a little," said the husband; " I set my line early this morning, and I'll look if anything is caught on it." He then pulled in the line, and behold, there was a hare hooked on to it!

" How extraordinary! " cries the good wife; " a hare in the water! "

" Why," says he, " don't you know there are hares in the water as well as rats? "

" No, indeed, I knew it not."

They now returned home, and the wife set about preparing all the nice eatables for supper. In a day or two the laborer learned from the talk of his acquaintances that his finding the treasure was no secret in the village, and in less than a week he was summoned to the castle.

" Is it true," says the lord, " that you have found a treasure? "

" It is not true," was the reply.

" But your wife has told me all."

" My wife does not know what she says — she is mad, my lord."

Hereupon the woman cries, " It is the truth, my lord! he has found a treasure and buried it beneath the floor of our cottage."

" When? "

" On the eve before the day when we went into the forest to look for fish."

" What do you say? "

" Yes; it was on the day that it rained cakes. We gathered a basketful of them, and coming home, my husband fished a fine hare out of the river."

My lord declared the woman to be an idiot; nevertheless he caused his servants to search under the laborer's cottage floor, but nothing was found there, and so the shrewd fellow secured his treasure.

(W. Clouston)

SUGGESTIONS FOR STUDY

1. How does the humor of this tale differ from that of the husband-and-wife situation in the Norwegian folk tale, page 581? Compare the story with " Women and Secrets," page 83.

2. Read other Russian folk tales. " Verlioka " is typical of the cruel-overseer type, " Kuzma Skorobogaty " of the talking-animal type. Compare the large part played by the forest in the Russian tales with that in German and Scandinavian stories. Why do surroundings of mountain and forest tend to promote folk literature? Is that true in the United States as well?

ALEXANDER SERGEYEVICH [1] PUSHKIN (1799–1837)

What Shakespeare is to English literature, Dante to Italian, and Goethe to German, Pushkin is to Russian literature — its greatest poet, the one who seems to embody more than any other the whole of Russia's past civilization and to bring to its highest point the glory of the language. The unfamiliarity of Europe with the Russian tongue and the difficulty of translating the full flavor of poetry have deprived Pushkin of a European reputation equal to that of the other great national poets, but Russians

---

[1] **Sergeyevich:** It is well for the student to understand the Russian system of names at the outset of this section. The middle name of a Russian is the patronymic, or " father " name. " Vich " means " son of " and " ovna,"

themselves regard him on a level with those great masters of the world. Before his day Russian poetry had imitated the French pattern without any native flavor of its own. Pushkin, though in many ways a romanticist, nevertheless opened up the great stores of material in the life and tradition of his native land in such a way as to stamp the quality of realism upon all later Russian literature.

Born into an aristocratic family, the boy Pushkin received the typical education of his time based on French models. When he was in the Lyceum (high school) one of the old poets of the day heard the boy's original work at a public examination and so great was his enthusiasm that young Pushkin even then was reputed to be the coming poet of Russia. Another famous Russian poet sent him his portrait inscribed " To a pupil from his defeated teacher." This promise of his school days was borne out by later writing, even while the young man plunged into the extravagant social life of the capital. But some verse expressing revolutionary ideas and satirizing the rulers brought about his banishment from St. Petersburg [2] and for several years he roamed through various Russian provinces, at one time escaping exile to Siberia by burning all his papers before the police could seize them. Later Tsar Nicholas I recalled him to court and made him a chamberlain. Here he led the irksome life of a courtier beset by the jealousies of those nobles who did not have his literary fame. His beautiful wife was not sympathetic with his work but entirely engrossed in society. It was on her account that the poet became involved in a duel with a French Royalist and was killed at the age of thirty-eight.

Pushkin produced in addition to innumerable short poems, several long works on which his fame really rests. The best known of these are: *Poltava,* a long historical poem; *Eugene Onegin,* a novel in verse, still studied in Soviet schools; *Boris Gudonov,* historical drama in blank verse; and *The Bronze Horseman,* a verse story celebrating the glories of Peter the great and St. Petersburg, including a fine description of the great inundation of the city in 1823.

" daughter of." This suffix is attached to the first name of the father. This Pushkin was the son of Sergey Pushkin. If the poet had had a son, this boy would have had Alexandrovich for his middle name; a daughter would have had Alexandrovna. Through the nineteenth century it was customary to address a person by both his first and second names without any titles prefixed. This imaginary daughter of Pushkin's would have been addressed as Marya Alexandrovna, not as Miss Pushkin, except that for an introduction the French Mlle. Pushkin would have been used. It is this custom which makes Russian proper names so confusing to foreigners. Modern Russia is tending to disregard the patronymic and thus simplify the names.

[2] St. Petersburg: The capital has had three names. St. Petersburg, from the time of Peter the Great to the first revolution; Petrograd during the first troubled period after the overthrow of the empire; and Leningrad since the beginning of the Soviet régime. In this section the name is used that was current at the time referred to.

It is hard to realize through the few short selections possible to include in this collection, the significant place of Pushkin in Russian literature or the thought which one critic says arises in every Russian's mind on reading him, "How beautifully this has been told! It could not, it ought not, to be told in a different way."

THE BRONZE HORSEMAN

The passage is the opening of the long poem, *The Bronze Horseman,* referring to the equestrian statue of Peter the Great in St. Petersburg. Peter was the monarch who first brought Russia into the European political circle. This description of the city of St. Petersburg shows Pushkin as the bard of his Nation.

> He stood upon the lonely shore,
> In thought deep as the waves' deep roar,
> And gazed into the distance. Grandly
> The Neva rolled her width before;
> A solitary boat skimmed swiftly. 5
> Just here and there against the green
> And swampy moss there could be seen
> Black dots of Finnish dingy hovels.
> The sunshine hid by misty screen
> In the dark forest held no revels; 10
> The trees moaned, murmuring.
>   He thought:
> " Hence Sweden's might shall we o'ershadow,
> Here build a town — thorn in the side
> To vex our haughty neighbor's pride.
> Nature herself wills that our window 15
> Should here be cut through Europe's wall;
> Firm on the Baltic shores, we shall
> See foreign ships each other follow
> With fluttering flags to the new port,
> And, joyful, feast our guests at Court." 20
>
> A hundred years — a city new,
> The northern lands fair pride and wonder,
> Rose from the swamps where forest grew;

1. **He:** Peter the Great. 4. **Neva:** the river at whose mouth St. Petersburg lies. 12. **Sweden's might:** In the seventeenth century, Sweden owned Finland and was a more powerful state in European politics than at present.

A stately, gorgeous beauty! Yonder,
Where hitherto a lonely Finn,   25
Nature's sad stepson, cast his fish net
Into the virgin waves, whose din
Alone broke silence round his hamlet
Upon the bleak, low shore — there throng
Gay crowds the busy streets along;   30
And, shouldering each other, masses
Of towers and palaces now stand;
Long file of ships passes, re-passes
Through harbors, by the wealth-strewn strand.
Herself in granite Neva clad,   35
Hung themselves bridges o'er her waters,
Decked themselves out her island daughters
With many a garden green and glad.
Bows now her head old Moscow, drooping
Before the younger capital,   40
As to a new Tsaritsa stooping
A dowager Queen in purple pall.
I love thee, Peter's own creation;
I love thy stiff and stately sight,
Broad Neva's powerful fluxation,   45
Her great embankments' granite might,
Inwrought designs of iron gateways,
Thy still, transparent, thoughtful nights
When soft and silvery moonless glimmer
Enters my room — and, without lights,   50
I read and write past midnight chiming,
While, clear cut, sleep the giant buildings
Along the empty streets, and higher
Soars bright, the Admiralty spire.
And, the deep dark of night not letting   55
Touch the gold skies, the dawn of day
To take the twilight's place is fretting,
Just yielding night one half-hour's sway.
I love thy cruel winter bright,
On Neva's ice the sleigh's fleet races,   60
The glow of frost on maidens' faces,

35–40. The construction of these lines is peculiar, after the Russian style.
In direct order they would be "Neva clad herself in granite," "bridges hung
themselves," "islands decked themselves," "Moscow bows her head."
41. **Tsaritsa:** daughter or wife of a Tsar.

Motionless space of ice-nipped height;
The ball-rooms' talk, their buzz and dazzle,
And, at the hour when young men razzle,
The foamy punch-bowl hissing blue.   65
I love the warlike clash and clamor
Of spring maneuvers in Mars Square,
The footmen and the horsemen there
In rhythmical and even glamour;
Over each stately rippling line   70
The captured colors torn and tattered,
And of those helmets bright, shot-shattered
In former frays, the brazen shine.
I love the cannons' smoke and thunder
The martial capital will see   75
When in the northern Palace yonder
Tsaritsa bears the heir-to-be;
Or when a war in triumph past
Rus' celebrates with joyous voices,
Or when Broad Neva breaks at last   80
Her ice and whirls it seaward fast,
And, scenting the spring days, rejoices.

                              (*Mme. N. Jarintzov*)

  79. **Rus'**: Russia.

AUTUMN — A FRAGMENT

"What then does not enter my drowsy mind . . . ?"
                              Derzhavin.

October comes at last. The grove is shaking
The last reluctant leaves from naked boughs.
The Autumn cold has breathed, the road is freezing, —
The brook still sounds behind the miller's house,
But the pond's hushed; now with his pack my neighbor   5
Makes for the distant field, — his hounds will rouse
The woods with barking, and his horse's feet
Will trample cruelly the winter wheat.

This is my time! What is Spring to me?
Thaw is a bore: mud running thick and stinking —   10
Spring makes me ill: my mind is never free
From dizzy dreams, my blood's in constant ferment.

Give me instead Winter's austerity,
The snows under the moon, — and what is gayer
Than to glide lightly in a sleigh with her   15
Whose fingers are like fire beneath the fur?

And oh, the fun! steel-shod to trace a pattern
In crystal on the river's glassy face!
The shining stir of festivals in Winter!
But there's a limit — nobody could face   20
Six months of snow, — even that cave dweller,
The bear, would growl " enough " in such a case.
Sleigh-rides with young Armidas pall, by Jove,
And you turn sour with loafing by the stove.

Oh, darling Summer, I could cherish you,   25
If heat and dust and gnats and flies were banished.
These dull the mind, the heart grows weary, too.
We, like the meadows, suffer drought; thought withers.
Drink is our only hope, and how we rue
Old woman Winter, at whose funeral banquet   30
Pancakes and wine were served, but now we hold
Memorial feasts of ices, sweet and cold.

They say ill things of the last days of Autumn;
To me, reader and friend, she is most dear.
Her quiet beauty shines for me as meekly   35
As an unloved child, with its stern parents near.
She can rejoice me more, I tell you frankly,
Than all the other seasons of the year.
I am a humble lover, and I could
Find, singularly, much in her that's good.   40

How shall I make it clear? I find her pleasing
As you perhaps may like a sickly girl,
Condemned to die, and shortly, who is drooping
Without a murmur of reproach to hurl
At life, forsaking her — upon her paling   45
Young lips a little smile is seen to curl.
She does not hear the grave's horrific yawn.
Today she lives — tomorrow she is gone.

Oh, mournful season that delights the eyes,
Your farewell beauty captivates my spirit.　　50
I love the pomp of Nature's fading dyes,
The forests, garmented in gold and purple,
The rush of noisy wind, and the pale skies
Half-hidden by the clouds in darkling billows,
And the rare sun-ray and the early frost,　　55
And threats of grizzled Winter, heard and lost.

Each time that Autumn comes I bloom afresh;
For me, I find, the Russian cold is good;
Again I go through life's routine with relish:
Sleep comes in season, and the need for food;　　60
Desire seethes — and I am young and merry,
My heart beats fast with lightly leaping blood.
I'm full of life — such is my organism
(If you will please excuse the prosaism).

My horse is brought; far out onto the plain　　65
He carries his glad rider, and the frozen
Dale echoes to his shining hooves, his mane
Streams in the keen wind like a banner blowing,
And the bright ice creaks under him again.
But day soon flickers out. At the forgotten　　70
Hearth, where the fire purrs low, or leaps like wind,
I read, or nourish long thoughts in my mind.

And I forget the world in the sweet silence,
While I am lulled by fancy, and once more
The soul oppressed with the old lyric fever　　75
Trembles, reverberates, and seeks to pour
Its burden freely forth, and as though dreaming
I watch the children that my visions bore,
And I am host to the invisible throngs
Who fill my reveries and build my songs.　　80

And thoughts stir bravely in my head, and rhymes
Run forth to meet them on light feet, and fingers
Reach for the pen, and the good quill betimes
Asks for the foolscap. Wait: the verses follow.

Thus a still ship sleeps on still seas. Hark: Chimes!   85
And swiftly all hands leap to man the rigging,
The sails are filled, they belly in the wind —
The monster moves — a foaming track behind.

It sails, but whither is it our ship goes?
What ports most beckon us? Colossal Nile's,   90
The bluffs of Scotland, or the eternal snows? . . .

(Babette Deutsch and Avrahm Yarmolinsky)

MY MONUMENT

It is hard for a poet who has received great acclaim in his heyday to
feel popular favor cooling in his later years. Pushkin was keenly sensitive to the waning of his vogue and consoled himself with the feeling that
posterity, at least, would appreciate him. This poem was written just the
year before his death. Do not regard this, however, as an old man's
poem, for Pushkin was only thirty-eight when he died.

I've reared myself a monument not made with hands;
The path to it shall ne'er be overgrown with grass,
Where it with high, unbending head shall tower
Above Napoleon's column.

Not wholly shall I die: the soul that nursed my muse   5
My dust shall long outlive and shall defy decay;
And men shall love to chant my lays, whilst on our earth
A single bard doth breathe or sing.

My fame shall live and be a Russian household word,
And all who speak our tongue my name shall whisper soft,   10
The Slav of ancient race, the Finn, the wild Tungese,
And Calmuck born on barren steppe.

And long shall I the people's favorite be held,
Since ne'er my lyre has failed to stir all feelings pure;
My verse the general cause has single pleaded,   15
And pity for the fallen taught.

4. **Napoleon's column:** i.e., his fame will be greater than Napoleon's.
11. **Slav:** a race name of one of the Aryan branches comparable to Teuton and
Latin. The Slavs include not only Russians but also Poles and most of the
inhabitants of the Balkan states.   11. **the Finn:** Finland at the time belonged
to Russia.   11. **Tungese:** member of the Tungus tribe in the Ural mountains.
12. **Calmuck:** or Kalmuck, a Mongol of the Volga valley.

To God's high will, my muse, in lowly meekness bow;
Let no rebuff offend, nor laurel crown demand;
Take praise or calumny with like indifference;
And never argue with the fool.   20

(*Charles Edward Turner*)

SUGGESTIONS FOR STUDY

1. Read a historical account of Peter the Great and the building of St. Petersburg. What light does the poem throw on the difficulties of building a city on this spot, and on Peter's reason for choosing it? If possible, obtain pictures of the city (now Leningrad) and the bronze statue. See reading list, page 894.

2. Does the poet make you feel his affection for his city? Does he emphasize the appearance or the mood of the city? Compare with poems on other cities, such as Whitman's "Mannahatta" and Sandburg's "Chicago." What details in Pushkin's poem could apply to cities you know? Which are distinctly Russian?

3. How does "Autumn" compare with "The Bronze Horseman" in its general emotional tone? How does the poet's preference in seasons compare with your own? What seasonal details mentioned in the poem resemble the climate in which you live? Which differ? Compare this with Keats' "Ode to Autumn," Carman's "Vagabond Song," and other autumn pieces. Consider also descriptions of the various seasons which you have read.

4. How does the mood of "My Monument" differ from that of the preceding poems? Do you consider it conceited? Discuss the difference between pride and conceit. Was his prophecy fulfilled? When you come to page 794, note evidence that he also had eventually a monument "made with hands."

5. Write a tribute either to your own city or your favorite season of the year, following Pushkin's method of the vivid detail.

NIKOLAY VASILIEVICH GOGOL (1809–1852)

Gogol, "the father of modern Russian realism," was a native of the Ukraine, or Little Russia. Both his grandfather and his father, petty country squires, could tell comic stories inimitably, and to his grandfather he owed the plots of many of his early tales. At school the boy showed himself a poor scholar but an excellent mimic of elderly or comic characters. The same traits were later revealed when he failed miserably as a history professor but succeeded admirably as a novelist and playwright.

Before fame arrived, however, he had experienced at St. Petersburg the depressing life of a petty clerk with ambitions which could not be realized. Thus he acquired the background to give actuality to the panorama of Russian characters which he immortalized in his remarkable comedy, *The Government Inspector,* and his great novel, *Dead Souls.* Both are considered classics of Russian literature. The novel is based on the get-rich-quick scheme of an unscrupulous official. " Soul " was the common term for a serf before the days of emancipation. The hero conceived the idea of buying at a small price the names of " souls " who had died since the last tax collection but on whom taxes had to be paid during the year. With this mythical list of serfs he planned to colonize a mythical estate and on this security obtain a large loan from a bank of the nobility. The adventures of the hero in search of his " dead souls " gives wide scope for Gogol's genius in drawing vivid and varied characters.

Though Gogol is considered the greatest Russian humorist, the underlying vein of sadness and misery common to all Russian literature is detected in his work. Pushkin said, " Behind his laughter you feel the unseen tears," and Gogol himself wrote, " I became a prey to fits of melancholy which were beyond my comprehension. In order to get rid of them I invented the funniest things I could think of. I invented funny characters in the funniest situations imaginable."

Because he could not face the hostility aroused by his satires on officialdom, Gogol spent most of his life outside of Russia wandering from country to country. The longest periods were spent in Rome, which he called his " true homeland." It was here that he wrote most of *Dead Souls.*

During his last years, he developed a strange obsession that his writings were a great sin in his life and twice he burned the second part of *Dead Souls.* He seemed torn by inner conflict and desolated by complete loneliness. He wrote, " If I could find one soul only! If only one soul would wish to speak to me! Everything seems to have died out. I think only dead souls still exist in Russia. It is dreadful."

A journey to Palestine failed to give him the religious comfort he sought. After his return to his native land, about four years before his death, he restlessly roamed from one spot to another. Finally he died in Moscow, as a result of refusing to eat during a period of mental depression.

THE GOVERNMENT INSPECTOR

No comedy has ever attained the popularity on the Russian stage of Gogol's *The Government Inspector,* nor has its performance been confined to that country. In fact it holds a unique place in the history of Russian drama. It was begun in 1834 after Gogol had abandoned his first attempt at a comedy because he feared it would not escape the censor. One of Gogol's poet friends showed the new play to Tsar Nicholas, who ordered that it be produced on the stage in 1836, laughed heartily at the first performance, and said, "Every one has received his due, and I most of all."

The plot of the story was first suggested to Gogol by Pushkin, who once at an inn had been taken for a government official coming secretly to inspect the town. On this mistaken identity theme, Gogol built up a complete satirical picture of Russian official life of his day, with its inefficiency, graft, and self-seeking held up to hilarious ridicule. Unfortunately though the play drew crowded houses, it also drew unpopularity upon its plainspeaking author, and Gogol voluntarily exiled himself to western Europe for about twelve years. Act I could almost be used as a one-act play because of its well-rounded presentation of the consternation in officialdom at the thought of an inspection.

ACT I

CHARACTERS [1] APPEARING IN THIS ACT

ANTON ANTONOVICH, *the Mayor*
AMMOS FYODOROVICH, *the Judge*
ARTEMY FILIPPOVICH, *the Charity Commissioner*
LUKA LUKICH, *the School Inspector*
CHRISTIAN IVANOVICH IIUBNER, *the Doctor*
IVAN KUZMICH, *the Postmaster*
PYOTR IVANOVICH BOBCHINSKY ⎫
PYOTR IVANOVICH DOBCHINSKY ⎬ *Policemen*
STEPAN ILYICH UHOVYORTOV, *the Police Commissioner*
SVISTUNOV, *the Mayor's servant*
ANNA ANDREYEVNA, *the Mayor's wife*
MARYA ANTONOVNA, *the Mayor's daughter*

A room in the Mayor's house.

The Mayor. I have called you together, gentlemen, to communicate to you a most unpleasant piece of news: an Inspector is coming to visit us.

Ammos Fyodorovich. An Inspector?

Artemy Filippovich. An Inspector?

The Mayor. A Government Inspector, from Petersburg, incognito; and with secret orders.

Ammos Fyodorovich. That's a pleasant surprise!

Artemy Filippovich. As though we hadn't trouble enough!

[1] **Characters:** See page 754 for explanation of Russian patronymics. The surnames are not given here for any of the characters except the policemen and servant.

Luka Lukich. Good heavens! And with secret orders!

The Mayor. I had a sort of foreboding of it: all night I was dreaming of two extraordinary rats. I assure you I never saw rats like them: black and unnaturally large! They came and sniffed about. — and went away. Here, I'll read you the letter I've received from Andrey Ivanovich Tchmyhov, whom you know, Artemy Filippovich. This is what he writes: " Dear friend and benefactor! " [*Mutters in an undertone, hastily looking through the letter.*] " and to inform you " . . . Ah, here it is: " I hasten to inform you, among other things, that an official has arrived with instructions to inspect the whole province, and especially our district. [*Lifts up his finger significantly.*] I have learned this from the most reliable sources, though he passes himself off for a private person. As I know that you have your little failings like everybody else, for you are a sensible man and don't like to let things slip through your fingers " [2] . . . [*Pausing.*] Well, we are all friends here . . . " I advise you to take steps in time, for he may arrive any minute, if, indeed, he has not come already and is not living among you incognito. . . . Yesterday I . . ." Well, here he goes on to family affairs, " My sister Anna Kirillovna and her husband have come to stay with us; Ivan Kirillovich has grown much stouter, and is always playing the fiddle " . . . and so on and so on. So that's the position!

Ammos Fyodorovich. Yes, it's an extraordinary position, simply extraordinary. There must be some reason for it.

Luka Lukich. What is it for, Anton Antonovich, how do you account for it? Why should an Inspector come here?

The Mayor. What for! It seems it was to be! [*With a sigh*] Hitherto, and thank God for it, they have pried into other towns, now our turn has come.

Ammos Fyodorovich. I imagine, Anton Antonovich, that there is a subtle and chiefly political reason. I'll tell you what it means: Russia . . . yes . . . is meaning to go to war, and the ministers, you see, have sent an official to find out whether there is any treason here.

The Mayor. Pooh, what next! And you a sensible man, too! Treason in a district town! Is it on the frontier, pray? Why, you might gallop for three years and not reach any foreign country.

Ammos Fyodorovich. No, I tell you, you are wrong there . . . you are . . . they have all sorts of schemes in Petersburg; they may be far away, but they take stock of everything.

[2] **slip through your fingers:** to miss the chance of some petty graft.

The Mayor. They may or they may not; anyway, I have warned you, gentlemen. Mind you, I have taken measures in my own department, and I advise you to do the same. And especially you, Artemy Filippovich! Our visitor is pretty certain to want to inspect the charitable institutions under your supervision first of all, and so you take care that everything is as it should be: see that the night-caps are clean and that the patients don't look like sweeps [3] as they do on ordinary days.

Artemy Filippovich. Oh, that's no great matter. Of course they can put on clean nightcaps.

The Mayor. Yes; and over every bed put an inscription in Latin or some other language . . . that's for you to decide, Christian Ivanovich . . . the name of each disease, when each patient was taken ill, the day of the week and the month. . . . It's a pity your patients smoke such strong tobacco that it makes one sneeze when one goes in. And it would be better if there were fewer of them; he will suspect at once that there is something wrong with the management, or that the doctor does not know his business.

Artemy Filippovich. Oh, as to doctoring, Christian Ivanovich and I came to the conclusion long ago that the nearer to nature the better — we don't make use of expensive medicines. They are simple people: if they die, they'll die anyhow; if they recover, they recover anyhow. And it would be difficult for Christian Ivanovich to interview the patients; he does not know a word of Russian.[4] [HUBNER *emits a sound intermediate between* e *and* a.]

The Mayor. I should advise you too, Ammos Fyodorovich, to look after the law-court. In the hall where the applicants come with complaints and petitions the porters have taken to keeping geese with a lot of young goslings, which are always waddling about under one's feet. Of course poultry-keeping is a most laudable pursuit, and why shouldn't the porter keep them? Only it's not the thing, you know, in a public office. . . . I meant to mention it to you before, but I always forgot it somehow.

Ammos Fyodorovich. I'll order them all to be taken to my kitchen today. Won't you come to dinner with me?

The Mayor. It's a pity, too, that you have all sorts of rubbish hanging up to dry in the court itself, and there's a hunting-whip on the top of the case where deeds are kept. I know you are fond of sport, but it would be better to take it away for a time, and when the

---

[3] sweeps: chimney-sweeps, who were naturally grimy.
[4] he does not know a word of Russian: He was a German doctor.

Inspector has gone you can hang it up again if you like. And then your Assessor too . . . of course he is a man who understands his business, but he smells as though he had just come out of a distillery — that's not the thing either. I meant to speak about it long ago, but my attention was always called off to something else, I don't know what. Something can be done for it if, as he says, it is his natural smell; he might be advised to try onion or garlic or something. Christian Ivanovich might give him some drug for it. [HUBNER *gives vent to the same inarticulate sound.*]

Ammos Fyodorovich. No, there is no getting over it: he says his nurse dropped him as a baby and he has smelt a little of vodka [5] ever since.

The Mayor. Oh well, I only just mentioned it. As for the way that the business of the court is conducted, and what Andrey Ivanovich in his letter calls " failings," I can say nothing. And indeed, what is there to say? There is no man entirely free from sin. . . . That is ordained by God Himself, and it is no use the Voltairians [6] disputing it.

Ammos Fyodorovich. What do you mean by sin, Anton Antonovich? There are sins and sins. I tell every one openly that I take bribes, but what bribes? Wolfhound puppies. That's a very different matter.

The Mayor. Well, puppies or anything else, it's bribes just the same.

Ammos Fyodorovich. Oh no, Anton Antonovich. If a man takes a fur coat worth five hundred rubles [7] or a shawl for his wife . . .

The Mayor. Well, what of it if the only bribes you take are puppies? You don't believe in God; you never go to church; while I am firm in the faith, anyway, and go to church every Sunday. But you . . . oh, I know you. When you begin talking about the creation of the world, it makes my hair stand on end.[8]

Ammos Fyodorovich. But I came to my views of myself, by my own thinking.

The Mayor. Well, in some cases too much thinking is worse than none at all. I spoke of the district court — but there, to tell the truth it is not likely that any one will peep into it; it's a spot to be envied indeed, it's under the special protection of Providence. But

---

[5] **vodka:** a strong native liquor of Russia.
[6] **Voltairians:** followers of Voltaire, who believed that Reason rather than God governed the universe. See page 89.
[7] **rubles:** A ruble is worth about fifty cents.
[8] **makes my hair stand on end:** that is, because Ammos is so unorthodox.

you, Lukich, as the Inspector of Schools, must be particularly careful about the teachers. Of course they are learned men and have been educated at all sorts of colleges, but they have very strange peculiarities, naturally, inseparable from their vocation. One of them, for instance, the one with a fat face . . . I can't recollect his name, never seems able to go into his desk without making a grimace like this [*makes a grimace*] and then begins smoothing his beard from under his cravat. Of course, if he makes a face like that at one of the boys it does not matter; it may be necessary, I can't judge; but just think if he does it to a visitor — that might be a dreadful thing: the Inspector or some one else might think it was meant for him. Goodness only knows what it might lead to.

Luka Lukich. What am I to do with him? I've spoken to him over and over again. Only the other day, when our marshal of nobility came into the classroom, he made a face worse than anything I've ever seen. He did it with the best intentions, but I got a talking-to for letting free-thinking notions be put into the boys' heads.

The Mayor. And I must say a word to you about the history teacher. He is a brainy fellow, one can see, and has any amount of learning, but he lectures with such fervor that he forgets himself. I heard him once. So long as he was talking about the Assyrians and the Babylonians it was not so bad, but when he came to Alexander the Great, I can't describe how he went on. I thought the house was on fire, I did indeed! He jumped out of his desk and banged a chair on the floor with all his might. Of course Alexander the Great was a hero, but why smash the chairs? It's destroying Government property.

Luka Lukich. Yes, he is excitable. I've mentioned it to him several times. He answers: " You may say what you like, but in the cause of learning I am ready to give my life."

The Mayor. Yes, such is the mysterious dispensation of Providence; clever men are either drunkards or they make such faces that you don't know where to look.

Luka Lukich. I wouldn't wish my worst enemy to serve in the department of education! One is afraid of every one; every one interferes; every one wants to show what a clever person he is.

The Mayor. There would be nothing to mind — but it's the damnable incognito! He'll look in all of a sudden: " Aha! so you are here, my pets! And who is Judge here? " he will say. " Lyapkin-

Tyapkin." [9] — " Hand him over! And who is Charity Commissioner? " — " Zemlyanika." [10] — " Hand him over! " That's what's so awful!

Enter the POSTMASTER.

The Postmaster. Do explain, gentlemen, what's this, what official's coming?

The Mayor. Why, haven't you heard?

The Postmaster. I have heard from Pyotr Ivanovich Bobchinsky. He was in the post office just now.

The Mayor. Well, what do you think about it?

The Postmaster. What do I think? There'll be war with the Turks.[11]

Ammos Fyodorovich. My very words! Just what I thought.

The Mayor. Yes, you're both completely out of it!

The Postmaster. Indeed, but it's war with the Turks. It's all those nasty French.

The Mayor. War with the Turks! It's we who are going to catch it, not the Turks. That's certain — I have a letter.

The Postmaster. Oh, in that case, there won't be war with the Turks.

The Mayor. Well, what do you say, Ivan Kuzmich?

The Postmaster. What do I matter? How about you, Anton Antonovich?

The Mayor. Me? Well, I'm not alarmed — but there, just a bit. . . . The shopkeepers and townspeople make me uneasy. They say I am the plague of their lives; though God is my witness, if I have taken something here and there, it has been with no ill-feeling. Indeed, I fancy . . . [*Takes him by the arm and leads him aside.*] . . . I wonder whether there hasn't been some secret report against me. Why should an Inspector be sent to us? Listen, Ivan Kuzmich, couldn't you, for our common benefit, just unseal and read every letter which reaches your post office, going or coming; just to see whether there is any tale-bearing or correspondence going on. If not, you can seal it up again; or, indeed, you can deliver it open.

The Postmaster. I know, I know. . . . You need not teach me, I do that already, not so much by way of precaution as from curi-

---

[9] **Lyapkin-Tyapkin:** surname of the judge.

[10] **Zemlyanika:** surname of the charity commission.

[11] **war with the Turks:** a constant fear at this time. Later it came to actual hostilities in what we know as the Crimean War.

osity: I do like to know what's going on in the world. I assure you, it makes capital reading. It is a pleasure to read some letters — all sorts of incidents are so well described . . . and so instructive . . . better than *The Moscow News!*

The Mayor. Well, tell me, haven't you read anything about an official from Petersburg?

The Postmaster. No, nothing about a Petersburg one, but a lot about those at Saratov and Kostroma.[12] But it is a pity you don't read the letters: there are fine passages in them. For instance, a lieutenant was writing to a friend the other day, and he described a ball in a most amusing way . . . very, very nice it was. " My life, dear friend," he writes, " is passed in Elysium: Young ladies in plenty, bands playing, banners flying." . . . **It's** written with great feeling. I have kept it on purpose. Would you like me to read it?

The Mayor. Oh, it's not the moment for that now. Well then, Ivan Kuzmich, do me the favor, if any sort of complaint or report comes into your hands, keep it without hesitation.

The Postmaster. I shall be pleased.

Ammos Fyodorovich. You had better look out; you will get into trouble for that one of these days!

The Postmaster. Oh, I dare say!

The Mayor. Nonsense, nonsense. It would be a very different thing if you made public use of it, but this is a private affair.

Ammos Fyodorovich. Yes, there is mischief afoot! And I must tell you, Anton Antonovich, I was coming to offer you a present — a dog, own sister to the hound that you know. You are aware, of course, that Tcheptovich is taking proceedings against Varhovinsky, and now I'm in clover. I am coursing hares on the lands of both.[13]

The Mayor. Holy saints! I don't care about your hares now: I can't get that damned incognito out of my head. One keeps expecting that the door will open — and in will walk . . .

BOBCHINSKY *and* DOBCHINSKY *enter, breathless.*

Bobchinsky. An extraordinary incident!
Dobchinsky. A surprising piece of news!
All. What? What is it?
Dobchinsky. An unforeseen occurrence: we went to the inn . . .
Bobchinsky. [*Interrupting*] Pyotr Ivanovich and I went to the inn.

12 **Saratov and Kostroma:** provinces of that part of Russia.
13 **coursing hares on the lands of both:** receiving bribes from both.

Dobchinsky. [*Interrupting*] Oh, allow me, Pyotr Ivanovich, I'll tell the story.

Bobchinsky. Oh no, allow me . . . allow me, allow me . . . you will never find words to tell it . . .

Dobchinsky. And you will get muddled and forget something.

Bobchinsky. I shan't, upon my soul I shan't. Don't interrupt, let me tell it, don't interrupt! Gentlemen, do please tell Pyotr Ivanovich not to interfere.

The Mayor. For goodness' sake, do tell us what has happened! My heart's in my mouth. Sit down, gentlemen! Take a chair, Pyotr Ivanovich, here is a chair. [*They all sit down round the two* Pyotr Ivanoviches.] Well, now, what is it?

Bobchinsky. Allow me, I will begin at the beginning. As soon as I had the pleasure of leaving your company, when you seemed somewhat perturbed by the letter you had received . . . yes, I ran then . . . Oh, please don't interrupt, Pyotr Ivanovich! I know it all perfectly well — So, you see I ran in to Korobkin's. And not finding Korobkin at home, I called at Rastakovsky's; and not finding Rastakovsky at home, I went on to see Ivan Kuzmich here, so as to tell him the news you had received, and as I came away I met Pyotr Ivanovich . . .

Dobchinsky. [*Interrupting*] Near the stall where they sell pies.

Bobchinsky. [*Waving him aside*] Near the stall where they sell pies. Yes, when I met Pyotr Ivanovich I said to him, " Have you heard the news Anton Antonovich has from a trustworthy Correspondent? And Pyotr Ivanovich had heard it already from your housekeeper, Avdotya, who had been sent to Filip Antonovich Potchetchuev's on some errand, I don't know what . . .

Dobchinsky. [*Interrupting*] To get a keg for French vodka.

Bobchinsky. [*Waving him aside*] To get a keg for French vodka. So we went, Pyotr Ivanovich and I, to Potchetchuev's. Please, Pyotr Ivanovich . . . er . . . don't interrupt, please don't interrupt! We were going to Potchetchuev's, and on the way Pyotr Ivanovich said, " Let us go into the inn. My stomach . . . I've had nothing to eat all day, and there is a quaking in my stomach." Yes, in Pyotr Ivanovich's stomach. . . . " And they have just got in a new lot of smoked salmon," he said, " so let's have lunch." No sooner had we walked into the inn than a young man . . .

Dobchinsky. [*Interrupting*] Of pleasant appearance, not wearing official uniform . . .

Bobchinsky. Of pleasant appearance, not wearing official uniform, was walking about the room like this, and in his face such a look of deliberation, so to speak. . . . A physiognomy . . . gestures, and here [*twirls his hand about his forehead*] a vast deal of everything. I had a sort of foreboding, and said to Pyotr Ivanovich, " There is something behind this." Yes, and Pyotr Ivanovich had already beckoned to the innkeeper . . . to Vlass, the innkeeper; his wife was brought to bed three weeks ago, and a smart little baby too, he will keep an inn like his father. Calling Vlass up, Pyotr Ivanovich asks him on the quiet: " Who is that young man? " he says, and Vlass answers: " That," he says . . . Oh, don't interrupt me, Pyotr Ivanovich, please don't interrupt me, you can't tell it, you really can't; you lisp, it's one of your teeth, I know, makes you lisp. . . . " That young man," he says, " is an official, yes, and has come from Petersburg, and his name," he says, " is Ivan Alexandrovich Hlestakov, and he is going," he says, " to the province of Saratov, and he's very strange in his deportment," he says, " he has been here nearly a fortnight, he goes on staying in the house, takes everything on tick [14] and won't pay a penny." As he was saying this, an inspiration dawned upon me. " Ah! " I said to Pyotr Ivanovich . . .

Dobchinsky. No, Pyotr Ivanovich, it was I who said " Ah! "

Bobchinsky. You said it first, and then I said it. " Ah! " we cried, Pyotr Ivanovich and I. " But what is his object in staying here when he has to go to Saratov? " Yes. Why, he is that official, not a doubt of it!

The Mayor. Who? What official?

Bobchinsky. The official that you have had warning of — the Government Inspector.

The Mayor. [*In alarm*] Good God, what are you saying? It can't be!

Dobchinsky. It is! He pays no money and he does not go away. Who can it be if not he? And his traveling pass is for Saratov.

Bobchinsky. It is he, upon my word, it is. So keenly observant; looked into everything. He saw that Pyotr Ivanovich and I were eating smoked salmon, — chiefly on account of Pyotr Ivanovich's stomach — yes; so he peeped into our plates. It gave me quite a turn.

The Mayor. Lord have mercy on us sinners! What room is he in?

Dobchinsky. Number five, under the stairs.

Bobchinsky. The very room in which the officers who were here last year had a fight.

[14] **takes everything on tick:** has everything charged to his bill.

The Mayor. And has he been here long?

Dobchinsky. A fortnight already. He came on St. Vassily's day.[15]

The Mayor. A whole fortnight! [*Aside.*] Saints alive! Holy martyrs, get me out of this! Within this fortnight the sergeant's wife has been flogged! The prisoners have not had their rations! The streets . . . like a regular pothouse! and the filth! Disgrace! Ignominy! [*Clutches his head.*]

Artemy Filippovich. What do you think, Anton Antonovich? Should we all go in a body to the inn?

Ammos Fyodorovich. No, no! Let the provost, the clergy, and the merchants go first; in the book of John the Mason [16] it says . . .

The Mayor. No, no; allow me to decide. I have had difficulties before and they have passed off safely, and I have been thanked into the bargain. Maybe God will pull us through this time too. [*Turning to* BOBCHINSKY.] You say he is a young man?

BOBCHINSKY. Yes, he is — not more than twenty-three or twenty-four.

The Mayor. That's as well; it is easier to see through a young man. It is hard work with an old devil, but a young man is all on the surface. You see to your own departments, gentlemen, while I'll go round myself, alone, or with Pyotr Ivanovich here, privately, as though taking a walk, to see that visitors to the town are suffering no inconvenience. Hey, Svistunov?

Svistunov. What is your pleasure?

The Mayor. Go at once for the Police Superintendent; but no, I shall want you. Tell some one to fetch the Police Superintendent as quick as he can, and then come here. [SVISTUNOV *runs off post-haste.*]

Artemy Filippovich. Come along, come along, Ammos Fyodorovich. There really may be trouble.

Ammos Fyodorovich. But what have you to fear? Put clean nightcaps on your patients and there is no finding anything amiss.

Artemy Filippovich. Nightcaps! The patients are ordered clear soup, and there is such a stink of cabbage in all my corridors that you have to hold your nose.

Ammos Fyodorovich. My mind is at rest. When you come to think of it, whoever would look into the district court? And if he does peep into some document, God help him! Here I have been sitting in the Judge's seat for fifteen years, but if ever I look into the

[15] St. Vassily's day: the Russian form of St. Basil (329–379 A.D.) whose day is celebrated by the Greek church January 1.

[16] book of John the Mason: Probably John Desaguliers, a Frenchman, one of the organizers of the Masonic Order in the eighteenth century.

statement of a case I chuck it away in despair! Solomon himself could not make out the rights and wrongs of it.

The JUDGE, *the* CHARITY COMMISSIONER, *the* SCHOOL INSPECTOR, *and the* POSTMASTER *go out, and in the doorway run into* SVISTUNOV.

The Mayor. Well, is the chaise there?

Svistunov. Yes, sir.

The Mayor. Go into the street . . . but no, stay! Go and fetch . . . But where are the others? Surely you haven't come back alone? I sent word that Prohorov [17] was to be here. Where is Prohorov?

Svistunov. Prohorov is at the police station, but he can't be put to any use.

The Mayor. How's that?

Svistunov. Well, he was brought in this morning dead drunk. They have poured two buckets of water over him, but he's not come to himself yet.

The Mayor. [*Clutching his head*] Oh, my God! my God! Make haste into the street . . . no, run into the other room first and bring me my sword and new hat. Well, Pyotr Ivanovich, let us be off!

Bobchinsky. Me too, me too! Do let me go too, Anton Antonovich!

The Mayor. No, no, Pyotr Ivanovich, you can't! It would be awkward, and besides, there is not room in the chaise.[18]

Bobchinsky. Never mind, never mind, I'll manage: I'll hop along after the chaise. If only I can have a peep through the door or something, to see what he will do and all that . . .

The Mayor. [*Taking his sword from* SVISTUNOV] Go at once and get the watchmen. Let each one of them take . . . Ah, what scratches there are on the sword! That confounded blackguard Abdulin — sees his Mayor with an old sword and never thinks of sending me a new one from his shop. Ah, deceitful wretches! And I'll be bound the rascals are getting up petitions on the sly. Every one of them is to take a street . . . oh, dash it, street! I mean, a broom — and sweep the street leading to the inn, and sweep it clean too . . . Do you hear? And you mind, now! I know you; you are hand in glove [19] with all sorts of people and slipping silver spoons into your boots — you had better look out, I have a sharp eye! What have you been up to with Tchernyaev, the draper, eh? He was giving you two

---

[17] **Prohorov:** one of the police officials.
[18] **chaise:** carriage.
[19] **hand in glove:** on intimate terms.

yards of cloth for your uniform and you walked off with the whole piece! You'd better be careful! You take more than's due to your rank. Go along!

Enter UHOVYORTOV, *the* POLICE COMMISSIONER

The Mayor. Ah, Stepan Ilyich! Kindly tell me, where had you vanished to? It's beyond everything.

Uhovyortov. I was just here by the gate.

The Mayor. Well, listen, Stepan Ilyich! The official from Petersburg has arrived. What arrangements have you made?

Uhovyortov. According to your instructions, I have sent Constable Pugovitsin with the watchmen to sweep the pavements.

The Mayor. And where is Derzhimorda?

Uhovyortov. He has done with the fire-hose.

The Mayor. And Prohorov's drunk?

Uhovyortov. Yes, sir.

The Mayor. How could you allow it?

Uhovyortov. Goodness only knows. There was a fight just outside the town yesterday — he went to settle it and came back drunk.

The Mayor. I tell you what, you do this: Constable Pugovitsin . . . he is a tall fellow, so let him stand on the bridge to make a good appearance. And look sharp and pull down the old fence beside the cobbler's and stick in a pole with a wisp of straw tied at the top, as though new streets were being laid out. The more destruction there is everywhere, the more it shows the activity of the town authorities. Ah, I forgot that beside that fence there is a rubbish heap it would take forty wagons to shift. What a nasty town it is, to be sure! Wherever you put up a monument, or even a plain fence, people shoot rubbish there of all sorts — I don't know where they get it from! [*Sighs.*] And if the official asks the police whether they are satisfied, they are all to say, " Perfectly satisfied, your honor "; and if anybody is dissatisfied, I'll give him something to satisfy him afterwards. . . . Och, och, och! I am to blame, very much to blame. [*Takes up the hat-box instead of the hat.*] God grant it all goes off well — and soon too, and I'll put up a candle [20] such as no one has ever put up before. I'll make every scoundrelly shopkeeper produce a hundred-weight of wax. Oh, my God, my God! Let us go, Pyotr Ivanovich! [*Is putting the cardboard box on his head instead of the hat.*]

---

[20] **put up a candle:** burn a candle before a shrine in the church.

Uhovyortov. Anton Antonovich, that's the box and not your hat.
The Mayor. [*Flinging down the box*] If it's a box, it's a box,
damn it! Oh, and if he should ask why the almshouse church has not
been built, though a grant was made for it five years ago, don't forget
to say that the building was begun, but it was burnt down. I sent
in a report about it. Or some one may forget like a fool and say it
was never begun. And tell Derzhimorda not to be too free with his
fists; he keeps order by giving every one a black eye — innocent and
guilty. Come along, Pyotr Ivanovich, come along! [*Goes out and
comes back.*] And don't let the soldiers go into the street without
anything on; those wretched fellows in the garrison put their coats
on over their shirts and nothing on their legs. [*All go out.*]

ANNA ANDREYEVNA *and* MARYA ANTONOVNA *run on the stage.*

Anna. Where are they, where are they? Oh dear! [*Opening the
door.*] Papa! Antosha! [21] Anton! [*Speaking quickly to* MARYA]
And it's all your doing, it's all because of you. You would be daw-
dling, first a pin, then a fichu! [*Runs to the window and calls.*]
Anton, Anton, where are you off to? Well, has he come? The Inspector? Has he a moustache? What sort of a moustache?
The Mayor's Voice. Presently, presently, my dear!
Anna. Presently? That's a nice thing! Presently! I don't want
it to be presently. . . . One thing you might tell me, what is he — a
colonel? Eh? [*Scornfully.*] He is gone! I won't let him forget it!
And it's all because of her: " Mamma, Mamma, do wait. I'll just pin
my fichu behind, I won't be a minute! " This is what comes of your
minute! Here we have heard nothing! And it's all your confounded
vanity: you heard the Postmaster was here, so you had to go prinking
before the looking-glass, turning this way and that way. She fancies
he is sweet on her, and all the time he is making faces at you behind
your back.
Marya. Well, it can't be helped, Mamma. We shall know all
about it in another hour or two.
Anna. In an hour or two! Thanks very much. A nice answer!
I wonder you didn't tell me we shall know better still in a month.
[*Leans out of window.*] Hey, Avdotya? Eh? I say, Avdotya, have
you heard that somebody has arrived? . . . You haven't? What a
silly girl! He waved you off? Let him wave; you should have got
it out of him all the same. Couldn't find that out! Her head's full
of nonsense, thinks of nothing but young men. What? They went

21 **Antosha:** pet name for Anton

off so quickly! But you should have run after the chaise. Run now, run along! Do you hear, run and ask where they are going: and mind you find out what kind of gentleman he is, what he is like — do you hear? Look through the door and find out everything, and what color his eyes are, whether they are black — and come back at once, do you hear? Make haste, make haste, make haste, make haste! [*Goes on shouting till the curtain falls.*]

The curtain falls upon them both standing at the window.

(*Constance Garnett*)

SUMMARY OF THE REST OF THE PLAY

In a scene at the inn we discover that the supposed Inspector Hlestakov is really only a petty official who has lost all his money gambling. Because he cannot pay for the meals he has eaten, he is expecting to be arrested, and so when the Mayor enters to pay his humble respects there is a laughable misunderstanding. As soon as Hlestakov realizes the situation, he assumes the rôle thrust upon him and gladly accepts the hospitality of the Mayor's home, is fêted by all the town, is shown all the public institutions and meets all the officials, who do their best to impress him. The false Inspector tells the most extravagant lies about the balls and dinners given in his St. Petersburg mansion. He makes love to the Mayor's daughter and finally becomes engaged to her, whereupon the Mayor is so overcome with his importance as to antagonize many of the townspeople. Hlestakov, fearing discovery, borrows money from all the fawning merchants and officials, and leaves town supposedly for a day only. Before going, however, he writes a long letter to a friend of his describing his experience and ridiculing all the officials of the place, and mails it in the postoffice. The Postmaster, to forestall what he supposes an unfavorable report of his department to the government, opens the letter and discovers the truth. The letter is carried to the Mayor and read before a group of officials, to the astonishment of all and the complete humiliation of the pretentious Mayor. He is in the midst of an angry tirade against the imposter, when a messenger announces that the real Inspector is at the inn and requests the Mayor's attendance at once. Upon the whole assemblage completely petrified by this unexpected news the final curtain falls.

SUGGESTIONS FOR STUDY

1. Point out the nature of the graft or incompetence in each department of the city government. How does Gogol make us laugh at this situation instead of denouncing it seriously? Where do you find " unseen tears " which Pushkin said were behind Gogol's laughter?

2. Select some good example of the Russian fatalism derived from the Orient; that is, accepting things as they exist, considering that they are destined to be so.

3. Do you see any conditions which parallel some in America today? If so, which?

4. Where in this act do you find some of the typical " stage business " of farce? Show how the Mayor works himself into a perfect frenzy.

5. In the speeches of Anna note carefully where her speeches are addressed to various characters, and when a form of talking to herself. How does she remind you of the Lady in *No Smoking?*

6. Consider the acting possibilities of this scene for an amateur group. Plan costumes and stage business.

MIKHAIL IRIEVICH LERMONTOV (1814–1841)

Strangely enough Lermontov's name was derived from the Scotch name Learmont, for one of his seventeenth-century ancestors was a Scottish adventurer who entered the Russian service. Upon the death of his mother, when the boy was only three years old, his grandmother took him away from his father and brought him up in preparation for the best Russian society. He early developed poetic tendencies and was greatly influenced by Byron and Shelley, whom he somewhat resembled in fire and intensity of disposition. At the age of twenty-two his first fame came with a poem upon the death of Pushkin, so revolutionary in its character as to bring about Lermontov's banishment to the Caucasus. But this proved fortunate, for the beauty of this mountain region inspired his greatest poetry. Upon his return to St. Petersburg he mingled in the gay military society of the capital for about two years until he was again banished to the Caucasus for participation in a duel. Only a year later he became involved in a second duel in which he was fatally shot at the age of twenty-seven.

His greatest long poems are *The Demon, A Novice,* which represents the dying confession of a rebellious young man, and *The Song of the Merchant Kalashnikov* based on the old epic folk tales. He also wrote a prose novel *A Hero of Our Times* in which he painted " a portrait composed of the vices of the generation of which he was a contemporary." When we consider that his work was all produced in about eight years by a youth in his twenties, it is remarkable that he should have attained the place he holds. One is reminded of the meteoric careers of Shelley and Keats, who had died about twenty years before him. The attitude of Russians toward his poetry is suggested in the words of one of their critics: " Pushkin is the day-luminary of Russian poetry, and Lermontov the night-luminary."

CAPTIVE KNIGHT

Silent I sit by the prison's high window,
Where through the bars the untamed blue is breaking.
Flecks in the azure, the free birds are playing;
Watching them fly there, my shamed heart is aching.

But on my sinful lips never a prayer,   5
Never a song in the praise of my charmer;
All I recall are far fights and old battles,
My heavy sword and my old iron armor.

Now in stone armor I hopelessly languish,
And a stone helmet my hot head encases,   10
This shield is proof against arrows and sword-play,
And without whip, without spur, my horse races.

Time is my horse, the swift-galloping charger,
I've for a visor this bleak prison grating,
My prison walls are my heavy stone armor;   15
Shielded by cast-iron doors, I am waiting.

Hurry, O fast-flying Time, go more quickly!
In my new armor I suffocate, reeling.
I shall alight, with Death holding my stirrup,
And raise this visor, my cold face revealing.   20

(Babette Deutsch and Avrahm Yarmolinsky)

ALEXEY TOLSTOY (1817–1875)

Though Count Alexey Tolstoy, the poet, belonged to the same general family (tracing its roots to the thirteenth century) as Count Leo Tolstoy, the novelist, nevertheless the two were only distant relatives. Alexey Tolstoy was a physical giant — reputed to have been able to unbend horseshoes — with a great love of the wild spaces of the steppes, and of the bear hunt. Yet at the age of six, he says he began " soiling paper with his verses," and the ambition to be a literary artist dominated his life. So eager was he to perfect his style that he did not send any of his poems to publishers until he was thirty-seven. His poetry is distinguished from that of the other Russians in that he writes in a major key of heartiness, humor, and health, whereas the minor key is the prevailing Russian choice. His work falls into three classes: the nationalist poetry celebrating the Old Russia, humorous poetry, and pure lyrics, many of which have been set to music. An example of the first is a long ballad about a hero Potok who falls asleep in the tenth century and awakens in Moscow in the sixteenth century, then again in St. Petersburg in the nineteenth. Through the eyes of this ancient visitor the poet shows the weaknesses and absurdities of modern life. However, Tolstoy, being neither an extreme radical nor an extreme conservative, pleased neither side, and spent most of his life away from the court though Tsar Alexander II was always his warm personal friend. Much of Tolstoy's humorous poetry centers around the character Kosina Prutkov, a complacent and naïve clerk in the Ministry of Finance, who parodies other Russian poets. In Tolstoy's lyric poetry there is delicacy, fervor, and rhythmic swing hard to convey in translation.

IT WAS IN EARLY–EARLY SPRING

It was in early-early spring;
New blades of grass were peering,
Rivulets ran, the warmth was soft,
Wood's greenness was transparent.
The shepherd's horn at break of day   5
Was yet unheard in village;
The forest ferns still had their fronds
In spikes of laces curling.
It was in early-early spring
White gleamed the silver birches —   10
When I beheld thine eyes to smile
From under drooping eyelids. . . .
It was in answer to my love
Thine eyelashes did tremble —
O life! O woods! O sunshine clear!   15
O youth! O hopes high soaring! . . .
And tears rose up into my eyes
As I adored thy features. . . .
It was in early-early spring —
White gleamed the silver birches —   20
It was the morning of our life!
O happiness! O tears!
O life! O woods! O sunshine clear!
Fresh breath of silver birches!

(Mme. N. Jarintzov)

NO WORD FROM YOU

No word from you, no answer and no greeting. . . .
A desert lies the world between us two.
My troubled thought, inquiring and unanswered,
Weighs on my heart, and heavy fear throbs through.
But can it be, that 'midst the hours of anger   5
Our past is gone, not leaving any trace?
A subtle sound of melody forgotten,
A falling star that plunges into space? . . .

(Mme. N. Jarintzov)

MY NATIVE LAND

Hail to thee, my native land!
Steeds in prairies straying,
Eagles screaming in the sky,
Wolves through snowstorms baying!

Hail, beloved motherland!   5
Hail, thou dreaming forest!
Midnight song of nightingale
Clouds and steppes and tempest!

(Mme. N. Jarintzov)

IF THOU LOVEST

If thou lovest, reason scatter;
If thou threat'nest, make it matter;
If thou swearest, make it hot;
If thou hittest, miss him not!
Dost thou argue, do it boldly;   5
Dost thou punish, do it coldly;
In forgiving, hold not back;
And in feasting, have no lack!

(Mme. N. Jarintzov)

NIKOLAY ALEXEYEVICH NEKRASOV (1821–1877)

In contrast to Alexey Tolstoy, Nekrasov is the poet of the down-and-out. Though he was born of good family, his youth, especially during his three-year stay at the University of St. Petersburg, was spent in most abject poverty. At times he lived on about eight cents a day, slept in the streets, and, to avoid starvation, turned his hand to any work that offered. But these experiences gave him knowledge of the dregs of the city, which he turned to good account, picturing for the first time in Russian poetry cabmen or convicts, printers or pickpockets as they came into his ken. The titles of some of his long poems are in themselves suggestive of the contents: *Frost — the Red-Nose, The Unfortunate, Peasant's Children, Russian Women, The Thief, The Pedlars,* and perhaps his most famous, *Who Lives Happily in Russia?*

Nekrasov is significant in Russian literature not only for ushering in the proletarian element, which has figured so largely since in the work of Dostoevsky, Gorki, and others, but also for introducing a rougher, more vigorous metrical form than was fashionable in his day. Thus in both subject matter and style he anticipated the moderns, and for that reason has gained in reputation since his death more than many of his contemporaries. He was also a determining literary force in his own time through the review which he edited for many years, and in which he introduced Turgenev, Dostoevsky, and many others to the Russian intellectual world.

AT TWILIGHT

This little poem might be taken as a dedication of Nekrasov's pen to the wretched and the unfortunate that he saw about him. The incident might be compared to that in Lincoln's life, when he saw the slaves being sold at the block, and determined that if he ever had opportunity to hit that evil, he would hit it hard.

At twilight as I crossed the market place,
　I heard the cracking of a wielded whip;
There did I see a little peasant girl,
　Head bowed, back bent, beneath a powerful grip.

She made no outcry as the lashes fell.　　　　　　　　5
　Only the hisses of the outraged air
Were heard in protest, but I called my Muse:
　" Behold! That is your sister over there."

　　　　　　　　　　　　　　　　　(*Anonymous Translation*)

THE SALT SONG

Who Lives Happily in Russia?, from which this song is taken, is Nekrasov's most famous poem. It relates the adventures of seven peasants who, falling into a dispute over this question, determine to answer it by going about and interviewing all the types of people that any of them have envied as being happy. The priest, the soldier, the wife of a prosperous peasant, and many others are asked the question. All give a negative answer, elaborating upon their misfortunes to prove their point. The inquirers finally come to the conclusion that there is no such thing as a happy person in Russia. But the poem ends with a note of confidence in the future of the nation in spite of present conditions. "The Salt Song" gives a poignant picture of a famine so terrible that no salt is to be had to give taste to the bread, which the mother literally salts with her tears. The abrupt meter follows the original closely.

God's will be done!
No food he'll try,
The youngest son —
Look, he will die.

Two bites, or one —
He pouts, he sighs,
The little son.   15
" More salt! " he cries.

A crust I got,   5
Another bit —
He touched it not:
" Put salt on it! "

The bit appears
Again all floured,
And wet with tears,
It is devoured.   20

Of salt no shred,
No pinch I see!   10
" Take flour instead,"
God whispered me.

The mother said
She'd saved her dear . . .
Salt was the bread —
How salt the tear!

(Babette Deutsch and Avrahm Yarmolinsky)

SUGGESTIONS FOR STUDY

1. In the lyrics of Lermontov, Alexey Tolstoy, and Nekrasov, indicate the mood or emotional tone of each. Which have the most marked singing qualities, the greatest vigor, the greatest originality?

2. Wherein do these poems show different aspects of the Romantic Movement? Explain the meaning of " Captive Knight." What English romantic poets does it suggest?

3. How do Tolstoy's poems illustrate the heartiness and happiness of his life in contrast to that of most Russian writers?

4. In what way are Nekrasov's poems different from the others in this group? How does his place in Russian poetry show some resemblance to Whitman's in American? What marked difference is there in their style?

IVAN SERGEYEVICH TURGENEV (1818–1883)

It was through Turgenev that western Europe first became aware of Russian literature. Even so great a critic as the Frenchman Renan once said that mute Russia had become vocal in Turgenev, whereas in truth, even before the days of Pushkin, Russia had produced a large body of literature. But in a sense Renan was right, for the translation of Turgenev's writings into various European languages opened communication with that apparently voiceless region, and led to the great vogue which the Russian novel had during the late nineteenth century throughout the Western world.

Turgenev's life presents striking contrasts of tragedy and triumph. Though born into a wealthy, aristocratic family of Orel, in central Russia, his childhood was darkened by the quarrels between his corrupt father and his shrewish mother. Later, after the death of the father, the young man and his mother were in constant disagreement about his love affairs and his preference for literature over a government career. In 1845 she cut off her son's income, and for five years he mingled with impecunious writers and artists both in Russia and abroad. At the death of his mother in 1850 he came into his inheritance and returned to his Russian home. Two years later he first made his name generally known through the publication of *A Sportsman's Sketches*, short stories of the peasant life he observed while on hunting expeditions. The sympathetic portrayal of the wrongs and hardships of the serfs brought Turgenev under government suspicion, which was only increased by his fervent obituary notice of Gogol soon after. Banished to his estate for almost two years, he celebrated his final freedom by leaving Russia permanently, except for occasional brief visits. Thus through long years of residence in European capitals, especially Paris, he became the literary link between his native land and the Western nations. For, expatriate though he was, his writing was always of Russia and the Russians.

He had a gift for catching, between the covers of his novels, characters that revealed certain native traits with startling clarity, such as Rudin, in the novel of that name, the charming cultivated gentleman incapable of action and decision, and Bazarov, in *Fathers and Sons*, the unconventional but high-minded "nihilist," from whom the radical group in Russia later adopted the appellation. All of his novels are fraught with social significance for they reflect the impulses and questionings of the intellectual groups which led to the emancipation of the serfs and other government reforms of the mid-nineteenth century. Not that his novels were in any sense propaganda, but rather that his rich pictures of native life covering the forties through the eighties were inevitable reflections of public thought. Turgenev is also particularly skillful in painting the varied landscape of Russia, seen often of course in retrospect, and therefore surprising in its clearness. In fact for a total and objective view of Russian life of his day, Turgenev has never been excelled, though in psychological intensity and analysis of the inner life of man he must yield the crown to Dostoevsky and Tolstoy. His six great novels are *Rudin, A Nobleman's Retreat, On the Eve, Fathers and Sons, Smoke,* and *Virgin Soil.* Besides, he has written many sketches and stories.

In person Turgenev was a giant of a man with a gentle, rather melancholy expression. In later years the dignity of his appearance was increased by his white hair and beard. He was invariably the aristocrat, polished and punctilious.

BIRYUK [1]

An ardent hunter, Turgenev spent many days in his youth roaming through the countryside and forest. But unlike the ordinary hunter he observed and bagged more than his game, for the insight into peasant life which he caught and fashioned into his *A Sportsman's Sketches* not only brought him personal fame, but brought to a focus that latent conscience about the wrongs of the serfs which had already troubled many thinking Russians. It is said that Tsar Alexander II was influenced by this book toward the emancipation of the serfs, which he proclaimed in 1861. Since the freeing of our American slaves so nearly coincides with this date, some writers have drawn a parallel between *A Sportsman's Sketches* and *Uncle Tom's Cabin,* but the two books have little resemblance to each other. Turgenev had none of the reformer's zeal of Mrs. Stowe, but simply recorded his experiences in an artistic form, and the facts spoke for themselves.

I was coming back from hunting one evening alone in a racing droshky.[2] I was six miles from home; my good trotting mare galloped bravely along the dusty road, pricking up her ears with an occasional snort; my weary dog stuck close to the hind wheels, as though he were fastened there. A tempest was coming on. In front, a huge, purplish storm cloud slowly rose from behind the forest; long gray rain clouds flew over my head and to meet me; the willows stirred and whispered restlessly. The suffocating heat changed suddenly to a damp chilli-

---

[1] **Biryuk:** Russian for wolf. In the province of Orel it is used to denote a lone, misanthropic man.

[2] **droshky:** four-wheeled carriage commonly used at that time for country travel.

ness; the darkness rapidly thickened. I gave the horse a lash with the reins, descended a steep slope, pushed across a dry watercourse overgrown with brushwood, mounted the hill, and drove into the forest. The road ran before me, bending between thick hazel bushes, now enveloped in darkness; I advanced with difficulty. The droshky jumped up and down over the hard roots of the ancient oaks and limes, which were continually intersected by deep ruts — the tracks of cart wheels; my horse began to stumble. A violent wind suddenly began to roar overhead; the trees blustered; big drops of rain fell with slow tap and splash on the leaves; there came a flash of lightning and a clap of thunder. The rain fell in torrents. I went on a step or so, and soon was forced to stop; my horse foundered; I could not see an inch before me. I managed to take refuge somehow in a spreading bush. Crouching down and covering my face, I waited patiently for the storm to blow over, when suddenly, in a flash of lightning, I saw a tall figure on the road. I began to stare intently in that direction — the figure seemed to have sprung out of the ground near my droshky.

" Who's that? " inquired a ringing voice.

" Why, who are you? "

" I'm the forester here."

I mentioned my name.

" Oh, I know! Are you on your way home? "

" Yes. But, you see, in such a storm . . ."

" Yes, there is a storm," replied the voice.

A pale flash of lightning lit up the forester from head to foot; a brief crashing clap of thunder followed at once upon it. The rain lashed with redoubled force.

" It won't be over just directly," the forester went on.

" What's to be done? "

" I'll take you to my hut, if you like," he said abruptly.

" That would be a service."

" Please to take your seat."

He went up to the mare's head, took her by the bit, and pulled her up. We set off. I held on to the cushion of the droshky, which rocked " like a boat on the sea," and called my dog. My poor mare splashed with difficulty through the mud, slipped and stumbled; the forester hovered before the shafts to right and to left like a ghost. We drove rather a long while; at last my guide stopped. " Here we are home, sir," he observed in a quiet voice. The gate creaked; some puppies barked a welcome. I raised my head, and in a flash of lightning I made out a small hut in the middle of a large yard, fenced in with hurdles.[3] From the one little window there was a dim light. The forester led his horse up to the steps and knocked at the door. " Coming, coming! " we heard in a little shrill voice; there was the patter of bare feet, the bolt creaked, and a girl of twelve, in a little old smock tied round the waist with list,[4] appeared in the doorway with a lantern in her hand.

" Show the gentleman a light," he said to her, " and I will put your droshky in the shed."

The little girl glanced at me, and went into the hut. I followed her.

The forester's hut consisted of one room, smoky, low-pitched, and empty, without curtains or partition. A tattered sheepskin hung on the wall. On the bench lay a single-barreled gun; in the corner lay a heap of rags; two great pots stood near the oven. A pine splinter was burning on the table, flickering up and dying down mournfully. In the very middle of the hut hung a cradle, suspended from the end of a long horizontal pole. The little girl put out the lantern, sat down on a tiny stool, and with her right hand began swinging the cradle, while with her left she attended to the smoldering pine splinter. I looked round — my heart sank within me; it's not cheering to go into a peasant's hut at night. The baby in the cradle breathed hard and fast.

" Are you all alone here? " I asked the little girl.

" Yes," she uttered, hardly audibly.

" You're the forester's daughter? "

" Yes," she whispered.

The door creaked, and the forester, bending his head, stepped across the threshold. He lifted the lantern from the floor, went up to the table, and lighted a candle.

" I dare say you're not used to the splinter light? " said he, and he shook back his curls.

I looked at him. Rarely has it been my fortune to behold such a comely creature. He was tall, broad-shouldered, and in marvelous proportion. His powerful muscles stood out in strong relief under his wet homespun shirt. A curly, black beard hid half of his stern and manly face; small brown eyes looked out boldly from under broad eyebrows which met in the middle. He stood before me, his arms held lightly akimbo.

I thanked him, and asked his name.

---

[3] **hurdles:** twigs interwoven to form a fence.
[4] **list:** a piece of cloth.

" My name's Foma," he answered, " and my nickname's Biryuk."
" Oh, you're Biryuk."

I looked with redoubled curiosity at him. From my Yermolaï [5] and others I had often heard stories about the forester Biryuk, whom all the peasants of the surrounding districts feared as they feared fire. According to them there had never been such a master of his business in the world before. " He won't let you carry off a handful of brushwood; he'll drop upon you like a fall of snow, whatever time it may be, even in the middle of the night, and you needn't think of resisting him — he's strong, and as cunning as the devil. . . . And there's no getting at him, anyhow; neither by brandy nor by money; there's no snare he'll walk into. More than once good folks have planned to put him out of the world, but no — it's never come off."

That was how the neighboring peasants spoke of Biryuk.

" So you're Biryuk," I repeated; " I've heard talk of you, brother. They say you show no mercy to any one."

" I do my duty," he answered grimly; " it's not right to eat the master's bread for nothing."

He took an axe from his girdle and began splitting splinters.

" Have you no wife? " I asked him.

" No," he answered, with a vigorous sweep of the axe.

" She's dead, I suppose? "

" No . . . yes . . . she's dead," he added, and turned away. I was silent; he raised his eyes and looked at me.

" She ran away with a traveling peddler," he brought out with a bitter smile. The little girl hung her head; the baby waked up and began crying; the little girl went to the cradle. " There, give it him," said Biryuk, thrusting a dirty feeding-bottle into her hand. " Him, too, she abandoned," he went on in an undertone, pointing to the baby. He went up to the door, stopped, and turned round.

" A gentleman like you," he began, " wouldn't care for our bread, I dare say, and except bread, I've — "

" I'm not hungry."

" Well, that's for you to say. I would have heated the samovar,[6] but I've no tea. . . . I'll go and see how your horse is getting on."

He went out and slammed the door. I looked round again. The hut struck me as more melancholy than ever. The bitter smell of stale smoke choked my breathing unpleasantly. The little girl did not stir from her place, and did not raise her eyes; from time to time she

---

5 **Yermolaï:** his servant.
6 **samovar:** Russian tea-urn heated by charcoal fire.

jogged the cradle, and timidly pulled her slipping smock up onto her shoulder; her bare legs hung motionless.

" What's your name? " I asked her.

" Ulita," she said, her mournful little face drooping more than ever.

The forester came in and sat down on the bench.

" The storm's passing over," he observed, after a brief silence; " if you wish it, I will guide you out of the forest."

I got up; Biryuk took his gun and examined the fire pan.

" What's that for? " I inquired.

" There's mischief in the forest. . . . They're cutting a tree down on Mares' Ravine," he added, in reply to my look of inquiry.

" Could you hear it from here? "

" I can hear it outside."

We went out together. The rain had ceased. Heavy masses of storm cloud were still huddled in the distance; from time to time there were long flashes of lightning; but here and there overhead the dark blue sky was already visible; stars twinkled through the swiftly flying clouds. The outline of the trees, drenched with rain, and stirred by the wind, began to stand out in the darkness. We listened. The forester took off his cap and bent his head. . . . " Th — . . . there! " he said suddenly, and he stretched out his hand: " see what a night he's pitched on." I had heard nothing but the rustle of the leaves. Biryuk led the mare out of the shed. " But, perhaps," he added aloud, " this way I shall miss him."

" I'll go with you . . . if you like? "

" Certainly," he answered, and he backed the horse in again; " we'll catch him in a trice, and then I'll take you. Let's be off."

We started, Biryuk in front, I following him. Heaven only knows how he found out his way, but he only stopped once or twice, and then merely to listen to the strokes of the axe.

" There," he muttered, " do you hear? do you hear? "

" Why, where? "

Biryuk shrugged his shoulders. We went down into the ravine; the wind was still for an instant; the rhythmical strokes reached my hearing distinctly. Biryuk glanced at me and shook his head. We went farther through the wet bracken and nettles. A slow muffled crash was heard. . . .

" He's felled it," muttered Biryuk. Meantime the sky had grown clearer and clearer; there was a faint light in the forest. We clambered at last out of the ravine.

" Wait here a little," the forester whispered to me. He bent down, and, raising his gun above his head, vanished among the bushes. I began listening with strained attention. Across the continual roar of the wind faint sounds from close by reached me; there was a cautious blow of an axe on the brushwood, the crash of wheels, the snort of a horse. . . .

"Where are you off to? Stop! " the iron voice of Biryuk thundered suddenly. Another voice was heard in a pitiful shriek, like a trapped hare. . . . A struggle was beginning.

"No, no, you've made a mistake," Biryuk declared, panting; "you're not going to get off. . . ."

I rushed in the direction of the noise, and ran up to the scene of the conflict, stumbling at every step. A felled tree lay on the ground, and near it Biryuk was busily engaged holding the thief down and binding his hands behind his back with a kerchief. I came closer. Biryuk got up and set him on his feet. I saw a peasant drenched with rain, in tatters, and with a long, disheveled beard. A sorry little nag, half covered with a stiff mat, was standing by, together with a rough cart. The forester did not utter a word; the peasant too was silent; his head was shaking.

"Let him go," I whispered in Biryuk's ears; "I'll pay for the tree."

Without a word Biryuk took the horse by the mane with his left hand; in his right he held the thief by the belt. "Now turn round, you rat! " he said grimly.

"The bit of an axe there, take it," muttered the peasant.

"No reason to lose it, certainly," said the forester, and he picked up the axe. We started. I walked behind. . . . The rain began sprinkling again, and soon fell in torrents. With difficulty we made our way to the hut. Biryuk pushed the captured horse into the middle of the yard, led the peasant into the room, loosened the knot in the kerchief, and made him sit down in a corner. The little girl, who had fallen asleep near the oven, jumped up and began staring at us in silent terror. I sat down on the locker.

"Ugh, what a downpour! " remarked the forester; "you will have to wait till it's over. Won't you lie down? "

"Thanks."

"I would have shut him in the store loft, on your honor's account," he went on, indicating the peasant; "but you see the bolt — "

"Leave him here; don't touch him," I interrupted.

The peasant stole a glance at me from under his brows. I vowed inwardly to set the poor wretch free, come what might. He sat without stirring on the locker. By the light of the lantern I could make

out his worn, wrinkled face, his overhanging yellow eyebrows, his restless eyes, his thin limbs. . . . The little girl lay down on the floor,
just at his feet, and again dropped asleep. Biryuk sat at the table,
his head in his hands. A cricket chirped in the corner . . . the rain
pattered on the roof and streamed down the windows; we were all
silent.

" Foma Kuzmich," said the peasant suddenly in a thick, broken
voice; " Foma Kuzmich! "

" What is it? "

" Let me go."

Biryuk made no answer.

" Let me go . . . hunger drove me to it; let me go."

" I know you," retorted the forester severely; " your set's all alike
— all thieves."

" Let me go," repeated the peasant. " Our manager . . . we're
ruined, that's what it is — let me go! "

" Ruined, indeed! . . . Nobody need steal."

" Let me go, Foma Kuzmich. . . . Don't destroy me. Your manager, you know yourself, will have no mercy on me; that's what it is."

Biryuk turned away. The peasant was shivering as though he were
in the throes of fever. His head was shaking, and his breathing came
in broken gasps.

" Let me go," he repeated with mournful desperation. " Let me go;
by God, let me go! I'll pay; see, by God, I will! By God, it was
through hunger! . . . the little ones are crying, you know yourself.
It's hard for us, see."

" You needn't go stealing, for all that."

" My little horse," the peasant went on, " my poor little horse, at
least . . . our only beast . . . let it go."

" I tell you, I can't. I'm not a free man; I'm made responsible.
You oughtn't to be spoilt, either."

" Let me go! It's through want, Foma Kuzmich, want — and
nothing else — let me go! "

" I know you! "

" Oh, let me go! "

" Ugh, what's the use of talking to you! sit quiet, or else you'll
catch it. Don't you see the gentleman, hey? "

The poor wretch hung his head. . . . Biryuk yawned and laid his
head on the table. The rain still persisted. I was waiting to see
what would happen.

Suddenly the peasant stood erect. His eyes were glittering, and his face flushed dark red. " Come, then, here; strike yourself, here," he began, his eyes puckering up and the corners of his mouth dropping; " come, cursed destroyer of men's souls! drink Christian blood, drink."

The forester turned round.

" I'm speaking to you, Asiatic, blood-sucker, you! "

" Are you drunk, or what, to set to being abusive? " began the forester, puzzled. " Are you out of your senses, hey? "

" Drunk! not at your expense, cursed destroyer of souls — brute, brute, brute! "

" Ah, you — I'll show you! "

" What's that to me? It's all one; I'm done for; what can I do without a home? Kill me — it's the same in the end; whether it's through hunger or like this — it's all one. Ruin us all — wife, children . . . kill us all at once. But, wait a bit, we'll get at you! "

Biryuk got up.

" Kill me, kill me," the peasant went on in savage tones; " kill me; come, come, kill me. . . ." The little girl jumped up hastily from the ground and stared at him. " Kill me, kill me! "

" Silence! " thundered the forester, and he took two steps forward.

" Stop, Foma, stop," I shouted; " let him go. . . . Peace be with him."

" I won't be silent," the luckless wretch went on. " It's all the same — ruin, anyway — you destroyer of souls, you brute; you've not come to ruin yet. . . . But wait a bit; you won't have long to boast of; they'll wring your neck; wait a bit! "

Biryuk clutched him by the shoulder. I rushed to help the peasant. . . .

" Don't touch him, master! " the forester shouted to me.

I should not have feared his threats, and already had my fist in the air; but to my intense amazement, with one pull he tugged the kerchief off the peasant's elbows, took him by the scruff of the neck, thrust his cap over his eyes, opened the door, and shoved him out.

" Go to the devil with your horse! " he shouted after him; " but mind, next time. . . ."

He came back into the hut and began rummaging in the corner.

" Well, Biryuk," I said at last, " you've astonished me; I see you're a splendid fellow."

" Oh, stop that, master," he cut me short with an air of vexation; " please don't speak of it. But I'd better see you on your way now," he added; " I suppose you won't wait for this little rain. . . ."

In the yard there was the rattle of the wheels of the peasant's cart.
" He's off, then! " he muttered; " but next time! "
Half an hour later he parted from me at the edge of the wood.

(Constance Garnett)

SUGGESTIONS FOR STUDY

1. By what details does the author transport the reader into a Russian atmosphere? Where is his descriptive power especially strong?

2. What is your opinion of Biryuk? What is typical of his character in the way he frees the peasants and receives the praise of the young master?

3. Can you see from this story why Turgenev had so much effect on social conditions in Russia? Read others of *A Sportsman's Sketches* to strengthen your first impression of this. If you read only one novel by this author, choose *Fathers and Sons*.

4. A great deal has been written about Turgenev's influence on other European literature. If you wish to read on this subject see reading list, page 893.

FEDOR MIKHAILOVICH DOSTOEVSKY (1821–1881)

Dostoevsky is one of the great trilogy of Russian novelists along with Turgenev and Tolstoy. Unlike the other two he did not belong to the nobility but to the middle or professional class. His father was a doctor in one of the large public hospitals of Moscow and it was in this hospital that Fedor was born. Loneliness and tragedy seemed to dog the boy's footsteps from youth. At the Military Engineer's school where he was prepared for an army commission he found the mathematics course uncongenial to his literary tastes, and the hearty manners of his schoolmates unsympathetic to his own more thoughtful disposition. While Fedor was still a youth his father, who had retired from the medical service and become a heavy-drinking, tyrannical landowner, was murdered by his own serfs, and soon after this tragedy the son developed epilepsy, which weakened all the middle years of his life. After completing his required military service in 1844 Dostoevsky decided to devote himself to literature, and the happiest day of his life, as he declared many years after, came when his novel *Poor Folks* was accepted with enthusiasm by the foremost critic of St. Petersburg. The public also hailed him as the great successor to Gogol, but unfortunately his popularity was short-lived and the many novels which he produced in the next three years fell flat.

Then in 1849 came the greatest tragedy of his life. He became involved in a socialist plot against the government which led to his arrest, a wearisome trial, and final sentence to death along with a score of other conspirators. The Tsar refused to let the young men be executed, but to play a grim jest in punishment he allowed preparation for the execution in the public square to be carried to the final moment of firing the shot. Then dramatically a messenger rode in with the news that the death sentence had been commuted to banishment to Siberia. The psychological effect on the prisoners was disastrous. One went mad on the spot and all were physically weakened.

Then for eight or nine years Dostoevsky was lost to literature, but his mental and emotional forces were gathering for the second creative period which far outshone his first. It was during these hard years of exile that his sympathy for the poor derelicts of life was intensified, and that his own philosophy of forgiveness, submission without bitterness, and brotherly love were fully developed. After his release, his reminiscences of prison life, *The House of the Dead,* portrayed the characters he knew in Siberia and proved influential in molding the public attitude toward criminals. In 1859 he returned to St. Petersburg, and once more entered the literary field. But still troubles pressed upon him in the form of debts, the failure of two magazines he edited, a marriage with a cold, unscrupulous woman, and the responsibilities of orphaned nieces and nephews. Always unpractical in money matters, Dostoevsky entered into a contract with a publisher by which he was to turn over the copyright on all his books if his new novel was not completed by a certain date. With failing eyesight he would have been unable to meet the situation had he not been aided by a young secretary whom he later married. Her devotion and practical sense brought to the last fourteen years of his life a happiness and security which he had never known before. His fame increased as one after another of his powerful novels appeared. In 1880 his greatest personal triumph came when his address at the unveiling of the monument to Pushkin in Moscow brought him unprecedented acclaim. But like a quick curtain after a climax on the stage, a sudden illness ended his life the next year.

Besides the books already mentioned the most significant works of Dostoevsky are *Memoirs from Underground,* dealing largely with distorted mental states; *Crime and Punishment,* involving the great problem of expiating crime both mentally and legally; *The Idiot,* the portrayal of a naïve and strangely impressive young man whose Christianity is literal and innate; and *The Brothers Karamazov,* often called his masterpiece, in which the three widely differing brothers present many of the aspects of the author's own family life and experience. Dostoevsky's books penetrate to the depths of human misery and despair, but infuse into all life a spiritual significance which lifts them above the sordid and purely pessimistic. Like Greek drama, his tragedy has cleansing power.

THE THIEF

One morning, just as I was about to leave for my place of employment, Agrafena (my cook, laundress, and housekeeper all in one person) entered my room, and, to my great astonishment, started a conversation.

She was a quiet, simple-minded woman, who during the whole six years of her stay with me had never spoken more than two or three words daily, and those in reference to my dinner — at least, I had never heard her.

" I have come to you, sir," she suddenly began, " about the renting out of the little spare room."

" What spare room? "

" The one that is near the kitchen, of course; which should it be? "

" Why? "

" Why do people generally take lodgers? Because."

" But who will take it? "

" Who will take it! A lodger, of course! Who should take it? "

" But there is hardly room in there, mother mine, for a bed; it will be too cramped. How can one live in it? "

" But why live in it! He only wants a place to sleep in; he will live on the window seat."

" What window seat? "

" How is that? What window seat? As if you did not know! The one in the hall. He will sit on it and sew, or do something else. But maybe he will sit on a chair; he has a chair of his own — and a table also, and everything."

" But who is he? "

" A nice, worldly-wise man. I will cook for him and will charge him only three rubles [1] in silver a month for room and board — "

At last, after long endeavor, I found out that some elderly man had talked Agrafena into taking him into the kitchen as lodger. When Agrafena once got a thing into her head that thing had to be; otherwise I knew I should have no peace. On those occasions when things did go against her wishes, she immediately fell into a sort of brooding, became exceedingly melancholy, and continued in that state for two or three weeks. During this time the food was invariably spoiled, the linen was missing, the floors unscrubbed; in a word, a lot of unpleasant things happened. I had long ago become aware of the fact that this woman of very few words was incapable of forming a

[1] **rubles:** coins worth about fifty cents.

decision, or of coming to any conclusion based on her own thoughts; and yet when it happened that by some means there had formed in her weak brain a sort of idea or wish to undertake a thing, to refuse her permission to carry out this idea or wish meant simply to kill her morally for some time. And so, acting in the sole interest of my peace of mind, I immediately agreed to this new proposition of hers.

" Has he at least the necessary papers, a passport,[2] or anything of the kind? "

" How then? Of course he has. A fine man like him — who has seen the world — He promised to pay three rubles a month."

On the very next day the new lodger appeared in my modest bachelor quarters; but I did not feel annoyed in the least — on the contrary, in a way I was glad of it. I live a very solitary, hermitlike life. I have almost no acquaintance and seldom go out. Having led the existence of a moor-cock [3] for ten years, I was naturally used to solitude. But ten, fifteen years or more of the same seclusion in company with a person like Agrafena, and in the same bachelor dwelling, was indeed a joyless prospect. Therefore, the presence of another quiet, unobtrusive man in the house was, under these circumstances, a real blessing.

Agrafena had spoken the truth: the lodger was a man who had seen much in his life. From his passport it appeared that he was a retired soldier, which I noticed even before I looked at the passport. As soon as I glanced at him in fact.

Astafi Ivanich, my lodger, belonged to the better sort of soldiers, another thing I noticed as soon as I saw him. We liked each other from the first, and our life flowed on peacefully and comfortably. The best thing was that Astafi Ivanich could at times tell a good story, incidents of his own life. In the general tediousness of my humdrum existence, such a narrator was a veritable treasure. Once he told me a story which has made a lasting impression upon me; but first the incident which led to the story.

Once I happened to be left alone in the house, Astafi and Agrafena having gone out on business. Suddenly I heard some one enter, and I felt that it must be a stranger; I went out into the corridor and found a man of short stature, and, notwithstanding the cold weather, dressed very thinly and without an overcoat.

" What is it you want? "

" The government clerk Alexandrov? Does he live here? "

---

[2] **passport:** The elaborate Russian police system required passports of natives as well as foreigners.   [3] **moor-cock:** prairie bird.

" There is no one here by that name, little brother; [4] good day."

" The porter told me he lived here," said the visitor, cautiously retreating toward the door.

" Go on, go on, little brother; be off! "

Soon after dinner the next day, when Astafi brought in my coat, which he had repaired for me, I once more heard a strange step in the corridor. I opened the door.

The visitor of the day before, calmly and before my very eyes, took my short coat from the rack, put it under his arm, and ran out.

Agrafena, who had all the time been looking at him in openmouthed surprise through the kitchen door, was seemingly unable to stir from her place and rescue the coat. But Astafi Ivanich rushed after the rascal, and, out of breath and panting, returned empty-handed. The man had vanished as if the earth had swallowed him.

" It is too bad, really, Astafi Ivanich," I said. " It is well that I have my cloak left. Otherwise the scoundrel would have put me out of service altogether."

But Astafi seemed so much affected by what had happened that as I gazed at him I forgot all about the theft. He could not regain his composure, and every once in a while threw down the work which occupied him, and began once more to recount how it had all happened, where he had been standing, while only two steps away my coat had been stolen before his very eyes, and how he could not even catch the thief. Then once more he resumed his work, only to throw it away again, and I saw him go down to the porter, tell him what had happened, and reproach him with not taking sufficient care of the house, that such a theft could be perpetrated in it. When he returned he began to upbraid Agrafena. Then he again resumed his work, muttering to himself for a long time — how this is the way it all was — how he stood here, and I there, and how before our very eyes, no farther than two steps away, the coat was taken off its hanger, and so on. In a word, Astafi Ivanich, though he knew how to do certain things, worried much over trifles.

" We have been fooled, Astafi Ivanich," I said to him that evening, handing him a glass of tea,[5] and hoping from sheer ennui [6] to call forth the story of the lost coat again, which by dint of much repetition had begun to sound extremely comical.

---

4 **little brother:** The Russians are fond of diminutive terms and use them much more freely in conversation than we do.

5 **glass of tea:** It is the Russian custom to drink hot tea from tall glasses.

6 **ennui:** boredom.

"Yes, we were fooled, sir. It angers me very much, though the loss is not mine, and I think there is nothing so despicably low in this world as a thief. They steal what you buy by working in the sweat of your brow — Your time and labor — The loathsome creature! It sickens me to talk of it — pfui! It makes me angry to think of it. How is it, sir, that you do not seem to be at all sorry about it? "

"To be sure, Astafi Ivanich, one would much sooner see his things burn up than see a thief take them. It is exasperating — "

"Yes, it is annoying to have anything stolen from you. But, of course, there are thieves and thieves — I, for instance, met an honest thief through an accident."

"How is that? An honest thief? How can a thief be honest, Astafi Ivanich? "

"You speak truth, sir. A thief cannot be an honest man. There never was such. I only wanted to say that he was an honest man, it seems to me, even though he stole. I was very sorry for him."

"And how did it happen, Astafi Ivanich? "

"It happened just two years ago. I was serving as house steward at the time, and the baron whom I served expected shortly to leave for his estate, so that I knew I should soon be out of a job, and then God only knew how I should be able to get along; and just then it was that I happened to meet in a tavern a poor forlorn creature, Emelian by name. Once upon a time he had served somewhere or other, but had been driven out of service on account of tippling. Such an unworthy creature as he was! He wore whatever came along. At times I even wondered if he wore a shirt under his shabby cloak; everything he could put his hands on was sold for drink. But he was not a rowdy. Oh, no; he was of a sweet, gentle nature, very kind and tender to every one; he never asked for anything, was, if anything, too conscientious — Well, you could see without asking when the poor fellow was dying for a drink, and of course you treated him to one. Well, we became friendly; that is, he attached himself to me like a little dog — you go this way, he follows — and all this after our very first meeting.

"Of course he remained with me that night; his passport was in order and the man seemed all right. On the second night also. On the third he did not leave the house, sitting on the window seat of the corridor the whole day, and of course he remained over that night too. Well, I thought, just see how he has forced himself upon you. You have to give him to eat and to drink and to shelter him. All a poor man needs is some one to sponge upon him. I soon found out that once before he had attached himself to a man just as he had now attached himself to me; they drank together, but the other one soon died of some deep-seated sorrow. I thought and thought: What shall I do with him? Drive him out — my conscience would not allow it — I felt very sorry for him: he was such a wretched, forlorn creature, terrible! And so dumb he did not ask for anything, only sat quietly and looked you straight in the eyes, just like a faithful little dog. That is how drink can ruin a man. And I thought to myself: Well, suppose I say to him: ' Get out of here, Emelian; you have nothing to do in here, you come to the wrong person; I will soon have nothing to eat myself, so how do you expect me to feed *you?* ' And I tried to imagine what he would do after I'd told him all this. And I could see how he would look at me for a long time after he had heard me, without understanding a word; how at last he would understand what I was driving at, and, rising from the window seat, take his little bundle — I see it before me now — a red-checked little bundle full of holes, in which he kept God knows what, and which he carted along with him wherever he went; how he would brush and fix up his worn cloak a little, so that it would look a bit more decent and not show so much the holes and patches — he was a man of very fine feelings! How he would have opened the door afterward and would have gone forth with tears in his eyes!

" Well, should a man be allowed to perish altogether? I all at once felt heartily sorry for him; but at the same time I thought: And what about me, am I any better off? And I said to myself: Well, Emelian, you will not feast overlong at my expense; soon I shall have to move from here myself, and then you will not find me again. Well, sir, my baron soon left for his estate with all his household, telling me before he went that he was very well satisfied with my services, and would gladly employ me again on his return to the capital. A fine man my baron was, but he died the same year.

" Well, after I had escorted my baron and his family a little way, I took my things and the little money I had saved up, and went to live with an old woman I knew, who rented out a corner of the room she occupied by herself. She used to be a nurse in some well-to-do family, and now, in her old age, they had pensioned her off. Well, I thought to myself, now it is good-by to you, Emelian, dear man, you will not find me now! And what do you think, sir? When I returned in the evening — I had paid a visit to an acquaintance of mine — whom should I see but Emelian sitting quietly upon my trunk with his red-checked bundle by his side. He was wrapped up in his poor little cloak, and was awaiting my home-coming. He must have been quite lonesome, because he had borrowed a prayer-book of the old woman and held it upside down. He had found me after all! My hands fell helplessly at my sides. Well, I thought, there is nothing to be done, why did I not drive him away first off? And I only asked him: 'Have you taken your passport along, Emelian?' Then I sat down, sir, and began to turn the matter over in my mind: Well, could he, a roving man, be much in my way? And after I had considered it well, I decided that he would not, and, besides, he would be of very little expense to me. Of course, he would have to be fed, but what does that amount to? Some bread in the morning and, to make it a little more appetizing, a little onion or so. For the midday meal again some bread and onion, and for the evening again onion and bread, and some kvas,[7] and, if some cabbage soup should happen to come our way, then we could both fill up to the throat. I ate little, and Emelian, who was a drinking man, surely ate almost nothing; all he wanted was vodka.[8] He would be the undoing of me with his drinking; but at the same time I felt a curious feeling creep over me. It seemed as if life would be a burden to me if Emelian went away. And so I decided then and there to be his father-benefactor. I would put him on his legs, I thought, save him from perishing, and gradually wean him from drink. Just you wait, I thought. Stay with me, Emelian, but stand pat now. Obey the word of command!

"Well, I thought to myself, I will begin by teaching him some work, but not at once; let him first enjoy himself a bit, and I will in the meanwhile look around and discover what he finds easiest, and would be capable of doing, because you must know, sir, a man must have a calling and a capacity for a certain work to be able to do it properly. And I began stealthily to observe him. And a hard subject he was, that Emelian! At first I tried to get at him with a kind word. Thus and thus I would speak to him: 'Emelian, you had better take more care of yourself and try to fix yourself up a little.

"'Give up drinking. Just look at yourself, man; you are all ragged, your cloak looks more like a sieve than anything else. It is not nice. It is about time for you to come to your senses and know when you have had enough.'

"He listened to me, my Emelian did, with lowered head; he had

---

[7] kvas: Russian non-intoxicating drink.
[8] vodka: highly intoxicating drink.

already reached that state, poor fellow, when the drink affected his tongue and he could not utter a sensible word. You talk to him about cucumbers, and he answers beans. He listened, listened to me for a long time, and then he would sigh deeply.

" ' What are you sighing for, Emelian? ' I ask him.

" ' Oh, it is nothing, Astafi Ivanich, do not worry. Only what I saw today, Astafi Ivanich — two women fighting about a basket of huckleberries that one of them had upset by accident.'

" ' Well, what of that? '

" ' And the woman whose berries were scattered snatched a like basket of huckleberries from the other woman's hand, and not only threw them on the ground, but stamped all over them.'

" ' Well, but what of that, Emelian? '

" ' Ech! ' I think to myself, ' Emelian! You have lost your poor wits through the cursed drink! '

" ' And again,' Emelian says, ' a baron lost a bill on the Gorokhova Street — or was it on the Sadova? A mujik [9] saw him drop it, and says, " My luck," but here another one interfered and says, " No, it is my luck! I saw it first. . . ." '

" ' Well, Emelian? '

" ' And the two mujiks started a fight, Astafi Ivanich, and the upshot was that a policeman came, picked up the money, handed it back to the baron, and threatened to put the mujiks under lock for raising a disturbance.'

" ' But what of that? What is there wonderful or edifying in that, Emelian? '

" ' Well, nothing, but the people laughed, Astafi Ivanich.'

" ' E-ch, Emelian! What have the people to do with it? ' I said. ' You have sold your immortal soul for a copper. But do you know what I will tell you, Emelian? '

" ' What, Astafi Ivanich? '

" ' You'd better take up some work, really you should. I am telling you for the hundredth time that you should have pity on yourself! '

" ' But what shall I do, Astafi Ivanich? I do not know where to begin and no one would employ me, Astafi Ivanich.'

" ' That is why they drove you out of service, Emelian; it is all on account of drink! '

" ' And today,' said Emelian, ' they called Vlass the barkeeper into the office.'

[9] **mujik:** a peasant.

" ' What did they call him for, Emelian? ' I asked.

" ' I don't know why, Astafi Ivanich. I suppose it was needed, so they called him.'

" ' Ech,' I thought to myself, ' no good will come of either of us, Emelian! It is for our sins that God is punishing us! '

" Well, what could a body do with such a man, sir!

" But he was sly, the fellow was, I tell you! He listened to me, listened, and at last it seems it began to tire him, and as quick as he would notice that I was growing angry he would take his cloak and slip out — and that was the last to be seen of him! He would not show up the whole day, and only in the evening would he return, as drunk as a lord. Who treated him to drinks, or where he got the money for it, God only knows; not from me, surely! . . .

" ' Well,' I say to him, ' Emelian, you will have to give up drink, do you hear? you will have to give it up! The next time you return tipsy, you will have to sleep on the stairs. I'll not let you in! '

" After this Emelian kept to the house for two days; on the third he once more sneaked out. I wait and wait for him; he does not come! I must confess that I was kind of frightened; besides, I felt terribly sorry for him. What had I done to the poor devil! I thought. I must have frightened him off. Where could he have gone to now, the wretched creature? Great God, he may perish yet! The night passed and he did not return. In the morning I went out into the hall, and he was lying there with his head on the lower step, almost stiff with cold.

" ' What is the matter with you, Emelian? The Lord save you! Why are you here? '

" ' But you know, Astafi Ivanich,' he replied, ' you were angry with me the other day; I aggravated you, and you promised to make me sleep in the hall, and I — so I — did not dare — to come in — and lay down here.'

" ' It would be better for you, Emelian,' I said, filled with anger and pity, ' to find a better employment than needlessly watching the stairs! '

" ' But what other employment, Astafi Ivanich? '

" ' Well, wretched creature that you are,' here anger had flamed up in me, ' if you would try to learn the tailoring art. Just look at the cloak you are wearing! Not only is it full of holes, but you are sweeping the stairs with it! You should at least take a needle and mend it a little, so it would look more decent. E-ch, a wretched tippler you are, and nothing more! '

" Well, sir! What do you think! He did take the needle — I had told him only for fun, and there he got scared and actually took the needle. He threw off his cloak and began to put the thread through; well, it was easy to see what would come of it; his eyes began to fill and redden, his hands trembled! He pushed and pushed the thread — could not get it through: he wetted it, rolled it between his fingers, smoothed it out, but it would not go! He flung it from him and looked at me.

" ' Well, Emelian! ' I said, ' you served me right! If people had seen it I would have died with shame! I only told you all this for fun, and because I was angry with you. Never mind sewing; may the Lord keep you from sin! You need not do anything, only keep out of mischief, and do not sleep on the stairs and put me to shame thereby! '

" ' But what shall I do, Astafi Ivanich; I know myself that I am always tipsy and unfit for anything! I only make you, my be — benefactor, angry for nothing.'

" And suddenly his bluish lips began to tremble, and a tear rolled down his unshaven, pale cheek, then another and another one, and he broke into a very flood of tears, my Emelian. Father in Heaven! I felt as if some one had cut me over the heart with a knife.

" ' E-ch, you sensitive man; why, I never thought! And who *could* have thought such a thing. No, I'd better give you up altogether, Emelian; do as you please.'

" Well, sir, what else is there to tell! But the whole thing is so insignificant and unimportant, it is really not worth while wasting words about it; for instance, you, sir, would not give two broken groschen [10] for it; but I, I would give much, if I had much, that this thing had never happened! I owned, sir, a pair of breeches, blue, in checks, a first-class article, the devil take them — a rich landowner who came here on business ordered them from me, but refused afterward to take them, saying that they were too tight, and left them with me.

" Well, I thought, the cloth is of first-rate quality! I can get five rubles for them in the old-clothes market-place, and, if not, I can cut a fine pair of pantaloons out of them for some St. Petersburg gent, and have a piece left over for a vest for myself. Everything counts with a poor man! And Emelian was at that time in sore straits. I saw that he had given up drinking, first one day, then a second, and a third, and looked so downhearted and sad.

[10] **groschen**: cents.

" Well, I thought, it is either that the poor fellow lacks the necessary coin, or maybe he has entered on the right path, and has at last listened to good sense.

" Well, to make a long story short, an important holiday came just at that time, and I went to vespers. When I came back I saw Emelian sitting on the window seat, as drunk as a lord. Eh! I thought, so that is what you are about! And I go to my trunk to get out something I needed. I look! The breeches are not there. I rummage about in this place and that place: gone! Well, after I had searched all over and saw that they were missing for fair, I felt as if something had gone through me! I went after the old woman — as to Emelian, though there was evidence against him in his being drunk, I somehow never thought of him!

" ' No,' says my old woman; ' the good Lord keep you, gentleman, what do I need breeches for? can I wear them? I myself missed a skirt the other day. I know nothing at all about it.'

" ' Well,' I asked, ' has any one called here? '

" ' No one called,' she said. ' I was in all the time; your friend here went out for a short while and then came back; here he sits! Why don't you ask him? '

" ' Did you happen, for some reason or other, Emelian, to take the breeches out of the trunk? The ones, you remember, which were made for the landowner? '

" ' No,' he says, ' I have not taken them, Astafi Ivanich.'

" ' What *could* have happened to them? ' Again I began to search, but nothing came of it! And Emelian sat and swayed to and fro on the window seat.

" I was on my knees before the open trunk, just in front of him. Suddenly I threw a sidelong glance at him. Ech, I thought, and felt very hot round the heart, and my face grew very red. Suddenly my eyes encountered Emelian's.

" ' No,' he says, ' Astafi Ivanich. You perhaps think that I — you know what I mean — but I have not taken them.'

" ' But where have they gone, Emelian? '

" ' No,' he says, ' Astafi Ivanich, I have not seen them at all.'

" ' Well, then, you think they simply went and got lost by themselves, Emelian? '

" ' Maybe they did, Astafi Ivanich.'

" After this I would not waste another word on him. I rose from my knees, locked the trunk, and after I had lighted the lamp I sat down to work. I was remaking a vest for a government clerk, who lived on the floor below. But I was terribly rattled, just the same. It would have been much easier to bear, I thought, if all my wardrobe had burned to ashes. Emelian, it seems, felt that I was deeply angered. It is always so, sir, when a man is guilty; he always feels beforehand when trouble approaches, as a bird feels the coming storm.

" ' And do you know, Astafi Ivanich,' he suddenly began, ' the leach [11] married the coachman's widow today.'

" I just looked at him; but, it seems, looked at him so angrily that he understood. I saw him rise from his seat, approach the bed, and begin to rummage in it, continually repeating: ' Where could they have gone, vanished, as if the devil had taken them! '

" I waited to see what was coming; I saw that my Emelian had crawled under the bed. I could contain myself no longer.

" ' Look here,' I said. ' What makes you crawl under the bed? '

" ' I am looking for the breeches, Astafi Ivanich,' said Emelian from under the bed. ' Maybe they got here somehow or other.'

" ' But what makes you, sir (in my anger I addressed him as if he was somebody), what makes you trouble yourself on account of such a plain man as I am; dirtying your knees for nothing! '

" ' But, Astafi Ivanich — I did not mean anything — I only thought maybe if we look for them we may find them yet.'

" ' Mm! Just listen to me a moment, Emelian! '

" ' What, Astafi Ivanich? '

" ' Have you not simply stolen them from me like a rascally thief, serving me so for my bread and salt? ' I said to him, beside myself with wrath at the sight of him crawling under the bed for something he knew was not there.

" ' No, Astafi Ivanich.' For a long time he remained lying flat under the bed. Suddenly he crawled out and stood before me — I seem to see him even now — as terrible a sight as sin itself.

" ' No,' he says to me in a trembling voice, shivering through all his body and pointing to his breast with his finger, so that all at once I became scared and could not move from my seat on the window. ' I have not taken your breeches, Astafi Ivanich.'

" ' Well,' I answered, ' Emelian, forgive me if in my foolishness I have accused you wrongfully. As to the breeches, let them go hang; we will get along without them. We have our hands, thank God, we will not have to steal, and now, too, we will not have to sponge on another poor man; we will earn our living.'

" Emelian listened to me and remained standing before me for some

[11] **leach**: doctor.

time, then he sat down and sat motionless the whole evening; when I lay down to sleep, he was still sitting in the same place.

" In the morning, when I awoke, I found him sleeping on the bare floor, wrapped up in his cloak; he felt his humiliation so strongly that he had no heart to go and lie down on the bed.

" Well, sir, from that day on I conceived a terrible dislike for the man; that is, rather, I hated him the first few days, feeling as if, for instance, my own son had robbed me and given me deadly offence. Ech, I thought, Emelian, Emelian! And Emelian, my dear sir, had gone on a two weeks' spree. Drunk to bestiality from morning till night. And during the whole two weeks he had not uttered a word. I suppose he was consumed the whole time by a deep-seated grief, or else he was trying in this way to make an end to himself. At last he gave up drinking. I suppose he had no longer the where-withal to buy vodka — had drunk up every copeck [12] — and he once more took up his old place on the window seat. I remember that he sat there for three whole days without a word; suddenly I see him weep; sits there and cries, but what crying! The tears come from his eyes in showers, drip, drip, as if he did not know that he was shedding them. It is very painful, sir, to see a grown man weep, all the more when the man is of advanced years, like Emelian, and cries from grief and a sorrowful heart.

" ' What ails you, Emelian? ' I say to him.

" He starts and shivers. This was the first time I had spoken to him since that eventful day.

" ' It is nothing — Astafi Ivanich.'

" ' God keep you, Emelian; never you mind it all. Let bygones be bygones. Don't take it to heart so, man! ' I felt very sorry for him.

" ' It is only that — that I would like to do something — some kind of work, Astafi Ivanich.'

" ' But what kind of work, Emelian? '

" ' Oh, any kind. Maybe I will go into some kind of service, as before. I have already been at my former employer's, asking. It will not do for me, Astafi Ivanich, to use you any longer. I, Astafi Ivanich, will perhaps obtain some employment, and then I will pay you for everything, food and all.'

" ' Don't, Emelian, don't. Well, let us say you committed a sin; well, it is all over! The devil take it all! Let us live as before — as if nothing had happened! '

[12] copeck: cent.

" ' You, Astafi Ivanich, you are probably hinting about *that*. But I have not taken your breeches.'

" ' Well, just as you please, Emelian! '

" ' No, Astafi Ivanich, evidently I cannot live with you longer. You will excuse me, Astafi Ivanich.'

" ' But God be with you, Emelian,' I said to him; ' who is it that is offending you or driving you out of the house? Is it I who am doing it? '

" ' No, but it is unseemly for me to misuse your hospitality any longer, Astafi Ivanich; 'twill be better to go.'

" I saw that he had in truth risen from his place and donned his ragged cloak — he felt offended, the man did, and had got it into his head to leave, and — basta.[13]

" ' But where are you going, Emelian? Listen to sense: what are you? Where will you go? '

" ' No, it is best so, Astafi Ivanich, do not try to keep me back,' and he once more broke into tears; ' let me be, Astafi Ivanich, you are no longer what you used to be.'

" ' Why am I not? I am just the same. But you will perish when left alone — like a foolish little child, my Emelian.'

" ' No, Astafi Ivanich. Lately, before you leave the house, you have taken to locking your trunk, and I, Astafi Ivanich, see it and weep — No, it is better you should let me go, Astafi Ivanich, and forgive me if I have offended you in any way during the time we have lived together.'

" Well, sir! And so he did go away. I waited a day and thought: Oh, he will be back toward evening. But a day passes, then another, and he does not return. On the third — he does not return. I grew frightened, and a terrible sadness gripped at my heart. I stopped eating and drinking, and lay whole nights without closing my eyes. The man had wholly disarmed me! On the fourth day I went to look for him; I looked in all the taverns and pot-houses in the vicinity, and asked if any one had seen him. No. Emelian had wholly disappeared! Maybe he has done away with his miserable existence, I thought. Maybe, when in his cups, he has perished like a dog, somewhere under a fence. I came home half dead with fatigue and despair, and decided to go out the next day again to look for him, cursing myself bitterly for letting the foolish, helpless man go away from me. But at dawn of the fifth day (it was a holiday) I heard the door creak. And whom should I see but Emelian! But in

---

[13] **basta**: Italian exclamation meaning *Enough!*

what a state! His face was bluish and his hair was full of mud, as if he had slept in the street; and he had grown thin, the poor fellow had, as thin as a rail. He took off his poor cloak, sat down on my trunk, and began to look at me. Well, sir, I was overjoyed, but at the same time felt a greater sadness than ever pulling at my heart-strings. This is how it was, sir: I felt that if a thing like that had happened to me, that is — I would sooner have perished like a dog, but would not have returned. And Emelian did. Well, naturally, it is hard to see a man in such a state. I began to coddle and to comfort him in every way.

" ' Well,' I said, ' Emelian, I am very glad you have returned; if you had not come so soon, you would not have found me in, as I intended to go hunting for you. Have you had anything to eat? '

" ' I have eaten, Astafi Ivanich.'

" ' I doubt it. Well, here is some cabbage soup — left over from yesterday; a nice soup with some meat in it — not the meager kind.[14] And here you have some bread and a little onion. Go ahead and eat; it will do you good.'

" I served it to him; and immediately realized that he must have been starving for the last three days — such an appetite as he showed! So it was hunger that had driven him back to me. Looking at the poor fellow, I was deeply touched, and decided to run into the near-by dram-shop. I will get him some vodka, I thought, to liven him up a bit and make peace with him. It is enough. I have nothing against the poor devil any longer. And so I brought the vodka and said to him: ' Here, Emelian, let us drink to each other's health in honor of the holiday. Come, take a drink. It will do you good.'

" He stretched out his hand, greedily stretched it out, you know, and stopped; then, after a while, he lifted the glass, carried it to his mouth, spilling the liquor on his sleeve; at last he did carry it to his mouth, but immediately put it back on the table.

" ' Well, why don't you drink, Emelian? '

" ' But no, I'll not, Astafi Ivanich.'

" ' You'll not drink it! '

" ' But I, Astafi Ivanich, I think — I'll not drink any more, Astafi Ivanich.'

" ' Is it for good you have decided to give it up, Emelian, or only for today? '

" He did not reply, and after a while I saw him lean his head on his hand, and I asked him: ' Are you not feeling well, Emelian? '

---

[14] **meager kind:** plain soup without meat or vegetables in it.

" ' Yes, pretty well, Astafi Ivanich.'

" I made him go to bed, and saw that he was truly in a bad way. His head was burning hot and he was shivering with ague. I sat by him the whole day; toward evening he grew worse. I prepared a meal for him of kvas, butter, and some onion, and threw in it a few bits of bread, and said to him: ' Go ahead and take some food; maybe you will feel better! '

" But he only shook his head: ' No, Astafi Ivanich, I shall not have any dinner today.'

" I had some tea prepared for him, giving a lot of trouble to the poor old woman from whom I rented a part of the room — but he would not take even a little tea.

" Well, I thought to myself, it is a bad case. On the third morning I went to see the doctor, an acquaintance of mine, Dr. Kostopravov, who had treated me when I still lived in my last place. The doctor came, examined the poor fellow, and only said: ' There was no need of sending for me, he is already too far gone, but you can give him some powders which I will prescribe.'

" Well, I didn't give him the powders at all, as I understood that the doctor was only doing it for form's sake; and in the meanwhile came the fifth day.

" He lay dying before me, sir. I sat on the windowseat with some work I had on hand lying on my lap. The old woman was raking the stove. We were all silent, and my heart was breaking over this poor, shiftless creature, as if he were my own son whom I was losing. I knew that Emelian was gazing at me all the time; I noticed from the earliest morning that he longed to tell me something, but seemingly dared not. At last I looked at him, and saw that he did not take his eyes from me, but that whenever his eyes met mine, he immediately lowered his own.

" ' Astafi Ivanich! '

" ' What, Emelian? '

" ' What if my cloak should be carried over to the old clothes market, would they give much for it, Astafi Ivanich? '

" ' Well,' I said, ' I do not know for certain, but three rubles they would probably give for it, Emelian.' I said it only to comfort the simple-minded creature; in reality they would have laughed in my face for even thinking to sell such a miserable, ragged thing.

" ' And I thought that they might give a little more, Astafi Ivanich. It is made of cloth, so how is it that they would not wish to pay more than three rubles for it? '

" ' Well, Emelian, if you wish to sell it, then of course you may ask more for it at first.'

" Emelian was silent for a moment, then he once more called to me.

" ' Astafi Ivanich! '

" ' What is it, Emelian? '

" ' You will sell the cloak after I am no more; no need of burying me in it, I can well get along without it; it is worth something, and may come handy to you.'

" Here I felt such a painful gripping at my heart as I cannot even express, sir. I saw that the sadness of approaching death had already come upon the man. Again we were silent for some time. About an hour passed in this way. I looked at him again and saw that he was still gazing at me, and when his eyes met mine he immediately lowered his.

" ' Would you like a drink of cold water? ' I asked him.

" ' Give me some, and may God repay you, Astafi Ivanich.'

" ' Would you like anything else, Emelian? '

" ' No, Astafi Ivanich, I do not want anything, but I — '

" ' What? '

" ' You know that — '

" ' What is it you want, Emelian? '

" ' The breeches — You know — It was I who took them — Astafi Ivanich — '

" ' Well,' I said, ' the great God will forgive you, Emelian, poor, unfortunate fellow that you are! Depart in peace.'

" And I had to turn away my head for a moment because grief for the poor devil took my breath away and the tears came in torrents from my eyes.

" ' Astafi Ivanich! — '

" I looked at him, saw that he wished to tell me something more, tried to raise himself, and was moving his lips — He reddened and looked at me — Suddenly I saw that he began to grow paler and paler; in a moment he fell with his head thrown back, breathed once, and gave his soul into God's keeping."

(*Lizzie B. Gorin*)

SUGGESTIONS FOR STUDY

1. By what details is the social and financial status of the characters made clear at the beginning of the story?

2. After finishing the story how do you feel toward Emelian and toward Astafi Ivanich? How does the story show Dostoevsky's attitude toward human derelicts? Compare Emelian's state with that of the peasant in "Biryuk." Which seems worse to you?

3. Dostoevsky's books had great influence in shaping events leading up to the Russian Revolution, but his books have been condemned by many Soviet critics. Can you see from this story how both of these situations have come about?

4. The rambling, repetitious, conversational style is typical of Dostoevsky's novels. How does this very style add to the effect produced on the reader? Do you like the "story-within-a-story" method? Why or why not? Does this confuse you at any point?

5. *The Brothers Karamazov* is the best novel of Dostoevsky's to read. This has also been made into play, opera, and movie. The man himself is as interesting to read about as a novel. A good brief account is in Myer's *Fighters of Fate.* An intimate picture is given in the biography written by his daughter Aimée Dostoevsky, and in the diary kept by his second wife. There are several other good lives of the author. See reading list.

LEO NIKOLAEVICH TOLSTOY (1828–1910)

Like Turgenev, Tolstoy belonged to the nobility, but unlike him, instead of living many years abroad, his life for the most part was spent on the great estate in south-central Russia where he was born. By the age of nine he had lost both parents, and his education was directed by an aunt. Fortunately, the affection and understanding of this intelligent woman gave Tolstoy a more favorable home environment than either of his two great contemporary novelists experienced. In the early trilogy of novels, *Childhood, Boyhood,* and *Youth,* which are thinly disguised autobiography, Tolstoy has given us a full picture of his inner life through those stages, and since the greatest significance lies in the development of his mental attitudes rather than in his outward acts, these books are a valuable contribution toward understanding him. At fifteen he went to the University of Kazan, but left three years later without a degree and for a time studied law at the University of St. Petersburg. Still unsatisfied in a career he turned at the age of twenty-three to the military service, and with his brother went to the Caucasus. Here his life shows a curious mixture of the dissipations typical of the young officers of his time and an inner seriousness as revealed in his diary and *Childhood* which he wrote while on active duty. In 1855 in the midst of the dangers of the Crimean War he read Dickens in English, wrote *Boyhood,* and developed that horror of warfare and devotion to the Christian ideal which colored his later thinking. His books, *Sevastopol Stories* and *The Cossacks* picture vividly the experiences of these turbulent years. The former, published originally as a series of sketches in a Russian review, brought him recognition from the literary critics of St. Petersburg and also from the Tsar, who ordered a French translation of the stories. *The Cossacks,* though not published till 1860, was begun before the Crimean War and shows the life of the soldiers in peace times.

Between 1857 and 1861 Tolstoy traveled extensively through western Europe accompanied part of the time by Turgenev, whose admiration for the rising author had been expressed in these words: " When this new wine is ripened there will be a drink fit for the gods." Later the two men unfortunately quarreled, and in spite of occasional reconciliations and meetings, they never could establish a permanent friendship because of fundamental differences of disposition. The suave and gentle Turgenev and the intense and probing Tolstoy were mentally irritating to each other.

In 1861, the year of the liberation of the serfs, Tolstoy returned to his estate, Yasnaya Polyana, where he lived, except for brief intervals, during the remaining fifty years of his life. Here he married, reared his family, and wrote his two greatest novels, which his wife painstakingly copied after their many revisions. The first of these was a monumental historical novel covering the period of the Napoleonic Wars, *War and Peace,* which ran as a serial for four years in *The Russian Messenger.* The panoramic effect of the many scenes, the philosophic interpretation of the meaning of war, the interplay of destiny and human will all combine to make this one of the world's masterpieces. The second great novel, *Anna Karenina,* is an intense study of the emotional life and personal problems of a group of Russian aristocrats of Tolstoy's own time. One of the characters, Levin, is Tolstoy himself, and through the mouth of this man we learn the questionings of life which had agitated the author over a period of years. These came to a definite head soon after the publication of *Anna Karenina* when Tolstoy was about fifty years old. He determined that the evils of life came through ambition, property, and selfishness, and that the only way to bring meaning into life was to break down all such barriers, to live simply as the peasants and workers lived, and to follow the teachings of Christ in their literal form unconfused by the dogma and ritual of the Church. These teachings he reduced to a few plain principles of conduct, one which he particularly emphasized being never to resist evil by violence. He renounced his previous novels and wrote only religious and philosophical tracts, or novels with the definite purpose of conveying his theories. He dressed and labored like a peasant, ignored his fortune, and practically severed the sympathy of his wife and family. In 1910 he wandered off on some contemplated pilgrimage and died suddenly and alone in an obscure railroad station.

Tolstoy's influence on his own and later times has been tremendous. He was the great seeker and questioner, restless and unsatisfied because of contradictions within himself. His intense pride he sought to humble by heroic measures, but it remained with him to the end, and he never attained by discipline the beautiful and forgiving character which Dostoevsky had by nature. Two of his fellow countrymen saw the drama of Tolstoy's inner conflict from different angles. Said Turgenev, " He never loved any one but himself." But Merezhkovsky said: " He has never loved any man, *not even himself.*"

SPRING

This is the second chapter of Tolstoy's third autobiographical novel called *Youth*. It is followed by " Reveries," the third chapter. Together they give an intimate impression of the young man's thoughts which throw light on his later attitude toward life. So closely does his novel follow the author's life that except for disguised names, it is practically an autobiography.

On the year when I entered the university, Easter fell so late in April that the examinations were set for St. Thomas' Week,[1] and I was obliged to fast in preparation for the Holy Communion, and make my final preparations, during Passion Week.

The weather had been soft, warm, and clear for three days after the wet snow which Karl Ivanich had been in the habit of calling " the son followed the father." Not a lump of snow was to be seen in the streets; dirty paste had given way to wet, shining pavements and rapid rivulets. The last drops were thawing from the roofs in the sun. The buds were swelling on the trees within the enclosures. The path in the courtyard was dry. In the direction of the stable, past the frozen heaps of manure, and between the stones about the porch, the moss-like grass was beginning to turn green. It was that particular period of spring which acts most powerfully upon the soul of man, — the clear, full, brilliant but not hot sun, the brooks and snow-bare places, perfumed freshness in the air, and the tender blue sky, with its long transparent clouds. I do not know why, but it seems to me that the influence of this first period of birth of the spring is even more powerful and perceptible in a great city; one sees less, but foresees more. I stood by the window, through whose double frames the morning sun cast dusty rays of light upon the floor of the school-room [2] which bored me so intolerably, solving a long algebraic equation on the blackboard. In one hand I held a soft, tattered copy of Franker's Algebra, in the other a small bit of chalk,

[1] **St. Thomas' Week:** in honor of St. Thomas Aquinas, March 7.
[2] **school-room:** in his own home, where he was tutored.

with which I had already smeared both hands, my face, and the elbows of my coat. Nikolai,[3] wearing an apron, and with his sleeves rolled up, was chipping off the cement, and extracting the nails of the window which opened on the front yard. His occupation, and the noise he made, distracted my attention.

Besides I was in a very evil and dissatisfied state of mind. Nothing would go right with me. I had made a mistake at the beginning of my calculation, so that I had had to begin all over again. I had dropped the chalk twice. I was conscious that my hands and face were dirty. The sponge had disappeared somewhere or other; the noise which Nikolai made shook my nerves painfully. I wanted to get into a rage, and growl. I flung aside the chalk and algebra, and began to pace the room. But I remembered that today I must go to confession, and that I must refrain from all evil; and all at once I fell into a peculiar, gentle mood, and approached Nikolai.

" Permit me; I will help you, Nikolai," said I, trying to impart the gentlest of tones to my voice. The thought that I was behaving well, stifling my vexation, and helping him, heightened this gentle disposition of mind still further.

The cement was cut away, the nails removed; but although Nikolai tugged at the cross-frame with all his might, the frame would not yield.

" If the frame comes out immediately now, when I pull on it," I thought, " it will signify that it is a sin, and that I need not do any more work today." The frame leaned to one side, and came out.

" Where is it to be carried? " said I.

" If you please, I will take care of it myself," replied Nikolai, evidently amazed and seemingly displeased with my zeal; " it must not be mixed up, but they belong in the garret in my room."

" I will mark it," said I, lifting the frame.

It seems to me that if the garret were two versts [4] away, and the window-frame were twice as heavy, I should be very much pleased. I wanted to exhaust myself by performing this service for Nikolai. When I returned to the room, the tiles and the cones of salt were already transferred to the window sills, and Nikolai, with a wing, had brushed off the sand and drowsy flies through the open window. The fresh, perfumed air had already entered and filled the room. From the window the hum of the city and the twittering of the sparrows in the yard were audible.

---

[3] **Nikolai**: his servant.
[4] **versts**: A verst in Russia is about two-thirds of a mile.

Every object was brilliantly illuminated; the room had grown cheerful; the light spring breeze fluttered the leaves of my algebra, and Nikolai's hair. I approached the window, sat down in it, bent toward the yard, and began to think.

A certain new, exceedingly powerful, and pleasant sensation penetrated my soul all at once. The wet earth, through which, here and there, bright green spears of grass with yellow stalks pushed their way; the rivulets, sparkling in the sun, and whirling along little clods of earth and shavings; and reddening twigs of syringa with swollen buds which undulate just beneath the window; the anxious twittering of the birds thronging the bush; the blackish hedge wet with the melted snow: but chiefly the damp, fragrant air and cheerful sun, — spoke to me intelligibly, clearly, of something new and very beautiful, which, though I cannot reproduce it as it told itself to me, I shall endeavor to repeat as I received it: everything spoke to me of beauty, happiness, and virtue, said that both were easy and possible to me, that one could not exist without the other and even that beauty, happiness, and virtue are one and the same. " How could I fail to understand this? How wicked I was before! How happy I might have been, and how happy I may be in the future! " I said to myself. " I must become another man as quickly, as quickly, as possible, this very moment, and begin to live differently." But, in spite of this, I still sat for a long time in the window, dreaming and doing nothing.

Has it ever happened to you, in summer, to lie down to sleep, during the daytime, in gloomy, rainy weather, and, waking up at sunset, to open your eyes, to catch sight through the wide square window, from under the linen shade which swells and beats its stick against the window sill, of the shady, purpling side of the linden alley, wet with rain, and the damp garden walks, illuminated by the bright, slanting rays; suddenly to catch the sound of merry life among the birds in the garden, and to see the insects which are circling in the window aperture, transparent in the sun, and become conscious of the fragrance of the air after rain, and to think, " How shameful of me to sleep away such an evening! " and then to spring up in haste, in order to go to the garden and rejoice in life? If this has happened to you, then that is a specimen of the powerful feeling which I experienced then.

REVERIES

" Today I shall confess, I shall purify myself of all my sins," I thought, " and I shall never commit any more." (Here I recalled all the sins which troubled me most.) " I shall go to church, without fail, every Sunday, and afterwards I shall read the Gospels for a whole hour; and then, out of the white bank-bill which I shall receive every month when I enter the university, I will be sure to give two rubles and a half (one-tenth) to the poor, and in such a manner that no one shall know it — and not to beggars, but I will seek out poor people, an orphan or old woman, whom no one knows about.

" I shall have a room to myself (probably St. Jerome's), and I shall take care of it myself, and keep it wonderfully clean; and I shall leave the man nothing to do for me, for he is just the same as I am. Then I shall go every day to the university on foot (and if they give me a droshky,[5] I shall sell it, and give that money also to the poor), and I shall do everything with the greatest precision. (What this " everything " was, I would not have told, in the least, then; but I vividly realized and felt that this " everything " meant an intellectual, moral, and irreproachable life.) " I shall prepare my lectures, and even go over the subjects beforehand, so that I shall be at the head in the first course, and write the dissertation; [6] in the second course, I shall know everything beforehand, and they can transfer me directly to the third course, so that at eighteen I shall graduate as first candidate, with two gold medals; then I shall stand my examination for the degree of Master, then Doctor, and I shall become the leading savant in Russia; I may be the most learned man in Europe, even." " Well, and afterwards? " I asked myself. But here remembered that these were dreams, — pride, sin, which I should have to recount to the priest that evening; and I went back to the beginning of my argument. " As a preparation for my lectures, I will walk out to the Sparrow Hills; there I will select a spot beneath a tree, and read over the lesson. Sometimes I shall take something to eat with me, cheese or cakes from Pedotti,[7] or something. I shall rest myself, and then I shall read some good book, or sketch views, or play on some instrument (I must not fail to learn to play the flute). Then She [8] will also take a walk on the Sparrow Hills, and

[5] **droshky**: four-wheeled carriage.
[6] **dissertation**: long, scholarly paper required for special honors.
[7] **Pedotti**: an Italian confectioner.
[8] **She**: an imaginary sweetheart.

some day she will come up to me and ask who I am. And I shall look at her so mournfully, and say that I am the son of a priest, and that I am happy only here when I am alone, quite, quite alone. Then she will give me her hand, and say something, and sit down beside me. Thus we shall come there every day, and we shall become friends, and I shall kiss her, — no, that is not well; on the contrary, from this day forth, I shall never more look at a woman. Never, never will I go into the maids' room, I will try not to pass by it, even; and in three years I shall be free from guardianship, and I shall marry, without fail. I shall take as much exercise as possible with gymnastics every day, so that when I am twenty-five I shall be stronger than Rappeau.[9] The first day, I will hold half a pood [10] in my outstretched hand for five minutes; on the second day, twenty-one pounds; on the third day, twenty-two pounds, and so on, so that at last I can support four poods in each hand, and I shall be stronger than all the men-servants; and when any one undertakes to insult me, or express himself disrespectfully of Her, I will take him thus, quite simply, by the breast, I will lift him an arshin [11] or two from the ground with one hand, and only hold him long enough to let him feel my power, and then I will release him. — But this is not well: no, I will not do him any harm, I will only show him. . . ."

Reproach me not because the dreams of youth were as childish as the dreams of childhood and boyhood. I am convinced that if I am fated to live to extreme old age, and my story follows my growth, as an old man of seventy I shall dream in exactly the same impossibly childish way as now. I shall dream of some charming Marie, who will fall in love with me as a toothless old man, as she loved Mazeppa; [12] of how my weak-minded son will suddenly become a Minister [13] through some unusual circumstance; or of how a treasure of millions will fall to me all of a sudden. I am convinced that there is no human being or age which is deprived of this beneficent, comforting capacity for dreaming. But, exclusive of the general traits of impossibility, — the witch-craft of reverie, — the dreams of each man and of each stage of growth possess their own distinctive character. During that period of time which I regard as the limit of boyhood and the beginning of youth, four sentiments formed the founda-

---

9 **Rappeau:** famous athlete of the day.
10 **pood:** a weight slightly more than thirty-six pounds.
11 **arshin:** a distance of two feet.
12 **Mazeppa:** one of Pushkin's heroes, whom Byron has celebrated in "Mazeppa's Ride." Marie was the young girl in love with Mazeppa.
13 **Minister:** important government official, not a clergyman.

tion of my dreams: love for her, the ideal woman, of whom I thought always in the same strain, and whom I expected to meet somewhere at any moment. This She was a little like Sonitchka; [14] a little like Mascha, Vasily's wife, when she washes the clothes in the tub; and a little like the woman with pearls on her white neck, whom I saw in the theater very long ago, in the box next to ours. The second sentiment was love of love. I wanted to have every one know and love me. I wanted to pronounce my name, Nikolai Irteneff, and have every one, startled by this information, surround me, and thank me for something. The third feeling was the hope of some remarkable, glorious good fortune, — so great and firm that it would border on madness. I was so sure that I should become the greatest and most distinguished man in the world very soon, in consequence of some extraordinary circumstance or other, that I found myself constantly in a state of agitated expectation of something enchantingly blissful. I was always expecting that it was about to begin, and that I was on the point of attaining whatever a man may desire; and I was always hastening about in all directions, supposing that it was already beginning in the place where I was not. The fourth and principal feeling was disgust at myself, and remorse, but a remorse so mingled with hope of bliss that there was nothing sorrowful about it. It seemed to me so easy and natural to tear myself away from all the past, to reconstruct, to forget everything which had been, and to begin my life with all its relations quite anew, that the past neither weighed upon nor fettered me. I even took pleasure in my repugnance to the past, and began to see it in more somber colors than it had possessed. The blacker was the circle of memories of the past, the purer and brighter did the pure, bright point of the present and the rainbow hues of the future stand out in relief against it. This voice of remorse and of passionate desire for perfection was the chief new spiritual sentiment at that epoch of my development; and it marked a new era in my views with regard to myself, to people, and the world. That beneficent, cheering voice has, since then, so often boldly been raised, in those sad hours when the soul has silently submitted to the weight of life's falsehood and vice, against every untruth, maliciously convicting the past, pointing to the bright spot of the present and making one love it, and promising good and happiness in the future, — the blessed, comforting voice! Is it possible that thou wilt ever cease to sound?

(Isabel Hapgood)

[14] **Sonitchka:** " little Sonia," a young girl he knew.

SUGGESTIONS FOR STUDY

1. What in this account shows Tolstoy's strong religious bent? His introspective turn of mind? His humanitarian sympathies? His principles of human equality? His intellectual ambitions?

2. Since a ruble is about fifty cents, figure how much his monthly allowance was to be at the university (first paragraph of "Reveries"). How does this compare with the allowance of an American college student of aristocratic family?

3. Discuss the subject of good resolutions and day dreams — their value and their discouraging aspects. Do Tolstoy's resemble those of young people today, or do you consider them unusual in any way?

4. All three biographical novels, *Childhood, Boyhood, Youth,* make excellent reading. The first gives an especially true picture of a Russian aristocratic country home, interesting to compare with Selma Lagerlöf's *Mårbacka.*

5. Do you know any other autobiographies which give a full picture of a young man's thoughts? If so, compare with this.

HOW MUCH LAND DOES A MAN NEED? [1]

I

An elder sister came to visit her younger sister in the country. The elder was married to a tradesman in town, the younger to a peasant in the village. As the sisters sat over their tea talking, the elder began to boast of the advantages of town life: saying how comfortably they lived there, how well they dressed, what fine clothes her children wore, what good things they ate and drank, and how she went to the theater, promenades, and entertainments.

The younger sister was piqued, and in turn disparaged the life of a tradesman, and stood up for that of a peasant.

"I would not change my way of life for yours," said she. "We may live roughly, but at least we are free from anxiety. You live in better style than we do, but though you often earn more than you need, you are very likely to lose all you have. You know the proverb, 'Loss and gain are brothers twain.' It often happens that people who are wealthy one day are begging their bread the next. Our way is safer. Though a peasant's life is not a fat one, it is a long one. We shall never grow rich, but we shall always have enough to eat."

[1] Sometimes translated with the title "Three Arshins of Land."

The elder sister said sneeringly:

" Enough? Yes, if you like to share with the pigs and the calves! What do you know of elegance or manners? However much your goodman may slave, you will die as you are living — on a dung heap — and your children the same."

" Well, what of that? " replied the younger. " Of course our work is rough and coarse. But, on the other hand, it is sure; and we need not bow to any one. But you, in your towns, are surrounded by temptations; today all may be right, but tomorrow the Evil One may tempt your husband with cards, wine, or women, and all will go to ruin. Don't such things happen often enough? "

Pahóm, the master of the house, was lying on the top of the oven,[2] and he listened to the women's chatter.

" It is perfectly true," thought he. " Busy as we are from childhood tilling mother earth, we peasants have no time to let any nonsense settle in our heads. Our only trouble is that we haven't land enough. If I had plenty of land, I shouldn't fear the Devil himself! "

The women finished their tea, chatted a while about dress, and then cleared away the tea-things and lay down to sleep.

But the Devil had been sitting behind the oven, and had heard all that was said. He was pleased that the peasant's wife had led her husband into boasting, and that he had said that if he had plenty of land he would not fear the Devil himself.

" All right," thought the Devil. " We will have a tussle. I'll give you land enough; and by means of that land I will get you into my power."

2

Close to the village there lived a lady, a small landowner, who had an estate of about three hundred acres. She had always lived on good terms with the peasants, until she engaged as her steward an old soldier, who took to burdening the people with fines. However careful Pahóm tried to be, it happened again and again that now a horse of his got among the lady's oats, now a cow strayed into her garden, now his calves found their way into her meadows — and he always had to pay a fine.

Pahóm paid up, but grumbled, and, going home in a temper, was rough with his family. All through that summer Pahóm had much

---

[2] **lying on the top of the oven:** The stove in a peasant's house was like a large box of brick with a flat top, which made a comfortable place to be in cold weather. From peasant stories it seems to be the special privilege of the man in the house to be on the oven.

trouble because of this steward; and he was even glad when winter came and the cattle had to be stabled. Though he grudged the fodder when they could no longer graze on the pasture land, at least he was free from anxiety about them.

In the winter the news got about that the lady was going to sell her land, and that the keeper of the inn on the high road was bargaining for it. When the peasants heard this they were very much alarmed.

" Well," thought they, " if the innkeeper gets the land, he will worry us with fines worse than the lady's steward. We all depend on that estate."

So the peasants went on behalf of their Commune,[3] and asked the lady not to sell the land to the innkeeper; offering her a better price for it themselves. The lady agreed to let them have it. Then the peasants tried to arrange for the Commune to buy the whole estate, so that it might be held by them all in common. They met twice to discuss it, but could not settle the matter; the Evil One sowed discord among them, and they could not agree. So they decided to buy the land individually, each according to his means; and the lady willingly agreed to this plan as she had to the other.

Presently Pahóm heard that a neighbor of his was buying fifty acres, and that the lady had consented to accept one-half in cash and to wait a year for the other half. Pahóm felt envious.

" Look at that," thought he, " the land is all being sold, and I shall get none of it." So he spoke to his wife.

" Other people are buying," said he, " and we must also buy twenty acres or so. Life is becoming impossible. That steward is simply crushing us with his fines."

So they put their heads together and considered how they could manage to buy it. They had one hundred rubles[4] laid by. They sold a colt, and one-half of their bees; hired out one of their sons as a laborer, and took his wages in advance; borrowed the rest from a brother-in-law, and so scraped together half the purchase money.

Having done this, Pahóm chose out a farm of forty acres, some of it wooded, and went to the lady to bargain for it. They came to an agreement, and he shook hands with her upon it, and paid her a deposit in advance. Then they went to town and signed the deeds; he paying half the price down, and undertaking to pay the remainder within two years.

[3] **Commune:** the smallest unit of government in Russia, which owned and administered the common property of the group.

[4] **one hundred rubles:** fifty dollars.

So now Pahóm had land of his own. He borrowed seed, and sowed it on the land he had bought. The harvest was a good one, and within a year he had managed to pay off his debts both to the lady and to his brother-in-law. So he became a landowner, plowing and sowing his own land, making hay on his own land, cutting his own trees, and feeding his cattle on his own pasture. When he went out to plow his fields, or to look at his growing corn, or at his grass meadows, his heart would fill with joy. The grass that grew and the flowers that bloomed there, seemed to him unlike any that grew elsewhere. Formerly, when he had passed by that land, it had appeared the same as any other land, but now it seemed quite different.

3

So Pahóm was well-contented, and everything would have been right if the neighboring peasants would only not have trespassed on his cornfields and meadows. He appealed to them most civilly, but they still went on: now the Communal herdsmen would let the village cows stray into his meadows; then horses from the night pasture would get among his corn. Pahóm turned them out again and again, and forgave their owners, and for a long time he forbore from prosecuting any one. But at last he lost patience and complained to the District Court. He knew it was the peasants' want of land, and no evil intent on their part, that caused the trouble; but he thought:

"I cannot go on overlooking it, or they will destroy all I have. They must be taught a lesson."

So he had them up, gave them one lesson, and then another, and two or three of the peasants were fined. After a time Pahóm's neighbors began to bear him a grudge for this, and would now and then let their cattle on to his land on purpose. One peasant even got into Pahóm's wood at night and cut down five young lime trees for their bark. Pahóm passing through the wood one day noticed something white. He came nearer, and saw the stripped trunks lying on the ground, and close by stood the stumps, where the trees had been. Pahóm was furious.

"If he had only cut one here and there it would have been bad enough," thought Pahóm, "but the rascal has actually cut down a whole clump. If I could only find out who did this I would pay him out." [5]

He racked his brains as to who it could be. Finally he decided:

[5] **pay him out**: get even with him.

" It must be Simon — no one else could have done it." So he went to Simon's homestead to have a look round, but he found nothing, and only had an angry scene. However, he now felt more certain than ever that Simon had done it, and he lodged a complaint. Simon was summoned. The case was tried, and re-tried, and at the end of it all Simon was acquitted, there being no evidence against him. Pahóm felt still more aggrieved, and let his anger loose upon the Elder and the Judges.

" You let thieves grease your palms," [6] said he. " If you were honest folk yourselves you would not let a thief go free."

So Pahóm quarreled with the Judges and with his neighbors. Threats to burn his building began to be uttered. So though Pahóm had more land, his place in the Commune was much worse than before.

About this time a rumor got about that many people were moving to new parts.

" There's no need for me to leave my land," thought Pahóm. " But some of the others might leave our village, and then there would be more room for us. I would take over their land myself and make my estate a bit bigger. I could then live more at ease. As it is, I am still too cramped to be comfortable."

One day Pahóm was sitting at home, when a peasant, passing through the village, happened to call in. He was allowed to stay the night, and supper was given him. Pahóm had a talk with this peasant and asked him where he came from. The stranger answered that he came from beyond the Volga, where he had been working. One word led to another, and the man went on to say that many people were settling in those parts. He told how some people from his village had settled there. They had joined the Commune and had had twenty-five acres per man granted them. The land was so good, he said, that the rye sown on it grew as high as a horse, and so thick that five cuts of a sickle made a sheaf. One peasant, he said, had brought nothing with him but his bare hands, and now he had six horses and two cows of his own.

Pahóm's heart kindled with desire. He thought:

" Why should I suffer in this narrow hole, if one can live so well elsewhere? I will sell my land and my homestead here, and with the money I will start afresh over there and get everything new. In this crowded place one is always having trouble. But I must first go and find out all about it myself."

[6] **grease your palms: bribe you.**

Toward summer he got ready and started. He went down the Volga on a steamer to Samára, then walked another three hundred miles on foot, and at last he reached the place. It was just as the stranger had said. The peasants had plenty of land; every man had twenty-five acres of Communal land given him for his use, and any one who had money could buy, besides, at two shillings an acre, as much good freehold land [7] as he wanted.

Having found out all he wished to know, Pahóm returned home as autumn came on, and began selling off his belongings. He sold his land at a profit, sold his homestead and all his cattle, and withdrew from membership of the Commune. He only waited till the spring, and then started with his family for the new settlement.

4

As soon as Pahóm and his family arrived at their new abode he applied for admission into the Commune of a large village. He stood treat to the Elders and obtained the necessary documents. Five shares of Communal land were given him for his own and his son's use: that is to say, 125 acres (not all together, but in different fields) besides the use of the Communal pasture. Pahóm put up the buildings he needed and bought cattle. Of the Communal land alone he had three times as much as at his former home, and the land was good corn-land. He was ten times better off than he had been. He had plenty of arable land and pasturage and could keep as many head of cattle as he liked.

At first, in the bustle of building and settling down, Pahóm was pleased with it all, but when he got used to it he began to think that even here he had not enough land. The first year he sowed wheat on his share of the Communal land and had a good crop. He wanted to go on sowing wheat, but had not enough Communal land for the purpose, and what he had already used was not available; for in those parts wheat is only sown on virgin soil or on fallow land. It is sown for one or two years, and then the land lies fallow till it is again overgrown with prairie grass. There were many who wanted such land, and there was not enough for all; so that people quarreled about it. Those who were better off wanted it for growing wheat, and those who were poor wanted it to let to dealers, so that they might raise money to pay their taxes. Pahóm wanted to sow more wheat; so he rented land from a dealer for a year. He sowed much wheat and had a fine crop, but the land was too far from the village

[7] **freehold land:** land which would be his personal property.

— the wheat had to be carted more than ten miles. After a time Pahóm noticed that some peasant-dealers were living on separate farms and were growing wealthy; and he thought:

"If I were to buy some freehold land and have a homestead on it, it would be a different thing altogether. Then it would all be nice and compact."

The question of buying freehold land recurred to him again and again.

He went on in the same way for three years, renting land and sowing wheat. The seasons turned out well and the crops were good, so that he began to lay money by. He might have gone on living contentedly, but he grew tired of having to rent other people's land every year and having to scramble for it. Wherever there was good land to be had the peasants would rush for it and it was taken up at once, so that unless you were sharp about it you got none. It happened in the third year that he and a dealer together rented a piece of pasture land from some peasants; and they had already plowed it up, when there was some dispute, and the peasants went to law about it, and things fell out so that the labor was all lost.

"If it were my own land," thought Pahóm, "I should be independent and there would not be all this unpleasantness."

So Pahóm began looking out for land which he could buy, and he came across a peasant who had bought thirteen hundred acres, but having got into difficulties, was willing to sell again cheap. Pahóm bargained and haggled with him, and at last they settled the price at 1,500 rubles, part in cash and part to be paid later. They had all but clinched the matter when a passing dealer happened to stop at Pahóm's one day to get a feed for his horses. He drank tea with Pahóm, and they had a talk. The dealer said that he was just returning from the land of the Bashkirs,[8] far away, where he had bought thirteen thousand acres of land, all for one thousand rubles. Pahóm questioned him further, and the tradesman said:

"All one needs to do is to make friends with the chiefs. I gave away about one hundred rubles' worth of dressing-gowns and carpets, besides a case of tea, and I gave wine to those who would drink it; and I got the land for less than two-pence an acre." And he showed Pahóm the title-deeds, saying:

"The land lies near a river, and the whole prairie is virgin soil."

Pahóm plied him with questions, and the tradesman said:

"There is more land there than you could cover if you walked a

[8] **Bashkirs:** people of the Ural Mountains.

year, and it all belongs to the Bashkirs. They are as simple as sheep, and land can be got almost for nothing."

"There now," thought Pahóm, "with my one thousand rubles, why should I get only thirteen hundred acres and saddle myself with a debt besides. If I take it out there I can get more than ten times as much for the money."

5

Pahóm inquired how to get to the place, and as soon as the tradesman had left him he prepared to go there himself. He left his wife to look after the homestead and started on his journey, taking his man with him. They stopped at a town on their way and bought a case of tea, some wine, and other presents, as the tradesman had advised. On and on they went until they had gone more than three hundred miles, and on the seventh day they came to a place where the Bashkirs had pitched their tents. It was all just as the tradesman had said. The people lived on the steppes,[9] by a river, in felt-covered tents. They neither tilled the ground nor ate bread. Their cattle and horses grazed in herds on the steppe. The colts were tethered behind the tents, and the mares were driven to them twice a day. The mares were milked, and from the milk kumiss [10] was made. It was the women who prepared kumiss, and they also made cheese. As far as the men were concerned, drinking kumiss and tea, eating mutton, and playing on their pipes was all they cared about. They were all stout and merry, and all the summer long they never thought of doing any work. They were quite ignorant and knew no Russian, but were good-natured enough.

As soon as they saw Pahóm they came out of their tents and gathered round their visitor. An interpreter was found, and Pahóm told them he had come about some land. The Bashkirs seemed very glad; they took Pahóm and led him into one of the best tents, where they made him sit on some down cushions placed on a carpet, while they sat round him. They gave him tea and kumiss, and had a sheep killed, and gave him mutton to eat. Pahóm took presents out of his cart and distributed them among the Bashkirs, and divided amongst them the tea. The Bashkirs were delighted. They talked a great deal among themselves, and then told the interpreter to translate.

"They wish to tell you," said the interpreter, "that they like you, and that it is our custom to do all we can to please a guest and to repay him for his gifts. You have given us presents; now tell us

[9] steppes: plains.   [10] kumiss: a distilled drink.

which of the things we possess please you best, that we may present them to you."

"What pleases me best here," answered Pahóm, " is your land. Our land is crowded, and the soil is exhausted; but you have plenty of land and it is good land. I never saw the like of it."

The interpreter translated. The Bashkirs talked among themselves for a while. Pahóm could not understand what they were saying, but saw that they were much amused, and that they shouted and laughed. Then they were silent and looked at Pahóm while the interpreter said:

" They wish me to tell you that in return for your presents they will gladly give you as much land as you want. You have only to point it out with your hand and it is yours."

The Bashkirs talked again for a while and began to dispute. Pahóm asked what they were disputing about, and the interpreter told him that some of them thought they ought to ask their chief about the land and not act in his absence, while others thought there was no need to wait for his return.

6

While the Bashkirs were disputing, a man in a large fox-fur cap appeared on the scene. They all became silent and rose to their feet. The interpreter said, " This is our Chief himself."

Pahóm immediately fetched the best dressing-gown and five pounds of tea and offered these to the Chief. The Chief accepted them, and seated himself in the place of honor. The Bashkirs at once began telling him something. The Chief listened for a while, then made a sign with his head for them to be silent, and addressing himself to Pahóm, said in Russian:

" Well, let it be so. Choose whatever piece of land you like; we have plenty of it."

" How can I take as much as I like? " thought Pahóm. " I must get a deed to make it secure, or else they may say, 'It is yours,' and afterwards may take it away again."

" Thank you for your kind words," he said aloud. " You have much land, and I only want a little. But I should like to be sure which bit is mine. Could it not be measured and made over to me? Life and death are in God's hands. You good people give it to me, but your children might wish to take it away again."

" You are quite right," said the Chief. " We will make it over to you."

" I heard that a dealer had been here," continued Pahóm, " and that you gave him a little land, too, and signed title-deeds to that effect. I should like to have it done in the same way."

The Chief understood.

" Yes," replied he, " that can be done quite easily. We have a scribe, and we will go to town with you and have the deed properly sealed."

" And what will be the price? " asked Pahóm.

" Our price is always the same: one thousand rubles a day."

Pahóm did not understand.

" A day? What measure is that? How many acres would that be? "

" We do not know how to reckon it out," said the Chief. " We sell it by the day. As much as you can go round on your feet in a day is yours, and the price is one thousand rubles a day."

Pahóm was surprised.

" But in a day you can get round a large tract of land," he said.

The Chief laughed.

" It will all be yours! " said he. " But there is one condition: If you don't return on the same day to the spot whence you started, your money is lost."

" But how am I to mark the way that I have gone? "

" Why, we shall go to any spot you like and stay there. You must start from that spot and make your round, taking a spade with you. Wherever you think necessary, make a mark. At every turning dig a hole and pile up the turf; then afterwards we will go round with a plow from hole to hole. You may make as large a circuit as you please, but before the sun sets you must return to the place you started from. All the land you cover will be yours."

Pahóm was delighted. It was decided to start early next morning. They talked a while, and after drinking some more kumiss and eating some more mutton, they had tea again, and then the night came on. They gave Pahóm a feather-bed to sleep on, and the Bashkirs dispersed for the night, promising to assemble the next morning at daybreak and ride out before sunrise to the appointed spot.

7

Pahóm lay on the feather-bed but could not sleep. He kept thinking about the land.

" What a large tract I will mark off! " thought he. " I can easily do thirty-five miles in a day. The days are long now, and within a circuit of thirty-five miles what a lot of land there will be! I will sell the poorer land, or let it to peasants, but I'll pick out the best and farm it. I will buy two ox-teams, and hire two more laborers. About a hundred and fifty acres shall be plow-land, and I will pasture cattle on the rest."

Pahóm lay awake all night, and dozed off only just before dawn. Hardly were his eyes closed when he had a dream. He thought he was lying in that same tent and heard somebody chuckling outside. He wondered who it could be, and rose and went out, and he saw the Bashkir Chief sitting in front of the tent holding his sides and rolling about with laughter. Going nearer to the Chief, Pahóm asked: " What are you laughing at? " But he saw that it was no longer the Chief, but the dealer who had recently stopped at his house and had told him about the land. Just as Pahóm was going to ask, " Have you been here long? " he saw that it was not the dealer, but the peasant who had come up from the Volga, long ago, to Pahóm's old home. Then he saw that it was not the peasant either, but the Devil himself with hoofs and horns, sitting there and chuckling, and before him lay a man barefoot, prostrate on the ground, with only trousers and a shirt on. And Pahóm dreamt that he looked more attentively to see what sort of a man it was that was lying there, and he saw that the man was dead, and that it was himself! He awoke horror-struck.

" What things one does dream! " thought he.

Looking around he saw through the open door that the dawn was breaking.

" It's time to wake them up," thought he. " We ought to be starting."

He got up, roused his man (who was sleeping in his cart), bade him harness; and went to call the Bashkirs.

" It's time to go to the steppe to measure the land," he said.

The Bashkirs rose and assembled, and the Chief came, too. Then they began drinking kumiss again, and offered Pahóm some tea, but he would not wait.

" If we are to go, let us go. It is high time," said he.

8

The Bashkirs got ready and they all started; some mounted on horses, and some in carts. Pahóm drove in his own small cart with his servant, and took a spade with him. When they reached the steppe the morning red was beginning to kindle. They ascended a hillock (called by the Bashkirs a *shikhan*) and dismounting from their carts and their horses, gathered in one spot. The Chief came up to Pahóm and stretching out his arm toward the plain,

" See," said he, " all this, as far as your eye can reach, is ours. You may have any part of it you like."

Pahóm's eyes glistened: it was all virgin soil, as flat as the palm of your hand, as black as the seed of a poppy, and in the hollows different kinds of grasses grew breast high.

The Chief took off his fox-fur cap, placed it on the ground and said: " This will be the mark. Start from here and return here again. All the land you go round shall be yours."

Pahóm took out his money and put it on the cap. Then he took off his outer coat, remaining in his sleeveless under-coat. He unfastened his girdle and tied it tight below his stomach, put a little bag of bread into the breast of his coat, and tying a flask of water to his girdle, he drew up the tops of his boots, took the spade from his man, and stood ready to start. He considered for some moments which way he had better go — it was tempting everywhere.

" No matter," he concluded, " I will go toward the rising sun."

He turned his face to the east, stretched himself, and waited for the sun to appear above the rim.

" I must lose no time," he thought, " and it is easier walking while it is still cool."

The sun's rays had hardly flashed above the horizon, before Pahóm, carrying the spade over his shoulder, went down into the steppe.

Pahóm started walking neither slowly nor quickly. After having gone a thousand yards he stopped, dug a hole, and placed pieces of turf one on another to make it more visible. Then he went on; and now that he had walked off his stiffness he quickened his pace. After a while he dug another hole.

Pahóm looked back. The hillock could be distinctly seen in the sunlight, with the people on it, and the glittering tires of the cart-wheels. At a rough guess Pahóm considered that he had walked three miles. It was growing warmer; he took off his under-coat, flung it across his shoulder, and went on again. It had grown quite warm now; he looked at the sun, it was time to think of breakfast.

" The first shift is done, but there are four in a day, and it is too soon yet to turn. But I will just take off my boots," said he to himself.

He sat down, took off his boots, stuck them into his girdle, and went on. It was easy walking now.

" I will go on for another three miles," thought he, " and then turn to the left. This spot is so fine, that it would be a pity to lose it. The further one goes, the better the land seems."

He went straight on for a while, and when he looked round, the hillock was scarcely visible and the people on it looked like black ants, and he could just see something glistening there in the sun.

" Ah," thought Pahóm, " I have gone far enough in this direction, it is time to turn. Besides I am in a regular sweat and very thirsty."

He stopped, dug a large hole and heaped up pieces of turf. Next he untied his flask, had a drink, and then turned sharply to the left. He went on and on; the grass was high, and it was very hot.

Pahóm began to grow tired: he looked at the sun and saw that it was noon.

" Well," he thought, " I must have a rest."

He sat down and ate some bread and drank some water; but he did not lie down, thinking that if he did he might fall asleep. After sitting a little while, he went on again. At first he walked easily: the food had strengthened him; but it had become terribly hot, and he felt sleepy; still he went on, thinking: " An hour to suffer, a life-time to live."

He went a long way in this direction also and was about to turn to the left again, when he perceived a damp hollow. " It would be a pity to leave that out," he thought. " Flax would do well there." So he went on past the hollow and dug a hole on the other side of it before he turned the corner. Pahóm looked toward the hillock. The heat made the air hazy; it seemed to be quivering, and through the haze the people on the hillock could scarcely be seen.

" Ah! " thought Pahóm, " I have made the sides too long; I must make this one shorter." And he went along the third side, stepping faster. He looked at the sun: it was nearly half way to the horizon, and he had not yet done two miles of the third side of the square. He was still ten miles from the goal.

" No," he thought, " though it will make my land lop-sided, I must hurry back in a straight line now. I might go too far, and as it is I have a great deal of land."

So Pahóm hurriedly dug a hole and turned straight toward the hillock.

9

Pahóm went straight toward the hillock, but he now walked with difficulty. He was done up with the heat, his bare feet were cut and bruised, and his legs began to fail. He longed to rest, but it was impossible if he meant to get back before sunset. The sun waits for no man, and it was sinking lower and lower.

" Oh dear," he thought, " if only I have not blundered trying for too much! What if I am too late? "

He looked toward the hillock and at the sun. He was still far from his goal, and the sun was already near the rim.

Pahóm walked on and on; it was very hard walking, but he went quicker and quicker. He pressed on, but was still far from the place. He began running, threw away his coat, his boots, his flask, and his cap, and kept only the spade, which he used as a support.

" What shall I do," he thought again, " I have grasped too much and ruined the whole affair. I can't get there before the sun sets."

And this fear made him still more breathless. Pahóm went on running, his soaked shirt and trousers stuck to him, and his mouth was parched. His breast was working like a blacksmith's bellows, his heart was beating like a hammer, and his legs were giving way as if they did not belong to him. Pahóm was seized with terror lest he should die of the strain.

Though afraid of death, he could not stop. " After having run all that way they will call me a fool if I stop now," thought he. And he ran on and on, and drew near and heard the Bashkirs yelling and shouting to him, and their cries inflamed his heart still more. He gathered his last strength and ran on.

The sun was close to the rim, and cloaked in mist looked large and red as blood. Now, yes, now, it was about to set! The sun was quite low, but he was also quite near his aim. Pahóm could already see the people on the hillock waving their arms to hurry him up. He could see the fox-fur cap on the ground, and the money on it, and the Chief sitting on the ground holding his sides. And Pahóm remembered his dream.

" There is plenty of land," thought he, " but will God let me live on it? I have lost my life, I have lost my life! I shall never reach that spot! "

Pahóm looked at the sun, which had reached the earth; one side of it had already disappeared. With all his remaining strength he rushed on, bending his body forward so that his legs could hardly follow fast enough to keep him from falling. Just as he reached the hillock it suddenly grew dark. He looked up — the sun had already set! He gave a cry: " All my labor has been in vain," thought he, and was about to stop, but he heard the Bashkirs still shouting, and remembered that though to him, from below, the sun seemed to have set, they on the hillock could still see it. He took a long breath and ran up the hillock. It was still light there. He reached the top and saw the cap. Before it sat the Chief laughing and holding his sides. Again Pahóm remembered his dream, and he uttered a cry; his legs gave way beneath him, he fell forward and reached the cap with his hands.

" Ah, that's a fine fellow! " exclaimed the Chief. " He has gained much land! "

Pahóm's servant came running up and tried to raise him, but he saw that blood was flowing from his mouth. Pahóm was dead!

The Bashkirs clicked their tongues to show their pity.

His servant picked up the spade and dug a grave long enough for Pahóm to lie in it, and buried him in it. Six feet from his head to his heels was all he needed.

(Aylmer Maude)

SUGGESTIONS FOR STUDY

1. How are realism and allegory blended in this story? What is the point of allegory? The significance of the title?

2. How does this story tally with Tolstoy's personality as shown in the extract from *Youth,* and in his later philosophy of life?

3. What shows that a certain form of Communism was practiced in Russia long before the days of the Soviet Republic?

4. Discuss the suspense and climax in this story. Compare with Browning's " How They Brought the Good News from Ghent to Aix." Do you know other stories where working against time plays a large part? This is a common device in the movies. Would this story make a good movie? Why or why not?

5. Do you know any other stories in which a man's greed is his own undoing?

6. Love of land is an important element in many of the world's great peasant novels. If you have read any of the following, discuss how this enters into the story: Hamsun's *Growth of the Soil,* Rölvaag's *Giants in the Earth,* Pearl Buck's *The Good Earth.*

7. Tolstoy has written many short stories which are worth reading. Of his long novels *Anna Karenina* and *War and Peace* are the best to read. *The Death of Ivan Ilyich* is a powerful novelette. *Anna Karenina* and *Resurrection* have both been made into operas and moving pictures.

ANTON PAVLOVICH CHEKHOV (1860–1904)

The father of Anton Chekhov had originally been a serf, but by industry had obtained his freedom before the general emancipation of 1861. Craving for his four children the education denied himself, the father sent Anton first to school in his native city of Taganrog on the sea of Azov, and later to the School of Medicine at the University of Moscow. The young man received his doctor's degree, but aside from a year in a hospital and active work during a cholera epidemic he engaged in little formal practice. As early as the age of nineteen, five years before obtaining his degree, he had begun to write, and in the field of literature he decided to put his real effort. But he never regretted his medical training, for it brought him into contact with diversified types of characters, and awakened his interest in mental abnormality which he used in many of his stories. Chekhov's understanding of human suffering was heightened by the fact that he himself was a victim of tuberculosis which caused his death at a German health resort while he was still in the early forties.

Chekhov's writing falls into two classes — his many short stories and eleven plays, five of which are full-length plays, the others one-act farces. Characteristic of the Russian stage, the plays are rambling and almost plotless, in some instances without the supposed essential to drama, a struggle. But they displayed Russian character with a fidelity which pleased Moscow audiences, and the opening night of his greatest play, *The Cherry Orchard,* brought him the ovation of his career. Five months later he was dead.

In his innumerable short stories Chekhov showed a careful artistry and economy of detail in contrast to the prolixity of the Russian novelists. Many of these stories are only a few pages long. Most of them portray the intellectual middle class, though no class of society has been omitted from this rich picture gallery. Not only by brevity, but also by humor, are these stories set off from the main trend of Russian fiction. The humor, however, is for the most part grim, and the effect on a reader of a succession of Chekhov stories is far from merry, for this supposed humor lies often enough in the futility of life and the discrepancies between one's dreams and the petty meannesses of actuality which destroy them. What begins with light-hearted laughter is likely to close with a wry ironic smile. Others of his stories are black tragedies, as the well-known "Ward No. 6," in which a doctor who lacks the will power to bring about needed reforms in his insane asylum is eventually himself shoved into Ward No. 6 and dies in intense mental agony.

Chekhov's mastery lies in the highly selected power of his details, the clear spotlight which he throws on a certain situation or quirk of character, leaving the rest in shadow. In this sense he is dramatic even when handling commonplace incidents and ordinary men.

THE SLANDERER

Chekhov's output of short stories has been tremendous, and most of them have been translated into English. One list shows twenty-four volumes containing two hundred and seventy-four individual stories. The following story is typical of Chekhov's manner in that it is very short, deals with middle-class people, and its humor is a cross between a merry smile at human foibles and a grim smile at the tricks of fate. Chekhov was greatly influenced by Maupassant, and this story was directly suggested to the author's mind by the French writer's "A Piece of String." A comparison of the two stories makes an interesting study.

Sergey Kapitonich Akhineyev, the teacher of calligraphy,[1] gave his daughter Natalya in marriage to the teacher of history and geography, Ivan Petrovich Loshadinikh. The wedding feast went on swimmingly. They sang, played, and danced in the parlor. Waiters, hired for the occasion from the club, bustled about hither and thither like madmen, in black frock coats and soiled white neckties. A loud noise of voices smote the air. From the outside people looked in at the windows — their social standing gave them no right to enter.

Just at midnight the host, Akhineyev, made his way to the kitchen to see whether everything was ready for the supper. The kitchen was filled with smoke from the floor to the ceiling; the smoke consisted of the odors of geese, ducks, and many other things. Victuals and beverages were scattered upon two tables in artistic disorder. Marfa, the cook, a stout, red-faced woman, was busying herself near the loaded tables.

"Show me the sturgeon," said Akhineyev, rubbing his hands and licking his lips. "What a fine odor! I could just devour the whole kitchen! Well, let me see the sturgeon!"

Marfa walked up to one of the benches and carefully lifted a greasy newspaper. Beneath that paper, in a huge dish, lay a big fat sturgeon, amid capers, olives, and carrots. Akhineyev glanced at the sturgeon and heaved a sigh of relief. His face became radiant, his eyes rolled under. He bent down, and, smacking his lips, issued a sound of a creaking wheel. He stood a while, then snapped his fingers for pleasure, and smacked his lips once more.

"Bah! The sound of a hearty kiss. Whom have you been kissing there, Marfusha?"[2] some one's voice was heard from the adjoining

---

[1] **calligraphy:** penmanship.
[2] **Marfusha:** nickname for Marfa.

room, and soon the closely cropped head of Vankin, the assistant school instructor, appeared in the doorway. " Whom have you been kissing here? A-a-ah! Very good! Sergey Kapitonich! A fine old man indeed! A pretty tête-a-tête! "

" I wasn't kissing at all," said Akhineyev, confused; " who told you, you fool? I only — smacked my lips with regards to — in consideration of my pleasure — at the sight of the fish."

" Tell that to some one else, not to me! " exclaimed Vankin, whose face expanded into a broad smile as he disappeared behind the door. Akhineyev blushed.

" The devil knows what may come out of this! " he thought. " He'll go about tale-bearing now, the rascal. He'll disgrace me before the whole town, the brute! "

Akhineyev entered the parlor timidly and cast futive glances to see what Vankin was doing. Vankin stood near the piano and, deftly bending down, whispered something to the inspector's sister-in-law, who was laughing.

" That's about me! " thought Akhineyev. " About me, the devil take him! She believes him, she's laughing. My God! No, that mustn't be left like that. No. I'll have to make it so that no one should believe him. I'll speak to all of them, and he'll remain a foolish gossip in the end."

Akhineyev scratched his head, and, still confused, walked up to Padekoi.

" I was in the kitchen a little while ago, arranging things there for the supper," he said to the Frenchman. " You like fish, I know, and I have a sturgeon of that length. About two yards. Ha, ha, ha! Yes, by the way, I have almost forgotten. There was a real anecdote about that sturgeon in the kitchen. I entered the kitchen a little while ago and wanted to examine the food. I glanced at the sturgeon and, for pleasure, I smacked my lips — it was so piquant! And just at that moment the fool Vankin entered and says — ha, ha, ha — and says: ' A-a! A-a-ah! You have been kissing here? ' — with Marfa; just think of it, with the cook! What he invented, that blockhead! The woman is ugly, she looks like a monkey, and he says we were kissing. What a queer fellow! "

" Who's a queer fellow? " asked Tarantulov as he approached them.

" I refer to Vankin. I went out into the kitchen — "

The story of Marfa and the sturgeon was repeated.

" That makes me laugh. What a queer fellow he is. In my opinion it is more pleasant to kiss the dog than to kiss Marfa," added Akhineyev, and, turning around, he noticed Mzda.

"We have been speaking about Vankin," he said to him. "What a queer fellow. He entered the kitchen and noticed me standing beside Marfa, and immediately he began to invent different stories. 'What?' he says, 'you have been kissing each other!' He was drunk, so he must have been dreaming. 'And I,' said I, 'I would rather kiss a duck than kiss Marfa. And I have a wife,' said I, 'you fool.' He made me appear ridiculous."

"Who made you appear ridiculous?" inquired the teacher of religion addressing Akhineyev.

"Vankin. I was standing in the kitchen, you know, and looking at the sturgeon—" And so forth. In about half an hour all the guests knew the story about Vankin and the sturgeon.

"Now let him tell," thought Akhineyev, rubbing his hands. "Let him do it. He'll start to tell them, and they'll cut him short: 'Don't talk nonsense, you fool! We know all about it.'"

And Akhineyev felt so much appeased that he drank, for joy, four glasses of brandy over and above his fill. Having escorted his daughter to her room, he went to his own and soon slept the sleep of an innocent child, and on the following day he no longer remembered the story of the sturgeon. But, alas! Man proposes and God disposes. The evil tongue does its wicked work, and even Akhineyev's cunning did not do him any good. One week later, on a Wednesday, after the third lesson, when Akhineyev stood in the teachers' room and discussed the vicious inclinations of the pupil Visyekin, the director approached him, and, beckoning to him, called him aside.

"See here, Sergey Kapitonich," said the director. "Pardon me. It isn't my affair, yet I must make it clear to you, nevertheless. It is my duty—You see, rumors are on foot that you are on intimate terms with that woman—with your cook—It isn't my affair, but—You may be on intimate terms with her, you may kiss her—You may do whatever you like, but, please, don't do it so openly! I beg of you. Don't forget that you are a pedagogue."

Akhineyev stood as though frozen and petrified. Like one stung by a swarm of bees and scalded with boiling water, he went home. On his way it seemed to him as though the whole town stared at him as at one besmeared with tar—At home new troubles awaited him.

"Why don't you eat anything?" asked his wife at their dinner. "What are you thinking about? Are you thinking about Cupid, eh?

You are longing for Marfushka. I know everything already, you Mahomet. Kind people have opened my eyes, you barbarian! "

And she slapped him on the cheek.

He rose from the table, and staggering, without cap or coat, directed his footsteps toward Vankin. The latter was at home.

" You rascal! " he said to Vankin. " Why have you covered me with mud before the whole world? Why have you slandered me? "

" How? What slander? What are you inventing? "

" And who told everybody that I was kissing Marfa? Not you, perhaps? Not you, you murderer? "

Vankin began to blink his eyes, and all the fibers of his face began to quiver. He lifted his eyes toward the image and ejaculated:

" May God punish me, may I lose my eyesight and die, if I said even a single word about you to any one! May I have neither house nor home! "

Vankin's sincerity admitted of no doubt. It was evident that it was not he who had gossiped.

" But who was it? Who? " Akhineyev asked himself, going over in his mind all his acquaintances, and striking his chest. " Who was it? "

(Herman Bernstein)

SUGGESTIONS FOR STUDY

1. How do you answer the question at the end of the story? What point is the author trying to make in this story? Is it a surprise ending, or not?

2. Compare the story with Maupassant's " The Piece of String," page 145. Wherein does the chief point of similarity lie? The chief point of difference? Which seems to you the greater story? Why?

3. Chekhov has been called a Russian O. Henry. Can you see any justification for the comparison? Read others of Chekhov's stories and observe a marked difference between his manner and O. Henry's.

MAXIM GORKI (1868–1936)

" Bitter " is the meaning of Gorki, the name assumed by Alexey Maximovich Peshkov and so entirely identified with him that one biographer has said his real name " will remain forever buried in the parish register." Bitter indeed were the circumstances surrounding the child from whom the writer grew, and bitter the picture of life coming from the pen of the mature man. Like Tolstoy, Gorki has given us a complete survey of his early life in a three-part biography (but without the fictional disguise of Tolstoy's) called *Childhood, In the World,* and *My Universities.* But the only marked parallel in their early lives is that both lost their parents in childhood. In all other circumstances the aristocrat Tolstoy and the proletarian Gorki represent opposite extremes. After the death of his parents Gorki lived with his maternal grandparents in Nizhni-Novgorod, the city in which he had been born. The grandfather was a close-fisted old dyer who apprenticed the boy to a shoemaker. At twelve Alexey ran away and took service as a pantry boy on a Volga River steamer. While assisting a drunken but well-read cook, the boy had access to a trunk full of good French and Russian fiction, and under this rough tutor first became interested in reading. In search of further education he went to Kazan under the impression that the university gave away free learning, but he soon found that he could do nothing without money and was forced to work in a wretched unsanitary bakeshop of which he has given a vivid picture in the short story "Twenty-six Men and One Girl." All kinds of odd jobs followed, until the youth became practically a tramp. At nineteen he tried unsuccessfully to shoot himself. During these years of wandering and abject poverty he was gathering the experience which he later turned into literature. At twenty-three his first sketches appeared in newspapers; with the help of an older writer he was soon accepted by the magazines; in the next few years he took his place with the leading writers of the day. His short stories opened up the world of the "down-and-outs" as seen from the inside, and Gorki fascinated his readers by the relentlessness of his realism. For all their miseries, his vagabonds had a sturdiness of will and power of action which most of the earlier heroes of Russian literature had lacked, and this in itself seemed to strike a new note of energy in the national fiction.

Gorki's background naturally made him a revolutionist and he was often imprisoned for his ideas. In 1906 at the height of his fame he came to the United States to raise money for his cause. At first he was honored at a literary banquet at which he and Mark Twain exchanged compliments, but afterwards the Americans were displeased by his unconventional ways and his mission was a failure. At the time of the Revolution of 1917 Gorki threw in his lot with the Bolsheviks and wrote many articles in their defense but disapproved of their destruction of all the arts of civilization and used his influence to moderate their treatment of creative artists and scholars. After 1922 on account of poor health he lived outside of Russia, for the most part in Italy. On occasional return visits he was greatly honored by the Russians. In 1932 the name of the most important street in Moscow and also that of his birthplace, Nizhni-Novgorod, were both officially changed to Gorki.

Gorki's most important field is the short story, but in addition he wrote several plays, which, however, proved inferior to Chekhov's. He was better suited to the realm of biography. Besides the three autobiographies mentioned above, he wrote excellent reminiscences of Tolstoy and Andreyev, and a curious "book of Russian eccentrics" called *Fragments from a Diary*. The most marked difference between Tolstoy's autobiography and Gorki's is that where the former is principally introspective, the latter is distinctly objective, giving the intricate pattern of persons and circumstances surrounding him without revealing to any great extent his own personality. During his years in Italy he wrote a three-volume novel, *The End and the Beginning*, which covers the forty years preceding the Revolution of 1917. The three parts are *Bystander* (1930), *The Magnet* (1931), and *Other Fires* (1933).

IN THE STEPPE [1]

This tale is really a story within a story, being told by a man in a hospital to his neighbor in the next bed. At the end we return to the hospital for the significant comment on the tale.

It was in the worst possible humor that we turned our backs upon Perekop, hungry as wolves and savage at the whole human race. For twelve hours we had been vainly using all our wits and putting forth our efforts to steal or beg something, and it was only when at last the truth was borne in upon us that neither method was likely to be successful, that we resolved to move on further. But whither? Further generally.

That was a resolution put by each to all and carried unanimously; but over and above this we were likewise prepared to go further in all respects, in the direction of the life-path on which we had been journeying so long, and that resolution was also formed by each of us, but in silence, and although not uttered aloud, it peered through the cheerless luster of our hungry eyes.

There were three of us, all told, and our acquaintance was of recent date; it was struck up when we were thrown together in a little tavern on the bank of the river Dnieper.

One of our trio — a muscular, red-haired fellow, with cold gray eyes — had been a soldier with the railway battalion, and then — if his own story was to be believed — a station-master on one of the Vistula [2] lines. He could speak German, and was remarkably well versed in the ins and outs of prison life.

People of our ilk are not given to talking about their past, having always grounds for this coyness which are more or less solid; for this

---

[1] **Steppe:** Russian for *prairie*.
[2] **Vistula:** river flowing through Poland into the Baltic Sea.

reason, we are all prone to take every man's word on trust, at least outwardly; in the depths of our consciousness, however, each of us had his doubts even about himself.

When therefore our second chum — a hard-featured, diminutive specimen of the human kind, with very thin lips always sceptically pursed up — gave himself out for an ex-student of the Moscow University, the soldier and I received the statement as a genuine fact. At bottom we did not care a fig whether he had been a student, a detective, or a thief; the main point was that at the moment when we made his acquaintance he was our equal, being just as hungry as ourselves, as much an object of watchfulness to the police in cities and of suspicion to the peasants in villages, hating the one and the other with the hate of the powerless, the hounded-down, hungry wild beast, and as eager for universal vengeance on one and all; in a word, his standing among the lords of nature and masters of life, as well as his own disposition, made him a bird of the same feather as ourselves.

Now there is no cement like misfortune for joining firmly together two or more natures — even though they be diametrically opposed to each other — and we were all convinced of the justice of our claim to consider ourselves miserable.

I was the third. Modesty, ingrained in my nature from my earliest days, forbids me to dwell upon my own merits, and a dislike to be taken for a greenhorn impels me to be silent as to my defects. Still, by way of supplying materials for classifying me, I don't mind saying that I have always looked upon myself as better than other people, and I continue cheerfully to do so to this day.

Well, as I was saying, we had turned our backs to Perekop and were moving forward, intending in the course of the day to come up with the shepherds, of whom one can always beg a piece of bread, for they seldom say nay to a request of that nature made by passers-by.

I was trudging along by the side of the soldier, the "student" jogging on behind us. On his shoulders hung something suggestive of a morning coat; his head, sharp, angular, and closely cropped, was encircled by the remnant of a broad-brimmed hat; gray trousers mottled with patches of many hues draped his legs, and to the soles of his feet he had fastened a pair of bootlegs picked up on the road, with twine which he had himself manufactured, using the lining of his costume as strains; this arrangement he called sandals. He plodded on in silence, raising clouds of dust, and his little green eyes kept twinkling as he moved.

The soldier was dressed in a blouse of red fustian [3] of which, according to his own account, he had become possessed " by his own hands " in Kherson; [4] over this blouse he wore a warm wadded vest; his headgear consisted of a soldier's kepi [5] of doubtful color, donned according to military usage on the side of his head; around his legs fluttered loose trousers of red fustian. His feet were bare.

I, too was dressed and barefoot.

And in this plight we trudged on, and the steppe, outspread around us in gigantic stretches, overarched by the deep blue sultry vault of the cloudless summer sky, looked like a huge platter, round and black. The gray dusty road, like a broad stripe, cut it in two and burned our feet. Here and there we passed through patches of reaped corn curiously resembling the cheeks of the soldier, which no razor had touched for many a day.

The Warrior marched singing in a somewhat hoarse voice: " And Thy holy Resurrection do we chaunt and praise." When serving in the army he had discharged the duties of chanter in the church of the battalion, learning by heart countless hymns and eulogies; and this knowledge he was now wont to abuse whenever conversation flagged.

In front of us, on the horizon, certain shapes caught our eye, shapes of soft shadowy outline and mellow hues, from lilac to a tender rose.

" It's clear that those are the Crimean mountains," remarked the " student," in a grating voice.

" Mountains? " exclaimed the soldier; " it's a bit too soon for you to see them yet, my lad. Clouds — mere clouds. See how they look for all the world like huckleberry jelly smothered in milk. . . ."

Here I chimed in with the remark that it would be very comforting if the clouds were indeed made of jelly. This comment at once aroused our appetite — the sore point of our lives for the moment.

" Oh the devil take it! " cried the soldier, easing his feelings in a flow of bad language, and spitting out, " not a living soul will come our way! Not one. . . . We are as hard set as bears in winter; we must suck our own paws."

" I told you we had better make for inhabited districts," observed the student in a magisterial tone.

" You told us! " repeated the soldier tauntingly. " It's easy to see you're a scholar and your business is to talk. Where are the inhabited districts in these parts, I'd like to know? The devil only knows where they're to be found."

---

[3] **fustian:** coarse cotton cloth.   [4] **Kherson:** city on the Black Sea.
[5] **kepi:** a military cap with a round crown sloping toward the front, and a visor.

The student answered nothing, merely screwing his lips together. The sun was going down and the cloud masses on the horizon were suffused with gorgeous tints for which language possesses no names. There was a scent of fresh earth and of salt in the atmosphere.

And the edge of our appetite was made keener still by this dry savory smell.

The void in our stomachs was aching. This was in truth a strange and unpleasant sensation; it was as though from all the muscles of the body juices were slowly ebbing away, one knew not whither, were evaporating, leaving the muscles bereft of their living suppleness. A feeling of prickly dryness came over the cavity of the mouth and throat, the brain was seized with dizziness and dark spots floated and twittered before the eyes. Sometimes these blurs would take the form of pieces of smoking meat or loaves of bread; fancy supplied "those visions of the past, those silent dreams" with their own appropriate odors, and then it seemed as if a knife were being turned in the stomach.

None the less we still kept pushing forwards, describing to each other our sensations, keeping a sharp lookout the while on every side in the hope of descrying somewhere a flock of sheep, and pricking up our ears for the shrill screak of the tilted cart of a Tartar carrying fruit to the Armenian bazaar.

But the steppe was deserted and silent.

On the eve of this dreary day we three had eaten among us four pounds of rye bread and five watermelons, but then we had covered about sixteen miles — an outlay of forces out of all proportion to the income! — and having fallen asleep in the market place of Perekop we woke up with hunger.

The student had wisely advised us not to go to sleep at all but to devote the night hours to "labor" [6] . . . but in decent society it is not correct to talk aloud about schemes for infringing the rights of property, wherefore I shall be silent on this matter. I merely wish to be just and it is not to my interest to be rude. I know that in our days of high culture, people wax milder and gentler in soul, and even when engaged in clutching their neighbor by the throat, for the manifest purpose of strangling him, they endeavor to accomplish this in the most loving-kind manner conceivable and with the strictest observance of all the proprieties befitting the occasion. The experience of my own throat, indeed, compels me to note this progress of morals and I affirm, with the agreeable feeling of certitude, that all

[6] "labor": irony for *thieving*.

things are progressing and growing more perfect in this world of ours. In particular this remarkable process is strikingly confirmed by the yearly growth of prisons, taverns, and lupanars.[7]

And thus swallowing our hunger spittle, and striving by means of friendly tattle to stifle the pangs in our stomachs, we marched on through the silent and tenantless steppe, in the rose-tinted rays of sunset, filled with vague hopes of we knew not what. Before us the sun was dipping downwards, gently sinking in the fleecy clouds, which were richly dyed with his glories; behind and on each side of us a light blue haze, floating up from earth to heaven, kept narrowing the sullen horizons which environed us.

" Brothers, get together stuff for the campfire," exclaimed the soldier, picking up from the ground something like a log. " We shall have to spend the night in the steppe . . . dew. Dry dung, twigs, everything you can lay your hands on! "

We went apart to different sides of the road, and began to gather dry steppe-grass and everything capable of burning. Each time that we had to stoop down to the earth a passionate desire seized us to fall down upon it, to lie there without budging and to eat it, that black greasy earth, to gorge ourselves with it, to feed on it till we collapsed, and then to sleep. Ay, even though it were the sleep that is breathless and everlasting, it mattered not, so that we could but eat, chew, and feel the warm thick mess slipping down slowly from the mouth through the parched gullet into the hungering, shrunken stomach, which was burning with a longing to take in any kind of food.

" If we could even light upon some roots! " sighed the soldier. " There are such eatable roots . . ."

But there were no such roots to be had in the black plowed soil. And meanwhile the veil of southern night was falling quickly; hardly had the last ray of sunlight faded from the west when the stars began to twinkle tremulously in the deep blue vault of heaven, and the gloomy shadows around us commingled and grew denser, narrowing the boundless dead level of the all-embracing steppe. . . .

" Brothers! " exclaimed the student in a whisper, " there, on the left, see, there's a man lying! "

" A man? " whispered the soldier doubtfully. " What would he be lying there for? "

" You'd better go and ask him. Anyhow, he is sure to have bread, if he has planted himself in the steppe . . ." reasoned the " student."

The soldier looked fixedly towards the spot where the man was

[7] lupanars: tuberculosis hospitals.

lying, and having spit out, in token of his determination, exclaimed:
" Let us make for him! "

None but the keen green eyes of the student could have recognized the form of a human being in the dark heap that bulged out of the earth some hundred yards or more to the left of the road. We shaped our course towards him, striding swiftly over great clods of plowed land, feeling as we neared him how the newborn hope of food within us sharpened the pains of hunger. We were already quite close to him, but the man lay motionless.

" Perhaps it isn't a man at all," moodily observed the soldier, giving utterance to the thought shared by all of us. But at that same instant our doubts were dispelled, the bundle on the earth suddenly stirred, waxed larger, and we could now see for ourselves that it was a real live man in kneeling posture, stretching out his arm towards us.

Then he broke the silence, speaking in a muffled, tremulous voice:
" Don't advance or I'll fire! "

A dry short click was wafted to our ears through the hazy air.

We pulled up as if in obedience to a word of command, and for a few seconds held our breath, dumfounded by this unfriendly reception.

" There's a scoundrel for you! " murmured the soldier expressively.

" Ye-es! " replied the student pensively. " Carries a revolver too . . . it's clear he is a fish with hard roe.[8] . . ."

" Ho! " ejaculated the soldier, who had evidently made up his mind to do something.

The man without changing his position continued to keep silence.

" Hello! there, we don't want to touch you . . . only let's have some bread . . . to eat, will you? Give it, brother, for Christ's sake! . . . may you be accursed, you hellhound! " The last words were muttered by the soldier in an aside.

The man spoke no word.

" Do you hear? " the soldier began anew, quivering with bitterness and despair.

" All right," said the man laconically. Now it was open to him to address us as " my dear brethren," and even if he had done so, infusing into those three Christian words all the holiest and purest sentiments, they would not have thrilled and humanized us in anything like the same degree as those two muffled monosyllables " all right! "

---

[8] **fish with hard roe:** slang comparable to our " hard-boiled."

" You need not be afraid of us, my good man," the soldier recommenced with a soft sweet smile on his face, although the " good man " could not perceive this smile, being at least twenty paces distant from us.

" We are peaceable men . . . on our way from Russia to the Kuban District [9] . . . we and our money got parted on the way, we ate the very clothes off our backs . . . and now this is the second day we have been fasting. . . ."

" Here! " cried the good man, with a sweep of his arm in the air. Something black flew aloft and fell on the plowland hard by. The student darted up to it.

" Here's another! And another! I've got no more! "

As soon as the student had gathered up this alms, it turned out that we had about four pounds weight of stale wheat bread. It had been rubbed into the earth and was very stale. But we paid no heed to the former drawback, while we were delighted at the latter. Stale bread is more filling than soft, contains less moisture.

" Take this, you . . . you take this . . . and you this . . ." said the soldier, intently bent on doling out our shares. " Stop! . . . that's not fair! Here, you, scholar! you must let another piece be nipped off your chunk, else your mate there won't have enough . . ."

The student submitted to the loss of this piece of his bread — a little over half an ounce in weight — without a murmur. It was given to me, and I stuffed it into my mouth.

Then I began to chew it, to chew it slowly, checking with great difficulty convulsive spasms in my jaws, which were craving to crunch a stone to powder. It was a keen pleasure to me to feel the spasmodic twinges of my gullet and to satisfy them little by little, dropwise as it were. Mouthful by mouthful, warm and delicious, delicious, delicious beyond words, beyond imaginings, they passed into my burning stomach and seemed to be metamorphosed there, instantaneously as it were, into blood and marrow. Joy, unwonted, gentle, life-giving joy warmed my heart as the void in my stomach was being gradually filled, and my general condition might in some sort be likened to that of one in a light slumber. I forgot all about those accursed days of chronic hunger and cold, I forgot even my comrades, so absorbed was I by the sensations which I was now experiencing.

But when I had jerked in from the palm of my hand the last

[9] **Kuban District:** the Kuban river flows northwest from the Caucasus Mountains into the Black Sea.

crumbs of bread there, I was overcome by a torturing desire to eat.

"The hellhound has got suet there still, or some kind of meat . . ." muttered the soldier, squatting on the earth beside me, and rubbing his stomach with his hands.

"Of course he has; the bread he gave us had the smell of meat about it . . . Ay, he has more bread left, too, you may be sure," remarked the student, adding in a whisper: "If it were not for his revolver . . ."

"Who is he, anyhow? Eh?"

"You can see he is one of our brethren, Isaac. . . ."

"He's a dog," the soldier declared in a tone of conviction.

We were sitting in a close group and looking obliquely towards the place where our benefactor with his revolver was seated. Not a word reached us from there, no faint sign of life or movement.

Night had gathered round us her wealth of gloom. The silence of the grave hung over the steppe, we could hear only each other's breathing. Now and again the melancholy squeak of the marmot's whistle was wafted to our ears. . . . The stars, heaven's living flowers, glistened over our heads. . . . We were dying to eat.

I say it with pride — I was neither worse nor better than my mates during this somewhat strange night. And it was I who put it to them that we ought to rise up and make for the man there. We need not hurt him, I pointed out, but we might devour every scrap of food we should find in his possession. He might, of course, fire on us. Well, let him. Of the three of us he would at worse hit one, if he hit at all, and if his aim did take effect, well, a revolver bullet would hardly inflict a deadly wound.

"Yes, let's go," exclaimed the soldier, starting to his feet. The student rose up more slowly than he. And we went forward, rushed indeed would be more correct. The student lagged behind us.

"Mate!" cried the soldier in a tone of reproach to him. We were conscious on our way of a faint murmur and then of the sharp click of a creaking pistol cock. All at once fire flashed and was almost instantaneously followed by an explosive sound.

"Missed!" shouted the soldier gleefully, reaching the man with one bound. "Now, you devil, I'll pummel you!" . . . The student flung himself upon the wallet.

But the devil, who was on his knees, fell backwards, upon his spine and throwing out his arms, was already choking as if with the rattle of death. . . .

" What sort of a devil is he? " wondered the soldier, who had already raised his foot to administer a kick to the man. " Can it be that he has really put some lead into himself? D'ye hear? Have you shot yourself, eh? "

" There's meat here and some kind of unleavened cakes and bread . . . quite a lot, brothers! " the student announced with jubilation.

" Well then, devil take you, burst! . . . Let us eat, friends! " cried the soldier. Meanwhile, I took the revolver out of the hand of the man, who had by this time ceased snorting, and lay motionless. In the drum there was but one more cartridge.

And we began to eat again in silence. The man, too, lay still, not stirring a limb. So we paid no heed to him whatever.

" Is it possible, dear brothers, that you have done all this only for the sake of bread? " a hoarse, quivering voice asked out of the darkness.

We shuddered at the sound, all three of us. Indeed, the student well-nigh choked himself and bending down to the ground, was seized with a violent fit of coughing.

The soldier, having chewed his mouthful to pulp, became abusive.

" Ah, you soul of a hound, may you split asunder like a dry stump! Do you think it's your skin that we want to peel off your body? What good would it be to us? Your muzzle is that of a fool, you heathen! Nothing will satisfy him but he must arm himself with a revolver and shoot at people! You hellhound, you . . ."

And he went on pouring out invectives and eating; wherefore his abuse lost all its expression and force. . . .

" You just wait a bit until we've finished eating and we'll settle our accounts with you," promised the student with malice. . . .

And then the silence of the night was broken with a woeful whining that terrified us.

" Brothers . . . how did I know? I fired . . . because I was afraid. I am on my way from New Athos . . . to the Government of Smolensk.[10] . . . Oh, good Lord! This fever harasses me to death . . . after sundown comes my torture! It was the fever that drove me from Athos . . . I was a carpenter there . . . that's my trade. . . . At home I have a wife . . . and two little girls. Three years have gone, this is the fourth since I last saw them. . . . Brothers, eat up every morsel! "

[10] **Smolensk:** city about 225 miles southwest of Moscow.

" We'll take very good care we do, so don't you be begging for any,"
broke in the student.

" Oh, Lord God! if I had only known that you were peaceful, good
fellows. . . . Do you think I'd have fired on you? But here in the
steppe, brothers, in the dead of the night . . . am I to blame? Eh? "

He wept as he spoke, or rather uttered a sort of tremulous, fearsome
howl.

" There, he's whining! " exclaimed the soldier contemptuously.

" He's certain to have money on him," remarked the student.

The soldier blinked his eyes, turned them on the student, and
grinned. " You are a cute one. . . . But look here, let us up and
make a fire and turn in for the night. . . ."

" And what about him? " inquired the student.

" Oh, the devil take him! You don't want us to roast him, do
you? "

" Well, it wouldn't be more than his deserts," replied the student,
with a shake of his angular head.

We started off accordingly to fetch the materials we had gathered.
We had flung them down on the spot where the carpenter had arrested
our progress with his threatening cry, and now we got them together
and were soon seated round the campfire. It burned gently in the
breathless night, lighting up the narrow space occupied by ourselves.
A feeling of drowsiness was stealing over us although we were still
ready to begin our supper over again.

" Brothers," . . . the carpenter called out to us. He was stretched
out on the ground three paces from us, and at times I fancied that he
was whispering something.

" Well? " exclaimed the soldier.

" May I come to you . . . to the fire? Death is creeping over me.
All the bones in my body are racked with pain . . . Oh Lord! I see
now I shall never reach home again. . . ."

" Crawl up here! " said the student patronizingly.

Slowly, as if he feared to lose a hand or a foot, the carpenter
dragged himself along the earth to the campfire. He was a tall, terribly emaciated man; every shred of clothing hung loosely and fluttered about him, and his large glazed eyes told the story of the pain
that was gnawing him. His face, wrenched out of shape, was long,
and his complexion, even in the red glare of the campfire, was of a
yellowish, earthy, corpse-like hue. He was trembling all over, and
the sight of him aroused a feeling of contemptuous pity. Stretching

out his long, skinny hands towards the blazing fire he rubbed his bony fingers, whereat the joints bent slowly, lifelessly. In truth it was sickening to look upon him.

"How did you come to be in that plight and trudging along on foot? You're tight-fisted, eh?" asked the soldier sullenly.

"That was the advice they gave me . . . don't make the journey, they said, by water . . . but take the Crimean [11] route . . . the air is wholesome . . . they said . . . And here I am unable to move . . . I shall die, brothers! I shall die alone in the steppe . . . the birds will pick my bones and no one will ever know. . . . My wife . . . my little daughters . . . will be watching for my home-coming — I wrote to them . . . but the rains of the steppe will be washing my bones . . . Oh Lord! Oh Lord!"

He set up a dismal howl like that of a wounded wolf.

"The devil!" shouted the soldier, working himself into a rage and springing to his feet. "Whatever are you whining for? Why don't you let us have peace? You are kicking the bucket? [12] Well then, kick it and shut up. . . . Who is in the need of the likes of you? Shut up!"

"Give him a rap on the head," suggested the student.

"Let's turn in and sleep," said I. . . . "And as for you, if you want to stay here by the fire, you'll have to stop your howling."

"D'ye hear?" chimed in the soldier savagely. "Very well, bear it in mind, then. You fancy we are going to pity you and nurse you because you flung us some bread and fired a bullet at us? You sour devil! Others in our place would have . . . Phew! . . ."

The soldier fell silent and stretched himself out at full length on the earth. . . . I too lay down. The terrified carpenter rolled himself up in a heap, and having crept nearer to the fire, began to gaze into it fixedly and in silence. I was lying on his right and could hear his teeth chatter. The student was couched on his left, and, drawing himself together in a bundle, had seemingly fallen fast asleep at once. The soldier, putting his arms under his head for a pillow, lay on the broad of his back and stared at the sky.

"What a night! eh? No end of stars . . . lukewarm air." It was he who addressed those words to me after the lapse of a little time. "What a sky! It's a blanket and not a sky, it is! I do love this roving life, my boy! It's cold and hungry to be

[11] **Crimean:** the Crimean peninsula juts into the northern part of the Black Sea.

[12] **kicking the bucket:** slang for "dying."

sure, but free enough in all conscience. . . . A fellow has no superiors over him. You are master of your own existence. You may, if you want to, bite off your own head, and no one dares haul you over the coals for it. Glorious! . . . I did have a hungry time of it those last few days and I felt cross about it . . . but here I'm lying now looking up at the heavens. . . . The stars are winking down at me . . . just as if they were saying: ' Never mind, Lakootyin, tramp about the earth and knuckle down to no man.' . . . Yes! And my heart feels light. . . . And you . . . how do you feel about it? Hello there! you carpenter. You mustn't feel angry with me, and don't you fear anything either! . . . We've eaten your bread — but that's nothing; you had bread and we had none, so we ate it up. . . . But you, like a savage, let fly a bullet at us. . . . Can't you see that you may hurt a fellow with a bullet? My! I was in a towering rage with you then, and if you hadn't flopped down as you did, I'd have given you a sound drubbing for your impudence. But as for the bread — you'll get into Perekop tomorrow and you can buy some there — you have cash about you . . . that I know. . . . Have you had that fever long? "

For a considerable time after this the bass voice of the soldier and the quivering tones of the sick carpenter continued to hum in my ears. The night, dark, almost black, descended lower and lower upon the earth and the fresh sappy air was flowing in soothing waves into my breast.

The campfire gave forth an even light and quickening warmth. . . . My eyes were glued together, and floating before them, athwart my dreams, hovered I know not what that calmed and purified them.

" Get up! Be alive! Let's be off! "

With a feeling of dread I opened my eyes and jumped quickly to my feet, the soldier lending me a helping hand by seizing my arm and jerking me violently from the earth.

" Make haste! March! "

Gloom and dismay were written in his face. I looked all around me. The sun had risen, and the roseate hues of its beams suffused the face of the carpenter, motionless and livid. His mouth was gaping wide, his eyes bulging far out of their sockets and fixed in a glassy stare of horror. The clothes on his chest were all torn into shreds and he lay there in a posture that was cramped and unnatural. There was no student.

" Well, have you made your survey? Come on, I tell you! " exclaimed the soldier authoritatively, dragging me by the arm.

" Is he dead? " I asked, shivering with the freshness of the morning.

" Of course he's dead. And you'd be dead, too, if you had been strangled in his place," he explained.

" He was . . . The student . . . ? " I ejaculated.

" Why, who else do you suppose? Perhaps you did it yourself? Or may be I did? Ye-es. There's a scholar for you . . . He settled the man most cleverly . . . and he's left his mates in a nice hole, too. . . . If I'd had any inkling of this, I'd have snuffed the life out of that same student yesterday. . . . I'd have put him out of pain in a twinkling, I would! A whack of my fist on his temples . . . and there'd have been one scoundrel less in the world! Can't you see what he's done? Now we must scamper off without letting the eye of man light on us in the steppe. Do you grasp the situation? Because they'll discover the carpenter's corpse today; they'll find him strangled and robbed. And they'll keep an eye on the brethren of our guild . . . asking, ' Where may you have come from? Where did you sleep last night? ' Well, and then they'll nab us . . . Although you and I have nothing on us . . . oh, yes, I've got his revolver in my breast! A nice fix! "

" Throw it away! " was my advice to the soldier.

" Throw it away? " he repeated thoughtfully. . . . "It's an article of value. . . . And perhaps they won't claw us yet. . . . No, I won't throw it away. . . . It's worth three rubles.[13] . . . There's a bullet in it, too. . . . Phew! Wouldn't I have sent that same bullet straight into the ear of our dead comrade! How much money did the hound scoop up, I wonder? Eh? The cursed dog! "

" It's hard on the carpenter's poor little daughters . . ." I observed.

" Daughters? Whose? Oh, the daughters of this . . . Oh, they'll grow up and get married, not to one of us though. . . . Oh, they're all right. . . . But let us clear out of this, mate, as quickly as we can. . . . Where are we to go to? "

" I haven't an idea. . . . It doesn't matter."

" And I don't know either, and I'm aware that it doesn't signify. Let us turn to the right — the sea ought to be over there."

And to the right we went.

I turned round. Far from us away in the steppe a dark mound stood out against the horizon, and overhead beamed the sun.

" You're looking to see whether he will rise again, eh? Don't be

[13] **three rubles:** about a dollar and a half.

uneasy, he won't get up to give us chase. . . . The scholar, you can see, is an adroit customer, he did the work with thoroughness. . . . And he's a choice comrade, to boot! He let us in for a soft thing! Ah, brother! People arc getting worse year after year, worse and worse," repeated the soldier in sorrowful tones.

The steppe silent and tenantless, flooded with the dazzling light of the morning sun, spread itself out before us, mingling at the horizon with the sky; and so pure was the light, so caressing and so abundant, that no dark, unjust deed seemed possible in the limitless space of that unbroken plane overarched by the azure vault of heaven.

" I'm dying for something to munch, brother! " exclaimed my mate, rolling a cigarette of the coarsest tobacco. . . .

" What shall we eat today, and where and how? "

" A puzzle."

And here the narrator — my neighbor in the hospital — brought his tale to an end, adding:

" That's all. That soldier and I became great friends and we journeyed on together as far as the District of Kars. He was a good-natured fellow who had seen a great deal of the world, and was a typical barefoot tramp. I held him in esteem. Right up to Asia Minor we kept together, and there we got parted from each other."

" And do you ever think of the carpenter? " I inquired.

" As you see — or rather as you have heard. . . ."

" And it doesn't trouble you? "

He began to laugh.

" Why, how ought I to feel about the matter? I am not to blame for what befell him just as you are not answerable for what happened to me. . . . And nobody is to blame for anything, because, one and all, we are brutes."

(*E. J. Dillon*)

SUGGESTIONS FOR STUDY

1. Characterize briefly each of the four men in the story. Which is the worst of the lot? Why? Are there any good traits in any of them? Discuss.

2. What in the story convinces the reader that the author had had first-hand knowledge of the life he portrays? What is the value of reading a story like this? Where do we find the philosophy of the tramp condensed in a few sentences? What do you think of it? Discuss the opinion of human nature expressed in the last line of the story.

3. Do we have similar situations in America today? Discuss. How do these men compare with the American " hitch-hiker "? How do labor conditions affect situations such as described in this story? What American writers picture the " down-and-out "?

4. What would you say of this story as to plot construction? Use of nature as a background? Use of conversation?

IVAN ALEXEYEVICH BUNIN (1870–1953)

Bunin has won a number of distinctions which mark him off from other Russian writers. When in 1933 he was awarded the Nobel prize in literature, he became the first Russian author to be thus honored. But Bunin had won prizes before. At nineteen he was granted the Pushkin prize, the highest academic distinction during the Empire, and a few years later he won it a second time for his translation of Longfellow's *Hiawatha* into Russian. Through this and other translations he was one of the first to open up the field of American literature, which soon proved highly popular in Russia. He is about the only one of the pre-Revolutionary writers whose literary reputation has really increased since 1917.

During these years Bunin lived in exile. Belonging to an old noble family, whose wealth remained intact to the time of the Revolution, he found it necessary to emigrate when the Bolsheviks invaded his province, north of the Black Sea. The escape to Constantinople was effected picturesquely but uncomfortably in a rotting old ship, and the author took nothing with him but his manuscripts and a small satchel of clothes. He soon joined the colony of exiled Russians in Paris but lived on the French Riviera.

Bunin's early writings portrayed the Russian peasant in a different light from the idealized " moujik " popular in Russian fiction during the late nineteenth and early twentieth centuries. His peasants are primitive, untamed creatures, ridden with superstition. *The Village,* a series of sketches published in 1910 not long after the unsuccessful revolution, is the most important of his analytical studies of peasant brutality, a work praised by Gorki as the best treatment in existence of the peasant. Bunin's own favorite among his stories as well as that of the general public is *The Gentleman from San Francisco,* of special interest to us because the central character is an American. This wealthy Californian, sailing for a European tour with every expectation of enjoying the utmost luxury that money can buy, dies on the day of his arrival at Capri, Italy, and thus becomes an unwanted corpse to be shipped back ignominiously in the hold of a vessel. During his exile Bunin wrote *The Rose of Jericho,* a collection of stories and poems, and *The Life of Arsenjenv,* a three-volume autobiographical novel.

Bunin has always considered his readers a limited group. " You will never see people reading my books in railway carriages," he once said. But by the discriminating his excellence is quickly recognized. It is significant that Gorki, who represents the opposite extreme in social background and political sympathies, has said of him: " I regard Bunin as the only Russian emigrant writer worthy of attention."

IN AN EMPTY HOUSE

From the walls the paper's blue is vanished,
The daguerreotypes, the ikons banished.
Only there the deepened blue appears
Where these hid it, hanging through the years.

From the heart the memory is perished,
Perished all that long ago it cherished!
Those remain, of whom death hides the face,
Leaving their yet unforgotten trace.

2. **ikons:** holy pictures usually painted on wood. They were placed not only in Greek Orthodox churches but also in the homes of all devout members.

THE BRIDE

On the yellow card with a nobleman's coronet the young porter at the Hotel Versailles [1] somehow managed to read the Christian name and patronymic: [2] Kasimir Stanislavovich; there followed something [3] still more complicated and still more difficult to pronounce. The porter turned the card this way and that in his hand, looked at the passport which the visitor had given him with it, shrugged his shoulders — none of those who stayed at the Versailles gave their cards — then he threw both on the table and began again to examine himself in the silvery, milky mirror which hung above the table, whipping up his thick hair with a comb. He wore an overcoat and shiny top boots; the gold braid on his cap was greasy with age — the hotel was a bad one.

Kasimir Stanislavovich left Kiev [4] for Moscow on April 8th, Good Friday, on receiving a telegram with the one word: " tenth." Some-

[1] **Hotel Versailles:** a cheap hotel in Moscow.
[2] **patronymic:** the middle or " father " name. For explanation see footnote, page 754.
[3] **something:** this was the third or family name.
[4] **Kiev:** important city of the Ukraine. about 500 miles southwest of Moscow.

how or other he managed to get the money for his fare and took his seat in a second-class compartment, gray and dim, but really giving him the sensation of comfort and luxury. The train was heated, and that railway-carriage heat and the smell of the heating apparatus and the sharp tapping of the little hammers in it reminded Kasimir Stanislavovich of other times. At times it seemed to him that winter had returned, that in the fields the white, very white drifts of snow had covered up the yellowish bristle of stubble and the large leaden pools where the wild ducks swam. But often, the snowstorm stopped suddenly and melted; the fields grew bright, and one felt that behind the clouds was much light, and the wet platforms of the railway stations looked black, and the rooks called from the naked poplars. At each big station Kasimir Stanislavovich went to the refreshment room for a drink, and returned to his carriage with newspapers in his hands; but he did not read them; he only sat sunk into the thick smoke of his cigarettes which burned and glowed, and to none of his neighbors — Odessa [5] Jews who played cards all the time — did he say a single word. He wore an autumn overcoat of which the pockets were worn, a very old black top hat, and new, but heavy, cheap boots. His hands, the typical hands of an habitual drunkard and an old inhabitant of basements, shook when he lit a match. Everything else about him spoke of poverty and drunkenness: no cuffs, a dirty linen collar, an ancient tie, an inflamed and ravaged face, bright-blue watery eyes. His side whiskers, dyed with a bad, brown dye, had an unnatural appearance. He looked tired and contemptuous.

The train reached Moscow the next day not at all on time; it was seven hours late. The weather was neither one thing nor the other, but better and drier than in Kiev, with something stirring in the air. Kasimir Stanislavovich took a cab without bargaining with the driver, and told him to drive straight to the Versailles. " I have known that hotel, my good fellow," he said, suddenly breaking his silence, " since my student days." As soon as his little bag, tied with stout rope, had been taken up to his room, he immediately went out.

It was nearly evening: the air was warm, the black trees on the boulevards were turning green; everywhere there were crowds of people, cars, carts. Moscow was trafficking and doing business, was returning to the usual, pressing work, was ending her holiday, and unconsciously welcomed the spring. A man who has lived his life and ruined it feels lonely on a spring evening in a strange, crowded city. Kasimir Stanislavovich walked the whole length of the Tverskoy

---

[5] **Odessa**: city about 250 miles south of Kiev, on the Black Sea.

Boulevard; he saw once more the cast-iron figure of the musing Pushkin, the gold and lilac top of the Strasnoy Monastery. . . . For about an hour he sat at the Café Filippov, drank chocolate, and read old comic papers. Then he went to a cinema,[6] whose flaming signs shone from far away down the Tverskaya through the darkling twilight. From the cinema he drove to a restaurant on the boulevard which he had also known in his student days. He was driven by an old man, bent in a bow, sad, gloomy, deeply absorbed in himself, in his old age, in his dark thoughts. All the way the man painfully and wearily helped on his lazy horse with his whole being, murmuring something to it all the time and occasionally bitterly reproaching it — and at last, when he reached the place, he allowed the load to slip from his shoulders for a moment and gave a deep sigh, as he took the money.

" I did not catch the name and thought you meant ' Prague,' " he muttered, turning his horse slowly; he seemed displeased, although the Prague was farther away.

" I remember the Prague too, old fellow," answered Kasimir Stanislavovich. " You must have been driving for a long time in Moscow."

" Driving? " the old man said. " I have been driving now for fifty-one years."

" That means that you may have driven me before," said Kasimir Stanislavovich.

" Perhaps I did," answered the old man dryly. " There are lots of people in the world; one can't remember all of you."

Of the old restaurant once known to Kasimir Stanislavovich there remained only the name. Now it was a large, first-class, though vulgar, restaurant. Over the entrance burnt an electric globe which with its unpleasant, heliotrope light, illuminated the smart, second-rate cabmen, impudent, and cruel to their lean, short-winded animals. In the damp hall stood pots of laurel and tropical plants of the kind which one sees carried on to the platforms from funerals to weddings and vice versa. From the porter's lodge several men rushed out together to Kasimir Stanislavovich, and all of them had just the same thick curl of hair as the porter at the Versailles. In the large greenish room, decorated in rococo [7] style, were a multitude of broad mirrors, and in the corner burnt a crimson ikon lamp. The room was still empty and only a few of the electric lights were on.

---

[6] **cinema:** moving picture theater.
[7] **rococo:** the elaborate style prevalent in the seventeenth and eighteenth centuries.

Kasimir Stanislavovich sat for a long time alone, doing nothing. One felt that behind the windows with their white blinds the long, spring evening had not yet grown dark; one heard from the street the thudding of hoofs; in the middle of the room there was the monotonous splash-splash of the little fountain in an aquarium round which goldfish, with their scales peeling off, lighted somehow from below, swam through the water. A waiter in white brought the dinner things, bread, and a decanter of cold vodka.[8] Kasimir Stanislavovich began drinking the vodka, held it in his mouth before swallowing it, and, having swallowed it, smelt the black bread as though with loathing. With a suddenness which gave even him a start a gramophone began to roar out through the room a mixture of Russian songs, now exaggeratedly boisterous and turbulent, now too tender, drawling, sentimental. . . . And Kasimir Stanislavovich's eyes grew red and tears filmed them at that sweet and snuffling drone of the machine. . . .

On the tenth of April Kasimir Stanislavovich woke up early. He had got back after four in the morning. As soon as he lay down, everything began to turn round him, to rush into an abyss, and he fell asleep instantly. In his sleep all the time he was conscious of the smell of the iron washstand which stood close to his face, and he dreamt of a spring day, trees in blossom, the hall of a manor house, and a number of people waiting anxiously for the bishop to arrive at any moment; and all night long he was wearied and tormented with that waiting. . . . Now in the corridors of the Versailles people rang, ran, called to one another. Behind the screen, through the double, dusty windowpanes, the sun shone; it was almost hot. Kasimir Stanislavovich took off his jacket, rang the bell, and began to wash. There came in a quick-eyed boy, with fox-colored hair on his head, in a frock coat and pink shirt.

" A loaf, samovar,[9] and lemon," Kasimir Stanislavovich said without looking at him.

" And tea and sugar? " the boy asked with Moscow sharpness.

And a minute later he rushed in with a boiling samovar in his hands held out level with his shoulders; on the round table in front of the sofa he quickly put a tray with a glass and a battered brass slop-basin,[10] and thumped the samovar down on the tray. . . . Kasimir Stanislavovich, while the tea was drawing,[11] mechanically opened

---

[8] **vodka:** highly intoxicating Russian liquor.
[9] **samovar:** Russian tea urn.
[10] **slop-basin:** into which to pour remains of tea before refilling the glass.
[11] **drawing:** steeping.

the *Moscow Daily* which the page boy had brought in with the samovar. His eye fell on a report that yesterday an unknown man had been picked up unconscious. . . . " The victim was taken to the hospital," he read, and threw the paper away. He felt very low and unsteady. He got up and opened the window — it faced the yard — and a breath of freshness and of the city came to him; there came to him the melodious shouts of hawkers, the bells of horse trams humming behind the house opposite, the blended rap-tap of the cars, the musical drone of church bells. . . . The city had long since started its huge, noisy life in that bright, jolly, almost spring day. Kasimir Stanislavovich squeezed the lemon into a glass of tea and greedily drank the sour, muddy liquid; then he went again behind the screen. The Versailles was quiet. It was pleasant and peaceful; his eye wandered leisurely over the hotel notice on the wall: " A stay of three hours is counted as a full day." A mouse scuttled in a chest of drawers, rolling about a piece of sugar left there by some visitor. . . . Thus half asleep Kasimir Stanislavovich lay for a long time behind the screen, until the sun had gone from the room and another freshness was wafted in from the window, the freshness of evening.

Then he carefully got himself in order: he undid his bag, changed his underclothing, took out a cheap, but clean handkerchief, brushed his shiny frock coat, top hat, and overcoat, took out of its torn pocket a crumbled Kiev newspaper of January 15 and threw it away into the corner. . . . Having dressed and combed his whiskers with a dyeing comb, he counted his money — there remained in his purse four rubles, seventy kopecks [12] — and went out. Exactly at six o'clock he was outside a low, ancient little church in the Molchanovka. Behind the church fence a spreading tree was just breaking into green; children were playing there — the black stocking of one thin little girl, jumping over a rope, was continually coming down — and he sat there on the bench among perambulators [13] with sleeping babies and nurses in Russian costume. Sparrows prattled all over the tree; the air was soft, all but summer — even the dust smelled of summer — the sunset sky behind the houses melted into a gentle gold, and one felt that once more there was somewhere in the world joy, youth, happiness. In the church the chandeliers were already burning, and there stood the pulpit, and in front of the pulpit was spread a little carpet. Kasimir Stanislavovich cautiously took off his top hat, trying not to untidy his hair, and entered the church nervously; he went

---

[12] **four rubles, seventy kopecks:** about $2.50.
[13] **perambulators:** baby carriages.

into a corner, but a corner from which he could see the couple to be married. He looked at the painted vault, raised his eyes to the cupola, and his every movement and every gasp echoed loudly through the silence. The church shone with gold; the candles sputtered expectantly. And now the priests and choir began to enter, crossing themselves with a carelessness which comes of habit; then old women, children, smart wedding guests, and worried stewards. A noise was heard in the porch, the crunching wheels of the carriage; every one turned their heads towards the entrance and a hymn burst out: " Come, my dove." Kasimir Stanislavovich became deathly pale, as his heart beat, and unconsciously he took a step forward. And close by him there passed — her veil touching him and a breath of lily-of-the-valley — she who did not know even of his existence in the world; she passed, bending her charming head, all flowered and transparent gauze, all snow-white and innocent, happy and timid, like a princess going to her first communion. . . . Kasimir Stanislavovich hardly saw the bridegroom who came to meet her, a rather small, broad-shouldered man with yellow, close-cropped hair. During the whole ceremony only one thing was before his eyes: the bent head, in the flowers and the veil, and the little hand trembling as it held a burning candle tied with a white ribbon in a bow. . . .

About ten o'clock he was back again in the hotel. All his overcoat smelled of the spring air. After coming out of the church, he had seen near the porch the car lined with white satin, and its window reflected in the sunset, and behind the window there flashed on him for the last time the face of her who was being carried away from him forever. After that he had wandered about in little streets and had come out on the Novensky Boulevard. . . . Now slowly and with trembling hands he took off his overcoat, put on the table a paper bag containing two green cucumbers which for some reason he had bought at a hawker's stall. They too smelled of spring even through the paper, and springlike through the upper pane of the window the April moon shone silvery, high up in the not-yet-darkened sky. Kasimir Stanislavovich lit a candle, sadly illuminating his empty, casual home, and sat down on the sofa, feeling on his face the freshness of evening. . . . Thus he sat for a long time. He did not ring the bell, gave no orders, locked himself in — all this seemed suspicious to the porter who had seen him enter his room with his shuffling feet and taking the key out of the door in order to lock himself in from the inside. Several times the porter stole up on tiptoe to the door and looked through the keyhole. Kasimir Stanislavovich was sitting on the sofa, trembling and wiping his face with a hand-kerchief, and weeping so bitterly, so copiously that the brown dye came off and was smeared over his face.

At night he tore the cord off the blind, and, seeing nothing through his tears, began to fasten it to the hook of the clothes-peg. But the guttering candle flickered and terrible dark waves swam and flickered over the locked room: he was old, weak — and he himself was well aware of it. . . . No. It was not in his power to die by his own hand!

In the morning he started for the railway station about three hours before the train left. At the station he quietly walked about among the passengers, with his tear-stained eyes on the ground; and he would stop unexpectedly before one and another, and in a low voice, even, but without expression, he would say rather quickly: " For God's sake . . . I am in a desperate position. . . . My fare to Briansk . . . If only a few kopecks . . ."

And some passengers, trying not to look at his top hat, at the worn velvet collar of his overcoat, at the dreadful face with the faded violet whiskers, hurriedly and with confusion gave him something.

And then, rushing out of the station on to the platform he got mixed in the crowd and disappeared into it, while in the Versailles in the room which for two days had, as it were, belonged to him, they carried out the slop pail, opened the windows to the April sun and fresh air, noisily moved the furniture, swept up and threw out the dust — and with the dust there fell under the table, under the table-cloth which slid down to the floor, his torn note, which he had for-gotten with the cucumbers:

" I beg that no one be accused of my death. I was at the wedding of my only daughter, who . . ."

(Leonard Woolf and S. S. Koteliansky)

SUGGESTIONS FOR STUDY

1. Is the ending a surprise to you? If so, how does it explain Kasimir's previous actions? If not, what preceding details suggested the outcome to you? Reread the story and note details which take on added signifi-cance after you know the outcome.

2. Fill in the details of the picture of Kasimir's life, here suggested by only a few strokes. Why was he attending his daughter's wedding in such a strange manner? Why didn't his daughter know him? Why did he want to commit suicide? Why did he not succeed? Discuss how our

total impression of Kasimir is aided by such details as the card presented at the hotel, his dyed whiskers, his top hat, etc.

3. Compare this derelict with Gorki's tramps in " In the Steppe." What marked differences do you note in background, type of character, and method of constructing the story? Which story impresses you more? Why?

4. Try writing a sketch in a modern American setting about a man or a woman who has seen better days. Consider carefully the use of the significant detail.

LEONID NIKOLAEVICH ANDREYEV (1871–1919)

Andreyev was one of those men whose outer personality presented a strange contrast to the tone of his writings. Those who knew him witnessed to his witty conversation and sense of humor, to his boyish enthusiasm for certain hobbies such as sailing, painting, and color photography, to his love of magnificence and his zest for having a house full of company. Yet to judge by his writings alone one would suppose him the most melancholy and pessimistic of men, for his favorite themes were death, disappointed hopes, and man's loneliness in the presence of fate.

He was born in Orel, which was also Turgenev's native home. His family were of the educated middle class, and he was sent to the Law School of the University of Moscow. Though admitted to practice, he soon found himself unsuited to the legal profession and devoted his energies to writing. The praise of Gorki and other critics brought him into early prominence which he maintained throughout his life by a long series of stories and dramas, though there was considerable controversy as to their merits. At the time of the Revolution Andreyev and his family fled into Finland. Here it was that they experienced the terrors of a Bolshevik air raid, which Andreyev has vividly chronicled in his diary. Soon after, he died of a heart attack, still a comparatively young man.

Andreyev's writings, while showing the usual Russian realism and preoccupation with the tragedy of life, are somewhat different in treatment, having a greater symbolism and, in one period of his work at least, a more lyrical style than the other Russian novelists use. His characters often seem less like actual individuals and more like human pawns illustrating some point in the author's mind. Three of his most striking stories or novelettes are *The Red Laugh* picturing the horrors of war; *The Governor* showing the rulers, at the time of the revolt of 1905, overwhelmed by the fate of popular uprising; *The Seven Who Were Hanged* revealing the emotions of seven widely differing types of persons preceding their execution. Among the plays *The Life of Man* is highly symbolical, portraying a mysterious Man in Gray holding the slowly burning candle of human life; *King Hunger* reflects the terrible famine conditions following the 1905 attempt at revolution; and *He Who Gets Slapped,* the most frequently presented in America, tells the poignant story of a circus clown who is repeatedly slapped in the face by fate. Perhaps in the outer merriment of the buffoon contrasted to the inner misery of his hidden soul, the author may have come the closest to an allegory of his own life.

THE LITTLE ANGEL

I

At times Sashka wished to give up what is called living: to cease to wash every morning in cold water, on which thin sheets of ice floated about; to go no more to the grammar school, and there to have to listen to every one scolding him; no more to experience the pain in the small of his back and indeed over his whole body when his mother made him kneel in the corner all the evening. But, since he was only thirteen years of age, and did not know all the means by which people abandon life at will, he continued to go to the grammar school and to kneel in the corner, and it seemed to him as if life would never end. A year would go by, and another, and yet another, and still he would be going to school, and be made to kneel in the corner. And since Sashka possessed an indomitable and bold spirit, he could not supinely tolerate evil, and so found means to avenge himself on life. With this object in view he would thrash his companions, be rude to the Head, impertinent to the masters, and tell lies all day long to his teachers and to his mother — but to his father only he never lied. If in a fight he got his nose broken, he would purposely make the damage worse, and howl, without shedding a single tear, but so loudly that all who heard him were fain to stop their ears to keep out the disagreeable sound. When he had howled as long as he thought advisable, he would suddenly cease, and, putting out his tongue, draw in his copybook a caricature of himself howling at an usher [1] who pressed his fingers to his ears, while the victor stood trembling with fear. The whole copybook was filled with caricatures, the one which most frequently occurred being that of a short stout woman beating a boy as thin as a lucifer match with a rolling pin. Below in a large scrawling hand would be written the legend: " Beg my pardon, puppy! " and the reply, " Won't! blow'd if I do! "

Before Christmas Sashka was expelled from school, and when his mother attempted to thrash him he bit her finger. This action gave

---

[1] **usher:** an under-teacher in a school.

him his liberty. He left off washing in the morning, ran about all day bullying the other boys, and had but one fear, and that was hunger, for his mother entirely left off providing for him, so that he came to depend upon the pieces of bread and potatoes which his father secreted for him. On these conditions Sashka found existence tolerable.

One Friday (it was Christmas Eve) he had been playing with the other boys, until they had dispersed to their homes, followed by the squeak of the rusty frozen wicket gate as it closed behind the last of them. It was already growing dark, and a gray snowy mist was traveling up from the country, along a dark alley; in a low black building, which stood fronting the end of the alley, a lamp was burning with a reddish, unblinking light. The frost had become more intense, and when Sashka reached the circle of light cast by the lamp he saw that fine dry flakes of snow were falling slowly on the air. It was high time to be getting home.

" Where have you been knocking about all night, puppy? " exclaimed his mother, doubling her fist, without, however, striking. Her sleeves were turned up, exposing her fat white arms, and on her forehead, almost devoid of eyebrows, stood beads of perspiration. As Sashka passed by her he recognized the familiar smell of vodka. His mother scratched her head with the short dirty nail of her thick forefinger, and since it was no good scolding, she merely spat, and cried: " Statisticians! that's what they are! "

Sashka shuffled contemptuously, and went behind the partition, from whence might be heard the heavy breathing of his father, Ivan Sarvich, who was in a chronic state of shivering, and was now trying to warm himself by sitting on the heated bench of the stove, with his hands under him, palms downwards.

" Sashka! the Svetchnikovs have invited you to the Christmas tree. The housemaid came," he whispered.

" Get along with you! " said Sashka with incredulity.

" Fact! The old woman there has purposely not told you, but she has mended your jacket all the same."

" Nonsense," Sashka replied, still more surprised.

The Svetchnikovs were rich people, who had put him to the grammar school, and after his expulsion had forbidden him their house.

His father once more took his oath to the truth of his statement, and Sashka became meditative.

" Well then, move, shift a bit," he said to his father, as he leapt upon the short bench, adding:

" I won't go to those devils. I should prove jolly well too much for them, if I were to turn up. Depraved boy," drawled Sashka in imitation of his patrons. " They are none too good themselves, the smug-faced prigs! "

" Oh! Sashka, Sashka," his father complained, sitting hunched up with cold, " you'll come to a bad end."

" What about yourself, then? " was Sashka's rude rejoinder. " Better shut up. Afraid of the old woman. Ba! old muff! "

His father sat on in silence and shivered. A faint light found its way through a broad chink at the top, where the partition failed to meet the ceiling by a quarter of an inch, and lay in bright patches upon his high forehead, beneath which the deep cavities of his eyes showed black.

In times gone by Ivan Sarvich had been used to drink heavily, and then his wife had feared and hated him. But when he had begun to develop unmistakable signs of consumption, and could drink no longer, she took to drink in her turn, and gradually accustomed herself to vodka. Then she avenged herself for all she had suffered at the hands of that tall narrow-chested man, who used incomprehensible words, had lost his place through disobedience and drunkenness, and who brought home with him just such long-haired, debauched and conceited fellows as himself.

In contradistinction to her husband, the more Feoktista Petrovna drank, the healthier she became, and the heavier became her fists. Now she said what she pleased, brought men and women to the house just as she chose, and sang with them noisy songs, while he lay silent behind the partition huddled together with perpetual cold, and meditating on the injustice and sorrow of human life. To every one with whom she talked, she complained that she had no such enemies in the world as her husband and son, and they were stuck-up statisticians!

For the space of an hour his mother kept drumming into Sashka's ears:

" But I say you shall go," punctuating each word with a heavy blow on the table, which made the tumblers, placed on it after washing, jump and rattle again.

" But I say I won't! " Sashka coolly replied, dragging down the corners of his mouth with the will to show his teeth — a habit which had earned for him at school the nickname of Wolfkin.

" I'll thrash you, won't I just! " cried his mother.

" All right! thrash away! "

But Feoktista Petrovna knew that she could no longer strike her son now that he had begun to retaliate by biting, and that if she drove him into the street he would go off larking, and sooner get frost-bitten than go to the Svetchnikovs; therefore she appealed to her husband's authority.

" Calls himself a father, and can't protect the mother from insult! "

" Really, Sashka, go. Why are you so obstinate? " he jerked out from the bench. " They will perhaps take you up again. They are kind people." Sashka only laughed in an insulting manner.

His father, long ago, before Sashka was born, had been a tutor at the Svetchnikovs', and had ever since looked on them as the best people in the world. At that time he had held also an appointment in the statistical office of the Zemstvo,[2] and had not yet taken to drink. Eventually he was compelled through his own fault to marry his landlady's daughter. From that time he severed his connection with the Svetchnikovs, and took to drink. Indeed, he let himself go to such an extent that he was several times picked up drunk in the streets and taken to the police station. But the Svetchnikovs did not cease to assist him with money, and Feoktista Petrovna, although she hated them, together with books and everything connected with her husband's past, still valued their acquaintance, and was in the habit of boasting of it.

" Perhaps you might bring something for me too from the Christmas tree," continued his father. He was using craft to induce his son to go, and Sashka knew it, and despised his father for his weakness and want of straightforwardness; though he really did wish to bring back something for the poor sickly old man, who had for a long time been without even good tobacco.

" All right! " he blurted out; " give me my jacket. Have you put the buttons on? No fear! I know you too well."

2

The children had not yet been admitted to the drawing-room, where the Christmas tree stood, but remained chattering in the nursery. Sashka, with lofty superciliousness, stood listening to their naïve talk, and fingering in his breeches pocket the broken cigarettes which he had managed to abstract from his host's study. At this moment there came up to him the youngest of the Svetchnikovs, Kolya, and stood motionless before him, a look of surprise on his face, his toes turned in, and a finger stuck in the corner of his pout-

2 **Zemstvo**: local provincial government.

ing mouth. Six months ago, at the instance of his relatives, he had given up this bad habit of putting his finger in his mouth, but he could not quite break himself of it. He had blond locks cut in a fringe on his forehead and falling in ringlets on his shoulders, and blue, wondering eyes; in fact, he was just such a boy in appearance as Sashka particularly loved to bully.

" Are 'oo weally a naughty boy? " he inquired of Sashka. " Miss said 'oo was. I'm a dood boy."

" That you are! " replied Sashka, considering the other's short velvet trousers and great turndown collar.

" Would 'oo like to have a dun? There! " and he pointed at him a little pop-gun with a cork tied to it. The Wolfkin took the gun, pressed down the spring, and, aiming at the nose of the unsuspecting Kolya, pulled the trigger. The cork struck his nose, and rebounding, hung by the string. Kolya's blue eyes opened wider than ever, and filled with tears. Transferring his finger from his mouth to his reddening nose he blinked his long eyelashes and whispered:

" Bad — bad boy! "

A young lady of striking appearance, with her hair dressed in the simplest and most becoming fashion, now entered the nursery. She was sister to the lady of the house, the very one indeed to whom Sashka's father had formerly given lessons.

" Here's the boy," said she, pointing out Sashka to the bald-headed man who accompanied her. " Bow, Sashka, you should not be so rude! "

But Sashka would bow neither to her, nor to her companion of the bald head. She little suspected how much he knew. But, as a fact, Sashka did know that his miserable father had loved her, and that she had married another; and, though this had taken place subsequent to his father's marriage, Sashka could not bring himself to forgive what seemed to him like treachery.

" Takes after his father! " sighed Sofia Dmitrievna. " Could not you, Plutov Mikhailovich, do something for him? My husband says that a commercial school would suit him better than the grammar school. Sashka, would you like to go to a technical school? "

" No! " curtly replied Sashka, who had caught the offensive word " husband."

" Do you want to be a shepherd, then? " asked the gentleman.

" Not likely! " said Sashka, in an offended tone.

" What then? "

Now Sashka did not know what he would like to be, but upon reflection replied: " Well, it's all the same to me, even a shepherd if you like."

The bald-headed gentleman regarded the strange boy with a look of perplexity. When his eyes had traveled up from his patched boots to his face, Sashka put out his tongue and quickly drew it back again, so that Sofia Dmitrievna did not notice anything, but the old gentleman showed an amount of irascibility that she could not understand.

" I should not mind going to a commercial school," bashfully suggested Sashka.

The lady was overjoyed at Sashka's decision, and meditated with a sigh on the beneficial influence exercised by an old love.

" I don't know whether there will be a vacancy," dryly remarked the old man, avoiding looking at Sashka, and smoothing down the ridge of hair which stuck up on the back of his head. " However, we shall see."

Meanwhile the children were becoming noisy, and in a great state of excitement were waiting impatiently for the Christmas tree.

The excellent practice which the pop-gun made in the hands of a boy who commanded respect both for his stature and for his reputation for naughtiness, found imitators, and many a little button of a nose was made red. The tiny maids, holding their sides, bent almost double with laughter, as their little cavaliers with manly contempt of fear and pain, but all the same wrinkling up their faces in suspense, received the impact of the cork.

At length the doors were opened, and a voice said: " Come in, children; gently, not so fast! " Opening their little eyes wide, and holding their breath in anticipation, the children filed into the brightly illuminated drawing-room in orderly pairs, and quietly walked around the glittering tree. It cast a strong, shadowless light on their eager faces, with rounded eyes and mouths. For a minute there reigned the silence of profound enchantment, which all at once broke out into a chorus of delighted exclamation. One of the little girls, unable to restrain her delight, kept dancing up and down in the same place, her little tress braided with blue ribbon beating meanwhile rhythmically against her shoulders. Sashka remained morose and gloomy — something evil was working in his wounded breast. The tree blinded him with its red, shrieking insolent glitter of countless candles. It was foreign, hostile to him, even as the crowd of small pretty children which surrounded it. He would have liked to give it a shove, and topple it over on their shining heads. It seemed as though some iron hand were gripping his heart, and wringing out of it every drop of blood. He crept behind the piano, and sat down there in a corner unconsciously crumpling to pieces in his pocket the last of the cigarettes, and thinking that though he had a father and mother and a home, it came to the same thing as if he had none, and nowhere to go to. He tried to recall to his imagination his little penknife, which he had acquired by a swap not long ago, and was very fond of; but his knife all at once seemed to him a very poor affair with its ground-down blade and only half of a yellow haft. Tomorrow he would smash it up, and then he would have nothing left at all!

But suddenly Sashka's narrow eyes gleamed with astonishment, and his face in a moment resumed its ordinary expression of audacity and self-confidence. On the side of the tree turned towards him — which was the back of it, and less brightly illuminated than the other side — he discovered something such as had never come within the circle of his existence, and without which all his surroundings appeared as empty as though peopled by persons without life. It was a little angel in wax carelessly hung in the thickest of the dark boughs, and looking as if it were floating in the air. His transparent dragon-fly wings trembled in the light, and he seemed altogether alive and ready to fly away. The rosy fingers of his exquisitely formed hands were stretched upwards, and from his head there floated just such locks as Kolya's. But there was something here that was wanting in Kolya's face, and in all other faces and things. The face of the little angel did not shine with joy, nor was it clouded by grief; but there lay on it the impress of another feeling, not to be explained in words, nor defined by thought, but to be attained only by the sympathy of a kindred feeling. Sashka was not conscious of the force of the mysterious influence which attracted him towards the little angel, but he felt that he had known him all his life, and had always loved him, loved him more than his penknife, more than his father, more than anything else. Filled with doubt, alarm, and a delight which he could not comprehend, Sashka clasped his hands to his bosom and whispered:

"Dear — dear little angel!"

The more intently he looked the more fraught with significance the expression of the little angel's face became. He was so infinitely far off, so unlike everything which surrounded him there. The other toys seemed to take a pride in hanging there, pretty and decked out, upon the glittering tree, but he was pensive, and fearing the intrusive light purposely hid himself in the dark greenery, so that none might see him. It would be a mad cruelty to touch his dainty little wings.

" Dear — dear! " whispered Sashka.

His head became feverish. He clasped his hands behind his back, and in full readiness to fight to the death to win the little angel, he walked to and fro with cautious, stealthy steps. He avoided looking at the little angel, lest he should direct the attention of others towards him, but he felt that he was still there, and had not flown away.

Now the hostess appeared in the doorway, a tall, stately lady with a bright aureole of gray hair dressed high upon her head. The children trooped round her with expressions of delight, and the little girl — the same that had danced about in her place — hung wearily on her hand, blinking heavily with sleepy eyes.

As Sashka approached her he seemed almost choking with emotion.

" Auntie — auntie! " said he, trying to speak caressingly, but his voice sounded harsher than ever, " Auntie, dear! "

She did not hear him, so he tugged impatiently at her dress.

" What's the matter with you? Why are you pulling my dress? " said the gray-haired lady in surprise. " It's rude."

" Auntie — auntie, do give me one thing from the tree; give me the little angel."

" Impossible," replied the lady in a tone of indifference. " We are going to keep the tree decorated till the New Year. But you are no longer a child; you should call me by name — Maria Dmitrievna."

Sashka, feeling as if he were falling down a precipice, grasped the last means of saving himself.

" I am sorry I have been naughty. I'll be more industrious for the future," he blurted out. But this formula, which had always paid with his masters, made no impression upon the lady of the gray hair.

" A good thing, too, my friend," she said, as unconcernedly as before.

" Give me the little angel," demanded Sashka, gruffly.

" But it's impossible. Can't you understand that? "

But Sashka did not understand, and when the lady turned to go out of the room he followed her, his gaze fixed without conscious thought upon her black silk dress. In his surging brain there glimmered a recollection of how one of the boys in his class had asked the master to mark him 3,[3] and when the master refused he had knelt down before him, and putting his hands together as in prayer, had begun to cry. The master was angry, but gave him 3 all the same. At the time Sashka had immortalized this episode in a caricature, but now his only means left was to follow the boy's example. Accordingly he plucked at the lady's dress again, and when she turned round, dropped with a bang onto his knees, and folded his hands as described above. But he could not squeeze out a single tear!

" Are you out of your mind? " exclaimed the gray-haired lady, casting a searching look round the room; but luckily no one was present.

" What is the matter with you? "

Kneeling there with clasped hands, Sashka looked at her with dislike, and rudely repeated:

" Give me the little angel."

His eyes, fixed intently on the lady to catch the first word she should utter, were anything but good to look at, and the hostess answered hurriedly:

" Well, then, I'll give it to you. Ah! What a stupid you are! I will give you what you want, but why could you not wait, till the New Year?

" Stand up! And never," she added in a didactic tone, " never kneel to any one: it is humiliating. Kneel before God alone."

" Talk away! " thought Sashka, trying to get in front of her, but merely succeeding in treading on her dress.

When she had taken the toy from the tree, Sashka devoured her with his eyes, but stretched out his hands for it with a painful pucker of the nose. It seemed to him that the tall lady would break the little angel.

" Beautiful thing! " said the lady, who was sorry to part with such a dainty and presumably expensive toy. " Who can have hung it there? Well, what do you want with such a thing? Are you not too big to know what to do with it? Look, there are some picture-books. But this I promised to give to Kolya; he begged so earnestly for it." But this was not the truth.

Sashka's agony became unbearable. He clenched his teeth convulsively, and seemed almost to grind them. The lady of the gray hair feared nothing so much as a scene, so she slowly held out the little angel to Sashka.

" There now, take it! " she said in a displeased tone; " what a persistent boy you are! "

---

[3] 3: high grade in the Russian marking system.

Sashka's hands as they seized the little angel seemed like tentacles, and were tense as steel springs, but withal so soft and careful that the little angel might have imagined himself to be flying in the air.

" A-h-h! " escaped in a long diminuendo [4] sigh from Sashka's breast, while in his eyes glistened two little tear-drops, which stood still there as though unused to the light. Slowly drawing the little angel to his bosom, he kept his shining eyes on the hostess, with a quiet, tender smile which died away in a feeling of unearthly bliss. It seemed, when the dainty wings of the little angel touched Sashka's sunken breast, as if he experienced something so blissful, so bright, the like of which had never before been experienced in this sorrowful, sinful, suffering world.

" A-h-h! " sighed he once more as the little angel's wings touched him. And at the shining of his face the absurdly decorated and insolently growing tree seemed to be extinguished, and the gray-haired, portly dame smiled with gladness, and the parchmentlike face of the bald-headed gentleman twitched, and the children fell into a vivid silence as though touched by a breath of human happiness.

For one short moment all observed a mysterious likeness between the awkward boy who had outgrown his clothes and the lineaments of the little angel, which had been spiritualized by the hand of an unknown artist.

But the next moment the picture was entirely changed. Crouching like a panther preparing to spring, Sashka surveyed the surrounding company, on the lookout for some one who should dare wrest his little angel from him.

" I'm going home," he said in a dull voice, having in view a way of escape through the crowd, " home to father."

3

His mother was asleep; worn out with a whole day's work and vodka-drinking. In the little room behind the partition there stood a small cooking lamp burning on the table. Its feeble yellow light, with difficulty penetrating the sooty glass, threw a strange shadow over the faces of Sashka and his father.

" Is it not pretty? " asked Sashka in a whisper, holding the little angel at a distance from his father, so as not to allow him to touch it.

" Yes, there's something most remarkable about him," whispered the father, gazing thoughtfully at the toy. And his face expressed the same concentrated attention and delight as did Sashka's.

---

[4] **diminuendo:** musical term for diminishing sound.

" Look, he is going to fly."

" I see it, too," replied Sashka in an ecstasy. " Think I'm blind?
But look at his little wings! Ah! don't touch! "

The father withdrew his hand, and with troubled eyes studied the
details of the little angel, while Sashka whispered with the air of a
pedagogue:

" Father, what a bad habit you have of touching everything! You
might break it."

There fell upon the wall the shadows of two grotesque, motionless
heads bending towards one another, one big and shaggy, the other
small and round.

Within the big head strange torturing thoughts, though at the
same time full of delight, were seething. His eyes unblinkingly regarded the little angel, and under his steadfast gaze it seemed to
grow larger and brighter, and its wings to tremble with a noiseless trepidation, and all the surroundings — the timber-built, soot-
stained wall, the dirty table, Sashka — everything became fused
into one level gray mass without light or shade. It seemed to the
broken man that he heard a pitying voice from the world of wonders, wherein once he dwelt, and whence he had been cast out forever. There they knew nothing of dirt, of weary quarreling, of the
blindly cruel strife of egotism, there they knew nothing of the tortures of a man arrested in the streets with callous laughter, and
beaten by the rough hand of the night-watchman. There everything
is pure, joyful, bright. And all this purity found an asylum in the
soul of her whom he loved more than life, and had lost — when he
had kept his hold upon his own useless life. With the smell of wax,
which emanated from the toy, was mingled a subtle aroma, and it
seemed to the broken man that her dear fingers touched the angel,
those fingers which he would fain have caressed in one long kiss, till
death should close his lips forever. This was why the little toy was
so beautiful, this was why there was in it something specially attractive, which defied description. The little angel had descended
from that heaven which her soul was to him, and had brought a ray
of light into the damp room, steeped in sulphurous fumes, and to
the dark soul of the man from whom had been taken all: love, and
happiness, and life.

On a level with the eyes of the man, who had lived his life, sparkled
the eyes of the boy, who was beginning his life, and embraced the
little angel in their caress. For them present and future had disappeared: the ever-sorrowful, piteous father, the rough, unendurable

mother, the black darkness of insults, of cruelty, of humiliations, and of spiteful grief. The thoughts of Sashka were formless, nebulous, but all the more deeply for that did they move his agitated soul. Everything that is good and bright in the world, all profound grief, and the hope of a soul that sighs for God — the little angel absorbed them all into himself, and that was why he glowed with such a soft divine radiance, that was why his little dragonfly wings trembled with a noiseless trepidation.

The father and son did not look at one another; their sick hearts grieved, wept, and rejoiced apart. But there was a something in their thoughts which fused their hearts in one, and annihilated that bottomless abyss which separates man from man and makes him so lonely, unhappy, and weak. The father with an unconscious motion put his arm around the neck of his son, and the son's head rested equally without conscious volition upon his father's consumptive chest.

" She it was who gave it to thee, was it not? " whispered the father, without taking his eyes off the little angel.

At another time Sashka would have replied with a rude negation, but now the only reply possible resounded of itself within his soul, and he calmly pronounced the pious fraud: " Who else? of course she did."

The father made no reply, and Sashka relapsed into silence.

Something grated in the adjoining room, then clicked, and then was silent for a moment, and then noisily and hurriedly the clock struck " One, two, three."

" Sashka, do you ever dream? " asked the father in a meditative tone.

" No! Oh, yes," he admitted, " once I had one, in which I fell down from the roof. We were climbing after the pigeons, and I fell down."

" But I dream always. Strange things are dreams. One sees the whole past, one loves and suffers as though it were reality."

Again he was silent, and Sashka felt his arm tremble as it lay upon his neck. The trembling and pressure of his father's arm became stronger and stronger, and the sensitive silence of the night was all at once broken by the pitiful sobbing sound of suppressed weeping. Sashka sternly puckered his brow, and cautiously — so as not to disturb the heavy trembling arm — wiped away a tear from his eyes. So strange was it to see a big old man crying.

" Ah! Sashka, Sashka," sobbed the father, " what is the meaning of everything? "

" Why, what's the matter? " sternly whispered Sashka. " You're crying just like a little boy."

" Well, I won't then," said the father with a piteous smile of excuse. " What's the good? "

Feoktista Petrovna turned on her bed. She sighed, cleared her throat, and mumbled incoherent sounds in a loud and strangely persistent manner.

It was time to go to bed. But before doing so the little angel must be disposed of for the night. He could not be left on the floor, so he was hung up by his string, which was fastened to the flue of the stove. There it stood out accurately delineated against the white Dutch tiles. And so they could both see him, Sashka and his father.

Hurriedly throwing into a corner the various rags on which he was in the habit of sleeping, Sashka lay down on his back, in order as quickly as possible to look again at the little angel.

" Why don't you undress? " asked his father as he shivered and wrapped himself up in his tattered blanket, and arranged his clothes, which he had thrown over his feet.

" What's the good? I shall soon be up again."

Sashka wished to add that he did not care to go to sleep at all, but he had no time to do so, since he fell to sleep as suddenly as though he had sunk to the bottom of a deep, swift river.

His father presently fell asleep also. And gentle sleep and restfulness lay upon the weary face of the man who had lived his life, and upon the brave face of the boy who was just beginning his life.

But the little angel hanging by the hot stove began to melt. The lamp, which had been left burning at the entreaty of Sashka, filled the room with the smell of kerosene, and through its smoked glass threw a melancholy light upon a scene of gradual dissolution. The little angel seemed to stir. Over his rose fingers were rolled thick drops which fell upon the bench. To the smell of kerosene was added the stifling scent of melting wax. The little angel gave a tremble as though on the point of flight, and — fell with a soft thud upon the hot flags.

An inquisitive cockroach singed its wings as it ran round the formless lump of melted wax, climbed up the dragonfly wings, and twitching its feelers went on its way.

Through the curtained window the gray-blue light of coming day crept in, and the frozen water carrier was already making a noise in the courtyard with his iron scoop.

(*W. H. Lowe*)

SUGGESTIONS FOR STUDY

1. What details of the story make it seem like an American situation? Which details have a distinctly Russian flavor?

2. How does Sashka resemble Tom Sawyer, Huckleberry Finn, Penrod, and other American boy characters in fiction?

3. What saves the story from undue sentimentality? Are the moments of tenderness in the boy made convincing?

4. How does the story show Andreyev's combination of typical Russian realism with an element of symbolism? What is the symbol? What does it signify? How does the ending of the story enhance the meaning of the symbol?

5. Compare the use of symbol with that in some of Hawthorne's stories. What do you find in common between the Andreyev and Bunin stories?

DEMYAN BEDNEY (1883–   )

The poetry of Demyan Bedney (assumed name of Yefim Alexeyevich Pridvorov) is representative of that produced since the Revolution in that it is vigorous, homely, untutored, with many of the same qualities as folklore. He was born in the province of Khersov, the son of a church warden. His schooling was rather scattered, though he was for a time at the University of St. Petersburg. In 1909 his verses were first published in a Socialist monthly. He served in the war as an assistant surgeon and with the Revolution joined the Red Army. Later he was honored by the Soviet Government for his poetry of a semiofficial nature such as the memorial inscription on the grave of dead soldiers in the Red Square.

NO ONE KNEW

APRIL 22, 1870

It was a day like any other,
The same dull sky, the same drab street.
There was the usual angry pother
From the policeman on his beat.
Proud of his new calotte's fine luster,   5
The arch-priest strutted down the nave;
And the pub rocked with brawl and bluster,
Where scamps gulped down what fortune gave.

5. **calotte:** a skullcap worn by the clergy.   7. **pub:** British slang for public house, a saloon.

The market women buzzed and bickered
Like flies above the honeypots.
The burghers' spouses danced and dickered,
Eyeing the drapers' latest lots.
An awe-struck peasant stared and stuttered,
Regarding an official door
Where yellow rags of paper fluttered: 15
A dead ukase of months before.
The fireman ranged his tower, surveying
The roofs, like the chained bears one sees;
And soldiers marched like slaves, obeying
The drill sergeant's obscenities.   20
Slow carts in caravans went winding
Dockward, where floury stevedores moiled;
And, under convoy, in the blinding
Dust of the road, a student toiled.
Berating some good pal and brother,   25
A drunken hand was loud in scorn. . . .
Russia was aching with the thorn
And bearing her old cross, poor mother,
That day, a day like any other,
And not a soul knew that — *Lenin was born!*   30

  (*Babette Deutsch and Avrahm Yarmolinsky*)

  16. **ukase:** an edict of the Russian government.

MIKHAIL PROKOFYEVICH GERASIMOV (1889–)

 Gerasimov belongs to a group of Moscow writers whose title of " The Smithy " suggests that they celebrate the industrial life of the city. Gerasimov is distinctly a proletarian. He was born in a log cabin at a small railroad station where his father was a switchman. He helped work on the railroad embankments and attended the company's technical school for a time. During the uprising of 1905 he was imprisoned and two years later escaped from Russia to roam about Europe working at any odd jobs he could find. He tasted prison life also in France, Belgium, and Italy, enlisted in the French army in 1914, was sent back to Russia because of his pacifist doctrines, and occupied several positions under the Soviet Government. He is a prolific writer, having published sixteen collections of poetry within seven years after the beginning of the Soviet régime.

THE FIRST BULB IS TURNED ON

From what nebula
Has a star rolled
Down among these slimy reeds?
The crowd of peasants sways —
Pressed by electric fingers   5
Of light that crumple
These men of stone.
Smiles stream forth
Through their straw beards.
They swallow the new light, gulping,   10
And scoop up handfuls
From the spring of light
Bared by the hand of man.
The floodgate with a desperate sob
Hides under leaping foam.   15
To vertebral trees,
To skeletal posts,
We fasten nerves of light.
The wooden bones of the village,
Its log ribs,   20
Are worked by copper muscles.
Hundreds of electric fangs
Sink into izba hearts,
Into the hearts of peasants.
On windows blind with centuries,   25
Black with splinter soot,
Constellations burst.
New eyes are hatched to seize the world.

(Babette Deutsch and Avrahm Yarmolinsky)

23. **izba:** a peasant's cottage or hut.

SERGEY ALEXANDROVICH ESSENIN (YESENIN)
(1895–1925)

Essenin was a peasant boy with no education beyond the village school.
His natural lyrical gift was evident when he was still in his teens. By
nineteen his first volume of poetry was published and in the twenties he

became a conspicuous leader among the "Imagist" school of poets who frequented the Moscow cafés. Through his marriage to Isadora Duncan, the dancer, he had opportunity to travel through Europe and America. But he remained the overemotional and untamable peasant boy, and feeling like a trapped wolf, he hanged himself at the age of thirty in a Leningrad hotel room. That very day he had given a friend a poem, written, he said, in his own blood. His pictures of peasant life, of the fields and steppes are his best. Wild horses, with which he seemed to feel an underlying kinship, figure in several of his poems as in the one here printed.

UPON GREEN HILLS

Upon green hills wild droves of horses blow
The golden bloom off of the days that go.

From the high hillocks of the blue-ing bay
Falls the sheer pitch of heavy manes that sway.

They toss their heads above the still lagoon
Caught with a silver bridle by the moon.

Snorting in fear of their own shadow they,
To screen it with their manes, await the day.

(Babette Deutsch and Avrahm Yarmolinsky)

SUGGESTIONS FOR STUDY

1. In what ways do these poems bring out significant changes in modern life? Where is the realistic method used? Where the symbolical?

2. How many different types of persons are described in "No One Knew"? Does the author describe them impersonally or can you detect his attitude toward them? How has the Revolution affected these different types? Do you consider this poem propaganda? Why or why not?

3. Why is a scientific development like electric lighting difficult to put into poetry? Compare "The First Bulb Is Turned On" with Snoilsky's "Birds on a Telegraph Wire." What similarity is there in the significance of the two? Which poem makes the significance back of it more impressive to you?

4. "Wild Horses" may be interpreted simply as a picture, or as a symbol of a human mood, or of the Russian Revolution. Which interpretation do you prefer? Why?

5. To what different types of pictorial art would these three poems lend themselves for illustration?

6. Try your hand at writing (in either poetry or prose) a "No One Knew" situation about some other historical character who has brought about great changes in life, choosing details to suggest the nature of the change. Try showing the poetic significance of some far-reaching scientific invention.

EFIM ZOZULYA (1891–   )

Zozulya fills a unique place among the writers recognized by the Soviet Republic. He is a satirist rather than a propagandist, and while he sometimes follows the pattern of realism, his quirk of ridicule always gives it individuality. His mask of laughter with possible tears behind it reminds us of Gogol; his symbolism recalls Andreyev; yet he is fundamentally like neither — only himself. The following tale departs from the usual method of the short story and becomes a grotesque fantasy, calling to mind the mood of much of our modern painting and music. In a remarkably vivid and condensed form it seems to crystallize the whole Revolutionary process as it has gone on in Russia. Ak immediately suggests Lenin to the imagination, and Ak's change of policy has its counterpart in actual occurrences. But beyond that, the story opens up the whole philosophy of human values, and thus gains true universality.

A TALE ABOUT AK AND HUMANITY

I. THE PLACARDS

The houses and the streets had an ordinary appearance. And, above them, the unchanging sky was azure. And the gray masks of the pavement stone were, as always, impenetrable and indifferent, while maddened men, from whose faces tears dropped into pails of paste, were adorning the walls with placards.

Their text was simple, pitiless and irrevocable.

Here it is:

"To all without exclusion:

"An examination of the inhabitants of the town with regard to their right to live is being carried out by districts by special commissions consisting of three members of the Courts of the Higher Decisions. Inhabitants, acknowledged to be superfluous (unnecessary), are obliged to depart from life within twenty-four hours. The right of appeal is allowed within that time. The appeal must be made in writing and will be delivered to the Central Court of the Higher Decisions. A reply will be given within three hours. Superfluous human beings, unable either from weakness of will or from love of living to depart from life, will be dealt with by the

Courts of the Higher Decisions, who will call on friends, neighbors, or special armed companies to execute the sentence.

" Remarks. 1. The inhabitants of the town, with complete obedience, are obliged to submit to the acts and regulations of the members of the Courts of the Higher Decisions. Truthful answers must be given to all questions. An official report will be given of the characteristics of every person judged to be superfluous.

" 2. This decree will be carried out with irrevocable severity. Human rubbish, hindering the reconstruction of life on the basis of justice and happiness, must be pitilessly destroyed. This decree concerns, without exclusion, all citizens — men and women, rich and poor.

" 3. The departure from town of any person whatsoever while the examination with regard to the right to live is in progress is absolutely forbidden."

II. THE FIRST WAVES OF PERTURBATION

" Have you read? "

" Have you read? "

" Have you read? ! "

" Have you read? ! !   Have you read? ! ! "

" Have you seen? ! !   Have you heard? ! ! "

" Have you read? ! ! "

Crowds began to gather all over the town. Traffic became congested. From sudden weakness pedestrians leaned against house walls. Many wept. Some had fainting spells. Towards evening their number reached a tremendous figure.

" Have you read? ! ! "

" How terrible? Who's ever heard of such a thing! "

" Why, we ourselves elected the Courts of the Higher Decisions! We ourselves gave them full powers! "

" Yes, that's true."

" We ourselves are to blame for the monstrous situation."

" Yes, that's true. We are to blame. That's because we ourselves wanted to create a better life. But who could have thought that the Courts would approach the question in so simple and terrible a manner? "

" But what names have been chosen for the composition of the Courts! Oh, what names! "

" How do you know? Have they published a list of the members? "

" I've heard from an acquaintance. Ak has been chosen Chairman."

" Oh, you don't say! Ak? That's a piece of good fortune! "

" Yes. Yes. It's a fact! "

" What good fortune! He's a magnificent personality."

" Of course! We must not be too anxious: he's sure to weed out the human rubbish. We need not fear injustice."

" Dear citizen, what do you think? Will I be left among the living? I am a decent sort of man. Do you know, once during the wreck of a ship twenty passengers saved themselves in a boat. But the boat could not stand such a huge load, and all were threatened with death. In order that fifteen might be saved, it was necessary that five should fling themselves into the sea. I was one of the five. I volunteered to do it. Don't look so incredulously. Now I'm old and feeble. Haven't you really heard of this happening? The papers were full of it at the time. My four comrades perished. A chance saved me. What do you think? Will they spare me? "

" And me, citizens? And me? I gave away all my possessions to the poor. That was long ago. I have documents to prove it."

" I don't know, really. All depends on the point of view of the Courts of the Higher Decisions."

" Allow me to inform you, esteemed citizens, that primitive usefulness to neighbors by no means justifies the existence of human beings on earth. Why, in that case, every stupid wet nurse would have the right to live. That's an old notion. You're behind the times! "

" What, then, is the value of a human being? "

" Yes, what is his value? "

" I don't know."

" Oh, you don't know! Why do you poke your muzzle here with your opinions if you don't know? "

" I'm sorry. I only said what I thought."

" Citizens! Citizens! Look! Look! They're running! What a confusion! A panic! "

" Oh, heavens! Heavens! . . . Ah! . . . Save yourselves! Save yourselves! "

" Stop! Don't run! "

" Don't make the panic worse! "

" Stop! "

III. THE FUGITIVES

The crowds ran in the streets. Red-cheeked young men ran, with terror-stricken faces. Modest clerks serving in offices and establishments. Bridegrooms in clean cuffs. Choir singers from amateur societies. Dandies. Tellers of anecdotes. Billiard players. Evening visitors to the moving pictures. Career-pursuers, evildoers, sharpers, with white foreheads and curly hair. Hypocritical rakes. Wicked drunkards. Jolly fellows, hooligans, Adonises, visionaries, lovers, cyclists. Broad-shouldered squabblers, squabbling from having nothing else to do, talkers, deceivers, long-haired hypocrites, petty grief indulgers, with dark sad eyes, behind whose sadness, concealed by youth, lay cold emptiness. Young churls with full, smiling lips, vainglorious adventurers, scandalmongers, good-hearted failures, clever profligates.

Corpulent, voracious, lazy women also ran. And lean shrews, nagging, boring women, tedious females, wives of fools and wise men, gossipers, betrayers, the envious and the greedy, now distorted with fear. Proud she-fools, the good-for-nothing good, those who from boredom dyed their hair, the colorless libertines, the lonely, the helpless, the brazen, the begging, the supplicating, who, from terror, had lost all outward decorum.

Stooped old men ran. And squat men, small men, tall men, and handsome and malformed men.

Men who managed houses, pawnbrokers, ironmongers, carpenters, artisans, jailers, grocers, good-natured publicans, decorous gray-haired lackeys, respectable fathers of families, those who had battened up dupes of their baseness, venerable sharps and fat scoundrels.

They ran in a dense, impetuous, ruthless mass. Loads of rags enveloped their bodies and extremities. Hot steam poured from their mouths. Curses and wails resounded through the concealed indifference of the abandoned edifices.

Many ran carrying possessions. With twisted fingers they dragged pillows, boxes, drawers. They seized their precious gems, their children, their money. They shouted, then returned, lifting their arms in terror, and then ran again.

But they were all turned back. All. Such beings as themselves shot at them, ran in front of them, beat them with sticks, fists, stones; there was biting too, and terrible outcries; the crowds fell back, leaving behind their killed and wounded.

Towards evening the town resumed its normal appearance. The trembling bodies of the inhabitants returned to their homes and flung themselves on their beds. A brief poignant hope desperately struggled in tight, feverish skulls.

IV. A SIMPLE PROCEDURE

" Your name? "

" Boss."

" How old are you? "

" Thirty."

" Occupation? "

" I make cigarettes."

" Tell the truth! "

" I am telling the truth. I've worked honestly at my trade for fourteen years and supported my family."

" Where is your family? "

" Here they are. This is my wife. This is my son."

" Doctor, examine the Boss family."

" I have done so."

" Well, what can you tell us about them? "

" Citizen Boss is anaemic. General condition, average. His wife suffers with headaches and rheumatism. The boy is healthy."

" Good. You may go, doctor. Citizen Boss, what are your pleasures? What do you love? "

" I love people and life generally."

" Be more precise, citizen Boss. To the point."

" I love. . . . Well, what do I love? . . . I love my son. . . . He is so clever with the fiddle. . . . I love my meals, though to be sure, I'm not a glutton. . . . I am fond of women. . . . It is pleasant to look at handsome women and girls passing in the street. I love, when I'm tired in the evening, to rest. . . . I love making cigarettes. . . . I can make five hundred an hour. . . . I love life."

" Be calm, citizen Boss! Stop whimpering. What do you say, psychologist? "

" Claptrap, colleague! Rubbish! The most ordinary creatures. A poor existence. Temperament semi-phlegmatic, semi-sanguine. Activity feeble. Class — the last. Hope for betterment — none. Passivity — seventy-five per cent. Mrs. Boss — still lower. The boy is commonplace, but perhaps. . . . How old is your son, citizen Boss? Stop whimpering! "

" Thirteen."

" Don't be alarmed. For the time being your son will remain among the living. As for you. . . . In any case, that is none of my affair. Render your decision, colleague! "

" In the name of the Courts of the Higher Decisions, with the object of cleansing life of superfluous human rubbish, of indifferent beings, I order you, citizen Boss, and your wife, to depart from this life within twenty-four hours. Be quiet! Don't bawl! Sanitary officer, calm the woman! Call the guard! It doesn't look as if they'll manage it without assistance."

V. CHARACTERISTICS OF THE SUPERFLUOUS PRESERVED IN THE GRAY CABINET

The Gray Cabinet was situated in the corridor in the department of the Courts of the Higher Decisions. This cabinet had the usual appearance: it was a solid, pensively stupid affair, like most cabinets. It was neither in width nor in height more than seven feet, but it was the grave of several thousand human beings. It was marked with the brief inscription:

" Catalogue of the Superfluous."

The catalogue was divided into several sections, and among others were:

" The Indiscriminately Impressionable."
" Petty Partisans."
" The Passive."
" Without Equilibrium."

and so forth.

The characteristics were stated briefly and objectively. In some instances, to be sure, there were sharp remarks, but these were, inevitably, red-penciled by Ak, who added his commentary to the effect that it was not necessary to abuse the superfluous.

Here are some specimen records of the characteristics of the superfluous:

" Superfluous Male No. 14,741.

" Health average. He visits acquaintances, without being either useful or interesting to them. He is free with advice. In the bloom of his strength he had seduced a girl, then cast her off. He regards the acquisition of furniture after marriage as the most important function in life. His brain is drowsy, lymphatic. He has no capacity for work. To the question what he considered to be the most interesting thing he had encountered in life, he told of his visit to the restaurant ' Quisisana ' in Paris. A common creature. Category of the lower strata. Heart feeble. Within 24 hours."

" Superfluous Male No. 14,623.

"A worker in a cooper's shop. Class — mediocre. Has no love for his work. His mind in everything works along lines of least resistance. Physically, well; but spiritually, he suffers from a common disease: the fear of life. The fear of freedom. When free, during holidays, he stupefies himself with alcohol. During the revolution he exhibited some energy: he wore a red ribbon, and hoarded potatoes and everything else he could get hold of. He was afraid of falling short. He prided himself on his proletarian origin. He took no active share in the revolution: he was afraid. He loves sour cream. He beats children. The tempo of his life is uniformly dispirited. Within 24 hours."

" Superfluous Male No. 15,201.

" He knows eight languages, but says that it is tedious to listen even to one. He is fond of ingenious trifles. Very self-confident. His self-confidence is based on his knowledge of languages. Demands esteem. Indulges in gossip. Towards real animate life indifferent, like an ox. Afraid of beggars. Sweet-tempered in his relations out of fear. Is fond of killing flies and other insects. Rarely experiences joy. Within 24 hours."

" Superfluous Female No. 4,356.

" Scolds her servants out of boredom. Secretly skims the cream from the milk and the fat top layer from the bouillon. Reads shilling-shockers. For days on end lounges on the couch. Her greatest dream: to have a frock with yellow sleeves and slit sides. For twelve years she was loved by a gifted inventor. She did not know his occupation, and thought he was an electrician. She abandoned him and married a tradesman in leather. No children. Is often capricious and hysterical without cause. Wakes in the night to order a samovar and a snack. A wholly superfluous creature. Within 24 hours."

VI. AT WORK

An army of specialists had gathered round Ak and the Courts of the Higher Decisions. It consisted of doctors, psychologists, observers and writers. They all worked with extraordinary speed. There were occasions when at a given hour the specialists speeded a good hundred persons on the way to the other world. And into the Gray Cabinet there flew a hundred records of characteristics, in which the lucidity of expression vied with the firm assurance of the authors.

From morning till night the work went on apace in the chief department. House commissions came and went. Companies of executors of sentences came and went, while behind the desks, as in an immense editorial office, dozens of human beings were sitting and writing, with quick, firm, unreflecting hands.

Ak looked at all this with narrow, strong, impenetrable eyes, and thought his own thoughts, from which his body grew more and more hunched, and his large, impetuous, stubborn head more and more gray.

Something rose up between him and his servants, something erected itself as it were between his tense, sleepless thought and the blind, unreflecting hands of the executors.

VII. AK'S DOUBTS

One day the members of the Courts of the Higher Decisions came into the department with the intention of delivering their reports.

They did not find Ak in his usual place. They sought and did not find him. They sent out messengers, called on the telephone without success.

Only after two hours they found him by chance in the Gray Cabinet.

Ak was sitting in the Cabinet on the death warrants of the superfluous, with an intense expression of thought in his eyes, unusual even for him.

" What are you doing here? " they asked Ak.

" As you see, I am thinking," answered Ak, wearily.

" But why in the Cabinet? "

" It's the most fitting place. I am thinking of human beings, and to think of human beings profitably it is best to do it in the immediate proximity of the decrees of their destruction. Only sitting on the documents of the destruction of man is it possible to learn something of his extraordinary strange life."

Some one laughed shallowly and emptily.

" Don't you laugh! " said Ak warningly, waving some one's record of characteristics in his hand. " Don't you laugh! I think the Courts of the Higher Decisions are passing through a crisis. An examination of the records of those who have perished has led me to seek new paths towards progress. You have all learned, quickly and malignantly, to prove the superfluity of this or that existence. Even the least gifted among you is ready, in a few phrases, to demonstrate this with conviction. And here am I sitting and thinking, ' Is your way just? ' "

Once more Ak lapsed into thought, then sighed bitterly, and said quietly:

" What's to be done? Where's the issue? When one examines the lives of the living, one arrives at the conclusion that three-fourths of them should be rooted out of existence. But when one examines those who have perished, a doubt comes; wouldn't it have been better if one had loved them and pitied them? That's where, in my opinion, is the blind alley of the human question, the blind alley of human history."

Again Ak lapsed into a sad silence, and he dug into the mountain of records of the condemned dead, and unhealthily began to pore over their officially painful brevity.

The members of the Courts departed. No one contradicted. In the first place, because it was useless to contradict Ak; in the second, because no one dared to contradict him. But they all felt that a new decision was ripening, and they nearly all felt dissatisfied: here was a matter which had become a matter of custom, everything was clear and definite, and now it looked as if it all would have to be changed for something else. But for what?

What else has this man's brain contrived, this brain which had such a fabulous power over the town?

VIII. THE CRISIS

Ak vanished.

He always vanished when he fell into meditation. They sought him everywhere and did not find him. Some one said that Ak was sitting outside the town and weeping. Others said that Ak was running about his garden on all fours and gnawing the earth.

The activity of the Courts of the Higher Decisions weakened. The work ceased to run smoothly with the disappearance of Ak. The inhabitants simply put up iron bars across their doors and would not let the servants of the Courts in. In some districts the questions of the members of the Courts as regards the right to live were answered with laughter, and it even happened that the superfluous seized the members of the Courts of the Higher Decisions and examined them as to their right to live and wrote mock records of characteristics, which in no wise differed from those preserved in the Gray Cabinet.

Chaos possessed the town. Superfluous, good-for-nothing inhabitants who had not yet been executed became so brazen as to appear in the streets and to make good cheer with their neighbors, to give themselves up to all sorts of diversions, and even to enter into marriage.

Congratulations were exchanged in the streets:

" Ended! Ended! Hurrah! "

" The examinations of the right to live have come to an end! "

" Don't you think, citizen, life's become very pleasant? There's less human rubbish about. Why, one can breathe now! "

" Aren't you ashamed, citizen? You really think that those who've left this life hadn't a right to it? Oh, I know some who haven't the right to live even a single hour, but they're still alive and will go on living! On the other hand, how many really decent people have perished? If you only knew! "

" That's nothing. Mistakes are unavoidable. Tell me, do you know what's become of Ak? "

" I don't know."

" Ak is sitting on a tree outside town and weeping."

" Ak is running about on all fours and gnawing the earth."

" Let him weep."

" Let him go on gnawing."

" You are rejoicing prematurely, citizens! Prematurely, I say. Ak is returning this evening, and the Courts of the Higher Decisions will resume their work."

" How do you know? "

" I know. There's still an awful lot of human rubbish left. It's necessary to clean up things thoroughly. Thoroughly."

" You're very hard, citizen."

" Fiddlesticks! "

" Citizens! Citizens! Look! Look! "

" New placards are being put up."

" Look! "

" Citizens! What a joy! What good fortune! "

" Citizens, read! "

" Read! "

" Read! Read! "

" Read! "

IX. THE NEW PLACARDS

Men were running breathlessly round the streets, with pails full of paste. Packets of huge rose-tinted placards were being unfurled and, with a joyous crackle, were being pasted onto walls of houses. Their text was precise, clear and simple:

" To all without exclusion:

" From the moment of the publication of this decree all inhabitants of the town are allowed to live. Live, multiply and fill the earth. The

Courts of the Higher Decisions have fulfilled their stern obligations and will hereafter be called the Courts of the Higher Delicacy. You are all excellent citizens, and your rights to life are indisputable.

"The Courts of the Higher Delicacy will appoint special commissions consisting of three members whose duty it shall be to pay daily visits to homes and to congratulate their occupants on the fact of their existence and to note their observations in special 'Joyous Records.'

"The members of these commissions shall have the right to question citizens as to the manner of their life, and citizens, if they so desire, may answer in detail. The latter is desirable. The joyous observations shall be preserved in the Rose-tinted Cabinet for posterity."

X. NORMAL LIFE RESUMED

The doors, the windows, the balconies were all opened. Loud human voices, laughter, singing and music resounded from them. Stout, incapable girls began to play on the piano. Gramophones dinned from morning till night. Fiddles, clarinets and guitars also made themselves audible. In the evening men took off their coats, sat themselves on the balconies, and, stretching out their legs, sighed with pleasure. The traffic in the streets grew animated. Young men, taking young women out with them, went driving in cabs and motorcars. The cafés and confectionery shops were full of customers enjoying pastries and cool drinks. Trinket shops which sold mirrors did a bustling business. Men and women bought mirrors and enjoyed their reflections. Artists and photographers were overrun with orders for portraits. The portraits were put into frames and adorned the walls. In one instance they caused a murder, which the newspapers made much of. It happened like this. A young man hired a furnished room and demanded that the portraits of the parents of his landlord and landlady be removed. The landlord and the landlady were offended and killed the young man, and threw him out of a fifth-story window onto the street.

Feelings of personal dignity and self-love developed tremendously. Collisions and quarrels became a common occurrence. Such colloquies as the following became the rule:

"It is evident that you're alive only because of some mistake. The Courts of the Higher Decisions did their work carelessly."

"Yes, very carelessly, when they left such as you alive."

Generally speaking, these quarrels went unnoticed in the normal course of life. Human beings improved their table, cooked all sorts of jams. Warm knit apparel became in demand, as every one held his health in high regard.

The members of the Courts of the Higher Delicacy regularly visited homes and asked their occupants how they managed.

Many replied that they managed very well, and even tried to convince their questioners of this.

" Just look! " they said, smiling with self-satisfaction and rubbing their hands. " We are pickling some cucumbers, he-he! And we have some pickled herrings, too. Our larder is better than it was, thank heavens. . . ."

Others complained of inconveniences and lamented the fact that the work of the Courts of the Higher Decisions had been cut prematurely short.

" Last evening I was in a tram, and just think of it! There wasn't a single unoccupied place. . . . What a disgrace! Both my wife and I had to stand up. There're a good many superfluous people left. They nudge you everywhere — the devil take them! A pity they weren't removed when there was the chance! "

Still others were perturbed for different reasons.

" Just consider! Neither on Wednesday nor on Thursday did any congratulate me on my existence. Shameless, I say! And what will you say to that? Is it, then, necessary for me to come to you to be congratulated, eh? "

XI. THE END OF THE TALE

In Ak's office, as before, the work went on apace: men were sitting there and writing. The Rose-tinted Cabinet was full of joyous records and observations. Carefully and in detail were described the birthdays, the marriages, the journeys, the dinners and the suppers, the love stories, indeed all manner of happenings, and some of the records bore the character and appearance of short stories and novels. The inhabitants requested the members of the Courts of the Higher Delicacy to publish them in the form of books, and they had plenty of reading.

Ak was silent.

He grew only more and more hunched and more and more gray.

Sometimes he got into the Rose-tinted Cabinet and remained sitting there a long time, just as he had done before in the Gray Cabinet.

Once he jumped out of the Rose-tinted Cabinet with the cry:

" It's necessary to kill them! To kill them! To kill them! "

But, on seeing the white fingers of his servants hurrying speedily across the paper, describing the living with the same zeal with which they had formerly described the dead, Ak waved a hand, ran out of the office and disappeared.

He disappeared forever.

There were many legends concerning the disappearance of Ak, and all sorts of rumors, but Ak was never again found.

And the human beings, of whom there were so many in town, whom at first Ak wanted to kill and afterwards pitied, and whom later he again wanted to kill, human beings among whom are many good people and not a little rubbish, continue to this day to live as if there had been no Ak at all, as if there had been no one to raise the question as regards one's right to live.

(John Cournos)

SUGGESTIONS FOR STUDY

1. Mention two or three ways in which this tale differs from the typical short story. Point out how it combines realism, fantasy, and satire. State the point of the allegory in a few words.

2. What specific parallels to events in this story can you find in the Russian Revolution? In what ways do the Courts of the Higher Decisions remind you of the French Revolution courts as described in *A Tale of Two Cities?* How is their procedure in marked contrast? How do these differences satirize modern efficiency?

3. What elements does this tale have in common with much ultramodern painting and music? Can you give any specific examples from these arts as illustrations? What parts of the tale might be particularly suggestive of subjects for creators in these other mediums?

4. Write some anonymous " case histories " of persons you have encountered in life who are " superfluous " for the common good. Observe Zozulya's method of suggesting teeming masses of humanity. Write a description of some situation you have observed involving crowds, using his method.

READING LIST

TRANSLATIONS FROM RUSSIAN LITERATURE

Poetry

Chadwick, N. K.: *Russian Heroic Poetry*

Coxwell, C. F.: *Russian Poems*

Deutsch, B. and Yarmolinsky, A.: *Modern Russian Poets*

Jarintzov, Nadine: *Russian Poets and Poems*

Metheson, P. E.: *Holy Russia*

Saminsky, Lillian: *Poems and Adaptions*

Selver, P.: *Anthology of Modern Slavonic Literature in Prose and Verse*

Modern Russian Poetry

Drama

Gogol, N.: *The Government Inspector and Other Plays*, trans. by Constance Garnett

Chekhov, A.: *The Cherry Orchard*
The Marriage Proposal

Andreyev, L.: *Plays: He Who Gets Slapped*
An Incident
Love of One's Neighbor (See general collections of one-act plays for both Chekhov and Andreyev).

Noyes, G. R.: *Masterpieces of Russian Drama*

Lyons, E.: *Six Soviet Plays*

Fiction

Houghton, Louise: *The Russian Grandmother's Wonder Tales*

Nisbet-Bain, R.: *Russian Fairy Tales*

Wheeler, Post: *Russian Wonder Tales*

Wratislav, A. H.: *Sixty Folk Tales from Slavonic Sources*

Gogol, N.: *Dead Souls*
Evening on a Farm
The Cloak

Turgenev, Ivan: *Sportsman's Sketches*
Fathers and Sons
On the Eve

Dostoevsky, F.: *Memories from the Dead House*
Crime and Punishment
The Brothers Karamazov

Tolstoy, L.: *Childhood, Adolescence, Youth* (fictional autobiography)
War and Peace
Anna Karenina

Bunin, I.: *The Gentleman from San Francisco*
The Village

Chekhov, A.: Short Stories (each name is the title story in a collection of his stories in translation): *The Bishop, The Chorus Girl, The Cook's Wedding, The Darling, The Duel, The Grasshopper, The Horse-Stealers, The Shooting Party, The Wife, The Witch*

Andreyev, L.: *The Little Angel and Other Stories*

Gorki, M.: *Twenty-Six Men and A Girl and Other Stories*

Merezhkovsky, D. S.: *The Romance of Leonardo da Vinci*

Ossorgin, M.: *Quiet Street*

Schweikert, H. C.: *Russian Short Stories*

Graham, S.: *Great Russian Short Stories*

Cournos, J.: *Short Stories out of Soviet Russia*

Beckhofer, C. E.: *Russian Anthology in English*

Wiener, L.: *Anthology of Russian Literature*, 2 vols.

Selver, P.: *Anthology of Modern Slavonic Literature in Prose and Verse*

Struve, Gleb: *Soviet Russian Literature*

Non-Fiction

Dostoevsky, F.: *Prison Life in Siberia*

Dostoevsky, Aimee: *Fedor Dostoevsky* (life written by his daughter)

Dostoevsky, Anna: *Diary of Dostoevsky's Wife*

Solovev, E.: *Dostoevsky*

Yarmolinsky, A.: *Dostoevsky*

Merezhkovsky, D. S.: *Tolstoy as Man and Artist*

Gorki, M.: *My Childhood*
My University Days
Fragments from My Diary

BOOKS ABOUT RUSSIA

Criticism and History of Literature

Baring, M.: *Landmarks in Russian Literature*
Outline of Russian Literature
Brandes, G.: *Impressions of Russia* (trans. from the Danish)
Bruckner, A.: *Literary History of Russia*
Hapgood, Isabel: *Survey of Russian Literature*
Kropotkin, P. A.: *Russian Literature*
Ideals and Realities in Russian Literature
Mirsky, D.: *Modern Russian Literature*
Olgin, M. J.: *Guide to Russian Literature*
Phelps, W. L.: *Essays on Russian Novelists*
Turner, C. E.: *Modern Novelists of Russia*
Vogüé, E.: *The Russian Novel* (trans. from the French)
Persky, S.: *Contemporary Russian Novelists* (trans. from the French)
Reavey, G.: *Soviet Literature*
Trotsky, L.: *Literature and the Revolution*
Freeman, J.: *Voices of October*
Patrick, G. Z.: *Popular Poetry in Soviet Russia*
Yarmolinsky, A.: *Russian Literature* (brief outline)

Biography

Lavrin, J.: *Gogol*
Maude, C.: *Life of Tolstoy*
Murry, J. M.: *Fedor Dostoevsky*

Myers, J. A.: *Dostoevsky* (in *Fighters of Fate*)
Meier-Graefe, J.: *Dostoevsky, the Man and the Work*
Yarmolinsky, A.: *Dostoevsky*
Dillon, E. J.: *Life of Gorki*

Art and Music

Kouzmin, M. and Voinov, V.: *Russian Graphic Art*
Newmarch, Rosa: *The Russian Arts*
Russian Opera
Walker, Conway: *German and Russian Opera*
Davidson, Gladys: *Stories from the Russian Operas*

Travel, Social Life and Custom

Baring, M.: *The Russian People*
Chamberlain, W. K.: *Russia's Iron Age*
Chesterton, Mrs. Cecil: *My Russian Venture*
Darling, J. N.: *Ding Goes to Russia* (a cartoonist's visit)
Davis, Jerome: *The New Russia* (14 contributors)
Fischer, L.: *Machines and Men in Russia*
Duranty, Walter: *Duranty Reports Russia*
Hindus, M.: *Red Bread*
The Great Offensive
Palmer, F. H. E.: *Russian Life in Town and Country*
Sayler, O. M.: *Inside the Moscow Art Theater*
Viollis, Andrée: *A Girl in Soviet Russia*
Walsh, E. A.: *The Last Stand* (interpretation of five-year plan)

Greek Literature

Greek Literature

THE Greeks, or as they called themselves, the Hellenes, are a branch of the Indo-European family who from very early times have occupied the territory of present-day Greece, the neighboring islands, and a part of the mainland of Asia Minor. Greek literature, in the usually accepted sense, is what was produced by them from the age of the Homeric poems (about tenth century B.C.) down to the time of Lucian in the second century of the Christian era. More particularly we associate this literature with the period from about 475 to 300 B.C. when Athens was the center of universal enlightenment.

Greek literature is not only the oldest in Europe, it is also the most original and spontaneous. It has the highest intrinsic significance and it is extremely important as a determining factor in shaping the course of Roman literature. It has also fixed most of the literary types in modern times. Directly or indirectly, therefore, it is the source and origin of much of our modern culture. It is not surprising that in the minds of many cultivated people Greek literature, Greek art, and the Greek view of life constitute our most precious human heritage.

This literature has suffered severe losses from the ravages of time. It has been estimated, for example, that probably not more than a tenth part of the tragedies of Aeschylus, Sophocles and Euripides has survived. But enough has been preserved to convince us of the unique genius of the Greeks and to give us an adequate idea of the scope and quality of their minds.

The Greeks had no effective political unity until it was forced upon them by the conquests of Alexander the Great. For hundreds of years the various city-states were often at odds with one another. But the Greeks did have a unity of race and of religion and looked upon outsiders as barbarians. They possessed also a common language, even though it differed in dialect forms. Most of the literature was written in the Ionic dialect, which was the one used in Athens. The Doric dialect was spoken in the peninsula of the Peloponnesus.

We shall follow the usual custom of dividing Greek literature into five periods. It will be observed that, as is always the case, poetry precedes prose.

The Iliad and the Odyssey preëminent among world's epics

1. The Age of Epic Poetry (to the sixth century B.C.). The *Iliad* and the *Odyssey*, the greatest of the world's epic poems, were cast into their present form in Ionia, Asia Minor, by the end of the eighth century B.C. They are ascribed to Homer and may indeed have been composed by him, or at least by one man, though there are some indications of composite authorship. They represent the culmination and perfection of a long development of epic poetry, the earlier stages of which are lost. Matthew Arnold described the Homeric poems as rapid in style, plain in thought and diction, and noble in action. The *Iliad* deals with the events leading to the final defeat of the Trojans by the Greeks. The *Odyssey* is a sort of sequel, narrating the adventures of Odysseus (Ulysses) on his return from Troy to his own kingdom, the island of Ithaca. The historical basis of these epics is very likely some struggle that took place between the Greeks and the earlier Phrygian inhabitants of the coast of Asia Minor.

To Homer was also attributed a mock-epic, the *Battle of the Frogs and the Mice,* of which only a small fragment remains. But this ascription is false. Also the so-called Homeric hymns, sung by the bards in praise of the gods, are of a later date. Very little is left of the minor epics, in which the various tribes celebrated their national heroes. The only other writer of the age whose name we know is Hesiod, a poet of minor importance. His *Works and Days,* a didactic poem on husbandry, influenced Virgil's *Georgics.*

Surviving lyric poetry only a fragment of the original

2. The Age of Lyric Poetry (sixth to fifth century B.C.). Lyric poetry is subjective in its nature; it expresses the thoughts or sentiments of the writer; it does not attempt to tell a story. It is a later development than epic poetry, since it presupposes the increased importance of the individual as well as a certain amount of reflective thought and of refined feeling. The Greeks called this sort of poetry *melic* because it was meant to be sung, either by one person or by a chorus. They distinguished various kinds of melic poetry according to the musical instrument which accompanied it or according to the nature of the subject matter. Thus lyric poetry (in their restricted meaning) was poetry accompanied by the lyre; elegiac poetry was mournful in tone, usually on death, but occasionally on love. Only a small amount of this early lyric poetry has survived. Simonides of Keos (556?–468? B.C.) is remembered chiefly for his epitaphs on the Greek heroes who fell in the Persian Wars. Greater than Simonides was Sappho (sixth century B.C.), the only Greek poetess of whom we have any knowledge. The few fragments of her work that have been saved show unusual emotional intensity and great beauty of form. The lyric poet whose work has been most fully preserved is Pindar (522–448? B.C.). His odes celebrate the victors in the Greek national games.

Greek literature and art culminates at Athens

3. *The Attic Period* (475–300 B.C.). The period derives its name from Attica, the state in which Athens is situated. It is the greatest period in Greek literature and art, and represents perhaps the finest flowering of the human spirit that the world has ever seen. Poetry, drama, history, oratory, and philosophy all flourished.

Greek drama marked by four great names

The Greek drama had a religious origin; it sprang from the worship of Dionysus. Tragedy developed first. From a chorus of worshipers a single character first stepped out and spoke. Then other characters were added, the chorus being all the while retained. The subject matter was taken from the epic cycle, which contained stories and personages familiar to all. Of Aeschylus (525–456 B.C.), the first great writer of tragedies, seven plays have been preserved out of the large number that he wrote. The best of these are *Prometheus Bound* and *Agamemnon*. One of his plays, the *Persians,* is unique in that the subject is taken from contemporary history. The general practice in Greek tragedy was to choose themes fairly remote in time and place and so preserve an "ideal distance." Aeschylus is distinguished for his imagination, his profound religious feeling and his lofty style. In comparison with him, his successor Sophocles (496?–406 B.C.) is less austere and more interested in the great human emotions. He fulfills admirably the Greek ideal of the golden mean and is also a consummate artist. The best of his seven plays that have survived are *Oedipus* and *Antigone.* The last of the great tragedy writers, Euripides (480–406 B.C.), was ranked below the other two, but his influence on Roman and French tragedy was even greater than theirs. He was more realistic than his predecessors and at the same time skeptical, sentimental and humanitarian. Nineteen of his plays have come down to us, of which *Alcestis*, the *Trojan Women* and *Medea* are among the most esteemed.

Comedy came a little later and appears also to have had its origin in religious ritual. A distinction is generally made between the Old Comedy, which was satirical, and the New Comedy, which was a mirror of life. Both kinds were in verse. Aristophanes (448?–380? B.C.) was stanchly conservative, satirizing Socrates in the *Clouds* and Euripides in the *Frogs*, his objection to both being that they were radical innovators. His keen wit was paired with a poetic sense of beauty. The New Comedy is represented by Menander (342–291 B.C.), of whom, however, no complete play has survived. He had a decisive influence on the Roman comedy writers, Plautus and Terence.

History, oratory, and philosophy written in distinguished prose

Prose literature had already made its appearance. Herodotus (484?–425 B.C.), sometimes called " the father of history," wrote about the struggle between the Greeks and the Persians. He was a delightful narrator, full of charming anecdotes, who utilized the information and the personal observations gathered on his travels. Xenophon (434?–355? B.C.) described in the *Anabasis* the adventures of a force of Greek mercenaries in the heart of the Persian Empire. He has also left in the *Memorabilia* an interesting account of the personality and teachings of Socrates, of whom he was an admiring disciple. The most philosophic of the Greek historians was Thucydides (471?–400? B.C.), who wrote about the Peloponnesian War between Athens and Sparta.

Oratory also flourished, especially in Athens. Demosthenes (384?–322 B.C.) is probably the greatest of all the world's orators. The political insight he showed and his zeal for Athenian liberty give him the elevated tone of a prophet who transcends merely local and temporary interests.

Philosophic speculation had been cultivated by the Greeks since the time of Thales in the seventh century B.C. The works of the early philosophers, some of them in verse, have been for the most part lost. Fortunately the writings of the two greatest Greek thinkers have been wonderfully well preserved. Both Plato and Aristotle have their rightful place in any account of Greek literature, the former because he was a great artist, the latter by sheer weight of intellect and because he was destined to be a literary influence two thousand years after his death. Plato (427–347 B.C.) was the ablest of the pupils of Socrates (469–399 B.C.). Socrates himself wrote nothing, but he led many to seek wisdom and righteousness. Plato is the greatest master of prose style among the Greeks. His dialogues develop the ideas of Socrates, besides adding many of his own. Aristotle (384–322 B.C.), in turn a pupil of Plato, was the great systematizer. He mapped out the various provinces of human knowledge and applied the scientific method to the investigation of their contents. With no particular literary skill himself, he nevertheless influenced the course of much later literature by his treatise on *Poetics*.

Center of culture shifts to Alexandria

4. The Alexandrian Age (300–146 B.C.). The great age of Athens was now over, never to return. But through the conquests of Alexander the Great, Hellenic culture spread through Egypt and many parts of Asia. New Greek cities sprang up, of which the most famous was Alexandria at the mouth of the Nile. It became a center of learning, but the literature produced there had no great originality, being imitative rather than truly creative. This is often called the Hellenistic period, since the impulse did not proceed directly from the Greeks themselves, but from the foreigners who had adopted their language and absorbed their culture. The outlook was essentially cosmopolitan. The outstanding writer of the period was Theocritus (310?–245? B.C.), who lived in Sicily and Alexandria. He wrote the most famous pastoral idylls of literature, which were of great influence on Virgil's *Eclogues*.

Rome conquers politically, but Greece culturally

5. The Graeco-Roman Age (146 B.C.–527 A.D.). Greece was conquered by Rome in 146 B.C., but the captive imposed his culture on the conqueror. So far as Greek literature is concerned, the spirit of the preceding age is continued. Prose was the prevailing medium. Polybius (205–123 B.C.) wrote about the course of Roman conquest. Plutarch (46?–120 A.D.) composed his *Parallel Lives*, the best-known collection of biographies in the world. The last of the great Greek writers was Lucian (120?–180? A.D.), a Syrian by birth but a master of classic Greek. His satirical dialogues in prose show his complete skepticism regarding the old mythology. His *True History* is a prose romance which has frequently been imitated by writers of extravagant fiction since his time. The lyric poetry collected in what is known as the Greek Anthology was mostly written during this period, though some of it is much earlier and some even later.

For more than a thousand years after the removal of the capital from Rome (330 A.D.), Constantinople (Byzantium) was the metropolis of an empire whose language and culture were Greek. But during this long Byzantine Age, which ended in the capture of Constantinople by the Turks in 1453, almost no literature of any value was produced.

HOMER

Greek literature begins with Homer, about whom we know nothing. He is the reputed author of the *Iliad* and the *Odyssey*, but we are completely ignorant of any facts about his life. Even the century in which he lived is uncertain, the estimates varying within a range of nearly three hundred years. Seven cities have claimed to be his birthplace, with no shred of reliable evidence for any one of them. There exist eight biographical accounts of him, all of them late inventions. There are legends to the effect that he was a blind, wandering bard, who begged his bread from door to door, that he lived to a very old age, and even that he committed suicide. So entirely are we in the dark about him that certain scholars have advanced the theory that he is a purely mythical figure, and that the poems which bear his name are really compilations in which many people have had a hand. The tendency of recent investigation is to discredit this view. Although the Homeric poems undoubtedly had many predecessors, since they are obviously the fulfillment and not the beginning of a poetic movement, there is enough unity and individuality in them to warrant the belief that they are in their present form essentially the work of a single man, whom we are free to call by his traditional name, Homer. He may have lived about the ninth century B.C., possibly in one of the islands of the Aegean or on the eastern mainland. The *Iliad* and the *Odyssey* were not committed to writing until the latter part of the sixth century B.C. Previous to that, they had been recited by rhapsodists or minstrels.

If there is such absolute uncertainty regarding Homer the man, there is no question whatsoever about the status of the Homeric poems. Not only is their meaning clear and the text clean and free from gaps, but the poetic merit is of the very highest. On this last point there has been remarkable unanimity of opinion from the time of the ancient Greeks to the present. For Aristotle, as for all the Greeks, Homer was the peerless poet. Sainte-Beuve, the sanest of modern critics, has said: "The work of Homer is the most admirable product of human poetry." There has been no dissenting voice from these two verdicts of the most authoritative critics of ancient and modern times respectively. To be sure, Homer, like nearly all Greek writers, was forgotten in the early Middle Ages, but since the Renaissance he has resumed his place along with Dante and Shakespeare in the highest group of the world's poets. The characteristics that are most admired in the Homeric poems are simplicity of sentiment and language, swiftness of narrative movement and nobility of outlook on life. Though the characters are simple and their motives uncomplicated, they are vividly realized and their actions are true to the fundamentals of human nature. Homer viewed life as an heroic enterprise to be undertaken with cheerful courage, but he did not blink the hazards of it. The joy of living is matched with the tragic sense of life. The Greek verse admirably expresses this union of apparent opposites: it is light without suffering loss of dignity. Perhaps naturalness and fresh spontaneity are the most striking qualities of the poems. It is unpremeditated art, which is art of the highest order.

The *Iliad* and the *Odyssey* are both connected with the story of the Fall of Troy, the former telling of the final fighting which preceded the capture of the city, and the latter, in a sort of sequel, narrating the adventures of Odysseus (Ulysses) on his return home from Troy. The theme of Troy and its fate has supplied inspiration for writers in all ages and countries. Some of the greatest Greek tragedies are connected, directly or indirectly, with the subject. Virgil's *Aeneid* gives the Roman version of the story. Even in the Middle Ages, when Homer was not read, the tale of Troy still lived on in romances. This non-Homeric material was used by Boccaccio, Chaucer, and Shakespeare — the last two in connection with the episode of Troilus and Cressida. And it must be remembered that in the Renaissance movement which changed the whole trend of European thought back to Greek ideals, the epics of Homer played a leading part.

The historical basis for this cycle of legends appears to have been a war waged about 1200 B.C. between the Greeks and the inhabitants of the northwestern promontory of Asia Minor. The site of Troy (called by the Greeks Ilium) has been excavated in recent times.

The original Greek meter of both the Homeric poems is hexameter, but the English translations are commonly in iambic pentameter, which conforms to the tradition of our literature. Our most famous translations have been made by men who were poets in their own right: John Chapman in the sixteenth century, Alexander Pope in the eighteenth century, and William Cullen Bryant in the nineteenth century. Our own century has added two poetic translations of interest: one by Caulfeild and the other by Bates. Prose translations are also numerous. The best known of the *Iliad* are those by Lang, Leaf, and Myers; of the *Odyssey*, by Butcher and Lang, Palmer, and T. E. Lawrence. In this last the famous English soldier has attempted to instill new vigor into the old story by a striking modernization of the language.

THE ILIAD

The story of the *Iliad* opens in the tenth year of the siege of Troy by the Greeks. The cause of the war has been the abduction of Helen, wife of Menelaus, King of Sparta, by Paris, son of Priam, King of Troy. The

Greeks under the leadership of Agamemnon, brother of Menelaus, have for nine years been vainly endeavoring to regain possession of Helen. This is the situation at the opening of the poem. Its theme is announced in the opening line, " Wrath." It is the wrath of Achilles, the doughtiest of the Greek warriors, against his leader, Agamemnon, for having taken away from him the captive maiden, Briseis. Achilles sulks in his tent, refusing to fight, and as a result the war goes badly for the Greeks. He is, however, induced to allow his friend Patroclus to don his armor and fight in his place. Patroclus is killed by Hector, the son of Priam and the bravest of the Trojans. Achilles, stung at last to action, avenges the death of his friend by killing Hector and dragging his body around the walls of Troy at the wheels of his chariot. The poem ends as Achilles, at the entreaty of Priam, yields up the body of Hector. But the doom of Troy is sealed with the loss of its most formidable champion. The story is diversified by various episodes such as the exploits of Diomedes, one of the Greek warriors, and the funeral games of Patroclus, but the central plot is never obscured by the minor incidents. Though the gods and goddesses frequently intervene in the struggle, the interest is always primarily in the human contestants.

THE DEATH OF HECTOR

Now when the advancing chiefs stood face to face,
The crested hero, Hector, thus began:
" No longer I avoid thee as of late,
O son of Peleus! Thrice around the walls
Of Priam's mighty city have I fled,   5
Nor dared to wait thy coming. Now my heart
Bids me encounter thee; my time is come
To slay or to be slain. Now let us call
The gods to witness, who attest and guard
The covenants of men. Should Jove bestow   10
On me the victory, and I take thy life,
Thou shalt meet no dishonor at my hands;
But, stripping off the armor, I will send
The Greeks thy body. Do the like by me."
    The swift Achilles answered with a frown: 15
" Accursèd Hector, never talk to me
Of covenants. Men and lions plight no faith,
Nor wolves agree with lambs, but each must plan
Evil against the other. So between
Thyself and me no compact can exist,   20

4. **son of Peleus**: Achilles.

Or understood intent. First, one of us
Must fall and yield his life-blood to the god
Of battles. Summon all thy valor now.
A skillful spearman thou hast need to be,
And a bold warrior. There is no escape,　　　　25
For now doth Pallas doom thee to be slain
By my good spear. Thou shalt repay to me
The evil thou hast done my countrymen, —
My friends whom thou hast slaughtered in thy rage."
　　He spake, and, brandishing his massive spear,　　30
Hurled it at Hector, who beheld its aim
From where he stood. He stooped, and over him
The brazen weapon passed, and plunged to earth.
Unseen by royal Hector, Pallas went
And plucked it from the ground, and brought it back　　35
And gave it to the hands of Peleus' son,
While Hector said to his illustrious foe:
　"Godlike Achilles, thou hast missed thy mark;
Nor hast thou learned my doom from Jupiter,
As thou pretendest. Thou art glib of tongue,　　40
And cunningly thou orderest thy speech,
In hope that I who hear thee may forget
My might and valor. Think not I shall flee,
That thou mayest pierce my back: for thou shalt send
Thy spear, if God permit thee, through my breast　　45
As I rush on thee. Now avoid in turn
My brazen weapon. Would that it might pass
Clean through thee, all its length! The tasks of war
For us of Troy were lighter for thy death,
Thou pest and deadly foe of all our race! "　　50
　　He spake, and brandishing his massive spear,
Hurled it, nor missed, but in the center smote
The buckler of Pelides. Far away
It bounded from the brass, and he was vexed
To see that the swift weapon from his hand　　55
Had flown in vain. He stood perplexed and sad;
No second spear had he. He called aloud
On the white-bucklered chief, Deiphobus,
To bring another; but that chief was far,

---

26. **Pallas:** Pallas Athene, goddess of wisdom.　53. **buckler:** small round shield.　53. **Pelides:** son of Peleus.

And Hector saw that it was so and said: —　　　　　60
"Ah me! the gods have summoned me to die.
I thought my warrior-friend, Deiphobus,
Was by my side; but he is still in Troy,
And Pallas has deceived me. Now my death
Cannot be far, — is near; there is no hope　　　　65
Of my escape, for so it pleases Jove
And Jove's great archer-son, who have till now
Delivered me. My hour at last is come;
Yet not ingloriously or passively
I die, but first will do some valiant deed,　　　　70
Of which mankind shall hear in after time."
　　He spake, and drew the keen-edged sword that hung,
Massive and finely tempered, at his side,
And sprang — as when an eagle high in heaven,
Through the thick cloud, darts downward to the plain　75
To clutch some tender lamb or timid hare,
So Hector, brandishing that keen-edged sword,
Sprang forward, while Achilles opposite
Leaped toward him, all on fire with savage hate,
And holding his bright buckler, nobly wrought,　　80
Before him. On his shining helmet waved
The fourfold crest; there tossed the golden tufts
With which the hand of Vulcan lavishly
Had decked it. As in the still hours of night
Hesper goes forth among the host of stars,　　　　85
The fairest light of heaven, so brightly shone,
Brandished in the right hand of Peleus' son,
The spear's keen blade, as, confident to slay
The noble Hector, o'er his glorious form
His quick eye ran, exploring where to plant　　　90
The surest wound. The glittering mail of brass
Won from the slain Patroclus guarded well
Each part, save only where the collar-bones
Divide the shoulder from the neck, and there
Appeared the throat, the spot where life is most　　95
In peril. Through that part the noble son
Of Peleus drave his spear; it went quite through
The tender neck, and yet the brazen blade

---

67. **archer-son:** Phoebus Apollo, god of the sun.　83. **Vulcan:** god of fire.
85. **Hesper:** the evening star.

Cleft not the windpipe, and the power to speak
Remained. The Trojan fell amid the dust,   100
And thus Achilles boasted o'er his fall:
  " Hector, when from the slain Patroclus thou
Didst strip his armor, little didst thou think
Of danger. Thou hadst then no fear of me,
Who was not near thee to avenge his death.   105
Fool! there was left within the roomy ships
A mightier one than he, who should come forth,
The avenger of his blood, to take thy life.
Foul dogs and birds of prey shall tear thy flesh;
The Greeks shall honor him with funeral rites."   110
  And then the crested Hector faintly said:
" I pray thee by thy life, and by thy knees,
And by thy parents, suffer not the dogs
To tear me at the galleys of the Greeks.
Accept abundant store of brass and gold,   115
Which gladly will my father and the queen,
My mother, give in ransom. Send to them
My body, that the warriors and the dames
Of Troy may light for me the funeral pile."
  The swift Achilles answered with a frown: 120
" Nay, by my knees entreat me not, thou cur,
Nor by my parents. I could even wish
My fury prompted me to cut thy flesh
In fragments, and devour it, such the wrong
That I have had from thee. There will be none   125
To drive away the dogs about thy head,
Not though thy Trojan friends should bring to me
Tenfold and twentyfold the offered gifts,
And promise others, — not though Priam, sprung
From Dardanus, should send thy weight in gold.   130
Thy mother shall not lay thee on thy bier,
To sorrow over thee whom she brought forth;
But dogs and birds of prey shall mangle thee."
  And then the crested Hector, dying, said:
" I know thee and too clearly I foresaw   135
I should not move thee, for thou hast a heart
Of iron. Yet reflect that for my sake
The anger of the gods may fall on thee,

130. **Dardanus:** mythical ancestor of the Trojans.

When Paris and Apollo strike thee down,
Strong as thou art, before the Scaean gates."   140
   Thus Hector spake, and straightway o'er him closed
The night of death; the soul forsook his limbs,
And flew to Hades, grieving for its fate,
So soon divorced from youth and youthful might.
Then said the great Achilles to the dead: 145
   " Die thou; and I, whenever it shall please
Jove and the other gods, will meet my fate."
   He spake, and, plucking forth his brazen lance,
He laid it by, and from the body stripped
The bloody mail. The thronging Greeks beheld   150
With wonder Hector's tall and stately form,
And no one came who did not add a wound;
And, looking to each other, thus they said:
   " How much more tamely Hector now endures
Our touch than when he set the fleet on fire! "   155
   Such were the words of those who smote the dead.
But now, when swift Achilles from the corpse
Had stripped the armor, he stood forth among
The Achaian host, and spake these wingèd words:
   " Leaders and princes of the Grecian host!   160
Since we, my friends, by favor of the gods,
Have overcome the chief who wrought more harm
To us than all the rest, let us assault
The town, and learn what they of Troy intend; —
Whether their troops will leave the citadel   165
Since he is slain, or hold it with strong hand,
Though Hector is no more. But why give thought
To plans like these while yet Patroclus lies
A corpse unwept, unburied, at the fleet?
I never will forget him while I live   170
And while these limbs have motion. Though below
In Hades they forget the dead, yet I
Will there remember my belovèd friend.
Now then, ye youths of Greece, move on and chant
A paean, while returning to the fleet,   175
We bring great glory with us; we have slain
The noble Hector, whom, throughout their town,

---

140. **Scaean:** the gate of Troy nearest the shore.   159. **Achaian:** from
Achaia or Achaea in Greece.   175. **paean:** song of triumph.

The Trojans ever worshiped like a god."
He spake, and, planning in his mind to treat
The noble Hector shamefully, he bored   180
The sinews of his feet between the heel
And ankle; drawing through them leathern thongs
He bound them to the car, but left the head
To trail in dust. And then he climbed the car,
Took in the shining mail, and lashed to speed   185
The coursers. Not unwillingly they flew.
Around the dead, as he was dragged along,
The dust arose; his dark locks swept the ground.
That head, of late so noble in men's eyes,
Lay deep amid the dust, for Jove that day   190
Suffered the foes of Hector to insult
His corse in his own land.
                 His mother saw,
And tore her hair, and flung her lustrous veil
Away, and uttered piercing shrieks. No less
His father, who so loved him, piteously   195
Bewailed him; and in all the streets of Troy
The people wept aloud, with such lament
As if the towery Ilium were in flames
Even to its loftiest roofs. They scarce could keep
The aged king within, who, wild with grief,   200
Struggled to rush through the Dardanian gates,
And, rolling in the dust, entreated all
Who stood around him, calling them by name:
  " Refrain, my friends, though kind be your intent.
Let me go forth alone, and at the fleet   205
Of Greece will I entreat this man of blood
And violence. He may perchance be moved
With reverence for my age, and pity me
In my gray hairs; for such a one as I
Is Peleus, his own father, by whose care   210
This Greek was reared to be a scourge to Troy,
And, more than all, a cause of grief to me,
So many sons of mine in life's fresh prime
Have fallen by his hand. I mourn for them,
But not with such keen anguish as I mourn   215
For Hector. Sorrow for his death will bring

192. **corse:** corpse.

My soul to Hades. Would that he had died
Here in my arms! this solace had been ours, —
His most unhappy mother and myself
Had stooped to shed these tears upon his bier."   220
  He spake, and wept, and all the citizens
Wept with him. Hecuba among the dames
Took up the lamentation, and began: —
  " Why do I live, my son, when thou art dead,
And I so wretched? — thou who wert my boast   225
Ever, by night and day, where'er I went,
And whom the Trojan men and matrons called
Their bulwark, honoring thee as if thou wert
A god. They glory in thy might no more,
Since fate and death have overtaken thee."   230
Weeping she spake.
                     Meantime Andromache
Had heard no tidings of her husband yet.
No messenger had even come to say
That he was still without the gates. She sat
In a recess of those magnificent halls,   235
And wove a twofold web of brilliant hues,
On which were scattered flowers of rare device;
And she had given her bright-haired maidens charge
To place an ample caldron on the fire,
That Hector, coming from the battlefield,   240
Might find the warm bath ready. Thoughtless one!
She knew not that the blue-eyed archer-queen,
Far from the bath prepared for him, had slain
Her husband by the hand of Peleus' son.
She heard the shrieks, the wail upon the tower,   245
Trembled in every limb, and quickly dropped
The shuttle, saying to her bright-haired maids:
  " Come with me, two of you, that I may learn
What now has happened. 'Tis my mother's voice
That I have heard. My heart leaps to my mouth;   250
My limbs fail under me. Some deadly harm
Hangs over Priam's sons; far be the hour
When I shall hear of it. And yet I fear
Lest that Achilles, having got between

---

222. **Hecuba:** wife of Priam and mother of Hector.   231. **Andromache:**
wife of Hector.   242. **archer-queen:** Artemis or Diana, goddess of the chase.

The daring Hector and the city gates,   255
May drive him to the plain alone, and quell
The desperate valor that was ever his;
For never would he keep the ranks, but ranged
Beyond them, and gave way to no man's might."
    She spake, and from the royal mansion rushed   260
Distractedly, and with a beating heart.
Her maids went with her. When she reached the tower
And throng of men, and, standing on the wall,
Looked forth, she saw her husband dragged away
Before the city. Toward the Grecian fleet   265
The swift steeds drew him. Sudden darkness came
Over her eyes, and in a breathless swoon
She sank away and fell. The ornaments
Dropped from her brow, — the wreath, the woven band,
The net, the veil which golden Venus gave   270
That day when crested Hector wedded her,
Dowered with large gifts, and led her from her home,
Eëtion's palace. Round her in a throng
Her sisters of the house of Priam pressed,
And gently raised her in that deathlike swoon.   275
But when she breathed again, and to its seat
The conscious mind returned, as in their arms
She lay, with sobs and broken speech she said:
    " Hector, — O wretched me! — we both were born
To sorrow; thou at Troy, in Priam's house,   280
And I at Thebè in Eëtion's halls,
By woody Placos. From a little child
He reared me there — unhappy he, and I
Unhappy! O that I had ne'er been born!
Thou goest down to Hades and the depths   285
Of earth, and leavest me in thine abode,
Widowed, and never to be comforted.
Thy son, a speechless babe, to whom we two
Gave being, — hapless parents! cannot have
Thy loving guardianship now thou art dead,   290
Nor be a joy to thee. Though he survive
The cruel warfare which the sons of Greece
Are waging, hard and evil yet will be

273. **Eëtion:** father of Andromache.   281. **Thebè:** town in Asia Minor.
282. **Placos:** mountain near Thebè.

His lot hereafter; others will remove
His landmarks and will make his fields their own.   295
The day in which a boy is fatherless
Makes him companionless; with downcast eyes
He wanders, and his cheeks are stained with tears.
Unfed he goes where sit his father's friends,
And plucks one by the cloak, and by the robe   300
Another. One who pities him shall give
A scanty draught, which only wets his lips,
But not his palate; while another boy,
Whose parents both are living, thrusts him thence
With blows and vulgar clamor: ' Get thee gone!   305
Thy father is not with us at the feast.'
Then to his widowed mother shall return
Astyanax in tears, who not long since
Was fed, while sitting in his father's lap,
On marrow and the delicate fat of lambs.   310
And ever when his childish sports had tired
The boy, and sleep came stealing over him,
He slumbered, softly cushioned, on a couch
And in his nurse's arms, his heart at ease
And satiate with delights. But now thy son   315
Astyanax, — whom so the Trojans name
Because thy valor guarded gate and tower, —
Thy care withdrawn, shall suffer many things.
While far from those who gave thee birth, beside
The roomy ships of Greece, the restless worms   320
Shall make thy flesh their banquet when the dogs
Have gorged themselves. Thy garments yet remain
Within the palace, delicately wrought
And graceful, woven by the women's hands;
And these, since thou shalt put them on no more,   325
Nor wear them in thy death, I burn with fire
Before the Trojan men and dames; and all
Shall see how gloriously thou wert arrayed."
  Weeping she spake, and with her wept her maids.

                                              (*W. C. Bryant*)

316. **Astyanax:** son of Hector and Andromache

SUGGESTIONS FOR STUDY

1. What qualities are displayed by Achilles and Hector both in words and action? Can you detect any difference in their personalities? Do they show magnanimity and chivalry? What episode throws most light on this question?

2. Though Homer's sympathies would be expected to lie with the Greeks, the modern reader is more likely to sympathize with the Trojans. Why is this the case? What is your own feeling in the matter?

3. In what lines is the sense of fate expressed? How great a part do the gods and goddesses play in the action? Find out from a Greek mythology why the various deities favored the side they did.

4. The German critic Lessing said that Homer, as a true poet, was primarily concerned with narration and that he instinctively substituted action for description. Does that apply to the passage you have read? Cite instances to prove your point.

5. Point out some of the characteristics of the Homeric style in the use of adjectives and comparisons. How does the metrical effect of this epic differ from that of the *Song of the Nibelungs* (page 422)? Of *Beowulf?*

6. Read the passage in Book 11 of the *Odyssey* where Odysseus converses with the ghost of the dead Achilles. How does Achilles feel about death? If you have never read the *Iliad* before, you should read the rest of the famous story in one of the major translations; or, if pressed for time, at least in summary. See Guerber's *Book of the Epic.*

THE ODYSSEY

Matthew Arnold called the *Iliad* the most important poetical monument in existence. Most modern readers prefer the *Odyssey*, which James Russell Lowell characterized as " The only long poem which is never dull." The *Iliad* deals mainly with fighting, the *Odyssey* with wanderings and romantic adventures. The hero of the *Odyssey* is Ulysses (in Greek, Odysseus), the most prudent and crafty of the Greek chieftains. Driven out of his course after he leaves Troy, he undergoes for ten years all kinds of perils and temptations before he is able to return to his own kingdom, the island of Ithaca. He visits the land of the Lotus Eaters, the island of the one-eyed Cyclops, and the home of Circe, the sorceress; he descends into the lower world and speaks with the shade of Achilles; he resists the lure of the sirens; he navigates successfully the strait between Scylla and Charybdis; he loses all his followers at sea and is himself shipwrecked on the island of the enchantress Calypso, who detains him for nine years. Once more launched on his way, he again founders and drifts to the island of the Phaeacians. Here, in one of the most charming episodes in the poem, the king's daughter Nausicaa takes pity on him and leads him to her father, who, after hearing his story, enables him to return home at last to Ithaca. At home, he finds his wife Penelopé beset by the chieftains of the island who are suitors for her hand. Disguised as a beggar, he gains admittance to the palace and with the aid of his son Telemachus slays all the suitors and is reunited to the faithful Penelopé. Ulysses enlists our admiration for his boldness and resourcefulness. Many of his experiences are told in the first person as he narrates his adventures to others. For all its romantic atmosphere, the *Odyssey* has many realistic touches, and it is precisely this union of the strange and the familiar which constitutes one of the chief delights of the poem.

PENELOPÉ RECOGNIZES ODYSSEUS

But the old dame, meanwhile, had gone to the room of her mistress,
Laughing aloud with joy, to tell of her husband's arrival:
Strode she along so fast that her feet did seem in a twinkle:
And, by the head of her mistress, she stood, and thus she addressed
    her:
" Wake, Penelopé, wake, dear child, and see with your own eyes   5
What you have longed to see, and prayed for days without number.
He has come back to his home at last, the godlike Odysseus,
And he has killed those men, the haughty suitors, who long time
Rudely coerced his son, and robbed his house and possessions."
    And, unto her in reply, the prudent Penelopé answered: 10
" Nurse dear, the Gods must have made you mad, for indeed they
    will sometimes
Utterly rob of his mind a person of good understanding,
As they have now, it appears, set Folly astride of your senses,
Though, hitherto, there was no one more sober of judgment than you
    were.
Why do you mock me thus, who have so much to distress me,   15
Saying such random words? for you woke me up from a slumber
Sweeter than ever closed my tired eyes in oblivion:
For I had never enjoyed a sleep like that, since Odysseus
Sailed to the siege of Troy, that name too hateful to mention.
But you had better go down, and back to the hall that you came   20
    from,
For had it been some other of these my women attendants
Brought me a tale like this, and waked me up from my slumber,
I should have sent her off very soon with something to cry for
Into the servants' room: but, for once, your age shall excuse you."
    And, unto her in reply, thus spoke the nurse Eurycleia: 25

" I am not speaking in jest, dear child, but really and truly
He has come back to his home, and is now in the house as I tell you.
He was the stranger whom all those men in the hall were insulting.
Yes, and a long time ago, Telemachus knew of his coming,
But he had kept concealed the designs of his father from prudence 30
That he might fitly requite the deeds of these insolent suitors."
    So did she speak: but, in joy, Penelopé sprang to her feet, and
Threw both arms round the neck of the dame, while a tear from
        her eyelid
Stole down her cheek, and words from her lips flowed fast and un-
        bidden:
    " Tell me the truth, dear nurse; whatever it be I can bear it. 35
If he has really come back, and is now in his home, as you tell me,
How did he lay strong hands on the shameless and insolent suitors,
All by himself, while the others remained indoors in a body? "
    And, unto her in reply, thus spoke dear nurse Eurycleia:
" Nothing at all have I seen or been told; but only a groaning 40
Reached us, of men being slain; but we all sat huddled together,
Quaking with fear, shut in by the doors of the women's apartments
Which were kept tightly closed, till at last Telemachus entered,
Sent from the hall by his father to summon us into his presence.
Then did I find Odysseus, erect in the midst of the corpses, 45
Standing alone: and the corpses were strewn on the pavement around
        him,
Heaps upon heaps; 'twould have warmed the heart in your breast to
        have seen it.
Now have the bodies been piled, in a row, at the gates of the court-
        yard,
While that with fumes of sulphur, Odysseus is cleansing the palace,
Kindling a red-hot fire; and he sent me forward to call you. 50
But come, follow me now, that your dear hearts newly united
May be refreshed and glad; for many a trial have you suffered.
For, now at last, your prayer, so long delayed, is accomplished.
He has come back to his hearth, and has found, alive and in safety,
Both yourself and his son; and, to all those insolent suitors 55
Who were destroying his house, he has dealt well-merited vengeance."
    And, unto her in reply, the prudent Penelopé answered:
    " It is too soon, dear nurse, for exaltation and laughter;
But you must know how welcome, to all, would be his appearance
Here in his halls, but chiefly, to me and the son whom I bore him. 60
Nevertheless 'tis not really true, this story you tell me,

But some immortal God has killed those men overbearing,
Angered against their pride and deeds of criminal outrage.
Seeing they paid respect to never a man or a woman,
Neither to good nor bad, who by ill luck happened to meet them; 65
So, in their insolent folly, they died. But Odysseus has perished,
Far from his native land, and will never return to Achaia."

And, in reply, thus spoke the dear old nurse Eurycleia:
"What is the thoughtless word, my child, from your lips has
    escapèd,
That he will come no more, though even now he is standing 70
Safely beside his hearth? Your mind was incredulous always.
Come, I will give you a proof which even yourself will acknowledge:
Do you remember the scar where the tusk of the wild boar gashed
    him?
When I was washing his feet, I noticed this, and I wanted
Sorely to tell you; but this he perceived in an instant, and firmly 75
Closed my mouth with his hand, that not one word could I utter.
But, if you follow me now, I will pledge myself as a surety,
And, if I play you false, then put me to death without mercy."

And, unto her in reply, the prudent Penelopé answered:
"Nurse dear, though clever you be and wise, you cannot unravel 80
All these wiles of the Gods who never have known a beginning.
Nevertheless we will go to find my son and to gaze on
These proud men who are slain, and see the man who has killed them."

So she went down the stairs, and much in her mind did she ponder
Whether to stay at a distance, and ply her husband with questions, 85
Or to take hold of his hands, and cover his head with kisses.
But, when she entered the hall, and had crossed the stone-paved
    threshold,
Then she sat down by herself, in the firelight, facing Odysseus,
Close to the opposite wall; but her lord was sitting in silence
Hard by a pillar, with downcast eyes, and wondering whether 90
Ever a word would come from his wife when at last she had seen him.
Long did she sit without speaking, by contrary impulse bewildered.
Sometimes she met his eye, and then, with sudden revulsion,
Could not believe that this ill-clothed man was really her husband.
Then did Telemachus speak in reproof, and thus he addressed her: 95
"Mother! strange mother indeed, with spirit so stern and unfeeling;
Why do you stay like this, so far from my father, and do not
Sit by his side and ask him of all his trials and adventures?

67. **Achaia:** or Achaea, a district on the northern coast of the Peloponnesus.

No other woman than you, with such unnatural coldness,
Would keep away from her husband, who, worn with hardships 100
 uncounted,
Now, in the twentieth year, had come to the land of his fathers.
But it was always so: your heart is more hard than a millstone."
 And, unto him in reply, the prudent Penelopé answered:
" Patience, my son, for the heart in my breast is bewildered and
 doubtful,
Nor can I make up my mind to address him or ask him a question, 105
Neither to look in his face: but if he is really Odysseus
Safely returned, why then we shall soon understand one another:
For we have signs, we two, which none but ourselves may discover."
 So did she speak; but he smiled, the divine much-enduring Odys-
 seus;
And, to Telemachus, gave he a hint, though playfully spoken: 110
" Leave your mother, my son, to ask me what questions she pleases:
For she will quickly be able to see the truth of the matter.
But, as I now am dirty and clothed in villainous garments,
Therefore she does not respect me nor own me as really her husband.
But let us think how best we may meet the dangers that face us. 115
For, if a man, by chance, should kill one citizen neighbor,
One whose companions are few, that might possibly help or avenge
 him,
Yet must he leave his kinsmen, and flee from his country for safety;
But we have killed those men on whom the city depended,
Lords in the Ithacan isle; and this gives cause for reflection."   120
 And, unto him in reply, the prudent Telemachus answered:
" Think this out for yourself, dear father, for you have the wisest
Judgment in all the world, for so they tell me: nor is there
One, among mortal men, who in this respect is your rival."
 And, unto him in reply, thus spoke the resourceful Odysseus: 125
" That being so, I will tell you the course that I think we must follow.
First, do you all have a bath, and clothe yourselves neatly in tunics:
Then bid the maids in the house put on their holiday dresses:
And let the heaven-sent bard, as he fingers his clear-toned lyre,
Play us a merry tune, to guide our steps in the dancing.   130
So that the neighbors may say, or any who chance to be passing,
' There is a wedding on hand in our lady Penelopé's palace.'
Thus the report of the slaughter will not spread over the city
Ere we have time to retreat to our sheltered farm in the forest.
Then we shall see what plan great Zeus will put in our power."   135

So did he speak; and they took good heed and did as he bade them.
First did they bathe themselves, and clothe themselves neatly in
    tunics;
Also the women put on their smartest frocks; and the minstrel,
Bringing his clear-toned lyre, did rouse their passionate longing
Both for delightful song, and the measured movements of danc-   140
    ing.
And, from the floor to the roof, as the dance was in progress, the big
    house
Rang with the merry tramp of men and of beautiful women.
You may be sure some man outside thus spoke when he heard it:
  " One of those men in there must have married the queen they are
    courting:
She is of no account, for she had not the spirit or courage   145
Even to guard that great big house till her husband should come
    back."
  Thus would some passer speak; but, what really had happened,
    they knew not.
Meanwhile, the housekeeper dame had washed great-hearted Odys-
    seus,
Clothed him in tunic, and thrown a beautiful cloak o'er his shoulders;
But 'twas Athené who poured, on his head, such power and 150
    beauty,
Making him taller and stouter to see, and, down on his shoulders,
Clustering locks to fall as it might be some hyacinth blossom.
And, as a skillful man, whom Hephaestus and Pallas Athené
Various arts have taught, may overlay gold upon silver,
And by his cunning skill, bring beautiful works to perfection, 155
So, o'er his head and shoulders, was dignity poured by Athené:
And, as he came from the bath, he was like an Immortal in presence.
Then he sat down once more on the seat from which he had risen,
Facing his wife, and thus, in courteous words, he addressed her:
  " Madam, it seems that the Gods, the dwellers in blessèd 160
    Olympus,
Made you more hard of heart than the race of womanly women.
Where could you find a wife who thus would, cold and constrained,
Hold aloof from her husband, who after incredible hardships,
Had, in the twentieth year, come back to the land of his fathers.
But I depend on you, good nurse, to make me a nice bed 165

---

150. **Athené:** Pallas Athena, called by the Romans Minerva, goddess of
wisdom. 153. **Hephaestus:** god of fire, same as the Roman Vulcan.

Where I may sleep; for I think your mistress's heart is of iron."

And, unto him in reply, the prudent Penelopé answered:

" I am not haughty, my lord, nor too obsequious either,

Nor do I wish to slight you, for well indeed I remember

What you were like when your long-oared ship sailcd out of the 170 harbor.

But come, nurse Eurycleia, make ready the massive old bedstead

Outside the door of the room which his own hands builded so strongly:

Carry the bedstead outside, and spread soft bedding upon it,

Wrappers and fleeces of sheep, and glistening rugs for his comfort."

So did she speak to test what her lord might know; but 175 Odysseus,

Answered in anger and spoke to his wife too cautiously minded:

" Lady, it grieves me much to hear the word you have spoken.

Who, I must ask you, has moved that bed?   'Twere a difficult matter

E'en for a skillful man; though of course an Immortal from heaven

Could put it where he liked, and with ease, if so he desired.   180

But not a mortal man could move that bed with a crowbar,

Though in the prime of life: because there's a wondrous contrivance

Hid in that well-wrought bed, which myself and no other invented.

Once, in the courtyard, there grew a leafy and wide-spreading olive,

Flourishing and full-grown, and like to a pillar in thickness.   185

Round it, I built a wall with great stones fitted together,

Making a chamber, and then, on top, I roofed it securely.

And I made folding doors of solid construction to guard it.

Then I cut off the boughs of the leafy and wide-spreading olive;

Then I cut off the trunk, and smoothed the stump with the 190 hatchet,

As a good craftsman should, and shaped it true with the T-square

So as to form a post, and bored in it holes with an auger;

And, from the trunk, I hewed a bedstead and wrought as a finish

Inlaid patterns of gold, and ivory varied with silver;

And, for a mattress, I laced it across with strippets of leather.   195

And I am telling you this as a token. But, lady, I know not

Whether the bed is still where I fixed it, or whether already

Some one has moved it away, after cutting the pedestal olive."

So did he speak: but her knees gave way, and her heart was a-flutter,

As she recalled the tokens which could by no chance be mistaken.   200

And, as she burst into tears, she ran to her husband, Odysseus,

191. **T-square:** instrument shaped like a T for obtaining right angles.

Throwing her arms round his neck, and she kissed his head and she
    sobbed out:
" Won't you forgive me Odysseus, for you know, better than all
    men,
What I have suffered, and how the Gods have begrudged us the bless-
    ing
That, till we reached old age, we should joyfully live with each   205
    other.
But be not angry now, or indignant because that I did not,
When I beheld you first, at once thus fondle and love you:
Seeing the heart in my breast would always shrink with a shudder,
Lest 'twere some other man, who had come with wily professions
Trying to lead me astray; for evil schemers are many.   210
Never had Argive Helen, that daughter of Zeus of the aegis,
Yielded herself to love, and the bed of the prince of the Trojans,
If she had known from the first that the warlike sons of Achaia
Would, by the force of arms, conduct her back to her homeland.
But 'twas a Power divine that inspired that action unseemly,   215
Else would she never have harbored a thought so mad and so deadly,
One that has proved unto us the source of all our troubles.
But now, since you have told me of tokens surely convincing
As to our marriage bed, which not a mortal can know of
But you and I alone, and one of our women attendants,   220
Actoris, who was in charge of the close-fitting doors of our chamber:
(She, when I left my home, was a present to me from my father)
Though I be stubborn indeed, my heart can no longer resist you."
    Thus did she speak, and roused still more his passion for groaning:
And, as he clasped in his arms his wife so wise and so lovely,   225
Fast flowed his tears. And as land is delightful and welcome to
    look on
Unto the struggling swimmers whose ship has been smashed by
    Poseidon,
Driven before the blast and swept by the great green billows:
And but a few have escaped to the shore from the rage of the waters,
Swimming for life, and their limbs with the salt sea brine are   230
    encrusted,
And, from the jaws of death, they climb to the land with rejoicing,
So 'twas a gladsome sight when Penelopé looked on her husband.

                                    (F. Caulfeild)

    211. **Argive:** from Argos, a city in the eastern Peloponnesus.   211. **aegis:**
shield.   227. **Poseidon:** god of the sea, same as the Roman Neptune.

SUGGESTIONS FOR STUDY

1. Why does Penelopé refuse to believe the nurse and Telemachus? How is she finally persuaded of the identity of Odysseus? How is her character brought out in this selection? Why do you think she has become one of the most famous women characters in literature?

2. What meter is employed in this translation? What famous American poem is in the same measure? What difference in general effect is there between this meter and the iambic pentameter? How would the meter here used suit a description of a fight, as in the *Iliad* selection? Find out if possible which meter is nearer the Greek original.

3. Point out striking epithets (adjectives), especially those applied to Odysseus and Penelopé. What do you observe in regard to compound words and reiterated epithets?

4. The whole of the *Odyssey* is recommended for reading. Among the most enjoyable parts are Book 6, on the meeting of Odysseus with Nausicaa, Book 9, on the adventure with Polyphemus the Cyclops, and Book 22, on the slaying of the suitors.

5. Two famous English sonnets should be read: Keats' "On First Looking into Chapman's Homer" and Andrew Lang's "The Odyssey."

6. A later tradition pictures Odysseus as dissatisfied with the uneventful life in Ithaca and seeking adventure anew. Is this in keeping with his character as delineated in the *Odyssey?* Tennyson's "Ulysses" is based on this legend, and his "The Lotus Eaters" on an adventure in the *Odyssey.* Can you name any other modern literature suggested by the *Odyssey?*

7. Vocabulary: coerced, oblivion, requite, surety, obsequious.

AESOP

Aesop is an even more shadowy figure than Homer. He is said to have been a deformed Greek slave of the sixth century B.C., who won his liberty by his skill in telling fables; but it is a matter of grave doubt whether he ever existed. In any case, the fables that pass under his name are of Oriental origin. For the history and significance of the fable see page 81.

THE COUNTRY MOUSE AND THE TOWN MOUSE

Once upon a time a Country Mouse who had a friend in town invited him, for old acquaintance sake, to pay him a visit in the country. The invitation being accepted in due form, the Country Mouse, though plain and rough and somewhat frugal in his nature, opened his heart and store, in honor of hospitality and an old friend. There was not a carefully stored up morsel that he did not bring forth out of his larder, peas and barley, cheese-parings and nuts, hoping by quantity to make up what he feared was wanting in quality, to suit the palate of his dainty guest. The Town Mouse, condescending to pick a bit here and a bit there, while the host sat nibbling a blade of barley-straw, at length exclaimed, " How is it, my good friend, that you can endure the dullness of this unpolished life? You are living like a toad in a hole. You can't really prefer these solitary rocks and woods to streets teeming with carriages and men. On my honor, you are wasting your time miserably here. We must make the most of life while it lasts. A mouse, you know, does not live forever. So come with me and I'll show you life and the town." Overpowered with such fine words and so polished a manner, the Country Mouse assented; and they set out together on their journey to town. It was late in the evening when they crept stealthily into the city, and midnight ere they reached the great house, where the Town Mouse took up his quarters. Here were couches of crimson velvet, carvings in ivory, everything, in short, that denoted wealth and luxury. On the table were the remains of a splendid banquet, to procure which all the choicest shops in town had been ransacked the day before. It was now the turn of the courtier to play the host; he places his country friend on purple, runs to and fro to supply all his wants, presses dish upon dish and dainty upon dainty, and, as though he were waiting on a king, tastes every course ere he ventures to place it before his rustic cousin. The Country Mouse, for his part, affects to make himself quite at home, and blesses the good fortune that had wrought such a change in his way of life; when, in the midst of his enjoyment, as he is thinking with contempt of the poor fare he has forsaken, on a sudden the door flies open, and a party of revelers, returning from a late entertainment, bursts into the room. The affrighted friends jump from the table in the greatest consternation and hide themselves in the first corner they can reach. No sooner do they venture to creep out again than the barking of dogs drives them back in still greater terror than before. At length, when things seemed quiet, the Country Mouse stole out from his hiding place, and, bidding his friend good-bye, whispered in his ear, " Oh, my good sir, this fine mode of living may do for those who like it; but give me my barley-bread in peace and security before the daintiest feast where Fear and Care are in waiting."

(John Smith)

SUGGESTIONS FOR STUDY

1. This fable is the first of a long line of literary pieces contrasting country and city manners. The theme lends itself especially well to humorous treatment. Sir Roger de Coverley is a good example in English literature. A variation is the countryman who tries unsuccessfully to ape city manners, as Bob Acres in Sheridan's *The Rivals*. Can you name other examples?

2. This story has been retold with various adaptations by modern fable writers. See La Fontaine's fable, and also George Ade's Fable in Slang called "The Wonderful Meal of Vittles" (in *Adventures in American Literature*).

3. Write a modern fable based on the idea of contrasting manners, either of city and country, or of different nations, as suggested by your study of their literature.

SAPPHO (Early Sixth Century B.C.)

Sappho is regarded as the greatest woman poet of antiquity, if not of all time. She was a native of the island of Lesbos, where she was the leader of a group of women devoted to music and poetry. In other respects, we know nothing of her life. The many later stories which were current about her are without historical warrant. Only a few complete poems and some scattered fragments have survived. Her chief theme was love. Emotional intensity and technical perfection are the distinguishing marks of her work. Plato wrote of her the epigram:

> " Some thoughtlessly proclaim the Muses nine;
> A tenth is Lesbian Sappho, maid divine."

HYMN TO VENUS

Immortal Venus, throned above
In radiant beauty, child of Jove,
O skilled in every art of love
    And artful snare;
Dread power, to whom I bend the knee,   5
Release my soul and set it free
From bonds of piercing agony
    And gloomy care.
Yet come thyself, if e'er, benign,
Thy listening ears thou didst incline   10

To my rude lay, the starry shine
    Of Jove's court leaving,
In chariot yoked with coursers fair,
Thine own immortal birds that bear
Thee swift to earth, the middle air   15
    With bright wings cleaving.
Soon they were sped — and thou, most blest,
In thine own smiles ambrosial dressed,
Didst ask what griefs my mind oppressed —
    What meant my song —   20
What end my frenzied thoughts pursue —
For what loved youth I spread anew
My amorous nets — " Who, Sappho, who
    Hath done thee wrong?
What though he fly, he'll soon return —   25
Still press thy gifts, though now he spurn;
Heed not his coldness — soon he'll burn,
    E'en though thou chide."
— And saidst thou thus, dread goddess? O,
Come then once more to ease my woe;   30
Grant all, and thy great self bestow,
    My shield and guide!

                (*J. H. Merivale*)

14. birds: the doves of Venus.   **18. ambrosial:** divine.

THE MOON AMID THE LESSER LIGHTS

The stars around the lovely moon
Fade back and vanish very soon,
When, round and full, her silver face
Swims into sight, and lights all space.

                (*Edwin Arnold*)

TO AN UNCULTURED LESBIAN WOMAN

Yea, thou shalt die,
    And lie
        Dumb in the silent tomb;
Nor of thy name
Shall there be any fame   5

In ages yet to be or years to come:
For of the flowering Rose
Which on Pieria blows,
Thou hast no share:
But in sad Hades' house, **10**
Unknown, inglorious
'Mid the dim shades that wander there
Shalt thou flit forth and haunt the filmy air.

(John Addington Symonds)

8. **Pieria:** an abode of the Muses on Mount Olympus.

A GIRL IN LOVE

" Oh, my sweet mother, 'tis in vain,
I cannot weave as once I wove,
So 'wildered is my heart and brain
With thinking of that youth I love."

(Thomas Moore)

ONE GIRL

1

Like the sweet apple which reddens upon the topmost bough,
A-top on the topmost twig, — which the pluckers forgot, somehow, —
Forgot it not, nay! but got it not, for none could get it till now.

2

Like the wild hyacinth flower which on the hills is found,
Which the passing feet of the shepherds forever tear and wound,
Until the purple blossom is trodden in the ground.

(Dante Gabriel Rossetti)

TO EVENING

O Hesperus! Thou bringest all things home;
All that the garish day hath scattered wide;
The sheep, the goat, back to the welcome fold;
Thou bring'st the child, too, to his mother's side.

(William Hyde Appleton)

1. **Hesperus:** evening star.   2. **garish:** dazzling.

SUGGESTIONS FOR STUDY

1. Express in your own words the content of the "Hymn to Venus."
2. What is the prevalent emotion in each separate lyric? Where is Sappho speaking for herself and where for another person?
3. What was the Greek conception of the life after death? How does this affect the poem "To an Uncultured Lesbian Woman"?
4. What is the significance of the lines entitled "One Girl"?
5. Who are the most famous women poets of England and America? Compare these fragments of Sappho with what you know of the writings of any of them. Have you found women poets in any of the other sections of this book? If so, where? Would you offer the name of any other woman as a rival to Sappho for the title of "greatest woman poet of all time"? If so, justify your choice.

ANACREON (563?–478? B.C.)

Little is known about the life of Anacreon except that he was born in an Ionian city on the coast of Asia Minor, sought the favor and protection of many patrons during his years of wandering, and lived to a ripe old age. Only a few fragments of his authentic verse have been preserved. His name has become almost a symbol of the glorification of wine and love. Many graceful little poems were later circulated under his name, and some of them are fair copies of Anacreon's style. It is probable that the example here given is a later imitation rather than an original. The term "anacreontic" is still given to a short light lyric that praises wine, woman, and song.

DRINKING

I care not for the idle state
Of Persia's king, the rich, the great!
I envy not the monarch's throne,
Nor wish the treasured gold my own.
But oh! be mine the rosy braid,   5
The fervor of my brows to shade;
Be mine the odors, richly sighing,
Amid my hoary tresses flying.
Today I'll haste to quaff my wine,
As if tomorrow ne'er should shine;   10
But if tomorrow comes, why then —
I'll haste to quaff my wine again.

And thus while all our days are bright,
Nor time has dimmed their bloomy light,
Let us the festal hours beguile   15
With mantling cup and cordial smile;
And shed from every bowl of wine
The richest drop on Bacchus' shrine!
For Death may come, with brow unpleasant,
May come when least we wish him present,   20
And beckon to the sable shore,
And grimly bid us — drink no more!

(Thomas Moore)

15. beguile: amuse.   16. mantling: foaming.

SOPHOCLES (496?–406 B.C.)

Sophocles was born in the village of Colonus near Athens. He was a patriotic Athenian who rendered good service to the state both in peace and in war. But his chief concern was with the theater, first as actor and then as dramatist. Of more than a hundred plays, only seven have survived, all belonging to the period of his maturity. As is usual in Greek tragedy, the subjects are taken from legends of the heroes of Greece. His three greatest plays, for example, are concerned with the fate of the ruling house of Thebes. These are *Oedipus the King, Oedipus in Colonus,* and *Antigone.* Technically, Sophocles made important innovations by the introduction of a third actor in a scene and by the use of painted scenery. As compared with his great predecessor Aeschylus, he made his characters more human and less like puppets of fate. Because of his broad humanity his moderation and restraint, his even-balanced soul, as well as his skill in construction and expression, he seems like the embodiment of serene classic perfection. Matthew Arnold spoke of him as one " who saw life steadily, and saw it whole."

THE GREEK DRAMA

The Greek drama differed from the modern drama in several important respects. In the first place, the Greek theater was outdoors in the form of a circular amphitheater. The performances took place in broad daylight and were attended by all classes, even by the slaves. During a tragedy, a religious solemnity prevailed. The actors were always males; they dressed in a conventional garb and wore buskins, or high-heeled shoes, to give them a heroic stature. Gestures and movements of the body were stately. The effect of a stage-scene was, therefore, statuesque. The dialogue seemed more like declamation than conversation. Often the important characters wore masks, inside which were fitted mouthpieces like small megaphones to give resonance to the voice. An indispensable part of the Greek drama was the chorus, which has been abandoned in the modern play, but still forms an important part of opera. The Greek chorus, however, consisted of a group of performers, who, during the entire representation, were on the stage witnessing the drama. In the intervals of the action, the chorus chanted songs relating to the theme of the play. The chorus was thus conceived as an ideal audience, giving voice to the feelings of the spectators, though sometimes it took a more direct part by advising or exhorting. It was frequently divided into two parts, one half singing a strophe and the other responding with an antistrophe, both to the accompaniment of a flute. The music was apparently very simple.

ANTIGONE

The situation at the opening of *Antigone* is that after the death of Oedipus, former King of Thebes, his daughters Antigone and Ismene were living in the palace with their brother Eteocles. Polyneikes, their second brother, who had been unjustly exiled, returned to attack the city. The two brothers fought and were killed, and Creon, their uncle, was made king. Creon ordered that Eteocles should be buried with religious rites, but that Polyneikes, having been an enemy to the city, should lie unburied. The play turns on the determination of Antigone, "the most perfect female character in Greek poetry," to resist the King's decree and to follow the divine law by burying her brother.

DRAMATIS PERSONAE

CREON, *King of Thebes*　　　　　　*Second Messenger*
HAEMON, *son of Creon*　　　　　　EURYDIKE, *wife of Creon*
TEIRESIAS, *a seer*　　　　　　　　ANTIGONE ⎫
Guards　　　　　　　　　　　　　ISMENE　⎬ *daughters of* OEDIPUS
First Messenger　　　　　　　　　*Chorus of Theban Elders*

SCENE: *Thebes, in front of the Palace. Early morning. Hills in the distance on the left; on the right the city.*

Enter ANTIGONE *and* ISMENE

Antig. Ismene, mine own sister, darling one!
Is there, of ills that sprang from Oedipus,
One left that Zeus will fail to bring on us,
The two who yet remain? Nought is there sad,
Nought full of sorrow, steeped in sin or shame,

5

But I have seen it in thy woes and mine.
And now, what new decree is this they tell,
Our Captain has enjoined on all the State?
Know'st thou? Hast heard? Or are they hid from thee,
The ills that come from foes upon our friends? 10

  Ism. No tidings of our friends, Antigone,
Pleasant or painful, since that hour have come,
When we, two sisters, lost our brothers twain,
In one day dying by a twofold blow.
And since in this last night the Argive host 15
Has left the field, I nothing further know,
Nor brightening fortune, nor increasing gloom.

  Antig. That knew I well, and therefore sent for thee
Beyond the gates, that thou may'st hear alone.

  Ism. What meanest thou? It is but all too clear 20
Thou broodest darkly o'er some tale of woe.

  Antig. And does not Creon treat our brothers twain
One with the rites of burial, one with shame?
Eteocles, so say they, he interred
Fitly, with wonted rites, as one held meet 25
To pass with honor to the dead below.
But for the corpse of Polyneikes, slain
So piteously, they say, he has proclaimed
To all the citizens, that none should give
His body burial, or bewail his fate, 30
But leave it still unwept, unsepulchered,
A prize full rich for birds that scent afar
Their sweet repast. So Creon bids, they say,
Creon the good, commanding thee and me, —
Yes, me, I say, — and now is coming here, 35
To make it clear to those who know it not,
And counts the matter not a trivial thing;
But whoso does the things that he forbids,
For him there waits within the city's walls
The death of stoning. Thus, then, stands thy case; 40
And quickly thou wilt show, if thou are born
Of noble nature, or degenerate liv'st,
Base child of honored parents.

  Ism.   How could I,
O daring in thy mood, in this our plight,

---

15. **Argive:** from Argos, a city in the Peloponnesus.

Or breaking law or keeping, aught avail? 45
 Antig. Wilt thou with me share risk and toil? Look to it.
 Ism. What risk is this? What purpose fills thy mind?
 Antig. Wilt thou help this my hand to lift the dead?
 Ism. Mean'st thou to bury him, when law forbids?
 Antig. He is my brother; yes, and thine, though thou 50
Would'st fain he were not. I desert him not.
 Ism. O daring one, when Creon bids thee not?
 Antig. He has no right to keep me from mine own.
 Ism. Ah me! remember, sister, how our sire
Perished, with hate o'erwhelmed and infamy, 55
From evils that himself did bring to light,
With his own hand himself of eyes bereaving,
And how his wife and mother, both in one,
With twisted cordage, cast away her life;
And thirdly, how our brothers in one day 60
In suicidal conflict wrought the doom,
Each of the other. And we twain are left;
And think, how much more wretchedly than all
We twain shall perish, if, against the law,
We brave our sovereign's edict and his power. 65
This first we need remember, we were born
Women; as such, not made to strive wth men.
And next, that they who reign surpass in strength,
And we must bow to this, and worse than this.
I then, entreating those that dwell below, 70
To judge me leniently, as forced to yield,
Will hearken to our rulers. Over-zeal
That still will meddle, little wisdom shows.
 Antig. I will not ask thee, nor though thou should'st wish
To do it, should'st thou join with my consent. 75
Do what thou wilt, I go to bury him;
And good it were, in doing this, to die.
Loved I shall be with him whom I have loved,
Guilty of holiest crime. More time is mine
In which to share the favor of the dead, 80
Than that of those who live; for I shall rest
Forever there. But thou, if thus thou please,

---

56. **bring to light:** Oedipus, discovering that he had unwittingly married his mother, Jocasta, put out his own eyes. This is the subject of Sophocles' tragedy, *Oedipus the King.* 59. **cordage:** Jocasta hanged herself.

Count as dishonored what the Gods approve.

Ism.   I do them no dishonor, but I find
Myself too weak to war against the State.   85

Antig.   Make what excuse thou wilt, I go to rear
A grave above the brother whom I love.

Ism.   Ah, wretched me! how much I fear for thee!

Antig.   Fear not for me. Thine own fate raise to safety.

Ism.   At any rate, disclose this deed to none;   90
Keep it close hidden: I will hide it too.

Antig.   Speak out! I bid thee. Silent, thou wilt be
More hateful to me, if thou fail to tell
My deed to all men.

Ism.   Fiery is thy mood,
Although thy deeds the very blood might chill.   95

Antig.   I know I please the souls I ought to please.

Ism.   Yes, if thou canst; thou seek'st the impossible.

Antig.   When strength shall fail me, then I'll cease to strive.

Ism.   We should not hunt the impossible at all.

Antig.   If thou speak thus, my hatred wilt thou gain,   100
And rightly wilt be hated of the dead.
Leave me and my ill counsel to endure
This dreadful doom. I shall not suffer aught
So evil as a death dishonorable.

Ism.   Go then, if so thou wilt. Of this be sure,   105
Wild as thou art, thy friends must love thee still.

                                        [*Exeunt.*

Enter Chorus of Theban Elders.

STROPHE I

Chor.   O light of yon bright sun,
Fairest of all that ever shone on Thebes,
    Thebes with her seven high gates,
    Thou didst appear that day,   110
    Eye of the golden dawn,
    O'er Dirké's streams advancing,
    Driving with quickened curb,
    In haste of headlong flight,
The warrior who, in panoply of proof,   115
From Argos came, with shield of glittering white;

112. **Dirké:** a river near Thebes.   115. **panoply of proof:** well-tested armor

Whom Polyneikes brought,
Roused by the strife of tongues
Against our fatherland,
As eagle shrieking shrill,   120
He hovered o'er our land,
With snow-white wing bedecked,
Begirt with myriad arms,
And flowing horsehair crests.

ANTISTROPHE I

He stood above our towers,   125
Encircling, with his spears all blood-stained,
  The portals of our gates;
  He went, before he filled
  His jaw with blood of men,
  Ere the pine-fed Hephaestos   130
  Had seized our crown of tow
  So loud the battle din
That Ares loves was raised around his rear,
A conflict hard e'en for his dragon foe.
  For breath of haughty speech   135
  Zeus hateth evermore;
  And seeing them advance,
  With mighty rushing stream,
  And clang of golden arms,
  With brandished fire he hurls   140
  One who rushed eagerly
  From topmost battlement
  To shout out, " Victory! "

STROPHE 2

Crashing to earth he fell,
Down-smitten, with his torch,   145
Who came, with madman's haste,
Drunken, with frenzied soul,
And swept o'er us with blasts,
The whirlwind blasts of hate.
Thus on one side they fare,   150

130. **Hephaestos:** god of fire. 133. **Ares:** god of war, same as Roman Mars.

And Ares great, like war-horse in his strength,
　Smiting now here, now there,
　Brought each his several fate.
For seven chief warriors at the seven gates met,
　Equals with equals matched,　　　　　　　　155
　To Zeus, the Lord of War,
　Left tribute, arms of bronze;
　All but the hateful ones,
Who, from one father and one mother sprung,
　Stood wielding, hand to hand,　　　　　　　　160
　Their two victorious spears,
And had their doom of death as common lot.

ANTISTROPHE 2

　But now, since Victory,
　Of mightiest name, hath come
　To Thebes, of chariots proud,　　　　　　　　165
　Joying and giving joy,
　After these wars just past,
　Learn ye forgetfulness,
And all night long, with dance and voice of hymns,
　Let us go round in state　　　　　　　　170
　To all the shrines of Gods,
While Bacchos, making Thebes resound with dance,
　Begins the strain of joy;
　But, lo! our country's king,
　Creon, Menoekeus' son,　　　　　　　　175
　New ruler, by new change,
　And providence of God,
Comes to us, steering on some new device;
　For, lo! he hath convened,
　By herald's loud command,　　　　　　　　180
This council of the elders of our land.

Enter CREON.

　Creon. My friends, for what concerns our commonwealth,
The Gods who vexed it with the billowing storms
Have righted it again; and I have sent
By special summons calling you to come　　　　　　　　185

172. **Bacchos:** god of wine and revelry.

Apart from all the others. This, in part,
As knowing ye did all along uphold
The might of Laios' throne, in part again,
Because when Oedipus our country ruled,
And, when he perished, then towards his sons   190
Ye still were faithful in your steadfast mind.
And since they fell, as by a double death,
Both on the selfsame day with murderous blow,
Smiting and being smitten, now I hold
Their thrones and all their power of sov'reignty   195
By nearness of my kindred to the dead.
And hard it is to learn what each man is,
In heart and mind and judgment, till he gain
Experience in princedom and in laws.
For me, whoe'er is called to guide a State,   200
And does not catch at counsels wise and good,
But holds his peace through any fear of man,
I deem him basest of all men that are,
And so have deemed long since; and whosoe'er
As worthier than his country counts his friend,   205
I utterly despise him. I myself,
Zeus be my witness, who beholdeth all,
Would not keep silence, seeing danger come,
Instead of safety, to my subjects true.
Nor could I take as friend my country's foe;   210
For this I know, that there our safety lies,
And sailing while the good ship holds her course,
We gather friends around us. By these rules
And such as these do I maintain the State.
And now I come, with edicts, close allied   215
To these in spirit, for my citizens,
Concerning those two sons of Oedipus.
Eteocles, who died in deeds of might
Illustrious, fighting for our fatherland,
To honor him with sepulture, all rites   220
Duly performed that to the noblest dead
Of right belong. Not so his brother; him
I speak of, Polyneikes, who, returned
From exile, sought with fire to desolate
His father's city and the shrines of Gods,   225

188. **Laios:** father of Oedipus.

Yes, sought to glut his rage with blood of men,
And lead them captives to the bondslave's doom;
Him I decree that none shall dare entomb,
That none shall utter wail or loud lament,
But leave his corpse unburied, by the dogs   230
And vultures mangled, foul to look upon.
Such is my purpose. Ne'er, if I can help,
Shall the vile have more honor than the just;
But whoso shows himself my country's friend,
Living or dead, from me shall honor gain.   235

   Chor. This is thy pleasure, O Menoekeus' son,
For him who hated, him who loved our State;
And thou hast power to make what laws thou wilt,
Both for the dead and all for us who live.

   Creon. Be ye then guardians of the things I speak.   240
   Chor. Commit this task to one of younger years.
   Creon. Nay, watchmen are appointed for the corpse.
   Chor. What other task then dost thou lay on us?
   Creon. Not to consent with those that disobey.
   Chor. None are so foolish as to seek for death.   245
   Creon. Yet that shall be the doom; but love of gain
Hath oft with false hopes lured men to their death.

Enter Guard.

   Guard. I will not say, O king, that I have come
Panting with speed, and plying nimble feet,
For I had many halting-points of thought,   250
Backwards and forwards turning, round and round;
For now my mind would give me sage advice:
" Poor wretch, why go where thou must bear the blame?
Or wilt thou tarry, fool? Shall Creon know
These things from others? How wilt thou 'scape grief? "   255
Revolving thus, I came in haste, yet slow,
And thus a short way finds itself prolonged;
But, last of all, to come to thee prevailed.
And though I tell of nought, yet I will speak;
For this one hope I cling to, might and main,   260
That I shall suffer nought but destiny.

   Creon. What is it then that causes such dismay?
   Guard. First, for mine own share in it, this I say,
The deed I did not, do not know who did,

Nor should I rightly come to ill for it.　　　265
 Creon.　Thou feel'st thy way and fencest up thy deed
All round and round.　'Twould seem thou hast some news.
 Guard.　Yea, news of fear engenders long delay.
 Creon.　Wilt thou not speak, and then depart in peace?
 Guard.　Well, speak I will.　The corpse . . . Some one has　270
 been
But now and buried it, a little dust
O'er the skin scattering, with the wonted rites.
 Creon.　What say'st thou?　What man dared this deed of guilt?
 Guard.　I know not.　Neither was there stroke of axe,
Nor earth cast up by mattock.　All the soil　　　275
Was dry and hard, no track of chariot wheel;
But he who did it went and left no sign.
And when the first day-watchman showed it us,
The sight caused wonder and sore grief to all;
For he had disappeared; no tomb indeed　　　280
Was over him, but dust all lightly strown,
As by some hand that shunned defiling guilt;
And no sign was there of wild beast or dog
Having come and torn him.　Evil words arose
Among us, guard to guard imputing blame,　　　285
Which might have come to blows, and none was there
To check its course, for each to each appeared
The man whose hand had done it.　Yet not one
Had it brought home, but each disclaimed all knowledge;
And we were ready in our hands to take　　　290
Bars of hot iron, and to walk through fire,
And call the Gods to witness none of us
Were privy to his schemes who planned the deed,
Nor his who wrought it.　Then at last, when nought
Was gained by all our searching, some one speaks,　　　295
Who made us bend our gaze upon the ground
In fear and trembling; for we neither saw
How to oppose it, nor, accepting it,
How we might prosper in it.　And his speech
Was this, that all our tale should go to thee,　　　300
Not hushed up anywise.　This gained the day;
And me, ill-starred, the lot condemns to win
This precious prize.　So here I come to thee

---

275. **Mattock:** pickaxe.　293. **were privy to:** had knowledge of.

Against my will; and surely do I trow
Thou dost not wish to see me. Still 'tis true   305
That no man loves the messenger of ill.
   Chor. For me, my prince, my mind some time has thought
If this perchance has some divine intent.
   Creon. Cease then, before thou fillest me with wrath,
Lest thou be found, though full of years, a fool.   310
For what thou say'st is most intolerable,
That for this corpse the providence of Gods
Has any care. What! have they buried him,
As to their patron paying honors high,
Who came to waste their columned shrines with fire,   315
To desecrate their offerings and their lands,
And all their wonted customs? Dost thou see
The Gods approving men of evil deeds?
It is not so; but men of rebel mood,
Lifting their head in secret long ago,   320
Still murmured thus against me. Never yet
Had their neck beneath the yoke, content
To bear it with submission. They, I know,
Have bribed these men to let the deed be done.
No thing in use by man, for power of ill,   325
Can equal money. This lays cities low,
This drives men forth from quiet dwelling-place,
This warps and changes minds of worthiest stamp,
To turn to deeds of baseness, teaching men
All shifts of cunning, and to know the guilt   330
Of every impious deed. But they who, hired,
Have wrought this crime, have labored to their cost,
Or soon or late to pay the penalty.
But if Zeus still claims any awe from me,
Know this, and with an oath I tell it thee,   335
Unless ye find the very man whose hand
Has wrought this burial, and before mine eyes
Present him captive, death shall not suffice,
Till first, hung up still living, ye shall show
The story of this outrage, that henceforth,   340
Knowing what gain is lawful, ye may grasp
At that, and learn it is not meet to love
Gain from all quarters. By base profit won
You will see more destroyed than prospering.

Guard.	May I then speak? Or shall I turn and go?	345
Creon.	See'st not e'en yet how vexing are thy words?	
Guard.	Is it thine ears they trouble, or thy soul?	
Creon.	Why dost thou gauge my trouble where it is?	
Guard.	The doer grieves thy heart, but I thine ears.	
Creon.	Pshaw! what a babbler, born to prate art thou!	350
Guard.	May be; yet I this deed, at least, did not.	
Creon.	Yes, and for money; selling e'en thy soul.	
Guard.	Ah me!	

How dire it is, in thinking, false to think!

 Creon. Prate about thinking; but unless ye show   355
To me the doers, ye shall say ere long
That scoundrel gains still work their punishment.

[Exit.

 Guard. God send we find him! Should we find him not,
As well may be (for this must chance decide),
You will not see me coming here again;   360
For now, being safe beyond all hope of mine,
Beyond all thought, I owe the Gods much thanks.

[Exit.

STROPHE I

 Chor. Many the forms of life,
Wondrous and strange to see,
But nought than man appears   365
More wondrous and more strange.
He, with the wintry gales,
O'er the white foaming sea,
'Mid wild waves surging round,
Wendeth his way across: 370
Earth, of all Gods, from ancient days the first,
Unworn and undecayed.
He, with his ploughs that travel o'er and o'er,
Furrowing with horse and mule,
Wears ever year by year.   375

ANTISTROPHE I

The thoughtless tribe of birds,
The beasts that roam the fields,
The brood in sea-depths born,

350. prate: chatter.

He takes them all in nets
Knotted in snaring mesh. 380
Man, wonderful in skill.
And by his subtle arts
He holds in sway the beasts
That roam the fields, or tread the mountain's height;
And brings the binding yoke 385
Upon the neck of horse with shaggy mane,
Or bull on mountain crest,
Untamable in strength.

STROPHE 2

And speech, and thought as swift as wind,
And tempered mood for higher life of states, 390
These he has learnt, and how to flee
Or the clear cold of frost unkind,
Or darts of storm and shower,
Man all-providing. Unprovided, he
Meeteth no chance the coming days may bring; 395
Only from Hades, still
He fails to find escape,
Though skill of art may teach him how to flee
From depths of fell disease incurable.

ANTISTROPHE 2

So, gifted with a wondrous might, 400
Above all fancy's dreams, with skill to plan,
Now unto evil, now to good,
He turns. While holding fast the laws,
His country's sacred rights,
That rest upon the oath of Gods on high, 405
High in the State; an outlaw from the State,
When loving, in his pride,
The thing that is not good;
Ne'er may he share my hearth, nor yet my thoughts,
Who worketh deeds of evil like to this. 410

Enter Guards, bringing in ANTIGONE.

As to this portent which the Gods have sent,
I stand in doubt. Can I, who know her, say

That this is not the maid Antigone?
O wretched one of wretched father born,
Thou child of Oedipus,
What means this? Surely 'tis not that they bring   415
Thee as a rebel 'gainst the king's decree,
And taken in the folly of thine act?
   Guard.   Yes! She it was by whom the deed was done.
We found her burying. Where is Creon, pray?   420
   Chor.   Back from his palace comes he just in time.

Enter CREON.

Creon.   What chance is this, with which my coming fits?
   Guard.   Men, O my king, should pledge themselves to nought;
For cool reflection makes their purpose void.
I surely thought I should be slow to come here,   425
Cowed by thy threats, which then fell thick on me;
But now persuaded by the sweet delight
Which comes unlooked for, and beyond our hopes,
I come, although I swore the contrary,
Bringing this maiden, whom in act we found   430
Decking the grave. No need for lots was now;
The prize was mine, and not another man's.
And now, O king, take her, and as thou wilt,
Judge and convict her. I can claim a right
To wash my hands of all this troublous coil.   435
   Creon.   How and where was it that ye seized and brought her?
   Guard.   She was in act of burying. Thou knowest all.
   Creon.   Dost know and rightly speak the tale thou tell'st?
   Guard.   I saw her burying that self-same corpse
Thou bad'st us not to bury. Speak I clear?   440
   Creon.   How was she seen, and taken in the act?
   Guard.   The matter passed as follows: — When we came,
With all those dreadful threats of thine upon us,
Sweeping away the dust which, lightly spread,
Covered the corpse, and laying stript and bare   445
The tainted carcase, on the hill we sat
To windward, shunning the infected air,
Each stirring up his fellow with strong words,
If any shirked his duty. This went on
Some time, until the glowing orb of day   450

435. **coil:** disturbance.

Stood in mid heaven, and the scorching heat
Fell on us. Then a sudden whirlwind rose,
A scourge from heaven, raising squalls on earth,
And filled the plain, the leafage stripping bare
Of all the forest, and the air's vast space   455
Was thick and troubled, and we closed our eyes,
Until the plague the Gods had sent was past;
And when it ceased, a weary time being gone,
The girl is seen, and with a bitter cry,
Shrill as a bird's, when it beholds its nest   460
All emptied of its infant brood, she wails;
Thus she, when she beholds the corpse all stript,
Groaned loud with many moanings, and she called
Fierce curses down on those who did the deed.
And in her hand she brings some fine, dry dust,   465
And from a vase of bronze, well wrought, upraised,
She pours the three libations o'er the dead.
And we, beholding, give her chase forthwith,
And run her down, nought terrified at us.
And then we charged her with the former deed,   470
As well as this. And nothing she denied.
But this to me both bitter is and sweet,
For to escape oneself from ill is sweet,
But to bring friends to trouble, this is hard
And painful. Yet my nature bids me count   475
Above all these things safety for myself.
   Creon. [*To* ANTIGONE] Thou, then — yes, thou, who bend'st thy
    face to earth —
Confessest thou, or dost deny the deed?
   Antig. I own I did it, and will not deny.
   Creon. [*To* Guard] Go thou thy way, where'er thy will may   480
    choose,
Freed from a weighty charge.
                         [*Exit Guard.*

[*To* ANTIGONE]   And now for thee.
Say in few words, not lengthening out thy speech,
Knew'st thou the edicts which forbade these things?
   Antig. I knew them. Could I fail? Full clear were they.
   Creon. And thou did'st dare to disobey these laws?   485
   Antig. Yes, for it was not Zeus who gave them forth,

      467. **libations:** drink-offerings to the gods.

Nor Justice, dwelling with the Gods below,
Who traced these laws for all the sons of men;
Nor did I deem thy edicts strong enough,
That thou, a mortal man, should'st over-pass   490
The unwritten laws of God that know not change.
They are not of today nor yesterday,
But live forever, nor can man assign
When first they sprang to being. Not through fear
Of any man's resolve was I prepared   495
Before the Gods to bear the penalty
Of sinning against these. That I should die
I knew (how should I not?) though thy decree
Had never spoken. And, before my time
If I shall die, I reckon this a gain;   500
For whoso lives, as I, in many woes,
How can it be but he shall gain by death?
And so for me to bear this doom of thine
Has nothing painful. But, if I had left
My mother's son unburied on his death,   505
In that I should have suffered; but in this
I suffer not. And should I seem to thee
To do a foolish deed, 'tis simply this, —
I bear the charge of folly from a fool.
    Chor. The maiden's stubborn will, of stubborn sire   510
The offspring shows itself. She knows not yet
To yield to evils.
    Creon.   Know then, minds too stiff
Most often stumble, and the rigid steel
Baked in the furnace, made exceeding hard,
Thou see'st most often split and shivered lie;   515
And I have known the steeds of fiery mood
With a small curb subdued. It is not meet
That one who lives in bondage to his neighbors
Should think too proudly. Wanton outrage then
This girl first learnt, transgressing these my laws;   520
But this, when she has done it, is again
A second outrage, over it to boast,
And laugh as having done it. Surely, then,
She is the man, not I, if, all unscathed,
Such deeds of might are hers. But be she child   525
Of mine own sister, or of one more near

Than all the kith and kin of Household Zeus,
She and her sister shall not 'scape a doom
Most foul and shameful; for I charge her, too,
With having planned this deed of sepulture.   530
Go ye and call her. 'Twas but now within
I saw her raving, losing self-command.
And still the mind of those who in the dark
Plan deeds of evil is the first to fail,
And so convicts itself of secret guilt.   535
But most I hate when one found out in guilt
Will seek to gloze and brave it to the end.
   Antig. And dost thou seek aught else beyond my death?
   Creon. Nought else for me. That gaining, I gain all.
   Antig. Why then delay? Of all thy words not one   540
Pleases me now (and may it never please!)
And so all mine must grate upon thine ears.
And yet how could I higher glory gain
Than placing my true brother in his tomb?
There is not one of these but would confess   545
It pleases them, did fear not seal their lips.
The tyrant's might in much besides excels,
And it may do and say whate'er it will.
   Creon. Of all the race of Cadmos thou alone
Look'st thus upon the deed.
   Antig.   They see it too   550
As I do, but their tongue is tied for thee.
   Creon. Art not ashamed against their thoughts to think?
   Antig. There is nought base in honoring our own blood.
   Creon. And was he not thy kin who fought against him?
   Antig. Yea, brother, of one father and one mother.   555
   Creon. Why then give honor which dishonors him?
   Antig. The dead below will not repeat thy words.
   Creon. Yes, if thou give like honor to the godless.
   Antig. It was his brother, not his slave that died.
   Creon. Wasting this land, while *he* died fighting for it.   560
   Antig. Yet Hades still craves equal rites for all.
   Creon. The good craves not the portion of the bad.
   Antig. Who knows if this be holy deemed below?
   Creon. Not even when he dies can foe be friend.

527. **Household Zeus:** Zeus was the god of the family. 537. **gloze:** explain away. 549. **Cadmos:** legendary founder of Thebes.

Antig. My nature leads to sharing love, not hate. 565
Creon. Go then below; and if thou must have love,
Love them. While I live, women shall not rule.

Enter ISMENE, *led in by Attendants.*

Chor. And, lo! Ismene at the gate
Comes shedding tears of sisterly regard,
And o'er her brow a gathering cloud 570
Mars the deep roseate blush,
Bedewing her fair cheek.

Creon. [*To* ISMENE] And thou who, creeping as a viper creeps,
Did'st drain my life in secret, and I knew not
That I was rearing two accursèd ones, 575
Subverters of my throne, — come, tell me, then,
Wilt thou confess thou took'st thy part in this,
Or wilt thou swear thou did'st not know of it?

Ism. I did the deed, if she did, go with her.
Yes, share the guilt, and bear an equal blame. 580

Antig. Nay, justice will not suffer this, for thou
Did'st not consent, nor did I let thee join.

Ism. Nay, in thy troubles, I am not ashamed
In the same boat with thee to share thy fate.

Antig. Who did it, Hades knows, and those below. 585
I do not love a friend who loves in words.

Ism. Do not, my sister, put me to such shame,
As not to let me join in death with thee,
And so to pay due reverence to the dead.

Antig. Share not my death, nor make thine own this deed 590
Thou had'st no hand in. My death shall suffice.

Ism. What life to me is sweet, bereaved of thee?

Antig. Ask Creon there, since thou o'er him dost watch.

Ism. Why vex me so, is nothing bettered by it?

Antig. 'Tis pain indeed, to laugh my laugh at thee. 595

Ism. But now, at least, how may I profit thee?

Antig. Save thou thyself. I grudge not thy escape.

Ism. Ah, woe is me! and must I miss thy fate?

Antig. Thou mad'st thy choice to live, and I to die.

Ism. 'Twas not because I failed to speak my thoughts. 600

Antig. To these did'st thou, to those did I seem wise.

Ism. And yet the offense is equal in us both.

Antig. Take courage. Thou dost live. My soul long since
Hath died to render service to the dead.

Creon. Of these two girls, the one goes mad but now, 605
The other ever since her life began.

Ism. E'en so, O king; no mind that ever lived
Stands firm in evil days, but goes astray.

Creon. Thine did, when, with the vile, vile deeds thou choosest.

Ism. How could I live without her presence here? 610

Creon. Speak not of presence. She is here no more.

Ism. And wilt thou slay thy son's betrothèd bride?

Creon. Full many a field there is which he may plough.

Ism. None like that plighted troth 'twixt him and her.

Creon. Wives that are vile I love not for my sons. 615

Ism. Ah, dearest Haemon, how thy father shames thee!

Creon. Thou with that marriage dost but vex my soul.

Chor. And wilt thou rob thy son of her he loved?

Creon. 'Tis Death, not I, shall break the marriage off.

Chor. Her doom is fixed, it seems, then. She must die. 620

Creon. Fixed, yes, by me and thee. No more delay,
Lead them within, ye slaves. These must be kept
Henceforth as women, suffered not to roam;
For even boldest natures shrink in fear
When they see Hades overshadowing life. 625

     [*Exeunt Guards with* ANTIGONE *and* ISMENE.

STROPHE I

Chor. Blessed are those whose life no woe doth taste!
 For unto those whose house
The Gods have shaken, nothing fails of curse
Or woe, that creeps to generations far.
  E'en thus a wave, (when spreads, 630
  With blasts from Thrakian coasts,
  The darkness of the deep,)
  Up from the sea's abyss
Hither and thither rolls the black sand on,
  And every jutting peak, 635
  Swept by the storm-wind's strength,
  Lashed by the fierce wild waves,
Re-echoes with the far-resounding roar.

ANTISTROPHE 1

I see the woes that smote, in ancient days,
   The seed of Labdacos,
Who perished long ago, with grief on grief   **640**
Still falling, nor does this age rescue that;
    Some God still smites it down,
    Nor have they any end:
    For now there rose a gleam,   **645**
    Over the last weak shoots,
That sprang from out the race of Oedipus;
    Yet this the blood-stained scythe
    Of those that reign below
    Cuts off relentlessly,   **650**
And maddened speech, and frenzied rage of heart.

STROPHE 2

Thy power, O Zeus, what haughtiness of man,
   Yea, what can hold in check?
Which neither sleep, that maketh all things old,
Nor the long months of Gods that never fail,   **655**
    Can for a moment seize.
    But still as Lord supreme,
    Waxing not old with time,
Thou dwellest in Thy sheen of radiancy
    On far Olympos' height.   **660**
Through future near or far as through the past,
   One law holds ever good,
Nought comes to life of man unscathed throughout by woe.

ANTISTROPHE 2

For hope to many comes in wanderings wild,
   A solace and support;
To many as a cheat of fond desires,   **665**
And creepeth still on him who knows it not,
    Until he burns his foot
    Within the scorching flame.
    Full well spake one of old,   **670**
That evil ever seems to be as good

640. **Labdacos:** grandfather of Oedipus.

To those whose thoughts of heart
  God leadeth unto woe,
And without woe, he spends but shortest space of time.

And here comes Haemon, last of all thy sons: 675
  Comes he bewailing sore
The fate of her who should have been his bride,
  The maid Antigone,
    Grieving o'er vanished joys?

Enter HAEMON

Creon. Soon we shall know much more than seers can tell   680
Surely thou dost not come, my son, to rage
Against thy father, hearing his decree,
Fixing her doom who should have been thy bride;
Or dost thou love us still, whate'er we do?
  Haemon. My father, I am thine; and thou dost guide   685
With thy wise counsels, which I gladly follow.
No marriage weighs one moment in the scales
With me, while thou dost guide my steps aright.
  Creon. This thought, my son, should dwell within thy breast,
That all things stand below a father's will;   690
For so men pray that they may rear and keep
Obedient offspring by their hearths and homes,
That they may both requite their father's foes,
And pay with him like honors to his friend.
But he who reareth sons that profit not,   695
What could one say of him but this, that he
Breeds his own sorrow, laughter to his foes?
Lose not thy reason, then, my son, o'ercome
By pleasure, for a woman's sake, but know,
A cold embrace is that to have at home   700
A worthless wife, the partner of thy bed.
What ulcerous sore is worse than one we love
Who proves all worthless? No! with loathing scorn,
As hateful to thee, let that girl go wed
A spouse in Hades. Taken in the act   705
I found her, her alone of all the State,
Rebellious. And I will not make myself
False to the State. She dies. So let her call
On Zeus, the lord of kindred. If I rear

Of mine own stock things foul and orderless,   710
I shall have work enough with those without,
For he who in the life of home is good
Will still be seen as just in things of state;
I should be sure that man would govern well,
And know well to be governed, and would stand   715
In war's wild storm, on his appointed post,
A just and good defender. But the man
Who by transgressions violates the laws,
Or thinks to bid the powers that be obey,
He must not hope to gather praise from me.   720
No! we must follow whom the State appoints
In things or just and trivial, or, may be,
The opposite of these. For anarchy
Is our worst evil, brings our commonwealth
To utter ruin, lays whole houses low,   725
In battle strife hurls firm allies in flight;
But they who yield to guidance — these shall find
Obedience saves most men. Thus help should come
To what our rulers order; least of all
Ought men to bow before a woman's sway.   730
Far better, if it must be so, to fall
By a man's hand, than thus to bear reproach,
By woman conquered.
    Chor.   Unto us, O king,
Unless our years have robbed us of our wit,
Thou seemest to say wisely what thou say'st.   735
    Haem. The Gods, my father, have bestowed on man
His reason, noblest of all earthly gifts;
And that thou speakest wrongly these thy words
I cannot say (God grant I ne'er know how
Such things to utter!) yet another's thoughts   740
May have some reason. 'Tis my lot to watch
What each man says or does, or blames in thee,
For dread thy face to one of low estate,
Who speaks what thou wilt not rejoice to hear.
But I can hear the things in darkness said,   745
How the whole city wails this maiden's fate,
As one " who of all women most unjustly,
For noblest deed must die the foulest death,
Who her own brother, fallen in the fray,

Would neither leave unburied, nor expose **750**
To carrion dogs, or any bird of prey,
May she not claim the meed of golden praise? "
Such is the whisper that in secret runs
All darkling. And for me, my father, nought
Is dearer than thy welfare. What can be **755**
A nobler prize of honor for the son
Than a sire's glory, or for sire than son's?
I pray thee, then, wear not one mood alone,
That what thou say'st is right, and nought but that;
For he who thinks that he alone is wise, **760**
His mind and speech above what others have,
Such men when searched are mostly empty found.
But for a man to learn, though he be wise,
Yea to learn much, and know the time to yield,
Brings no disgrace. When winter floods the streams, **765**
Thou see'st the trees that bend before the storm,
Save their last twigs, while those that will not yield
Perish with root and branch. And when one hauls
Too tight the mainsail rope, and will not slack,
He has to end his voyage with deck o'erturned. **770**
Do thou then yield; permit thyself to change.
Young though I be, if any prudent thought
Be with me, I at least will dare assert
The higher worth of one, who, come what will,
Is full of knowledge. If that may not be **775**
(For nature is not wont to take that bent),
'Tis good to learn from those who counsel well.

Chor. My king! 'tis fit that thou should'st learn from him,
If he speaks words in season; and, in turn,
That thou [*to* HAEMON] should'st learn of him, for both speak
    well. **780**

Creon. Shall we at our age stoop to learn from him,
Young as he is, the lesson to be wise?

Haem. Learn nought thou should'st not learn. And if I'm young,
Thou should'st my deeds and not my years consider.

Creon. Is that thy deed to reverence rebel souls? **785**

Haem. I would bid none waste reverence on the base.

Creon. Has not that girl been seized with that disease?

Haem. The men of Thebes with one accord say, No.

Creon. And will my subjects tell us how to rule?

Haem. Dost thou not see thou speakest like a boy?   790
Creon. Must I then rule for others than myself?
Haem. That is no State which hangs on one man's will.
Creon. Is not the State deemed his who governs it?
Haem. Brave rule!   Alone, and o'er an empty land!
Creon. This boy, it seems, will be his bride's ally.   795
Haem. If thou art she, for thou art all my care.
Creon. Basest of base, against thy father pleading!
Haem. Yea, for I see thee sin a grievous sin.
Creon. And do I sin revering mine own sway?
Haem. Thou show'st no reverence, trampling on God's laws.   800
Creon. O guilty soul, by woman's craft beguiled!
Haem. Thou wilt not find me slave unto the base.
Creon. Thy every word is still on her behalf.
Haem. Yea, and on thine and mine, and theirs below.
Creon. Be sure thou shalt not wed her while she lives.   805
Haem. Then she must die, and, dying, others slay.
Creon. And dost thou dare to come to me with threats?
Haem. Is it a threat against vain thoughts to speak?
Creon. Thou to thy cost shalt teach me wisdom's ways,
Thyself in wisdom wanting.
Haem.   I would say   810
Thou wast unwise, if thou wert not my father.
Creon. Thou woman's slave, I say, prate on no more.
Haem. Wilt thou then speak, and, speaking, listen not?
Creon. Nay, by Olympos!   Thou shalt not go free
To flout me with reproaches.   Lead her out   815
Whom my soul hates, that she may die forthwith
Before mine eyes, and near her bridegroom here.
Haem. No!   Think it not!   Near me she shall not die,
And thou shalt never see my face alive,
That thou may'st storm at those who like to yield.   820
                                                     [*Exit.*

Chor. The man has gone, O king, in hasty mood.
A mind distressed in youth is hard to bear.
Creon. Let him do what he will, and bear himself
As more than man, he shall not save those girls.
Chor. What!   Dost thou mean to slay them both alike?   825
Creon. Not her who touched it not; there thou say'st well.
Chor. What form of death mean'st thou to slay her with?

794. **brave:** the word is used ironically.

Creon. Leading her on to where the desert path
Is loneliest, there alive, in rocky cave
Will I immure her, just so much of food   830
Before her set as may avert pollution,
And save the city from the guilt of blood;
And there, invoking Hades, whom alone
Of all the Gods she worships, she, perchance,
Shall gain escape from death, or then shall know   835
That Hades-worship is but labor lost.

[*Exit.*

STROPHE

Chor. O Love, in every battle victor owned;
    Love, rushing on thy prey,
Now on a maiden's soft and blooming cheek,
    In secret ambush hid;   840
Now o'er the broad sea wandering at will,
    And now in shepherd's folds;
Of all the Undying Ones none 'scape from thee,
    Nor yet of mortal men
Whose lives are measured as a fleeting day;   845
And who has thee is frenzied in his soul.

ANTISTROPHE

Thou makest vile the purpose of the just,
    To his own fatal harm;
Thou hast stirred up this fierce and deadly strife,
    Of men of nearest kin;   850
The charm of eyes of bride beloved and fair
    Is crowned with victory,
And dwells on high among the powers that rule,
    Equal with holiest laws;
For Aphrodite, she whom none subdues,   855
Sports in her might and majesty divine,

    I, even I, am borne
    Beyond the appointed laws;
    I look on this, and cannot stay
    The fountain of my tears.   860
    For, lo! I see her, see Antigone

855. **Aphrodite:** Venus, goddess of love.

Wend her sad, lonely way
To that bride-chamber where we all must lie.

Antig. Behold, O men of this my fatherland,
  I wend my last lone way,
Seeing the last sunbeam, now and nevermore;   865
  He leads me yet alive,
  Hades that welcomes all,
  To Acheron's dark shore,
  With neither part nor lot   870
  In marriage festival,
  Nor hath the marriage hymn
  Been sung for me as bride,
But I shall be the bride of Acheron.

Chor. And hast thou not all honor, worthiest praise,   875
Who goest to the home that hides the dead,
Not smitten by the sickness that decays,
  Nor by the sharp sword's need,
But of thine own free will, in fullest life,
  Alone of mortals, thus
  To Hades tak'st thy way?   880

Antig. I heard of old her pitiable end,
  On Sipylos' high crag,
The Phrygian stranger from a far land come,
  Whom Tantalos begat;   885
  Whom growth of rugged rock,
  Clinging as ivy clings,
  Subdued, and made its own:
  And now, so runs the tale,
  There, as she melts in shower,   890
  The snow abideth aye,
And still bedews yon cliffs that lie below
  Those brows that ever weep.
With fate like hers God brings me to my rest.

Chor. A Goddess she, and of the high Gods born;   895
And we are mortals, born of mortal seed.
And lo! for one who liveth but to die,
To gain like doom with those of heavenly race,
  Is great and strange to hear.

869. **Acheron**: a river of Hades. 883. **Sipylos**: mountain in Phrygia. 884. **Phrygian stranger**: Niobe, who was married to the king of Thebes. After all her children were slain, she was turned to stone. 885. **Tantalos**: an ancestor of Oedipus. 891. **aye**: ever.

Antig.   Ye mock me then. Alas! Why wait ye not,   900
By all our fathers' Gods, I ask of you,
   Till I have passed away,
   But flout me while I live?
   O city that I love,
   O men that claim as yours   905
   That city stored with wealth,
   O Dirkè, fairest fount,
O grove of Thebes, that boasts her chariot host,
   I bid you witness all,
   How, with no friends to weep,   910
   By what stern laws condemned,
I go to that strong dungeon of the tomb,
   For burial strange, ah me!
Nor dwelling with the living, nor the dead.
   Chor.   Forward and forward still to farthest verge   915
   Of daring hast thou gone,
And now, O child, thou hast rushed violently
   Where Right erects her throne;
Surely thou payest to the uttermost
   Thy father's debt of guilt,   920
   Antig.   Ah! thou hast touched the quick of all my grief,
The thrice-told tale of all my father's woe,
   The fate which dogs us all,
The old Labdakid race of ancient fame.
   Woe for the curses dire   925
   Of that defilèd bed,
   With foulest incest stained,
   My mother's with my sire,
Whence I myself have sprung, most miserable.
   And now, I go to them,   930
   To sojourn in the grave,
   Accursèd, and unwed;
   Ah, brother, thou did'st find
   Thy marriage fraught with ill,
And thou, though dead, hast smitten down my life.   935
   Chor.   Acts reverent and devout
   May claim devotion's name,
But power, in one to whom power comes as trust,
   May never be defied;
   And thee, thy stubborn mood,   940

Self-chosen, layeth low.

Antig.   Unwept, without a friend,
Unwed, and whelmed in woe,
I journey on this road that open lies
No more shall it be mine (O misery!)
To look upon yon daylight's holy eye;   945
   And yet, of all my friends,
   Not one bewails my fate,
   No kindly tear is shed.

Enter CREON.

Creon.   And know ye not, if men have leave to speak   950
Their songs and wailings thus to stave off death,
That they will never stop?   Lead, lead her on,
Without delay, and, as I said, immure
In yon cavernous tomb, and then depart.
Leave her to choose, or drear and lonely death,   955
Or, living, in the tomb to find her home.
Our hands are clean in all that touches her;
But she no more shall dwell on earth with us.

Antig.   [*Turning towards the cavern*] O tomb, my bridal chamber,
   vaulted home.
Guarded right well forever, where I go   960
To join mine own, of whom the greater part
Among the dead doth Persephassa hold;
And I, of all the last and saddest, wend
My way below, life's little span unfilled.
And yet I go, and feed myself with hopes   965
That I shall meet them, by my father loved,
Dear to my mother, well-beloved of thee,
Thou darling brother: I, with these my hands,
Washed each dear corpse, arrayed you, poured libations,
In rites of burial; and in care for thee,   970
Thy body, Polyneikes, honoring,
I gain this recompense.   [And yet in sight
Of all that rightly judge the deed was good;
I had not done it had I come to be
A mother with her children, — had not dared,   975
Though 'twere a husband dead that moldered there,

962. **Persephassa:** more commonly Persephone or Proserpine, queen of
the lower world.

Against my country's will to bear this toil.
And am I asked what law constrained me thus?
I answer, had I lost a husband dear,
I might have had another; other sons   980
By other spouse, if one were lost to me;
But when my father and my mother sleep
In Hades, then no brother more can come.
And therefore, giving thee the foremost place,
I seemed in Creon's eyes, O brother dear,   985
To sin in boldest daring.   Therefore now
He leads me, having taken me by force,
Cut off from marriage bed and marriage song,
Untasting wife's true joy, or mother's bliss,
With infant at her breast, but all forlorn,   990
Bereaved of friends, in utter misery,
Alive, I tread the chambers of the dead.]
What law of Heaven have I transgressed against?
What use for me, ill-starred one, still to look
To any God for succor, or to call   995
On any friend for aid?   For holiest deed
I bear this charge of rank unholiness.
If acts like these the Gods on high approve,
We, taught by pain, shall own that we have sinned;
But if these sin, [*looking at* CREON] I pray they suffer not   1000
Worse evils than the wrongs they do to me.
   Chor.   Still do the same wild blasts
Vex her who standeth there.
   Creon.   Therefore shall these her guards
Weep sore for this delay.   1005
   Chor.   Ah me! this word of thine
Tells of death drawing nigh.
   Creon.   I cannot bid thee hope
For other end than this.
   Antig.   O citadel of Thebes, my native land,   1010
Ye Gods of ancient days,
   I go, and linger not.
Behold me, O ye senators of Thebes,
The last, lone scion of the kingly race,
What things I suffer, and from whom they come,   1015
Revering still the laws of reverence.
             [*Guards lead* ANTIGONE *away.* . . .

1014. **scion:** descendant.

Enter TEIRESIAS, *guided by a Boy.*

Teir.   Princes of Thebes, we come as travelers joined,
One seeing for both, for still the blind must use
A guide's assistance to direct his steps.
   Creon.   And what new thing, Teiresias, brings thee here?   1020
   Teir.   I'll tell thee, and do thou the seer obey.
   Creon.   Of old I was not wont to slight thy thoughts.
   Teir.   So did'st thou steer our city's course full well.
   Creon.   I bear my witness from good profit gained.
   Teir.   Know, then, thou walk'st on fortune's razor-edge.   1025
   Creon.   What means this?   How I shudder at thy speech!
   Teir.   Soon shalt thou know, as thou dost hear the signs
Of my dread art.   For sitting, as of old,
Upon my ancient seat of augury,
Where every bird finds haven, lo! I hear   1030
Strange cry of winged creatures, shouting shrill,
With inarticulate passion, and I knew
That they were tearing each the other's flesh
With bloody talons, for their whirring wings
Made that quite clear; and straightway I, in fear,   1035
Made trial of the sacrifice that lay
On fiery altar.   And Hephaestos' flame
Shone not from out the offering; but there oozed
Upon the ashes, a trickling from the bones,
A moisture, and it smoldered, and it spat,   1040
And, lo! the gall was scattered to the air,
And forth from out the fat that wrapped them round
The thigh-bones fell.   Such omens of decay
From holy sacrifice I learnt from him,
This boy, who now stands here, for he is still   1045
A guide to me, as I to others am.
And all this evil falls upon the State,
From out thy counsels; for our altars all,
Our sacred hearths are full of food for dogs
And birds unclean, the flesh of that poor wretch   1050
Who fell, the son of Oedipus.   And so
The Gods no more hear prayers of sacrifice,
Nor own the flame that burns the victim's limbs;
Nor do the birds give cry of omen good,
But feed on carrion of a slaughtered corpse.   1055

Think thou on this, my son: to err, indeed,
Is common unto all, but having erred,
He is no longer reckless or unblest,
Who, having fallen into evil, seeks
For healing, nor continues still unmoved.   1060
Self-will must bear the charge of stubbornness.
Yield to the dead, and outrage not a corpse.
What prowess is it fallen foes to slay?
Good counsel give I, planning good for thee,
And of all joys the sweetest is to learn   1065
From one who speaketh well, should that bring gain.

   Creon.   Old man, as archers aiming at their mark,
So ye shoot forth your venomed darts at me;
I know your augur's tricks, and by your tribe
Long since am tricked and sold.   Yes, gain your gains,   1070
Get Sardis' amber metal, Indian gold;
That corpse ye shall not hide in any tomb.
Not though the eagles, birds of Zeus, should bear
Their carrion morsels to the throne of God,
Not even fearing this pollution dire,   1075
Will I consent to burial.   Well I know
That man is powerless to pollute the Gods.
But many fall, Teiresias, dotard old,
A shameful fall, who gloze their shameful words
For lucre's sake, with surface show of good.   1080

   Teir.   Ah me! Does no man know, does none consider . . . ?

   Creon.   Consider what?   What trite poor saw comes now?

   Teir.   How far good counsel is of all things best?

   Creon.   So far, I trow, as folly is worst ill.

   Teir.   Of that disease thy soul, alas! is full.   1085

   Creon.   I will not meet a seer with evil words.

   Teir.   Thou dost so, saying I divine with lies.

   Creon.   The race of seers is ever fond of gold.

   Teir.   And that of tyrants still loves lucre foul.

   Creon.   Dost know thou speak'st thy words of those that   1090
     rule?

   Teir.   I know.   Through me thou rul'st a city saved.

   Creon.   Wise seer art thou, yet given o'ermuch to wrong.

   Teir.   Thou'lt stir me to speak out my soul's dread secrets.

1071. **Sardis:** capital of Lydia in Asia Minor.   The "amber metal" is gold.
1082. **saw:** proverbial saying.

Creon. Out with them; only speak them not for gain.
Teir. So is 't, I trow, in all that touches thee. 1095
Creon. Know that thou shalt not bargain with my will.
Teir. Know, then, and know it well, that thou shalt see
Not many winding circuits of the sun,
Before thou giv'st as quittance for the dead,
A corpse by thee begotten; for that thou 1100
Hast to the ground cast one that walked on earth,
And foully placed within a sepulchre
A living soul; and now thou keep'st from them,
The Gods below, the corpse of one unblest,
Unwept, unhallowed, and in these things thou 1105
Can'st claim no part, nor yet the Gods above;
But they by thee are outraged; and they wait,
The sure though slow avengers of the grave,
The dread Erinnyes of the mighty Gods,
For thee in these same evils to be snared. 1110
Search well if I say this as one who sells
His soul for money. Yet a little while,
And in thy house the wail of men and women
Shall make it plain. And every city stirs
Itself in arms against thee, owning those 1115
Whose limbs the dogs have buried, or fierce wolves,
Or wingèd birds have brought the accursèd taint
To region consecrate. Doom like to this,
Sure darting as an arrow to its mark,
I launch at thee (for thou dost vex me sore), 1120
An archer aiming at the very heart,
And thou shalt not escape its fiery sting.
And now, O boy, lead thou me home again,
That he may vent his spleen on younger men,
And learn to keep his tongue more orderly, 1125
With better thoughts than this his present mood.

[*Exit.*

Chor. The man has gone, O king, predicting woe,
And well we know, since first our raven hair
Was mixed with gray, that never yet his words
Were uttered to our State and failed of truth. 1130
Creon. I know it too, 'tis that that troubles me.

1099. **quittance:** payment. 1109. **Erinnyes:** the Furies, or avenging deities.

To yield is hard, but, holding out, to smite
One's soul with sorrow, this is harder still.

   Chor. We need wise counsel, O Menoekeus' son.

   Creon. What shall I do? Speak thou, and I'll obey.   1135

   Chor. Go then, and free the maiden from her tomb,
And give a grave to him who lies exposed.

   Creon. Is this thy counsel? Dost thou bid me yield?

   Chor. Without delay, O king, for lo! they come,
The Gods' swift-footed ministers of ill,   1140
And in an instant lay the self-willed low.

   Creon. Ah me! 'tis hard; and yet I bend my will
To do thy bidding. With necessity
We must not fight at such o'erwhelming odds.

   Chor. Go then and act! Commit it not to others.   1145

   Creon. E'en as I am I'll go. Come, come, my men,
Present or absent, come, and in your hands
Bring axes: come to yonder eminence.
And I, since now my judgment leans that way,
Who myself bound her, now myself will loose,   1150
Too much I fear lest it should wisest prove
Maintaining ancient laws to end my life.

                      [Exit. . . .

Enter Messenger.

   Mess. Ye men of Cadmos and Amphion's house,
I know no life of mortal man which I
Would either praise or blame. 'Tis Fortune's chance   1155
That raiseth up, and Fortune bringeth low,
The man who lives in good or evil plight;
And prophet of men's future there is none.
For Creon, so I deemed, deserved to be
At once admired and envied, having saved   1160
This land of Cadmos from the hands of foes;
And, having ruled with fullest sovereignty,
He lived and prospered, joyous in a race
Of goodly offspring. Now, all this is gone;
For when men lose the joys that sweeten life,   1165
I cannot deem they live, but rather count
As if a breathing corpse. His heaped-up stores
Of wealth are large, so be it, and he lives
With all a sovereign's state; and yet, if joy

Be absent, all the rest I count as nought,　1170
And would not weigh them against pleasure's charm,
More than a vapor's shadow.
　Chor.　　　　　What is this?
What new disaster tell'st thou of our chiefs?
　Mess.　Dead are they, and the living cause their death.
　Chor.　Who slays, and who is slaughtered?　Tell thy tale.　1175
　Mess.　Haemon is dead, slain, weltering in his blood.
　Chor.　By his own act, or by his father's hand?
　Mess.　His own, in wrath against his father's crime.
　Chor.　O prophet! true, most true, those words of thine.
　Mess.　Since things stand thus, we well may counsel take.　1180
　Chor.　Lo!　Creon's wife comes, sad Eurydike.
She from the house approaches, hearing speech
About her son, or else by accident.

Enter EURYDIKE.

　Euryd.　I on my way, my friends, as suppliant bound,
To pay my vows at Pallas' shrine, have heard　1185
Your words, and so I chanced to draw the bolt
Of the half-opened door, when lo! a sound
Falls on my ears, of evil striking home,
And terror-struck I fall in deadly swoon
Back in my handmaids' arms; yet tell it me,　1190
Tell the tale once again, for I shall hear,
By long experience disciplined to grief.
　Mess.　Dear lady, I will tell thee: I was by,
And will not leave one word of truth untold.
Why should we smooth and gloze, where all too soon　1195
We should be found as liars?　Truth is still
The only safety.　Lo!　I went with him,
Thy husband, in attendance, to the edge
Of yonder plain, where still all ruthlessly
The corpse of Polyneikes lay exposed,　1200
Mangled by dogs.　And, having prayed to her,
The Goddess of all pathways, and to Pluto,
To temper wrath with pity, him they washed
With holy washing; and what yet was left

1185. **Pallas:** Pallas Athene, goddess of wisdom.　1202. **Goddess:** Hecate
who haunted the places where roads met.　1202. **Pluto:** god of the lower
world.

We burnt in branches freshly cut, and heaped   1205
A high-raised grave from out his native soil,
And then we entered on the stone-paved home,
Death's marriage-chamber for the ill-starred maid.
And some one hears, while standing yet afar,
Shrill voice of wailing near the bridal bower,   1210
By funeral rites unhallowed, and he comes
And tells my master, Creon. On his ears,
Advancing nearer, falls a shriek confused
Of bitter sorrow, and with groaning loud,
He utters one sad cry, " Me miserable!   1215
And am I then a prophet? Do I wend
This day the dreariest way of all my life?
My son's voice greets me. Go, my servants, go,
Quickly draw near, and standing by the tomb,
Search ye and see; and where the stone torn out   1220
Shall make an opening, look ye in, and say
If I hear Haemon's voice, or if my soul
Is cheated by the Gods." And then we searched,
As he, our master, in his frenzy bade us;
And, in the furthest corner of the vault,   1225
We saw her hanging by her neck, with cord
Of linen threads entwined, and him we found
Clasping her form in passionate embrace,
And mourning o'er the doom that robbed him of her,
His father's deed, and that his marriage bed,   1230
So full of woe. When Creon saw him there,
Groaning aloud in bitterness of heart,
He goes to him, and calls in wailing voice,
" Poor boy! what hast thou done? Hast thou then lost
Thy reason? In what evil sinkest thou?   1235
Come forth, my child, on bended knee I ask thee."
And then the boy, with fierce, wild-gleaming eyes,
Glared at him, spat upon his face, and draws,
Still answering nought, the sharp two-handled sword.
Missing his aim (his father from the blow   1240
Turning aside) in anger with himself,
The poor ill-doomed one, even as he was,
Fell on his sword, and drove it through his breast,
Full half its length, and clasping, yet alive,
The maiden's arm, still soft, he there breathes out   1245

In broken gasps, upon her fair white cheek,
Swift stream of bloody shower. So they lie,
Dead bridegroom with dead bride, and he has gained,
Poor boy, his marriage rites in Hades home,
And left to all men witness terrible,   1250
That man's worst ill is want of counsel wise.

                                                            [*Exit* EURYDIKE.
   Chor.   What dost thou make of this? She turneth back,
Before one word, or good or ill, she speaks.
   Mess.   I too am full of wonder. Yet with hopes
I feed myself, she will not think it meet,   1255
Hearing her son's woes, openly to wail
Out in the town, but to her handmaids there
Will give command to wail her woe at home.
Too trained a judgment has she so to err.
   Chor.   I know not. To my mind, or silence hard,   1260
Or vain wild cries, are signs of bitter woe.
   Mess.   Soon we shall know, within the house advancing,
If, in the passion of her heart, she hides
A secret purpose. Truly dost thou speak;
There is a terror in that silence hard.   1265
   Chor.   [*Seeing* CREON *approaching with the corpse of* HAEMON
    in his arms.]
And lo! the king himself is drawing nigh,
And in his hands he bears a record clear,
No woe (if I may speak) by others caused,
   Himself the great offender.

Enter CREON, *bearing* HAEMON's *body.*

   Creon.   Woe! for the sins of souls of evil mood,   1270
   Stern, mighty to destroy!
O ye who look on those of kindred race,
   The slayers and the slain,
Woe for mine own rash plans that prosper not!
Woe for thee, son; but new in life's career,   1275
   And by a new fate dying!
    Woe! woe!
   Thou diest, thou art gone,
Not by thine evil counsel, but by mine.
   Chor.   Ah me! Too late thou seem'st to see the right.   1280
   Creon.   Ah me!

I learn the grievous lesson. On my head,
God, pressing sore, hath smitten me and vexed,
In ways most rough and terrible (Ah me!)
Shattering my joy, as trampled under foot.
Woe! woe! Man's labors are but labor lost.   1285

Enter Second Messenger.

   Sec. Mess. My master! thou, as one who hast full store,
One source of sorrow bearest in thine arms,
And others in thy house, too soon, it seems,
Thou need'st must come and see.
   Creon.   And what remains
Worse evil than the evils that we bear?   1290
   Sec. Mess. Thy wife is dead, that corpse's mother true,
Ill-starred one, smitten with a blow just dealt.
   Creon. O agony!
Haven of Death, that none may pacify,
   Why dost thou thus destroy me?   1295
[*Turning to* MESSENGER.] O thou who comest, bringing in thy train
   Woes horrible to tell,
Thou tramplest on a man already slain.
What say'st thou? What new tidings bring'st to me?
   Ah me! ah me!   1300
Is it that now there waits in store for me
My own wife's death to crown my misery?
   Chor. Full clearly thou may'st see. No longer now
Does yon recess conceal her.

The gates open and show the dead body of EURYDIKE.

   Creon.   Woe is me!
This second ill I gaze on, miserable,   1305
What fate, yea, what still lies in wait for me?
Here in my arms I bear what was my son;
And there, O misery! look upon the dead.
Ah, wretched mother! ah, my son! my son!
   Sec. Mess. In frenzy wild she round the altar clung,   1310
And closed her darkening eyelids, and bewailed
The noble fate of Megareus, who died
Long since, and then again that corpse thou hast;

   1312. **Megareus:** one of the chief warriors of Thebes.

And last of all she cried a bitter cry
Against thy deeds, the murderer of thy sons.   1315
   Creon. Woe! woe! alas!
I shudder in my fear. Will no one strike
A deadly blow with sharp two-edgèd sword?
   Fearful my fate, alas!
And with a fearful woe full sore beset.   1320
   Sec. Mess. She in her death charged thee with being the cause
Of all their sorrows, these and those of old.
   Creon. And in what way struck she the murderous blow?
   Sec. Mess. With her own hand below her heart she stabbed,
Hearing her son's most pitiable fate.   1325
   Creon. Ah me! The fault is mine. On no one else,
Of all that live, the fearful guilt can come;
I, even I, did slay thee, woe is me!
I, yes, I speak the truth. Lead me, ye guards,
Lead me forth quickly; lead me out of sight,   1330
More crushed to nothing than is nothing's self.
   Chor. Thou counsellest gain, if gain there be in ills,
For present ills when shortest then are best.
   Creon. Oh, come thou then, come thou,
The last of all my dooms, that brings to me   1335
Best boon, my life's last day. Come then, oh come,
That never more I look upon the light.
   Chor. These things are in the future. What is near,
That we must do. O'er what is yet to come
They watch, to Whom that work of right belongs.   1340
   Creon. I did but pray for what I most desire.
   Chor. Pray thou for nothing then; for mortal man
There is no issue from a doom decreed.
   Creon. [*Looking at the two corpses.*] Lead me then forth, vain
     shadow that I am,
Who slew thee, O my son, unwillingly,   1345
And thee too — (O my sorrow!) — and I know not
Which way to look or turn. All near at hand
Is turned to evil; and upon my head
There falls a doom far worse than I can bear.
   Chor. Man's highest blessedness,   1350
   In wisdom chiefly stands;
And in the things that touch upon the Gods,
   'Tis best in word or deed

To shun unholy pride;
Great words of boasting bring great punishments, 1355
And so to gray-haired age
Teach wisdom at the last.

(E. H. Plumtre)

SUGGESTIONS FOR STUDY
On the Characters and General Import of the Play

1. Show how the opening speech of Antigone is typical of her character and attitude. What is the essential core of her character? What is "the higher law" to which she appeals? Study carefully lines 486–494 and also line 565 as the most valuable clues to her conduct.

2. Compare the behavior of Ismene with that of Antigone throughout the play. What traits of character does the latter possess which her sister lacks?

3. Account as fully as you can for the motives which actuate Creon. Why does he insist that Polyneikes shall lie unburied? Why does he enforce the strictest observance of his edict? Look up the Greek idea of life after death.

4. Since they admired, above all, moderation and prudence, the Greeks believed that overconfidence and insolence toward gods and men — *hybris,* as they called it — inevitably brought about its *nemesis* or retribution. Do you think that Creon was guilty of *hybris* and thus incurred a just punishment?

5. Explain the first speech of Haemon in view of his subsequent conduct. What is the rôle of Teiresias in the play?

6. In view of the fact that the Greeks believed a tragedy should search and purify, consider these questions: To what extent is the course of the action determined by destiny? Does fate absolve the characters of responsibility for their acts? What is the final "moral" of the drama? How would it differ for an ancient Greek and for a modern reader?

7. The speeches in Greek tragedies abound in generalizations and sententious sayings about life and human relations. Pick out some of these in the speeches of Antigone, Ismene, and Haemon. Debate any of these which seem to you false or open to question.

8. What is Creon's attitude toward women? How far does Ismene accept it? To what extent is Antigone a rebel at this point? What does Creon say about money? About anarchy? How do his ideas on these subjects agree with your own?

On the Technique of the Play

9. How much of the action takes place off stage? What was Shakespeare's practice in this matter? In general what is modern practice?

How did the Greeks differ from us in what they considered suitable for action on the stage? How have the movies affected present technique in the matter of off-stage action?

10. Study the nature and function of the chorus (page 928). Where does the chorus in *Antigone* confine itself to comment and where does it participate more actively? Do you find the chorus helpful or detrimental to your enjoyment of the play?

11. Express in your own words the essential thought of each of the four choric songs beginning lines 107, 363, 626, and 837, respectively. Indicate any change in the point of view and sympathy of the chorus during the course of the play. Where does the change occur? What reasons can you suggest for it?

12. It was the practice in Greek tragedies to intersperse the longer speeches of the actors with a quick interchange of short speeches, often of only one line each. Select examples of this in *Antigone*. What is the advantage of this method?

On Collateral Reading

13. Revival of the Greek method of presenting plays has been undertaken in many colleges. Have you witnessed such a performance? If so, discuss it. Plan the costuming and setting for a presentation of this play. Consult books on Greek theater, art, and architecture.

14. If you have derived interest and enjoyment from *Antigone,* read also a good translation of Sophocles' *Oedipus the King,* Euripides' *The Trojan Women,* or other Greek plays. Read Swinburne's *Atalanta in Calydon* as an excellent modern imitation of the Greek tragedy. The choric songs are especially fine.

15. Vocabulary: sepulture, rites, trow, portent, wanton, unscathed, subverters, sheen, requite, flout, immure, trite, meed, darkling, succor, augury, dotard, lucre.

THUCYDIDES (471?–400? B.C.)

Thucydides was the greatest of Greek historians. The material for a biography is scanty, but we do know that he was born in Athens of a wealthy and prominent family, that he held high command in the Athenian army in the Peloponnesian War but was exiled because of dissatisfaction with his conduct of affairs. He has been called the first great war correspondent, but he was in reality much more than that. His mental grasp enabled him to seize the general significance of particular events. The Peloponnesian War (431–404 B.C.) which he narrates in his *History,* was fought between Athens and her allies on the one side and Sparta and her allies on the other. It resulted in the defeat of Athens and the end of her dominion. Thucydides, who had seen the war as an active participant and from various points of view, was convinced of its tremendous importance. He hoped to glean lessons from it which would be profitable, as he expressed it, for " those who desire an exact knowledge of the past as a key to the future, which in all probability will repeat or resemble the past. The work is meant to be a possession forever, not the rhetorical triumph of an hour." The *History* is graphically written and contains some famous passages, such as the description of the plague at Athens and the narrative of the ill-fated Athenian expedition to Sicily. Nearly a quarter of it is made up of speeches, which Thucydides freely composed from memory or report. The best known of these is the Funeral Oration of Pericles. It amounts to a glorification of the free, liberal spirit of Athens. Pericles (495?–429 B.C.) was the Athenian statesman and orator after whom the most brilliant period of Greek culture is often named.

THE FUNERAL ORATION OF PERICLES

In the same winter the Athenians gave a funeral at the public cost to those who had first fallen in this war. It was a custom of their ancestors, and the manner of it is as follows. Three days before the ceremony, the bones of the dead are laid out in a tent which has been erected; and their friends bring to their relatives such offerings as they please. In the funeral procession cypress coffins are borne in cars, one for each tribe; the bones of the deceased being placed in the coffin of their tribe. Among these is carried one empty bier decked for the missing, that is, for those whose bodies could not be recovered. Any citizen or stranger who pleases, joins in the procession: and the female relatives are there to wail at the burial. The dead are laid in the public sepulcher in the beautiful suburb of the city, in which those who fall in war are always buried; with the exception of those slain at Marathon, who for their singular and extraordinary valor were interred on the spot where they fell. After the bodies have been laid in the earth, a man chosen by the state, of approved wisdom, and eminent reputation, pronounces over them an appropriate panegyric,[1] after which all retire. Such is the manner of the burying; and throughout the whole of the war, whenever the occasion arose, the established custom was observed. Meanwhile these were the first that had fallen, and Pericles, son of Xanthippus, was chosen to pronounce their eulogium.[2] When the proper time arrived, he advanced from the sepulcher to an elevated platform in order to be heard by as many of the crowd as possible, and spoke as follows:

" Most of my predecessors in this place have commended him who

---

[1] **panegyric:** discourse of praise.   [2] **eulogium:** eulogy.

made this speech part of the law, telling us that it is well that it should be delivered at the burial of those who fall in battle. For myself, I should have thought that the worth which had displayed itself in deeds, would be sufficiently rewarded by honors also shown by deeds; such as you now see in this funeral prepared at the people's cost. And I could have wished that the reputations of many brave men were not to be imperiled in the mouth of a single individual, to stand or fall according as he spoke well or ill. For it is hard to speak properly upon a subject where it is even difficult to convince your hearers that you are speaking the truth. On the one hand, the friend who is familiar with every fact of the story, may think that some point has not been set forth with that fulness which he wishes and knows it to deserve; on the other, he who is a stranger to the matter may be led by envy to suspect exaggeration if he hears anything above his own nature. For men can endure to hear others praised only so long as they can severally persuade themselves of their own ability to equal the actions recounted: when this point is passed, envy comes in and with it incredulity. However, since our ancestors have stamped this custom with their approval, it becomes my duty to obey the law and to try to satisfy your several wishes and opinions as best I may.

" I shall begin with our ancestors: it is both just and proper that they should have the honor of the first mention on an occasion like the present. They dwelt in the country without break in the succession from generation to generation, and handed it down free to the present time by their valor. And if our more remote ancestors deserve praise, much more do our own fathers, who added to their inheritance the empire which we now possess, and spared no pains to be able to leave their acquisitions to us of the present generation. Lastly, there are few parts of our dominions that have not been augmented by those of us here, who are still more or less in the vigor of life; while the mother country has been furnished by us with everything that can enable her to depend on her own resources whether for war or for peace. That part of our history which tells of the military achievements which gave us our several possessions, or of the ready valor with which either we or our fathers stemmed the tide of Hellenic or foreign aggression, is a theme too familiar to my hearers for me to dilate [3] on, and I shall therefore pass it by. But what was the road by which we reached our position, what the form of government under which our greatness grew, what the national habits out of which it sprang — these are questions which I may try to solve before I pro-

---

[3] **dilate**: enlarge.

ceed to my panegyric upon these men; since I think this to be a subject upon which on the present occasion a speaker may properly dwell, and to which the whole assemblage, whether citizens or foreigners, may listen with advantage.

"Our constitution does not copy the laws of neighboring states; we are rather a pattern to others than imitators ourselves. Its administration favors the many instead of the few; this is why it is called a democracy. If we look to the laws, they afford equal justice to all in their private differences; if to social standing, advancement in public life falls to reputation for capacity, class considerations not being allowed to interfere with merit; nor again does poverty bar the way; if a man is able to serve the state, he is not hindered by the obscurity of his condition. The freedom which we enjoy in our government extends also to our ordinary life. There, far from exercising a jealous surveillance over each other, we do not feel called upon to be angry with our neighbor for doing what he likes, or even to indulge in those injurious looks which cannot fail to be offensive, although they inflict no positive penalty. But all this ease in our private relations does not make us lawless as citizens. Against this fear is our chief safeguard, teaching us to obey the magistrates and the laws, particularly such as regard the protection of the injured, whether they are actually on the statute book, or belong to that code which, although unwritten, yet cannot be broken without acknowledged disgrace.

"Further, we provide plenty of means for the mind to refresh itself from business. We celebrate games and sacrifices all the year round, and the elegance of our private establishments forms a daily source of pleasure and helps to banish the spleen; [4] while the magnitude of our city draws the produce of the world into our harbor, so that to the Athenian the fruits of other countries are as familiar a luxury as those of his own.

"If we turn to our military policy, there also we differ from our antagonists. We throw open our city to the world, and never by alien acts exclude foreigners from any opportunity of learning or observing, although the eyes of an enemy may occasionally profit by our liberality; trusting less in system and policy than to the native spirit of our citizens; while in education, where our rivals from their very cradles by a painful discipline seek after manliness, at Athens we live exactly as we please, and yet are just as ready to encounter every legitimate danger. In proof of this it may be noticed that the Lacedaemonians [5] do not invade our country alone, but bring with them

---

[4] **spleen:** low spirits.   [5] **Lacedaemonians:** Spartans.

all their confederates; while we Athenians advance unsupported into the territory of a neighbor, and fighting upon a foreign soil usually vanquish with ease men who are defending their homes. Our united force was never yet encountered by any enemy, because we have at once to attend to our marine and to dispatch our citizens by land upon a hundred different services; so that, wherever they engage with some such fraction of our strength, a success against a detachment is magnified into a victory over the nation, and a defeat into a reverse suffered at the hands of the entire people. And yet if with habits not of labor but of ease, and courage not of art but of nature, we are still willing to encounter danger, we have the double advantage of escaping the experience of hardships in anticipation and of facing them in the hour of need as fearlessly as those who are never free from them.

" Nor are these the only points in which our city is worthy of admiration. We cultivate refinement without extravagance and knowledge without effeminacy; wealth we employ more for use than for show, and place the real disgrace of poverty not in owning to the fact but in declining the struggle against it. Our public men have, besides politics, their private affairs to attend to, and our ordinary citizens, though occupied with the pursuits of industry, are still fair judges of public matters; for, unlike any other nation, regarding him who takes no part in these duties not as unambitious but as useless, we Athenians are able to judge at all events if we cannot originate, and instead of looking on discussion as a stumbling-block in the way of action, we think it an indispensable preliminary to any wise action at all. Again, in our enterprises we present the singular spectacle of daring and deliberation, each carried to its highest point, and both united in the same persons; although usually decision is the fruit of ignorance, hesitation of reflection. But the palm of courage will surely be adjudged most justly to those who best know the difference between hardship and pleasure and yet are never tempted to shrink from danger. In generosity we are equally singular, acquiring our friends by conferring not by receiving favors. Yet, of course, the doer of the favor is the firmer friend of the two, in order by continued kindness to keep the recipient in his debt; while the debtor feels less keenly from the very consciousness that the return he makes will be a payment, not a free gift. And it is only the Athenians who, fearless of consequences, confer their benefits not from calculations of expediency, but in the confidence of liberality.

" In short, I say that as a city we are the school of Hellas; while I doubt if the world can produce a man, who where he has only himself to depend upon, is equal to so many emergencies, and graced by so happy a versatility as the Athenian. And that this is no mere boast thrown out for the occasion, but plain matter of fact, the power of the state acquired by these habits proves. For Athens alone of her contemporaries is found when tested to be greater than her reputation, and alone gives no occasion to her assailants to blush at the antagonist by whom they have been worsted, or to her subjects to question her title by merit to rule. Rather, the admiration of the present and succeeding ages will be ours, since we have not left our power without witness, but have shown it by mighty proofs; and far from needing a Homer for our panegyrist, or other of his craft whose verses might charm for the moment only for the impression which they gave to melt at the touch of fact, we have forced every sea and land to be the highway of our daring, and everywhere, whether for evil or for good, have left imperishable monuments behind us. Such is the Athens for which these men, in the assertion of their resolve not to lose her, nobly fought and died; and well may every one of their survivors be ready to suffer in her cause.

" Indeed if I have dwelt at some length upon the character of our country, it has been to show that our stake in the struggle is not the same as theirs who have no such blessings to lose, and also that the panegyric of the men over whom I am now speaking might be by definite proofs established. That panegyric is now in a great measure complete; for the Athens that I have celebrated is only what the heroism of these and their like have made her, men whose fame, unlike that of most Hellenes, will be found to be only commensurate with their deserts. And if a test of worth be wanted, it is to be found in their closing scene, and this not only in the cases in which it set the final seal upon their merit, but also in those in which it gave the first intimation of their having any. For there is justice in the claim that steadfastness in his country's battles should be as a cloak to cover a man's other imperfections; since the good action has blotted out the bad, and his merit as a citizen more than out-weighed his demerits as an individual. But none of these allowed either wealth with its prospect of future enjoyment to unnerve his spirit, or poverty with its hope of a day of freedom and riches to tempt him to shrink from danger. No, holding that vengeance upon their enemies was more to be desired than any personal blessings, and reckoning this to be the most glorious of hazards, they joyfully determined to accept the risk, to make sure of their vengeance and to let their wishes wait; and while committing to hope the uncertainty of final success, in the business before them they thought fit to act boldly and trust in themselves. Thus choosing to die resisting, rather than to live submitting, they fled only from dishonor, but met danger face to face, and after one brief moment, while at the summit of their fortune, escaped, not from their fear, but from their glory.

" So died these men as became Athenians. You, their survivors, must determine to have as unfaltering a resolution in the field, though you may pray that it may have a happier issue. And not contented with ideas derived only from words of the advantages which are bound up with the defense of your country, though these would furnish a valuable text to a speaker even before an audience so alive to them as the present, you must yourselves realize the power of Athens, and feed your eyes upon her from day to day, till love of her fills your hearts; and then when all her greatness shall break upon you, you must reflect that it was by courage, sense of duty, and a keen feeling of honor in action that men were enabled to win all this, and that no personal failure in an enterprise could make them consent to deprive their country of their valor, but they laid it at her feet as the most glorious contribution that they could offer. For this offering of their lives made in common by them all, they each of them individually received that renown which never grows old, and for a sepulcher, not so much that in which their bones have been deposited, but that noblest of shrines wherein their glory is laid up to be eternally remembered upon every occasion on which deed or story shall call for its commemoration. For heroes have the whole earth for their tomb; and in lands far from their own, where the column with its epitaph declares it, there is enshrined in every breast a record unwritten with no tablet to preserve it, except that of the heart. These take as your model, and judging happiness to be the fruit of freedom and freedom of valor, never decline the dangers of war. For it is not the miserable that would most justly be unsparing of their lives; these have nothing to hope for. It is rather they to whom continued life may bring reverses as yet unknown, and to whom a fall, if it came, would be most tremendous in its consequences. And surely, to a man of spirit, the degradation of cowardice must be immeasurably more grievous than the unfelt death which strikes him in the midst of his strength and patriotism!

" Comfort, therefore, not condolence, is what I have to offer to the parents of the dead who may be here. Numberless are the chances to which, as they know, the life of man is subject; but fortunate indeed are they who draw for their lot a death so glorious as that which has caused your mourning, and to whom life has been so exactly measured as to terminate in the happiness in which it has been passed. Still I know that this is a hard saying, especially when those are in question of whom you will constantly be reminded by seeing in the homes of others blessings of which once you also boasted; for grief is felt not so much for the want of what we have never known, as for the loss of that to which we have been long accustomed. Yet you who are still of an age to beget children must bear up in the hope of having others in their stead; not only will they help you to forget those whom you have lost, but will be to the state at once a reinforcement and a security; for never can a fair or just policy be expected of the citizen who does not, like his fellows, bring to the decision the interests and apprehensions of a father. While those of you who have passed your prime must congratulate yourselves with the thought that the best part of your life was fortunate, and that the brief span that remains will be cheered by the fame of the departed. For it is only the love of honor that never grows old; and honor it is, not gain, as some would have it, that rejoices the heart of age and help-lessness.

"Turning to the sons or brothers of the dead, I see an arduous struggle before you. When a man is gone, all are wont to praise him, and should your merit be ever so transcendent,[6] you will still find it difficult not merely to overtake, but even to approach their renown. The living have envy to contend with, while those who are no longer in our path are honored with a good will into which rivalry does not enter. On the other hand, if I must say anything on the subject of female excellence to those of you who will now be in widowhood, it will be all comprised in this brief exhortation. Great will be your glory in not falling short of your natural character; and greatest will be hers who is least talked of among the men whether for good or for bad.

"My task is now finished. I have performed it to the best of my ability, and in word, at least, the requirements of the law are now satisfied. If deeds be in question, those who are here interred have received part of their honors already, and for the rest, their children will be brought up till manhood at the public expense. The state thus offers a valuable prize, as the garland of victory in this race of valor, for the reward both of those who have fallen and their survivors.

[6] **transcendent:** surpassing.

And where the rewards for merit are greatest, there are found the best citizens.

" And now that you have brought to a close your lamentations for your relatives, you may depart."

(Richard Crawley)

SUGGESTIONS FOR STUDY

1. Describe the funeral rites which called forth this oration. What part of the ceremony has had its counterpart in our own time?

2. How does Pericles define a democracy? What kind of liberty do the Athenians possess? What are some of its results? Modern critics of democratic liberty sometimes assert that it makes men self-centered and indifferent to the public welfare. What is the contention of Pericles about this matter?

3. What specific virtues does he think the free exercise of liberty has bred in the Athenians? How much mention is made of discipline? Discuss the question whether liberty should not be accompanied by discipline, and how and by whom the latter should be exercised.

4. Pericles says nothing about the existence of slaves, who nevertheless constituted a fairly large proportion of the inhabitants of Athens. How does this situation affect the picture he paints?

5. What does Pericles say about the treatment of foreigners in Athens? The use of wealth? The greatest glory of a woman? How do all of these comments compare with present American ideas?

6. What would you say of the reasoning power shown in this oration? Of the eloquence? Pick out the sentences which you think are particularly memorable.

7. Compare the situation and the speech as a whole with Lincoln's " Gettysburg Address." With Webster's " Bunker Hill Speech." Compare the Athenians' attitude toward liberty with that of the Americans, as described in Burke's " Speech on Conciliation." How does the emotional tone compare with Patrick Henry's famous speech before the Virginia convention? Compare the ideas on liberty and the eloquence of Pericles with those shown by current speeches of note which you gather from magazines or newspapers.

8. Write an original oration interpreting American democracy as Pericles did Athenian.

ARISTOPHANES (448?–380? B.C.)

Aristophanes, the greatest comic poet of antiquity, was an Athenian of the Athenians. He was very conservative by temperament and opposed to changes of all sorts, particularly to manifestations of democracy. He employed his polished wit to satirize Socrates, in *The Clouds,* as a disturber of men's thoughts, and to attack Euripides, in *The Frogs,* as an innovator in the tragic drama. Other comedies of his, among the eleven that have been preserved, are *The Birds, The Wasps,* and *Lysistrata.* The essence of the Old Comedy, of which he is the supreme representative, was to criticize unsparingly persons and institutions, both for the sake of furnishing amusement and in order to curb misconduct and folly. A great drawback to the enjoyment of Aristophanes is the difficulty of understanding his numerous references to contemporary matters.

THE FROGS

In *The Frogs,* Bacchus, accompanied by his slave Xanthias, has descended to the lower world to get a tragic poet to take back to Athens. As the following scene opens, Charon is waiting by the river Styx to ferry Bacchus across. The play ends in a dramatic contest between Aeschylus and Euripides. Bacchus awards the prize to the former and takes him back to the world of living men. The Chorus in the play was made up of men dressed to represent frogs. The region near the theater in Athens was marshy.

Charon. Hoy! Bear a hand, there. — Heave ashore.
Bacchus. What's this?
Xanthias. The lake it is, the place he told us of.
By Jove! and there's the boat, and here's old Charon.
Bacchus. Well, Charon! Welcome, Charon! Welcome kindly!
Charon. Who wants the ferryman? Anybody waiting   5
To remove from the sorrows of life? A passage anybody
To Lethe's wharf? — to Cerberus's Reach?
To Tartarus? — to Taenarus? — to Perdition?
Bacchus. Yes, I.
Charon. Get in then.
Bacchus. [*Hesitatingly*] Tell me, where are you going?
To Perdition really — ?
Charon. [*Not sarcastically, but civilly, in the way of business*]
Yes, to oblige you, I will.   10
With all my heart — Step in there.
Bacchus. Have a care!
Take care, good Charon! Charon, have a care!

---

7. **Lethe:** the river of forgetfulness in the lower world. 7. **Cerberus:** the dog that guarded the lower world. 8. **Tartarus:** place of punishment of the wicked. 8. **Taenarus:** town in the Peloponnesus.

BACCHUS *gets into the boat.*

Come, Xanthias, come!

Charon.   I take no slaves aboard
Except they've volunteered for the naval victory.

Xanthias.   I could not: — I was suffering with sore eyes.   15
Charon.   You must trudge away then, round by the end of the lake
there.

Xanthias.   And whereabouts shall I wait?
Charon.   At the Stone of Repentance,
By the Slough of Despond beyond the Tribulations;
You understand me?

Xanthias.   Yes, I understand you;
A lucky, promising direction, truly.

Charon. [*To* BACCHUS] Sit down at the oar.   20
Come quick, if there's more coming!

[*To* BACCHUS *again*] Holloh! what's that you're doing? [BAC-
CHUS *is seated in a buffoonish attitude on the side of the boat
where the oar was fastened.*]

Bacchus.   What you told me.
I'm sitting at the oar.

Charon.   Sit *there,* I tell you,
You Fatguts; that's your place.

Bacchus. [*Changes his place*].
Well, so I do.   25

Charon.   Now ply your hands and arms.
Bacchus. [*Makes a silly motion with his arms*] Well, so I do.
Charon.   You'd best leave off your fooling. Take to the oar.
And pull away.

Bacchus.   But how shall I contrive?
I've never served on board. — I'm only a landsman;
I'm quite unused to it. —

Charon.   We can manage it.
As soon as you begin you shall have some music   30
That will teach you to keep time.

Bacchus.   What music's that?
Charon.   A chorus of Frogs — uncommon musical Frogs.
Bacchus.   Well, give me the word and the time.
Charon.   Whooh up, up; whooh up, up.

---

14. **victory:** slaves who volunteered for military or naval service were
given their freedom.   17. **Slough of Despond:** an expression from Bunyan's
Pilgrim's Progress, here used appropriately by the translator.

CHORUS

Brekeke-kesh, koash, koash,
Shall the Choral Quiristers of the Marsh   35
Be censured and rejected as hoarse and harsh;
   And their Chromatic essays
    Deprived of praise?
No, let us raise afresh
Our obstreperous Brekeke-kesh;   40
The customary croak and cry
   Of the creatures
    At the theaters,
In their yearly revelry.
Brekeke-kesh, koash, koash.   45
  Bacchus. [*Rowing in great misery*] How I'm mauled.
     How I'm galled;
    Worn and mangled to a mash —
    There they go! " *Koash, koash!* "
  Frogs. Brekeke-kesh, koash, koash.   50
  Bacchus. Oh, beshrew
    All your crew;
You don't consider how I smart.
  Frogs. Now for a sample of the Art!
    Brekeke-kesh, koash, koash.   55
  Bacchus. I wish you hanged, with all my heart.
    Have you nothing else to say?
" *Brekeke-kesh, koash* " all day!
  Frogs. We've a right, we've a right;
    And we croak at ye for spite.   60
    We've a right, we've a right;
    Day and night, day and night;
    Night and day,
    Still to creak and croak away.
Phoebus and every Grace   65
Admire and approve of the croaking race;
And the egregious guttural notes
That are gargled and warbled in their lyrical throats.
    In reproof of your scorn

35. Quiristers: Choristers.   37. Chromatic: in music, employing semi-tones. The translator's use of capitals here and elsewhere is somewhat arbitrary. 65. Phoebus: Apollo. 67. egregious: notable.

Mighty Pan nods his horn; 70
Beating time to the rhyme
With his hoof, with his hoof.
Persisting in our plan
We proceed as we began,
Breke-kesh, breke-kesh, koash, koash. 75
Bacchus. Oh, the Frogs, consume and rot 'em,
I've a blister on my bottom
Hold your tongues you tuneful creatures.
Frogs. Cease with your profane entreaties
All in vain for ever striving: 80
   Silence is against our natures.
With the vernal heat reviving,
   Our aquatic crew repair
From their periodic sleep,
In the dark and chilly deep, 85
To the cheerful upper air;
Then we frolic here and there
All amidst the meadows fair;
Shady plants of asphodel
Are the lodges where we dwell; 90
Chanting in the leafy bowers
All the livelong summer hours,
Till the sudden gusty showers
Send us headlong, helter-skelter,
To the pool to seek for shelter; 95
Meager, eager, leaping, lunging,
From the sedgy wharfage plunging
To the tranquil depth below,
There we muster all a-row;
Where, secure from toil and trouble, 100
With a tuneful hubble-bubble,
Our symphonious accents flow
Brekeke-kesh, koash, koash.
Bacchus. I forbid you to proceed.
Frogs. That would be severe indeed; 105
Arbitrary, bold, and rash —
Brekeke-kesh, koash, koash.

---

70. **Pan:** god of shepherds, flocks and forests. 82. **vernal:** of springtime.
89. **asphodel:** the asphodel of the Greek poets is supposed to be a variety of
narcissus. 97. **sedgy wharfage:** resting-place on the sedge, or water-grass.

Bacchus. I command you to desist —
   —- Oh, my back, there! oh, my wrist!
     What a twist!   110
     What a sprain!

Frogs. Once again —
   We renew the tuneful strain.
   Brekeke-kesh, koash, koash.

Bacchus. I disdain — (Hang the pain!)   115
   All your nonsense, noise, and trash.
   O, my blister! O, my sprain!

Frogs. Brekeke-kesh, koash, koash.
   Friends and Frogs, we must display
   All our powers of voice today;   120
   Suffer not this stranger here,
   With fastidious foreign ear,
   To confound us and abash.
   Brekeke-kesh, koash, koash.

Bacchus. Well, my spirit is not broke,   125
   If it's only for the joke,
   I'll outdo you with a croak.
   Here it goes, [*Very loud*] " Koash, koash."

Frogs. Now for a glorious croaking crash,
   [*Still louder*] Brekeke-kesh, koash, koash.   130

Bacchus. [*Splashing with his oar*] I'll disperse you with a splash.

Frogs. Brekeke-kesh, koash, koash.

Bacchus. I'll subdue
   Your rebellious, noisy crew —
   Have amongst you there, slap-dash. [*Strikes at*   135
    them.]

Frogs. Brekeke-kesh, koash, koash.
   We defy your oar and you.

Charon. Hold! We're ashore just — shift your oar. Get out. —
Now pay your fare.

Bacchus. There — there it is — the twopence.

                        (*John Hookham Frere*)

SUGGESTIONS FOR STUDY

1. Does this scene appeal to you as funny? Discuss the question
whether its humor is of an irreverent character. Would it seem more or
less so to an Athenian than to us? Why?

2. How much does this scene tell you of the Greek idea of the world of the dead? Compare with Ulysses' journey to Hades in the Odyssey.

3. Note the metrical effects achieved by the Chorus. Do you think the imitation of the sound made by frogs is a good one? How does this Chorus satirize the Chorus in a tragedy?

4. Could this scene be effectively presented on the stage? If so, discuss how you would costume the characters and arrange the stage. Would the idea lend itself to a Walt Disney cartoon?

5. Compare this scene with those in Barrie's *Peter Pan* in which water and forest creatures appear on the stage. Do you know other comic fantasies of a similar nature?

6. Vocabulary: perdition, obstreperous, beshrew, aquatic, symphonious, fastidious, abash.

PLATO (427–347 B.C.)

Plato was, with the possible exception of his pupil Aristotle, the greatest of the Greek philosophers. He was born in Athens of a wealthy and aristocratic family. In his youth he is said to have distinguished himself in athletics and to have had ambitions as a poet. When he was about twenty years old he met Socrates and became his devoted disciple. After the death of Socrates in 399 B.C., he traveled widely for twelve years in order to gain a knowledge of the world. We are not certain of his movements, but he seems to have visited Sicily twice, presumably in the hope of seeing some of his schemes for political reforms put in practice. In 387 B.C. he settled again in Athens and gathered about him a group of followers, whom he taught in the garden or grove of Academus, henceforth known as Plato's Academy. He died in Athens at the age of eighty, hard at work until the last.

Socrates (469–399 B.C.), the master of Plato, left no writings. Books, he said, could not answer questions, but men might. So he preferred to talk with men on the street and in the market-place, and, by dint of skillful questioning, induce them to think. He attracted in time a group of enthusiastic followers, and to two of these, Plato and Xenophon, we owe most of our knowledge of him. Some of the young men who had associated with him became involved in dubious political enterprises, and the Athenians vented their resentment upon Socrates, whom they condemned to death for corrupting the youth and introducing new divinities. The second charge referred to the conviction of Socrates that he possessed an in-dwelling spirit which often guided him aright. Various things combined to make Socrates an unforgettable figure — his physical and moral courage, his frank, modest friendliness, his humor, and even his physical ugliness. He is perhaps more truly alive today than any other man of antiquity. His teaching was of an ethical and practical nature and was exemplified in his own life. It seemed to him that the beginning of wisdom was to know oneself and to admit ignorance of other matters. But since for him wisdom was synonymous with virtue, an increase in knowledge was in every way desirable for the good life.

Plato's writings consist of dialogues which, with a single exception, are built up around the figure of Socrates. Their simplicity and beauty of expression have given them an assured place in literature as well as in philosophy. It is generally believed that the earlier dialogues represent pretty faithfully the teaching of Socrates, while the later ones develop Plato's own philosophy. Among the most noted are the *Apology, Crito,* and *Phaedo,* which are concerned with the trial and death of Socrates, the *Symposium* and *Phaedrus,* which expound certain of Plato's most characteristic doctrines, and his masterpiece, the *Republic,* a description of an ideal state, the most famous of all Utopias. Plato's special contribution to philosophy was the doctrine of ideas. He taught that ideas were more real than things, that they furnished the perfect models, of which particular things were but faulty copies. But ideas, though infinite in number, vary greatly in worth. At the top of the scale of values, supreme over all, are the eternal ideals of the True, the Good, and the Beautiful. Plato's influence has never ceased to be felt and is still potent today.

THE APOLOGY OF SOCRATES

There are many reasons why I am not grieved, O men of Athens, at the vote of condemnation. I expected this, and am only surprised that the votes are so nearly equal; for I had thought that the majority against me would have been far larger; but now, had thirty votes gone over to the other side, I should have been acquitted. And I may say that I have escaped Meletus.[1] And I may say more; for without the assistance of Anytus and Lycon, he would not have had a fifth part of the votes, as the law requires, in which case he would have incurred a fine of a thousand drachmae,[2] as is evident.

And so he proposes death as the penalty. And what shall I propose on my part, O men of Athens? Clearly that which is my due. And what is that which I ought to pay or to receive? What shall be done to the man who has never had the wit to be idle during his whole life; but has been careless of what the many care about — wealth, and family interests, and military offices, and speaking in the assembly, and magistracies, and plots, and parties. Reflecting that I was really too honest a man to follow in this way and live, I did not go where

---

[1] **Meletus:** the chief accuser of Socrates. He was assisted by Anytus and Lycon.

[2] **drachmae:** Greek silver coins of various values.

I could do no good to you or to myself; but where I could do the greatest good privately to every one of you, thither I went, and sought to persuade every man among you, that he must look to himself, and seek virtue and wisdom before he looks to his private interests, and look to the state before he looks to the interests of the state; and that this should be the order which he observes in all his actions. What shall be done to such a one? Doubtless some good thing, O men of Athens, if he has his reward; and the good should be of a kind suitable to him. What would be a reward suitable to a poor man who is your benefactor, who desires leisure that he may instruct you? There can be no more fitting reward than maintenance in the prytaneum,[3] O men of Athens, a reward which he deserves far more than the citizen who has won the prize at Olympia in the horse or chariot race, whether the chariots were drawn by two horses or by many. For I am in want, and he has enough; and he only gives you the appearance of happiness, and I give you the reality. And if I am to estimate the penalty justly, I say that maintenance in the prytaneum is the just return.

Perhaps you may think that I am braving you in saying this, as in what I said before about the tears and prayers. But that is not the case. I speak rather because I am convinced that I never intentionally wronged any one, although I cannot convince you of that — for we have had a short conversation only; but if there were a law at Athens, such as there is in other cities, that a capital cause should not be decided in one day, then I believe that I should have convinced you; but now the time is too short. I cannot in a moment refute great slanders; and, as I am convinced that I never wronged another, I will assuredly not wrong myself. I will not say of myself that I deserve any evil, or propose any penalty. Why should I? Because I am afraid of the penalty of death which Meletus proposes? When I do not know whether death is a good or an evil, why should I propose a penalty which would certainly be an evil? Shall I say imprisonment? And why should I live in prison, and be the slave of the magistrates of the year — of the eleven? Or shall the penalty be a fine, and imprisonment until the fine is paid? There is the same objection. I should have to lie in prison, for money I have none, and cannot pay. And if I say exile (and this may possibly be the penalty which you will affix), I must indeed be blinded by the love of life, if I were to consider that when you, who are my

---

[3] **prytaneum:** public hall in Athens for the entertainment of ambassadors and honored citizens.

own citizens, cannot endure my discourses and words, and have found them so grievous and odious that you would fain have done with them, others are likely to endure me. No indeed, men of Athens, that is not very likely. And what a life should I lead, at my age, wandering from city to city, living in ever-changing exile, and always being driven out! For I am quite sure that into whatever place I go, as here so also there, the young men will come to me; and if I drive them away, their elders will drive me out at their desire: and if I let them come, their fathers and friends will drive me out for their sakes.

Some one will say: Yes, Socrates, but cannot you hold your tongue, and then you may go into a foreign city, and no one will interfere with you? Now I have great difficulty in making you understand my answer to this. For if I tell you that this would be a disobedience to a divine command, and therefore that I cannot hold my tongue, you will not believe that I am serious; and if I say again that the greatest good of man is daily to converse about virtue, and all that concerning which you hear me examining myself and others, and that the life which is unexamined is not worth living — that you are still less likely to believe. And yet what I say is true, although a thing of which it is hard for me to persuade you. Moreover, I am not accustomed to think that I deserve any punishment. Had I money I might have proposed to give you what I had, and have been none the worse. But you see that I have none, and can only ask you to proportion the fine to my means. However, I think that I could afford a mina,[4] and therefore I propose that penalty; Plato, Crito, Critobulus, and Apollodorus, my friends here, bid me say thirty minae, and they will be the sureties. Well, then, say thirty minae, let that be the penalty; for that they will be ample security to you.

Not much time will be gained, O Athenians, in return for the evil name which you will get from the detractors of the city, who will say that you killed Socrates, a wise man; for they will call me wise even although I am not wise when they want to reproach you. If you had waited a little while, your desire would have been fulfilled in the course of nature. For I am far advanced in years, as you may perceive, and not far from death. I am speaking now only to those of you who have condemned me to death. And I have another thing to say to them: You think that I was convicted through deficiency of words — I mean, that if I had thought fit to leave nothing undone,

4 **mina**: perhaps about twenty-five dollars in our money.

nothing unsaid, I might have gained an acquittal. Not so; the deficiency which led to my conviction was not of words — certainly not. But I had not the boldness or impudence or inclination to address you as you would have liked me to address you, weeping and wailing and lamenting, and saying and doing many things which you have been accustomed to hear from others, and which, as I say, are unworthy of me. But I thought that I ought not to do anything common or mean in the hour of danger: nor do I now repent of the manner of my defense, and I would rather die having spoken after my manner, than speak in your manner and live. For neither in war nor yet at law ought any man to use every way of escaping death. For often in battle there is no doubt that if a man will throw away his arms, and fall on his knees before his pursuers, he may escape death; and in other dangers there are other ways of escaping death if a man is willing to say and do anything. The difficulty, my friends, is not in avoiding death, but in avoiding unrighteousness; for that runs faster than death. I am old and move slowly, and the slower runner has overtaken me, and my accusers are keen and quick, and the faster runner, who is unrighteousness, has overtaken them. And now I depart hence condemned by you to suffer the penalty of death, and they too go their ways condemned by the truth to suffer the penalty of villainy and wrong; and I must abide by my award — let them abide by theirs. I suppose that these things may be regarded as fated — and I think that they are well.

And now, O men who have condemned me, I would fain prophesy to you; for I am about to die, and that is the hour in which men are gifted with prophetic power. And I prophesy to you who are my murderers, that immediately after my death punishment far heavier than you have inflicted on me will surely await you. Me you have killed because you wanted to escape the accuser, and not to give an account of your lives. But that will not be as you suppose: far otherwise. For I say that there will be more accusers of you than there are now; accusers whom hitherto I have restrained; and as they are younger they will be more severe with you, and you will be more offended at them. For if you think that by killing men you can avoid the accuser censuring your lives, you are mistaken; that is not a way of escape which is either possible or honorable; the easiest and the noblest way is not to be crushing others, but to be improving yourselves. This is the prophecy which I utter before my departure to the judges who have condemned me.

Friends, who would have acquitted me, I would like also to talk with you about this thing which has happened, while the magistrates are busy, and before I go to the place at which I must die. Stay then a while, for we may as well talk with one another while there is time. You are my friends, and I should like to show you the meaning of this event which has happened to me. O my judges — for you I may truly call judges — I should like to tell you of a wonderful circumstance. Hitherto the familiar oracle [5] within me has constantly been in the habit of opposing me even about trifles, if I was going to make a slip or error about anything; and now as you see there has come upon me that which may be thought, and is generally believed to be, the last and worst evil. But the oracle made no sign of opposition, either as I was leaving my house and going out in the morning, or when I was going up into this court, or while I was speaking, at anything which I was going to say; and yet I have often been stopped in the middle of a speech, but now in nothing I either said or did touching this matter has the oracle opposed me. What do I take to be the explanation of this? I will tell you. I regard this as a proof that what has happened to me is a good, and that those of us who think that death is an evil are in error. This is a great proof to me of what I am saying, for the customary sign would surely have opposed me had I been going to evil and not to good.

Let us reflect in another way, and we shall see that there is great reason to hope that death is a good, for one of two things: either death is a state of nothingness and utter unconsciousness, or, as men say, there is a change and migration of the soul from this world to another. Now if you suppose that there is no consciousness, but a sleep like the sleep of him who is undisturbed even by the sight of dreams, death will be an unspeakable gain. For if a person were to select the night in which his sleep was undisturbed even by dreams, and were to compare with this the other days and nights of his life, and then were to tell us how many days and nights he had passed in the course of his life better and more pleasantly than this one, I think that any man, I will not say a private man, but even the great king will not find many such days or nights, when compared with the others. Now if death is like this, I say that to die is gain; for eternity is then only a single night. But if death is the journey to another place, and there, as men say, all the dead are, what good, O my friends and judges, can be greater than this? If indeed when the

---

[5] **familiar oracle**: the *daimonion* or in-dwelling spirit which frequently **warned** Socrates not to do certain things.

pilgrim arrives in the world below, he is delivered from the professors of justice in this world, and finds the true judges who are said to give judgment there, Minos [6] and Rhadamanthus and Aeacus and Triptolemus,[7] and other sons of God who were righteous in their own life, that pilgrimage will be worth making. What would not a man give if he might converse with Orpheus [8] and Musaeus [9] and Hesiod [10] and Homer? Nay, if this be true, let me die again and again. I, too, shall have a wonderful interest in a place where I can converse with Palamedes,[11] and Ajax the son of Telamon,[12] and other heroes of old, who have suffered death through an unjust judgment; and there will be no small pleasure, as I think, in comparing my own suffering with theirs. Above all, I shall be able to continue my search into true and false knowledge; as in this world, so also in that! I shall find out who is wise, and who pretends to be wise, and is not. What would not a man give, O judges, to be able to examine the leader [13] of the great Trojan expedition; or Odysseus [14] or Sisyphus,[15] or numberless others, men and women too! What infinite delight would there be in conversing with them and asking them questions! For in that world they do not put a man to death for this; certainly not. For besides being happier in that world than in this, they will be immortal, if what is said is true.

Wherefore, O judges, be of good cheer about death, and know this of a truth — that no evil can happen to a good man, either in life or after death. He and his are not neglected by the gods; nor has my own approaching end happened by mere chance. But I see clearly that to die and be released was better for me; and therefore the oracle gave no sign. For which reason, also, I am not angry with my accusers or my condemners; they have done me no harm, although neither of them meant to do me any good; and for this I may gently blame them.

Still I have a favor to ask of them. When my sons are grown up,

[6] **Minos:** one of the judges of the lower world, along with Aeacus and Rhadamanthus.

[7] **Triptolemus:** mythical inventor of agriculture.

[8] **Orpheus:** in Greek legend, the chief representative of the art of song and playing on the lyre.

[9] **Musaeus:** son of Orpheus.

[10] **Hesiod:** father of Greek didactic poetry (eighth century B.C.).

[11] **Palamedes:** a hero of the Trojan War, along with Ajax.

[12] **Telamon:** a Greek hero in his own right.

[13] **leader:** Agamemnon.

[14] **Odysseus:** or Ulysses, hero of the *Odyssey.*

[15] **Sisyphus:** He was compelled in the under world to roll a heavy stone forever up a steep hill.

I would ask you, O my friends, to punish them; and I would have you trouble them, as I have troubled you, if they seem to care about riches, or anything, more than about virtue; or if they pretend to be something when they are really nothing — then reprove them, as I have reproved you, for not caring about that for which they ought to care, and thinking that they are something when they are really nothing. And if you do this, I and my sons will have received justice at your hands.

The hour of departure has arrived, and we go our ways — I to die, and you to live. Which is better God only knows.

(Benjamin Jowett)

PHAEDO

The dialogue receives its name from Phaedo, a disciple of Socrates, who tells his friend Echecrates about the death of the master. Socrates, who has been arguing for the immortality of the soul and giving his views about the nature of the after life, is still speaking when this last section of the dialogue opens.

" Wherefore, Simmias, seeing all these things, what ought not we to do in order to obtain virtue and wisdom in this life? Fair is the prize, and the hope great.

" I do not mean to affirm that the description which I have given of the soul and her mansions is exactly true — a man of sense ought hardly to say that. But I do say that, inasmuch as the soul is shown to be immortal, he may venture to think, not improperly or unworthily, that something of the kind is true. The venture is a glorious one, and he ought to comfort himself with words like these, which is the reason why I lengthen out the tale. Wherefore, I say, let a man be of good cheer about his soul, who has cast away the pleasures and ornaments of the body as alien to him, and rather hurtful in their effects, and has followed after the pleasures of knowledge in this life; who has adorned the soul in her own proper jewels, which are temperance, and justice, and courage, and nobility, and truth — in these arrayed she is ready to go on her journey to the world below, when her time comes. You, Simmias and Cebes, and all other men, will depart at some time or other. Me already, as the tragic poet would say, the voice of fate calls. Soon I must drink the poison; and I think that I had better repair to the bath first, in order that the women may not have the trouble of washing my body after I am dead."

When he had done speaking, Crito said: " And have you any commands for us, Socrates — anything to say about your children, or any other matter in which we can serve you? "

" Nothing particular," he said, " only, as I have always told you, I would have you to look to yourselves; that is a service which you may always be doing to me and mine as well as to yourselves. And you need not make professions; for if you take no thought for yourselves, and walk not according to the precepts which I have given you, not now for the first time, the warmth of your professions will be of no avail."

" We will do our best," said Crito. " But in what way would you have us bury you? "

" In any way that you like; only you must get hold of me, and take care that I do not walk away from you." Then he turned to us, and added with a smile: " I cannot make Crito believe that I am the same Socrates who have been talking and conducting the argument; he fancies that I am the other Socrates whom he will soon see, a dead body — and he asks, ' How shall he bury me? ' And though I have spoken many words in the endeavor to show that when I have drunk the poison I shall leave you and go to the joys of the blessed — these words of mine, with which I comforted you and myself, have had, as I perceive, no effect upon Crito. And therefore I want you to be surety for me now, as he was surety for me at the trial: but let the promise be of another sort; for he was my surety to the judges that I would remain, but you must be my surety to him that I shall not remain, but go away and depart; and then he will suffer less at my death, and not be grieved when he sees my body being burned or buried. I would not have him sorrow at my hard lot, or say at the burial, ' Thus we lay out Socrates,' or, ' Thus we follow him to the grave or bury him ': for false words are not only evil in themselves, but they infect the soul with evil. Be of good cheer then, my dear Crito, and say that you are burying my body only, and do with that as is usual, and as you think best."

When he had spoken these words, he arose and went into the bath-chamber with Crito, who bid us wait; and we waited, talking and thinking of the subject of the discourse, and also of the greatness of our sorrow; he was like a father of whom we were being bereaved, and we were about to pass the rest of our lives as orphans. When he had taken the bath, his children were brought to him — (he had two young sons and an elder one); and the women of his family also came, and he talked to them and gave them a few directions in the presence of Crito; and he then dismissed them and returned to us.

Now the hour of sunset was near, for a good deal of time had passed while he was within. When he came out, he sat down with us again after his bath, but not much was said. Soon the jailer, who was the servant of the eleven, entered and stood by him, saying: " To you, Socrates, whom I know to be the noblest and gentlest and best of all who ever came to this place, I will not impute the angry feelings of other men, who rage and swear at me when, in obedience to the authorities, I bid them drink the poison — indeed I am sure that you will not be angry with me; for others, as you are aware, and not I, are the guilty cause. And so fare you well, and try to bear lightly that must needs be; you know my errand." Then bursting into tears he turned away and went out.

Socrates looked at him and said: " I return your good wishes, and will do as you bid." Then turning to us, he said: " How charming the man is; since I have been in prison he has always been coming to see me, and at times he would talk to me, and was as good as could be to me, and now see how generously he sorrows for me. But we must do as he says, Crito; let the cup be brought, if the poison is prepared; if not, let the attendant prepare some."

" Yet," said Crito, " the sun is still upon the hilltops, and many a one has taken the draught late, and after the announcement has been made to him, he has eaten and drunk, and indulged in sensual delights; do not hasten then, there is still time."

Socrates said: " Yes, Crito, and they of whom you speak are right in doing thus, for they think that they will gain by the delay; but I am right in not doing thus, for I do not think that I should gain anything by drinking the poison a little later; I should be sparing and saving a life which is already gone; I could only laugh at myself for this. Please then to do as I say, and not to refuse me."

Crito, when he heard this, made a sign to the servant; and the servant went in, and remained for some time, and then returned with the jailer carrying the cup of poison. Socrates said: " You, my good friend, who are experienced in these matters, shall give me directions how I am to proceed." The man answered: " You have only to walk about until your legs are heavy, and then to lie down, and the poison will act." At the same time he handed the cup to Socrates, who in the easiest and gentlest manner, without the least fear or change of color or feature, looking at the man with all his eyes, Echecrates, as his manner was, took the cup and said: "What do you say about making a libation [1] out of this cup to any god? May I, or not? "

The man answered: "We only prepare, Socrates, just so much as we deem enough."

" I understand," he said; " yet I may and must pray to the gods to prosper my journey from this to that other world — may this then, which is my prayer, be granted to me."

Then holding the cup to his lips, quite readily and cheerfully he drank off the poison. And hitherto most of us had been able to control our sorrow; but now when we saw him drinking, and saw too that he had finished the draught, we could not longer forbear, and in spite of myself my own tears were flowing fast; so that I covered my face and wept over myself, for certainly I was not weeping over him, but at the thought of my own calamity in having lost such a companion. Nor was I the first, for Crito, when he found himself unable to restrain his tears, had got up and moved away, and I followed; and at that moment, Apollodorus, who had been weeping all the time, broke out into a loud cry which made cowards of us all. Socrates alone retained his calmness. " What is this strange outcry? " he said. " I sent away the women mainly in order that they might not offend in this way, for I have heard that a man should die in peace. Be quiet then, and have patience."

When we heard that, we were ashamed, and refrained our tears; and he walked about until, as he said, his legs began to fail, and then he lay on his back, according to the directions, and the man who gave him the poison now and then looked at his feet and legs; and after a while he pressed his foot hard and asked him if he could feel; and he said, No; and then his leg, and so upwards and upwards, and showed us that he was cold and stiff. And he felt them himself, and said: " When the poison reaches the heart, that will be the end." He was beginning to grow cold about the groin, when he uncovered his face, for he had covered himself up, and said (they were his last words) — he said: " Crito, I owe a cock to Asclepius; [2] will you remember to pay the debt? "

" The debt shall be paid," said Crito; " is there anything else? "

There was no answer to this question; but in a minute or two a movement was heard, and the attendants uncovered him; his eyes were set, and Crito closed his eyes and mouth.

[1] libation: drink-offering to the gods.

[2] Asclepius: more commonly Aesculapius, god of medicine. It was the custom for those who had been healed to offer a cock to him.

Such was the end, Echecrates, of our friend, whom I may truly call the wisest, and justest, and best of all the men whom I have ever known.

(Benjamin Jowett)

SUGGESTIONS FOR STUDY

1. Explain the words of Socrates: " The life which is unexamined is not worth living." To what extent did he exemplify his precept?

2. One of the Socratic dialogues of Plato deals with the abstract question of courage, and the argument is not entirely satisfying. In the *Apology* and in *Phaedo* we have an *example* of courage presented direct to us. Why is that more effective? What gave Socrates his courage? Can you think of any other books where moral courage is concretely depicted?

3. How does Socrates consider the avoiding of death compared with the avoiding of unrighteousness? Why is unrighteousness hard to avoid? What argument does he advance to show that we may regard death as a good?

4. To what extent does he seem conscious of supernatural guidance?

5. What do you mean by a sense of humor? Can you find any indications of such a thing in Socrates?

6. What did Socrates mean by his last words to Crito?

7. From what you have read about Socrates, does he seem to you to have deserved the tribute which Phaedo paid him? Compare him with other great moral leaders of the world's history.

8. Read Plato's short and masterly dialogue *Crito* for further proof of Socrates' devotion to his principles.

XENOPHON (434?–355? B.C.)

Xenophon is the only other Greek historian of the great period besides Herodotus and Thucydides whose works have survived. He was an Athenian by birth. Early in life he came under the influence of Socrates, for whom he conceived the warmest admiration and affection. In 401 B.C., he accompanied Cyrus the Younger on his campaign to wrest the throne of Persia from his brother Artaxerxes. Cyrus fell in battle, whereupon Xenophon took command of the ten thousand Greek mercenaries in Cyrus' army and led them with daring and skill back to the Black Sea. This exploit he recorded in his most celebrated work, *The Anabasis* or *March to Babylon,* which achieved a sort of immortality in modern times by being used as a textbook in beginning Greek. After his return from the expedition, Xenophon fell into disfavor at Athens and was formally banished.

The decree was subsequently revoked, but he seems not to have cared to live again in his native city. He died at Corinth. His most interesting book is the collection of *Memorabilia* or *Recollections,* in which he describes, soberly but sympathetically, the character and beliefs of Socrates. His literary style is simple and attractive.

THE MEMORABILIA

The opening chapters and the concluding paragraph of the work which Xenophon devoted to the memory of Socrates are here given. The bulk of the book consists of dialogues between Socrates and persons engaged in different occupations upon the subjects which most occupied his attention — piety toward the gods, temperance, friendship, the duties of children to parents, the political virtues, the useful arts, etc.

I have often wondered by what arguments those who drew up the indictment against Socrates could persuade the Athenians that his life was forfeit to the state. The indictment against him was to this effect: *Socrates is guilty of rejecting the gods acknowledged by the state and of bringing in strange deities: he is also guilty of corrupting the youth.*

First then, that he rejected the gods acknowledged by the state — what evidence did they produce of that? He offered sacrifices constantly, and made no secret of it, now in his home, now at the altars of the state temples, and he made use of divination [1] with as little secrecy. Indeed it had become notorious that Socrates claimed to be guided by " the deity." [2] It was out of this claim, I think, that the charge of bringing in strange deities arose. He was no more bringing in anything strange than are other believers in divination, who rely on augury, [3] oracles, coincidences and sacrifices. For these men's belief is not that the birds or the folk met by accident know what profits the inquirer, but that they are the instruments by which the gods make this known; and that was Socrates' belief too. Only, whereas most men say that the birds or the folk they meet dissuade or encourage them, Socrates said what he meant; for he said that the deity gave him a sign. Many of his companions were counseled by him to do this or not to do that in accordance with the warnings of the deity; and those who followed his advice prospered, and those who rejected it had cause for regret. And yet who would not admit that

---

[1] divination: discovery of the unknown or future by supernatural means.
[2] " the deity ": the divine oracle which Socrates claimed as his peculiar possession.
[3] augury: divination by flight of birds, etc.

he wished to appear neither a knave nor a fool to his companions? But he would have been thought both, had he proved to be mistaken when he alleged that his counsel was in accordance with divine revelation. Obviously, then, he would not have given the counsel if he had not been confident that what he said would come true. And who could have inspired him with that confidence but a god? And since he had confidence in the gods, how can he have disbelieved in the existence of the gods?

Another way he had of dealing with intimate friends was this: if there was no room for doubt, he advised them to act as they thought best; but if the consequences could not be foreseen, he sent them to the oracle to inquire whether the thing ought to be done. Those who intended to control a house or a city, he said, needed the help of divination. For the craft of carpenter, smith, farmer or ruler, and the theory of such crafts, and arithmetic and economics and generalship might be learned and mastered by the application of human powers; but the deepest secrets of these matters the gods reserved to themselves; they were dark to men. You may plant a field well; but you know not who shall gather the fruits. You may build a house well; but you know not who shall dwell in it. Able to command, you cannot know whether it is profitable to command. Versed in statecraft, you know not whether it is profitable to guide the state. Though, for your delight, you marry a pretty woman, you cannot tell whether she will bring you sorrow. Though you form a party among men mighty in the state, you know not whether they will cause you to be driven from the state. If any man thinks that these matters are wholly within the grasp of the human mind and nothing in them is beyond our reason, that man, he said, is irrational. But it is no less irrational to seek the guidance of heaven in matters which men are permitted by the gods to decide for themselves by study: to ask, for instance, Is it better to get an experienced coachman to drive my carriage or a man without experience? Is it better to get an experienced seaman to steer my ship or a man without experience? So too with what we may know by reckoning, measurement or weighing. To put such questions to the gods seemed to his mind profane. In short, what the gods have granted us to do by help of learning, we must learn; what is hidden from mortals we should try to find out from the gods by divination; for to him that is in their grace the gods grant a sign.

Moreover, Socrates lived ever in the open; for early in the morning he went to the public promenades and training grounds; in the forenoon he was seen in the market; and the rest of the day he passed just where most people were to be met. He was generally talking, and any one might listen. Yet none ever knew him to offend against piety and religion in deed or word. He did not even discuss that topic so favored by other talkers, " the Nature of the Universe; " and avoided speculation on the so-called " Cosmos " of the Professors, how it works, and on the laws that govern the phenomena of the heavens. Indeed he would argue that to trouble one's mind with such problems is sheer folly. In the first place, he would inquire, did these thinkers suppose that their knowledge of human affairs was so complete that they must seek these new fields for the exercise of their brains; or that it was their duty to neglect human affairs and consider only things divine? Moreover, he marveled at their blindness in not seeing that man cannot solve these riddles; since even the most conceited talkers on these problems did not agree in their theories, but behaved to one another like madmen. As some madmen have no fear of danger and others are afraid where there is nothing to be afraid of, as some will do or say anything in a crowd with no sense of shame, while others shrink even from going abroad among men, some respect neither temple nor altar nor any other sacred thing, others worship stocks and stones and beasts, so is it, he held, with those who worry with " Universal Nature." Some hold that *What is* is one, others that it is infinite in number; some that all things are in perpetual motion, others that nothing can ever be moved at any time; some that all life is birth and decay, others that nothing can ever be born or ever die. Nor were those the only questions he asked about such theorists. Students of human nature, he said, think that they will apply their knowledge in due course for the good of themselves and any others they choose. Do those who pry into heavenly phenomena [4] imagine that, once they have discovered the laws by which these are produced, they will create at their will winds, waters, seasons and such things to their need? Or have they no such expectation, and are they satisfied with knowing the causes of these various phenomena?

Such, then, was his criticism of those who meddle with these matters. His own conversation was ever of human things. The problems he discussed were, What is godly, what is ungodly; what is beautiful, what is ugly; what is just, what is unjust; what is prudence, what is madness; what is courage, what is cowardice; what is a state, what is a statesman; what is government, and what is a governor; — these

---

[4] **phenomena:** plural of phenomenon, whatever may be perceived.

and others like them, of which the knowledge made a " gentleman," in his estimation, while ignorance should involve the reproach of " slavishness."

2

No less wonderful is it to me that some believed the charge brought against Socrates of corrupting the youth. In the first place, apart from what I have said, in control of his own passions and appetites he was the strictest of men; further, in endurance of cold and heat and every kind of toil he was most resolute; and besides, his needs were so schooled to moderation that having very little he was yet very content. Such was his own character; how then can he have led others into impiety, crime, gluttony, lust, or sloth? On the contrary, he cured these vices in many, by putting into them a desire for goodness, and by giving them confidence that self-discipline would make them gentlemen. To be sure he never professed to teach this; but, by letting his own light shine, he led his disciples to hope that they through imitation of him would attain to such excellence. Furthermore, he himself never neglected the body, and reproved such neglect in others. Thus overeating followed by overexertion he disapproved. But he approved of taking as much hard exercise as is agreeable to the soul; for the habit not only insured good health, but did not hamper the care of the soul.

On the other hand, he disliked foppery and pretentiousness in the fashion of clothes or shoes or in behavior. Nor, again, did he encourage love of money in his companions. For while he checked their other desires, he would not make money himself out of their desire for his companionship. He held that this self-denying ordinance insured his liberty. Those who charged a fee for their society he denounced for selling themselves into bondage; since they were bound to converse with all from whom they took the fee. He marveled that any one should make money by the profession of virtue, and should not reflect that his highest reward would be the gain of a good friend; as though he who became a true gentleman could fail to feel deep gratitude for a benefit so great. Socrates indeed never promised any such boon to any one; but he was confident that those of his companions who adopted his principles of conduct would throughout life be good friends to him and to one another. How, then, should such a man " corrupt the youth "? Unless, perchance, it be corruption to foster virtue.

All who knew what manner of man Socrates was and who seek

after virtue continue to this day to miss him beyond all others, as the chief of helpers in the quest of virtue. For myself, I have described him as he was: so religious that he did nothing without counsel from the gods; so just that he did no injury, however small, to any man, but conferred the greatest benefits on all who dealt with him; so self-controlled that he never chose the pleasanter rather than the better course; so wise that he was unerring in his judgment of the better and the worse, and needed no counselor, but relied on himself for his knowledge of them; masterly in expounding and defining such things; no less masterly in putting others to the test, and convincing them of error and exhorting them to follow virtue and gentleness. To me then he seemed to be all that a truly good and happy man must be. But if there is any doubter, let him set the character of other men beside these things; then let him judge.

(*Anonymous Translation*)

SUGGESTIONS FOR STUDY

1. How does Xenophon's picture of Socrates harmonize with Plato's? Which brought him more clearly before you as a man?

2. What was the attitude of Socrates in regard to augury, oracles, and sacrifices? Find an example in Plato's account of his death which proves that he offered sacrifice.

3. How did he usually spend the day? What subjects did he discuss? What topics did he avoid? Why?

4. Sum up Xenophon's refutation of the two charges in the indictment against Socrates.

5. Cite other examples in history where persons of high character and service to humanity have been unjustly executed. Write a defense of some one of them.

THE GREEK ANTHOLOGY

The *Greek Anthology* is the name given to a large collection of short lyric poems written by many authors over a period of more than twelve hundred years. The earliest specimens go back to nearly 700 B.C. and the latest are as recent as the sixth century A.D. The word "anthology," which meant in Greek a collection of flowers, is peculiarly applicable to these dainty and delicate blossoms of verse. The poems treat of all kinds of subjects, notably those stock themes of lyric poetry — love, death, and nature. They display antiquity on its most human side and often reveal a depth of tenderness which we should not suspect from reading some of the more famous writers. The term "epigram" is sometimes applied to them, but it should be observed that the word originally had a meaning different from the present one. It signified a pithy statement suitable for an epitaph. Some of the most admired poems in the *Greek Anthology* are actual inscriptions for gravestones, as, for example, this restrained epitaph on the Spartans who fell at Thermopylae:

> " Tell at Sparta, passer-by,
> Here, at her command, we lie."

The terse charm of these poems has attracted many translators. Their influence can be detected in such modern volumes of verse as *A Shropshire Lad* by A. E. Housman and *The Spoon River Anthology* of E. L. Masters.

The selections here given are arranged in chronological order. It is not necessary to consider the authors, about whom at best we know very little.

I

Must I not die? What matter if I go
To Pluto's mansion with a gouty toe?
Whether I totter lame or run all day
I shall not want for bearers on my way.
And so, my boys, as sure as I'm a sinner   5
I don't intend to miss a single dinner.

2

Beauty's but a painted fly.
    If to keep a man you wish,
Charm's the hidden mystery
    That will hook your fish.

3

It is not love to love the fair
And feast one's eyes on beauty rare,
For beauty all men's gaze enthrals,
Nor for a lover's rapture calls.

Nay, he alone true love doth know   5
Who pays no heed to outward show,
And though his mistress homely be
Still finds in her the perfect she.

4

Now the white violets bloom, and now
    The bluebells drink the rain,

And straying o'er the mountain's brow
　The lilies flower again.
Spring perfumes sweet men's hearts enthral.　　　5
But Zeno's sweeter far than all.

In vain ye smile, O meadows gay!
　The allurement of the rose
Outshines the blossoms ye display,
　Her beauty warmer glows.　　　10
Lovers must choose my Zeno fair,
The rose of love beyond compare.

5

Touch with your lips this cup, and I
　My sober vows will break,
Not for the wine but that your kiss
　The thirst of love may slake.
A bowl so sweet I may not fly　　　5
　E'en though it drunken make;
It tells me of its new-won bliss
　And lo, my share I take.

6

A lad knows nothing of the woes
　That we poor lasses bear,
Among his comrades blithe he goes
　And friends his sorrows share.

He has his games, whene'er he please,　　　5
　He strolls from street to street,
He finds delight in all he sees,
　His eyes bright colors meet.

But we poor girls are hid away
　We never see the light,　　　10
We brood in solitude by day
　And weep alone at night.

We live as though in dungeons sealed
　Where no men ever come:
Unkissed, uncourted, unrevealed,　　　15
　Pale prisoners of the home.

7

Ye passers by, Eubulus lieth here,
The foe of wine who never knew good cheer.
Come then and drink our fill while we have breath,
For all too soon we make the port of death.

8

Say not the good are dead.
    It is a mystic sleep
    That now they keep.
The grave is but their bed.

9

My Heliodora, in the earth beneath,
    Tears still to thee I send;
Poor relics of my heart, a gift to Death,
    From Love that knows no end.

With tender offerings to thy grave I come;   5
    My tears libation make;
My longing eyes gaze fondly on thy tomb,
    For our dear love's dear sake.

Useless my gifts, my anguish, and my pain;
    In death thou dost abide.   10
Thy Meleager cries, and cries in vain,
    By that dark river side.

Ah me, ah me! where's now the cherished flower,
    That His fierce fingers crushed?
The blossom scarce had reached perfection's hour;   15
    He cast it to the dust.

Kind earth, all mother, on my knees I pray,
    Guard her whom still I weep;
Her gentle body on thy bosom lay,
    And let her softly sleep.   20

11. **Meleager:** one of the compilers of the Greek Anthology and the author of this poem.

10

" Sing the wrath " — I learnt at school:
" Sing the wrath," I teach my boys.
Wrath indeed! alas, poor fool,
   These your married joys!
When I took myself a wife   5
Naught I gained but wrath and strife.

All day long her tempers fret,
   Every hour she burns with rage;
Never respite can I get,
   Nightlong battle wage.   10
Strife she brought instead of dower,
Battlefield for marriage bower.

Though no railing words I speak,
   Though I bow before her pride,
Silent sit in patience meek,   15
   She's not satisfied.
Finds new reasons for her spite
Just because I will not fight.

(F. A. Wright)

1. **"Sing the wrath":** the opening words of Homer's *Iliad*.

SUGGESTIONS FOR STUDY

1. Characterize, as far as possible, each of the supposed speakers in the poems.

2. Which of the poems may properly be called epitaphs?

3. Read other poems in the *Greek Anthology*. Many of them appear in modern collections, especially in Van Doren's *Anthology of World Poetry*.

4. What famous English lyric was suggested by poem 5? In what different ways do these poems remind you of various ones in Housman's *A Shropshire Lad*, Master's *The Spoon River Anthology*, Emily Dickinson's *Poems*, Wordsworth's " Lucy " poems, and others.

THEOCRITUS (310?–245? B.C.)

Our scanty knowledge of the life of Theocritus is mostly inferred from his writings. He was born in Sicily, was educated at Alexandria in Egypt, and returned to Sicily to end his days. He is the creator of pastoral or bucolic poetry. He called his poems "idyls," which meant in Greek "little pictures," and the term is still applied to short descriptions of scenes or incidents from rustic life. Theocritus was a city-bred man who wished to return to nature and the simple life. This desire imparted a certain amount of genuineness to his idyls. Unfortunately, the literary tradition which he established degenerated later into something very frigid and artificial. Virgil's *Eclogues*, which were undoubtedly influenced by Theocritus, are very fine poems indeed. But when the pastoral convention was resumed in Italy in the sixteenth century and from there spread to other countries, it became a mere make-believe. In the poems, plays, and prose romances of this type, the shepherds and shepherdesses were idealized beyond any resemblance to actuality, they were adorned with fancy names, and were pictured as leading a care-free existence in some innocent Arcadia. By the end of the eighteenth century, genuine love of nature and fidelity to truth put an end to these absurdly artificial conventions. The modern story or poem of country life is, as a rule, of a very different type.

THE CYCLOPS

And so an easier life our Cyclops drew,
   The ancient Polyphemus, who in youth
Loved Galatea while the manhood grew
   Adown his cheeks, and darkened round his mouth.
No jot he cared for apples, olives, roses;   5
   Love made him mad; the whole world was neglected,
The very sheep went backward to their closes
   From out the fair green pastures, self-directed.
And singing Galatea, thus, he wore
   The sunrise down along the weedy shore,   10
And pined alone, and felt the cruel wound
Beneath his heart, which Cypris' arrow bore,
   With a deep pang: but, so, the cure was found;
And, sitting on a lofty rock, he cast
   His eyes upon the sea, and sang at last: 15
" O whitest Galatea, can it be
   That thou shouldst spurn me off who love thee so?
More white than curds, my girl, thou art to see,
More meek than lambs, more full of leaping glee
   Than kids, and brighter than the early glow   20

1. **Cyclops:** one-eyed giant. 2. **Polyphemus:** the most famous of the Cyclops. The adventures of Odysseus with him are related in Book 9 of the *Odyssey*. 3. **Galatea:** a sea-nymph. 7. **closes:** inclosed places. 12. **Cypris':** of Aphrodite or Venus.

On grapes that swell to ripen, — sour like thee!
Thou comest to me with the fragrant sleep,
  And with the fragrant sleep thou goest from me;
Thou fliest . . . fliest as a frightened sheep
  Flies the gray wolf! — yet love did overcome me,   25
So long! — I loved thee, maiden, first of all,
  When down the hills (my mother fast beside thee)
I saw thee stray to pluck the summer-fall
  Of hyacinth-bells, and went myself to guide thee;
And since my eyes have seen thee, they can leave thee   30
  No more, from that day's light! But thou . . . by Zeus,
Thou wilt not care for *that*, to let it grieve thee!
  I know thee, fair one, why thou springest loose
From my arm round thee. Why? I tell thee, dear!
  One shaggy eyebrow draws its smudging road   35
Straight through my ample front, from ear to ear;
  One eye rolls underneath; and yawning, broad,
Flat nostrils feel the bulging lips too near.
  Yet . . . ho, ho! — *I*, — whatever I appear, —
Do feed a thousand oxen! When I have done,   40
I milk the cows, and drink the milk that's best!
  I lack no cheese, while summer keeps the sun;
And after, in the cold, it's ready prest!
  And then, I know to sing, as there is none
Of all the Cyclops can, . . . a song of thee,   45
Sweet apple of my soul, on love's fair tree,
  And of myself who love thee . . . till the west
Forgets the light, and all but I have rest.
  I feed for thee, besides, eleven fair does,
And all in fawn; and four tame whelps of bears.   50
Come to me, sweet! thou shalt have all of those
  In change for love! I will not halve the shares.
Leave the blue sea, with pure white arms extended
  To the dry shore; and, in my cave's recess,
Thou shalt be gladder for the noon-light ended;   55
  For here be laurels, spiral cypresses,
Dark ivy, and a vine whose leaves infold
Most luscious grapes; and here is water cold,
  The wooded Aetna pours down through the trees
From the white snows, which gods were scarce too bold   60

50. in fawn: pregnant.

To drink in turn with nectar. Who with these
  Would choose the salt wave of the lukewarm seas?
Nay, look on me! If I am hairy and rough,
  I have an oak's heart in me; there's a fire
In these gray ashes which burns hot enough;   65
  And, when I burn for *thee*, I grudge the pyre
No fuel . . . not my soul, nor this one eye, —
Most precious thing I have, because thereby
I see thee, fairest! Out, alas! I wish
My mother had borne me finnèd like a fish,   70
That I might plunge down in the ocean near thee,
  And kiss thy glittering hand between the weeds,
If still thy face were turned; and I would bear thee
  Each lily white, and poppy fair that bleeds
Its red heart down its leaves! — one gift, for hours   75
  Of summer, — one for winter; since to cheer thee,
I could not bring at once all kinds of flowers
Even now, girl, now, I fain would learn to swim,
  If stranger in a ship sailed nigh, I wis,
  That I may know how sweet a thing it is   80
To live down with you in the deep and dim!
Come up, O Galatea, from the ocean,
  And, having come, forget again to go!
As I, who sing out here my heart's emotion,
  Could sit forever. Come up from below!   85
Come, keep my flocks beside me, milk my kine;
  Come, press my cheese, distrain my whey and curd!
Ah, mother! she alone . . . that mother of mine . . .
  Did wrong me sore! I blame her! Nor a word
Of kindly intercession did she address   90
Thine ear with for my sake; and ne'ertheless
  She saw me wasting, wasting, day by day;
  Both head and feet were aching, I will say,
All sick for grief, as I myself was sick.
  O Cyclops, Cyclops! whither hast thou sent   95
  Thy soul on fluttering wings? If thou wert bent
On turning bowls, or pulling green and thick
  The sprouts to give thy lambkins, thou wouldst make thee
  A wiser Cyclops than for what we take thee.
Milk dry the present! Why pursue too quick   100

61. **nectar:** the drink of the gods. 79. **wis:** know. 87. **distrain:** seize.

That future which is fugitive aright?
Thy Galatea thou shalt haply find,
Or else a maiden fairer and more kind;
For many girls do call me through the night,
And, as they call, do laugh out silverly.   105
I, too, am something in the world, I see! "

While thus the Cyclops love and lambs did fold,
Ease came with song, he could not buy with gold.

(*Elizabeth Barrett Browning*)

102. **haply**: perhaps.   107. **fold**: take to the fold.

SUGGESTIONS FOR STUDY

1. Show that this idyl is a variant of the story of Beauty and the Beast.
2. Show how " Ease came with song " to the Cyclops.
3. How does the Cyclops try to commend himself to Galatea?
4. What is the significance of the final line in the speech of the Cyclops?
5. Select the lines of Mrs. Browning's rendering of the poem which you consider particularly beautiful or effective.
6. What English or American poems do you know which may be called " idyls "?

PLUTARCH (46?–120 A.D.)

Plutarch is the author of the most famous series of biographies in the world. He was born at Chaeronea in Greece, studied in Athens, and stayed some time in Rome, where he lectured on philosophy. The Emperors Trajan and Hadrian honored him with titles and appointments. His *Parallel Lives* of celebrated Greeks and Romans are arranged in pairs; for example, Demosthenes and Cicero, Alexander the Great and Julius Caesar. Much learning and research went into the writing of them. His concern with moral questions did not prevent him from telling an interesting and at times dramatic story. He became immensely popular at the Renaissance. Amyot made a translation of the *Lives* into French which reads like an original work. Sir Thomas North, in turn, translated Amyot into English and his version supplied Shakespeare with materials for his Roman plays — *Julius Caesar, Antony and Cleopatra,* and *Coriolanus.* Plutarch is still one of the most read of the ancient authors.

LIFE OF ALEXANDER

Alexander the Great (356–323 B.C.), one of the world's great conquerors, was the son of King Philip of Macedonia. He succeeded his father in 336 shortly after the latter had made himself master of Greece, and in 334 set out on his great expedition from which he never returned. In the course of a very few years he completely subdued the Persian Empire, secured the submission of Egypt, and proceeded in his explorations and conquests as far as northern India, beyond which his soldiers refused to follow him. He died at Babylon at the age of thirty-three, having made greater conquests than were ever achieved by any European before or after him. Although the empire which Alexander won by his sword soon fell to pieces, the effects of his career were enduring. He and his successors were great builders of cities in Asia Minor, Syria, and Egypt, and some of these cities, like Alexandria and Antioch, developed into important centers of Greek culture. The Greek language became the common speech of the civilized world. In this Alexandrian Age there was neither the political freedom nor the original genius of the great statesmen and writers of old Greece, but learning and science flourished as they had never done before.

Alexander was born the sixth of Hecatombaeon,[1] which month the Macedonians call Lous, the same day that the temple of Diana[2] at Ephesus was burnt; which Hegesias[3] of Magnesia makes the occasion of a conceit,[4] frigid enough to have stopped the conflagration. The temple, he says, took fire and was burnt while its mistress was absent, assisting at the birth of Alexander. And all the Eastern soothsayers who happened to be then at Ephesus, looking upon the ruin of this temple to be the forerunner of some other calamity, ran about the town, beating their faces, and crying that this day had brought forth something that would prove fatal and destructive to all Asia.

Just after Philip had taken Potidaea, he received these three messages at one time, that Parmenio had overthrown the Illyrians in a great battle, that his race horse had won the course at the Olympic games, and that his wife had given birth to Alexander; with which being naturally well pleased, as an addition to his satisfaction, he was assured by the diviners that a son, whose birth was accompanied with three such successes, could not fail of being invincible.

---

[1] **Hecatombaeon:** the latter half of July and the first half of August.

[2] **Diana:** goddess of the chase; her temple at Ephesus in Asia Minor was one of the " wonders of the world."

[3] **Hegesias:** Greek historian of the fourth century B.C.

[4] **conceit:** fanciful notion.

The statues that gave the best representation of Alexander's person were those of Lysippus [5] (by whom alone he would suffer his image to be made), those peculiarities which many of his successors afterwards and his friends used to affect to imitate, the inclination of his head a little on one side towards his left shoulder, and his melting eye, having been expressed by this artist with great exactness. But Apelles,[6] who drew him with thunderbolts in his hand, made his complexion browner and darker than it was naturally; for he was fair and of a light color, passing into ruddiness in his face and upon his breast. Aristoxenus [7] in his Memoirs tells us that a most agreeable odor exhaled from his skin, and that his breath and body all over was so fragrant as to perfume the clothes which he wore next him; the cause of which might probably be the hot and adust [8] temperament of his body. For sweet smells, Theophrastus conceives, are produced by the concoction of moist humors by heat, which is the reason that those parts of the world which are driest and most burnt up afford spices of the best kind and in the greatest quantity; for the heat of the sun exhausts all the superfluous moisture which lies in the surface of bodies, ready to generate putrefaction. And this hot constitution, it may be, rendered Alexander so addicted to drinking, and so choleric.[9] His temperance, as to the pleasures of the body, was apparent in him in his very childhood, as he was with much difficulty incited to them, and always used them with great moderation; though in other things he was extremely eager and vehement, and in his love of glory, and the pursuit of it, he showed a solidity of high spirit and magnanimity far above his age. For he neither sought nor valued it upon every occasion, as his father Philip did (who affected to show his eloquence almost to a degree of pedantry, and took care to have the victories of his racing chariots at the Olympic games engraven on his coin), but when he was asked by some about him, whether he would run a race in the Olympic games, as he was very swift-footed, he answered, he would, if he might have kings to run with him. Indeed, he seems in general to have looked with indifference, if not with dislike, upon the professed athletes. He often appointed prizes, for which not only tragedians and musicians, pipers and harpers, but rhapsodists [10] also, strove to outvie one another;

---

[5] **Lysippus:** Greek sculptor of the fourth century B.C.
[6] **Apelles:** greatest of Greek painters, fourth century B.C.
[7] **Aristoxenus:** Greek philosopher of the fourth century B.C.
[8] **adust:** parched.
[9] **choleric:** angry.
[10] **rhapsodists:** reciters.

and delighted in all manner of hunting and cudgel-playing,[11] but never gave any encouragement to contests either of boxing or of the pancratium.[12]

While he was yet very young, he entertained the ambassadors from the King of Persia, in the absence of his father, and entering much into conversation with them, gained so much upon them by his affability, and the questions he asked them, which were far from being childish or trifling (for he inquired of them the length of the ways, the nature of the road into inner Asia, the character of their king, how he carried himself to his enemies, and what forces he was able to bring into the field), that they were struck with admiration of him, and looked upon the ability so much famed of Philip to be nothing in comparison with the forwardness and high purpose that appeared thus early in his son. Whenever he heard Philip had taken any town of importance, or won any signal victory, instead of rejoicing at it altogether, he would tell his companions that his father would anticipate everything, and leave him and them no opportunities of performing great and illustrious actions. For being more bent upon action and glory than either upon pleasure or riches, he esteemed all that he should receive from his father as a diminution and prevention of his own future achievements; and would have chosen rather to succeed to a kingdom involved in troubles and wars, which would have afforded him frequent exercise of his courage, and a large field of honor, than to one already flourishing and settled, where his inheritance would be an inactive life, and the mere enjoyment of wealth and luxury.

The care of his education, as it might be presumed, was committed to a great many attendants, preceptors, and teachers, over the whole of whom Leonidas, a near kinsman of Olympias,[13] a man of austere temper, presided, who did not indeed himself decline the name of what in reality is a noble and honorable office, but in general his dignity, and his near relationship, obtained him from other people the title of Alexander's foster-father and governor. But he who took upon him the actual place and style of his pedagogue was Lysimachus the Acarnanian, who, though he had nothing specially to recommend him, but his lucky fancy of calling himself Phoenix,[14] Alexander Achilles, and Philip Peleus,[15] was therefore well enough esteemed, and ranked in the next degree after Leonidas.

[11] cudgel-playing: contest with short, thick sticks.
[12] pancratium: athletic contest of boxing and wrestling.
[13] Olympias: mother of Alexander.
[14] Phoenix: fabulous sacred bird of the Egyptians.
[15] Peleus: father of Achilles.

Philonicus the Thessalian brought the horse Bucephalus to Philip, offering to sell him for thirteen talents; but when they went into the field to try him, they found him so very vicious and unmanageable, that he reared up when they endeavored to mount him, and would not so much as endure the voice of any of Philip's attendants. Upon which, as they were leading him away as wholly useless and untractable, Alexander, who stood by, said, "What an excellent horse do they lose for want of address [16] and boldness to manage him!"

Philip at first took no notice of what he said; but when he heard him repeat the same thing several times, and saw he was much vexed to see the horse sent away, "Do you reproach," said he to him, "those who are older than yourself, as if you knew more, and were better able to manage him than they?"

"I could manage this horse," replied he, "better than others do."

"And if you do not," said Philip, "what will you forfeit for your rashness?"

"I will pay," answered Alexander, "the whole price of the horse."

At this the whole company fell a-laughing; and as soon as the wager was settled amongst them, he immediately ran to the horse, and taking hold of the bridle, turned him directly towards the sun, having, it seems, observed that he was disturbed at and afraid of the motion of his own shadow; then letting him go forward a little, still keeping the reins in his hands, and stroking him gently when he found him begin to grow eager and fiery, he let fall his upper garment softly, and with one nimble leap securely mounted him, and when he was seated, by little and little drew in the bridle, and curbed him without either striking or spurring him. Presently, when he found him free from all rebelliousness, and only impatient for the course, he let him go at full speed, inciting him now with a commanding voice, and urged him also with his heel. Philip and his friends looked on at first in silence and anxiety for the result, till seeing him turn at the end of his career, and come back rejoicing and triumphing for what he had performed, they all burst out into acclamations of applause; and his father shedding tears, it is said, for joy, kissed him as he came down from his horse, and in his transport said, "O my son, look thee out a kingdom equal to and worthy of thyself, for Macedonia is too little for thee."

After this, considering him to be of a temper easy to be led to his duty by reason, but by no means to be compelled, he always endeavored to persuade rather than to command or force him to any-

---

[16] **address: skill.**

thing; and now looking upon the instruction and tuition of his youth to be of greater difficulty and importance than to be wholly trusted to the ordinary masters in music and poetry, and the common school subjects, and to require, as Sophocles says —

"The bridle and the rudder too,"

he sent for Aristotle,[17] the most learned and most celebrated philosopher of his time, and rewarded him with a munificence proportionable to and becoming the care he took to instruct his son. For he repeopled his native city Stagira, which he had caused to be demolished a little before, and restored all the citizens, who were in exile or slavery, to their habitations. As a place for the pursuit of their studies and exercise, he assigned the temple of the Nymphs, near Mieza, where, to this very day, they show you Aristotle's stone seats, and the shady walks which he was wont to frequent. It would appear that Alexander received from him not only his doctrines of Morals and of Politics, but also something of those more abstruse and profound theories which these philosophers, by the very names they gave them, professed to reserve for oral communication to the initiated, and did not allow many to become acquainted with. For when he was in Asia, and heard Aristotle had published some treaties of that kind, he wrote to him, using very plain language to him in behalf of philosophy, the following letter. "Alexander to Aristotle, greeting. You have not done well to publish your books of oral doctrine; for what is there now that we excel others in, if those things which we have been particularly instructed in be laid open to all? For my part, I assure you, I had rather excel others in the knowledge of what is excellent, than in the extent of my power and dominion. Farewell." And Aristotle, soothing this passion for pre-eminence, speaks, in his excuse for himself, of these doctrines as in fact both published and not published: as indeed, to say the truth, his books on metaphysics [18] are written in a style which makes them useless for ordinary teaching, and instructive only, in the way of memoranda, for those who have been already conversant in that sort of learning.

Doubtless also it was to Aristotle that he owed the inclination he had, not to the theory only, but likewise to the practice of the art of medicine. For when any of his friends were sick, he would often prescribe them their course of diet, and medicines proper to their

---

[17] **Aristotle:** (384–322 B.C.) pupil of Plato and along with him the greatest philosopher of antiquity.

[18] **metaphysics:** philosophy of ultimate reality or of first principles. The term was coined by Aristotle's pupils.

disease, as we may find in his epistles. He was naturally a great lover of all kinds of learning and reading; and Onesicritus [19] informs us that he constantly laid Homer's *Iliad*, according to the copy cor-. rected by Aristotle, called the casket copy, with his dagger under his pillow, declaring that he esteemed it a perfect portable treasure of all military virtue and knowledge. When he was in the upper Asia, being destitute of other books, he ordered Harpalus to send him some; who furnished him with Philistus's [20] History, a great many of the plays of Euripides,[21] Sophocles, and Aeschylus, and some dithyrambic [22] odes, composed by Telestes and Philoxenus.[23] For a while he loved and cherished Aristotle no less, as he was wont to say himself, than if he had been his father, giving this reason for it, that as he had received life from the one, so the other had taught him to live well. But afterwards, upon some mistrust of him, yet not so great as to make him do him any hurt, his familiarity and friendly kindness to him abated so much of its former force and affectionate-ness, as to make it evident he was alienated from him. However, his violent thirst after and passion for learning, which were once im-planted, still grew up with him, and never decayed; as appears by his veneration of Anaxarchus,[24] by the present of fifty talents [25] which he sent to Xenocrates,[26] and his particular care and esteem of Dan-damis and Calanus.

While Philip went on his expedition against the Byzantines, he left Alexander, then sixteen years old, his lieutenant in Macedonia, committing the charge of his seal to him; who, not to sit idle, reduced the rebellious Maedi, and having taken their chief town by storm, drove out the barbarous inhabitants, and planting a colony of several nations in their room, called the place after his own name, Alexan-dropolis. At the battle of Chaeronea,[27] which his father fought against the Grecians, he is said to have been the first man that charged the Thebans' sacred band. And even in my remembrance,

[19] **Onesicritus:** biographer of Alexander.
[20] **Philistus:** (432–356 B.C.) Greek historian of Sicily.
[21] **Euripides:** Aeschylus, Sophocles, and Euripides were, in chronological order, the greatest Greek writers of tragedies.
[22] **dithyrambic:** in a wild, irregular strain.
[23] **Philoxenus:** Greek poet who flourished about 400 B.C.
[24] **Anaxarchus:** Greek philosopher and companion of Alexander in his Asiatic campaigns.
[25] **talents:** the talent was a weight and denomination of money of con, siderable value.
[26] **Xenocrates:** Greek philosopher of the fourth century B.C.
[27] **Chaeronea:** the battle there took place 338 B.C. and resulted in the defeat of the Thebans and Athenians and the overthrow of Greek liberty.

there stood an old oak near the river Cephisus, which people called Alexander's oak, because his tent was pitched under it. And not far off are to be seen the graves of the Macedonians who fell in that battle. This early bravery made Philip so fond of him, that nothing pleased him more than to hear his subjects call himself their general and Alexander their king.

(Dryden–Clough)

SUGGESTIONS FOR STUDY

1. What qualities did Alexander display in his youth? Which of these showed his power of leadership?

2. What was the attitude of Philip to Alexander? Was this a wise one for a father to take? Discuss the question of how a gifted child should be treated.

3. What did Alexander learn from Aristotle? How did his education compare with that of a young man of today? What caused the estrangement between Alexander and Aristotle?

4. Compare Plutarch's manner of writing with that of the Renaissance biographer Vasari (page 364); with the modern biographers Maurois (page 220) and Ludwig (page 545); with English and American biographers whom you have read.

5. What use of the story of Alexander was made in literature during the Middle Ages? By Dryden? Do you know any modern literature in which he is a character?

6. Vocabulary: pedantry, austere, pedagogue, untractable, munificence, abstruse.

LUCIAN (120?–180? A.D.)

Lucian, the last of the Greek writers who can be termed classical, has also been called "the first of the moderns." He was not a native Greek but a Syrian, born at Samosata near Antioch. He is the most striking example in antiquity of a writer who achieved perfect command of an acquired language. In our own time, the novelist Joseph Conrad, a Pole by birth, attained a similar mastery of English. Lucian took up the profession of sophist, or teacher of philosophy and rhetoric, in which capacity he traveled widely, delivering lectures with great success. His last days were spent in Egypt.

Lucian was a man without convictions. He had no belief in religion, whether pagan or Christian, and mocked at all schools of philosophy. He satirized these things in his dialogues, which are the prose equivalents of the poetic dramas of Aristophanes. The best of them are the *Dialogues of the Gods,* in which he derides the ancient deities, and the *Dialogues of the Dead,* filled with ridicule of all types of humanity. His literary model was the Platonic dialogue, but where Plato strove with all the fervor of his being to penetrate to ultimate reality, Lucian concluded that there was no such thing as truth. As for men, he felt that their conduct always fell far short of their professions and that they were therefore hopelessly hypocritical. " I make it my business," he said, " to hate quacks, hate trickery, hate lies, and hate conceit and I hate every such class of wicked men."

Quite different from his dialogues is his *True History,* a novel describing a voyage to the moon. He says of it himself that the only true statement in it is that it contains nothing but lies from beginning to end! It influenced Rabelais' *Pantagruel* and Swift's *Gulliver's Travels* and may still be read with pleasure by any one who likes extravagant stories.

THE JUDGMENT OF PARIS

This is one of the *Dialogues of the Gods.*

According to the Greek legend, Paris was the son of Priam, King of Troy. His mother having dreamed that her child would ruin his country, when Paris was born he was exposed on Mt. Ida in Phrygia. But his life was saved by the herdsmen and he grew up among them, distinguished for beauty and strength. When the goddesses Hera, Athena, and Aphrodite quarreled as to which one of them was the most beautiful, Paris was selected as the judge. He decided in favor of Aphrodite, who had promised him the most beautiful woman in the world as his wife. In order to obtain his bride, Paris went to Lacedaemon where he was hospitably received by Menelaus, whose kindness he repaid by persuading Helen, the wife of Menelaus, to flee with him to Troy. The siege of Troy by the united Greeks followed. Hera and Athena, the unsuccessful rivals of Aphrodite, naturally became the bitter enemies of the Trojans.

It should be observed that the Greek names of the divinities differ from the Latin names which are more familiar to us. Jupiter appears as Zeus, Mercury as Hermes, Juno as Hera, Minerva as Athena, Venus as Aphrodite, Mars as Ares.

Persons: ZEUS, HERMES, PARIS, HERA, ATHENA, APHRODITE

Zeus. Hermes, take this apple and go to Phrygia,[1] to Priam's son, the cowherd — he is pasturing his drove on Ida — and say to him that since he is handsome himself, and a connoisseur in matters of love, he has been appointed by Zeus to judge which is the fairest of the three goddesses. The apple is to be the victor's prize. [*To the goddesses.*] It is time now that you ladies were off to the judge. I

---

[1] **Phrygia:** a district in Asia Minor.

have delegated the office of umpire because I am equally attached to you all, and if it were possible I should gladly see you all win. Moreover, the man who gives the prize of beauty to one must in the nature of things be detested by the others. These reasons disqualify me as umpire; but the young man in Phrygia to whom you are going is of a royal house — being in fact a cousin of Ganymede,[2] whom you know — and he has the simple manner of the mountains.

Aphrodite. For my part, Zeus, you might make Momus [3] himself the umpire and I should still go confidently to trial; for what could he find to criticize in me? And the others must needs put up with the man.

Hera. We are not afraid either, Aphrodite, even if your Ares were to settle the question. We are satisfied with this man, whoever he is, — this Paris.

Zeus. [*To* ATHENA] Well, daughter, are you of the same mind? What do you say? You turn away blushing? It is natural for you virgins to be coy in such matters. But you might at least nod. [ATHENA *nods.*] Off with you, then; and the defeated, mind you, are not to be angry with the judge nor to do any harm to the young man. It is impossible for all to be equal in beauty. [*They start.*]

Hermes. Let us make straight for Phrygia. I will go first, and do you follow smartly. And don't be uneasy. I know Paris; he is a handsome young fellow, a lover by temperament, and a most competent judge in such cases as this. His decision will certainly be correct.

Aphrodite. That is good news, and all in my favor. [*To* HERMES, *apart.*] Is this person a bachelor, or has he a wife?

Hermes. Not exactly a bachelor.

Aphrodite. What do you mean?

Hermes. Apparently a woman of Ida is his mate, a good enough creature, but crude and extremely rustic. He does not seem to care much about her. But why do you ask?

Aphrodite. Oh, I just asked.

Athena. [*To* HERMES] This is a breach of trust, sirrah. You are having a private understanding with Aphrodite.

Hermes. It's nothing terrible, and has nothing to do with you. She was asking me whether Paris is a bachelor.

Athena. Why is that any business of hers?

---

[2] Ganymede: cup-bearer of the gods.
[3] Momus: in Greek mythology, the lampooner of the gods. Lucian frequently refers to him.

Hermes. I don't know; she says she asked casually, without any object.

Athena. Well, is he a bachelor?

Hermes. Apparently not.

Athena. Has he any leaning towards war? Is he an ambitious person, or a cowherd merely?

Hermes. I can't say certainly; but it is safe to guess that a man of his age will hanker after fighting and long to distinguish himself in the field.

Aphrodite. See now, I don't find any fault with you for talking apart with her. Fault-finding is not natural to Aphrodite.

Hermes. She was asking me almost exactly what you did, so don't take it amiss or think you are badly treated. I answered her just as simply as I did you.

— But while we are talking we have come a long way. We have left the stars behind and almost reached Phrygia. I see Ida and the whole range of Gargarus clearly; and unless I am mistaken, I can even make out Paris, your judge.

Hera. Where is he? I don't see him.

Hermes. Look off to the left — not at the summit of the mountain, but along the flank where the cave is. There you see the herd.

Hera. But not the herdsman.

Hermes. What? Look along my finger, so. Don't you see the cows coming from among the rocks, and a man with a crook running down the bluff to hem them in and keep them from scattering further?

Hera. I see now, if that is he.

Hermes. That's he. When we are close at hand we will take to the ground, if you please, and come up to him walking, so as not to frighten him by dropping from the unseen.

Hera. Very good, we will do so. [*They alight.*] Now that we are on earth, Aphrodite, you had better go ahead and lead the way. You are probably familiar with the spot. The story goes that you have visited Anchises [4] here more than once.

Aphrodite. Those jokes don't bother me very much, Hera.

Hermes. I will lead the way myself. Here is the umpire close by; let us address him. [*To* PARIS.] Good morning, cowherd!

Paris. Good morning, my lad. Who are you? And who are these women whom you are escorting? — not mountain-bred: they are too pretty.

[4] **Anchises:** Trojan hero, connected on both sides with the royal family of Troy. Aphrodite bore him a son, Aeneas.

Hermes. And not women. Paris, you see before you Hera and Athena and Aphrodite; and I am Hermes, bearing a message from Zeus. Why do you tremble and lose color? Don't be frightened; it's nothing bad. He bids you judge which of them is fairest; " for," says Zeus, " you are fair yourself and wise in lover's love, so I turn over the case to you. You will know what the prize is when you read the legend on the apple." [*Hands him the apple.*]

Paris. Let me see what it all means. FOR THE FAIREST, the apple says. How in the world, Lord Hermes, can I, a mortal man and a rustic, be judge of this marvelous spectacle, which is beyond a cowherd's powers? Judgment in such matters belongs rather to the dainty folk in towns. As for me, I have the art to judge between goat and goat, as between heifer and heifer, in point of beauty. But these ladies are beautiful alike. I do not know how a man could drag his sight from one to rest it on another. Wherever my eye falls first, there it clings and approves what it finds. I am fairly bathed in their beauty. It surrounds me altogether. I wish I were all eyes, like Argus.[5] I think I should judge wisely if I gave the apple to them all. And here is something to consider too: one of them is sister and wife of Zeus, while the others are his daughters. Doesn't this make the decision hard?

Hermes. I can't say. I only know that you can't shirk what Zeus commands.

Paris. Make them promise one thing, Hermes: that the losers will not be angry with me, but only consider my sight defective.

Hermes. They say they will do so; but it is time you made your decision.

Paris. I will try; for what else can I do? Good heavens, what a sight! What beauty! How fair the maiden goddess [6] is! and how queenly, glorious, and worthy of her station is the wife of Zeus! [7] and how sweet is Aphrodite's glance, with her soft, winning smile! — Bah! I can hold no more pleasure. If you please, I should like to study each separately; as it is, I look two ways at once.

Aphrodite. Yes, let us do it that way.

Paris. Go off, then, two of you. Hera, do you stay.

Hera. I will; and when you have considered me carefully you had better consider something else — whether you like the results of a verdict in my favor. For if you decide, Paris, that I am the fairest, you shall be lord of all Asia.

[5] **Argus:** a mythological being with countless eyes.
[6] **maiden goddess:** Athena.　　　　[7] **wife of Zeus:** Hera.

Paris. My justice is not for sale. Go now; I am satisfied. Come next, Athena.

Athena. Here I am, Paris; and if you decide that I am fairest, you shall never be beaten in battle. I will make you a victorious warrior.

Paris. I have no use for war and battle, Athena. Peace reigns, as you see in Phrygia and Lydia, and my father's realm is undisturbed. ‾ut cheer up; you shall not suffer for it, even if my justice is not for sale. I have finished with you; it is Aphrodite's turn.

Aphrodite. At your service, Paris, and I shall bear careful inspection. And if you like, my dear lad, listen to me too. I have had an eye on you for some time; and seeing you so young and handsome — does Phrygia hold such another? — I congratulate you on your looks, but I blame you for not leaving these rocks and living in the city. Why do you waste your beauty in the desert? What good do you get of the mountains? How are your cattle the better because you are handsome? You ought to have had a wife before this; not a wild country girl like the women of Ida, but a queen from Argos or Corinth, or a Spartan woman like Helen, for instance. She is young and lovely, in no way inferior to me, and what is most important, made for love. If that woman should but see you, I know she would surrender herself, and leave everything to follow you and be your wife; but of course you have heard about her yourself.

Paris. Not a word. But I should love to listen if you will tell me the whole story.

Aphrodite. She is the daughter of that fair Leda [8] whom Zeus loved.

Paris. And what does she look like?

Aphrodite. She is blond, soft, and delicate, yet strong with athletic sports. She is so sought after that men fought for her sake when Theseus stole her, yet a little girl. And when she was grown up, all the noblest of the Greeks came courting her; and Menelaus was chosen, of the family of Pelops. But if you like, I will make her your wife.

Paris. What do you mean? She is married already.

Aphrodite. You are a young provincial, to be sure. But I know how to manage an affair like that.

Paris. How? I should like to know myself.

Aphrodite. You will set out on your travels, ostensibly to see Greece; and when you come to Lacedaemon, Helen will see you.

[8] **Leda:** the mother, not only of Helen, but of Castor and Pollux as well.

The rest shall be my affair, to arrange that she fall in love with you and follow you.

Paris. Ah, that is what seems impossible to me — that a woman should be willing to leave her husband and sail away with a stranger to a strange land.

Aphrodite. Don't worry about that. I have two fair children, Longing and Love, whom I shall give you as guides on your journey. And Love shall enter into the woman and compel her to love, while Longing shall invest you with the charm in her eyes. I will be there myself, and I will ask the Graces to come too, so that we may make a joint attack upon her.

Paris. How all this is to come about remains to be seen; but I am already in love with Helen. Somehow or other I see her with my mind's eye, and my voyage to Greece and my visit to Sparta and my return with her. It oppresses me that I am not carrying it out this minute.

Aphrodite. Don't fall in love, Paris, until you have given me the matchmaker's fee in the shape of a verdict. It would be nice if we could have a joint festival in honor of your marriage and my victory. It all rests with you. You can buy love, beauty, a wife, with that apple.

Paris. I am afraid you will forget me after the award is made.

Aphrodite. Do you want my oath?

Paris. By no means; only your promise.

Aphrodite. I promise that I will give you Helen to be your wife, that she shall follow you to Troy, and that I will attend in person and help you in every way.

Paris. And you will bring Love and Longing and the Graces?

Aphrodite. Trust me, and I will have Desire and Hymen [9] there into the bargain.

Paris. On these conditions I award the apple to you. Take it!

(Emily James Smith)

SUGGESTIONS FOR STUDY

1. Be sure you know the Latin names of all the divinities here represented and understand the attributes and functions of each.

2. How do the goddesses reveal their respective personalities in their conversation, and in their attempted means of influencing Paris?

3. What impression do you get of the character of Paris? Would you

[9] **Hymen:** god of marriage.

expect him to play a heroic part in the Trojan War? How does the *Iliad* bear out your supposition on this point?

4. What has Lucian in common with the mythical Momus to whom an allusion is made in the dialogue? With Aristophanes? With Rabelais? With Jonathan Swift? What modern satirists do you know?

5. What is the essential difference between a dialogue and a play? Name some good modern specimens of the dialogue as a literary form. Where else in this book have you found a dialogue?

6. Vocabulary: connoisseur, casually, ostensibly.

READING LIST

TRANSLATIONS FROM GREEK LITERATURE

Readings from the Literature of Ancient Greece, ed. by Dora Pym
Masterpieces of Greek Literature, ed. by J. H. Wright
The Girdle of Aphrodite, trans. from the *Greek Anthology* by F. A. Wright
Homer: *Iliad,* verse trans. by W. C. Bryant
Homer: *Iliad,* prose trans. by Lang, Leaf, and Meyer
Homer: *Odyssey,* verse trans. by F. Caulfeild
Homer: *Odyssey,* prose trans. by Butcher and Lang
Homer: *Odyssey,* prose trans. by T. E. Lawrence

Plato: *Dialogues,* trans. by B. Jowett
Herodotus: *History* (Everyman's Library)
Thucydides: *Peloponnesian War* (Everyman's Library)
Xenophon: *Memorabilia*
Theocritus: *Idyls,* trans. by C. S. Calverley
Lucian: *Dialogues,* trans. by A. M. Harmon
Plutarch: *Lives* (Everyman's Library)
Four Greek Plays (Modern Library); contains Aeschylus' *Agamemnon,* Sophocles' *Oedipus the King,* Euripides' *Medea* and Aristophanes' *The Frogs*

BOOKS ABOUT GREEK HISTORY, LITERATURE, ART, CIVILIZATION, ETC.

Lavell, C. F.: *A Biography of the Greek People*
Botsford, G. W.: *Hellenic History*
Bowra: C. M.: *Ancient Greek Literature*
Dickinson, G. L.: *The Greek View of Life*
Livingstone, R. W.: *The Greek Genius and Its Meaning to Us*
Toynbee, A. J.: *Greek Civilization and Character*

Bulfinch, Thomas: *The Age of Fable*
Gayley, C. M.: *The Classic Myths in English Literature*
Cornford, F. M.: *Greek Religious Thought from Homer to the Age of Alexander*
Zielinski, Thaddeus: *The Religion of Ancient Greece*
Walters, H. B.: *The Art of the Greeks*

Roman Literature

Roman Literature

THE term Latin literature is applied to all the literature written in the Latin language. The expression Roman literature is generally employed to designate that portion of Latin literature which was produced during the time when Rome was a nation; that is to say, down to the fall of the Roman Empire in 476 A.D. This is by far the most important body of Latin literature, but it is well for us to remember that the Latin language continued to be a vehicle for certain kinds of literature during the Middle Ages and at the time of the Renaissance, and that it is still the official language of the Roman Catholic Church. Latin is a dead language only in the sense that it is not now the mother tongue of any living person. In parts of the ecclesiastical world and among certain scholars it is still very much alive.

Roman literature is unquestionably inferior to Greek literature in spontaneity, originality, and imagination. The Romans were by comparison with the Greeks a sober-minded, practical people. Their earliest attempts at literary expression seem to have been made in connection with communal religious rites and country festivals. How far they would have succeeded in evolving a literature of their own, it is difficult to say, for it was the influence of Greek culture, with which the Romans came into early contact through their conquest of the Greek cities in southern Italy, that determined the whole subsequent development of their literature. In a large sense, therefore, Roman literature is derivative; but that statement should not imply that it has not qualities peculiarly its own, which reflect the character and outlook of the people who produced it. It has sanity, gravity and a close touch with everyday reality. The Latin language, though greatly inferior to the Greek in flexibility and expressiveness, offsets these defects to some extent by a remarkable sonority and a clean-cut precision.

Roman literature introduced by comedy, soon followed by epic and oratory

As with other nations, poetry appears before prose but in the form of comedy rather than epic. The earliest Roman writer of whom we have any sure knowledge was Plautus (254?–184 B.C.), whose comedies were imitated from the Greek dramatist Menander. His plays, of which a number are extant, were written to supply amusement and not to satirize individuals or institutions. After the Renaissance, his influence can be detected in much Elizabethan drama and in Molière's plays. Shakespeare's *The Comedy of Errors* is a good example of a famous play based on Plautus. A later writer of comedies was Terence (190?–159? B.C.), superior to Plautus in dramatic construction and elegance of language, but with less spontaneous fun. Terence deserves to be remembered if only for one famous line: " I am a man, and nothing that concerns a man do I deem a matter of indifference to me." In connection with these two dramatists, it is worth noting that the Romans, like the modern Italians, were greatly interested in acting and probably held the art of impersonation in higher esteem than the story or structure of the play.

Epic poetry begins with Ennius (239–169 B.C.) who has been called the " Father of Roman Poetry." But only a fragment of his epic on the history of the Roman race has been preserved and his fame has been entirely overshadowed by that of Virgil. Prose now makes its appearance, with oratory and history taking the first place in importance. Cato the Censor (234–149 B.C.) is the first orator of note, but his speeches have unfortunately been lost. The Romans had a native talent for oratory, though the amount of it that has survived is small compared with what we have from the Athenians. Jurisprudence also became a favorite study to which the Romans were able to make contributions of the greatest importance. Rome is still thought of as the law-giver of the nations.

The Golden Age marks change from Republic to Empire

The Golden Age of Roman literature coincides with the last days of the Republic and the beginning of the Empire. Rome sought and acquired world power and became increasingly cosmopolitan. In this, her best period of literature, she was less an imitator of Greek literature than a continuator of it in new surroundings. She added her own earnestness and sense of human values. Cicero (106–43 B.C.) was the first great prose writer and remains to this day the model of elegant Latin. Fifty or more orations are his most famous compositions, but his colloquial letters and reflective treatises (" essays " we should call them today) are at least of equal interest to us moderns. Julius Caesar (100–44 B.C.), the greatest military genius of antiquity — perhaps, indeed, of all time — has his place in literature as a historian on a small scale, who narrated events in a simple, straightforward, objective fashion. A later historian, Livy (59 B.C.–17 A.D.), told the story of Rome in a masterly style. Only about a quarter of his work is preserved, but we have outlines of the rest.

Meanwhile Roman poetry was also entering upon its great period. The first outstanding Roman poet is Lucretius (96?–55 B.C.), who was the author of the most famous didactic poem in the world, *On the Nature of Things.* He wished to free men from the fear of death by demonstrating that the soul would perish with the body, developing his argument from the ideas of the Greek philosophers Democritus and Epicurus. His contemporary Catullus (87–54 B.C.) was the finest lyrical genius ever to use the Latin language. Endowed with strong emotional instincts, he was unrivaled among the Romans in the spontaneity and sincerity of his utterance. Tibullus and Propertius were lesser lyric lights. Ovid (43 B.C.–17 A.D.), who, like the last two writers, used the form of the elegy, with alternate hexameter and pentameter lines, is best remembered for his attractive versions of Graeco-Roman mythology. Virgil (70–19 B.C.) is the greatest Roman poet, if we take universal fame as a criterion. His *Aeneid* became at once the national epic of Rome, and it has remained to this day the most widely known of Latin poems. His other poems, the *Georgics* and *Eclogues,* though considerably less celebrated, are hardly inferior in inspiration or technique. Horace (65–8 B.C.), by reason of his having become the favorite poet of many men of the world and of affairs, ranks second only to Virgil in fame. He exhibits the highest perfection of style and technical mastery of lyric forms achieved by any of the Roman poets. In genuineness and depth of feeling he is not the equal of Catullus. This great period is also frequently referred to as the Augustan Age because it coincides with the reign of the first Roman emperor, himself a patron of letters.

The Silver Age shows wane of literary power

For more than a hundred years after the death of Augustus in 14 A.D. we have the so-called Silver Age. With the loss of political liberty went a decline in manliness of character and independence of utterance. Flattery of the emperor, the court, or high-placed patrons introduced a note of cringing subserviency which had been wholly lacking in the writers of republican Rome. The number of poets and prose writers increases and technical skill improves, but originality sadly wanes. Compared with the Golden Age, this Silver Age is much like the Alexandrian period in Greek literature when contrasted with the great Athenian period. Many of the authors of the Silver Age were natives of Spain, which by this time had become pretty thoroughly Romanized. Such, for example, were Seneca (4 B.C.–65 A.D.) and his nephew, the epic poet Lucan. Seneca preached the Stoic philosophy, that virtue is the highest good and that the passions should be controlled even to the point of indifference to pleasure and pain. He was also the only Roman writer of tragedies. His plays were freely imitated from Euripides and were not intended for the stage. They were revived, however, at the time of the Renaissance and exercised an important influence on the European drama. Petronius wrote a realistic novel *Satiricon,* unique of its kind, of which only a part has been preserved. Martial (40?–102? A.D.) was the author of epigrams, short poems with witty turns of thought and expression. Quintilian (35?–100? A.D.) wrote a treatise on the training of an orator. The tyranny of Nero, under which Seneca and other writers had suffered, was followed by the more liberal policy of the Emperors Nerva and Trajan. Therefore, Tacitus (55?–120? A.D.), who ranks with Livy as the greatest Roman historian, was able to express his mind and utter moral condemnations with impunity. In Juvenal (60?–140? A.D.) satirical poetry, which had always been a favorite form with the Romans, reached its highest point. Tacitus and Juvenal between them paint a very dark picture of their age. The letters of Pliny the Younger (62?–114? A.D.) to the Emperor Trajan brighten this picture to some extent. African writers now came to the fore, among them Apuleius, the author of a long romance, the *Golden Ass,* which contains among other things the graceful story of Cupid and Psyche. Suetonius (75?–160? A.D.), the last of the more famous historians, wrote the *Lives of the Caesars.*

Latin literature of late Empire and Middle Ages declines in style and variety

In the later Empire there was a constant decline in culture and consequently in literature. The Emperor Marcus Aurelius, who reigned from 161 to 180 A.D., wrote his *Meditations,* which are maxims of Stoic philosophy, in Greek. Saint Augustine (354–430 A.D.), the ablest of the Fathers of the Church, was the first Christian writer of genius. We may consider him also the last great Latin writer of antiquity, since he sang the dirge of the Roman Empire in his *City of God*.

After the fall of the Roman Empire, which may be conveniently dated 476 A.D., Latin continued to be the vehicle of thought for many centuries, but it was frequently a barbarous Latin when judged by Ciceronian standards. Occasionally works appeared which might be classed as pure literature. Boethius (475?-525?) wrote the *Consolation of Philosophy*, a mixture of prose and verse, which enjoyed a high reputation in medieval times. In the tenth century a German monk named Ekkehard wrote the *Song of Walter*, which is perhaps the high-water mark of good Latin in the Middle Ages. But for us today the medieval Latin writings which seem most alive are, on the one hand, the hymns of the Church and, on the other, the very worldly songs of the wandering students. At the time of the Renaissance, Latin was restored to something of its ancient purity by Petrarch and later scholars. Erasmus (1466?-1536) may be taken as the last great example of a man who wrote Latin with all the gusto of a living language. His *Praise of Folly* remains one of the classics of world literature.

Except in minor forms, Roman literature clearly outshone by Greek

A few profitable generalizations may be made in comparing Greek literature with Roman literature. The superiority of the former in originality, profundity and range is obvious. The Romans virtually admitted their own inferiority by their open imitation of Greek models. Virgil, for example, who had the Homeric poems constantly in mind when he composed the *Aeneid*, by no means attained to the stature of Homer. The Roman lyric poets, notably Catullus and Horace, fare better in comparison, though that is partly because so much of the earlier Greek lyric poetry has been lost. In the drama the Greeks tower immeasurably above the Romans. The Romans contributed nothing to philosophy. On the other hand, Livy and Tacitus are not so markedly inferior to Herodotus and Thucydides. Rome triumphed only in certain minor branches of literature, such as the familiar letter, the poetic satire, and some types of prose romance. In these, if we can judge by extant remains, the Romans actually excelled the Greeks.

LUCRETIUS (96?–55? B.C.)

We know very little about the life of Lucretius, who was not only one of the greatest of the Roman poets but also one of the few Romans who were genuinely interested in philosophy. All we can be sure of is that he came of a distinguished family and lived during the later Roman Republic, when civil wars were sapping the foundations of the state. The stories of his madness and suicide have never been completely substantiated. The dignified sadness which he displays may have been native to him or may have been produced by the constant spectacle of bloodshed and misery.

His poem *On the Nature of Things* is an outstanding example of the Roman genius for didactic poetry. Lucretius wrote it with the definite purpose of freeing men's minds from the fear of death by proving that their souls are as mortal as their bodies. Religion to him was synonymous with superstition. He believed it had filled men with nameless terrors of a life after death and thus had prevented them from being happy.

The philosophy of Lucretius may be called materialism or naturalism. His master in thinking was the Greek philosopher Epicurus, who taught the pursuit of reasonable happiness. Lucretius employs for his argument the doctrine of atoms, first proclaimed by another Greek philosopher, Democritus. Everything, human beings included, is made up of ultimate particles of matter. At death these particles disperse and consciousness ceases forever. Hence there is nothing to dread after death.

Lucretius is more read and appreciated today than he was during his life. That is partly because, unlike most of his fellow countrymen, he had a scientific habit of mind, but it is also due in large measure to his passion for his subject and the poetic eloquence which this fervor engenders.

ON THE NATURE OF THINGS

The following passages are taken from the opening book of the poem. In the first one, Lucretius adopts the epic convention of beginning with an invocation. He addresses Venus (in whom he did not actually believe) because she was reputed to be the mother of Aeneas, from whom the Romans traced their origin. The second passage is meant to illustrate the atrocities that are perpetrated in the name of religion. Agamemnon, having offended the goddess Diana, can only appease her wrath by offering up his own daughter, Iphigenia, as a sacrifice. Such, says Lucretius, are the crimes to which religion leads!

I

Parent of Rome! sweet Venus! source of love!
Delight of mortals and the Blest above!

Who gladst the earth, the sea, all things that lie
Beneath yon gliding spheres that beam on high;
From thee all pleasure, beauty, being, flows, 5
Life springs to light, and pregnant nature glows.
Thee, Goddess! thee the winds and tempests fly,
Clouds at thy presence quit the brightening sky;
The teeming Earth exerts her genial powers,
In fair profusion spreads her sweetest flowers; 10
The smiling seas in gentle waves appear,
And glory gilds the tranquil atmosphere.
    When youthful Spring salutes the cheerful vales,
And soft Favonius wakes his balmy gales,
Pierced by thy flame, gay birds in every bower 15
Feel thy approach, and hail thy sacred power;
Exulting herds o'er laughing verdure play,
Rush through the rapid streams, and boundless stray.
Rapt into bliss by thy inspiring charms,
Thy sweet allurements, and thy soft alarms, 20
All beings burn thy pleasure to fulfil,
And wait, enraptured, on thy heavenly will.
Through seas and streams thy kindly power prevails,
O'erspreads the mountains and pervades the dales,
The bowery mansions of melodious birds, 25
And open pastures of rejoicing herds;
Darts through each kindling breast love's melting rage,
And all things renovates from age to age.

                              (*Thomas Busby*)

14. **Favonius:** the west wind.

2

    Too long to bondage Reason was consigned,
Chained by Religion, tyrant of the mind.
From heaven itself she showed her baleful head,
With aspect horrible and menace dread,
Frowned on mankind; but a bold Grecian rose, 5
To face her terrors, and her reign oppose.
Nor Gods could awe, nor their immortal fame,
Nor Jove's dread thunder, nor his forky flame.

    5. **Grecian:** Epicurus (342–270 B.C.).

In vain his purpose heavenly wrath reproves,
His dauntless soul no sacred murmur moves. 10
By Nature's bounds he scorns to be confined,
And calls forth all his energy of mind;
His vivid power awakes! and soaring flies
Beyond the flaming portals of the skies;
In might of thought the vast expanse surveys, 15
Returns triumphant, and no man displays
What beings *may*, what being *ne'er* shall rise,
And where their power's eternal limit lies.
Hence stern Religion, our dismay before,
By him subjected, and our plague no more, 20
Humbled in turn, beneath our feet is driven,
And his brave victory equals us to heaven.

But ah! I tremble, lest you still suppose
From Reason's elements seduction flows.
Yet at Religion, and her ruthless deeds, 25
What soul but shudders, and what heart but bleeds,
Behold fair Iphigenia's cruel doom! —
By the first chiefs of Greece, in youthful bloom,
To Death she's led! what tears of pity flowed,
While Dian's altar streamed with guiltless blood! 30
The attending nymphs the holy crown prepare,
The sacred fillet binds her virgin hair,
Before the shrine her sire in sorrow stands,
The thirsty poignard lurks in priestly hands,
The mournful citizens are bathed in tears, 35
In silent agony the fair appears;
Now, humbly kneeling, pleads with streaming eyes,
And now, with piteous voice, for mercy cries.
That first the king a father's name she gave,
In vain she pleads; nor prayers, nor tears, can save. 40
Lo! from her palace and her friends she's torn,
Strait to the sanguine altar sanguine borne;
Not as when blissful Hymen wakes his rites
Of mutual vows and solemnized delights,
But in the roseate hour of nuptial prime 45
A victim falls to bigotry and crime.
A parent's hands his suppliant child destroy,

32. **fillet**: head-band.   42. **sanguine**: bloody.

Her life the purchase of a wind for Troy.
Such mighty evils holy phrenzy brings!
Such direful outrage from Religion springs!　　　50

(Thomas Busby)

48. **wind:** Agamemnon, by sacrificing his daughter to Diana, obtained from the goddess a favorable wind to carry him to Troy.

SUGGESTIONS FOR STUDY

1. Look up the teachings of Epicurus, whose philosophy Lucretius followed. How may Epicurus be said to have overcome Religion? How does the first selection reflect Epicurean ideas? How does the second?

2. Comment on the last line of the second passage. It is the most quoted line of the poem. What is lacking in Lucretius' conception of religion? Is the last line ever illustrated in modern life?

3. How does the first selection remind you of English nature poetry? Of what authors or poems in particular? What is there in the style of the second which reminds you of Pope? Why is this style suitable for a translation of Lucretius rather than a more modern type of rhythm?

CATULLUS (87–54 B.C.)

Gaius Valerius Catullus was born at Verona. He ran through his paternal inheritance and spent most of his short life in Rome, where he mingled with the younger social set and frequented the literary circle. He had a country seat on the peninsula of Sirmio on beautiful Lake Garda. He was a contemporary of the philosophical poet Lucretius but totally unlike him in that he seems to have had no general interests. He interpreted everything in terms of personal emotions. He has been called the only Roman poet who possessed the passionate heart of a genuine lyric poet. In comparison with him, Horace, in spite of his superior range, appears detached and intellectual. Catullus is, indeed, Rome's greatest lyric poet precisely because of his intensity of feeling and the unsought beauty of his expression. Much of his best verse was inspired by his love affair with " Lesbia," a fickle, unworthy woman, who has been identified as the notorious social siren Clodia. The various stages through which he passed in his infatuation with her are recorded in his poems — devotion and confidence, suspicion and jealousy, bitter resentment, attempts at renunciation, and finally scornful indifference. He loved and hated, and sometimes did both at the same time. But the note of happiness in his love is rare; he experienced mainly its bitterness.

TO LESBIA

Oh! let us love and have our day,
All that the bitter graybeards say
Appraising at a single mite.
My Lesbia, suns can set and rise;
For us the brief light dawns and dies   5
Once only, and the rest is night.
A thousand kisses, then five score,
A thousand and a hundred more,
Then one for each you gave before.
Then, as the many thousands grow,   10
We'll wreck the counting lest we know,
Or lest an evil eye prevail
Through knowledge of the kisses' tale.

(Hugh McNaghten)

ON LESBIA

Lesbia forever on me rails.
To talk of me she never fails.
Now, hang me, but for all her art,
I find that I have gained her heart.
My proof is this: I plainly see
The case is just the same with me;
I curse her every hour sincerely,
Yet, hang me, but I love her dearly.

(Jonathan Swift)

ON LESBIA

I love and hate. Ah! never ask why so!
I hate and love. . . . and that is all I know.
I see 'tis folly, but I feel 'tis woe.

(W. S. Landor)

ON THE DEATH OF LESBIA'S SPARROW

Mourn Loves and Graces all, and you
Of men the lovelier chosen few.
The sparrow of my love is dead,
The playmate of my love is sped,

Her sparrow, prized beyond her eyes,   5
So honey-sweet was he, and wise
To know her as a girl her mother.
He would not leave her for another,
Would on her lap be still astir
And chirping still for none but her.   10
And now he journeys whence they say
No steps retrace the darkling way.
Cursed shades, I curse you, swallowing
In Orcus every dainty thing:
The dainty pet ye ravished here!   15
Fie, fie, for shame! ah, birdie dear!
Flushed, heavy eyelids are the due
My love is paying, all for you.

                (*Hugh McNaghten*)

14. **Orcus:** Hades.

FAREWELL TO BITHYNIA[1]

A balmy warmth comes wafted o'er the seas,
    The savage howl of wintry tempests drear
In the sweet whispers of the western breeze
    Has died away; the spring, the spring is here!

Now quit, Catullus, quit the Phrygian plain,   5
    Where days of sweltering sunshine soon shall crown
Nicaea's fields with wealth of golden grain,
    And fly to Asia's cities of renown!

Already through each nerve a flutter runs
    Of eager hope, that longs to be away;   10
Already 'neath the light of other suns
    My feet, new-winged for travel, yearn to stray.

And you, ye band of comrades tried and true,
    Who side by side went forth from home, farewell!
How far apart the paths shall carry you   15
    Back to your native shore, ah, who can tell?

                (*Theodore Martin*)

[1] **Bithinia:** in Asia Minor, where Catullus held an official position for a short time.

HOME TO SIRMIO

Dear Sirmio, that art the very eye
Of islands and peninsulas, that lie
Deeply embosomed in calm inland lake,
Or where the waves of the vast ocean break;
Joy of all joys, to gaze on thee once more!　　　　5
I scarce believe that I have left the shore
Of Thynia, and Bithynia's parching plain,
And gaze on thee in safety once again!
Oh, what more sweet than when, from care set free,
The spirit lays its burden down, and we,　　　　10
With distant travel spent, come home and spread
Our limbs to rest along the wished-for bed!
This, this alone, repays such toils as these!
Smile, then, fair Sirmio, and thy master please, —
And you, ye dancing waters of the lake,　　　　15
Rejoice; and every smile of home awake!

(Theodore Martin)

TO HIS BROTHER

From land to land, o'er many waters borne,
Brother, I come to these thy rites forlorn,
The latest gift, the due of death, to pay,
The fruitless word to silent dust to say.
Since death has reft thy living self from me,　　　　5
Poor brother, stolen away so cruelly,
Ye this the while, which ancient use decrees
Sad ritual of our sires for obsequies,
Take, streaming with a brother's tears that tell
Of a last greeting, brother, a last farewell.　　　　10

(Hugh McNaghten)

NUPTIAL SONG

The nuptial song or epithalamium was developed into a special literary form by the Greeks. The finest specimen preserved is an idyl of Theocritus which celebrates the marriage of Menelaus and Helen. Catullus wrote several nuptial songs of great beauty and dignity, and his example was followed by many later Roman writers. The burden of these ancient marriage songs consisted of invocations of blessing and predictions of happiness. This species of poem is less common in modern literature, though Ronsard in France and Edmund Spenser and Ben Jonson in England contributed to it. Spenser's "Epithalamium" (1595) is perhaps the most admired of all nuptial songs. Its grave Christian spirit forms an interesting contrast to the sensuous paganism of Catullus.

Youths. Lo, Hesper is at hand! Rise, youths! His light
Expected long now harbingers the night.
'Tis time to quit the feast. We must away.
Swell high with me the hymeneal lay.
Anon the virgin comes in blushes by.   5
Oh Hymen, Hymenaeus, be thou nigh!

Maidens. Mark you the youths? Rise up, rise up, each maid!
Already hath the evening star displayed
In the dim welkin his Oetaean flame.
Mark you their nimbleness? Then know their aim!   10
Anon they'll sing a lay we must outvie.
Oh Hymen, Hymenaeus, be thou nigh!

Youths. No easy triumph, comrades, shall we gain.
See how the maids are practicing their strain!
Nor vainly so. With undivided care   15
Their task is wrought — what marvel, if 'tis fair?
Whilst we, who labor with distracted wit,
Are like to lose the palm, and so 'tis fit,
Bestowing here our voice and there our ear.
Well studied work to victory is dear —   20
Pains undivided, toil that will not tire;
Then kindle to your task with answering fire!
Anon they will begin; we must reply.
Oh Hymen, Hymenaeus, be thou nigh!

Maidens. Say, Hesper, say, what fire of all that shine   25
In Heaven's great vault more cruel is than thine?
Who from the mother's arms her child can tear —
The child that clasps her mother in despair;

1. **Hesper:** the evening star. 2. **harbingers:** heralds. 4. **hymeneal:** adjective from Hymen or Hymenaeus, the god of marriage. 9. **Oetaean:** of Mt. Oeta, where the funeral pyre of Hercules was built.

And to the youth, whose blood is all aflame,
Consigns the virgin sinking in her shame!⁣   30
When towns are sacked, what cruelty more drear?
Oh Hymen, Hymenaeus, Hymen, hear!

Youths. Say, Hesper, say, what fire of all that shine
In Heaven's great vault more jocund is than thine?
Who with thy flame dost ratify the bond   35
Of wedlock-troth first vowed by lovers fond,
By parents vowed, but consummated ne'er,
Until thy star hath risen upon the air?
What choicer hour sends heaven our life to cheer?
Oh Hymen, Hymenaeus, Hymen, hear!   40

Maidens. Woe, my companions, woe, that Hesper thus
Hath reft the fairest of our mates from us!
Why were we heedless of thy coming — why?
For most it fits to watch, when thou art nigh.
To stolen delights by night the lover hies,   45
And him wilt thou, oh Hesper, oft surprise,
When thou in other name dost reappear.
Oh Hymen, Hymenaeus, Hymen, hear!

Youths. Heed not the railing of the virgin choir!
They joy to chide thee with fictitious ire.   50
How, if within their secret soul they long
For what they so vituperate in song?
Then to their chiding turn a heedless ear.
Oh Hymen, Hymenaeus, draw thou near!

Maidens. As in a garden grows some floweret fair,   55
Safe from the flocks, safe from the ploughman's share,
Nursed by the sun, by gentle breezes fanned,
Fed by the showers, admired on every hand,
There as it coyly blossoms in the shade,
Desired by many a youth, by many a maid;   60
But pluck that flower, its witchery is o'er,
And neither youth nor maid desires it more.
So is the virgin prized, endeared as much,
Whilst yet unsullied by a lover's touch;

But if she lose her chaste and virgin flower,   65
Her beauty's bloom is blighted in an hour;
To youths no more, no more to maidens dear.
Oh Hymen, Hymenaeus, be thou near!

Youths. As grows a widowed vine in open fields,
It hangs its head, no mellow clusters yields;   70
So droops the fragile stem, its topmost shoot
With nerveless tendril hangs about its root;
That vine no husbandman nor rustic swain
Hath cared to tend or cultivate or train;
But if by happier chance that self-same vine   75
Around a husband elm its tendrils twine,
Then many a husbandman and rustic swain
Its shoots will tend and cultivate and train.
Even such the virgin, and unprized as much,
That fades, untended by a lover's touch;   80
But when, in fulness of her maiden pride,
Some fitting mate has won her for his bride,
She's loved as never was she loved before,
And parents bless her and are stern no more.

Youths and Maidens. Then spurn not, oh ye virgins, such a   85
      groom!
Unmeet it is to spurn the man to whom
Thy father gave thee, and thy mother too;
For unto them is thy obedience due.
Not wholly thine is thy virginity;
Thy parents own some part of it in thee.   90
One third thy father's is by right divine,
One third thy mother's; one alone is thine.
Then war not with these twain, who with thy dower
Have given their son-in-law their rights and power.

                                    (*Theodore Martin*)

SUGGESTIONS FOR STUDY

1. Show how each of these poems has a peculiarly personal note. What were the things that interested Catullus? What subjects are lacking in his verse?

2. What is his attitude toward death? Where is it revealed?

3. What do you gather from these poems about his feelings toward Lesbia? What does he mean by " I love and hate "?

4. Show how the Youths and Maidens try to outvie each other in the " Nuptial Song." What is the attitude assumed by the Maidens? Is it fictitious or sincere? What is the conclusion on which the Youths and Maidens jointly agree? How is the relationship between parents and children shown to be different from that of our day?

5. It has been said that Burns is the British poet most like Catullus. Point out any resemblances. Do any of the poems remind you of other English poets?

6. Read Tennyson's poem " To Catullus." What is the justification for Tennyson's designation of Catullus as the " tenderest of Roman poets "?

7. Vocabulary: appraising, reft, obsequies, bourne, welkin, jocund, vituperate.

CICERO (106–43 B.C.)

Marcus Tullius Cicero was Rome's most famous orator and one of her most revered statesmen. He was also a writer on philosophic subjects. He came from a well-to-do family and received the best education the age could afford. Beginning his public career early, he held in succession various offices until he was made consul in 66 B.C. During his term as consul he thwarted the conspiracy of Catiline to overthrow the government and was voted by the Senate the honorable title of " father of his country." Incurring the enmity of a powerful political faction, he went into voluntary exile for a year in Greece. On being allowed to return to Rome he ceased for a time active opposition to those in power. But when the civil war broke out between Pompey and Caesar, he took the side of the former. Caesar, after defeating Pompey, magnanimously refused to molest Cicero, who now withdrew temporarily from affairs and devoted himself to philosophy, thus appearing to acquiesce in the dictatorship of Caesar. When Caesar was assassinated in 44 B.C., Cicero made another valiant effort to save the Republic. He thundered his denunciations of Mark Antony, who, less generous than Caesar, had him put to death.

Cicero's orations are his best-known writings. He perfected himself with the utmost care in the art of public speaking. Our great American orators such as Webster, Clay, and Wendell Phillips, modeled themselves largely on him. His philosophic essays on *The Nature of the Gods, Old Age, Friendship,* and others are of livelier interest to us, even though he was not so much an original thinker as an interpreter of other men's thoughts. He was also a prolific writer of letters, which seem to have been genuinely private and not intended for publication. As a result of these, hardly another man of antiquity is personally as well known to us.

Cicero was little read during the Middle Ages, but Petrarch and other scholars of the Renaissance revived the study of him and regarded his diction and style as the true criterion of good classical Latin. This tradition of Ciceronian Latin continued almost to the present day.

SPEECH FOR MARCELLUS

The following extracts are from the first oration which Cicero delivered after the overthrow of the Republic and one of the last he was ever to make. The occasion was the generous pardon extended by Julius Caesar to Marcellus, his irreconcilable opponent. Cicero, who like Marcellus had opposed Caesar and favored the cause of Pompey, was profoundly moved by Caesar's magnanimity and rose in the Senate to congratulate him. The speech was made in 46 B.C. and is said to have been impromptu.

It is true, Gaius Caesar, that the fame of your military glory will be celebrated not by our lips and our literature alone, but by practically the whole world; nor shall any age ever be silent concerning your renown. And yet somehow it seems to me that great deeds of war are drowned even in the pages of history by the shouts of soldiers and the blare of trumpets. But when we hear or read of some act of mercy, of kindness, of justice, of self-control, or of wisdom, especially if it be done in the heat of passion, the foe of counsel, or by a conqueror, who naturally tends to pride and arrogance, how our hearts burn with love for men we have never seen, whether they be real men or only heroes of fiction! How great then shall be our praise for you, how great our loyalty and devotion to you — you whom we see among us, whose thoughts and feelings we see reflected in your face, your wish to save all that the fortune of war has left of the Republic! I swear that the very walls of this council-chamber seem to long to thank you. . . .

This day you are right to rank above all your great days of triumph and thanksgiving. For this deed belongs to Caesar alone; all those other victories, great as they were, you won as leader, but there was a great multitude to follow you. In this action you are both leader and follower; and it is a great action. Time will bring to an end your trophies and monuments (for old age destroys all the works of men's hands), but this justice and clemency [1] of yours gains day by day a greater glory, so that even if passing years diminish your material achievements they add more and more to your honor. Indeed, you had already surpassed all previous victors in civil war in justice and mercy; but today you have conquered yourself. . . .

[1] **clemency:** mercy.

You seem to have been victorious over victory, since you have not exacted from the conquered all that victory had won for you. For although by the laws of victory we, the conquered, should all have been ruined, by the judgment of your clemency we have been spared. Rightly therefore are you named " Unconquered," for you have been victorious over the very nature and strength of victory itself. . . .

Think not that your life consists only in the union of body and spirit; nay, that is your true life, that which shall live in the memory of all the centuries, which posterity shall cherish, which eternity itself shall ever protect. To the future you must look, to the future you must turn; you have long given it much to admire; now it waits also for something to honor. It is true that men in ages to come will marvel when they hear and read of your commands, both in the army and the provinces, of the Rhine, the Northern Ocean, the Nile, your numberless battles, your incredible victories, your monuments, your gifts to the people, your triumphs. But, unless this city is firmly established by your policy and your laws, it may be that your name will wander far and wide, but it will not have a certain home and a sure abiding-place.

Among those, too, who come after us, there will be, as there has been among us, a great division of opinion about you; for some will praise your achievements to the skies, while others perhaps will look for something more and that not the least important thing — unless you quench the smoldering fires of civil war by preserving the Republic, so that your military success may seem to be due to good fortune, while your home policy is your own work. Mold your actions therefore to please those critics who will pass judgment on your work many centuries hence; and, indeed, I believe their judgment will be fairer than ours; for it will not be colored by affection or greed, hatred or envy. And furthermore, even if, as some think, it will not matter to you then, now in truth it does matter that you should so act that oblivion will never blot out your glory.

(Dora Pym)

LETTER TO HIS FAMILY

This letter was written by Cicero to his wife, Terentia, and his two children, on the eve of his departure from Italy. Political intrigue had driven him into exile. He sailed from Brindisi, on the east coast of Italy, and was in banishment for a year and a half.

BRINDISI

[April 30th, 58 B.C.]

MY DARLING TERENTIA, MY LITTLE TULLIA, AND
MY BOY CICERO,

I do not send you as many letters as I might, because I am always wretched; but when I write to you or read your letters I weep so bitterly that I cannot bear it. Ah, if only I had been less greedy of life! Then I should truly have seen nothing or but little of the evil of life. But if Fate has preserved me for some hope of regaining one day a measure of prosperity, I have not made so great a mistake; but if my present unhappy plight is fixed forever, I would honestly like to see you again, my darling, as quickly as possible — and then to die in your arms; for we have received no gratitude either from the gods, whom you have worshiped so piously, or from men whom I have always served.

I have been staying thirteen days at Brindisi with Marcus Laenius Flaccus, a splendid man, who sets my safety far above danger to his own life and fortunes; the penalty of that iniquitous decree has not prevented his offering me everything which hospitality and friendship could demand. I hope I shall be able to show my gratitude some day.

I leave Brindisi on April 30th; I am making for Cyzicus [1] by way of Macedonia. Oh, how lonely and wretched I am! But what can I do? Ask you to come? A woman ill and worn-out in mind and body? Of course not. Then must I do without you? This, I think, is what I will do; if there is hope of my recall, you must promote it and help it on; but if, as I fear, it is all over and done with, do your very best to come to me somehow. You can be quite sure of one thing: if I have you I shall not feel I am entirely done for. But what will become of my little Tullia? . . . Certainly at all costs we must preserve the poor child's married happiness and not allow her to come under a cloud. How will my Cicero manage? He is always in my heart and my loving thoughts.

I cannot write more now; my grief prevents me. I do not know how you have managed, whether you have still some of my property, or whether it has all been confiscated. . . . You need not be worried about the freeing of the slaves. A promise was made to your slaves that you would treat each one according to his merits. Now Orpheus so far has been satisfactory, but no one of the others is

---

[1] **Cyzicus:** a town in Asia Minor.

specially so. The arrangement made with the other slaves is this, that if my property went out of my hands they should be my freed slaves, if they could make good their claim to it; but if I were allowed to keep it they should remain my slaves except a very few of them.

You tell me to keep my heart up and hope for a return of prosperity; I only wish there were some ground for that hope. Now I am miserable about getting your letters. Who will bring them to me? I should wait for them at Brindisi, but the sailors will not allow it because they don't want to lose the favorable breeze.

For the rest, Terentia mine, give yourself, as you can, honorable consolation. I have lived my life, I have been successful; not my faults, but my virtues have ruined me. . . . Take care of yourself as well as you can, and remember that I am much more troubled by your unhappiness than by my own.

Good-by, Terentia, best and most faithful of wives; good-by, my darling little daughter, and Cicero, the only hope left to me.

Your loving husband and father,
M. T. C.
(*Dora Pym*)

SUGGESTIONS FOR STUDY

1. What, according to Cicero, is the greatest victory Caesar has gained? Why? See Proverbs 16:32 for a good summary of the point. What does Cicero mean by the words, "the heat of passion, the foe of counsel"?

2. What does he think is the great work Caesar has ahead of him? What prophecy does Cicero make of posterity's attitude toward Caesar? Has it been fulfilled?

3. Does this speech seem to you sincere? What do you think of Cicero as an impromptu speaker? Read others of Cicero's orations and compare him with Pericles (see page 967) and with famous orators not in this book, such as Burke, Webster, Clay.

4. What light does Cicero's letter throw on his character and disposition? How does it change the impression you might have from reading the speech alone?

5. Cicero and Pliny are the most famous Roman letter writers; Madame de Sévigné and Voltaire are among the most pleasing of the French; Goethe and Nietzsche, among the best-known of the German. Who are the most celebrated English and American letter writers? What was the great period of letter writing in modern times? From one of the many collections of miscellaneous letters in school editions read letters by some of these writers.

HORACE (65–8 B.C.)

Quintus Horatius Flaccus was born of humble parents in the south of Italy. He was given the best education the age afforded, at Rome and at Athens. After the assassination of Caesar, he joined the army of Brutus and was in command of a legion in the battle of Philippi. The defeat of the republicans rendered Horace's position precarious. Fortunately, through the friendship of Virgil he was introduced to the wealthy Maecenas, who acted as his patron and gave him the celebrated Sabine farm where he could live free from care and devote himself to poetry. Horace now accepted the imperial rule without too many qualms and even became one of its most eloquent defenders. His charming personality and broad humanity endeared him to people and no doubt explain his intimacy with the austere Virgil, who was his opposite in temperament and disposition.

The *Odes* are by far his most famous poems. They have been as widely read as Virgil's *Aeneid*. His *Satires* reveal the critical bent of his mind, while his mellow *Epistles* express his soberer reflections on life. All his poems are perfect in metrical structure and felicitous phrasing. His profundity and orginality are more open to question. He did not plumb the depths nor scale the heights of human emotions; as a practical man of the world he was content with the middle range. There is evidence that he sometimes described emotions which he did not really feel. But at least his patriotism and his loyal devotion to his friends were genuine. His philosophy of life, which he had learned from the Epicureans, was to pursue pleasure rationally. Observe the golden mean, be moderate in all things, do not despise the pleasures of the moment, such as love and wine, but remember that a contented mind is the greatest of all boons — such was his counsel to all men. The passionate conviction of Lucretius, the emotional intensity of Catullus, the majestic manner of Virgil were beyond his powers. He was essentially the poet of sound judgment and good taste and as such he has delighted innumerable readers in all countries since his time.

A list of his translators in English reads like a roll call of the poets, as witness Ben Jonson, Milton, Dryden, Pope, Cowper, Matthew Arnold, Austin Dobson, Eugene Field, Louis Untermeyer. Even statesmen like John Quincy Adams and Gladstone have turned poet in his behalf. There is something in the neatness and completeness of his phrasing which goads his reader into attempting to express it in his own tongue. And we have the results in all styles, ranging from the eighteenth-century precision of Pope to the twentieth-century chuckles of the columnist F. P. A. Today Horace seems the most alive of any poet in a dead language.

TO THE FOUNTAIN OF BANDUSIA

O fountain of Bandusia!
Whence crystal waters flow,
With garlands gay and wine I'll pay
The sacrifice I owe;
A sportive kid with budding horns   5
I have, whose crimson blood
Anon shall dye and sanctify
Thy cool and babbling flood.

O fountain of Bandusia!
The Dog-star's hateful spell   10
No evil brings into the springs
That from thy bosom well;
Here oxen, wearied by the plow,
The roving cattle here
Hasten in quest of certain rest,   15
And quaff thy gracious cheer.

O fountain of Bandusia!
Ennobled shalt thou be,
For I shall sing the joys that spring
Beneath yon ilex-tree.   20
Yes, fountain of Bandusia,
Posterity shall know
The cooling brooks that from thy nooks
Singing and dancing go.

(Eugene Field)

1. **Bandusia:** a fountain in southern Italy near Horace's birthplace. 10. **Dog-star:** the conjunction of the rising of the Dog-star (Sirius) with the rising of the sun was regarded by the ancients as a cause of the sultry heat of summer. We still use the term "dog days." 20. **ilex-tree:** a kind of oak tree.

THE SHIP OF STATE

The exact occasion of this poem is unknown. It might have been written at any time during the troubled period before the final establishment of the Empire. Though no politician himself, Horace followed public events with the most fervent patriotic interest. One of his most famous lines is " Good 'tis and fine for fatherland to die."

O ship of state,
Shall new winds bear you back upon the sea?
What are you doing? Seek the harbor's lee
    Ere 'tis too late!

Do you bemoan   5
Your side was stripped of oarage in the blast?
Swift Africus has weakened, too, your mast;
    The sailyards groan.

Of cables bare,
Your keel can scarce endure the lordly wave.   10
Your sails are rent; you have no gods to save,
    Or answer prayer.

Though Pontic pine,
The noble daughter of a far-famed wood,
You boast your lineage and title good, —   15
    A useless line!

The sailor there
In painted sterns no reassurance finds;
Unless you owe derision to the winds,
    Beware — beware!   20

My grief erewhile,
But now my care — my longing! shun the seas
That flow between the gleaming Cyclades,
    Each shining isle.

                              (*R. M. Field*)

7. **Africus:** the southwest wind.   13. **Pontic:** from Pontus, a tract of Asia Minor bordering on the Black Sea.   23. **Cyclades:** a group of islands in the Greek Archipelago.

TO LEUCONÖE

What end the gods may have ordained for me,
    And what for thee,
        Seek not to learn, Leuconöe; we may not know.
Chaldean tables cannot bring us rest.
    'Tis for the best   5
        To bear in patience what may come, or weal or woe.

4. **Chaldean tables:** the calculations of Chaldean (Babylonian) astronomers. Rome was full of Oriental fortune tellers in Horace's day.

If for more winters our poor lot is cast,
Or this the last,
  Which on the crumbing rocks has dashed Etruscan seas,
  Strain clear the wine; this life is short, at best.   10
Take hope with zest,
    And, trusting not Tomorrow, snatch Today for ease!

(R. M. Field)

TO MISTRESS PYRRHA

What dainty boy with sweet perfumes bedewed
Has lavished kisses, Pyrrha, in the cave?
For whom amid the roses, many-hued,
Do you bind back your tresses' yellow wave?

How oft will he deplore your fickle whim,   5
And wonder at the storm and roughening deeps,
Who now enjoys you, all in all to him,
And dreams of you, whose only thoughts he keeps.

Wretched are they to whom you seem so fair; —
That I escaped the storms, the gods be praised!   10
My dripping garments, offered with a prayer,
Stand as a tablet to the sea-god raised.

(R. M. Field)

TO CHLOE

Chloe, you shun me like a hind
  That, seeking vainly for her mother,
Hears danger in each breath of wind,
  And wildly darts this way and t'other;

Whether the breezes sway the wood   5
  Or lizards scuttle through the brambles,
She starts, and off, as though pursued,
  The foolish, frightened creature scrambles.

But, Chloe, you're no infant thing
  That should esteem a man an ogre;   10
Let go your mother's apron-string,
  And pin your faith upon a toga!

(Eugene Field)

A PARAPHRASE OF THE PRECEDING ODE

How happens it, my cruel miss,
   You're always giving me the mitten?
You seem to have forgotten this:
   That you no longer are a kitten!

A woman that has reached the years   **5**
   Of that which people call discretion
Should put aside all childish fears
   And see in courtship no transgression.

A mother's solace may be sweet,
   But Hymen's tenderness is sweeter;   **10**
And though all virile love be meet,
   You'll find the poet's love is meter.

                      (Eugene Field)

SUGGESTIONS FOR STUDY

1. What are the various interests which Horace manifests in these odes? Which lines best express his philosophy of life?

2. What is his general attitude toward women? What differences do you find in the various poems on the subject?

3. Which of the poems do you like best? For what reasons? Why have the poems of Horace appealed so strongly to "men of the world"? Read some translations made by famous personages. A good selection is to be found in Van Doren's *Anthology of World Poetry*.

4. Comparing these odes of Horace with the poems of Catullus, what is the chief difference you note? How do these differ from the typical English ode form?

5. What modern poems do you know which resemble the odes of Horace in sentiment, tone, or style? In what American poem is the image of the Ship of State employed?

VIRGIL (70–19 B.C.)

Publius Vergilius Maro was born of peasant stock near Mantua. The love of country life and the knowledge of farming which he shows in his writings may be traced to his early experiences. He was educated in the schools of the neighboring towns and afterwards in Rome and Naples. He secured the patronage of the rich and powerful Maecenas and thus was enlisted in the service of the Emperor Augustus. His tranquil and secluded life was spent chiefly in Rome and in the vicinity of Naples. He died at Brindisi on his return from a journey to Athens and was buried at Naples, where his tomb was long regarded with religious veneration. Horace and others have testified to the great affection and esteem in which he was held by all who knew him.

Virgil occupies a central and commanding position in Roman literature and is preëminently the national poet. His literary career falls into two parts. In the earlier period he composed his pastoral poems known as the *Eclogues* or *Bucolics* and a set of didactic poems called the *Georgics*. These poems proclaim the charm of Italy. In his second period he wrote his epic, the *Aeneid,* which declares the glory of Rome. The *Aeneid* was greeted at once as the unapproached masterpiece of Roman literature and as the equal of the Homeric poems. It is only during the last hundred years or so that Virgil's claim to be ranked among the world's supremely great poets has been seriously disputed. In any case he is certainly the most finished literary artist that Rome produced. He excels in "that subtle fusion of the music and the meaning of language which touches the deepest and most secret springs of emotion." He touches especially the emotions of wonder, admiration, and reverence. His influence on all the literatures of Western Europe has been incalculably great.

THE AENEID

Whether or not the *Aeneid* was written at the request of Augustus, as has been reported, it was plainly intended to be the national epic of Rome. Though the hero, Aeneas, is a purely mythical figure, he embodies the Roman ideal of character and it is his definite mission in life to found Rome. Moreover, Virgil assumes in the poem the tone of a prophet: Rome has equally a mission to fulfill, which is to establish peace and order and to rule the world through law. The *Aeneid* consists of twelve books. The first six, influenced by the *Odyssey,* narrate the wanderings of Aeneas after the fall of Troy; the last six, patterned on the *Iliad,* tell of the fighting in Latium which led up to the founding of Rome. Though he took Homer as a model, Virgil was essentially original in the shaping of his material and in his imaginative interpretation. Aeneas is represented not only as the founder of Rome but as the personal ancestor of the Caesars as well. He is the son of Anchises and Venus — half-Trojan and half-divinity. Fleeing with a small band of followers from Troy, which the Greeks have taken and destroyed, he comes, after many adventures on land and sea, to Carthage and tells to Queen Dido the story of the fall of Troy. The love episode of Aeneas and Dido is the most romantic passage in the poem. When he leaves her at the call of duty, she takes her own life. Arriving in Italy, he first visits the lower world to consult with the spirit of his father. On his return to the upper world, he is cordially received by King Latinus. But a local prince, Turnus, becomes his mortal enemy and fighting ensues with varying shifts of fortune. Finally Aeneas slays Turnus in single combat, and so the story ends.

Compared with the primitive simplicity of the Homeric poems, the *Aeneid* seems sophisticated. It substitutes conscious artistry for native inspiration. As a hero, the " pious " Aeneas does not enlist our sympathies in the way that Achilles and Hector and Ulysses do. Some moderns have even called him a prig. But Virgil felt the necessity of holding up to his age the ideal of filial obedience and steadfast purpose. There was something of the same priestlike quality in his own character, which explains in part why the Middle Ages regarded him as supernaturally endowed and why Dante chose him to represent human wisdom and to act as his guide through the Inferno.

BOOK II

Aeneas relates to Queen Dido of Carthage how Troy was finally captured.

All were attentive to the godlike man,
When, from his lofty couch, he thus began:

" Great queen! what you command me to relate
Renews the sad remembrance of our fate,
An empire from its old foundations rent,   5
And every woe the Trojans underwent;
A peopled city made a desert place;
All that I saw, and part of which I was,
Not ev'n the hardest of our foes could hear,
Nor stern Ulysses tell without a tear.   10
And now the latter watch of wasting night,
And setting stars, to kindly rest invite.
But, since you take such interest in our woe,
And Troy's disastrous end desire to know,
I will restrain my tears, and briefly tell   15
What in our last and fatal night befell.

" By destiny compelled, and in despair,
The Greeks grew weary of the tedious war;
And, by Minerva's aid, a fabric reared,
Which, like a steed of monstrous height, appeared;   20

10. **Ulysses:** one of the Greek leaders and hero of Homer's *Odyssey*
19. **Minerva:** goddess of wisdom, called by the Greeks Pallas.

The sides were planked with pine, they feigned it made
For their return, and this the vow they paid.
Thus they pretend; but in the hollow side
Selected numbers of their soldiers hide.
With inward arms the dire machine they load,   25
And iron bowels stuff the dark abode.
In sight of Troy lies Tenedos, an isle
(While fortune did on Priam's empire smile)
Renowned for wealth; but since a faithless bay,
Where ships exposed to winds and weather lay.   30
There was their fleet concealed; we thought for Greece
The sails were hoisted, and our fears release.
The Trojans, cooped within their walls so long,
Unbar their gates, and issue in a throng,
Like swarming bees, and with delight survey   35
The camp deserted where the Grecians lay.
The quarters of the several chiefs they showed,
' Here Phoenix, here Achilles made abode,
Here joined the battles, there the navy rode.'
Part on the pile their wondering eyes employ   40
(The pile by Pallas raised to ruin Troy).
Thymaetes first ('tis doubtful whether hired,
Or so the Trojan destiny required)
Moved that the ramparts might be broken down,
To lodge the monster fabric in the town.   45
But Capys, and the rest of sounder mind,
The fatal present to the flames designed;
Or to the watery deep; at least to bore
The hollow sides, and hidden frauds explore.
The giddy vulgar, as their fancies guide,
With noise say nothing, and in parts divide.   50
Laocoön, followed by a numerous crowd,
Ran from the fort; and cried, from far, aloud:
' O wretched countrymen! what fury reigns?
What more than madness has possessed your brains?   55
Think you the Grecians from your coasts are gone,
And are Ulysses' arts no better known?

---

28. **Priam:** King of Troy.   38. **Phoenix:** teacher of Achilles.   38. **Achilles:** the most formidable of the Greek warriors.   42. **Thymaetes:** one of the aged counselors.   46. **Capys:** companion of Aeneas.   50. **giddy vulgar:** fickle mob. 52. **Laocoön:** brother of Anchises and uncle of Aeneas.

This hollow fabric either must enclose,
Within its blind recess, our secret foes;
Or 'tis an engine raised above the town,   60
'T' o'erlook the walls, and then to batter down.
Somewhat is sure designed, by fraud or force;
Trust not their presents, nor admit the horse.'
Thus having said, against the steed he threw
His forceful spear, which, hissing as it flew,   65
Pierced through the yielding planks of jointed wood,
And trembling in the hollow belly stood.
The sides transpierced return a rattling sound,
And groans of Greeks enclosed come issuing through the wound.
And had not Heaven the fall of Troy designed,   70
Or had not men been fated to be blind,
Enough was said and done, t' inspire a better mind;
Then had our lances pierced the treacherous wood,
And Ilian towers and Priam's empire stood.
Meantime, with shouts, the Trojan shepherds bring   75
A captive Greek in bands before the king;
Taken, to take; who made himself their prey,
T' impose on their belief, and Troy betray;
Fixed on his aim, and obstinately bent
To die undaunted, or to circumvent.   80
About the captive, tides of Trojans flow;
All press to see, and some insult the foe.
Now hear how well the Greeks their wiles disguised,
Behold a nation in a man comprised.
Trembling the miscreant stood, unarmed and bound.   85
He stared, and rolled his haggard eyes around;
Then said, ' Alas! what earth remains, what sea
Is open to receive unhappy me!
What fate a wretched fugitive attends,
Scorned by my foes, abandoned by my friends! '   90
He said and sighed, and cast a rueful eye;
Our pity kindles, and our passions die.
We cheer the youth to make his own defense,
And freely tell us what he was, and whence.
What news he could impart, we long to know,   95
And what to credit from a captive foe.

74. **Ilian:** of Ilium or Troy.   77. **Taken, to take:** destined to capture his captors.

" His fear at length dismissed, he said, ' Whate'er
My fate ordains, my words shall be sincere.
I neither can, nor dare, my birth disclaim;
Greece is my country, Sinon is my name.   100
Though plunged by fortune's power in misery,
'Tis not in fortune's power to make me lie.
If any chance has hither brought the name
Of Palamedes, not unknown to fame,
Who suffered from the malice of the times,   105
Accused and sentenced for pretended crimes,
Because the fatal wars he would prevent,
Whose death the wretched Greeks too late lament,
Me, then a boy, my father, poor and bare
Of other means, committed to his care,   110
His kinsman and companion in the war.
While fortune favored, while his arms support
The cause, and ruled the counsels of the court,
I made some figure there; nor was my name
Obscure, nor I without my share of fame.   115
But when Ulysses, with fallacious arts,
Had made impression in the people's hearts;
And forged a treason in my patron's name
(I speak of things too far divulged by fame),
My kinsman fell; then I, without support,   120
In private mourned his loss, and left the court.
Mad as I was, I could not bear his fate
With silent grief, but loudly blamed the state;
And cursed the direful author of my woes.
'Twas told again, and hence my ruin rose.   125
I threatened, if indulgent Heaven once more
Would land me safely on my native shore,
His death with double vengeance to restore.
This moved the murderer's hate, and soon ensued
Th' effects of malice from a man so proud.   130
Ambiguous rumors through the camp he spread,
And sought, by treason, my devoted head;
New crimes invented, left unturned no stone
To make my guilt appear, and hide his own,
Till Calchas was by force and threatening wrought.   135

104. **Palamedes:** messenger sent to persuade Ulysses to join the Greeks in the war against Troy.   135. **Calchas:** priest of Apollo.   135. **wrought:** worked upon.

But why — why dwell I on that anxious thought?
If on my nation just revenge you seek,
And 'tis t' appear a foe, t' appear a Greek,
Already you my name and country know,
Assuage your thirst of blood, and strike the blow.   140
My death will both the kingly brothers please,
And set insatiate Ithacus at ease.'
This fair unfinished tale, these broken starts,
Raised expectations in our longing hearts,
Unknowing as we were in Grecian arts.   145
His former trembling once again renewed,
With acted fear, the villain thus pursued:

" ' Long had the Grecians (tired with fruitless care,
And wearied with an unsuccessful war)
Resolved to raise the siege, and leave the town;   150
And, had the gods permitted, they had gone.
But oft the wintery seas and southern winds
Withstood their passage home, and changed their minds.
Portents and prodigies their souls amazed;
But most, when this stupendous pile was raised.   155
Then flaming meteors, hung in air, were seen,
And thunders rattled through a sky serene.
Dismayed, and fearful of some dire event,
Eurypylus, t' inquire their fate, was sent;
He from the gods this dreadful answer brought: 160

" ' O Grecians! when the Trojan shores you sought,
Your passage with a virgin's blood was bought!
So must your safe return be bought again,
And Grecian blood once more atone the main! '
The spreading rumor round the people ran;   165
All feared, and each believed himself the man.
Ulysses took th' advantage of their fright;
Called Calchas, and produced in open sight;
Then bade him name the wretch, ordained by fate
The public victim, to redeem the state.   170
Already some presaged the dire event,

141. kingly brothers: Agamemnon and Menelaus, leaders of the Greeks.
142. insatiate: never satisfied.   142. Ithacus: Ulysses, whose home was
Ithaca.   162. virgin's blood: the reference is to the sacrifice of Iphigenia by
her father Agamemnon.   164. main: high seas.   171. presaged: foreshadowed.

And saw what sacrifice Ulysses meant.
For twice five days the good old seer withstood
Th' intended treason, and was dumb to blood.
Till, tired with endless clamors, and pursuit   175
Of Ithacus, he stood no longer mute;
But, as it was agreed, pronounced that I
Was destined by the wrathful gods to die!
All praised the sentence, pleased the storm should fall
On one alone, whose fury threatened all.   180
The dismal day was come, the priests prepare
Their leavened cakes, and fillets for my hair.
I followed nature's laws, and must avow
I broke my bonds, and fled the fatal blow.
Hid in a weedy lake all night I lay,   185
Secure of safety when they sailed away.
But now what further hopes for me remain,
To see my friends or native soil again?
My tender infants, or my careful sire,
Whom they returning will to death require?   190
Will perpetrate on them their first design,
And take the forfeit of their heads for mine!
Which, oh, if pity mortal minds can move,
If there be faith below, or gods above,
If innocence and truth can claim desert,   195
Ye Trojans, from an injured wretch avert.'
False tears true pity move. The king commands
To loose his fetters, and unbind his hands;
Then adds these friendly words: ' Dismiss thy fears,
Forget the Greeks, be mine as thou wert theirs.   200
But truly tell, was it for force or guile,
Or some religious end, you raised this pile.'
Thus said the king. He, full of fraudful arts,
This well invented tale for truth imparts:
' Ye lamps of Heaven! ' he said, and lifted high   205
His hands now free, ' thou venerable sky,
Inviolable powers, adored with dread,
Ye fatal fillets, that once bound this head,
Ye sacred altars, from whose flames I fled,
Be all of you abjured; and grant I may,   210
Without a crime, th' ungrateful Greeks betray!

182. **fillets:** head-bands.   202. **pile:** the wooden horse.

Reveal the secrets of the guilty state,
And justly punish whom I justly hate!
But you, O king! preserve the faith you gave,
If I, to save myself, your empire save.   215
The Grecian hopes, and all th' attempts they made,
Were only founded on Minerva's aid.
But from the time when impious Diomede,
And false Ulysses, that inventive head,
Her fatal image from the temple drew,   220
The sleeping guardians of the castle slew,
Her virgin statue with their bloody hands
Polluted, and profaned her holy bands.
From thence the tide of fortune left their shore,
And ebbed much faster than it flowed before.   225
Their courage languished, as their hopes decayed,
And Pallas, now averse, refused her aid,
Nor did the goddess doubtfully declare
Her altered mind, and alienated care.
When first her fatal image touched the ground,   230
She sternly cast her glaring eyes around,
That sparkled as they rolled, and seemed to threat;
Her heavenly limbs distilled a briny sweat.
Thrice from the ground she leaped, was seen to wield
Her brandished lance, and shake her horrid shield!   235
Then Calchas bade our host for flight prepare,
And hope no conquest from the tedious war,
Till first they sailed for Greece; with prayers besought
Her injured power, and better omens brought.
And now their navy ploughs the watery main,   240
Yet, soon expect it on your shores again,
With Pallas pleased, as Calchas did ordain.
But first, to reconcile the blue-eyed maid,
For her stolen statue, and her tower betrayed,
Warned by the seer, to her offended name   245
We raised, and dedicate this wondrous frame,
So lofty, lest through your forbidden gates
It pass, and intercept our better fates.
For, once admitted there, our hopes are lost;
And Troy may then a new Palladium boast.   250

218. **Diomede:** one of the foremost of the Greek heroes.   243. **blue-eyed maid:** Pallas.   250. **Palladium:** statue of Pallas in Troy.

For so religion and the gods ordain,
That if you violate with hands profane
Minerva's gift, your town in flames shall burn
(Which omen, O ye gods, on Graecia turn)!
But if it climb, with your assisting hands,   255
The Trojan walls, and in the city stands,
Then Troy shall Argos and Mycenae burn,
And the reverse of fate on us return.'

" With such deceits he gained their easy hearts,
Too prone to credit his perfidious arts,   260
What Diomede, nor Thetis's greater son,
A thousand ships, nor ten years' siege had done.
False tears and fawning words the city won.
A greater omen, and of worse portent,
Did our unwary minds with fear torment,   265
Concurring to produce the dire event.
Laocoön, Neptune's priest by lot that year,
With solemn pomp then sacrificed a steer.
When, dreadful to behold, from sea we spied
Two serpents ranked abreast, the seas divide,   270
And smoothly sweep along the swelling tide.
Their flaming crests above the waves they show,
Their bellies seem to burn the seas below,
Their speckled tails advance to steer their course,
And, on the sounding shore, the flying billows force.   275
And now the strand, and now the plain they held,
Their ardent eyes with bloody streaks were filled;
Their nimble tongues they brandished as they came,
And licked their hissing jaws that sputtered flame.
We fled amazed; their destined way they take,   280
And to Laocoön and his children make;
And first around the tender boys they wind,
Then with their sharpened fangs their limbs and bodies grind.
The wretched father, running to their aid
With pious haste, but vain, they next invade.   285
Twice round his waist their winding volumes rolled,
And twice about his gasping throat they fold.
The priest, thus doubly choked, their crests divide,
And, towering o'er his head, in triumph ride.

261. **Thetis:** mother of Achilles.

With both his hands he labors at the knots, 290
His holy fillets the blue venom blots.
His roaring fills the flitting air around.
Thus, when an ox receives a glancing wound,
He breaks his bands, the fatal altar flies,
And, with loud bellowings, breaks the yielding skies. 295
Their tasks performed, the serpents quit their prey,
And to the tower of Pallas make their way.
Couched at her feet, they lie protected there,
By her large buckler, and protended spear.
Amazement seizes all; the general cry 300
Proclaims Laocoön justly doomed to die,
Whose hand the will of Pallas had withstood,
And dared to violate the sacred wood.
All vote t' admit the steed, that vows be paid,
And incense offered, to th' offended maid. 305
A spacious breach is made, the town lies bare,
Some hoisting levers, some the wheels prepare,
And fasten to the horse's feet; the rest
With cables haul along th' unwieldy beast.
Each on his fellow for assistance calls. 310
At length the fatal fabric mounts the walls,
Big with destruction. Boys with chaplets crowned,
And choirs of virgins, sing and dance around.
Thus raised aloft, and then descending down,
It enters o'er our heads, and threats the town. 315
O sacred city! built by hands divine!
O valiant heroes of the Trojan line!
Four times he stuck; as oft the clashing sound
Of arms was heard, and inward groans rebound.
Yet, mad with zeal, and blinded with our fate, 320
We haul along the horse in solemn state;
Then place the dire portent within the tower.
Cassandra cried, and cursed the unhappy hour;
Foretold our fate; but, by the god's decree,
All heard, and none believed, the prophecy. 325
With branches we the fanes adorn, and waste
In jollity the day ordained to be the last.
Meantime the rapid heavens rolled down the light,

---

299. **protended:** outstretched. 323. **Cassandra:** daughter of Priam and
a prophetess doomed never to be believed. 326. **fanes:** temples.

And on the shaded ocean rushed the night.
Our men secure, nor guards nor sentries held,   330
But easy sleep their weary limbs compelled.
The Grecians had embarked their naval powers
From Tenedos, and sought our well-known shores,
Safe under covert of the silent night,
And guided by th' imperial galley's light.   335
When Sinon, favored by the partial gods,
Unlocked the horse, and oped his dark abodes;
Restored to vital air our hidden foes,
Who joyful from their long confinement rose.
Tysander bold, and Sthenelus their guide,   340
And dire Ulysses, down the cable slide.
Then Thoas, Athamas, and Pyrrhus haste;
Nor was the Podalirian hero last;
Nor injured Menelaus, nor the famed
Epeus, who the fatal engine framed.   345
A nameless crowd succeed; their forces join
T' invade the town, oppressed with sleep and wine.
Those few they find awake first meet their fate,
Then to their fellows they unbar the gate.
'Twas in the dead of night, when sleep repairs   350
Our bodies worn with toils, our minds with cares,
When Hector's ghost before my sight appears;
A bloody shroud he seemed, and bathed in tears.
Such as he was, when, by Pelides slain,
Thessalian coursers dragged him o'er the plain.   355
Swollen were his feet, as when the thongs were thrust
Through the bored holes, his body black with dust.
Unlike that Hector, who returned from toils
Of war triumphant, in Aeacian spoils,
Or him, who made the fainting Greeks retire,   360
And launched against their navy Phrygian fire.
His hair and beard stood stiffened with his gore;
And all the wounds, he for his country bore,
Now streamed afresh, and with new purple ran.
I wept to see the visionary man,   365

343. **Podalirian hero:** leader of the Thessalians against the Trojans.
346. **succeed:** follow.   352. **Hector:** son of Priam and greatest of the Trojan
heroes.   He was slain by Achilles.   354. **Pelides:** Achilles, son of Peleus.
359. **Aeacian:** named after Aeacus, grandfather of Achilles.   361. **Phrygian:**
Trojan.

And, while my trance continued, thus began:
' O light of Trojans, and support of Troy,
Thy father's champion, and thy country's joy!
O long expected by thy friends! from whence
Art thou so late returned for our defense?   370
Do we behold thee, wearied as we are,
With length of labors, and with toils of war?
After so many funerals of thy own,
Art thou restored to thy declining town?
But say, what wounds are these?   What new disgrace   375
Deforms the manly features of thy face? '
To this the specter no reply did frame;
But answered to the cause for which he came,
And, groaning from the bottom of his breast,
This warning, in these mournful words, expressed: 380
' O goddess-born! escape, by timely flight,
The flames and horrors of this fatal night.
The foes, already, have possessed the wall,
Troy nods from high, and totters to her fall.
Enough is paid to Priam's royal name,   385
More than enough to duty and to fame.
If by a mortal hand my father's throne
Could be defended, 'twas by mine alone.
Now Troy to thee commends her future state,
And gives her gods companions of thy fate: 390
From their assistance happier walls expect,
Which, wandering long, at last thou shalt erect.'
He said, and brought me, from their blest abodes,
The venerable statues of the gods.
With ancient Vesta from the sacred choir   395
The wreaths and relics of th' immortal fire.

" Now peals of shouts come thundering from afar,
Cries, threats, and loud laments, and mingled war!
The noise approaches, though our palace stood
Aloof from streets, encompassed with a wood.   400
Louder, and yet more loud, I hear th' alarms
Of human cries distinct, and clashing arms!
Fear broke my slumbers; I no longer stay,

381. **goddess-born**: Aeneas was the son of Venus.   395. **Vesta**: goddess of
the hearth.   396. **immortal fire**: the fire of Vesta was supposed never to go out.

But mount the terrace, thence the town survey,
And hearken what the fruitful sounds convey! 405
Thus when a flood of fire by wind is borne,
Crackling it rolls, and mows the standing corn;
Or deluges, descending on the plains,
Sweep o'er the yellow year, destroy the pains
Of laboring oxen, and the peasant's gains, 410
Unroot the forest oaks, and bear away
Flocks, folds, and trees, an undistinguished prey!
The shepherd climbs the cliff, and sees, from far,
The wasteful ravage of the watery war.
Then Hector's faith was manifestly cleared; 415
And Grecian frauds in open light appeared!
The palace of Deïphobus ascends
In smoky flames, and catches on his friend's;
Ucalegon burns next; the seas are bright
With splendor not their own, and shine with Trojan light. 420
New clamors and new clangors now arise,
The sound of trumpets mixed with fighting cries!
With frenzy seized, I run to meet th' alarms,
Resolved on death, resolved to die in arms!
But first to gather friends, with them t' oppose, 425
If fortune favored, and repel the foes;
Spurred by my courage, by my country fired,
With sense of honor, and revenge inspired!

" Pantheus, Apollo's priest, a sacred name,
Had 'scaped the Grecian swords, and passed the flame; 430
With relics loaden, to my doors he fled,
And, by the hand, his tender grandson led.
' What hope, O Pantheus whither can we run?
Where make a stand? and what may yet be done? '
Scarce had I said, when Pantheus, with a groan, 435
' Troy is no more, and Ilium was a town!
The fatal day, th' appointed hour, is come,
When wrathful Jove's irrevocable doom
Transfers the Trojan state to Grecian hands.
The fire consumes the town, the foe commands! 440
And armed hosts, an unexpected force,

417. **Deïphobus:** brother of Hector and next to him the bravest of the
Trojans.   419. **Ucalegon:** the house of Ucalegon.

Break from the bowels of the fatal horse!
Within the gates proud Sinon throws about
The flames, and foes for entrance press without,
With thousand others, whom I fear to name, 445
More than from Argos or Mycenae came.
To several posts their parties they divide;
Some block the narrow streets, some scour the wide.
The bold they kill, th' unwary they surprise;
Who fights finds death, and death finds him who flies. 450
The warders of the gate but scarce maintain
Th' unequal combat, and resist in vain.'
I heard; and Heaven, that well-born souls inspires,
Prompts me, through lifted swords and rising fires,
To run, where clashing arms and clamor calls, 455
And rush undaunted to defend the walls!
Ripheus and Iphitus by my side engage,
For valor one renowned, and one for age.
Dymas and Hypanis by moonlight knew
My motions and my mien, and to my party drew; 460
With young Choroebus, who by love was led
To win renown, and fair Cassandra's bed;
And lately brought his troops to Priam's aid,
Forewarned in vain by the prophetic maid.
Whom, when I saw, resolved in arms to fall, 465
And that one spirit animated all.
' Brave souls,' said I, ' but brave, alas! in vain,
Come, finish what our cruel fates ordain;
You see the desperate state of our affairs,
And Heaven's protecting powers are deaf to prayers. 470
The passive gods behold the Greeks defile
Their temples, and abandon to the spoil
Their own abodes; we, feeble few, conspire
To save a sinking town involved in fire.
Then let us fall, but fall amidst our foes; 475
Despair of life, the means of living shows.'
So bold a speech encouraged their desire
Of death, and added fuel to their fire!

" As hungry wolves, with raging appetite,
Scour through the fields, nor fear the stormy night, 48¢

461. **Choroebus:** son of the King of Phrygia.

Their whelps at home expect the promised food,
And long to temper their dry chaps in blood,
So rushed we forth at once, resolved to die,
Resolved in death the last extremes to try!
We leave the narrow lanes behind, and dare   485
Th' unequal combat in the public square.
Night was our friend, our leader was Despair.
What tongue can tell the slaughter of that night!
What eyes can weep the sorrows and affright!
An ancient and imperial city falls,   490
The streets are filled with frequent funerals.
Houses and holy temples float in blood,
And hostile nations make a common flood.
Not only Trojans fall, but, in their turn,
The vanquished triumph, and the victors mourn.   495
Ours take new courage from despair and night;
Confused the fortune is, confused the fight.
All parts resound with tumults, plaints, and fears,
And grisly death in sundry shapes appears!
Androgeos fell among us, with his band,   500
Who thought us Grecians newly come to land.
' From whence,' said he, ' my friends, this long delay?
You loiter, while the spoils are borne away.
Our ships are laden with the Trojan store,
And you, like truants, come too late ashore.'   505
He said, but soon corrected his mistake,
Found by the doubtful answers which we make.
Amazed he would have shunned th' unequal fight,
But we, more numerous, intercept his flight.
As when some peasant, in a bushy brake,   510
Has, with unwary footing, pressed a snake,
He starts aside, astonished, when he spies
His rising crest, blue neck, and rolling eyes;
So from our arms surprised Androgeos flies!
In vain; for him and his we compass round,   515
Possessed with fear, unknowing of the ground;
And of their lives an easy conquest found.
Thus Fortune on our first endeavor smiled;
Choroebus then, with youthful hopes beguiled,
Swollen with success, and of a daring mind,   520

482. temper: soothe. 482. chaps: chops, jaws.

This new invention fatally designed.
' My friends,' said he, ' since Fortune shows the way,
'Tis fit we should th' auspicious guide obey.
For what has she these Grecian arms bestowed,
But their destruction, and the Trojans' good? 525
Then change we shields, and their devices bear,
Let fraud supply the want of force in war.
They find us arms.' This said, himself he dressed
In dead Androgeos' spoils, his upper vest,
His painted buckler, and his plumy crest. 530
Thus Rypheus, Dymas, all the Trojan train,
Lay down their own attire, and strip the slain.
Mixed with the Greeks, we go with ill presage,
Flattered with hopes to glut our greedy rage;
Unknown, assaulting whom we blindly meet, 535
And strew, with Grecian carcases, the street.
Thus while their straggling parties we defeat,
Some to the shore and safer ships retreat;
And some, oppressed with more ignoble fear,
Remount the hollow horse, and pant in secret there. 540

" But ah! what use of valor can be made,
When Heaven's propitious powers refuse their aid!
Behold the royal prophetess, the fair
Cassandra, dragged by her dishevelled hair;
Whom not Minerva's shrine, nor sacred bands, 545
In safety could protect from sacrilegious hands:
On Heaven she cast her eyes, she sighed, she cried
('Twas all she could), her tender arms were tied.
So sad a sight Choroebus could not bear;
But, fired with rage, distracted with despair, 550
Amid the barbarous ravishers he flew;
Our leader's rash example we pursue;
But storms of stones, from the proud temple's height,
Pour down, and on our battered helms alight.
We from our friends received this fatal blow, 555
Who thought us Grecians, as we seemed in show.
They aim at the mistaken crests, from high,
And ours beneath the ponderous ruin lie.
Then, moved with anger and disdain, to see
Their troops dispersed, the royal virgin free, 560

The Grecians rally, and their powers unite,
With fury charge us, and renew the fight.
The brother-kings with Ajax join their force,
And the whole squadron of Thessalian horse.

" Thus, when the rival winds their quarrel try,   565
Contending for the kingdom of the sky,
South, east, and west, on airy coursers borne,
The whirlwind gathers, and the woods are torn:
Then Nereus strikes the deep, the billows rise,
And, mixed with ooze and sand, pollute the skies.   570
The troops we squandered first again appear
From several quarters, and enclose the rear.
They first observe, and to the rest betray,
Our different speech; our borrowed arms survey.
Oppressed with odds, we fall; Choroebus first,   575
At Pallas's altar, by Peneleus pierced.
Then Rypheus followed, in th' unequal fight,
Just of his word, observant of the right.
Heaven thought not so: Dymas their fate attends,
With Hypanis, mistaken by their friends.   580
Nor Pantheus, thee, thy miter, nor the bands
Of awful Phoebus, saved from impious hands.
Ye Trojan flames, your testimony bear
What I performed, and what I suffered there,
No sword avoiding in the fatal strife,   585
Exposed to death, and prodigal of life.
Witness, ye Heavens! I live not by my fault;
I strove to have deserved the death I sought.
But when I could not fight, and would have died,
Borne off to distance by the growing tide,   590
Old Iphitus and I were hurried thence,
With Pelias wounded, and without defense.
New clamors from th' invested palace ring;
We run to die, or disengage the king.
So hot th' assault, so high the tumult rose,   595
While ours defend, and while the Greeks oppose,
As all the Dardan and Argolic race

563. **Ajax**: one of the most valiant of the Greek heroes. 569. **Nereus**: a sea-god. 579. **Dymas**: object, not subject, of attends. 581. **miter**: bishop's cap. 582. **Phoebus**: Apollo. 593. **invested**: besieged. 597. **Dardan**: Trojan. 597. **Argolic**: from Argos in Greece.

Had been contracted in that narrow space;
Or as all Ilium else were void of fear,
And tumult, war, and slaughter only there.   600
Their targets in a tortoise cast, the foes
Secure advancing, to the turrets rose.
Some mount the scaling ladders; some, more bold,
Swerve upwards, and by posts and pillars hold.
Their left hand gripes their bucklers in th' ascent,   605
While with the right they seize the battlement.
From the demolished towers the Trojans throw
Huge heaps of stones, that, falling, crush the foe.
And heavy beams and rafters from the sides
(Such arms their last necessity provides),   610
And gilded roofs come tumbling from on high,
The marks of state and ancient royalty.
The guards below, fixed in the pass, attend
The charge undaunted, and the gate defend.
Renewed in courage, with recovered breath,   615
A second time we ran to tempt our death,
To clear the palace from the foe, succeed
The weary living, and revenge the dead.
A postern door, yet unobserved and free,
Joined by the length of a blind gallery,   620
To the king's closet led, a way well known
To Hector's wife, while Priam held the throne:
Through which she brought Astyanax, unseen,
To cheer his grandsire and his grandsire's queen.
Through this we pass, and mount the tower from whence,   625
With unavailing arms, the Trojans make defense.
From this the trembling king had oft descried
The Grecian camp, and saw their navy ride.
Beams from his lofty height with swords we hew;
Then, wrenching with our hands, th' assault renew.   630
And, where the rafters on the columns meet,
We push them headlong with our arms and feet.
The lightning flies not swifter than the fall,
Nor thunder louder than the ruined wall.
Down goes the top at once; the Greeks beneath   635
Are piecemeal torn, or pounded into death.

601. **targets:** shields.   601. **tortoise:** screen formed with overlapping shields.
619. **postern door:** rear door.   623. **Astyanax:** son of Hector and Andromache.

Yet more succeed, and more to death are sent;
We cease not from above, nor they below relent.
Before the gate stood Pyrrhus, threatening loud,
With glittering arms conspicuous in the crowd.   640
So shines, renewed in youth, the crested snake,
Who slept the winter in a thorny brake;
And, casting off his slough, when spring returns,
Now looks aloft, and with new glory burns.
Restored with poisonous herbs, his ardent sides   645
Reflect the Sun, and, raised on spires, he rides;
High o'er the grass, hissing he rolls along,
And brandishes, by fits, his forky tongue.
Proud Periphas, and fierce Automedon,
His father's charioteer, together run   650
To force the gate; the Scyrian infantry
Rush on in crowds, and the barred passage free.
Entering the court, with shouts the skies they rend,
And flaming firebrands to the roofs ascend.
Himself, among the foremost, deals his blows,   655
And, with his ax, repeated strokes bestows
On the strong doors; then all their shoulders ply,
Till from the posts the brazen hinges fly.
He hews apace, the double bars at length
Yield to his ax, and unresisted strength.   660
A mighty breach is made; the rooms concealed
Appear, and all the palace is revealed:
The halls of audience, and of public state,
And where the lonely queen in secret sat.
Armed soldiers now by trembling maids are seen,   665
With not a door, and scarce a space between.
The house is filled with loud laments and cries,
And shrieks of women rend the vaulted skies.
The fearful matrons run from place to place,
And kiss the thresholds, and the posts embrace.   670
The fatal work inhuman Pyrrhus plies,
And all his father sparkles in his eyes.
Nor bars, nor fighting guards, his force sustain;
The bars are broken, and the guards are slain.
In rush the Greeks, and all th' apartments fill;   675

---

639. **Pyrrhus:** son of Achilles.   643. **slough:** skin.   The word is pronounced
sluff.   651. **Scyrian:** from Scyros, an island in the Aegean.

Those few defendants whom they find they kill.
Not with so fierce a rage, the foaming flood
Roars, when he finds his rapid course withstood,
Bears down the dams with unresisted sway,
And sweeps the cattle and the cots away.   680
These eyes beheld him, when he marched between
The brother-kings. I saw th' unhappy queen,
The hundred wives, and where old Priam stood,
To stain his hallowed altar with his blood.
The fifty nuptial beds (such hopes had he,   685
So large a promise of a progeny).
The posts of plated gold and hung with spoils
Fell the reward of the proud victor's toils.
Where'er the raging fire had left a space,
The Grecians enter, and possess the place.   690
Perhaps you may of Priam's fate inquire.
He, when he saw his regal town on fire,
His ruined palace, and his entering foes,
On every side inevitable woes,
In arms disused, invests his limbs decayed   695
Like them, with age — a late and useless aid.
His feeble shoulders scarce the weight sustain;
Loaded, not armed, he creeps along with pain,
Despairing of success, ambitious to be slain!
Uncovered but by Heaven, there stood in view   700
An altar; near the hearth a laurel grew,
Doddered with age, whose boughs encompass round
The household gods, and shade the holy ground.
Here Hecuba, with all her helpless train
Of dames, for shelter sought, but sought in vain.   705
Driven like a flock of doves along the sky,
Their images they hug, and to their altars fly.
The queen, when she beheld her trembling lord,
And hanging by his side a heavy sword,
' What rage,' she cried, ' has seized my husband's mind; 710
What arms are these, and to what use designed?
These times want other aids; were Hector here,
Even Hector now in vain, like Priam, would appear.
With us, one common shelter thou shalt find,

680. cots: cottages.   702. doddered: trembling with frailty.   704. Hecuba:
wife of Priam.

Or in one common fate with us be joined.'   715
She said: and with a last salute embraced
The poor old man, and by the laurel placed.
Behold Polites, one of Priam's sons,
Pursued by Pyrrhus, there for safety runs.
Through swords and foes, amazed and hurt he flies   720
Through empty courts, and open galleries.
Him Pyrrhus, urging with his lance, pursues,
And often reaches, and his thrusts renews.
The youth transfixed, with lamentable cries,
Expires, before his wretched parents' eyes.   725
Whom, gasping at his feet, when Priam saw,
The fear of death gave place to nature's law.
And, shaking more with anger than with age,
' The gods,' said he, ' requite thy brutal rage,
As sure they will, barbarian; sure they must,   730
If there be gods in Heaven, and gods be just;
Who tak'st in wrongs an insolent delight,
With a son's death t' infect a father's sight.
Not he, whom thou and lying fame conspire
To call thee his; not he, thy vaunted sire,   735
Thus used my wretched age; the gods he feared,
The laws of nature and of nations heard.
He cheered my sorrows, and, for sums of gold,
The bloodless carcase of my Hector sold,
Pitied the woes a parent underwent,   740
And sent me back in safety from his tent.'

" This said, his feeble hand a javelin threw,
Which, fluttering, seemed to loiter as it flew;
Just, and but barely, to the mark it held,
And faintly tinkled on the brazen shield.   745

" Then Pyrrhus thus: ' Go thou from me to fate;
And to my father my foul deeds relate.
Now die.' With that he dragged the trembling sire,
Sliddering through clottered blood and holy mire
(The mingled paste his murdered son had made),   750
Hauled from beneath the violated shade,
And on the sacred pile the royal victim laid.

        749. **sliddering:** sliding.   749. **clottered:** clotted.

His right hand held his bloody falchion bare;
His left he twisted in his hoary hair.
Then, with a speeding thrust, his heart he found.   755
The lukewarm blood came rushing through the wound,
And sanguine streams distained the sacred ground.
Thus Priam fell, and shared one common fate
With Troy in ashes, and his ruined state;
He, who the scepter of all Asia swayed,   760
Whom monarchs, like domestic slaves, obeyed.
On the bleak shore now lies th' abandoned king,
A headless carcase, and a nameless thing.

" Then, not before, I felt my curdled blood
Congeal with fear, my hair with horror stood.   765
My father's image filled my pious mind,
Lest equal years might equal fortune find.
Again I thought on my forsaken wife,
And trembled for my son's abandoned life.
I looked about, but found myself alone,   770
Deserted at my need, my friends were gone.
Some spent with toil, some with despair oppressed,
Leaped headlong from the heights; the flames consumed the rest.
Thus, wandering in my way, without a guide,
The graceless Helen in the porch I spied   775
Of Vesta's temple; there she lurked alone;
Muffled she sat, and, what she could, unknown.
But, by the flames, that cast their blaze around,
That common bane of Greece and Troy I found.
For Ilium burnt, she dreads the Trojan's sword;   780
More dreads the vengeance of her injured lord;
Even by those gods, who refuged her, abhorred.
Trembling with rage, the strumpet I regard;
Resolved to give her guilt the due reward.
' Shall she triumphant sail before the wind,   785
And leave in flames unhappy Troy behind?
Shall she her kingdom and her friends review,
In state attended with a captive crew;
While unrevenged the good old Priam falls,

753. falchion: curved sword. 775. Helen: wife of Menelaus. Her abduction by Paris was the cause of the war. 777. what she could: as far as possible. 779. bane: cause of ruin. 783. strumpet: prostitute.

And Grecian fires consume the Trojan walls?   790
For this the Phrygian fields and Xanthian flood
Were swelled with bodies, and were drunk with blood!
'Tis true, a soldier can small honor gain,
And boast no conquest from a woman slain;
Yet shall the fact not pass without applause,   795
Of vengeance taken in so just a cause.
The punished crime shall set my soul at ease,
And murmuring manes of my friends appease.'
Thus while I rave, a gleam of pleasant light
Spread o'er the place, and, shining heavenly bright,   800
My mother stood revealed before my sight.
Never so radiant did her eyes appear;
Nor her own star confessed a light so clear.
Great in her charms, as when the gods above
She looks, and breathes herself into their love.   805
She held my hand, the destined blow to break;
Then, from her rosy lips, began to speak:

[Venus reproves Aeneas for his rage against Helen, since not she but
the gods have caused the destruction. At Venus's command, Aeneas goes
to rescue his family. The aged father, Anchises, at first refuses to leave,
but suddenly a miraculous flame lights the forehead of his grandson,
Ascanius, and he takes this as a sign from the gods.]

" The good old man with suppliant hands implored
The gods' protection, and their star adored.
' Now, now,' said he, ' my son, no more delay,   810
I yield, I follow where Heaven shows the way.
Keep (O my country gods!) our dwelling place,
And guard this relic of the Trojan race,
This tender child; these omens are your own;
And you can yet restore the ruined town.   815
At least accomplish what your signs foreshow.
I stand resigned, and am prepared to go.'

" He said; the crackling flames appear on high,
And driving sparkles dance along the sky.
With Vulcan's rage the rising winds conspire;   820

791. **Xanthian:** of Xanthus, a river near Troy. 798. **manes:** spirits. Both
syllables of the word are pronounced. 801. **mother:** Venus. 820. **Vulcan:** god
of fire.

And near our palace rolls the flood of fire.
' Haste, my dear father ('tis no time to wait)
And load my shoulders with a willing freight.
Whate'er befalls, your life shall be my care,
One death, or one deliverance we will share,   825
My hand shall lead our little son; and you,
My faithful consort, shall our steps pursue.
Next, you, my servants, heed my strict commands:
Without the walls a ruined temple stands,
To Ceres hallowed once, a cypress nigh   830
Shoots up her venerable head on high;
By long religion kept; there bend your feet;
And, in divided parties, let us meet.
Our country gods, the relics, and the bands,
Hold you, my father, in your guiltless hands.   835
In me 'tis impious holy things to bear,
Red as I am with slaughter, new from war:
Till, in some living stream, I cleanse the guilt
Of dire debate, and blood in battle spilt.'
Thus, ordering all that prudence could provide,   840
I clothe my shoulders with a lion's hide,
And yellow spoils; then, on my bending back,
The welcome load of my dear father take.
While, on my better hand, Ascanius hung,
And, with unequal paces, tript along.   845
Creüsa kept behind; by choice we stray
Through every dark and every devious way.
I, who so bold and dauntless, just before,
The Grecian darts and shocks of lances bore,
At every shadow now am seized with fear,   850
Not for myself, but for the charge I bear.
Till near the ruined gate arrived at last,
Secure, and deeming all the danger past,
A frightful noise of trampling feet we hear;
My father, looking through the shades with fear,   855
Cried out, ' Haste, haste, my son, the foes are nigh!
Their swords and shining armor I descry.'
Some hostile god, for some unknown offense,
Had sure bereft my mind of better sense;
For while, through winding ways, I took my flight,   860

830. **Ceres:** goddess of agriculture.   846. **Creüsa:** wife of Aeneas.

And sought the shelter of the gloomy night,
Alas! I lost Creüsa; hard to tell
If by her fatal destiny she fell,
Or weary sat, or wandered with affright;
But she was lost for ever to my sight.   865
I knew not, or reflected, till I met
My friends, at Ceres' now deserted seat.
We met; not one was wanting, only she
Deceived her friends, her son, and wretched me.
What mad expressions did my tongue refuse!   870
Whom did I not of gods or men accuse!
This was the fatal blow, that pained me more
Than all I felt from ruined Troy before.
Stung with my loss, and raving with despair,
Abandoning my now forgotten care,   875
Of counsel, comfort, and of hope bereft,
My sire, my son, my country gods, I left.
In shining armor once again I sheath
My limbs, not feeling wounds, nor fearing death.
Then headlong to the burning walls I run,   880
And seek the danger I was forced to shun.
I tread my former tracks; through night explore
Each passage, every street I crossed before.
All things were full of horror and affright,
And dreadful even the silence of the night.   885
Then to my father's house I make repair,
With some small glimpse of hope to find her there.
Instead of her, the cruel Greeks I met.
The house was filled with foes, with flames beset.
Driven on the wings of winds, whole sheets of fire,   890
Through air transported, to the roofs aspire.
From thence to Priam's palace I resort,
And search the citadel, and desert court.
Then, unobserved, I pass by Juno's church;
A guard of Grecians had possessed the porch.   895
There Phoenix and Ulysses watch the prey,
And thither all the wealth of Troy convey.
The spoils which they from ransacked houses brought,
And golden bowls from burning altars caught.
The tables of the gods, the purple vests,   900

869. deceived: disappointed.

The peoples' treasure, and the pomp of priests.
A rank of wretched youths, with pinioned hands,
And captive matrons, in long order stands.
Then, with ungoverned madness, I proclaim,
Through all the silent streets, Creüsa's name, 905
Creüsa still I call. At length she hears;
And, sudden, through the shades of night appears.
Appears no more Creüsa, nor my wife,
But a pale specter, larger than the life.
Aghast, astonished, and struck dumb with fear, 910
I stood; like bristles rose my stiffened hair,
Then thus the ghost began to soothe my grief:
'Nor tears, nor cries, can give the dead relief;
Desist, my much-loved lord, t' indulge your pain.
You bear no more than what the gods ordain. 915
My fates permit me not from hence to fly;
Nor he, the great comptroller of the sky.
Long wandering ways for you the powers decree:
On land hard labors, and a length of sea.
Then, after many painful years are past, 920
On Latium's happy shore you shall be cast,
Where gentle Tiber from his bed beholds
The flowery meadows, and the feeding folds.
There ends your toils; and there your fates provide
A quiet kingdom and a royal bride: 925
There fortune shall the Trojan line restore;
And you for lost Creüsa weep no more.
Fear not that I shall watch, with servile shame,
Th' imperious looks of some proud Grecian dame;
Or, stooping to the victor's lust, disgrace 930
My goddess-mother, or my royal race.
And now farewell. The parent of the gods
Restrains my fleeting soul in her abodes.
I trust our common issue to your care.'
She said, and gliding passed unseen in air. 935
I strove to speak, but horror tied my tongue;
And thrice about her neck my arms I flung;
And, thrice deceived, on vain embraces hung.

917. **comptroller**: controller. Jupiter is meant. 921. **Latium**: district of
Italy to which Aeneas eventually goes. 931. **goddess-mother**: Creüsa was
also of divine birth. 932. **parent of the gods**: Cybele, called the Great
Mother of the Gods.

Light as an empty dream at break of day,
Or as a blast of wind, she rushed away. 940

" Thus, having passed the night in fruitless pain,
I to my longing friends return again.
Amazed th' augmented number to behold,
Of men and matrons mixed, of young and old;
A wretched exiled crew together brought, 945
With arms appointed, and with treasure fraught;
Resolved and willing under my command,
To run all hazards both of sea and land.
The Morn began, from Ida, to display
Her rosy cheeks, and Phosphor led the day. 950
Before the gates the Grecians took their post:
And all pretence of late relief were lost.
I yield to fate, unwillingly retire,
And, loaded, up the hill convey my sire."

(John Dryden)

946. **appointed:** equipped. 946. **fraught:** laden. 950. **Phosphor:** the morning star.

SUGGESTIONS FOR STUDY

1. Several interesting comparisons may be made between the *Aeneid* and the *Iliad*. The latter ends with the funeral rites of Hector. Nothing is said about the capture of the city or the fate of Achilles. According to a later story, mentioned by Virgil in the sixth book of the *Aeneid*, Achilles was killed by Paris. What are the chief differences you notice in the accounts of fighting in the two epics?

2. What are the qualities displayed by Aeneas in both words and deeds?

3. What opinion does Virgil, through the words of Aeneas, wish to convey of the Greeks? Does he seem to you as fair to the Greeks as Homer is to the Trojans?

4. Tell in your own words the story which Sinon narrates to the Trojans. Does the story seem plausible? How do you explain the fact that even the ominous noises inside the wooden horse do not prevent the Trojans from admitting it into their city?

5. Describe the incident of Laocoön and his two sons. Look at a picture of the famous Laocoön statue, now in the Vatican, representing the three victims strangled by the serpents (see history or art books or sets of small prints on Greek art). The passage in Virgil and the statue were used by the German critic Lessing as the starting point for a comparison

between the essential natures of poetry and sculpture. (For Lessing, see page 449.)

6. Recount the episode of Helen. Why is she called the " common bane of Greece and Troy "?

7. How much fatalism appears in the narrative of Aeneas? In what lines is it most clearly expressed? To what extent do the gods and goddesses influence the course of events?

8. Where do departed spirits appear? With what results? Where does Virgil employ prophecy or other devices to connect the past and future?

9. There are a number of elaborate similes in Virgil. Select three or four examples of these, and explain the point of comparison. Do they add to your enjoyment or halt the action too much?

10. Read other parts of the *Aeneid,* especially the interesting Book 4 which recounts the love affair of Aeneas and Dido. Read Tennyson's fine poem " To Virgil." Tennyson calls Virgil the " Wielder of the stateliest measure ever molded by the lips of man." Does Dryden succeed in conveying that feeling in his translation?

11. In the Middle Ages Virgil was reputed to be a prophet and a necromancer. Can you detect anything in him (or in Aeneas) which would lend color to this belief?

12. What dramatic possibilities does this story have? Would it be suitable for stage or film production? Why, or why not? To help visualize the scene refer to books on Greek art and costume, page 1018.

13. Vocabulary: miscreant, haggard, rueful, fallacious, divulge, assuage, portents, prodigies, abjured, perfidious, grisly, auspicious, propitious, beguiled, descry, progeny, requite, dross.

LIVY (59 B.C.–17 A.D.)

Titus Livius was born at Padua in northern Italy of a patrician family. He received an excellent education in " the two languages," as they were called, that is, the literatures of Greece and Rome. After a life of comparative ease and independence in Rome, he retired shortly before his death to his native Padua.

Livy ranks among the greatest of the ancient historians. He conceived and carried out the ambitious design of writing the history of Rome from its foundation down to his own day. Of this monumental work, which is the first attempt to write the continuous history of a whole people, unfortunately only a small portion has survived, but this remnant has been sufficient to perpetuate Livy's reputation both as a spirited historian and a master of style. Most of the familiar stories of early Rome, such as that of Romulus and Remus, have come down to us through the writings of Livy.

Though Livy was not so much a philosophic historian as a masterly narrator of events, historical judgments are by no means lacking in his work. He remained a republican at heart, accepting the rule of Augustus with reluctance. Instead, therefore, of indulging in any roseate forecasts of imperial splendor, such as we find in Virgil and even in Horace, he tried in his history to show how the Romans rose to greatness through the practice of simple virtues and in what danger they were of degenerating when these virtues declined. He was, however, deeply convinced of the true grandeur of Rome and was consequently inclined to attribute her success in war to the essential justice of her cause. After the manner of Thucydides and other ancient historians, he composed freely the speeches which he attributed to the historical actors.

FROM SAGUNTUM TO THE TREBIA

The Carthaginian general Hannibal was one of the greatest military leaders of all history. Never was Rome so near destruction as when he invaded Italy by land in 218 B.C.

When Hannibal had made up his mind to go forward and lose no time in reaching Italy, his goal, he ordered a muster of his troops and addressed them in tones of mingled rebuke and encouragement. " I am astonished," he said, " to see how hearts that have been always dauntless have now suddenly become a prey to fear. Think of the many victorious campaigns you have gone through, and remember that you did not leave Spain before you had added to the Carthaginian empire all the tribes in the country washed by two widely remote seas. The Roman people made a demand for all who had taken part in the siege of Saguntum to be given up to them, and you, to avenge the insult, have crossed the Ebro to wipe out the name of Rome and bring freedom to the world. When you commenced your march, from the setting to the rising sun, none of you thought it too much for you, but now when you see that by far the greater part of the way has been accomplished; the passes of the Pyrenees, which were held by most warlike tribes, surmounted; the Rhone, that mighty stream, crossed in the face of so many thousand Gauls, and the rush of its waters checked — now that you are within sight of the Alps, on the other side of which lies Italy, you have become weary and are arresting your march in the very gates of the enemy. What do you imagine the Alps to be other than lofty mountains? Suppose them to be higher than the peaks of the Pyrenees, surely no region in the world can touch the sky or be impassable to man. Even the Alps are inhabited and cultivated, animals are bred and reared there, their gorges and ravines can be traversed by armies. Why, even the envoys whom you see here did not cross the Alps by flying through the air, nor were their ancestors native to the soil. They came into Italy as emigrants looking for a land to settle in, and they crossed the Alps often in immense bodies with their wives and children and all their belongings. What can be inaccessible or insuperable to the soldier who carries nothing with him but his weapons of war? What toils and perils you went through for eight months to effect the capture of Saguntum! [1] And now that Rome, the capital of the world, is your goal, can you deem anything so difficult or so arduous that it should prevent you from reaching it? Many years ago the Gauls captured the place which Carthaginians despair of approaching; either you must confess yourselves inferior in courage and enterprise to a people whom you have conquered again and again, or else you must look forward to finishing your march on the ground between the Tiber and the walls of Rome."

At length they came to a much narrower pass which descended over such sheer cliffs that a light-armed soldier could hardly get down it even by hanging on to projecting roots and branches. The place had always been precipitous, and a landslip had recently carried away the road for 1000 feet. The cavalry came to a halt here as though they had arrived at their journey's end, and whilst Hannibal was wondering what could be causing the delay he was informed that there was no passage. Then he went forward to examine the place and saw that there was nothing for it but to lead the army by a long circuitous route over pathless and untrodden snow. But this, too, soon proved to be impracticable. The old snow had been covered to a moderate depth by a fresh fall, and the first comers planted their feet firmly on the new snow, but when it had become melted under the tread of so many men and beasts there was nothing to walk on but ice covered with slush. Their progress now became one incessant and miserable struggle. The smooth ice allowed no foothold, and as they were going down a steep incline they were still less able to keep on their legs, whilst, once down, they tried in vain to rise, as their hands and knees were continually slipping. There were no stumps or roots about for them to get hold of and support themselves by, so they rolled about helplessly on the glassy ice and slushy snow. The baggage animals as they toiled along cut through occasionally into the lowest layer of snow, and when they stumbled they struck out their hoofs in their

[1] **Saguntum:** on northeast coast of Spain, modern Valencia.

struggles to recover themselves and broke through into the hard and congealed ice below, where most of them stuck as though caught in a gin.[2]

At last, when men and beasts alike were worn out by their fruitless exertions, a camp was formed on the summit, after the place had been cleared with immense difficulty owing to the quantity of snow that had to be removed. The next thing was to level the rock through which alone a road was practicable. The soldiers were told off to cut through it. They built up against it an enormous pile of tall trees which they had felled and lopped, and when the wind was strong enough to blow up the fire they set light to the pile. When the rock was red hot they poured vinegar upon it to disintegrate it. After thus treating it by the fire they opened a way through it with their tools, and eased the steep slope by winding tracks of moderate gradient,[3] so that not only the baggage animals but even the elephants could be led down.

Four days were spent over the rock, and the animals were almost starved to death, for the heights are mostly bare of vegetation and what herbage there is is buried beneath the snow. In the lower levels there were sunny valleys and streams flowing through woods, and spots more deserving of human inhabitants. Here the beasts were turned loose to graze, and the troops, worn out with their engineering, were allowed to rest. In three days more they reached the open plains and found a pleasanter country and pleasanter people living in it.

(*Anonymous Translation*)

SUGGESTIONS FOR STUDY

1. Livy, like other ancient historians, freely composed the speeches which he put into the mouths of his characters. Do you regard the sentiments attributed to Hannibal as probable or not? Does Livy appear to be fair to him? Give reasons for your answers.

2. Comment on the vividness of the account of the crossing of the Alps. What good descriptive or narrative passages do you know in the works of American and English historians? As a military exploit, compare this with Napoleon's crossing the Alps, with General Wolfe's scaling the rock of Quebec, and with other hazardous feats of historical significance.

3. Vocabulary: arduous, precipitous, disintegrate, gradient.

[2] **gin:** trap.   [3] **gradient:** slope.

OVID (43 B.C.–17 A.D.)

Publius Ovidius Naso was born in a mountainous district of Italy. He was educated at Rome and after a visit to Greece and Asia Minor took up his abode at the capital. There he led a gay, dissipated life, moving in the world of wealth and fashion and courting the society of the great. In 8 A.D. a decree of banishment was issued against him, ostensibly because he had written an immoral book, but more probably because of some unknown misdemeanor. He was exiled to a town near the mouth of the Danube, where he spent the rest of his life in a trying climate and among barbarians. All his supplications to be allowed to return to his family, his friends, and the only sort of life he loved or understood passed unheeded.

Of all the great Roman poets, Ovid had the least measure of Roman seriousness. He was indolent in habits, without ambition or deep convictions, and averse to all the severer processes of thought. He was fitted only for the sensuous enjoyment of life. But if he lacked character, he did possess a poetic temperament. His fertile fancy, his ready response to visual beauty, and his command of melodious language made him one of the most prolific of Roman poets. His best-known works are the *Art of Love* and the *Metamorphoses*. The former was characterized by Macaulay as " perhaps the most immoral book ever written." Love meant for Ovid only desire, not devotion. A certain amount of personal interest attaches also to the poems written in exile in which he pleads for forgiveness.

Ovid is extremely important both as a source of information and as an influence. Most moderns owe to him, directly or indirectly, what familiarity they have with the world of wonder created by Greek imagination. His subjects inspired many artists of the Italian Renaissance. English poets from Chaucer to Pope are greatly in his debt. The Romantic Movement got rid of classical mythology as poetic adornment, and since then the influence of Ovid on modern literature has largely ceased.

The *Metamorphoses* is Ovid's acknowledged masterpiece. It is a long narrative poem which recounts the legendary stories of miraculous transformations. It begins with the original change from Chaos to Cosmos and ends with the metamorphosis of Julius Caesar into a star. Some two hundred and fifty stories of these transformations are told. The Greek mind with its vivid imagination saw suggestions of personal life everywhere. A rustling tree, a bubbling spring, or a running brook was felt by them to possess an indwelling spirit. The myths were invented to account for the change from the animating spirit to the outward form. Ovid merely drew upon the common stock of these stories. He added nothing except the graceful manner of telling. His attitude toward these myths leaves one in doubt whether he really believed them. Certainly he manifests none of the awe or reverence of Virgil.

THE FLOOD

The floods, by nature enemies to land,
And proudly swelling with their new command,
Remove the living stones that stopped their way,
And, gushing from their source, augment the sea.
Then, with his mace, their monarch struck the ground.   5
With inward trembling earth received the wound;
And rising streams a ready passage found.
The expanded waters gather on the plain,
They float the fields, and overtop the grain;
Then rushing onwards, with a sweepy sway,   10
Bear flocks, and folds, and laboring hinds away.
Nor safe their dwellings were; for, sapped by floods,
Their houses fell upon their household gods.
The solid piles, too strongly built to fall,
High o'er their heads behold a watery wall.   15
Now seas and earth were in confusion lost;
A world of waters, and without a coast.
    One climbs a cliff; one in his boat is borne,
And ploughs above, where late he sowed his corn.
Others o'er chimney tops and turrets row,   20
And drop their anchors on the meads below;
Or downward driven, they bruise the tender vine,
Or tossed aloft, are knocked against a pine.
And where of late the kids had cropped the grass,
The monsters of the deep now take their place.   25
Insulting Nereids on the cities ride,
And wondering dolphins o'er the palace glide.
On leaves, and masts of mighty oaks, they browse;
And their broad fins entangle in the boughs.
The frighted wolf now swims among the sheep;   30
The yellow lion wanders in the deep;
His rapid force no longer helps the boar;
The stag swims faster than he ran before.
The fowls, long beating on their wings in vain,
Despair of land, and drop into the main.   35
Now hills and vales no more distinction know,
And leveled nature lies oppressed below.

11. **hinds:** farm servants.   21. **meads:** meadows.   26. **Nereids:** sea nymphs.

The most of mortals perish in the flood,
The small remainder dies for want of food.
A mountain of stupendous height there stands   **40**
Betwixt the Athenian and Boeotian lands,
The bound of fruitful fields, while fields they were,
But then a field of waters did appear.
Parnassus is its name; whose forky rise
Mounts through the clouds, and mates the lofty skies. **45**
High on the summit of this dubious cliff,
Deucalion wafting moored his little skiff.
He with his wife were only left behind
Of perished man; they two were human kind.
The mountain-nymphs and Themis they adore,   **50**
And from her oracles relief implore.
The most upright of mortal men was he;
The most sincere and holy woman, she.

When Jupiter, surveying earth from high,
Beheld it in a lake of water lie,   **55**
That, where so many millions lately lived,
But two, the best of either sex, survived,
He loosed the northern wind; fierce Boreas flies
To puff away the clouds, and purge the skies.
Serenely, while he blows, the vapors driven   **60**
Discover heaven to earth, and earth to heaven.
The billows fall, while Neptune lays his mace
On the rough sea, and smooths its furrowed face,
Already Triton, at his call, appears
Above the waves; a Tyrian robe he wears;   **65**
And in his hand a crooked trumpet bears.
The sovereign bids him peaceful sounds inspire,
And give the waves the signal to retire.
His writhen shell he takes, whose narrow vent
Grows by degrees into a large extent;   **70**
Then gives it breath; the blast, with doubling sound,
Runs the wide circuit of the world around.
The sun first heard it, in his early East,
And met the rattling echoes in the West.
The waters, listening to the trumpet's roar,   **75**

50. **Themis:** goddess of justice   58. **Boreas:** god of the north wind.
64. **Triton:** a sea-god.   65. **Tyrian:** from Tyre in Asia Minor, where purple
dyes were made; hence purple.   69. **writhen:** distorted.

Obey the summons, and forsake the shore.
   A thin circumference of land appears;
And Earth, but not at once, her visage rears,
And peeps upon the seas from upper grounds.
The streams, but just contained within their bounds,   8c
By slow degrees into their channels crawl;
And earth increases as the waters fall.
In longer time the tops of trees appear,
Which mud on their dishonored branches bear.
   At length the world was all restored to view,   85
But desolate, and of a sickly hue.
Nature beheld herself, and stood aghast,
A dismal desert, and a silent waste.
   Which when Deucalion, with a piteous look,
Beheld, he wept, and thus to Pyrrha spoke: 90
" Oh wife, oh sister, oh of all thy kind
The best and only creature left behind,
By kindred, love, and now by dangers joined;
Of multitudes, who breathed the common air,
We two remain; a species in a pair;   95
The rest the seas have swallowed; nor have we
E'en of this wretched life a certainty.
The clouds are still above; and, while I speak,
A second deluge o'er our heads may break.
Should I be snatched from hence, and thou remain,   100
Without relief, or partner of thy pain,
How couldst thou such a wretched life sustain?
Should I be left, and thou be lost, the sea,
That buried her I loved, should bury me.
Oh could our father his old arts inspire,   105
And make me heir of his informing fire,
That so I might abolished man retrieve,
And perished people in new souls might live!
But heaven is pleased, nor ought we to complain,
That we, the examples of mankind remain."   110
   He said: the careful couple join their tears,
And then invoke the gods, with pious prayers.
Thus in devotion having eased their grief,
From sacred oracles they seek relief;
And to Cephisus' brook their way pursue.   115
The stream was troubled, but the ford they knew.

With living waters in the fountain bred,
They sprinkle first their garments, and their head,
Then took the way which to the temple led.
The roofs were all defiled with moss and mire, 120
The desert altars void of solemn fire.
Before the gradual prostrate they adored,
The pavement kissed; and thus the saint implored:
" O righteous Themis, if the powers above
By prayers are bent to pity, and to love; 125
If human miseries can move their mind;
If yet they can forgive, and yet be kind;
Tell how we may restore, by second birth,
Mankind, and people desolated earth."
  Then thus the gracious goddess, nodding, said: 130
" Depart, and with your vestments veil your head;
And stooping lowly down, with loosened zones,
Throw each behind your backs your mighty mother's bones."
  Amazed the pair, and mute with wonder, stand,
Till Pyrrha first refused the dire command. 135
" Forbid it heaven," said she, " that I should tear
Those holy relics from the sepulcher."
They pondered the mysterious words again,
For some new sense; and long they sought in vain.
At length Deucalion cleared his cloudy brow, 140
And said: " The dark enigma will allow
A meaning, which, if well I understand,
From sacrilege will free the god's command.
This earth our mighty mother is; the stones
In her capacious body are her bones. 145
These we must cast behind." With hope, and fear,
The woman did the new solution hear.
The man diffides in his own augury,
And doubts the gods; yet both resolve to try.
  Descending from the mount, they first unbind 150
Their vests, and, veiled, they cast the stones behind.
The stones (a miracle to mortal view,
But long tradition makes it pass for true)
Did first the rigor of their kind expel,
And suppled into softness as they fell; 155
Then swelled, and, swelling, by degrees grew warm;

148. **diffides**: distrusts.

And took the rudiments of human form;
Imperfect shades, in marble such are seen,
When the rude chisel does the man begin;
While yet the roughness of the stone remains,   16c
Without the rising muscles, and the veins.
The sappy parts, and next resembling juice,
Were turned to moisture, for the body's use,
Supplying humors, blood, and nourishment.
The rest, too solid to receive a bent,   165
Converts to bones; and what was once a vein,
Its former name and nature did retain.
By help of power divine, in little space,
What the man threw, assumed a manly face;
And what the wife, renewed the female race.   170
Hence we derive our nature, born to bear
Laborious life, and hardened into care.

                                              (*John Dryden*)

SUGGESTIONS FOR STUDY

1. Read Genesis, chapters 6, 7, and 8, and compare the account of the Flood given there with Ovid's narrative. Considered purely as literature, which of the two makes a better tale as to action, vividness of presentation, poetic feeling?

2. The Greek divinities and oracles were frequently represented as speaking in riddles. Do you know any other instances of this?

3. Pick out words and phrases of a poetical character. How do you think this translation compares in general effectiveness with Dryden's translation of Virgil?

TACITUS (55?–120? A.D.)

Publius Cornelius Tacitus stands along with Livy in the first rank of Roman historians. He came of a family of good social position and held various offices. He lived through the reigns of many emperors. The times were troubled and there were frequent outbreaks of violence and periods of terrorism. Tacitus came to associate the degeneracy of his times with the imperial rule and to look back to the Roman Republic as the Golden Age. He viewed history from the standpoint of an austere moralist. "I regard it as history's highest function," he said, "to rescue merit from oblivion and to hold up as a terror to base words and actions the reprobation of posterity." It was in this spirit that he wrote his *Histories* and

Annals, which between them tell the story of the Empire up to the end of the first century, though less than half the original work has been preserved. Tacitus also wrote the biography of his father-in-law Agricola, a general and statesman, who was for several years governor of Britain.

The brevity of Tacitus is proverbial. There are no superfluous words in his sentences. His psychological insight makes him unusually successful in character painting.

GERMANY

Tacitus' *Germany* is perhaps his most widely read book today. It gives us the earliest information we have about a people who at a much later date were to play a tremendous part in history. Whether Tacitus had visited Germany, we do not know. He has been suspected of idealizing the Germans in order to show up, by contrast, the servility and degradation of the Romans. His attitude seems, rather, to have been a mixture of admiration for their independence and martial spirit and of dread of them as a standing menace to Rome. Certainly he did not hesitate to point out their vices of drunkenness, gluttony, and indolence.

Personally I associate myself with the opinions of those who hold that in the peoples of Germany there has been given to the world a race untainted by intermarriage with other races, a peculiar people and pure, like no one but themselves; whence it comes that their physique, in spite of their vast numbers, is identical: fierce blue eyes, red hair, tall frames, powerful only spasmodically, and impatient at the same time of labor and hard work, and by no means habituated to bearing thirst and heat; to cold and hunger, thanks to the climate and the soil, they are accustomed.

They take their kings on the ground of birth, their generals on the basis of courage. The authority of their kings is not unlimited or arbitrary; their generals control them by example rather than command, and by means of the admiration which attends upon energy and a conspicuous place in front of the line. But anything beyond this — capital punishment, imprisonment, even a blow — is permitted only to the priests, and then not as a penalty or under the general's orders, but as an inspiration from the god whom they supposed to accompany them on campaign: certain totems,[1] in fact, and emblems are fetched from groves and carried into battle. The strongest incentive to courage lies in this, that neither chance nor casual grouping makes the squadron or the wedge, but family and kinship. Close at hand, too, are their dearest, whence is heard the wailing voice of

---

[1] **totems:** natural objects taken as symbols of the clan.

woman and the child's cry. Here are the witnesses who are in each man's eyes most precious; here the praise he covets most. They take their wounds to mother and wife, who do not shrink from counting the hurts and demanding a sight of them: they minister to the combatants food and exhortation.

Tradition relates that some lost or losing battles have been restored by the women, by the incessance of their prayers and by the baring of their breasts; for so is it brought home to the men that the slavery, which they dread much more keenly on their women's account, is close at hand. It follows that the loyalty of those tribes is more effectually guaranteed from whom, among other hostages,[2] maids of high birth have been exacted.

On small matters the chiefs consult; on larger questions the community; but with this limitation, that even the subjects, the decision of which rests with the people, are first handled by the chiefs. They meet, unless there be some unforeseen and sudden emergency, on days set apart — when the moon, that is, is new or at the full; they regard this as the most auspicious herald for the transaction of business. They count not by days as we do, but by nights;[3] their decisions and proclamations are subject to this principle: the night, that is, seems to take precedence of the day.

It is a foible[4] of their freedom that they do not meet at once and when commanded, but a second and a third day is wasted by dilatoriness in assembling. When the mob is pleased to begin, they take their seats carrying arms. Silence is called for by the priests, who thenceforward have power also to coerce; then a king or a chief is listened to, in order of age, birth, glory in war, or eloquence, with the prestige which belongs to their counsel rather than with any prescriptive[5] right to command. If the advice tendered be displeasing, they reject it with groans; if it please them, they clash their spears. The most complimentary expression of assent is this martial approbation.

At this assembly it is also permissible to lay accusations and to bring capital charges. The nature of the death penalty differs according to the offense: traitors and deserters are hung from trees; cowards and poor fighters and notorious evil-livers are plunged in the mud of marshes with a hurdle on their heads. The difference of punishment has regard to the principle that crime should be blazoned[6]

---

[2] **hostages:** persons given as pledges.
[3] **nights:** the English word " fortnight " is a survival of this
[4] **foible:** weakness.
[5] **prescriptive:** prescribed by custom.
[6] **blazoned:** proclaimed.

abroad by its retribution, but abomination hidden. Lighter offences have also a measured punishment; those convicted are fined in a number of horses and cattle. Part of the fine goes to the king or the state; part is paid to the person himself who brings the charge or to his relatives. At the same gatherings are selected chiefs, who administer law through the cantons and villages. Each of them has one hundred assessors from the people to be his responsible advisers.

They do no business, public or private, without arms in their hands; yet the custom is that no one take arms until the state has endorsed his competence: then in the assembly itself one of the chiefs or his father or his relatives equip the young man with shield and spear. This corresponds with them to the toga,[7] and is youth's first public distinction; hitherto he seems a member of the household, now a member of the state. Conspicuously high birth, or signal services on the part of ancestors, win the chieftain's approbation even for very young men; they mingle with the others, men of maturer strength and tested by long years, and have no shame to be seen among his retinue. In the retinue itself degrees are observed, depending on the judgment of him whom they follow; there is great rivalry among the retainers to decide who shall have the first place with his chief, and among the chieftains as to who shall have the largest and keenest retinue. This means rank and strength, to be surrounded always with a large band of chosen youths — glory in peace, in war protection. Nor is it only so with his own people, but with neighboring states also it means name and fame for a man that his retinue be conspicuous for number and character. Such men are in request for embassies, and are honored with gifts, and often, by the mere terror of their name, break the back of opposition in war.

When the battlefield is reached it is a reproach for a chief to be surpassed in prowess; a reproach for his retinue not to equal the prowess of its chief; but to have left the field and survived one's chief, this means lifelong infamy and shame. To protect and defend him, to devote one's own feats even to his glorification, this is the gist of their allegiance; the chief fights for victory, but the retainers for the chief. Should it happen that the community where they are born be drugged with long years of peace and quiet, many of the high-born youth voluntarily seek those tribes which are at the time engaged in some war; for rest is unwelcome to the race, and they distinguish themselves more readily in the midst of uncertainties. Besides, you cannot keep up a great retinue except by war and violence, for it is to the free-

---

[7] **toga:** loose-flowing outer garment of the Romans.

handed chief that they look for that war-horse, for that murderous and masterful spear. Banquetings and a certain rude but lavish outfit take the place of salary. The material for this free-handedness comes through war and foray.[8] You will not so readily persuade them to plough the land and wait for the year's returns as to challenge the enemy and earn wounds. Besides, it seems limp and slack to get with the sweating of your brow what you can gain with the shedding of your blood.

When they are not entering on war, they spend much time in hunting, but more in idleness — creatures who eat and sleep, the best and bravest warriors doing nothing, having handed over the charge of their home, hearth, and estate to the women and the old men and the weakest members of the family; for themselves they vegetate, by that curious incongruity of temperament which makes of the same men such lovers of slumber and such haters of quiet.

No race indulges more lavishly in hospitality and entertainment; to close the door against any human being is a crime. Every one according to his property receives at a well-spread board; should it fail, he who had been your host points out your place of entertainment and goes with you. You go next door, without an invitation, but it makes no difference; you are received with the same courtesy. Stranger or acquaintance, no one distinguishes them where the right of hospitality is concerned. It is customary to speed the parting guest with anything he fancies. There is the same readiness in turn to ask of him. Gifts are their delight, but they neither count upon what they have given, nor are bound by what they have received.

The marriage tie with them is strict; you will find nothing in their character to praise more highly. They are almost the only barbarians who are content with a wife apiece. The very few exceptions have nothing to do with passion, but consist of those with whom polygamous marriage is eagerly sought for the sake of their high birth. To limit the number of their children, to make away with any of the later children is held abominable, and good habits have more force with them than good laws elsewhere.

(Maurice Hutton)

SUGGESTIONS FOR STUDY

1. Make lists of the good and the bad qualities of the Germans which Tacitus notes. Which of these do you think are still national characteristics of the Germans? Of the other nations of Teutonic blood — the

---

[8] **foray:** raid.

English and Scandinavians? Do you find any of these racial characteristics illustrated in the early German and Scandinavian literature?

2. What do you gather about the position of women among the Germans?

3. In what respects do you think the Romans of Tacitus' day differed
from the contemporary Germans? Are criticisms of the Romans implied
anywhere in the narrative?

4. Vocabulary: habituated, dilatoriness, coerce, prowess, dower, invio-
late.

PLINY THE YOUNGER (62?–114? A.D.)

Gaius Plinius, known as Pliny the Younger, to distinguish him from his
uncle, Pliny the Elder, author of the *Natural History,* was trained by his
uncle and by Quintilian, the writer on rhetoric. He entered public life,
rose to be consul, and was later made governor of a Roman province. He
was wealthy and philanthropic, one of the best representatives of the later
Roman nobility.

Along with Cicero, he is the best of Roman letter writers. His *Letters*
give a pleasing picture of society about the year 100 A.D., in sharp contrast
to the satires of Juvenal and the epigrams of Martial. They seem to have
been written with an eye to publication.

My dear Tacitus,

You ask me to write you an account of my uncle's death, in order
that you may hand it down accurately to posterity. I am grateful
to you, for I see that his death if celebrated by your pen, will attain
undying fame. For, though he perished along with whole peoples
and cities in a disaster which overwhelmed one of the fairest spots on
our coast, in a disaster so remarkable as to secure that at least he
will not be forgotten, though, besides this, he had written many books
that will be remembered, yet the undying fame of your writings will
help to keep his memory green. So I am ready, nay anxious, to do
what you ask.

My uncle was at Misenum [1] in supreme command of the fleet. On
August 24th, about one o'clock in the afternoon, my mother drew
his attention to the appearance of a cloud, unusually large and of a
strange shape. He had taken a sun-bath followed by a cold bath,
and was lying down after lunch, reading. He immediately put on his
shoes and climbed to a spot whence he could better see this phenomenon. None of the people who were looking at the cloud from
a distance were certain from which mountain it was coming (we

[1] **Misenum:** on the Bay of Naples.

found out afterward that it was Vesuvius); it was more like a pine-tree than anything else, for it shot up into a trunk of great height and then spread out into several branches. Sometimes it looked white, sometimes spotted, as though it had drawn up earth or cinders.

To a scholar like my uncle a natural phenomenon of this magnitude seemed worthy of closer study. So he ordered a launch and said I could go with him if I liked. But I said that I would rather go on with my studies, for, as it happened, he had given me some writing to do. Just as he was leaving the house a note came from Rectina, the wife of Bassus, who was terrified at the approaching danger; his villa stood just below ours, and there was no means of escape except by sea; she begged my uncle to save her from this perilous position. So he changed his mind and went out in the guise of a rescuer rather than a scientific observer. Large boats were launched, and he embarked with the intention of carrying help not only to Rectina, but to many others who lived along that shore because it was so picturesque. Therefore he hastened in the direction whence fugitives were coming and steered a straight course for the point of danger; so free from fear was he that he dictated and noted down all the motions and shapes of that terrible portent as he went along.

Already ashes were falling on the ships, and the nearer they drew the hotter and thicker grew the showers; then came pumice-stones and other stones, blackened and scorched and cracked by fire, while the sea ebbed suddenly and the shore was blocked by landslides. The steersman was for turning back, and my uncle hesitated for a moment, and then said to him, " Fortune favors the brave. Try to reach Pomponianus." Pomponianus was at Stabiae, right across the corner of the Bay (for the sea sweeps far into the curving shore just there), where the danger was not yet close at hand; but it was in full view and certain to come nearer as it spread, so he had packed up and gone into a boat, ready to push off directly the contrary wind fell. This wind blew my uncle into Stabiae, and he embraced Pomponianus, who was trembling with fright, cheering him up and encouraging him; in order to calm his friend's fears by showing how safe he felt himself, he ordered a bath, after which he sat down to dinner in high good humor, or at least he managed to assume a mask of good humor, which is equally wonderful.

Meanwhile, broad sheets of flame broke out all over Mount Vesuvius, rising high in the air and lighting up the sky, their brightness silhouetted [2] against the darkness of the night. My uncle tried to quiet people's fears by saying that fires had been left burning by ter-

[2] **silhouetted:** outlined.

rified peasants when they deserted their houses, which were now in flames and causing this light. Then he went to bed and really slept, for, being a stout man, he breathed heavily and loudly, so that he was heard by the people who were waiting about outside his door. But the courtyard which led to his room was covered to such a depth under a drift of ashes and pumice-stones that if he had stayed in bed any longer he would not have been able to get out of the door.

So he was wakened and joined Pomponianus and the others, who had been keeping watch. They consulted together as to whether it would be better to stay under cover or to go wandering about in the open. For the house was beginning to totter under the frequent and violent earthquakes, and it seemed to rock to and fro as though it had been shaken from its foundations. On the other hand, if they went outside they had the falling pumice-stones to fear, though, being porous, they were light. After comparing the two risks they chose the latter. They tied pillows on their heads with tablecloths; this was their only protection against the showers of stones and ashes.

Day had now dawned elsewhere, but with them was darkness, blacker and deeper than the deepest night, though here and there it was relieved by torches and other lights. They decided to go down to the shore in order to see from close at hand whether the sea would allow them to get away, but the waves were still high and contrary. There my uncle lay down on a disused sail and again and again called for cold water, which he drank. Then flames, heralded by a strong smell of sulphur, put the others to flight and roused him. Leaning on two slaves he managed to stand up, but instantly fell down again; I think his breathing was blocked by the thick fumes, which choked the narrow passage of his throat; it was never very strong and often got inflamed. When daylight returned — three days after his death — his body was found without any wound or scar, covered with the clothes he had been wearing. He looked more like a man asleep than dead.

Meantime, Mother and I were at Misenum. But you don't want to hear about anything but my uncle's death, so I will close. Let me add that I have related either what I witnessed myself or heard at the time, when one gets the truest accounts. You will pick out what you want. For it is one thing to write a letter to a friend, and quite another to write a history for the general public.

Good-by.

PLINY

(Dora Pym)

SUGGESTIONS FOR STUDY

1. Discuss the importance of this letter as a first-hand account of the eruption of Vesuvius. Does the fact that it was written twenty-seven years after the event lessen its value as a historical document?

2. Pliny elsewhere quotes his uncle as having said that no book was so bad as not to contain something of value. Do you agree with this assertion?

3. What constitutes a good letter? Why has letter writing declined as an art in recent times? Name some letter writers whom you have enjoyed reading. How does a collection of a person's letters give a somewhat different picture from an autobiography?

4. For further reading: (a) Bulwer-Lytton's *Last Days of Pompeii*, (b) J. Overbeck's " Pompeii," (c) Other letters by Pliny, (d) Miscellaneous letters from collections of letters.

MARTIAL (40?–102? A.D.)

The satirical element was very prominent in Roman literature and was in fact cultivated as a special branch of poetry. Horace wrote some clever satires as a by-product of his literary activity. Juvenal, a century later, devoted all his poetical talents to their composition. But the long satire is very likely to become dull as the conditions change which called it forth. That is why Martial with his gift of condensation was well advised to stick to the short form of the epigram where he could score his points without multiplying words.

Marcus Valerius Martialis was born at Bilbilis in Spain, whither he returned to spend his declining years after having passed more than half his life in Rome. He had a hard struggle with poverty and was often forced to stoop to flattery of the rich in order to sell his poems. He was a keen observer of life with an unusual power of seeing through shams. With no pretension of being a moralist, he directed the shafts of his wit at weaknesses and vices in which he himself shared. His special gift was his ability to " hit off " a character or a situation in a few lines. In this restricted field he is a master. He has been well called the " father of the epigram." The term epigram, which had been applied originally to an inscription on a monument or building, came in his hands to mean a short poem with a witty turn of expression. In modern times it is often used to denote a pointed saying in prose as well as in verse.

THE BEAU

You are everywhere thought just too lovely to live.
  You must be; I hear and believe it.
But, Cotilus, pray be so good as to say
  What's a lovely man, as you conceive it?

"Well, a lovely man must have his hair combed and curled   5
   Of perfumes he mustn't be chary,
Must hum the last strain from the Nile and from Spain,
   Must dance well and mustn't be hairy.

"He must linger all day by some lady friend's chair,
   With murmured remarks must regale her,   10
Must get billets doux and respond to them, too,
   Must be firm and precise with his tailor.

"He must always be posted on every intrigue
   And must whirl in the gay social vortex;
Each family tree through all years A.U.C.   15
   He must know from medulla to cortex."

That will do! This will make a man lovely, you say?
   I'm not in position to doubt it —
But when I want to pass for a thoroughbred ass
   I can see how I'd best set about it.   20

(*Paul Nixon*)

11. **billets doux**: love letters. 15. **A.U.C.**: *ante urbem conditam*, before the founding of the city. The Romans reckoned time before and after the founding of Rome which was supposed to have taken place in 753 B.C. 16. **medulla to cortex**: marrow to bark.

SUGGESTIONS FOR STUDY

1. Is this epigram of Martial applicable today? Compare Martial's picture of a beau with that drawn by Addison in the Spectator, "A Beau's Head." After consulting pictures of ancient Romans and eighteenth-century Englishmen, discuss notable differences in the external appearance of the two beaus. Compare also with a present-day beau. What in Martial's epigram is still applicable today?

2. Compare Martial with some modern poets who have drawn satirical portraits: Oliver Wendell Holmes, Bret Harte, Eugene Field, Edwin Arlington Robinson. What poems of theirs or others do you know which would come under this heading?

3. Vocabulary: regale, intrigue, vortex.

ANCIENT WORLD

MARCUS AURELIUS (121–180 A.D.)

Marcus Aurelius was a Roman emperor and a Stoic philosopher. He came of an ancient and honorable family and was adopted by the Emperor Antoninus Pius. He received an excellent education and never lost his thirst for knowledge. His self-discipline was remarkable. From the age of twelve he began to practice austerities in his life until these became habitual modes of conduct with him. In 161 he succeeded his adoptive father as emperor. His administration was not only prudent and efficient, but also marked by justice and humanity. " The noblest of pagan emperors," as he has been called, he seemed to embody Plato's ideal of a philosopher-king. The only blot on his record was his persecution of Christianity, but it must be remembered that he was deeply attached to the religion of his ancestors and regarded the Christians as fanatics who menaced the very foundations of the state. Although he chose to write in Greek, it would be absurd to consider him as anything but a representative of Roman literature. His *Meditations* are not a systematic treatise on Stoicism. They are casual observations which achieve their unity by a general attitude and tone. Their lofty sentiments are doubly effective because we know that Marcus Aurelius, like Socrates, practiced what he preached.

The Stoic philosophy came from Greece and dates from the end of the fourth century B.C., though some aspects of it may be traced farther back to Socrates. Rome, rather than Greece, however, was the place where Stoicism most profoundly affected men's thinking and lives. It was professed by Cicero and by Cato the Younger in the days of the Roman Republic, and flourished still more under the Empire when it was preached in the writings of the younger Seneca (4 B.C.–65 A.D.) and of the Greek slave Epictetus (60?–120? A.D.). It reached its climax in Marcus Aurelius. Although it developed a speculative side, it was more a theory of life than a philosophic system. The kernel of it was ethical. Its great rival was Epicureanism, which also originated in Greece. But the opposition between the two is not as complete as is commonly supposed. Both endeavored to free man from the dominion of circumstance, Stoicism by urging repression of desire, Epicureanism by recommending its wise regulation. Stoicism taught that pleasure is not to be pursued as an end. Pain is not an absolute evil because it may be triumphed over. If we are always inwardly prepared for the worst, nothing can seriously disturb us. All the ills of life may be endured with composure. It is the duty of every man to subordinate himself to more general interests — his family, his country, mankind. Stoicism was the first philosophy to teach cosmopolitanism and the universal brotherhood of men.

MEDITATIONS

Thou wilt find rest from vain fancies if thou doest every act in life as though it were thy last.

Thou seest how few be the things, the which if a man has at his command his life flows gently on and is divine.

Find time still to be learning somewhat good, and give up being desultory.

A man should *be* upright, not be *kept* upright.

Never esteem anything as of advantage to thee that shall make thee break thy word or lose thy self-respect.

Remember that man's life lies all within this present, as it were but a hair's breadth of time; as for the rest, the past is gone, the future yet unseen. Short, therefore, is man's life, and narrow is the corner of the earth wherein he dwells.

Nothing has such power to broaden the mind as the ability to investigate systematically and truly all that comes under thy observation in life.

By a tranquil mind I mean nothing else than a mind well ordered.

Think on this doctrine — that reasoning beings were created for one another's sake; that to be patient is a branch of justice, and that men sin without intending it.

The universe is change; our life is what our thoughts make it.

Be not as one that hath ten thousand years to live; death is nigh at hand: while thou livest, while thou hast time, be good.

Doth perfect beauty stand in need of praise at all? Nay; no more than law, no more than truth, no more than loving kindness, nor than modesty.

Observe always that everything is the result of a change, and get used to thinking that there is nothing Nature loves so well as to change existing forms and to make new ones like them.

Mark how fleeting and paltry is the estate of man — yesterday in embryo, tomorrow a mummy or ashes. So for the hairsbreadth of time assigned to thee live rationally, and part with life cheerfully, as drops the ripe olive, extolling the season that bore it and the tree that matured it.

Deem not life a thing of consequence. For look at the yawning void of the future, and at that other limitless space, the past.

Always take the short cut; and that is the rational one. Therefore say and do everything according to soundest reason.

If any man can convince me and bring home to me that I do not think or act aright, gladly will I change; for I search after truth, by which man never yet was harmed. But he is harmed who abideth on still in his deception and ignorance.

What is not good for the swarm is not good for the bee.

One Universe made up of all that is; and one God in it all, and one principle of Being, and one Law, the Reason, shared by all thinking creatures, and one Truth.

To a rational being it is the same thing to act according to nature and according to reason.

Be not careless in deeds, nor confused in words, nor rambling in thought.

A wrongdoer is often a man that has left something undone, not always he that has done something.

(Anonymous Translation)

SUGGESTIONS FOR STUDY

1. Compare these *Meditations* of Marcus Aurelius with the *Thoughts* of Pascal and the selections from Leonardo's *Note Books*.

2. Pick out the sayings of Marcus Aurelius which you consider typical of the Stoic philosophy. On the whole does this seem to you an admirable philosophy?

3. Do any of his ideas seem to you impracticable? If so, which? What kind of human beings does Marcus Aurelius presuppose if his ideas are to be carried out in practice?

4. Read some of the maxims of Epictetus, who expressed similar sentiments.

5. Memorize two or three of the sayings which appeal most strongly to you. Write some "Meditations" of your own which will bring out your own philosophy of life.

SAINT AUGUSTINE (354–430 A.D.)

Saint Augustine, the greatest of the Fathers of the Latin Church, was born in North Africa of a pagan father and a Christian mother. His mother, Monica, never ceased to work and pray for her son's conversion, which came with dramatic suddenness in 386 after years of irregular life and of spiritual wandering. Augustine was ordained a priest and finally rose to be bishop, in which capacity he zealously defended orthodoxy against all manner of heresy. As a theologian he has been revered by Catholics and Protestants alike.

Augustine's works, like the man himself, are distinguished by their ardor and sincerity. The most important, by all odds, are his *Confessions* and his *City of God.* The *Confessions* tell the story of his life down to his conversion. As an autobiography, the book ranks with the best in the world along with the lives of Benvenuto Cellini, Rousseau, Goethe, and Benjamn Franklin. The *City of God* is the first Christian philosophy of history. It was written shortly after the capture and pillage of Rome by the barbarians in 410, and was designed to refute the contention that Christianity was responsible for the calamity. Augustine draws a contrast between the City of God, which is the unseen community of true believers, and the city of this world, whose end is destruction.

THE CONFESSIONS

Saint Augustine's autobiography culminates in the supreme moment of his life — his conversion at the age of thirty-two. He had tried love and friendship in a vain endeavor to find peace for his soul, which nothing short of God could satisfy. Plunged in misery, he was seated beside his friend Alypius when the revelation came to him.

But when a deep consideration had from the secret bottom of my soul drawn together and heaped up all my misery in the sight of my heart; there arose a mighty storm, bringing a mighty shower of tears. Which that I might pour forth wholly, in its natural expressions, I rose from Alypius. Solitude was suggested to me as fitter for the business of weeping; so I retired so far that even his presence could not be a burthen [1] to me. Thus was it then with me, and he perceived something of it; for something I suppose I had spoken, wherein the tones of my voice appeared choked with weeping, and so had risen up. He then remained where we were sitting, most extremely astonished. I cast myself down I know not how, under a certain fig tree, giving full vent to my tears; and the floods of mine eyes gushed out, an *acceptable sacrifice to Thee.* And, not indeed in these words, yet to this purpose, spake I much unto Thee: *And Thou, O Lord, how long? how long, Lord, wilt Thou be angry, for ever? Remember not our former iniquities,* for I felt that I was held by them. I sent up these sorrowful words; How long? how long, " tomorrow, and tomorrow? " Why not now? why not is there this hour an end to my uncleanness?

So was I speaking, and weeping in the most bitter contrition [2] of my heart, when, lo! I heard from a neighboring house a voice, as of

[1] **burthen:** burden.   [2] **contrition:** penitence.

boy or girl, I know not, chanting, and oft repeating, " Take up and read. Take up and read." Instantly, my countenance altered, I began to think most intently, whether children were wont in any kind of play to sing such words; nor could I remember ever to have heard the like. So checking the torrent of my tears, I arose; interpreting it to be no other than a command from God, to open the book, and read the first chapter I should find. For I had heard of Antony,[3] that coming in during the reading of the Gospel, he received the admonition, as if what was being read, was spoken to him; *Go, sell all that thou hast, and give to the poor, and thou shalt have treasure in heaven, and come and follow me.* And by such oracle he was forthwith converted unto Thee. Eagerly then I returned to the place where Alypius was sitting; for there had I laid the volume of the Apostle,[4] when I arose thence. I seized, opened, and in silence read that section, on which my eyes first fell: *Not in rioting and drunkenness, not in chambering[5] and wantonness, not in strife and envying: but put ye on the Lord Jesus Christ, and make not provision for the flesh, in concupiscence.*[6] No further would I read; nor needed I; for instantly at the end of this sentence, by a light as it were of serenity infused into my heart, all the darkness of doubt vanished away.

Then putting my finger between, or some other mark, I shut the volume, and with a calmed countenance made it known to Alypius. And what was brought in him, which I knew not, he thus showed me. He asked to see what I had read. I showed him; and he looked even further than I had read, and I knew not what followed. This followed, *Him that is weak in the faith, receive;* which he applied to himself, and disclosed to me. And by this admonition was he strengthened; and by a good resolution and purpose, and most corresponding to his character, wherein he did always very far differ from me, for the better, without any turbulent delay he joined me. Thence we go in to my mother; we tell her; she rejoiceth; we relate in order how it took place; she leaps for joy, and triumpheth, and blesseth Thee, *Who art able to do above that which we ask or think;* for she perceived that Thou hadst given her more for me, than she was wont to beg by her pitiful and most sorrowful groanings. For Thou convertedst me unto Thyself, so that I sought neither wife, nor any hope of this world, standing in that rule of faith, where Thou hadst showed me unto her in a vision, so many years before. And

---

[3] **Antony:** Saint Anthony, the first Christian monk, third century A.D.
[4] **Apostle:** Saint Paul. The passage quoted is from *Romans* 13: 13 and 14.
[5] **chambering:** lewdness.
[6] **concupiscence:** worldly desire.

Thou didst *convert her mourning into joy,* much more plentiful than she had desired, and in a much more precious and purer way than she erst [7] required, by having grandchildren of my body.

　　　　　　　　　　　　　　　　　　　　　(*E. B. Pusey*)

　　[7] erst: formerly.

SUGGESTIONS FOR STUDY

1. Compare the conversion of St. Augustine with that of St. Paul. You will find an account of the latter in Acts 9:1–9. Compare St. Augustine's early life and his complete change of habits with those of St. Francis of Assisi (see page 331).

2. At the time of the Renaissance, scholars used often to turn at random to passages in Virgil in order to find oracles to guide them. What was the significance of the change from the Bible to Virgil? How does the use of the chance passage in the Bible for guidance play an important part in Tennyson's " Enoch Arden "? Why do most modern men not have recourse to oracles at all? What do they use for guidance instead?

3. What phrases of St. Augustine have been reflected in two of the mystic poems in the Spanish section?

Medieval Latin Poems

THE DAY OF WRATH

The supreme product of Latin hymn writing, the " Dies Irae " or " Day of Wrath," is commonly attributed to the Italian churchman Thomas of Celano (thirteenth century), though other possible authors have been suggested. At any rate, it is the most famous of the medieval hymns, voicing as it does the terrors of men at the thought of the Judgment Day. Sir Walter Scott's version, which is given here, is more a paraphrase than an exact translation. It is found in an appropriate setting at the end of his *Lay of the Last Minstrel.*

Other well-known Latin hymns are those ascribed to Bernard of Clairvaux (1091–1153), such as " Jerusalem the Golden " and " Jesus, the very Thought of Thee," which are devotional in tone and emphasize the consoling side of religion. The " Stabat Mater," on the vigil of Mary by the Cross, was probably written by Jacopone da Todi, an Italian mystic of the thirteenth century.

> That day of wrath, that dreadful day,
> When heaven and earth shall pass away,
> What power shall be the sinner's stay?
> How shall he meet that dreadful day?

When, shriveling like a parchèd scroll 5
The flaming heavens together roll;
When louder yet, and yet more dread
Swells the high trump that wakes the dead!

Oh! on that day, that wrathful day,
When man to judgment wakes from clay, 10
Be THOU the trembling sinner's stay,
Though heaven and earth shall pass away!

(*Sir Walter Scott*)

STUDENT DRINKING SONGS

In startling contrast to the medieval Latin hymns are the rollicking drinking songs of the wandering students or " goliards," as they were nick-named. There were apparently many of these students in England, France, and Germany during the twelfth and thirteenth centuries who were more interested in carousing than in scholarship. Those who think of the Middle Ages as being all gloom might revise their opinion considerably if they read a number of these songs. The tone is joyous and carefree, sometimes also coarse and almost sacrilegious. This is all the more remarkable since the great majority of the wandering students were " clerks " (i.e., clerics), ostensibly studying theology with a view to entering the service of the church. Some of their songs, like the one given here, are still used by the German students.

GAUDEAMUS IGITUR

Let us live, then, and be glad
While young life's before us!
After youthful pastime had,
After old age hard and sad,
Earth will slumber o'er us. 5

Where are they who in this world,
Ere we kept, were keeping?
Go ye to the gods above;
Go to hell; inquire thereof.
They are not; they're sleeping. 10

Gaudeamus Igitur: Let us then rejoice.

Brief is life, and brevity
    Briefly shall be ended.
        Death comes like a whirlwind strong,
        Bears us with his blast along;
None shall be defended.   15

Live this university,
    Men that learning nourish;
        Live each member of the same,
        Long live all that bear its name;
Let them ever flourish!   20

Live the commonwealth also,
    And the men that guide it!
        Live our town in strength and health,
        Founders, patrons, by whose wealth
We are here provided!   25

Live all girls! A health to you
    Melting maids and beauteous!
        Live the wives and women too,
        Gentle, loving, tender, true,
Good, industrious, duteous!   30

Perish cares that pule and pine!
    Perish envious blamers!
        Die the Devil, thine and mine!
        Die the starch-necked Philistine!
Scoffers and defamers!   35

                    (J. A. Symonds)

31. **pule and pine:** grieve and languish.   34. **starch-necked:** prim.
34. **Philistine:** The term is applied by the German students to anyone outside
the university.   Goethe and Heine in Germany and Matthew Arnold in England also used the word in the sense of an uncultured person.

SUGGESTIONS FOR STUDY

  1. Contrast, in a few phrases, the two Latin songs.

  2. The theme of man's facing the consequences of his life on a day of
judgment has been often used both in art and literature.   Michelangelo's
tremendous fresco on the wall of the Sistine Chapel is the most famous

of the many "Last Judgments" to be found in art galleries. Michael Wigglesworth's "Day of Doom" was the most famous poem of early Puritan America. Do you know of other treatments of the subject? How have modern ideas on the subject become considerably modified since the days of the composition of this hymn?

3. Compare "Gaudeamus Igitur" with the poem of Anacreon, page 926, or with such a modern poem as Richard Hovey's "Stein Song." What other drinking songs do you know?

READING LIST

TRANSLATIONS FROM ROMAN LITERATURE

Readings from the Literature of Ancient Rome, ed. by Dora Pym
Roman Literature in Translation, ed. by G. Howe and G. A. Harrer
Lucretius: *Of the Nature of Things,* trans. by W. E. Leonard

Virgil: *Aeneid,* trans. by W. C. Bryant
Virgil: *Georgics* and *Eclogues,* trans. by T. C. Williams
Horace: *Echoes from a Sabine Farm,* trans. by E. and R. W. Field
Catullus: *Poems,* trans. by F. A. Wright

BOOKS ABOUT ROMAN HISTORY, LITERATURE, ART, CIVILIZATION, ETC.

Showerman, G.: *Rome and the Romans*
Greene, W. C.: *The Achievement of Rome*
Lanciani, R.: *Ancient and Modern Rome*
Johnston, H. W.: *The Private Life of the Romans*
Davis, W. S.: *A Day in Old Rome*
Fowler, W. W.: *Social Life at Rome in the Age of Cicero*
Abbott, F. F.: *The Common People of Ancient Rome*
McDaniel, W. B.: *Roman Private Life and Its Survivals*
Fox, W. S.: *Greek and Roman Mythology*
Gremier, A.: *The Roman Spirit in Religion, Thought and Art*
Mackail, J. W.: *Latin Literature*

Duff, J. W.: *A Literary History of Rome*
Walters, H. B.: *The Art of the Romans*
Mackail, J. W.: *Virgil and His Meaning to the World Today*
Showerman, G.: *Horace and His Influence*
Harrington, K. P.: *Catullus and His Influence*

Fiction and Poetry

Bulwer-Lytton, E. G.: *The Last Days of Pompeii*
Davis, W. S.: *A Friend of Caesar*
Sienkiewicz, H.: *Quo Vadis*
Wallace, Lew: *Ben-Hur*
Macaulay, T. B.: *Lays of Ancient Rome*

Egyptian Literature

Egyptian Literature

"Time got his wrinkles reaping thee
Sweet herbs from all antiquity."

So might Sidney Lanier have sung of Egyptian literature, for this, the oldest of all national writings, reveals Time's wrinkles most astonishingly. Antiquarians are in doubt as to the exact date of the earliest writings, but approximately 4500 B.C. may be taken as a starting point.

The earliest remains are those carved on the durable stone of monuments. Had it not been for the importance attached by the Egyptians to a life after death, the most ancient literature would never have survived. The great tombs were the libraries in which the numerous writings were preserved, either as inscriptions on the walls or written on papyrus. This substance, from which our word *paper* is derived, was made from a certain kind of reed growing in the Nile. It is a curious fact that long after the living plant became extinct in the Nile valley, the dried pressed leaves bore silent witness to the ancient civilization. Many of these precious papyri are now scattered in libraries and museums throughout the world, some of the most important being in London, Berlin, and Leningrad.

Four thousand years of Egyptian dynasties leave literary record

The thirty-one dynasties of kings reigning in Egypt up to the conquest by Alexander the Great in 332 B.C. may be divided into three main groups:

1. *The Old Kingdom* (to 3000 B.C.) has left only stone inscriptions. One of the most interesting is a letter of thanks written by a boy Pharaoh to a general who had sent him a captive Ethiopian dwarf dancer.

2. *The Middle Kingdom* (3000–1600 B.C.) introduced the use of papyrus and has left many literary documents. One of the finest poems is the Hymn to Usertesen III (see page 1107).

3. *The New Kingdom* (1600–332 B.C.) included the time of the Exodus of the Israelites under Moses, about 1300 B.C. Up to the death-struggles with the Eastern conquering nations, Assyria, Persia, and Greece, this period produced the greatest body of literature of the three. After Alexander the Great, Egypt became just a Greek province. Her glory had become merely a tradition of the past.

Scholars trace evolution of Egyptian language

The language of ancient Egypt had three forms of writing:

1. *Hieroglyphic* is the oldest, and the most attractive to the eye since the characters are pictures of the idea expressed. Birds and animals, men, suns, trees, and other objects are easily recognizable. It was most commonly used in monumental inscriptions.

2. *Hieratic* is a later form, in which the pictures have been modified to simpler, more conventional figures. Most of the papyrus manuscripts use this form.

3. *Demotic,* a still later form (from about the seventh century B.C.) with a reduced number of symbols, was used largely for commercial records. After Alexander's conquest the language was transposed into Greek characters, with eight demotic signs retained.

The interpretation of these old writings was accomplished by means of the Rosetta Stone, discovered during the Napoleonic wars and now preserved in the British Museum. It is covered with an inscription written in three parallel sets of characters: hieroglyphic, demotic and Greek. By comparing the characters the meaning of the old forms could be ascertained, and thus the whole Egyptian literature was suddenly opened up for modern scholars. Since many of the old manuscripts were apparently the work of pupils taking dictation, and full of errors, there is endless opportunity for these scholars to compare and correct them.

Egyptian literature limited in scope and style

Extensive as this literature is in amount, it is rather limited in type — largely epitaphs, hymns in praise of monarchs and gods, religious and moral teachings, records, ledgers, and letters. A few tales remain — one of a shipwrecked sailor, another of a prince whose violent death was foretold. The most extensive work is *The Book of the Dead,* consisting of religious formulas for the conduct of the soul after death. If all parts from various existing manuscripts were combined, it would contain one hundred and sixty-five chapters.

The style of Egyptian literature, like that of its art, is stiff, pompous, and lacking in both grace and subtlety. The poets, like the

Pharaohs, seem to be constantly on parade to the accompaniment of brass trumpets. They love high-sounding titles and laudatory figures of speech drawn from the mighty forces of nature. These, for example, are typical phrases to describe a monarch:

"A victorious lion putting forth its claws while roaring loudly and uttering its voice in the Valley of the Gazelles."

"His mighty will seizeth on his enemies like a flame catching the ki-ki plant (castor-oil plant) with the storm behind it."

On the whole the interest of Egyptian literature lies in its astounding antiquity, and the light it throws on history, rather than in any personal satisfaction to the reader because of its charm or human verity.

HYMN TO USERTESEN III

One of the most interesting old manuscripts of the twelfth dynasty is the Prisse Papyrus of "Proverbs" discovered by Flinders Petrie in the ruins of a temporary town built for the workers on the pyramid of Usertesen II. In this manuscript appears a hymn to the son of the man buried in the pyramid, Usertesen III. This is probably the most complete and effective single poem of Egyptian literature. It is obvious that repetition was the basis of this ancient poetry. Since we know nothing of the sound values of the characters, it is impossible to tell whether either rhyme or regular rhythm was also involved, but the musical quality suggested is decidedly that of sounding brass and clashing cymbal.

The hymn contains many more stanzas, but a great deal of it cannot be deciphered.

Twice jubilant are the gods: thou hast established their offerings.
Twice jubilant are thy children: thou hast made their boundaries.
Twice jubilant are thy forefathers: thou hast increased their portions.
Twice jubilant is Egypt in thy strong arm: thou hast guarded the
    ancient order.
Twice jubilant are the Pat in thy administration: thy mighty spirit   5
    hath taken upon itself their provisionment.
Twice jubilant are the two regions in thy valor: thou has widened
    their possessions.
Twice jubilant are thy paid young troops: thou hast made them to
    prosper.
Twice jubilant are thy veterans: thou hast made them to renew their
    youth.

3. **portions:** offerings to the dead, often lavish.   5. **Pat:** the people.
6. **the two regions:** probably lower and upper Egypt.

Twice jubilant are the two lands in thy might: thou hast guarded their walls.

Twice jubilant be thou, O Horus, who hast widened his bound-   10
ary: thou art from everlasting to everlasting.

Twice great is the lord of his city, above a million arms: as for other rulers of men, they are but common folk.

Twice great is the lord of his city: he is as it were a dyke, damming the stream in its water flood.

Twice great is the lord of his city: he is as it were a cool lodge, letting every man repose unto full daylight.

Twice great is the lord of his city: he is as it were a bulwark, with walls built of the sharp stones of Kesem.

Twice great is the lord of his city: he is as it were a place of   15
refuge, excluding the marauder.

Twice great is the lord of his city: he is as it were an asylum, shielding the terrified from his foe.

Twice great is the lord of his city: he is as it were a shade, the cool vegetation of the flood-time in the season of harvest.

Twice great is the lord of his city: he is as it were a corner warm and dry in time of winter.

Twice great is the lord of his city: he is as it were a rock barring the blast in time of tempest.

Twice great is the lord of his city: he is as it were Sekhemt to foes   20
who tread upon his boundary.

(Francis Llewellyn Griffith)

10. **Horus:** the sun-god, represented over temple doors as a winged disk, and symbolizing protection.   12. **as it were:** This elaborated form of *like* is used to suggest the high-sounding phrases of the Egyptians.   14. **Kesem:** the name of a town.   20. **Sekhemt:** an avenging goddess with the head of a lioness.

SUGGESTIONS FOR STUDY

1. If you knew nothing of early Egyptian life, how many details of the country, the customs, and the religion could you glean from this poem?

2. What elements make this a poem rather than a piece of prose?

3. Compare this poem with the hymns of Moses and Miriam after the Israelites escaped from Egypt, Exodus 15:1–22. What similarities do you find in the style?

4. As background for this poem, study prints of Egyptian art, and read accounts of excavations made in recent years. In the opera *Aïda,* Verdi has attempted to reproduce the spirit of ancient Egypt. Do you think he has succeeded? Can you think of other traces which ancient Egypt has left upon modern life?

Babylonian-Assyrian Literature

WHILE the Egyptian kingdom dominated the valley of the Nile, there was gradually developing another civilization in the fertile valley of the Tigris and Euphrates rivers farther east. The earliest race, the Sumerians, were conquered about 2900 B.C. by Semitic tribes, and united under Sargon I. This great Babylonian empire reached the height of its power under the dynasty of Hammurapi. The laws issued by Hammurapi (about 2100 B.C.) are among the most important remains of that time, comparing favorably with the Mosaic law in high moral standard. About 1300 B.C. the Assyrians, who had been gradually strengthening themselves in the northern part of the valley, swept down on the Babylonians and made them tributary. Nineveh, the Assyrian capital, remained the most important city of western Asia until its fall in 606 B.C. before the Babylonians, who again established their supremacy, only to fall in their turn before the Persians in 538 B.C.

Babylonian books made of clay

The great Babylonian and Assyrian empires left a voluminous literature behind them. The ancient Sumerians had an aboriginal language with written symbols composed of wedge-shaped characters, from which the language of the two great empires developed. The reason for the wedge shapes was that clay tablets pressed by the sharp edge of a stylus were used for written records. These tablets varied in size from great blocks to small bricks. The smallest, about three by four inches, and one inch thick, were used for letters and even inclosed in clay envelopes for privacy. Such records, like the papyri of Egypt, resisted the inroads of time and exist today in great numbers. Assurbanipal, an Assyrian monarch of the seventh century B.C., assembled at Nineveh a tremendous library of about twenty-two thousand clay tablets; and had it not been for the destruction of many of these when Nineveh fell before the Persians, we might have had today a complete picture of Assyrian literature. Much, however, remains, both there and in temples of other cities. Religion dominates literature, for the priests were the only scholars. Their writing includes poetry, prayers, hymns, magic formulas, but most important of all many long epic poems preserving the myths of deities and the traditions of the past.

Great epics record lives of the gods

The great " Creation Epic of Babylon " centers around the sun-god Marduk who battles with Trainat, the salt-water ocean, from whose slain body he creates heaven and earth. Later Marduk creates man from the blood of another rebellious god. The other deities build a sanctuary to Marduk and hail him lord with a list of fifty honorary titles. The recital of this epic was part of the annual New Year's Festival of the Babylonians.

Ishtar, goddess of love, identified with the planet Venus, figures in many of the epics. One story of her " Descent into Hades " during half the year resembles the Greek myth of Persephone, in symbolizing the death of vegetation during winter and its revival with the return of the goddess in the spring.

But the most important of all the Babylonian epics is that of Gilgamesh, two-thirds god and one-third human. He is loved by the goddess Ishtar but because of her fickleness he rejects her. She in revenge creates a terrible bull to destroy the hero, but Gilgamesh slays the creature. Later the death of his friend reminds him that he too is mortal because he is one-third human, and he determines to win immortality. He consults his ancestor, Ut-napishtim, who has been translated to the garden of the gods without dying. It seems that the recipe is to remain awake for six days and seven nights, but Gilgamesh falls asleep in the attempt. His last hope is to bring the plant of eternal youth from the bottom of the ocean, but that too fails, for a serpent eats the plant. In despair the hero conjures the spirit of his friend from the dead and learns of the cheerless life of the spirits, especially those whose bodies have not been properly buried. Thus the epic ends on a tragic note. Ut-napishtim, the ancestor consulted by Gilgamesh, is the Babylonian Noah, and in telling his experiences he gives us a version of the Deluge which resembles in many of its details that of the Bible.

THE STORY OF THE DELUGE

From Tablet XI of the Epic of Gilgamesh

Ut-napishtim, in order to show Gilgamesh how he had obtained immortality, relates the story of the deluge. He tells first that after the gods have decided to send a flood to the earth, Ea, one of the leaders of the gods, mysteriously conveys to the mind of the mortal the coming event and instructs him to save himself and all life in a ship which he is to build according to the god's instructions. The story continues:

On the fifth day I designed its shape.
According to the design its sides were one hundred and twenty cubits
    high,
Correspondingly the edge of its roof was one hundred and twenty
    cubits.
I designed its forecastle and drew up the plan —
I gave it six decks;   5
I divided it outside seven times;
I divided its interior nine times.
I hammered water-plugs into its midst,
Selected an oar, and put in what was necessary.
Six sars of bitumen I poured into the furnace,   10
Three sars of bitumen I poured inside.
Three sars of oil the basket-carriers [of the ship] brought in —
Besides one sar of oil which [the sacrifices] consumed,
Two sars of oil which the shipman stowed away.

    .   .   .   .   .   .

Before sundown the great ship was completed.   15
Everything I owned I stowed into it,
All that I had of silver I stowed into it,
All that I had of gold I stowed into it,
All the seed of life that there was I loaded into it.
I caused to go up into the ship my whole family and clan,   20
The cattle of the field, animals of the field, all the craftsmen I brought
    up.
Shamash had fixed a time for me:

2. **one hundred and twenty cubits:** A cubit was the length of the forearm (about twenty inches); hence the ship was about two hundred feet high. 10. **sars:** A sar is a large measure, the exact size of which is not known. 13. **the sacrifices:** Throughout this selection the brackets indicate words supplied by the translator where the original could not be deciphered. 22. **Shamash:** the Sun-god.

" The sender of [darkness] will send a heavy rain at eventide;
Then go into the ship and close thy door."
That time arrived.

The sender of [darkness] sent a heavy rain at eventide;   25
I studied the appearance of the weather,
To look at the weather I was afraid.
I entered the ship and closed the door;
To the pilot of the ship, to Puzur-Amurru, the sailor,   30
I entrusted the great house along with its possessions.
As soon as a gleam of the dawn shone forth,
A black cloud rose up from the foundations of heaven.
Adad thundered in the midst of it,
Shullat and Hanish lead the van,   35
Travel as messengers over mountain and land.
Iragal tears out the [masts];
Ninurta proceeds, breaks down the dams.
The Anunnaki raised their torches,
With their brightness they illumine the land.   40
Adad's wrath reaches the heavens,
Turning to darkness everything that was bright;
The [breadth] of the land he shattered like a pot.
One day the southerly storm [roared unceasingly],
Quickly it blew and made the waters [reach] the mountains.   45
Like a battle [the floods] came upon men,
No one could see his fellow;
From the heavens men could not be seen at all.
The gods feared the deluge,
They withdrew and ascended to the heaven of Anu;   50
The gods cowered like a dog, they lay down at the outer walls.

· · · · · · · · ·

Six days and six nights
The wind blew, the deluge, the southerly storm overwhelmed the land.
When the seventh day arrived,
The southerly storm, the deluge, was defeated in the battle,   55
Which it had fought like an army.
The sea became quiet and calm, the hurricane, the deluge ceased,
And all mankind was turned to clay;
Level as a roof the field had become.

34. **Adad:** the Storm-god. The two mentioned in the next line are his attendants. 37. **Iragal:** god of Hades. 38. **Ninurta:** another god of the lower world. 39. **The Anunnaki:** gods of the lower world.

I opened the hatch, and light fell upon my countenance. 60
I knelt down, sat down, wept;
Over my countenance ran my tears.
I looked forth to the regions at the boundary of the sea;
Toward " the twelve " an island arose.
Upon Mount Nisir the ship landed, 65
Mount Nisir held the ship so that it did not move.
One day, a second day, Mount Nisir held the ship so that it did not
    move;
A third day, a fourth day, Mount Nisir held the ship so that it did not
    move;
A fifth day, a sixth day, Mount Nisir held the ship so that it did not
    move;
When the seventh day came, 70
I caused a dove to go forth, released it.
The dove went forth, it returned;
Since there was no resting place, it turned back.
I caused a swallow to go forth, released it.
The swallow went forth and returned; 75
Since there was no resting place, it turned back.
I caused a raven to go forth, released it;
The raven went forth, saw the subsiding of the water;
It eats, wades, [croaks], and does not return.
Thereupon I caused [everything] to go forth to the four winds 80
    and brought a sacrifice;
I made an incense offering on the top of the mountain.
Seven and seven [votive] pots I set out,
Poured into their bottom reeds, cedar wood, and myrtle.
The gods smelled the savor,
The gods smelled the sweet savor; 85
The gods gathered like flies above the sacrificer.

    •   •   •   •   •   •   •

As soon as Enlil came,
He saw the ship; then Enlil was enraged,
Was filled with anger against the Igigi-gods.
" Some one has escaped alive, 90
No man to remain alive in the destruction! "

    •   •   •   •   •   •

64. the twelve: the twelve signs of the zodiac; hence toward the sky.
87. Enlil: the warrior god who had determined to send the storm. He was
supposed to rule the northern hemisphere. 89. Igigi-gods: gods of the upper
world.

Ea opened his mouth and spoke,
Said to the warrior Enlil:
" Thou wise one among the gods, warrior!
Why, why didst thou, without considering, cause a flood?   95
Let the sinner bear his sin,
Let the evil-doer bear his crimes;
Give in, that he may not be cut off, be patient that he may not
     [perish]!
Instead of thy causing a deluge,
A lion should have come and diminished the people.   100
Instead of thy causing a deluge,
A wolf should have come and diminished the people.
Instead of thy causing a deluge,
A famine should have come and destroyed the land.
Instead of thy causing a deluge,   105
Irra should have come and destroyed the land.
I myself did not give away the decision of the great gods.
I caused the arch-wise one to see dreams, and [thus] he heard the
     decision of the gods."

Now Enlil's senses came back to him,
Enlil entered the ship.   110
He took my hand and brought me up,
Brought up my wife and caused her to kneel beside me.
Touched our foreheads, and standing between us, he blessed us.
" Formerly Ut-napishtim was a human being,
Now Ut-napishtim and his wife shall be like us gods.   115
Ut-napishtim, verily, shall dwell afar at the source of the rivers."
They took me, and in the distance at the source of the rivers they
     caused me to dwell.   *(Emil G. H. Kraeling)*

92. **Ea:** god who ruled the southern hemisphere, a milder and wiser god
than Enlil.   106. **Irra:** god of pestilence.

SUGGESTIONS FOR STUDY

1. Compare this version of the flood with that in the Bible, Genesis 6,
7, and 8.   List similar and dissimilar details.   Which predominate?

2. Read the Greek version of the flood in the story of Deucalion, page
1078.   Is the Babylonian story closer to the Hebrew or to the Greek?
Which of the three is most interesting merely from the point of view of
effective narrative?   Which has the most spiritual quality?

3. Name counterparts of some of the Babylonian gods among the Greek,
Roman, German, and Scandinavian gods.

WHILE the literature of the other ancient Semitic nations survives almost exclusively in the world of scholarship, that of the Hebrews, because of its religious significance, is the literary inheritance of the masses. The Old Testament is revered by Christian and Jew alike, and the Bible maintains its place as the best seller among books.

Marked variety of type present in Old Testament

The Old Testament is a rich library of literature. In it are to be found history, short story, poetry, proverb, and prophecy. The narratives concerning Noah, Abraham, Joseph, Moses, David, and Daniel are known (or should be) by all children. The Books of Ruth and Esther have the artistry of construction of the short story and novelette. The poetry of the Psalms and the Song of Solomon shows richness of imagery and balance of phrasing. Wisdom for daily guidance is packed into the Book of Proverbs. Job presents a powerful drama of human suffering and soul struggle. The books of prophecy include vision and invective, poetry and pleading. No student of literature can afford to be ignorant of the Old Testament, because of its intrinsic value and because the thread of its influence is visible throughout the literature of our own language. In fact, so intimately has the phrasing of the King James version of the Bible entered into our consciousness that we scarcely think of it as translation at all, but rather as a part of our own literary product like Shakespeare and Milton.

Hebrew rhythm based on repetition and balance

Ancient Hebrew poetry depends for its rhythm upon repetition and balance rather than on accents and rhymes. Perhaps its rich cadences have been more appreciated as poetry since free verse has come into its own. Then, too, modern printing of the Psalms in the form of poetry rather than in the solid prose formation of the standard Bible has helped the ear through the eye. The simplicity of Hebrew sentence structure gives a measured dignity to the succession of direct clauses unbroken by complexities. Common rhythmic devices are: (1) refrain, as in Psalm 136 with its reiterated " For his mercy endureth forever "; (2) repetition of idea with different phrasing, as in Psalm 5, " Give ear to my words, O Lord, consider my meditations " — these commonly run in pairs, but sometimes in a longer series; (3) questions and answers, as in Psalm 24, " Who is the King of Glory? The Lord of Hosts, he is the King of Glory "; (4) contrast, as in Psalm 1 between the godly and the ungodly carried throughout the Psalm. The highly metaphorical quality of the poetry is evident in almost any Psalm, and is particularly varied in the selections included in this section.

Josephus and the Talmud fill early centuries of our era

The New Testament, being written in Greek, does not come under Hebrew literature. In the early centuries of the Christian era, however, the Hebrew language is active in the historical works of Josephus (37?–95? A.D.) whose *War of the Jews,* in seven books, and *Antiquities of the Jews,* in twenty, give us our best picture of the interval between the Old and New Testaments, and the events leading up to the destruction of the Jewish state in 70 A.D., of which he was an eyewitness.

The second great Hebrew work of the early centuries of our era is the Talmud, a long series of maxims, instructions, and commentaries developed by the priesthood to explain the Old Testament and Mishna (body of laws supplementing those of the Old Testament). The word Talmud at first designated a method of study, but later came to be applied to the records themselves. Among the dry legal elaboration of this book there are frequent flashes of literary interest, particularly in the stories of the patriarchs and short moral tales. The Talmud was practically completed by the end of the sixth century, but between that time and the eleventh it was subject to considerable revision by scholars known as Geonim and thus the period is called the Gaonic age.

Hebrew secular literature developed from twelfth century on

Among the numerous Hebrew writers of the middle centuries, the greatest poet and philosopher is Judah ha-Levi (1086?–1140?), a Spanish Jew. Spain, in fact, became the chief center of medieval

Hebrew culture. By this time Jewish writers were reaching out beyond the limitations of religious teaching to produce a new secular literature in which nature and love were treated with grace and charm. Between the tenth and the eighteenth centuries distinguished Jewish writers were to be found in France, Germany, and Italy. In the last-named country their work showed the marked influence of the Renaissance, but in the others it suffered from the forced segregation of the race.

During the eighteenth and nineteenth centuries Hebrew literature was greatly affected by the changing standards of the Western world. In the eighteenth century the German Jews led a literary revival, but in the next century the center of activity changed to Russia. A movement known as the Haskalah urged the Jews to break away from traditional methods of thought and take an active part in the main stream of writing. The novel and short story began to flourish and were often used for Haskalah propaganda. Modern Hebrew poetry has thrived, with a host of poets carrying on the tradition of Judah ha-Levi. Of course modern Jewish literature is much more extensive than the limits of modern Hebrew literature, for many Jewish writers use entirely the vernacular of the country in which they live and therefore belong to the literature of that language. It is interesting to note, however, that outside of the Chinese-Japanese group, Hebrew is one of the few languages of the ancient world which is producing an active literature today.

PSALM 91

He that dwelleth in the secret place of the most High shall abide under the shadow of the Almighty.
I will say of the Lord, He is my refuge and my fortress: my God; in him will I trust.
Surely he shall deliver thee from the snare of the fowler, and from the noisome pestilence.
He shall cover thee with feathers, and under his wings shalt thou trust; his truth shall be thy shield and buckler.
Thou shalt not be afraid for the terror by night; nor for the   5 arrow that flieth by day;
Nor for the pestilence that walketh in darkness; nor for the destruction that wasteth at noonday.
A thousand shall fall at thy side, and ten thousand at thy right hand; but it shall not come nigh thee.

Only with thine eyes shalt thou behold and see the reward of the wicked.

Because thou hast made the Lord, which is my refuge, even the most High, thy habitation;

There shall no evil befall thee, neither shall any plague come nigh thy dwelling. 10

For he shall give his angels charge over thee to keep thee in all thy ways.

They shall bear thee up in their hands, lest thou dash thy foot against a stone.

Thou shalt tread upon the lion and the adder; the young lion and the dragon shalt thou trample under feet.

Because he hath set his love upon me, therefore will I deliver him; I will set him on high because he hath known my name.

He shall call upon me and I will answer him; I will be with him in trouble; I will deliver him and honor him. 15

With long life will I satisfy him and show him my salvation.

(King James Version)

PSALM 103

Bless the Lord, O my soul; and all that is within me, bless his holy name.

Bless the Lord, O my soul, and forget not all his benefits:

Who forgiveth all thine iniquities; who healeth all thy diseases;

Who redeemeth thy life from destruction; who crowneth thee with loving kindness and tender mercies;

Who satisfieth thy mouth with good things; so that thy youth is renewed like the eagle's. 5

The Lord executeth righteousness and judgment for all that are oppressed.

He made known his ways unto Moses, his acts unto the children of Israel.

The Lord is merciful and gracious, slow to anger, and plenteous in mercy.

He will not always chide; neither will he keep his anger for ever.

He hath not dealt with us after our sins; nor rewarded us according to our iniquities. 10

For as the heaven is high above the earth, so great is his mercy toward them that fear him.

As far as the east is from the west, so far hath he removed our transgressions from us.

Like as a father pitieth his children, so the Lord pitieth them that
fear him.

For he knoweth our frame; he remembereth that we are dust.

As for man, his days are as grass; as a flower of the field so he   15
flourisheth.

For the wind passeth over it and it is gone; and the place thereof
shall know it no more.

But the mercy of the Lord is from everlasting to everlasting upon
them that fear him, and his righteousness unto children's children.

To such as keep his covenant, and to those that remember his
commandments to do them

The Lord hath prepared his throne in the heavens; and his kingdom ruleth over all.

Bless the Lord, ye his angels that excel in strength, that do his   20
commandments, hearkening unto the voice of his word.

Bless ye the Lord, all ye his hosts; ye ministers of his, that do his
pleasure.

Bless the Lord, all his works in all places of his dominion; bless the
Lord, O my soul.

                                                  (*King James Version*)

A SPRING SERENADE

Song of Solomon 2:8-17

The voice of my beloved!

Behold, he cometh leaping upon the mountains, skipping upon the
hills.

My beloved is like a roe or a young hart.

Behold, he standeth behind our wall; he looketh forth at the windows
showing himself through the lattice.

My beloved spake and said unto me,   5

Rise up, my love, my fair one, and come away.

For, lo, the winter is past; the rain is over and gone.

The flowers appear on the earth;

The time of the singing of birds is come, and the voice of the turtle
is heard in our land.

                    9. **turtle:** turtle-dove.

The fig tree putteth forth her green figs, and the vines with the   10
   tender grapes give a good smell.
Arise, my love, my fair one, and come away.
O my dove that art in the clefts of the rock, in the secret places of
   the stairs,
Let me see thy countenance, let me hear thy voice;
For sweet is thy voice and thy countenance is comely.
Take us the foxes, the little foxes that spoil the vines, for our   15
   vines have tender grapes.
My beloved is mine and I am his.
He feedeth among the lilies.
Until the day break and the shadows flee away, turn, my beloved,
   and be thou like a roe or a young hart upon the mountains of
   Bether.

(King James Version)

AMOS (Eighth Century B.C.)

Though the Book of Amos appears in the last third of the Old Testament, in time of composition it is one of the earliest, having been written in the middle of the eighth century B.C. before the Pentateuch and Psalms were put into their present form, and before any of the so-called books of prophecy had appeared.

Amos was a herdsman of Tekoa. His great significance is that whereas earlier leaders had defended the Israelites as the " chosen people," Amos acted as a national conscience and denounced the social injustice he observed among his own people. To him religion was not a matter of formal rites and sacrifices but a social virtue and moral obligation. The following powerful denunciation put in the mouth of the Lord can strike home in the modern world as well as in 750 B.C.

These lines are from Amos 5:11-12, 21-24.

THE LORD DENOUNCES INJUSTICE

Forasmuch as ye trample on the poor,
And take from him exaction of wheat,
Though ye have built houses of hewn stone,
Ye shall not dwell in them,
Though ye have planted pleasant vineyards,   5
Ye shall not drink the wine thereof.
For I know how manifold are your transgressions

And how mighty are your sins,
Ye who afflict the just, who take bribes,
Who deprive the poor of their rights in courts of justice.   10

.   .   .   .

I hate, I despise your feasts,
I take no delight in your solemn assemblies.
Though you offer me your burnt offerings and cereal offerings,
I will not accept them;
The peace offerings of your fat beasts I will not regard   15
Take away from me the noise of thy songs;
The clang of thy viols I will not hear.
But let equity roll down as waters,
And justice as a perennial stream.

(English Revised Version)

SUGGESTIONS FOR STUDY

1. Characterize the differing moods of the selections from Psalms and the Song of Solomon here given. What other moods do you know in the Psalms not here represented?

2. Select some of the striking metaphors and explain the point of resemblance. Do you find any which seem exaggerated figures? Which ones seem to grow naturally out of climate or general conditions of Palestine?

3. Point out in these poems metrical devices common to Hebrew poetry. Do the poems seem musical to your ear?

4. What impression of the personality of the Lord is given by these Psalms? By the selection from Amos?

5. Where in Psalm 91 does the speaker seem to change? Study carefully the use of pronouns throughout this Psalm.

6. To throw further light on these Old Testament passages consult other well-known versions. How do you think the Revised Versions compare in poetic flavor with the King James?

7. The Old Testament is a rich field for additional reading. Interesting studies might be made of (1) the short stories, (2) drama based on Bible narrative, (3) the varying emotions of the Psalms, (4) prophets who mourn and denounce (see Sargent's famous "Frieze of the Prophets," original in Boston Public Library).

ABRAM AND THE IDOLS

In the Talmud, an accumulation of Hebrew religious lore made during the early centuries of our era, we find many narratives told with skill and vigor. The following tale of Abram (same as Abraham, founder of the Hebrew tribes) has within its brief limits sprightly dialogue, suspense, climax, and catastrophe. It is significant as showing the first advance beyond the primitive stage of idolatry. Abram, the fearless, independent thinker, is in contrast to his brother Haran, the trimmer.

Terah, the father of Abram, was a maker and seller of idols. One day he went out leaving his son in charge. And when a man came to buy an idol, Abram asked him, " How old are you? "

And the other replied, " Fifty years, sixty years . . ."

" Alas," said Abram. " You who are sixty years old will bow down before a thing that is only one day old! "

And the man was ashamed and left without buying an idol.

One day a woman came in, carrying a plateful of rye. She said to Abram, " Take this, and go before one of the idols, and offer this sacrifice." Abram arose and took a stick and broke the idols; then put the stick in the hand of the largest idol. When his father returned he asked, " Who has done this? "

And Abram replied, " There came a woman with a plateful of rye, and she approached me and said, ' Take this and go before one of the idols and offer sacrifice.' And I did so, and one of the idols said, ' I want to eat first,' and another said, ' I want to eat first.' And the biggest of them took this stick and broke the others."

And Terah said, " You are mocking me! " and he brought him before Nimrod.

Nimrod said to Abram, " We bow in worship to the fire."

Abram replied, " And we to water which extinguishes fire."

Nimrod said, " So be it, let us bow to water."

And Abram replied, " Then let us bow to the cloud which brings the water."

" So be it," said Nimrod, " let us bow to the cloud."

" Then," said Abram, " let us bow to the wind, which disperses the cloud."

" To the wind then," said Nimrod.

" Then," said Abram, " let us bow to the son of man who resists the wind."

" Since you make merry with words," said the king, " see, I bow to fire and you shall be thrown therein; and let the God to whom you bow come and save you."

And Haran was there, too, and his heart was divided between Abram and Nimrod. And he said, " If Abram gets the better of it, I will say I am with Abram; and if Nimrod gets the better of it, I will say I am with Nimrod."

Abram came forth alive from the furnace, and they asked Haran,
" With whom are you? "

And he said, " With Abram."

They threw him into the fire; but his entrails were burned, and
when he came out he died in front of his father Terah.

(Anonymous Translation)

JUDAH HA–LEVI (1086?–1140?)

During the Middle Ages when the Jews were an exiled people scattered
throughout Europe, Spain became the stronghold of Jewish culture. Here
at Toledo was born the greatest of medieval Hebrew poets, Judah ha-Levi.
He was a man of wide learning, versed in the Koran as well as the Old
Testament, in philosophy as well as in poetry. He studied medicine as a
pastime, according to his own comment in a letter, " In the hours which
belong neither to the day nor to the night, I occupy myself with the vanity
of medical science, although I am unable to heal. I physic Babel [1] but it
continues infirm." His youthful poems, said to have been begun at the
age of thirteen are light-hearted and romantic, but his mature poetry turns
to religion and the mourning of his race for the lost Jerusalem. It is in
these national themes that he reaches the climax of poetic fervor. At the
age of sixty he started alone to visit the Holy Land, which had been for
so many years the land of his dreams. After reaching Palestine records
of his life cease, but according to tradition, he was killed by a Muslim
for reciting his " Ode to Zion " before the walls of Jerusalem. A brief
counterpart of the famous Ode may be found in the little poem which
follows.

LONGING FOR JERUSALEM

O city of the world, with sacred splendor blest,
My spirit yearns to thee from out the far-off West;
A stream of love wells forth when I recall thy day;
Now is thy temple waste, thy glory passed away.
Had I an eagle's wing, straight would I fly to thee,   5
Moisten thy holy dust with wet cheeks streaming free.
Oh! how I long for thee! albeit thy King has gone,
Albeit where balm once flowed, the serpent dwells alone.
Could I but kiss thy dust, so would I fain expire,
As sweet as honey then, my passion, my desire!   10

(Emma Lazarus)

[1] physic Babel: doctor the miscellaneous races of the city.

Modern Hebrew Poetry

To illustrate the variety and power of modern Hebrew poetry, only a few examples can be given here. Jacob Cahan is noteworthy for the originality of his imagery. Yehoash (Solomon Bloomgarden) is one of the most able lyrists who writes in Yiddish. Yiddish is a modern dialect of Hebrew developed as a corruption of German when large numbers of Jews left Germany for Eastern Europe toward the end of the Middle Ages. With modified grammar and the introduction of words from various tongues it became practically a distinct language, and in the nineteenth century began to develop a literature of its own, principally in Russia and the United States.

JACOB CAHAN (1877–   )

DO YOU KNOW WHAT THE MOUNTAINS ARE?

Do you know what the mountains are?
The mountains are cries,
Cries of freedom, a wild shouting, vehement voices,
Which broke forth in tempestuous power
From the heart girdled with strength, thirsting for might and   5
    drunk with it,
The heart of life —
Broke forth, sprang out against the skies —
And were frozen.
And the frozen cries stand
Like memorials in the wastes of the world,   10
From eternity to eternity.
And the wind will not bear them away,
Never shall the wind bear them away.
The silent snow rests on them,
And the sun shines on them, and the moon shines on them,   15
And about them life pours onwards, a rushing of bubbles —
And they stand there, frozen,
From eternity unto eternity.

(Maurice Samuel)

YEHOASH (SOLOMON BLOOMGARDEN, 1870–1927)

AN OLD SONG (Yiddish)

In the blossom-land Japan
Somewhere thus an old song ran:

Said a warrior to a smith,
" Hammer me a sword forthwith.
Make the blade   5
Light as wind on water laid.
Make it long
As the wheat at harvest song.
Supple, swift
As a snake, without a rift,   10
Full of lightnings, thousand-eyed!
Smooth as silken cloth and thin
As the web that spiders spin.
And merciless as pain, and cold."

" On the hilt what shall be told? "   15

" On the sword's hilt, my good man,"
Said the warrior of Japan,
" Trace for me
A running lake, a flock of sheep
And one who sings her child to sleep."   20

(*Marie Syrkin*)

SUGGESTIONS FOR STUDY

1. What new light do you get on Abraham's character from the Talmud story? Read the stories about him given in Genesis 11:27 to chapter 24. Do these seem in keeping with his independence as indicated in the Talmud story?

2. What do the Ten Commandments say about idol worship? Exodus 22:3–6. On what famous occasion soon after the Commandments were given did the Israelites violate the law? What effect has the law about idols had on Hebrew art?

3. In the Hebrew secular poetry interpret the meaning of each poem. How does each show traces of the history of the race?

4. What differences do you realize in the metrical effect of these poems and that of the Psalms?

READING LIST

EGYPTIAN, BABYLONIAN-ASSYRIAN LITERATURE

Best studied in the general works on page 1244, and in histories of the ancient world. For art, consult Maspero, G.: *Art in Egypt.*

HEBREW LITERATURE

Old Testament

Cunliffe, J. W. and Battenhouse, H. M.: *Century Readings in the Old Testament*

Rhodes, C. E.: *Old Testament Narratives*

Miller, H. A.: *Readings from the Old Testament*

Moulton, R. G.: *The Modern Reader's Bible*
The Bible as Literature

Van Dyke, Henry: *The Poetry of the Psalms*

Famous Derivative Literature in English

Browning, Robert: *Saul*

Miracle plays: *Noah*
Abraham and Isaac

Milton, John: *Paradise Lost*
Samson Agonistes

Byron, Lord: *Hebrew Melodies*
The Destruction of Sennacherib
Jephthah's Daughter

About the Hebrews

Van Dyke, Henry: *The House of Rimmon* (drama)

Parker, L. N.: *Joseph and His Brethren* (drama)

Connelly, Marc: *Green Pastures* (drama)

Wallace, Lew: *Ben-Hur* (novel)

Kipling, Rudyard: *Pharaoh and the Sergeant*

Hebrew Literature Since the Old Testament

Fleg, Edmond: *The Jewish Anthology,* trans. by Maurice Samuel

Raskin, P. M.: *Anthology of Modern Jewish Poetry*

Music Based on Hebrew Literature

Handel, George Frederick: Oratorios: *The Messiah*
Esther
Saul
Israel in Egypt
Samson

Haydn, Josef: Oratorio: *The Creation*

Mendelssohn, Felix: Oratorio: *Elijah*

Saint-Saens, Charles: Opera: *Samson and Delilah*

No attempt is made to list the many settings of the Psalms.

Persian Literature

PERSIAN Literature, like the writings of the Egyptians, Babylonians, and Assyrians, belongs to the ancient world, but differs from them in being continued into modern times. Even so, its total existence of about twenty-seven hundred years does not equal the Egyptian of about four thousand, for it had a much later beginning. Its history falls into three main periods:

1. *The Ancient Iranian* (to third century A.D.) consists largely of inscriptions on the monuments of kings, especially on that of the conqueror Darius the Great, and of the sacred writings composing the *Avesta*, the teachings of Zoroaster. This great founder of the ancient Iranian religion lived between 660 and 583 B.C. according to Persian records, or as early as 1000 B.C. according to many scholars. He wrote voluminously. Pliny refers to two million verses of Zoroaster, and tradition agrees on there being twenty-one books. The originals, however, were destroyed when Alexander caused the palace at Persepolis to be burned in the fourth century B.C., and other copies were lost during the Greek conquest.

2. *The Medieval Period* (third to tenth centuries A.D.) followed a great revival of the Zoroastrian religion. Copies of the original writings which had been translated into other tongues were assembled and re-translated into Persian. Much of the old ceremonial which had been preserved only in the memory of priests was put into writing, and a great body of commentary appeared. Since *Zend* means *explanation,* the original with its later additions was usually called *Zend-Avesta*. In the seventh century the conquest of Persia by the Muslims again made Zoroastrianism a persecuted religion. Only a few copies of the *Avesta,* most carefully secreted by priests, survived the widespread destruction of sacred books. The manuscripts from which our present knowledge of the great work is derived are even later, dating back only to the thirteenth century. Five hundred years later these were obtained with great difficulty by a young French

scholar who lived among Zoroastrian priests for seven years. Finally in 1771 he published the first translation into a modern language. There was practically no creative writing done during the medieval period, unless some be discovered in the excavation being constantly carried on since 1890. Much of the material unearthed in recent years has not yet been translated.

3. *The New Persian Literature* (tenth century to present) was Muslim, for the Arabs had conquered Persia in 641. Though opposed to Zoroastrian philosophy, this new literature was not narrowly Muslim, but maintained its own marked individuality. Its poetry emphasized beauty of form rather than originality of idea. Its repeated theme of love and wine was partly mystic, symbolizing religious ecstasy, and partly sensuous. Besides innumerable minor poets, this period produced several great names: Firdausi (940?–1020?), Omar Khayyám (? –1123), Sa'di (1184?–1291), Hafiz (? –1389?), and Jami (1414–1492). Firdausi represents historical romance in his great epic, *Shah Namah* (*The Book of Kings*), from which Matthew Arnold drew his story of *Sohrab and Rustum*. Omar Khayyám, writer of mystic and didactic quatrains, is the best known to the English-speaking world through the excellent adaptation of the *Rubáiyát* made by Edward Fitzgerald. Sa'di was the greatest realist, picturing the world of men with sprightly humor. Hafiz is considered by Persians their greatest mystic poet, though he is not so well known to the Occidental world as Omar. Jami wrote excellent tales, odes, and lyrics.

On the whole Persian literature emphasizes poetry rather than prose. Its weakness is monotony of theme, over-elaboration, artificiality, and sentimentality. Its strength is its constant reaching out for beauty, its mystic interpretation of life and death, and its rich symbolism.

THE AVESTA

The *Avesta* is the sacred book of the ancient Persian religion founded by Zoroaster (flourished 1000? B.C.). The word might be translated either *law* or *wisdom*. When the title is written *Zend-Avesta*, it applies to the original sacred books with the Zend or commentary added from time to time over several centuries. The *Avesta* weathered two great conquests of Persia, that by Alexander the Great in the fourth century B.C. and that by the Muslims in the seventh century A.D. After each of these conquests the sacred books were destroyed, and it was only through the memories of the priests and retranslation from foreign copies that the lore of the ancient days is now extant. Western Europe gained translations

of the secretly guarded tomes through the discoveries of Anquetil du
Perron, a young French scholar, who lived for seven years among the
priests.

The *Avesta,* as it exists today, has six main divisions, one of the most
important of which is the *Yasna* (worship) consisting of prayers, hymns,
and ceremonies. The following is one of the most poetic passages, giving
part of the ritual of the fire worship. The priest in white robe and veil
invokes the power of the Sun-god, Ahura Mazda, consecrates the sacred
water, the offering, the bundle of twigs and the juice of a sacred plant,
the drinking of which is supposed to bring a blessing upon the worshiper.
As the fire is kindled, the chant arises to a climax with the flames.

TO THE FIRE

I offer my sacrifice and homage to thee, the Fire, as a good offering, and an offering with our hail of salvation, even as an offering of
praise with benedictions to thee, the Fire, O Ahura Mazda's son!
Meet for sacrifice art thou, and worthy of [our] homage. And as
meet for sacrifice, and thus worthy of our homage, may'st thou be in
the house of men [who worship Mazda]. Salvation be to this man
who worships thee in verity and truth, with wood in hand and *baresma*
[sacred twigs] ready, with flesh in hand and holding too the mor-
tars. And may'st thou be ever fed with wood as the prescription
orders. Yea, may'st have thy perfume justly, and thy sacred butter
without fail, and thine andirons regularly placed. Be of full age as
to thy nourishment, of the canon's age as to the measure of thy food.
O Fire, Ahura Mazda's son! Be now aflame within this house; be
ever without fail in flame; be all ashine within this house; for long
time be thou thus to the furtherance of the heroic [renovation], to
the completion of [all] progress, yea, even till the good heroic [mil-
lenial] time when that renovation shall have become complete. Give
me, O Fire, Ahura Mazda's son! a speedy glory, speedy nourishment
and speedy booty, and abundant glory, abundant nourishment, abundant booty, an expanded mind, and nimbleness of tongue and soul
and understanding, even an understanding continually growing in its
largeness, and that never wanders.

(*L. H. Mills*)

FIRDAUSI (940?–1020?)

Firdausi is the literary name of Abu'l-Kasim Hasan, bestowed on him, according to tradition, by Sultan Mahmud, and signifying " belonging to Paradise." Whether this was a tribute to the quality of his verse or derived from the garden in which the poet's father was gardener is hard to say. Firdausi's *Shah Namah* (*Book of Kings*) was literally his life work. He put in long years of preparatory study before writing this great epic of the ancient national heroes. He was about forty years old when he began the actual composition and more than seventy when he finished it.

The legends that have grown up around Firdausi's own life are as picturesque as any celebrated in his verse. When he first went from his native town of Tus to the Sultan's capital, his intrusion was resented by three well-established poets of the court. To get rid of him they proposed a trial of poetic skill common in those days. Each was to compose a line for a quatrain, the upstart being required to produce the difficult last line with proper rhyme. To catch him they chose words for which there was scarcely a rhyme in the language. But instantly the newcomer capped the quatrain, not only with a proper rhyme, but also with a historical allusion unknown to any of them. One English scholar has composed a quatrain to illustrate the idea and the difficult rhyme of the original:

> The glance of thy face rivals moonlight or silver;
> Thy cheek's downy bloom is as soft as the chilver;
> Thy eyelashes pierce through the warrior's cuirass;
> As Giv's spear in combat did Pushan harass.

Needless to say, the young poet won his spurs and became a favorite of the Sultan, who promised him a golden dirhem for each couplet upon the completion of his great epic. By the time, however, that a payment of sixty thousand dirhems was to be made many years later, the Sultan was induced by intriguing courtiers to send silver instead of gold dirhems — a much smaller sum. The story goes that Firdausi was in the bath when the money bags arrived, borne on the backs of elephants. So furious was he on discovering the deception that he divided the bounty among the bath steward, the elephant driver, and a third servant. He then vented his wrath in a vehement satire against the Sultan and fled the country to save his skin. After ten years he returned to his native city of Tus. The repentant Sultan, hearing this, sent him the originally promised gold dirhems, but by the time the money arrived the aged man was dead.

The *Book of Kings* in its sixty thousand rhymed couplets records the lives of fifty kings. From it Matthew Arnold derived his story for *Sohrab and Rustum*. The following description is characteristic of the nature of the exploits and the vigor of the style.

THE WARRIOR SAM KILLS A DRAGON

The dragon seemed a lofty mountain,
And trailed upon the ground its hairlike lassos.
Its tongue was like a tree-trunk charred; its jaws
Were open and were lying in my path.
Its eyes were like two cisterns full of blood.   5
It bellowed when it saw me and came on
In fury, seeming all afire, O Shah!
Within. . . . The world 'gan swim before mine eyes,
A black reek went up to the murky clouds,
Earth's surface shook beneath the bellowing,   10
The venom seemed to be a sea of Chin.

Then like a gallant warrior I roared
Against that dragon as a lion roareth,
And tarried not, but fitted to my bow
A poplar arrow tipped with adamant,   15
And shot it at the dragon's jaws, to pin
The tongue against the throat. The tongue lolled pinned;
The dragon was astound.

     Again I shot,
Again I pierced the mouth; — the creature writhed.
I shot a third shaft right adown its jaws;   20
Its heart's blood spouted seething.

     When it closed
And pressed me hard, I took mine ox-head mace,
And, in the strength of God, the Lord of all,
Urged on mine elephantine steed and smote
The dragon's head. Thou wouldst have said that heaven   25
Rained mountains down thereon.

     I smashed the skull,
As it had been a mighty elephant's,
And venom poured forth like the river Nile.
So struck I that the dragon rose no more,
While earth was leveled to the hills with brains,   30
Kasaf was flowing like a stream of gall,
And all was peace.

          (*A. G. and E. Warner*)

11. **Chin:** China.   31. **Kasaf:** a local river.

A SATIRE ON THE SULTAN MAHMUD

This is part of the satire written by Firdausi after the Sultan had sent him silver instead of gold dirhems upon completion of his great epic, the *Shah Namah*. The Sultan little realized the picture of himself which would go down to posterity as the revenge of the irate poet.

Oh, had thy father graced a kingly throne,
Thy mother been for royal virtues known,
A different fate the poet then had shared —
Honors and wealth had been his just reward;
But how remote from thee a glorious line!　　　5
No high, ennobling ancestry is thine;
From a vile stock thy bold career began —
A blacksmith was thy sire, of Isfahan.
Alas! from vice can goodness ever spring?
Is mercy hoped for in a tyrant king?　　　10
Can water wash the Ethiopian white?
Can we remove the darkness from the night?
The tree to which a bitter fruit is given
Would still be bitter in the bowers of heaven;
And a bad heart keeps on its vicious course —　　　15
Or if it changes, changes for the worse;
Whilst streams of milk, where Eden's flow'rets blow,
Acquire more honeyed sweetness as they flow.
The reckless king who grinds the poor like thee
Must ever be consigned to infamy!　　　20

.　　.　　.　　.　　.　　.

The toil of thirty years is now complete,
Record sublime of many a warlike feat,
Written 'midst toil and trouble; but the strain
Awakens every heart, and will remain
A lasting stimulus to glorious deeds;　　　25
For even the bashful maid who kindling reads,
Becomes a warrior. Thirty years of care,
Urged on by royal promise, did I bear,
And now deceived and scorned, the aged bard
Is basely cheated of his pledged reward!　　　30

(*J. Atkinson*)

OMAR KHAYYÁM (? –1123)

Though we do not know the exact date of Omar Khayyám's birth, we do have a record of seven names bestowed upon him by his parents, out of which Omar alone is used to designate him. Khayyám, signifying "Tentmaker," is his father's name. Young Omar, a native of Naishápúr, was educated in the learning of his day. It is said that when one of his friends arose to the position of Vizier to the Shah, Omar, instead of seeking political preferment, requested that he be granted a life of safe retirement to devote himself to "amassing the riches of learning." The request being granted with a proper pension, he thereafter gave himself to the study of mathematics and astronomy. He was one of a small group of scholars authorized to revise the Persian calendar. His books on algebra and geometry became standard works, and a Persian historian a century after his death called him the greatest scholar of his time.

In contrast to his learned productions, he wrote, from time to time, scattered philosophical quatrains. Just how many of the verses surviving in various manuscripts may be attributed to him cannot be told accurately. Out of the twelve hundred assigned to him by different scholars many are of doubtful origin, for the oldest manuscript extant was written more than three hundred years after his death and has no critical notes. From these many quatrains, Edward Fitzgerald, a Victorian poet and friend of Tennyson, selected and rendered freely into English poetry about a hundred, arranging them in a sequence of thought which the original never had. So popular has this poem become that Omar Khayyám's name is probably the best known to the English-speaking world among Oriental poets. Ironically enough, the Persians themselves class him as a great astronomer, but not as a particularly great poet, and are astonished at the Western verdict. Fitzgerald's rendering of the quatrains in English follows the Persian metrical form and conveys the rich symbolical quality of the original. The total impression, however, of a pessimistic view of human destiny is greater in Fitzgerald than in the original, for Omar's moods were varied, whereas the translator has selected only those verses which build up a unified impression of life and death.

THE RUBÁIYÁT OF OMAR KHAYYÁM

I

Wake! For the Sun, who scattered into flight
The Stars before him from the Field of Night,
   Drives Night along with them from Heaven and strikes
The Sultan's Turret with a Shaft of Light.

2

Before the phantom of False morning died,　　　　　5
Methought a Voice within the Tavern cried,
　"When all the Temple is prepared within,
Why nods the drowsy Worshiper outside?"

3

And, as the Cock crew, those who stood before
The Tavern shouted, "Open then the Door!　　　　　10
　You know how little while we have to stay,
And, once departed, may return no more."

7

Come, fill the Cup, and in the fire of Spring
Your Winter-Garment of Repentance fling;
　The Bird of Time has but a little way　　　　　15
To flutter — and the Bird is on the Wing.

8

Whether at Naishápúr or Babylon,
Whether the Cup with sweet or bitter run,
　The Wine of Life keeps oozing drop by drop,
The Leaves of Life keep falling one by one.　　　　　20

9

Each Morn a thousand Roses brings, you say;
Yes, but where leaves the Rose of Yesterday?
　And this first Summer month that brings the Rose
Shall take Jamshyd and Kaikobád away.

10

Well, let it take them! What have we to do　　　　　25
With Kaikobád the Great, or Kaikhosrú?
　Let Zal and Rustum bluster as they will,
Or Hátim call to Supper — heed not you.

---

5. **False morning:** In the Orient, a "false dawn" precedes the real dawn by about an hour. 24. **Jamshyd and Kaikobád:** These and the names in stanza 10 refer to ancient Persian kings and heroes. Rustum is the famous warrior in Arnold's *Sohrab and Rustum.*

11

With me along the strip of Herbage strown
That just divides the desert from the sown,   30
   Where name of Slave and Sultan is forgot —
And peace to Máhmúd on his golden Throne!

12

A Book of Verses underneath the Bough,
A Jug of Wine, a Loaf of Bread — and Thou
   Beside me singing in the Wilderness —   35
Oh, Wilderness were Paradise enow!

13

Some for the Glories of This World; and some
Sigh for the Prophet's Paradise to come;
   Ah, take the Cash, and let the Credit go,
Nor heed the rumble of a distant Drum!   40

14

Look to the blowing Rose about us — " Lo,
Laughing," she says, " into the world I blow,
   At once the silken tassel of my Purse
Tear, and its Treasure on the Garden throw."

15

And those who husbanded the Golden Grain,   45
And those who flung it to the winds like Rain,
   Alike to no such aureate Earth are turned
As, buried once, Men want dug up again.

16

The Worldly Hope Men set their Hearts upon
Turns Ashes — or it prospers; and anon,   50
   Like Snow upon the Desert's dusty Face,
Lighting a little hour or so — was gone.

---

   32. Máhmúd: famous Sultan who conquered India and upon whom
Firdausi wrote the satire on page 1132.

17

Think, in this battered Caravanserai
Whose Portals are alternate Night and Day,
   How Sultan after Sultan with his Pomp   55
Abode his destined Hour, and went his way.

.   .   .   .

19

I sometimes think that never blows so red
The Rose as where some buried Caesar bled;
   That every Hyacinth the Garden wears
Dropped in her Lap from some Once lovely Head.   60

20

And this reviving Herb whose tender Green
Fledges the River-Lip on which we lean —
   Ah! lean upon it lightly! for who knows
From what once lovely Lip it springs unseen!

21

Ah, my Belovèd, fill the Cup that clears   65
Today of past Regrets and future Fears;
   Tomorrow! — Why Tomorrow I may be
Myself with Yesterday's Seven Thousand Years.

22

For some we loved, the loveliest and the best
That from his Vintage rolling Time hath pressed,   70
   Have drunk their Cup a Round or two before,
And one by one crept silently to rest.

23

And we that now make merry in the Room
They left, and Summer dresses in new bloom,
   Ourselves must be beneath the Couch of Earth   75
Descend — ourselves to make a Couch — for whom?

53. **Caravanserai:** inn.

24

Ah, make the most of what we yet may spend,
Before we too into the Dust descend;
　　Dust into Dust, and under Dust to lie,
Sans Wine, sans Song, sans Singer, and — sans End!　　80

25

Alike for those who for TODAY prepare,
And those that after some TOMORROW stare,
　　A Muezzín from the Tower of Darkness cries,
" Fools! your Reward is neither Here nor There."

26

Why, all the Saints and Sages who discussed　　85
Of the Two Worlds so wisely — they are thrust
　　Like foolish Prophets forth; their Words to Scorn
Are scattered, and their Mouths are stopped with Dust.

27

Myself when young did eagerly frequent
Doctor and Saint, and heard great argument　　90
　　About it and about; but evermore
Came out by the same door where in I went.

28

With them the seed of Wisdom did I sow,
And with mine own hand wrought to make it grow;
　　And this was all the Harvest that I reaped —　　95
" I came like Water, and like Wind I go."

29

Into this Universe, and *Why* not knowing
Nor *Whence*, like Water willy-nilly flowing;
　　And out of it, as Wind along the Waste,
I know not *Whither*, willy-nilly, blowing.　　100

　　80. Sans: without.　83. Muezzín: summoner to prayer.

30

What, without asking, hither hurried *Whence?*
And, without asking, *Whither* hurried hence!
    Oh, many a Cup of this forbidden Wine
Must drown the memory of that insolence!

31

Up from Earth's Center through the Seventh Gate   105
I rose, and on the Throne of Saturn sate,
    And many a Knot unraveled by the Road;
But not the Master-knot of Human Fate.

32

There was the Door to which I found no Key;
There was the Veil through which I might not see.   110
    Some little talk awhile of ME and THEE
There was — and then no more of THEE and ME.

33

Earth could not answer; nor the Seas that mourn
In flowing Purple, of their Lord forlorn;
    Nor rolling Heaven, with all his Signs revealed   115
And hidden by the sleeve of Night and Morn.

57

Ah, but my Computations, People say,
Reduced the Year to better reckoning? — Nay,
    'Twas only striking from the Calendar
Unborn Tomorrow, and dead Yesterday.   120

63

Oh, threats of Hell and Hopes of Paradise!
One thing at least is certain — *This* Life flies;

---

105. **Seventh Gate:** The ancients believed that seven great planets moved
in concentric circles around the Earth. Saturn was the seventh or most
distant. The seventh heaven was the highest sphere of happiness or spiritual
exaltation. 117. **my Computations:** a reference to his work in revising the
Persian calendar.

One thing is certain and the rest is Lies;
The Flower that once has blown for ever dies.

64

Strange, is it not? that of the myriads who   125
Before us passed the door of Darkness through,
   Not one returns to tell us of the Road,
Which to discover we must travel too.

65

The Revelations of Devout and Learned
Who rose before us, and as Prophets burned,   130
   Are all but Stories, which, awoke from Sleep
They told their comrades, and to Sleep returned.

66

I sent my Soul through the Invisible,
Some letter of that After-life to spell;
   And by and by my Soul returned to me,   135
And answered, " I Myself am Heaven and Hell."

67

Heaven but the Vision of fulfilled Desire,
And Hell the Shadow from a Soul on fire,
   Cast on the Darkness into which Ourselves,
So late emerged from, shall so soon expire.   140

68

We are no other than a moving row
Of Magic Shadow-shapes that come and go
   Round with the Sun-illumined Lantern held
In Midnight by the Master of the Show;

69

But helpless Pieces of the Game He plays   145
Upon this Chequer-board of Nights and Days;
   Hither and thither moves, and checks, and slays,
And one by one back in the Closet lays.

143. **Sun-illumined Lantern:** the earth.

70

The Ball no question makes of Ayes and Noes,
But Here or There as strikes the Player goes;
   And He that tossed you down into the Field,
He knows about it all — HE knows — HE knows!   150

71

The Moving Finger writes; and, having writ,
Moves on; nor all your Piety nor Wit
   Shall lure it back to cancel half a Line,   155
Nor all your Tears wash out a Word of it.

72

And that inverted Bowl they call the Sky,
Whereunder crawling cooped we live and die,
   Lift not your hands to *It* for help — for It
As impotently moves as you or I.   160

.   .   .   .

99

Ah Love! could you and I with Him conspire
To grasp this sorry Scheme of Things Entire,
   Would not we shatter it to bits — and then
Re-mold it nearer to the Heart's desire!

.   .   .   .

(Edward Fitzgerald)

SA'DI (1184?–1291)

Sa'di's special field is the moral tale, the maxim, the fable, all of which he treats with lightness and charm. He said of his own work that " the pearls of salutary counsel are strung on the thread of diction, and the bitter medicine of advice is mingled with the honey of mirthful humor." It is the honey that has made his medicine in demand both in the East and in the West, where he is one of the most widely translated Persian poets. His writings are assembled in two volumes: the *Bustan (Orchard,* or *Garden of Perfume)* and the *Gulistan (Rose-Garden).* The first is in verse, the second in prose interspersed with verse.

Sa'di was a great traveler. The disastrous result of one of his youthful adventures is told in the following selection from the *Rose-Garden.* He had participated in the Sultan's defense against the European Crusaders, had been captured, ransomed, and as a result was forced into marriage with a shrewish wife. He ran away from her and made his way back to the Persian capital, but was not cured of either marriage or travel, for he took a second wife and is said to have made fourteen pilgrimages to the shrine at Mecca and to have scoured India, Asia Minor, and Africa.

His writing was done late in life and shows the seasoned philosopher and tolerant gentleman, with excellent common sense and a twinkle in his eye over the follies of humanity. Among the mystic and visionary Persian poets, Sa'di stands out as a realist picturing the teeming life of highway and bazaar.

Dr. R. A. Nicholson has thus characterized him in verse:

> O full of human wisdom, happy sage,
> A Persian Horace, mingling on thy page,
> Where childhood learns to read, age reads to learn,
> Moral with gay and tale with truth in turn;
> Which as we read, our fancy so beguile,
> The matter pleases for the golden style,
> A style that softly winning, simply dressed,
> Endears the topic and refines the jest.

THE CAPTIVE GETS A WIFE

Having become weary of the society of my friends at Damascus, I set out for the wilderness of Jerusalem, and associated with the brutes until I was made prisoner by the Franks, who set me to work along with Jews at digging in the fosse of Tripolis; till one of the principal men of Aleppo, between whom and myself a former intimacy had subsisted, passed that way and recognized me, and said, "What state is this? and how are you living?" I replied:

Stanza

> "From men to mountain and to wild I fled,
> Myself to heavenly converse to betake;
> Conjecture now my state that in a shed
> Of savages I must my dwelling make."

Couplet

> Better to live in chains with those we love,
> Than with the strange 'mid flow'rets gay to move.

He took compassion on my state, and with ten dinars [1] redeemed me from the bondage of the Franks, and took me along with him to

---

[1] **dinars:** Since the word *dinar* is applied to various Oriental coins, it is hard to estimate this value.

Aleppo. He had a daughter, whom he united to me in the marriage knot, with a portion of a hundred dinars. As time went on the girl turned out to be of a bad temper, quarrelsome and unruly. She began to give loose to her tongue, and to disturb my happiness as they have said:

Distichs

In a good man's house an evil wife
Is his hell above in this present life.
From a vixen wife protect us well;
Save us, O God! from the pains of hell.

At length she gave vent to reproaches, and said, "Art thou not he whom my father purchased from the Frank's prison for ten dinars?" I replied, "Yes! he redeemed me with ten dinars, and sold me into thy hands for a hundred."

Distichs

I've heard that once a man of high degree
From a wolf's teeth and claws a lamb set free.
That night its throat he severed with a knife;
When thus complained the lamb's departing life:
"Thou from the wolf didst save me then; but now,
Too plainly I perceive the wolf art thou."

(*E. B. Eastwick*)

A TALE IN PROSE AND VERSE

I saw an Arab sitting in a ring of jewel dealers at Basra, telling a story how once upon a time in the desert he had lost his road, and had not a morsel of food remaining, so that he had settled in his heart he must die. "Suddenly," said he, "I lighted upon a bag which felt to be full of grain. Never can I forget the relish and the joy of thinking that it was indeed parched corn, and then the agony and despair to find it only a bag of pearls."

The desert traveler mid the driving sands,
Sinking with thirst — what matter if his hands
Holds pearls or dust? His dried mouth curseth both!
So when a man with hunger falls to die,
What difference whether in his girdle cloth
He hideth gold or only frippery?

(*Sir Edwin Arnold*)

WISE SAYINGS

1

Money abides not in the palm
Of those who careless live,
Nor patience in the lover's heart,
Nor water in the sieve!

2

To door of king, or minister, or peer,
Draw not thou nigh unless with patrons girt;
For if a poor man at the gate appear,
Warders his collar seize, and dogs his shirt!

3

They who in youth to manners ne'er attend,
Will in advancing years small gain acquire.
Wood, while 'tis green, thou mayst with pleasure bend;
When dry, thou canst not change it save by fire.

(E. B. Eastwick)

HAFIZ (? –1389?)

For lack of a Boswell, the life of Hafiz, like that of so many other Oriental poets, is largely a matter of tradition. His pen name, Hafiz — convenient substitute for a ponderous actual name — means "one who knows the Koran by heart." This suggests that he had the highest form of education of his day. We know that he came of a good family and passed most of his life in his native city of Shiraz. We assume that he was married, from a pathetic poem which seems to refer to the death of his wife. We are entertained by legends of how he feared shipwreck and so sent a poem in place of his person when invited to visit the Sultan in India; how he was rebuked by the great conqueror Tamerlane for offering in one of his love poems to exchange two great cities ruled by that Tatar chief for the mole on his beloved's cheek; how at his death the priests, reluctant to perform rites over his body because of his unorthodox views, were finally won over by the line from one of his poems: "Though he be immersed in sin, he goeth to Paradise."

Hafiz is usually regarded by the Persians as their greatest lyric poet.

His favorite form is the *ghazal* (ode), a poem of about sixteen couplets. The rhyme scheme is peculiar. The opening couplet has the usual double rhyme, but thereafter the first line of each couplet has no rhyme and the second line rhymes with the first couplet, thus making only one rhyme throughout the poem. Hafiz wrote more than five hundred *ghazals* besides numerous quatrains and other lyrics. His greatness, however, is not a mere matter of volume, but of richness and delicacy of style. He follows the usual Persian themes of love and wine, and much critical argument has been expended as to how much is to be taken literally and how much is merely symbolical for divine inspiration and the oblivion of death.

QUATRAINS

1

O lovers, you whose happy hands enlace,
For whom Time's wheel, forgotten, flies apace,
When my time cometh, hail the endless round,
That other Aprils may recall my face.

2

O time of broken vows that none could mend,
The bitter foe was once a faithful friend.
So to the skirts of solitude I cling,
Lest friendship lure me to an evil end.

3

When tyrants rule, can gold redeem the earth?
When sorrow haunts the home, can joy have birth?
Not all the promised aeons of delight
These seven dull days of mortal care are worth.

4

O great of soul! How gladly would I give
All that I am to thee by whom I live!
If thou wouldst know the bitterness of hell,
Pour friendship's water through an empty sieve.

5

'Twere folly to thyself to be more kind,
Or from Creation call thyself to mind.
Learn wisdom from the pupil of the eye
That looks on all men, yet to self is blind.

6

One that should dwell in squalor for a space,
Of former pride will not retain a trace;
But some poor stranger in a foreign land
Sighs and remembers still his native place.

7

The way to Thee lies over grief and pain.
The soul gropes on, the darkness doth remain.
We only look upon the perfect face
When the lamp failing, shows the quest is vain.

(From translation of Syed Abdul Majid
Rendered into verse by L. Crammer-Byng)

LYRICS

I

The writing on the pages of the Rose
(For readers are not all interpreters)
Only the Nightingale may understand.

I murmured to my soul apart: " Suppose
Thy throne o'ercanopied the universe — "
" Love, love endures; the rest is crumbling sand."

O Love, in search of thee whoever goes
To Reason's school, goes further and fares worse;
For him no face-to-face or hand-in-hand!

2

The calm circumference of life
When I would fain have kept,
Time caught me in the tide of strife
And to the center swept.

Of this fierce glow which Love and You
Within my breast inspire.
The Sun is but a spark that flew
And set the heavens afire!

(Reynold A. Nicholson)

JAMI (1414–1492)

The pen name Jami, like Firdausi, has a possible double meaning. The poet came from a town called Jam, but he himself uses his name with the significance of "cup," meaning that he contains and pours out the divine spirit, which Persian poets hide under the metaphor of wine. He was a devout follower of the Dervishes, and a mystic philosopher whose orthodoxy was not questioned as was that of Omar Khayyám and Hafiz. From his many works (a hundred according to some accounts) seven of his best poems have been gathered into a collection called *The Seven Stars of the Great Bear*. One of these is an elaborated version of the story of Joseph and Potiphar's wife in the Bible. Another is called "Salaman and Absal," from which the following brief story is taken.

THE BEWILDERED ARAB

From the solitary desert
Up to Baghdad came a simple
   Arab; there amid the rout
Grew bewildered of the countless
People, hither, thither, running,   5
Coming, going, meeting, parting,
Clamor, clatter, and confusion,
   All about him and about.

Travel-wearied, hubbub-dizzy,
   Would the simple Arab fain   10
Get to sleep — "But then, on waking,
How," quoth he, "amid so many
   Waking, know myself again?"

So, to make the matter certain,
Strung a gourd about his ankle,   15
And, into a corner creeping,
Baghdad and himself and people
   Soon were blotted from his brain.

But one that heard him and divined
His purpose, slyly crept behind;   20
From the sleeper's ankle clipping,
   Round his own the pumpkin tied,
   And laid him down to sleep beside.

By and by the Arab, waking,
Looks directly for his signal —   25
Sees it on another's ankle —
Cries aloud, " Oh, good-for-nothing
Rascal to perplex me so!
That by you I am bewildered,
Whether I be I or no!   30
If I — the pumpkin why on you?
If you — then where am I, and who? "

(Edward Fitzgerald)

SUGGESTIONS FOR STUDY

1. What elements of true worship are to be found in the ritual " To the Fire "? What elements of poetry? How has the name Mazda been applied in modern times? Why so?

2. Compare the feats of the Warrior Sam with those of the heroes of other nations, especially Beowulf's fight with Grendel. If you have read Arnold's *Sohrab and Rustum,* discuss what elements it has in common with this.

3. Compare Firdausi's satire with some by Dryden and Pope. Why is the meter chosen by the translator especially suitable for this type of poem? Do you think the satire was deserved? See page 1153, the account of Tarafa, and note the result of another Oriental satire on a ruler.

4. Study the *Rubáiyát* stanza by stanza to get the meaning hidden under the figurative language. An interpretive sentence summary is helpful toward getting at the point of each. What symbols are frequently repeated? For what do they stand? What general impression of the poet's attitude toward life and death do you get from the whole? Wherein is it pessimistic? Where do you find familiar quotations? Memorize stanzas you particularly like.

5. What similarities and what differences do you note between Omar and Hafiz? Which seems more figurative? Which is easier to understand? Which seems to have more warmth of human experience?

6. Where in this Persian poetry does humor enter in? What elements do you find in Persian poetry which were missing in Egyptian, Babylonian, and Hebrew poetry? Which of the European literatures does it resemble in general flavor?

READING LIST

Translations from Persian Literature

A Persian Anthology, trans. by E. G. Browne

Early Persian Poetry, trans. by A. V. Williams-Jackson

The Shah-Namah of Firdausi, trans. by Alexander Rogers; also by A. and E. Warner; also by Edward Eastwick

The Rubáiyát of Omar Khayyám, trans. by Edward Fitzgerald; also by Richard Le Gallienne

The Bustan of Sa'di, trans. by A. Hart Edwards

The Gulistan of Sa'di, trans. by Edwin Arnold

Songs of Hafiz, tran. by Edna Underwood

Odes from the Divan of Hafiz, trans. by Richard Le Gallienne; also by Gertrude L. Bell

Eastern Poetry and Prose, trans. by R. A. Nicholson

World's Great Classics, Oriental Literature, Vol. II

About Persia

Levy, R.: *Persian Literature: An Introduction*

Browne, E. G.: *A History of Persian Literature,* 4 vols.

Arnold, Matthew: *Sohrab and Rustum*

Pope, A. U.: *An Introduction to Persian Art*

See also General Oriental Reading List, page 1244.

Arabic Literature

"WISDOM has alighted upon three things — the brain of the Franks, the hands of the Chinese, and the tongue of the Arabs." Thus ran an Arabic saying, and its boast justifies itself to the student of the richly varied language and engaging body of literature produced by the sons of the desert. The barrenness of the land and the isolation of its settlements developed an Arabian society based on the family and tribe rather than a unified nation. This is reflected in the early literature by the absence of a single great national epic. Instead, we find innumerable tales told by the Bedouin professional storyteller around the campfire. A large group of these stories centers around Antar, who holds a place in their tradition similar to that of King Arthur in English. Like many other national heroes he had his famous horse and sword, and in himself demonstrated the virtues dear to the Arabian heart — truthfulness, generosity, hospitality, and love of freedom. The life of a later day, when Mahomet had fired the Arabs to become conquerors, and thus brought them into contact with Persian wealth and sophistication, is caught for us in the collection of *The Thousand and One Nights* commonly called *The Arabian Nights*. This is, without doubt, the best-known group of Oriental stories in English translation. The Arabs were also given to anecdotes, brief fables, and pithy sayings, with which they pointed their arguments or enlivened their conversation. Thus the Arabic takes a pre-eminent place among Oriental languages for its prose narrative.

Poetry, too, has flourished. Often it is found embedded in a prose story, for the narrator easily dropped into rhythm; but most of it is separate composition. It is marked by brevity, wit, and highly lyrical quality. In comparing it with Persian poetry, one is struck by the greater variety of subject matter in the Arabic. Read in quantity, the Persian cloys and stifles like a too heavily perfumed atmosphere, but Arabic comes like a sweep of fresh air across a plain — individual, free, and identified with daily life. The Bedouin love of animals brings the horse, the camel, the gazelle into poetry. The sand dune and the storm are a relief after the reiterated rose and nightingale of the Persians. The pessimistic elegancies of the Persians are replaced by the ardors of the Arabs. Smiles and tears follow each other in quick succession.

Arabic poetry can be considered more anonymously than Persian; that is, among the tremendous number of identified poets there are few great individuals who must be mentioned, and consequently it seems unnecessary to confuse the mind by enumerating multisyllabled names.

The form of the poetry, however, deserves some attention. During the classical period from the sixth to the eighth century, the *Kasidah* (poem or ode) consisted of a series of distichs (couplets) ranging from seven or ten to more than a hundred. The early "trembling" meter of iambics rhyming throughout the poem was supposed to measure the trot of the she-camel. By the time of Mahomet there were about sixteen different meters in vogue. Each line was supposed to be a complete thought in itself — a fashion which lends itself to sharp satire and trenchant wit. Much Arabic verse is suggestive of eighteenth-century English poetry. On the whole, however, the poetry is notable for its originality of observation and vitality of emotion.

Arabic poetry cannot be left without mention of its close connection with the Spanish. During the seven hundred years of Moorish domination, Cordova, with its university and library of four hundred thousand volumes, became the cultural center of the West as Bagdad was of the East. A tenth-century anthology of Spanish-Arabic poetry contained twenty thousand verses. Several of the Moorish monarchs were poets, including the last king of Seville, Mu'tamid, who wrote elegies on his own misfortunes. Thus Arabic literature, like the sign of the prophet Mahomet, sweeps in a great crescent with one tip in Persia and the other in Spain.

Kahlil Gibran (1883–1931) was a Lebanese-born mystical poet and philosopher. His first plays and poems, written in Arabic, were cherished by the entire Arab world. At the age of twenty he adopted English as his medium of expression and came to live in New York. *The Prophet, The Garden of the Prophet,* and *The Death of the Prophet* are his best-known works. His very popular *Jesus, the Son of Man* is an attempt to reveal Christ through the consciousness of his contemporaries.

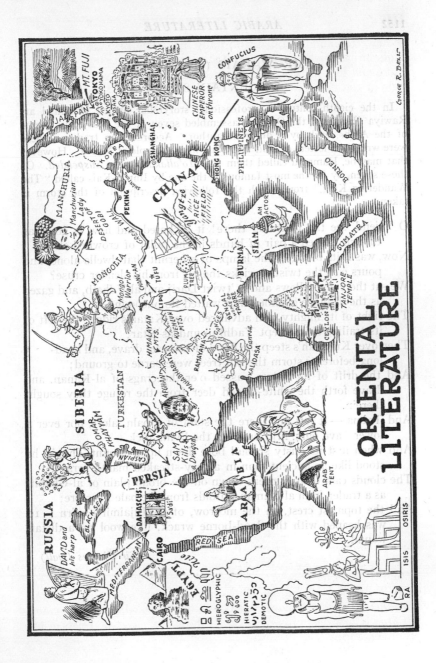

ORIENTAL LITERATURE

IMR AL–KAIS (Sixth Century)

A MOUNTAIN STORM

In the eighth century a professional storyteller named Hammad ar-Rawiya (Hammad the Quoter) assembled seven of the best early poems of the Arabs, each by a different author. According to tradition these were written in letters of gold and hung in the temple at Mecca. However that may be, Hammad called them the *Mo'allakat,* or the *Suspended.* Of these seven, by far the most famous is the one by Imr al-Kais called " The Wandering King," from which the following description of the storm is taken.

O Friend, see the lightning there! it flickered and now is gone, as
    though flashed a pair of hands in the pillar of crowned cloud.
Now, was it its blaze, or the lamps of a hermit that dwells alone, and
    pours o'er the twisted wicks the oil from his slender cruse?
We sat there, my fellows and I, 'twixt Darij and al-Udhaib, and gazed
    as the distance gloomed and waited its oncoming.
The right of its mighty rain advanced over Katan's ridge; the left of
    its trailing skirt swept Yadhbul and as-Sitar;
Then over Kutaifah's steep the flood of its onset drave, and head-   5
    long before its storm the tall trees were borne to ground;
And the drift of its waters passed o'er the crags of al-Kanan, and
    drave forth the white-legged deer from the refuge they sought
    therein.
And Taima — it left not there the stem of a palm aloft, nor ever a
    tower save ours, firm built on the living rock.
And when first its misty shroud bore down upon Mount Thabir, he
    stood like an ancient man in a gray-streaked mantle wrapt.
The clouds cast their burdens down on the broad plain of al-Ghabit,
    as a trader from al-Yaman unfolds from the bale his store;
And the topmost crest, on the morrow, of al-Mujaimir's cairn   10
    was heaped with the flood-borne wrack, like wool on a distaff
    wound.

                            (Sir Charles Lyall)

TARAFA (Sixth Century)

What little we know of Tarafa seems to represent him as a typical prodigal son. He belonged to a leading family of the tribe of Bakr on the Persian Gulf, but squandered his money recklessly, was driven away by his family, repented, was reconciled to them, but again squandered his money until he was reduced to the necessity of tending camels for his brother. Tarafa was accused by his brother of neglecting the camels to write poetry. "What good is poetry if the camels are lost?" he cried. To justify himself, Tarafa purposely allowed the camels to be stolen by a rival tribe, wrote a long poem containing the following description, and so impressed the chieftain that the stolen camels were returned with the added bounty of a hundred more. Besides that, Tarafa won permanent fame as the writer of one of the *Seven Suspended Poems,* the most celebrated in Arabian literature. But poetry proved his ultimate undoing, for he could not resist writing a satire on the king. The crafty monarch granted Tarafa leave to visit his old home, giving him a sealed letter to the governor. This proved to be an order to bury the poet alive, and the sentence was executed.

HE PRAISES HIS CAMEL

Yet I have means to fly from grief, when such pursues me, on a lean
    high beast, which paces swiftly by day and by night,
A camel sure of foot, firm and thin as the planks of a bier, whom I
    guide surely over the trodden ways, ways etched in earth as tex-
    ture is in cloth;
A she-camel, rival of the best, swift as an ostrich. When she trots, her
    hind feet fall in the marks of her forefeet on the beaten road.

With her white feathery tail she lashes backward and forward. Some-
    times the lash falls on her rider.
Firm and polished are her haunches as two worn jambs of a   5
    castle gate.
The bones of her spine are supple and well-attached, and her neck
    rises solidly.
When she raises her long neck it is like the rudder of a boat going up
    the Tigris.
She carries her strong thighs well apart, as a carrier of water holds
    apart his buckets.
Red is the hair under her chin. Strong she is of back, long of stride
    easily she moves her forelegs.

The marks of the girths on her sides are as the marks of water-   10
    courses over smooth rock.
Sometimes the marks unite and sometimes are distinct, like the gores
    in fine linen, well-cut and stitched.
Her long skull is like an anvil, and where the bones unite, their edges
    are sharp as the teeth of a file.
Her cheek is smooth as paper of Syria, and her upper lip like leather
    of Yemen, exactly and smoothly cut.
The two polished mirrors of her eyes gleam in the caverns of their
    sockets as water gleams in rocky pools.

Her ears are sharp to hear the low voices of the night, and not   15
    inattentive to the loud call,
Pricked ears, that show her breeding, like those of a lone wild bull
    in the groves of Haumel.
Her upper lip is divided and her nose pierced. When she stretches
    them along the ground her pace increases.
I touch her with my whip and she quickens her step, even though it
    be the time when the mirage shimmers on the burning sands.
She walks with graceful gait, as the dancing girl walks, showing her
    master the skirts of her trailing garment.

        (*Eunice Tietjens, after Sir W. Jones and F. E. Johnson*)

Miscellaneous Arabic Lyrics
ON OLD AGE
'AMR SON OF QAMI'AH (SIXTH CENTURY)

Now am I, that have passed the space of ninety years, as though on
    a day I had stripped off the cheek-straps of my bridle;
I raise myself painfully on three supports, by the help of my hands
    and a staff, and after that I stand upright.
The Daughters of Time have shot at me from a place which I could
    not see; and how should he fare who is shot at, while he cannot
    shoot in reply?
Yea, if it were an arrow that shot me, I could have defended myself
    against it; but I am shot with that which is not a shaft.
When men see me they say — " Art thou not he that but lately   5
    was bright with new arms and armor, no sluggish fighter? "
Yea, I perish: but of Time I cannot kill even a night; and that which

I slay of him amounts not even to a thread for stringing beads
upon.
I am slain by looking forward to day and night, and looking onward
to year after year.

(Sir Charles Lyall)

ON THE BURIAL OF HIS SON
ABU'L-ATAHIYA (748–828)

Full is my sorrow now that you are dead,
And I have thrown the dust upon your head.
In other days I preached unendingly,
But now, my little boy, you preach to me.

(Henry Baerlein)

THREE POEMS
MU'TAMID (KING OF SEVILLE, 1069–1091)

THE FOUNTAIN

The sea hath tempered it; the mighty sun
    Polished the blade,
And from the limpid sheath the sword leaps forth;
    Man hath not made
A better in Damascus — though for slaughter
Hath steel somewhat advantage over water.

A LETTER

Fain would I write to thee, and great display
Of reed and scroll have I — and naught to say
But that my heart is hotter than noonday.
Beloved, while the poor reed halts and lingers,
Tracing strange patterns in my heedless fingers,
    The long, slow tears,
Make bold to write upon my telltale cheek
In a clear hand the things I dare not speak.

WOO NOT THE WORLD

Woo not the world too rashly, for behold,
Beneath the painted silk and broidering,
It is a faithless and inconstant thing.
(Listen to me, Mu'tamid, growing old.)

And we — that dreamed youth's blade would never rust,
Hoped wells from the mirage, roses from the sand —
The riddle of the world shall understand
And put on wisdom with the robe of dust.

(Dulcie Lawrence Smith after Ismail Ali)

ONE PHYSICIAN TO ANOTHER

AN EPIGRAM ON A PHYSICIAN OF EGYPT
BY A PHYSICIAN OF ANTIOCH

Whoever has recourse to thee
Can hope for health no more,
He's launched into perdition's sea,
A sea without a shore.

Where'er admission thou canst gain,
Where'er thy phyz can pierce,
At once the doctor they retain,
The mourners and the hearse.

(J. D. Carlyle)

ON A LITTLE MAN WITH A VERY LARGE BEARD

ISAAC BEN KHALIF

How can thy chin that burden bear?
Is it all gravity to shock?
Is it to make the people stare?
And be thyself a laughing stock?

When I behold thy little feet   5
After thy beard obsequious run,
I always fancy that I meet
Some father followed by his son.

A man like thee scarce e'er appeared —
A beard like thine — where shall we find it?   10
Surely thou cherishest thy beard
In hopes to hide thyself behind it!

(J. D. Carlyle)

THE INCONSISTENT

An Anonymous Elderly Suitor

When I sent you my melons, you cried out in scorn
They ought to be heavy and wrinkled and yellow;
When I offered myself, whom those graces adorn,
You flouted and called me an ugly old fellow.

FROM THE " ARABIAN NIGHTS "

(Compiled about the thirteenth century)

ADMONITION

There is no writer that shall not perish, but what his hand hath
written endureth ever.
Write, therefore, nothing but what will please thee when thou shalt
see it on the day of judgment.

(Edward William Lane)

ON A SILVER TABLE

Cast down your eyes, lift up your souls,
Dig spoons into the great sauce bowls.
Eat roast and fried and boiled and grilled,
Eat jams and jellies, warmed and chilled.
Eat quails cooked golden to the minute,   5
Eat nut-fed lamb with raisins in it.
Who would the warm stout capon blame,
Date-colored with judicious flame,
Because he could not sing or fly?
(He eats the better).   Nor can I. . . .   10
The golds of man are manifold
But Allah made this kabab's gold;
He made this purslane salad sup
The soul of olives from a cup;
He set these twin and ponderous fish   15
To lie on mint leaves in a dish. . . .

12. **kabab:** roasted meat.
13. **purslane:** a plant of the portulaca family, prized for salads in the Orient.

I will be silent now and eat
A meal which poets shall repeat
In songs of cooking, sound and sage,
Down all the hungry roads of age.   20

(*Edward Powys Mathers*)

SUGGESTIONS FOR STUDY

1. What qualities distinguish Arabic poetry from that of the other Oriental nations you have read so far? Prove your point by examples. How does it compare in interest with them?

2. Show that Arabian poetry is close to the daily lives of the people. If you knew nothing of Arabian life, what details could you glean from this group of poems?

3. Which subjects of these poems seem unusual for poetic treatment? Which commonplace? Does there seem to be more or less variety in the subject matter of Arabian than of Hebrew and Persian poetry?

READING LIST

Translations from Arabic Literature

The Thousand and One Nights (*The Arabian Nights*) trans. by E. W. Lane; also by John Payne

The Singing Caravan, trans. by Henry Baerlein

The Divan of Abu'l-Ala, trans. by H. Baerlein

The Poems of Mu'tamid, King of Seville, trans. by Dulcie L. Smith

Eastern Poetry and Prose, trans. by R. A. Nicholson

Sung to Shahryar, poems from the Arabian Nights, trans. by E. Powys Mathers

About Arabia

Nicholson, R. A.: *A Literary History of the Arabs*

Huart, C.: *A History of Arabic Literature*

Lawrence, T. E.: *Revolt in the Desert*

Seven Pillars of Wisdom

Thomas, L. J.: *With Lawrence in Arabia*

Indian Literature

INDIA, with its long ages of history behind it, its intermingling of races, and its tangle of languages, presents a complicated problem for a brief discussion. As to government, the history may be divided into four major periods: (1) Hindu domination (up to 1001 A.D.); (2) Muslim domination (1001–1757); (3) British domination (1757–1949); (4) national independence (1949–   ). From a literary point of view there are also four divisions:

1. *The Ancient Vedic period* (to about 1000 B.C.). During this time the Brahman-Hindus, an Aryan people akin to the Greeks, Romans, and Teutons, were gradually migrating from their mountain fastnesses toward the southeast, following the courses of the Indus and Ganges rivers. They brought with them a body of religious literature, of which the most interesting parts are the *Rig-Veda*, a collection of hymns with a few secular poems, and the *Upanishads*, philosophical essays.

2. *The Middle Indian period* (tenth to fifth centuries B.C.). As the Brahmans became adjusted to the easy life of the lower river valleys, they ceased to be creative. This period marked the rise of Buddhism (sixth century B.C.) in opposition to Brahmanism. The definitely sectarian writing has little literary interest.

3. *The Classic Sanskrit period* (fifth century B.C. to sixteenth century A.D.). The Sanskrit language was also developed by the Brahmans, but differed markedly from the older Vedic. It was a language of refinement and elegance rather than of primitive power. It may be compared to Latin in that after it produced a classic literature over centuries, it became practically a dead language, being used today only for certain limited purposes and in a modified form.

Lack of time-sense evident in Indian literature

To the Hindu, time is a matter of indifference. He often seems to reproduce in life the vacuum of eternity which is his ideal of heaven.

This has affected literature in several ways. Before the fifth century B.C. nothing was put into writing, but the burden of an extensive literature was placed upon memory alone. Then after writing was employed, no records of exact dates were ever kept, so that an accurate history of Sanskrit literature is practically impossible. Even their most important early poet, Kalidasa, is left wandering through a maze of many centuries without a date on which to rest his head. In the third place, this early literature is storytelling at its most leisurely gait.

Great epics and story collections provide wealth of narrative in Sanskrit

The Indians have two major epics, and the *Mahabharata* alone is seven or eight times as long as the *Iliad* and the *Odyssey* put together. In fact, it is the longest poem in the world. Of course it has little unity. Though ostensibly an account of the wars of the Bharata comparable to the seige of Troy in the *Iliad*, the story is so overlaid with family histories and embroidered with love adventures and fantastic supernatural manifestations that the Western reader is lost in the labyrinth. The same is true of the *Ramayana*, recounting the adventures of Rama, the incarnation of a god, and his beautiful wife, who spend years of exile in the jungle, and later cover most of India in the course of their wanderings. A marked difference between the two poems is that the *Mahabharata* is truly a national epic, a product of centuries and of many narrators, while the *Ramayana* is the work of a poet, Valmiki. Because of the absence of dates, authorities differ as to which preceded the other in time. Probably the truth is that the *Mahabharata* was older in its beginning but later in its completed form, while the *Ramayana* was composed within a compact period of time. Both of these books are regarded as sacred by the devout Hindu and are carefully studied for his soul's salvation.

A third tremendous collection of stories is the *Panchatantra*, which probably dates back to the first century of our era. This consists of five books of fables and short tales interspersed with poetry. It has had an interesting history, having passed, in a continuous chain of translation, through the following languages: Persian, Arabic, Greek, Hebrew, Latin, and German. It was one of the first Oriental works to reach a modern European language, but it is a matter of conjecture how much of the original remained after roaming through six languages in succession.

Drama and lyric poetry prominent in classic Sanskrit period

Drama played an important part in Sanskrit. Kalidasa, " the Hindu Shakespeare," produced three masterpieces, of which *Sakuntala* is outstanding and has been produced on the English and American stages. Another classic is *The Little Clay Cart,* of unknown authorship, though attributed to King Sudraka. A third dramatic favorite is *Gita Govinda* by Jayadeva, which is typical of the mystic poem-drama with little plot or action.

Strangely enough, Indian literature, which seems to emphasize the extended narrative, has also produced some of the best brief, witty verse of any language. Bhartrihari of the seventh century A.D. is the prime master of this type.

Modern literature turns to vernacular

4. *The fourth period of Indian literature,* dating from about the sixteenth century, may be called the Modern, to cover a complication of Hindu, Muslim, and Christian elements. The numerous and different languages of India pose a problem in the creation of a national literature for modern India. Oral tradition still runs strong: popular are ballads of village events, songs composed for special family occasions, songs of religious feeling, and narrative poems that enunciate political propaganda. Written poetry tends to be either religious or political in subject matter. Drama mostly consists of a reworking of ancient Sanskrit plays; novels, new to the Indian literary scene, are imitative of English types.

Very popular have been the writings of India's two great twentieth-century leaders, Mahatma Gandhi (1869–1948) and Jawaharlal Nehru (1889–   ). Gandhi's autobiography, *The Story of My Experiments with Truth,* and his essays have been enthusiastically received; as have Nehru's writings, *Letters from a Father to His Daughter* (written while Nehru served a prison term as a political prisoner), *Glimpses of World History, Discovery of India,* and various speeches.

THE PANCHATANTRA (about Second Century, B.C.)

The *Panchatantra,* meaning *Book of the Five Headings,* is a widely read collection of tales, of which the authorship and original date of production are both lost in antiquity. Aside from the intrinsic merit of its many stories, it is interesting as the oldest example of a series of tales told within a framework narrative, such as we are familiar with in *The Arabian Nights,*

the *Decameron,* and *Canterbury Tales.* The primary story concerns the
attempt of a Brahman to teach within six months all the science of practical and political affairs to two rather stupid and willful princes. The
Five Headings under which he organizes his course are Loss of Friends,
Winning of Friends, Crows and Owls (international relations), Loss of
Gains, and Ill-Considered Action. He goes hunting with the boys, and
during intervals of rest recounts stories which engross their attention and
at the same time drive home a point. Since many of the illustrative stories
are beast tales, the book has strong kinship to Aesop's *Fables.* The stories
are interspersed with bits of trenchant verse. The following is taken from
the fifth part, on Ill-Considered Action.

THE LION–MAKERS

In a certain place there dwelt four Brahman youths in the greatest
friendship. Three of them had got to the further shore of the ocean
of science,[1] but were devoid of common sense; while the fourth had
common sense only, and no mind for science. Now once upon a time
these friends took counsel together, and said, " Of what profit is science, if we cannot go with it to some foreign country and win the
favor of the princes and make our fortune? Therefore to the Eastern
Country let us go." And so it came to pass.

Now after they had gone a little way, the eldest spoke: " There
is one among us, the fourth, who has no learning, but only common
sense; and a man can't get presents from kings by common sense
without learning. Not a whit will I give him of all that I gain; so
let him go home."

And the second said, " Ho there, Gumption! Get you homeward
for you have no learning! "

But the third made answer, " Alas, it is not fitting to do so; for
we have played together since we were boys. So let him come along
too. He's a noble fellow and shall have a share in the riches that
we win."

On then they went together, till in a jungle they saw the bones of
a dead lion. Then spoke the first: " Ha! now we can put our book-
learning to the test. Here lies some sort of a dead creature. By the
power of our learning we'll bring it to life. I'll put the bones together." And that then he did with zeal. The second added flesh,
blood, and hide. But just as the third was breathing the breath of
life into it, Gumption stopped him and said, " Hold! This is a lion
that you are turning out. If you make him alive, he will kill every one
of us."

---

[1] science: learning.

Thereupon answered the other, " Fie, stupid! is learning to be fruitless in my hands? "

" Well, then," said Gumption, " just wait a bit till I climb a tree."

Thereupon the lion was brought to life. But the instant this was done, he sprang up and killed the three. Afterward Gumption climbed down and went home.

Therefore (concluded the Gold-magician) therefore I say:

> Book-learning people rightly cherish,
> But gumption's best of all to me.
> Bereft of gumption you shall perish,
> Like to the Lion-makers three.

(Charles R. Lanman)

KINGS

In sensuous coil
And heartless toil,
In sinuous course
And armored force,
In savage harms   5
That yield to charms —
In all these things
Are snakes like kings.

Uneven, rough,
And high enough —   10
Yet low folk roam
Their flanks at home,
And wild things haunt
Them, hungry, gaunt —
In all these things   15
Are hills like kings.

The things that claw and the things that gore
Are unreliable things;
And so is a man with a sword in his hand,
And rivers, and women, and kings.   20

(Arthur W. Ryder)

FOOL AND FALSE

With the shrewd and upright man
  Seek a friendship rare;
Exercise with shrewd and false
  Superheedful care;
Pity for the upright fool
  Find within your heart;
If a man be fool and false,
  Shun him from the start.

(Arthur W. Ryder)

POVERTY

A beggar to the graveyard hied
And there " Friend corpse, arise," he cried;
" One moment lift my heavy weight
Of poverty; for I of late
Grow weary and desire instead
Your comfort; you are good and dead."
The corpse was silent. He was sure
'Twas better to be dead than poor.

(Arthur W. Ryder)

KALIDASA (probably Fifth Century A.D.)

Though Kalidasa is generally considered the greatest of the early poets
of the great Indian Renaissance, so little is known of him that even the
century in which he lived has been a matter of dispute between two groups:
the scholars, who assign him to the fifth century A.D., and the traditionalists,
who put him back into the first century B.C. Tradition has furnished all
the picturesque details of his life: that he was an ox-driver of sufficient
intelligence to enable the rejected suitors of a certain princess to trick her
into marrying him by representing him as a great scholar; that he was
murdered by a lady of the court to conceal the deception of her claim that
she had written some of his impromptu verses.

Kalidasa has been called " the Hindu Shakespeare " because of his pre-
eminence in the field of drama, and his versatility in producing also excellent lyric and descriptive poetry. He has left three great dramas, one
picturing court life, one representing the ancient gods, and most famous
of all *Sakuntala,* the romance of a king and a country maid. This particularly charmed the poet Goethe, who read it in a German translation of the

English translation of 1789. It is this play which, of the three, most suggests Shakespeare in its interweaving of poetic and comic scenes and its well-drawn characterizations. The story, taken with modifications from the *Mahabharata*, tells how a king married Sakuntala, the beautiful daughter of a hermit, but returned to court and, because of a curse which an enemy had pronounced, forgot about her completely. Sakuntala's only hope of recognition was through a ring, which she lost while bathing in a river. Years after, the king encounters his own son, now a child of six years, and is strangely moved by the beauty and fearlessness of the unknown boy. The ring is discovered by a fisherman inside a fish and is brought to the king, who then recognizes his wife and rejoices over his new-found son. It is interesting to note that this ancient Sanskrit play has had several productions on the modern stage. One of the first was at Smith College in 1904, and in 1919 simultaneous performances were given in London and New York.

THE UNION OF THE SEASONS

In this outstanding descriptive poem Kalidasa opens with the heat of summer, passes through the changes of autumn and winter, and finally concludes with the joyousness of spring. Only the first and last parts are here given.

THE SUMMER

Now the thirsty gazelle hastens after water, its palate dry, glowing with the mighty heat, when like a herd of elephants the clouds appear. The snake which, warmed by the sun's rays, once stretched himself in the burning hot sand, now hissing turns and seeks the shade. The lion, with thirsty throat, hunts the elephant no more. Courage fails him, his tongue trembles. . . . Forest fires have destroyed the young grass, the gust of the wind drives fiercely the dead leaves. The waters are dried up in every pool. In sighs ceases the song of the birds, as they cluster upon the trees decked only with faded leaves. The weary monkeys crawl slowly on the hill. The buffaloes wander about seeking for water. . . . But he that lives by the lotus-pond drinks the fragrance of the flowers, wets with cool streams the floors of his house, and by moonlight sports with his beloved in song and jest; he forgets the heat of the summer.

THE SPRING

The springtime god, the god of love, comes, beloved, to wound the hearts of happy men; the god who has made the bees his bowstring, and mango blossoms his arrow. The maiden loves, the light breeze blows fragrantly, the trees are in bloom, and the lotus adorns the pool. Peaceful is the night and refreshing is the day. How lovely is all in spring! When the lakes are bright with jewels, and like the moon in splendor shines every band of maidens; when mango trees wave amid flowers, then comes the joy of spring. The fair girls wander out, at the call of the love-god, with garlands on the breast, with cool sandals on the feet, and their breath fragrant with betel.[1] Fearless they go, and *karnikara* flowers make their earrings, while *açoka* buds are nestling in their dark locks; and the jasmine lies upon their heads. The heart of the young man is filled with joy, as the *atimuktas* open their fragrant buds, and the drunken bees kiss the shining flowers, while delicately back and forth sway the tendrils of every plant touched by the light zephyrs. But he that is repulsed by his love is pierced in his heart as by an arrow.

(Peter von Bohlen)

[1] **betel**: a species of pepper plant, the leaves and nuts of which some Asiatics like to chew. The flowers mentioned in italics in the next few lines are native plants for which there is no exact English equivalent.

A LYRIC

Thy face, a lovely lily,
Thine eyes, the lotus blue,
Thy teeth are jasmine blossoms,
Thy lips, the rosebud's hue.

The velvet touch of the champak
Thy tender skin doth own —
How comes it the Creator
Hath made thy heart a stone?

(A. V. Williams-Jackson)

5. **champak**: an East-Indian tree similar to a magnolia. The blossom is here meant.

BHARTRIHARI (Seventh Century A.D.)

Unfortunately no exact record remains of the poet who excelled in the writing of brief lyrics and wise sayings in verse, clear and sharp as a crystal stiletto. If tradition can be trusted, he suffered from conflicting forces within himself — a love of religion and a love of the world, for it is said that seven times he entered a monastery and underwent preliminary training as a monk, but seven times he forsook the restricted life. One legend has it that he kept a horse near at hand during his cloistered periods so that when the spirit moved him he might quickly escape into the world. Most of his lyrics are to be found in three volumes of *Centuries,* collections of a hundred poems, but others are in existence, besides some of doubtful origin ascribed to him.

LYRICS

I

She whom I worship night and day, she loathes my very sight,
And on my neighbor dotes, who in another takes delight;
A third, she in my humble self, nothing but good can see.
Now out upon the god of love, and him, and them, and me!

2

A bald man felt the sun's fierce rays
   Scorch his defenseless head,
In haste to shun the noontide blaze
   Beneath a palm he fled;
Prone as he lay a heavy fruit
   Crashed through his drowsy brain.
Whom fate has sworn to persecute
   Finds every refuge vain.

3

Snatch a jewel, if it please you, from the tiger's ravening throat;
Cross the ocean though its billows toss in foam-wreaths round your
   boat;
Fearless twine an angry cobra like a garland round your head;
But with fools forbear to argue — better strive to wake the dead.

4

The hermit's tattered patchwork robe, or courtier's silken weeds,
One wife to tend thy home, or troops of elephants and steeds,
One simple meal at close of day, or many a gorgeous feast,
It matters not, be but thy soul from earthly cares released.

5

When but a little I had learned, in my own partial eyes
I seemed a perfect Solon [1] and immeasurably wise;

---

[1] **Solon:** wise Athenian law-giver of the sixth century **B.C.**

But when a little higher I had climbed in wisdom's school,
The fever-fit was over and I knew myself a fool.

6

Not to swerve from truth or mercy, not for life to stoop to shame;
From the poor no gifts accepting, nor from men of evil fame
Lofty faith and proud submission — who on Fortune's giddy ledge
Firm can tread this path of duty, narrow as the saber's edge?

(1-6, *C. H. Tawney*)

7

I saw an ass who bore a load
Of sandal wood along the road,
And almost with the burden bent,
Yet never guessed the sandal scent;
So pedants bear a ponderous mass
Of books they comprehend not — like the ass.

8

I see a dog — no stone to shy at him;
Yonder a stone — no dog's in view;
There is your dog, here stones to try at him —
The king's dog! What's a man to do?

(7 and 8, *Paul Elmer More*)

9

Angling in life's river,
Cupid drops his line.
On the hook he fastens
Some fair maiden fine.

Men — those silly fishes —
Quick dart up above;
Out he pulls and fries them
In the fire of love.

(*A. V. Williams-Jackson*)

RABINDRANATH TAGORE (1861–1941)

When in 1913 the Nobel prize was awarded to Tagore, the Hindu poet and dramatist, it went for the first and only time in its history to an Oriental. True, in the list of Nobel prize winners Tagore is classed as a British poet, because technically he is a British subject, and the book of poems, *Gitanjali,* upon which the award was made had been read by the committee in the poet's own English translation. Tagore is, however, in every true sense a Hindu. He was born into a high-caste family of Calcutta, his grandfather having been a prince. In his autobiography, *My Reminiscences,* he has given a vivid picture of his boyhood home, his education by private tutors along with his brothers, his brief experiences in schools, his first trip to England at seventeen where he was sent to study law, and his return to India to devote himself to writing. When he was forty, he established a school at Bolpur, about ninety miles from Calcutta, in order to carry out his progressive ideas of education. The eight thousand pounds he received as the Nobel prize he turned over to the improvement of this school, which has since developed into an international university. In 1915 he was knighted by the British government, but four years later he resigned his title as a protest against the methods being used in the Punjab. The Sir, however, was still often used before his name without any special objection on his part.

Tagore's early writing was all done in the Bengali dialect of his native home. His thorough training in English, however, enabled him to make his own translations of his work, and later he did some of his creative work directly in that language, though by far the greater part has been composed in his native tongue. Among his many volumes of poetry are *The Gardener,* early poems which he dedicated to Queen Victoria with the request that he might be a gardener in her garden of poetry; *Gitanjali (Song Offerings),* already mentioned; *Fireflies,* modeled after the Japanese style; and *Sheaves,* one of his latest volumes. As a dramatist he also won a reputation with *The King of the Dark Chamber, Chitra,* a one-act play based on an incident in the *Mahabharata,* and *The Post-Office,* a two-act play of the dream world built up by an invalid child. In prose, besides his reminiscences, he has produced short stories and a great deal of miscellaneous writing on education, philosophy, and Indian nationalism. The great dignity and majesty of his appearance with his flowing white hair and beard, and the native costume which he has never discarded for European dress, contribute to the total effect of spiritual benignity produced by his life and work.

GITANJALI

1

My song has put off her adornments. She has no pride of dress and decoration. Ornaments would mar our union; they would come between thee and me; their jingling would drown thy whispers.

My poet's vanity dies in shame before thy sight. O master poet, I have sat down at thy feet. Only let me make my life simple and straight, like a flute of reed for thee to fill with music.

2

The child who is decked with prince's robes and who has jeweled chains round his neck loses all pleasure in his play; his dress hampers him at every step.

In fear that it may be frayed, or stained with dust he keeps himself from the world, and is afraid even to move.

Mother, it is no gain, thy bondage of finery, if it keep one shut off from the healthful dust of the earth, if it rob one of the right of entrance to the great fair of common human life.

3

Where the mind is without fear and the head is held high;
Where knowledge is free;
Where the world has not been broken up into fragments by narrow domestic walls;
Where words come out from the depth of truth;
Where tireless striving stretches its arms towards perfection.
Where the clear stream of reason has not lost its way into the dreary desert sand of dead habit;
Where the mind is led forward by thee into ever-widening thought and action —
Into that heaven of freedom, my Father, let my country awake.

4

When the heart is hard and parched up, come upon me with a shower of mercy.

When grace is lost from life, come with a burst of song.

When tumultuous work raises its din on all sides shutting me out from beyond, come to me, my lord of silence, with thy peace and rest.

When my beggarly heart sits crouched, shut up in a corner, break open the door, my king, and come with the ceremony of a king.

When desire blinds the mind with delusion and dust, O thou holy one, thou wakeful, come with thy light and thy thunder.

5

You came down from your throne and stood at my cottage door.

I was singing all alone in a corner, and the melody caught your ear. You came down and stood at my cottage door.

Masters are many in your hall, and songs are sung there at all hours. But the simple carol of this novice struck at your love. One plaintive little strain mingled with the great music of the world, and with a flower for a prize you came down and stopped at my cottage door.

6

On the day when death will knock at thy door what wilt thou offer to him?

Oh, I will set before my guest the full vessel of my life — I will never let him go with empty hands.

All the sweet vintage of all my autumn days and summer nights, all the earnings and gleanings of my busy life will I place before him at the close of my days when death will knock at my door.

(Rabindranath Tagore)

FIREFLIES

This volume (1928) was a result of Tagore's study of Japanese poetry, which fascinated him by its compressed and highly selective art. The significance of the title is explained in the first poem, and one is inclined to agree with the prophecy expressed in the second after reading this book of captivating phrases. They should be read in connection with Japanese poetry (pages 1224–1231).

I

My fancies are fireflies, —
Specks of living light
twinkling in the dark.

2

My words that are slight
may lightly dance upon time's waves
when my works heavy with import have
gone down.

3

Let my love, like sunlight, surround you
and yet give you illumined freedom.

4

From the solemn gloom of the temple
children run out to sit in the dust,
God watches them play
and forgets the priest.

5

In the mountain, stillness surges up
to explore its own height;
in the lake, movement stands still
to contemplate its own depth.

6

The freedom of the storm and the bondage
of the stem
join hands in the dance of swaying
branches.

7

While God waits for His temple to be built
of love,
men bring stones.

8

My heart today smiles at its past night of tears
like a wet tree glistening in the sun
after the rain is over.

9

My flower, seek not thy paradise
in a fool's buttonhole.

10

Trees are the earth's endless effort to speak
to the listening heaven.

11

The burden of self is lightened
when I laugh at myself.

12

The cloud gives all its gold
to the departing sun
and greets the rising moon
with only a pale smile.

13

He who does good comes to the temple gate,
he who loves reaches the shrine.

14

The clumsiness of power spoils the key,
and uses the pickaxe.

(*Rabindranath Tagore*)

SHEAVES

TO THE SONS OF INDIA

Before the glance of the West with its
Pride of power, its traders rolling in luxury,
And its pomp of wealth, do not,
O sons of Bharat,[1] feel ashamed to wear
Your plain white garb and to live   5
Your simple life with mien noble and calm.
Listen not to what they say, keep your priceless treasure
In your heart, let it rest
On your smooth brow as an invisible crown.
That which looks large and has been heaped high,   10

---

[1] **Bharat:** supposed ancestor of the Hindus, about whom and his immediate descendents the *Mahabharata* was written.

Let it not overwhelm you, and do not
Prostrate yourselves before it.
Place your free soul on the throne
Of poverty, filling your mind
With the leisure of want.   15

SONG OF THE TREE

My moonlight,
On this April eve you are caught
In my branches and leaves;
The song that in the stream of your tune
Floods the stars   5
Sounds now in my courtyard
While my heart keeps time
All my buds burst into blossom
To the hint of your laughter;
The south wind drunk with the scent   10
Of my flowers has lost its way.
O White, you have sent a wave of color
Into my soul;
My murmurous heart has been entangled
In the net of your laughter.   15

(Nagendranath Gupta)

SUGGESTIONS FOR STUDY

1. Which of the selections in this section illustrate the mystic and spiritual qualities of the Hindus; which the practical and witty? Which appeal to the senses rather than to the mind or the soul?

2. Since the meaning of these poems is often hidden under a metaphor, interpret in plain language those of which this is true.

3. Read other stories from the *Panchatantra* and compare them with the wise tales of other Oriental countries, with Aesop's Fables, and the Uncle Remus stories.

4. Read condensed versions of the two great epics such as are to be found in Guerber's *Book of the Epic*. In what way are these stories more difficult to follow than the *Iliad* and *Odyssey*? Wherein do their moral concepts differ from those of Greek, Hebrew, and Christian?

5. Read one of the translations of *Sakuntala*, preferably that of Arthur Ryder in the Everyman's Library series and also in Eliot's *Little Theater Classics* (the acting version). An older and more formal translation is that of Sir Monier Monier-Williams also found in Clark's *World Drama*.

Would you enjoy seeing this on the stage? Does it have emotional appeal for you? Dramatic force? Does Kalidasa deserve the title of " the Hindu Shakespeare"? Discuss.

READING LIST

Translations from Indian Literature

Specimen of Old Indian Poetry, trans. by R. T. H. Griffith

Indian Poetry, trans. by Edwin Arnold

The Ramayana and the Mahabharata, condensed in English verse by Romesh C. Dutt

The Panchatantra, trans. by Arthur W. Ryder

Indian Wisdom, trans. by Monier-Williams

A Century of Indian Epigrams, trans. by Paul Elmer More

Two Centuries of Bhartrihari, trans. by C. H. Tawney

Sakuntala, trans. by Arthur W. Ryder; also by Monier-Williams; also by Lawrence Binyon

The Little Clay Cart, trans. by Arthur W. Ryder

Anthology of Modern Indian Poetry, trans. by Gwendoline Goodwin

Poems by Indian Women, trans. by M. G. C. Macnicol

Songs from Prison, trans. by Mahatma Ghandi

Tagore, Rabindranath:
Poetry: *The Gardener*
*Gitanjali
*Fireflies
Sheaves

Drama: *King of the Dark Chamber*
Chitra
*The Post-Office
Stories:
*The Hungry Stones and Other Stories
Non-fiction: **Reminiscences*
Glimpses of Bengal
Letter to a Friend

About India

Gowen, H. H.: *History of Indian Literature*

Horrwitz, E.: *A Short History of Indian Literature*
The Indian Theater

Macdonell, A. A.: *A History of Sanskrit Literature*
*India's Past

Bonsels, Waldemar: *An Indian Journey*

Mayo, Katherine: *Mother India*

Mukerji, Dhan Gopal: *Visit India with Me*

Thompson-Seton, Grace: *" Yes, Lady Saheb "*

Kipling, Rudyard: **Kim*
Soldiers Three
Under the Deodars

Roy, B. K.: *Rabindranath Tagore: The Man and His Poetry*

Thompson, E. J.: *Rabindranath Tagore: His Life and Work*

Solomon, W. E. G.: *The Charm of Indian Art*

* Books marked with an asterisk are recommended for purchase for the library on a limited budget.

Chinese Literature

Chinese Literature

THE student of Chinese literature is awed by two of its aspects — its volume and its antiquity.

China is a vast realm, more than eighteen hundred miles from north to south, and thirteen hundred from east to west. Like any great sweep of territory, it has within its boundaries every variation of climate and topography. Symbolical of this variety is the course of the Yangtze river, "The River of Golden Sand," the great bond between widely separated regions. This river rises in the high plateaus of Thibet, passes through deep-hewn gorges, breaks into turbulent spring floods, but eventually winds placidly through long stretches of level rice fields and tamely submits to becoming the commercial highway of the country. North China, cold, rugged, subject to famine, has produced warlike hordes against whom the Great Wall, fifteen hundred miles long was originally built, but who eventually ruled the land. South China, warm, smiling, and friendly to cultivation both of soil and civilization, has preserved the charm of handicraft, art, and poetry. In addition to these two actual backgrounds, Chinese literature often describes an imaginary paradise of the far west beyond the mountains, where the details of landscape are set down with as calm assurance as if the poet were looking out from his own window.

Ancient China still present as an influence

In antiquity Chinese literature rivals that of Egypt. While authentic history opens with the Emperor Yu's accession in 2205 B.C., the earliest songs go back much further. Unlike Egypt, China has preserved her literature as a continuous and living influence up to the present time. A striking example of this is that when the Chinese republic was established in 1911, one of these songs of the twenty-fourth century B.C., was adopted as the national anthem. And Mei Sheng, who died in 140 B.C. has been called " the father of *modern* Chinese poetry." Though China is, in many respects, breaking away from her past in this century, yet she is intimately bound to it in a way hard to realize by Americans bred to a young land.

The educational and governmental system of China throughout the ages has been designed to preserve the ancient classics. Qualifications for government positions were in former times entirely based on literary proficiency, largely a matter of memorizing the classics and showing ability at poetic composition. These classics were all written long before the Christian era, and are contained in two sets of books usually referred to as the Five Classics and the Four Books.

The Five Classics include:

1. The Book of Change, sixty-four divinations.

2. The Book of History (2356–620 B.C.). Modern scholarship has proved much of this to be unreliable, especially the early part; but compared with that of other Oriental nations, Chinese history on the whole is accurate.

3. The Book of Poetry, consisting of three hundred and five odes, most of which were written between 1000 and 600 B.C. Tradition said that these were assembled by Confucius from an earlier collection of three thousand, but it is now known that this book existed before his day, and that he arranged only the music, long since lost.

4. Spring and Autumn, a history by Confucius of his native state, and the only extant work of his own composition.

5. A Book of Ceremonies.

The Four Books are of later composition. They include:

1. The Analects or Discourses of Confucius recorded by his disciples and published after his death.

2. The Great Learning, a book of commentary.

3. The Doctrine of the Mean (middle way, moderation) supposedly written by the grandson of Confucius.

4. The Book of Mencius, a disciple of Confucius whose philosophy resembles his, but with a different emphasis.

With this library as the entire curriculum of education, with a premium put upon mere memory, and with original thinking regarded as an insult to the ancient masters, it is easily understood how these classics dominated intellectual life for centuries. In Chinese literature the ideal hero is not the man of muscle, but the man of memory — not the warrior, but the scholar.

Poetry inherent to Chinese disposition

The Chinese are poets at heart. Even their advanced degrees of stereotyped learning were designed by the terms Flowering Talent, Promoted Man, Entered Scholar, and Forest of Pencils. Educated men wrote poetry as a pastime. When they met together they played games based on the writing of poetry just as they played chess. Poetry was written in the classic language and therefore fitted to intellectual pursuit. The later developments of drama and novel, being written in the colloquial language, were regarded scornfully by scholars as suited only to the uneducated or to women.

Chinese poets are innumerable. Chinese poems are brief. Therefore they are as uncounted as the stars. The Chinese themselves have no complete history of their poetry, though one is now being written. The beauty of these scattered verses has made special appeal in recent years to English translators, many of whom are poets in their own language, such as Amy Lowell, Witter Bynner, A. Cranmer-Byng, and Arthur Waley. Yet the many volumes which have appeared have scarcely scratched the surface of the native verse.

Golden Age of poetry during T'ang dynasty

Certain periods of Chinese life have been more productive of poetry than others. It was during the Han dynasty (206 B.C.– 220 A.D.) that Buddhism was introduced into China from India, and much creative work resulted from this new impetus. The Golden Age, however, was during the T'ang dynasty (618–905 A.D.). In the middle of the eighth century, the three greatest poets of the race were writing contemporaneously. Of these, the most famous name to Westerners is Li Po, who has been widely translated; but Chinese scholars consider him distinctly inferior to Tu Fu, who, because of idiomatic difficulties, is less frequently attempted in English. The third poet is Po Chu-i. A further listing of names in so brief a history would seem futile.

Chinese poetry written in unique form

To understand the unique construction of a Chinese poem, some knowledge of the form of language is necessary. It is essentially a picture language. Each character represents a definite object or idea. Though the original ideographs have been considerably modified, they are still to a certain extent pictures, and thus a beautiful poem makes an appeal to the eye as well as to the imagination _n a way almost impossible for a Westerner to grasp. It is the selection of the ideographs with the proper connotations, and their arrangement into an intricate pattern which constitutes the art of the poet. For example, of the different characters representing sunrise, one shows the sun peeping above the horizon, another represents it above an armed head, and a third as seen through a mist. If the poet wishes to say *sunrise*, he must select the word which gives the right suggestion to harmonize with the total impression of the poem. Except for the ancient odes, most poems are written in four lines. Each line consists of the same number of characters, most commonly either five or seven. Thus a poem contains only twenty or twenty-eight words. There are two tones in which Chinese words may be pronounced, the meaning being different according to the tone used. In the neat little rectangle of a poem these tones must be alternated in such a way as to form a rhythmic pattern. An example of one of the many meters is here given. *Ping* represents the even tone, *tse* the variable.

> ping, tse, ping, tse, tse,
> tse, ping, tse, ping, ping,
> ping, tse, tse, ping, tse,
> tse, ping, ping, tse, ping.

Since Chinese has no " little " words, such as pronouns, conjunctions, prepositions, or auxiliaries to indicate tense, it is hard to determine sometimes whether the poem should be translated in the first or third person, the present or past tense. Thus it is possible for the same poem to have quite different translations into English, all of them legitimate interpretations. These complications are the despair of the translator and at the same time his challenge.

The Chinese poet leaves a great deal more to the imagination than the English. The reader must also be a poet, whose reflective mood is enhanced by the picture or the experience, which he must supplement from his own inner life. The subject matter of Chinese poetry is different in emphasis from the English. There is comparatively little love poetry, but a great deal on friendship between men. Much of this is " farewell " poetry, since officials were frequently transferred to another part of the country, and banishment for political reasons was common. It was also fashionable for a guest to present his host with a farewell poem upon leaving. Nature is ever present, as with all nations, but is treated more objectively than in English. A poem is simply a little sketch of something the writer has observed. It is this type which has most engaged the attention of translators.

The drama arose in China from the cult of ancestor worship, being originally a ceremonial accompanied by music and dancing. By the time of the Golden Age of Poetry in the T'ang dynasty, it had become an established and beautiful form. In the much later Mongol dynasty, when poetry was declining, drama reached its climax of popularity, and today practically every Chinese town has its theater. The style of the play and its method of production is similar to the Japanese, which developed from it and is fully described on page 1231.

The novel was a gradual development from the love of storytelling which dominates all Oriental life. Much scorned by the scholars of officialdom, novels nevertheless flourished among the populace as a whole from the thirteenth century on, and several of the shorter ones have been translated into English. Russian influence has been notable in the books of the last century.

Chinese novels flourish after 1920

Since 1920 China has developed a flourishing school of novelists writing in the modern spoken language. Mao Dun (1896–   ) is China's leading novelist. His *Eclipse* (1927–28) deals with events of the 1926–27 revolution. The most influential work is *The Story of Ah Q* by Lu Hsün (1881–1936). Ah Q has become the symbol of everything that is contemptible in the Chinese character. Pa Ching (1905–   ) in *Torrent of Life* draws a realistic indictment of the traditional Chinese family system. These novelists represent an important phase of the Communist revolution.

CONFUCIUS (551–478 B.C.)

The doctrines of Confucius have molded Chinese thinking for twenty-four hundred years, yet he was not an original thinker or an inspired prophet. Confucianism is not a religion, for it is silent on the subject of God and immortality; rather it is a philosophy of living, an ethical code, and a political doctrine. Confucius was really the person by whom the conceptions and standards of conduct developed by the Chinese through preceding centuries were assembled and put into concrete form.

He was born in the province of Lu, now Shantung. Like many great men, Confucius was a precocious child. He mastered the learning of his day at an early age, and became the manager of a large estate at seventeen. During twenty-seven months of seclusion after the death of his mother, he formulated much of his philosophy. The Chinese had always venerated ancestors, but the young man's devotion was exceptional, and the emphasis he laid upon honoring the dead has resulted in practically a worship of ancestors. Some one has said that China is a land in which ten million living men are held in subservience to a hundred million dead ones.

From the age of twenty-two to the end of his life, Confucius was a scholar and teacher. He collected the materials which constitute the Five Classics, and thus became the founder of Chinese literature. During his fifties he also had practical experience as governor of his province for four years. Political intrigue caused him to withdraw in disgust, and his later years were saddened by the death of his son and some of his favorite disciples, as well as by his feeling that he had failed to establish his teachings, which were his life work. Little did he dream that after his death he would be deified, and that centuries later a temple in his honor would be found in every Chinese village.

THE ANALECTS OF CONFUCIUS

The precepts of Confucius have been handed down through the *Analects* written by his disciples. The only extant piece of writing done by the master himself is the history of his province which is one of the Five Classics. His teachings were largely by word of mouth and were recorded after his death.

Confucius had no belief in anything supernatural. He refused to discuss the immortality of the soul, but he created an earthly immortality for the dead through the ancestor worship which perpetuates their names and influence. In the complete absence of mysticism and entire devotion to the intellectual and practical, Confucianism shows its chief difference from the other great doctrines which have swayed mankind. The five cardinal principles of Confucius were humanity, uprightness, decorum, wisdom, and truth. His great ideal was the prosperity of the state and its government in such a way as to serve the best interests of all its citizens. The desires of the individual were completely subservient to the standards of the family and state. Ardent emotion had no place in a philosophy based on calm deliberation. Society was poured into a mold of ceremonial and left to cool for centuries. That is why the breaking up of this mold in the twentieth century through Western contacts has caused such internal rending of China. The following are selections from the *Analects*:

The Master said —

A plausible tongue and a fascinating expression are seldom associated with true virtue.

Let loyalty and truth be paramount with you. Have no friends not equal to yourself. If you have faults, shrink not from correcting them.

Learning without thought is labor lost. Thought without learning is intellectual death.

In mourning, it is better to be sincere than to be punctilious.

The faults of men are characteristic of themselves. By observing a man's faults you may infer what his virtues are.

The commander-in-chief of an army can be carried captive, but the convictions of even the meanest man cannot be taken from him.

A youth should be filial at home, respectful abroad. He should be earnest and truthful. He should overflow in love to all, but cultivate the friendship of the good. Then, whatsoever of energy may be left to him, he should devote to the improvement of his mind.

(A disciple having asked for a definition of charity, the Master said:) LOVE ONE ANOTHER!

(Having been further asked for a definition of knowledge, the Master said:) KNOW ONE ANOTHER!

(Someone asked Confucius, " Master, what think you concerning the principle that good should be returned for evil? " The Master replied:) What then will you return for good? No, RETURN GOOD FOR GOOD; FOR EVIL, JUSTICE.

(A Disciple having asked for a rule of life in a word, the Master said:) Is not Reciprocity that word? WHAT YOU WOULD NOT OTHERS SHOULD DO UNTO YOU, DO NOT UNTO THEM.

(Herbert A. Giles)

CHINESE PROVERBS

Deal with the faults of others as gently as with your own.

If you bow at all, bow low.

A man thinks he knows, but a woman knows better.

If Fortune smiles, who doesn't? If Fortune doesn't, who does?

Only imbeciles want credit for the achievements of their ancestors.

Long visits bring short compliments.

The faults which a man condemns when out of office, he commits when in.

Every one gives a shove to the tumbling wall.

If you can't draw a tiger, draw a dog.

Gold is tested by fire; man, by gold.

Man dies and leaves a name. The tiger dies and leaves a skin.

Those who have not tasted the bitterest of life's bitters, can never appreciate the sweetest of life's sweets.

The Tongue is a sharp sword which slays, though it draws no blood.

Better a dog in peace than a man in war.

(Herbert A. Giles)

SUGGESTIONS FOR STUDY

1. Where in the teachings of Confucius do you find similarities to the teachings of Socrates? of Christ? What impression of Confucius do you form from the selections here given? Compare him with other teachers of moral precepts such as Pascal, Marcus Aurelius, etc.

2. Explain in plain English the significance of the Chinese proverbs which are expressed figuratively. Do you know English proverbs which correspond to any of them? How do they compare in wit with Franklin's *Sayings of Poor Richard?* What other countries have produced famous collections of proverbs?

The Folk Tale

Out of the mists of antiquity there have come down to us innumerable tales of the common people which are rich in the local color of the country. "The Wonderful Pear Tree" illustrates the love of magic which permeates all Oriental lands, and is part of the universal folk theme of the outwitting of a stupid or stingy person.

THE WONDERFUL PEAR TREE

Once upon a time a countryman came into the town on market-day, and brought a load of very special pears with him to sell. He set up his barrow in a good corner, and soon had a great crowd round him; for every one knew he always sold extra fine pears, though he did also ask an extra high price. Now, while he was crying up his fruit, a poor, old, ragged, hungry-looking priest stopped just in front of the barrow, and very humbly begged him to give him one of the pears. But the countryman, who was very mean and very nasty-tempered, wouldn't hear of giving him any, and as the priest didn't seem inclined to move on, he began calling him all the bad names he could think of. " Good sir," said the priest, " you have got hundreds of pears on your barrow. I only ask you for one. You would never even know you had lost one. Really, you needn't get angry."

" Give him a pear that is going bad; that will make him happy," said one of the crowd. " The old man is quite right; you'd never miss it."

" I've said I won't, and I won't! " cried the countryman; and all the people close by began shouting, first one thing, and then another, until the constable of the market, hearing the hubbub, hurried up;

and when he had made out what was the matter, pulled some cash out of his purse, bought a pear, and gave it to the priest. For he was afraid that the noise would come to the ears of the mandarin who was just being carried down the street.

The old priest took the pear with a low bow, and held it up in front of the crowd, saying, " You all know that I have no home, no parents, no children, no clothes of my own, no food, because I gave up everything when I became a priest. So it puzzles me how any one can be so selfish and so stingy as to refuse to give me one single pear. Now I am quite a different sort of man from this countryman. I have got here some perfectly exquisite pears, and I shall feel most deeply honored if you will accept them from me."

" Why on earth didn't you eat them yourself, instead of begging for one? " asked a man in the crowd.

" Ah," answered the priest, " I must grow them first."

So he ate up the pear, only leaving a single pip. Then he took a pick which was fastened across his back, dug a deep hole in the ground at his feet, and planted the pip, which he covered all over with earth. " Will some one fetch me some hot water to water this? " he asked. The people, who were crowding round, thought he was only joking, but one of them ran and fetched a kettle of boiling water and gave it to the priest, who very carefully poured it over the place where he had sowed the pip. Then, almost while he was pouring, they saw, first a tiny green sprout, and then another, come pushing their heads above the ground; then one leaf uncurled, and then another, while the shoots kept growing taller and taller; then there stood before them a young tree with a few branches with a few leaves; then more leaves; then flowers; and last of all clusters of huge, ripe, sweet-smelling pears weighing the branches down to the ground! Now the priest's face shone with pleasure, and the crowd roared with delight when he picked the pears one by one until they were all gone, handing them round with a bow to each man present. Then the old man took the pick again, hacked at the tree until it fell with a crash, when he shouldered it, leaves and all, and with a final bow, walked away.

All the time this had been going on, the countryman, quite forgetting his barrow and pears, had been in the midst of the crowd, standing on the tips of his toes, and straining his eyes to try to make out what was happening. But when the old priest had gone and the crowd was getting thin, he turned round to his barrow, and saw with horror that it was quite empty. Every single pear had gone! In a moment he understood what had happened. The pears the old priest had been so generous in giving away were not his own; they were the countryman's! What was more, one of the handles of his barrow was missing, and there was no doubt that he had started from home with two! He was in a towering rage, and rushed as hard as he could after the priest; but just as he turned the corner he saw, lying close to the wall, the barrow-handle itself, which without any doubt was the very pear tree which the priest had cut down. All the people in the market were simply splitting their sides with laughter; but as for the priest, no one saw him any more.

(Herbert A. Giles)

TAO YUAN–MING (365–427 A.D.)

ONCE MORE FIELDS AND GARDENS

Even as a young man
I was out of tune with ordinary pleasures.
It was my nature to love the rooted hills,
The high hills which look upon the four edges of Heaven.
What follow to spend one's life like a dropped leaf
Snared under the dust of streets,   5
But for thirteen years it was so I lived.

The caged bird longs for the fluttering of high leaves.
The fish in the garden pool languishes for the whirled water
Of meeting streams.
So I desired to clear and seed a patch of the wild Southern moor.   10
And always a countryman at heart,
I have come back to the square enclosures of my fields
And to my walled garden with its quiet paths.

Mine is a little property of ten *mou* or so,   15
A thatched house of eight or nine rooms.
On the North side the eaves are overhung
With the thick leaves of elm-trees,
And willow-trees break the strong force of the wind.
On the South in front of the great hall,   20
Peach-trees and plum-trees spread a net of branches
Before the distant view.

The village is hazy, hazy,
The mist sucks over the open moor.
A dog barks in the sunken lane which runs through the village.   25
A cock crows perched on a slippery mulberry.

There is no dust or clatter
In the courtyard before my house.
My private rooms are quiet,
And calm with the leisure of moonlight through an open door.   30

For a long time I have lived in a cage;
Now I have returned.
For one must return
To fulfil one's nature.

(Florence Ayscough and Amy Lowell)

LI PO (701?–762 A.D.)

"He is the lofty peak of Tai towering above ten thousand mountains and hills; he is the sun in whose presence a billion stars of heaven lose their scintillating splendor." With typical Chinese hyperbole, an admirer thus described Li Po. He has undoubtedly received more publicity in the Western world than any other of the innumerable Chinese poets, partly because of the merit of his work, partly because of rather picturesque details of his personality.

He was a native of the western mountains of China. The brilliance of his mind, which enabled him to assimilate many of the classics at the age of ten, was offset by lack of industry and fondness for wine-drinking with good companions, so that he neglected to continue his studies to the advanced degrees expected of a successful scholar. Instead he tossed off poems with surprising ease. At about the age of forty he went to Chang-an, the great cosmopolitan center where the Emperor Hsuan Tsung held brilliant court. Li Po immediately won royal favor through his wit and conviviality. Three years later he lost it through jealous intrigues and returned to the mountains. During his stay in the metropolis he became a great friend of Tu Fu, who is ranked higher as a poet by Chinese critics. The two men bantered each other good-naturedly in poetry. Li Po rallied Tu Fu on the seriousness with which he took his poetic art in these words:

> " Behold! On the summit of Fan-ko mountain
> Is this my friend in the shade of his wide sun-hat?
> You are looking painfully thin and wan today.
> Have you been having another attack of poetry? "

But Tu Fu was equal to retaliation, for in his long poem called "Eight Immortals of the Wine-Cup" he opens his description of Li Po's bibulous habits with the lines:

> "Then there's Li Po! Give him a tankard of wine
> And he will pour forth a hundred poems."

The last years of Li Po's life were given to wandering and various adventures. Once he was sentenced to death for his part in a revolt, but was reprieved at the last minute. No account of Li Po fails to omit the picturesque legend of his death. One night — probably after several wine-cups — while floating on a lake in a canoe, he attempted to embrace the beautiful image of the moon reflected in the water — and was drowned!

POEMS OF LI PO

The first poem here given is one of his most famous and appears in many translations. It is symbolical of sorrow, as the second is of happiness. Both of these poems have been set to music. The first six are pictures of women, each symbolical of a different mood. Other poems suggest the mountain district from which the poet came.

I

A SIGH FROM A STAIRCASE OF JADE

Her jade-white staircase is cold with dew;
Her silk soles are wet, she lingered there so long. . . .
Behind her closed casement why is she still waiting,
Watching through its crystal pane the glow of the autumn moon?

2

A SONG OF PURE HAPPINESS

Her robe is a cloud, her face a flower;
Her balcony glimmering with the bright spring dew,
Is either the tip of earth's Jade Mountain
Or a moon-edged roof of paradise.

(1 and 2, *Witter Bynner*)

3

SPRING THOUGHTS

The grass of Yen grows green and fine as silk;
Low hangs the mulberry branch in the state of Chin.

And in the remembering time of day my heart is broken,
For then I know you think of me.
O strange Spring wond, I know you not at all.
Why do you pass through the silken curtain of my bower?

(3, Arthur Christy)

4

ON THE RIVER

She is gathering lotus in the river of Yeh.
She spies a passer-by and turns round,
Singing her boat song.
She laughs and hides away among the lilies;
And seeming shy, she will not show her face again.   5

5

ON THE LAKE

The water of the Mirror Lake
Is clear like the moon.
The girl of Yeh-chi
Has a face white as snow.
Her silvery image   5
Trembles in the silvery ripple.

6

NOCTURNE

Blue water . . . a clear moon . . .
In the moonlight the white herons are flying.
Listen! Do you hear the girls who gather water-chestnuts?
They are going home in the night, singing.

7

THE SUMMIT TEMPLE

Tonight I stay at the Summit Temple.
Here I could pluck the stars with my hand,
I dare not speak aloud in the silence,
For fear of disturbing the dwellers of heaven.

(4–7, Shigeyoshi Obata)

8

ALONE WITH CHING MOUNTAIN

Flocks of birds fly high and are gone,
Just a solitary piece of cloud sails slowly by,
I sit alone, communing with the towering summit of Chin Ting.
Long we commune, but we never grow weary of each other.

9

A SPRING SONG IN SOLITUDE

The air of the world is changed by the East wind!
Water and woods luxuriantly welcome the Spring;
A white moonlight is shining on the grass;
The falling petals of Spring flowers fly one by one through the air;
The mountain tops have emptied themselves of clouds,
And all the birds are seeking places for their nests.
Everything has a place to call its own,
But I am alone.
I gaze on this moonlit world,
And singing, I drink in the fragrance of the Spring flowers.

10

AUTUMN THOUGHTS

The God of Heaven seems to have no heart,
Permitting thus the beauty of the Summer world to be Autumnal.
But everything has its own season.
Southward flying birds do not care for human beings.
And the fish has his time.
Looking up — the snow is falling;
Looking down — the green grass and beautiful trees
Are becoming more withered each day.
But the garden's beautiful chrysanthemums stand tall and bloom luxuriantly.
Why should we not drink a cup of wine to celebrate their beauty,
Or rather should we sing a song for this flower?

(8–10, *Arthur Christy*)

TU FU (713-770 A.D.)

Tu Fu stands out among Chinese poets as having the greatest fame since his death, and probably the greatest misfortunes during his lifetime. He was born into the military-literary class of the Shensi province. With birth and brains in his favor, we might presuppose for him an easy life, but instead fate dealt him fortune like this:

When he went to the capital, Chang-an, for his examinations, he was refused a degree because of some unorthodox views. When after several years he became established in a position, a revolution took place, Tu Fu was banished, was captured by brigands, and was held prisoner for a year or so. When he recovered from that disaster and again was given a government position as censor, he incurred the displeasure of the Emperor and was demoted to a post in an insignificant town. He resigned this position and suffered in abject poverty for several years. The family lived in a grass hut, which he has described in several poems. Some of his children died of hunger. Later he was caught in a flood and had to spend days in a ruined temple without any food. When finally rescued and given a feast of honor by some officials, the final irony came upon him — he died of overeating.

Tu Fu's many poems have had few translators because of their highly idiomatic and difficult style. But the great number of a highly personal nature have enabled the Chinese scholar, Florence Ayscough, to build up two volumes of biography of the poet with literal translations of his poems. These are called *Tu Fu, The Autobiography of a Chinese Poet* (1929) and *Travels of a Chinese Poet* (1934). The original intention had been a work in collaboration with Amy Lowell similar to their anthology *Fir-Flower Tablets*, in which only a few of Tu Fu's poems had appeared. But Miss Lowell's death prevented the final rendering into rhythmic English, and the literal versions are more valuable as biographic notes than as poems.

The example here given, taken from their earlier collaborated efforts, represents the homesickness of Tu Fu while away from his family at the capital, Chang-an. In Chinese poetry the moon is usually suggestive of sadness. Jade symbolizes something highly beautiful and precious. The two are often used in conjunction to create a mood of melancholy.

MOON NIGHT

Tonight — the moon at Fou Chou.
In the center of the Women's Apartments
There is only one to look at it.
I am far away, but I love my little son, my daughter.
They cannot understand and think of Chang-An.   5

The sweet-smelling mist makes the cloud head-dress damp,
The jade arm must be chilly
In this clear, glorious shining.
When shall I lean on the lonely screen?
When shall we both be shone upon, and the scars of tears be dry?   10

(*Florence Ayscough and Amy Lowell*)

THE LITTLE RAIN

Oh! she is good, the little rain! and well she knows our need
Who cometh in the time of spring to aid the sun-drawn seed;
She wanders with a friendly wind through silent nights unseen,
The furrows feel her happy tears, and lo! the land is green!

Last night cloud-shadows gloomed the path that winds to my abode,
And the torches of the river-boats like angry meteors glowed.
Today fresh colors break the soil, and butterflies take wing
Down broidered lawns all bright with pearls in the garden of the
    king.

(*L. Cranmer-Byng*)

CHINESE LYRICS BY VARIOUS POETS

I

CHAN FANG-SHENG (FOURTH CENTURY A.D.)

SAILING HOMEWARD

Cliffs that rise a thousand feet
Without a break,
Lake that stretches a hundred miles
Without a wave,
Sands that are white through all the year,   5
Without a stain,
Pine-tree woods, winter and summer
Ever-green,
Streams that forever flow and flow
Without a pause,   10
Trees that for twenty thousand years
Your vows have kept,

You have suddenly healed the pain of a traveler's heart,
And moved his brush to write a new song.

(*Arthur Waley*)

2

CHIN TAO-YU (T'ANG DYNASTY)

A POOR GIRL

Living under a thatch roof, never wearing fragrant silk,
She longs to arrange a marriage, but how could she dare?
Who would know her simple face the loveliest of them all
When we choose for worldliness, not for worth?
Her fingers embroider beyond compare,
But she cannot vie with painted brows;
And year after year she has sewn gold thread
On bridal robes for other girls.

(*Witter Bynner*)

Chinese Poems in English Rhyme

The following translations are unusual in two ways: they are the only translations of any note in English made by a native of China, and they are turned into typical English meter, because the translator feels that the rhythms to which English ears are most accustomed will best convey the poetic mood. Admiral Ts'ai T'ing-Kan has been working on these translations for many years in the midst of a busy public life. In his *Chinese Poems in English Rhyme*, the poem in the original Chinese precedes each translation so that the Western reader may see the appearance of the poem in Chinese character. They are all four-line poems with either five or seven characters to the line. The poets here represented are from the Sung dynasty (960–1279).

I

CHENG HAO

IMPROMPTU LINES ON A SPRING DAY

In days when clouds are light and breezes softly blow,
I cross to yonder stream where flowers and willows grow.
Some worldlings, knowing not my heart's deep inward joy,
May say I snatch these hours to play the truant boy.

2

LIN CH'I

THE PALACE EXAMINATION

In gorgeous dress the monarch took the throne,
Like sun or moon his countenance appeared.
The royal standards in my ink-slab shone
With imaged snakes and 'broidered dragons weird.
Our theme was ancient rites and music old,
In lengthy essays each must then unfold.
When singled out at court, I answer made,
Ere yet the slanting rays could westward fade.

3

YEH SHIH

TRYING TO VISIT A GARDEN

Though knocks I give, no owner at the gate is seen,
I fear my pointed clogs may mar his mossy green.
But charms of spring within a garden who can keep?
A spray of apricot across the wall doth peep!

4

SU SHIH

SHADOWS OF FLOWERS

The shadows up the terrace crept in thick array,
In vain the lad was told to sweep them all away.
And when the setting sun their forms withdrew,
Then lo! the silver moonlight brought them forth anew.

5

YEH LI

DEPARTED SPRING

From roofs the sparrows on my desk their shadows cast,
Into my ink-stand willow-down was falling fast,
While I, in leisure, by the window read the *Yi*,[1]
Nor noted when the spring had taken leave of me.

[1] **Yi**: The Book of Change, oldest of the Five Classics, see page 1180.

6

TU MU

AN AUTUMN EVE

Against the painted screen the moon projects its light,
With silken fan the flitting glowworms I evade.
Upon the garden roof, where cool as liquid seems the night,
I lie and watch the Herdboy and his Weaving-Maid.[2]

7

TS'AI CH'IO

A PAVILION BY THE WATER

Well screened on bamboo couch, and pillowed on a stone,
I doze at noon, the volume fallen by my side.
And when I wake, o'er queerest dreams I laugh alone,
And hear the fisher's flute along the rippling tide.

8

LU MEI-PO

THE SNOW AND PLUM FLOWER'S RIVALRY

Plum and snow in beauty oft have vied.
A pen is stayed; the bard can scarce decide.
In whiteness flow'rs to flakes three parts must yield;
In sweetness flakes to flow'rs must grant the field.

9

LU MEI-PO

THE SNOW AND THE PLUM FLOWERS

How impotent are flowers without the snow!
And without verse how vain the human show!
At eve with falling snow and poetry
And flowers, spring is a perfect trilogy.

(1–9, *Admiral Ts'ai T'ing-Kan*)

---

[2] **the Herdboy and his Weaving-Maid:** two stars which meet only once every year, being separated the rest of the time by the Milky Way. The Chinese call them the two lovers of heaven. The former is known to us as Altair, the latter as Vega.

SUGGESTIONS FOR STUDY

1. As you read the Chinese poems try to put yourself completely in the poet's mood and visualize as far as you can the picture he presents. Study as many Chinese prints as you can find to enter into the spirit of their art. A visit to a museum of Chinese art, if possible, is a great aid to the fuller realization of the significance of the poetry.

2. Investigate further the peculiar form of Chinese poetry. Good explanations are given in the introductions of the books starred on the reading list. Look at the originals of the poems given in *Chinese Poems in English Rhyme*.

3. Try writing some original poetry in the Chinese manner. While it may look easy at first, you will find that it is not so simple to produce a really effective bit of poetic observation.

4. If you have a flair for poetry, try making a smooth rhythmical version of some of the literal translations given by Florence Ayscough in her books on Tu Fu.

LIU CHI (1311-1375)

OUTSIDES

The short moral tale is a favorite with the Chinese as with other Orientals. The following throws considerable light on social conditions of six hundred years ago, many of which are only too true in modern life as well.

At Hangchow there once lived a costermonger who understood how to keep oranges a whole year without letting them spoil. His fruit was always fresh-looking, firm as jade, and of a beautiful golden hue; but inside — dry as an old cocoon.

One day I asked him, saying, " Are your oranges for altar or sacrificial purposes, or for show at banquets? Or do you make this outside display merely to cheat the foolish? as cheat them you most outrageously do."

" Sir," replied the orangeman, " I have carried on this trade now for many years. It is my source of livelihood. I sell; the world buys. And I have yet to learn that you are the only honest man about and I am the only cheat. Perhaps it never struck you in this light. The baton-bearers of today, seated on their tiger-skins, pose as the martial guardians of the State; but what are they compared with the Captains of old? The broad-brimmed, long-robed ministers of today pose as pillars of the constitution; but have they the wisdom of our ancient counsellors? Evil doers arise and none can subdue them. The people are in misery and none can relieve them. Clerks are corrupt and none can restrain them. Laws decay, and none can renew them. Our officials eat the bread of the State and know no shame. They sit in lofty halls, ride fine steeds, drink themselves drunk with wine, and batten on the richest fare. Which of them but puts on an awe-inspiring look, a dignified mien? — all gold and gems without, but dry cocoons within. You pay, sir, no heed to these things, while you are very particular about my oranges."

I had no answer to make. I retired to ponder over this costermonger's wit. Was he really out of conceit with the age, or only quizzing me in defense of his fruit?

(*Herbert A. Giles*)

THE TWIN SISTERS

Though fiction has been looked upon superciliously by the scholarly officials of China, it has flourished among those who had no intellectual reputation to maintain. To the Occidental reader much of this is of interest not only as entertainment, but also as an indication of social concepts and customs which differentiate the East from the West. The following story is an old tale of uncertain date and authorship translated more than a hundred years ago by Sir John Davis, the first English scholar to introduce Chinese works into that language. Though the plot is somewhat farcical, it nevertheless reflects certain customs which were ordinary enough in China, such as the formal arrangement of marriage by the parents, the common admiration for the scholar as a hero, and the social recognition of polygamy. It is interesting to note that another much longer story based on practically the same plot has been translated under the title "The Twins" in *Chinese Stories* by Robert K. Douglas. In that story, however, the two girls are secretly in love with two young scholars, one of whom is clever, the other rather slow-witted. By a clever trick the girls induce the Mandarin to tell them the subject of the examination beforehand, and by this advance warning both suitors are able to win their brides. The following story presents a different complication.

Early in the reign of an Emperor of the Ming dynasty,[1] there dwelt, in a city of the province of Hoo-kwang, a merchant, named Siaou-kiang, who had the misfortune to live on very indifferent terms with his wife. They were for a long while without any family, until, after a lapse of many years, two daughters, twins, were born to them. It

---

[1] **Ming dynasty:** (1368–1644) the last great Chinese dynasty before the rule of the Manchus.

is a popular remark that sons generally resemble the father, and daughters the mother; but these two sisters, contrary to what is usually the case, did not inherit the features of either of their parents; and they seemed like the children of some other family. Neither was the difference confined to their persons, for their dispositions were quite as dissimilar. As the father and mother were extremely plain and very stupid, so, on the contrary, the daughters were very handsome and particularly clever. After ten years of age, they began to resemble fair flowers glittering with dew, or fragrant herbs agitated by the breeze; and their beauty every day increased, until, having reached the age of fourteen or fifteen, no one could behold them without emotion. Not only were the young men in love with them, but even those of a more advanced age, when they beheld them, confessed the power of their charms.

Their dispositions were extremely docile, but notwithstanding this, they had learned but little, and the whole extent of their knowledge was confined to figures. As to the use of the needle and other female accomplishments, they needed but little instruction in order to acquire them. Their dress and ornaments were (from their station in life) coarse and ordinary, but yet, when these two girls were compared with the daughters of more wealthy and dignified persons, it was allowed by all that they need not change their homely dress, and metal ornaments, for the silks and jewels of the others.

As they were so very handsome and engaging, it naturally followed that the young men of fortune and family should seek them.

The good man and his dame were more like enemies than husband and wife. The former wanted to marry his daughters without the interference of the latter; and his wife, on the other hand, wished to obtain two sons-in-law without the knowledge of her husband. With this principle of mutual deceit, they each of them secretly engaged with their separate friends.

Though the father was severe in his own house, he was naturally of a kind and friendly disposition; not like his wife, whose turbulence led her, when provoked, to make the neighborhood ring with her violence. People therefore said to themselves that it would be an easier thing to dupe him than her, and that of the two, it was better to aid the wife than the husband. Hence it was that the latter was more successful in her adherents than the former, and after a little while, for each of her daughters, a husband was selected.

A fortunate day was chosen for the marriage, and the bridegrooms were desired to send the wedding presents; but with a view to prevent her husband's disapprobation and rejection of the match, he was kept in ignorance of the whole.

There were some sensible persons who said that the propriety of a daughter's marriage ought to be determined by the father, and that if the mother would not consent, the matter should be referred to the magistrate, who would never side with an obstinate woman, nor put aside the husband for the sake of favoring the wife. These persons wanted to get somebody to make their proposals to the former; but unfortunately, all those whom they asked proved to be as ready to deceive him as they were afraid of his wife, and when invited to act against her, they immediately made some pretext for declining. They dared not to incur her resentment, saying that if they offended the husband, they had nothing to do but to wait until he broke out, and then reason with him; and if he was violent, they might still go and complain to the magistrate. But if they offended his wife, and her anger was excited, it was not fit for them to contend with a woman; and should she abuse, and even chastise them, they must bear it, and could do nothing in return.

Thus it was that no one would consent to assist those who wished to make proposals to the good man, and they were accordingly obliged to open the subject to him in person. He had been very much nettled at seeing people in the first instance go to his wife, without coming to consult him, and therefore, on the present occasion, when the marriage of his daughters was proposed to him, he echoed his consent with great satisfaction, and made not the slightest objection.

The suitors told him that every one was afraid of his wife, and that, for this reason, none would act as mediators. What, therefore, was to be done? He replied, " When the parties are unknown to each other, it is necessary to make use of such agents; but when I have already given my consent, what more is required? " The suitors, hearing this, were very glad, and a lucky day was chosen on the spot for the transmission and reception of the marriage presents.

The husband's plan was similar to his wife's, inasmuch as he would make no disclosure beforehand, but left the matter to be developed by the occasion. It happened that the lucky day fixed upon by both parties was the same, and the gifts of all the four bridegrooms arrived at the door together. The gongs made a great din, and the different articles composing the presents were spread out profusely, so that there was no telling to what names they belonged.

The first idea was that the bridegrooms, knowing the bad understanding which existed between the parents of the bride, and fearful of offending either party, had each caused a pair of ceremonial tickets to be made out, one for Siaou-kiang, and the other for his wife, thinking it better to be too ceremonious, than not enough so. When, however, the tickets were examined a little closer, it turned out, to the great astonishment of either party, that no two names were the same, but all four of the cards had a different title.

The father and mother stared at each other, and both broke out at once. Said one, " In addition to my two sons-in-law, whence come these two wretched pretenders? "

Said the other, " Who has sent all these things to be placed by the side of my presents? "

He exclaimed to his wife, " Who will have the audacity to receive one of these gifts, without the consent of me, the master of the house? "

His wife replied, " Without leave from me, the mistress of the family, who will venture to take anything that is here? "

Upon this, the good man said, " It is a maxim, that a woman, before her marriage, must obey her father, and after it, her husband. Now with respect to my daughters, I being their father, it is their duty to be guided by me, and with respect to yourself, I being the husband have a right to control you. What is the reason, then, of your behaving in this manner? "

She immediately replied, " It is also a maxim, that in the marriage of a son, the father is to have the direction, but in the marriage of a daughter, the mother. If the former were our case at present, then indeed you might do as you pleased, but as we are now concerned about the latter, I, as a matter of course, have the sole right to command. Under what pretense, then, do you meddle with my affairs? "

From words they would very soon have proceeded to blows, but those who were standing by prevented them, and kept them apart from each other. The wife would not listen to another word. She took the presents which belonged to her two favorites, and receiving them all as they were inserted in the list, told the people to go back with her answer. At the same time, she ordered all the rest to be thrown out of doors, and would not let one of them remain in the house.

Her husband was of course greatly enraged at this. He, in his turn, had them all brought back, and emptying the boxes and bowls, wrote an answer himself, and sent it.

He was well aware that this double espousal must ultimately come before the magistrate; but deferred the presentation of a written report, and was resolved to try what prompt and forcible measures would do in the first instance. The parents of his intended sons-in-law were desired by him to choose a fortunate day, and having made a grand preparation of lanterns and torches, to engage a number of sturdy fellows to support them in carrying off his daughters by force. Should this measure fail, it would not be too late to present an address.

Those two persons readily adopted the suggestion, and chose an early day for the nuptials. They hired a number of ruffians to follow the chairs,[2] with a hope that they might carry everything by numbers.

It remained for them to discover that such a plan might answer well enough against men, but that a female opponent was not so easily discomfited. The wife placed herself at her door, with one of the bars in her hands, and by her resolution plainly showed that she would have no mercy on those who attempted to cross the threshold. They all dispersed like mice to their hole, and left half of the chairs, lanterns and torches behind them; which might be called levying "contributions from the vanquished." All these were seized and detained by the lady for her own use.

Her husband, greatly incensed at this, immediately urged his two friends to present an address without delay. These persons, however, knew very well that such an address on this occasion was not likely to be very successful, and that it was not usual for persons, so closely connected, to proceed to law against each other. They therefore determined not to oppose her openly, but to state they had been repulsed with such violence from Siaou-kiang's door, and lay the whole blame upon him in the first instance. They resolved to resort to the Chy-foo, the first magistrate of the district, instead of the Chy-hien. When their address had been presented, the husband sent in a statement of the facts as they really happened, by way of answer. The two friends also sent in particular statements, and, as if they deemed it inexpedient to bring a married woman too much forward on such an occasion, merely placed her at the head of the witnesses, saying that she was the mother of the two girls who had been betrothed, and should be examined by the magistrate.

At that time the office of chief magistrate was exercised by a deputy. This person had not long been in the situation, but bore the character of a very upright man, and possessed high literary rank at an early age. When he had received the address, he ordered a notice to be put up, fixing the period of trial within a few days. He previously sent

---

[2] **chairs:** similar to sedan chairs, borne on the shoulders of coolies.

for the husband in order to examine him, and afterwards for all the four persons, as well as every one whose name was mentioned in the address, with the exception of the woman; for he supposed, that as she had a husband to guide her, any evidence which she could give must be the same as his, since it was not customary for husband and wife to differ on such points.

He was very little aware that on this occasion the mother of the betrothed daughters was the enemy of the intended fathers-in-law. He had heard of litigations between friends, but seldom of any between such near connections as these. When the wife observed that she was not called upon for her evidence, she complained loudly of the injustice that was done her, and that the Mandarin was therefore obliged to send for her up.[3]

She pointed to her husband, and said, " Though he may pretend to the character of a man, he has very little of the sense of one, and anybody that pleases can make a fool of him. He has no regard to his daughters' happiness, and those whom he has chosen to be their husbands are the most disreputable persons in the neighborhood. It was for this reason that I endeavored to provide somewhat better for them, and would not permit him to have the control. I have to beg that your worship will condescend to give me your instructions."

When the Mandarin had heard what she had to say, he observed it was reasonable enough. He then sent for the husband, to examine him again. The latter stated that his wife was of a very turbulent disposition, and on every occasion endeavored to browbeat and get the better of her husband. That on common occasions, he was ready to submit to this, but the marriage of his daughters was a thing of such importance that he could never think of giving up his right into her hands.

The judge, seeing that what he said was also reasonable, felt himself at a loss to decide between them. He then addressed himself to both, saying, " According to rule, the husband has a right to be arbitrator on such an occasion as that in dispute, but in family matters it is sometimes not possible to adhere strictly to general rules, nor to consider things too much in the abstract. Wait until I call your daughters before me, and hear what they have to say: whether they think that their father or their mother is doing what is best for them."

Both the husband and the wife prostrated themselves, and said they were quite satisfied with this arrangement. The Mandarin then issued a written order, and sent persons to summon the daughters.

[3] **send for her up:** call for her testimony.

When these were gone, he said to himself that as the parents were both so plain and ordinary in their appearance, it was not likely that fair flowers should be produced from reeds; but if the daughters were still more ugly than the parents, there was no telling where it would end! He then, with a countenance on which surprise was ready depicted, waited their arrival in his hall.

As soon as they were arrived, all the inferior officers and attendants, without their usual regard to decorum, pressed forward in a crowd to gaze, as if some prodigy had dropped down from the skies. As for the Mandarin himself, he was altogether amazed, and could not guess whence two such divine persons could have flown thither. Luckily for him, his emissaries at the same moment announced that " such a person's daughters were arrived." He then knew that flowers of extraordinary beauty had for once been produced from reeds, and that the daughters were not only an improvement on their parents, but that they retained no resemblance whatever to them.

When he had recovered from his surprise, he addressed them thus, " Your father and mother, being unable to agree together, have, it appears, betrothed you two to four different persons, and at last refer their dispute to my decision. Your father says that your mother is in the wrong, and she, in her turn, complains of him. It has been observed of old that ' an upright magistrate can ill interfere with family affairs.' I have accordingly sent for you to ask whether, in general, your father or your mother has acted with most discretion? "

Both the girls were naturally shy and bashful, and would at any time have run away at the sight of one man, but now, when several hundred pairs of eyes were fixed, and as it were nailed, upon them, they were ready to hide themselves under the table.

The judge's eyes were clearer than other people's. Having observed them for some time, he asked them how they could give answers if they were so bashful? When they replied not a word, though he repeated his question several times, he began to draw his evidence from their looks. These seemed to say that both of their parents were a little in the wrong, but it did not become them, as their daughters, to mention it.

The judge inwardly understood their meaning, and said to himself, " Two such charming young women ought not to be given to ordinary husbands. I shall not now ask whether the father or the mother be in the right, but send for all four of the intended bridegrooms, and compare them together. Should the girls consent to marry any of them, I shall award to them the same." Having this resolved, he was on the point of issuing a written order for their appearance, when the four fathers-in-law kneeled down before him, and said, " It is not necessary for your worship to send out the order. Our sons are all of them waiting outside, each hoping that his wife may be awarded to him. May we proceed to call them in? "

The judge said, " If that is the case, make haste and tell them to come in."

They all four went out, and presently returned, each leading in his son, saying, " This is my boy: I hope your worship will award to him his wife."

The latter however shook his head, and observed the four youths narrowly. They looked as if they had all come from the same stock, being very strange and uncouth in their appearance. Far from being good looking, there was not one without some defect in his limbs or features. The judge said to himself. " To choose them husbands from among these four would be like searching for a hero among dwarfs. How can I possibly select one! — I did not think that so much beauty and such ill-fortune could be combined."

He then sighed, and calling on the father's favorites to kneel down on the left side, and on the mother's to do the same on the right, he told the two girls to kneel down in the midst, and spoke to them as follows: " All those who were engaged by your father and mother to marry you are now present. I have already asked you for your real sentiments. Since you would not speak, I suppose that, in the first place, shame prevented you, and, in the second, the difficulty of mentioning your parents' faults. I do not now call on you to speak a word, but merely to turn your heads a little on one side, and thereby evince your real wishes. If you wish to marry your father's favorites, turn yourselves to the left; if your mother's, to the right. But remember that in this slight movement is involved the welfare of your whole life, and your choice should therefore be a good one."

When he had said this, the whole assembly anxiously fixed their eyes upon the two damsels, to see them turn their heads. They, however, on the first entrance of the four suitors, had looked at them, and observing their uncouth appearance, they hung down their heads, and closed their eyes, and let fall their tears in silence. When the judge had spoken to them, they turned neither to the right, nor to the left, but remaining fixed, with their faces towards him, began to weep aloud. The more he pressed them to speak the more violently did they cry; until all those who were present began to weep in sympathy with them, and everyone felt the extent of their hardship.

The judge then said, " It would seem from this, that the persons chosen by both your parents are exceptionable.[4] You need not think of marrying any of them; I will provide for you myself. There is no good reason why two such persons should be given as wives to booby clowns. Place yourselves on one side; I have arranged it all for you already. Call up the father and mother." They both appeared and knelt down before the table, on which the judge, striking with his hand, cried out in great anger, " You two must be devoid of all principle to regard your daughters' welfare as mere child's play. If you wanted to give them in marriage, you should have consulted together, and seen that the parties were suited to each other; not having endeavored to unite persons so dissimilar. You may have learned, from what has here passed, the probable result of the union had it taken place. It is fortunate that the affair was referred to me, who shall decide it in a manner quite different from what is customary. Had you gone to another officer, he would have adhered to the usual track, and awarded them to one or other of the suitors; and thus the happiness of these two young women would have been destroyed by a single stroke of his pencil. They shall now marry neither of the parties to whom they were betrothed. I will depute persons to provide a suitable match for them. Do not suppose that, in taking this step, I am going to consult my private views or to violate justice. On the contrary, I am adhering to the strictest reason and propriety. Wait till I have made out an adjudication, by which you will all be satisfied."

He then took up his pencil and wrote the following document: " It appears that Siaou-kiang and his wife, having daughters, twins, of extraordinary beauty, many persons were desirous of obtaining them in marriage, and each has endeavored to effect his views in a different way. As the father and mother were at variance, and the agents of one party endeavored to deceive the husband, while those of the other aimed at keeping the wife in ignorance, mistakes and confusion were the consequence. There were four husbands provided for the two brides, and as the latter could not divide themselves, it was not possible for the union to take place. As the daughters appear disgusted with those whom it was intended they should marry, I have pitied their distress, and departed from what is usually considered as the proper course, for the sake of performing an act of benevolence; but at the same time, without infringing the laws for my own private views. In all contracts of marriage, the consent of both father and

4 **cxceptionable:** undesirable.

mother, and the intervention of negotiators, are indispensable. Now, in the case of the mother's favorites, though there have been negotiators, there was no father's consent. Were I to sanction their claim, it would be a dangerous precedent. In the case of Siaou-kiang's favorites, though there was the father's consent, there were no negotiators, and were I to permit them to succeed, the precedent would be equally pernicious. Both cases, then, would at once violate ancient law and modern opinion. The four suitors must seek brides elsewhere, for these two cannot be given to any of them. It is better that they should be separated now, than that, by being united, they should become miserable hereafter. Though, therefore, I do this out of compassion for the one party, it is at the same time the most beneficial course than can be pursued for the other. Nobody need again address me on the subject; this judgment is decisive."

When it was written, a crier was ordered to read it aloud; after which, every one was sent out, nor was anybody permitted to make further remark. Persons were then dispatched to those whom the judge employed as agents for procuring proper matches for the two damsels. These were ordered, in the event of succeeding in their search, to repair to the judge, who, if he approved of the persons, would permit the marriage to take place.

After continuing their search for some time, those agents brought a number of youths, who, though they were said to be suitable, did not please the judge. He therefore hit upon another expedient, and determined to choose for the two daughters husbands according to literary merit; that they might excel in talent, as well as in personal accomplishments.

It happened that some country people had lately caught a couple of live deer, which they had presented to him, and which suited very well with his present scheme. He issued a notice, fixing a particular day for a literary examination; and required of the competitors, that instead of writing on the outside of their essays (as was the custom) the particulars of their age, they should state merely whether they were married, or single. He said that as the periodical examination for literary degrees was not far distant, he wished to be previously acquainted in some measure with the abilities of the candidates, and that he had provided, as the subject of contention for the unmarried, two beautiful damsels; and for those who were already married, a brace of curious deer. Those who won the prizes would be the first literary candidates of the year.

At the place of examination there was a vacant building. The judge sent for the mother and her two daughters, to live in the upper part, and kept the deer in a place below. When the notice was once issued, it roused the candidates in all the surrounding districts. Those who were already married were inspired chiefly by the desire of success, and regarded the deer as merely tokens of this. The young men who were unmarried were extremely rejoiced at having a chance of obtaining a handsome bride, together with their literary honors.

When the day of examination arrived, they exerted themselves to the utmost for the sake of obtaining so desirable a reward. When it was over, they never thought of returning home, but all remained in a body on the spot, for the sake of hearing the decision.

After three days, a list was published, in which about ten persons from each district appeared selected for re-examination. Those who were thus chosen suspected that this second examination was not so much to determine their literary merit, as to ascertain their personal appearance, and such of them as were good looking began to entertain great hopes. When the appointed day arrived, they dressed and adorned themselves with scrupulous nicety, and when they appeared before the judge, assumed their best looks, with a hope that he might be pleased with their appearance and place them at the head of the candidates.

The judge was as able to distinguish between their respective personal qualifications, as their abilities and knowledge; and being desirous of ascertaining the first, he made his remarks upon them when their names were called over. He observed whether their appearance denoted persons of respectability and wealth, or otherwise. When the examination was concluded, he desired his officer, before he had come out to his audience hall, next morning, to collect the musicians, and proceeding to the place where the two ladies and the deer were stationed, to conduct them to his office. The deer were to be placed on one side of the hall; and the two ladies, seated in ornamented sedans, used at weddings, were to be stationed on the other. The flowered lanterns and the music were to be in readiness to proceed to the marriage.

When his orders were given, the judge returned to his house to examine the essays. At daylight the next morning he issued a list, containing the names of the four successful candidates, the two married, and the two bachelors. The rest, ranged according to their merits, were to have inferior marks of distinction conferred upon them.

There is no occasion to notice the two who obtained the deer as their reward, and therefore we shall not mention their names. Of the two who won the ladies, one was a graduate, named Sze-tsin, and the other a younger candidate, whose name was Chy-yuen.

All those whose names had been noticed at the examination entered the Hall of Audience to learn the result. When they observed on which side the two ladies were, they all crowded thither to see the damsels whose beauty was so famous; and that part of the hall was filled with spectators. On the side where the deer were stationed, a single person only, in the dress of a graduate, stood, apparently in sorrow, and without a desire to go and behold the two beauties. Some of those in the hall, who observed him, said that this must be one of the successful candidates who was married, and who, knowing that neither of the ladies would come to his share, but that he had obtained one of the deer, had previously come to make his selection, that he might take the best when the time for choosing arrived.

To the surprise of these persons, however, some of the candidates from the other side of the hall went over to him, and paying their respects, said, " We congratulate you, sir; one of these fair ladies is yours."

That graduate however waved his hand in token of denial, and said, " I have nothing to do with them."

They all exclaimed, " You are the first of the four successful competitors, and are also unmarried. How then can you say that you have nothing to do with them? "

He answered, " We shall soon see the judge, and if you will listen you will then be informed." They could not understand his meaning, but supposed that these words were nothing more than a little modesty on his part.

When the drum had been struck three times, the judge came into his hall, and those whose names had been distinguished went to pay him their respects. He then asked, " Which are the four successful candidates? I request them to stand aside, that I may address them." When his officer heard this, he read aloud the list. Besides Sze-tsin, there should have appeared three others; but two only were present, both of whom were married, and the absent one was the unmarried candidate.

The judge upon this exclaimed, " How happens it that on such an occasion as the present, he is not here? "

Sze-tsin replied, " He is a friend of mine, and lives in the same district. Not being aware of the business of today, he has not come."

The judge said, " Is this the graduate Sze-tsin? Sir, I have admired your abilities and learning. There could be no doubt of your succeeding at the present examination. These two ladies are certainly very beautiful and their having obtained two such husbands is a just dispensation of Heaven."

Sze-tsin bowed at this, and answered, " Your worship is very gracious; but I am a man of an infelicitous destiny, and unworthy to enjoy such great good. I request you will select a substitute in my room; for I am unwilling to mar the happiness of my intended bride."

The judge exclaimed, " How is this! What is the reason of your thus strangely declining? Tell the officer to ask the two ladies which of them is the eldest, and request her to come to her husband."

Sze-tsin again bowed, and stopping the officer, requested that he would not go. The judge said, " What is the reason of this? "

Sze-tsin replied, " It is my unhappy fate to be condemned to celibacy, as I am never to be paired with a wife. All those to whom I have made overtures of marriage, no sooner were they engaged to me than they became seized with a mortal sickness and died; and in this manner, by the time I was twenty, I had been the innocent cause of the death of six different ladies. All the fortune-tellers whom I have consulted say that I am never to have a wife, and that I ought therefore to become a priest of the religion of either Fo or Taou. Although now of the literary order, I must soon forsake letters and become a priest. I will not venture again to hazard the life of any young woman, and thereby add to the list of my sins."

The judge, having heard him, replied, " Why should you do thus? There is little faith to be put in such predictions. They were but unskillful diviners who told you this, and if you have been unfortunate in your former addresses, it must have been by mere chance. Why should you behave like a man who has a stoppage at the throat, and cannot eat? Though you seem bent upon your resolution, I will not consent to it. I have, however, one thing to observe: how happens it that the candidate Chy-yuen is not present? In the first place, I had chosen an auspicious day, on purpose that he might come and be married; and secondly, as the hand-writing of his second essay did not correspond with that of his first, I wished to question him a little on the subject. What is the meaning of this non-arrival? "

Sze-tsin, hearing this, answered, " I am possessed of a secret, which by right I should not have divulged; but since your worship has said thus much, it might be still more culpable in me to conceal it. This candidate is a particular friend of mine. As he was very poor, and had not wherewithal to wed, I formed an intention of assisting him. The two essays were both of my composition. The first was in his handwriting, but the second, because he did not come, was written by me for him. I resolved, that should the first place be allotted to myself, I would yield up the prize to him; but did not expect, that by very extraordinary luck, we should both of us have been preferred. Since your worship has, through your great penetration, discovered the truth, my endeavor to serve my friend has turned out very much to his prejudice. I therefore am now compelled to entreat your pardon in his behalf, and to request that you will extend to him, by your kindness, what I meditated for him."

The judge replied, " Is this the state of the case? Had I not fortunately discovered the truth from you, a great injustice would have been done to one of the ladies. As the matter now stands, both the first and the second place are yours, and each of the ladies belongs to you. Any one may make pretensions to riches and honors, but such beauty as they possess is not to be found everywhere, and none should obtain, but such as deserve them; certainly not a false pretender. Tell the officer immediately to request both the ladies to come thither, that the marriage may be concluded."

Sze-tsin obstinately and repeatedly declined, observing that a man whose destiny it was never to be paired with a wife, and who could not have one — how much less possible was it for him to have two?

The judge laughed at this, and said, " What has happened today is in exact conformity with your fortune. To be paired with a wife meant that there never could be two of you. Were you to marry one wife, there would then be a pair, and you might fear that your destiny would oppose some obstacle; but now, since you marry two, there will be one more than a pair, and this will agree very well with the prediction. It would appear from this, that such was its very intention, and therefore you need not apprehend a recurrence of your former fortune."

When he had done speaking, the whole number of persons present expressed their approbation, saying that the decision of the judge this day had, as it were, created a new destiny for Sze-tsin, and that the explanation he had given was admirable. They advised Sze-tsin to relinquish his pertinacity, and return thanks to the judge, with the two ladies.

Sze-tsin therefore had no alternative: he was obliged to yield. Standing up before the judge, in company with the two ladies they all bowed down four times before their benefactor, Sze-tsin then called for his horse, and accompanied the two ornamented sedans home.

When he was gone, the inferior rewards were distributed. All those who had witnessed the good fortune of Sze-tsin exclaimed that the happiness of the immortal gods was not superior to his. The regard of the judge for talent and merit had caused it all. At this examination, three only had succeeded, but the fourth was a mere pretender, and it was just that he who had helped him should have the reward.

Some time after, Sze-tsin was promoted to higher literary rank. The name of the judge became celebrated in consequence of his decision, until it reached the court, when the emperor called him to Peking, and gave him a situation in the Military Tribunal. Sze-tsin was advanced to a place in the Literary College, and continued to live with his friend the judge on the terms of father and son.

The ancient saying is very true, that " none but the worthy can discern the worthy."

(*Sir John Davis*)

SUGGESTIONS FOR STUDY

1. What do you think of this story as to (1) interest as a narrative, (2) reflection of Chinese life, (3) technique of construction?

2. If you have access to Douglas' *Chinese Stories*, read " The Twins," and compare it on the above points with this story. The fact that it is developed more through conversation makes it a much longer story. Do you like Douglas' manner of handling the story better?

3. Do you think that this story would be more or less amusing to an Occidental reader than to a Chinese? Why?

4. Would this story lend itself well to dramatizing? to a motion picture? Discuss.

READING LIST

Translations from Chinese Literature

Lotus and Chrysanthemum, ed. by J. L. French

Fir-Flower Tablets, trans. by Florence Ayscough and Amy Lowell

Images in Jade, trans. by Arthur Christy

Jade Mountain, trans. by Witter Bynner

A Canticle by Pan, trans. by Witter Bynner

* Books marked with an asterisk are recommended for purchase for the library on a limited budget.

A Lute of Jade, trans. by L. Cranmer-Byng

A Feast of Lanterns, trans. by L. Cranmer-Byng

*A Hundred and Seventy Chinese Poems, trans. by Arthur Waley

More Translations from the Chinese, trans. by Arthur Waley

The Temple, trans. by Arthur Waley

*Chinese Poems in English Rhyme, trans. by Admiral Ts'ai T'ing-Kan

The Works of Li Po, trans. by Shigeyoshi Obata

Tu Fu, the Autobiography of a Chinese Poet, trans. by Florence Ayscough

Travels of a Chinese Poet, trans. by Florence Ayscough

Cathay, trans. by Ezra Pound

Gems of Chinese Literature, ed. by H. A. Giles

Chinese Novels, trans. by Sir John Francis Davis

The Tragedy of Ah Qui, and Other Modern Chinese Stories, ed. by Kyn Yn Yn

*Chinese Stories, trans. by Robert K. Douglas

Stanton, William: *The Chinese Drama* (contains 3 plays)

World's Great Classics, Vol. IV. *China.*

Plays in English after the Chinese Manner

Hazelton, Jr., George C.: *The Yellow Jacket*

Hsiung, Cheng Chin: *The Thrice-*

Promised Bride, (in Shay, F.: *Twenty-Five Short Plays*)

Oliver, Margaret: *The Turtle Dove* (in several collections of one-act plays)

About China

Giles, H. A.: *A History of Chinese Literature*

Arlington, L. C.: *The Chinese Drama* (summaries of many plays)

Buss, Kate: *Studies in Chinese Drama*

Chia-Chien, Chu: *The Chinese Theater* (excellent illustrations) (trans. from the French)

**Zucker, A. E.: *The Chinese Theater* (contains also a modern one-act play)

Werner, E. T. C.: *Myths and Legends of China*

Brown, Brian: *The Story of Confucius*

Carpenter, Frank: *China*

Kendall, Elizabeth: *A Wayfarer in China*

Wilhelm, Richard: *The Soul of China* (trans. by John Holroyd Reece and Arthur Waley)

Buck, Pearl: *The Good Earth*
Sons
A House Divided (called **House of Earth* in one-vol. ed. of the three)
East Wind: West Wind
The Mother

Morant, G. S.: *A History of Chinese Art*

Ferguson, J. C.: *Chinese Painting*

Waley, Arthur: *Introduction to the Study of Chinese Painting*

---

* Books marked with an asterisk are recommended for purchase for the library on a limited budget.

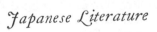
Japanese Literature

Japanese Literature

THOUGH Japanese literature is an outgrowth of Chinese and bears certain resemblances to it, nevertheless both the language and the literature of Japan have a marked individuality. In the first place, considered beside the antiquity of Chinese writing, Japanese literature seems youthful indeed. While Chinese literature is forty-five hundred years old, Japanese counts a mere twelve hundred years.

Japanese literature opens with the eighth century

Tradition places the founding of the Japanese empire at 660 B.C., but there are no actual historical records until the fifth century A.D., and no literature until the eighth century. Chinese influence molded the early history of Japan, especially after the acceptance of Buddhism in 552 A.D. The younger nation used the ideographs of the older for written records, but their oral language was quite different. By the eighth century the characters had become considerably modified to express the phonetic distinctions, and a national language and literature emerged. The striking difference in the two tongues is that Chinese words are monosyllabic, while Japanese are polysyllabic. Every syllable in a Japanese word ends in a vowel except those ending in *n*. This in itself creates a flowing rhythm somewhat comparable to the Italian among European languages.

The beginning of an individual Japanese literature can be placed at 712 A.D., with the *Kojiki* (*Record of Ancient Matters*) compiled at the command of the Emperor to give an account of the creation of the world and of the ancient Japanese empire. This is the repository of the native religion, Shintoism. But more interesting from a literary point of view are the early anthologies: the *Manyoshu* (*Collection of Myriad Leaves*) and the *Kokiushu* (*Ancient and Modern Songs*) made in the eighth and ninth centuries respectively.

Brevity and beauty the hall-mark of Japanese poetry

In these anthologies is established the form which has remained a standard poetic mold up to the present time. This is the *tanka*, limited to thirty-one syllables, divided into five lines in the order 5, 7, 5, 7, 7. Because of the structure of the language with its vowel endings, rhyme is not used, nor do we find the rhythmic devices of alliteration and accent common to English poetry. Nevertheless, a good poem has a distinct rhythmic quality which the Japanese consider attuned to " the pulse-beat of the universe." A later development, the *hokku* or *haiku*, is even more abbreviated, having only seventeen syllables, arranged 5, 7, 5. Naturally these restricted forms give opportunity for only a tiny glimpse of beauty in each poem. Like Japanese prints, they show merely a carefully selected detail and omit all which would distract attention from it. The Japanese have a word to characterize the poetic temperament which suggests a combination of surprise, wonder, awe, and delight. Literally it might be translated " Ah!-ness." The poet must be aware of the " Ah!-ness " of the world and transmit it to the reader. The writing of poetry is almost a national pastime in Japan, and few individuals can be set above the many as great enough to warrant special mention in a condensed account. Even today a national poetry contest at the Imperial palace is an annual event anticipated with great interest. As many as twenty-five thousand poems will be received in response to an assigned topic such as " New Snow on Mount Fuji," or " Pines Reflected in Limpid Water." To have one's poem read before the Emperor is a coveted honor.

Classic Age marked by verse compilations and prose romances

The Classic Age of Japanese literature was between the ninth and twelfth centuries, with a firmly established Imperial family at Kyoto giving patronage to all the arts. By the end of this period there had appeared seven great compilations of verse and a surprising number of prose romances and tales. In the eleventh century women took the lead in literature, and novel writing reached its climax in *The Romance of Prince Genji* by Lady Murasaki, whose given name was Skikibu. This has in recent years been translated into English by Arthur Waley in six volumes, and has aroused great interest through its astoundingly modern tone in picturing the people of the Imperial palace.

A series of dynastic wars put an end to the high development of

civilization, and the twelfth to the seventeenth centuries are called
the Dark Ages of Japan. But during this time (1350) a curious book
of brief essays or running commentary on life with the fantastic title
Tsure-zure Gusa (Weeds of Idleness) was written by a monk named
Kenko. From this we gain a vivid picture of medieval Japan.

The Nō lyrical drama becomes an important element in literature

Another important type arising in this period is the Nō drama.
These lyrical, semireligious plays in which music, dancing, and
costume play an essential part, were developed from the older religious rites at about the same time the morality plays in England were
supplanting the earlier miracle plays. But the Nō drama is still
commonly presented on the stage in Japan in its original form, some
of the actors even wearing priceless ancestral costumes, whereas the
English morality play has only an occasional revival. The continuous
influence of the Nō plays is rather to be compared to that of Shakespeare in English, though the plays themselves bear no resemblance
to his.

Japan has produced one playwright who has been called the
Shakespeare of his country, Chikamatsu Monzaemon (1653–1724).
He broke away from the classics and revitalized the *jōruri,* or puppet
drama, in which he intermingled comedy and tragedy. Some of his
plays are historical; others portray the manners of his day.

Two popular novelists enliven the eighteenth century

The eighteenth century brought a general revival of the novel,
marked by two writers of special interest. The prolific Kyokutei
Bakin (1767–1848) wrote two hundred and sixty volumes, one of
which ran to three thousand pages. His masterpiece, *New Moon,*
and many others, in spite of their artificialities, still maintain popularity in Japan. Jippensha Ikku (1763–1831), " the Japanese Mark
Twain," produced a humorous novel with a title usually translated
Shank's Mare, which is first cousin to *Huckleberry Finn, Pickwick
Papers, Don Quixote,* and *Dead Souls* in its lively picture of varied
characters seen through the eyes of comic roamers. Ikku was also
a great practical joker. When dying he told his friends that his spirit
would speak to them after his death if they would cremate his body
without changing the clothes. The spirit of laughter spoke indeed,
for he had concealed fireworks in his pockets, which went off as soon
as the flame touched his body.

Foreign influence modifies trend of current literature

In the middle of the nineteenth century Japan, after many years of isolation from Western nations, opened her door to foreign trade, and a new period of literature began under this new influence. Since then, there have been intervals of marked reaction against foreign life, but Japan is inevitably permeated with the modern mood and cannot escape. Russian and English influences are especially strong in literature, women are beginning to write once more, and fiction is taking an honored place and becoming more realistic. The Japanese are avid readers and know foreign languages so well that they do not wait for translators to extend their acquaintance with foreign literatures. Present-day Japanese poetry is a strange blend of modern freedom and industrialism seen with the quaint " Ah!-ness " of the Japanese mind.

Modern Japanese literature deeply affected by war dislocations

The impetus for the creation of a modern Japanese literature came from a book published by Tsubouchi Shoyo (1859–1935) in 1885, entitled *The Essence of the Novel*. The author's thesis was that Japanese writers should adopt the philosophy expressed in contemporary Western literature.

Many novelists, accepting the advice as gospel, began to treat realistically problems of social and individual adjustment, often those of soldiers fighting in the undeclared war with China. Himo Ashihei's series of soldiers' diaries describe in minute detail the wretched life of a common soldier. Hori Tatsuo's *The Wind Rises* is a husband's sensitive, day-by-day account of his wife's death.

The Drifting Cloud (symbol of an aimless life) is the work of a women novelist, Hayashi Fumiko (1904–1951). It is an accumulation of repulsive facts which created the gloom and misery of Japan at the end of World War II, seen by a woman returning from a life of luxury and passion in Indo-China.

The most important novel to appear in Japan in the years of rehabilitation was Tanizaki's *The Thin Snow*. Like *The Drifting Cloud*, it is a photographic report of commonplace details, many of them repulsive, in the life of a family in the years of wretchedness, 1936–1941. Occasionally these naturalistic passages are interrupted by lyrical descriptions of nature in the manner of Japanese painting. *A Fool's Love* by the same author is a direct imitation of the theme and action of Somerset Maugham's *Of Human Bondage*.

The Communists also developed a propagandist school of writing whose best-known novel is *The Crab Canning Boat* by Kobayashi Takiji (1903–1933). The work is the description of a voyage to Kamchatka by a fleet of fishing and canning boats. The author depicts the terrible conditions under which the men work. When the expedition meets a crew of Soviet subjects, the men, filled with admiration for the efficiency and contentment of everyone on the Russian ship, are converted to Marxism. Although the work is artistically crude, it displays some of the raw power of American propaganda works of the same period.

Although all these works are in the stream of modern European and American literature, they reflect the dislocations and suffering that afflicted Japan during World War II and its aftermath.

The Folk Tale

THE SEVEN PLEAS

Japanese folk tales, like those of other nations, reach far back into the memories of the race and bring us sudden realization of how certain human characteristics persist throughout the centuries. In addition to those which illustrate the pure exuberance of fancy, characteristic of children and childish stages in the development of a race, we often come across tales which bear considerable relationship to the short story of today with its realistic pictures of men and women in their daily lives. "The Seven Pleas" is significant in that it shows a greater regard for the intelligence and the importance of women than we usually credit to the Oriental point of view. Strangely enough, there was a period in Japanese history during the Heian dynasty (ninth to thirteenth centuries) when women maintained literary leadership over the men, and wrote the most important works of the day. Perhaps this story dates back to that time. Later with a long series of dynastic wars, women dropped back into a position of intellectual inferiority from which only modern education has enabled them to emerge.

Japanese fairy tales show some unique conventionalities of form. Their opening is " In the olden, olden time," comparable to our " Once upon a time," and their ending, if happy, is " Congratulation! Congratulation! " But the sad story ends " Sorrowful! Sorrowful! " The story invariably has a moral, though it is not always definitely expressed as a " moral tag."

This story is taken from a collection made by Chiyono Sugimoto, daughter of Etsu Sugimoto, author of the well-known book, *A Daughter of the Samurai.* The tales are written just as she heard them in childhood from her grandmother.

In the olden, olden time there was an old man who had seven daughters. The youngest, who was his favorite, was the most beautiful as well as the cleverest of them all.

One spring day when the old man was in his field, planting rice, he grew very tired. Straightening his bent back he looked at his unfinished work and was discouraged.

"Ah, I am blessed with many daughters," he sighed aloud, "but I have no son. If only some young man would come and help me, I would gladly give him one of my daughters as bride."

Now in the very next rice patch was a young man busily working. He overheard the old man's words, and, hastily pushing down in the water his handful of green shoots, he stepped up on the narrow path between the two fields.

"Old man, old man," he called, "do you want strong help?"

"Yes, yes," eagerly cried the old man. "If you will help me plant my field by sunset, I will give you my daughter for a bride!"

The young man at once stepped down into the water beside the old man and worked so rapidly, sticking the plants in straight rows five plants long, that before sunset the field was finished.

The old man bowed his thanks and started home, but the young man hurried after him.

"Old man, old man, do not walk so fast," he called. "When shall I expect my bride?"

Then the old man began to be troubled, for the youth was one known throughout the village as "Taro Silly."

Stopping, he slowly pulled his pipe from his girdle, as an old man does when he is puzzled, then, fumbling in his tobacco case for stone and metal, he struck fire, letting the sparks fall on a bit of dried grass-cotton held in the hardened palm of his hand. Blowing it into a blaze with his breath, he lighted his pipe, and after three whiffs looked at the youth.

"This is the greatest thing in life for my daughter," he said deliberately. "I must consult with her before I reply."

"Yes, yes, so be it," said the young man, going contentedly back to his work.

The old man walked slowly homeward, thinking of his bargain with regret, now that it was too late, and wondering with dread how he was to gain courage to propose the subject to his daughters.

He was a mild old man and day after day he thought and hesitated; and when he looked upon his growing field he slowly shook his head from side to side. Finally from much brooding he fell sick and one morning did not get up, but lay sighing and groaning.

His eldest daughter came to him.

" Father, Father, what is your ailing? " she asked anxiously. " Do you want medicine or hot water? "

" No, I want neither medicine nor hot water," he replied, " but I have one plea."

" What is it? " she asked.

" That you will consent to be the bride of Taro Silly."

" Oh, Father! Bride to that foolish young man? Oh no, Father, I cannot! "

She bowed very politely, but she went away.

The next morning the old man was no better, and the second daughter went to him and asked,

" Father, Father, what is your ailing? Do you want medicine or hot water? "

" No, I want neither medicine nor hot water," he replied, " but I have one plea."

" What is it? " she asked.

" That you will consent to be the bride of Taro Silly."

" Oh, Father! Bride of that foolish young man! " she exclaimed, " Oh no, I cannot! " She bowed politely, but she went away as her sister had done.

The third morning the third daughter came with the same question, and after hearing her father's plea, she also made the same answer, then bowed politely and went away. So it was with the fourth, fifth, and sixth daughters. On the seventh morning, when his youngest daughter came, the old man was almost distracted with sleeplessness and worry.

" Father, Father, what is your ailing? " she asked. " Can I bring you medicine or hot water? "

" No, daughter! " the old man replied as before. " I want neither medicine nor hot water, but I have one plea."

" What is it? " she asked. " Anything I can do for you I will."

Then he told her of his rash promise to the young man, and asked if she would consent to be the bride of Taro Silly. This dutiful daughter drooped her head for a moment then made a deep bow.

" Whatever you have promised," she gently replied, " must of course be done." Then she went away to prepare herself to be a bride.

Finally the day came, and she went to the home of Taro Silly and was married. On the third day, as is the custom, the groom and bride made their first visit to the bride's family. All morning the sisters were busy preparing the dinner of welcome, and they talked of nothing else but how they could endure to entertain their stupid brother-in-law.

Finally the young couple were seen coming along between the trees which lined the road, the groom walking first and the bride dutifully following just three steps behind.

The husband was a stupid young man, but he was good-natured and very anxious to make a favorable impression on his bride's family, so he carefully obeyed all the instructions which she had given him before they left home. The father-in-law's house had been recently built and he was very proud of it, but the carpenter had put in one piece of faulty lumber, which was a source of great annoyance to the old man, and for which he never failed to apologize to a guest. The bride had told her husband that when he looked at the tokonoma[1] post and praised its beauty, her father would at once point out a large knot and lament over the defect. Then the son-in-law was to say,

" Why not hang a post-roll picture[2] over the knot? It will hide the defect and also add to the beauty of the room."

All happened just as the bride had said. When the groom made his suggestion, the father was delighted at so simple a remedy, and the sisters thought, " The fellow is not so stupid as we imagined! "

There was also a cup missing from a valuable tea-set, for which the old man always made lament, saying, " It seems as if nothing can be perfect! " The groom had been given careful instructions what he was to say in this case also, and all happened just as the bride had said. Tea was served and the cup was lamented.

" Why not remove the empty cup-holder? " the young man quickly suggested. " Then no one will miss the broken cup."

Again the father was delighted, and again the sisters thought, " The fellow is not so stupid after all."

Everything was a matter of form, and the young man conducted himself so well that the father congratulated himself on having found an excellent husband for his favorite daughter.

[1] **tokonoma**: an alcove in a Japanese home reserved as a shrine of beauty. The carefully chosen picture or flower arrangement placed here is frequently changed.

[2] **post-roll picture**: a picture painted on a roll of paper or fabric and hung lengthwise.

After dinner was over the two men went out to the shed where the horse was kept.

" That is a fine horse," said the old man as he pointed to the animal, " but it seems as if nothing can be perfect. His blind eye is a sad defect."

" Why not hang a roll picture over it and so cover the defect and at the same time add to the beauty of the horse? " said the silly boy.

" Ah," thought the surprised old man, " I fear my son-in-law is only his wife's parrot." But as he walked along, there came a second thought. " Nevertheless, she has married well, for he has the sense to know that his wisdom lies in his wife, and allows her mind to be his guide."

The young couple lived long and gathered many rice bales; for it is a true saying, " The house where wisdom dwells in the head of the wife, is always successful and prosperous."

Congratulation! Congratulation!

(Chiyono Sugimoto)

SUGGESTIONS FOR STUDY

1. Compare this tale with the Chinese tale. Do you find any details which show the close relationship between the two races? What qualities do you find in them which you have observed in the folk tales of other nations?

2. Compare " The Seven Pleas " with the Russian tale " Fish in the Forest " and the Norwegian " The Husband Who Was to Mind the House," as pictures of relations between husband and wife.

3. Read other Japanese tales. Sugimoto's *Picture Tales from the Japanese* is especially recommended as conveying the spirit of the original.

Japanese Poetry

Since the names of individual poets play a less important rôle in Japanese literature than in others, and since some books of translation do not even indicate the author's names, the poems have here been arranged according to subject matter, with the name of the poet, where known, following each poem. Authors of the original poems are printed in roman type, translators in italics. With the exception of the few poems labeled " modern " these *tanka* and *hokku* are from medieval collections.

HUMAN EMOTIONS

I

Come and gone is the year,
   No tidings yet of my love.
My silk sleeve is damp with tears.
   Like silkworm curled in cocoon
   My heart is hidden in darkness.

2

Mount Fusi has fires,
   But they are hidden from sight.
Mount Fusi I said,
   But I meant myself — Few see [1]
   The fires of my secret heart.

3

Dead leaves whirling
   In the heartless autumn gust!
Still more fleeting
   Have I found (as all men must)
   Man's short life from dust to dust.

(Chisato)

4

" What starts the growth
   Of the Weed of Forgetfulness? "
I asked my soul.
   " Its seeds are in the stony soil
   Of the heart that is without tenderness."

(Sosei)

5

An avenue of blossoms —
   The same soft colors as in other springs —
And perfumes still the same —
   But he who planted them no longer here —
   Then never say this whiff of spring's the same.

(Tsurayuki)

---

[1] **Few see:** an attempt to show the punning which is characteristic of even serious poems in Japanese.

6

I longed to say something good
Of someone.
I had grown tired
Of my own selfishness.

7

Feeling inclined toward charity,
I agreed with a friend of mine
Who is conceited.

(6 and 7 by Takuboku Ishikawa — modern)
(*Glenn Hughes and Yozan Iwasaki*)

NATURE POEMS

BUTTERFLIES

I

Like a woman slipping off her haori [1] — that is the appearance of a butterfly.

2

Perched upon the temple-bell, the butterfly sleeps.

3

Even while sleeping, its dream is of play — ah! the butterfly of the grass!

4

Wake up! wake up! — I will make thee my comrade, thou sleeping butterfly.

5

Ah! the sad expression in the eyes of that caged bird! — envying the butterfly!

6

When I saw the fallen flower return to the branch — lo! it was only a butterfly!

[1] haori: a cloak lined with bright-colored silk.

7

Ah, the butterfly!   Even when chased, it never has the air of being
in a hurry.

8

As for butterflies, they all have the appearance of being about seventeen or eighteen years old.

9

How the butterfly sports — just as if there were no enmity in this
world.

10

If (in our next existence) we be reborn as butterflies upon the moor,
then perchance we may be happy together!

(Lafcadio Hearn)

INSECTS

1

Today united in love —
we who can meet so rarely;
Hear how the insects sing!
Their trill to our heart keeps time.

2

Hark to the tones that tinkle,
the chant of the suzumushi! [2]
If a jewel of dew could sing,
it would tinkle with such a voice.

3

Changed is my childhood's home —
all but the insect voices;
I think they are trying to sing
of the happier days that were.

(1–3, J. I. Bryan)

[2] **suzumushi:** a little insect like a cricket.

LAUGH ME TO SCORN

Laugh me to scorn if you please;
Call me your frog in the well.
Blossoms bend over my well;
And its water mirrors the moon!

(J. I. Bryan)

THE ISLAND IN THE OFFING

A lark rises
From an island in the offing.
Where the lark lives
There is farm-land;
Where there is farm-land
There is man;
Where there is man
There is love.

(Doppo Kunikita — modern)
(Glenn Hughes and Yozan Iwasaki)

THE SEASONS

SPRING

The nightingale sings
　　Though snow yet silvers the branches.
Does he foretell the spring,
　　Or does he mistake that whiteness
　　For the soft down of young plum blossoms?

(Sosei)

SUMMER

Today wisteria buds broke
　　In waves of color on my garden wall.
But the waters of my lake
　　Are still lonesome for waves of melody.
　　When will the mountain-cuckoo come?

(Attributed to Hitomaro)

AUTUMN

Have I been dreaming?
But yesterday, it seems, knee-deep in water
We planted rice-shoots;
    Today across a yellow plain
    The autumn breeze beckons us to the harvest.

WINTER

Snow has fallen in the night.
    Lo! My garden has budded anew.
Every bare twig and branch
    Bends with new blossoms, quite unnamed
    Among the myriad flowers of spring.

(Tsurayuki)

MISTS

Spring wears mist-garments.
    They are delicate — too delicate indeed —
For these rough zephyrs
    Have torn them, and the shreds
    Are fluttering to earth.

(Yukihira)

MOUNT FUJI

Less lofty summits
    Vanish in the vaulted blue.
Fuji rears her head
    Alone in peerless brightness,
    Like snow in dazzling whiteness!

(Empress Dowager Sadako)
(J. I. Bryan)

THE RISING MOON

Clinging to the clothes
    Which now the white waves lend her,
The full moon arose
    Above the shore-line slender
    In Autumn's stately splendor!

(Yosano Akiko)
(J. I. Bryan)

THE SUNFLOWER

Thou burstest from mood;
Marvel of thy every atom burning in life,
How fully thou livest!
Passionate lover of sunlight,
Symbol of youth and pride; 5
What absorption of thy life's memory,
Wonder of thy consciousness —
Mighty sense of thy existence!

(Yone Noguchi — modern. Author and translator.)

A LONE PINE TREE

I heard you singing in chorus with the birds yesterday.
Last evening, too, I heard you singing together with the moon.
I saw how your burning rhythm of fire
Fused with the minds of others into a piece of perfect song.
Your modest bearing, your discerning knowledge of the others, 5
Your power of self-criticism is beautiful indeed.
(I am but a fragment of flesh, I confess, when facing Nature.)
Ah, lone pine tree at the summit,
You will readily take part in singing at any time,
With a stream or clouds or even a rock out of shape, 10
As with birds or moon.
(I feel ashamed I am only a wilful human being fastidious in choice.)

Today under the blue sky where not one bird flies,
You are singing all alone. . . .
Ah, you are a soloist of ringing voice! 15
I see for the first time your beauty reaching the climax,
When listening to your solo.
There's dignity of independence in your bearing as a soloist,
That is reared in the divine air of solitude and silence.
Ah, solo that makes you only to be yourself, 20
Ah, your solo ringing in silvery voice,
What a solemn glory I feel,
What a tear-inspiring emotion I receive!
One's individuality is more or less impaired in chorus with the others
But in solo we find a perfect expression of self. 25
Ah, lone pine tree at the summit,

Your worth as a soloist
Makes me understand a silence and solitude.
How I wish to earn a dignity of independence that is all my own!
Let me listen from a distance to your solo,   30
Lone pine tree, my beloved,
Sing! Sing!

> (Yone Noguchi — modern. Author and translator.)

SUGGESTIONS FOR STUDY

1. Japanese poetry must be read with the same spirit as Chinese poetry,
but with even more imagination, for less is told in words. Do not try to
read these poems hastily. In order to get anything from them, you must
let your mind play with the picture suggested or the idea, until you feel
that you are creating something along with the poet. Study Japanese
prints in connection with the reading. See reading list for books on
Japanese art.

2. Study Tagore's poems from *Fireflies,* page 1171, in connection with
these. Did he catch the spirit of Japanese poetry? Do you find anything
in them that suggests they were written by a Hindu rather than a Japanese?

3. Try writing poems similar to the *tanka* or *hokku* about your own
observations of nature or human beings. In what way do you find this
good discipline in observation? In word selection?

Japanese Drama

Up to the present century when Western ideas invaded Eastern Asia,
the drama of both China and Japan retained its fixed character, and even today in Japan the *Nō* plays dating back to the fifteenth century are popular
with people of literary and artistic tastes. The exact meaning of the word
Nō differs according to various authorities, some translating it *talent,* and
others *unity.* There are about 250 of the *Nō* plays in existence today, and
many of them have been translated into English. This type of play is
essentially serious, those treating of gods and warriors having a patriotic or
pious lesson, those picturing romantic or mother love having lyrical beauty
or sadness. In contrast to the *Nō* play is the *kyogen* (wild words), a farcical piece, often a parody on a specific *Nō* play. Since the *Nō* without the
music, dancing, and picturesque costuming which add to its charm in presentation is likely to become somewhat tedious on the printed page because
of its mythological references, the example of a Japanese play here given
is a *kyogen,* which appeals more directly through its dialogue.

Before reading, it is well to visualize the way in which these plays are presented in Japan. The theaters are small and the seats for the audience often uncovered to the sky. The stage is a rectangular raised platform open to the audience on three sides, with a straight backdrop usually painted with pine trees to suggest those before a famous temple. The stage has its own roof supported by four slender pillars. At the back a passage screened by pine trees leads to the actors' dressing room. The stage can be comparatively small because there is no scenery, but instead the imagination of the audience interprets certain fixed symbols. An open framework is a boat; four posts and a roof, a house; flags painted like wheels, a carriage; a few branches, a forest; a bamboo pole, a bridge. The actor's fan, which unfurled adds grace and charm to the dance, may, when closed, become a writing brush or a dagger. With no curtain to break up the acts, and no changes of scenery except what the property man manages neatly before the eyes of the audience, a play is without limitations of time and space. By stepping through an imaginary door the actor goes from house to garden; by running around the stage he transports himself from one end of the world to the other; and by climbing a ladder he goes to heaven.

The costuming of the actors, however, is as elaborate as the staging is simple. Medieval in style, often actual heirlooms, and stiff with embroidery, these costumes are a delight to the eye. The wide sleeves play an important part in the action. They may be spread like wings to represent flight, flung over the arm in the gayety of the dance, drooped to represent weariness, or held across the face for mourning. The leading actors wear masks of elaborate design, and since the women's parts are played by men and the Emperor is always played by a young boy, the mask creates the necessary illusion. Gods, dragons, and demons, who are the chief characters in many of the plays, are fearsome masterpieces of costume and make-up. The masks are of wood, and some precious ones are said to be more than a thousand years old.

The appeal to the eye is further carried out by the dancing, which is an essential part of the acting. A great actor must also be a great dancer. The steps are of course quite different from those familiar to the West. Gliding, shuffling, and occasional stamping work themselves up to a rhythmic climax as the play reaches its dénouement. To add to the resonance of the dance, earthenware pots are placed under the stage.

The appeal to the ear which the play undoubtedly has for the native may be missing to the Occidental, since Japanese music is based on a different scale from ours. The orchestra sits at the back of the stage. It numbers four instruments: a flute and three drums of varying size and tone. Besides the uncouth notes of these instruments, the players themselves utter sharp cries as the action works up to an emotional climax. Eight to ten men in ceremonial costume sit on the floor at one side of the stage and form the chorus to explain the action in song or accompany the actors' words in low monotone. All the gradations of speaking and singing voice used in the play form a rhythmic pattern which has a special meaning to the Japanese audience not comprehensible to the Western visitor.

The program of plays bears a closer resemblance to that of our motion pictures than of our legitimate stage, for it is a continuous program of varying entertainment lasting for at least seven hours and sometimes running all day. The conventional order in which the plays are presented is (1) a divine play of the gods; (2) a warrior play; (3) a love play, or a "flower" play — chief character, the soul of a flower; (4) a "mad" play — chief character, usually a woman, insane from grief — or a play of manners; (5) a *kyogen*, a farce in which demons and comic human characters strive to outwit one another. This is supposed to rest the audience after the strain of the serious plays.

The following *kyogen* parodies a *Nō* play in which a coromorant fisher has been condemned to eternal punishment because of his cruelty in trapping innocent creatures. He pleads, however, that as a compensating virtue he has given lodging to a priest, and upon proof of this the fisher is forgiven and transported to Buddha's heaven. To the Japanese mind this teaches a lofty moral lesson. The parody is obvious in the following farce.

THE BIRD–CATCHER IN HELL

Anonymous KYŌGEN

PERSONS

YAMA, *King of Hell*
KIYOYORI, *the Bird-Catcher*
DEMONS
CHORUS

Yama. Yama, the King of Hell, comes forth to stand
At the Meeting of the Ways. [*Shouting*]
Yai, yai. Where are my minions?
Demons. Haa! Here we are.
Yama. If any sinners come along, set upon them and drive them off to Hell.
Demons. We tremble and obey.

Enter the bird-catcher, KIYOYORI

Kiyoyori. "All men are sinners." What have I to fear
More than the rest?

My name is Kiyoyori the Bird-Catcher.   I was very well known on
the Terrestrial Plane.   But the span of my years came to its ap-
pointed close; I was caught in the Wind of Impermanence; and
here I am, marching to the Sunless Land.
Without a pang
I leave the world where I was wont to dwell,
The Temporal World.
Whither, oh whither have my feet carried me?
To the Six Ways already I have come.
Why, here I am already at the meeting of the Six Ways of Existence.
I think on the whole I'll go to Heaven.
>   *Demon.*   Haha!   That smells like a man.   Why, sure enough here's
>   a sinner coming.   We must report him.   [*To* YAMA] Please,
>   sir, here's the first sinner arrived already!
>   *Yama.*   Then bustle him to Hell at once.
>   *Demon.*   I tremble and obey.   Listen, you sinner!

" Hell is ever at hand," which is more than
Can be said of Heaven.   [*Seizing* KIYOYORI]
Come on, now, come on!   [KIYOYORI *resists.*]
Yai, Yai!
Let me tell you, you're showing a great
Deal more spirit than most sinners do.
What was your job when you were on the
Terrestrial Plane?
>   *Kiyoyori.*   I was Kiyoyori, the famous bird-catcher.
>   *Demon.*   Bird-catcher?   That's bad.   Taking life from morning
>   to night.   That's very serious, you know.   I am afraid you will
>   have to go to Hell.
>   *Kiyoyori.*   Really, I don't consider I'm as bad as all that.   I should
>   be very much obliged if you would let me go to Heaven.
>   *Demon.*   We must ask King Yama about this.   [*To* YAMA]
Please sir — !
>   *Yama.*   Well, what is it?
>   *Demon.*   It's like this.   The sinner says that on the Terrestrial
>   Plane he was a well-known bird-catcher.   Now that means taking
>   life all the time; it's a serious matter, and he certainly ought to
>   go to Hell.   But when we told him so, he said we'd entirely mis-
>   judged him.   What had we better do about it?
>   *Yama.*   You'd better send him to me.
>   *Demon.*   Very well.   [*To* KIYOYORI] Come along, King Yama
>   says he'll see you himself.

Kiyoyori. I'm coming.

Demon. Here's that sinner you sent for.

Yama. Listen to me, you sinner. I understand that when you were in the world you spent your whole time snaring birds. You are a very bad man and must go to Hell at once.

Kiyoyori. That's all very well. But the birds I caught were sold to gentlemen to feed their falcons on; so there was really no harm in it.

Yama. " Falcon " is another kind of bird, isn't it?

Kiyoyori. Yes, that's right.

Yama. Well then, I really don't see that there was much harm in it.

Kiyoyori. I see you take my view. It was the falcons who were to blame, not I. That being so, I should be very much obliged if you would allow me to go straight to Heaven.

Yama. [*Reciting in the Nō style*] Then the Great King of Hell —
Because, though on the Hill of Death
Many birds flew, he had not tasted one,
" Come, take your pole," he cried, and here and now
Give us a demonstration of your art.
Then go in peace.

Kiyoyori. Nothing could be simpler.
I will catch a few birds and present them to you.
Then he took his pole, and crying
" To the hunt, to the hunt! . . ."

Chorus. " To the bird-hunt," he cried,
And suddenly from the steep paths of the southern side of the Hill of
Death
Many birds came flying.
Then swifter than sight his pole
Darted among them.
" I will roast them," he cried.
And when they were cooked,
" Please try one," and he offered them to the King.

Yama. [*Greedily*] Let me eat it, let me eat it. [*Eats, smacking his lips.*]
Well! I must say they taste uncommonly good!

Kiyoyori. [*To the* DEMONS] Perhaps you would like to try some?

Demons. Oh, thank you! [*They eat greedily and snatch.*] I want that bit! No, it's mine! What a flavor!

Yama. I never tasted anything so nice. You have given us such

a treat that I am going to send you back to the world to go on
bird-catching for another three years.

Kiyoyori. I am very much obliged to you, I'm sure.

Chorus. You shall catch many birds,
Pheasant, pigeon, heron and stork.
They shall not elude you, but fall
Fast into the fatal snare.
So he, reprieved, turned back towards the World;
But Yama, loth to see him go, bestowed
A jeweled crown, which Kiyoyori bore
Respectfully to the Terrestrial Plane,
There to begin his second span of life.

(Arthur Waley)

OKAKURA KAKUZO (1863–1913)

Artist, archaeologist, philosopher, teacher, and author, Okakura Kakuzo
did signal service in presenting to the Western world the ideals which have
governed Japanese art and philosophy for centuries. The span of his life
was almost the same as the period of Japan's contact with the Western
nations, for Commodore Perry had opened the door of Japan just a decade
before Okakura was born. But Western ideas had not permeated the country sufficiently during his childhood to alter the education of a boy born
into an aristocratic family of the old feudal régime. Okakura was a product of ancient Japan brought into contact through later experience and
travel with Occidental civilization. While in many respects he was a modern, eager for new ideas, he never lost certain fundamental conceptions of
life and art deeply ingrained in his nature.

In his own country he was President of the Imperial Academy of Fine
Arts of Tokio, one of the founders of the Imperial Archaeological Committee, and organizer of the Japan Art Institute, a private school in a
suburb of Tokio. In our country, where he spent a number of years during
the first decade of this century, he was connected with the Boston Museum
of Fine Arts. During this period, in 1906, he wrote *The Book of Tea*
as an explanation for his American friends of the elements of Japanese
thought which he felt to be inadequately understood in this country. So
popular did this little book of essays prove that, although it is not a
translation from the Japanese language but a composition in English, it
seems almost an essential to an American who would taste the full flavor
of Japanese literature. The following essay is taken from it.

THE TEA–ROOM

To European architects brought up on the tradition of stone and brick construction, our Japanese method of building with wood and bamboo seems scarcely worthy to be ranked as architecture. It is but quite recently that a competent student of Western architecture has recognized and paid tribute to the remarkable perfection of our great temples. Such being the case as regards our classic architecture, we could hardly expect the outsider to appreciate the subtle beauty of the tea-room, its principles of construction and decoration being entirely different from those of the West.

The tea-room (the *Sukiya*) does not pretend to be other than a mere cottage — a straw hut, as we call it. The original ideographs for Sukiya mean the Abode of Fancy. Latterly the various tea-masters substituted various Chinese characters according to their conception of the tea-room, and the term Sukiya may signify the Abode of Vacancy or the Abode of the Unsymmetrical. It is an Abode of Fancy inasmuch as it is an ephemeral structure built to house a poetic impulse. It is an Abode of Vacancy inasmuch as it is devoid of ornamentation except for what may be placed in it to satisfy some esthetic need of the moment. It is an Abode of the Unsymmetrical inasmuch as it is consecrated to the worship of the Imperfect, purposely leaving something unfinished for the play of the imagination to complete. The ideals of Teaism [1] have since the sixteenth century influenced our architecture to such degree that the ordinary Japanese interior of the present day, on account of the extreme simplicity and chasteness of its scheme of decoration, appears to foreigners almost barren. . . .

The early tea-room consisted merely of a portion of the ordinary drawing-room partitioned off by screens for the purpose of the tea-gathering. The portion partitioned off was called the Kakoi (enclosure), a name still applied to those tea-rooms which are built into a house and are not independent constructions. The Sukiya consists of the tea-room proper, designed to accommodate not more than five persons, a number suggestive of the saying " more than the Graces and less than the Muses," an anteroom (*midsuya*) where the tea utensils are washed and arranged before being brought in, a portico (*machiai*) in which the guests wait until they receive the summons to enter the tea-room, and a garden path (the *roji*) which connects

[1] Teaism: a cult founded on the adoration of the beautiful.

the machiai with the tea-room. The tea-room is unimpressive in appearance. It is smaller than the smallest of Japanese houses, while the materials used in its construction are intended to give the impression of refined poverty. Yet we must remember that all this is the result of profound artistic forethought, and the details have been worked out with care perhaps even greater than that expended on the building of the richest palaces and temples. A good tea-room is more costly than an ordinary mansion, for the selection of its materials, as well as its workmanship, requires immense care and precision. Indeed, the carpenters employed by the tea-masters form a distinct and highly honored class among the artisans, their work being no less delicate than that of the makers of lacquered cabinets. . . .

All our great tea-masters were students of Zen [2] and attempted to introduce the spirit of Zennism into the actualities of life. Thus the room, like the other equipments of the tea-ceremony, reflects many of the Zen doctrines. The size of the orthodox tea-room, which is four mats and a half, or ten feet square, is determined by a passage in the Sutra of Vikramadytia. In that interesting work, Vikramadytia welcomes the Saint Manjushiri and eighty-four thousand disciples of Buddha in a room of this size — an allegory based on the theory of the non-existence of space to the truly enlightened. Again, the roji, the garden path which leads from the machiai to the tea-room, signified the first stage of meditation — the passage into self-illumination. The roji was intended to break connection with the outside world, and to produce a fresh sensation conducive to the full enjoyment of estheticism in the tea-room itself. One who has trodden this garden path cannot fail to remember how his spirit as he walked in the twilight of evergreens over the regular irregularities of the stepping stones, beneath which lay dried pine needles, and passed beside the moss-covered granite lanterns, became uplifted above ordinary thoughts. One may be in the midst of a city, and yet feel as if he were in the forest far away from the dust and din of civilization. Great was the ingenuity of the tea-masters in producing these effects of serenity and purity. The nature of the sensations to be aroused in passing through the roji differed with different tea-masters. Some, like Rikiu, aimed at utter loneliness, and claimed the secret of making a roji was contained in the ancient ditty:

---

[2] **Zen**: a cult introduced in the twelfth century which rejected all scriptures and substituted meditation.

> " I look beyond;
> Flowers are not,
> Nor tinted leaves.
> On the sea beach
> A solitary cottage stands
> In the waning light
> Of an autumn eve."

Others, like Kobori-Enshiu sought for a different effect. Enshiu said the idea of a garden path was to be found in the following verses:

> " A cluster of summer trees,
> A bit of the sea,
> A pale evening moon."

It is not difficult to gather his meaning. He wished to create the attitude of a newly awakened soul still lingering amid shadowy dreams of the past, yet bathing in the sweet unconsciousness of a mellow spiritual light, and yearning for the freedom that lay in the expanse beyond.

Thus prepared, the guest will silently approach the sanctuary, and if a samurai,[3] will leave his sword on the rack beneath the eaves, the tea-room being pre-eminently the house of peace. Then he will bend low and creep into the room through a small door not more than three feet in height. This proceeding was incumbent on all guests — high and low alike — and was intended to inculcate humility. The order of precedence having been mutually agreed upon while resting in the machiai, the guests one by one enter noiselessly and take their seats, first making obeisance to the picture or flower arrangement on the *tokonoma*.[4] The host will not enter the room until all the guests have seated themselves and quiet reigns with nothing to break the silence save the note of the boiling water in the iron kettle. The kettle sings well, for pieces of iron are so arranged in the bottom as to produce a peculiar melody in which one may hear the echoes of a cataract muffled by clouds, of a distant sea breaking among the rocks, a rainstorm sweeping through a bamboo forest, or of the soughing of pines on some faraway hill.

Even in the daytime the light of the room is subdued, for the low eaves of the slanting roof admit but few of the sun's rays. Everything is sober in tint from the ceiling to the floor; the guests themselves have carefully chosen garments of unobtrusive colors. The

---

[3] **samurai:** member of the military caste.
[4] **tokonoma:** alcove of beauty. See page 1223.

mellowness of age is over all, everything suggestive of recent acquirement being tabooed save only the one note of contrast furnished by the bamboo dipper and the linen napkin, both immaculately white and new. However faded the tea-room and the tea-equipment may seem, everything is absolutely clean. Not a particle of dust will be found in the darkest corner, for if any exists the host is not a tea-master. One of the first requisites of a tea-master is the knowledge of how to sweep, clean, and wash, for there is an art in cleaning and dusting. A piece of antique metal work must not be attacked with the unscrupulous zeal of the Dutch housewife. Dripping water from a flower vase need not be wiped away, for it may be suggestive of dew and coolness.

In this connection there is a story of Rikiu which well illustrates the ideas of cleanliness entertained by the tea-masters. Rikiu was watching his son Shoan as he swept and watered the garden path. "Not clean enough," said Rikiu, when Shoan had finished his task, and bade him try again. After a weary hour, the son turned to Rukiu: "Father, there is nothing more to be done. The steps have been washed for the third time, the stone lanterns and the trees are well sprinkled with water, moss and lichens are shining with a fresh verdure! Not a twig, not a leaf have I left on the ground."

"Young fool," chided the tea-master, "that is not the way a garden path should be swept." Saying this, Rikiu stepped into the garden, shook a tree and scattered over the garden gold and crimson leaves, scraps of the brocade of autumn! What Rikiu demanded was not cleanliness alone, but the beautiful and the natural also.

The name, Abode of Fancy, implies a structure created to meet some individual artistic requirement. The tea-room is made for the tea-master, not the tea-master for the tea-room. It is not intended for posterity and is therefore ephemeral. The idea that every one should have a house of his own is based on an ancient custom of the Japanese race, Shinto superstition ordaining that every dwelling should be evacuated on the death of its chief occupant. Perhaps there may have been some unrealized sanitary reason for this practice. . . . In the tea-room fugitiveness is suggested in the thatched roof, frailty in the slender pillars, lightness in the bamboo support, apparent carelessness in the use of commonplace materials. The eternal is to be found only in the spirit which, embodied in these simple surroundings, beautifies them with the subtle light of its refinement.

That the tea-room should be built to suit some individual taste is an enforcement of the principle of vitality in art. Art, to be fully appreciated, must be true to contemporaneous life. It is not that we should ignore the claims of posterity, but that we should seek to enjoy the present more. It is not that we should disregard the creations of the past, but that we should try to assimilate them into our consciousness. Slavish conformity to traditions and formulas fetters the expression of individuality in architecture. We can but weep over those senseless imitations of European buildings which one beholds in modern Japan. . . .

The term, Abode of Vacancy, besides conveying the Taoist theory of the all-containing, involves the conception of a continued need of change in decorative motives. The tea-room is absolutely empty, except for what may be placed there temporarily to satisfy some esthetic mood. Some special art object is brought in for the occasion, and everything else is selected and arranged to enhance the beauty of the principal theme. One cannot listen to different pieces of music at the same time, a real comprehension of the beautiful being possible only through concentration upon some central motive. Thus it will be seen that the system of decoration in our tea-rooms is opposed to that which obtains in the West, where the interior of a house is often converted into a museum. To a Japanese accustomed to simplicity or ornamentation and frequent change of decorative method, a Western interior permanently filled with a vast array of pictures, statuary, and bric-a-brac gives the impression of mere vulgar display of riches. It calls for a mighty wealth of appreciation to enjoy the constant sight of even a masterpiece, and limitless indeed must be the capacity for artistic feeling in those who can exist day after day in the midst of such confusion of color and form as to be often seen in the homes of Europe and America.

" The Abode of the Unsymmetrical " suggests another phase of our decorative scheme. The absence of symmetry in Japanese art objects has been often commented upon by Western critics. This, also, is a result of working out through Zennism of Taoist [5] ideals. . . . True beauty could be discovered only by one who mentally completed the incomplete. The virility of life and art lay in its possibilities for growth. In the tea-room it is left for each guest in imagination to complete the total effect in relation to himself. Since Zennism has become the prevailing mode of thought, the art of the extreme Orient has purposely avoided the symmetrical in expressing not only com-

[5] **Taoist:** Taoism is a Chinese system of philosophy which points the way toward happiness and peace of mind.

pletion, but repetition. Uniformity of design was considered as fatal to the freshness of imagination. Thus landscapes, birds, and flowers became the favorite subjects for depiction rather than the human figure, the latter being present in the person of the beholder himself.

In the tea-room, the fear of repetition is a constant presence. The various objects for the decoration of a room should be so selected that no color or design shall be repeated. If you have a living flower, a painting of flowers is not allowable. If you are using a round kettle, the water pitcher should be angular. A cup with a black glaze should not be associated with a tea-caddy of black lacquer. In placing a vase on an incense burner on the *tokonoma,* care should be taken not to put it in the exact center, lest it divide the space into equal halves. The pillar of the *tokonoma* should be of a different kind of wood from the other pillars, in order to break any suggestion of monotony in the room.

Here again the Japanese method of interior decoration differs from that of the Occident, where we see objects arranged symmetrically on mantelpieces and elsewhere. In Western houses we are often confronted with what appears to us useless reiteration. We find it trying to talk to a man while his full length portrait stares at us from behind his back. We wonder which is real, he of the picture or he who talks, and feel a curious conviction that one of them must be a fraud. Many a time have we sat at a festive board contemplating, with a secret shock to our digestion, the representation of abundance on the dining-room walls. Why these pictured victims of chase and sport, the elaborate carvings of fishes and fruit? Why the display of family plates, reminding us of those who have dined and are dead?

The simplicity of the tea-room and its freedom from vulgarity make it truly a sanctuary from the vexations of the outer world. There and there alone can one consecrate himself to undisturbed adoration of the beautiful. In the sixteenth century the tea-room afforded a welcome respite from labor to the fierce warriors and statesmen engaged in the unification and reconstruction of Japan. In the seventeenth century, after the strict formalism of the To-kugawa rule had been developed, it offered the only opportunity possible for the free communion of artistic spirits. Before a great work of art there was no distinction between daimyo,[6] samurai, and commoner. Nowadays industrialism is making true refinement more and more difficult all the world over. Do we not need the tea-room more than ever?

---

[6] **daimyo:** one of the chief nobles.

SUGGESTIONS FOR STUDY

1. What new understanding of Japanese thought has the author brought you? What does this philosophy have in common with Christianity? In what ways does it differ from social practice and religious worship in this country? In what ways are you reminded of some of the ideas of Emerson and Thoreau?

2. Discuss the author's comment on American interior decoration. Find some pictures of typical American homes about 1906 when this was written and decide whether we are nearer the Japanese ideal of simplicity or farther from it than we were then. Are American tea-rooms in any way comparable to Japanese tea-rooms?

3. Discuss the tea-master's lesson to his son on the art of cleaning. What principles does this open up concerning the relation between beauty and neatness? Find in the Chinese section a poem which is another illustration of the tea-master's lesson.

4. Discuss the author's query in his last line: Do we need the tea-room?

READING LIST

Translations from Japanese Literature

Lotus and Chrysanthemum, ed. by J. L. French

Japanese Lyrics, trans. by Lafcadio Hearn

An Anthology of Haiku, ed. by Asataro Miyamori (gives parallel translations)

Hokkus, trans. by Yone Noguchi

Little Poems from the Japanese, trans. by Lawrence Binyon

Moons of Nippon, trans. by Edna W. Underwood

Japanese Poetry, trans. by Arthur Waley

The Master Singers of Japan, trans. by Clara Walsh

Sword and Blossom Poems from the Japanese, trans. by S. Kimura and Charlotte Peake

Fifteen Poets of Modern Japan, trans. by Glenn Hughes and Yozan Iwasaki

Miyamori, Asataro: *Tales of the Samurai*

Murasaki, Lady: *The Tale of Genji*, trans. by Arthur Waley (6 vols.)

The Nō Plays of Japan, trans. by Arthur Waley

Nogaku, Japanese Drama, trans. by Beatrice L. Suzuki

Written in English by Japanese Authors

Kakuzo, Okakura: *The Book of Tea*

Sugimoto, Etsu: *A Daughter of the Samurai*

Sugimoto, Chiyono: *Picture Tales from the Japanese*

Noguchi, Yone: *The Story of Yone Noguchi*

The Spirit of Japanese Poetry

* Books marked with an asterisk are recommended for purchase for the library on a limited budget.

Tsurumi, Yusuke: *Present–Day Japan*

About Japan

Bryan, J. I.: *The Literature of Japan*

Aston, W. G.: *A History of Japanese Literature*

Page, C. H.: *Japanese Poetry*

Chamberlain, B. H.: *Japanese Poetry*

Carpenter, Frank: *Japan and Korea*

Hearn, Lafcadio: *Kokoro*
 Out of the East

Wildes, H. E.: *Japan in Crisis*

Blacker, J. F.: *The A B C of Japanese Art*

Hartmann, Sadakichi: *Japanese Art*

Bowei, H. P.: *On the Laws of Japanese Painting* (for correlation with poetry)

GENERAL ORIENTAL LITERATURE

Translations

Columbia University Course in Literature, Vol. I, *Wisdom of the East*

The Garden of Bright Waters, trans. by E. Powys Mathers

*Poetry of the Orient, ed. by Eunice Tietjens

Colored Stars, trans. by E. Powys Mathers

History of General Oriental Literature

*Holliday, Carl: *The Dawn of Literature*

GENERAL WORLD LITERATURE

Translations

Cunliffe, J. W. and Showerman, G.: *Century Readings in Ancient Classical and Modern European Literature*

Copeland, C. T.: *The Copeland Translations*

*Houston, P. H. and Smith, R. M.: *Types of World Literature*

*Van Doren, M.: *An Anthology of World Poetry*

*Van Doren, C.: *An Anthology of World Prose*

Longfellow, H. W.: *Poets and Poetry of Europe*

Clark, B. H.: *World Drama*

Bercovici, K.: *Best Short Stories of the World*

*Clark, B. H. and Lieber, M.: *Great Short Stories of the World*

*Lee, F. H.: *Folk Tales of All Nations*

*Borrow, G. H.: *Ballads of All Nations*

Jones, L. and Gaul, C. C.: *131 Best Stories*

Columbia University Course in Literature

World's Best Literature

World's Great Classics

*Guerber, H. A.: *The Book of the Epic*

History and Criticism

*Richardson, W. L. and Owen, J. M.: *Literature of the World*

*Gunn, S.: *The Story of Literature*

Rose, W. and Isaacs, J.: *Contemporary Movements in European Literature*

* Books marked with an asterisk are recommended for purchase for the library on a limited budget.

Recent European and Latin American Poetry

HARRY MARTINSON (1904–   )

Harry Martinson, poet, novelist, and author of travel sketches, is one of the most original and powerful of modern Swedish writers. His principal works are two autobiographical novels, *Flowering Nettles* and *The Way Out;* two sketches of travel impressions based on his six years at sea, *Aimless Journeys* and *Cape Farewell;* and two semi-philosophical nature studies, *Dreams and Daddy Long Legs* and *Midsummer Valley.*

VISUAL MEMORY

Thin birches stood on Stockholm's nesses,
I saw them nod one spring —
With brittle lines swaying in the water
Broken, rocking zigzag — white, water
Like optic water-lilies.   5
And white gulls in keeping with it all,
And white terns —
When — plop — our black barge came in
So useful
With chug-chug and belly-cough and sixteen barrels of oil.   10

And the rainbow shimmer of the oozing oil
— A spectrum saga —
Began to fight with the swaying white rods of the optic lilies.

1. **nesses:** promontories; overhanging cliffs.   7. **terns:** sea birds.

They fought, they fought like China's exotic dragons!
They fought and they wearied the eye   15
Till evening came with wind and billows —
And the woman of love tarried forever.

(*Erik Wahlgren and Martin S. Allwood*)

ILYA EHRENBURG (1891–   )

Ehrenburg's life has been closely related to the development of Communism in Russia. He spent time in political prisons, wandered in exile over Europe, suffered poverty to an unbelievable extent; but despite all the threats to his survival, he managed to exist and to become a writer popular in Russia and approved by the state officials. His main ability lies in the area of reporting, but he has done much to acquaint Soviet Russia with the merit of foreign writers whom he has translated. His travels have been worldwide. Novelist, poet, journalist, and short-story writer, he is enormously gifted. His best-known novels include *The Love of Jeanne Ney, The Racketeer, A Street in Moscow*, and *Out of Chaos*, which is considered to be his best. He has also written for the films.

THE TREE

The meek dew shone, the grass lay prostrate
As humbly as a slave will lie,
And veering from the roof the swallow
Had sought the wide and tender sky.

And you alone, great tree, remaining   5
There at your post, stood straight and still,
Lonely and stubborn as a soldier
Whose duty was to hold the hill.

And under fire you tossed and twisted,
As through your boughs the torment ran,   10
And when you met your mortal moment
You died as gravely as a man.

(*Babette Deutsch*)

"The Tree" by Ilya Ehrenburg. Reprinted from *A Treasure of Russian Verse* by Avrahm Yarmolinsky. Copyright, 1949, by The Macmillan Company and reprinted with their permission.

GABRIELA MISTRAL (1889–1957)

This Chilean poet is noted for her sensitivity to the problems facing women in the home and in the school. She is gentle in her understanding of children. Her poetry has a simplicity that underscores the feeling expressed. Most of her adult life was spent in Mexico and the United States.

NIGHT

Sleep, my child; because of you
The western skies their light efface;
There is no glitter save the dew,
Nor any whiteness, save my face.

My little son, because you dream,   5
The road lies hushed, in peace unfurled,
Nothing murmurs save the stream;
I am alone in a sleeping world.

A slow mist drowns the silent land,
A blue sigh fades in darkening skies;   10
Like a gentle, soothing hand
Upon the earth a quiet lies.

Not my child alone I've sung,
Cradling him, to easy sleep;
The earth too, as my cradle swung,   15
Drifted into slumber deep.

(*Alice Jane McVan*)

2. **efface:** obliterate; wipe out.

SUGGESTIONS FOR STUDY

VISUAL MEMORY
1. Explain the phrases " optic water-lilies " and " spectrum saga."
2. Everything moves and changes in the poem. The last line seems out of keeping with the rest of the poem, but as all moves and loses identity, the woman in the memory of the speaker still seems to be standing there. What other contrasts are there in the poem?

THE TREE

   1. What kinds of things may have destroyed the tree?
   2. What is the significance of the swallow's leaving?

NIGHT

   1. Describe the mother's mood as she rocks the cradle of her sleeping child.

   2. Explain the meaning, in the last stanza, of the phrase, " Not my child alone I've sung. . . ."

Recent European Prose

ALBERT SCHWEITZER (1875–)

Schweitzer has won the acclaim of the world for his life of dedicated service to the suffering natives of Africa and for his deliberate choice of the kind of career that most men with his varied talents would reject as being too hard. Theologian, musicologist, missionary, professor, philosopher, surgeon, and writer, Schweitzer might have devoted his life to any one of these varied professions. Instead he selected the life of the missionary-doctor.

At the age of thirty Schweitzer gave up a successful professorship and began a study of medicine that required six years for completion. Then, at Lambaréné in French Equatorial Africa, he set up a hospital for the natives and carried on research into the causes and cures of leprosy and sleeping sickness. At Lambaréné he found the peace and happiness of the inner life. During the first World War he was interned by the French as a German national. While living in a series of prison camps, he wrote *Paul and His Interpreters* and *The Mysticism of Paul the Apostle.* His principal works are *J. S. Bach: Musician and Poet, The Quest of the Historical Jesus,* and *Out of My Life and Thought.*

It is Schweitzer's hope that men will rise above the differences of race and nationality and work together for the best that mankind is capable of achieving. The one great need in the civilized world, he believes, is " reverence for life." His ideas are set forth in his philosophical writings, *The Decay and Restoration of Civilization* and *Civilization and Ethics.* For his continuous efforts to persuade people around the world to learn to understand each other, he was awarded the Nobel Peace Prize in 1952.

The excerpts that follow, taken from his autobiography, reveal the momentous decision that determined the whole course of his future life. He describes his friends' negative reaction to his announced intention to forsake Europe and go to Africa. He could not believe that they could have faith in the philosophy of the Bible and yet be aghast at his decision to put into practice the New Testament teaching that men should help their less fortunate fellow men.

DEDICATION

THE RIGHT TO HAPPINESS

The thought that I had been granted such a specially happy youth was ever in my mind; I felt it even as something oppressive, and ever more clearly there presented itself to me the question whether this happiness was a thing that I might accept as a matter of course. Here, then, was the second great experience of my life, viz., this question about the right to happiness. As an experience it joined itself to that other one which had accompanied me from my childhood up; I mean my deep sympathy with the pain which prevails in the world around us. These two experiences slowly melted into one another, and thence came definiteness to my interpretation of life as a whole, and a decision as to the future of my own life in particular.

It became steadily clearer to me that I had not the inward right to take as a matter of course my happy youth, my good health, and my power of work. Out of the depths of my feeling of happiness there grew up gradually within me an understanding of the saying of Jesus that we must not treat our lives as being for ourselves alone. Whoever is spared personal pain must feel himself called to help in diminishing the pain of others. We must all carry our share of the misery which lies upon the world. Darkly and confusedly this thought worked in me, and sometimes it left me, so that I breathed freely and fancied once more that I was to become completely the lord of my own life. But the little cloud had risen above the horizon. I could, indeed, sometimes look away and lose sight of it, but it was growing nevertheless; slowly but unceasingly it grew, and at last it hid the whole sky.

" WHOSOEVER SHALL LOSE HIS LIFE "

The plan which I meant now to put into execution had been in my mind for a long time, having been conceived so long ago as my student days. It struck me as incomprehensible that I should be allowed to lead such a happy life, while I saw so many people around me wrestling with care and suffering. Even at school I had felt stirred whenever I got a glimpse of the miserable home surroundings of some of my schoolfellows and compared them with the absolutely ideal conditions in which we children [1] of the parsonage of Günsbach lived. While at the University [2] and enjoying the happiness of being able to study and even to produce some results in science and art, I could not help thinking continually of others who were denied that happiness by their material circumstances or their health. Then one brilliant summer morning at Günsbach, during the Whitsuntide [3] holidays — it was in 1896 — there came to me, as I awoke, the thought that I must not accept this happiness as a matter of course, but must give something in return for it. Proceeding to think the matter out at once with calm deliberation, while the birds were singing outside, I settled with myself before I got up that I would consider myself justified in living till I was thirty for science and art, in order to devote myself from that time forward to the direct service of humanity. Many a time already had I tried to settle what meaning lay hidden for me in the saying of Jesus, " Whosoever would save his life shall lose it, and whosoever shall lose his life for My sake and the Gospel's shall save it." Now the answer was found. In addition to the outward, I now had inward happiness.

DEEDS INSTEAD OF WORDS

I wanted to be a doctor that I might be able to work without having to talk. For years I had been giving myself out in words, and it was with joy that I had followed the calling of theological [4] teacher and of preacher. But this new form of activity I could not represent to myself as talking about the religion of love, but only as an actual putting it into practice. Medical knowledge made it pos-

---

[1] **we children:** Schweitzer and his brothers and sisters; their father was the parson in the village of Günsbach.

[2] **the University:** Strasbourg University in Alsace where Schweitzer was both an undergraduate and a graduate student and later a professor.

[3] **Whitsuntide:** the week beginning on Whitsunday, the seventh Sunday after Easter. This is a regular holiday in most European schools and universities.

[4] **theological:** refers to *theology,* the study of the history and nature of religious doctrines.

sible for me to carry out my intention in the best and most complete way, wherever the path of service might lead me. In view of the plan for Equatorial Africa,[5] the acquisition of such knowledge was especially indicated, because in the district to which I thought of going, a doctor was, according to the missionaries' reports, the most needed of all needed things. They were always complaining in their magazine that the natives who visited them in physical suffering could not be given the help they desired. To become one day the doctor whom these poor creatures needed, it was worth while, so I judged, to become a medical student. Whenever.I was inclined to feel that the years I should have to sacrifice were too long, I reminded myself that Hamilcar and Hannibal [6] had prepared for their march on Rome by their slow and tedious conquest of Spain.

[5] One evening in 1904 Schweitzer happened to read a magazine issued by the Paris Missionary Society in which a call was made for missionary-doctors to aid the mission's work among the natives of Gabun, one of the four French colonies of French Equatorial Africa, bordering on the Atlantic. Schweitzer's decision to train himself for this work is the " plan " he refers to.

[6] **Hamilcar and Hannibal:** the famed generals of Carthage in North Africa, who spent years achieving their goal — the invasion of Italy.

SUGGESTIONS FOR STUDY

1. Why did Schweitzer deliberately decide against what most men would call a " happy life? "

2. What plan did he make for dividing his life into areas for work till thirty? after thirty?

3. What is the meaning of the quotation " Whosoever would save his life shall lose it " in terms of Schweitzer's decision?

JEAN GIRAUDOUX (1882–1944)

Jean Giraudoux, the greatest French dramatist of the 1930's, wrote his plays in poetical prose. Of his dramas, those produced and published in this country are *The Madwoman of Chaillot*, *The Enchanted*, *Ondine*, and Christopher Fry's adaptation of *Tiger at the Gates*.

In *The Enchanted* a ghost brings justice of an unusual sort to a small town. Petty officialdom, confused by the turn in events, is represented by the mayor; the inspector, who has come to prove the nonexistence of any ghost in *his* territory; and the supervisor of the town, who realizes that normalcy has departed from the village way of life.

Inspector. I must tell you in all seriousness, the Administration considers your report utterly ludicrous. Spirits don't exist. Consequently they don't haunt towns. Not in my district.

Mayor. They haunt this town.

Inspector. Let's not be childish, Mr. Mayor. We know what ghosts are. Ghosts are a mysterious clashing of pots and pans at midnight in an apartment where they want to get the tenants out in order to raise the rent. Ghosts are a walking bedsheet that frightens away the night watchman just before a burglary.

Supervisor. Not in this town, Inspector.

Inspector. No? And just how are you haunted in this town?

Supervisor. We are haunted by an occult [1] presence which is clearly bent on sapping the foundation of civilized society. I may add, incidentally, that I find myself in complete sympathy with its aims. . . .

Inspector. Really! And by what means is this power sapping the foundation of civilized society?

Supervisor. We don't know the means. But we know the result. Take, for example, the behavior of animals. Formerly, when a man beat a dog, the dog would cringe and lick his hand. Now he bites it. It's the same with the children.

Inspector. They bite their parents?

Supervisor. When children are mistreated, instead of crying and begging pardon, they simply leave the house and refuse to return. As for the women . . . !

Inspector. They've stopped chattering?

Supervisor. Within the last month, our most desperate domestic problems have suddenly been solved — in the simplest imaginable way. The women have quietly left their husbands and gone off with attractive men.

Mayor. I will add a few details. In the civic lottery, last Sunday, for the first time in history, the big cash prize went to the neediest couple in town, and not as always to Monsieur Dumas, the millionaire. The motorcycle was won by the young captain of the football team, and not as usual by the Mother Superior of the convent. On Wednesday, two people were run over by a motor truck.

[1] **occult:** mysterious or obscure.

Not, as you might expect, the youngest and healthiest of our citizens, but the oldest and most decrepit — who happened to be also the stingiest and most venomous. You see what is happening? For the first time in the memory of man, fortune is displaying some intelligence, and chance seems to know what it is about.

Inspector. What you are describing, my friend, is the nullification [2] of human liberty.

Doctor. While you're on the subject, Mr. Mayor, you might say a word about the census returns.

Mayor. I must confess I haven't had the courage to send in the forms, Inspector.

Inspector. Your constituents have been telling lies, have they?

Mayor. Quite the contrary. They have been telling the truth in so outrageous a manner that it amounts to indecency. Under section two, for instance, instead of giving the names of their children, many of them insist on putting down the names of cats, dogs, birds, and even rubber plants — the things they really love and consider part of themselves.

Inspector. They're mad.

Mayor. Under "name of spouse," they put down the names of movie stars, heroines of romance, and even occasionally the name of an automobile or boat.

Inspector. And how long have these scandals been going on?

Mayor. Since the ghost appeared.

[At the end of the play, the ghost is trapped by the officials and shot. The teacher who has fallen in love with the ghost is thus freed from her " delusion," and she turns to a flesh-and-blood reality for her lover. The moral seems to be that men of small importance resent and will fight any change that threatens the security of their comfortable lives.]

---

2 **nullification:** destruction or annihilation.

SUGGESTIONS FOR STUDY

1. What examples of irony are present in this scene? With what aspects of modern life is Giraudoux concerned?

2. One of the author's themes in *The Enchanted* is the petty injustices in contemporary life. How does he believe the problems of basic dishonesty and moral unconcern should be resolved?

3. What elements of humor appear in this scene?

4. Giraudoux writes often of a modern, imaginary utopia as it would exist in his own country. Usually a utopia (a place of ideal perfection)

is created to point out the weaknesses in society. To illustrate this point, compare his utopia with that of Sir Thomas More or George Orwell.

JUAN RAMÓN JIMÉNEZ (1881–   )

The poet Jiménez was born in the town of Moquer in Andalusian Spain. After attending the University of Seville, he moved to Madrid, where he came under the influence of the literary movement led by Rubén Darío. His travels in France led to an interest in French literature. He also lived in Switzerland, in New York, and, after the Spanish Civil War began in 1936, in Puerto Rico. In 1956 he won the Nobel prize for literature. Because so much of his writing is based on personal observation, his poetry is personal and impressionistic.

In Spain one of Jiménez' most popular books has been *Platero and I*, an anecdotal and imaginative series of conversations between the author and his donkey. They are unusual in that they are actually poems presented in prose form.

FROM PLATERO AND I

PLATERO

Platero is a small donkey, a soft, hairy donkey; so soft to the touch that he might be said to be made of cotton, with no bones. Only the jet mirrors of his eyes are hard like two black crystal scarabs.[1]

I turn him loose, and he goes to the meadow, and, with his nose, he gently caresses the little flowers of rose and blue and gold. . . . I call him softly, " Platero? " and he comes to me at a gay little trot that is like laughter of a vague, idyllic [2] tinkling sound.

He eats whatever I give him. He likes mandarin oranges,[3] amber-hued muscatel grapes, purple figs tipped with crystalline drops of honey.

He is as loving and tender as a child, but strong and sturdy as a rock. When on Sundays, I ride him through the lanes in the outskirts of the town, slow-moving countrymen, dressed in their Sunday clean, watch him a while, speculatively.

" He is like steel," they say.

Steel, yes. Steel and moon silver at the same time.

---

[1] **scarabs:** beetles.
[2] **idyllic:** pleasant.
[3] **mandarin oranges:** tangerines.

" Platero," " The Cart," " Peep Show," " Fireworks," from *Platero and I* by Juan Ramón Jiménez, translated by Eloise Roach. Reprinted with permission of the publishers, the University of Texas Press.

THE CART

In the big creek, which the rains had swollen as far as the vine-yard, we found an old cart stuck in the mud, lost to view under its load of grass and oranges. A ragged, dirty little girl was weeping over one wheel, trying to help the donkey, who was, alas, smaller and frailer than Platero. And the little donkey was spending him-self against the wind, trying vainly at the sobbing cry of the child to pull the cart out of the mire. His efforts were futile, like the efforts of brave children, like the breath of those tired summer breezes which fall fainting among the flowers.

I patted Platero, and as well as I could, I hitched him to the cart in front of the wretched little donkey. I encouraged him then with an affectionate command, and Platero, at one tug, pulled cart and beast out of the mud and up the bank.

How the little girl smiled! It was as if the evening sun, setting among the yellow-crystal rainclouds, had kindled a dawn of joy be-hind her dirty tears.

With tearful gladness, she offered me two choice oranges, perfect, heavy, round. I took them gratefully, and I gave one to the weak little donkey, to comfort him; the other to Platero as a golden reward.

PEEP SHOW

Suddenly, monotonously, the silence of the street is broken by the harsh rolling of a little drum. Then a cracked voice spasmodically [4] sends forth a long, trembling cry. The sound of running feet is heard down the street. Children cry:

"The peep show man! The peep-show man!"

In the corner a small green box with four little red flags waits in-vitingly on its stand. The old man beats and beats his drum. A group of penniless children, hands in pockets or clasped behind, silently surround the little box. Presently another one arrives run-ning, his penny clutched tightly in the palm of his hand. He steps forward, looks eagerly into the disc.

"Now . . . General Prim . . . on his white horse! . . ." says the old peep-show man wearily, and he beats his drum.

"The port of Barcelona! . . ." And more rolling.

Other children arrive with pennies ready and hand them at once

---

[4] **spasmodically:** intermittently.

to the old fellow, regarding him with rapt attention, impatient to buy his make-believe.

" Now . . . the castle of Havana! . . ." And the drum rolls. Platero, who has gone with a neighbor's little girl and her dog to see the show, puts his head playfully between the children's heads. The old man, with sudden good humor, says to him: " Where is your penny? "

And the empty-handed children laugh cheerlessly, looking at the peep-show man with humble, flattering solicitude.[5]

FIREWORKS

On September watch nights we would go to the hill behind the orchard house to enjoy, from the fragrant peacefulness that the pond lilies distilled there, the noise of the festive town. Pioza, the old vineyard watchman, drunk on the threshing floor, played his cornet hour after hour, face to the moon.

Quite late the fireworks came. First there were dull, short explosions; then single skyrockets, which, high above, opened with a sigh and were like a starry eye that might, for a moment, see the countryside in red, purple, blue; and there were others whose splendor fell like a naked maiden bowing low, like a blood-red willow dripping flowers of light. Oh, what flaming peacocks, what aerial masses of clear roses, what fiery pheasants in gardens of stars.

Platero, at each explosion, would shudder, all blue, purple, red, in the sudden illumination of space; and in the wavering brightness that enlarged and shortened his shadow on the hilltop, I could see his big black eyes looking at me in fright.

When, as a climax, the revolving golden castle wreath — the one that bursts in a deep thunderclap, at which women close their eyes and stop their ears — rose to the constellated sky amid the distant clamor of the town, Platero, braying in a crazed manner, would run among the vine stumps toward the tranquil pines in shadow, like a soul pursued by the devil.

[5] **solicitude:** concern.

SUGGESTIONS FOR STUDY

1. What unusual comparisons or similes does the author use to provide imagery?

2. How are colors used for contrast? Note the author's careful use of colors and sounds to heighten the effect of his little scenes of life in Spain.

3. In " Peep Show " why does the author describe the peep-show man as talking " wearily " and the children laughing " cheerlessly "? Why do the children look at the man with " solicitude "? What sort of comfort do they receive from the fact that the peep-show man asks Platero, the donkey, for a penny?

4. As a writing exercise, describe in terms of colors or sounds a scene that is familiar to you — a scene at a state fair or a circus, in a city street, at a highway accident, from your bedroom window, or in a local hangout.

GIOVANNI GUARESCHI (1908–)

Guareschi has established a reputation for viewing the Communist position in Italy with humor and detachment. During World War II he was imprisoned for his outspoken attacks upon the government. In his humorous magazine, *Candido,* he often voices his views obliquely. His literary fame rests on his characterization of the priest Don Camillo, a whimsical fellow who fights a constant battle with the Communist mayor of his town.

THE NEW LOOK

When the official news came through, along with the first directives, Peppone was staggered. In the good old days he had fought like a lion to have one of the village streets called after Joseph Stalin and had even given his name to the consumers' cooperative. As if this were not enough, the great hall of this emporium [1] and meeting place was decorated with a bigger-than-life-size portrait of the great man.

Such was Peppone's discomfiture,[2] that when he had called his henchmen together he found himself for the first time with nothing to say. All he did was toss the sheet of paper containing the directives onto the table and throw out his arms in a helpless and disconsolate manner. Then Smilzo summed up the situation.

" What fault have we, chief, if we believed what the higher-ups told us? Anyhow, it's all perfectly simple. We take down the street sign, change the cooperative's name and splash a bucket of whitewash over the wall. Stalinism has gone down the drain."

They had met in the cooperative, and on the wall in front of them

[1] **emporium:** store.
[2] **discomfiture:** frustration.

was the gigantic portrait of the mustachioed, posthumously [3] purged leader. Peppone looked at it very sadly. He himself had insisted that it be a fresco because, as he had declared at the unveiling, " It must endure as long as the glory of the father of all peoples, that is, forever and ever."

Don Camillo's voice suddenly boomed forth in their midst. " Good evening," he said heartily, and went to sit down. " Is there some celebration? " he asked.

" When a visitor sees that he's not wanted," put in Peppone, " the least he can do is go away without stopping to argue."

" Certainly," said Don Camillo. " But when a visitor is taking advantage of his last chance to admire a masterpiece of art which is about to be destroyed, then wanted or not wanted, it's his duty to remain."

He scrutinized the painting on the wall and then added, " Because it's a fresco, you'll have to scrape and replaster the wall. Twelve yards of plastering is no joke. Oh, well, politics is politics. I don't run the same risk, thank heaven. My Leader's held His own for nearly two thousand years."

Peppone jumped to his feet. " Father," he said, " if you want to pick a fight, you've come to the right place."

Don Camillo shook his head. " Never again, Mr. Mayor, never again! We've fought quite enough over that fellow with the bushy mustache. I came simply to indulge in the legitimate satisfaction of seeing you destroy the image of your former god."

Peppone brought his fist down on the table and shouted, " You shan't have that satisfaction. As long as I live, that face won't be touched."

" Then you're disobeying the higher-ups. You're running afoul of Party discipline."

" No, I'm not," shouted Peppone. " The Party doesn't order me to give satisfaction to a rascally priest or other such garbage."

Peppone got into real hot water because the reactionary papers took up the story and carried pieces about " deviations," [4] " Stalinist factions," and " possible splits." Very soon a trouble shooter was sent from national headquarters. He addressed the henchmen as follows: " The only answer is to go ahead and get rid of the painting and the street sign and the name on the façade of the building, as originally intended."

---

[3] **posthumously:** after the death of (here, of Stalin).

[4] **deviations:** policies that indicate a departure from Party doctrines.

" My personal prestige is at stake," Peppone told him. " We're not getting rid of anything. I won't hear of giving that miserable priest such satisfaction."

" Very well, then," the trouble shooter concluded, " I'll make a report on your objections." He did exactly this. As a result Peppone received an ultimatum.

Peppone went to the rectory and threw the letter in front of Don Camillo. Don Camillo read it over and then came out with the single word, " Garibaldi." [5]

" Garibaldi? " muttered Peppone suspiciously. " Where does he come in? "

" Because he has the same first name as Stalin, and you can leave the first half of the inscription on the façade of the cooperative the way it is. As for the painting, you don't need to deface it. You can just pierce a hole and put in a glass door connecting the great hall with the bowling alley. As for the street sign, never mind about that. One day it will fall, all by itself."

Peppone pounded his fist on the table. " I said I wasn't going to give you any satisfaction."

" I don't want any. I'd rather have a live Peppone than a dead Stalin. It's better to thumb a nose at Stalin than at you. Just think it over and see if you don't agree."

Peppone thought for a moment, and then said, " From my point of view, you're quite right."

" From mine too. Lambrusco wine or Fontanella? "

" Lambrusco," said Peppone without hesitation.

It was a fine bottle and so were the two that followed. At a certain point Peppone raised his glass and shouted, " Hurrah for Garibaldi! "

"' Hurrah! " said Don Camillo, clinking his glass against the other.

[5] **Garibaldi**: Giuseppe Garibaldi (1807–1882), Italian patriot.

SUGGESTIONS FOR STUDY

1. How is the friendship of the priest Don Camillo and the Communist mayor Peppone sustained even though the two men represent two opposing ways of life?

2. What clues to the personalities of the two men are given in this chapter?

3. Why does Don Camillo work out a solution for the mayor?

4. What literary means does Guareschi use to get his point of political satire across to his readers?

5. For more amusing tales of these two men, read *The Little World of Don Camillo, Don Camillo and His Flock,* or *Don Camillo's Dilemma.* In these books Guareschi portrays Italian life in the confused and difficult years following World War II. Why were postwar conditions in Italy conducive to the inroads of Communism?

MIKHAIL ZOSHCHENKO (1895–   )

Because his anecdotal stories often bared the underlying confusion and general discomfort of the Russian man of the street, who was trying so hard to understand the superior Russian efficiency, Zoshchenko was purged in 1946 for his outspoken views. His whereabouts at the present time are unknown. His stories are snapshots of life taken at close range. Although he occasionally tried to write seriously, he soon found that his popularity rested upon his humorous tales, told lightly and with pointed satire and subtle irony. His criticism, veiled in ridicule, won him praise from readers but eventually forced him into silence. His style is colloquial, natural, and extremely condensed. He writes of the life he saw about him, a life he knew well, for he had had many jobs and had traveled broadly in his native land. His short-story collections are entitled *Russia Laughs, The Woman Who Could Not Read,* and *The Wonderful Dog.*

A SLIGHT MISTAKE

"What day is it today?" asked Gregory Ivanovich. "Wednesday, it seems. . . . Of course. Wednesday. It happened on Monday. On Monday the workers in our factory nearly died of laughing. It was too funny for words. A little error had occurred.

"Of course you know the people in our factory are all literate. Wake anyone up in the middle of the night and ask him to sign his name. He'll do it. That is because the Troika [1] sent to our factory was a very strenuous one. In three months they liquidated [2] all illiteracy. Of course there were some quite incapable fellows who would always mix up their names. Youseff, for instance, never got it straight. He would write the S in the wrong place, put the flourish on too early, or forget the letter Y. But the others got on all right. Now, remembering this, imagine what happened!

"It was only by chance that Yeremei Mironovich noticed the slip. Saturday, say, is pay day. And on Monday the cashier checks up

---

[1] **Troika** (troi'kå): here, a committee of three.

[2] **liquidated:** The Russians use *liquidate* to mean to correct, to abolish, and even to execute (a person).

"A Slight Mistake" from *Russia Laughs* by Mikhail Zoshchenko. Reprinted by permission of Lothrop, Lee & Shepard Co., Inc.

the pay cards to see whether the accounts are correct. There he is, clicking on the abacus,[3] and all of a sudden he spots a cross on the pay roll. All around, signatures; but in one field a cross. 'Why a cross?' thinks the cashier. Why this cross, when all illiteracy has been fundamentally liquidated and everybody knows how to sign his name?

"The cashier looks and sees that the cross is placed against the name of Hlebnikoff. He says to the bookkeeper, 'Just look, there's a cross!' The bookkeeper to the secretary; the secretary passes it on. Soon it is all around the workroom. What was the Troika about, if in all that time they couldn't liquidate illiteracy? The chairman runs to the cashier and asks for the pay roll. The Troika stands around with a sheepish grin on its three faces. They all look and see the cross against Hlebnikoff's name.

"'Who is this Hlebnikoff?' they all ask. 'Why is this Hlebnikoff not liquidated? Why is everybody else enlightened and literate and only Hlebnikoff perishing in abysmal darkness? How can this be possible? What was the Troika doing, and what organ did it use for its thinking?'

"The Troika stands and shrugs its shoulders. They call for Hlebnikoff. He is a skilled wood turner. He comes very reluctantly. They ask him, 'Are you literate?'

"'Literate,' he replies.

"'Can you sign your name?'

"'Of course I can. Three months they spent liquidating me.'

"The chairman spreads out his arms. The Troika shrugs shoulders. The cashier produces the pay roll. They hand it to Hlebnikoff and ask, 'Who signed this cross?'

"Hlebnikoff looks and looks. 'The handwriting,' he says, 'is mine. I wrote this cross, I was dead drunk. Couldn't sign my name.'

"Shouts of laughter. Every one congratulates the Troika. It is absolved of every doubt. They shake hands with Hlebnikoff. 'This,' they say, 'is a mountain lifted from our shoulders. Why, we almost thought that you, Hlebnikoff, even now, like a blind man, were still lost in abysmal darkness.'

"For the next half month's pay Hlebnikoff, for all his literacy, signed once more with a cross. Drunk again! But nobody was astonished now. They had become used to it. They knew he was a literate man."

---

[3] **abacus:** an ancient device, consisting of strings and beads, for calculating sums.

SUGGESTIONS FOR STUDY

1. What phases of Russian bureaucracy are satirized in this story?
2. How does the author succeed in making his point through humor whereas a serious treatment of the same situation might well fail?
3. Select the lines that illustrate Zoshchenko's use of irony and satire.
4. Can you recall, from your own experience, examples of overzealous officials defeating their own aims?

Recent Oriental Poetry

Oriental verse since World War II has shown the influence of both European and American writers. New experiments have been carried out in form, style, and the use of words. The innate ability of Chinese and Japanese writers to express much feeling in words has, however, not changed. The postwar problems of Japan under occupation and of China under Communist domination have played a major role in the shaping of the subject matter of contemporary poetry. Modern Oriental poets, finally beginning to escape from the confinement of propaganda writing, are casting about for an expression of their own personal feelings as poets and human beings — feelings divorced from the political consequences of the times.

KAHLIL GIBRAN (1883–1931)

Gibran has been labeled " the Blake of the twentieth century," because like the English artist and poet William Blake, he excelled in the arts of poetry and painting. Born in Lebanon, Gibran lived for a time in Paris, studying Rodin's technique in sculpture, and then moved to the United States, where he remained for the last twenty years of his life. Although he could speak many languages, Gibran chose to write in English. *The Prophet,* which appeared in 1923, is his most popular work. In this long poem Gibran states his philosophy of life: a glorious enjoyment of the good things in life, a high moral regard for his fellow men, and an awareness of the importance of the least of things in existence. This poem represents the last conversations between a prophet and his disciples. The disciples ask about the meaning of the various phases of life; the poem is the prophet's answer.

Other writings by Gibran include *The Garden of the Prophet, The Death of the Prophet, Jesus, the Son of Man, Secrets of the Heart,* and *Tears and Laughter.* In all of his poems, Gibran attempts to explain man's relationship to God, to other men, and to himself.

FROM THE PROPHET

ABOUT WORK

You work that you may keep pace with
the earth and the soul of the earth.

For to be idle is to become a stranger
unto the seasons, and to step out of life's
procession, that marches in majesty and   5
proud submission toward the infinite.

When you work you are a flute through
whose heart the whispering of the hours turns
to music.

Which of you would be a reed, dumb and   10
silent, when all else sings together in
unison?

Always you have been told that work is
a curse and labor a misfortune.

But I say to you that when you work   15
you fulfill a part of earth's furthest
dream, assigned to you when that dream was
born.

And in keeping yourself with labor
you are in truth loving life,   20
And to love life through labor is to
be intimate with life's inmost secret.

But if you in your pain call birth an
affliction and the support of the flesh a
curse written upon your brow, then I answer   25
that naught but the sweat of your brow shall
wash away that which is written.

You have been told also that life is
darkness, and in your weariness you echo

what was said by the weary.

And I say that life is indeed darkness
save when there is urge,

And all urge is blind save when there
is knowledge,

And all knowledge is vain save when
there is work,

And all work is empty save when there
is love;

And when you work with love you bind
yourself to yourself, and to one another,
and to God.

And what is it to work with love?

It is to weave the cloth with threads
drawn from your heart, even as if your beloved were to wear that cloth.

It is to build a house with affection,
even as if your beloved were to dwell in that
house.

It is to sow seeds with tenderness and
reap the harvest with joy, even as if your
beloved were to eat the fruit.

It is to charge all things you fashion
with a breath of your own spirit,

And to know that all the blessed dead
are standing about you and watching.

Often have I heard you say, as if
speaking in sleep, " He who works in marble,
and finds the shape of his own soul in the
stone, is nobler than he who plows the
soil.

" And he who seizes the rainbow to lay
it on a cloth in the likeness of man, is
more than he who makes the sandals for our
feet."

But I say, not in sleep but in the
overwakefulness of noontide, that the wind
speaks not more sweetly to the giant oaks
than to the least of all the blades of grass;

30

35

40

45

50

55

60

65

And he alone is great who turns the voice
of the wind into a song made sweeter by his 70
own loving.

Work is love made visible.
And if you cannot work with love but only
with distaste, it is better that you should
leave your work and sit at the gate of the 75
temple and take alms of those who work with
joy.
For if you bake bread with indifference,
you bake a bitter bread that feeds but half
man's hunger. 80
And if you grudge the crushing of the
grapes, your grudge distils a poison in the
wine.
And if you sing though as angels and
love not the singing, you muffle man's ears 85
to the voices of the day and the voices of
the night.

SUGGESTIONS FOR STUDY

1. What does Gibran mean by " keep pace with the earth " and " become
a stranger unto the seasons "?
2. How does love for work change the nature and significance of work?
3. How do the metaphors in lines 43–51 relate to Gibran's idea of working with love? Does he place emphasis upon work itself or upon the
spirit with which work is done?
4. Do various types of work have different values? Is a sculptor, for
example, more important than a farmer or a painter more than a shoemaker? How does Gibran explain his point of view through his imagery
of the wind (lines 65–68)?

NAKANO SHIGEHARU (1902–   )

SONG

Don't sing
Don't sing of scarlet blossoms or the wings of dragonflies
Don't sing of murmuring breezes or the scent of a woman's hair.

" Song " by Nakano Shigeharu, in *Modern Japanese Literature: From 1868 to Present
Day,* compiled and edited by Donald Keene. Published by Grove Press, Inc., 1956. Reprinted by permission.

All of the weak, delicate things
All the false, lying things
All the languid things, omit.   5
Reject every elegance
And sing what is wholly true,
Filling the stomach,
Flooding the breast at the moment of desperation,   10
Songs which rebound when beaten
Songs which scoop up courage from the pit of shame.
These songs
Sing in a powerful rhythm with swelling throats!
These songs   15
Hammer into the hearts of all who pass you by!

(Donald Keene)

KITAGAWA FUYUHIKO (1900–   )

EARLY SPRING

Midnight
A rain mixed with snow fell,
It trickled desolately on the bamboo thicket.
The dream dealt with another's heart.
When I awoke   5
The pillow was cold with tears.
— What has happened to my heart?
The sun shines in mildly from tall windows,
A humming rises from the steelworks,
I got out of bed   10
And poked with a stick the muck in the ditch;
The turbid water slowly began to move.
A little lizard had yielded himself to the current.
In the fields
I push open black earth.   15
The wheat sprouts greenly grow. —
You can trust the earth.

(Donald Keene)

"Early Spring" by Kitagawa Fuyuhiko, in *Modern Japanese Literature: From 1868 to Present Day*, compiled and edited by Donald Keene. Published by Grove Press, Inc., 1956. Reprinted by permission.

WÊN I-TO (1898–1946)

THE DEAD WATER

Here is a ditch of dead and hopeless water,
No breeze can raise a ripple on its skin;
Better cast into it scraps of brass and iron
And pour the refuse of your dishes in.

Maybe emeralds on the brass will grow,   5
And rust on the iron turn to ruby flowers,
Let rank oil weave a layer of silky gauze
And microbes broider cloudy patterns there.

Let it ferment into a ditch of wine,
Green wine with opal froth upon the brim,   10
A lustrous pearl will spring and swell in a laugh
To be burst by gnats that come to rob the vintage.

And thus a ditch of dead and hopeless water
May boast of vivid color.
If frogs cannot endure the deathly silence,   15
The water may have songs.

There is a ditch of dead and hopeless water:
The region where no beauty ever is.
Better abandon it to ugliness —
See from it what a world may still be wrought!   20

(Harold Acton and Ch'en Shih-Hsiang)

SUGGESTIONS FOR STUDY

SONG
  1. What is the tone of this poem?
  2. According to this poem, what kinds of songs should the poet write?

EARLY SPRING
  1. What is the mood of the poet?
  2. Explain the last line. What does the poet feel one *cannot* trust?

THE DEAD WATER
  1. What kind of world may be wrought from the dead water?

" The Dead Water " by Wên I-to. Reprinted from *Modern Chinese Poetry*, translated by Harold Acton and Ch'en Shih-Hsiang, published by Gerald Duckworth & Co. Ltd. Used by permission.

Acknowledgments

The editors are indebted to the following authors, periodicals, and publishers for permission to use the selections indicated, all rights in which are in all cases reserved by the owner of the copyright.

The American-Scandinavian Foundation: "Half a Sheet of Paper" by August Strindberg from *Sweden's Best Stories;* "The Brothers" and "Life and Song" by Björnstjerne Björnson from *Told in Norway;* "Valborg Song" by Holger Drachmann, "Song" by Adam Oehlenschläger, and "Sunlight in the Room" by Ludvig Holstein from the *Book of Danish Verse;* "Old China" and "Birds on a Telegraph Wire" by Carl Snoilsky, "Song after Harvest" by Erik Axel Karlfeldt from *The Anthology of Swedish Lyrics.*

D. Appleton-Century Company, Inc.: Selection from *Byron* by André Maurois; "Roderick's Soliloquy" from *The Cid* by Pierre Corneille, reprinted in *Chief European Dramatists.*

Ivan Bunin: "In an Empty House."

The University of Chicago Press: "Kings," "Fool and False," and "Poverty" from *The Panchatantra,* translated by Arthur Ryder; nine Chinese lyrics from *Chinese Poems in English Rhyme,* translated by Admiral Ts'ai T'ing-Kan.

P. F. Collier & Son Corporation: "The Thief" by Fedor Dostoevsky, translated by Lizzie B. Gorin, reprinted from Volume One of *Short Story Classics, Foreign.*

Columbia University Press: Parts II and III of "Hymn to Usertesen III," translated by Francis L. Griffith; "The Story of the Deluge," translated by Émile G. H. Kraeling; "A Mountain Storm" by Imr al-Kais, translated by C. J. Lyall; "To the Fire," translated by L. H. Mills; "The Warrior Sam Kills a Dragon," by Firdausi, translated by A. G. and E. Warner; "A Satire on the Sultan Mahmud" by Firdausi, translated by J. Atkinson; "The Captive Gets a Wife" by Sa'di, translated by E. B. Eastwick; nine short lyrics by Bhartrihari, translated by C. H. Tawney; "The Union of the Seasons" by Kalidasa, translated by Peter von Bohlen; "A Lyric" by Kalidasa, translated by A. V. W. Jackson; "The Lion-Makers" from *The Panchatantra,* translated by Charles R. Lanman; all from *Columbia University Course in Literature, Volume One, Wisdom of the East,* copyright by the Columbia University Press.

Dodd, Mead & Company, Inc.: " The Tea Room " from *The Book of Tea* by Okakura; " Crainquebille " by Anatole France; " The Ox " by Carducci, " If, Lord, Thy Love for Me Is Strong " by Saint Teresa, translated by Arthur Symons; " February Dialogue " and " Nature " by Herman Wildenvey. All are used by permission of the publishers, Dodd, Mead & Company, Inc.

Doubleday, Doran & Company, Inc.: " The Story of a Story " from *The Girl from the Marsh Croft* by Selma Lagerlöf, copyright, 1910, by Doubleday, Doran and Company, Inc.; three poems by Antonio Machado from *Rosinante to the Road Again* by John Dos Passos, copyright, 1922, by Doubleday, Doran and Company, Inc.

E. P. Dutton & Co., Inc.: " The Jar " taken from *Better Think Twice about It* by Luigi Pirandello, published and copyrighted by E. P. Dutton & Co., Inc., " An Enemy of the People " taken from *Ghosts, An Enemy of the People, and Warriors of Helgeland* by Henrik Ibsen, translated by R. Farquharson Sharp, published by E. P. Dutton & Co., Inc., in the Everyman's Library; selection from Snorri Sturluson's *Heimskringla*, translated by Samuel Laing, published by E. P. Dutton & Co., Inc., in the Everyman's Library; " A Tale about Ak and Humanity " by Efim Zozulya, taken from *Short Stories out of Soviet Russia*, translated by John Cournos, published and copyrighted by E. P. Dutton & Co., Inc.; fifty-four lines taken from *The Girdle of Aphrodite*, translated by F. A. Wright, published by E. P. Dutton & Co., Inc., in the Broadway Translations Series; forty-six lines taken from *The Poets of the Greek Anthology*, translated by F. A. Wright, published by E. P. Dutton & Co., Inc., in the Broadway Translations; seven quatrains taken from *Rubáiyát* of Hafiz, translated by Syed Abdul Majid, adapted by L. Cranmer-Byng, published by E. P. Dutton & Co., Inc., in the *Wisdom of the East Series;* " The Sunflower " and " A Lone Pine Tree " taken from *The Spirit of Japanese Poetry* by Yone Noguchi, published by E. P. Dutton & Co., Inc., in the *Wisdom of the East Series;* " On the Burial of His Son " by Abu'l-atahiya, taken from *The Singing Caravan* by Henry Baerlein, " The Fountain," " A Letter," " Woo Not the World " taken from *The Poems of Mu'tamid, King of Seville,* translated by Dulcie Smith, both published by E. P. Dutton & Co., Inc., in the *Wisdom of the East Series;* " On the River," " Nocturne," " The Summit Temple," and " On the Lake " taken from *The Works of Li Po* translated by Shigeyoshi Obata, published and copyrighted by E. P. Dutton & Co., Inc.; " The Little Rain " by Tu Fu taken from *A Lute of Jade,* translated by L. Cranmer-Byng, published and copyrighted by E. P. Dutton & Co., Inc.; " Spring Thoughts," " Autumn Thoughts," " A Spring Song in Solitude," and " Alone with Ching Mountain " by Li Po taken from *Images in Jade,* translated by Arthur Christy, published and copyrighted by E. P. Dutton & Co., Inc., New York.

Constance Garnett: For her translation of Nikolay Gogol's *The Government Inspector*, Act I.

W. F. Hapgood: "Spring" and "Reveries" from *Youth* by Leo Tolstoy, translated by Isabel Hapgood.

Harcourt, Brace and Company, Inc.: Cicero's "Speech for Marcellus" and "Letter to His Family" and Pliny's letter, "The Eruption of Vesuvius," from *Readings from the Literature of Ancient Rome,* edited by Dora Pym; "Farewell to Hamburg," "A Pine Tree Stands So Lonely," "To My Sister," "I Pass Your Little Window," "Child, You Are Like a Flower," "You've Pearls and You've Diamonds," "By the Sea," "Lightly Swinging Bells Are Ringing," "The Weavers," and "Where?" from *Poems of Heinrich Heine,* translated by Louis Untermeyer, copyright, 1917, by Harcourt, Brace and Company, Inc.; "The Loreley" from *Blue Rhine - Black Forest* by Louis Untermeyer, copyright, 1930, by Harcourt, Brace and Company, Inc.

Harper & Brothers: The first three parts of Chapter One of *Giants in the Earth* by Ole E. Rölvaag.

The Harvard University Press: "Germany" by Tacitus reprinted in the Loeb Classical Library.

The Hispanic Society of America: "The Bull and the Picador" by José Zorrilla, "Sonatina" and "To Roosevelt" by Rubén Darío, "Throttle the Swan" by Enrique González Martínez from the *Hispanic Anthology.*

Henry Holt and Company: "Insects," "Laugh Me to Scorn," "Mount Fuji," "The Rising Moon" from J. I. Bryan's *The Literature of Japan;* selection from *Jean-Christophe* by Romain Rolland, translated by Gilbert Cannan; stanzas from *The Nibelungenlied,* translated by G. H. Needler; a scene from *Cyrano de Bergerac* by Edmond Rostand, translated by Brian Hooker.

Houghton Mifflin Company: Saint Teresa's "Lines Written in Her Breviary," Luis de Góngora's "Let Me Go Warm," Lope de Vega's "Tomorrow," Johann von Goethe's "Wanderer's Night Song," Ludwig Uhland's "The Luck of Edenhall" and "The Castle by the Sea" translated by Henry W. Longfellow; Pío Baroja's "The Abyss" from *Great Spanish Short Stories,* translated by W. B. Wells; two selections from *A Century of Indian Epigrams* by Paul Elmer More; ten butterfly poems from *Japanese Lyrics* by Lafcadio Hearn; "Once More Fields and Gardens" by Tao-Yuan-Ming and "Moon Night" by Tu Fu from *Fir-Flower Tablets,* translated by Ayscough and Lowell. These selections are used by permission of, and by arrangement with, Houghton Mifflin Company. This permission is granted for use of this material in books published and sold only by Harcourt, Brace and Company. No permission is given or implied that this material may be used in books printed from plates sold or leased by them to another person, corporation, city, state or other entity.

Mildred Howells: W. D. Howells' translation of Leopardi's "Ode to

Italy " from *Modern Italian Poets*, copyright, 1887, by Harper & Brothers, copyright, 1914, by W. D. Howells.

Glenn Hughes: Kunikita's " The Island in the Offing," Ishikawa's " I longed to say," etc. and " Feeling inclined," etc. all translated by Glenn Hughes and Yozan Iwasaki, reprinted from *Fifteen Poets of Modern Japan*, published by University of Washington Book Store.

International Publishers Company, Inc.: " Autumn " by Alexander Pushkin, " Captive Knight " by Mikhail Lermontov, " The Salt Song " by Nikolay Nekrasov, " No One Knew " by Demyan Bedney, " The First Bulb Is Turned On " by Mikhail Gerasimov, " Upon Green Hills " by Sergey Essenin, all translated by Deutsch and Yarmolinsky in the *Russian Poetry Anthology*.

Alfred A. Knopf, Inc.: the selection from *Pan* by Knut Hamsun; Tarafa's " He Praises His Camel " reprinted from *Poetry of the Orient* by Eunice Tietjens; " The Bride " reprinted from *The Elaghin Affair* by Ivan Bunin; " The Little Angel " by Leonid Andreyev; selection from *Kristin Lavransdatter* by Sigrid Undset; Li Po's " A Sigh from the Staircase of Jade " and " A Song of Pure Happiness," Chin Tao-yu's " A Poor Girl " reprinted from *Jade Mountain* by Witter Bynner; all by permission of and special arrangement with Alfred A. Knopf, Inc., authorized publishers.

Liveright Publishing Corporation: " The Goose-Herd " from *Iolanthe's Wedding* by Hermann Sudermann, copyright, 1919; " Spleen " and " Sunset " from *Poetry and Prose Poems* by Charles Baudelaire; " The Coronation " and " In Exile " from *Napoleon* by Emil Ludwig, copyright, 1926, all by permission of the Liveright Publishing Corporation.

The Macmillan Company: Anton Chekhov's " A Slander " from *Horse-Stealers*, translated by Constance Garnett; Ivan Turgenev's " Biryuk " from *Sportsman's Sketches*, translated by Constance Garnett; " A Good Will " from *Selections from Kant* by John Watson; " To the Sons of India " and " Song of the Tree " from *Sheaves*, fourteen lyrics from *Fireflies*, and six lyrics from *Gitanjali* by Rabindranath Tagore, all by permission of The Macmillan Company, publishers.

Salvador de Madariaga: coplas from *Spanish Folksongs*.

The Menorah Journal: the translation by Maurice Samuel of Jacob Cahan's " Do You Know What the Mountains Are? " and the translation by Marie Syrkin of Solomon Bloomgarden's " An Old Song."

Paul Nixon: his translation of Martial's " The Beau " from *A Roman Wit*.

Philip Nutt: " The Horse Thief " from *The Merry Tales of Hans Sachs*.

Mrs. Sophia Patterson: her translation of Goethe's " The Elf King."

Poet Lore: Rainer Maria Rilke's " The Cloud " and " Prayer of the Maidens to Mary," translated by Jessie Lemont; " Little Meret " from *Green-Coated Henry* by Gottfried Keller; " The Fabliau of the Three Hunchbacks " translated by Frederick Luquiens.

G. P. Putnam's Sons: Maupassant's " The Piece of String " translated by George Burnham Ives in *Little French Masterpieces;* " How the Thelemites Were Governed " and " How Panurge Asketh Counsel " by François Rabelais from *Selections from Rabelais;* " Letter to Posterity " from Robinson's *Petrarch.*

Ezra Pound: his translation of Lope de Vega's " Song of the Virgin Mother."

H. C. Schweikert: his translation of Ibáñez' " In the Sea."

Charles Scribner's Sons: Benavente's " No Smoking "; Horace's " To the Fountain of Bandusia," " The Ship of State," " To Leuconöe," " To Mistress Pyrrha," " To Chloe," " A Paraphrase of the Preceding Ode " from *Echoes from the Sabine Farm* by Eugene Field.

Frederick A. Stokes Company: " The Seven Pleas " reprinted by permission from *Picture Tales from the Japanese* by Chiyono Sugimoto, copyright, 1928, by Frederick A. Stokes Company.

The Viking Press, Inc.: Verlaine's " My Familiar Dream " and " Late Wisdom," Rimbaud's " The Sleeper of the Valley," Verhaeren's " The Mill," De Regnier's " On the Shore," Jammes' " That Thou Art Poor," Fort's " Bell of Dawn " from *The Poets of Modern France* by Ludwig Lewisohn, copyright, 1918, published by The Viking Press, Inc., New York.

George Allen & Unwin, Ltd.: " The Oil Merchant's Donkey " from Monteiro's *Tales of Old Lusitania;* " Sailing Homeward," translated by Arthur Waley, reprinted from *The Temple;* " The Bird Catcher in Hell," translated by Arthur Waley from *The Nō Plays of Japan.*

G. Bell & Sons, Ltd.: Arthur Schopenhauer's " On Thinking for Oneself," translated by Belfort Bax.

Basil Blackwell & Mott, Ltd.: Pushkin's " Description of St. Petersburg " from *The Bronze Horseman;* Alexey Tolstoy's " It Was in Early-Early Spring," " No Word from You," " My Native Land," " If Thou Lovest " from *Russian Poets and Poems* by Mme. N. Jarintzov.

Cambridge University Press: Catullus' " To Lesbia," " To His Brother," and " On the Death of Lesbia's Sparrow " from Macnaghten's *Poems of Catullus;* Hafiz' " The Writing on the Pages of the Rose " and " The Calm Circumference of Life " from Nicholson's *Eastern Poetry and Prose;* " On Old Age " from Lyall's *The Poems of 'Amr Son of Qami'ah.*

Chapman & Hall, Ltd.: selections from *Chanson de Roland.*

Chatto and Windus: " Gaudeamus Igitur " from J. A. Symonds' *Wine, Women and Song.*

Gerald Duckworth & Co., Ltd.: selections from Leonardo da Vinci's *Note Books.*

The Golden Cockerel Press and Havelock Ellis: three coplas from *Sonnets and Folk Songs* by Havelock Ellis.

Gowans and Gray, Ltd.: the folk tale, " The Wonderful Pear Tree."

William Heinemann, Ltd.: Edward Marsh's translation of " Women and

Secrets " and " The Crow and the Fox " by La Fontaine; and *The Attack on the Mill* by Émile Zola.

Oxford University Press: " The Ballad of Count Arnaldos " and Juan Ruiz's " On the Power of Money " from *Spanish Prose and Poetry, Old and New* by Miss Ida Farnell; Aylmer Maude's translation of Tolstoy's " How Much Land Does a Man Need? " reprinted from Mr. and Mrs. Aylmer Maude's *Twenty-three Tales*.

Kegan Paul, Trench, Trubner & Co., Ltd.: Sa'di's " The Captive Gets a Wife " and " Wise Sayings," translated by E. B. Eastwick.

Kelly and Walsh, Ltd.: Confucius' " Selections from the *Analects*," " Chinese Proverbs," and Liu Chi's " Outsides," translated by H. A. Giles, reprinted from *Gems of Chinese Literature*.

Elliot Stock: " Fish in the Forest " from the *Book of Noodles*.

Williams & Norgate Ltd.: " A Mountain Storm " by Imr al-Kais from Sir Charles Lyall's *Ancient Arabic Poetry*.

Pronunciation Dictionary

In the following dictionary the student will find the names of authors, titles, characters, places, and foreign quotations within the selections which present any pronunciation difficulty. Authors are alphabetized by their surnames except in a few cases where they are commonly called by their given names, like Michelangelo, or by assumed names, like Voltaire. If the author's full name is given in the text, the pronunciation of all his names is given; if he is mentioned only by surname, that alone is here given.

PRONUNCIATION KEY

The pronunciation has been indicated by the simple key familiar to the student from his general use of dictionaries.

Vowels

ā māte   ō tōne
å senåte   ŏ ŏbey
â dâre   ô ôrb
ă căt   ŏ nŏd
ä fäther   ŏ cŏnnect
à àsk   o͞o mo͞od
à Elbà   o͝o co͝ok
ē ēve   oi oil
ê êvent   ou out
ĕ mĕt   ū ūnit
ĕ novĕl   ů ůnite
ē pērhaps   û ûrn
ī bīte   ŭ ŭp
ĭ hĭt   *ŭ* focŭs

Foreign sounds

ü   menü (French u)
'   non-existent vowel as in *tabl'*, *autr'* (French)

Consonants

b, d, f, l, m, n, p, r, t with their usual English sounds
k   *k*ill, *c*ase
s   *s*ell, *c*ell
(Note that c does not appear in the phonetic transcript.)
z   si*z*e, burn*s*
g   *g*et
h   *h*as
j   *j*oy

w   *w*ant
y   *y*et (used only as a consonant)
v   *v*ote. In Russian words has value of vf
ch   *ch*ur*ch*
sh   *sh*ow
zh   a*z*ure
ks   a*x*
kw   *qu*ick
th   *th*in
t̶h̶   *th*en

Foreign sounds

N   French nasal as in bo*n*, e*n*fi*n*
K   German guttural, as in i*ch*, köni*g*
(Note that only the capital letters indicate the foreign sounds; n and k represent their normal English sounds.)

CHARACTERISTICS OF THE LANGUAGES

This is simply a brief summary of a few of the most conspicuous differences between each of the languages and English, which may be helpful for the student to know. The continental values of the vowels referred to are as follows:

Spelling	Long	Short
a	ä	à
e	ā	ĕ
i	ē	ĭ
o	ō	ŏ
u	ōō	ŏŏ

French

Accent: each syllable distinctly pronounced with no marked accent, but a rising inflection at the end usually indicated by the accent mark on the last syllable.

Vowels: continental values. The sounds of the vowels are changed by the accent marks: ´ ` ^ . The nasalized vowels are indicated by äN, ôN, ăN, ĕN, and the French u by ü. These sounds are best learned by imitation of someone who knows the language.

Consonants: Ç gives c the sound of s before a or o where it would otherwise have the sound of k. J and sometimes g have the sound of zh. Th has the sound of t; ch of sh; gn of ny. There are often silent consonants, especially at the ends of words.

Spanish

Accent: most commonly on penult; often indicated by an accent mark to prevent confusion. Note that in Spanish the mark ´ is a definite accent mark, not a modification of the vowel sound, as in French.

Vowels: continental values.

Consonants: C before e and i has the sound of th; s has the sound of s or z; j and sometimes x have the sound of h; ñ has the sound of ny.

Italian

Accent: most commonly on penult. Each syllable is distinctly pronounced, and double consonants are definitely pronounced with both syllables.

Vowels: continental values, pure tone, almost no modifications.

Consonants: Ch and cch have the sound of k; c before e and i has sound of ch; g before e and i has the sound of j; gn of ny; j of y.

German

Accent: Tends toward the beginning of the word.

Vowels: continental values except when modified by umlaut, thus: ä has the sound of ĕ; ö of û; ü same as French u. Final e is pronounced as a separate syllable, ē.

Consonants: guttural ch as in ich, represented by κ. G always has either the hard sound or the guttural; j has the sound of y; final d sounds like t, and final b like p; w has the sound of v; v of f; z of tz or ts; th of t; st of sht and sp of shp at the beginning of syllables; sch of sh.

Scandinavian Languages

Since each of the three has its own peculiarities, only very general points can be mentioned.

Accent: Tends toward the beginning of the word.

Vowels: continental values, modifications by umlaut similar to German; å or aa has the sound of ô.

Consonants: many similarities to German, especially the sound of g, y, th, and the guttural represented phonetically by к.

Russian

Since the Russian words have been transliterated from a different alphabet, they are spelled almost phonetically and therefore except for their length are not as difficult as many from other languages.

Accent: Tends toward the penult, but shows considerable variation.

Vowels: continental values except that Russian long o is nearer ô than ō.

Consonants: V has the sound of vf. Some pronunciation tables indicate this by f or ff, but as the sound is really a combination of v and f, it is here indicated by v to agree with the spelling. Final d and b have the same sounds as in German.

Greek and Latin

The Anglicized pronunciations in common use are given. In Greek ch has the sound of k, ph of f. Final e and es are pronounced as separate syllables.

Oriental Languages

All the Oriental languages have been transliterated from entirely different alphabets, and the names are therefore practically phonetic as they stand, and accent is equally distributed. The vowels have their continental values; hence, Sa'di (sä-dē) and Li Po (lē pō). The apostrophe appearing in some of the Oriental names stands for varying symbols representing aspirates usually disregarded in English pronunciation. In Chinese the u is always ōō or ŏŏ, never ū; Tu Fu (tōō fōō). Since Chinese names are all monosyllabic with equally distributed accent and phonetic spelling, they present no pronunciation difficulty and with a few exceptions are omitted from this list. Japanese names are also omitted, since they are phonetic and the accent is equally balanced among all the syllables. An American, however, being used to accent is inclined to place it on the penult thus: Okakura Kakuzo (ō-kà-kōō'rà kà-kōō'zō).

Abeillard or Abélard, Fr. ä-bä-lär′

Abu'l-Atahiya, Ar. ä-bōōl′-ä-tä-hē′yà

Achilles, Gr. à-kĭl′ēz

Aeneas, Lat. ē-nē′as

Agrafena, R. ä-grä-fä′nà

Alarcón, Pedro Antonio de, Sp. ä-lär-kōn′, pä′drō àn-tō′nĭ-ō dä

Alegría, Ciro, Sp. ä′lä-grē′ä, sē′rŏ

Alemán, Mateo, Sp. ä-lä-män′, mä-tä′ō

Alicante, Sp. ä-lē-kän′tä

Alvaro, Corrado, It. äl-vä′rō, kŏr-rä′dŏ

Ammos Fyodorovich, R. à′môs fyŏ-dôr′ŏ-vēch

'Amr, son of Qami'ah, Ar. ämr′, kä-mē′hà

Anchises, Gr. ăn-kī′sēz

Andreyev, Leonid, R. än-drä′yĕv, lä-ō-nēd′

Andromache, Gr. ăn-drŏm′à-kĕ

Anna Andreyevna, R. än′à än-drä′-yĕv-nà

Annunzio, Gabriele d', It. dän-nōōn′dzĕ-ō, gä-brē-ā′lä

Anouilh, Jean, Fr. ă-nü′y, zhäN

Antigone, Gr. ăn-tĭg′ō-nĕ

Anton Antonovich, R. än-tôn′ än-tôn′ŏ-vēch

Arc de Triomphe, Fr. ärk dē trē-ôNf′

Arnaldos, Sp. är-näl′dŏs

Artemy Filippovich, R. är-tä′mĭ fē-lēp′ŏ-vēch

Asbjörnsen and Moe, Nor. äs-byûrn′sĕn, mō

Assisi, It. äs-sē′zē

Astafi Ivanich, R. äs-tä′fē ē-vän′ēch

Astyanax, Gr. ăs-tī′à-năks

Attayda, Catharina de, Por. ä-tī′-dà, kä-tä-rē′nä dä

Aucassin and Nicolette, Fr. ō-kà-säN′, nē-kō-lĕt′

Azuela, Mariano, Sp. ä-swä′lä, mä-ryä′nŏ

Balzac, Honoré de, Fr. bäl-zäk′, ō-nō-rä′ dē

Bandusia, Lat. băn-dōōz′yà

Baroja, Pío, Sp. bä-rŏ′hà, pē′ō

Baudelaire, Charles, Fr. bō-d′lâr′, shärl

Bayard, Madame, Fr. bà-yàr′, mà-däm′

Bazán, Emilia Pardo, Sp. bä-thän′, ä-mē′lĭ-à pär′dō

Beaumarchais, Fr. bō-mär-shĕ′

Bécquer, Gustavo Adolfo, Sp. bĕk′âr, gōō-stäv′ō à-dôl′fō

Bedney, Demyan, R. bĕd′nē, dĕm-yän′

Benavente, Jacinto, Sp. bä-nä-vĕn′tä, hä-thēn′tō

Béranger, Pierre Jean de, Fr. bā-räN-zhä′, pē-âr′ zhäN dē

Berceo, Gonzalo de, Sp. bĕr-thä′ō, gŏn-thä′lō dä

Bergman Hjalmar, Sw. băr′y′-màn, yàl′màr

Bhartrihari, Sanskrit b′här-trē-hä′rē

Biryuk, R. bēr-yōōk′

Björnson, Björnstjerne, Nor. byûrn′-sōn, byûrn′styĕrn-à

Blasco Ibáñez, Vicente, Sp. bläs′kō ē-bä′nyäth, vĕ-thĕn′tä

Blazon, Thibaud de, Fr. blà-zôN′, tē-bō′ dē

Boccaccio, Giovanni, It. bŏk-kä′chō, jŏ-vän′nĕ

Boileau, Fr. bwä-lō′

Bojer, Johan, Nor. bō′yĕr, yō′hän

Bossuet, Fr. bŏ-swĕ′

Bucephalus, Gr. bū-sĕf′à-lŭs

Bunin, Ivan Alexeyevich, R. bōō′-nĭn, ē-vàn′ à-lĕk-sä′yĕ-vēch

Bürger, Gottfried August, Ger. bür′gĕr, gŏt′frēt ou′gōost

Calderón de la Barca, Pedro, Sp. käl-dä-rōn′ dä lä bär′kà, pä′drō

Camoëns, Luis de, Port. kä-moinsh′, lŏō-ēs dä; Eng. kăm′ŏ-ĕns

Camus, Albert, Fr. kà′mü′, àl′bâr′

Cellini, Benvenuto, It. chĕl-lē′nĕ, bĕn-vä-nōō′tō

Cervantes, Miguel de, Sp. thĕr-vän′täs, mē-gĕl′ dä; Eng. sĕr-văn′tēz

Champs-Élysées, Fr. shäNs-ā-lē-zā′

chanson de gestes, Fr. shäN-sôN′ dē zhĕst

Charon, Gr. kā'rŏn

Chateaubriand, Fr. shȧ-tō-brē-äɴ'

Chekhov, Anton Pavlovich, R. chĕ'ᴋôv, ȧn-tôn' päv'lô-vēch

Chénier, Fr. shā-nyā'

Christian Ivanovich Hubner, R. and Ger. krĭst-ĭ-än' ē-vän'ō-vēch hōōb'nâr

Cicero, Lat. sĭs'ēr-ō

Claudel, Paul, Fr. klō'dĕl', pôl

Cocteau, Jean, Fr. kôk'tō', zhäɴ

Corneille, Pierre, Fr. kôr-nā'y', pē-âr'

Crainquebille, Jérome, Fr. kräɴ-k'bēl', zhā-rôm'

Creüsa, Gr. krē-ū'sȧ

Croce, Benedetto, It. krō'chȧ, bā'nȧ-dāt'tô

Crito, Gr. krī'tō

Cyrano de Bergerac. *Also* Savinien-Hercule, Fr. sē-rä-nō' dē bâr-zhĕr-äk'. *Also,* sȧ-vē-nyäɴ'-âr-kül'

damoiseau, Fr. dȧ-mwȧ-zō'

Dante Alighieri, It. dän'tä ä-lē̇-gyả'rē

Dantès, Edmond, Fr. däɴ-tĕs', ȧd-môɴ'

Darío, Rubén, Sp. dȧ-rē'ō, rōō-bĕn'

Daudet, Alphonse, Fr. dō-dĕ', ȧl-fôɴz'

De Guiche, Fr. dē-gēsh'

Dei nomine, Lat. dā'ē nŏ'mĭ-nā

Deledda, Grazia, It. dȧ-lĕd'dä, grä'tsyä

Deucalion, Gr. dū-kā'lĭ-ŏn

de trop, Fr. dē trō'

Diderot, Fr. dēd-rō'

Djinn, Ar. jĭn

Don Quixote, Sp. dŏn kē̇-hō'tä; Eng. dŏn kwĭk'sŏt

Drachmann, Holger, Dan. dräᴋ'mȧn, hôl'gēr

Dumas, Alexandre, Fr. dü-mä', ȧ-lĕk-säɴ'dr'

Duun, Olav, Nor. dōōn, ō'läv

Echegaray José, Sp. ā-chä-gä-rī', hō-zā'

Edda, Nor. ĕd'dȧ

Edenhall, Ger. ā'dĕn-häl

Ehrenburg, Ilya, R. ā'rĕn-bōōrᴋ, ĭl-yȧ'

esprit gaulois, Fr. ĕs-prē' gōl-wä'

Espronceda, José de, Sp. äs-prŏn-thā'dȧ, hō-zā' dä

Essenin, Sergey Alexandrovich, R. yĕ-sän'nĭn, sēr-gā' ȧ-lĕk-sän'drō-vēch

Eurycleia, Gr. ū-rĭ-klē'yȧ

Eurydike, Gr. ū-rĭd'ĭ-kė̆

Eystein, Nor. ī'shtän

fabliau; plural, fabliaux, Fr. fȧ-blĭ-ō', both the same

Falkberget, Johan, Nor. fälk'bĕr'gĕ, yô-hän'

Faust, Ger. foust

Feoktista Petrovna, R. fā-ŏk-tēs'tȧ pā-trôv'nȧ

Firdausi, Per. fēr-dou'sē

Flaubert, Fr. flō-bâr'

Fort, Paul, Fr. fôr, pôl

Françoise, Fr. fräɴ-swäz'; feminine form of François fräɴ-swä'

Gagny, Fr. gȧ-nyē'

Galatea, Gr. găl-ȧ-tē'ȧ

Galdós, Benito Pérez, Sp. gäl-dōs', bā-nē'tō pā'räth

Gallegos, Rómulo, Sp. gä-yä'gōs, rô'mōō-lō

Gálvez, Manuel, Sp. gäl'väs, mä-nwĕl'

Gandhi, Mahatma, Ind. gän'dē, mȧ-hät'mȧ

García Lorca, Federico, Sp. gär-thē'ä lôr'kä, fä'thȧ-rē'kō

Garin de Biaucaire, Fr. gȧ-răɴ' dē byō-kâr'

Gautier, Fr. gō-tyä'

Gerasimov, Mikhail Prokofyevich, R. gĕr-ȧ-sē'môv, mē-hȧ-ēl' prŏ-kôf'yä-vēch

Géronte, Fr. zhā-rôɴt'

Gianetto, It. jȧ-nĕt'tō

Gibran, Kahlil, Ar. jōōb-rän', kȧ-lēl'

Gide, André, Fr. zhēd, äɴ'drä'

Gil Blas, Fr. zhēl blȧs

Giovanna, It. jo-vän'nȧ; feminine of Giovanni jô-vän'nė̆

Giraudoux, Jean, Fr. zhē'rō'dōō', zhäN

Gitanjali, Bengali jē-tän-jä-lē

Giuseppa, It. jōō-sĕp'pà; feminine of Giuseppe jōō-sĕp'pā

Goethe, Johann Wolgang von, Ger. gú'tē, yō'hän vŏlf'gäng fŏn

Gogol, Nikolai Vasilievich, R. gô'-gôl, nē-kō-lī' và-sēl'ya-vēch

Goncharov, R. gôn-chär-ŏv'

Góngora, Luis de, Sp. gōn'gō-rà, lwēs dä

González Martínez, Enrique, Sp. gōn-thä'läth màr-tē'nāth, ĕn-rē'kä

Gorki, Maxim, R. gôr'kē, mäk-sēm'

Guareschi, Giovanni, It. gwä-rĕs'kē, jŏ-vän'nĕ

Guzman de Alfarache, Sp. gōōth'-màn dä àl-fà-rä'chä

Haemon, Gr. hē'mŏn

Hafiz, Per. hä'fīz

Hallström, Per, Sw. häl'strĕm, pâr

Hamsun, Knut, Nor. häm'sōōn, knōōt

Hauchecorne of Bréauté, Fr. ōsh-kôrn', brā-ō-tā'

Heidenstam, Verner von, Sw. hĕ'ī-dĕn-stàm, vär'nēr fôn

Heimskringla, Nor. hāms'krĭng-là

Heine, Heinrich, Ger. hī'nē, hīn'rĭK

Hellström, Gustaf, Sw. hĕl'strĕm, gŭs'täv

Héloïse, Fr. ā-lō-ēz'

Hernani, Fr. ĕr-nà-nē'

Herzeleide, Ger. hĕrt-zĕ-lī'dē

Hesse, Hermann, Ger. hĕs'ĕ, hĕr'män

Hippius, Zinaida, R. hĕp'ĭ-ŭs, zē-nà-ē'dà

Hofmannsthal, Hugo von, Ger. hōf'mäns-täl, hōō'gō fŏn

Holstein, Ludvig, Dan. hōl'stān, lōŏd'vĕg

Houlbrcque uf Mannville, Fr. ōōl-brĕk', màn-vēl'

Hugo, Victor, Fr. ü-gŏ', vēk-tôr'; Eng. hū'gō

Imr Al-Kais, Ar. ēmr' äl-kä'ēs

Iriarte, Tomás de, Sp. ē-ryär'tä, tō-mäs' dä

Ismene, Gr. ĭs-mē'nĕ

Ivan Kuzmich, R. ē-vän' kōōz-mēch'

Ivan Petrovich Loshadinikh, R. ē-vän' pā'trō-vēch lôsh-à-dē'nēK

Jacqueline, Fr. zhàk'lēn'

Jami, Per. jä'mē

Jammes, Francis, Fr. zhäm, frän-sēs'

Jean Christophe, Fr. zhäN krēs-tŏf'

Jean Michel, Fr. zhäN mē-shĕl'

Jiménez, Juan Ramón, Sp. hĕ-mā'nāth, hwän rä-môn'

Jongleurs, Fr. zhöN-glēr'

Josephus, Heb. jō-sē'fŭs

Jötunheim, Nor. yē'tōōn-hām

Jouve, Fr. zhōōv

Judah ha-Levi, Heb. jōō'dà hà-lä'vĕ

Karlfeldt, Erik Axel, Sw. kärl'fĕlt, ā'rēk äk'sĕl

Kasimir Stanislavovich, R. kà-zē-mēr' stàn-ĭs-lä'vô-vēch

Kristin Lavransdatter, Nor. krĭs'tĭn läv'räns-dät-tēr

La Fontaine, Jean de, Fr. là fôN-tĕn', zhäN dē

Lagerkvist, Pär Fabian, Sw. lä'-yèr-kvĭst, pâr fä'bĭ-ăn

Lagerlöf, Selma, Sw. lä'gēr-lûf, sĕl'mà

Lamartine, Fr. là-màr-tēn'

Landsmaal, Nor. läns'mōl'

Laocoön, Gr. lä-ŏk'ō-ŏn

La Rochefoucauld, Fr. là rŏsh-fōō-kō'

Lazarillo de Tormes, Sp. là-thà-rē'lyō dä tŏr'mäs

Léandre, Fr. lā-äN'dr'

Leconte dc Lisle, Fr. lē-kôNt' dē lēl

Leonardo da Vinci, It. lä-ō-när'dō dä vēn'chē

Leonov, Leonid, R. lyĭ-ô'nôf, lyĕ-ô-nyēt'

Leopardi, Giacomo, It. lä-ŏ-pär'dĕ, jä'kŏ-mō

Le Sage, Fr. lē säzh

Leuconoë, Gr. lū-kō'nō-ḗ
Levi, Carlo, It. lâ've, kär'lȯ
Li Po, Chin. lē pō
Loti, Fr. lō-tē'
Lucinde, Fr. lü-sănd"
Lucretius, Lat. lōō-krē'shŭs
Ludwig, Emil, Ger. lōōt'vĭκ, ä-mēl'
Luka Lukich, R. lōō-kä' lōō-kēch'

Machado, Antonio, Sp. mä-chä'dō, än-tō'nē-o
Machiavelli, Nicolo, It. mä-kyä-vĕl'lē, nēk-kō-lō'
Maeterlinck, Maurice, Fr. mä-tĕr-lăn', mō-rēs'; Eng. mä'tēr-lĭnk
Malandain, Fr. mȧ-làn-dăn'
Malraux, André, Fr. màl'rō', än'drä'
Manon Lescaut, Fr. mȧ-nȯn' lĕs-kō'
Manzoni, Alessandro, It. män-dzō'nē, ä-lĕs-sän'drō
Mårbacka, Sw. môr'bäk-ȧ
Marcellus, Lat. mär-sĕl'ŭs
Marcus Aurelius, Lat. mär'kŭs ō-rē'lĭ-ŭs
Marivaux, Fr. mä-rē-vō'
Martine, Fr. mär-tēn'
Martínez Sierra, Gregorio, Sp. mär-tē'nāth syĕr'rä, grȧ-gō'ryō
Martínez Zuviría, Gustavo, Port. mär-tē'näs sōō've-rē'ä, gōōsh-tȧ'-vōō
Marya Antonovna, R. mȧ-rē'ȧ än-tôn'ȯv-nȧ
Mateo Falcone, It. mȧ-tä'ō fȧl-kō'nä
Maupassant, Guy de, Fr. mō-pȧ-sän', gē dē
Maurois, André, Fr. mô'rwȧ', än'drä'
Mazzini, Giuseppe, It. mät-zē'nē, jōō-sĕp'pä
Mephistopheles, Gr. mĕf-ĭs-tŏf'ḗ-lēz
Mérimée, Prosper, Fr. mä-rē-mä', prȯ-spâr'
Merlier, Fr. mârl-yä'
Metamorphoses, Gr. mĕt-ȧ-môr'fō-sēz
Michelangelo Buonarroti, It. mē-kĕl-än'jä-lō bwô-när-rô'tē; Eng., mī-kĕl-ăn'jĕ-lō

Miranda, Señor Don Diego de, Sp. mē-rän'dȧ, sän-yōr' dōn dyä'gō dä
Misère de misère, Fr. mē-sâr' dē mē-sâr'
Mistral, Gabriela, Sp. mēs-träl', gä'brḗ-ä'lä
Molière, Jean Baptiste Poquelin, Fr. mȯ-lyâr', zhän bȧ-tēst' pōk'-lăn'
Monstrum horrendum et ingens, Lat. mŏn'strŭm hŏr-rĕn'dŭm ĕt ĭn-gĕns'
Montaigne, Michel de, Fr. môn-tàn'y', mē-shĕl' dē; Eng., mŏn-tān'
Montesquieu, Fr. môn-tĕs-kē-û'; Eng., mŏn-tĕs-kū'
Montijo, Count of, Sp. mŏn-tē'hō
Moravia, Alberto, It. mō-rä'vyä, äl-bĕr'tȯ
Mort aux vaches, Fr. môrt ō väsh
Musset, Alfred de, Fr. mü-sĕ', ȧl-frĕd' dē

Natalya, R. nȧ-täl'yȧ
Nehru, Jawaharlal, Ind. nä'rōō, jȧ-wä'hȧr-läl
Nekrasov, Nikolai Alexeyevich, R. nĕk-rä'sŏv, nē'kō-lī ȧ-lĕk-sā'yȧ-vēch
Neruda, Pablo, Sp. nä-rö'thä, pä'blō
Nibelungs, Ger. nē'bĕ-lōōngz
Nizhni-Novgorod, R. nēzh'nē nȯv'-gȯ-rôt

Odin, Nor. ō'dĭn
Odysseus, Gr. ō-dĭs'ūs
Oehlenschläger, Adam Gottlob, Dan. ē-lĕn-shlä'gĕr, ä'dȧm gōt'lŏp
Omar Khayyám, Per. ō'màr κī-yäm'
Ortega y Gasset, José, Sp. ôr-tä'gä ḗ gä-sĕt', hō-zā'

Panquer, Dominique, Fr. pȧn-kä', dō-mē-nēk'
Paolo and Francesca, It. pä'ō-lō, frän-chĕs'kä
Parzival, Ger. pär'tzē-fäl
Pascal, Blaise, Fr. pȧs-käl', blâz
Patroclus, Gr. pȧ-trō'klŭs
Pavese, Cesare, It. pä-vĕ'sĕ, chä'-zä-rä

Peleus, Gr. pē'lūs

Pereda, José María de, Sp. pä-rä'-thȧ, hō-zā' mȧ-rē'ȧ dā

Pérez de Ayala, Ramón, Sp. pä'rāth dā ä-yä'lä, rä-môn'

Pericles, Gr. pĕr'ĭ-klēz

Peshkov, Alexey Maximovich, R. pĕsh'kŏv, ȧ-lĕk'sā-ē mȧk sēm'ŏ-vēch

petit verre, Fr. p'tē' vâr

Petrarch, Eng. pē'trärk; or Petrarca, Francesco, It. pä-trär'kȧ, frän-chĕs'kō

Petrograd, R. pĕt'rō-grȧd (English form)

Phaedo, Gr. fē'dō

Pilnyak, Boris, R. pyĭl-y'-nyȧk', bŭ-ryēs

Pirandello, Luigi, It. pē-rän-dĕl'lō, lōō-ē'jē

Pléiade, Fr. plä-yäd'

Plutarch, Gr. plōō'tärk

Polyneikes, Gr. pŏl-ĭ-nī'kēz

Polyphemus, Gr. pŏl-ĭ-fē'mŭs

Portocarraro, Señor Don Eugenio, Sp. pōr-tō-kȧ-rä'rō, sän-yōr' dōn ā-ōō-hā'nyō

Porto Vecchio, It. pŏr'tō vĕk'ē-ō

Prévost, Fr. prä-vō'

Proust, Marcel, Fr. prōōst, mȧr'sĕl'

Pushkin, Alexander Sergeyevich, R. pōōsh'kĭn, ȧ-lĕk-sän'dĕr sĕr-gā'yĕ-vēch

Pyotr Ivanovich Bobchinsky, R. pē-ō'tr' ē-vän'ŏ-vēch bôb-chĭn'skĭ

Quintero, Serafín and Joaquín, Sp. kĕn-tā'rō, sä'rä-fēn' and hwä-kēn'

Rabelais, François, Fr. rȧ-b'-lĕ', frän-swä'

Racine, Fr. rȧ-sēn'

Régnier, Henri de, Fr. rā-nyä', än-rē' dē

Remarque, Erich Maria, Ger. rĕ-märk', ā'rĭk mä-rē'ä

Renan, Fr. rē-näN'

Rilke, Rainer Maria, Ger. rĭl'kē, rī'nĕr mä-rē'ȧ

Rimbaud, Jean Arthur, Fr. răN-bō', zhän ȧr-tür'

Robert M. (Monsieur), Fr. rō-bĕr', mē-syû

Rocinante, Sp. rō-thē-nän'tä; Eng. rŏz-ĭ-năn'tĕ

Rocreuse, Fr. rō-krûz'

Rolland, Romain, Fr. rō-läN', rō-măN'

Rölvaag, Ole, Nor. rŭl'vôg, ō'lȧ

Rostand, Edmond, Fr. rō-stäN', äd-môN'

Rousseau, Jean-Jacques, Fr. rōō-sō', zhäN-zhäk'

Rubáiyát, Per. rōō-bī-yät'

Rueda, Lope de, Sp. rwä'thȧ, lō'pä dā

Ruiz, Juan, Archpriest of Hita, Sp. rwēth, hwän, ē'tȧ

Sachs, Hans, Ger. zäĸs, häns

Sa'di, Per. sä-dē'

Sainte-Beuve, Fr. săNt-bûv'

Saga, Nor. sä'gȧ

Saguntum, Lat. sä-gōōn'tōōm; Eng. sä-gŭn'tŭm

Sancho Panza, Sp. sän'chō pän'thä Eng. sănk'ō păn'zȧ

Sartre, Jean-Paul, Fr. sär'tr', zhäN-pôl'

Schopenhauer, Arthur, Ger. shō-pĕn-hou'ēr, är-tōōr'

Schweitzer, Albert, Ger., schvī'tsēr, äl'bērt

Sergey Kapitonich Akhineyev, R. sĕr-gā' kä-pē-tô'nech ȧ-kēn-ā'yĕv

Sganarelle, Fr. sgä-nä-rĕl'

Sholokhov, Mikhail, R. shô'lŭ-ĸôf, myĭ-ĸŭ-ēl'

Siegfried, Ger. zēĸ'frēt; Eng. sēg'-frēd

Sigurd, Nor. sē'gûrd

Sillanpää, Frans Eemil, Finn. sĭl'län-pä', fräns â'mĭl

Silone, Ignazio, It. sē-lō'nȧ, ē-nyä'tsyŏ

Siwertz, Sigfrid, Sw. sē'vērts, sēg'-frēd

Socrates, Gr. sŏk'rȧ-tēz

Söderberg, Hjalmar, Sw. sû'dēr-bȧr'y', yȧl'mȧr

Sofia Dmitrievna, R. sôf'ĭ-ȧ dmē'-trē-ĕv-nȧ

Sologub, Fedor, R. sŭ-lŭ-gōōp', fyô'dēr

Sophocles, Gr. sŏf'ō-klēz

Staël, Madame de, Ger. stä'ĕl; Fr. stä-ĕl', màdäm' dē

Stepan Ilyich Uhovyortov, R. stĕp-àn' ēl-yēch' ōō-hŏv'yôr-tŏv

Sturluson, Snorri, Nor. stōōr'lē-sōn, snŏr'rĕ

Svetchnikovs, R. svĕch'nē-kŏvs

Svistunov, R. svēst'ōō-nŏv

Tacitus, Lat. tăs'ĭ-tŭs

Tagore, Rabindranath, Bengali tä-gōr', rà-bĭn'drà-nàth

Te Deum Laudamus, Lat. tā dā'ōŏm lou-dä'mōŏs

Tegnér, Esaias, Sw. tĕng-nâr' ĕ-sī'às

Teiresias, Gr. tī-rē'sĭ-às

Telemachus, Gr. tĕl-ĕm'à-kŭs

Teresa, Sp. tä-rā'sä; Eng. tĕ-rē'sà

Thor, Nor. tôr; Eng. thôr

Thucydides, Gr. thū-sĭd'ĭ-dēz

Tiodoro Gamba, It. tē-ō-dō'rō gäm'bà

Toggenburg, Ger. tŏg'gĕn-bōōrg

Tolstoy, Alexey, R. tŏl-stoi', à-lĕk'sä-ē

Tolstoy, Leo, R. tŏl'stoi, lē'ō (English form)

Troyes, Chrétien de, Fr. trwä', krä-tyăN' dē

Tu Fu, Chin. tōō fōō

Uhland, Ludwig, Ger. ōō-länt', lōōt'vĭK

Unamuno, Miguel de, Sp. ōō'nä-mōō-nō, mĕ-gĕl' dä

Undset, Sigrid, Nor. ōōnd'sĕt, sē'grĕd

Utgaard-Loki, Nor. ōōt'gôrd-lō'kē

Ut-napishtim, Bab. ŭt-nă-pĭsh'tĭm

Valborg, Dan. vàl'bôrg

Valère, Fr. và-lâr'

Värmland, Sw. vĕrm'länd

Vega, Lope de, Sp. vä'gà, lō'pä dä

Ventadour, Bernard de, Fr. väN-tà-dōōr', bĕr-när' dē

Verhaeren, Émile, Fr. vĕr-hä'rĕn, ä-mēl'

Verlaine, Fr. vĕr-lân'

Verrocchio, Andrea del, It. vĕr-rōk'kē-ō, än-drā'à dĕl

Vigny, Fr. vē-nyē'

Villon, François, Fr. vē-yôN' or vē-lôN', fräN-swä'

Virgil, Lat. vûr'jĭl

Vogelweide. See Walther von der Vogelweide.

Volsunga Saga, Nor. vôl'sōŏng-à sä'gà

Voltaire, François Marie Arouet de, Fr. vôl-târ', fräN-swä' mä-rē' à-rōō-ĕ' dē

Walther von der Vogelweide, Ger. vältĕr fŏn dĕr fō'gĕl-vī-dē

Werfel, Franz, Ger. vĕr'fĕl, fränts

Wildenvey, Herman, Nor. vĭl-dĕn-vā, hĕr'màn

Wolfram von Eschenbach, Ger. vôlf'räm fŏn ĕsh'ĕn-bäK

Xanthias, Gr. zăn'thĭ-às

Xenophon, Gr. zĕn'ô-fŏn

Yehoash, Heb. yĕ-hō'ăsh

Yvetot, Fr. ēv-tō'

Zamyatin, Yevgeny, R. zä-myä'tĭn, yĭv-gä'nyē

Zi' Dima Licasi, It. tzē dē'mà lē-kä'sē

Zirafa, Don Lollo, It. tzē-rä'fà, dŏn lōl'lō

Zola, Émile, Fr. zô-lä', ä-mēl'

Zorrilla, José, Sp. thôr-rēl'yà, hō-zä'

Zoshchenko, Mikhail, R. zô'shchĕn-kô, myĭ-Kŭ-ēl'

Zozulya, Efim, R. zô-zōōl'yà, yĕ'fēm

INDEX